INTRODUCTION TO
SOCIOLOGY
FOURTH EDITION

Mike O'Donnell

SENIOR LECTURER IN SOCIOLOGY
UNIVERSITY OF WESTMINSTER, LONDON

Nelson

Thomas Nelson and Sons Ltd
Nelson House
Mayfield Road
Walton-on-Thames
Surrey KT12 5PL
United Kingdom

© Mike O'Donnell 1997

First published by Thomas Nelson and Sons Ltd 1997

I(T)P® Thomas Nelson is an International Thomson Publishing
Company
I(T)P® is used under licence

ISBN 0-17-490019-8
NPN 9 8 7 6 5 4 3

Publication team:
Acquisitions: Chris Coyer
Administration: Jenny Goode
Editorial Management: Sonia Clark, Simon Tanner-Tremaine,
Simon Bell, Helen King
Freelance Editorial: Collette Biggs, Mary Korndorffer
Marketing: Jane Lewis
Production: Liam Reardon
Picture Research: Image Select
Design: Earl & Thompson Marketing Ltd

Typeset in 10/12pt Minion by DP Press Ltd
Printed in China

Contents

Acknowledgements

I owe debts of gratitude to many people for the help and patience they have extended to me through the various editions of this book. I am especially grateful to Anne Vellender and Caroline Riddle. I would like to thank Chris Coyer, Sonia Clark, Mary Korndorffer, Simon Tanner-Tremaine and Brenda Curtis of Thomas Nelson for their work on this edition and for their support, and Collette Biggs for her editorial heroics. Thanks also to my friend and colleague Penri Griffiths for his kindness and understanding.

The book is dedicated to Saisha and Tara, Michael and Christopher, with love from Dad.

Preface

How to use this book

The fourth edition of *Introduction to Sociology* marks a break with previous editions. The three editions to date were organised mainly in terms of the various sociological perspectives, notably, Functionalism, Marxism and Symbolic Interactionism. These perspectives do not, of course, disappear in this edition but they are placed within a larger theoretical framework. The sociological framework now adopted here is a three-part typology of societies:

- Traditional
- Early Modern
- Late Modern (or Postmodern).

There is sound precedent for such an approach. After all, the founders of sociology were centrally concerned with issues of transition from traditional – agricultural, to modern – industrial society, or, as, Marx preferred it, to modern – capitalist society.

The division of the modern period into early and late modernity requires more explanation. Both early nineteenth century and late twentieth century Britain can be classified as 'modern societies' but the great differences between them necessitate that a distinction be made between early and late modernity. The various 'post' theories – postindustrial society theory, post-Fordism, poststructuralism and postmodernism – represent one loosely related attempt to describe the character of late modernity.

A main difference between a traditional/modern framework of analysis and the perspectives approach is that the former reasserts the strong relationship between sociology and history and also with the other social sciences. However, I do not wish to claim too much for adopting a more historically based approach to sociology, still less that it is original. What an historical framework of sociological analysis does is shift the focus away from sometimes rather abstracted theory to the context in which social change and issues emerge. Accordingly, this textbook is now somewhat less a record of the development of various theoretical perspectives and more a critical account of various analyses of key changes from the traditional to the modern and from the early modern to the late modern. In making this emphasis I am following Marx, Weber and Durkheim themselves who were primarily motivated by an interest in social developments, issues and events. Nevertheless, time has moved on – by roughly a century – and in introducing a second historical break between the modern and late modern, in addition to that between the traditional and the modern, a whole range of new questions is raised. These questions are introduced in the first two chapters and come increasingly into play in the course of this book. The extended final chapter includes a review of recent theoretical developments in the subject.

Given that this book has always had a strong historical and comparative emphasis, the above reshaping has been relatively straightforward. The intention behind this edition, then, is not so much to present (still) more theory but to explain further what has been happening in a fast changing world. I am appreciative of recent developments in 'A' level syllabuses, which I have taken as an invitation to do this.

This edition of *Introduction to Sociology* incorporates, in slimmed down form, the *New Introductory Reader in Sociology*. This is to sharpen the relationship between text and readings/stimulus materials and to increase the amount of the latter in the core text itself. In recognition of the increased importance of stimulus materials in examinations, successive editions of this textbook have used more and lengthier quotations. A useful exercise is for students themselves to think up appropriate questions to quotations – which is basically what the Chief Examiner does. This exercise can work well in groups. The additional incorporation of readings and questions at the end of chapters carries the provision of stimulus material a stage further. However, the readings are also intended to give a sense of the development of the subject by providing access to original sources and also to illustrate the relevance of sociology to the contemporary world by using some non-sociological data.

In addition to the questions which follow readings, questions also occur at intervals throughout, and at the end of chapters. I remain convinced that sociology at advanced level is as much about asking questions as about giving explanations. Sociology should not be a static monologue but a constant interrogation of a constantly changing society.

Although the following chapters can be read in any order, it may be helpful to point out that some are arranged in sequential clusters. This applies to the theory/method chapters (1, 2 and 21); the chapters covering socialisation (3 and 4); stratification (5, 6, 7 and 8); social policy and health (13 and 14); and perhaps least obviously, the 'culture' chapters (15, 16, 17 and 18).

As with previous editions, this book tends to become slightly more demanding as it progresses. Given a reasonably early grounding in the course on theory and method, this should cause no problems. The added material on tradition, modernity and late modernity in Chapters 1, 2 and 21 is intended to be user-friendly. However, it is a matter of judgement when best to phase in aspects of these matters and some will prefer to do so later rather than sooner in a course.

Mike O'Donnell
London 1997

Credits

The author and publishers are grateful to the following for kind permission to reproduce photographs:

Allsport: pages 233 (Tony Duffy), 475 left (Steve Morton), 495
Carlos Friere/Rapho/Network Photographers: page 368
Caroline Forbes: page 18
Caroline Penn/Save The Children: page 512
Frank Spooner Pictures: pages 332 (Gavin Smith), 506 top (Ollerenshaw)
Guardian Newspaper: pages 220, 223, 567
Hulton Deutsch Collection: pages 34, 137, 373
Hulton Getty Collection: page 5 left
Hutchison Library: pages 501 left (Melanie Friend), 575
Image Select: page 161
Kobal Collection: page 452
Len Cross: pages 23, 59, 90, 217, 249 left & right, 297, 399, 415
Mark Edwards/Still Pictures: pages 1 left, 501 right, 549
MSI: pages 339 right, 377, 488
News Team Birmingham: page 541 (R. Leon)
Nigel Dickinson/Still Pictures: page 317
Popperfoto: pages 3, 305 left (Henner Frankenfeld), 305 right (Gary Cameron), 339 left, 565
Rex Features: pages 167 right (Adrian Sherratt), 367 (Eric Den), 445 left (Merrin), 445 right, 470 left (Today Newspaper), 506 bottom
Simon Hoggart: page 482
Thomas Nelson Archive: pages 5 right, 470 right, 529 right
Tom Smith/Daily Express/Press Association: page 511
Tony Stone Images: pages 1 right (Lonnie Duka), 151 (Joseph Pobereskin), 167 left (Christopher Pillitz), 258 (Andrew Errington), 285 (Greg Pease), 460 (Penny Tweedie), 475 right (Wayne Eastep), 519 (Rohan), 529 left, 547 (Paul Chesley), 561 (Janet Gill), 564 (Alan Bedding), 623 (Earth Imaging)
Tracey Grannum: page 85
Yaroslava: page 315

The author and publishers wish to thank the following for permission to use copyright material:

Blackwell Publishers for permission to reprint extracts from: Krishan Kumar, *Post-industrial to Post Modern Society*, 1995; from U Beck, A Giddens and S Lash, *Reflexive Modernisation: Politics Tradition and Aesthetics in the Modern Social Order*, 1994; from E Barker, *The Making of a Moonie: Choice or Brainwashing*, 1984; Zygmunt Bauman, *Thinking Sociologically*, 1990 (three extracts); R Delmar in J Mitchell and A Oakley eds., *What is Feminism?*, 1986; Sylvia Walby, *Theorising Patriarchy*, 1990.
The Controller of Crown Copyright for permission to reproduce material from the following HMSO publications: *Regional Trends*, 1995; *Britain: A Handbook*, published annually; *Social Trends*, 1991, 1994, 1995, 1996; *Home Office Research Findings* number 24, 1995.
George Braziller Inc. for permission to reproduce extracts from C Wright Mills, *Images of Man*, 1960.
HarperCollins Publishers for permission to reproduce material from A Bryman, *Quantity and Quality in Social Research*, © A Bryman 1988; from P Cooke, 'Locality, Economic Restructuring and World Development', in P Cooke ed., *The Changing Face of Urban Britons: Localities*, 1989.
Houghton Mifflin Company for extracts from Rose, Arnold M ed., *Human Behaviour and Social Processes*, Copyright © 1962 by Houghton Mifflin Company, excerpted with permission.
JAI Press for permission to reproduce material from Walter W Powell, *Research in Organisational Behaviour*, 1990.

Macmillan for permission to reprint an extract from D Lockwood, 'Sources of Variation in Working Class Images of Society', reprinted in Anthony Giddens and David Held eds., *Classes Power and Conflict: Classical and Contemporary Debates*, 1982; and for permission to reprint an extract from P Thompson, *The Nature of Work: An Introduction to Debates on the Labour Process*, 1989.
Open University Press for permission to reproduce material from M Banks et al., *Careers and Identities*, 1992; from A McGrew, 'A Global Society', in S Hall et al. eds., *Modernity and its Futures*, 1992; from I Bates and G Riseborough, *Youth and Inequality*, 1993; from R Scase, *Class*, 1992; from E Martin, *The Woman in the Body*, 1987; from M Mac an Ghaill, *The Making of Men: Masculinities, Sexualities and Schooling*, 1994; from D103 SS Workbook 5; *Running The Country*, D212, Unit 1-7.
Oxford University Press for permission to reproduce an extract from C Wright Mills, *The Power Elite*, 1956.
Oxford University Press Inc. for extracts from *The Sociological Imagination* by C Wright Mills, Copyright © 1959 by C Wright Mills, used by permission of Oxford University Press Inc.; for extracts from *Max Weber: Essays in Sociology* by Max Weber, Copyright © 1946 by Max Weber, used by permission of Oxford University Press Inc.
Polity Press for permission to reproduce material from A Giddens, *Modernity and Self-identity: Self and Society in the Late Modern Age*, 1991; from F R Elliot, 'Private Arena or Adjunct to the State', in *Social and Cultural Forms of Modernity*, 1992; from W Connell, *Gender and Power*, 1987, and two extracts from W Connell, *Masculinities*, 1995.
Routledge for permission to reproduce material from Jan Pahl ed., *Private Violence and Public Policy*, 1985; from S Bowles and H Gintis, *Schooling in Capitalist America*, 1976; from R Bowe and S Ball with A Gold, *Reforming Education and Changing Schools: Case Studies in Policy Sociology*, 1992; from J Obelkevich and P Catterall eds., *Understanding Post-War British Society*, 1994; from D Strinati, 'What is Postmodernism?', in *An Introduction to Theories of Popular Culture*, 1995; from D Morley and K Robins, *Spaces of Identity*, 1995; from J Curran, 'Rethinking the media as public sphere', in P Dahlgren and C Sparks eds., *Communication and Citizenship*, 1991; for extracts from G Davie, 'Religion in Post-War Britain', in *Understanding Post-War British Society*, 1994.
Sage Publications Ltd for permission to reprint extracts from J Young, 'The Future of Criminology: The Need for Radical Realism', in R Matthews and J Young eds., *Confronting Crime*, Copyright © R Matthews and J Young, 1986; for permission to reprint extracts from J Clarke, A Cochrane and E McLaughlin, *Managing Social Policy*, © J Clarke, A Cochrane and E McLaughlin, 1994.
The Free Press for permission to reproduce material from Emile Durkheim, *The Rules of Sociological Method*, 1964.
Social Studies Review for permission to reproduce a graphic from the Volume 3, Issue 1, September 1987.
The Sociological Review for permission to reprint an extract from F Devine, 'Social Identities, Class Identity and Political Perspectives', 1992.
The Times, *Financial Times*, *Daily Telegraph*, *Guardian*, *Observer* and *Independent* for permission to reproduce illustrations and extracts from articles.
UCL Press for permission to reproduce an extract from Bob Coles, *Youth and Social Policy, Youth Citizenship and Young Careers*, 1995.
Zed Books for permission to reproduce an extract from R Cohen, *Contested Domains: Debates in International Labour Studies*, 1991.

Every effort has been made to trace all the copyright holders, but if any have been inadvertently overlooked the publishers will be pleased to make the necessary arrangements at the first opportunity.

1

What is Sociology? Concepts and Theory

Sociology in a changing world

Aims of this chapter

1 To introduce the subject of sociology and some basic sociological concepts.

2 To examine the relationship between sociology and the social context in which it was established.

3 To introduce the main structural and interpretive sociological perspectives and some questions they seek to address.

4 To discuss some of the main influences on contemporary sociology.

5 To introduce the concepts of tradition, modernity and postmodernity and contemporary debates about them.

What is sociology?

Sociology is the systematic study of societies. Societies may vary in size from a small tribe of Amazonian Indians to the whole of Western society. Today, we even speak of 'global society'. A society consists of individuals belonging to groups which may vary in size, from, for instance, the family to the total population of a given area. Sociology studies interaction between the self (or individual) and groups, and interaction between groups. The self may both affect certain groups (and so society) and be affected by these groups. Social interaction between the self and others (or, at least, another) begins at birth, and usually continues until death. Or to put it more poetically, 'from the rocking of the cradle to the rolling of the hearse', individuals are part of society.

Perhaps the main contribution of sociology is that it can help people to better understand their own lives. It does so by explaining the relationships between personal experience and 'external' events, between self and society. Thus, the loss of a job or the closure of a local school may be seen by a given individual as a purely personal problem or even a tragedy, with perhaps little thought being given to the underlying causes of such occurrences. Sociology can help to explain such experiences by exploring who is responsible for it – perhaps politicians, planners, investors or trade unionists – and, perhaps, whether or not what has happened is part of a wider social trend in, say, unemployment or school closures. Often, through making sense of society we can begin to make more sense of our own lives.

Charles Wright Mills (1916-62) described the links between self and society in terms of 'personal troubles' – such as losing one's job or being wounded in combat – and 'public issues' – such as rising unemployment or war:

> *Perhaps the most fruitful distinction with which the sociological imagination works is between 'the personal troubles of milieux' and 'the public issues of social structure'. This distinction is an essential tool of the sociological imagination and a feature of all classic work in social science.*
>
> *(Mills, 1959:8)*

Mills argued that it requires imagination to see that the immediate 'milieu' or social context of one's own life is often (perhaps always) linked to much wider developments. He urged that sociologists try to connect biography – personal life history – with social change and structure – history and sociology. He claimed that the 'classic' sociologists such as Marx, Durkheim and Weber – have always done this (see pp. 10-12). It remains true that a better understanding of the 'personal/public' axis is, as Mills put it, the purpose of 'the sociological imagination'. (Reading 1)

Basic sociological concepts

Self and society

This section further examines the relationship between self and society introduced above. It briefly describes how the self is socialised into a given culture or way of life and then examines the relationship between culture and social structure. Explanations of these key concepts are kept to a minimum here, as they are all discussed in greater detail later.

Self, socialisation and culture

Self

Manford Kuhn defines the concept of self as 'denoting the core of the personality system ... organised around its awareness of itself and its conscious and unconscious orientation toward its most vital interests and values, involving identity, status, commitment, and desire' (in J Gould and W Kolb, eds, 1964: 628-9). Kuhn suggests that the term 'ego' is interchangeable with that of self within sociology. The important aspects to note from this definition is that the self is conscious of itself and has a sense of its own identity. In so far as personalities and identities are unique, we can speak of 'individuality'.

In considering the nature of the self, it is necessary to introduce a still more fundamental social scientific issue – the extent to which human beings are formed by biological inheritance, i.e. genetically, or through socialisation, i.e. culturally; the celebrated 'nature-nurture debate'. Another way of putting this is the difference between instinct and learned behaviour, the former being inherited, the latter being acquired through socialisation. In general, sociologists take a minimal view of what is instinctive behaviour (broader terms are 'drivers' or 'needs'). Thus, most would accept that there are innate (inborn) needs of food, shelter and sex. Beyond this, sociologists prefer to explore the possibility that behaviour is shaped by social experience rather than that it is simply a biological 'given'. However, although the orientation of sociology is towards social explanation, there is no contradiction between social and biological explanations of behaviour. It is a matter for empirical research by biologists, sociologists, social biologists and by other relevant subject specialists to establish explanations of human behaviour.

One approach to studying the role of society in forming human behaviour is to examine the development of individuals who were either wholly or largely excluded from social interaction for a period of their lives. Such cases include those who apparently spent much of their childhood isolated from others 'in the wild' and those who were cut off from others through confinement at a similarly early age. Examples of the former are the 'Wild boy of Aveyron', and two girls, the 'Wolf children of Bengal'. A more recent case is that of a 14-year-old boy found by Bedouins in the Syrian desert apparently long since abandoned by his mother. The boy had exceptional speed (50 miles per hour!), and generally behaved like the gazelles he was found living with. His hands and feet had to

Figure 1.1 A 'lost boy' found in the Syrian desert. Can there be culture without socialisation?

be tied to prevent him escaping (Figure 1.1). A case of the latter is the girl, Genie, who was locked in her room between the ages of one-and-a-half and thirteen.

The effects of 'growing up' in such unsocial conditions in these and similar cases seem consistent. Immediately on emerging into society, the children were typically described by observers as 'primitive' and 'hardly human'. Despite efforts to resocialise them, none of the children developed social and communication skills beyond a rudimentary level. Above all, their limited ability to learn language prevented them from functioning fully in adult society.

The above examples of unsocialised childhood do not have the status of controlled scientific experiments (see pp. 24-6). However, collectively they do suggest that human development, including the acquisition of basic social and communication skills, requires substantial contact with others. It is only in a social context that the self can develop. Self and society are, therefore, complementary concepts rather than in opposition as they are sometimes presented. You cannot have individuals without society or society without individuals.

Socialisation

Socialisation is the process by which human behaviour is shaped through experience in social situations. Through socialisation the individual learns the values, norms (formal and informal 'rules'), and beliefs of a given society.

The American sociologist Charles Cooley (1864-1929) distinguished two types of socialisation: primary and secondary. These two forms of socialisation are defined partly in terms of the particular groups or 'agencies' in which they occur. Primary groups are small, involve face-to-face relationships and allow the individual to express the whole self, both feelings and intellect. The family, peer groups of close friends and closely-knit groups of neighbours are primary groups. Within these groups the individual learns, by personal experience, the primary values such as love, loyalty, justice, and sharing. Freud emphasised that the first few years of a person's life – those usually spent amongst primary groups – are the most important in forming the framework of his or her character. Secondary groups are larger, more impersonal, more formally organised, and exist for specific purposes. Secondary socialisation involves learning how to organise and conduct oneself in formal contexts and how to behave towards people who have different degrees of status and authority. The school is an important example of an agency of secondary socialisation, but all formal organisations influence their members to some degree and, to that extent, can be included within this category. Trade unions and professional associations are relevant examples: membership is granted to the individual on the assumption that s/he will conform to the beliefs, aims and regulations of the organisation. In allowing the organisation to affect her or his behaviour in this way, the individual necessarily accepts a socialising influence on her or his conduct. In addition to primary and secondary groups, the mass media – the press, radio, television, the cinema, records, tapes and various other forms of communication which comprise them – play a socialising role whose effects we will consider in more detail later.

The distinction between primary and secondary socialisation parallels that between informal and formal socialisation. Informal socialisation usually takes place as a part of everyday activity: it affects us unconsciously and must be distinguished from the formal acquisition of specific skills such as reading and writing. In primary socialisation, certain values and customs will be formally taught to a child (formal socialisation) but much else will be informally 'picked up' by imitating parents, siblings, and other children.

Culture

Culture is the way of life of a particular society: it refers to all aspects of human behaviour that are learnt rather than genetically transmitted. It includes the values, norms and beliefs of a particular society as well as the way these are expressed through actions, words and symbols. Socialisation is the means through which cultural transmission occurs and, as we have seen, it is a continuous process. Cultures vary, although cultural similarities also occur to a greater or lesser extent. Generally, the greatest cultural differences occur between non-industrial and non-literate societies such as the African pygmies and industrial (or perhaps now, postindustrial) and literate societies such as those of Western Europe. When two very different cultures come into significant contact, one or both are invariably changed. Where change is swift or great, it can be a disruptive and difficult process. This was (and still is) true of the impact of Western, capitalist, Christian culture on much of the rest of the world.

Values, norms, status and role

Values

Values are general but fundamental standards of a given society which have a wide influence on social conduct and organisation. Thus, the value of individualism has had greater influence in capitalist societies and that of collectivism (commitment to the community) more influence in communist societies. The values of hard work and achievement are often associated with capitalist societies, and Margaret Thatcher's attempt to foster an 'enterprise culture' may be considered as an effort to reinforce this value orientation. It is not easy to clarify the fundamental values of a given society because of their sheer breadth. To do so is to define the basic nature of a particular culture. In attempting such a definition, it is worth considering whether certain cultural values clash with or even contradict each other – such as achievement and community or individualism and equality.

Norms

Norms are precepts or guidelines to behaviour. They may be formal – such as the written rules of an organisation – or highly informal such as what kind of dress it is more or less acceptable to wear on a very hot day. As with values, norms vary between

cultures but, equally, they can change within a culture. You can probably think of a dozen ways in which norms in contemporary Britain differ from those of a more traditional society.

Status and role

Values provide a general guide, and norms a rather more specific guide, to behaviour. The concepts of status and role describe aspects of behaviour itself. A status is a particular position in society. Thus, there are a range of statuses within the family, such as mother and daughter, and within the occupational system, such as doctor or shop-assistant. A role is the behaviour expected of a person occupying a given status or social position and the rights associated with it. Thus, doctors play a role in relation to health and disease and shop-assistants in relation to selling goods. Roles are governed by certain norms or expectations (we 'know' how doctors are supposed to behave) but are also, to some extent, interpreted by the individuals playing them (no two doctors behave in exactly the same way). Robert Merton has suggested that where a status involves more than one social relationship, the term role-set be used rather than role. Thus, the role-set of a shop-assistant includes relationships with a manager, customers and perhaps other shop-assistants. Of course, roles are not played by robots but by humans. How a person plays a role will reflect his or her individuality.

Values, norms, statuses and roles can be thought of within the broader concepts of culture and socialisation. Their specific nature or 'content' is created within given cultures and they vary between cultures. Socialisation is the means by which specific values, norms, statuses and roles are learnt.

Negotiated order

According to the Penguin Dictionary of Sociology:

> *Negotiated order theory regards social phenomena, particularly organisational arrangements, as emerging from the ongoing process of interaction between people. The interaction process involves constant negotiations and renegotiation …* (280)

Thus, the social order of a classroom is partly the outcome of the negotiation between the pupils and teacher (negotiated orders vary between classes).

The concepts of negotiation and negotiated order are 'liberating' in the respect that they imply that they are not imposed from 'outside' but are created by individuals interacting with each other.

Sociological concepts and theories

This chapter has so far examined a number of key sociological concepts: self, society, socialisation, culture, values, norms, status and role. Other key sociological concepts examined in this book are structure, interaction, power and authority, ideology, community and alienation. These key concepts, or to adopt Robert Nisbet's phrase, 'unit ideas', are too limited to provide an adequate definition of sociology but they do clearly indicate its central concerns. This is even more the case when concepts are related in clusters such as 'self, socialisation and culture' and 'status and role'.

Like individual building bricks, sociological concepts are of limited usefulness in isolation. It is only when concepts are used in creating theories that they play a part in explaining as well as describing social processes. Thus, there are several theories of alienation and a variety of theories focusing on the concept of community. In the next section, we discuss some of the major theoretical issues of sociology.

The founding of sociology: sociological theory

Sociology is an attempt to understand society: how it operates and the experiences and purposes of its members. One way of approaching sociology is to appreciate some of the key questions it raises. The questions and problems raised by the founders of sociology remain in essence those asked by sociologists and, indeed, other interested people today. Here I first briefly introduce the thoughts of the founders of sociology in order to give an idea of the framework and scope of the discipline. We then look at some key sociological questions. This prepares the way for consideration of the main sociological approaches or perspectives which can be seen as attempts to answer the fundamental questions of sociology. The chapter concludes with an examination of some of the main contemporary trends in sociology.

The founding of modern sociology: Marx, Durkheim and Weber

Marx (1818-1883), Durkheim (1858-1917), and Weber (1864-1920) have had a major and lasting impact on the discipline of sociology. They were among the first to look at society in what we have come to think of as a specifically sociological way.

Although contemporary sociologists ask additional and sometimes different questions to those of Marx, Weber and Durkheim, the continuing relevance of their work reflects two things. First, the general questions they asked are similar to some which sociologists ask today. Second, the frameworks of social analysis and explanation or sociological perspectives they worked out have been developed and modified rather than wholly replaced. However, in the concluding section of Chapter 2 we will consider a range of more recently developed concepts which arguably have particular relevance to the second half of the twentieth century and beyond, sometimes referred to as late modernity.

The nineteenth century context

The nineteenth century was a period of rapid change as great as today's. Industrial and political revolutions, sometimes known as the 'dual revolutions', tore apart the fabric of society. The agricultural revolution forced peasants off the land, and the industrial revolution provided jobs for them in the cities. Often the new industrial workers – and at first these included women and children – lived and worked in conditions of squalid exploitation. By contrast, the manufacturing, commercial and financial middle class prospered in an industrial boom. The traditional landed aristocracy also generally thrived, party because of its great hereditary wealth and power, and partly because many of its members invested in industrial expansion.

Figure 1.2 Karl Marx (1818-1883) and Max Weber (1864-1920): who 'won' their 'debate' about social change and social class?

Politically the new middle class struggled successfully to share power with the aristocracy. In Britain, it managed to acquire the vote and other political rights without revolution, but France and other European countries experienced almost a century of political turmoil. As the century progressed, the claims of the working class for political rights and social justice were more and more strongly asserted. In 1848 Europe was swept by revolution. In this, the working class and its supporters played a prominent part. Marx himself participated in an unsuccessful uprising in Germany in that year.

Marx, Durkheim and Weber were interested in, and wanted to understand, the major changes that were occurring in Europe during their own time. Even though they were of different nationalities, Marx and Weber being German and Durkheim being French, the scale and scope of change was such that they were confronted by much the same problems. Our interest arises from the fact that our own period reflects both continuity with and contrast to theirs, and society today can be partly explained by past events and developments. Ours is a society in which, at last, the working class and women have political rights, but in which class, gender and other conflict is by no means dead. The nineteenth century was a battleground between the old regime and the new, the traditional and the modern. Along with the study of class relations, the contrast and conflict between the traditional and the modern remains an axial consideration of sociology. Britain is still cloaked in tradition: witness the continuation of the monarchy and the House of Lords. Further, the conflict between traditional, rural society and modern, industrial society has been partly 'exported' from Europe to the wider world, in which the developing countries are the new battleground. Marx, Durkheim and Weber's writings are of relevance to all these matters. It may be that Western society has more recently moved beyond the traditional and modern into a 'third age' – so called 'postmodernity' or 'late modernity'. If so, it is certain that postmodernity was born in the womb of modernity and that to understand it, we must first understand modernity.

The founders of sociology wanted to do more than just tell the tale of their times and perhaps offer a few unsystematic interpretations of events. They went deeper than that in their search for explanations, and in doing so created the foundation of a new discipline, sociology. Separately, they attempted to develop ways of examining society and social change which would account not only for how their own societies functioned and changed but which would explain the nature and functioning of society itself. They believed that a scientific approach would assist them greatly in this enterprise. Indeed, perhaps they put too much faith in science, and many sociologists have since argued that, as well as being affected by society, people also help to create it – perhaps to a greater extent than Marx and Durkheim, though possibly not Weber, allowed. In their faith in science, the founders of sociology reflected the spirit of their period. Charles Darwin's exciting new scientific theory of evolution seemed to offer a biological explanation of the origin of humanity, and Marx, Weber and Durkheim sought to explain social life in similarly scientific terms. They were aware, however, that human consciousness and creativity raise issues that do not occur in the non-human sciences and we return to these later. Marx and Durkheim in particular built up distinctive perspectives or general models of how society works. Since their deaths, other perspectives have been developed within sociology, some of which address themselves more specifically to the problems of the individual in modern society. These are introduced later in this chapter and the next.

The next section will tend to emphasise the differences rather than the similarities between the perspectives of Marx, Weber and Durkheim. However, we attempt to convey the common central concerns of sociology by examining their perspectives in the form of answers to a number of fundamental sociological questions. Sociology is better understood as a series of questions on the nature of society with no set answers, than as a set of agreed findings (although such findings do exist). Mills suggests that the questions asked by the founders of sociology as much as the models they produced are what established a classic tradition of sociological enquiry. (Reading 2)

Sociological theory: structural and interpretive perspectives

At this stage, all that we mean by sociological theory is the body of ideas, tested and untested, making up sociological thought.

We can best understand the disagreements among contemporary sociologists, many of which have their roots in the thought of Durkheim, Marx and Weber, by examining some basic questions of sociological theory to which, in one way or another, all three gave answers. It would not be possible to construct an adequate sociological perspective without answering the following questions, although other major questions could also be asked:

1 How is society constructed?
2 How does society 'operate' or function?
3 Why are some groups in society more powerful than others?
4 What causes social change?
5 Is society normally in orderly balance or in conflict?
6 What is the relationship of the individual to society?
7 What is the primary purpose of sociological study?

The answers given to these questions by Durkheim, Marx and Weber helped to produce three distinct traditions of sociological thought or perspectives: functionalism which owes much to Durkheim, Marxism (Marx), and social action theory (Weber). We will examine separately these three traditions and the answers they give to the above questions of theory. All three of these sociological perspectives are structural in nature. Structural sociology is primarily concerned with how society affects individual and group behaviour, rather than with how individuals and groups create society. Thus, the sort of issue a structural sociologist would be interested in is how the class and family background of an individual (the individual's social-structural position) affect his or her chances of doing well at school and getting a good job. Functionalism is referred to as consensus structuralism because it emphasises the central role that agreement (consensus) between people on moral values has in maintaining social order. Marxism and social action theory, on the other hand, stress conflict in society rather than consensus. It is a further crucially important feature of the structuralist theories that they tend to seek scientific or positivist explanations of social behaviour.

Interpretive sociology, in contrast to structuralism, is primarily concerned with how individuals and groups create, find meaning in, and experience society, rather than in how society affects them. Examples of the kind of matters that have interested interpretive sociologists are what it 'feels like' to be labelled a 'criminal' or 'mad', or simply 'not very bright' at school work. Interpretive sociology is, in part, a reaction against the scientific or positivist approach associated with the structural perspectives. Interpretive sociology is further explained later in this chapter (see pp. 9-11). Immediately, the structural sociologies of functionalism, Marxism and social action theory are described by reference to the seven key questions stated above. It can be seen that the answers given to the questions by the various perspectives differ, sometimes to the point of contradiction. It needs to be stressed that the following section on functionalism reflects the work of later functionalists, besides Durkheim, particularly that of Talcott Parsons (1902-1979).

Structural perspectives

Functionalism (consensus structuralism): Durkheim

1 How is society constructed?

Society or the social system is constructed of various institutions, the most basic of which is the family. A social institution is a group of people organised for a specific purpose (or purposes) – the nuclear family, for example, is organised in order to produce and rear children. As societies develop, the number and complexity of social institutions increases. This process is referred to as differentiation. The civil service and industrial corporations are examples of complex, modern institutions. They developed, respectively, from the King's adviser and small-scale cottage industries.

Institutions are grouped together into four sub-systems:

- Economic (factories, offices)
- Political (political parties)
- Kinship (families)
- Cultural and community organisations (schools, churches)

2 How does society 'operate' or function?

Functionalists consider that society 'operates' in a way comparable to the functioning of a biological organism. This comparison is referred to as the organic analogy (or organismic analogy). So social institutions function in combination with one another and for the benefit of society as a whole, just as the various parts of the human body function in relation to one another and to the whole body. For example, schools function in relation to work because they prepare people for work. And, like the human body, society is more than the sum of its individual parts.

Although the structure and functioning of society can be separated for the purpose of theoretical consideration, in reality they are inseparable. Obviously, a society or organisation has to exist (have structure) before it can do anything (function).

3 Why are some groups in society more powerful than others?

The unequal possession of power in society has tended to interest Marxists and social action theorists more than functionalists. The latter tend to assume that it is practically necessary that some individuals and groups be more powerful than others, because only a limited number can take important decisions. Thus, they argue that there must be leaders in organisations and in society, otherwise there would be chaos.

4 What causes social change?

According to functionalists, social change occurs when it is functionally necessary for it to do so. For example, in modern societies educational systems tend to expand because such societies require a more literate and numerate population than less 'advanced' societies.

Change may occur through adaptation or integration. Adaptation occurs when an existing institution readjusts to meet new needs – as in the example given in the last paragraph. Integration occurs when a society adopts a new element and makes it part of itself. Thus, a society may successfully integrate (or fail to integrate) a group of immigrants. Functionalists tend to think of change as evolutionary (gradual), not revolutionary.

5 Is society normally in orderly balance or in conflict?

Functionalists consider that order and equilibrium (balance) are normal to society. Disequilibrium (civil war, for example) is an abnormal social state. They compare disequilibrium in society to sickness in a living organism.

The basis of social equilibrium is the existence of moral consensus. Moral consensus means that everybody, or nearly everybody in a society shares the same values. Thus, a high level of consumption of goods might be a value in American society, but not in many economically and technologically more 'primitive' societies. As we shall see in a later chapter, functionalists stress the importance of the effective teaching of social values in maintaining order and conformity. The role of parents and teachers in passing on values to the younger generation is stressed.

6 What is the relationship of the individual to society?

Functionalists regard the individual as formed by society through the influence of such institutions as the family, school and workplace. They leave little room for the view that the individual can significantly control her or his own life, let alone change society. Durkheim stated that, for him, the individual is the point of arrival, not of departure. In other words, in his view sociology is not about the individual. As we shall see, not all sociologists agree with this.

7 What is the primary purpose of sociological study?

The primary purpose of sociology is to analyse and explain the normal (and abnormal) functioning of society. This involves studying the relationship of the different parts of society to one another, and of the parts to the whole. Thus, the relationship between education and work is studied, but so too is the (necessary) contribution of both to the functioning of the social system as a whole. Durkheim insisted that sociologists should discover and explain the relationship between social facts, just as natural scientists do with physical facts.

Marxism (conflict structuralism 1)

1 How is society constructed?

According to Marx, society is constructed from classes. In all societies except the most simple, there are two major social classes. It is people's relationship to the means of production that determines which class they are in. The most powerful class is that which owns the means of production (land, factories) and the least powerful is that which has to sell its labour in order to make a living. In capitalist society (a society based on a private enterprise economy), the capitalist class or bourgeoisie as Marx called it, is the ruling class and the working class or proletariat, the subordinate class. In other words, in his view, business controls labour.

2 How does society 'operate' or function?

In Marx's view, society operates mainly through class conflict. Each class normally pursues its own interest, and this brings it into conflict with other classes. In particular, he argued that in capitalist society the bourgeoisie and proletariat are fundamentally opposed. This point is developed and explained later.

3 Why are some groups in society more powerful than others?

For Marx, class is the basis of power. Some classes are more powerful than others because they own more property and wealth, and this gives them the means to defend and keep what they hold. Unlike functionalists, Marx did not consider that this state of affairs is inevitable and necessary. He believed that socialism could achieve a more equal sharing of power, property and wealth.

4 What causes social change?

Social change occurs as a result of class conflict. Class conflict is the dynamo of history. In the later middle ages, there was conflict between the landed aristocracy and the rising bourgeoisie, and in capitalist society the major conflict is between the bourgeoisie and the proletariat. The victory of a new class introduces a new historical period, thus the rise of the bourgeoisie introduced the capitalist epoch. Such was the dynamic search of capitalists for resources and markets that the capitalist system became worldwide. (Reading 3)

5 Is society normally in orderly balance or in conflict?

Society is in a state of fundamental conflict between the classes. Marx recognised, however, that periods of social order and equilibrium can occur, in which class conflict is temporarily submerged. He argued that such periods benefit the rich and powerful more than others.

6 What is the relationship of the individual to society?

There are two major schools of thought amongst Marxists about the relationship of the individual to society, and these reflect an ambiguity in Marx's work itself. One tradition of Marxist thought tends to see the individual as powerless to affect either her or his own life or that of others. Those who hold this view regard class conflict and socialist revolution as inevitable regardless of what any single individual may do. Some Marxists, however, see a much greater role for the individual in society even though they still see the prime source of individual identity as coming from class membership (see pp. 146-7).

7 What is the primary purpose of sociological study?

The purpose of sociology is to describe, analyse and explain class conflict. Marxists also want to change the world in a Marxist direction. However, in the late 1980s and early 1990s, the 'Marxist' societies of Eastern Europe experienced crisis and change (see p. 13). The main practical alternative model to capitalism began to fragment. Even so, this does not necessarily mean that Marxist sociological analysis of capitalism is wholly wrong.

Social action theory (conflict structuralism 2): Weber

1 How is society constructed?

Society is created through social interaction. Social interaction is the behaviour of people consciously relating to one another. In the process of interaction, people form institutions. Although people create institutions such as schools, factories and churches, these institutions in turn influence people. This is partly because pressure exists to observe the rules and procedures of institutions.

Weber felt that Marx overemphasised the importance of class groupings. He recognised that classes are important but considered political parties and status groups (social and friendship groups) to be further powerful and important forces in society, not necessarily dependent on class (as Marx contended they essentially were). This major point of difference between Marx and Weber is explained fully in Chapter 5. Weber also stressed the power of large organisations or bureaucracies over the life of the individual.

2 How does society 'operate' or function?

Again, Weber's answer to this question shows his keen awareness of both the individual's influence on society and of society's influence on the individual. On the one hand, he stresses that the ideas and feelings people have do sometimes inspire action and affect history. For example, he argued that certain powerful and dynamic figures, or charismatic leaders as he called them, such as Christ and Napoleon, really can change the course of events. On the other hand, he realised that most people's lives are formed and limited by the society they live in, and particularly by the immediate institutions they come in contact with, such as schools and places of work. He was personally concerned that large-scale institutions of modern societies (factories or government bureaucracies, for example) would limit the scope of individual freedom and creativity. It seems to worry Weber more than it does the strict functionalists that many people may be only 'small cogs in large machines' as far as their work is concerned.

3 Why are some groups in society more powerful than others?

Power is one of Weber's central concepts. He combines elements of consensus and conflict sociology in his treatment of this matter. He agreed with the functionalists that for society to function efficiently some people have to have more power than others. He pointed out that in modern bureaucratic organisations (the civil service, for example) there are always more powerful people at the top, and less powerful people at the bottom; that is, bureaucracies are organised hierarchically. But Weber also accepted, with Marx, that those groups which do gain a powerful position in society tend to use it primarily in their own interest. Thus, in medieval society the king and nobility used power for their own ends, even though they may also have sometimes used it for the general good as well.

4 What causes social change?

Weber considered that social change can occur for many reasons, or, more technically, according to his analysis, social change is multifactoral. Ideas, new inventions, war, the rise and fall of power groups, influential individuals and other factors all contribute to, and are part of, historical change. In insisting on the possible variety of causes of change, Weber wished to distinguish his position from that of Marx, whom he thought overemphasised class conflict as an explanation for change.

5 Is society normally in orderly balance or in conflict?

This issue of equilibrium and conflict in society is posed to contrast functionalism and Marxism, and is of less central concern to social action theorists. Weber considered that society is not normally either in balance or in conflict – the state of society varies from case to case. A society may be untroubled for centuries and then be plunged into decades of turmoil. Weber preferred to study specific cases rather than make sweeping generalisations about what is 'normal'.

6 What is the relationship of the individual to society?

The relationship of the individual to society is of central importance in social action theory. Although Weber fully realised that individuals are affected by social institutions such as the family, school, the workplace and the mass media, he did not consider analysis of the operation and effect of these influences to be the only or primary purpose of sociology. It is more important, in his view, to understand the meanings that individuals experience in their own social lives than simply to analyse what 'causes' or 'influences' them to act as they do. Although Weber appreciated that individual action is uniquely experienced by the social actor, he still felt able to generalise about social action, because in practice there are widely-shared patterns of social behaviour. For instance, people may act rationally, emotionally or idealistically, and it is possible to categorise and generalise their actions accordingly. Despite Weber's emphasis on interpreting the quality and potential variety of individual experience and meaning, he was committed to scientific sociology. Nevertheless, although we have termed him a

conflict structuralist in this section, he was also a founding father of interpretive sociology.

The interpretive approach has become popular, and has developed in a number of forms in the twentieth century.

7 What is the primary purpose of sociological study?

The purpose of sociology is to understand and explain the meaning of social action and interaction.

Interpretive perspectives

There have been other attempts besides Weber's to 'build in' individual meaning and intention into sociological theory. These include symbolic interactionism, ethno-methodology and the basically philosophical perspective of phenomenology. The most influential and easiest to understand of these is symbolic interactionism, or simply interactionism. This is dealt with first and at some length. Ethnomethodology is only briefly dealt with in this chapter and phenomenology is not presented until Chapter 21.

Interactionism

The structural (or systems) theories so far examined tend to approach the relationship of self and society from the point of view of the influence of society on the self. Interactionists tend to work from the self 'outwards', stressing that people create society. The perspective is sometimes referred to as symbolic interactionism because of its emphasis on the importance of the symbolic means of communication, including language, dress and gesture. Interactionists fully accept that society does constrain and form individuals, although they consider that there is invariably opportunity for some 'creative' action – to use a favourite word of W I Thomas, an early interactionist. Interactionism developed mainly at the University of Chicago during the inter-war years. The social psychologist George Mead (1880-1949) was probably the most influential figure among interactionists.

Mead describes two general stages in the development of the self: the play and game stages. Prior to these stages the child's relationship to others is one of imitation without conscious awareness of the meaning of actions.

At the play stage, the child begins to try out certain familiar roles such as parent, teacher or doctor. The child's 'let's pretend to be …' is a powerful in-built learning device. It is, however, limited. At this stage, the child does not see beyond individual roles to a more generalised view of social situations. S/he only attempts to perform the roles of certain 'significant others' seen at first hand or perhaps through the media. It is as if in the early stages of learning a play, the child 'gets to know' some leading parts but has little sense of the 'plot' as a whole.

The game stage involves virtually a double progression. Firstly, in Mead's words, 'the child must have the attitude of all the others involved in that game' or situation. Perhaps children play team games so badly because they have not fully developed an awareness of the various roles in the team or a competent way of fitting in with other roles. Gradually, the child becomes more socially aware, not only at games, of course, but in other group situations such as meals and outings. However, the full development of self depends not only on the awareness of all other roles in a situation but on the further ability to realise that the group, community or society as a whole 'exercises control over the conduct of its individual members'. In this sense, Mead refers to the group as a whole as the 'generalised other'. Only in so far as the child learns to take the attitude of the other does s/he become a full member of society. Essentially, Mead is saying the same thing as Parsons. Both recognise the need for the child to learn 'the rules of the game' or of society. Crucially, Mead gives more emphasis to the capacity of the individual to 'play the game' actively and creatively. This is apparent in the aspect of his thought to which we now turn and which complements the above.

Mead divided the self into the 'I' and the 'me'. The 'I' is the active part of the self whereas the 'me' is passive, that is, the 'me' is the part that others (significant and generalised) act upon (see figure below). Charles Cooley, a colleague of Mead's, used the term 'looking-glass self' to describe how we see an image or get an impression of ourselves through the responses of others. As the individual becomes aware of the 'me', he or she is also able to act upon him or herself, by controlling it. As Mead put it, the individual becomes an object to him or herself. Human consciousness extends to other things and people as well as oneself. Mead used the term 'making indications' to describe the operation of consciousness. Making indications is central in the specifically human process of constructing meanings and actions. (Reading 4)

Figure 1.3 Symbolic interactionist model of socialisation (and social experience generally)

More than Cooley, Mead wanted to stress that the 'I' can control or direct the self not only to conform but to act independently. As he put it: 'The 'I' gives the sense of freedom, of initiative'. Mead noted that the dynamic 'I' often dominates over the conformist 'me' in highly creative people such as artists and brilliant sportsmen but that we all have moments of originality (or, at least, moments that feel original). In providing a framework of analysis in which the social actor could indeed be conceived of as acting, often unpredictably and with uncertain consequences, Mead made an outstanding contribution to social science.

Mead's awareness of both the constraints on (controls and limits) and creativity of social interaction is apparent in his analysis of language – a central feature of symbolic interactionism. Language is the major vehicle of social communication. Its purpose is to express meaning. Of necessity, the young child is, at first, only the object of linguistic communication, but gradually begins to use language for her or his own purposes. Mead

strenuously rejects the notion that language is simply a matter of imitation (except, he concedes, in the parrot). Nearly all the meanings that an individual could want to express are available in the stock of words of most languages, but even so, scientists and poets operating at the limits of available meaning and language do create new words and linguistic forms. This is what language is for: to provide meaningful symbolism. When necessary, new verbal symbols are created. Because the main concern of symbolic interactionists is with meaningful communication, they have a primary interest in language. Interactionists frequently stress that (by means of language) people negotiate the various social roles they are expected to play. This means that they bargain with others, often those in authority, about how exactly they will perform them. This suggests the further concept of negotiated order. For example, certain students or workers may be able to 'get away with' doing less work than others because, over time, they have managed to establish or 'negotiate' a lower level of performance with whoever is in charge. Others may also try to do so but for some reason fail. Order exists but it reflects the complexities and negotiations of interaction. Similarly, interactionists note that different individuals interpret the same role in different ways. Roles are seen as less binding than functionalists suggest. Thus, as a glance around your classroom or lecture hall will verify, the role of student can be interpreted in many different and contrasting ways.

Before concluding this section, we need to be clear about how interactionists approach the analysis of social institutions. For them, an institution is not a 'thing' separate from the people that make up its structure, but is considered as the product of interaction; this is true of the family, the school, the peer group. Indeed, any institution can be viewed as the product of the interaction of the people of whom it is composed. As we shall see when we examine specific topics, such as education and work, this perspective is extremely fruitful.

The nature of modern symbolic interactionist theory is well illustrated by the metaphors interactionists use to describe social life. Erving Goffman has compared social interaction with the dramatic action of a play, and Eric Berne, the founder of transactional psychoanalysis, entitled one of his books *Games People Play*. For Goffman, the main difference between acting in a play and 'acting' in life is that there is more scope for role interpretation in life itself; nor is the social actor tied to a formal script but can improvise freely. He recognises that social change greatly depends on such original and creative 'improvisation'. Yet the essential similarity between drama and life remains and Goffman adopts a dramaturgical model of social interaction. Social life, like a play, is 'made up': it is a human construction that has the meaning and 'reality' that human beings give it.

Criticisms of interactionism

Two related criticisms of interactionism can be made at this point. Despite the perspective's emphasis on the interaction of self and society, it does not adequately deal with macro (large-scale) issues of power and structure. For instance, the question of which group or class controls society is not one that is central to interactionism. It is as though the approach of working out through the self via interaction with others loses direction before it reaches the issues of control and power that affect, perhaps, millions. Nevertheless, as we shall see, interactionism provides great insight into issues of power and control at the group or small organisation level. Thus, interactionism has become essential in understanding the detailed processes of teacher-pupil interaction and the 'labelling' of certain individuals as 'deviant'.

A second criticism of interactionism is that it suffers from a certain naive, liberal optimism. This criticism does not obviously emerge from the above account of Mead's key concepts, but Chicago interactionists tended to believe that given the 'freedom' to interact and learn through experience, people would reach rational and humane conclusions, and therefore create a rational, humane society. This view reflects both nineteenth century belief in progress and the American dream of self and societal achievement. Of course, this view of human nature is just as valid as the conservative emphasis of functionalism on the need for constraint and control and the more sombre view of Marxists that it is natural for people to act first and foremost in their own self (i.e. class) interest. However, post-Second World War interactionists have not quite maintained the optimism of their precursors. For Goffman and the deviancy theorist Howard Becker, it is not the ordinary but the extraordinary person that is the 'hero' – the 'outsider' who wittingly or otherwise challenges 'society'. If, in turn, this orientation has drawn the criticism of romanticism, it is, at least, an antidote to the conformism implicit in the structural perspectives.

Ethnomethodology

The Californian sociologist, Harold Garfinkel, founded ethnomethodology in the late 1950s and early 1960s. The cumbersome term ethnomethodology in fact accurately describes the approach.

'Ethnic' means 'people' or 'cultural group' and the term, therefore, means methods used by people – specifically, to create meaning and order in social life. Garfinkel considers that the basic method social actors use to create meaning is 'commonsense reasoning'. He argues that inter-subjective (i.e. personally shared) communication and reasoning can lead to shared interpretations of experience (i.e. people achieve a common understanding of things). Thus, typically, groups of people from, say, jurors to teachers develop their own ways of thinking and behaving and it is these that sociologists should study.

Garfinkel stresses that social order is created and recreated by actors reasoning and communicating and it is not the product of externally imposed norms. He has devised a number of 'natural' situations in which normal expectations of participants are not met and yet in which they continue to try to make orderly sense out of what is happening. Thus, he contrived a situation in which a student counsellor gave entirely arbitrary answers to clients. Nevertheless, the student-clients did struggle to make sense and

order out of the nonsense. Garfinkel's view of order as a negotiated process rather than as 'something' externally imposed is a major contribution to sociology and, in particular, has greatly influenced organisational and institutional analysis.

Structuration theory: beyond the structure/ interpretive dualism

None of the theory we have looked at so far was produced in the last quarter of a century and much of it is 50 or 100 years old. There is a danger that the above account of the earlier development of sociological theory might suggest a misleading picture of the state of sociological theory today. Up to the 1960s and perhaps a little later, sociological theory developed as something of a 'ding dong' battle between the structural theorists, especially functionalism but also Marxism, and the interpretive theories. The structural theories emphasise society as something external to the individual which influences or even determines her or his behaviour. These external forces are social structure. On the other hand, the interpretive theories stress individual action or agency which is taken to be meaningful and purposeful. This opposition is often referred to as a dualistic approach with one 'side' of the debate committed to the structural pole of the dualism and the other to the agency/action pole. Even though leading sociologists from one or other 'side' did sometimes recognise that the other 'side' was also contributing usefully to the subject, the popular impression of sociology was of a deeply divided discipline.

In the last quarter of a century, there have been many attempts to theorise the relationship between structure and agency in a way that overcomes the notion that they are two opposites. We will discuss some of these theories later. Here it is enough briefly to introduce perhaps the best known of them – Anthony Giddens' structuration theory.

Giddens proposes that instead of thinking of structure and agency as dualisms, we should think of them as two aspects of the same phenomenon – a duality rather than a dualism. Giddens' concept of the duality of structure involves both structure and agency (though the term agency is not directly used). Social structure would not exist unless human agency created it but human agency requires social structure to occur at all. This should become clearer when we have explained what Giddens means by 'structure'.

By structure, Giddens means rules and resources (the material and cultural means that enable people to act). Thus, schools and factories and other social institutions have their own rules and resources, the use of which reproduces these institutions. Schools and factories do not reproduce themselves, people or human agents reproduce them. By using institutional rules and resources, people reproduce an institution over time and space. Social structure, then, does not exist apart from the human action which creates it. Thus, observing school rules and using school equipment (resources), employing factory procedures and plant is structuration. The term used by Giddens to indicate the seamless nature of structure/agency is practice. Social practice is simultaneously action and structure.

It is worth giving a more extended example to illustrate Giddens' theory of structuration. Let us take Rupert Murdoch, the media mogul, and his International News Corporation (INC). There is no difficulty in conceiving of Murdoch as a powerful agent – he is a hands-on proprietor, appointing and dismissing television and newspaper editors as he sees fit. What should be equally clear by now is that the rules and resources of INC – its structure – enable Murdoch to act so powerfully and that in acting, he reproduces (or (re)structures) the company. Others at INC are involved in the process of structuration but it is Murdoch who is best positioned in terms of the rules and resources (money, power, etc.). As this example shows, it is a simple matter to relate Giddens' concept of structuration to that of inequality.

Giddens' theory of structuration is introduced at this early point partly because it is a major sociological theory and partly because it illustrates a strong tendency in contemporary sociology to get beyond the either/or structural/interpretive approaches. Giddens and others have already produced an impressive and interesting body of theory and analysis which we begin to examine in Chapter 2 and which has given a new relevance and vitality to the subject. The poststructuralist, Foucault, has also attempted to break down the structure/agency dualism, and his contribution is considered at several points in this book.

Important contemporary influences on sociology

In addition to the development of sociology through the major perspectives discussed above, there are a number of contemporary movements whose origin lies largely outside sociology, which nevertheless have greatly influenced the development of the discipline. Among the most influential of such movements are feminism, anti-racism, the new right ('Thatcherism') and the environmental or 'green' movement. These are briefly discussed below but they frequently recur in this book as strands of influence across specific sociological topics. The possible effects of the decline of communism on Marxist sociology and the emergence of a radical alternative perspective are also discussed.

Feminism

In the 1950s women were, if not quite 'invisible' within sociology, certainly in a secondary and subordinate position to men. This was true both in terms of who had power and prestige within the discipline – overwhelmingly men – and in terms of the presentation and content of the subject – 'masculinised' language

and illustrations told about a world dominated by male concerns. Sociology has probably been more open to change than most areas of society in respect to gender (male/female relations). Today, the world is still largely dominated by males but there appears to have been a greater increase in the proportion of women in higher status positions within sociology than in other areas – although they are still in a minority even there. However, the presentation and content of the subject is undergoing radical change if not revolution because of the feminist movement. Certainly, most sociology textbooks and probably the majority of all sociology books are now written in gender-neutral language (at least, their authors attempt to do so!). The content of sociology has been substantially 'feminised'. Gender relations, including the (continuing) emancipation of women, is a topic in itself, but the issue of patriarchy (male domination) and the problems and priorities of women have become part of every sociological topic. The research, redefining and theorising involved in this have made sociology a vastly more enlightening and potentially liberating discipline for both sexes.

Anti-racism

Anti-racism is one of several terms which could be used to indicate the movements of opposition to racism and in favour of racial equality that have been a feature of the post-war world. Looked at in total, these movements have had both a cultural and structural dimension. Culturally, they have asserted the reality of black achievement – often missing from official syllabuses, including sociology ones – and have opposed racial prejudice by attacking racist stereotypes and 'humour'. Many sociologists have attempted to 'deracialise' the subject of sociology, and this has also happened in other academic areas, such as history. Black achievements and issues relating to black culture and its relations with white culture have been increasingly covered, although there remain large areas of inadequate understanding.

The structural dimension of anti-racism focuses on the lack of black power within institutions: business, education, etc. In this sense, institutional racism has been widely adopted as a concept within sociology. Whether sociologists have effectively applied anti-racist values to the organisation of their own discipline is more debatable. There appear to be as few black people in leading positions in sociology as in other professions. A partial exception to this is the sociology of race itself but perhaps this merely reinforces the stereotype.

The new right

At the core of new right philosophy is a belief in a particular version of individualism and a converse scepticism about state control and interference. New right philosophers, such as Roger Scruton, and politicians, such as Norman Tebbitt, are radical individualists in the sense that they believe in the maximum possible freedom for the individual. This ideology has had its most influential application in economics, where the 'free market' approach has had a world-wide impact in the last decade or so. However, the new right is equally a moral and cultural movement. Its rhetoric has, at times, had almost a revivalist fervour and, indeed, the extent to which this philosophy has revived from its low ebb in the 1960s is remarkable. The new right strongly contends that capitalism is the only socio-economic system which adequately allows for individual freedom.

The impact of new right thinking on sociology has taken some time to develop. In the late 1980s, David Marsland wrote highly critically about what he perceived as a distinct left-wing bias in sociology textbooks. However, he did not himself produce a general account of sociology which presumably would have incorporated new right perspectives. In his introductory text *Social Class and Stratification*, Peter Saunders does include precisely such an analysis and leaves the distinct impression that he favours it over other accounts (see p. 153). However, it remains to be seen what the overall impact of new right thinking on sociology will be and whether or not a new right 'school' of sociology develops. (For a fuller account of Saunders' own perspective, see Chapter 21, pp. 635-6.)

The effect of the decline of communism on Marxist sociology

At the time of writing in early 1997, it is too soon to be sure what effects the apparent collapse of communism in the Soviet Union and Eastern Europe will have on Marxist sociology. The effects may be profound but it is unlikely that Marxist sociology will either be wholly discredited or abandoned. Marxist sociology is very different from communist political and social practice. Marxist sociology is a theory about how society 'works' and its most detailed application is to capitalist society. Marxist analysis of capitalism can be considered quite separately from the attempts to build communist societies. The Mexican writer Octavio Paz puts the point well: 'the failure of communism to provide a satisfactory answer to society's questions does not mean that the questions are wrong' (quoted in the *Times*, October 1991). Marxism continues to offer explanation and comment on poverty and inequality, urban squalor, rising crime and consumer culture in capitalist society.

However, Marxist sociology cannot remain a purely critical perspective, unresponsive to historical events. I suggest that the failure of Soviet communism (perhaps of twentieth century communism) offers at least two main 'lessons' to Marxists who have not already learnt them. First, to be worthwhile at all, communism and/or socialism must be democratic. Totalitarianism is a human evil not to be risked again. The Marxist critique of capitalism might acquire greater bite and conviction if it had more to say about democracy and participation. Second, it is now virtually self-evident that in terms of both choice and efficiency 'free markets' must operate in respect to most goods and services (although, of course, co-operatives as well as capitalist enterprises can compete in free markets and, further, certain goods

or services, such as health, might be provided on the basis of need rather than individual purchasing power). It may be that a 'communism' which is radically democratic and which broadly accepts economic markets won't be different to democratic socialism. Similarly, to the extent that Marxist sociology adopts these assumptions, it too may begin to lose its distinctive character and become absorbed within a more general radical sociological perspective or approach.

Radical sociology

It is highly arguable that, in practice, Marxism is no longer the main alternative sociology to 'functionalist/capitalist' sociology. As has already been indicated, a large body of sociology reflecting feminist and anti-racist perspectives has emerged since the 1960s. Further, much sociological analysis of class inequality has not been based on precise Marxist assumptions (about which, in any case, Marxists disagree). Concern with the triple inequalities of gender, race and class provides the focus for what can be referred to as a radical sociology of the left. Crucially, in claiming the existence of a broad radical sociology, there is a clear tendency for sociologists concerned with one of these inequalities also to be concerned, to a greater or lesser extent, with the other two.

Two of the main characteristics of radical sociology are that it is critical of the inequalities of present society and it is concerned to show that change is possible. Howard Sherman and James Wood make these points effectively in their book, *Sociology: Traditional and Radical Perspectives*:

> Radical sociology attempts to view social arrangements from the perspective of oppressed groups – groups such as the poor, the unemployed, workers, blacks and other minorities, and women. From this point of view it carefully analyses the major institutions of capitalist society. It asks how these institutions – social, political and economic – evolved into their present forms. It asks who benefits by these institutions and if a major change in society is possible and necessary. Finally, radical sociology considers possible alternatives to present social organisation.
>
> *(1982: Preface)*

It should be added that any radical sociology must be as concerned with human freedom as with achieving greater equality. The failure of Eastern European communism, particularly the oppression and denial of human and civil rights, should make it clear that attempts to bring about greater equality at the expense of basic freedom are likely to achieve neither. There needs to be careful analysis of the relationship between freedom and equality and of the desirable balance between the two.

Finally, the concern of radical sociologists with oppression and inequality is increasingly on a global rather than narrowly national scale. This reflects the increasingly inter-related nature of global society. This issue is briefly examined in the following section.

Environmentalism

Like the other movements discussed in this section, environmental awareness and concern occur outside of sociology. Indeed, until recently, sociology has been slower in incorporating an environmental perspective than, for instance, a feminist or an anti-racist perspective. This may be because whereas the latter focus on specific social groups, the state of the environment is not the concern of any group in particular – although it affects everybody. Nevertheless, environmentalism has impinged on sociology in the area of economic and related social change. Thus, sociologists increasingly analyse economic investment and disinvestment both in Britain and internationally in terms not only of its effect on people but also on the environment. Community analysis now routinely locates people within environmental as well as social contexts. Both are related to economic development or lack of it. Thus, the decline and possible revival of inner urban areas is envisaged as a complex economic, social and environmental issue. Urban decay has meant unemployment, a wasted industrial environment, and consequent lack of opportunity, demoralisation and discontent. What a revival will mean is not yet clear.

Integration of economic, social and environmental analysis similarly occurs in the area of international development and underdevelopment. For instance, it is increasingly appreciated that multi-national companies can make or break whole communities and that unless governments control them and hold them to account, they may do so irresponsibly. Further, there is a growing awareness of the environmental damage sometimes caused by economic 'development' in terms of both people and their planet and of the dangers of leaving this damage as a huge 'debt' to future generations.

Globalisation

Sociology is well suited to grapple with accelerating globalisation. This phenomenon is occurring politically (for instance, in the moves to greater European co-operation); culturally, in the way that both the media and religions cross international boundaries; and, of course, economically. Sociology has always sought to explain and make sense of change and is increasingly impelled to do so in the context of an interdependent world or, in Marshall McLuhan's words, 'a global village'.

The 'post' theories (putting up the posts)

The prefix 'post' comes from the Latin word 'post' which means 'after'. There are four main sociological theories with 'post' in their title each one announcing the end of something and the beginning of something else. These are

- postindustrial society theory
- post-Fordist theory
- poststructualism
- postmodernism

Postindustrial society theory was developed by Daniel Bell in his book *The Coming of Post Industrial Society: A Venture in Social Forecasting*, (1973). Bell argued that the production and dissemination of information had replaced industrial production as the central economic process in Western societies. He further argued that a new class of scientific, technological and professional experts now 'ran' society. Bell was also one of the first to observe that Western societies had shifted from being primarily producers of goods to service production, and that knowledge and culture had become relatively more important than material matters in these societies.

Post-Fordist theory argues that there has been a sharp decline in the organisation of production along the Henry Ford, assembly-line model. Like Bell, post-Fordists consider that the use of information technology is having a huge impact on the organisation of production, requiring fewer but more flexible and better-educated employees. Post-Fordists observe that this trend towards a more flexible, slimmed-down organisation is happening in many other areas of society, including government and the welfare state (see pp. 252-5). Critical commentators on postindustrial society and post-Fordist theory point out that these developments occur within and are shaped by capitalism and that they have involved job loss and social dislocation. It has been observed that these changes are not the result of the 'inevitable' march of technology and knowledge but can be implemented and structured according to human priorities.

The distinction between poststructuralism and postmodernism will be explained later in this book. We will refer to them both under the movement of postmodernism. Postmodernism has two basic tenets, one negative and one positive. The negative idea of postmodernism is that the Marxist and liberal philosophies of progress, indeed all such utopian philosophies, have been guilty of a naive miscalculation. They have grossly underestimated the destructiveness of human beings, to each other and to the natural world. This bleak observation is counteracted by the positive idea of postmodernism: that, freed of the illusions of big ideologies, people, as individuals and groups, can get on with developing their own distinctive identities and projects. In the absence of a big plan, people are free to make their own plans. Ironically, this view leads back not to utopian liberalism but to the liberalism of compromise – respect for other people's freedom requires that we limit our own; others have the right to their identity; we should accept plurality (variety) and difference. Postmodernism is, then, partly a modest philosophy of anti-utopian caution, and as such it coincides with a mood of subdued realism as we approach the millennium. On the other hand, it also coincides with an interesting period of cultural innovation, unexpectedness and eccentricity.

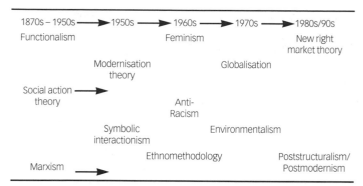

Figure 1.4 Sociology: theoretical perspectives and influences

Note: The dates in the diagram are intended to give only an approximate idea of the growth and development of a particular perspective/influence.

Types of society: traditional, modern and late modern

Categorising society into broad types is fraught with problems. Such typologies have often tended to carry implicit value judgements about which societies are more 'advanced' or 'civilised'. Thus, the term 'primitive' to describe non-literate societies is discredited as it has come to carry naive connotations of 'savagery' and lack of 'civilisation'.

Problematic though typing societies may be, it has not stopped sociologists from attempting to do so. Indeed, it is difficult to see how they could avoid it. Comparing different aspects of societies, sometimes at different stages in their history, is essential in understanding how social institutions are operated and change (see pp. 25-6). However, even the very broad typology of societies presented below and used, with qualifications, throughout this book, would not gain universal agreement among sociologists. Some of these disagreements are indicated by alternative typological terms given in brackets. The meaning of the terms is given following Figure 1.5.

		Examples
TRADITIONAL (Pre-Industrial)	Preliterate	Zulus
	Literate	Medieval European States
MODERN (Industrial) (Capitalist/Communist)		England, 1900 USA/USSR, 1950
LATE MODERN (Late Capitalist) (Postmodern)		United States, 1996 Hong Kong?

Figure 1.5 Types of society

Traditional society

Traditional society is often referred to simply as pre-industrial society because the term 'traditional' is sometimes associated with

similar criticisms as 'primitive'. However, the term traditional, shorn of any negative connotations, is coming back into favour among some sociologists as it provides a useful basis of comparison with modern society or modernity. Traditional societies are based on established values and authority, and are often rooted in religion (see pp. 40-1).

Modern society (capitalist/communist societies)

Modern society and the age of modernity is characterised by the rise of science and technology, industrialisation and bureaucracy, and a widespread belief (or ideology) in the possibility of human and social progress. This ideology had its roots in the eighteenth century European enlightenment. Although Weber had his doubts about 'the march of progress', he is the sociologist most responsible for developing theory of modern society and bureaucracy.

Marxists usually prefer to categorise industrial societies as either capitalist or communist rather than use the term 'modern' to describe both. For them the current epoch is best described as capitalist, and communism offers a possible alternative form of development from it.

Much of the current interest in modernity among social scientists reflects the fact that many consider

either

1 that modernity is radically changing

or

2 that modernity is coming to an end and (to over simplify somewhat) being replaced by late modernity or postmodernity.

Either way, many sociologists are indicating that global society is undergoing profound change. Whether this is so (or whether perhaps sociologists are undergoing an extended bout of pre-millenarian excitability!) is one of the main questions addressed throughout this book.

Late modern society (or postmodern or late capitalist society)

What, then, are the characteristics of 'late modernity', as Anthony Giddens has termed the current period, or postmodernity as some others prefer to call it. As is discussed in the Chapter 2, Giddens suggests that one of the main characteristics of late modernity is a heightened awareness of the failures of modernity, especially in relation to the damage done to the environment and the species danger this could represent. Linked to this is a decline in the belief in progress and a turning away from political and public issues to individual, more personal, concerns. However, this analysis, large scale and ambitious though it is, arguably falls short of providing an adequate theory of late modernity.

Krishan Kumar approaches the problem of understanding what

he prefers to term 'post-modern society' in a rather different way. In his *From Post-industrial to Post-Modern Society*, (1995), Kumar argues that the four 'post' theories – postindustrial society theory, post-Fordism, and postmodernism (in which he includes poststructuratism) are highly complementary. He suggests that taken critically together, they might provide the basis of an integrated theory of the contemporary world (for basic definitions of the 'post' theories, see p. 14). Again, Kumar's thinking will be discussed later. The following quotation does no more than indicate his view of the potential of these theories and their relationship to modernity:

> *(W)hat seems to me remarkable is how much of the present state of the world they manage to capture. We do live in a world saturated with information and communication. The nature of work and industrial organisation is truly changing with unnerving speed. Modern societies have indeed reached a point where, even if they have not given up on modernity, many of its classic attitudes and assumptions have become seriously questionable.*
>
> *(1995: 201)*

Kumar recognises that it is too early to conclude that these newish theories will supersede the classic theories of the late nineteenth and early twentieth century – the theories of modernity – on which, in any case, they partly build. On the other hand, Marx, Weber, Durkheim and Mead were not evangelists. Their texts are not biblical but are open to critical revision, development and, where demonstrated inadequate, rejection.

Many contemporary Marxists, like the postmodernists, regard the current period as one of great and rapid change. They see capitalism as increasingly, and comprehensively, triumphant throughout the globe – especially with its apparent 'conquest' of China, Russia and even Cuba.

Even the swing back to communism in Russia and other Eastern European countries in 1995 crucially occurred within the framework of democratic elections and a continuing commitment to investment from capitalist countries. Accordingly, Marxists tend to refer to the current period as one of 'late capitalism' rather than late modernity or postmodernity. Yet, the analysis of late capitalism by Marxists such as Jameson and Harvey has much in common with postmodernism. Both perspectives see a much enhanced role for communication, culture and consumerism in the contemporary world. However, whereas postmodernists tend to see possibilities for choice and creativity in these developments, Marxists are more inclined to see capitalist manipulation and the profit motive. It may be clever fun to play around with designer products but doesn't the last laugh (and the profits) go to Calvin Klein and George Armani?

Types of society and types of social explanation

Table 1.1 – suggests a strong relationship between types of society – traditional, modern and late modern – and the way members of these societies understand and explain the meaning of their own and others lives (i.e. their social explanations). People tend to explain their lives using the types of theories dominant in their own societies (although there are many exceptions). As Table 1.1 – should make clear, this point is more obvious than might at first seem to be the case.

Table 1.1 Types of society and social explanations

Type of society	Dominant types of social explanation
TRADITIONAL	Magic Religion
MODERN	Scientific Rational Social Scientific
LATE MODERN/POSTMODERN	Science and Reason (including Social Science) but more informed by Moral, Emotional and Personal Values

Dominant types of social explanation in traditional society

The belief systems of traditional societies have been and, for those that remain, generally still are based on magic and/or religion. For most people in these societies, religion explains society. No need is perceived for a separate study of society or sociology. In the West, religion has declined fairly slowly as science has provided an alternative basis of explanation, and the impact of the West on many traditional societies has been traumatic and disruptive. The Muslim, Hindu and Buddhist cultures of the Near and Far East arguably retained their essential traditional identities as they struggled to absorb the impact of the West. However, the West's effect on African and native American Indian cultures was more deeply damaging and disruptive. The collective psychological and cultural trauma to these people is only now beginning fully to be explored.

Dominant types of social explanation in modern society

In modern societies there has been a move towards secular and scientific explanations of all forms of existence although some people retained an exclusively religious view of the world and others, including the scientist Isaac Newton, felt able to hold both religious and scientific explanations of the universe. As has already been explained, the nineteenth century founders of sociology attempted to construct a science of society (which does not necessarily mean that they lacked a humanistic perspective).

Not surprisingly, the founding sociologists were greatly concerned to describe and explain the change from traditional, agricultural society to modern, capitalist industrial society. For instance, Durkheim described the almost automatic conformity to social norms, beliefs and bonds of members of traditional society as 'mechanical solidarity'. The more complex weave of modern social interconnection and interdependence, he described as 'organic solidarity'. He argued that the basis of organic solidarity was the division of labour in which virtually every worker depended for doing her or his own work on the work of someone else. Durkheim's contemporary, Ferdinand Tönnies described the change from traditional to modern society as one from social association based on community to that based on contract (i.e. regulated association based on mutual self-interest).

In attempting to explain the development of modern society, the founders of sociology used the methods of modernity – the scientific approach. Durkheim and Marx perhaps especially, aspired to produce a science of society. Durkheim attempted to spell out 'the rules of sociological method' in a book of that title. In some of his writings Marx appeared to claim that he had discovered the scientific logic of historical development. Weber was as rigorous as any in insisting on a scientifically neutral analysis of society, although within this approach he sought to understand people's feelings and meanings. He also considered that modern industry and bureaucracy produced dehumanising effects as well as material progress.

Weber was not alone in his awareness of the negative effects – 'the dark side' – of modernity. As Krishan Kumar has illustrated, the protest against the excesses of modernity – industrial filth and human exploitation – is as old as modernity itself. It is a protest that has been more strongly expressed in the arts and literature than in the social sciences. In the 1820s and 1830s, the romantic poets decried the degradation of nature (what we would now call the environment) wrought by 'dark, satanic mills'; in the late Victorian period Dickens described and decried urban squalor; and in the 1940s, Picasso captured the destructive power of military technology in his painting of the bombing of Guernica. Sociologists, too, have often shown sensitivity to the moral and emotional side of human experience but have less often effectively expressed this in their writings. This may be changing. The impact of postmodernism on sociology seems to be generating a range of concepts and methods which promise to take sociology a little closer to the human heart (see pp. 551-2).

Dominant types of social explanation in late modern societies

The dominant type of social or sociological explanation in late modernity is still based on rational, social scientific analysis. The battery of sociological theory already briefly described in this chapter and the methods described in the next are virtually certain to remain at the core of the sociological enterprise.

Nevertheless, changes are occurring. A determined and sustained attempt is underway to deal with the moral, emotional and personal aspects of members of society and of sociological authors themselves. A list of some of the contents of the journal *Sociology* between early 1993 and late 1995 illustrates the point:

'Special Issue: Auto/Biography in Sociology'

'Reading Lives: How the Personal Might be Social'

'Weaving Stories: Personal Auto/Biographies in Feminist Research'

'Even Sociologists Fall In Love: An Exploration in the Sociology of Emotions'

'Love and Intimacy: The Gender Division of Emotion and 'Emotion Work''

'Towards a Sociology of Nature'

'Heroic Death'

'Cultural Identity: Disclosing Commonality and Difference in In-Depth Interviewing'

'Consumption, Identity – Formation and Uncertainty'

'Forget Postmodernism? Notes from de Bunker'

'Love', 'Death', 'Identity', 'the Personal'

These are areas not traditionally much associated with sociology. They are more usually thought of as the subject matter of psychology or literature. So what is happening? Put simply, many sociologists are increasingly beginning to suggest that classic sociology, including even interpretive perspectives, has not done justice to the full range of human experience. A new effort is being made – as witnessed by the titles of the above articles – to understand the subjectivity (personal perspectives/feelings) of both the people studied by sociologists and of the sociologists themselves. In the next chapter an indication is given of how this is occurring (see pp. 42-5) and throughout this book sections drawing on late modern or postmodern analysis will make reference to issues of subjectivity. Concern with personal perspective and feeling is not new in sociology but is currently flourishing to an extent that has already had a major effect on the discipline and may well further do so.

What has caused this renewed emphasis on subjectivity within sociology? The recent source of influence goes back to the protest movements of the 1960s which argued that mainstream political and public life had become remote from the experience and values of the majority. The feminist movement probably developed this sentiment further than any other. The feminist slogan 'the personal

Figure 1.6 Feminist sociologists, such as Ann Oakley, have often made links between the personal and the social

is political' was not only an ideological expression but a programme for social change. Within sociology and other disciplines, females in particular have sought to bring personal issues to the surface and to show their relationship to wider contexts.

Conclusion

What Charles Wright Mills referred to as the 'classic tradition' of sociological theory remains the main source of sociological insight into societies – traditional, modern and late modern. This is especially so if interpretive theory, particularly symbolic interactionism, is included within the classic tradition. The social 'structures' of class, gender, race/ethnicity, age and global inequality remain at the centre of most sociological analysis. However, the emphasis of much recent sociology, on linking the personal to the social and in charting how identity is forged in a media-saturated world of commercial consumer culture, is not only opening up less familiar areas of sociological concern, it is beginning to change how we see the established ones. For those who find such sentiments somewhat modish, Charles Wright Mills' words of nearly 40 years ago, may come as a shock:

We are at the end of what is called the Modern Age. Just as Antiquity was followed by several centuries of Oriental ascendancy which westerners provincially call the Dark Ages, so now the Modern Age is being succeeded by the postmodern period …

The ending of one period and the beginning of another is, to be sure, a matter of definition. But definitions, like everything social, are historically specific. And now our basic definitions of society and of self are being overtaken by new realities. I do not mean merely that we feel we are in an epochal kind of transition, I mean that too many of our explanations are derived from the great historical tradition from the Medieval to the Modern Age; and that when they are generalised for use today, they become unwieldy, irrelevant and not convincing. And I mean also that our major orientations – liberalism and socialism – have virtually collapsed as adequate explanations of the world and of ourselves.

(The Listener, 1959)

Questions

1 Make a list of the purposes of sociological study. Has your view of what sociology is about changed having read this chapter? If so, how?

2 What are the main types of society as described in this chapter? What are the main features of late modern (or high modern) society? In what ways, if any, do early (late eighteenth/early nineteenth century) modern and late modern society differ?

Summary

1 Sociology is the systematic study of societies. Society is made up of individuals and groups. Sociology can help the self or individual better to understand her or his life by explaining how 'external' events affect personal experience.

2 'Self, socialisation and culture' are a related 'cluster' of basic sociological concepts. Socialisation is the process by which the self learns the culture or way of life of his or her society.

3 'Values and norms' are a related pair of concepts. Values are standards which underlie the norms or rules of a society.

4 'Status and role' are a related pair of concepts. A status is a particular position in society and a role is the behaviour expected of a person in a particular status.

5 The sociology of Marx, Durkheim and Weber can be viewed as attempts to understand the great developments of their epoch such as capitalism, industrialisation, urbanisation, and the emergence of new forms of social conflict. Their perspectives or models of society were structural in nature in that they mainly

described how social forces and developments 'bear down on' or 'structure' the lives of individuals and groups.

6 Functionalism is based on the perspective that major social institutions and 'sub-systems' (such as kinship and economic) exist to meet fundamental human needs (such as procreation and production/consumption). Modern functionalism is particularly associated with the American sociologist Talcott Parsons, but Parsons was himself greatly influenced by Durkheim.

7 Marxism is based on the perspective that class conflict is the fundamental social force or dynamic. Marxist theory states that in capitalist society the main social classes are the capitalist class and the working class.

8 Weber's work cannot be categorised under a single label but is sometimes referred to as social action theory. Weber tried to integrate (bring together) both structural perspective and what later came to be known as interpretive perspective.

9 Interactionism is the main interpretist perspective. George Mead considered that society forms and structures the self's experience but that the self also helps to create its own social experience.

10 Ethnomethodology is the study of the 'commonsense reasoning' of people by which they achieve a meaningful understanding of society and social events.

11 Structuration theory rejects polarised theoretical approaches to sociology and conceptualises structure and agency as a single process – structuration.

12 Several movements and theories have recently influenced the development of sociology. These include:
   • Feminism
   • Anti-racism
   • The new right
   • Environmentalism
   • Globalisation
   • The 'Post' theories

13 Societies may be categorised into three broad types and associated types of explanation:
   Traditional
   Modern
   Late Modern (or Postmodern)
   For further reading and questions, see the end of Chapter 21.

Readings

Reading 1
Personal troubles and public issues

From C Wright Mills, *The Sociological Imagination* (Oxford University Press, 1990), pp. 9-10

(Personal troubles of 'milieux' and public issues of social structure refer to the individual's own experience within a social context.)

Perhaps the most fruitful distinction with which the sociological imagination works is between 'the personal troubles of milieu' and 'the public issues of social structure'. The distinction is an essential tool of the sociological imagination and a feature of all classic work in social science.

Troubles occur within the character of the individual and within the range of his immediate relations with others; they have to do with his self and with those limited areas of social life of which he is directly and personally aware. Accordingly, the statement and the resolution of troubles properly lie within the individual as a biographical entity and within the scope of his immediate milieu – the social setting that is directly open to his personal experience and to some extent his wilful activity. A trouble is a private matter: values cherished by an individual are felt by him to be threatened.

Issues have to do with matters that transcend these local environments of the individual and the range of his inner life. They have to do with the organisation of many such milieux into the institutions of an historical society as a whole, with the ways in which various milieux overlap and interpenetrate to form the larger structure of social and historical life. An issue is a public matter: some value cherished by publics is felt to be threatened. Often there is a debate about what the value really is and about what it is that really threatens it. This debate is often without focus if only because it is the very nature of an issue, unlike even widespread trouble, that it cannot very well be defined in terms of the immediate and everyday environments of ordinary men. An issue, in fact, often involves a crisis in institutional arrangements, and often too it involves what Marxists call 'contradictions, or 'antagonisms'.

In these terms, consider employment. When in a city of a hundred million only one man is unemployed, that is his personal trouble, and for its relief we properly look to the character of the man, his skills and his immediate opportunities. But when in a nation of fifty million employees, fifteen million men are unemployed, that is an issue, and we may not hope to find its solution within the range of opportunities open to any one individual. The very structure of opportunities has collapsed. Both the correct statement of the problem and the range of possible solutions require us to consider the economic and political institutions of the society, and not merely the personal situation and character of a scatter of individuals.

Consider war ...

Consider marriage ...

Or consider the metropolis – the horrible, beautiful ugly, magnificent sprawl of the great city ...

Questions

1 How does Mills show that unemployment can be both a public issue and a personal trouble?
2 Consider either war or marriage or the metropolis – or any other matter – in terms of it being both a possible cause of personal trouble and as a public issue of social structure.

Reading 2
Sociological models or perspectives

From C Wright Mills, *Images of Man* (George Braziller, Inc., 1960), pp. 3-4

In short, the classic sociologists construct models of society and use them to develop a number of theories. What is important is the fact that neither the correctness nor the inaccuracy of any of these specific theories necessarily confirms or upsets the usefulness or the adequacy of the models. The models can be used for the construction of many theories. They can be used for correcting errors in theories made with their aid. And they are readily open: they can themselves be modified in ways to make them more useful as analytic tools and empirically closer to the run of fact.

It is these models that are great – not only as contributions to the history of social reflection and inquiry, but also as influences on subsequent sociological thinking. They, I believe, are what is alive in the classic tradition of sociology. And I think, too, that they are the reason why so persistently there have been, under quite varied circumstances, so many 'revivals' of the thinkers presented in these pages; in short, why their works are 'classic.'

The classic tradition, then, may not be defined by any one specific method, certainly not by the acceptance of any one theory of society, history, or human nature. Once that is acknowledged, a usable definition is simple enough – although its application in selecting a book of illustrative readings is by no means automatic. The classic tradition is most readily defined by the character of the questions that have guided and do now guide those who are part of it. These questions are generally of wide scope: they concern total societies, their transformations, and the varieties of individual men and women that inhabit them. The answers given by classic sociologists provide conceptions about society, about history and about biography, and in their work these three are usually linked closely together. The structure of society and the mechanics of history are seen within the same perspective, and within this perspective changes in human nature are also defined.

Questions

1 Suggest two questions asked by Marx, Durkheim and Weber about society in constructing their sociological models or perspectives.
2 Give reasons why the sociological model or perspective developed by either Mark *or* Weber *or* Durkheim remains of interest and use to sociologists today. Are there any ways in which you think their perspectives are now outdated?

Reading 3
Class conflict

From Karl Marx and Friedrich Engels, *The Communist Manifesto* (Penguin, 1981), pp. 79-80

The history of all hitherto existing society is the history of class struggles.

Freeman and slave, patrician and plebeian, lord and serf, guild-master and journeyman, in a word, oppressor and oppressed stood in constant opposition to one another, carried on an uninterrupted, now hidden, now open fight that each time ended, either in a revolutionary reconstitution of society at large, or in the common ruin of the contending classes.

In the earlier epochs of history, we find almost everywhere a complicated arrangement of society into various orders, a manifold gradation of social rank. In ancient Rome we have patricians, knights, plebeians, slaves; in the Middle Ages, feudal lords, vassals, guild-masters, journeymen, apprentices, serfs; in almost all of these classes, again, subordinate gradations.

The modern bourgeois society that has sprouted from the ruins of feudal society has not done away with class antagonisms. It has but established new classes, new conditions of oppression, new forms of struggle in place of the old ones.

Our epoch, the epoch of the bourgeoisie, possesses, however, this distinctive feature. It has simplified the class antagonisms. Society as a whole is more and more splitting up into two great hostile camps, into two great classes directly facing each other – bourgeoisie and proletariat.

From the serfs of the Middle Ages sprang the chartered burghers of the earliest towns. From these burgesses the first elements of the bourgeoisie were developed.

The discovery of America, the rounding of the Cape, opened up fresh ground for the rising bourgeoisie. The East-Indian and Chinese markets, the colonisation of America, trade with the colonies, the increase in the means of exchange and in commodities generally, gave to commerce, to navigation, to industry, an impulse never before known, and thereby, to the revolutionary element in the tottering feudal society, a rapid development.

Questions

1 In what ways do Marx and Engels suggest that the 'bourgeois' epoch differed from previous epochs of class conflict?
2 Do you consider that society is still divided into 'two great classes' – bourgeoisie and proletariat – or are we in a new 'epoch' perhaps not foreseen by Marx and Engels?

Reading 4
Self, self-consciousness and self-indication in the theory of G H Mead

From Herbert Blumer, 'Symbolic Interaction', in Arnold M Rose ed., *Human Behaviour and Social Process* (Houghton-Mifflin, 1962), pp. 180-81

The key feature in Mead's analysis is that the human being has a self. This idea should not be cast aside as esoteric or glossed over as something that is obvious and hence not worthy of attention. In declaring that the human being has a self, Mead has in mind chiefly that the human being can be the object of his own actions. He can act toward himself as he might act toward others. Each of us is familiar with actions of this sort in which the human being gets angry with himself, rebuffs himself, takes pride in himself, argues with himself, tries to bolster his own courage, tells himself that he should 'do this' or not 'do that,' sets goals for himself, makes compromises with himself, and plans what he is going to do. That the human being acts towards himself in these and countless other ways is a matter of easy empirical observation. To recognise that the human being can act toward himself is no mystical conjuration.

Mead regards this ability of the human being to act toward himself as the central mechanism with which the human being faces and deals with his world. This mechanism enables the human being to make indication to himself of things in his surroundings and thus to guide his actions by what he notes. Anything of which a human being is conscious is something which he is indicting to himself – the ticking of a clock, a knock at the door, the appearance of a friend, the remark made by a companion, a recognition that he has a task to perform, or the realisation that he has a cold. Conversely, anything of which he is not conscious is, *ipso facto*, something which he is not indicating to himself. The conscious life of the human being, from the time that he awakens until he falls asleep, is a continual flow of self-indications – notations of the things with which he deals and takes into account. We are given, then, a picture of the human being as an organism which confronts its world with a mechanism of making indications to itself. This is the mechanism that is involved in interpreting the actions of others. To interpret the actions of another is to point out to oneself that the action has this or that meaning or character.

Now, according to Mead, the significance of making indications to oneself is of paramount importance. The importance lies along two lines. First, to indicate something is to extricate it from its setting, to hold it apart, to give it a meaning or, in Mead's language, to make it into an object. An object – that is to say, anything that an individual indicates to himself – is different from a stimulus; instead of having an intrinsic character which acts on the individual and which can be identified apart from the individual, its character or meaning is conferred on it by the individual. The object is a product of the individual's disposition to act …

The second important implication of the fact that the human being makes indications to himself is that his action is constructed or built up instead of being a mere release … His action is built up step by step through a process of such self-indication. The human individual pieces together and guides his action by taking account of different things and interpreting their significance for his prospective action. There is no instance of conscious action of which this is not true.

Questions

1 Summarise in your own words what Mead considers are the main characteristics of the self (approximately 100 words).
2 See Reading 1, Question 2, Chapter 2.

Sociological Methods and Theory: Tradition, Modernity and Postmodernity

Is this science? A sociological interview

Aims of this chapter

1   To compare sociological and natural scientific methods.
    To introduce the comparative method.
    To discuss whether or not sociology is a science (see pp. 38-40).

2   To introduce the main types of sociological methods – quantitative and qualitative – and sources of data – primary and secondary

3   To discuss the relationship between sociological theory/perspectives and methods.

4   To introduce the terms tradition, modernity and postmodernity as descriptions of three distinct types of society.

5   To discuss the relationship of sociology to modernity and postmodernity.

Sociology and science

There is a long-running debate on the nature of sociology as a discipline. Part of this debate is about whether or not sociology can be called a science. There are two main aspects to this question. The first is whether or not the subject matter of sociology – social interaction – is best understood by scientific methods. We will return to this later in the chapter. The second is whether or not the methods that sociologists use and the results they produce can be termed scientific. To make the comparison between social scientific and scientific methods, it is first necessary briefly to describe the latter.

Natural science

This section offers a simple introduction to natural science. More problematic issues are considered later in the chapter.

Natural science describes those sciences concerned with researching and explaining the 'world of nature', the natural world. These include physics, chemistry and biology. Science is concerned with the accumulation of *verifiable* (capable of being proved true) knowledge. It has traditionally used two methods: observation and experimentation. For reasons outlined below, laboratory experimentation is often considered the most accurate and therefore the ideal method of testing an hypothesis. In practice, all the sciences also use observation. Biologists observe, record and attempt to explain aspects of organic life. The same applies to astronomers in respect of their field of enquiry. It is important that observations are precisely and accurately made. To establish the truth of an observation, it helps to repeat it. Sociologists make full use of observation but very little of the laboratory experiment. Instead, they have developed a battery of methods of their own. How these compare to the laboratory method we consider below. Invariably, experiment involves some observation, but observation need not involve experiment.

Scientific research of an explanatory kind often involves establishing whether the scientist's initial idea of hypothesis is true or false. The research is the means by which the hypothesis becomes a proven theory. Thus, we can very simply present the process of explanatory scientific enquiry in several stages:

1   Observation of phenomena ('facts').
2   Hypothesis (formulated so that it can be tested).
3   Collection of data using systematic method(s) (usually experiment or observation or both).
4   Analysis of data.
5   Test of hypothesis against data.
6   Confirmation or Refutation of hypothesis (if the latter, 'return to 3' to reformulate or produce a new hypothesis).
7   Theory – a generalisation built upon a repeatedly confirmed hypothesis (or hypotheses).

In the natural sciences, a repeatedly confirmed hypothesis (or series of related hypotheses) is known as a theory or law. Two well known laws of natural science are Newton's law of gravity and Einstein's law of relativity. Laws state that given precisely the same conditions, specific factors or elements will interact in the same way. An important consequence of this is that natural science provides a basis of prediction, i.e. it provides a logical means of establishing what will happen to certain 'things' in given conditions (e.g. how two chemicals will react in given conditions). Few social scientists claim that their methods enable them to produce laws which provide precise predictions.

The laboratory experiment

The most common method used by natural scientists such as chemists or physicists to test a hypothesis is the *laboratory-controlled experiment*. We discuss this method now because its ability to give precise findings and the relative lack of its use in sociology are often cited to undermine the claims of sociology to be scientific. Natural scientists, like social scientists, often want to measure the effect of one 'thing' on another. A biologist might want to measure the effect that being deprived of light has on the growth of a plant; a sociologist might want to measure the effect of class background on educational attainment. Let us see how a biologist might set up an experiment. S/he may hypothesise that light deprivation will slow growth, but is not sure by how much. S/he is likely to use two plants that for reasons for precise comparability are as similar as possible. One will be deprived of light and the other (the control) will not. Here we must introduce the concept of a variable, something that varies. Relevant variables that can affect plant growth are moisture, warmth, soil quality and, of course, light. All of the variables apart from light must be held constant between the two plants. This means that both plants must receive the same amount of moisture, warmth, and so on, but not, of course, light. If this were not so, it would be impossible to tell whether light variation or some other variable accounted for the difference in growth. Another way of putting this point is that the conditions in which the experiment takes place must be controlled. In this experiment, light is referred to as the independent variable (because it is assumed to be the causal factor, not the affected factor, in the experiment) and growth is the dependent variable (because it is affected by the independent variable). The biologist can calculate the result of the experiment by measuring the difference between the plants. S/he will then be able to confirm, discard or reformulate the original hypothesis in more precise terms. A reliable and valid experiment is repeatable and so its findings are open to further verification (proof). A repeatedly verified experiment adds to the growing body of scientific knowledge.

The impact of natural science on sociology

The nineteenth and early twentieth century sociologists so far discussed were understandably greatly impressed by the achievements of natural science – physics, chemistry and biology – and wanted, as far as possible, to apply the same methods of research and analysis to society. Auguste Comte (1798-1857), arguably the founder of sociology, strongly reflected this influence and actually referred to sociology as 'social physics'. He advocated the use of experiment and systematic observation as the methods for the study of society, and believed that by their use 'laws' of society could be established just as there are laws of physics or chemistry. He referred to sociology as a 'positive science' and sometimes used the term positivism to describe this approach. The positivist approach is based on the assumption that there are 'social facts' which interact with other social facts in ways which can be observed and measured. If it can be established that social facts repeatedly interact together in the same way, then it becomes possible to predict that they will do so in the future. Within the positivist model, 'external' social facts are seen as causing human responses. On this point, Durkheim agreed with Comte, arguing that there is 'a category of social facts', including ways of 'acting, thinking and feeling, external to the individual ... which ... control him'. (Reading 1)

Few sociologists since Comte have believed that either the methods or precise aims of the natural sciences could be applied wholesale to sociology. In practice, sociologists have adapted some of the methods of natural science for their own use, as well as developing some that would rarely, if ever, be used in the natural sciences. A full discussion of this point is given later in this chapter (see pp. 38-9). (See also Reading 2)

The comparative-historical method: 'the only alternative to experiment'

It is rarely either practical or appropriate for sociologists to employ the laboratory experiment. Human beings cannot be treated like guinea-pigs. This means that they have to adopt some other method for observing and measuring social relationships. Both Durkheim and the more contemporary sociologist Ronald Fletcher argue that the only way to do this is by employing what Durkheim termed the 'comparative historical method' and what Fletcher simply calls the 'comparative method':

> *In sciences dealing with inanimate subject-matter, and with organic, physiological facts, some interconnections of which an explanation is sought can be artificially isolated from their normal contexts and examined in precisely measurable laboratory conditions. In sociology, except perhaps in the case of some small group interactions, this is completely impossible. We cannot put Great Britain, the Kwakiutl Indians, or the complex development of, say, Babylonian law, into laboratories. Furthermore, we know that any 'part' of a social system can only be understood in its essential interconnectedness with others. Quite apart, then, from any ethical considerations (of which there are many) laboratory techniques are simply not appropriate to the nature and level of human associational facts.*
>
> *We must, however, have some procedures for testing our theories, and the simple truth is that a careful formulation and use of the comparative method is sociology's only alternative to experimentation.*
>
> (Fletcher, 1981:77)

The comparative method involves systematic comparison of apparently similar phenomena in separate social contexts such as the development of the family in two or more societies. To give another example, the apparent relationship between high social class origin and high educational attainment has been demonstrated by comparative research repeatedly to occur both within particular societies and between societies. Such a relationship is referred to as a concomitant variation or, more usually now, as a correlation which means there is some kind of relationship between the two factors – possibly a causal one. Thus, it may be that there is a causal relationship between high educational attainment and high social class origin.

Durkheim stressed the importance of systematic comparison. This could be done in terms of comparisons between similar types of society, comparisons within a society, (e.g. between areas or groups), and comparisons between different types of society (e.g. between 'traditional' and 'modern' societies). Such comparisons help explain why a correlation does or does not occur in particular circumstances. Thus, research both within Britain and internationally has produced a number of explanations about the relationship between class and educational attainment (see pp. 87-98).

Durkheim himself attempted a major piece of comparative research on suicide partly to demonstrate the application of his methodological approach. He wanted to show that even so apparently personal an act as suicide reflects 'external' social conditions. He argued that what he called the 'social suicide-rate' is the product of these 'collective' social 'forces'.

The 'Ideal type' and the comparative method

Max Weber used the concept of ideal type particularly in the context of the comparative method. He used it to refer to concepts or models which attempt to describe the essential or main elements of a social phenomenon. Thus, using an ideal type description of capitalism as a system operating on the profit motive, Weber was then able to look at particular cases of capitalist societies to see what concrete forms profit-seeking took in each of them. Thus, the abstract or 'pure' ideal type description facilitates the analysis of individual cases. Another example of an ideal type is Weber's description of social action as rational, affective and traditional. This typology enabled Weber better to organise his examination of action in various societies in which action would differ to a greater or lesser extent from the ideal typology. By now it should be obvious that the concept of ideal type has nothing at all to do with 'perfection' in any religious or other sense.

The comparative method and contemporary sociology

The comparative method has not quite come to occupy the place in sociology which Durkheim and, more recently, Fletcher have advocated. This is partly because of the rise of interpretive sociology which does not seek to explain social action in terms of 'external' causes. In addition, sociologists have become much more aware of the problems of the comparability of statistics.

The comparative method has been presented here in some detail to exemplify the enormous influence on early sociologists of the natural science method. Nevertheless, the meticulous methodology of Durkheim and Weber remains as an object lesson and much of the theory and concepts they employed in pursuing comparative research are still useful.

The current fast-growing interest in globalisation or world sociology has again increased sociologists' sensitivity to social comparison. The categorisation of societies into (mainly) traditional, modern and post or late modern provides a general but useful basis for this type of comparison of societies and is used as such – more or less explicitly – by many sociologists.

In today's 'global village' of a world in which so many trends are international or transnational, the need for a comparative perspective – 'specialised generalists' as Stanislav Andreski put it – is indisputable, even if comparison is not always pursued with quite the same scientifically systematic intent of Durkheim. More systematic studies require sophisticated methodology, usually an

international social survey of some kind. The social survey is presented in a later section of this chapter (see pp. 28-9).

Discussion issues

Why are sociological research studies never 'repeatable' in the sense that laboratory studies are? Is it true to say that all laboratory experiments are, in fact, precisely 'repeatable'? Why or why not?
How effective do you consider the comparative method to be as an alternative to the laboratory experiment?

Sociological methods

Before discussing sociological methods in detail, it will be useful to present some key general aspects of methodology. These can be conveniently listed into several pairs: descriptive and explanatory research; quantitative and qualitative research; subjectivity and objectivity; reliability and validity; and primary and secondary data. Finally, the relationship between the terms structural/ interpretist and positivist/anti-positivist is briefly discussed.

Descriptive and explanatory research

In general, sociological research may be descriptive or explanatory, or both. Descriptive research is aimed at finding out and presenting 'facts' (for instance, the trend in the birth rate over a period of time) or at describing social processes (for example, how a gang operates). Explanatory research seeks to give sociological reasons why something happens. Thus a possible sociological explanation for the downward trend in the birth-rate for most of the 1970s might be that more couples wanted to have a higher standard and quality of life rather than have a first or further child (like all hypotheses, this would have to be tested by research). 'Attitude surveys' are sometimes classified as a third type of survey. However, they can be regarded as descriptive, although what they attempt to describe are subjective states of mind rather than more concrete social facts.

Quantitative and qualitative research

Sociological methods are divided into two broad types: quantitative and qualitative. Quantitative methods are used to produce numerical or statistical data. They are usually employed in sociology in research into social relationships such as that between social class and social mobility. A now classic study in which a mainly quantitative approach was adopted was the *Oxford Social Mobility Survey* (1982). The study used a sample of 10,000 men from across the full range of social classes. The main quantitative techniques are questionnaires and structured interviews.

Qualitative methods are mainly used to produce data about the personal experience and meanings of social actors. They are usually based on the social actor's own words or on observations (sometimes filmed) of the actor's behaviour. There are now many pieces of qualitative research which explore the experience of school pupils. These include several accounts of anti-school subcultures, including Stephen Ball's *Beachside Comprehensive* (1981). The main qualitative methods are observation and unstructured interviews.

Later in this chapter, the relationship between quantitative and qualitative methods and the perspectives – structural and interpretist, discussed in Chapter 1, are explored. Broadly, quantitative methods are more suitable for structural research, and qualitative methods for interpretist research.

However, because sociologists often seek both types of information, there is considerable overlap in their usage. Many, probably the majority of sociologists, employ both types – often to provide complementary data.

Alan Bryman makes this point particularly strongly. (Reading 3)

Objective and subjective data in sociology

Objective data refers to facts and information about 'social reality' 'outside' or 'beyond' the individual. Durkheim stated that the task of sociology is to establish how objective 'social facts' affect social behaviour. Thus, he argued that certain 'social facts' affect the suicide rate (see pp. 361-2). Subjective data is information about the specific feelings and experience of individuals: it is less about how society affects the individual than about how the individual feels, thinks and acts towards society. In this sense, structural sociology deals more with objective data and interpretist sociology more with subjective data.

Structural/interpretist theories and positivist/anti-positivist methods

In many sociology books the mainly structural theories of functionalism, Marxism and Weber are described as positivist in their methodology. What is meant by this is that, like Comte (see p. 25), these theoretical approaches adopt the assumed methodological premises of natural science, i.e. that there are factors external to social actors which determine their social behaviour. In contrast, interpretist theories are described as anti-positivist because they reject the positivist methodological premise and instead use methods aimed at describing and understanding the meanings of social actors. While these distinctions are helpful, it should be stressed that there are no rigid links between structural theories and quantitative methods, and interpretive theories and qualitative methods. For instance, Weber is sometimes said to be a

positivist yet he developed the influential concept of 'verstehen' – a process of understanding subjectivity found in the social sciences but scarcely at all in the natural sciences. (Reading 2). In general, the term structuralist rather than positivist will be used here to indicate the approach that there are factors or 'structures' external to social actors which influence their actions. One good reason for this is that many sociologists described as positivist, including Durkheim and Parsons, reject the term as a description of their approach.

Reliability and validity

An experiment or piece of research is reliable if when replicated (repeated under exactly the same conditions) it produces the same result. Reliability in the social sciences is not as high as in the natural sciences. This is because it is not possible to control the conditions of sociological research to the extent of those of natural science. A laboratory experiment is generally more precisely repeatable, and so more reliable, than a piece of sociological research.

A piece of research is valid if it produces the type of data the researcher is seeking, i.e. if it measures or illustrates what the researcher intends. Thus, a researcher wanting to know the voting intentions of the national electorate will probably conduct a large-scale sample survey, whereas a researcher wanting to understand teacher-pupil interaction will probably seek to observe particular examples. Both researchers have chosen valid approaches for what they want to find out.

It is sometimes argued that quantitative research is more likely to be reliable, and qualitative more likely to be valid. This is because the former tends to be highly structured and controlled whereas the latter is more open-ended and receptive to respondents' subjectivity. Structure and control are associated with reliability, whereas sensitivity to the subjects' own responses is considered more likely to produce a valid account of them.

Primary and secondary sources

Primary sources of information refer to data produced by the sociologist's original research. The use of observation, interviews and questionnaires produces primary data. Secondary sources of data are those which already exist, such as official statistics, newspapers, and research already carried out by other sociologists. Although these two sources of data are discussed separately, they are often used to complement each other.

Primary sources: the social survey

Quantitative methods are virtually synonymous with the social survey. Sociologists who want to produce original statistical data, usually conduct a social survey. A social survey collects standardised data usually about a large population. Questionnaires and standardised (pre-set) interviews are the most frequent techniques used in implementing social surveys. The main purpose of a social survey is to produce data which provides a basis for generalising about the survey population or target group. This means that survey responses must be able to be turned into quantitative or numerical form. Social surveys – often of a simple, descriptive kind – regularly appear in the press, indicating that a certain percentage of people are 'for' or 'against' a given proposition.

Cross-sectional and longitudinal surveys

The two main types of survey are the cross-sectional and longitudinal. The cross-sectional survey gives information about a group (usually a sample) at a particular point in time. It is usually relatively cheap and quick to do. The longitudinal survey studies a selected group (or groups) over a period of time. It enables the effect of the variables to be studied over the longer term.

The famous television survey *Seven Up* is an example in point. A group of children from different social backgrounds have been interviewed at regular intervals of seven years (so far, the group has been interviewed at seven, and on four other occasions). It is quite clear that social class has had a great effect on the lives of these children and particularly on their educational career and cultural opportunities.

Social surveys, can, then, help to establish regularities or tendencies in human behaviour, but not social scientific laws. Taken together, established tendencies provide a basis for the cumulative (gradually increasing) development of social scientific theory and knowledge, just as scientific experiment and law provides a similar basis for science.

Sampling

The target population of a social survey is often very large. It may be working class families in East London, the electorate, or striking school teachers. Practicalities of time and money, therefore, usually require that only part of, or a sample of, the total population is surveyed – thus the term 'sample survey'.

It is important to select an accurate sample. If the sample is faulty in some way, it will not provide an adequate basis on which to draw conclusions about the target population. Often, sociologists test their chosen method of research by implementing a 'pilot study' prior to a full-scale survey. A pilot survey could show whether or not respondents fully understand and are comfortable with the questions in the survey, and may also provide practical insights on such matters as the time and expense involved.

The first stage in the sampling process requires identifying the relevant population for sampling, i.e. the target population referred to above. The term sampling unit refers to the individuals, groups or other phenomena (the survey may be of newspapers, households, and so on) which could provide part of a relevant sample for the survey.

The next stage is usually to obtain a or produce a 'sampling frame' which is a list from which the sample will be taken (although this stage may not occur in less structured, and usually less accurate, sampling procedures). Examples of possible sampling frames are local electoral rolls, school rolls or the *National Census*. Although official records such as electoral rolls and the Census aim to be fully comprehensive, they rarely completely achieve this. However, such inadequacies are not usually on a scale likely to affect the statistical significance of survey findings.

Representative and non-representative sampling

The next stage in sampling – selecting the sample itself – involves the choice of a sampling technique or techniques. Usually, the function of these techniques is to ensure that the sample is as representative as possible of the members of the sampling frame and so of the relevant population, i.e. it contains (or 'represents') their typical characteristics in the same proportion. Thus, a sample taken from a given school roll which is serving as the sampling frame should contain the same proportion of females and males and ethnic minority members as the roll itself if it is intended to be fully representative of these groups. Sample size is another factor which affects representativeness. The right size for a sample varies according to the population being surveyed and the issue being researched – it is not always a case of the larger the better.

Non-representative sampling also occurs in sociology. The logic of this approach is that a non-representative sample may provide the most demanding and rigorous test of the researcher's hypothesis. Thus, Goldthorpe and Lockwood were sceptical of the view of hypothesis which was widely held in the late 1950s, that better-off members of the working class were becoming more middle class as a result of their affluence – the 'embourgeoisement hypothesis'. To give the hypothesis every chance of being confirmed and their own doubts confounded, they tested it against an untypically affluent sample of workers in Luton. However, their findings did not confirm the embourgeoisement hypothesis. They found that in a number of important ways the affluent workers could not be considered middle class (see pp. 172-4).

Random and systematic sampling

A random sample or probability sample allows each member of the group being sampled a known and equal chance of being selected. Thus, a sample of 50 students from a total of five hundred could be randomly selected by putting the names of the whole group into a hat and drawing out 50. It is more usual, however, to take a systematic sample. This involves selecting names at regular intervals, depending on how big the sample is to be. In the case of our 500 students a school or college list could be used from which every tenth name would be selected up to the five hundredth to get a sample of 50. The same technique could be used in the case of electoral registers or other lists appropriate to particular areas of research. Usually, systematic sampling leads to greater precision than totally random sampling as it produces a more even sample spread over the population list.

It is important to appreciate the limits of random sampling. The technique depends on the mathematical probability that a number of members carefully selected from a larger group will be more or less representative of that group. Sometimes the improbable happens and the sample is unrepresentative of the target population. One way in which it is sometimes appropriate to increase the precision of sampling is through stratification.

Stratified random sampling

Stratification means that before any sample selection takes place, the population is divided into a number of mutually exclusive groups or 'strata'. Each stratum is then sampled – either randomly or systematically. Thus, a researcher wanting to select from a school list a sample which contained the same proportion of male and female pupils as the list itself would stratify the list according to sex and take two separate, proportionate sub-samples. Or the process of stratification could be carried further by dividing the male and female lists into black and white males and black and white females, and then taking sub-samples of each of the four groups. In the example below a sample of one in ten has been taken from each stratified group:

Table 2.1 A stratified random sample

	Stratum size	Sub-sample
white male	60	6
black male	20	2
white female	80	8
black female	40	4

This example clearly shows that a stratified random sample has a greater chance of being representative of the total population than one which is merely random.

Quota sampling

Moser and Kalton describe quota sampling as 'a method of stratified sampling in which selection within strata is non-random'. Thus, once the researcher has decided which groups or strata to

survey, the required number (quota) of respondents within each group is then selected either by the researcher or an assistant. Moser and Kalton go on to emphasise that the 'essential difference' between probability and quota samples lies in the selection of the final sampling units.

A quota sample replaces randomness with human judgement. A researcher seeking quotas of, say, six white male, two black male, eight white female, and four black female pupils would select them rather than draw them from a sampling frame. However, since the characteristics of a given quota are predetermined (e.g. black male pupil), the possibility of human error in sample selection can be limited. But not all quota controls (characteristics) can be clearly defined. Thus, deciding which class someone belongs to may be difficult, even with the help of guidelines.

Cluster and multi-stage sampling

A cluster sample is a sample drawn only from selected parts or clusters of the total target population. Cluster sampling design is sometimes adopted when the target population is too large for a random sample to be drawn (e.g. a sample of 20,000 from a population of 50,000,000) or where no satisfactory sampling frame exists (e.g. as in some undeveloped regions). In such circumstances, separate groups or clusters of urban, rural and, perhaps, suburban areas might be used to draw the sample from.

A multi-stage sample occurs when one sample is drawn from another. A cluster sample is a specific example. Thus, selected constituencies, wards and polling districts, could be, respectively, the second, third, and fourth stages of cluster sampling. Multi-stage sampling can save time and money, although in certain respects it increases the chances of the final sample being unrepresentative.

Snowball sampling

A snowball 'sample' – if it can be so-called – is a sample of a particular group built up from an initial member (or 'contact') of that group. Research into youth gangs or criminal gangs may involve this technique. Snowball sampling lacks any statistical basis of randomness or representativeness but can make for interesting and illuminating reading. It perhaps better belongs to qualitative rather than quantitative research.

Discussion issues

What 'sampling frames' other than those suggested on p. 28 can you think of? What are their likely advantages and disadvantages?

Questionnaires

Questionnaires are the most frequent means by which a social survey is carried out. A questionnaire is a list of pre-set questions asked by the researcher of members of the sample (the respondents).

Closed and open-ended questions

Questions may be closed or fixed-choice, or open-ended. Figure 2.1 shows some examples of closed questions on the theme of gender treatment in school 'x'.

Closed questions enable ease of quantification but they limit freedom of response. They can also lead to a false sense of precision when quantified: quantification only reflects the adequacy of the questions asked and of the response choices. How adequate do you think the questions and response choices are in the figure?

Examples

1 Do you consider that female and male pupils are treated equally? Tick *one* of the boxes.

☐ Yes ☐ No

2 Score school x on the extent to which it has achieved gender equality between female and male pupils. Ring one number only.

1	2	3	4	5	6	7	8	9	10
Low									High

3 How would you rate school x on the achievement of gender equality between male and female pupils? Tick *one* of the boxes.

☐ Poor   ☐ Satisfactory   ☐ Good   ☐ Excellent

Figure 2.1 Questions with response choices

Open-ended questions are designed to allow more freedom of response – sometimes complete freedom of response. Freer responses can vary greatly and can rarely be quantified with a high level of precision as can closed ones. They are often primarily intended to provide depth and complexity – perhaps to complement numerical data. An example of an open-ended question is:

How do you think female pupils in school x are affected by the school's equal opportunity policies?

Operationalising concepts: codification

Two further matters in relation to quantification require consideration: concept operationalisation and coding. Sociologists often seek to measure such abstractions as alienation or inequality. The first requirement in operationalising a concept is to define precisely what is meant by it. This may involve breaking it down into sub-concepts, termed components, as Blauner did with alienation (see pp. 263-4). It is then necessary to establish concretely measurable characteristics or indicators of the concept. Thus, indicators of inequality may be considered to be differentials of income, health and education. These can be measured and compared.

Codification involves giving a symbolic – usually numerical – value to responses to questions. As we saw above, there is little practical difficulty in doing this in the case of closed questions which are often pre-coded on the questionnaire. Coding open-ended questions is more complex. Responses have to be put into similar categories and these categories can then be numbered for statistical comparison. Thus, answers to the example of an open-ended question given below could be categorised as follows:

How do you think female pupils in school x are affected by the school's equal opportunity policies?

(Categories used by researcher to quantify open-ended responses)

1 More females now choose scientific subjects.
2 There has been less sexual harassment of female pupils.
3 The policies have had little effect.
4 The policies have made matters worse by making people over-conscious of gender issues.

Quantifying essentially qualitative responses is not only often difficult but sometimes inappropriate. Individuals may not want their free speech subjected to cumbersome quantification, and in any case such treatment may distract from appreciation of its personal meaning.

Administering questionnaires

Questionnaires can be administered in a variety of ways including personally (by the researcher or an assistant), by post, by phone, or with a newspaper or magazine. Each of these methods has particular problems and advantages.

A questionnaire administered by an interviewer in which the latter merely reads out and, if necessary, clarifies questions for the respondent is the same as a completely structured interview (see p. 34). A personal approach of this kind usually achieves a better response rate than administering a questionnaire through the post. Difficulties in understanding the questionnaire, lack of interest or forgetfulness mean that postal questionnaires often receive a low response rate. However, postal questionnaires have the advantages of being relatively cheap compared to interviews and of being able easily to access a large sample who are perhaps geographically widely spread. Follow-up letters or visits where possible, improve postal questionnaire response rate. A low-response rate can affect the representativeness of the final sample by making it less typical of the target population.

Advantages and disadvantages of questionnaires

The main advantage of questionnaires is that they provide a wide range of data on which to base generalisations. They are an essential part of the methodological tool-kit of structural sociology.

Often a questionnaire survey is used, in traditional social scientific fashion, specifically to test an hypothesis. A celebrated example of a study which used questionnaires (as well as other techniques) has already been referred to: Goldthorpe and Lockwood's testing of the embourgeoisement hypothesis by means of their survey of affluent workers in Luton (see pp. 172-4).

The disadvantages of questionnaires partly reflect the limitation of the form itself and partly the nature of the structuralist assumptions underlying their use. The form of a questionnaire is such that the researcher 'imposes' questions on the respondent who may or may not answer them, or if s/he does, may or may not tell the truth. Low response rate, possible lies, 'jokes' and inaccuracies can all undermine the reliability of a questionnaire survey. Even a well-designed questionnaire can fall foul of these problems. The limitations of the questionnaire arguably reflect the limitations of the structural approach itself. Structuralists, sometimes by means of the use of questionnaires, attempt to build up explanations of behaviour largely in terms of external social factors. For interpretists, this misses out the most important aspect of people – their capacity to initiate meaningful and even original action. In practice most contemporary sociologists are well aware of the pitfalls of a rigidly structural approach and, even more, of the limitations of research based exclusively on a questionnaire survey. Many combine both quantitative and qualitative methods, as did Willmott and Young over 30 years ago in carrying out their survey of family and kinship in East London:

> *But the statistical material [from mainly structured interviews], essential though it was, had its obvious limitations. We had set out from the beginning with the deliberate intention to combine statistical analysis with the kind of detailed description and individual illustration that could come only from fairly free and lengthy interviews and from personal observation, because we thought that this would give a more rounded – and more accurate – account than either method alone.*
>
> (Willmott and Young, 1969:210)

Interviews

There are three types of interview: structured, semi-structured and unstructured. They vary according to the types of question asked and the data generated. A totally structured interview is a questionnaire by another name. Its main purpose is to provide quantifiable data. The semi-structured and unstructured interview produce progressively more qualitative data. In the case of the unstructured interview the researcher will invariably use only a schedule made up of general areas or topics to be covered which can serve as a checklist if responses become highly discursive. The schedule for a semi-structured interview gives more details and

direction but still allows considerable freedom of response. Two separate pieces of research into the experience of housework used schedules of this kind: Hannah Gavron's *The Captive Wife,* and Ann Oakley's *The Sociology of Housework.* A practical aspect of conducting unstructured interviews is that the researcher cannot be sure how long each one will last. Ann Oakley's interviews in the above study varied from one and a quarter to three and a half hours.

Conducting interviews

In conducting interviews, it is important that the interviewer does not say or do anything that is likely to distort responses. Inadvertently intimidating or confusing the interviewee or seeming to imply that a particular answer is correct is likely to have an adverse effect on the data produced by the interview. In general, it is good practice politely to introduce oneself and the purposes of the research. In the case of long, unstructured interviews, considerable effort may be required to lay the ground for the interview – perhaps through using an intermediary-contact or by writing or phoning. In the interview situation itself, the brief, factual questions on such matters as the age and status of the respondent with which most interviews of whatever type usually begin provide a further opportunity to establish interviewer-interviewee rapport before more probing or demanding questions are asked. When possible, it is usually good practice to check responses with the interviewee, prior to concluding the interview. This is not only a check on accuracy but recognises that the data 'belong' first and foremost to the respondent.

Recording interviews

It is sometimes preferable to record an interview rather than attempt to take a written record during the course of the interview. The tape can be transcribed later prior to analysis. It can be particularly convenient to record unstructured and group interviews (i.e. interviews with two or more respondents) when the attention, sensitivity and skill of the interviewer is likely to be needed exclusively in conducting the interview. An interviewer who is busily writing in an attempt to 'keep up with' what is being said may well interfere with the natural flow of responses and so inhibit free and unselfconscious expression of feeling and opinion. It is easier for respondents to 'forget about' a tape-recorder or even a video-camera than a frantically scribbling interviewer. However, a film or video camera is potentially distracting – especially if respondents are tempted to 'play to the camera'. A visual recording can show gestures and expressions which may clarify respondents' meanings but the degree to which this is so may be marginal.

During the 1970s and 1980s, a number of studies of secondary school pupils using tape-recorded unstructured interviews were conducted. These included Paul Willis's *Learning to Labour* – a study of a group of working class 'lads' and M Mac an Ghaill's *Young, Gifted and Black* – a study of several single-sex groups of black students.

What is noticeable in both cases in reading the transcribed texts of the group interviews is the brief and infrequent nature of the prompts and questions of the interviewers. Often, the respondents seem to 'take off' into their own conversation – which is precisely what an interviewer would generally hope for. Thus, in each of three transcripts with a group of young women referred to as 'the sisters', Mac an Ghaill makes only a single intervention – in each case further to prompt a line of thought already being pursued by a respondent. These are the interventions – all that occur in well over a thousand words of transcribed text:

1 'What do you mean? Compared to black women?'
2 'What about your brothers?'
3 'You changed your style and they didn't?'

A general indicator of a skilled in-depth interviewer is one who says little but says it effectively and creates space for the respondent(s) to reply.

Advantages and disadvantages of interviews

The advantages and disadvantages of interviews vary according to the type of interview. Those of the totally structured interview are the same as those of the questionnaire discussed above: it generates quantifiable data which provide a basis for generalisation. At the other extreme, the unstructured interview is potentially one of the most sensitive tools of qualitative research. By allowing such freedom of response, it enables the researcher to understand the feelings, motives and thinking of the respondent – always assuming that some form of misconception or miscommunication is not occurring. The nature of the data produced by unstructured interviews tends to be different in one significant way from that produced by participant observation, another key method of qualitative research (discussed below). Participant observation usually provides information about the research subject in natural, everyday action. The structured interview gives an opportunity for subjects to reflect on and explain action – their own or others. It is quite common, therefore, to find the two methods used in a complementary way. Thus, in his study of homosexuals, Laud Humphreys first played the participant observational role of 'voyeur' (an accepted one within the homosexual community). He then went on to interview twelve of the group.

Observation can be divided into non-participant and participant observation. In both cases, the observation may be overt (open, not hidden) or covert (hidden, secret). These different circumstances raise different problems.

Observations

Non-participant observation

Non-participant observation involves the sociologist in an exclusively observational role in relation to the subject of the research. At least that is the theory. In fact, however, one of the earliest examples of the use of observational technique showed how difficult it is for the researcher to remain entirely separate from the subject. This was in Elton Mayo's overt observation of the Hawthorne electricity plant in Chicago. Mayo and his team were asked to examine the effects of various changes in working conditions on the productivity of the work force at the Hawthorne factory. Mayo found that virtually any change in variables affecting working conditions – even those that made conditions worse than they were originally – seemed to result in an improvement in productivity! At last, he was forced to conclude that what caused the improvement in production was the presence of the research team itself. It had stimulated the workforce to greater efforts! The Hawthorne experiment provides a strong warning to sociologists to be aware of the effect they themselves can have on their findings. Researcher effect of this kind is sometimes referred to as 'Hawthorne effect'. Taking their cue from Mayo's experience, some sociologists have preferred to 'factor out' the effect of their own presence by observing their subject matter covertly.

One such piece of research is Valerie Yule's covert observation of adult-child interaction. Yule observed 85 adult-child pairs for three minutes each, all of them matched with another pair of people for comparison (the 'control' pairs were highly varied in terms of age and included male-female, all-female and all-male). Yule's interesting findings were that all-adult pairs tend to interact much more positively than adult-child pairs.

Non-participant observation often lends itself to a structured, quantitative analysis and presentation of findings, even though as in Yule's research the subject matter of the enquiry may be about the quality of human interaction. Yule observed that whereas four fifths of the all adult pairs 'had some speech together, or at least a glance or a smile', over half of the adults in the adult-child pairs 'took no notice of the children they were with' during the three minutes period of observation. For two-fifths of the adult-child sample, the interaction was negative. She quantifies those interactions that did occur in a simple, descriptive way. Here are some examples:

> *Seven adults crossed roads telling their children to look out or hurry up, but none of them looked at the children they were speaking to. Five yanked the child by arm or hand.*
>
> *Six children cried in pushers. Three were smacked, two given sweets round the side of the pusher without a glance at them, and one was ignored.*

> *Four children in shops were told to behave themselves in varying degrees of severity, and one was then pacified with sweets.*
>
> *Four children on buses were scolded or smacked for misbehaviour, following complete inattention.*
>
> *Four children at bus stops were told to behave or keep still, and one was cuffed.*
>
> *Four children tried to talk to adults who paid no attention.*
>
> *Three children tried to talk to adults and were rejected.*
>
> (Yule, 1986:445)

As far as achieving objectivity, non-participant observation, particularly covert, has certain advantages. The time and energy of the researcher can be devoted exclusively to precise observation (and recording). In contrast to participant observation, the judgement of the researcher cannot be biased or distorted by relationships with research subjects built up during the course of research. On the other hand, there is a limitation on the nature of explanation possible in research based exclusively on non-participant observation. This is that the views and feelings the actors have about their actions cannot be systematically accessed by the researcher and may not be expressed at all unless they happen to come up during the course of observation. To acquire such qualitative information, non-participant observation can usefully be supported by in-depth interviews, with at least a sub-sample of those observed or by some other form of qualitative method.

Participant observation

Participant observation involves the sociologist taking part in the social action which s/he seeks to describe and understand. It is perhaps the most qualitative of all sociological methods but, as is always the case, it is not possible to categorise, number and tabulate all the data produced by this form of research. Participant observation has been particularly widely employed since the 1960s by interactionists and ethnomethodologists.

Ethnography

The origins of participant observation within social science go back at least to the early part of the twentieth century when anthropologists (researchers into non-literate societies) sometimes adopted it as part of the ethnographic approach. Ethnography is research based on closely observing and recording the way of life of a particular culture or subculture, and participant observation was seen as a way of getting as close as possible to the subjects of the research. The method was notably employed by Bronislow Malinowski and Margaret Mead (see Chapter 15 for further reference to Mead's work). One of the societies that Malinowski examined was the Trobriand Islanders of the Western Pacific.

Malinowski used participant observation for the same purposes as more recent sociologists. He wanted to 'grasp the natives' point of view', to 'realise (their) vision of the world' and observe them 'acting naturally'. To do this he remained with them for over a year. In order for the participant observer to give people the opportunity to adjust to her or his presence and to show a typical range of behaviour, s/he must often be prepared to spend lengthy periods of time with them. It is crucial for the participant observer to win the confidence and acceptance of the people s/he is studying if they are to behave naturally. In the case of Margaret Mead, recent research suggests that she was not always taken entirely seriously by the subjects of her study, adolescent Samoan girls. In her book, *Coming of Age in Samoa*, first published during the 1920s, she reports that women were sexually remarkably free by Western standards. Freeman (1983) now argues that the girls were largely 'having her on' in this matter.

Participant observation within subcultures

More recent participant observational studies have often been of specific subcultures. In particular, there has been a large number of participant observational studies of gangs and other youth subcultural groups. One of the earliest and most influential of these was William Foote Whyte's *Street Corner Society*. Whyte studied a gang in a poor, largely Italian immigrant part of Chicago. He described himself as 'seeking to build a sociology based on observed interpersonal events'. The following quotation from Whyte states a major justification for the participant observational approach:

> *As I sat and listened, I learned the answers to questions that I would not even have had the sense to ask if I had been getting my information solely on an interviewing basis.*
>
> (Whyte, 1955:303)

In other words, participant observation teaches the social scientist what questions to ask as well as providing some of the answers.

In view of the apparent deception perpetrated on Margaret Mead, it is instructive that Whyte gained much of his information and insight from Doc, a gang leader with whom he struck up a friendship. Whyte confided overtly in Doc about the nature of his research although he was vague about it with others. Doc responded helpfully. This is a case when a strong subjective involvement of researcher and subject contributed positively to the research. Whyte suggests that he began his research as a participant observer and ended as an 'observing participant' and by doing so came to understand matters more deeply.

Figure 2.2 Typical members of a 'gang of lads': deviant male subcultures – a popular area for participant observation among (male) sociologists

Another study of a gang is James Patrick's *A Glasgow Gang Observed* (1973). Adopting a covert approach, Patrick joined a Glasgow gang. The result is a fascinating study of gang behaviour, and particularly of gang hierarchy and ritual. But was Patrick justified in keeping his identity secret? According to the author's own account, the members of the gang did not think so and would happily exact revenge on him for misleading them. No general moral rule can be laid down on this question of secrecy: each sociologist must make her or his own judgement on the matter. Patrick's study also raises another moral issue which can occur in the course of participant observation into areas of deviancy. Does 'the cause of research' justify the sociologist adopting a deviant identity and perhaps committing deviant acts?

Another study which was both covert (in part) and involved the adoption of a deviant role was Laud Humphreys' study of homosexuality in public toilets in the United States. Humphreys adopted the role of 'watcher' or 'voyeur' of the sexual activities of others. Only later, after he had become accepted, did he reveal his identity as a researcher and converse openly with some of the homosexuals. In this way he attempted to achieve the benefits of naturalistic observation and of direct questioning.

Ken Pryce's *Endless Pressure* (1979) – a study of the Afro-Caribbean community of the St Paul's area of Bristol – is now a classic of participant observation. Pryce adapted his approach to convenience and circumstances. Thus, he revealed his identity as a researcher to some but not to others. In an incidental but helpful meeting with a 'hustler', he concealed it 'not … to deceive, but merely to sustain … rapport'. However, with a more conventional group of contacts, he simply remarks that 'it was not necessary to be guarded about my true identity as a researcher'. Similarly, the precise focus of Pryce's study developed actively during the course of research. As he puts it, in terms similar to Whyte's: 'insights and hypotheses that later were to form the substance of the thesis, were developed in the actual process of investigation'.

Advantages and disadvantages of participant observation

The main advantage and disadvantage of participant observation are opposite sides of the same coin: the method can bring all the insight and understanding that comes with subjective involvement but also all the possible loss of objectivity. Ronald Frankenburg, himself the author of a participant observational study of life in a Welsh village, has usefully suggested three stages of research for the participant observer which offer some safeguard against excessive subjectivity. Each of these stages involves a different degree of involvement with the subject matter. Firstly, the research project must be set up – a relatively objective process. Secondly, the sociologist becomes subjectively (personally) involved with those s/he wishes to study. thirdly, s/he withdraws to consider and assess her/his experience and findings.

In her research into the 'Moonies' (Unification Church), Eileen Barker experienced three phases in what is basically the second stage of Frankenburg's model. These were:

1 passive (e.g. watching and listening)
2 interactive (e.g. conversing, explorative questions)
3 active (e.g. more insistent, 'awkward' questions)

This phasing in gave more structure and control to the process of participation. (Reading 4)

Authors of participant observational studies are not uncommonly accused of sentimentalising and over-romanticising the deviants, criminals and youth groups which have typically been the subjects of their research. Certainly, there is a strong suggestion of identification with 'the outsider' in a number of classic participant observational studies but on the credit side such studies often have an authenticity which could scarcely be achieved by survey work.

Discussions issues

What areas/topics of research can you think of which would lend themselves particularly to the use of participant observation and/or unstructured interviews? Why might quantitative methods produce less satisfactory results in such cases?

The relationship between perspectives and methods

There is a general, but by no means precise relationship between the theoretical perspectives described in Chapter 1 and the methods of primary research described above. This relationship is presented in Figure 2.3.

It is worth summarising three ways in which the structural/quantitative and interpretive/qualitative lines are

frequently crossed. First, methods generally thought of as of a particular type can in fact often be used to produce data of the other type. Thus, Valerie Yule used observation ('normally' thought of as a qualitative method) to quantify adult-child interactions. Second, the two types of theory-methods are often used to complement each other. Thus, John Goldthorpe collected personal autobiographical data of a qualitative kind from a sub-sample of his main sample of 10,000 respondents to a questionnaire on social mobility (see pp. 144-5). Third, although well-aware of the important general linkages along structural/quantitative and interpretive/qualitative lines, sociologists often adopt whatever approaches and techniques seem most effectively to meet the needs of their research, *Doing Sociological Research*, which generally show a considerable degree of methodological pragmatism and improvisation. In principle and in practice, they argue that methodological 'pluralism' (variety) is often more effective than an 'either/or' approach.

Structural theories	Interpretive theories
Marxism, functionalism, Weber/social action,	Interactionism, Ethnomethodology
Quantitative methods	**Qualitative methods**
Social surveys, questionnaires, comparative surveys, interviews	Unstructured interviews, observation (Non PO and PO)

Note: Max Weber's social action theory is presented as mainly structural but partly interpretive.

Figure 2.3 Relationships between theories and methods

Secondary sources

Secondary sources of data are those which already exist. This makes the field rather wide! Almost any data can be used in a study providing they are used relevantly and accurately.

Official statistics

The Census – a demographic survey of the whole population – was first conducted in 1801 and has been held at regular intervals ever since. From that time central government has been the major producer, user and disseminator of large-scale information. In addition to questions on 'established' areas such as occupation and residence, the 1991 Census was the first to ask a question about ethnic origin. Some were uneasy about this. What is your own view? Another issue in relation to the 1991 Census was the greater number of non-responses in inner-urban areas than elsewhere. This may have been because non-poll-tax payers in the inner-cities did not accept official assurances that census responses were wholly confidential, and feared that their returns might be accessed by local authorities to locate them. This matter could affect the overall reliability of the 1991 census data. Today each government department carries out its own research, which is co-ordinated by the Government Statistical Service. Two well-known annual digests of official statistics covering the main areas of public life are *Social Trends* and the *Annual Abstract of Statistics*. The former is designed for more popular consumption but each is based on the same sources.

There is lively debate among sociologists about the use of official statistics in research. Both interpretists and Marxists make radical criticisms of their validity and reliability. For instance, Cicourel and Garfinkel argue that, respectively, police and judicial stereotypes of offenders influence criminal statistics. Atkinson has made a similar case in relation to the taken-for-granted assumptions of coroners about what constitutes evidence of suicide. For their part Marxists argue that statistics collected by the capitalist state are generally framed and presented in a way which supports the capitalist system. In particular, they contend that there is a high degree of official tolerance to 'the crimes of the powerful'.

The accusation that official statistics were used in a biased, or at least suspect, fashion by government was made quite widely by opposition politicians and press in the 1980s and early 1990s. In particular, it was noted that nearly all of more than 30 changes in the way the official unemployment figures were computed resulted in a decrease in the total figure. In this case, part of the dispute centred on what constituted unemployment (being registered at a Job Centre? being unemployed for at least a month?), i.e. on how unemployment should be defined. The question of definition came to the fore even more sharply in a long-running debate on whether the numbers of those in poverty had increased or not under the Conservative government. Critics tended to argue that the numbers in relative poverty (i.e. allowing for changing standards) had increased whereas a number of Conservative politicians argued that precisely because standards of assessing poverty have changed, it is pointless to assess how many are 'in poverty'.

Issues relating to the use of official statistics are discussed in detail in relation to crime (see pp. 340-8), suicide (see pp. 361-3), and poverty (see pp. 381-3).

Other sources of statistics

In addition to the routine production of statistics, special government reports – often the work of 'Government commissions' – dealing with important areas of national interest or concern appear from time to time. Often these contain important statistical and other data. One such report was *Inequalities in Health*, sometimes referred to by the name of its chairman as the *Black Report*. The report provided a mine of information on social inequality and ill-health.

Many voluntary organisations and pressure groups regularly publish statistics in their specialist area. Unsurprisingly, their statistics often appear to be selected and presented to favour their own causes. Nevertheless, statistical data provided by, for example,

the Low Pay Unit and National Society for the Prevention of Cruelty to Children, frequently inform and enhance public awareness and debate on key social issues.

Historical sources

Historical references are important in providing a basis of comparison in sociology, and also of course in establishing patterns of social change. Inevitably, there are often issues of reliability and interpretation in relation to historical evidence. For instance, Friedrich Engels' still influential *The Origin of the Family, Private Property and the State* (1884) was based on a secondary source, Lewis Morgan's *Ancient Society*, which recent scholarship has challenged in relation both to aspect of factual accuracy and interpretation. Peter Laslett's study, *Household and Family in Past Time* (1972) is generally accepted as authoritative. Laslett used statistical data from parish records which largely exploded the 'myth' of the predominance of the extended family in pre-industrial Britain – a highly significant contribution to the framework of family analysis.

Historical study provides much pictorial, artistic and other data of a non-statistical and also non-printed kind. The proportion of such data to statistical and printed material becomes greater the further one goes back in history: Philip Ariès *Centuries of Childhood* (1973) makes telling use of family portraits in pursuing his case that childhood was not conceived of as a separate 'age stage' in medieval Europe. Children are depicted in such portraits as 'little adults'. Such evidence usually requires corroboration. Thus, Ariès also draws on written materials to substantiate his argument.

Local historical sources have the advantage of accessibility to students. For example, an examination of disused factory or dock records and sites and, particularly, interviews with long-time inhabitants of an area (oral history) can provide the basis of lively social history/sociology. The former Open University course, *Popular Culture* effectively used three 'official' (Blackpool Corporation) holiday brochures, from the late nineteenth century, the 1920s, and the current year to exemplify the changing nature of the seaside holiday in the cultural life of the north west, particularly for the working class. The 'story' was further brought up-to-date by student visits to five sites in Blackpool, including the Pleasure Beach and Coral Island, which were each subjected to cultural analysis. This kind of imaginative work can bring social science to light in a way that a textbook could not. For 'Blackpool', read 'Southend', 'Brighton' or 'Scarborough'!

Personal documents

A personal document gives a participant's own view of particular experiences. Such sources are used in sociology to represent the opinions and meaning of actors involved in given social situations. Examples of personal documents are diaries, letters and informal life-histories. Published autobiographies are still personal documents but they may be filtered by consideration of others' feelings and by legal requirements, such as libel laws.

1 Autobiographical data: research subject

Sometimes, researchers who have conducted large-scale social surveys encourage a number of respondents to produce some form of personal document to give qualitative depth to their quantitative data. Both Young and Willmott in their survey of the family in Bethnal Green and John H Goldthorpe *et al.*, in their survey of social mobility, did this. In the former case, some respondents kept personal diaries and in the latter some respondents provided life-histories. Goldthorpe and his colleagues provided eight questions for their respondents which were posed 'in an entirely open-ended form'. Here is a brief extract from the introductory *Life-History Notes Leaflet* with which respondents were provided:

> *Below we have a list of questions. If you would write a paragraph or so in answer to each of these, this would give us the kind of notes that we want. On the other hand, you may wish to arrange what you write in your own way, taking these questions simply as a guide to the points which chiefly interest us.*
>
> *(Goldthorpe et al., 1980:219)*

The more the sociologist tries to 'guide' or 'structure' responses, the less personally valid they are likely to be. Nevertheless, in general, personal documents tend to score high on validity, though there is no guarantee of their wider representativeness.

However, autobiographical data is not merely a way of putting human flesh on statistical bones. It can serve as a check on or, at least, provide another viewpoint to statistically-based findings. Thus, among Goldthorpe's respondents, there were some whom he categorised as being stable in class position who clearly considered that they had been socially mobile. It was fair and accurate to record these perceptions brought to light through the personal documents. They could perhaps provide data for a future research agenda.

2 Autobiographical data: research author

If autobiographical data on the subject(s) of research can be useful, can the reader of a piece of sociological research benefit from knowing something about its author and, if so, what? Current sociological opinion tends to the view that author and research are inextricably bound together. However, before examining why this is so, it is worth reiterating the classical sociological answer to this question viz., that the sociologist should try to be as 'objective' as possible in the course of research. Weber argued along these lines. Charles Wright Mills, aware of the difficulties in achieving objectivity, urged sociologists to clarify and state their values to their reading public, who could then judge whether or not these affected their research.

Much sociological research is motivated by the interests and values of those who undertake it. This is especially true of areas

recently opened up to examination such as gender and sexuality and ethnic identity. For instance, people who have experienced gender discrimination, or domestic or racial violence, or who have struggled to develop their cultural identity might want to research the wider context of these matters. Can their own experience be regarded as research data and, therefore, included in the write-up? The answer here is in the affirmative provided that the personal experience is relevant to the research and is incorporated effectively. Thus, the relationship between personal experience and public issues can be explored without undermining methodological rigour. Jane Ribbens puts the matter well in advocating that students be more frequently invited to use autobiographical writing as part of their sociology:

> *Society thus can be seen to occur 'inside' ourselves. To use ourselves as sources for sociological analysis is a challenging project requiring students to learn to regard their autobiographies in terms of how sociological audiences will receive them.*
>
> *(Sociology, 1993:81)*

There are two main ways in which bringing personal experience into sociological research can go wrong. First, the writer may become so emotional, biased or perhaps political (i.e. subjective) that any general relevance of the research is lost. A type of research which is particularly susceptible to this problem is action research – in which the research is aimed at solving a particular practical problem e.g. racism in a school. The second danger is that the research becomes simply trivial or anecdotal and again, therefore, of no wider relevance.

The mass media

The mass media provide an ever-growing potential source of material for sociologists. This material is of two types. First, is data routinely provided in programmes which may be supported by considerable research staff and resources. Thus, programmes such as *Panorama* and *World In Action* pour out a wealth of data which are often more up-to-date than anything else available. The problem is that the sociologist cannot be sure whether these data are accurate, so they need to be checked and the source clearly acknowledged in any published work.

More typically, sociologists use material from the printed and visual media for critical analysis. Thus, a variety of publications or broadcasts (more usually, a series of broadcasts) have been analysed for political or other ideological bias. The Glasgow Media Group has regularly published analyses of television news broadcasts in which the content has been scrutinised and quantified for bias (see pp. 510-11). This method is termed content analysis. Similar content analysis of sexism and racism in the media has also occurred. Another technique, often used in combination with content analysis, is semiological analysis. This involves working out or 'decoding' the meaning of mainly visual symbols and signs.

Like nearly all secondary source material, mass media material is not produced primarily for sociological use. It may, therefore, be incomplete or superficial from a sociologist's point of view. It may also be personally or politically biased and it is essential that the sociologist does not merely pass this on uncritically to readers.

Is sociology a science?

If science is defined broadly as the accumulation of verifiable knowledge, then sociology is a science. If it is defined narrowly as the testing of hypotheses by positivistic methodology, then sociology can hardly claim to be a science. Such a definition would also exclude much observational work in other disciplines. It is true, however, that sociology rarely produces results that are as precise and repeatable as those produced by the natural sciences. Nevertheless, Durkheim, Marx and Weber never stopped trying to be as scientific as possible and their work laid a rich theoretical and methodological basis for the further development of the discipline along scientific lines. More recently, the complex and rigorous empirical research of professional sociologists, such as John Goldthorpe and A H Halsey, goes far beyond the competence and commonsense understanding of lay people in its methodological basis and findings.

In contrast to self-consciously scientific approaches to sociology, interpretive sociology is often less concerned with causal explanation or factual description than with human understanding. Perhaps such work is closer to the humanities than to sciences. This does not make it unscientific but, perhaps, it is essentially non-scientific. Unlike functionalists and many Marxists, interpretative sociologists have often shown no great desire to have their work classified as scientific. C Wright Mills, a sociologist who does not admit to a simple label himself, refers disparagingly to the 'cook-book' appearance of some scientifically oriented sociological textbooks. Erving Goffman compares traditional positivist methodology to the instructions on a child's chemistry set: 'follow the rules and you, too, can be a real scientist'.

Interpretive sociologists willingly embrace what embarrasses the positivists: the subjective element in society and in sociological research. Subjectivity cuts two ways. Firstly, researchers have their own values: secondly, those being studied behave individually and therefore in a way that cannot be precisely predicted. Ethnomethodologists, such as Cicourel and Garfinkel, claim that it is impossible for sociologists to be passive observers of 'truth'. What they 'see' is bound, in some sense, to be the result of the interaction between themselves and what they study. Yet ethnomethodologists also claim to be in the business of discovering and describing how people act and interact. Given their emphasis upon the subjective element in perception, how can they be confident of the accuracy of their own observations and reports? Their answer is that they, at least, are aware of the problem and so better able to deal with it

than positivists, who may naively believe that they can 'factor themselves out' of their work. On the matter of the individuality of the subject of social research, Schütz, the phenomenologist, is relevant, and goes further than the ethnomethodologists. He points out that, whereas the natural sciences have concepts about objects, the social sciences have concepts about objects which have concepts about objects (including, perhaps, the researcher). In other words, people can think and, we must add, choose. They may even decide deliberately to mislead the researcher. Because of this, the level of accurate prediction in the social sciences can never be as high as in the natural sciences. Schütz, however, also points out that groups of people share common patterns of thought and behaviour, and that the researcher is able to check his or her descriptions of these with those of other observers. If there is agreement about what is observed, this is perhaps as close as achieving objectivity as is possible.

So much for what sociologists themselves think about the nature of their discipline. We now examine the opinions of two major philosophers of science upon the same issue (a philosopher of science is somebody who systematically attempts to clarify the principles underlying science). On the whole, these commentators from outside sociology have tended to take a reproving tone. Karl Popper's particular 'bogey man' is Marx. It is, however, Marx 'the prophet of revolution' that Popper admonishes – not Marx the sociologist – although, in fairness, Popper's argument is that the two are inseparable. He says that in 'prophesying' proletarian revolution, Marx is essentially unscientific in taking as given something that has not yet happened. In Popper's view, 'prophecy', religion and ideology have no place in science and, therefore, he declares Marxism to be unscientific. We do not have to accept Popper's conclusion to agree that Marxists' sociological theory and concepts must be open to the same criticism and testing as those of other perspectives. The fact that Marxist sociologists are likely to be politically Marxists does not free them from the constraints of the discipline. No sensible Marxist sociologist would want the kind of illusory freedom in which mere assertion replaces argument based on reason and evidence. It is Popper's soundest and central point that social science, like natural science, must constantly test and re-test its theories. The most rigorous way to do this is for the researcher to attempt to falsify, rather than verify, his or her own hypotheses – Popper's famous principle of falsification. He argues that Marxism cannot be scientific because many of its major theories refer to the future and are not, therefore, open to falsification. It is impossible to prove definitely that there will not be a proletarian revolution because the future is unknown. The statement that there will be one is, therefore, unscientific. In their own defence, some modern Marxists would argue that their immediate concern is less with proving or falsifying propositions than with providing a theoretical critique of capitalist society and with developing theoretical alternatives to it. Most of them would also dissociate themselves from the supposed prophetic element in Marx's writing and, to that extent Popper's criticisms become redundant.

A further point made by Popper is of particular interest to sociologists. It is that no hypothesis can be considered finally proven. For example, although thousands of white swans have been sighted, there remains the possibility of coming across a black one. Similarly, to do the same experiment 999 times with the same result may seem to prove something, but the thousandth experiment may produce a different result. The practice of science involves a sort of industrious scepticism and Popper would frankly like to see more evidence of it among social scientists. More research and less theorising seems to be his advice.

Ernest Gellner is a recent writer in the tradition of Popper. His particular objection is to Garfinkel's ethnomethodology. He condemns its obsession with subjectivism as mere romanticism and, like Popper, he advocates a staunchly empirical approach to the understanding of society. Although the Marxist Barry Hindess has little else in common with Popper and Gellner, he also attacks extreme ethnomethodological subjectivism in his critique of statistics.

There is much commonsense – if this is not too odd a word to use of such sophisticated work – in the thought of Popper and Gellner. Theoretical cloud castles in the sky must be brought to earth and examined for substance and content, a comment that applies to functionalism as much as to Marxism. Similarly, those who are so 'hung up' on subjectivism that they allow little hope of meaningful sociological discourse hardly help to further the development of the discipline as a collective enterprise. (For a further discussion of this point, see Chapter 21).

What is science?

Until now, we have tended to regard science as a standard by which to take the measure of social science. Apart from a simple distinction between a broad and narrow definition of science, we have assumed the concept of science itself to be unproblematic. In so doing, we are in danger of giving it the status of a sort of sacred cow, divine and inscrutable. The work of Thomas Kuhn, however, attempts to 'debunk' such a reverential view of science and to ask not only how true it is to its own professed principles of empiricism and objectivity, but also whether these principles are the ones by which the natural sciences actually operate. Subjectivity may be a spectre that haunts science as well as social science.

Kuhn dismisses the notion that science is merely a collection of theories, methods and factual findings. Instead, he suggests the view that scientists, like sociologists, make use of paradigms or perspectives about their specialist fields which influence the direction and nature of their experimental research. Thus, Einstein's theories can be said to have provided the basis of a new working paradigm for astro-physics. Many of his ideas were speculative, partial and unproven, but they have since inspired more detailed research into problems concerning space and time. To this extent, Einstein's thought seems to provide much the same function as a sociological perspective.

A central feature of Kuhn's argument is that scientific paradigms change radically at certain periods in history. Thus, his book is entitled *The Structure of Scientific Revolutions*. This revolutionary change occurs when a discovery cannot be made to fit into the dominant paradigm. We need an example here. For centuries, it was believed that the earth was the centre of the universe and that the sun revolved around it. This paradigm survived despite the increasing difficulty of accommodating newly discovered facts to it. Eventually, Copernicus produced evidence that overturned it. A new paradigm, that the earth revolves around the sun, became accepted.

Given paradigmatic changes and revolutions within the sciences, similar disagreements in sociology, expressed through the perspectives, appear less crippling to the claims of the subject to respectability and even scientific status. It is true that the natural sciences generate a greater 'sense' of consensus about theoretical and methodological approach than sociology does, but it is still a young discipline and it is possible that greater 'paradigmatic unity' may yet develop.

A further criticism may be offered against the notion of science as a monument to objectivity. Science, too, is haunted by the problem of subjectivity. First, a relatively minor point. Heisenberg's uncertainty principle points out that the light required to observe tiny particles will affect the way they behave. Thus, to a small degree, the scientist causes the behaviour he observes! That is a classic example of the dilemma of subjectivity. Second, a serious ethical point. Scientific research, like social research, takes place in society. Research provides knowledge which may be used constructively or destructively. Scientists who allow their skills to be used in a cause they believe to be morally wrong are in the same position as soldiers, administrators and others who do the same. Research findings do not exist in a social vacuum – some power is likely to use them. Einstein believed passionately that scientists should take responsibility for the work they do and its possible application to human life.

What is sociology?

By way of a long detour, we come again to this question. Sociology is the study of human social life by any means that are effective. These may be more or less scientific, depending on how that term is defined, or even non-scientific. All that is necessary is that their application contributes to our knowledge and understanding of social life. To do this, 'findings' must be presented sufficiently intelligibly to be communicable to the body of professional sociologists (and, ideally, via them to the interested public). C Wright Mills is surely correct when he argues that sociology is better practised with imagination and flexibility than with rigid adherence to the models of natural science. Sociology is a craft to be judged by its product: what works best is best. Whilst not rejecting the broadly scientific basis of sociology, Nisbet caps Mills in stressing the role of the creative imagination in sociology. This, he says, gives it the quality of an art form. Nisbet's observation brings the wheel full circle: sociology is both science and art. Given the complexity of its subject matter, it needs to be.

> ### Questions
>
> 1   Make a list of arguments for and against the view that sociology is a science. On balance, what is your own view? (Do individually or in groups.)
> 2   Briefly describe one method more appropriate to the social than to the natural sciences. What is the purpose of this method? (see Readings 2 and 4)

Tradition, modernity, postmodernity and sociology

The final section in Chapter 1 introduced the three main types of society and the main types of social explanations associated with each. The previous section in this chapter discussed whether or not sociology is a science. This section develops these themes more fully and particularly seeks to explain postmodernism and postmodernity.

Tradition and modernity

The terms traditional society, modernity and postmodernity are widely used in sociology to indicate three different types of society. This gives them first rank importance in the 'league-table' of sociological concepts. There is a rough consensus about the meanings of the first two terms but not about that of the third to which we will return later. The following definitions of tradition and modernity would probably command broad agreement:

Tradition is: 'A set of social practices which seek to celebrate and inculcate (socialise into) certain behavioural norms and values implying continuity (deep links) with a real or imagined past, and usually associated with widely accepted rituals or other forms of symbolic behaviour (e.g. sacrifices, holy feasts)' (*Oxford Dictionary of Sociology*: 537). (Author's brackets)

> *In short, modernity can be taken as a summary term, referring to that cluster of social, economic and political systems brought into being in the West from somewhere around the eighteenth century onwards.*
>
> *(Sarrup: 1993)*

Sarrup's short definition may be assumed to include under 'social', cultural and intellectual developments as well. It is on these that we will tend to concentrate in this chapter, given that the radical social, economic and political break made with the past in the eighteenth/early nineteenth century has already briefly been introduced (see pp. 5-6).

Stuart Hall: modernity and tradition

Consideration will now be given to the substantial break with traditional society that modernity represents. We can use Stuart Hall's outline of the distinctive characteristics of modern society as the basis of a comparison between modern and traditional society.

1   Political

The dominance of secular, political authority over the new nation-state and the marginalisation of church/religious influence from state/political matters.

2   Economic

The replacing of feudal and other precapitalist economies by an economy in which a developed monetary (money) system provides the medium for exchange (trade), 'based on the large-scale production and consumption of commodities for the market, extensive ownership of private property and the accumulation of capital on a systematic, long-term basis' (a description strongly reflecting Marx's work).

3   Social

The decline of the traditional social order (e.g. feudalism) and the development of new division of labour and the emergence of new classes and of changed but still patriarchal relations between men and women.

4   Religious

The decline of religion and the rise of a secular, materialist culture.

5   Intellectual

The rise of a scientific, rationalist way of categorising or looking at the world. Points 4 and 5 are closely linked (and reflect Max Weber's work).

6   Cultural

New communities are constructed – some ethnic or national – which challenge the traditional, transnational community of Christendom. Newly formed nations develop their own symbols and interpretations of history – a process which intensifies in the nineteenth century. Modern nations construct their own identities and traditions – selectively, to suit their own purposes. Thus, French national identity was forged partly in the rejection of aristocracy and monarchy whereas in Britain the monarchy became for many a symbol of nation.

As Hall says, these political, economic, social and cultural processes were the 'motors' which formed modernity. However, powerful though the transformation was, it was neither immediate nor ever complete. Tradition survives, especially in Britain. In Britain it continues not only in residues such as the monarchy and

House of Lords but in the efforts of all kinds of groups to find precedent and authority for their own beliefs and activities in the past.

For example, modern socialist, Tony Benn, though he renounced his hereditary peerage, still sought traditional precedent for his socialist beliefs in the activities of the radical seventeenth century group, the Levellers.

Anthony Giddens: tradition and modernity

In his essay, *Living in a Post-Traditional Society* (1994) Anthony Gidden's analyses: the nature of tradition and the continuing concern with tradition or inventing tradition in modern societies. Giddens defines tradition as follows (his definition is followed by a full explanation):

> *I shall understand 'tradition' in the following way. Tradition … is bound up with memory, specifically what Maurice Halbwachs terms 'collective memory'; involves ritual; is connected with what I shall call a 'formulaic notion of truth'; has guardians; and, unlike custom, has a binding force which has a combined moral and emotional content.*
>
> *Memory, like tradition – in some sense or another – is about organising of the past in relation to the present.*
>
> *(1994:95)*

Gidden's definition of tradition can be paraphrased as follows. He states that awareness of tradition is a kind of group memory or imagined memory of the past; tradition involves ritual; offers a recipe for the truth; has 'guardians' such as immams or priests; and unlike everyday customs, generates deep moral and emotional attachment.

Individual memory and collective tradition are both ways of recalling and making sense of the past or meaningfully relating the past to the present. He states elsewhere that tradition acts as a kind of 'glue' that holds society together. National saints' days, independence days, armistice day, and royal birthdays are relevant examples.

Although Giddens asserts starkly that 'modernity destroys tradition' (91) he argues that especially in *early* modernity, traditional attitudes and behaviour persisted and actually contributed to the earlier phases of modern social development. In the early nineteenth century, traditional political and religious authorities were still cited by central and local elites to encourage hard work and conformity albeit in an increasingly industrial and urban context. Like Hall, Giddens also stresses the invented nature of much tradition, particularly the growing emphasis on 'the nation' as a focus of loyalty and social solidarity. However, traditional *local* community did not break up overnight in the face of a growing sense of national identity. Even newer urban and suburban settlements often developed character and traditions partly independent of national, commercial and cultural trends.

According to Giddens, it is only in late modernity (or what some call postmodernity) that local communities and their established traditions are thoroughly undermined by modernity. What brings this about is *globalisation*. Modern audio-visual media have the potential to penetrate virtually every home and community in the world and with them comes the commercial imagery of contemporary capitalism. As Giddens puts it 'post-traditional society is the first *global society*' (96). Local communities are 'evacuated' (emptied of established tradition) by the process of globalisation. Even heritage areas often come under pressure to introduce ('tastefully'), say, McDonalds and while 'Mexican waves' are 'not cricket', on the other hand, they are!

Giddens is surely right about the disintegrative impact of globalisation on established traditions. However, he may underestimate the extent to which people hang onto or invent traditions, even in late modernity. Traditions not only strengthen group solidarity but they provide support and substance for individual and group identity. The search for identity in late modernity – be it national, ethnic, sexual or whatever – is, in fact, a major theme of this book. Invariably, part of asserting an identity involves finding a history – or like-minded others – a tradition. For instance, British Euro-enthusiasts and Euro-sceptics seem equally able to cite traditions of friendship or rivalry with Europe suitable to the identity they want to construct for Britain now. Again, a key contemporary question is whether 'the Muslim world' can retain its fundamental traditions and lifestyles against the disintegrative tide of global capitalisation.

Despite the frequent reworkings of tradition in modern societies, Giddens clearly contrasts modernity and tradition. We can now turn to his description of the main characteristics of modernity. This presentation can be brief as the passage from which these points are taken is included here as a reading. (Reading 5)

According to Giddens the two central characteristics of modernity are:

1 Industrialisation:
   a its physical aspects e.g. machinery.
   b its social relations e.g., primarily social classes.
2 Capitalism – the production of commodities using wage labour for the competitive market.

Other major characteristics of modernity are:

3 Surveillance – the capacity of organisations, including the state, to acquire information on and supervise individuals and groups.
4 Total war capacity – due to 'industrial' technology.

Giddens goes on to state that the most prominent social form of modernity is the nation-state (now in *late* modernity under some challenge from globalisation (see pp. 579-80)). Gidden's third and fourth points add significantly to Hall's list and we will discuss these matters more fully in the appropriate parts of this book (see also Reading 5).

Modernity and sociology

Modernity is a period during which science and reason have become the main means by which human beings seek to understand the world and solve problems. The modern age of enquiry and exploration began around the time of the Reformation but, as Sarrup indicates, gathered fresh impetus with the industrial and political revolutions of the late eighteenth/early nineteenth century (see pp. 5-6). We will examine the institutional and organisational aspects of modernity – economic, political, educational – in the appropriate sections of this book. Here, our concern is with the relationship of modernity as a cultural and intellectual phenomenon to early sociology. As such, modernity is driven by a belief in the power of human reason to understand and change, in short, to master the world.

Sociology has a dual relationship to modernity. On the one hand, sociology was a product of and reflects modernity, and, on the other, it is an attempt to describe and explain modern society.

Table 2.2 indicates how sociology was 'produced' or constructed within and shaped by modernity. When Auguste Comte stated that the purpose of sociology is 'to understand, in order to predict, in order to control' he was echoing the boldest claims of natural scientists of the period. Almost 150 years after his death, it would be difficult to find a sociologist to repeat this boast.

For Comte and Durkheim in France and later Radcliffe-Brown at the London School of Economics, successfully emulating the model of natural science – establishing universal social scientific laws – was the route to securing professional credibility and high status for sociology.

In their attempt to analyse modern society, many sociologists have adopted – sometimes rather uncritically – the approach of natural science. This includes model building. The structural theories described in Chapter 1 build elaborate 'scientific' models of society which are then used to explain social behaviour. In crude Marxist and Functionalist models, social structure constantly seems to determine the behaviour of individuals and groups, sometimes giving a mechanistic feel to these perspectives.

Just as romantic poetry, literature and art is a reaction against the predominance of science and reason, so the interpretive perspectives are, in part, a reaction against 'scientific', structural sociology. In the post-Second World War period up to the early 1980s, sociology tended to be divided into structuralist and interpretist camps. On the one hand, was Functionalism and Marxism, and, on the other, the various interpretive perspectives, including symbolic interactionism and ethnomethodology. The tendency to see the structural and interpretist levels as (often incompatible) opposites or as 'dualisms', as Giddens puts it, reflects the way in which in modern society science and reason are often opposed to the personal and emotional. More recently many sociologists have taken a complementary approach to structural and interpretive levels and largely abandoned the 'battle of the perspectives' of previous decades.

Table 2.2 Modernity and sociology

Modernity	Sociology (19th century)
Rise of Science	Sociology is defined as a Science (Comte, Durkheim, Marx)
Emphasis on Reason	Sociology adopts a rational approach
Belief in Progress	Belief in progress in much sociology
Scientists seen as 'objective' experts on the natural world	Sociologists see themselves as 'objective' experts on the social world
Science seeks to discover 'the laws of the universe'	Some sociologists (positivists) seek to discover 'the laws' of history and society
Science applies evolutionary theory: develops systems of evolutionary classification	Sociology classifies societies according to stages of development e.g. simple, traditional, modern
Human beings seen as capable of acquiring great control over nature and the environment	Sociologists confident that their knowledge of society can be applied to the practical running of it (planning/policy)
Science and Reason seen as able greatly to improve the human condition i.e. to achieve PROGRESS	Sociologists consider they can help to understand and solve 'social problems' i.e. to contribute to PROGRESS
Government and the State seen as essential in bringing about progress/ social improvement	Sociologists expect to *advise* government about how to achieve its objectives
BUT	BUT
Romantic movement defends nature against applied science (industrial 'development') and questions 'progress'	*Interpretive* sociology develops as an alternative to positivism emphasising meaning as distinct from functioning.

Modernity, postmodernity and sociology

It is a cliché that every historical period is one of change. However, there is a growing consensus among many sociologists that the last 30 or so years of the twentieth century are characterised by rapid and probably fundamental, social change. This change is variously referred to as a transition from modernity to postmodernity or, as Giddens prefers it, from modernity to late modernity. As we saw in a previous section, it is the process of globalisation, particularly of information and communication, which makes change in the current epoch so potentially radical and universal.

Madan Sarrup's definition of postmodernity conveys both the

usefulness and some of the uncertainties associated with the term:

> *Postmodernity suggests what came after modernity; it refers to the incipient or actual dissolution of those social forms associated with modernity. Some thinkers assume that it is a movement towards a postindustrial age, but there are many ambiguities: should the postmodern be regarded as a part of the modern? Is it a continuity or a radical break? Is it a natural change or does it indicate a mood, a state of mind?*
>
> *(1993:130)*

On the basis that sociology is about questions as well as answers, the above is an excellent definition of postmodernity. However, don't expect to be able to answer all the questions yet!

Anthony Giddens and Ulrich Beck are among those who prefer the term 'late' modernity and reject the view that society is now 'post' or 'after' modernity.

Giddens defines late modernity as a period when modern society has become much more critically aware of the consequences of modernity, particularly the negative ones. He believes that the modern project of improving the human condition i.e. of progress, is still achievable. It is not yet too late to learn from our mistakes. Giddens refers to the heightened critical awareness which he associates with late modernity as reflexivity and regards this as a central characteristic of late modernity. It is Giddens use of the term reflexivity that is adopted in this book rather than the interesting but complex use employed by Beck now discussed.

Ulrich Beck also considers that reflexivity is a key feature of late modernity but gives the term, a slightly different emphasis. In his definition of reflexivity, Beck particularly stresses the *unintended*, destructive consequences of modernity (e.g. of industry on the environment):

> *This new stage (late modernity), in which one kind of modernisation undercuts and changes another, is what I call the stage of reflexive modernisation.*
>
> *(Beck et al., 1994:2 – author's brackets)*

'Reflexive modernisation' – the unintended or thoughtless destruction and damage caused by modernisation – creates what Beck has famously called 'the risk society' and what Giddens refers to as 'manufactured uncertainty'. Global warming; the pollution and exhaustion of parts of the environment; the risks attached to mass fowl and animal production for food (such as immunity to some antibiotics); the proliferation of nuclear, chemical and other weapons of 'mass destruction,' are all examples of the unintended high risk consequences of modernity. In 'late modernity', the negative consequences of science, industrialisation and big government emerge as very real presences – no longer just pale spectres at the feast of modernity.

Table 2.3 Modernity and postmodernity

Modernity	Postmodernity (or Late modernity)
Belief in Science/Reason	*Reflexivity* (greater critical awareness) characterises postmodernity e.g. concern about the sometimes highly damaging effects of applied-science on nature, the environment and humanity. A concern which extends to the global (e.g. global warming, level of fish stocks) as well as other levels.
Belief in Social Progress	Growing awareness of the risks and unintended negative consequences of the pursuit of progress (Beck, Giddens) (e.g. car pollution/accidents).
Rise of Nationalism The nation state is seen as the boundary of 'society'.	Process of Globalisation occurs. The nation state – 'society' – is increasingly breached by global economic, cultural and political forces.
Emphasis on the Economic – production/development.	Increasing importance of the Cultural.
	1 Communication of information – a cultural process achieved via the media – is the defining feature of postindustrial society (Bell).
	2 Culture in the form of consumption and lifestyle rather than work defines identity.
Politics, government and the state are central to society.	Scepticism of traditional politics/government. Growth of 'life-politics' i.e. linking the personal and the public as in social movement such as feminism and environmentalism.
Tendency to see the world in terms of dualisms or opposites e.g. objective/subjective, male/female ('opposite numbers').	Tendency to see connections, similarities, unities e.g. the subjective and objective are inseparable; sexual identity envisaged more as a spectrum.
Nature largely taken for granted.	Emergence of a greater sense of responsibility for nature/environment.

Note: Table 2.2 – and the full text explain these points further.

Despite damaging 'side-effects', industrialisation has been immensely successful in increasing the production of goods and services. Neither Beck nor Giddens suggests that the process of material wealth creation should be reversed nor think that there would be much public support for such a reversal. Nevertheless, they regard it as imperative to address the plight of the 'losers' of late modern society – both in the West and globally. In late modernity, the 'losers' might include not just those impoverished or injured by 'development' but people of the rich world, too. In Beck's now famous words, 'poverty is hierarchic, smog is democratic'.

Further characteristics of late or postmodernity proposed by Giddens, Beck and others are presented in Table 2.3. Two characteristics not mentioned elsewhere in this chapter require brief explanation prior to fuller discussion later. First, there appears to be increased scepticism of conventional politics and a parallel growth of what Giddens refers to as 'life-politics'. This term refers to attempts to achieve large-scale change through personal and group-communal action rather than primarily through party politics and central government. This organic approach to change evolved in the feminist, environmental and other *social movements*. It is well encapsulated in the feminist slogan: 'the personal is political'. The second characteristic in the table, which only requires noting here, is the tendency of postmodernists to reject polarised or dualistic ways of thinking. Thus, perception is seen by postmodernists as a point of view not as an objective or 'expert' sight of 'the truth' or 'reality'. In everyday life, it is perhaps the area of gender and sexuality that have become most depolarised and 'ambiguous' (to quote the word used by a bishop to describe his own sexuality). Many people now view gender and sexual identities in terms of personal/social choice rather than as biological 'destiny'.

Just as the founders of sociology were influenced by modernity, so 100 years or so later, contemporary sociologists are influenced by postmodernity or late modernity. Table 2.4 indicates that the scope of this influence has been considerable. However, the core questions about the nature of society which engaged the founders of the subject remain much the same even if many contemporary sociologists would both present and answer them somewhat differently. The focus of subject disciplines can change as can the answers they provide, but the central concern of sociology with the relationship of the individual to social groups, with power relations of all kinds, and with the experience, causes and consequences of social change, is likely to persist.

Table 2.4 Postmodernity and sociology

Postmodernity	Sociology
Reflexive concern about the negative effects of applied science on nature, the environment and humanity.	*Reflexive* concern about the negative effects of applied science on nature, the environment and humanity.
Growing awareness of the risks and unintended negative consequences of the pursuit of progress.	Sociologists tend to distance themselves from perspectives that may imply progress e.g. Marxism, liberalism. Sociologists tend to be less moralistic but more aware of links between subjective values/ethics and research.
Process of Globalisation occurs.	Sociology of Globalisation is developed.
Increasing importance of the cultural: communication, consumption, lifestyle.	Sociology focuses increasingly on cultural issues but some insist that capitalism remains the key system to be analysed.
Scepticism of traditional politics/ government. Growth of 'life-politics'.	A shift in focus from central government to social movements and life-politics (e.g. Animal Rights Movement). Giddens refers to the attempt to link the personal and public as 'dialogic democracy' (implying two-way dialogue/ influence.
Tendency to reject a view of the world in terms of opposites but to seek connections.	Sociology increasingly presents supposed 'dualisms' such as individual/society, subjective/ objective as deeply interwoven. Thus, the relationship of the individual and society is seen as a process rather than in terms of the effect of one on the other.
Emergence of a greater sense of responsibility to nature/ environment.	Greater sociological interest in the environment and humans' relationship to it. A sociology of postmodernity begins to develop.

Note: Table 2.3 – and the full text explain points about postmodernity.

Postmodernity or late modernity?

There is much agreement in substance between many who employ the term postmodernity and those who prefer that of late modernity. Many postmodernists would agree with the propositions of Giddens and Beck described above which they put forward under the description of late modernity or reflexive modernity (among others!). Yet whereas postmodernists state that contemporary Western society is now 'after' or 'beyond' modernity, Giddens argues that it is still modern albeit at a late or advanced stage of modernity.

The difference in terminological usage, reflects, in part, a different evaluation of the changes in question rather than disagreement about what these changes are. Giddens sees the move from early to late modernity as one which does not involve a fundamental break in the nature of society. The capacity for self-criticism which was always a defining feature of modern society has simply become more heightened and better informed by experience in late modernity. There is more awareness of mistakes made and damage done in pursuit of material progress. In contrast, those who prefer the term postmodernity to that of late modernity do consider that the present period represents a radical break with modernity and the onset of a distinctive historical period. Thus, Zygmunt Bauman states:

> *The term 'postmodernity' renders accurately the defining traits of the social condition that emerged throughout the affluent countries of Europe and of European descent in the course of the twentieth century, and took its present shape in the second half of the century.*
>
> *(1993:187)*

Bauman describes the 'twin differences that set the postmodern condition apart from modern society' as follows:

1 Postmodern society is freed from the 'false consciousness' or optimistic illusions of modernity, and
2 Postmodern society is a new type of social condition which has built in or, to use Bauman's term, institutionalised a whole range of largely negative characteristics, such as environmental damage, which were generally unforeseen or disregarded in modernity.

Both these points echo Giddens's own analysis except that Giddens does not consider that they provide a case for arguing that Western society has moved beyond, or 'post' modernity. Whereas Giddens considers that the modernist project of controlled progress might yet be retrieved, Bauman asserts that this is impossible.

Partly, to avoid further terminological wrangling, Giddens suggests that the term 'reflexive modernity' could be routinely used to describe contemporary Western society. This runs the risk of

further complicating the picture. For the sake of simplicity, I shall use the terms postmodernism and postmodernity in this book while recognising that the question of whether or not Western society has moved beyond the modern remains unresolved.

Key questions about postmodernity

The core of Chapter 1 focused on some key questions asked by the founders of sociology about the nature of society, particularly modern society. I have not discussed postmodernism in relation to the same questions, partly because it is still so unfamiliar to many that it requires considerable contextualisation before subjecting it to some of the more searching questions of sociological theory. This will come later (see pp. 637-46). Here it is sufficient to indicate that postmodernism attempts to overcome the dualistic or either/or approach to structure and agency (subjective action/meaning) of the structural and interpretist perspectives. Immediately, it will be more useful to ask some of the more empirical questions of key interest to postmodernists, a number of which have been touched on above. However, the responses are to be looked for in the body of this text, much of which is focused on these questions:

Key questions of postmodernity

1 Is postmodernity a period when the 'price of progress' e.g. environmental damage, is more important than further material progress itself?
2 Have culture/knowledge issues largely replaced economic and material ones as definitive of society?
3 Has globalisation occurred i.e. is there a crucial sense in which forces of commerce and communication have produced a global society?
4 Have class questions declined in importance compared to those of gender, race/ethnicity, nationality and other bases of identity and action?
5 Have leisure/consumption become more significant than work/production?

You may already have some answers of your own to the above questions. In which case, the reading of this book could become a creative dialogue.

Question

Make a list of characteristics of:
i traditional societies;
ii modern societies.
Briefly, what are the main differences between the two?

Summary

1 Natural science, particularly the laboratory experiment, provided a model which early sociologists tended to imitate. However, because the possibility of experimenting with humans is restricted, the comparative method was developed as an alternative to experiment. The comparative method involves systematic comparison of apparently similar phenomena in separate social contexts, e.g. the development of the family in two or more societies. Weber's concept of the ideal type can be useful in comparative analysis. An ideal type is a model of the essential elements of a social phenomenon.

2 A variety of 'contrasting pairs' was introduced to indicate the scope and variety of sociology. The discipline seeks to explain both society's effect on people and people's contribution to and interpretation of society. This difference in emphasis produces distinctions between quantitative and qualitative research; objective and subjective data; structural/interpretist theories and positivist/anti-positivist methods; and partly that between reliability and validity.

3 Primary sources of information are produced by the sociologist's original research. Observation, interviews and questionnaires are major means of producing primary data.

4 A Social Survey collects standardised data usually about a large population. A social survey usually requires a sample to be taken.

5 A Sample is a part of a total population. Usually, every effort is made to select a sample which is as representative as possible of the total population but there are situations in which an unrepresentative sample can be effectively used. There are various types of samples, each with advantages and disadvantages.

6 Interviews are of three types: structured, semi-structured and unstructured. A structured interview asks 'closed' questions, an unstructured interview 'open' questions, and a semi-structured interview directs the respondent to address certain areas while allowing freedom as to how this is done. Some interviews use all the above techniques.

7 The advantages and disadvantages of the interview largely reflect the fact that it involves face-to-face interaction between the researcher (or representative) and respondent. Help and guidance can be given but bias can occur.

8 Observation can be divided into non-participant and participant observation. Non-participant observation has the potential advantage of greater objectivity as the researcher is not directly involved but for that reason lacks the benefit of subjective experience. The reverse is true of participant observation.

9 Structural sociology is associated particularly with the social survey and quantitative methods and particularly in the case of Marx, Durkheim and Weber with the comparative-historical method. Interpretive perspectives are strongly associated with qualitative methods. However, much sociological research and analysis freely draws on a variety of theory and method.

10 Secondary sources are data which already exist. There is a massive amount of secondary data and while some are of high quality, in general, they should be used critically.

11 Sociologists frequently think of societies in terms of the traditional, the modern and the postmodern. However, there can be great overlap between the three.

12 Sociology was founded in modern times and reflected the concerns and issues of the nineteenth and early twentieth century. Today, sociology reflects key issues and concerns of the so-called postmodern or late modern period. However, sociology's central focus on the relationship of the individual to social groups, with power relations, and with the experience, causes and consequences of social change, is continuous.

Research and coursework

Each topic area in this book is followed by a section titled 'Research and coursework'. As a general guide to research the point-by-point description of the stages of scientific enquiry on p. 24 should be useful. However, depending on whether the research inclines to the quantitative or qualitative, or both, the relevant later section(s) of the chapter should be read. An absolutely essential aspect of research beyond GCSE level is to link the theoretical and methodological aspects (see particularly p. 35, although this linkage is repeatedly explored throughout this book).

The overall design, implementation and writing up of a piece of research must be as methodologically rigorous as is possible. Examiners are not assessing 'a good idea' but award marks on the extent to which a piece of research meets given requirements or criteria (which, in this case, relate to good research practice). As well as using sound manuals of research method, it is wise to be armed with the relevant assessment criteria when doing a piece of coursework. These are published by examination boards which also often provide 'exemplars' of coursework and other guidance for research.

Having made the above essential points, it is worth briefly introducing a non-traditional type of research which may legitimately influence student researchers. This is action research. Action research is literally research which may provide findings which may guide future action. It has developed most strongly within education, where teachers have researched classroom, school, or school-community issues with a view to applying their findings to 'improving' matters. Students, as members of educational institutions, may also want to select a topic of research on which their findings may have practical relevance. There are many such issues including those involving gender, ethnicity and classroom interaction. However, these are sensitive areas and the choice of a topic will need to be negotiated with a tutor.

Further reading

Murray Morison's *Methods in Sociology* (Longman, 1986) and Patrick McNeill's *Research Methods* (Routledge, 1989) remain useful introductory texts. Nick Howe's *Advanced Practical Sociology* (Nelson, 1994) is among the best of several guides to producing coursework. My recommendation is to access some original sources – perhaps most conveniently in the form of collected readings. My *A New Introductory Reader in Sociology* (Nelson, 1993) has both theory and method sections. An up-to-date but quite demanding book on sociological theory is Derek Layder's *Understanding Social Theory* (Sage, 1994). Even more so, is Barry Barnes' *The Elements of Social Theory* (UCL Press, 1995).

Readings

Reading 1
'Social facts' – the object of sociological study

From Emile Durkheim, *The Rules of Sociological Method* (The Free Press, 1964), pp. 1-4

But in reality there is in every society a certain group of phenomena which may be differentiated from those studied by the other natural sciences. When I fulfil my obligations as brother, husband, or citizen, when I execute my contracts, I perform duties which are defined, externally to myself and my acts, in law and in custom. Even if they conform to my own sentiments and I feel their reality subjectively, such reality is still objective, for I did not create them; I merely inherited them through my education. How many times it happens, moreover, that we are ignorant of the details of the obligations incumbent upon us, and that in order to acquaint ourselves with them we must consult the law and its authorised interpreters! Similarly, the church-member finds the beliefs and practices of his religious life ready-made at birth; their existence prior to his own implies their existence outside of himself. The system of signs I use to express my thought, the system of currency I employ to pay my debts, the instruments of credit I utilise in my commercial relations, the practices followed in my profession, etc., function independently of my own use of them. And these statements can be repeated for each member of society. Here, then, are ways of acting, thinking, and feeling that present the noteworthy property of existing outside the individual consciousness.

These types of conduct or thought are not only external to the individual but are, moreover, endowed with coercive power, by virtue of which they impose themselves upon him, independent of his individual will. Of course, when I fully consent and conform to them, this constraint is felt only slightly, if at all, and is therefore unnecessary. But it is, nonetheless, an intrinsic characteristic of these facts, the proof thereof being that it asserts itself as soon as I attempt to resist it. If I attempt to violate the law, it reacts against me so as to prevent my act before its accomplishment, or to nullify my violation by restoring the damage, if it is accomplished and reparable, or to make me expiate it if it cannot be compensated for otherwise …

Here then, is a category of facts with very distinctive characteristics: it consists of ways of acting, thinking, and feeling, external to the individual, and endowed with a power of coercion, by reason of which they control him. These ways of thinking could not be confused with biological phenomena, since they consist of representations and of actions; nor with psychological phenomena, which exist only in the individual consciousness and through it. They constitute, thus, a new variety of phenomena; and it is to them exclusively that the term 'social' ought to be applied …

These ways of thinking and acting therefore constitute the

proper domain of sociology. It is true that, when we define them with this word 'constraint,' we risk shocking the zealous partisans of absolute individualism. For those who profess the complete autonomy of the individual, man's dignity is diminished whenever he is made to feel that he is not completely self-determinant. It is generally accepted today, however, that most of our ideas and our tendencies are not developed by ourselves but come to us from without. How can they become a part of us except by imposing themselves upon us? This is the whole meaning of our definition. And it is generally accepted, moreover, that social constraint is not necessarily incompatible with the individual personality.

Questions

1 Summarise in your own words what Durkheim considers are the main characteristics of social facts (approximately 100 words).
2 Do you consider that Mead's analysis of the self and Durkheim's analysis of social facts contradict each other or can they be seen as complementary? (See also Reading 4, Chapter 1).

Reading 2
'Verstehen' (understanding) – a method of the social but not of the natural sciences

From Eileen Barker, *The Making of a Moonie: Choice or Brainwashing* (Basil Blackwell, 1984), pp. 18-19

The concept of *Verstehen* is associated with Max Weber. It is the process of trying to understand the subjective meanings of others.

Although many of their interests and methods overlap, the social sciences are unlike the natural sciences in a number of ways. This is partly because they ask different kinds of questions. The chemist does not try to find out what molecules 'feel' when they are subjected to a particular process, but some degree of subject understanding is necessary for the sociologist if he is to describe, let alone understand or explain, what his data are doing. The method employed in the attempt to gain some kind of empathetic understanding of what the world looks like from other people's point of view is frequently referred to as *Verstehen*.

Although the two are frequently confused, empathy does not necessarily imply sympathy. *Verstehen* is a process of inquiry during which the researcher tries to put himself in other people's shoes or, to use another metaphor, to see the world through their glasses. He attempts to recognise the assumptions of 'filters' through which their world is seen, so that the actions and perceptions of the people he is studying begin to make sense. Obviously, this is an exercise which is much easier in some instances than in others. As a mother of teenage children, I found little difficulty in empathising fairly quickly with most of the parents I met. It took a bit longer

with some of my other subjects. The first time a young Californian Moonie rushed up and flung his arms around me with declarations of eternal love, I recoiled with truly British horror and only just managed to prevent myself from protesting that I did not think we had been introduced.

Questions

1 Why does Eileen Barker state that the sociologist needs to develop empathetic understanding or Verstehen.
2 Compare Barker's approach to studying society to that of Durkheim in Reading 1 and of Comte in the text.

Reading 3
Combining quantitative and qualitative research

From Alan Bryman, *Quantity and Quality in Social Research* (Unwin Hyman, 1988), pp. 127-28

The rather partisan, either/or tenor of the debate about quantitative and qualitative research may appear somewhat bizarre to an outsider, for whom the obvious way forward is likely to be a fusion of the two approaches so that their respective strengths might be reaped. The technical version of the debate more readily allows this solution to be accommodated because it is much less wedded than the epistemological version to a view that the two traditions reflect antagonistic views about how the social sciences ought to be conducted. In this chapter, the focal concern will be the ways in which the methods associated with quantitative and qualitative research can be, and have been, combined. As noted, there are examples of investigations carried out by investigators who locate their work largely within the tradition of qualitative research, but who have used survey procedures in tandem with participant observation (e.g. Woods, 1979; Ball, 1981). Such research will be employed as an example of the combination of quantitative and qualitative research, because the chief concern of the present chapter is with the *methods* with which each is associated.

The focus on methods of investigation should not lose sight of the significance of a distinction between quantitative and qualitative *data*. For example, some of the findings associated with an ethnographic study may be presented in a quantified form. In their research on the de-skilling of clerical work, Crompton and Jones (1988) collected much detailed qualitative information, in the form of verbatim reports, on the work of their respondents. In spite of considerable reservations about coding these data, they aggregated people's accounts of their work in terms of the amounts of control they were able to exercise in their work. Even among qualitative researchers who prefer to resist such temptations, the use of quasi-quantitative terms like 'many', 'frequently', 'some', and the like, is common (e.g. Gans, 1982, p.408). Further survey researchers provide the occasional verbatim quotation from an interview, or one or two case examples of respondents who exemplify a particular pattern. Sometimes, the reporting of qualitative data deriving from a survey can be quite considerable. In addition, researchers sometimes use a structured interview for the simultaneous collection of both quantitative and qualitative data. For example, Ford et al. (1982) employed such a structured interview schedule to investigate employers' recruitment practices. Quantitative data were collected on such topics as the frequency of use of particular methods of recruitment. The schedule also permitted qualitative data to be collected on employers' reasons for the use and non-use of particular recruitment channels. Such cases may be viewed as indicative of a slight limitation in discussing quantitative and qualitative research largely in terms of methods of data collection. However, there is little doubt that methods like surveys and participant observation are typically seen as sources of quantitative and qualitative data respectively, so that it is not proposed to challenge this convention but merely to alert the reader to the lack of a hard and fast distinction.

Question

What are the advantages of combining quantitative and qualitative data? (Reading and text)

Reading 4
Three stages in a participant observational study

From Eileen Barker, *The Making of a Moonie: Choice or Brainwashing* (Basil Blackwell, 1984), p.19

A perennial problem in participant observation is the ethical issue of whether it is justified to lie or hide the truth if it seems to help the research. The problem is even more difficult to escape in the case of covert (hidden) as opposed to overt (open) research.

I found that the role I played as a participant observer went through three distinct stages during the course of the study. First there was a passive stage during which I did very little except to watch and listen (doing the washing-up in the kitchen was always a good place for this). Next there was an interactive stage during which I felt familiar enough with the Unification perspective to join in conversations without jarring; Moonies no longer felt that they had to 'translate' everything for me, and those Moonies who did not know me would sometimes take me to be a member. Finally there was the active stage. Having learned the social language in the first stage and how to use it in the second, I began in the third stage to explore its range and scope, its potentialities and its limitations. I argued and asked all the awkward questions that I had been afraid to voice too loudly to an earlier stage lest I were not allowed to continue my study. I could no longer be told that I did not understand because, in one sense at least, I patently *did* understand quite a lot – and I was using Unification arguments

in my questioning. In this I angered some Moonies and saddened others, but there were those who not only tolerated my probing but actually discussed the problems that they and the movement were facing with an amazing frankness.

Of course, even in the interactive stage it was known that I was not a Moonie. I never pretended that I was, or that I was likely to become one. I admit that I was sometimes evasive, and I certainly did not always say everything that was on my mind, but I cannot remember any occasion on which I consciously lied to a Moonie.

Questions

1 What problems mentioned in the above extract does Eileen Barker encounter in her participant observational study or the Moonies?
2 How does she deal with these problems?

Reading 5
The main characteristics of modernity

From Anthony Giddens, *Modernity and Self-Identity Self and Society in the Late Modern Age* (Cambridge: Polity Press, 1991), pp. 14-15

… I use the term 'modernity' (here) in a very general sense, to refer to the institutions and modes of behaviour established first of all in post-feudal Europe, but which in the twentieth century increasingly have become world-historical in their impact. 'Modernity' can be understood as roughly equivalent to 'the industrialised world', so long as it be recognised that industrialism is not its only institutional dimension. I take industrialism to refer to the social relations implied in the widespread use of material power and machinery in production processes. As such, it is one institutional axis of modernity. A second dimension is capitalism, where this term means a system of commodity production involving both competitive product markets and the commodification of labour power. Each of these can be distinguished analytically from the institutions of surveillance, the basis of the massive increase in organisational power associated with the emergence of modern social life. Surveillance refers to the supervisory control of subject populations, whether this control takes the form of 'visible' supervision in Foucault's sense, or the use of information to co-ordinate social activities. This dimension can in turn be separated from control of the means of violence in the context of the 'industrialisation of war'. Modernity ushers in an era of 'total war', in which the potential destructive power of weaponry, signalled above all by the existence of nuclear armaments, becomes immense.

Modernity produces certain distinct social forms, of which the most prominent is the nation-state. A banal observation, of course, until one remembers the established tendency of sociology to concentrate on 'society' as its designated subject-matter. The sociologist's 'society', applied to the period of modernity at any rate, is a nation-state, but this is usually a covert equation rather than an explicitly theorised one. As a sociopolitical entity the nation-state contrasts in a fundamental way with most types of traditional order.

Questions

1 What are the main characteristics of modern society and how does it differ from traditional society? (see pp. 40-2)
2 What is 'modern' about the nation-state?

Households, Families and Marriage

A nuclear family – the 'cereal packet norm' – no longer so much the norm in 1997

Aims of this chapter

1   To present a variety of sociological and policy perspectives on families and households.

2   To illustrate that family and household structures change historically and to present the debate about family types.

3   To analyse the causes and effects of stresses on families.

4   To explain the character and causes of family diversity.

5   To analyse of the main relationships between families and social structure, including aspects of class, gender and age.

Households, families and marriage: terminology and trends

This section defines and gives some basic data on households, families and marriage. The statistics indicate great and rapid change in all these areas, although whether this amounts to a 'crisis' or merely adaptation to the nature and demands of modern society is debatable.

A household is a person or group of people living in a given dwelling. In *Social Trends 1990* it is remarked that:

> One of the most notable features of the period since the Second World War has been the increase in people living alone: in 1988, over a quarter of households in Great Britain contained only one person, compared with about one-eighth in 1961.
>
> (*Social Trends*, 1990)

If we add to the 27 per cent of single person households the 34 per cent in which only two people live, then, these account for over three-fifths of all households. Table 3.1 summarises this and related data.

Table 3.1 Households: by size

Great Britain	1961	1971	1981	1991	1995-96
			Percentages		
One person	14	18	22	27	28
Two people	30	32	32	34	35
Three people	23	19	17	16	16
Four people	18	17	18	16	15
Five people	9	8	7	5	5
Six or more people	7	6	4	2	2
All households (=100%)(millions)	16.2	18.2	19.5	22.4	23.5

(Source: *Social Trends*, 1997:40)

Table 3.2 Households: by type of household and family

Great Britain	1961	1971	1981	1991	1995-96
			Percentages		
One person					
Under pensionable age	4	6	8	11	13
Over pensionable age	7	12	14	16	15
Two or more unrelated adults	5	4	5	3	2
One family					
Married couple					
No children	26	27	26	28	29
1-2 dependent children	30	26	25	20	19
3 or more dependent children	8	9	6	5	4
Non-dependent children only	10	8	8	8	6
Lone parent					
Dependent children	2	3	5	6	7
Non-dependent children only	4	4	4	4	3
Two or more families	3	1	1	1	1
All households (=100%)(millions)	16.2	18.2	19.5	22.4	23.5

(Source: *Social Trends*, 1997:40)

While the circumstances and lifestyle of the small household majority must command increasing attention from sociologists, the above statistics could be misleading. If we consider people rather than households, then in 1995-96, 58 per cent lived in households headed by a married couple and one half of these had children either dependent or non-dependent (see Table 3.2). Susan McRae's research of 1993 shows that marriage still remains the ambition of the majority in England. However, people are now on average marrying later and in 1993, the number of marriages dropped below 300,000 for the first time while divorces continued to rise (see Figure 3.1). Overall, statistics seem to show the conventional family in decline.

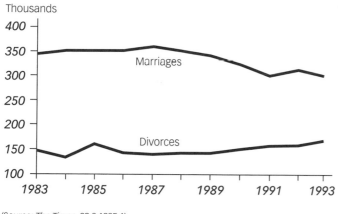

(Source: *The Times,* 23.8.1995:1)

Figure 3.1 Divorces rise and fewer get married

The most common family systems are the *nuclear family* and the *extended family.* A nuclear family is comprised of mother, father and child or children, either natural or adopted. The nuclear family is also sometimes referred to as the conjugal family. Usually members of a nuclear family share the same household. The extended family consists of the nuclear family and at least one relative living in the same household. The extended family is also sometimes referred to as the stem family. The classic extended family in Britain was a couple, their eldest son, and his wife and children living in the same household. It is helpful, however, to broaden our conception of the extended family. Sometimes relatives such as grandparents or elderly aunts live near a given nuclear family and participate in fairly intense social interaction with it. It is useful to think of such a situation as an extended family-type structure. We also include various communal structures within this broad description. Kinship is social relationship based on real or assumed (adopted) consanguinity (blood relationship).

A *reconstituted family* is a form of nuclear family in which one or both partners have had children from a previous relationship which become part of the 'new' family, i.e. there is at least one step-relationship within the family. In a society in which at least one out of three marriages involves a partner who is remarrying, the reconstituted family is becoming increasingly common. Issues raised by the reconstituted family, including non-blood relationships, are in need of further research.

It is debated whether the single parent family is a distinct family type or an incomplete nuclear family. In any case, there are well over a million such families in Britain, and it is urgent both that sociologists adequately analyse the phenomenon and that society and politicians respond constructively to it.

Different forms of marriage affect family structure. Monogamy allows one wife to one husband and is usually the only legally permitted form of marriage in societies in which the Christian tradition has predominated. Polygamy, which allows a person to have more than one spouse, is common in some traditional societies. Polygyny, where a man has more than one wife, is more

common than polyandry, where a wife has more than one husband. The former is common in some tribes but is also practised by some contemporary Muslims. It also occurs as a result of Mormon religious belief, particularly in the North American State of Utah. Polyandry occurs as a matter of practicality in parts of Tibet. It operates as a form of birth control in poorer regions. However many husbands a woman has, she is limited by nature to a certain number of children.

Marriage patterns are becoming more varied in contemporary British society. Monogamy remains the only legally permitted form of marriage, but a large and increasing number of people experience it more than once. About one in three marriages are remarriages for at least one of the partners. A minority pattern of serial monogamy in which a person marries two or more times – having divorced a previous spouse – is therefore developing.

Those who argue that continuity and conventionality characterise family and marriage patterns in Britain point to the fact that the majority are born into a nuclear family, marry and produce one themselves. Others are much more impressed by the variety and complexity of family and marriage practices. They perceive a *pluralistic* pattern rather than the dominance of the conventional or traditional nuclear family and marriage.

Perspectives on the family

For many, the family seems a familiar and comfortable institution. It can be a 'haven in a heartless world', a refuge from the impersonality and stress of work or school.

Sociologists have never accepted as adequate this simple and romantic view of the family. They have always considered that the influence of society penetrates deeply into the family, and some have argued that the family, in turn, can substantially influence society. Nevertheless, until quite recently the sociology of the family was predominantly functionalist. Broadly speaking, the literature dealt with the functions of the family in relation to society as a whole or to the various social subsystems. The functionalist approach has now been challenged from various directions. Even so, functionalist analysis of the family provides perhaps the clearest and easiest to understand application of this perspective.

Functionalist perspective
Murdock and Parsons

Functionalists regard the family as an important 'organ' in the 'body' of society. It is what the family 'does' or the functions of the family that most interest them. George Murdock, an early functionalist, considered the four basic functions of the family to be sexual, reproductive, educational or socialising and economic. Although these functions can evolve, he considered them to be 'universal'.

We can take sex and reproduction together. According to

Murdock, marriage and the nuclear family provide the best opportunity for the socially controlled expression of the sex drive. More importantly, they provide the necessary institutional stability for the reproduction and nurture (bringing up) of children. The bringing up of children requires considerable time and effort – human maturation takes longer than that of any other species relative to life-span. To be brought up effectively, children usually require the help of more than one person (for practical if not emotional reasons). In most societies the two people who produce a child are expected to co-operate in its socialisation and in providing for it economically. Practical commitment to children based on shared involvement and responsibility exists in polygamous as well as monogamous marriages. In polygamous Muslim societies a man is not expected to marry more wives and produce more children than he can afford.

Talcott Parsons argues that there are two 'basic and irreducible functions' universal to all families. These are primary socialisation and the stabilisation of the adult personality. Socialisation involves the internalisation of culture and the structuring of the personality so that the individual is socially acceptable. The stabilisation of adult personalities is achieved through the emotional security, including sexual expression, provided by marriage.

To argue that the nuclear family is a socially useful institution need not mean, as Murdock and Parsons imply, that it is biologically necessary and natural. Margaret Mead – while stressing the utility of the nuclear family contends that it is culturally, not biologically based. Comparisons with similar species by no means provide conclusive evidence, but males of other primates often do not remain with the female they have made pregnant. The fact that the human male usually does so is probably because this arrangement conveniently provides a secure context for the lengthy child-rearing necessary to the species. Another pointer in this direction is the fact that whilst many societies have allowed considerable sexual freedom before marriage, the widespread tendency is to curtail or abolish it afterwards. This, again, is a question of practicality not biology: it focuses energy and attention on spouse and children and, in particular, prevents the male from having more children than he is able to look after. Historically, the taboo (social disapproval) on sex outside marriage is a protective device for children and, to that extent, the human species. This argument loses much of its practical, if not emotional, force, however, in this age of effective and easily available contraception. The family's role in laying down the basis of culture through socialisation is universally stressed by functionalists.

Criticisms of Murdock and Parsons

As D H Morgan points out, Murdock's analysis suffers from a failure to consider whether or not other institutions could take over the functions he associates with the family, but other functionalists such as Parsons have explored this issue. Further, Murdock rather too readily assumes that the nuclear family functions harmoniously. More contemporary functionalists N W Bell and E F Vogel, as well as radical phenomenologists R D Laing and David

Cooper, have shown that the modern family can contain great tensions. Recent functionalists, however, still tend to assume a 'fit' between the nuclear family and society as a whole, even though they may concede that it may be internally under stress. Arguably, they are overinfluenced by the harmony implicit in the organic analogy in making this assumption. We examine functionalist analysis of how the family has 'adapted to the needs' of industrial society in a later section (see pp. 63-4).

Bell and Vogel: nuclear family and social system

As explained in Chapter 1, functionalists see each social institution in terms of its role within its own social subsystem (family/kinship) and in terms of its relationship to society as a whole. The model below illustrates this point in respect of the modern family.

Figure 3.2 is very simple to interpret. It shows that the family gives 'something' to and gets 'something' from each sub-system. Take the example of the economy. The family provides labour for which its members get paid. Money is then 'recycled' back into the economy through the purchase of goods which the family needs and through family savings. Thus, the family is seen as both dependent on and contributing to the economy. It is the same with the political system. In return for loyalty and obedience (compliance), family members get leadership from politicians (however confusing this may sometimes be!). From the community comes support and identity in return for participation and commitment (adherence). The only aspect of the model that might cause difficulty is calling the fourth sub-system the value system rather than kinship. The family is, of course, part of the kinship system and reflects and passes on the values of society. Other institutions are involved in value socialisation but the family's role is primary.

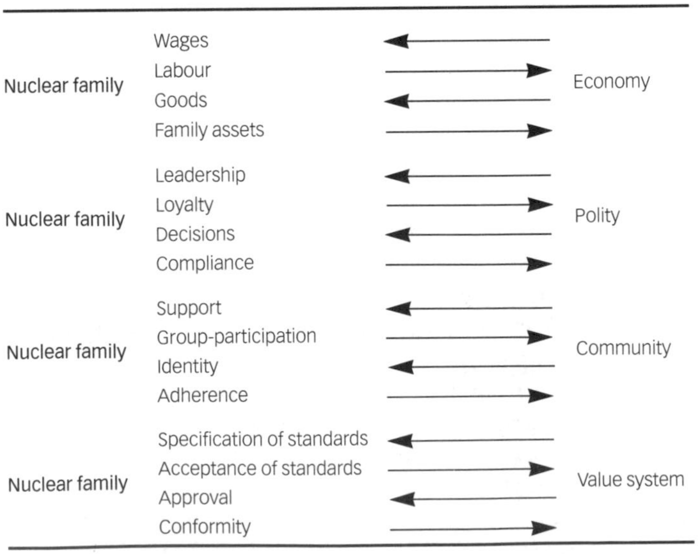

Nuclear family	Wages	←	Economy
	Labour	→	
	Goods	←	
	Family assets	→	
Nuclear family	Leadership	←	Polity
	Loyalty	→	
	Decisions	←	
	Compliance	→	
Nuclear family	Support	←	Community
	Group-participation	→	
	Identity	←	
	Adherence	→	
Nuclear family	Specification of standards	←	Value system
	Acceptance of standards	→	
	Approval	←	
	Conformity	→	

(Source: Adapted from Bell and Vogel, 1960)

Figure 3.2 The interchange between the nuclear family and the traditional sub-systems of society

Marxist and other class-based family analysis

Marxists also adopt a structural perspective on the family. They do not, however, regard the nuclear family as a universal feature of human society, but put it in the context of capitalist society and, particularly, the class nature of that society.

Friedrich Engels' (1820-1895) *The Origin of the Family: Private Property and the State* remains the starting point for most Marxist analysis of the family and of gender relations. Engels examines the emergence of the nuclear family and male dominance in an historical context. He hypothesised that in the nomadic stage of man's social development there was a substantial measure of sexual equality. Neither exclusive sexual possessiveness nor much private property existed. People and things were held in common although mothers had an immediate involvement with young children. Gradually, the male sphere of activity became more specialised and distinct: cattle breeding, mining and trade were added to their primary responsibility of hunting. This leads to the central point of Engels' argument. As men acquired greater control over wealth and property, they sought means to ensure that it stayed within their personal possession and was passed on to their offspring. To do this they had to know who their offspring were! This meant that the free sexual relations of the horde had to be replaced by monogamy, and a system of inheritance based on blood introduced. In a male-dominated society, the eldest male was established as inheritor. The state, also male-dominated, gave powerful legal support to male control over the family, women, and private property. Thus, in Engels' analysis, the growth of private property and male dominance or patriarchy evolved together. Marxists and Marxist feminists see the state as supporting capitalism and patriarchy whereas liberal or pluralist feminists argue that the state is not always oppressive and can be used to achieve reform.

Comment on Engels

As Rosalind Delmar puts it, the major contribution of Engels was to assert 'women's oppression as a problem of history, rather than of biology'. She uses the word 'assert' rather than 'prove' because the details of Engels' historical account are thought to be wrong. The precise historical truth on this issue is probably beyond proof but the point to appreciate is that Engels concluded that as the monogamous nuclear family and female subordination had developed historically, it is possible to change them. This is the basis of Marxist and most socialist analyses of the family. The opposite view, that the sexual division of labour which consigns the woman primarily to the home and the man to economic labour, is founded on the analysis that such an arrangement is biologically rooted and virtually immutable (unchangeable). It is the basis of the more crude functionalist analysis of the nuclear family. Although the patriarchal (male-dominated) nuclear family predated capitalist society, Engels and Marx considered that it fitted the needs of capitalism particularly well. Capitalist society was based on the accumulation of private wealth and property mainly controlled by

men. Accordingly, a patriarchal family structure linked to a system of primogeniture (in which the eldest son inherits) suited it very well. Primogeniture was primarily of significance among the upper and middle classes: the working class had little to pass on anyway. Marx and Engels did argue, however, that capitalism provided a limited opportunity for women to escape domestic bondage by finding employment outside the home and thus acquiring an independent source of income. Even so, they considered that, ultimately, the liberation of women depended on a change of social system from capitalism to socialism. Private property would then be abolished and the organisation of child-rearing and socialisation would be a matter for the community as a whole to determine.

Further Marxist analysis of families

More recent Marxist and socialist writers – particularly Marxist feminists – have tended to be sceptical of the supposed improvement in the status of women that more direct involvement in the economy brings. Blackburn and Stewart point out that women often play the kind of 'service' role in the work situation which can be regarded as an extension of their low domestic status rather than an improvement on it. Further, Engels has been somewhat criticised for a 'waiting for the revolution' approach to the solution of gender exploitation. Contemporary neo-Marxist and socialist feminists such as Juliet Mitchell and Ann Oakley tend to be much keener than he was in the search for immediate improvements in gender relations (see Chapter 7, pp. 190-1 where non-Marxist feminist perspectives on gender are also discussed).

Some Marxists regard the sexual possessiveness of marital partners as just one expression of the possessive and, in their view, selfish individualism of capitalist society. Marx himself claimed that marriage 'is incontestably a form of exclusive private property'. The female 'gives' sex in return for the economic security her husband provides. She gets the worst of the arrangement because she is the more dependent. Engels suggested that her position is one of glorified prostitution. Perhaps the cultural stereotyping embodied in such phrases as 'she's a real gold-digger' and 'she's out to get her man' bear out the view that the economic dependency of women under capitalism can undermine their dignity. Although not wholly out-of-date, this picture of the family is less applicable to the 1990s than in Marx and Engels' own day.

Marxists consider that the family socialises children to conform, even though, in the case of the working class, it is against their fundamental interests to do so (see Chapter 7, pp. 198-200). On the other hand, experience of exploitation can produce feelings critical of the system among the proletariat (working class) and these may also be passed on through the family as well as through workmates and friends. As we shall see, Marxists generally consider that the socialising and other functions of the nuclear family could, at least, be pared down and done more effectively by other institutions such as state nurseries.

It would be wrong to think that only Marxists are aware of the major influence of class on family life and, especially, of the way the family socialises children to 'belong' to a particular class. On the contrary, since the war a vast body of largely empirical work has contributed to our knowledge of the links between family and class. The writings of A H Halsey and J W Douglas are examples. Through the research of these and other scholars we later study the relationship between family, education and class, and that section (Chapter 4, pp. 87-92) should be regarded as a direct continuation of this chapter. Indeed, class pervades not only the family but many aspects of social life. The experience of class, however, begins in the family. (For an analysis of feminist family policy contributions, see Chapter 13, pp. 408-9).

A pluralist-feminist or multidimensional approach to family/gender relations

In the 1980s and 1990s, feminist commentators on the family have reflected other influences than Marxism while still focusing sharply on the link between how the division of labour is gendered and the wider subordination of females. The emerging new perspective contains a number of strands – some in tension with each other. However, there are some broad points of agreement in what can be referred to as a *pluralist-feminist* perspective on the family.

First, the gendered division of labour which allocates domestic work overwhelmingly to women is seen as *socially constructed*, not as the product of nature. Functionalist theories are rejected to the extent that they take a *naturalistic* approach. Feminists recognise that sex, reproduction, socialisation and economic production 'need' to occur but not necessary in ways that 'exploit' female labour and/or leave them relatively powerless. Rosalind Coward argues that females are 'seduced' by constructions of motherhood and domesticity which rarely deliver the pleasure-fantasy offered (e.g. in advertisements) but trap them into stereotypically female labour. Coward's concept of power owes more to the French social historian, Michel Foucault, than to Marx. Females are seen as *positioned* in subordinate situations in systems by being drawn into *discourses* ('stories', images, myths, ideologies) which place them there. Discourses such as the myth of domesticity or submissive femininity help to create real gender and other inequalities and can be self-reproducing in that both beneficiaries and victims believe in their 'reality'.

A second feature of the pluralist-feminist or multidimensional approach to family/gender relations is an attempt to analyse historically the changing relationship of the so-called *private* and *public* spheres of social existence and to link this to an understanding of the position of women. The view that the family is a sphere of personal autonomy and free affective expression is seen as a convenient myth which helps to subordinate women. Faith Robertson Elliot argues that the modern state has constantly attempted to influence if not control the supposed private realm of family and domesticity. Thus, in the nineteenth century, legislation banned women from most heavy manual work and most types of professional work, targeting them towards paid or unpaid domestic work. Although women were used in a wider range of paid labour during both world wars, after each, state policy directed them back towards stereotypical roles. (Sylvia Walby's

account of the relationship between public and private patriarch is discussed in Chapter 7, pp. 206-7.)

Thirdly, in general, pluralist-feminists believe that they can change things. They do not consider that the state operates either exclusively in the interests of capitalism or of males. Thus, women themselves can influence state policy, as can, for instance, ethnic or religious groups, i.e. the approach is genuinely multidimensional in considering that various groups can be meaningfully involved in policy formation. For example, Faith Robertson Elliot considers the achieving of state support for single parents to be a positive gain for the women's movement and supporting groups (see Reading 1 and also pp. 408-9).

Fourthly, like feminist social science in general, the pluralist-feminist approach is political. In particular it has the emancipation of women at its heart. Helen Crowley puts the matter very concretely:

> *Women have acquired a political voice which challenges, amongst other things, the politics of redistribution and resource alleviation … Questions are then raised – both politically and theoretically – about sexuality, intersexual relations, mothering, childhood, old age, wealth redistribution, individual freedom and social control. These social questions are becoming a real testing ground of modernity and its original pressure of liberty and equality for all – women as well as men.*
>
> *(Crowley in Bocock and Thomson eds., p. 101)*

The scope of this agenda well illustrates that contemporary feminists far from regarding the family as private and self-contained, see it as a focal point of wider issues.

Is the nuclear family universal or are other family types possible (and functional)?

The terms of the debate

We now examine the functionalist claim that the nuclear family is universal. First, Murdock's definition of the family needs to be noted:

> *The family is a social group characterised by common residence, economic co-operation and reproduction. It includes adults of both sexes, at least two of whom maintain a socially approved sexual relationship, and one or more children, own or adopted, of sexually cohabiting adults.*
>
> *(1949)*

Murdock's claim that the nuclear family is universal has an empirical and theoretical aspect. He supported it empirically by examining 250 varied types of society and concluding that the nuclear family occurred in all of them. Theoretically, he argues that the nuclear family, with its shared division of labour between the sexes, is the most efficient and convenient institution to accomplish the functions referred to above. This largely explains its universality. Functionalists, of course, recognise the widespread existence of the extended family but see the nuclear family as its essential core. Literally, the extended family is an extension of the nuclear family. The same argument is applied to polygamous families. One person may make several marriages but each separate coupling and offspring is regarded as a nuclear family.

Four categories of evidence can be cited against the functionalist position on the nuclear family. These are:

1 Comparative cultural evidence of non-nuclear families.
2 Deliberate attempts to produce collectively-based families.
3 Single parent families.
4 Lesbian and homosexual led families.

We will examine each of these categories in turn.

Comparative cultural evidence of non-nuclear families

The Nayar case

It can be argued that the Nayars of Malabar offer an example of a society in which the nuclear family did not exist. Until about the mid-nineteenth century, when their traditional social system began to break up under the impact of the British, the Nayar produced and reared children without the aid of the nuclear family. Young Nayar females went through a tali-rite or ritual marriage. However, after the tali-rite, the female and male involved were not required to have any further contact other than that the female was required to mourn at the male's funeral. After the tali-rite, the female was free to take up to several sexual partners. As a result, paternity was often uncertain. In practical terms this did not matter, as the mother's brother, not the natural father, was responsible for her and her offspring. When this was not possible the next nearest male relative on the mother's side was responsible.

Despite some opinion to the contrary, the Nayar case is surely an exception to the familiar nuclear family pattern. Kathleen Gough's point that a special and socially recognised tie existed between a woman and the man who first initiated her sexually, does not affect the argument at all. The 'couple' certainly did not constitute the basis of a nuclear family in terms of Murdock's definition in that the nuclear 'unit' had no continuous social existence. A necessary consequence of this is that inheritance was *matrilineal* in Nayar society (i.e. it occurred in the name of the mother). Further examination shows, however, that there was a sound functional reason for the Nayar form of child-rearing. The Nayars were a very warlike people. The women were able to assist

each other during the frequent absences of the men, and in the event of one male relative being killed, there would still be others left to provide for the woman and her children. The Nayar system of child-rearing was, then, functionally well adapted to the needs of that particular society. Regarded thus, it is quite consistent with functionalist perspectives about the need of children for a stable social environment. Perhaps this is more significant than the literal fact that the Nayar case does represent a rare exception to the 'universality' of the nuclear family.

However, a separation of biological and social parenthood is not unique to the Nayar. It occurred, in similar circumstances, among the Ashanti in Ghana. In different circumstances, it is also increasingly common in modern societies.

Deliberate attempts to produce collectively-based families

The Kibbutzim

There have been few attempts in modern society to abolish the nuclear family outright but many efforts to replace it partially by other institutions or to merge it within a larger extended family-type structure. Perhaps the best-known attempt to supplement the family by providing alternative institutions to assist parents with childrearing is the Israeli kibbutzim. In the early days of the Jewish settlement in the state of Israel, the kibbutzim stressed the collective values of the whole community against the more concentrated, limited, and it was thought sometimes selfish ties of the family. It was also part of the beliefs (or ideology) of the movement to release women from child-rearing and to enable them to have as much time for work and leisure as men. Young infants were taken to special children's houses after only a short time with their parents. They grew up together and were looked after by specially trained nurses (or metapalets) and teachers. They were allowed to see their parents for a few hours only each day, and they slept in the children's houses and not their parents' residence. Women were therefore free to do any work on the same terms as men. Gradually, there has been a reversion to a traditional sexual division of labour and family form: the separation between parents and children is less complete; in many kibbutzim, children return to spend the night at their parents' flat, and women are more involved than men in traditionally feminine roles such as working in the communal kitchen or laundry. The kibbutzim reduced but did not replace the role of the nuclear family.

Despite this partial return to nuclear family norms, some kibbutzim still thrive and are now well beyond the experimental phase. It is significant that children of the kibbutzim and adults from kibbutzim backgrounds are as psychologically well-adjusted as people from other backgrounds. Not unexpectedly, however, many have acquired values that express the importance of the group rather than individual achievement. The charge by Bruno Bettelheim, however, that adults brought up in the kibbutzim lack the capacity for leadership has not been found to be true. It does seem, therefore, that the role of the family in rearing children can be successfully reduced, as long as other effective institutions exist to do the job.

The Soviet 'experiment'

There has been only one attempt by a government to seriously undermine the nuclear family. This happened in the former Soviet Union in the period immediately following the revolution of 1917. Marriage, divorce and even abortion were made available on an almost casual basis. The ideological inspiration behind this attempt to undermine the family was the communist ideas of Marx, Engels and Lenin. They considered that in capitalist societies the family both expressed and helped to perpetuate the unequal and repressive nature of the capitalist system itself. In particular, they considered that the domination of husband over wife in the family reflected that of the capitalist manufacturer over the wage-labourer in economic and social life. But it was not simply ideology that motivated the communist revolutionaries. Practically, they wanted to release more women from domestic toil to enable them to assist in reconstructing the country's economy which had been badly damaged by revolution and civil war. To help achieve this, communal facilities were established for bringing up children, though at first these were quite inadequate.

In the mid 1930s, the government substantially changed major aspects of its policy towards the family. In 1935 a new law was passed, making parents legally responsible for the misbehaviour of their children. In 1936 much stricter marriage and divorce legislation was passed. This was partly because the previous approach had helped to produce considerable social problems, including a high rate of infant mortality and neglect and juvenile delinquency. In addition, the government was now keen to increase the birth rate and this was thought to require a stable family structure and fewer abortions. It is significant, however, that a progressively extending network of maternity homes, nurseries and kindergartens was also established both to assist population expansion and to allow women more freely to enter and remain in the labour force. As Professor Bronfenbrenner says, conditions were so unstable in post-revolutionary Russia that it would be unwise to regard the Soviet experiment to undermine the family as a serious test of whether or not it is possible for a society to do without the family. Nevertheless, certain less general conclusions do suggest themselves. Firstly, the Soviet experiment again makes it obvious that the crucial functions concerning the reproduction, nurture and socialisation of children, traditionally fulfilled by the family, cannot just be left to chance. If the family does not perform these functions, then some other institution or institutions must. Secondly, where adequate alternative institutions are established, they can, at least in part, replace the family. The Soviet Union, and indeed other Communist countries, recognised the need for planned alternative facilities for child-rearing if the traditional functions of the family were to be reduced. The former Soviet Union, East Germany and China were all much better equipped with nursery and pre-school facilities than Britain. In addition, the Soviet Union ran a state system of boarding schools which brought up millions of children and so freed their parents, particularly their mothers, from the need to do so.

The sixties commune movement

A much less organised effort to breach the limits of the nuclear family as the commune 'movement' of the late 1960s. Communes of one kind or another have existed for thousands of years – religious communities are one example – and will no doubt continue to exist, although they have a tendency to be short-lived. An interesting example of communal idealism which illustrates the fragility of the movement was the plan of the poets Wordsworth, Coleridge and Southey to establish a utopia (perfect society) in miniature on the banks of the Susquehanna River in the United States. Like most people's dreams of returning to nature, this one remained a dream, although Wordsworth and Coleridge did go to live in the more accessible English Lake District.

The ideological theorising which inspired many of the communes of the 1960s was rarely as well thought out as that of the kibbutzim pioneers. Ideas of 'togetherness' and of 'sharing things, feelings and experience' were enough to persuade thousands of young people, at one time or another, to spend a few weeks or months in a commune. Others pursued the ideal of alternative living more rigorously and attempted to live self-sufficiently, practising communist principles in respect of property. In many communes nuclear families or, quite often, single-parent families simply fitted in – sometimes benefiting from the help that single adults or childless couples gave them with their children. In others, more organised attempts to bring up children communally occurred and in such cases these arrangements were often consciously thought of as alternatives to the nuclear family. Likewise, serious attempts were sometimes made to share the burden of domestic work equally between men and women. In other cases, as feminists have pointed out, the power-structure of communes was, in practice if not in theory, highly patriarchal.

Even at its peak in the late 1960s the commune movement was never more than a marginal challenge to conventional family structures. The nature of modern society tends strongly to undermine the extended family type structure of communes. Geographical mobility – often caused by occupational change – is so great that the chances of the same group of people finding it convenient to stay together over a long period are small. Unless modern society itself breaks down and we return to a more localised agricultural pattern of living, communes seem likely to remain peripheral. Yet, for certain groups, especially students and young, unmarried adults, communal living can offer an enjoyable and practical social framework. It is also not uncommon for groups of one-parent families to live either together or close to one another in order to benefit from mutual co-operation and assistance.

Single-parent families

The possibility that the single-parent family is a distinct and viable family type requires discussion if for no other reason than that in

Great Britain

Percentages

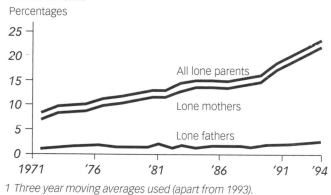

1 Three year moving averages used (apart from 1993).

Note: The proportion of families headed by a single parent increased from nearly eight per cent in 1971 to nearly 23 per cent in 1994.

(Source: Social Trends, 1997:43)

Figure 3.3 Families headed by lone parents as a percentage[1] of all families with dependent children

1994, one in five families with dependent children in Britain were headed by a single parent, over 90 per cent of whom were women. Any adequate sociological discussion of this issue should not be influenced by the social stigma which some still attach to single parenthood. This taint is perhaps implicit in the functionalist

Figure 3.4 Not so untypical: one family in five is headed by a single parent

model which defines certain social institutions, such as the nuclear family, as 'the norm' and others as 'deviant' or even 'pathological' ('sick'). More recently, certain thinkers on the New Right, notably Charles Murray, have seemed to pathologise single parenthood (see pp. 390-1). Given that there are tens of millions of single-parent families throughout the world an attempt at sociologically neutral enquiry into the issue will be made here.

The majority of single-parent families are headed by a divorced or separated female or by a female who is unmarried but 'ideally' might like to be married. In other words, most single parents regard the nuclear family – roughly as defined by Murdock – as the most desirable type of family. Ellis Cashmore's study of over 250 poorer single parents demonstrates that for many in this group, life can be hard and lonely (Cashmore, 1985). Yet, as the one-parent family continues to grow, it becomes increasingly necessary to understand it sociologically and to accommodate it in terms of social policy.

Some women do make a deliberate choice in favour of single-parenthood. Jean Renvoize's *Single Mothers By Choice* (1985) examines 30 mothers of this kind. Significantly, however, most of her sample are professionally qualified women who are able to afford a child independently. Cashmore's study finds few poorer women who regard single-parenthood as in itself liberating, although for some it is a better alternative than an oppressive relationship. Although the percentage of children born outside of marriage is increasing in all social class groups, the prevalence is of a much higher amount in the lower social class groups and realistically must be considered generally to add to their problems.

The majority of British Afro-Caribbean children have been born within marriage. However, a relatively high number are born to unmarried mothers. According to the 1982 PSI survey, 31 per cent of Afro-Caribbean households with children under sixteen were headed by a single parent compared to ten per cent of white households and five per cent of Asian. More recently (1989), Charles Murray, citing government statistics, states that about 48 per cent of live births to black women born in the West Indies occur outside marriage, and this is broadly in line with the general trend during the 1980s (the overall figure in 1994 was 33 per cent).

Similar statistics to the above in the United States have caused some to argue that the single-parent black family is a genuine adaptation to black experience and needs and so is merely a different type of family from the nuclear family but just as 'normal' in its context. Evidence cited to support this analysis includes the polygamous nature of marriage among many black people's West African predecessors and the highly disruptive effect of slavery on marital and family relationships. The contemporary situation of many British, as well as American, black people also provides possible explanations for a high rate of one-parent families. In particular, the high rate of unemployment among black males may deter some black females from marrying them on the grounds that they may be an economic deficit rather than an asset. Instead, family support is sought from within, particularly from female kin, although brothers, too, can be called upon. Indeed, it only seems possible to regard the one-parent black family as an effective family type in the context of the wider kinship system. A higher percentage of British Afro-Caribbean women than white women are in paid work and, given that a substantial minority are single parents, they could only achieve this on the basis of childcare offered by relatives. The lack of childcare facilities provided by local authorities in Britain reinforces this point. For those without such help, and given the high cost of private childcare, dependency on welfare might be the only alternative.

Ann Phoenix states that 'Afro-Caribbean families … are represented in every possible category of family' and warns against representing the single-parent family as typical of the black community or of negatively stereotyping 'the Afro-Caribbean family'. It is hoped that the above discussion avoids this. What it is intended to do is explore whether or not the single-parent family in general, and the Afro-Caribbean single-parent family in particular, can be regarded as an alternative to the nuclear family and as an exception to the nuclear family's universality. The answer seems to be a qualified 'yes' to both these questions. In no modern society has the single-parent family replaced the nuclear family as the dominant family form, but it is becoming increasingly common throughout Western society and is clearly a functional (if minimal) unit, particularly in the context of wider kinship networks.

Lesbian and homosexual led 'families'

The number of lesbian and homosexual couples who bring up children is small but increasing. The following description of lesbian parenthood suggests that they can face much the same problems as heterosexual couples and some more besides:

> ### Lesbian 'Parenthood'
>
> *Michelle G and Nancy S were lovers, lesbians who had been together for 11 years and wanted to fulfil their maternal instincts. They took a joint decision to have a baby, like a growing number of American lesbian couples. Ms G found a sperm donor and was present at the artificial insemination of Ms S and at the birth of their daughter in 1980.*
>
> *There followed happy years of parenthood. A boy was born four years later. Both women were actively involved in bringing up their children – changing nappies, comforting them when ill or unhappy, exalting in their progress. That was until the partnership turned sour. Now they are fighting one another every inch of the way through the Californian courts for custody of the children they love.*
>
> *It is a nasty battle, but one that is becoming increasingly common in the United States because of the number of gay couples having children, the ease with which they split up and the confusion surrounding the law on parenthood.*
>
> *In the past year, courts in Maryland, New York and Los Angeles have had to confront the tricky issue of whether to give access rights to 'mothers' who are not related by blood to their children, and who cannot legally marry the biological*

> *mother, but who have played the role of parent since the children were born.*
>
> *So far the courts have ruled that such de facto parents are not parents in law and therefore have no right to see their children once relationships have ended. In contrast to what happens in most divorces between biological parents, the children's best interests are not even an issue. In the case of Ms G and Ms S (their names are being withheld by court order for the sake of the children) the Californian courts have decided that the children are not Ms G's and that she has no right of access, despite having helped to bring them up. This ruling is now being challenged in an appeal and a hearing is expected next spring.*
>
> *(Lucy Hodges, 'When is a parent not a parent', The Independent, 28.9.1990:19)*

At about the same time as the above report was published, a British court of appeal reversed a decision which had given child custody to a man whose wife had declared herself a lesbian and from whom he was separated. Such cases are unlikely ever to be more than a small minority of those concerning 'the family' but they are common enough to require placing within 'the sociology of the family'.

Indeed, are such social units 'families? They do not fulfil Murdock's definition because they do not include 'adults of both sexes' and its is debatable whether the sexual relationships within them are 'socially approved'. As with the case of the single-parent family, a more limited definition of the family is required if lesbian and homosexual families can, in fact, be defined as families. Such a definition would be that a family is a social group characterised by common residence and co-operation, including at least one adult and child.

Conclusion: is the nuclear family universal?

It is clear that a stable and happy nuclear family is outstandingly well-equipped to perform the basic functions of the reproduction and rearing of children, although in many traditional societies it only functions efficiently as part of an extended kinship system. It is historical fact that in almost every society the nuclear family has been the basic social unit. However, it is not quite true that the nuclear family is universal to all societies. At least, it is strongly arguable that the Nayar and similar cases are exceptions. It is certainly not true that the nuclear family is universal in all societies, in the sense that it is the only type of family found.

The main exception is the single-parent family. Murdock, of course, was aware of the single-parent family 'exception', and the issue is really whether it should be regarded as a 'deviant' family form or simply as another family-type of equal status to the nuclear family.

It is well worth noting that of those cases in which a child's biological father is not involved in its upbringing, the families which function best enjoy some other form of regular and routine assistance for the mother. In the case of the Nayar and Ashanti, the mother relies on blood relatives. In the case of single-parent families in modern societies – particularly, perhaps black single-parent families – there may also be considerable reliance on kin. In lesbian families, a female couple provide mutual support.

A problem in most advanced societies is that many single parents do not have access to a significant network of kin support. There are two broad policy responses to this, not necessarily wholly contradictory. The first is to accept that modern family life is often unstable and fragmentary, and that the state ought to ensure that the basic needs of children are met, above all, by ensuring an adequate national system of pre-school nurseries. This would meet the needs not only of single parents who want to do paid work but also of the many married couples with children who both want to do paid work. The second policy response is to try to 'shore up' the nuclear family. For instance, divorce could be made more difficult to obtain, and absent fathers pursued and required to maintain their offspring. These issues recur throughout the remainder of this chapter.

The family and community in Britain from pre-industrial to modern times

It is used to be thought that the extended family was typical in pre-industrial England and that the nuclear family became predominant as a result of industrialisation. It was argued by Goode and Parsons that the industrial economy requires a more mobile population and that this tends to break up extended families; in particular, the urban, industrial areas drew in younger people. Historical and sociological research has shown this to be too simple a view. Nevertheless, as Edward Shorter and others argue, this new knowledge need not fundamentally change our perception of the difference between local community life in pre-industrial and modern times. Even though family structure has changed less than was thought, its relationship to the wider community has partly changed. We will divide our study of changes in the family into three historical phases: the pre-industrial, the early industrial and the modern.

The pre-industrial family

Peter Laslett has shown that, the nuclear family was, in fact, the norm in pre-industrial Britain, and other research strongly suggests that the same was true for North America. It is quite likely, however, that the extended family was more common in continental Europe, at least in the East. One important exception

to the nuclear family norm existed in Britain. It was usual for the eldest and inheriting son and his family to remain in his parents' home. This was to mutual benefit: the ageing parents could receive help from their eldest son, who was able to live in and look after the property he would eventually inherit. Although other children usually moved out of the parental home at marriage, they normally lived close by.

An interesting suggestion emerging from more recent research on the family further refutes the functionalist view that the predominance of the nuclear family occurred as a result of industrialisation. Harris argues that the very fact that non-inheriting children had to make their own way in the world helped to provide a mobile labour force and to foster the values of hard work and achievement necessary for capitalist activity. Seemingly, it was not necessary for the family to 'adapt' greatly to the early industrial society, as functionalists maintain. On the contrary, the single inheritance system may have helped foster industrialisation. The same system of inheritance exists in Japan and may have had a similar effect.

Talcott Parsons emphasises the multi-functional nature of the pre-industrial family. Whereas the modern nuclear family typically receives much assistance from the state in performing its basic functions, the pre-industrial family had to be more self-sufficient. At times of crisis, considerable help was often provided by kin and neighbours. If this help was essentially informal, it was also expected and needed.

Then, as now, the family was the major institution of sex, reproduction and nurture. As far as socialisation was concerned, the family, supported by church and community, taught traditional behaviour and morality. For the great majority there was no formal schooling and most could neither read nor write. Skills, including farming skills, were normally learnt through practical application, usually under the watchful eye of family or kin. The major economic function of most families was to produce enough for their members to survive – comfortably if possible. The better off and more successful produced a surplus which could then be sold in market towns – mainly for consumption by the urban minority. The function of job placement was more often performed by the family in pre-industrial times than it is now. This means that older members of the family would frequently place younger members in work.

Whatever the precise size and structure of the pre-industrial family, Edward Shorter seems to be right to suggest that both kin and community had greater control and influence on individual and nuclear family life than is the case now. This observation fits in with the view of some functionalists that family and community 'did' more for their members than they do today.

The early industrial family

With industrialisation and the movement of population to the towns, major changes began to take place in the functional relationship of the family to society. But just as sociologists have exaggerated the extent of the extended family in the pre-industrial past, so too have they often overstressed the speed and extent of the change to the nuclear family in industrial, urban areas. Obviously, if the nuclear family was the predominant form before industrialisation, there could hardly have been a massive shift towards it after industrialisation. There is some evidence that in industrial working class areas the extended family was, in fact, more common than in rural areas. This was the pattern found by Anderson in his research into households in the cotton-manufacturing town of Preston and a rural area nearby, in the mid-nineteenth century. Peter Willmott and Michael Young's famous study of working class family life in Bethnal Green in the 1950s showed the strength of extended family type structures at that time and it is likely that this pattern had existed for several generations. The usefulness of extended family type structures to the working class in the nineteenth century is apparent. Older women could help out domestically when the younger married women went out to work. People arriving from the rural areas would often stay with relatives, not only out of immediate necessity, but also in the hope of picking up tips about jobs, or even getting a specific recommendation and placement. Extended families in contemporary immigrant communities play much the same role.

There were also sound personal and social reasons for middle class families to stay close together in Victorian England. In particular, in the absence of a welfare state, the old still depended on their kin for help and companionship. Quite often, the large, three-floor Victorian middle class house was the home of three generations.

The pattern painted by modern scholarship is, then, of more continuity between pre-industrial and early industrial family structure and life than has been previously noted. The extended family and supportive community was often needed as much in industrial and dockland areas as it had been in rural areas. The real changes in family and community life occurred much closer to our own time, and these have more to do with family size and the break-up of families than with any marked change from the extended to the nuclear form.

The 'modern' family

The twentieth century, our third period for consideration, has seen substantial changes in the size of the family and in its relationship to society. Largely because of improved methods of birth control and the resultant decrease in the fertility rate, families tend to be much smaller than in Victorian times. A family of four, two parents and two children, has become typical of both the working and middle classes. Change in family size has probably had as much effect on family life as any supposed change in family structure. Nevertheless, it can be said that the post-Second World War period is the one in which the nuclear family has overwhelmingly predominated over the extended. Indeed, as early as 1971, the majority of households contained only one or two people – a fact

which suggests that even the nuclear family is suffering some fragmentation. According to functionalists such as Talcott Parsons, the modern nuclear family has adapted to fulfil more specialised functions. Further, the relationship of family to community has changed in certain respects, if perhaps less so than some authorities have previously thought.

Recent research by Peter Wilmott (1986) confirms that although kin are now less likely to live close to each other, contact often remains quite frequent. He describes three types of kinship arrangements in contemporary Britain:

1 The *local extended family* – two or three related nuclear families in separate but geographically close households (such as in 1950s Bethnal Green). This type of family pattern is on the decline (see p. 52).
2 The *dispersed extended family* – two or more related nuclear families which are not localised and consequently see each other less than in the case of the local extended family. However, visits are still quite frequent, occurring perhaps on a weekly or fortnightly basis. This type accounts for about half of families, and is probably now typical of both the working and middle classes (despite other differences discussed below).
3 The *attenuated extended family* – this is like the dispersed extended family but contact is much less frequent. This accounts for about three-eighths of families.

Overall, Willmott concludes that 'The most striking feature of British kinship, now and in the past, and in both rural and urban environments, is its resilience' (1988).

The debate about changing family functions and roles

Functionalist perspective

The classic functionalist 'position' on the changing functions of the family is that the state has largely taken over certain of its functions while the family has become more specialised in others. Talcott Parsons is perhaps the best-known proponent of this view. Ronald Fletcher, a British functionalist, sharply disagrees with Parsons on this matter (as on others). Fletcher argues that the modern family is more involved across a wide range of functions – essential and non-essential – than previously. Marxists agree with functionalists that the family performs essential functions in capitalist societies but argue that it does so in a way that results in the exploitation of its members, particularly women. A view expressed from the New Right is that inadequate family performance partly reflects a failure of individual responsibility, especially on the part of some male parents.

In general, functionalists consider that the basic functions of the modern nuclear family remain those that the family has traditionally fulfilled to a greater or lesser extent, but that all four functions have been modified. According to Murdock, these are:

sex, reproduction, socialisation, and the economic. Talcott Parsons, in particular, argues that as the basic functions have tended to be reduced, the family has acquired a still greater role in personal and emotional life. There has been a parallel decline in the involvement of the local community with the individual. Often there is a wall of privacy between family and neighbourhood community.

For the majority, marriage is still the main outlet for sexual activity and some consider it to be the only morally acceptable one. Many people, however, no longer exclusively associate sex with marriage. Michael Schofield's work shows a growth in permissive attitudes to sex before marriage among young people. In the United States, The Hite Report (1989) suggested that many women no longer regard sexual expression exclusively in terms of their marital relationship. If marriage is not as exclusively the outlet for sexual expression as in the past, it still provides the most popular basis of companionship and mutual assistance. The increase in the number of people suffering from AIDS does not appear to have greatly affected the above patterns of behaviour, and it is not even clear whether it has brought about 'safer sex' among heterosexuals although this now appears to have widely occurred among the homosexual community (1991).

Reproduction still occurs predominantly within a two-parent family context despite a steep increase in births outside marriage in recent years. There has been a corresponding rise in the number of children taken into local authority care, but most of these still received early nurture and socialisation within some sort of family situation, however unstable.

The state has come increasingly to intervene in child socialisation, particularly from the age of five when children usually start school. Even infants (and for that matter unborn children) can benefit from a variety of advice and assistance available from central, and sometimes local, government sources. A state system of pre-school nurseries is not, however, provided in Britain, and the responsibility for early childcare and socialisation falls more heavily on the family than in other European societies (see p. 79). Functionalists stress the continuing importance of 'the family' as the agency of primary socialisation. Here they are not merely referring to informal socialisation, which functionalists have always seen as necessary to passing on the values and norms of society, but to formal teaching too. Fletcher suggests that more teaching and learning take place in the family now than in the past. We live in a complex world in which 'the three Rs' are necessary rather than optional. Many parents play a large part in teaching these and other skills.

Although increasing numbers of individuals work wholly or partly from home, the family itself is rarely now a unit of economic production, although it is an important unit of consumption. Many goods, such as refrigerators, washing machines, and three-piece suites are manufactured largely for the family market. It hardly needs to be said that without this market there would be economic collapse. In addition, families collectively produce and maintain the labour force. Finally, the investment of family money in banks, building societies, unit trusts and stocks and shares provides necessary loan capital for industrial investment.

The protection and assistance traditionally afforded by kin and community is now commonly provided by the state. The logic of welfare is that social security, not the family, must remain the final safety net for people faced with poverty. The National Health Service plays a major role here. So, too, do the contributory national insurance schemes covering sickness and unemployment payments, and the social security system, which is supposed to be the ultimate 'security' against poverty if all else fails. Some have seen the apparent loss of the family's welfare function and its assumption by the state as an example of the growing impersonality of the modern world. Even caring for one's fellows has been taken over by 'big brother', and strugglers are assisted by salaried social workers rather than by friends. This is too simple a view. Firstly, the Welfare State provides many services, including necessary medical services to the poor, that people would not otherwise obtain. Secondly, help from family and friends does, and indeed should, supplement and overlap that provided by the welfare state. The state cannot usually supply the human and emotional support that people undergoing material or emotional crisis often need, although many social workers have made remarkable efforts to do so. The administration of social security payments has, however, often been obtusely bureaucratic – hardly a bracing recipe for 'clients' often already dispirited and suffering.

Talcott Parsons emphasises the importance of the contemporary family in 'stabilising' the adult personality. It provides a relatively secure and personally meaningful context for self-fulfilment, in contrast with the frequently stressful and impersonal nature of work. Parsons considers that the family has shed some of its less necessary functions and has adapted to become more specialised in two tasks: that of socialisation, and 'tension' or emotional management.

Ronald Fletcher agrees that the nuclear family remains a functionally necessary social unit but disagrees that it has lost its non-essential functions. In *The Family and Marriage in Britain* (1962) Fletcher lists the non-essential functions of the family as political participation (e.g. voting), economic, education, health, religious, and recreation. It is largely the increased leisure time and wealth available to families that enables them to be more involved in these areas. However, Fletcher fully acknowledges that in some of these areas, particularly education and health, the state has also become much more involved. On balance, he considers that both family and state devote more time to 'non-essential areas', and suggests that this reflects technological advance, greater leisure and more demanding standards. Although Fletcher recognises that the nuclear family is beset by a range of problems, these have intensified in the 30 or so years since he published his book. Although clearly a 'supporter' of the nuclear family, it is likely that he would paint a less positive picture of its performance in the light of some of the trends discussed elsewhere in this chapter.

As David Morgan observes in his article *Socialisation and the Family: Change and Diversity* (1988), the various perspectives on how the functions of the family have developed in the past two hundred years are not easy entirely to reconcile. He himself takes the view that it is not particularly helpful to describe changes in the family in terms of a 'loss of functions'. He comments that 'there does not seem to be any evidence of an overall decline in the family in terms of its centrality in the lives of individuals or its importance in many areas of social life'. However, within this broad pattern of continuing importance, some specialisation has occurred: '(I)t is possible to talk of a shift in the range of uses to which family relationships are put … with a particular sharper focus on the material relationship and with the business of child-rearing. To this extent the family may be described as a more specialised institution' (40).

The issues of family relationships – particularly that of wife and husband – and of childrearing are fully discussed below.

Marxist-feminist perspective

Marxists agree that the family performs a range of functions within capitalist society. However, they evaluate these in a negatively critical way, reflecting their overall view of capitalism. Marxists consider that in capitalist society, the working class family is subordinated to the needs of production. In early capitalism, high productivity could only be achieved if men, women and children were directly involved in industrial work. As machine productivity increased, it became economic and, in fact, potentially more productive to exclude children and women from industrial work. Children could then be educated and become more efficient producers, and women could better maintain male labour as full-time 'housewives'. Marxist-feminist Sue Sharpe (1972) has usefully conceptualised the role of women in industrial capitalist society in terms of 'reproduction'. Women reproduce a labour force both by giving birth to it and by socialising it into the normal required to achieve working class acceptance of and conformity to capitalist society. They also help to reproduce the existing male labour force by meeting its maintenance and sexual needs. Of course, Sharpe challenges the inevitability of this structuring of the family and of the role of working class women, while recognising that it is apparently highly functional for capitalist society at a given stage of its development.

Juliette Mitchell has analysed the role of women, and by implication that of the family in capitalist society in its current stage of development, in which the service rather than the industrial sector predominates (Mitchell 1986). Once again, economic expansion has increased the demand for women in paid employment, albeit typically in offices rather than factories. Mitchell points out that this development is not necessarily a wholly liberating one for women. They are on average less well paid than men, typically subject to male authority (frequently even when better qualified), and often overwhelmingly carry the burden of housework. In other words, women live within a patriarchal system. It is to the key issue of equality and democracy within the family that we now turn.

Symmetrical or patriarchal family? Conjugal roles

Peter Willmott and Michael Young make some interesting observations on changes in family roles and relationships in their book *The Symmetrical Family* (1973). Much of what they say continues and develops earlier British research on the family, including their own. In the 1950s, for instance, Elizabeth Bott found that, on the basis of an admittedly small sample (twenty families), working class spouses tended to divide tasks sharply and pursue separate leisure activities, whereas the opposite applied to the middle class. Thus, she describes these as, respectively, segregated and joint conjugal role relationships.

In *The Symmetrical Family*, Willmott and Young argue that 'the direction of change has, we believe, been from Bott's first to her second type' of family. By symmetrical, then, they mean a joint or shared approach to married life rather than one which is segregated into largely separate roles. The symmetrical family is not wholly egalitarian because a considerable degree of separate role allocation still occurs, but 'a measure of egalitarianism' does exist. They go on to say that 'In this context [egalitarianism], the essence of a symmetrical relationship is that it is opposite but similar'.

The data on which Willmott and Young developed their concept of the symmetrical family was a large-scale social survey of the adult population of the London Metropolitan Region. The interview responses show a large majority of husbands in all classes reporting that they help their wives at least once a week in a domestic task, although the majority is noticeably the smallest among the semi-skilled and unskilled category. Once a week is a very modest amount of help, and as Willmott and Young themselves comment, 'most married couples were obviously still a long way from the state of unisex that some young people had arrived at'. Despite the qualifications with which Willmott and Young constantly hedge their symmetrical family analysis, they appear at times to strain their data to support what they see as an emerging trend to symmetry.

Willmott and Young consider that the pattern of economic development underlies the move towards symmetry. Firstly, as more women are doing paid work, there is practical logic and fairness in men becoming more involved with domestic work. Secondly, immense improvements in household technology are assumed to have reduced the time committed to housework, to have removed much of the drudgery from it, and to have simplified it to the point where any member of a household can do it. Within this context the development of the symmetrical family seems almost 'natural'.

Mary Maynard: unequally gendered housework

Nevertheless, Mary Maynard represents the opinion of many feminists when she writes that 'despite the predominance of this view, a vast amount of empirical evidence suggests otherwise'. She goes on to cite two types of evidence which demonstrate that women still overwhelmingly carry the main burden and stress of housework: American time-budget surveys and mainly British sociological surveys and studies of housework and the housewife. These findings will be discussed in greater detail in Chapter 7 (see pp. 198-9) but need briefly to be referred to here. The time-budget studies measured time spent on housework and other activities, particularly paid work and leisure. They consistently show that although women tend to do less housework when they are also doing paid work, the overall length of their working week increases. In contrast, it is the husbands of wives who have the longest overall working week, that have the shortest working week themselves. The relatively little housework or childcare they do seems to be regarded as a form of back-up help.

Although the time-budget studies are American, Table 3.3 provides data which suggests their findings might apply equally to Britain. The table contrasts how household tasks and child-rearing were shared between men and women in 1983 and 1991. In the latter case, it provides data on how respondents thought the tasks ought to be shared, categorised for men and women. Unfortunately the data does not provide information on the paid-work status of respondents. The table merits close analysis but, in general, it shows that women do the more demanding household tasks and child-rearing, with men only approaching equal involvement in the lighter perhaps more 'symbolic' ones. The reality of sharing lags well behind what respondents tend to consider ought to happen, although there is perhaps a very slight overall trend to greater sharing between 1983 and 1991.

The second type of research cited by Maynard – British studies of housework and the housewife – confirms the highly gendered organisation of housework (i.e. it is organised on the basis of sexual difference). Studies show that although modern household technology has changed the content of housework, it has had little

effect on the amount women perform (although, as noted above, if they are also involved in paid work, some reduction in housework tends to occur). Whereas, in the past, basic housework took up more time, now the demands of quality child-rearing, and the selection, buying and other work involved in maintaining high standards of consumption, and, in some cases, entertaining, take up more time. Qualitative materials on the experience of being a housewife shows what Maynard refers to as 'a series of contradictions and conflicts'. She cites several reasons for this, including both that much of the work is routine, repetitive and boring – despite involving a degree of autonomy (independence) – and that men tend to underestimate and under-appreciate it.

Family privatisation and consumerism

Both Young and Willmott, and John Goldthorpe and David Lockwood in their 'affluent worker' study have noted a tendency towards family based – rather than community based social life, both among their main sample of affluent manual workers and the smaller, control group of white-collar employees. Spouses spent time together inside the home rather than in visiting friends and neighbours. Goldthorpe and Lockwood termed this trend the privatisation of family life (see pp. 172-5). It is a concept which chimes in well with Parson's notion of a more isolated, functionally-specialised nuclear family.

There are several reasons for the development of the privatised nuclear pattern of living. An underlying factor is the movement of population caused partly by the operation of a free labour market and government policy to disperse population from the declining inner city areas. This has undermined community and extended-family type social networks. Important, too, is the massive postwar

Table 3.3 Household division of labour of married couples: by sex and task, 1983 and 1991

	Actual allocation of tasks						How tasks should be allocated		
	1983			1991			1991		
	Mainly man	Mainly woman	Shared equally	Mainly man	Mainly woman	Shared equally	Mainly man	Mainly woman	Shared equally
		Percentages			Percentages			Numbers	
Household tasks (percentages)									
Household shopping	5	51	44	7	50	43	1	30	68
Makes evening meal	5	77	17	6	77	17	–	52	45
Does evening dishes	17	40	40	22	39	36	11	17	70
Does household cleaning	3	72	24	4	72	23	1	44	54
Does washing and ironing	1	89	10	2	88	9	–	69	30
Repairs household equipment	82	6	10	82	6	8	73	1	24
Money and bills	29	39	32	32	38	30	22	15	61

Note: Rounding can result in sequences not adding up to 100%.

(Source: Social and Community Planning Research)

boom in home-based, leisure consumer items such as televisions and hi-fis. Many married people, as well as aspiring to a high material standard of living, have great expectations of their marital relationship as well. Unlike many Eastern societies in which marriages are arranged by parents, Western societies allow people to marry for love and romance. Even after the first flush is over, couples tend to expect and demand much of each other, both in terms of everyday companionship and deeper emotional and physical commitment. With this in mind, some commentators have referred to modern marriage as companionate marriage. There is 'another side' to the high expectations and emotional demands of modern marriage, however. They can contribute to disillusionment if the reality fails to match up to the ideal (see p. 67).

Christopher Lasch, a radical American intellectual, gives a depressing view of the nuclear family in capitalist society. He puts quite a different value on family consumerism and even on the marital relationship from that of functionalists. He argues, as do many Marxists, that the family market is manipulated by capitalist advertisers and producers. People are persuaded to buy the 'latest' item, even when they neither need nor want it: this spending keeps the wheels of the capitalist economy turning. The stresses of a materialist society which lacks deeper spiritual or human values shows in marriage – and divorce. For Lasch, the family in 'bourgeois' society has ceased to be a private refuge. In his view the privatisation of the family is breached by the consumerist ideology of the media. These observations are examined more closely later (Chapter 17).

Some quarter of a century after the publication of Goldthorpe and Lockwood's work, it is arguable that the developments which produced the privatised nuclear family now undermine it. The dedicated pursuit of private satisfaction may partly explain why so many marriages break-up and why 27 per cent of households now have only a single resident.

Marriage and families: stress and adaptation

A wide range of data and developments are often cited to demonstrate that the family as a basic social institution is under stress and is even in danger of 'breaking up'. In this section several factors relevant to this issue will be discussed critically. However, it is important at the outset to appreciate that many sociologists wholly or largely reject the thesis that the family is breaking up, and favour instead a different model of analysis and interpretation. They adopt a broadly pluralist model of families and life-cycles in which it is stated that individuals adopt or develop a variety of family types and situations and also non-family life-styles. The latter include living as a couple (married or unmarried) without children or as a single person. These sociologists criticise the 'family

break-up' thesis as being based on a narrow view of families in which the nuclear family is considered the norm and sometimes specifically as the desirable norm both functionally and morally. Aspects of this debate have already been discussed in relation to the question of whether or not the nuclear family is universal as the most functional family type.

The key issues in relation to family change and adaptation discussed below are:

1 Divorce
2 Single-parent families
3 Co-habitation
4 Child neglect and abuse
5 Generational conflict: a crisis of authority?

Divorce

Arguably, the rise in the divorce rate is the most striking indicator of family stress, although it may also release married partners and their children from stress. Many thousands opt for separation rather than divorce, so the divorce figures underestimate the extent of marital breakdown. In 1993 the number of divorces was seven times that in 1961. In the latter year, the proportion of marriages to divorces was about three to one. Figure 3.5 gives details of the rising divorce rate between 1961 and 1993. Table 3.4 shows that the number of marriages per annum has been falling as steadily as the divorce rate has been rising.

United Kingdom

1 Including annulments.
2 For one or both partners.

(Source: Office of Population Censuses and Surveys; General Register Office (Scotland); General Register Office (Northern Ireland; Social Trends 1996:57)

Figure 3.5 Marriages and divorces

Table 3.4 Marriage and divorce rates: EC comparison, 1981 and 1993

	Marriages		Divorces	
	1981	1993	1981	1993
	Rates per 1,000 population			
United Kingdom	7.1	5.9	2.8	3.1
Denmark	5.0	6.1	2.8	2.5
Finland	6.3	4.9	2.0	2.5
Sweden	4.5	3.9	2.4	2.5
Belgium	6.5	5.4	1.6	2.1
Austria	6.3	5.6	1.8	2.0
Netherlands	6.0	5.8	2.0	2.0
France	5.8	4.4	1.6	1.9
Germany	6.2	5.5	2.0	1.9
Luxembourg	5.5	6.0	1.4	1.9
Portugal	7.8	6.9	0.7	1.2
Greece	6.9	6.0	0.7	0.7
Spain	5.4	4.0	0.3	0.7
Italy	5.6	5.1	0.2	0.4
Irish Republic	6.0	4.4		
EC average	6.1	5.3	1.5	1.7

(Source: *Social Trends* 1996:57)

Factors underlying the increase in the divorce rate

The decline of religion and changes in the divorce laws

Changes in cultural attitudes towards marriage have created a climate of public opinion in which it has been possible to pass laws which have made it increasingly easy to opt out of marriage. The long-term background to the erosion of marriage as a permanent and binding commitment is the decline in formal religious belief. Marriage is less often seen as a sacred, spiritual union, but more as a personal and practical commitment which can be abandoned if it fails. This attitude to marriage has resulted in a series of changes in the law, making the grounds for divorce less strict and the administrative procedure for obtaining it less complicated and time-consuming (for instance, in 1977 it became possible to get divorced by post in some circumstances). The Divorce Law Reform Act of 1969 (actually implemented in 1971) established that it was enough merely to prove 'irretrievable breakdown of marriage' to obtain a divorce. The 'irretrievable breakdown of marriage' was made the sole cause. The phrase is general enough to be interpreted to include virtually all conceivable reasons for divorce. Although there was an increase in the divorce rate following the Act, it would be crude to think of the Act as 'causing' this increase. Deeper reasons for it must be sought in the broader cultural factors mentioned above. Viewed in longer perspective, the statistical trend is that of a gradual increase in divorce with occasional sharp jumps when enabling legislation was passed. In addition to the 1969 Act, another such instance was the 1949 Legal Aid Act, which enabled women seeking divorce to obtain financial assistance in doing so.

Capitalism, the rise of individualism and romantic love

Edward Shorter in his book *The Making of the Modern Family* (1975) argues that the onset of capitalism promoted individualistic and sexually freer or 'romantic' behaviour (Shorter's view of the 'romantic' behaviour is distinctly unrosy).

Capitalism broke up traditional communities and set their populations 'free', in the limited sense that they could go to towns and compete for work. But they were free also from traditional family and community control, freer to have personal and sexual relations with whom they wished. In the long-term, this freedom evolved into the virtual right to choose and, within ever more generous limits, get rid of one's spouse. The question of romantic marriage must be seen against the background of a steady decline in family and community control of choice of partner, courtship and marriage. Traditionally, couples married (or had their marriages arranged) for down-to-earth material reasons, such as, to take a middle class example, joining two family estates or businesses together. Courtship was supervised closely, if more or less informally, within the community. During the last two hundred years, however, people have been increasingly marrying whom they want rather than whom they are told to. As Shorter points out, the danger in marrying for mainly romantic reasons is that when romantic love and attraction disappear, so too might marriage.

Although the sweep of Shorter's analysis covers several centuries of the influence of capitalism on cultural attitudes and behaviour, it is worth reading the following passage, bearing in mind the free-market revival of the 1980s and the accompanying pressures on families, all of which occurred after he had published his book:

> *How did capitalism help cause that powerful thrust of sentiment among the unmarried that I have called the romance revolution? To what extent may sleeping around before marriage and choosing partners on the basis of personal attraction rather than wealth be associated with economic change? The principal link here is the increased participation of young unmarried people, especially women, in the free-market labour force. The logic of the market-place positively demands individualism: the system will succeed only if each participant ruthlessly pursues his (sic) own self-interest, buying cheap, selling dear, and enhancing his own interests at the cost of his competitors (i.e. his fellow citizens … thus, the free market engraves upon all who are caught up in it the attitude: 'Look out for number one'.*
>
> (Shorter, 1977:253)

Improved birth-control technology may have further contributed to sexual attitudes and behaviour based on personal gratification rather than any wider norms or morality. The spread of AIDS has made it paramount that such behaviour should in any case be 'safe'.

Problems of inter-personal communication

A cluster of other factors – most of which are fairly self-evident – correlate with divorce. Partners who are dissimilar in culture, social background, or religion, or who are of very different age are more prone to divorce, as are those who marry young and may still be developing personally and emotionally. Barbara Thomas and Jean Collard in *Who Divorces?* (1984) suggest that for these and other divorced couples, a common underlying problem is often poor inter-personal communication. They agree with Young and Willmott that the small conjugal family has increasingly become the principal and sometimes sole source of deep emotional expression, and that this can put a strain on the marriages of those who have communication problems.

The changing status of women

Some observers associate the increase in divorce with the changing status of women. The female share of divorce petitions has generally outnumbered that of men in both Britain and the United States in recent years. In Britain the female share was about 70 per cent in the early 1990s. It may be that, as more women have entered the labour market, they have acquired the necessary economic independence to opt out of an unsatisfactory marriage if they choose to do so. Further, involvement in paid work also enables them to meet more prospective partners than if they remained full-time housewives. Interestingly, according to the US Bureau of Census Report (1972), better-paid female divorcees are more likely to delay remarriage or remain single than are low-paid ones. Whether or not women will be able to maintain their limited gains in the labour market of the late 1990s remains to be seen.

However, perhaps the main effect on the divorce rate of the increasing involvement of women in paid work is a result of the dual burden of housework and paid work discussed by Maynard (above). In *When Marriage Ends* (1976), Nicky Hart argues that the contradictory demands of these two roles can produce tension between wife and husband and in particular, lead the former eventually to seek divorce.

The rise in the number of single-parent families

This matter has been fully discussed elsewhere in this chapter (see pp. 59-60) and is further dealt with in the context of the 'underclass' in Chapter 13 (see pp. 390-1). Two points can be stressed here in relation to single parenthood and family stress. First, the majority of single-parent families occur because of divorce. To that extent, they are the product of stress on, or the failure of, what were originally nuclear families. Second, single parenthood is undoubtedly demanding and stressful for those many single parents without adequate income and resources. Policy issues relating to this are discussed on p. 59 and extensively on pp. 79-80.

The rise in the number of couples cohabiting

As Figure 3.6 shows, there has been a considerable rise in the percentage of non-married women aged between 18 and 49 cohabiting since 1981. It has risen from 12 to 23 per cent. However, the percentage cohabiting in Britain remains smaller than with that typical of the Scandinavian countries, which is over 40 per cent.

However, a report *The Relationship Revolution*, published by the charity One Plus One, suggests that the Scandinavian pattern of-term cohabitation – *instead of* rather than merely *prior to* marriage is emerging in Britain. Marriage 'could become irrelevant as an expression of commitment' once cohabitation is established as a basis for child-rearing, as it is in Scandinavia. The recent sharp decline in the annual number of marriages in Britain lends support to this view.

Child neglect and abuse

Essentially, contemporary sociological perspectives link the treatment of children, including child-abuse, with general cultural attitudes to children rather than merely with individual mental pathology (illness). There is growing evidence in the late 1980s and 1990s of a child-abuse problem of significant proportions. In particular, a series of cases involving the abuse of children in care seemed to indicate inadequate local authority supervision of child-care establishments. By 1996 there were increasing calls for a national enquiry into the issue. However, more everyday problems receive less media attention – on a daily basis, many young children and their mothers struggle to meet the practical demands of life.

Poorer children are more likely to experience a variety of problems. At a wider level, Britain is at the bottom of the European league in terms of the provision of child-care for three to five-year-olds. These facts offer a better starting point for analysis than moral panics about individuals characterised as 'monsters' or 'beasts'.

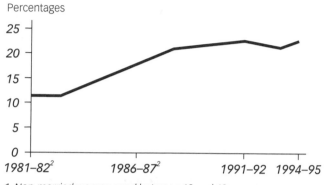

Great Britain

Percentages

1981–82²   1986–87²   1991–92   1994–95

1 *Non-married women aged between 18 and 49.*
2 *Calendar years up to 1988.*

(Source: *General Household Survey*, Office of Population Censuses and Surveys; *Social Trends*, 1996:55)

Figure 3.6 Percentage of women[1] (aged 18–49) cohabiting

Table 3.5 Percentage of women cohabiting: by age and marital status, 1993-94 to 1994-95

	Single[1]	Separated	Divorced	Widowed	All non-married women
Great Britain			Percentages		
16-24	14	8	–	–	14
25-34	33	17	29	–	30
35-49	18	7	25	14	19
50-59	6	5	12	3	8
All aged 16 to 59					

1 *Never married.*

(Source: *General Household Survey*, Office of Population Censuses and Surveys; *Social Trends*, 1996:58)

Generational conflict: a crisis of authority?

Again, the issue of generational conflict is one which is amply discussed elsewhere in this book (see Chapter 15 p. 448). In fact, surveys on the attitudes of teenagers repeatedly show that broadly they like their parents, get on reasonably well with them, and are generally fairly satisfied with life. On the other hand, there has been a continuous and now highly destructive and expensive problem of juvenile delinquency and often related drunkenness since the Second World War, for which a supposed decline in parental authority is sometimes blamed.

Specifically, the charge made is that the family is failing to act as an effective agency of social control. This accusation, however, could equally be made against the schools and police. The causes of juvenile delinquency must therefore be sought in the wider society rather than in the failure of any single institution such as the family. This we do in Chapter 12. Here, it need only be said that the more permissive and democratic ideals of the post-war period reduce the credibility of physical punishment as a means of maintaining control both within the family and within society. It is difficult to imagine a widespread reversion to more traditional forms of discipline within the family without some comparable broader change in society. Whether such a change would have much effect on juvenile delinquency is entirely debatable.

The dynamics of family violence: a view from radical psychiatry

One of the cult figures of the 1960s was the radical psychiatrist Ronald Laing. His analysis of the family illustrates aspects of the phenomenological perspective. His primary concern is with the 'self' but he does not separate the life of the self from that of others. For him 'madness' is not a personal deficiency but must be interpreted as a way of making sense of experience. Thus, he spoke of schizophrenic families rather than schizophrenic individuals – if the self is forced into fantasy escape, it is because there is something to escape from. Although Laing's primary focus on analysis is the micro-level of group interaction, the tension and psychological 'violence' he sees in family life persuaded him to look at the wider world:

> *Concerned as I am with this inner world, observing day to day its devastation, I ask why this has happened.*

If he finds an answer to this question, it is that the violence of the outside world – the Vietnam war was particularly in his mind – fuses with and reinforces the potential for violence within us. Corpses on a dead television screen are unreal, but slowly we learn not to care about them or each other, or the human consequences of what we do. The family cannot cope with all this or give it meaning. He suggests that for some, personal madness is a retreat from 'madness out there.' This recalls the pained cry of poet Allen Ginsberg: 'I have seen the best minds of my generation driven mad.'

David Cooper, a colleague of Laing, goes beyond the latter in taking explicitly political attitudes. His approach owes much to Marx, but, unlike him, Cooper wants to abolish the family itself – at least, as a hard and fast biological unit. Cooper's basic criticism of the family in bourgeois society is the peculiarly limiting and constraining role it plays:

> *The child, in fact, is taught primarily not how to survive in society but how to submit to it. Surface rituals like etiquette, organised games, mechanical learning operations at school replace deep experiences of spontaneous creativity, inventive play, freely developing fantasies and dreams.*

That, perhaps, is the nub of Cooper and Laing. They want a freer, less repressive society – always provided that what is freely expressed is love rather than selfishness or hate. Cooper's belief that spontaneous, 'wanted' relationships should take preference over biological and legal bonds is what leads him to attack the rational family.

In retrospect, Laing and Cooper's contributions have been less in the directly social and political dimension of their work than in nudging their sizeable audience, particularly among young, educated adults, further in the direction of experimental permissiveness in relationships, not only with children, but with each other. To that extent, they are not entirely out of tune with the genial liberal adviser on childbearing of the 1950s, Dr Benjamin Spock.

Another commentator on the family, anthropologist Edmund Leach, seems to capture the essence of the above criticisms of the family in his own description of it as 'a prison'. Although Leach intends the analogy to be derogatory, there is a sense in which the family must inevitably constrain the individual. Society itself is also sometimes compared to a prison, and for the same reason: it limits total freedom. If functionalists accept the need for social control too uncritically, perhaps the radical psychiatrists underestimate the potentially dangerous as well as positive effects of its absence.

Conjugal conflict: wife-battering

As is the case with child abuse, it is difficult to be sure whether the problem has become more widespread or whether it has merely come closer to public awareness. Dobash and Dobash (1980) cite the police records of Edinburgh and Glasgow, which show that the second most common form of violence is wife-assault, making up 25 per cent of recorded violent crime.

In her introduction to *Private Violence and Public Policy* (1985), Jan Pahl argues that wife-battering should be seen as 'the extension of the domination and control of husbands over wives'. Pahl rejects individualistic explanations of wife-battering in favour of a structural analysis of patriarchy – one aspect of which can be violence by males against females, specifically in a couple relationship. She is able to cite an impressive array of historical and comparative cultural data to demonstrate that male violence against women is typically embedded in a patriarchal context (see Reading 2).

Robert Chester – the nuclear family is 'normal'

Before concluding on the issue of whether 'the family' is breaking up or adapting, it is important to note the views of Robert Chester, who argues that the nuclear family and marriage remain the normative experience for the great majority of Britons. It can be plausibly argued that Chester gives voice to the opinions of this 'silent majority'. Chester complains that:

> *Much play is made of the supposed pluralism and diversity of contemporary family forms …*
>
> *Discontinuities in the family get more notice than continuities partly because they often involve stress or other grounds for social concern. Traditionalists point to them as signifying the decline of the family. Feminists and other objectors to the conventional family have an obvious interest in derogating it … lobbies for various minority forms of family life seek to legitimise what is often still regarded as deviant. But to win support for policies which help those who need it, it should not be necessary to obscure the factual prevalence of conventional family arrangements.*
>
> *(Chester, 1985:185,188)*

Chester's case for the 'prevalence of conventional family arrangements' is largely 'factual'; or statistical. Most people get married and live in nuclear families. Most children are bought up in nuclear families. Most marriages end with death, not divorce. Divorcees are usually keen to marry again. These facts were true when Chester wrote in 1985 and they remain true into the 1990s. However, he 'who lives by statistics, dies by statistics', and the fact is that the statistical trends since Chester wrote, show the continued erosion of the conventional nuclear family and marriage. Trends may reverse or level out, but they show little sign of doing so.

Nevertheless, in 1997, as in 1985, Chester would be able correctly to state that most people aspire to marriage and to form a nuclear family and actually achieve these goals. Functionalists would argue that in doing so, they are choosing the most practical and effective institution in which to bring up children.

Chester makes one minor qualification to his case for the 'prevalence of conventional family arrangements'. He recognises that increasingly married women do paid work and so the pattern of the male breadwinner and the housewife is changing somewhat. He suggests that the new pattern is established and accommodating enough to be dubbed 'the neo-conventional family'.

Conclusion: is 'the family' breaking up or adapting?

We have examined impressive evidence of stress on the nuclear family. This does not mean that the nuclear family is breaking up or, to use David Cooper's more dramatic word, 'dying'. Marriage remains fairly popular, and the majority of the population gets married. Moreover, the remarriage rates of divorcees are high, both in Britain and the United States, where three-quarters of divorced women and five-sixths of divorced men remarry. At current remarriage rates in Britain, nearly one in five people born around 1950 will have been married twice by the time they are 50. True, statistics show that young people are living together for more lengthy periods than previously, but most established couples do eventually get married. So stress on the family does not result in either the family or marriage being unpopular – they are not.

When people divorce, they are giving up a particular partner and not necessarily the idea of marriage. In any case, the majority of married people still do not get divorced but remain committed, more or less happily, to one partner for life. If present trends continue, however, a large minority will experience a different marital pattern from the traditional one. This pattern has been called serial monogamy. Less frequently, individuals have more than one family. These changes amount to a substantial adaptation of traditional marriage and the nuclear family, and cannot be described as a pattern of simple continuity. Nevertheless, serial monogamy does not seem an especially functional social adaptation. Rather, it represents what a large number of people seem to want, or at least accept, as sometimes necessary, regardless of considerable inconvenience. A United Kingdom survey in 1977 found that as many as 60 per cent of young people considered that divorce was something that might happen to them. So a recognition of the potential impermanence of marriage and even family commitment is now part of our cultural outlook.

Although the nuclear family survives and often flourishes still as the dominant family form, it is within the context of an increasingly pluralistic or varied pattern of family life. The single-parent family is the most common exception to the nuclear family.

Part of the variety and complexity of private and domestic life comes from the fact that the majority of households now contain only one or two people – some of whom have deliberately opted out of having a conventional family life. In the light of such developments, Jaber Gubrium and James Holstein in *What is Family?* (1990) answer the question in the title of their book by arguing that there is no longer a single answer. They suggest that a quasi-religious faith in the particular ideal of 'the family' can obscure the varied, complex and often difficult reality of creating families and relationships in which people are differently involved. Whatever one may think of it, it is the pluralist pattern of family life described earlier that is the trend in contemporary Britain (see pp. 56–61).

The above changes can give little obvious comfort to those who favour the extended family-type structures. The modern family is typically small, and second families especially so. No satisfactory general alternative to the nuclear family seems to exist. The nature of modern society works against extended family structures – attractive though these may be in principle. A less mobile, more localised society would no doubt produce a family system woven into kin and community but, for the moment, that is not the kind of society we have.

Questions

1 Which of its members benefit most and which least from the nuclear family?
2 Discuss the view that social change promoted an increase in single-parent families and therefore society should help to support them.

Family and household diversity

The theme of family and household diversity is a central one in this chapter, and direct consideration here will enable us to bring together and expand upon a number of points made in other contexts. In 1982, Rhona and Robert Rapoport stated that:

> *Families in Britain today are in a transition from coping in a society in which there was a single overriding norm of what family life should be like to a society in which a plurality of norms are recognised as legitimate and, indeed, desirable.*
>
> *(1982:476)*

The Rapoports' argument about the diversity of family life in Britain includes the development of 'alternative' family types to the nuclear family, such as the single-parent family discussed above, but adds a number of other important factors. They identify what they term five different types of diversity in contemporary families. These are:

- organisational
- cultural
- class
- life course
- cohort

We will discuss each of these types of diversity in turn, first making the Rapoports' views and adding further comment.

Organisational family and household diversity

Organisational diversity refers to different types of family structure (such as the reconstituted family and the single-parent family); the variety of households (including the increase in one and two person households); different types of kinship patterns; and the domestic division of labour (like Robert Chester, they remark on the development of 'dual-worker' families).

Most of the above points have been discussed elsewhere in this chapter, although they are, of course, equally relevant in this context. The references are: different types of family structure, pp. 56-61; different types of kinship patterns, pp. 61-3; and the domestic division of labour, pp. 56-7. A category which it would be useful to analyse further is one and two person households, which tend to be overlooked in the various debates about 'the family'.

Singles and couples: non-nuclear family households

As Table 3.1 shows, the majority of households contain only one or two residents. Yet this 'group' has attracted relatively little attention from sociologists. This is perhaps because it is not truly a group at all, but an aggregate made up of a variety of different categories of people. Nevertheless, these people are a large and increasing part of the mosaic of domestic and social life, and too much concentration on the nuclear family can obscure their lifestyles. If we focus on households rather than the nuclear family, then what we see is a diversity of lifestyles reflecting people at different points in their life course.

Who, then, are the single individuals who, in total, occupy more than a quarter of households? A small but growing minority are

I want to be alone...

The number of single-person households is set to rise from 6.8 million in 1995 to 8 million by the end of the century, according to a survey by Mintel. An increasing majority of Britain's singles are happy with their lot, it says, particularly valuing their freedom while a minority of 10 per cent still, find singledom lonely and expensive. The survey finds that single people under 55 have on average eight hours a week more leisure time than their counterparts in households of two or more, and more than 60 per cent usually eat in front of the television.

Alexander Garrett

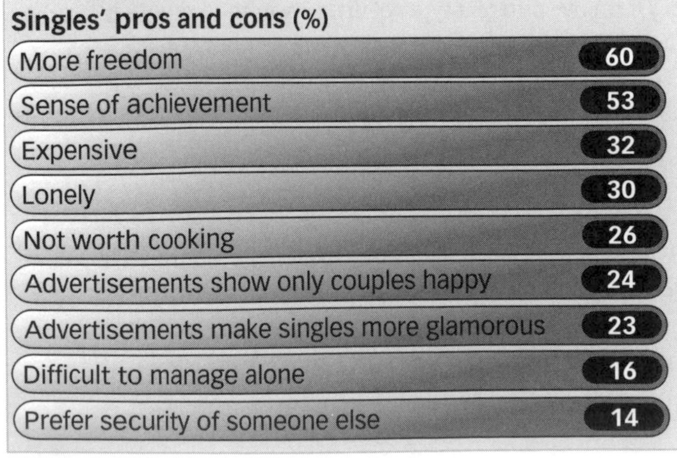

Singles' pros and cons (%)

More freedom	60
Sense of achievement	53
Expensive	32
Lonely	30
Not worth cooking	26
Advertisements show only couples happy	24
Advertisements make singles more glamorous	23
Difficult to manage alone	16
Prefer security of someone else	14

(Source: Mintel, *The Observer*, 24.3.1996:18)

Figure 3.7 Single-person households

better-off young adults, some of whom are part of the trend to marrying slightly later and who buy a house for convenience or as an investment. Another group – at any one time, hundreds of thousands, if not millions, in number – are separated or divorced individuals who temporarily or permanently are living on their own. Unlike the former, younger group, the social life of this group is relatively unstudied. Given the popularity of re-marriage, many in this situation are clearly highly concerned to find another partner. Where do they meet each other? Singles bars, over-30s nights, clubs and the personal sections of the classified 'ad' columns are all part of a communication network that has proliferated since the 1960s to meet this group's needs.

In some contrast to the previous two categories, are the several million middle-aged or elderly individuals who live alone, most of them as a result of losing their partner (see Figure 3.8). Figure 3.8 shows that women of pensionable age are the largest group living alone, but it is in younger age groups that the increase in living alone is occurring. Personal health and wealth are often the key to quality of life in their situation.

The rise in households of two people has been less spectacular than those of one, but at 35 per cent this is the largest category of all households. Their situation is fully considered in the following paragraphs.

What are the factors that have brought about this growth in small, non-family households? First, the rise of the individual and couple household has been accompanied by a reduction in the average number of children per family, which is now less than two. The majority of couples have only one or two children. Assuming these are born within a few years of each other, the couple may have an extended period of less committed time, either before the first child's birth or after the last child leaves home, or both. Simply, children take up a smaller proportion of their parents' lives than they used to when the average family size was bigger. However, working counter to this trend is the longer dependency on their parents of many teenagers and young adults. A second development reinforces the tendency to more uncommitted time. Average life expectancy has greatly increased during this century, creating what has been referred to as 'a third age' of relative freedom and choice, unhampered by dependent children. The creation of more 'free time' would be of dubious benefit, however, without a third development: the wealth to enjoy it. Wealth per capita in Britain has more than doubled since the Second World War, and with this a huge increase in leisure options has occurred. Single people, married couples without children, and the elderly have all become targeted as 'consumer' groups by advertisers and producers. Although 'the family market' is still the largest in terms of total people, the large minority groups mentioned above constitute lucrative niche leisure markets. Singles' holidays, commercial coach trips for senior citizens, and even one-cup tea-bags and six-packs of small bottles of wine all attest to the growing commercial attention paid to Britain's 'solos' and couples.

In fact, the trends towards consumerism and privatisation, often considered to characterise the nuclear family, seem no less

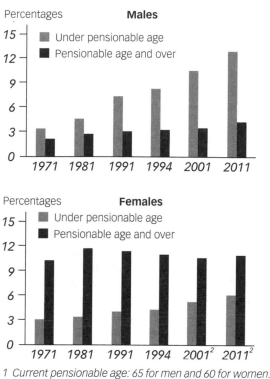

England and Wales

Figure 3.8 One-person households as a percentage of all households: by gender and whether under or over pensionable age[1]

1 Current pensionable age: 65 for men and 60 for women.
2 Projections.

(Source: Social Trends, 1996:50)

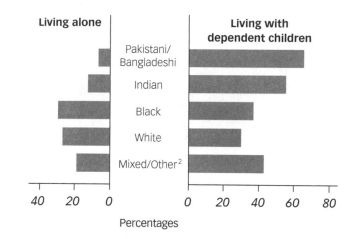

1 Percentage of heads of households in each ethnic group living in each household type.
2 Includes Chinese, other ethnic groups of non-mixed origin and people of mixed origin.

(Source: Social Trends, 1995:31)

Figure 3.9 Households: by ethnic group of head of household[1], spring 1994

true of the groups under discussion. Certainly, they generally have more uncommitted income to spend on leisure consumption than most married couples who have young children and high mortgages or rent bills. It is not possible to generalise about the extent of privatised living patterns across so broad a group. However, older and middle-aged people mostly have less incentive than children and teenagers to indulge in out-of-doors activity. Even young single adults who have done a hard day's work may more often prefer the comfort and amenity of their own home to going out. These are areas which merit further research.

The various organisational or structural charges referred to by the Rapoports are to a large extent complementary. Thus, the rise in one or two person households is partly a cause of the greater dispersal of kinship networks noted by Peter Wilmott. The most rapidly increasing group among those living alone is younger or middle-aged males – surely a reflection of wider changes in gender, marriage/divorce, and family patterns.

Cultural (ethnic)

Cultural differences can be caused by a variety of factors, including class, as well as ethnicity. However, Britain is a multi-ethnic society,

and this section provides an opportunity to discuss ethnic differences in relation to family life.

Figure 3.9 provides data on two types of households – heads of household living alone and heads of household living with dependent children. On the basis of these limited comparisons, Pakistani/Bangladeshi and Indian families are more dissimilar to white families than are black. However, it should be remembered that a higher proportion of Afro-Caribbean families than white are single-parent headed.

South-Asian families

The structure and culture of Asian families and communities have remained relatively stable since migration began in the 1950s, first from mainly Hindu India, and later from mainly Muslim Pakistan and Bangladesh. In the case of both these ethnic-religious communities, the family tends to be extended, traditional and patriarchal. Roger Ballard's study, published in 1982, comparing Asian families in Britain to families in South Asia and to white British families, found some adaptation but rather more continuity than change. Broadly, his findings remain valid today. Partly due to the expense and scarcity of large houses in Britain, Asian family households tend to be rather smaller in Britain than in South Asia, a trend strengthened by the apparent wish of more second and third generation British Asians to set up independent households (no doubt facilitated by improved economic circumstances).

Bhikhu Parekh has remarked that British society's attitude to Asian culture is often 'ambivalent'.

> *While it may admire the strength of the Asian family, it generally disapproves of Asian marriage customs, the caste system, the practice of untouchability, some religious rituals, food habits, attitudes to women, the apparent polytheism of the Hindus, and so on.*
>
> *(1982:20)*

There is little doubt that this attitude of ambivalence is routinely reciprocated. Asians were initially disgusted by the indigenous attitudes to the elderly, sexual explicitness, and teenage 'licence'.

Writing in 1992, Avtar Brah finds the basic solidarity of Asian family-life still to be strong. Interestingly, however, from her sample of white and Asian girls, it is the latter who tend to be more questioning of traditional gender roles within the home:

> *The strongest opposition to the sexual division of labour in the home came from Asian girls, with half of the sample rejecting the notion of nominal help from men and insisting that housework should be shared on an equal basis. Clearly both Asian and white women's views embody elements of collusion, resistance and opposition (to sexism -author's bracket).*
>
> *(1992:72)*

However, Brah goes on to stress the mutual confidence and respect between Asian adolescents and their parents:

> *The great majority of the Asian adolescents expected their marriages to be arranged – a prospect they accepted because, unlike the media portrayal of bullying Asian parents ramming arranged marriages down the throats of their children, many adolescents felt confident that they would not be forced into a marriage that they did not want.*
>
> *(72)*

The effectiveness of family support in the Asian community is further suggested by the educational and career achievements of, especially Indian, and to a lesser extent Pakistani young males and females. The impression of continuing inter-generational solidarity was confirmed in 1995, when virtually the whole British Pakistani community in Bradford seemed united in its opposition to the use of a local street for prostitution. What this episode showed was that there is, indeed, a traditional community, rooted in family and religion, in modern, secular Britain.

Afro-Caribbean families

The Afro-Caribbean family has been considered already in this chapter (see pp. 59-60) and will be further considered in the context of education in the next (see pp. 116-7). Here, it is relevant to point out that, as in the case of South Asians, Afro-Caribbean families in Britain reflect the societies from which they migrated.

Jocelyn Barrow suggests that there are three types of West Indian families in the Caribbean: the conventional nuclear family (often strongly Christian, respectable, and economically self-sufficient), the common-law family; and the mother household or single-parent family (1982). These family types are certainly observable in the Afro-Caribbean community in Britain. Given the tendency to stereotype the British Afro-Caribbean family as single-parent it is worth remembering that about half Afro-Caribbean families are two-parent.

Jean Breeze makes perhaps the key point about the Afro-Caribbean family – that it tends to be mother-centred or matrifocal. Afro-Caribbean females, with or without long-term partners, are more likely than white females to combine domestic work with paid work. Afro-Caribbean females often network for childcare purposes although this can be more difficult in Britain if there are few female relatives. This matrifocal pattern does not mean that the Afro-Caribbean community is not also patriarchal. The term matrifocal describes a pattern of work and sociability. Males can be the beneficiaries of female work in the Afro-Caribbean as in other communities. As far as the distribution of power between the two sexes is concerned, matters are complex and the issue will be considered elsewhere (see pp. 207-9).

Class

Working class families and communities

In this section we explore differences and similarities between working and middle class cultural and community life or 'social networks', to use Margaret Stacey's term. Although this section is following the Rapoport's theme of the diversity of family life, it will also be argued that there is convergence between lower middle and upper working class family life. However, at the very top and broad bottom of society, inequalities and lifestyle differences increased during the Thatcher-Major years.

Richard Hoggart's painstakingly detailed description of traditional working class life in 1950s Leeds is fully presented in Chapter 18 (see pp. 481-4). The fact that traditional working class community has largely broken up does not mean it never existed. Some recent commentators, failing to find thriving working class communities of the kind described 40 years ago by Young and Willmott and by Hoggart seem almost to assume that the whole phenomenon is a romantic fiction.

Coates and Silburn's late 1960s study of the lower class St Anne's district of Nottingham falls a little into this trap. The fact that they find St Anne's to be a fragmented community does not mean it was always so. As they, in fact, well illustrate, the decline of community was due partly to urban renewal policies – a factor also emphasised by Young and Willmott in their Bethnal Green study well over a decade previously.

Apart from those working class people who have chosen to leave inner city areas, many had to leave because of compulsory clearance orders and were offered public housing elsewhere. This was part of a national plan (which had considerable local variations) to divert industry and population away from the inner cities, which could then be used as the location for office blocks, major shops and stores, and as the centre of the leisure and entertainment industry. Public housing makes up about a quarter of residential property, and generalisations need to be made carefully. However, a consensus has emerged, which includes even their original designer, that high-rise flats have been a failure as a major means of providing cheap mass-accommodation. Incidents such as the collapse of the Ronan Point block, and the suicide jump of a depressed Birmingham mother, with her baby, from her high-storey flat have created the worst publicity, but myriad problems of design and functioning, such as block entrances leading out into garbage zones or lifts perpetually breaking down, have provided a daily diet of irritation and frustration for thousands. Nevertheless, it is, of course, a major contribution that the material conditions of living provided by many of these developments are vastly superior to that of the old-fashioned terraced houses they have often replaced. But this improvement can be achieved equally in smaller, low rise developments or still other kinds of accommodation at less cost to communal life. As potential communities, high-rise flats have limited possibilities. Living off the ground is not conducive to shared activity and most corridors in high-rise flats do not provide an environment that encourages friendly conversations with neighbours. Even Frank Lloyd Wright's imaginative idea of high-rise developments as 'vertical streets in the sky' with various shops, facilities and meeting places strategically scattered on all levels to facilitate interaction and communication seems expensive and artificial, though clearly the concept is better than the human filing cabinets that some blocks have become.

Working class housing estates make up most of the rest of public housing. These are often located on the outskirts of urban areas and replace traditional, more centrally situated housing. Living conditions on post-war, mainly working class housing estates vary from almost as bad as in the worst of the high-rise flats to very good indeed. John Stedman's estate at Corby and the prize-winning Handley Green development at Laindon, near Basildon, are spacious, well-designed and attractive. But in general, people have to travel to work from public housing estates and shopping, too, can require a journey. The separation of these basic functions is not conducive to an integrated community life in the old style. A seldom remarked-on-effect of the decrease in the fertility of working class mothers is that fewer children exist to establish inter-family social links and this must further reduce the numbers of friends within the neighbourhood. Community centres, which are a feature of some recently established estates, often fail to draw people together for leisure activities though teenagers do frequently use them. Even so, the streets and open areas of estates are often preferred by adolescents – especially by 'tougher' boys. Perhaps it is through their activity and that of younger children who still like to 'play out' that we see a glimpse of at least one continuous strand in the pattern of working class neighbourhood life.

As a result of the 'right to buy' policy of Margaret Thatcher, over 1.5 million council houses had been sold to former tenants by 1992. This policy has created or at least sharpened differences within the working class. Patrick Dunleavy goes so far as to argue that the differences between house-owners and non-house-owners can be as significant as those between people having 'middle' and 'working' class jobs. In particular, there is a correlation between house-ownership and voting Conservative. Critics of this view have pointed out that occupational status itself correlates with house-ownership and with characteristics associated with it (Marshall, 1988).

An important effect of the right to buy policy has been drastically to reduce the stock of public housing held by local councils. Partly because of cuts in support grants by central government, Councils are unable to build sufficient replacements to meet need. As a result, the number of families in temporary accommodation (e.g. bed and breakfast, cheap hotels) and the problem of homelessness visibly increased during the late 1980s and around the turn of the decade. Whether the longer term homeless are now so detached or cut-off from the more 'solid' working class as better to be considered part of an 'underclass' is debatable. The matter is discussed in Chapter 13 (see pp. 388-93).

Middle class families and communities

Despite the complexity of the overall picture, most middle class owner occupiers still tend to live in suburban neighbourhoods. The term suburban neighbourhood can cover a wide spectrum from, for instance, areas of inter-war semi-detached property, with upper working as well as lower middle class residents, to areas of high status, often detached property occupied mainly by professional, managerial and business groups. Generalisations therefore need to be cautious.

In dormitory suburbs, the very fact that people live and work in separate places is not conducive to the development of integrated community life. As Elizabeth Bott shows, middle class friendship networks tend to be more extended than those in traditional working class communities (1957). For instance, the middle class are more ready to join clubs and associations requiring commitment to activity beyond the immediate neighbourhood. Middle class parents are more likely to participate in organisations and activities concerning their children's educational welfare such as Parent-Teachers Associations or school open days.

The privatisation of middle class family life is highly compatible with extended friendship networks and relative lack of involvements in the immediate neighbourhood. Social life is more organised and friends are not expected to 'pop in and out' as they might do in a traditional working class neighbourhood. A telephone call can courteously pave the way for a visit, but it can as easily be instead, if one of the parties is occupied. Privacy and control of time can be virtually a necessity if work brought home from the office and children's homework is to be properly done.

Mutual concern with children is what brings middle class people most readily together. In their book about the Canadian suburb of Crestwood Heights, Seeley and his co-authors argue that the major institutional focus of the community is on child-rearing.

Interfamily social life is organised, mainly by mothers, around this central concern from the time when turns are taken to give children's tea parties, to when offspring depart for higher education. At this point the female parent often returns to paid work.

Family convergence

Despite the above contrasts, family and community life is more similar across the middle and working classes than, say, 50 years ago. Then, the majority of the working class was forced to live in rented accommodation. Now, the majority live in public housing or own their own houses. Indeed, over 65 per cent of families in Britain now own their own homes. This fact, in combination with the movement out of the urban areas means that the suburban ideal cuts across class lines to a considerable extent. A house of their own is what most families seem to want and many have already achieved it. Add to this the even more general processes of family privatisation, consumerism and, much more controversially, symmetrical gender role-playing already noted and a very real convergence in family lifestyle between, particularly, the lower middle and upper working class is apparent. The stable working class community networked by matrifocal extended families is an increasing rarity. Economic change and geographical and social mobility has reduced communal solidarity. Yet, as we shall see throughout the book, class and status differences still divide these groups and even more, those groups at the social extremes. In particular although the family roles played mainly by females have adapted to the family changes described above (and below), gender inequality within the family and in paid work appears largely to continue.

Life course

The life courses of families (and, therefore, the individuals within them) can vary greatly. This can reflect choice or circumstances. For instance, some families may have several children and experience a rearing period stretched over many years whereas for others, this stage may be half as long or less. Biology also plays a part in family diversity reflecting life course difference. Thus, while it is common for 30 year olds to have dependent children, it is much less common for 70 year olds to have them.

The life course cannot be considered alone, apart from the interplay of choice and social circumstances. Class, ethnic and other structural factors as well as government policy shape individual and family experience.

Cohort

A cohort of individuals refers to those born in the same year (or chosen band of years – say, within five years of each other). Families with children belonging to roughly the same cohorts share a common experience of historical events. These can range from unemployment, war, student revolution or whatever. Again, however, it is obvious that other factors such as class and ethnicity will mediate how each family responds.

Conclusion

The section above on family and household diversity is partly descriptive in nature. The causes of such a diverse picture are themselves likely to be diverse. Many of the causes have, in fact, been discussed in earlier sections of this chapter. Changing family structure and roles and stresses on the family all contribute to changing family and individual lifestyles. Here I will briefly present some of the main causes of family and household diversity, the substance of which can be gleaned from elsewhere in this book:

Causes of family/household diversity

1 The material condition of industrial-capitalist society

Greater affluence, greater geographical and occupational mobility and, more recently, the greater economic independence of (some) women make choice and diversity more possible. Increased longevity itself has had a major impact on patterns of residence and family life. In the Thatcher-Major period, increasing social inequality produced lifestyles, including patterns of residence of utter contrast – sometimes within a few dozen yards of each other.

2 The individualistic and liberal values of capitalist society

As Edward Shorter points out, the romantic and individualistic values of capitalist society encourage people to believe that they should be able to choose and, if they want, change their partners. As Anthony Giddens observes for many in the West, 'commitment' is 'for now', not necessarily 'for ever'. Relationships depend on feelings, not externally imposed moral frameworks (The Transformation of Intimacy, 1992). In the West, at least, religion has done little to stem this trend though it may sometimes have slowed it. Even Catholic Eire voted narrowly to legalise divorce in 1995.

3 Immigration

The cultural life of Britain has been greatly added to by the immigration of the 1950s and 1960s. Asian families often established extended families in a single house (or joined two adjacent houses together). Extended kinship patterns were also the norm among West Indian immigrants although many young women with children actually live without a partner.

It is perhaps not too fanciful to suggest that the above pattern of family and household diversity has something of a postmodern character about it. Indigenous Westerners seem to be operating not immorally but on the basis of their own judgements and choice rather than on somebody else's morality. If things don't work out, they try again – which tends to lead to new beginnings in new households. A great many, through choice or accident, live alone although this does not mean they are lonely. It may be that the logic of liberal capitalism drives ever further towards the fragmentation of individual lifestyles. Set against this, are the still traditional family patterns of immigrant groups drawn into an alien cultural setting through the workings of the capitalist labour market. Such contrasts are considered typical of the 'postmodern world'.

Whether, in particular, Asian family structures and norms will survive the lure of liberal capitalism is an intriguing question. Of course, it is possible, even likely, that the young will forge their own cultural variations drawing from both Western and Eastern traditions rather than make polarised either/or choices.

The family policy debate

The family is always likely to be a focus of concern in modern societies. There are two related reasons for this. First, the modern state, supported by public opinion, has come to regard the welfare, health and education of the nation's children as its ultimate responsibility. Second, the future of the nation depends on the physical, intellectual and moral quality of its children.

Policy is about public action in relation to particular matters. As far as the family is concerned, there is a large body of legislation regulating family life and this is constantly being changed and added to. Thus, the law regulating divorce has been changed many times since the Second World War, sometimes, quite radically. Disagreements about what *should* be done in relation to the family are considerable. Policy is the battle-ground of different ideologies and interest groups which have varying degrees of influence and power. Although Conservative governments were 'in power' between 1979 and 1997, it is highly arguable that family life did not develop according to their stated values. In a liberal society, personal and family relationships are not easy to influence, still less, control.

It is not surprising that a lively policy debate focusing on the family, developed during the late 1980s and 1990s. The main changes affecting family life in the post-war period, and particularly since the mid 1960s, have already been described. By the early 1990s one in three new births occurred out of wedlock, one in five families with dependent children were headed by a single parent, and the popularity of marriage had begun to plummet as that of cohabitation increased. Not surprisingly, it was widely perceived that a radical change had occurred in one of society's key institutions. While interpretations vary about what has 'gone wrong', 'the family' is perceived by many to be 'in trouble'.

The perspectives considered below are political and policy-oriented, rather than sociological although some are informed by sociological concepts and analysis. These perspectives are:

1 Conservative
2 Ethical Socialist
3 Pluralist

Conservative

To oversimplify somewhat, since the mid 1970s, there have been two main tendencies within the Conservative party: the traditionalist and the New Right. The traditionalists tend to support established institutions, authority and morality. The New Right believes that the fundamental force behind a free and efficient society is the operation of the free market and that the role of government should be limited and specific. The New Right or free marketeers believe that individuals should, where possible, succeed by dint of their own efforts. Often, Conservatives are

influenced by both these ideological perspectives although there is some tension between them.

From the late 1980s, the Conservatives increasingly highlighted the issue of single parenthood and so-called welfare 'dependency'. They are greatly influenced by the American social commentator, Charles Murray, whose arguments were later reflected in the speeches of Peter Lilley who became Secretary of State for Social Security in 1992. Murray's thinking combined New Right economics with a traditional moral tone. Both the American and British New Right made the cost of the welfare state a major public issue. Murray argued that the provision of 'generous' welfare made it economically rational for many females to become pregnant because this enabled them to acquire a higher living standard than otherwise. He suggested that a severe curtailment of their welfare rights would cause them to act differently and would save the tax-payer money. Murray made a big impact when he visited England in 1989 and forecast the development of an American style 'underclass' in Britain with single-parent females and dislocated young males at its core.

According to Hartley Dean and Peter Taylor-Goobey, Murray shifted from economic argument to more explicit moral censure in his later, post-1990, work:

> *Blame, Murray emphasises, is important …*
>
> *In every discourse, the consistent mark of the underclass stems, therefore, not from its objective relations with the state, the market or the social environment but from the acknowledgement of its culpability.*
>
> *(1992:43)*

Despite some initial moral posturing, Peter Lilley tended to revert to an emphasis on the cost of welfare when expressing concern at the explosion of single parenthood. Table 3.6 shows that in 1992, about one in two children in poverty were from lone parent families.

Table 3.6 Children in poverty

Estimated numbers of children in families dependent on Income Support or in families whose resources are below the level of Income Support although they do not meet the criteria to receive it. (Great Britain, 1992).

	Thousands by type of family
Unemployed couples:	1,075
Couples in full-time work:	410
Other couples:	365
Lone parent families:	1,840

(Source: *The Guardian*, 22.3.1995:5)

Some 1.8 million children of lone parents were, therefore in poverty, and in the great majority of cases the parent was dependent on income support.

The main measure taken by the Conservatives to lessen the cost of lone parents to the state and tax payer was the setting up of the Child Support Agency. The aim behind the Agency is to require the absent parent – in 90 per cent of cases, the male – to contribute to the upkeep of his children according to his means. So far, the Agency has saved only a tiny fraction of the amount of welfare benefit paid to single parents and much less than its own modest targets. In addition, both sets of parents – those with and without custody of children – have frequently expressed dissatisfaction with the financial assessments and operation of the Agency.

New Right thinker and politician, John Redwood addressed one aspect of the family shortly after his unsuccessful campaign for the Conservative leadership in 1995. He suggested that very young (e.g. fourteen to sixteen year olds) unmarried teenage mothers might be best-advised to put the children out for adoption rather than embark on a life of state dependency. However, the number of single-parent families to this age group is very small. After rising steadily for a decade, pregnancies to those under sixteen actually fell between 1990 and 1991 from 8,634 to 7,819. Whatever the merits or otherwise of Mr Redwood's suggestion, it bore no relevance to the larger issue of single parenthood which some Conservatives had earlier targeted.

Ethical socialist

The same trends in family life which concerned the Conservative New Right has also troubled many traditionally minded socialists and reformist liberals. In particular, a group termed ethical socialists have been vocal on this issue. Although this group use research data to back-up its support for the traditional family, it makes no secret of its moral position. Thus, A H Halsey states in the introduction to Norman Dennis and George Erdos's *Families without Fatherhood* (1992):

> *Whatever the character of society or state, policy or economy, religion or culture, parents cannot escape responsibility for the quality of their children as citizens.*
>
> *In the light of this political morality I see incontrovertible evidence of a weakening of the norms of the traditional family since the 1960s. It is not that I see a golden age of traditionalism. Nevertheless the traditional family system was a coherent strategy for the ordering of relations in such a way as to equip children for their own adult responsibilities.*
>
> *(xii)*

Halsey goes on to argue that the children of parents who do not follow the traditional norm 'are disadvantaged in many major aspects of their chances of living a successful life' (xiii). Among the evidence that Dennis and Erdos review which supports Halsey's claim is a study of Israel Kolvin and his colleagues at Newcastle

University. In 1979-80, they studied a random sample of 264 people born in May and June of 1947 and then aged 32-33. The researchers already had much of detailed information about the sample. Kolvin considered the relationship between fatherhood and a wide range of experiences members of the sample had in childhood and adulthood. Kolvin found correlations between the quality of home background, including fathering, and an astonishing range of factors from 'being physically smaller, stammering, being poor scorers in intelligence tests, or having a criminal record …' (58)

As socialists, Halsey and Dennis and Erdos believe that the state should substantially support families and are scathing of the Thatcher government's record in this respect. Nevertheless, they state a clear preference for the traditional child-centred working class family of the immediate post-war period to the ego-centre individualism which they see as emerging strongly in the 1960s and being reinforced by the ascendancy of the New Right under Margaret Thatcher (Reading 3).

Policies for family pluralism: universal childcare

Conservative and ethical socialist policies agree in wanting to strengthen the traditional nuclear family and in wanting to slow down its fragmentation – although their solutions vary considerably. However, there is a large body of opinion which considers that the relative decline of the traditional nuclear family is unlikely significantly to reverse and that society had better properly plan for the pluralistic family situation that has already developed. Foremost among this broad group are a wide range of feminists. In addition, many progressive politicians across the political spectrum would give some support to the kind of policies indicated below.

Feminist pluralists tend to point to two major recent developments in family life requiring government response. First, is the fact that one in five families in Britain is now headed by a single parent. Second, is the increasing participation of females in paid work. This trend includes mothers (Figure 3.10) but, interestingly, not single-parent mothers. A likely reason for the

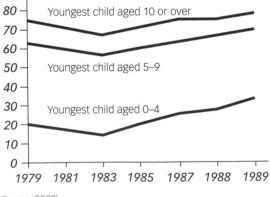

Percentage of women aged 16–59 years

(Source: OPCS)

Figure 3.10 Mothers in paid work in Britain

exclusion of single-parent mothers from this trend is the scarcity and expense of childcare in Britain. Their need is probably even greater than that of mothers in paid work generally, and the lack of childcare probably explains their decreasing participation in paid work compared to their better provided for European counterparts (see Figure 3.11).

Of women with a child under five, 41 per cent were in employment in 1989, twelve per cent of these full-time, compared to 28 per cent in 1979. Overall, the percentage of women with dependent children in employment rose from 52 per cent in 1979 to 59 per cent in 1989 (having fallen to 46 per cent in 1983 as a result of a recession). Twenty per cent of all women with dependent children are in full-time paid employment.

Juliet Mitchell (1986) and other feminists have warned of the tendency for females to be used as part of a reserve army of labour under capitalism – easily hired and fired. Just as in the nineteenth century women's labour was first required and then dispensed with in the factories and mines, there is an increasing demand for female labour in the service sector in the late twentieth century. However, as we have seen this has not been accompanied by any significant decrease in the proportion of domestic work done by women compared to men. In terms of a more equal sharing of domestic work, the 'symmetrical family' has largely not happened. Although there are obvious material advantages in both partners earning an income, the double load of work on the female partner can have adverse effects both for her and her children.

Trends in the British labour market, particularly towards more 'flexible' working hours lend support to Mitchell's concerns. In 1994 the Daycare Trust published a report, *Not Just Nine to Five* which argued that the increase in shift working had not been complemented by improved availability of childcare. The report was based on a survey of 442 shift workers with children under twelve. The report describes the great inconvenience experienced by many of the shift workers and the complexity of the arrangements many had to make in order to cope. 50 per cent had to use at least two forms of childcare as well as the help of a partner or relative. Some used up to seven or eight additional types of care!

Much of the extension in shift work has come in the low paid service sector in which female workers tend to be concentrated. Longer opening hours for shops are the main example but overall thirteen per cent of workers are on shift and about nine per cent more on 'atypical' hours.

Availability of childcare in Britain: a review

How well is Britain geared for the employment of women in terms of the needs of the women and children involved? Writing in *New Society* (5.2.88), Judy Dunn gives the startling statistic that between 1958 and 1984, the proportion of pre-school children cared for in day nurseries fell from seventeen per cent to three per cent. *Caring for children: the 1990 Report* states that public childcare for five to nine year-olds is available for 0.2 per cent in term time and 0.3 per cent during holidays (Family Policy Study Centre). However, during the second half of the 1980s there was an increase in the

(a) Births outside marriage

Live births outside marriage as a percentage of all births, 1988

(b) Care for the under-fives

Local authority provided and registered day-care places, per 100 under-fives, March 1988

(Source: *Regional Trends*, HMSO)

Figure 3.11 Births outside marriage and care for the under-fives

numbers of childminders although some would not consider this as an equally effective form of care. *Regional Trends, 1990*, gives figures for registered childminders, playgroups and local authority nurseries in the form of the percentage of places available to the total of under-fives in given regions. in England this varies from 14.7 in the north to 24.6 in the south west. By 1990, private and voluntary childcare provided more places than local authorities. In many areas, available places substantially fall short of meeting need. This must be made up by unregistered help including relatives and friends, or sometimes not made up at all.

The almost universally recognised inadequacy of childcare provision in Britain must greatly inconvenience many mothers and negatively affect their children – to put it mildly. For many – whether married or single parents – their only option is to manage as best they can. They 'juggle' their child or children with other domestic and employment commitments with energy and ingenuity – but at some risk to their health.

A group that is particularly hard hit by the cost and/or

inadequacy of childcare facilities is separated, divorced or single women with children. Many women on benefit would rather be in employment but the cost for child care plus employment related expenses often means that they are scarcely any better, or even slight worse off. This is largely because single parents can earn only fifteen pounds per week before a pound is deducted from benefit for each pound earned (1991). A clearer case of a poverty trap would be difficult to imagine. In 1990, two single parents took the British government to law on this issue on the grounds that it broke the European Community directives aimed at equalising access between the sexes to social security benefits and training facilities. The Court of Appeal referred the case to the European Court.

Given the increasing demand for female paid-labour, and the importance of producing well cared for and stimulated children, one is forced to wonder why a situation of inadequate childcare provision is allowed to persist. A possible reason may be ambivalence on the part of some politicians and members of the public about putting children under five in childcare at all. Margaret Thatcher herself seemed to see seeking informal help as the main solution to childcare in remarks made when answering a question about how she managed to combine a career with a family:

> *Yet no matter how hard you work or how capable you are, you can't do it all yourself. You have to seek reliable help – a relative, or what my mother would have called 'a treasure' someone who brought not only her work but her affections to the family.*

Margaret Thatcher then went on to mention the role of voluntary agencies in helping with childcare and mentioned forthcoming government legislation aimed at fathers who failed to pay maintenance. It has also been Conservative government policy to encourage the private provision of childcare facilities and the cost of childcare to parents was made exempt from tax in 1990. However, cuts in central government funding to local government has meant that public sector provision of childcare provision has often been cut itself. Some critics have suggested that the desire to cut public spending largely accounts for Conservative policy to childcare. In 1995 a pre-school voucher scheme, to be piloted in 1996 was announced. However, the £1,100 value of the voucher only covers a small part of the annual care of one child. So far it is unclear how poorer parents will make up the deficit.

There is now a considerable body of academic opinion which should allay any fears that under fives are disadvantaged in day-nurseries and 'would be better with their mothers'. Professor Bengt-Erick Andersson, head of developmental psychology at the Stockholm Institute of Education, went to far as to say that it 'seems the earlier children mix with others, the better'. He said that those who entered day care before the age of one performed better than other groups monitored at the age of thirteen – both academically and in terms of 'socio-emotional variables'. He

suggested that a major reason for this was the amount of interaction they experienced with adults and peers. However, he added the proviso that:

> *The research was done in Sweden and … it is a country with a very high-quality day care. If that situation differs, the findings might not be applicable.*

Harriet Harman of the Labour party has argued that there should be greater choice of childcare provision, more government resources for maintaining standards, and more community provision of childcare – especially for the less well-off. This seems to accept that while the sources of funding for childcare may vary, ultimately central government in partnership with local government should ensure the right of childcare to all children. Currently, the country is a long way from achieving this.

In their book *For the Children's Sake*, Caroline New and Miriam David suggest that of the three main demands of the women's movement – control of their own fertility, equal pay for equal work and universal provision of childcare – it is the last one that remains conspicuously unachieved. The result is great difficulties for many women and disadvantage for many children. If it is true that educational standards in Britain lag behind those of most other advanced countries, perhaps the explanation for this begins with inadequate childcare.

Conclusion: the family policy debate

Underlying the above policy debate on the family is a paradox, almost a scarcely recognised hypocrisy. On the one hand, the majority of the public appear to want much greater freedom in sexual, marital and other relationships than was available to most in the past. Certainly the law has made divorce much easier and pre-marital sexual experience and co-habitation before or even instead of marriage are common. On the other hand, there is a reluctance to face the need to deal with the consequences of such increased freedom and ability to withdraw from commitments. The main consequence is that large numbers of children do not reliably have the material and emotional support of two adults. What is the morally 'right' solution to this problem could be endlessly debated. What is undoubted the case is the need for an effective solution whether this lies in the direction of much greater publicly-financed collective care for children or greater in-put from parents whether separated or not – or both.

Questions

1 Why has there been a major increase in the numbers of one and two person households?
2 Compare and contrast South Asian and Afro-Caribbean households.

Summary

1 A household is a person or group of people living together. In the post-Second World War period, there has been an increase in the numbers of households with only one or two inhabitants. Nevertheless, a large majority of people experience a nuclear family at some stage in their lives. A nuclear family is comprised of mother, father and child or children, whether natural or adopted. The extended family consists of the nuclear family and at least one relative living in the same household.

2 There are various Perspectives on the Family. Functionalist perspective analyses the functions of the family in relation to society and the adaptation of the family to historical change. Marxist perspective analyses how the family helps to reproduce capitalist society by maintaining the current labour force and reproducing and socialising the next.

 Feminist perspective stresses the subordination and oppression of women within the family and society. Pluralists – feminist perspective recognises that while some groups (e.g. upper class males) have more power than others, many groups, including feminist organisations, can have a significant effect on state policy.

3 Non-Nuclear Families:

 Functionalists argue that the nuclear family is universal. However, there are several categories of evidence against this position. These are:

 • Comparative Cultural Evidence of Non-Nuclear Families e.g. The Nayar Case.
 • Deliberate Attempts to Produce Collectively-based Families e.g. The Kibbutzim; The Soviet 'Experiment'; 1960s Communes.
 • Single-Parent Families.
 • Lesbian and Homosexual Led Families.

 Whether or not the above cases are considered as 'true' families, it is clear that in those cases in which a child's biological father is not involved in its upbringing, some other form of regular and routine assistance is usually available for the mother.

4 Historically, it helps to think of the development of the family in three phases.

 ■ The Pre-Industrial Family:

 It is a 'myth' that the pre-industrial family was mainly extended. Laslett's research shows that it was mainly nuclear but it was often much bigger than the average contemporary family.

 ■ The Early Industrial Family:

 The movement of population to towns often temporarily 'broke up' families but, once settled, working class families, in particular, were often extended in type.

 ■ The 'Modern' Family:

 Functionalists and Marxists agree that the family performs a range of functions within capitalist society but whereas the former see these as 'necessary' the latter consider that they are often oppressive particularly in relation to working class families and to women. Another important debate centres on how 'symmetrical' male and female family roles have or have not become.

5 A key debate on the family is whether privatised patterns of family living have replaced previously more communal ones. As early as the 1950s, Bott's work indicated that segregated (distinct) conjugal roles and more community-oriented living characterised working class life and that joint (more equal and shared) conjugal roles and wider spread friendship networks characterised middle class life. Much research and discussion has occurred about the extent to which working class families, indeed, most families are privatised and consumer oriented and much less involved in local community life.

6 There are a number of signs that marriage and the family can experience great stress in contemporary society. The most obvious is the high divorce rate. Edward Shorter suggests that one reason for the break-up of modern marriage is the high expectation that accompanies the romanticism which often surrounds it.

7 A range of other issues surround marriage and the family. Some such as the rise in single parent families and in co-habiting are open to differing sociological (and moral) interpretation. Others such as child-abuse and wife-battering – although requiring careful analysis and understanding – belong to everybody's category of human misery.

8 Is the Family Breaking up or Adapting?

 Although the summary has used the term 'the family' for convenient' shorthand', the chapter itself suggests that there are a plurality of households and families. An alternative to the view that 'the family' is breaking up is that people are adapting quite variously to small-scale living.

9 Family and Household Diversity:

 Increased family diversity is apparent in organisational, cultural, class, life course and cohort terms.

10 The Family Policy Debate:

 Fierce debate focuses on the role of 'the Family' and the support which families require. Conservative, ethical socialist and pluralist feminists views are discussed here.

Research and coursework

There are many possible research areas on households, families and marriage, including family roles, functions, change, and stresses on the family. It could be interesting, however, to probe one of the less well-researched areas. Why, for instance, are there more single person households than previously? Are there big differences among single person householders? Some will be elderly and have lost a partner, some will be younger and may have divorced a partner or never had one. Given the limits on your research of time and resources, you may only be able to research into one group. Research into younger divorcees living alone might produce interesting findings. Do they live alone out of necessity or choice? Do they prefer living alone to marriage? Do they intend to marry again? Are there differences between the females and males in your sample (both economically and in terms of how they manage their social lives)?

Locating a sample (perhaps a quota) of younger divorcees may not be easy. However, it is worth noting that large samples are often not practical or required. Five males and five females could be enough if the research is of a more qualitative kind – perhaps involving a semi-structured or unstructured interview with each respondent.

Further reading

Current literature on households and families tends to have moved beyond rehearsing well-worn arguments about 'the functions of the family'. David H H Morgan's article *Socialisation and the Family: Change and Diversity* in M Woodhead and J McGrath eds., (Open University, 1988) is a useful overview of established and more recent research on the family. Diana Gittins' *The Family in Question: Changing Households and Familiar Ideologies* (MacMillan, 1985) brings a lively awareness of current issues to a staple topic. Adrian Wilson's *Family* (Routledge, 1991) remains a useful introduction to the topic.

Readings

Reading 1
The state and feminist goals

From F R Elliot, *Private Arena or Adjunct to the State in Social and Cultural Forms of Modernity* (Polity, 1992), pp.108-9

There are now a range of feminist commentators on state and family who appear to be neither Marxist-feminist nor radical-feminist and whose accounts of the state-family relation tend to be eclectic and descriptive rather than theoretical. However, considered as a whole, such accounts seem to suggest that the critical characteristic of the state is its diversity and multi-dimensionality. Diversity has been attributed to almost every aspect and level of the state. First, state institutions have been seen as having their own histories and logics, as complex, poorly articulated, and, in some measure, independent of each other. Second, it has been suggested that divergent interests – patriarchal and feminist, capitalistic and proletarian, racial and religious, local, national, and international – seek and hold state power and in varying degrees orchestrate state policies. There is recognition also of divergences in women's interests.

(Author's note: Elliot then goes on to further illustrate the 'diversity and multi-dimensionality' of the state in relation to women – showing that the state sometimes promotes and sometimes impedes the interests of women, or given groups of women. Thus, pre-1894, the state improved the property rights of women but denied them political rights.)

In this emergent 'pluralist-feminism', gender divisions remain a central feature of the social order and the primary object of study, and inequality, exploitation, conflict and contradictions are pervasive concepts. However, diverse and competing interest groups with the power to shape state action are recognised, and multiple contradictions are presumed. It is thus implied that no one group is able to orchestrate a unified set of policies through which it systematically oppresses other groups and, conversely, that no one grouping is subject to a unified system of control. At the same time, this 'pluralist-feminism' differs from 'classical pluralism' in that it does not see interest groups as equal in political strength and it does not see the state as neutral arbiter between interest groups. It recognises inequality and is concerned to show which interest groups make demands of the state and how they are differentially rewarded. …

Questions

1 In what ways does a pluralist-feminist account of state-family relations differ from a Marxist-feminist account?
2 What successes might pluralist-feminists claim that women have achieved through the state? (see also Chapter 7, pp. 205-6)

Reading 2
Why does domestic violence against women occur?

From Jan Pahl ed., *Private Violence and Public Policy* (Routledge and Kegan Paul, 1985), pp.4-6

Broadly speaking, there are two approaches to causal analysis of this problem. The first approach locates the problem within the individuals concerned and seeks to explain the violence in terms of deviant or pathological personalities. The work of Faulk, for example, which was concerned with men who had been convicted of wife-abuse, showed that a majority of them could be classified as being mentally ill in one way or another (Faulk, 1974). However, other studies have not so far confirmed this finding, which was, of course, carried out with an unusual group in that all the men had actually been convicted of assault. Several researchers have found a link between violence and excessive consumption of alcohol. In my own study, 52 per cent of the women said that their husbands often drank to excess, and this is similar to the proportions recorded by Gelles (1974) and Gayford (1975). However, it has been suggested that drunkenness should be seen not as a 'cause' of violence but as a condition which co-exists with it. Thus men who wish to carry out a violent act may become intoxicated in order to have the courage to perform the act. After violence has occurred both the man and his wife may excuse his behaviour on the grounds that since he had been drunk he could not be held responsible for what had happened.

Violent personalities are also seen as being a consequence of childhood experiences. The study carried out by Straus, Gelles and Steinmetz showed that people who grew up in violent homes were more likely to use violence than those who had not. Thus one in ten of husbands who grew up in violent families were wife beaters in the sense of serious assault, and this is over three times the rate for husbands who did not grow up in such homes. However, the researchers point out that it would be a mistake to put too great a burden on what is learned in the family. To see this one needs only to look at the violence rates for children of non-violent parents. These rates show that a considerable amount of violence is perpetrated by people whose parents were not violent to them and not violent to each other.

The second approach locates the problem in a broader social-structural context and focuses, not narrowly upon the individual, but upon the whole social situation within which the violence takes place. Here explanation is in terms of social context rather than in terms of individuals, and here new light can be thrown upon the behaviour of individuals. For example, this explanation would look beyond the link between drunkenness and battering to consider the way in which some cultures see both phenomena as symptoms of masculinity and male dominance. The social-structural explanation would, similarly, look beyond the fact that a drunken man committed an assault, to recognise that if he assaults a policeman he is likely to be prosecuted, while if he assaults his wife it is likely to be labelled a 'domestic dispute' for which police intervention is kept to a minimum. And this explanation would see the fact that some women return again and again to their violent husbands, not as a result of some sort of sado-masochism, but as a consequence of the inadequate help given to battered women and the hardships experienced by women who are trying to bring up children by themselves.

The legitimisation of violence by the wider society is an important part of this broader structural approach. This legitimisation is woven into a culture at every level, from the level of popular saying to the level of legislation. An important part of this legitimisation is the denial that wife abuse takes place, or the assertion that its occurrence is rare and is confined to unusual or deviant couples. In recent years, however, evidence has accumulated to confirm that violence against wives occurs in many very different societies, and at all social levels. It would be incorrect to see violence as confined to Britain and to the working class within Britain. Throughout this book reference is made to British and American studies. However, it is important to note the existence of studies of wife abuse in Germany (Hagemann-White, 1981), Israel (Saunders, 1982), the Mediterranean (Loizos, 1978), Amazonia (Chagnon, 1968) and Mexico (Roldan, 1982), and the existence of refuges or shelters for battered women in Britain, the United States, Holland, West Germany, Switzerland, Belgium, Canada, France, Australia, New Zealand and Israel (Dobash and Dobash, 1980). Schlegel rated forty-five societies and showed that three-quarters of them permitted husbands to be aggressive towards their wives (Schlegel, 1972).

Just as wife abuse takes place in the majority of societies, so it has been condoned throughout most of history. Historically the tradition of accepting wife assault is longer than the tradition of deploring it. Until the nineteenth century British law gave to husbands the right to beat their wives for what was called 'lawful correction', and it was only excessive beating that was frowned upon. The law reflected and upheld a hierarchical and patriarchal family structure.

Questions

1 Critically describe 'the two approaches to causal analysis' of the problem of 'wife' or 'women' battering.
2 Relate 'wife' or 'women' battering to the 'hierarchical and patriarchal family structure'.

Reading 3
The case for the traditional family

From A H Halsey, Introduction to N Dennis and G Erdos, *Families Without Fatherhood* (IEA Health and Welfare Unit, 1992), pp. xii-xiii (slightly adapted)

Whatever the character of society or state, polity or economy, religion or culture, parents cannot escape responsibility for the quality of their children as citizens.

In the light of this political morality I see incontrovertible evidence of a weakening of the norms of the traditional family since the 1960s. It is not that I see a golden age of traditionalism. Material deprivation, and inequality between the classes and the sexes were integral to British society in the first half of the century. There was no utopia. There was cruelty, a double standard of sexual morality, incest and child abuse, savage treatment of unmarried mothers, desertions and separations. Nevertheless the traditional family system was a coherent strategy for the ordering of relations in such a way as to equip children for their own eventual adult responsibilities.

The much-needed reform of the system required comprehensive strengthening of supporting health, education and security services if quality children were to be produced, women were to have freedom to combine motherhood with career and men were to be encouraged to take a fuller part in the domestic rearing of their offspring. Instead the evidence of more recent change is that the supporting services have deteriorated, the increment of economic growth has been transferred disproportionately to the individual pocket horizontally and to the rich vertically through the running down of family allowances, the raising of regressive national insurance contributions, the abandoning of joint taxation for spouses, the failure to fund adequate community care, and so on. In the 1980s the economic individual has been exalted and the social community desecrated. Paradoxically, Mrs Thatcher may well be seen by dispassionate future commentators as a major architect of the demolition of the traditional family.

Mrs Thatcher inadvertently found her central, (individualistic) principles powerfully supported in this crucial area (i.e. the family) by quite other social and personal forces in the creation of a new and indeed unprecedented wave of pro-individual, anti-social development of economy, polity and community.

No one can deny that divorce, separation, birth outside marriage and one-parent families as well as cohabitation and extra-marital sexual intercourse have increased rapidly. Many applaud these freedoms. But what should be universally acknowledged is that the children of parents who do not follow the traditional norm (i.e. taking on personal, active and long-term responsibility for the social upbringing of the children they generate) are thereby disadvantaged in many major aspects of their chances of living a successful life. On the evidence available such children tend to die earlier, to have more illness, to do less well at school, to exist at a lower level of nutrition, comfort and conviviality, to suffer more unemployment, to be more prone to deviance and crime, and finally to repeat the cycle of unstable parenting from which they themselves have suffered.

Questions

1 Halsey indicates several areas of evidence (e.g. divorce, separation) that show that the traditional family is under stress. Select two of these areas and find and discuss the relevant evidence (using this chapter).

2 Critically discuss Halsey's view that Mrs Thatcher 'may well be seen … as a major architect of the demolition of the traditional family'.

4

Education, Training and Education Policy

In the 1980s and 1990s education and business often got closer. A good thing? Or not?

Aims of this chapter

1 To analyse the main sociological perspectives on education and apply them to:

   i   socialisation and cultural reproduction (macro perspectives)
   ii the economy and the reproduction of a labour force
   iii the school and cultural and economic reproduction (micro perspectives)
   iv the role of ideology and discourse in education

2 To review sociological research and education policy in relation to inequalities of:

   i   class
   ii gender
   iii 'race'/ethnicity
   iv state and private-sector education

3 To analyse and interpret post-war education policy of the Labour and Conservative parties in relation to both education, training and industry and the organisation of the education system.

Educational issues and perspectives

This chapter should have personal relevance to all students who read it. The educational system claims a large portion of your life – a minimum of eleven years and probably thirteen or more, given that you are reading this book. It is certainly worth knowing what the educational system is 'doing' to you.

A major issue in the sociology of education is that of equality, particularly why working class children generally attain less (in terms of examinations) than middle class children of similar measured intelligence. This issue was hotly debated during the 1950s and 1960s. During the 1970s, issues relating to gender and education and 'race' and education came more strongly to the fore both in terms of sociological theory and educational policy.

With the Conservative general election victory of 1979, a new educational agenda began to take shape largely focusing on educational standards and the relationship between education and industry.

There are several perspectives on the sociology of education of which five are particularly important:

• Functionalist
• Marxist
• Liberal (Reformist)
• Free Market (New Right)
• Interactionist

Both functionalists and Marxists agree that education socialises people 'into' society by formal and informal processes. Because Marxists are opposed to capitalist society, however, they are highly critical of the ways in which young people are socialised to conform to it. Functionalists tend to take conformity for granted as normal. The liberal perspective reflects the reforming political orientation (inclination) which, as we noted in Chapter 1, characterises some sociologists. Liberal sociologists take their stand on the principle that everybody should have equal educational opportunity, even though they accept that fair competition will still result in inequality in examination results, and in career opportunities and rewards. The attempt to achieve the limited goal of equal opportunity has involved much political campaigning and legal change. The abolition of the eleven-plus examination in many areas owed something to the analyses and efforts of liberal sociologists. Both Marxists and liberals see the source of inequality of educational opportunity, in socio-economic background differences. Liberals tend to be much more optimistic that this inequality can be reduced by reform at the educational level itself, whereas Marxists argue that real change in the educational system requires a much more fundamental change in the structure of society. Thus, they contend that if there were more equality of income and if workers had more control of the places they work in, they would be able to afford to keep their children at school longer and also pass on greater confidence and experience to them.

The 'free market' approach to education is otherwise described as the New Right or Thatcherite approach. The belief behind this approach is that by allowing parents of pupils choice in education and so forcing schools to compete against each other, standards will be pushed upwards. This philosophy dominated Conservative ideology and policy in the late 1980s and into the mid 1990s.

Marxist, liberal and free market approaches to education are highly political and ideological although each cites social scientific data in support. The interactionist perspective is less obviously political. It focuses on classroom relationships and particularly on how classroom interaction can be affected by, and in turn, can affect external social factors. The ideological nature of education is another major theme of this chapter, particularly in the section on educational issues and policy.

The above perspectives should be regarded as 'ideal-type' descriptions rather than labels: reality is usually more complex than any description of it. Sociologists do not like being neatly labelled, any more than anyone else does. For instance, many functionalists take a liberal attitude to educational reform. Similarly, some Marxists carefully support certain educational reforms, even though these may not go as far as they might like. Both Marxists and liberals often adopt interactionist concepts and techniques in the process of research.

The sociology of education

There are three parts in this section: the first is on education and socialisation, the second is on the relationship of education to the economy, and the third examines the role of the school at the micro level in relation to cultural and economic reproduction.

1 Education, socialisation and cultural reproduction

Durkheim and Marx

Both Durkheim and Marx fully understood that in order to survive, societies need to socialise their young to accept dominant norms and values. The contemporary French Marxist, Pierre Bourdieu, has stressed the same point in referring to the need of capitalist society to 'culturally reproduce' itself. Reflecting the realities of this time, Marx himself concentrated relatively more on the role of religion in reinforcing cultural conformity whereas present-day Marxists see a greater role for education. Some of the major recent contributors to the sociology of education owe substantial debts to both Marx and Durkheim: this is particularly true of Althusser and Bourdieu.

We begin with Durkheim, partly because of the importance and detail of his work in this area and partly because of his continuing influence. The following quotation illustrates how great he considered the power of education over the individual to be:

> … each society, considered at a given stage of development, has a system of education which exercises an influence upon individuals which is usually irresistible.

Although Durkheim considered that the individual can hardly resist the effect of the educational system, his own historical studies of educational systems show that he also regarded the educational system itself as open to wider social influences. Basically, it must pass on society's values. For example, he argued that the competitive examination system came about precisely because modern society is itself individualistic and competitive. He contended that such a system would have been dysfunctional (disruptive) in the middle ages, when social status was generally ascribed (i.e. inherited). For the aristocracy to have to compete with others to maintain their social position would have risked overthrowing the whole social order, so such an idea was not entertained.

We need to give a more practical illustration of what Durkheim meant by the role of the educational system in producing conformity. Most obviously, teachers 'tell' pupils formally what to do. Formal socialisation can cover a great deal, such as telling pupils how to eat, dress and speak, as well as what values they should hold. Durkheim particularly emphasised the role of ritual in forming patterns of behaviour and in reinforcing values. Thus, school assemblies might involve rituals in which national patriotism is expressed and strengthened. He was also aware of the less obvious or 'unconscious' ways in which pupils are socialised. For example, schools are very hierarchical institutions (power is concentrated in the hands of given people), and it is precisely because hierarchy is assumed to be beyond question that children come to accept it as inevitable. They learn that some people, such as headteachers, can command more respect, politeness and obedience than others and, as a result, pupils are prepared to accept the same situation in society generally.

Althusser and Bourdieu: Marxist structuralists

The Marxist structuralists, Althusser and Bourdieu, have absorbed much of Durkheim's approach to analysing education, as well as that of Marx. It is worth explaining briefly how this dual influence has come about. Durkheim was French. His influence was passed on to Althusser and Bourdieu partly through an anthropologist called Lévi-Strauss, the founder of a school of thought known as 'structuralism'. An important aspect of structuralism is that by unconsciously learning ways and structures of thought, feeling and behaviour, people 'automatically' carry on the culture into which they have been born. Really, this is to say little more than that people are socialised to conform, except that it emphasises the extent to which this process occurs unconsciously. Now, the socialisation of the unconscious mind has been stressed by Durkheim and, via Lévi-Strauss, it surfaces again in the work of Althusser and Bourdieu. It is to their work that we now turn.

It must be remembered that although Althusser and Bourdieu reflect the influence of their compatriots, Durkheim and Lévi-Strauss, they are also neo-Marxists. Marx's thought, therefore, figures prominently in their writings. Following him, Althusser considers that the functioning of the educational system is largely determined by the needs of the capitalist socio-economic system. As far as the working class is concerned, this means that it must also be socialised to accept its position in the class system and the kind of work it has to do. Bourdieu has made a specialist study of education in capitalist society, and particularly in France. It is in his writings that we see most clearly the convergence (coming together) of certain concepts of Marx and Durkheim.

Whereas Durkheim emphasised that certain aspects of a common culture (for example, patriotism) are passed on to all members of a society, Bourdieu concentrates on how middle and working class cultures are reproduced. He analyses particularly the role of the educational system in this process. Like Althusser, he argues that schools are middle class institutions, run by middle class people (teachers), in which, in general, middle class pupils succeed. Working class culture does not fit well into the demands of such an educational system. In support of his case, he is able to point to substantial empirical evidence to show that in the United States and the Western European countries, middle class children tend to achieve better qualifications and to get better jobs than working class children of equal measured intelligence. He explains this further by use of the terms *habitus* and *cultural capital*.

Habitus is cultural background – the mesh of taste, style and manners that form cultural identity. He argues that because the educational system is middle class, middle class children come into it appropriately socialised to do well. Their values, attitudes and behaviour correspond closely with teachers' expectations and the demands of the examination system i.e. they have cultural capital. On the other hand, working class children suffer a *cultural deficit* (see Chapter 5 for a general view of class cultural differences). This observation does not mean that Bourdieu has a low opinion of working class culture, but that he regards it as largely non-academic. For instance, a working class novelist is a contradiction in terms because any such person who writes a novel employs middle class patterns of thought and expression and therefore starts to become middle class.

Bourdieu states that the examination system functions both as a formal and ritual ('ceremonial') occasion, in which the cultural ascendancy of the middle class child is legitimised (made to seem generally just and acceptable, and to *eliminate* working class children from academic education. In addition, many working class children *self-eliminate* themselves from academic advancement. The examination system is not a fair competition although it seems to be as there is a surface appearance of neutrality. Because it is accepted as fair by the middle and working class alike, it serves to *legitimise* what Bourdieu regards as the fundamentally unequal process of cultural reproduction. As a result, the middle class is generally considered to have earned its superior rewards and status and the working class, likewise, to have gained its desserts. Bourdieu sums up the means by which this 'illusion' is achieved in the term 'symbolic violence'. It is a powerful phrase and it means that the middle class cultural ascendancy and privilege is conserved and reproduced not by physical force but by a commanding superiority in the field of communication – particularly language. Thus, expertise in manipulation of cultural symbols and forms such as literature, art and logic in a way acceptable to the middle class is a weapon in the class struggle, whether consciously used as such or not. Untrained and inexperienced in this skill, working class children are often overawed and 'mystified' by it. The sense of injury and loss undoubtedly suffered by many working class 'failures' perhaps justifies Bourdieu's savage metaphor of symbolic violence. At any rate, to him, it provides the answer to the question of how working class people are ideologically persuaded to fit into their often boring and relatively unrewarding roles.

Criticism of Bourdieu

Bourdieu has been criticised both by more orthodox Marxists and by liberals. Of the former, Raymond Boudon argues that Bourdieu overstresses the cultural or, as Boudon calls them, the primary effects of stratification to the point of virtually ignoring the secondary, or material and practical effects. Boudon considers the secondary effects more important. These affect older working class pupils, who may find that they simply do not have enough money to stay on at school, or who may leave school just because their friends do. Boudon gets qualified support from the British sociologist, A H Halsey, whose refutation of Bourdieu we turn to shortly.

Bourdieu and his colleague Althusser, are also sometimes accused of a mechanical or deterministic view of cultural reproduction. Bourdieu in particular is arraigned as a 'cultural determinist.' Basically, the charge of determinism means that Bourdieu is thought to believe that class culture is inevitably passed on from generation to generation, changing only in response to deeper developments in the economic substructure (or base) of society. Thus, he would recognise that changes in economic production, such as wide-scale automation, might affect the way of life and the educational training of working people but, or so the accusation goes, he would not allow the possibility that working class people could change their own social position of cultural awareness outside the framework of such technological and socio-economic development. This charge seems broadly to be valid, although in defence of Bourdieu, he does allow that the educational system (and the cultural system generally) can operate in a 'relatively autonomous' (free) way. In other words, teachers, artists and other intellectuals and creative people have some freedom of thought and action. Bourdieu makes two major qualifications to this, however. First, such 'autonomy' does not ultimately change the class system; indeed, it may even provide a safety-valve for tensions within it. Second, teachers and artists, like other people, are in any case socialised 'into' the class system and, consequently, most unlikely to think beyond it. Such freedom as exists is, therefore, very limited for most individuals. Althusser's position is similar to that of Bourdieu. We return to him in Chapter 21.

Basil Bernstein: speech codes

The work of Basil Bernstein on class culture is complementary to that of Bourdieu. Bernstein is particularly noted for his contribution to the analysis of the relationship between class and language. He has proposed a distinction between what he calls restricted and elaborated language codes. Restricted codes are everyday, informal speech patterns which everybody uses. People using restricted codes are usually familiar with each other and consequently these codes often use language short-cuts and expression which take a lot as understood. In contrast, elaborated codes fully express meanings and use more conceptual language in doing so. Bernstein describes restricted codes as context bound whereas elaborated codes are of more universal application. Whereas middle class children learn elaborated codes at home, working class children tend not to do so. As schools use elaborated codes, this gives middle class children an educational advantage. Thus, a working class child will understand from concrete experience what it means to be 'diddled' or 'done' by paying too high a price in a shop or supermarket, but s/he will be less prepared than the middle class child to understand and talk about, say, the concept of injustice raised by the situation. According to Bernstein, this is not just a matter of unfamiliarity with the relevant vocabulary – although this must play a part – but it is due, more fundamentally, to lack of practised competence in elaborated (or more conceptual) codes of thought.

Criticism of Bernstein: Labov

Bernstein's hypothesis has been criticised by the American sociologist, William Labov, amongst others. Labov interviewed a number of black working class children and found that, once they felt confident and at ease with him, they were perfectly capable of expressing themselves in abstract conceptual terms, albeit in dialect rather than standard English. Interestingly, from the point of view of the effect of research method on findings, Labov stresses the importance of establishing an interview situation in which the subjects can behave normally. He suggests that formal interviews can sometimes have the opposite effect and produce misleading data. In defence of Bernstein, it still remains quite possible that middle class children have more practice in conceptual thought and expression. Further, differences of dialect, whether based on race or class, would tend to disfavour working class children and to favour middle class children in communicating with middle class teachers. Both points are acceptable within Bourdieu's broad capital-deficit model of cultural reproduction. He himself relates his scheme to the whole range of cultural expression: it is not just the language and modes of thought but also the style and manners, sentiments and forms of emotional expression of teachers that accord better with those of middle class children. For example, behaviour that seems 'nice and well-mannered' to a middle class child may seem 'posh and snobby' to a working class child. Neither view is more correct than the other, but the middle class child is more likely to fit in with the middle class methods of most schools.

How working class 'lads' get working class jobs: a Marxist analysis: Paul Willis, 1977

Paul Willis' book is entitled *Learning to Labour*, but its real concern is manifested in its sub-title: 'How working class 'lads' get working class jobs.' Willis describes a harsh collision between the tough working class 'lads' who are the subject of his study and the highly middle class world of the educational system. Willis' work provides concrete examples of some of the theoretical points made by Bourdieu. The lads seldom even begin to struggle for examination success which not only requires a kind of mental discipline foreign to their experience but is unlikely to be of much use in the kind of manual jobs most of them expect to get. The lads tend to find the conformist behaviour of the 'lobes', as they call more hard-working pupils, a matter for mockery and amusement.

The school experience of the lads fails significantly to alter the course of their lives. Schools are middle class institutions in that they are run by middle class people (teachers) and because success in them requires conformity to middle class values, such as academic commitment, and middle class goals, such as a career. Comparing the lads to the lobes, Spansky, one of the lads, says:

> *I mean, what will they remember of their school life? What will they have to look back on? Sitting in a classroom, sweating their bollocks off, you know, while we've been … I mean look at the things we can look back on, fighting on the Pakis, fighting on the JA's (Jamaicans). Some of the things we've done on teachers, it'll be a laff when we look back on it.*
>
> (Willis, 1977:4)

School seems to be good for a 'laff' and not much else. Judging by the following reactions of the lads to a lecture on the need for discipline at school and work, they obviously see little connection between school and the type of work they will do.

> *Spansky: He makes the same points all the time.*
> *Fuzz: He's always on about if you get a job, you've got to do this, you've got to do that. I've done it. You don't have to be none of that. Just go to a place, ask for a man in charge. Nothing like what he says.*
> *Joey: It's ridiculous …*
>
> (92)

Paul Willis notes that in later years, some of the lads do come to regret their failure to realise that education did offer a possible escape from life as a manual labourer. But to what extent does the school system give the lads a fair chance? Basically, Willis sympathises with their spirited rejection of the label of 'failures'. He appreciates, far more than Bourdieu seems to, that, in terms of their own class position, their way of life makes sense, or, it did so as long as the lads did, in fact, get jobs. Now, in 1997, things have changed but have the current generation of lads changed with them?

The lads in the 1990s: 'The gobbo barmy harmy'

The anti-school culture of the lads in the early 1970s made a degree of sense in that they nearly all got jobs regardless of school performance. In the near quarter of a century since then, the number of jobs in manufacturing has almost halved and jobs in other areas of manual work have tended to decrease. The economy has changed but has the anti-school subculture of the lads?

There have always been a substantial number of working class boys who have achieved upward mobility out of the working class. That remains true (see Mac an Ghaill pp. 195-6). However, throughout the late 1980s and 1990s there has been a steady stream of publications, some sociological, expressing concern that 'macho' anti-school working class youth culture has remained frozen in time while the rest of the world has changed. Sometimes this phenomenon is seen as a crisis of youthful working class masculinity (see p. 90) and sometimes more specifically as a crisis of schooling and the transition to work.

Chris Woodhead, Chief Inspector of Schools, has commented on the 'failure of boys, and in particular white working class boys'.

> *Research shows that white working-class boys are the least likely to participate in full-time further education after the age of 16, and … are the most likely to be completely unqualified on leaving compulsory education.*
>
> (The Times, 6.3.1996:18)

In attempting to explain this situation, Woodhead tends towards individualistic interpretations – such as inadequate parental support and poor teaching. A more sociological explanation would be that a time lag might be expected to occur before members of a culture can fully respond to a change in the economic basis of that culture (i.e. the collapse of traditional working class jobs). In any case, it would be naive to imagine that the lads would react positively to a sharp decline in their job prospects. For many working class lads school and training schemes are seen as 'a waste of time'. In their fathers' time, qualifications were not essential in order to get a job but now they often do not even lead to a job. George Riseborough's study *GBH – The Gobbo Barmy Harmy: one day in the life of the YTS boys* contains many comments from the lads which show some awareness and resentment of their predicament. Here, in typically, robust language, is one about YTS schemes:

> *I don't mind doin' borin' things, so long as it pays reet! It's great, i'n't it? It's like the programme, that advertisement on the tele with these YTS people. 'I was in the YTS and I got a job at the end of it.' The lyin bastards! I wandered 'ow much the bastards get paid for that! They're all fucking actors, getting paid. Real YTS would say, 'This is a load of bollocks and y' go on for them t' rip ya off!'*
>
> (In 'Youth and Inequality', 1993:225)

Authorities have always tended to see the lads as 'disruptive'. It is difficult to imagine that they will become any less so without a revival of their prospects for 'real' jobs – whatever these may turn out to be.

Young women from school to the job market: Christine Griffin

Like many studies of young people of school age carried out in the 1960s and 1970s, Paul Willis' was exclusively about young males. Since then, there have been several about young females. One of the most interesting of these is Christine Griffin's *Typical Girls? Young Women from School to the Job Market* (1985). Griffin studied a group of young white working class women from Birmingham fifth forms into their first two years in the local employment market. The first stage involved interviewing 180 students and the second stage concentrated on 25 young women from five schools who had few,

White dropouts in cycle of failure

Anti-school bias 'blights boys for life'

The Times, 6.3.1996

Figure 4.1 Educational underperformance of some young males, especially working class, is currently causing concern

or no qualifications. Like Willis, Griffin focuses primarily on the issue of cultural reproduction influentially explored by Bourdieu.

Griffin found that the young women differed significantly from the young men of Willis's study in their attitudes and behaviour. First, the female 'gang' did not occur among the young women – small friendship groups of two, three or four being much more common. Second, deviance for females was defined in terms of 'loose' sexuality rather than 'troublemaking'. Third, the strong identification the 'lads' made with factory work scarcely occurred among the females. A few referred to office work as 'snooty' but in practice most of them applied for jobs in the following order of preference: office, shop, factory. There was no clear division, therefore, of the kind that Willis found between the 'lads' and the 'ear 'oles' (or 'lobes'). The young working class women did not 'predestine' themselves to factory work as the 'lads' largely did.

The model Griffin offers to explain the situation and behaviour of the young women combines elements of gender and class analysis. She suggests that they are simultaneously moving in three markets:

• the labour market
• the marriage market
• the sexual market.

To less-qualified women the labour market offers either manual work or, increasingly, routine office work – and this is what the young females sought. The relationship between the marriage and sexual markets is the key arena in which most of the young women negotiate their main future identity. To behave in a sexually loose manner could damage their 'marriage prospects'. Even though paid-work is becoming a larger part of women's lives, many young women still seek their identity chiefly through romance, marriage and, 'inevitably', a man. In a complementary study, Sue Lees examines the language of female sexual insult – particularly the use of the term 'slag' – which she describes as functioning 'to control the social and autonomous behaviour of girls and steer them into marriage'.

Angela McRobbie describes how 'girls magazines' spin an 'ideology of romance' which is the opposite side of the 'slag' stereotype but perhaps just as ensnaring (see p. 513). However, Griffin notes that a minority of the young women, particularly black females are sceptical of both 'mythologies' and seek more independent identities. In a later study of 249 mainly working class West London fourth form girls (1991), Sue Sharpe found them to be less gullible about romance and relationships than the previous generation (1972). However, they have less realistic expectations about their working lives in a world that remains largely patriarchal. Sharpe comments that 'they look forward to a future in which they are likely to end up juggling paid work and domestic life, like their mothers before them'.

A H Halsey's critique of the theory of cultural reproduction: a liberal response to Bourdieu

A H Halsey's approach is more liberal than those discussed above. He draws heavily on a survey study of social change in Britain between 1913 and 1972, known as the Oxford Mobility Study. the original sample was of 10,000 men between the ages of 20 and 64.

Before describing the points on which Halsey differs from Bourdieu, it is important to be clear on their fundamental points of agreement. They are at one in stressing and lamenting the fact that many working class children do not reach anything approaching their full educational potential and, therefore, tend to get jobs below their capacity. Both want to change this situation, although they have different views about how this might be done (Chapter 5).

A substantial and important point of emphasis, rather than a total disagreement, divides Halsey from Bourdieu and other theorists of 'cultural reproduction'. To explain this, we need first to introduce the difference between materials and cultural factors affecting educational attainment. Material factors are physical and environmental, such as the standard of housing, clothes and food. Virtually, they amount to 'the things money can buy'. Cultural factors refer to less tangible matters of values, norms and attitudes.

We have already seen that Bourdieu argues that it is the possession of 'cultural capital' which accounts for the educational success of middle class children; school merely plays a part, albeit an important one, in the reproduction of cultural advantage.

In his major work, *Origins and Destinations*, with A F Heath and J M Ridge (1980). Halsey tends to emphasise material rather than cultural factors in explaining class differences in educational attainment. He makes a number of points. Firstly drawing on data from the Oxford study, he shows that there has been a substantial and progressive tendency for children to improve on the formal educational attainment of previous generations, and that even in state selective schools (mainly grammar schools selecting at eleven), the 'overwhelming feature' was that the majority of pupils came from social backgrounds in which neither parent had an education of grammar school quality. Clearly, therefore, these first generation 'selected-school' pupils could not have inherited their cultural advantage from parents who did not have it to pass on.

A second point in Halsey's case is his critique of Jackson and Marsden's *Education and the Working Class* (1962), a piece of research that seems to support Bourdieu's thesis. Out of a sample of 88 working class boys who went to grammar school, Jackson and Marsden found that a much higher number (34) than would have been expected purely on the basis of chance, came from 'sunken' middle class backgrounds. By 'sunken' middle class, they mean working class families with middle class relatives or families whose head had previously owned a small business. Halsey's data force him to work with a slightly different definition of sunken middle class; even so, his findings lead in the opposite direction from those of Jackson and Marsden. His evidence is that the relative chances of obtaining selective education declined for those from educated backgrounds compared to those from non-educated backgrounds from the pre- to the post-war period. This was true of the sunken middle class as well as others. Thus, while Halsey agrees that to have an educated relative tends to help a child educationally, it mattered less in the expanded post-war educational system than it had previously.

Halsey makes two further points. First, the group of middle class children that did benefit disproportionately from selective education did not have selectively educated parents, and so could not have inherited cultural capital in this way. Second, although Halsey fully accepts that most working class children come from educationally disadvantaged backgrounds, he makes much of the fact that those who did get places at grammar school and survived there to take 'O' levels did almost as well as children from middle class backgrounds. The problem of course, as Halsey recognises, is that relatively few working class children got into grammar schools in the first place.

Although Halsey emphasises material rather than cultural factors in explaining the educational under-attainment of working class children, he does not exclude the role of the latter. Indeed, he suggests that class cultural, as well as material factors, may account for the fact that, under the tripartite system, a much higher proportion of middle class children sat 'O' levels. Cultural disadvantage took effect particularly at the eleven-plus examination, failure at which prevented a large number of able working class children, as well as 'border-line' children from all classes, from obtaining an academic education, and going on to take 'O' levels.

Halsey is aware of the need to consider the change in the secondary system from tripartite to comprehensive when analysing the continuing relatively low attainment of working class children. In doing this, he uses the terminology of Raymond Boudon, who categorises the educational effects of class stratification into the primary and the secondary. As interpreted by Halsey and applied to British education, primary effects are cultural and material differences that hamper educational success in early schooling, and secondary effects are those that govern performance at secondary school level. Halsey suggests that, under the tripartite system, primary effects probably predominated, but that with the widespread abolition of the eleven-plus examination and the introduction of comprehensive education, secondary effects may be more potent. Their operation could well prevent the improvement in educational opportunity and attainment of working class children that comprehensivisation was widely expected to bring about (see pp. 101-4).

Halsey stresses that class is 'a major' factor affecting educational attainment, but he avoids sweeping generalisation in favour of closely reasoned argument supported by detailed evidence. The following quotation, taken from one of his reviews, perhaps reveals his complex spirit:

> *Life, including the life of the ... examination room, is understood better by gamblers than by mechanistic theoreticians. The dice are loaded - by class, by sex, by date of birth and even, perhaps ... by genes. Among these, the force of class is a major one: it affects deeply the structure of opportunity. The force of stratification is still wider and deeper. But neither make it possible to deduce automatically the fate of particular individuals.*

2 Education, the economy and the reproduction of a labour force

The preparation of a labour force requires not only the teaching of specific skills, such as the three 'Rs,' technology or computing, but also the more general socialisation of individuals to accept the discipline of work and, to some extent, their own likely place within the occupational structure. We will begin this section by presenting a functionalist perspective on these points, and then introduce other perspectives.

Functionalism: occupational selection and social mobility

Talcott Parsons gives a highly functionalist description of how he considers the educational system operates in relation to the occupational structure. He suggests that elementary (primary) schools sort out pupils according to their general level of ability (capacity), that secondary schools establish the more specific abilities and, accordingly, direct some to work and others on to further education:

> *Very broadly we may say that the elementary school phase is concerned with the internationalisation in children of motivation to achievement. The focus is on the level of capacity ...*
>
> *In approaching the question of the types of capacity differentiated, it should be kept in mind that secondary school is the principal springboard from which lower-status persons will enter the labour force, whereas those achieving higher status will continue their formal education in college, and some of them beyond.*

Parsons, then believes that the educational system actually does what is generally claimed for it – that is, selects people according to their ability and qualifies them accordingly. He and other functionalists tend to assume that there is a rough correspondence between individual intelligence, individual attainment (a pupil's measured performance) at school, and the job eventually obtained. Parsons sees the allocation of occupational status on the basis of 'achievement' as strongly characteristic of modern capitalist societies and particularly of the United States. More traditional societies allocated people to occupations on the basis of 'ascription' (by birth). Ralph Turner also considers that genuine and intense competition operates in the American educational system through comprehensive high schools, and he calls the resulting social mobility (movement up and down the social scale) 'contest' mobility. By contrast, he regards mobility of talented lower class children in Britain as 'sponsored' – through the grammar school system. This distinction, made in the1950s, has been blurred as a result of comprehensivisation in England and Wales. In any case, Turner's argument is severely weakened by the fact that he failed adequately to consider that lower social class membership substantially hinders social mobility in both countries.

The relationship between functionalism and the hereditary view of intelligence

It is clear that the functionalist case rests on whether intelligence, academic attainment and occupational position do in fact correlate strongly with one another. In particular, if intelligence and occupational status do not correlate strongly, then the functionalist model is largely discredited and the possibility must be examined that other factors are more relevant in determining occupational status. The functionalist position has recently acquired support from the work of a number of psychologists on both sides of the Atlantic though, as these scholars are not sociologists, it would be misleading to think of them as functionalists when their work merely complements the functionalist position. In Britain, Hans Eysenck is the foremost of these, and in the United States Arthur Jensen and Carl Bereiter have been prominent. Before briefly summarising their major points, something must be said about what is meant by intelligence. Intelligence refers to general cognitive ability, or the ability to reason, comprehend and make judgements. It is produced by heredity and environment. Psychologists do not agree on the precise relative importance of these two factors: some put the influence of heredity as low as 50 per cent, whilst others put it at 80 per cent, or even slightly higher.

As one might expect, those psychologists who consider that intelligence and occupational status strongly correlate estimate the hereditary element of intelligence at the high end. The 'high-estimate' viewpoint received a blow when it was demonstrated that the methodology of Sir Cyril Burt, on whose work the hereditarian case partly rested, was unscientific. Nevertheless, the debate continues. The psychologists who stress heredity – we may call them 'the hereditarians' – explain the fact that the children of parents of high occupational status also tend to achieve similar status in terms of their relatively higher level of inherited intelligence. The same applies, in reverse, to people of low social origin. Of course, although the hereditarians argue that there is a strong link between the level of intelligence of parents and children, they accept that this correspondence is not complete. For the minority of less intelligent middle class children and more intelligent working class children, the possibility of downward or upward mobility respectively, occurs by reason of the level of their intelligence. The hereditarians regard the fact that there is only a fairly small amount of long-range upward or downward mobility in both Britain and the United States as evidence for, not against, their argument. Like functionalists, the hereditarian psychologists consider that the educational system 'does the job'. It qualifies people according to their ability and directs them towards appropriate occupations.

New Right perspective, education and the economy

Functionalist perspective on education has probably had no direct influence on the New Right free market philosophy dominant in the Conservative party in the 1980s and1990s. Nevertheless, there are substantial parallels between the two. First, the Conservatives have emphasised individual competition between pupils (testing), between teachers (appraisal – which may be related to promotion), and between schools (open enrolment) (see p. 127 for more detail on Conservative policy). Thus, competition is seen as the driving force behind individual and, ultimately, national achievement. Second, again like the Functionalists, Conservatives tend to set aside the evidence that class factors greatly distort fair competition partly on the basis that education can directly do little about class inequalities.

A third parallel between many Conservatives and Functionalists is the tendency to see the function of education as closely tied to the needs of the economy. Throughout the 1980s, the government made a variety of attempts to increase the influence of the business world in education. More school governorships were allocated to business people. The business-dominated Manpower Services Commission (MSC) took over much of the vocational training of young people, including the majority of Youth Training Schemes (YTSs) from further education colleges. Even within schools, the Technical and Vocational Educational Initiative (TVEI) was funded by the MSC. There was a sustained attempt to spread the spirit of the 'enterprise culture' throughout the whole of the educational system. TVEI has become TVE – Technical and Vocational Extension – and vocational training is now controlled by the business dominated TECs (Training and Enterprise Councils) (1991).

Marxism, occupational selection and social mobility

A major refutation of the arguments of Functionalists and hereditarian psychologists comes from the American Marxists, Herbert Bowles and Samuel Gintis. We will present their refutation first and then describe the broader theoretical context of their position. On the basis of detailed statistical analysis, Bowles and Gintis show that, in the United States, the probability of obtaining economic success is considerably greater for those born of parents of high socio-economic status than for those of high intelligence. Put plainly, socio-economic background is generally a much more significant factor in obtaining economic success than is intelligence. They show that a man born in the bottom decile (tenth) in terms of socio-economic background has only 4.2 per cent probability of being in the top fifth of income distribution, whereas a person born in the top decile in terms of socio-economic backgrounds has a 43.9 per cent probability of being in the top fifth of income distribution as an adult. That this extreme inequality of outcome is due to socio-economic background and not to the differential distribution of intelligence is shown by a further sophisticated statistical calculation. This calculation is hypothetical (rests on supposition) and demonstrates how income would be distributed on the basis of measured intelligence only. Because the general level of measured intelligence is somewhat higher for those born into higher socio-economic backgrounds, those born into the top decile have, in this hypothetical model, a marginally better chance of reaching the top fifth of income distribution than those born into the bottom decile on the basis of 'the genetic inheritance of IQ' (Bowles and Gintis). Those born in the bottom decile would have an 18.7 per cent probability of being in the top fifth in income, and those born in the top decile a 21.4 per cent probability on the basis of differences in intelligence alone. These figures are so far from the actual patterns described above that we have to agree with Bowles and Gintis' insistence on the relative unimportance of IQ and the prime importance of socio-economic background in explaining economic success. The best hope for obtaining high income, then, is to be born into a high socio-economic background. As Bowles and Gintis say succinctly: 'the power and privilege of the capitalist class are often inherited, but not through superior genes'.

Another American, Christopher Jencks, has also written with authority in this area. He sums up the matter effectively when he writes that although the heredity-environment argument is likely to rage indefinitely, the best evidence:

> ... *does not, however, suggest that variations in cognitive skill account for much of the inequality among American adults. There is nearly as much economic inequality among individuals with identical test scores as in the general population.*

Jencks further points out that schools themselves cannot make an unequal and hierarchical society equal. For that to happen, income, wealth, cultural opportunity and status would have to be more equally distributed. This observation is obvious but nonetheless true.

It is a strength of Bowles and Gintis's case that they use their opponents' data on the relationship between heredity and intelligence. Other authorities also see this relationship as less strong than Jensen and Eysenck do, and point out that not only does the relative level of educational attainment of a child vary over time but so too do scores in intelligence tests. Indeed, it is actually possible to prepare successfully for intelligence tests, so they can hardly be regarded as neutral instruments of measurement. J W B Douglas, whose work we refer to below, regards intelligence tests in this more sceptical light. He argues that scores achieved in them, as well as academic performance, are considerably influenced by social background.

A reformer's response to Marxist and functionalists: A H Halsey

Halsey rejects what he sees as the pessimism of Marxists and the conservatism of many functionalists. Yet, in arguing that educational reform can facilitate upward mobility from the working class, he has to work hard with the facts produced by his own research and that of his colleagues. The data he presents in *Origins and Destinations* largely confirm the established view that in Britain, as in America, the offspring of the middle class have a very much greater chance of remaining middle class than the offspring of the working class have of becoming middle class, (over six times greater, depending on precisely how middle and working class are defined). What is more, this situation did not substantially change between 1913 and 1972. What did happen is that because of the expansion of the service sector and the contraction of the industrial sector of the economy, more middle class jobs became available. All classes benefited, but the working class did not do so any more than others. Indeed, in the years following the immediate

post-Second World War period, its members did relatively less well.

In the face of such evidence, Halsey is determinedly hopeful rather than optimistic. He conceded that so far the middle class has benefited proportionately more from the expansion of state education than the working class has, but he argues that this would be unlikely to continue if further expansion took place. In fact, figures for 1994 show the better-off retaining their advantage in terms of money spent by the state. (see Figure 4.2) Given that middle class youth is now largely catered for, an additional increase in educational opportunity would be bound to benefit the working class. He also hopes that as (and if) the comprehensive system becomes better established, it will reduce class inequalities in education. His own research, however, does not provide data on whether or not this is happening (see Chapter 6). The section of Halsey's book on future educational policy is inevitably, more speculative than the rest of *Origins and Destinations*. Perhaps its implied corollary is that in his view, there is, in any case, no practical alternative to reform.

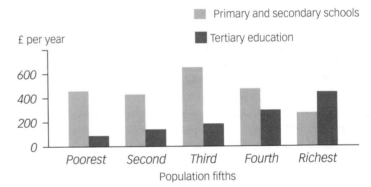

Note: *To obtain total state spending on education for each fifth grouping, both columns should be added together. Thus, the richest fifth receive more expenditure than the poorest fifth because more children of the rich go on to tertiary education.*

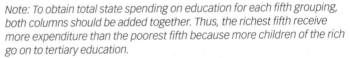

(Source: *Fiscal Studies*)

Figure 4.2 Education benefits

Marxism, economy, education and class

Marxists do not consider that the educational systems of advanced capitalist societies effectively and fairly match people to jobs. They believe that education in capitalist society contributes to the continuance of the class system and class inequality; in particular, it reproduces a labour force which is socialised to accept its lot and has, in any case, no adequate alternative means of survival. By 'socialised' we mean that the majority of working class children who 'fail' academically tend to accept their own 'failure' and the 'success' of most middle class children as legitimate. The fact that a small minority of working class children do 'make it' helps to foster the illusion that the educational system is fair and 'neutral,' and a highly unequal society presupposes that most children will fail academically and fill the lower occupations. In a sense, these matters become 'facts of life' for them, although for many an underlying sense remains that circumstances could be different.

Bowles and Gintis: the correspondence principle

Like Bourdieu, Bowles and Gintis give many examples of how social relationships in the educational system correspond to those of the economic system and thus prepare children for working life. They refer to these structural parallels between the education and the economic system as the *correspondence principle*. (Reading 1). They argue that it is mainly through the invisible (or informal curriculum) that pupils are socialised for their position in the workplace. They stress especially that educational institutions, like factories and offices, are intensely hierarchical. Like workers, pupils, are expected to obey authority and have little or no control over the content of their work. This results in a feeling of non-involvement in, or alienation from, work. Only a minority of mainly middle class children go on to experience relative freedom and responsibility in study: fewer still are educated for leadership.

Braverman: education for conformity: storage

The American Marxist, Harry Braverman, also argues that, far from being primarily involved in teaching working class children specific occupational skills, it is one of the hidden functions of schools to prepare children for the tedium of work (by being tedious themselves!): 'In school, the child and the adolescent practice what they will later be called upon to do as adults: the conformity to routines'. (Labour and Monopoly Capital, 287). Braverman's critique, however, is more complex than this suggests and deserves fuller presentation. He sees the educational system as subordinate to the economic, but not, perhaps, as might be anticipated. He makes a powerful argument that most unskilled, semi-skilled and even many so-called skilled manual and non-manual jobs can be done with little or no skill at all (see Chapter 9). He therefore eliminates occupational preparation as a major function of education for the majority. Indeed, it is true that most jobs at these levels are learnt at work itself, not at school. He agrees that the three basic communication skills of reading, writing and arithmetic are learnt in schools, but he considers these to be necessary in the general context of modern life, rather than specifically at work (where, of course, they also help!). Braverman's thesis is supported by estimates that in Britain between two and five million adults are not fully literate; yet they obviously manage to do their jobs, despite this handicap. He also differentiates between the kind of work just described and professional, managerial and other work of a similar level, for which lengthy training is necessary. Some critics have suggested that even with these occupations, the length of time spent in studying in institutions could be profitably shortened. Thus, Robert Dore suggests that engineers could be well-trained through a combination of supervised experience 'on-the-job' and part-time or short, full-time courses.

Braverman also considers that schools fulfil another function – that of 'child minding' or 'child storage' while parents are at work. He points out that the raising of the minimum age for compulsory education has coincided with the increase in the number of working mothers. His comments on the relationship between educational expansion and the rate of unemployment are echoed by the British social historian, Harold Silver. They both claim that in the 1930s this relationship served to reduce unemployment amongst the young by removing large numbers of them from the job market. In addition, it provides jobs in teaching and administration for many thousands of middle class people. The steady increase in those staying on for further education or training in Britain from the late 1970s has similarly 'mopped up' some of the unemployed. However useful or not qualifications may be, the pursuit of them occupies the time and energy of young people. Significantly, provision has been made increasingly for less qualified sixteen and seventeen year olds, who are weakest in the job market, to stay on in education. Braverman's remark that 'there is no longer any place for the young in society than school' refers to the role of schools generally, but it has a particular application to the less employable.

Braverman not only argues that few job-specific skills are learnt in pre-sixteen education, but also that the 'qualification paper-chase' is in itself unnecessary and futile. Whilst there is empirical support for the first position, the second depends very much more on point of view. It is true, however, that pupils and the general public are sometimes unaware of the extent to which the job-market value of qualifications has become substantially less now that more people have them at all levels. To take two examples, teacher training and librarianship; the qualifications required for entry into both these courses have risen. This does not guarantee that the people now entering them will be better than in the past or that they will do the job more effectively, but they will appear more impressive on paper. Braverman suggests that employers use qualifications as a screening device to ensure a minimum quality of entrant and, to maintain the same standard over time, they tend to adjust their requirement upwards. He cites some interesting survey evidence from Berg that there is now chronic over-qualification in many areas of employment, particularly at the clerical level. Berg's data also showed that over-educated employees tended to do a worse job, and to be more dissatisfied than the less well-qualified.

Conclusion

Although the functional relationship between the educational and economic systems in Britain and America is in some respects rather obscure, its importance should not be underestimated. Modern nations require, at least, a highly educated minority, particularly in the areas of scientific and technological research, and a generally literate and numerate population. Accordingly, education is a major item of government expenditure in all such societies. As we have seen, some argue that the educational system in Britain ought to be more closely directed to serve the needs of the economy. Japan is a country that has had a recent tradition of centralised planning in education: its 'economic miracle' would not have been possible without the efficiency of its educational system. Great emphasis is placed on the development of mathematical and scientific skills; although this has achieved results, it has often been at the price of putting extreme pressure on teenagers.

3 The role of the school in cultural and economic reproduction

Much has already been written in this chapter about the role of schools in socialising pupils (cultural reproduction) and the preparation of a labour force (economic reproduction). These two processes are intimately connected in that the way an individual is socialised greatly determines the job s/he will obtain.

This section briefly examines two aspects of the role of the school. First, a closer analysis is given of how teachers categorise or label pupils at the micro-level, i.e. the level of classroom interaction. Second, the question is asked whether, given the influence of external factors such as class and gender socialisation or educational performance, schools can 'make a difference' to the level of their pupils' achievements. The first sub-section tends to stress the extent to which schools reinforce external social factors whereas the second suggests that 'good' schools can make a significant difference despite social disadvantage.

Schools, 'labelling' and cultural reproduction

We have already seen how the Marxists, Bourdieu and Bernstein, see the educational system as a middle class agency which helps to produce middle class cultural ascendancy. A number of interactionists in Britain and America have reached similar conclusions. Their theoretical focus is, however, in some cases narrower than that of the Marxists, and their method of research is on a smaller scale and largely participant-observational.

A pioneering study in this area is David Hargreaves' *Social Relations in a Secondary School* (1967). The secondary school in question was an all boys' secondary modern school in which Hargreaves took on the participant observational role of teacher. His study was concerned with the factors within the school context which contribute to the creation of two sub-cultures, 'the academic and the delinquescent'. He emphasises how academic streaming greatly affects the membership of these two sub-cultures. Those who were placed in the lowest ('E') stream were the most likely to become part of the delinquescent (or delinquency-prone) sub-culture, whereas those in the 'A' stream tended to conform. Hargreaves attributes the formation of these peer-group sub-cultures directly to the school's policy of streaming which, he claims, results in an increasing feeling of inferiority on the part of the lower stream boys as they progress into the third and fourth forms. We can, then, conveniently think of the streaming process as a form of labelling which, in this instance and presumably often, has unintended consequences. It must be said that other sources show that social class factors mediated through the home and neighbourhood also contributed to the formation of youth peer-groups, although these were beyond the practical limits of Hargreaves' research.

Colin Lacey's *Hightown Grammar* (1971) is a parallel study to that of Hargreaves, concerned with the effect of streaming in a grammar school. His findings complement those of Hargreaves

and he adds the observation that when frustrated expectations at school coincide with problems at home, 'the worst cases of emotional disturbance occur'.

Stephen Ball's study of polarised pupil sub-culture in a comprehensive school completes a trilogy (*Beachside Comprehensive: a Case-study of Secondary Schooling 1981*). Ball finds that 'banding' contributes to the formation of what he terms 'pro-school' and 'anti-school' sub-cultures. Interestingly, however, he found that when Beachside did convert to mixed ability teaching, labelling of pupils largely on the basis of class stereotyping continued to occur. This suggests that a high level of skill and commitment is needed by teachers if they are to avoid stereotyping (see also Spender, pp.112-3).

Ball's observations lead him to produce the following typology to explain the nature of pro- and anti-school groups.

Pro-School:
1 Supportive (conformers because they believe they ought to be.
2 Manipulative (conformers because it suits their self-interest).

Anti-school:
1 Passive ('drifters' into nonconformist or apathetic (behaviour).
2 Rejecting (active nonconformers/rebels).

In Paul Willis' study, *Learning to Labour*, the role of the school, including the labelling of working class 'lads' and the formation of what he calls anti-school sub-cultures, is put in a wide socio-economic context. In pointing out that the academic failure of the 'lads' provides new recruits to manual labour, and so helps to maintain the capitalist system, Willis shows himself to be a structural sociologist as well as a detailed ethnographer (social scientist who studies cultural activity through detailed observation – see p. 89). His strong emphasis on structure differentiates him from interactionists such as Hargreaves and Woods.

In the 1980s and 1990s, sociologists influenced by the interactionist approach, have increasingly emphasised the *variety* and *difference* of student adaptation and response to the school context, including teacher labelling. Peter Woods identifies eight modes of adaptation to the school situation ranging from *ingratiation* ('keeping in' with teachers), through *ritualism* (going through the motions of conformity) to *rebellion*. John Furlong finds even this typology inadequate to the complexity and individuality of student adaptation. Mac an Ghaill has attempted to link school adaptation with gender orientation, particularly with male students self-concepts of masculinity (see pp. 195-8).

Like Willis, Nell Keddie draws on both interactionist and structural perspectives in her detailed examination of how cultural reproduction occurs in the classroom through the labelling process. She argues that sometimes intelligent working class children may be labelled, or mis-labelled, stupid because of 'troublesome' behaviour. This label can become a 'self-fulfilling prophecy,' if the child accepts it and loses the motivation to compete academically. Keddie rejects any implication that working class culture is inferior: she refers to this view as 'the myth of cultural deprivation'. She argues that the educational system should build on working class culture rather than ignore or repress it – a view that Bernstein himself accepts as having clarified his own position. One problem is that nobody has yet explained in detail what a curriculum based on, or even substantially reflecting, working class culture might be like, or how it would help working class children to function better in capitalist society (if, indeed, that were its aim). In fact, classroom organisation and curriculum have not moved as Keddie hoped. By 1997, a large majority of Maths, Science, French and English classes for fifteen to sixteen year olds were grouped by ability.

The quality of schools: Michael Rutter

A piece of research which contrasts markedly with those described in the previous sections is that of Michael Rutter et al., *Fifteen Thousand Hours*. Rutter's methods were highly empirical and statistical and both his methods and his findings have attracted strong criticism, but he has stood by his main conclusions. *Fifteen Thousand Hours*, published in 1979, summarised several years' research into the performance of twelve Inner London secondary schools. The aim of the research was to discover why some schools 'succeeded' and others did not. The team looked at four factors: attendance, academic achievement, behaviour in school, and the rate of delinquency outside it.

Rutter found that schools obtained very varied ratings on all the above counts, even when difference in social class background and intelligence in intake was allowed for. Those schools that scored well on one factor tended to do well on others. What, then, on Rutter's evidence, makes for a successful school? Pupil performance on the above four points is associated with a certain school 'ethos' of which sound teaching and professional behaviour is the keynote. Teachers who are punctual, well-organised and patient, who encourage pupils, share extracurricular activities with them, and can inspire by example, are likely to get the best from pupils. Whatever the teacher's style and values, consistency helps. This applies as much to senior as to junior staff, and Rutter adds that an established system of rewards and punishments improves pupils' performance. Because some schools were successful on all four points, the researchers sought an underlying reason. These successful schools varied in their approach from the traditional to the progressive but the researchers concluded that what they had in common was a consistent commitment to their own values and rules. This consistency created an atmosphere or ethos that was secure and purposeful and in which effective work could take place and good human relationships prosper.

Fifteen Thousand Hours was initially well-received both by the press and by many influential academics. Like many books that elicit such a response, it clarified and built upon a body of sentiment that had been growing for some time. In the mid 1970s, a concern for academic standards and quality in education, which had been simmering for some time, rose to the surface. The *Bennet Report* in 1976, comparing various kinds of teaching methods in primary schools, found amongst other things that whatever method of teaching was used, the ability, experience and commitment of the individual teacher was a crucial variable. Formal and informal teaching methods could both be successful – provided that they were done well. Again, themes of consistency and commitment are stressed.

Criticism of Rutter

We can divide Rutter's critics into those who attack the quality of his research in its own terms and those who argue that, in addition to the limitations of his methodology, he also asks inadequate, if not wrong, questions. Of the former, several are especially concerned with the limitations of his statistical method. Amongst these are Anthony Heath and Peter Clifford of Oxford University, who argue that the effect on performance which Rutter attributes to secondary school factors might well have been caused by the carry-over effect of primary schooling or by the interest of parents. In brief, Rutter has not controlled for the various non-school factors that are known to affect children's school attainment.

The second group of Rutter's critics put their criticisms of his methodology within a broad critique of his whole theoretical approach. Michael Young rejects the assumption that social relations in school can be adequately understood on the basis of a model that assumes value consensus within the school. He finds it inconceivable that a school could 'function' or be properly analysed without reference to class, gender and racial divisions. To him, it is ludicrous to applaud consistency without raising the question of 'consistency in the pursuit of what purposes?' Rutter's answer to Young was that his research was only concerned with school performance in relation to the four factors mentioned above.

A further criticism of the report is that it tells us nothing about the fate of the children when they leave school. Rutter does not even present data on the question of whether, because children in some schools do better in public examinations than others, their occupational prospects are improved – a point which cannot be assumed, given that most of the children in the study were highly disadvantaged and that even 'the examination successes' were moderate by national standards.

Perhaps Rutter cannot be condemned for asking a particular set of questions, but clearly these questions are limited in scope and context and, to judge by the current state of debate, the answers to them need to be treated with caution. Even so, it is worth recalling that, if interpreted cautiously and in the light of other relevant data, Rutter's findings appear neither startling nor particularly original. Writing in 1968 of lower manual working class pupils, J W Douglas said:

> *Although (they) … are at a disadvantage relative to the middle class in all types of school, those at schools with a good record are far less handicapped.*

Much more recent data in the form of government published league tables of schools' results confirms both Rutter's research findings *and* the strong correlation between social class and educational attainment established by much sociological research. Similar schools with similar pupils do occasionally produce significantly different examination results but generally there remains a clear relationship between class and educational attainment – however that may be interpreted.

4 Foucault: ideology, discourse and power

It is useful here to examine the concepts of ideology, discourse and power in relation to education. We are at a point in the chapter between considering sociological perspectives on education and analysing education policy. The concepts of ideology, discourse and power can be used to link the two.

We will first deal with ideology, power and education. Gregor McLennan provides a definition of ideology which links ideologies to power:

> *Ideologies are sets of ideas, assumptions and images by which people make sense of society, which give a clear social identity, and which serve in some way to legitimise relations of power in society.*
>
> *(1991:111)*

We have already seen that Marxists consider that education in capitalist societies socialises pupils into 'sets of ideas, assumptions and images' (i.e. ideologies) by which they participate in, and believe in the capitalist system. The other perspectives we have so far considered likewise argue that education socialises pupils into society although interactionists argue that young people play a more active part in socialisation than certain Marxists suggest. We have also seen that the education system plays a role in selecting individuals for particular positions in society. Different positions offer varying degrees of power and rewards. In terms of McLennan's definition, the education system 'legitimises' (*appears to provide a fair basis for*) the reproduction of class, gender and ethnic inequality.

In the second part of this chapter we consider the political ideologies and policies associated with attempts to change or reform the education system. These include the introduction of the comprehensive system by the Labour party and the introduction of an education 'market' by the Conservatives under Margaret Thatcher. The Labour party reforms were motivated by an ideology of equality of opportunity, and the Thatcherite reforms largely by the capitalist free-market ideology of competititon applied to education. Both sets of educational reforms were intended to bring about great social change although it is arguable that both have achieved less than their supporters hoped.

The link between *ideology, power and position* is so well established in sociology and so useful in analysis that there may seem little need of alternative concepts in this area. However, the French post-structuralist Michel Foucault has developed a range of influential concepts which cover similar ground to those of ideology, power and position. Whereas Marxism tends to treat ideology and action as distinct, though deeply related phenomena, Foucault regards them as inseparable. What people do, say and think is for Foucault a seamless whole. This is because he considers that individuals are part of wider *fields of power* which shape their ideas and actions. The prison system and the education system itself are examples of fields of power. Both these systems impact powerfully on individuals, structuring their lives. Foucault used the term *power-knowledge* to describe how powerful ideas shape or generate a framework of *discipline* for organisational systems – for instance, the penal service or education system. Thus, when the comprehensive system was being introduced, the power-knowledge that was dominant was *egalitarian* whereas the Conservative educational reforms were shaped by a *competitive* power-knowledge. (Note: I have selected my own examples to illustrate Foucault's ideas.) During these respective periods, the thinking and behaviour of teachers, pupils and others in education was saturated by the relevant power-knowledge – everyone, as it were, operated within the same field of power even though some resisted or tried to modify its effects. The two systems, then, generate their own *regimes of truth*, to use Foucault's term. However, in the latter's view such regimes of truth reflected their adherents' values, philosophies and interest rather than any objective reality.

Foucault uses his key concept of *discourse* to describe common assumptions which underlie particular patterns of language use. The term applies particularly to 'expert jargon'. Its meaning is similar to that of ideology but it includes an emphasis on the power of language as well as the ideas language expresses. Thus, discourses occur about what constitutes the educationally 'subnormal' and who should be categorised as such. There are discourses about the 'single-parent' family and the educational performance of the Afro-Caribbean child; about why males perform better than females in the natural sciences and worse in languages; about the effects of competitive tests on young children; and so on. Often, 'experts' have the power or authority to establish a particular discourse which then can be difficult to challenge without the help of an alternative set of 'experts'. The following quotation from Derek Layder should further clarify what Foucault meant by the term discourse:

A discourse here refers to all that can be thought, written or said about a particular thing such as a product (like a car, or a washing detergent), or a topic of specialist knowledge (such as sport or medicine) (or education). In this sense, the ability to employ a discourse reflects a command of knowledge of a particular area. It also implies that this facility is employed in relation to people who lack such command and have no legitimate claim to such knowledge. For instance, command of a particular discourse, such as that of medicine or law (or education), also allows control over those who do not, such as patients and clients (and pupils/students).

(Layder, 1994:97)

(Note: the education references are the author's additions).

Foucault and Marxism

How significant is the Foucault's contribution to our understanding of how educational and other organisational processes work? It would be very surprising if many of Foucault's insights had not been achieved within other theoretical frameworks. There are obvious similarities between Foucault's analysis of discourse and that of labelling theory described in the previous section (see pp. 96-8). Both see labels as socially constructed rather than as 'objectively true' and stress that some have more power to define than others. Along with the power of definition comes control and discipline.

As already suggested above, the Marxists' concepts of ideology and power cover similar ground to that of power-knowledge. Many ex- or neo-Marxists have adopted some of Foucault's concepts while retaining Marxist ones as well. Thus, Tom Hulley and Tom Clarke use the (Marxist) concept of ideology 'to refer to wide-ranging systems of ideas' (e.g. capitalist ideology) whereas they define discourses as more 'local' in that they are 'associated with specialised knowledge or expertise and tend to be the province of 'experts'' (1991:16) (e.g. Youth Training Advisor). This does seem a viable combination of the terms ideology and discourse.

Foucault and the sociology of educational knowledge and control

In the early 1970s, Michael F D Young and his colleagues analysed school curricula and organisation in terms of its ideological content. Like Marxists, Bernstein and Bourdieu, they argued that the alienating nature of much of the curriculum and the hierarchical structure of schools socialised pupils to accept a similar experience in paid-work. Accepting these things is passed off as 'realism' or 'just commonsense'. On the other hand, school did not provide alternative knowledge critical of the schooling and organisation of work in capitalist society.

Despite its broadly Marxist framework, Young *et al.*'s analysis foreshadows an important aspect of Foucault's thought in its emphasis on the role of 'experts' in defining, selecting and managing relevant knowledge. Young *et al.* stated that experts (inspectors, advisors, teachers), determined what was 'high status' and what was 'low status' knowledge. The former was comprised mainly of academic subjects – often taken by middle class pupils – and excluded vocational or less academic subjects – often taken by working class pupils. The Thatcherite education reforms did engage with these issues but cannot be said to have solved them (see pp. 120-5).

Differences between Foucault and Marxism

Notwithstanding the above similarities, two major differences between Foucault and Marxism need to be noted. First, Foucault rejects the class conflict theory of history which is fundamental to Marxism. In Foucault's view power has many possible sources and operates in many different ways. Although Foucault himself did not analyse education in details, his approach would suggest a focus on power-knowledge in relation to gender, 'race', disability and other differences as well as class. Second, Foucault's widely adopted concept of discourse arguably provides a 'missing tool' in Marxism for analysis of how power or, rather, power-knowledge works, particularly at the small and medium scale levels of organisational and professional 'expertise'.

Foucault and Ivan Illich: a brief comparison

Ivan Illich (1971) argued that both the formal and informal or *hidden curriculum* produced conformity among pupils. So-called educational experts determined what pupils should 'know', smothering pupils' own interests and choice. Schools functioned to inculcate discipline, grade and select pupils, rather than to stimulate freely motivated learning. This analysis is compatible with Foucault's theory of power-knowledge and the discipline it creates, although it lacks the latter's theoretical scope and attention to historical detail.

What Illich offers that Foucault does not, is alternatives to social conformity. In the case of education, this lies in 'deschooling'. Deschooling involves the voluntary setting up of *skill exchanges* in which people teach each other life-skills, and of *learning webs* in which people meet and explore common problems. In the early 1970s, Illich's ideas were often received sympathetically but in the mid 1990s the gloomier vision of Foucault holds greater sway. However, the concept of 'webs' or networking does have some current relevance particularly as use of internet and the world-wide web – both based on relatively non-controlled access to computerised communication – spreads internationally. However, at the moment access to such networks is limited and does not yet greatly reflect Illich's ideal of mass popular self-learning.

Conclusion: Foucault and the sociology of education

There is much more to Foucault than the above application of his thought to education can even indicate. However, there are suggested absences and defects in his theoretical approach, too. Anthony Giddens mentions two of these (1995). First, Foucault tends to present power as operating impersonally whereas for Giddens power should be linked to people and resources. Those groups with more resources – either cultural or material – are better able to pressure their own self/group interest. Gidden's point has particular application to education, given the advantage that those with material and cultural resources often win for their children. Second, Giddens argues that Foucault disregards human agency or the power of human beings to make events rather than simply be their victims. This is a common criticism of French structuralists and poststructuralists. In this respect, it is interesting that Stephen Ball finds that in his very late writings, Foucault himself regretted his own determinism (Ball, 1991). Ball quotes Foucault in the final year of his life to the effect that 'the real political task' is to criticise the working of institutions, including the education system, 'in such a manner that the political violence which has always exercised itself obscurely through them will be unmasked, so that one can fight them.'

Questions

1 To what extent does the education system reflect society rather than provide the means of individual opportunity or social change?
2 Does the application of Foucault's ideas to education add anything new to the sociology of education?

Educational issues and policy: 1944-1997

A period of over 50 years is a long one to cover in relation to an area as controversial and subject to change as education. Yet, conveniently the post-war period falls into two clearly identifiable parts with a brief time of uncertainty and transition in between. The first period is from 1994 to 1976, the second from 1979 to the present (1997) and perhaps beyond, and the transition was roughly between 1976 and 1979. All these dates must, of course, be regarded as approximate, particularly the last (the new government of 1997 may begin a new epoch in educational policy and reform).

The key theme of the first period was that of equality of opportunity in relation particularly to class disadvantage and later gender and 'race'/ethnicity. Upward mobility through the eleven-plus exam was of the limited, 'sponsored' variety referred to earlier by Turner (see p. 92). It was initiated by the Butler Education Act of

1944 and partly brought to a close by Prime Minister James Callaghan's Ruskin College speech of 1976 when new priorities were signalled at the top of the educational agenda. These priorities were the relationship of education to industry and the standards attained by pupils and students in the state sector. Callaghan's brief premiership, 1976-79 – our 'transitional' period – saw these problems discussed rather than acted upon. They became the main points in the educational agenda of 'Thatcherism', along with the issue of curriculum content, in particular what is culturally appropriate for 'British' pupils to learn. Even so, it was not until Margaret Thatcher's third period in office that the main Conservative educational reforms were passed in law via the Educational Reform Act (ERA) of 1988.

Table 4.1 Educational Ideologies and policies: 1944-90s

1940s/1950s	1960s/1970s	1970s/1980s	1980s/1990s
Market Liberalism (within a paternalistic framework)	Reformist Liberalism	'Equality;' for Minorities	Market Liberalism (and central curricular control)
Tripartite System	Comprehensive System	Impacted on the Whole of the Educational System	1988 Educational Reform Act
	Compensatory Education (Sole Quasi-socialist Measure)	Feminism	National Curriculum
		Multi-culturalism/ Anti-Racism	Competing Schools
		Special Needs	
Private Education			

Class, equality and opportunity

Much of the earlier part of this chapter examined the effect of social class on educational attainment. Both the Butler Education Act of 1944 and the systematic introduction of comprehensive education from 1965 were attempts to widen equality of opportunity albeit very different in kind. They were both essentially liberal measures although, for reasons discussed below, supports of the comprehensive system regarded it as much more egalitarian than the tripartite system introduced by the 1944 Act (see below). A third measure discussed below is compensatory education. This policy, which only affected a small percentage of the school population, was more genuinely socialist than comprehensivisation as it attempted to compensate for the material and cultural disadvantages experienced by working class children by enriching their home and community experience.

Before discussing various policy measures it is worth briefly examining again the issue with which they were largely concerned – the under-achievement of working class children. In the 1960s, J W Douglas compared the attainment level of high ability students from different social backgrounds and found that success at 'O' level and staying on at school after the fifth year were strongly correlated with class (see Table 4.2).

Table 4.2 A comparison of pupils of different social class background but of similar high ability

	Upper middle class	Lower middle class	Upper working class	Lower working class
% Gaining good GCEs	77	60	53	37
% Leaving school in their 5th year	10	22	33	50

(Source: Adapted from J W B Douglas, *All Our Future*, 1968)

Douglas found the difference between intelligence and attainment was even greater among pupils of less measured intelligence from a similar wide range of social backgrounds. According to Anthony Heath (1987), and despite the reforms we are about to discuss, much the same pattern of working class under-achievement persisted into the 1980s (see p. 102). Social class, then, makes a substantial contribution to academic attainment. A number of sociologists, including the American, Jencks, have raised another important question of educational inequality. They argue that even when children of different social backgrounds do achieve similar levels of attainment, their life-chances, in terms of careers and acquiring wealth, are not fully equalised as a result: higher classes still do better. Research by Gordon Marshall demonstrates that this is also true in Britain (1988).

The tripartite system

There was a sizeable political and public consensus behind the Butler Act. It raised the school leaving age to fifteen and made state education entirely free. The Act stated the government's commitment in principle to providing an educational system suited to each child's 'age, aptitude and ability'. In pursuit of this objective, local authorities were required to organise education in three progressive stages; primary, secondary and further (most post-school education excluding higher education, which was based mainly in universities). Although it was not specifically laid down in the Act, most local authorities divided secondary education into grammar, secondary modern and technical schools. This threefold division became known as the tripartite system. Grammar schools were for more 'academic' children and

secondary modern schools for virtually all the rest. Nationally, only a very small percentage of students went to technical schools which provided practical, vocationally-oriented courses. Most local authorities used an eleven-plus examination to select pupils for specific types of schools. Very few offered grammar school places to even as much as 30 per cent of their secondary intake and many offered far fewer. Critics of the tripartite system soon began to argue that it was inadequate to meet the aptitudes and abilities of all children. While this was true, the Act did open up secondary education to all and this in itself ensured that the general educational level of the population would improve.

The problems and related policy debates which we deal with below must be understood in the post 1944 Act educational context. Of course, the broader social context is also relevant, particularly the class nature of British society. It became clear in the 1950s and early 1960s that the educational system as it had developed under the 1944 Act was not ensuring equality of opportunity between social classes and was failing to bring out the potential of many children, particularly those from disadvantaged backgrounds. American sociologist, Ralph Turner astutely observed that the upward social mobility sponsored via the eleven-plus was sufficient to replenish Britain's elite without much changing its inegalitarian class structure. The 1944 Act did not effectively confront the issue of quality education for all. Halsey's early work with Floud and Martin, and Jackson and Marsden's, and J W B Douglas's studies already referred to were a significant sociological contribution to this growing awareness. The major issue at secondary level focused on the eleven-plus exam and the system to which it paved the way.

The comprehensive system

The major criticism against the tripartite system, put forward particularly by the Labour party, was that the eleven-plus examination discriminated against working class children. Details of the examination results were kept secret and relatively few working class children were offered grammar school places even among those who were of comparable intelligence to successful middle class children. However, shortage of places meant disappointment for some middle class families too (thirteen per cent of eleven-year-olds were offered places in London, 29 per cent in Wales). Unless their families could afford to send them to private school, unsuccessful middle class children, too, had to share the common fate of 'failures' – and 'failure' was the term used. An educational system that had many more 'losers' than 'winners' was likely to cause widespread resentment.

It was not long before specific and detailed arguments against the tripartite system began to be presented. Criticism also focused on the content of the exam itself, as well as on the divisive effects of the tripartite system. Some authorities cast doubts on the validity of the aptitude and attainment tests frequently used in the exam. In local authorities in which teachers' reports were also used as a basis of selection, it was an easy matter to suggest that unfair and subjective judgement might decide a child's future. 'Deciding a child's future at eleven' was at the nub of the debate: eleven was widely considered to be too early to determine this issue. A child might have an 'off day' during the eleven-plus examination period; might not realise the importance of the exam; or be a 'late developer'. For those who accepted them, these arguments suggested the alternative to tripartite was of a non-selective or comprehensive system of secondary schooling. Those who favoured comprehensivisation did so because they believed that it would remove the damaging and unfair stigma of eleven-plus 'failure'.

Further, by enabling pupils of different social backgrounds to mix with each other, it was thought that a cultural 'rub-off' effect would occur, of particular benefit to working class children. The Labour government elected in 1964, issued Circular 10.65, inviting those local authorities which had not yet done so – still, in 1965, the large majority – to draw up schemes for comprehensive education. By the end of 1978, just over 80 per cent of state secondary education was organised along comprehensive lines, although some observers seriously doubt whether much more than 60 per cent are 'genuinely' comprehensive.

In assessing the performance of the comprehensive system, it must be realised that the term comprehensive covers many different types of school. The Leicestershire system, for instance, involves separate institutions for the eleven to fourteen age group, and for the fourteen to eighteen age group. More typically, south east Essex has 10 schools for eleven to sixteen year-olds which 'feed into' a single-site sixth form college. Despite the popularity of the sixth form colleges and of other 'sixteen-plus' colleges, the most common form of comprehensive is still the school for eleven to eighteen year-olds.

Has the comprehensive system improved the attainment levels of working class children? A H Heath

Supporters of comprehensivisation argued that the eleven-plus exam discriminated particularly against working class children. They believed that effective comprehensive education might partly reverse social class disadvantage so that by sixteen the public examination results of working class children might be better than under the tripartite system. Early comparisons of the overall performance of comprehensive schools and grammar/secondary schools in similar socio-economic situations showed little difference between the two (Eggleston 1975, National Children's Bureau, 1980). More recently (1987), Anthony Heath concludes that 'one of the most widespread myths in contemporary education is that comprehensive schools have sacrificed standards on the altar of equality' ('Class in the Classroom', *New Society*, July 17, 1987).

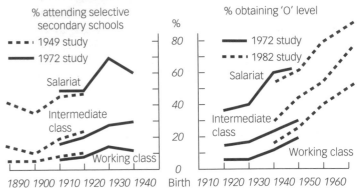

Notes:

1 *The reason why the lines for the 1949 and 1972 and the 1972 and 1982 studies are not continuous is that the studies used slightly different definitions of class.*

2 *The decade dates in the figure refer to birth groups – their examination results come eleven years (eleven-plus (a)) or sixteen years ('O' level (b)) later.*

3 *Each social class is given a percentage score to indicate the overall performance of its members in eleven-plus and 'O' level (in the case of each class grouping, the score has progressively improved but the difference in performance between class groupings has remained roughly the same).*

Figure 4.3 Social background and selective schooling

Heath specifically examines the issue of whether the attainment level of working class children has improved under the comprehensive system. Using data from three different studies (including, most recently, his own) he compares the attainment level of the children of the 'salariat' (higher class), intermediate class and working class from the beginning of the century to the early 1980s (Figure 4.3). The left hand side of the figure (a) compares the findings of the 1949 (Glass) on class origin and selective schooling with those of the 1972 (Halsey) study. The right hand side of the figure (b) compares the findings of the 1972 study on social class and 'O' levels obtained with those of the 1982 study (Heath). The figure looks somewhat complicated but its main message is simple. It is in Heath's words that:

> *... class inequalities first in access to selective secondary schools, then at O and next perhaps at A-level, have shown no overall tendency to decline ... (T)hey seem to reappear in a new guise but fundamentally unchanged as the educational environment changes around them.*

According to Heath's analysis, first the 1944 Act and then comprehensivisation has failed to shift the relative inequalities of attainment according to class:

> The evidence of the 1972 study showed that the social engineering of the 1944 Act had no measurable impact on class inequalities ... and in the mainly comprehensive period, the 1982 study showed that the inequalities in examination success are very similar to those already documented in access to selective schools.

Heath offers two explanations for the stubbornness of relative educational inequalities. First, the reforms were not as radical as they were sometimes presented. Second, educationally ambitious families are generally able to 'play the system', whatever it happens to be, especially those who are able to afford private education for their children.

It is worth elaborating on the first point. The 1944 Act did nothing directly to equalise class inequalities except require all children to remain in full-time education until fifteen and to make state education free. Indeed, the eleven-plus represented a built-in disadvantage for working class children. Often, too, comprehensive reform was too mild to affect class disadvantage

Very important in judging where a school is genuinely comprehensive is its internal system of academic organisation. These vary widely. Some schools 'stream' pupils rigidly – 'tripartite under the same roof' as their critics would say – whilst others use mixed ability teaching for most, if not all, classes. Many would say the former are not really comprehensive. Similarly, pastoral or tutor systems (concerned with general pupil welfare and discipline) can vary greatly in quality. Tutor groups which contain children from a variety of social and, where relevant, racial backgrounds are closest to the comprehensive spirit. However, a study of Julienne Ford suggested that children are more likely to make friends on the basis of academic rather than pastoral groupings. Middle class children, who were a majority in the upper academic groupings, tended to associate with each other, and the same applied to the working class children in the lower academic groupings.

A refutation of Heath: A McPherson and J Willms

On the basis of their own separate research, Andrew McPherson and J Douglas Willms disagree with Heath's conclusion about the ineffectiveness of the comprehensive system in equalising attainment between working and middle class children:

> Anthony Heath says that research has shown that comprehensive reorganisation, in common with other educational reforms this century, has made little impact on social-class inequalities in British education (New Society, 17 July 1987). He is not correct to say this about comprehensive reorganisation, nor to conclude that, 'in the face of this remarkable resilience of class inequalities, educational reforms seem powerless, whether for good or ill'.
>
> (A McPherson and J Willms, 1988)

McPherson and Willms carried out their research in Scotland. They state that although social class differences in attainment remained roughly stable in Scotland (as well as in England) for several decades after 1945, their own more recent research (1987) 'has a different and more up-to-date story to tell about comprehensive schooling'. If anything, the statistical aspects of their study are more complex than those of Heath's, but, again, their findings are straightforward and can be listed as follows:

1 Average attainment between 1976 and 1984 increased across all social class groups.
2 There are still large social class differences in attainment.
3 Attainment has been rising faster among lower groups. For Example:
   i The skilled manual improved their performance in relation to the intermediate by roughly half an ordinary grade.
   ii Overall, working class pupils improved their performance in relation to middle class schools by about half an ordinary grade.
   iii Pupils of average socio-economic background attained higher, the longer the school had been an all-through comprehensive.

Importantly, McPherson and Willms also argue that Heath's data can also be interpreted as showing the beginnings of an improvement at 'O' level in the performance of working class children in relation to the children of the salariat. What is clear, therefore, is the need for further research on the effects of established comprehensive schools and local comprehensive systems on pupils' attainment.

The comprehensive system and attainment: conclusion

The following points can be made reflecting current research on the comprehensive system:

1 Average attainment across all social classes has continued to improve under the comprehensive system as it did prior to comprehensivisation (since 1945).
2 The rate of improvement in pupil attainment in other industrialised nations (e.g. Germany, France, Japan) has tended to be greater than in Britain.

3 It is possible, even likely, that the relative attainment of working class to middle class children has recently begun to improve as a result of comprehensivisation.

4 Attempts radically to change the comprehensive system or reverse further progress towards it *may* occur just as it appears to be beginning to increase its effectiveness.

Compensatory education: an example of positive discrimination

The principle behind compensatory education is to provide additional educational or education-related help to those who are socially disadvantaged.

Like many recent progressive initiatives in post-war education and social work, compensatory education was first tried in the United States. There, the major motive was to compensate those who had been deprived for racial reasons, whereas in Britain, the focus has been on compensating for general social disadvantage (though in the inner cities this has included large numbers of black people). Compensatory education was often justified by *cultural deprivation theory*. Some who put forward this view, such as Charlotte K Brooks, seem to assume the inferiority of working class culture, and not surprisingly have been criticised. On the other hand, growing evidence that much of the cause of the relative educational under-achievement of working class children lay in their social background argued for intervention. Socialist, Eric Butterworth expressed his objection to being 'put into jackboots' for supporting pre-school nurseries and school-home contact for the disadvantaged.

As early as 1956, a 'demonstration guidance project' was established in New York, to provide extra educational support for intelligent children of the deprived racial minorities. It seemed a success and similar programmes followed, but with the difference that they included the whole ability range. In 1965, the Johnson government included a 'Head Start' programme in its policies of social reform. As its name suggests, the purpose of 'Head Start' was mainly to prepare disadvantaged minority children for school by giving them special pre-school help.

Assessments of Head Start vary. The principle criteria used in the follow-up studies in evaluating success were gains in IQ and improvement in academic performance. On both counts the results of the initial follow-up studies were disappointing. IQ gains tended to be short-term, and there was little difference in attainment between the Head Start children and others of similar background. The hereditarians in the nature-nurture debate have cited this as evidence that intelligence and even educational performance cannot be significantly improved by 'environmental engineering'. Others have viewed the matter differently. Hunt argues that some schemes in the Head Start programme were inappropriate to the needs of the children they were supposed to help. Apparently, the curricula adopted often assumed considerable competence in the verbal and numerical skills that it

was the object of the programmes to teach! This was because available curriculum material reflected the needs and attainment of middle class children who normally had virtually exclusive access to pre-school education. Several better-designed pre-school programmes have, in fact, achieved lasting gains. A prominent feature of some of these has been the close involvement of the children's mothers, but Bereiter and Engelmann report several successful projects not involving direct maternal participation. Frequently, these involved a special stress on developing linguistic skills. A later (1976-77) and more comprehensive follow-up of Head Start by Lazar and Darlington showed an average reduction of academic failure in project children of 36.4 per cent. It must be noted, however, that their findings were based on better pre-school projects, and not from a random sample of Head Start projects. They are not, therefore, representative of the whole original Head Start population.

In a useful review of the evidence relating to Head Start, Harry McGurk adds a cautionary note. He points out that both mothers and children often got considerable pleasure out of Head Start schemes and increased their confidence as a result of being involved in the programmes. This is important in itself. As McGurk says, there are other values than that of improving IQ scores.

The Educational Priority Area (EPA) programme, has been Britain's major effort in the field of compensatory education. The EPAs embodied the principle of positive discrimination (that extra help should be given to the socially disadvantaged) advocated by the Plowden Report of 1967. The EPA projects were set up by the Labour Secretary of State for Education and Science, Anthony Crosland. They were located in London, Birmingham, Liverpool and the West Riding of Yorkshire. On the basis of their exploratory work, they recommended positive discrimination, especially in the form of pre-schooling, in their report to government in 1971. Plowden aside, the main propagandist and theorist of positive discrimination in Britain has been A H Halsey. The policy of positive discrimination has not been short of critics however and we will briefly review their comments before returning to Halsey's defence.

Criticism and defence of compensatory education

First is a powerful criticism of the limited scope of positive discrimination based on analysis initially put forward by Barnes and Lucas, but later reiterated by Peter Townsend. They correctly point out that although particular areas of geographical concentration of poverty do exist, the majority of the poor are scattered throughout the country and outside these areas. As a result, positive discrimination can miss the needs of the majority and serve as a smoke screen for penny-pinching by government. Barnes and Lucas refer to the 'ecological fallacy' underlying the EPA approach: a policy that is generated through area analysis rather than the needs of specific social groups.

The above observations partly provide the basis for a more

fundamental criticism by Townsend. He argues that policies of positive discrimination tend to be merely cosmetic whilst the real causes of disadvantage and poverty remain untouched. In his view, these causes are national in scope and structural in nature. He demands industrial, employment, housing and land policies which will radically redistribute wealth and systematically reduce, if not abolish, poverty. In order to illustrate his point, he draws on the experience of an exercise in positive discrimination outside education, the Community Development Project. In particular, the Coventry CDP group argued that in the face of national or even international factors which affected the local context in which they worked, they could do relatively little. For example, a few community workers could not deal with the consequences of thousands being thrown out of work as a result of a recession in car production. They contended that only a national policy of economic redevelopment and social justice could cope. This kind of analysis has received support from the American, Christopher Jencks, in his book *Inequality*.

Basil Bernstein's controversial article, *Education Cannot Compensate for Society* (1970), was concerned with the cultural aspects rather than socio-economics of positive discrimination. The essence of his criticism is that compensatory education implies that working class culture is in some sense inferior. The policy implications of this are to direct attention away from the quality of schools and curricula towards supposed inadequacies in working class families. Bernstein suggests that is the wrong emphasis. He argues that it is more important to put right the mainstream of the educational system than to over-concentrate on marginal 'compensatory' reforms. He argues that curriculum reform is needed to take into account the way working class children live their lives – the 'conditions' and 'contexts' of their culture should affect everyday education as much as do those of the middle class. Bernstein is surely correct in this central point. Educational change that does not affect the main curriculum is likely to be of only peripheral influence.

A H Halsey has consistently defended compensatory education against its critics. The starkly assertive title of an article he published in 1980 is *Education Can Compensate*, and it is clearly intended as a reply to Bernstein's piece of ten years before. He especially emphasises the reassuring American evidence of Lazar and Darlington. He stresses that, given enthusiasm and careful organisation, a pre-school programme of compensatory education can be a 'crucial weapon' of government policy. He fully accepts, however, that the mainstream of the educational system must also be fair and effective as well. Thus, he continues passionately to support comprehensive education. For their part, his Marxist critics continue to wonder whether educational reform can significantly help the disadvantaged in the absence of fundamental social and economic change.

Private education, inequality and elite reproduction

It remains substantially true that Britain is run by middle aged or older white males of upper or upper middle class origins. This section proposes to examine the role of private schools, particularly so-called public schools such as Eton and Harrow, in the system of elite reproduction, and their wider effect on British culture and society. This is a controversial and under-researched area but it is quite central to understanding British education and society.

Private education: the facts

According to Geoffrey Walford (1993), there were 2,287 registered private schools in England in 1991. These educated about 7.4% of the school population although for the sixteen-plus age group, the figure was 19.6% (no doubt reflecting the importance of 'A' levels for university entrance). About 53 per cent of private school pupils are male and 47 per cent female with co-educational establishments growing somewhat at the expense of single sex schools in recent years. There is considerable variety in the private school sector, including some progressive schools in which students usually participate in the running of the institution. The most radical of these is Summerhill founded by the libertarian, A S Neill.

However in terms of national influence it is the misleadingly named public schools which matter. These schools educate less than one per cent of the total school population, but as Walford says, they have had an 'historic position in educating the nation's elite'. Public school status is acquired through membership of the Headmasters' Conference (HMC) and in 1993, the HMC had 233 members. In practice, it is the top 20 or so public schools such as Winchester, Marlborough, Eton and Harrow which provide privileged access to future power, position and wealth. Many children attending private schools outside this elite group are not from especially wealthy backgrounds nor greatly advantaged by their private education. An increasing number of HMC schools are co-educational. In 1995 Rugby appointed its first female head-girl – amid an explosion of protest from some male students! In girls' private education, the Girls Schools Association (GSA) is considered roughly equivalent to the HMC. However, despite the impressive academic performance of many girls in private education, there is no major sign yet that they will challenge ex-public school boys in national power and influence – even in a modest way. The days may be gone when privately educated girls were taught mainly to think in terms of equipping themselves with the skills necessary for a 'good marriage' but equality of access to privilege and power with males is not apparent either.

Public schools and elite domination: a gendered elite

The very high representation of ex-public school males in the so-called 'great' professions, in politics and in finance is striking. Not only are the percentages high but as Table 4.3 suggests, they have remained so over a long period of time. The data is from various sources and about different elite professions but provides a useful general picture.

Table 4.3 Ex-public school males in the 'great' professions

Occupations	1971	1984	1990s
	Percentage from public schools		
Conservative Cabinet	77.7	N/A	85 (1990)
Navy	88.9	N/A	N/A
Army	86.1	N/A	N/A
Top Judiciary	80.2	84	84 (1991)
Bank Directors	N/A*	70	N/A
Top Civil Servants	N/A	49	N/A

N/A: not available

(Sources: Figures for 1971 (Scott, 1991); for 1984 (Reid *et al.*, 1991); for 1990s – judiciary (Byers, 1991; *The Guardian*, 12.10.1992). *Not available from these sources)

As Geoffrey Walford points out, just because ex-public school males tend to dominate occupational elites today does not mean that they will do so 20 or 50 years hence. However, as about 50 per cent of home-undergraduate places at Oxford and Cambridge are taken up by students from public schools, it is a reasonable guess that matters will not greatly change. Gerard McCrum has referred to 'a growing take-over of the 'old' universities by public schools' (TES, 14.3.95:7). What seems to be happening, then, is that the better off middle class are securing a route to the elite occupations via the independent schools and the 'older' universities – particularly Oxford and Cambridge but also, notably, Durham and Bristol. Interestingly, McCrum notes that since 1972 the numbers of females from independent schools entering university arts courses increased four-fold and it may be that larger numbers of them will be established in the elite occupations in a generation or so. However, what will certainly limit elite penetration by privately educated females is the continuing higher attainment level of boys over girls schools in this sector (see Table 4.4). The top 4 schools (all boys) have 'led the league' since it was established in 1992. Thus inequality of attainment between females and males from public schools is even greater at degree level at Oxford and Cambridge – which remain the main conduit to the British elite.

Table 4.4 Independent school A level results = Top 20 1994-95 (*ranked by UCAS points where A = 10, B = 8, ... E = 2. AS grades count half, e.g. A = 5. First figure is number of candidates*)

Gender	School	Pupils	Points
B	Winchester College, Winchester	136	31.9
B	St Paul's School, London	141	31.8
B	Westminster School, London	132	31.4
B	Eton College, Windsor	240	29.5
B	Royal Grammar School, Guildford	107	29.0
B	King's College School, London	131	28.7
G	North London Collegiate School, The, Edgware	106	28.6
G	Lady Eleanor Holles School, The, Hampton	87	28.3
B	Haberdashers' Aske's School, The, Borehamwood	152	28.2
G	St Paul's Girls' School, London	101	28.2
B	Manchester Grammar School, Manchester	200	27.8
G	King Edward VI High School for Girls, Birmingham	73	27.4
B	Radley College, Abingdon	127	27.2
C	Sevenoaks School (IB exams), Sevenoaks	69	27.1
G	Wycombe Abbey School, High Wycombe	55	27.0
G	Haberdashers' Askes School for Girls, Elstree	114	26.9
G	Perse School for Girls, Cambridge	51	26.9
G	St Mary's School, Calne	43	26.9
C	King's School, Canterbury	139	26.5
B	Royal Grammar School, Newcastle-upon-Tyne	147	26.5

Average points per pupil
B: boys, G: girls, C: co-educational
(Source: *The Guardian*, 26.8.1995:6 – adapted)

How public schools contribute to elite reproduction

Three ways in which the public schools contribute to elite reproduction can be suggested.

1 They offer academic advantage.
2 They provide suitable general socialisation for elite participation.
3 They provide useful contacts.

1 Academic advantage

In general, independent schools offer better facilities and equipment and a better teacher-pupil ratio than state schools. They do so because they can afford these advantages. Gerard McCrum observes that 'independent secondary schools now spend two-thirds more on educating each pupil than state schools and were able to increase their fees well above the inflation rate in the 1980s. This may help to explain their growing dominance'. (TES, 1995)

2 General socialisation: character formation

The 'public school type' has provoked both ridicule and admiration, hatred and jealousy. It is not surprising that the traditionally tough academic and physical regimes of public schools should have generated strong reactions both among those who have been subject to them and among a wider public. Observation would suggest that the public schools are often successful in engendering confidence and an inclination if not necessarily a capacity for leadership. The adage that 'the battle of Waterloo was won on the playing fields of Eton' may be a cliché but it indicates the link between the public schools and British military and imperial leadership. The ex-public school boys who have largely led Britain in its imperial and post-imperial periods may often have been self-interested but they were often formidable. Their successors today may have toned down the public school style somewhat but it would be naive to underestimate their determination to maintain their access to power.

In general, the ethos of public schools is socially and politically conservative. That is to be expected given their pivotal role in converting social/cultural capital into occupational and political power and position. The zaniness and creative nonconformity of some public school pupils rarely leads them ultimately to forsake the route to renewed wealth and high status that their elders have mapped out for them. The public school comic humour of Peter Cooke and Dudley Moore and of Monty Python may nibble but won't bite the hand that feeds it. Similarly, the innumerable novels and plays that criticise, the more sadistic and macho side of public school life may, at best, have contributed to some humanisation of the institution without affecting its basic function of elite reproduction.

3 Contacts: the old boy network

In addition to the character attributes inculcated by public schools, the more elite ones often provide a formidable network of contacts. It is difficult empirically to measure the value of contacts or to demonstrate precisely how they work to advantage because they often operate informally and discreetly. However, friendships and associations made at public school may well give a crucial career edge to some of the 50 per cent of Oxbridge home-undergraduates of public-school background compared to those from state schools. This hypothesis is not proven but is strongly suggested by the dominance of ex-public school boys in elite areas of national life. Discrimination in favour of a contact in, say, a job appointment may occur unconsciously. Impersonal and fair interview procedures may be formally observed but at the level of personal rapport perhaps those in position tend to prefer people of similar cultural background to themselves. This may be 'justified' on the basis of 'the right kind of person' getting the job. Walter Ellis, author of *The Oxbridge Conspiracy* (1994) argues that in the 1990s, Oxbridge students are still 'apprenticed rigorously to the Establishment' (5). For instance, whatever the explanation, in 1993-94, Oxbridge put in 904 of the applications for the Civil Service fast stream and got 40 per cent of the places.

In practice, however, the old boy network seems generally to operate in a taken-for-granted way without much need for self-justification. Figure 4.4 shows the location of most of the principal London clubs for those of varying elite backgrounds and occupations. There the line between sociability, business and helping one's fellow man must be as blurred as the view from the smoking rooms.

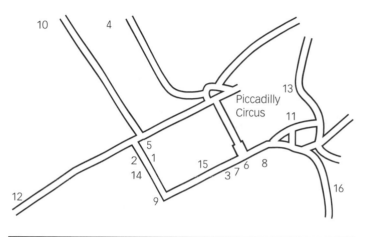

Clubs ranked by fees	Founded	Address
1 Boodle's	1762	St James's St SW1
2 Brooks's	1764	St James's St SW1
3 Reform	1836	Pall Mall, SW1
4 Buck's	1919	Clifford St, W1
5 White's	1693	St James's, SW1
6 Athenaeum	1824	Pall Mall, SW1
7 Travellers'	1819	Pall Mall, SW1
8 Turf	1868	Carlton House Terr., SW1
9 Carlton	1832	St James's St., SW1
10 Savile	1868	Brook St, W1
11 City of London	1832	Old Broad St, EC2
12 Cavalry and Guards	1893	Piccadilly, W1
13 Beefsteak	1876	Irving St, WC2
14 Pratt's	1841	Park Place, SW1
15 Army and Navy	1837	Pall Mall, SW1
16 National Liberal	1882	Whitehall Place, SW1

The clubs are ranked in approximate order of their annual subscriptions. All except the City of London Club are shown by number on the sketch map.

Figure 4.4 Principal London clubs: the networking of the British elite

Class, power and the public schools

The public schools function to reproduce upper class wealth, power and status but they do not create them. The basis of the position of the upper class is its material and cultural capital. It is the wealth of the upper class which enables it to create the public school system which serves to maintain its position.

It is relevant here only to touch on the nature of upper class power as this issue is discussed elsewhere (see pp. 165-8 and pp. 312-4). Marxists consider that the upper class is also a ruling class (see Miliband, 1969). Liberal pluralists recognise that the upper class occupies disproportionate economic and political power and position but nevertheless consider that it does so within a society which is fundamentally a representative democracy. Earlier in this section, we looked at the domination of ex-public school males in elite occupations, including top political careers (although far fewer Labour than Conservative MPs have attended public school). This domination is in itself a striking inequality in Britain's national life and we will shortly consider what, if anything, should be done about it.

Immediately, however, we will examine some other possible direct effects of the public school system on British society and culture.

Effects of the public school system

Two arguable effects of the public school system are discussed below: the role of the public schools in the development of an anti-industrial culture in Britain and their contribution to a culture of deference and parochialism in the rest of the population.

The Weiner thesis: the public schools and anti-industrialisation

Martin Weiner's *English Culture and the Decline of the Industrial Spirit* (1981) argues that aristocratic values and influence prevented the development of a full-blooded industrial culture in Britain. He states that the self-made industrial bourgeoisie sent their sons to the Victorian public schools not to learn to be industrialists but to be gentlemen:

> *The ethos of the schools, in keeping with their surroundings, exalted the careers coloured by the aristocratic ideals of honour and public leadership - the military, politics, the civil service, and the higher professions. Public school boys made excellent administrators of a far-flung empire, but the training so admirably suited for that task ill-fitted that for economic leadership. The public schools nurtured the future elite's political, not economic, abilities and a desire to maintain stability and order far outweighed the desire to maximise individual or national wealth.*
>
> (Weiner, 1981:21)

Weiner does not find the same opposition among the newly rich to their offspring working in banking and finance in the City of London as to their working in industry (Table 4.3 suggests this is also true of later generations). In this context, W B Rubinstein points out that the financial bourgeoisie was more significant economically and socially than the industrial bourgeoisie – before, after and during the industrial revolution. In this respect, he finds the emphasis of the Weiner thesis somewhat biased and argues that elite preference for finance over industry has much wider origins than the snobbishness of the industrial bourgeoisie or the aristocratic obsessions of the public schools. Rubinstein's historical interpretation of the place of industry in the national economy may be correct but it is also clear that the public schools contributed little to improving the long term relative weakness of Britain's manufacturing industry. Later, we discuss the attempts under Margaret Thatcher to confront this issue (see pp. 120-5).

Elite leadership and popular deference and parochialism

The argument discussed in this section is that the conservative culture of England's elite, notably as expressed through the public schools and Oxbridge, is largely responsible for the creation of a conservative national culture in England. Weiner himself develops this analysis in relation to the broad middle classes in England and I suggest that it can be extended – with modifications – to the working class.

As far as the middle classes were concerned the effect of the public schools and lifestyle was that of imitation. Weiner points out that although in the inter-war years only about one in twenty Englishman passed through them, the public schools 'became an archetypal national institution'. He quotes Roy Lewis and Angus Maude's observation that the public schools 'enjoyed an invisible empire among the middle classes, who avidly read the new genre of public school literature' (for instance, Billy Bunter and Biggles books). Weiner goes on to say: 'Those who could afford it, sent their sons (to public schools); those who could not, sought a grammar school as close as possible to the public school model.' (21)

The children of the large majority of the population did not go to grammar schools, however. After the second world war, most of them went instead to secondary modern schools from which they progressed into manual or routine non-manual work. Direct imitation of the upper and upper middle classes – even in watered down form – was not an option for them. Nevertheless, they were and are influenced by the dominant traditional and conservative upper class culture. Two strands of response among the working class can briefly be indicated here.

First, a sizeable minority of working class people have long been impressed by the upper class. Marxists would refer to this as a form of 'false consciousness'. Some regard the upper class as their 'natural leaders' and, politically, make up what is sometimes referred to as the deferential working class Tory vote. Second, a larger proportion of the working class developed an authentically original class culture which reacted self-defensively and protectively against the upper classes (aristocratic and bourgeois). Politically, the main expression of this reaction was support for the Labour party and, industrially, for the trade unions. The progressive minority of the middle class tended to support the labour movement and supplied many of its political leaders (sometimes diluting the movement's socialist philosophy in the process).

However, despite the above opposition, the dominant social and political culture in Britain has remained conservative. In contrast to the Scandinavian and several other Western European countries in which the labour movement and reforming middle classes have produced a progressive, modernising culture, Britain retains a huge and expensive monarchy, an unrepresentative House of Lords, and is run to a great extent by a privileged elite generally opposed to the kind of participatory institutions the rest of Western Europe largely takes for granted. Ironically, the strongest recent challenge to Britain's traditional elite has come from the free-market wing of the Conservative party rather than from the left, which since 1979 has been preoccupied with its own internal problems. Under Margaret Thatcher, the free marketeers or New Right attempted to generate a new 'entrepreneurial culture' to replace both 'labourism' and traditional elitism/defence. Aided by the right-wing press, the Thatcherites attacked both socialism and, less systematically, certain citadels of ex-public school domination such as the higher reaches of the civil service. However, although the Thatcherite reforms may have opened up Britain's elites to some new talent (see pp. 165-7), particularly talent with a business orientation, the signs are that Britain's traditional elite and traditionally conservative national culture remains largely intact.

The continuing power and status of the ex-public school elite is not difficult to understand in that the institutional and social links from boyhood to manhood are, as described above, quite obvious. Less easy to explain is the ideological and cultural hegemony (decisive sway) of the ex-public school elite over much of the rest of the population. Two reasons for this can briefly be offered here. First, the Conservative party has quite effectively presented itself as the party of 'one nation' as opposed to merely a class-based party. Historically, the Conservatives have used the ideology of nation and empire to appeal beyond class boundaries. Such an approach was notably successful when the Falklands war reversed Margaret Thatcher's declining fortunes and gained her an electoral landslide. Nationalism remains a potent force in English culture and politics and almost inevitably has the effect of distancing the English from wider currents of European and global concern. To that extent nationalism has a parochial, narrowing effect on English culture and society. Second, and relatedly, given that a country must have leaders, then, ex-public school males are in a highly advantageous position to present themselves as well-equipped and trained to lead. Whether the image of 'natural leader' still carries much weight with the electorate is a moot point but surveys often show that the Tories are generally regarded as economically more competent and stronger on law and order.

End them, mend them or leave them alone?

The arguments for abolishing the public schools can be briefly stated. They are highly inegalitarian and make the development of a society based on equality of opportunity impossible. Second, as described above, they spawn an enormous cultural influence utterly disproportionate to their size.

The introduction of the Assisted Places Scheme by the Conservatives in 1981 perhaps implies tacit acceptance of their inegalitarian nature and effects. The scheme was designed to allow selected clever children who otherwise could not afford to do so, to attend academically selective, fee-paying schools. The scheme costs over £100 million a year, involves 350 schools, and in 1995 paid for the fees of 33,000 pupils. Research suggests that the scheme most benefits 'sunken' or less well-off middle class families but some working class families also benefit. So, of course, do the schools themselves who acquire able students, reliably paid for, and are able to claim a slightly wider social basis to their in-take. As APS pupils are only a small fraction of one per cent of state sector pupils, the effects on the state sector would seem to be a slight creaming of its most academically able pupils and the implied slur that the state sector is second best.

It is Labour party policy to abolish the Assisted Places Scheme. Labour would also withdraw charitable status from independent schools from which they gain considerable tax advantages. However, it is not Labour party policy to abolish the independent sector itself. One argument for this position is the libertarian one – enshrined in European law – that citizens should have the right to set up alternative educational institutions to those provided by the state. A second argument is more pragmatic. It is that if the public schools were abolished, the rich and well-connected would simply seek privileged education for their children outside of Britain and perhaps also take their expertise and wealth elsewhere. Third, is perhaps the fear that a country so long run largely by a privileged elite would not prosper so well if it were replaced by a less experienced more meritocratic one.

In 1995 several commentators suggested that Labour tackle the 'problem' of the public schools by enticing as many as possible back into the state sector. However, it seems to be assumed that the price needed to be paid for this, would be to allow the schools thus enticed, to retain selective status. Such a policy might advantage academically able children from less privileged backgrounds but would do nothing for the majority.

One can see why there is only limited public and political support for the abolition of the public schools. They are formidable institutions and their abolition would have profound consequences. However, there are precedents for putting controversial issues on the political agenda and then doing something about them. Margaret Thatcher's privatisation programme is one example. It remains to be seen whether the abolition of the public schools will be another.

Question

What is the relationship of the public schools to British society?

Gender in education

This section is divided into two parts. First, the academic attainment of females and males is compared and explanations for the differences briefly discussed. Second, the main perspectives on gender and education are introduced and discussed. Each perspective is based on a particularly ideological approach which is reflected in both analysis of the current situation and policy suggestions for change.

Percentages

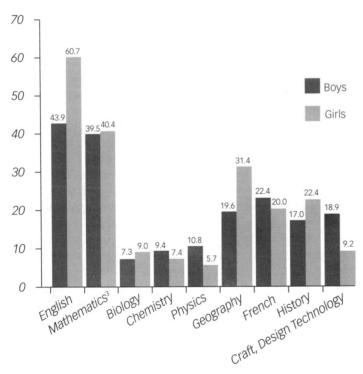

1 16-year-olds (year 4 in Scotland)
2 SCE standard grades in Scotland
3 Excluding Computer Science (England) and Computer Studies and Statistics (Wales) (in which boys do better)

(Source: *Regional Trends*, 1995)

Figure 4.5 Pupils[1] achieving GCSE[2] grades A–C: by selected subject and sex, 1992–1993, GB

Number of full-time university undergraduates (UK domiciled)

English	Males 3,200 / Females 6,800
Mathematics	Males 5,900 / Females 3,000
Biology	Males 3,300 / Females 4,400
French	Males 900 / Females 3,000
History	Males 6,400 / Females 5,600
Chemistry	Males 5,900 / Females 3,200
Physics	Males 5,900 / Females 1,300
Computer Studies	Males 6,600 / Females 900

■ Males
■ Females

(Source: *Some Facts About Women*, 1994)

Figure 4.6 Full-time undergraduates at GB universities, selected subjects, 1992-1993, by sex

Gender and educational attainment

Concern about gender and educational attainment focuses mainly on the extent to which females and males perform differently in different subjects and their tendency to study different subjects, given the choice. However, it is not true that males generally attain more qualifications or higher grades than females at school. In fact, the reverse is the case. In 1987/88, 62 per cent of females left school in the United Kingdom with at least one GCSE grade A-C or equivalent whereas the figure for males was 54 per cent. On the basis of similar figures, females now also perform slightly better at 'A' level but not by some other measures (see Figure 4.8).

Figure 4.5 shows the percentage of school levers with grade A-C at GCSE by subject and sex in 1992-93. The stronger performance of females in languages, including English, and Biology, and the stronger performance of males in Maths, Physics and Chemistry has been long entrenched but has changed during the late 1980s and 1990s with girls closing the maths, 'hard' sciences gap.

Figure 4.6 gives the breakdown of national curriculum subjects studied at university by sex. It frequently goes unnoticed that differential subject specialisation is actually much greater at university than school level. Figure 4.7 gives subject specialisation at degree level for a slightly earlier period but provides more details. Females makes up about five per cent of those studying engineering and 22 per cent of those studying mathematical sciences. In contrast, they represent over 60 per cent of students in languages, librarianship, biological sciences, creative arts, studies allied to medicine and about 80 per cent of those in education.

The subject specialisms in which females predominate, especially the more vocational ones such as education and librarianship, parallel the tendency of better qualified women to enter the lower professions rather than the better paid higher professions (see p. 201). This is by no means always because they are not qualified to study subjects likely to lead to higher paid occupations. Even within the lower professions, females disproportionately occupy less senior posts (see Chapter 7, p. 201). To what extent the educational and vocational paths typical of better qualified females reflect the way they think of themselves is discussed below. It is also relevant to consider whether a country short of engineers and scientists, can afford to 'lose' able females to these areas (see Table 4.5).

Note: In some professions, current recruitment to training (see Figure 4.7) suggests a somewhat more equal gender balance will gradually develop e.g. in architecture, and medicine and dentistry.

It is not only better qualified females who experience occupational stereotyping. Females with minimal or no qualifications are likely to do unskilled manual work in particular occupational areas and those somewhat better qualified are likely to do routine office work (see p. 202). How education can contribute to occupational sex stereotyping is a major theme in the following pages.

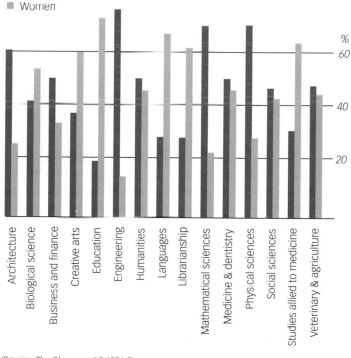

(Source: *The Observer*, 4.2.1991:9)

Figure 4.7 Degrees of difference: how the gender divide affected subjects studied by full-time university undergraduates in 1989-90

Table 4.5 Women in professions

	Men	Women		Men	Women
	Percentages			Percentages	
Accountants	90.3	9.7	Engineers	99.5	0.5
Architects	92.2	7.8	Solicitors	78.6	21.4
Barristers	79.8	21.2	Surveyors	94.3	5.7
Dentists	76.8	23.2	Vets	73.5	26.5
Doctors (GPs)	77.6	22.4			
(Surgeons)	96.8	3.2			

(Source: UK Inter-professional Group, 1990)

Gender, education and the curriculum: perspectives

Sandra Acker usefully suggests that there are three main Western feminist theoretical frameworks – liberal, radical and socialist – each of which have an application to education. However, this typology does not include some traditional and/or politically conservative thinking on gender and education which, for convenience, will be referred to here simply as 'conservative' – with a small 'c'. We will also briefly look at Gaby Weiner's recent suggestions that a poststructuralist feminism can both unify and guide the practical application (praxis) of feminism in education (1994).

The five theoretical areas to be considered are, then:

• liberal
• radical
• socialist
• conservative
• poststructuralist

Gaby Weiner and Madeleine Arnot have suggested that as far as teacher's practice is concerned a simple polarity between an equal opportunities/girl friendly approach and an anti-sexist/girl-centred approach occurs. However, as we shall see later, Weiner and Arnot do not consider their own and Acker's typology to be mutually exclusive.

Liberal feminism and education

The basis of liberal feminism is a commitment to equal opportunities for males and females. The Sex Discrimination Act of 1975 has generally been interpreted to mean that females are entitled to the same treatment as males in the main areas of public life including education. The Equal Opportunities Commission (EOC) has responsibility for implementing the Sex Discrimination Act, including taking relevant cases to law.

With the passing of the 1975 Act, it was made clear for the first time that the formal, public and legal position in Britain was opposed to sex discrimination just as the Race Relations Acts had done so in respect to racial discrimination (sport and single sex schools were exempt from the terms of the Sex Discrimination Act). Since the Act was passed, the previously widespread practice whereby schools required females to study certain subjects and males to study others became illegal and virtually ceased. The Act not only banned sexual discrimination (direct and indirect or unintended) but also encouraged the active promotion of equal opportunity. Some commentators such as A Dora (1985) have stressed the potential of the Act to legitimate strong policies of equal opportunity.

Others have been more critical of what they consider to be the limited practical effect of the Act on gender equality in schools. Thus, Madeleine Arnot considers that while the EOC has often effectively intervened with local education authorities to prevent curriculum differentiation between the sexes, it has done relatively little to promote anti-sexist projects and has been 'disappointing for those who wish to see greater evidence of sex equality in schooling – i.e. improvements in the quality of schooling for girls and in the experience of women teachers' ('Political lip-service or radical reform' in M Arnot and G Weiner eds., *Gender and the Politics of Schooling* (Hutchinson, 1987)). As we shall see, these kind of initiatives have occurred more through individual teachers, groups, schools and sometimes local education authorities.

The terms of the Sex Discrimination Act applicable to education did represent an important clarification of principle and guide to practice. Previous major pronouncements by government on gender and education had been at best ambiguous and, at worst, reinforced a highly traditional version of roles and expectations. Ann Marie Wolpe's analysis of the 'gender content' of three government reports on aspects of secondary education – *The Norwood Report* (1943), *The Crowther Report* (1959) and *The Newson Report* (1963) – makes this point strongly:

> *In conclusion it can be said that none of the three reports considered the reality of the situation which applies to such a large proportion of women, viz as workers outside the home. Their focus on women and marriage provides them with a means of extricating themselves from this situation. The stated overriding concern of girls with their future marriages provides them with the means of legitimation for this omission. Having established this dichotomy between the world of work and marriage all three reports are able to provide an ideological basis for the perpetuation of an education system which does not open up new vistas or possibilities to the majority of girls.*
>
> *(Wolpe in Flude and Ahier, 1976:141)*

Radical-feminism and education

Radical-feminists consider that patriarchy – the system of domination of females by males – is the central issue for women. In their view, patriarchy permeates the whole of society and the whole of the educational system. They therefore address and attempt to confront sex-bias not only in the allocation of the subject curriculum to females and males but in all aspects of the educational system. It will be helpful to look at this in terms of the cultural reproduction of patriarchy and the structure of patriarchy in each case both within education and society.

Dale Spender has analysed the cultural reproduction of patriarchy in several publications of which perhaps the most relevant to education is *Invisible Women: The Schooling Scandal* (Writers and Readers Co-operative, 1982). She finds patriarchal assumptions in both the formal and hidden curriculum. About the former, she writes:

> *What is considered inherently interesting is knowledge about men. Because men control the records, and the value system, it is generally believed that it is men who have done all the exciting things: it is men who have made history, made discoveries, made inventions and performed feats of skill and courage – according to men. These are the important activities and only men have engaged in them, so we are led to believe. And so it is that the activities of men become the curriculum.*
>
> *(Spender, 1982:58)*

Spender is equally concerned to uncover the processes within the hidden or informal curriculum that maintain and reproduce patriarchy. She finds that teachers, often unconsciously, behave towards males and females in ways which reinforce the self-concepts of the former as dominant and the latter is submissive. Thus, her video-tapes of lessons frequently show teachers paying substantially more attention to boys (partly in response to boys' demands) even when boys are in a minority in the class.

Radical-feminists seek to raise girls' awareness of the structure of patriarchy in schools, the workplace and within families. One strategy for doing this is establishing female discussion and support groups in which patriarchy can be examined, and the confidence and skills of females to combat it, developed. Support groups and also less formal networking among female teachers can be helpful in dealing with such matters as female career advancement in male dominated institutions, 'routine' sexism and sexual harassment.

Some radical feminists, including Dale Spender, have argued that single-sex schools or classes can be beneficial to girls as they remove the negative influence of boys referred to above (see Figure 4.8). There is some debated evidence that more females chose to study scientific subjects in single sex institutions and that their attainment is better (however, the EOC cites data to suggest that other factors – such as selection – account for these trends). Others argue that separating females from males is hardly a good

Percentage entering university arts courses with AAA/AAB grades, with performance of state boys held constant

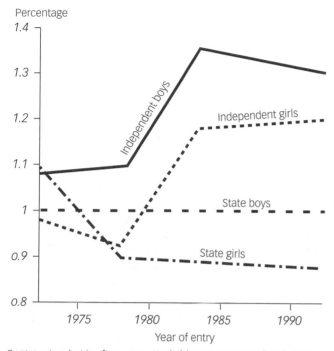

Contrary to what is often suggested girls are not outperforming boys academically by all or even most significant measures. Matters are complex. In a twenty year period to the early 1990s, state school boys improved their relative position to state school girls at the very top end of those who went on to enter university arts courses (stereotypically considered a 'female' subject area for females). Independent schools girls – more often educated in single sex schools – did much better.

This trend among high achievers has important implications for entry in Britain's national and local elites – which look likely to remain significantly upper and upper middle class in origin – and patriarchal – for the foreseeable future.

(Source: G McCrum, *The Times*, 7.3.1994:37)

Figure 4.8 The relative decline of state-educated girls entering university arts courses. Is single sex education a solution?

preparation for dealing with them after leaving school. They contend that raising teachers' awareness, changing the 'male-centred' nature of science curricula and other measures can be effective in improving the performance of females in scientific subjects in a co-educational environment. The *Girls into Science and Technology project* (GIST) achieved promising results on the basis of such strategies.

Socialist-feminism and education

Socialist-feminists consider that gender inequality is deeply linked to the class nature of capitalist society and that for female liberation to be achieved both inequalities must effectively be dealt with. However, socialist-feminists have increasingly tended to adopt the same kind of immediate reforms as those favoured by radical-

feminists except that they consistently seek to raise class as well as gender issues, and particularly to link the two. They see the educational system as reproducing gender inequalities in a way that broadly suits the needs of capitalism. Thus, Christine Griffin attempted to show how it is that working class girls get working class jobs – if routine office as well as factory work is assumed to be working class (see pp. 90-1).

Certainly, socialist-feminists have been able convincingly to show that gender identity is greatly affected by the class experience of a particular female or male i.e. that gender identity is mediated by class. In this respect a telling study is Katherine Clarricoates' *The Importance of Being Ernest ... Emma ... Tom ... Jane: The Perception and Categorisation of Gender Conformity and Gender Deviation in Primary Schools.*

Clarricoates examined gender socialisation in four different types of school of which two will be considered here:

- A traditional working class school, 'Dock Side'.
- A modern suburban rural middle class school 'Applegate'.

In Dock Side the behaviour and norms considered 'typical' of the two sexes were 'sharply differentiated'. 'Toughness' and 'masculinity' were expected of the boys (as described by Willis p. 89) whereas the girls were expected to be co-operative and helpful. When girls did do well academically this tended to be 'explained away' and seen as 'wanting to please rather than being intelligent'. Separation and even segregation was imposed on the two sexes – emphasising difference, polarity and even opposition – 'separate playgrounds, separate toilets, separate games, even separate lists on registers'.

Whereas in Dock Side high academic achievement was 'neither highly valued nor expected', the opposite applied at Applegate – for both sexes. Sex-separation was considerably less rigid at Applegate although not to the point where complete role symmetry occurred. Thus, when a male pupil dressed-up as a female, the ridicule of his peers went unchecked by the teacher.

Aggression was not approved of for either sex but more tolerated in the case of boys. Clarricoates' findings appear to complement Elizabeth Bott's much earlier (1957) in which she found that conjugal roles in middle class families tended to be joint (more similar) and those in working class families to be more segregated. Already, in primary school differential class and gender influences seem to be shaping future patterns of behaviour.

The very scope of socialist-feminist analysis, embracing patriarchy, capitalism and their inter-relations, makes the task of describing, let alone producing, an alternative education for females all the more daunting. Sheila Miles and Chris Middleton argue that much more than equal opportunities is needed and that 'education to make children aware of their social and political environment, including anti-sexist and anti-racist work, has to be built into the foundations of the curriculum, not added as an afterthought' in (M Hammer and M Flude: 1988, p. 204).

At a more preliminary level, the right-hand column of Table 4.6 contains some socialist influenced-strategies of an egalitarian and participatory kind.

Table 4.6 Liberal and radical/socialist feminist educational strategies

Equal opportunities/girl friendly	Anti-sexist/girl-centred
Persuading girls into science and technology.	Recognising the importance of girl-centred study; for example, what is 'herstory', or girl- and woman-centred science or technology.
Providing a compulsory common core of subject, to include 'hard' sciences for girls and humanities for boys.	Providing girls with skills and knowledge to challenge the male system in the workplace and the home.
Rearranging option blocks to reduce stereotyped choices.	Giving girls a sense of solidarity with other members of their sex, and hence greater confidence and motivation..
Analysing sexism in textbooks, readers and resources.	Widening girls' horizons while not denigrating the lives and work of their mothers, female friends and women in the community.
Reviewing school organisation – for example, registers, assemblies, uniform, discipline.	Changing the nature of schooling: replacing hierarchy, competitiveness, authoritarianism and selection with co-operation, democracy, egalitarianism and community.
Producing in-service courses and policy guidelines.	Exploring the relationship between sexuality, women's oppression and sexual harassment in school and the workplace.
Establishing mixed-sex working parties to develop and monitor school policy.	Establishing schoolgirls' and women's support groups.
Creating posts for equal opportunities.	Decision-making through wide consultation and collective working.

(Source: Arnot and Weiner, 1987:356)

Conservative perspectives on feminism in education

At the time of writing (1997), Conservative administrations have been in power for eighteen consecutive years. Until the Education Reform Act of 1988, Conservative central government intervened little in gender matters in education. Thus local authorities and individual teachers and schools were largely left to pursue their own policies within the existing framework of legislation. To that extent, Conservative administrations accepted the liberal framework of equal opportunities set up by the 1975 Sex Discrimination Act.

The establishing of a legally compulsory national curriculum did have profound implications for gender and education. Henceforward girls (as well as boys) would be required to take science to sixteen and boys would be required to take a foreign language as well as English to sixteen. These requirements remained in place even when the compulsory national curriculum for the years fourteen to sixteen was trimmed back to five subjects in 1991. Ironically, these reforms could be interpreted as a move in the direction of the firm action demanded of central government by many socialist-feminists to establish a compulsory curriculum in which girls could not 'opt out of' and avoid 'hard' sciences and maths. However, there is a proviso in the Act referring to science which allows students to study this area of the curriculum for either twenty per cent or 12.5 per cent of their timetable, with only the former providing an adequate route to 'A' level. Miles and Middleton have commented on the 12.5 per cent route that 'pupils taking this option, the majority of whom will undoubtedly be girls, will face severe constraints on their choice of jobs'. However, Miles and Middleton themselves make the point that there is no basis for devaluing or undervaluing the subjects in which females currently out-perform males.

It remains to be seen how the science provisions of the national curriculum evolve. However, it may be that the government introduced them less in a spirit of sex equality and more because it perceived a 'national economic need' to do so. It may have decided that the reduction in the number of young people (due to low birth rates in the1970s/1980s) and the shortage of scientists and engineers has made it necessary to foster latent female scientific talent. This interpretation is lent plausibility by the absence of any more general concern about sexism in the Act.

Some traditionalists have attacked the awareness (of patriarchy and sexism) raising and other activities of radical- and socialist-feminists referred to above. Mervyn Hiskett suggests that these feminists are attempting to 'hi-jack' the minds of young people whose parents would often not approve if they were really aware of what was happening (*Should Sons and Daughters be Brought Up Differently?* Radical-Feminism in Schools in D Anderson, *Full Circle?* (The Social Affairs Unit, 1988). Hiskett argues that girls should be allowed to decide for themselves how they want to balance domestic and paid-work commitments. Perhaps Hiskett is being a little simplistic. The national curriculum itself substantially prescribes what the young should learn. That said, all education should be critical.

Conclusion: poststructural feminism and education

Gaby Weiner's *Feminism in Education: An Introduction* (1994) accepts that in future, feminism is likely to be of various ideological hues. Even so, she considers that feminists are likely to be more effective in education if they share certain broad strategies and goals. 'It is crucial', she argues, 'the feminist educators both maintain their critique of existing school practices and offer new challenges to meet the ever-changing circumstances of educational practice' (118).

She goes on to suggest a number of possibilities for feminist action in education. I will deal with these one by one, giving examples for each:

1 'Challenging the universalities and certainties of predominant curriculum epistemologies' e.g. challenging the understanding/assumption (epistemology) which Weiner sees in the history national curriculum, that history is *man*-made.

2 Adopting feminist teaching/learning approaches 'which allow for the possibilities of feminist counter-discourses in education' e.g. developing independent learning approaches, collaborative investigative work, or small group discussion of contentious issues.

3 Consciously positioning feminist educators within educational practices e.g. working with parents or colleagues to change school curricula or organisation.

As reference to Arnot and Weiner's list of feminist educational strategies published in 1987 shows, Weiner's thoughts above are not new. What is clearer in her 1994 book is an awareness that what had seemed like fragmentation in the feminist movement can, instead, be viewed positively as variety and difference (i.e. in a poststructuralist way). Nevertheless, her suggestions summarised above indicate a continuing concern to maintain collective and cumulative progress in the area of gender education.

'Race' and ethnicity in education

Two main issues have emerged in the context of 'race' and ethnicity in education. The first concerns the attainment level of the children of more recent immigrant minorities, particularly of black minorities. The second concerns the nature of the curriculum in a society in which a number of minorities live.

Black minorities and educational attainment

In the 1960s and 1970s, the most frequently expressed educational concern in relation to black minorities was about the low average attainment level of children of Afro-Caribbean origin. Although this concern continues, it has developed into a more general awareness of the variety of levels of attainment of the children of various minorities. Differences between the performances of ethnic groups is shown in the research of Florisse Kysel into the 'O' levels and CSE results in 1985 of children from twelve groups (including 'other') in the former Inner London Education Authority. As can be seen from Table 4.7 the performance of the children of certain minorities, notably Indian and African Asian, exceeds that of English, Scottish, Welsh and Irish (ESWI), while that of others, notably Bangladeshi and Turkish, is considerably worse. The performance score is arrived at by giving a specific number of points for each grade from 7 for an 'O' level, to 1 for a CSE5. Before attempting any explanation of the performance differences between groups, it will be helpful to compare the rate of improvement between groupings over time.

It is noticeable that whereas the improvement rate of ESWI pupils and Asian pupils has slowed, that of 'Caribbean' and pupils of other minority groups has been substantial (Table 4.8).

Before considering the reasons behind the pattern of attainment of minority children in schools, it is important to draw attention to the relatively large presence of ethnic minority students in higher education. The situation here is complex but offers some grounds for optimism (see p. 125).

A considerable range of sociological explanations has been put forward for why some minority groups perform well academically and others do not. We discuss these below. First, however, it needs to be stated that for those who consider that black people are genetically less intelligent than Caucasian (Indo-European) people, no problem is presented by the evidence of their comparatively low achievement. Jensen, for instance, believes that the fact that 'Negroes' (sic) score, on average, twelve to fifteen points less on general intelligence tests than whites is a clear indication that they are innately substantially less intelligent. From his point of view, the kindest course would be to accept this and to cease trying to make them achieve levels of academic attainment that are generally beyond them. A variety of arguments can be cited against Jensen's view, but here we will concentrate exclusively on the social factors which might affect the performance of blacks in attainment and in intelligence tests. In view of the exploitation and racism experienced by Afro-Caribbean people, it is perhaps ill-judged if not highly racist, to suggest they are intellectually inferior when convincing social explanations for their educational performance, including the effects of white racism, have not yet been fully explored. We consider these explanations now. In doing so, a comparison is frequently made between Afro-Caribbean and Indian children as there is a wide gap between their average levels of attainment. The discussion occurs under the following headings:

- Class and minority attainment
- Family (class and gender)
- Racism in society and minority group responses
- Racism in the educational system

Table 4.7 Average performance scores

	Average performance score	Number of pupils
African	16.9	426
African Asian	22.7	162
Arab	14.0	91
Bangladeshi	8.7	333
Caribbean	13.6	2,981
ESWI*	15.2	10,685
Greek	17.6	243
Indian	24.5	398
Pakistani	21.3	231
SE Asian	19.1	300
Turkish	11.9	268
Other	21.3	940

ESWI = English, Scottish, Welsh and Irish

(Source: *Flirisse Kysel, Ethnic Background and Examination Results,* Educational Research, Vol 30, No.1, June, 1988)

Table 4.8 Changes in performance scores

		Performance score	Number of pupils
Asian[1]	1976	18.4	389
	1985	18.9	1,124
Caribbean	1976	10.3	2,381
	1985	13.6	2,981
ESW[1]	1976	14.0	19,820
	1985	15.2	10,685
Other[2]	1976	14.5	1,808
	1985	18.4	2,268
All	1976	13.7	24,398
	1985	15.6	17,058

1 *Includes African Asian, Bangladeshi, Indian and Pakistani pupils*
2 *Includes all groups other than Asian Caribbean and ESWI*

Class and minority attainment

Part of the explanation for the high average attainment level of Indian minority children is that the Indian minority is a relatively middle class group. The same is true of African Asians – many of whom were business people prior to their expulsion from Kenya and Uganda in the late 1960s. During the 1950s and early 1960s, thousands of Indian doctors, chemists and nurses answered the call of the National Health Service. Others set up small businesses –

shops and restaurants – sometimes as a response to being passed over for promotion by white employees. In time, some of these businesses have become medium and even large-scale. In contrast, many more immigrants from Bangladesh and parts of Pakistan were rural peasants and this is reflected particularly in the educational performance of the children of the former group, most of whom are relatively recent immigrants.

Most Afro-Caribbean male immigrants took up manual jobs, mostly skilled or semi-skilled, on immigrating to Britain. Females, who tended to come later, were typically employed in unskilled manual work and, increasingly, routine office work. Their children were, therefore, overwhelmingly working class. Some commentators (Mabey, 1981), argue that this fact alone largely explains why the educational performance of Afro-Caribbean children tends to lag behind that of Indian and white children (both of which groups contain more children from middle class families). Marxists and socialists certainly incline to favour this explanation. However, research by Craft and Craft (1983) does seem to show that Afro-Caribbean working class children attain significantly less than white working class children and that the same is true of middle class children of the two groups (Table 4.9). So, while class may explain some of the under-attainment of Afro-Caribbean children, we are still left with the need for further explanation.

Family (class and gender)

The high value put on educational achievement in the Asian community and the active support given by families to children in their studies, partly accounts for the high attainment levels of certain Asian minorities, including Indian. Again, however, the class factor may be relevant in that effective support seems to come particularly from more middle class families. There is a long established higher education network in Indian, and middle class (or higher caste) females as well as males are often motivated by family expectation to compete academically.

There is also great enthusiasm for educational achievement in the Afro-Caribbean community (Tizzard, 1988). However, relatively few Afro-Caribbean families have the experience and tradition of seeking higher education and once more this largely reflects their class. Their concern tends to be focused on problems of primary and secondary education. Further, for the large minority of lone parent families in the Afro-Caribbean community, there are inevitable practical problems of time and money in supporting their children's education (see p. 60). However, perhaps the main contrast between the Indian and Afro-Caribbean experience of British education is that there appears to have been a relatively easy 'cultural fit' in the first case but not in the second (see below). Something of a vicious circle of mutual near-rejection has occurred between some Afro-Caribbean children and the educational system. In frustration, many Afro-Caribbean parents have sought extra education for their children outside the state system:

Table 4.9 Fifth-form examination performance by ethnicity and social class

Examination Performance	White Percentages		Asian Percentages		West Indian Percentages		Other Percentages		All Percentages		Totals Percentages
	MC[1]	WC	MC	WC	MC	WC	MC	WC	MC	WC	
High[2]	31	18	32	16	20	9	26	16	30	16	21
Medium	55	62	8	64	49	51	59	63	56	61	59
Low	14	20	10	21	31	41	16	21	14	23	20

1 *MC = Middle Class, WC = Working Class. These categories are based on OPCS classification. See original paper for further details.*
2 *High, Medium Low. These categories are based on number of GCE 'O' level and/or CSE passes.*

(Source: Craft and Craft (1983) in *The Swan Report*, 1985:60)

> *In every city with a sizeable black population, Saturday schools exist, organised by black community activists, educationalists and parents, running them with a great deal of energy, inspiration and very little else. Parents pay what they can.*
>
> *(Reva Klein, 'Saturday is the only alternative',*
> *TES, 15.3.1991:26)*

It is relevant at this point to refer to some limited evidence that Afro-Caribbean females tend to perform better academically than males. Barbara Tizzard *et al.*'s *Young Children At School In The Inner City* (1988) addresses both the issue of the influence of the home on educational attainment and the relative performance of black (Afro-Caribbean) and white girls and boys. Tizzard *et al.* tested 343 children, of whom 171 were white and 106 were black, across 30 schools. The study was longitudinal and was carried out between 1982 and 1985. The children were mainly working class.

The study found that parents of both black and white children were interested in and practically supportive of their children's education and that this was especially true of black parents. These findings are reported emphatically:

> *There is another widely held belief amongst teachers, that black parents are particularly likely to fail to provide adequate educational support for their children. This, too, proved to be a myth. We found that black parents gave their children even more help with school work than white parents, and had a more positive attitude towards giving this help ...*
>
> *Both black and white parents read aloud to their children with equal frequency – during the reception year 40 per cent said that they read to them every day. The great majority of parents provided their children with books – at school entry, as we saw for ourselves, only a quarter of the children had as few as ten or less books – and similar proportions of black and white parents said that they borrowed children's books from the public library, and attended school meetings.*
>
> *(Tizzard et al., 1988:176)*

On the matter of the relative performance of black and white girls and boys, it is again worth quoting Tizzard at length:

> *One of the main aims of our study was to look for factors that might account for differences in the school attainments of boys and girls, and black and white children. At the pre-school stage, we found no significant ethnic differences in early reading, writing and maths skills, or in scores on the WPPSI vocabulary test. The only sex differences at this stage was that both black and white girls were superior to boys in writing. This superiority continued throughout the infant school. At the end of infant school, there was still no overall ethnic difference in attainment, but the black girls had emerged as ahead of all other groups in both reading and writing, whilst black boys were doing worst. Both black and white boys made more progress than girls at maths, with white boys making the most progress. When we retested the children at the end of the first year of junior school, there were still no significant overall ethnic differences in attainment. By now there was a significant sex difference in reading, with girls definitely ahead of boys.*
>
> *(Tizzard et al., 1988:180-1)*

Tizzard goes on to suggest that racism might play an increased role in the under-achievement of Afro-Caribbean children in later schooling and this is discussed below. Even so, there is fragmentary evidence that black girls may continue to maintain an edge over black boys into secondary school. Geoffrey Driver's survey of school leavers in five multi-racial inner-city schools showed that Afro-Caribbean pupils and, especially, the girls achieved results that were generally better than those of English boys and girls. Driver attributes the success of the girls to the strength derived from the matrifocal family tradition in Jamaica and carried over, out of practical necessity, to England. A major problem with Driver's research is that he does not control for social class variables and it may be that he is comparing groups of white and black children of different socio-economic background.

Another limited piece of evidence that Afro-Caribbean females attain at higher educational levels than Afro-Caribbean males is provided by Mary Fuller (1982) who in a single case study found that in the 'academic' band of the fifth form of a mixed comprehensive school, black girls averaged 7.6 'O' level and CSE exam passes as against 5.6 for the black boys. Fuller's study is full of illuminating detail. She observes that the girls 'formed a discernible subculture within the school' which emerged 'from the girls' positive acceptance of the fact of being black and female'. They were committed to achieving academic success but were not pro-school. Academic and ultimately career success were necessary both materially and psychologically: the first because many black women have to be major breadwinners, the second to give them a sense of self-worth. However, they had no normative commitment to general conformity at school. There are three aspects to this attitude. First, to appear too keen might attract the ridicule of black boys with whom they saw themselves as partly in competition. Second, their self-image tended to be that of fun-lovers not 'goody-goodies'. Third, they realised that public examinations were not assessed by their teachers so there was no undue need to please them.

On the basis of her data, Tizzard is able to offer no explanation for the apparent difference between the attainment of Afro-Caribbean females and males. However, both Driver and Fuller hypothesise that the relatively independent and central role of women in the Afro-Caribbean community both domestically and in paid work may act as a motivation to achievement. They are particularly accustomed to hard work and coping. What, then, explains the under-achievement of Afro-Caribbean males? Several studies suggest that the process of rejection of Afro-Caribbean males by white society and their response to rejection may, among other effects, result in educational under-achievement. The next two sections are largely concerned with this issue.

Racism in society and minority youth responses

Chapter 8 presents evidence that substantial racism occurs against black minorities in Britain. Indian and Afro-Caribbean minorities have coped with racism in some ways similarly, and in others quite differently. A common reaction in both communities, especially among the second and third generations since immigration, is anger. This seems a psychologically healthy response to prejudice and discrimination. As far as Afro-Caribbean youth is concerned anger seems a less self-damaging reaction than the low self-esteem reported in earlier research among black children in both the United States and Britain. In the course of research in the Southern United States, Robert Coles noted that the drawings of black children contained some strange features. They tended to picture themselves as small, dowdy and, sometimes, with various features missing, whereas they portrayed white children in a large and positive way. Even the weather and landscape on the pictures depicting the white children were better! More recently, Bernard Coard came across a similar phenomenon in Britain (*Urban*

Education, 1971). However, since the 1960s positive images of 'black power' and 'black is beautiful' have been readily available to black youth and judging from black youth culture, these are the ones that have been imitated.

It is arguable that the response of Afro-Caribbean youth, especially males, to racism differs from that of Indian youth in the way and perhaps the extent to which they reject white institutions, including education, and pursue alternative means of opportunity and expression (see pp. 207-9 and pp. 226-7). Stuart Hall goes so far as to refer to a culture of resistance to dominant power structures among Afro-Caribbean youth. Indian middle class youth, despite common resentment at racism and a willingness to defend themselves against intimidation, are able to use the professional and business resources of their own community and their own qualifications to make socio-economic progress. Because of different circumstances, they have tended to 'negotiate' a different 'solution' to the problems posed by British society.

Racism in the educational system

A distinction must be made here between individual and institutional racism although these terms are discussed at greater length in Chapter 8 (see pp. 218-9). Individual racism refers to the racial prejudice or discrimination of one person against another. Institutional racism occurs when a set of rules or an organisational system operates in a racist way. Both individual and institutional racism may be intentional or unintentional although some definitions of institutional racism assume it to be unintentional. How far is the educational system characterised by individual or institutional racism?

The analysis that the British educational system is institutionally racist is as much a political as a sociological one in that it is aimed at changing the system in an anti-racist direction. Chris Mullard argues that the relatively small number of black Head Teachers and other more senior teachers, the relatively high number of Afro-Caribbean children in lower streams and designated educationally sub-normal and the racially biased (in his view) curriculum demonstrate that the British educational system is structurally racist. What Mullard suggests should be done about this is discussed shortly.

There are no nationally representative social surveys which quantify the extent of individual racism among teachers. However, a relatively large scale study by P A Green (unpublished PhD thesis) is reported by Cohen and Manion. Green observed and recorded 70 white British teachers in multi-ethnic teaching situations. He then asked them to complete an attitude inventory in which a scale designed to measure their prejudice had been 'hidden'. Twelve highly prejudiced teachers, and twelve who scored low on prejudice were identified. Cohen and Manion summarise Green's findings on the differences between these two groups in classroom interaction – established through analysis of his recordings:

1 Highly intolerant teachers gave significantly less time to accepting the feelings of children of West Indian origin.
2 Highly intolerant teachers gave only minimal praise to children of West Indian origin.
3 Highly intolerant teachers gave significantly less attention to the ideas contributed by children of West Indian origin.
4 Highly intolerant teachers used direct teaching of individual children significantly less with pupils of West Indian origin.
5 Highly intolerant teachers gave significantly more authoritative directions to children of West Indian origin.
6 Highly intolerant teachers gave significantly less time to children of West Indian origin to initiate contribution to class discussions.

Cohen and Manion comment that what is now needed is qualitative data on teacher-pupil interaction in the multi-ethnic classroom to complement Green's more quantitative approach.

Mac an Ghaills' *Young, Gifted and Black* (1988) provides qualitative data on this issue not in the form of observed classroom interaction but in the form of interviews with members of various pupil peer groups, including an anti-school group of Afro-Caribbean males calling itself the 'Rasta-Heads'. The interviews clearly show that the Rasta-Heads feel they are negatively labelled by teachers. Interestingly, the Rasta-Heads are supported in their view by members of a mainly Indian working class peer group, the Warriors:

> *MM: Do you think that West Indians cause more trouble than Asians?*
>
> *Ashwin: No, don't be stupid, that's what teachers think. The Indians cause just as much trouble.*
>
> *Raj: The West Indians are more obvious some 'ow. They're seen more easily ...*
>
> *MM: Do you think they are more dumber?*
>
> *Raj: No I don't.*
>
> *Iqbal: No, because they can do as well as Indian kids, better than at lot of them. The ones who have been in most trouble were the brainy ones, like Kevin and Michael, in the first year they were the brainy ones, really brainy.*
>
> (Mac an Ghaill, 1988:122-3)

Although something is clearly going badly wrong for many young Afro-Caribbeans in school, it may not be the educational system alone or primarily that is causing it. Tizzard (1988) leaves open the possibility that it is factors in the wider society that may be decisive in alienating many young Afro-Caribbeans, especially males. A highly statistical analysis by David Drew and John Gray questions whether schools have a major negative effect on the attainment of Afro-Caribbean children arguing that their performance at sixteen can be roughly predicted at twelve without reference to any 'racist factor' (*The Black-White Gap in Exam Achievement* (Sheffield University, 1990)).

Conclusion

The average attainment of children of minority groups varies greatly. It seems likely that class is a more important variable than ethnicity or racism in explaining average levels of attainment. However, the tradition and resources of an ethnic group may play a part in how its members negotiate the educational system. The attainment levels of Afro-Caribbean children, especially males, continue to give cause for concern, despite improvement. Whether the cause of their relatively strong resistance to the educational system lies within education, or the wider society, or both is open to debate.

Minorities and the curriculum: perspectives

What is the appropriate curriculum for a society which is multi-ethnic and in which substantial racism occurs. We will briefly review four approaches:

- The Assimilationist
- The Multi-Cultural (Pluralist)
- The Anti-Racist (Radical/Marxist)
- Educational Needs

The assimilationist approach was the general 'commonsense' of the 1950s and early 1960s. It was widely assumed that black immigrants and their children would eventually learn to behave like white Britons. This applied to education as to other matters. A more sophisticated version of this approach was put forward by the New Right in the1980s. Thus, Ray Honeyford, a Head Teacher in Bradford, argued that it is the role of the schools to teach a common national culture – whatever particular minorities might wish to do privately. A modified version of this approach is apparent in some aspects of the national curriculum as it has been developed under Conservative governments. The emphasis on British history, English literature, the Christian religion in the curriculum exemplifies this. However, the Educational Reform Act (1988) also requires the multicultural nature of British society to be recognised across the curriculum – although some have doubted the strength of this commitment.

The multicultural approach argues that minorities are part of British society and culture and that this should be fully reflected in the curriculum, which should therefore be multicultural. The multicultural movement has helped to broaden and enliven the curriculum but has been criticised as superficial and 'merely' concerned with culture – 'saris, samosas and steel bands'! In particular, anti-racists have argued that multiculturalism fails to address the central problem of racism.

Anti-racists want to rid the British educational system, including the curriculum, of racism (see p. 232). Given that they consider that the educational system is 'structured' in a racist way, this is a sizeable task. It would require the appointment of many more black teachers and educational administrators, particularly at a senior level, and confrontation of the 'racist' nature of much of British imperial history and contemporary society. When the borough of Brent attempted to embark on such a policy, it attracted massive negative coverage from the popular media and a visit from the national educational inspectorate.

Maureen Stone's *The Education of the Black Child in Britain* (Fontana, 1981) argues that the priority of black parents is that the educational system should meet the educational needs of their children, particularly the three 'Rs'. Multiculturalism, especially if incompetently handled by white liberals, could detract from this. Black children respond best to straightforward teaching and discipline, not lax progressivism. Smith and Tomlinson's study of twenty urban comprehensive schools between 1981-1988 can be interpreted to support Stone (Policy Studies Institute, 1988). They conclude that schools which are effective for white children are also effective for black children. In other words, both benefit from good teaching. Of course, multiculturalism and anti-racism are compatible with good teaching but should not occur at its expense.

A conservative revolution in education and training?

The rest of this chapter is concerned with Conservative education policy from 1979 to 1997. It divides into two main but overlapping parts. First, is an analysis of the Conservatives' attempt to reshape the relationship between education, vocational training and industry. Second, is an examination of the content, objectives and consequences of the 1988 Educational Reform Act. One objective of the Act, was to relate education more closely to industry and to create a more entrepreneurial culture among the young. The Act also aimed to promote a more integrated *national culture* – through the national curriculum.

The aims of Conservative education and training policies were, then, extremely ambitious. These policies were very different in their ideological inspiration from the educational policies of the Labour governments but comparable in their scope and intention to change English society as well as its education system. They test the truth of A H Halsey's dictum: 'education cannot change society'.

Industry, education and training

This section deals with the relationship between two major sub-systems of society: the economy and education/training. The focus is particularly on how the new emphasis (on training) under Thatcherism affected both the education system and the economy. This is a wide scope and requires some introduction.

Prior to 1979, education and training had been seen as two largely distinct activities. Yet by 1995 the Department of Education had been merged with that of Employment to create the Department for Education and Employment (DEE). In 1979, the purpose of the schools system was generally considered to be education. Vocational preparation was carried out at different levels through apprenticeships, through Further Education courses such as RSA and BTEC, and through professional courses often based in Higher Education. Most of these courses did have a general or liberal educational element. The view behind this was that life is about more than just doing a job and that 'the whole person' should be educated. It was sometimes difficult to convince students on vocational courses of the value of the liberal humanist aspect of the courses. Novelist Tom Sharpe's depictions of the demoralised F E lecturer, Wilt, making his desultory way to teach poetry criticism to Meat Packers 2, must ring true for many who have faced comparable challenges.

The reforms of the Thatcher-Major period sought to change the relationship between education and industry in three main ways:

1 To change the 'culture' of the education system so that it became more favourable to industry.
2 To reduce the control of the unions over apprenticeships and to establish a new system of youth training.
3 To establish a new system of national vocational qualifications (NVQs) and general national vocational qualifications (GNVQs) which would run alongside and to some extent overlap with academic (non-vocational) education.

These aims were not stated on 'day one' of Margaret Thatcher's first administration but developed gradually. The third only came clearly into focus in the Major period. However, the concept of NVQs and GNVQs was developed in the latter half of the1980s. NVQs are vocationally highly specific e.g. mechanical engineering, whereas GNVQs are much more general in nature, referring to a broad vocational area e.g. business. The stated purpose of the GNVQ initiative is to provide a framework of vocational qualifications, equivalent in value and quality to academic qualifications, from foundation to postgraduate level. Figure 4.10 describes the plan.

Given the wide scope of the Thatcher-Major reforms in the area of education/training, it is useful to have a framework within which to interpret their significance. Geoff Watts' 'functional breakdown' of the relationship between education and employment provides this (1985). In this respect, he suggests four functional relationships:

• Selection
• Socialisation
• Orientation
• Preparation

These functions need briefly to be described although selection and socialisation have already been dealt with at length (see pp. 87-92 and pp. 96-8). Selection is achieved by certificating people at various levels of attainment and the information is then used by employers. Socialisation for employment involves informal and formal learning of values, norms and behaviour relevant to work. Orientation is more specific than socialisation and includes aspects such as careers education and work experience. Preparation for work is specifically vocational training. The Thatcher-Major reforms affected all these functions and sought to change the culture of education (socialisation/orientation) as well as vocational training (preparation).

Higher Education is dealt with in separate sub-section but many of the issues in fourteen to eighteen education/training also arose in relation to higher education. Both sectors were subject to similar central government policies in the Thatcher-Major period.

Finally, it should be noted that no distinction is made here between training and vocational education (although the latter is more often used elsewhere to refer to higher level courses).

Issues and perspectives

The main reason why the quality of vocational training in Britain is so urgent a matter is the country's long term relative economic decline and, in particular, the decline of its manufacturing industry. Even recent 'bright spots' in British manufacturing such as electronics in South Wales and car production in the north east and midlands tend to have been achieved by overseas inward-investors who use their own methods of labour organisation and training. In his Ruskin speech of 1976, James Callaghan, expressed deep concern about the effectiveness of the relationship between the education/training system and industry. This concern has remained central to public debate ever since because matters have failed significantly to improve. Between 1990 and 1991, Britain slipped from tenth to thirteenth in world competitiveness and was twenty first in the availability of skilled workers in the latter year (Management Development Institute, 1992). By 1995, Britain had dropped further back, to eighteenth.

Critics of the relationship between education and industry tend to make two basic points. First, in a number of commercial areas industry is not being supplied with the skilled employees it needs. Second, the education system is, certainly until recently, characterised by an anti-industrial and anti-entrepreneurial spirit with the result that pupils and students develop negative attitudes to working in industry.

Evidence suggests that it is at the intermediate (e.g. BTEC, RSA) and lower levels of vocational/professional education rather than the graduate or post-graduate level where there has been an endemic problem.

Alan Smithers has been a major critic of the alleged failure of the education/vocational training system to provide the skills needed by British industry. He illustrates two areas where this has happened: the intermediate vocational (see Table 4.10) and the technician and craftsmen (sic) level in qualifications in engineering and technology (see Table 4.11). The twenty per cent of the UK workforce with intermediate vocational qualifications compares particularly unfavourably with Germany and the Netherlands. It is also with Germany that comparison in respect to qualified technicians is most unfavourable. Despite a fall in the proportion of young people with science 'A' levels, there is 'little solid evidence of a shortfall in recruitment to science based-careers' (Council for

Industry and Higher Education, 1995). Smithers's data supports this comment.

Table 4.10 Vocational qualifications of workforce

Vocational qualifications	France (1988)	Germany (1989)	Netherlands (1985)	UK (1988)
		Percentages		
Degree and Higher Diplomas[1]	14	18	18	17
Intermediate Vocational Qualifications[2]	33	56	44	20
None[3]	53	26	38	63

1 Degrees, HND, HNC, teaching, nursing and equivalent.
2 BTEC National, City and Guilds and equivalent.
3 General education only (below HE)

(Source: Mason, Prais and van Ark, 1990. Discussion Paper No.191, London: NIESR, reprinted in Smith and Robinson, 1991)

Table 4.11 Qualifications in engineering and technology in selected countries, 1985

Level	UK	France	Germany	Japan	USA
			Thousands		
Doctorate	0.7	0.3	1.0	0.3	0.5
Master's degree	2	–	–	5	4
Bachelor's degree	14	15	21	30	19
Technician	29	35	44	27	17
Craftsman	35	92	120	44	n/a

Raw numbers for Japan and USA reduced in proportion to UK population. Populations of France and West Germany taken as sufficiently similar to UK not to require adjustment.

(Source: Prais, 1988. National Institute Economic Review, February, 76-83, reprinted in Smith and Robinson, 1991)

It is obvious that Britain lags in the provision of foundation (lower) level vocational qualifications as well as at the intermediate. The 63 per cent with no vocational qualifications puts the UK well adrift of competitor countries. In the post-war period, this situation can be traced back to the failure to develop technical schools as part of the tripartite system and the fact that the secondary modern schools seldom provided courses with vocational qualifications. Initially, the secondary modern schools did not offer formal qualifications and when they introduced the Certificate for Secondary Education (CSE), it was widely regarded as an inferior version of the academic 'O' level (GCE).

Prior to the election of Margaret Thatcher in 1979, concern about the quality of Britain's vocational education and about the relationship between education and industry was widespread across the political spectrum. However, ideological perspectives and solutions varied greatly. Among Conservatives two broad approaches were apparent. First, the New Right wanted to revitalise education with the 'entrepreneurial spirit' and to forge more effective links with industry. More traditional Conservatives were often more cautious, unwilling to risk any dilution of academic standards. Some of the latter shared what can be termed a *liberal-humanist* approach common across the centre of the political spectrum as well as within the education system itself. Typically, this second view accepted that there were inadequacies in the education/training system but insisted that the *prime* purpose of education (as distinct from training) was not to prepare or train people for work but to develop the whole personality-intellect, emotions and character. This perspective was common in the Labour Party and among social democrats generally.

A third view, tended to be sceptical about the nature of the relationship between education and industry in capitalist society. This approach, common among radicals and Marxists, is presented particularly in the criticisms of the Youth Training Scheme and, later, of Youth Training given below.

Education and training policies under Margaret Thatcher: 1979-90

A cluster of policies were implemented during the Thatcher period of government which can be referred to as the 'new vocationalism'. The New Right wing of the Conservative Party was uppermost in the formulation and implementation of these policies although the more traditionalist wing had the greater influence on the 1988 Education Reform Act. Policies and institutions associated with the new vocationalism were:

The Technical and Vocational Educational Initiative (TVEI) (1982-1997)

The Certificate of Prevocational Education (Now defunct)

The Youth Training Scheme (YTS) (Replaced by Youth Training (YT) in 1990 and later by the Training Credits (TC) scheme).

The Manpower Services Commission (MSC) (Now defunct)

The City Technology Colleges

The National Council for Vocational Qualifications

The new vocationalism

Both Keith Joseph, Secretary of State for Education, 1981-86, and David Young, Chairman of the Manpower Services Commission and former businessman, were convinced exponents of the New Right approach to education described above. Young was the more practical of the two and it was the MSC which funded both TVEI

and YTS. This gave Young and the MSC influence in schools through TVEI, and in further education through YTS. It was Young rather than Joseph who imparted the philosophy and practice of the new vocationalism throughout the education system and its influence continues strong into the second half of the1990s.

TVEI provided central funding for initiatives in educational institutions which introduced teaching/learning experiences which employed new technology and/or were oriented to the world of work. In the spirit of Thatcherite entrepreneurialism and cost-consciousness, institutions were required to 'bid' for funding. Despite this, it was not possible for the MSC to ensure that what happened in practice precisely reflected the terms of the bids. Some teachers introduced initiatives – in, say, history or environmental studies – in which they pointed out negative as well as positive aspects of industry. Thus, in some cases, the initiative was negotiated in a way that ensured it was a progressive learning experience and not the uncritical vehicle for entrepreneurial propaganda that some enthusiasts were in danger of making it. The various responses to TVEI, illustrate that social actors – in this case

(a) Numbers leaving school, 1989-91

('000s)

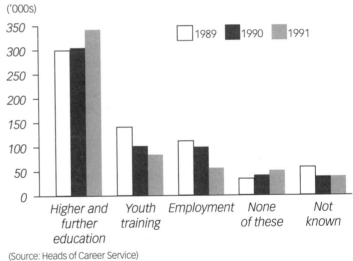

(Source: Heads of Career Service)

(b) Destination as percentage of total, 1989-91

Note: *Generally young people avoided youth training schemes if they could.*

(Source: Focus in Britain, Perennial)

Figure 4.9 Figure trends in post-school activity, 1989-91

teachers – can negotiate and even subvert the purpose of the powerful.

The Youth Training Scheme, eventually replaced by Youth Training, provided trainees with a small grant and subsidised training (paid to the 'employer') with back-up from a College of Further Education. However, the back-up was to be exclusively job-related. General education – for instance, social or environmental – was not included. The quality of training varied greatly. Some larger businesses such as department stores and banks had the resources to make the training experiences meaningful but, in many cases, 'trainees' learnt little and felt they were being used as 'cheap labour'. In 1987, the government required unemployed school leavers to take up a training place. The option of the 'dole' was removed other than in exceptional circumstances. By 1993, there were 76,000 school leavers who were neither on a training scheme nor receiving income support. Norman Fowler, then Chairman of the Conservative party, suggested that many were probably at home but equally many appeared to be 'on the road'.

Critical comment on the new vocationalism

Robert Moore presents the new vocationalism as in ideological conflict with the liberal-humanist approach to education (1987). In Moore's (and Gramsci's) terms, the new vocationalism achieved hegemony (ascendancy) over other educational ideologies, including liberal humanism, in the 1980s and 1990s. Moore sees the contest of educational ideologies as 'relatively autonomous' and considers that a move away from the 'possessive individualist' assumptions underlying the new vocationalism could occur. Moore gives 'the skills approach to learning' as a main example of the thinking behind the new vocationalism. Unlike the liberal humanist approach which is based on acquiring a critical appreciation of subject knowledge for its own sake, the skills or competency-based approach fragments or reduces areas of knowledge or practical activity into specific skills or procedures. The learning, assessment and certification of skills becomes the main aim of 'education/training'. Interestingly, Moore includes GCSE as an example of a course reflecting the skills approach and, by the same token, it could be argued that some 'A' levels (Sociology?) are being developed in the same direction. Moore refers to the new vocationalism as 'an ideology of production regulating education' but one whose hegemony is open to challenge. He states that:

> *Occupationalism (the new vocationalism) can be seen as more precisely reflecting the interests of that fragment of the middle class based in industry and commerce than did the humanist education of the professions.*
>
> *(241)*

Some commentators have referred to the more traditional Marxist theoretical framework of Bowles and Gintis to explain the relationship between the new vocationalism and industry rather than adopting, as Moore does, a Gramscian approach (Abercrombie *et al.*, 1994). Bowles and Gintis see a tight functional fit or correspondence between the education system (part of the superstructure) and the economy (part of the base) (see p. 95). The main means by which pupils are channelled towards positions in the occupational hierarchy is the hidden curriculum. Thus, the hidden curriculum of the new vocationalism is competitiveness within an overall framework of hierarchy and conformity. As Denis Gleeson points out, however:

> *With reference to the behavioural objectives associated with life skills training, it is argued that the hidden curriculum has now surfaced as the official curriculum.*
>
> *(1986:382)*

In contrast, Robert Moore's argument is that education does not inevitably function to service production – rather education is an area of serious hegemonic struggle.

Two of the most frequently made criticisms of YTS and YT are that they were set up to massage the unemployment figures and to control and 'store' young people (Gleeson, 1986; Finn, 1993). Many YTS schemes certainly seemed to be makeshift and underfunded. Tales of some YTS supervisors making money out of 'cheap labour' were difficult to prove but, for whatever reason, most trainees were not offered full-time jobs in the places where they trained. This has been especially the case for young Afro-Caribbean males (see below).

Youth training and equal opportunities

Youth Training operates under equal opportunity regulations in relation to gender and ethnicity. In practice, however, much training has been gendered and/or racialised in a variety of ways. Just as, under the influence of gender socialisation, females and males in mainstream education often 'choose' subjects for gender stereotypical reasons, so they do also in Youth Training. Several of the case studies in the 16 to 19 Initiative Study describe certain courses, such as a 'Care' course as still swamped by girls, whereas a 'Building Operatives Scheme' had only one female on it (see, for instance I Bates and G Roseborough *eds*, *Youth and Inequality*, 1993, especially Chapters 1 and 8). Such examples argue ill for any significant breakdown in gender stereotyping in the lower status occupations in which Youth Training still generally operates. In one respect, however, females may be advantaged by gender, and that is segmentation in employment. Whereas in a primarily manufacturing economy, job segmentation favoured males, statistics are increasingly showing that in the current service-oriented British economy, more females than males are obtaining full-time jobs (Labour Force Survey, Winter 1994/5). This is a radical change in the post-war pattern in which the majority of full-time jobs have previously gone to males. A survey of those who took Youth Training courses between December 1992 and January 1994 found that while 28 per cent of males were unemployed, only 25 per cent of females were left without work (D of E).

In the case of Afro-Caribbean males, gender and 'racial' factors reinforce each other to their great disadvantage. Negative stereotyping by both careers advisors and employers contributes to disproportionate numbers of young Afro-Caribbean males being directed to unsuitable training courses and being refused jobs (Report, *Observer* 12.2.95:5). The Department of Employment survey for 1992-94 referred to above found 62 per cent of black males between sixteen and 24 in London to be unemployed, compared to twenty per cent of whites in the same age group. Some black community leaders claim that black males are more likely to be advised to do college-based courses with little work experience as opposed to employee-based courses which are more likely to lead to jobs (Observer Report). Black females find employment more easily than black males largely because of the developments in the occupational structure referred to above. For them, discrimination is apparently more likely to occur when they seek promotion or higher status jobs.

TECS and (G)NVQS: 1990 Onwards

The youth training programmes and many of the other vocational education/training initiatives of the 1980s often had an improvised quality about them. They bore the mark of either a hasty response to circumstances – escalating youth unemployment in the case of YTS – or of being driven by ideological enthusiasm rather than long term analysis and planning – such as, arguably, the City Technology Colleges initiative.

By the early 1990s a framework for training and vocational education was in place although it is not yet clear how effective it will be. The main aspects of this framework are the Training and Enterprise Councils (TECS) and the setting up of the G/NVQ system throughout the whole education system, as described above.

In 1992, the 82 Training and Enterprise Councils took over the co-ordination of employment training, including the provision of Youth Credits. Early evidence of their performance is very mixed. South West Thames TEC closed in 1994 after becoming bankrupt but other TECs ran surpluses and claimed to be successfully meeting the demands of their local employment markets. The TECs are run predominantly by business people. As a *Times Educational Supplement* editorial stated in 1991:

> *The TECs will be a critical test-bed of the Government ideology that a skilled workforce should be trained according to the ideas and cash of local businessmen, rather than through government agencies or education departments.*
>
> *(TES, 22.3.1991:23)*

It is likely that the Labour party would add local authority and union representation to the TECs governing boards but maintain the system itself.

The impact of the new vocationalism on higher education has already been substantial and is certain to increase further. Figure 4.10 shows the recent sharp increase in vocationally qualified entrants into higher education and the even steeper increase that is projected. Nevertheless, of the more than 260,000 who started GNVQs between 1992 and 1994, only 100,000 had achieved even a partial award by 1995. Professor Alan Smithers commented that the Joint Council of National Vocational Awarding Bodies were 'oddly complacent', when fewer than half the students who

NVQs	GNVQs	Academic
5 (Professional, managerial)		
4 (Higher technician, junior management)		Higher education
3 (Technician, supervisor)	Advanced	2 GCE 'A'-levels
2 (Craft)	Intermediate	5 GCSEs, Grades A-C
1 (Foundation)	Foundation	Other GCSEs

Qualified for university entrance

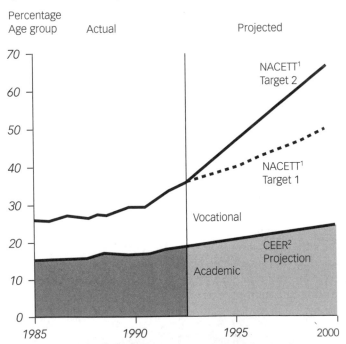

1 *National Advisory Council for Education and Training Targets.*
2 *Centre for Education and Employment Research, University of Manchester.*

(Source: A Smith and P Robinson, Post-18 Education: Growth, Change, Prospect, CIHE, 1995:7)

Figure 4.10 Equivalence of qualifications

registered on to courses have either completed an award or passed any units at all. Smithers also criticised the quality of the awards themselves. So far, neither the performance of the TECs nor of the Vocational Awarding Bodies suggests that the 'British problem' of the low priority given to training and to vocational education has yet been solved. The latest intervention in this area was the Dearing Report of 1996. Dearing recommended genuine parity of esteem between vocational, (NVQs), general vocational (GNVQs) and academic courses and much easier 'mixing and matching' between them. A government white paper of 1996 stated that Britian did extremely well in producing science graduates but was well behind leading European countries, especially Germany, in intermediate and basic education. Despite all the rhetoric and reform, the relative position of British education was little changed in twenty years.

From an 'elite' to a 'mass' system of higher education

Against a background of rising youth unemployment, the expansion of youth training and of sixteen to eighteen education in general, had been widely expected. Less predicted was the extremely rapid expansion of the numbers of students in higher education between 1990 and 1994. The age participation rate for eighteen-year-olds in higher education increased from thirteen per cent in 1978 to nineteen per cent in 1990 up to 31 per cent in 1993. (see Figure 4.10). There was a similar sharp increase in non 'A' level entrants, largely as a result of Access courses which gave adults with limited academic backgrounds a crash-preparation for higher education. The expansion in student numbers was far from matched by an increase in resources and put considerable strain on the higher education system. Why, then, was the policy of rapid expansion implemented?

Reasons for the expansion of higher education

One reason why the expansion of higher education occurred was to improve the cultural level and professional and practical skills of the population. In particular, the expansion of the service sector stimulated a long term demand for better educated employees. Further, better educated people tend to be more effective in civil life as well as in economic activity. However, these points do not fully explain why the expansion of higher education accelerated precisely when it did.

To explain the timing of expansion, more immediate factors must be considered. First, it is no coincidence that the rapid expansion of higher education occurred at the same time as unemployment was also rapidly rising, particularly among the eighteen to 24 year-old age group. There had been enough social discontent in the 1980s and, again, in the early 1990s (the poll tax protests, urban disorders) to suggest to government that people might be better occupied and less likely to become disaffected in higher education than otherwise.

However, there was also a genuine increase in demand for higher education mainly from females, particularly middle class females. By 1993 the percentage of females in universities, albeit disproportionately in the newer rather than the older ones, was almost 50 per cent. Despite continued stereotypical subject specialisation (see p. 111), this trend clearly strengthens females in the struggle for gender equality.

Equal opportunities and access to higher education! Ethnicity, class and age

The representation of Britain's ethnic minorities in higher education varies but overall is now greater than might be anticipated. Research by the Commission for Racial Equality (1990-91) found that Asians and Orientals were over-represented and Afro-Caribbeans not under-represented on the basis of the national population. However, the CRE stated that there is a bias in the selection procedures against non-white candidates which results in Afro-Caribbeans and Bangladeshis being significantly under-represented in the 'older' universities, but not in the former polytechnics (now known as 'new' universities and which were responsible for most of the recent expansion of higher education). It cannot simplistically be assumed that these differential acceptance rates were due to racism – either intentional or institutional – in the old universities, nevertheless, as Tariq Modood wrote: 'the issue of discrimination is a real one' (THES, 16.7.1993). Modood also commented on the relatively weaker correlation between class position and achieving entry into higher education in relation to non-whites compared to whites: 'It is striking that most ethnic minority groups have worse class profiles than whites, but produce much larger proportions of applications and admissions in the higher education system.'

However, it needs to be said that well-qualified as well as less well-qualified non-whites can be discriminated against in the job market. Equality of educational achievement would not guarantee equality in the labour market or in society.

The data on the social class origins of entrants into higher education indicates that, at last, in the 1990s the percentage of entrants from lower class, relative to higher class groups, began significantly to increase. This follows a period in the late 1980s when the reverse was true. Again, it is notable that the greater proportion of this increase has occurred in the new universities but latterly a similar, if less marked, trend has occurred in the old universities. Trends can change, however, and it may be that the slowing of the expansion of higher education in the mid 1990s will contribute to the reversal of this trend – as, perhaps, traditional, better qualified, often young, middle class applicants are favoured.

As we saw above, it was mainly middle class females who benefited from the more limited expansion of the late 1980s. Finally, it is worth reiterating that the traditional working class has greatly reduced in size during the post-war period with the result that the *absolute* number of working class children experiencing disadvantaged access to higher education has fallen – even if relative disadvantage has decreased little.

The final change in the higher education student population to be mentioned here is that increasing numbers of students over 21 years of age. Again, this change has occurred much more in the new than in the old universities. Whereas in 1993, ten per cent of entrants to the new universities were by non-traditional (non-'A' level) routes, the percentage for the older universities was ten per cent. Arguably, the changing age structure of the student population is producing more substantial educational and social consequences than has been widely observed. The learning experience itself is now much more likely to be multi-generational and less age-separated. The generations are having to adjust and get to know each other in an equal context. Further, the concept of education as continuing or recurrent throughout the life course seems better to fit both the employment and leisure patterns of contemporary society. Employment increasingly involves change and reskilling and education also opens up more leisure options at a time when many older people have more leisure.

Higher education: the meaning of the trends

The previous section deals with trends in recruitment to higher education of certain social groups. It is impossible to make sense of these trends without bearing in mind two major changes in the organisation and purposes of the higher education system. First, is that the universities are no longer primarily concerned with providing traditional, academic degree courses and are likely be increasingly less so up to the year 2000 and beyond. In 1993, vocational diplomas and degrees together made up 56 per cent of all undergraduate work (see Figure 4.10). Second, and relatedly, is the fact that it is the new universities which put on the larger proportion of non-degree undergraduate work and, as we saw above, take on by far the largest numbers of female, minority and older students. There is, then, a deepening division of labour between the old and new universities.

The differentiation between the old and new universities has great social significance. The older universities, particularly Oxbridge but also institutions such as Bristol and Durham, are likely to continue to recruit substantially (at about 50 per cent) from the public schools. Walter Ellis also argues that privilege persists at the point of exit

The present system is not just unfair, it is almost criminally wasteful. We now have 123 universities in Britain ... Some are struggling. Some may never quite make it. Others, though, are splendid institutions ... Employers, seeking the leaders of tomorrow, have for years short-circuited the weary business of selection by placing too much reliance of the Oxbridge gene poll. Today, with more graduates than ever jostling for position, it would be impossible for Oxbridge to cream off all the best jobs, even in its traditional core professions. Yet, perversely, (Oxbridge) ... have in our 'meritocratic age' come to be valued even more, so that the modern milk round frequently excludes some universities altogether ....

(326)

Even the recent trend to equalisation in the gender balances of these universities comes largely from an increasing proportion of public school girl entrants. With the new universities, shouldering most of the burdens of recent expansion, it is possible that the old universities will function to reproduce a privileged national elite (and professional elites) even more than in the past. It is true that the elite will be refreshed by some new talent, some of it rising via the old universities, but the process of strengthening an established elite with a modest influx of meritocrats is hardly new. It may be that the power and privilege of Britain's upper class will be strengthened rather than weakened by the development of a mass higher education system. Within the mass system – and somewhat obscured by it – the old elite system remains firmly in place.

However, 'massed' below is a greatly expanded higher education system. The extended system should certainly sustain and extend occupational opportunity for entry into the lower and middle reaches, if, much more rarely, the higher reaches of business, central and local government civil service, and the professions. A H Halsey's comment about the recent expansion of the university system Europe-wide applies no less to Britain. He writes of recent changes as 'replacing the older idea of the university ... by a much more expansive and, as many would argue, a diluted conception of tertiary rather than higher education'. (1995:168)

Universities, especially the new universities are increasingly recruiting vocationally qualified entrants and an increasing proportion are doing vocational or professional courses. Some Marxists might see this as the preparation of a 'new working class' (see Braverman pp. 95-6). This may be too simple. What will affect events will be how the 'new students' see themselves and how, long term, they want to employ the cultural capital and practical power and position that may be available to them. However, many are unlikely to experience a relatively straight-forward progress into middle class income, security and status that seemed almost a birthright of the highly educated in the 1960s and 1970s. In 1993, the Council for Industry and Higher Education reported that fourteen per cent of graduates remained unemployed six months after graduation. The Council's comment that 'graduates will have to adjust their expectations towards a wider range of jobs' was not altogether encouraging.

Conclusion: education and the 'enterprise culture'

Did the Thatcherite aim of achieving a more entrepreneurially-oriented culture in education succeed? Certainly in Geoff Watts' terms, much more socialisation and orientation of pupils and students towards industry occurred in the mid 1990s than twenty years previously, The proportion of students opting for vocational courses (preparation in Watt's model) also increased dramatically during the Thatcher-Major period.

However, the evidence that young Britains have become more enthusiastically disposed to industry is scant. Many appear to take vocational courses as a practical and even defensive measure – they see such courses as a means of getting a job. Similarly, the increase in self-employment in the 1980s probably reflected necessity as much as choice – for many it was self-employment or nothing. Many young people experienced relative poverty as students, difficulty in getting a job, short or long term dependency on state benefits or unemployment. The undoubted desire of most of them for a good, secure job probably fell short of enthusiasm for the 'enterprise culture' Indeed there is evidence that young people might yet be receptive to some of the principles which underlie humanistic education.

The 1988 Education Reform Act

The Education Reform Act (ERA) of 1988 is widely regarded as the most significant piece of legislation since the Butler Act of 1944. The main points of the Act are summarised below. However, it should be noted that some of the policies stipulated in the Act were already in operation prior to when it was passed. In part, the Act codified and clarified existing Conservative measures, bringing them into a major new educational framework for five to sixteen year-olds.

Main terms of the 1988 Education Reform Act

- The establishment of a national core curriculum (subjects that must be studied by all pupils).
- The introduction of national standardised tests in certain key subjects at ages seven, eleven, fourteen and sixteen.
- Local management of schools (LMS) – headteachers and governors allowed greater control of budgets and able to decide how much to spend on such matters as heating, books and teachers.
- Open enrolment: this means that schools are able to expand their numbers if there is the demand without the local authority being able to stop them.

- Opting out: parents and governors are given the right to receive money directly from the Government and so 'opt out' of local authority control. 'Opted out' or 'direct grant' schools run their own affairs, including the hiring and firing of teachers and hiring certain services e.g. catering.
- Inner London Education Authority was abolished.
- City Technology Colleges: to specialise in technology education (though later, other specialisms were allowed). Again, LEAs were by-passed – funding coming from central government and private industry sponsorship.

After the Act: evaluating the education system after the Conservative reforms

It was the intention of the Conservatives that the 1988 Education Act would be as important in shaping the educational system as the 1944 Act had been. The 1944 Act had established a system which, with the crucial addition of the comprehensive reforms, had lasted for almost 50 years. Presumably, both Labour and the Conservatives both wanted the best education system possible in terms of results and efficiency but they went about achieving this in different ways. Labour wanted equality of opportunity. In particular, it wanted to tap what was seen as a vast reservoir of wasted talent among the working class and ethnic minority groups. The Conservatives wanted to raise standards and to improve education's service to industry. They believed that competition is what produces the best results. Accordingly, they introduced what is termed an *internal market* into education. An internal market introduces a simulated or quasi market system into the public sector. Thus, in the case of education, the 1988 Act set up a framework in which schools were required to compete against schools and, often, parents/pupils against each other to get the school of their 'choice'.

Almost a decade after the passing of the 1988 Act, it is still somewhat too early to gauge its effects or to determine whether or not its goals have been achieved. However, some matters are becoming clearer and a provisional review of the Act can be offered.

Objectives of the 1988 Education Reform Act

1 To reduce the power of local education authorities and of the teachers' unions in running education and to increase that of parents and business.
2 To subject the education system to market forces and to place it more directly under central state control.
3 To use the national curriculum as a means to foster national culture, identity and cohesion.

4 To raise standards (by means of the national curriculum and testing).

5 In combination with other reforms, to relate education more closely to industry, to improve science and technology education and vocational training.

6 To change the educational culture in Britain – making it more competitive and entrepreneurial and less egalitarian and progressive.

Objectives 1 and 2: To reduce the power of local authorities and teacher unions and to subject the education system to market forces

Objectives 1 and 2 of the 1988 Education Reform Act were ideologically and politically motivated. This is not in itself a criticism because it is inevitable that any education policy should reflect the ideology of those who promote it. However, whereas the 1944 Education Act was passed by a coalition government and reflected a broad cross-party consensus, the 1988 Act was based on Conservative ideology and was passed against some fierce opposition in parliament and in the country.

The shift in power from the local education authorities and teacher unions to central government, individual schools and parents seems unlikely ever to be fully reversed. In particular, it seems improbable that either a Conservative or a Labour government would ever give up the power to determine the content of the national curriculum or the right to shape the education system and intervene in its running. The 1993 Education Act substantially extended the practical powers of the Secretary of State for Education to intervene in the running of the education system, including the right to appoint a special team to take over the running of schools in the state sector deemed to be failing badly (a power first used in 1995 – Hackney Downs School being closed down). The 1993 Act also set up a government quango – the Schools Funding Agency – to promote opting out and to provide the means for some co-ordination among opted out schools.

Geoff Whitty has commented on the seeming contradiction between the centralising aspects of the 1988 Act and its free market aspects (1992). Whitty particularly has in mind the national curriculum and tests when he refers to as centralising tendencies. He suggests that this national curriculum and tests may be given less importance once a competitive, free-market system is fully in place. In Whitty's view a highly competitive and selective education system geared particularly to the needs of the middle class is what the New Right section of the Tory party wanted. It is certainly true that some of the radical New Right free marketeers in the Tory party would prefer schools to compete on the basis of different 'goods' (curriculum) offered as well as on relative standards. Whitty quotes Dennis O'Keefe as saying:

> If you do not like the groceries at one supermarket, try another. The system which has utterly outperformed all others in history in the production of a wide range of goods and services needs trying out in the field of education too.
>
> (quoted Whitty:293)

Certain policy developments since 1988 lend some support to Whitty's view. There have been sizeable cut-backs in the compulsory national curriculum and in the amount of testing. This did allow for more variety or 'market diversity' in the curriculum. However, it was done mainly because the initial curriculum and tests were widely seen as too bureaucratic and time-consuming, not as a result of any retreat from a national curriculum and testing system. The government made another move towards 'market diversity'; in allowing specialist schools to develop. These included schools specialising in the arts and sport as well as the City Technology Colleges. The latter were partially exempt from national curriculum and testing. Even so, by 1996 there were fewer than 100 such schools in a state system of nearly 25,000.

Despite the above developments, in practice, it seems likely that the majority of the Conservative party will remain committed to a national curriculum and testing system designed to measure and compare the competitive performances between schools and individual pupils. The Labour party and the Liberal Democrats also support a national curriculum (although the former might have preferred the more socialist sounding title of 'common curriculum' had they introduced it). There are two main reasons for this broad support for a national curriculum. First, as Andy Green says, the national curriculum is regarded as mechanism for further 'modernising' Britain (see objectives 4, 5 and 6). Second, the national curriculum is seen by many politicians and intellectuals as a means of promoting a national culture and social integration. Labour and the Liberal Democrats may have different notions than Conservatives about the content of the national curriculum and national culture but they are most unlikely to give up the power to define and mould them, established by the 1988 Act.

The operation of the education market in practice

1 Parents

So far, one of the main empirical studies of the workings of the new education market established by the 1988 Act is Stephen Ball *et al. Educational Reform and its Consequences* (1994). Stephen Ball, Richard Bowe and Sharon Gerwitz sought to establish the effects of competition between schools and parental choice of school on the education system and especially on the opportunities of children from different social groups. Between 1991 and 1994, they studied fifteen schools in three neighbouring local education authorities. The schools were varied in type, including local authority schools, opted out grant maintained schools, as well as two voluntary aided church schools and a City Technology College. Their pupil intake was also varied, both in terms of social class and ethnic group.

Ball *et al.* found that the schools had changed to reflect competitive values and ways of operating. Competition between schools for the most able pupils had increased. On the other hand, children with Special Education Needs were given lower priority. Some schools went back to streaming and setting. More money was spent on advertising including the design and printing of glossy brochures. Co-operation between schools decreased as they competed for the 'best customers'. Schools did pay more attention to parents but within a competitive framework that advantaged middle class rather than working class parents.

Ball *et al.* found that the material and cultural resources of middle class parents gave them, as a group, a decisive advantage over working class parents in participating in and manipulating the education market. Money is the key to a number of practical advantages, including geographical mobility. Middle class parents were better able to afford transport to take their children to the school of their choice or even to move house. In contrast, working class parents were more likely to send their children to a nearby school – for both financial and social reasons. Middle class parents were also better able to afford coaching for their children and to pay for childcare and domestic assistance, thus giving themselves more time to concentrate on their children's educational and general welfare.

The cultural capital (see pp. 87-8) of middle class parents comes into play in their greater ability to inform themselves about and manipulate the new education market place. They also pass on cultural capital to their children who are able to draw on it in the interviews which selective schools increasingly adopt.

In so far as children from ethnic minority backgrounds are more likely to be working class, they are disadvantaged accordingly. In addition, they may also face a range of other social and linguistic disadvantages as well as the possibility of racism.

None of the above findings of Ball *et al.* on class and ethnic disadvantage are new or particularly surprising. What is new is that the educational system has been changed from one which attempted, in a limited way, to equalise educational opportunity to one which is manifestly based on competition between unequal contestants. What Ball *et al.* find is that in the new situation, inequality is increasing. Again, this is hardly surprising. Kenneth Baker who introduced the 1988 Act has commented that 'the age of egalitarianism is over' – a sentiment with which many of his colleagues would have concurred. Along with other Conservative policies in the Thatcher-Major period, the Baker Act contributed to an increase in inequality.

2 Business

In addition to seeking to increase the participation of parents in education, the Conservatives sought to increase the power and involvement of business. As early as 1980, both groups had their representation on school boards of governors enhanced at the expense of local education and teacher representatives. (see Figure 4.11) The extent of business involvement, especially in CTCs

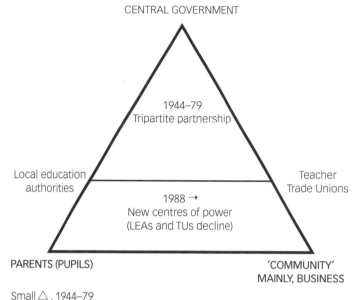

Figure 4.11 The old and new balance of power in education

remained less than the Conservatives had hoped for. Where it did occur, it often combined self interest with public service. In early 1993, the *Observer* ran a story on 'the Burger King Academy' in London's Tower Hamlets to be opened later in that year (17.2.1993:2). Burger King stated that their intention was to help truants and low achievers. The company would take on some of the school's costs and the borough would keep others. A giant Burger King red and white logo was placed above the school entrance. The borough's Chief Education Officer stated that the venture was a partnership between local government, community organisations and local business in a joint effort to do something for children at risk. Although not typical in the scale of private sector involvement, the Burger King Academy typifies a trend. Stephen Ball's own comment on the development was 'it is part of a gradual privatisation of aspects of education provision' (quoted, *The Observer*). Business companies often combined education – say, the provision of information packs in their area of expertise – along with self-advertisement (the packs would have their logos printed on them). Critics felt that this was mixing capitalist ideology, values and influence too closely with education. (Reading 2)

In the absence of a massive infusion of business funds into state education – which has not so far happened – the acid test of business involvement is on the training side of the Thatcher-Major reforms. Business people have decisive power under central government in the Training and Enterprise Councils. At the moment it is not clear that they are achieving the quality revolution in training hoped for by the Major government (see pp. 124-5).

3 The effects of the education market on comprehensive schools

The aim of the tripartite system was to select pupils on the basis of 'ability' at eleven and educate them in one of three different types of schools considered appropriate to them. The aim of the comprehensive system was to educate students with a fully balanced range of abilities in a single school (see pp. 101-4). For various reasons, many comprehensives were never truly comprehensive in the sense of achieving an acceptable balance. Even in 1979, the first year of Margaret Thatcher's premiership, school inspectors found only just under 50 per cent of 'comprehensives' to have a genuine 'mix' of pupils from the top, middle and bottom ends of the ability scale.

During the debate around the time of the 1988 Act, government emphasised that the Act was not intended to be an attack on the comprehensive system – it was stated to be a measure to raise standards in all schools. In the light of this, it is particularly interesting to examine what has happened to the ability mix in comprehensive schools during the Thatcher-Major years. According to research by Caroline Benn and Clyde Chitty (*Thirty Years On*, 1996) the number of genuine comprehensive schools declined substantially during this period. They consider that for a school to be genuinely comprehensive, between ten and twenty per cent of its pupils must be in the top twenty per cent ability range. On this basis only 27% of so-called comprehensive schools were genuinely comprehensive by the mid 1990s (see Table 4.12). On the other hand, eighteen per cent were effectively grammar schools.

Table 4.12 Ability range in comprehensive schools

Percentage of schools	Percentage of pupils in top 20% ability range	Type of school
18	20%+	Effectively grammar
27	10-20%	Fully comprehensive
16	10% or less	Not fully comprehensive
38	Less than 5%	Not fully comprehensive

Why has this happened? Benn and Chitty argue that it is largely the effect of the education market that has produced this polarisation in schools. In this respect, their statistics complement the work of Ball *et al.* discussed above. Middle class parents choose and are selected by 'better' (i.e. more academic) schools. The rest, disproportionately working class pupils and families, are left with less sought after schools most of which are now closer in type to the old secondary moderns than genuine comprehensives. The increasing powers of selection announced for schools in 1996 are likely to intensify this trend. Market processes, then, are largely responsible for producing what Benn and Chitty refer to as the most polarised education system in Europe – an educational system which they believe is no less polarised than the country's class system.

Objective 3: national curriculum, national culture, identity and cohesion

The purposes (or functions) of state education have always included socialisation, social integration and social control. The aim of developing a shared national culture and identity through the national curriculum is an intensification of these purposes. That such an aim did underlie the 1988 Act is clear from the following statement of Kenneth Baker the history curriculum working party: 'the programmes of study should have at the core the history of Britain, the record of its past and, in particular, its political, constitutional and cultural heritage' (quoted Whitty:295). In the event, the compulsory reading tests for the national curriculum in English as well as History focused overwhelmingly on English culture. Similarly, the Religious Education curriculum is centrally concerned with Christianity. However, while the national curriculum reflects a strong concern with national culture, the substantial increase in non-national curriculum time brought about by the Dearing review of the national curriculum (1994-95) allowed more scope for exploring other cultures in addition to indigenous British.

Notwithstanding the aspiration to cultural integration underlying the national curriculum, in practice, no single consensual (agreed) version of 'British culture' has emerged which is taught in British schools. There are several reasons for this. First, neither educationalists nor the public generally agree on the precise values, core content and interpretation of British culture. Different teachers will inevitably make differences of emphasis and evaluation even when teaching from the same text. Second, and relatedly, many educationalists and others would consider that any attempt to inculcate a single cultural tradition through the curriculum would probably reflect the dominant culture of England's conservative elite. Third, individuals and groups seem to interpret their 'Britishness' and 'Englishness' in different ways – to an extent that it is not easy to establish clear, central cultural values on which they agree (see pp. 238-42). 'Nation' and 'national identity' are imagined differently by different people and some do not even find them wholly attractive concepts.

Notwithstanding the above difficulties, in 1995, Dr Nick Tate, the chief executive of the School Curriculum and Assessment Authority, revived the debate about the role of schools in fostering a national identity. Tate's main objective is that the national curriculum should act to achieve social integration and cohesion. He stated: 'What I am concerned about is that the centre should hold …' He argues that instead of a watered down multiculturalism, schools should teach what he describes as a 'fairly clear majority culture which is distinguished by the fact that its roots are European, Christian, classical … going back centuries' (TES, 18.7.1995:7).

Dr Tate refers approvingly to the French national curriculum, the main purpose of which he sees as providing 'all French children', of whatever ethnic background, 'with a common entitlement to a French identity'. However, Anne Corbett, a British journalist domiciled in France for over twenty years, sees matters rather differently. She describes how the French national system of education was conceived:

> *The system was obligatory, free and secular. The militantly secular and public approach, bringing together the Republican commitment to equal rights and to advancement by merit in the public service, along with the insistence on respect for the French language, are the basis of a cultural identity.*
>
> *(TES, 28.7.1995:7)*

What Corbett is emphasising is the equal rights and opportunities which the French system aspires to, not a specific cultural content. In France, it is shared rights which 'are the basis of a cultural identity'. In contrast, Tate seems to be searching for a core of traditions and practices, as well as values, which should be taught to everybody. A cultural identity based on shared rights and opportunities is much easier to establish than one based on supposedly shared tradition and behaviour. The way the two national curriculums treat religion is indicative. The French remove it altogether from the curriculum as being potentially divisive and because it is a private matter, whereas, the Conservative national curriculum has tried to make the teaching and practice of the Christian religion central to the process of social integration. These issues are pursued again in a later section (see pp. 238–42). It may be that the French values of 'liberty, equality and fraternity' provide a more widely acceptable basis of 'national identity' than the arguably more sectional conservative and religious values which underpin much of the English national curriculum.

Keith Sharpe has suggested another reason why the national curriculum in England may be failing to inculcate a shared national identity among the young (TES, 11.8.1995:10). He argues that the education market tends to set schools against each other and encourages them to stress their differences rather than what they have in common. This militates against the development of cultural consensus. Sharpe's point here is really an application of Whitty's argument referred to earlier: that the 1988 Act contains two contradictory tendencies – one is to emphasise national culture, the other is to promote individual competition and market forces. Sharpe implies that an educational system based on a mechanism which creates winners and losers is not best suited to the creation of shared values and community.

A Times Educational Supplement editorial takes the latter point up. It refers to the rising rate of crime among teenagers, the falling wages of eighteen year-olds and the fact that 150,000 seventeen year-old school leavers have never been in paid work (TES, 28.7.1995:10). The editorial concludes: 'If Britain's children are to feel that they belong and that they share a national identity, their country has got to give something in return.' In other words, a society that does not create a sense of fairness and justice is unlikely to create a shared national culture and community. In this respect,

the jury is still out on the effects of the new education market.

In 1996, Dr Tate developed and clarified his position in relation to the moral aspects of the shared culture in which he considered that the national curriculum should play a major role in inculcating. He suggested a more formal aim for personal and social education including an emphasis on 'contributing to society's efforts to maintain structures centred on the two-parent family'. (*Times*, 15.1.1996) However, would this mean that those who held different views would not gain equal respect or an equal hearing for their principles? There is a potential clash here between the prescriptive morality of traditionalists such as Dr Tate and the free speech ideals of liberal education.

There is no doubt that Dr Tate intends that the curriculum should be morally prescriptive rather than that it should merely explore moral issues. He argued that once the content of a moral code had been agreed to be taught in schools it should be non-negotiable. His own suggested 'commandments' are:

- Honesty
- Respect for others
- Politeness
- A sense of fair play
- Forgiveness
- Punctuality
- Non-violent behaviour
- Patience
- Faithfulness
- Self-discipline

(Source: *The Times*, 15.1.1996:1)

What do you think?

From a sociological point of view, it needs to be reiterated that there is nothing new in schools socialising pupils to think and behave in given ways. Much of the sociology of education has been about uncovering the *hidden* or *informal* ideological and moral content of education (see pp. 87–92). However, Dr Tate's proposal is to prescribe an overt, formal moral content to the curriculum. He particularly suggests that Personal and Social Education – which is a compulsory part of the National Curriculum – should be used for this purpose. This goes against the longer term post-war trend in state sector education which has been to present moral issues as matters for discussion and personal judgement although it is consistent with the more prescriptive nature of the post 1988 national curriculum. Dr Tate is advocating a change that could fundamentally affect British society. Might his suggestions improve attitudes and standards of behaviour among the young? Or are they a threat to the value of free moral choice?

Objective 4: raising standards

It is still too early to say whether the national curriculum and testing system has in itself yet raised educational standards. However, it appears that the long-term improvement in standards (as measured by examination results) which has been occurring

'O' level/GCSE performance of boys and girls
Percentage of those gaining five places

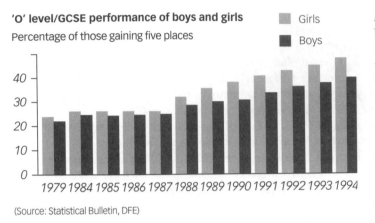

(Source: Statistical Bulletin, DFE)

Figure 4.12 Level best

throughout the post-war period has continued since the 1988 Education Act, at least, at sixteen-plus level. This improvement is reflected both in the increasing numbers of students who pass exams and in the numbers who receive grade 'C' or above at GCSE. Figure 4.12 shows a steady increase in the percentage of students receiving 5 GCSEs at grade 'C' or above from 1987.

However, as with all statistics it is important to be aware of the 'lies' and 'damn lies' they may tell as well as the truths. 1988 – the year when the recent gradual improvement started – was not only the year when the national curriculum was introduced (so it can have had little effect on the 1988 GCSE results) but was also the year in which 'O' levels became GCSEs. It is not easy to prove but it has been widely suggested that GCSEs are 'easier' then 'O' levels because they generally employ a greater amount of coursework. If so, this would account for some of the improvement from that date. However, why did the steady improvement continue (at an average annual rate of two per cent)? It may be that teachers simply got used to and became better at teaching to the new examination system (whereas results for the previously familiar 'O' level system had been at a fairly level plateau for some years). Further, the 1995 GCSE results indicate that they, too, may now have begun to plateau. In that year the increase in the proportion of students gaining C grades or above in 5 subjects increased by 0.1 percentage points. As Figure 4.13 shows, the percentage gaining grade C or

Percentage of candidates getting grade C and above

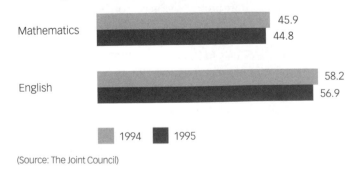

(Source: The Joint Council)

Figure 4.13 Falling standards?

above in two of the three core subjects actually fell but it remains to be seen whether or not this will be a continuing trend.

A feature of the result trends discussed so far is that they deal with only about the top 50 per cent of pupils. Do the other 50 per cent or so not matter? In fact, there is some evidence based on government statistics to suggest that in the new education market system many of these pupils do come to matter less. There are two types of evidence for this. First, in about half of those local authorities in which an increase in the percentage of students gaining 5 GCSEs grade A-C occurred, an increase also occurred in those achieving no GCSEs. It may be that those pupils who had little likelihood of contributing positively to a school's league position (i.e. of gaining 5 GCSEs grade A-C) received less attention from teachers than those likely to do so. The second type of evidence relates to school exclusions. The sharp increase during the 1990s in pupils excluded from schools (see Figure 4.14) suggests that some schools had decided to give less time and commitment to 'problem' pupils. this may have been motivated by a concern for the 'image' of the school in the competitive education market as well as by anxiety about examination results.

Permanent exclusions, England

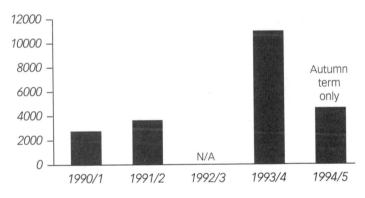

(Source: Department of Education and Employment)

Figure 4.14 Exclusions from school

In the above brief excursion into the standards debate, we have only considered standards at GCSE level. At other levels, from primary to degree, the debate is at least as complex and inconclusive. However, at all levels and in most academic and vocational areas, attainment standards in Britain give cause for concern when compared to those of key competitor nations such as Germany and Singapore (see p. 121). Unsurprisingly, as we approach the new century, both major political parties are emphasising the need to improve educational standards. Thus, the thrust of Labour's 'Excellence for Everyone' (1995) is on establishing and monitoring both teaching standards and those of pupils' academic attainment rather than on the provision of more resources. The Conservatives continue to look for an improvement in standards through the effects of their market reforms and a steady increase in selection.

Both Labour and the Conservatives are linking the drive to

improve standards with the firming up of social control and integration discussed in the previous section. Thus, in 1996 Labour outlined a plan for home-school contracts in which parents would be required to ensure that their children would complete work given. Should parents consistently break the contract, a 'mentor' would take over this responsibility. Not dissimilarly, Conservative appointee, Dr Nick Tate, chief executive of SCAA has stressed the role of education in inculcating moral standards in pupils which according to a Times report, 'should be agreed nationally and set in stone'. (15.1.1996)

Objectives 5 and 6: to relate education more closely to industry and to remove it from egalitarian influences

These objectives of the Conservatives were pursued by a variety of policies and measures in addition to the 1988 Education Reform Act. Their effectiveness has been analysed in a previous section (see especially, pp. 120-5).

Although it is doubtful that the Conservative reforms have produced a genuinely deep-rooted entrepreneurial culture in British education, the negative side of their agenda – the dilution of teacher union and local authority influence in education looks likely to survive the passing of the Conservatives from government. While there has been an increase in the involvement of individual business people and business corporations in education, neither they nor the Conservative government seem to have won the hearts and minds of pupils and parents to an entrepreneurial culture. Two recessions and consistently high unemployment in the Thatcher-Major period may have blunted popular entrepreneurial enthusiasm. In addition, the widespread perception that business people themselves – particularly at the top – were mainly concerned with their own wealth and preferment further inhibited the spread of entrepreneurial ideology (see p. 166).

Nevertheless, by 1997 there existed many more links between education and industry than at the time of the Ruskin speech twenty years previously. Education itself was organised much more along business-type lines. These institutional changes have required teachers and academics, pupils and students to behave in a more business-type way. Whether, in time, they will also begin to think and believe in a more entrepreneurial way remains to be seen. While some of the more immediate effects of the new market-style system of education are apparent, it will be several more years yet before a measured assessment of its longer term effects can be made.

Question

Choose any major area of post-war education policy (e.g. in relation to class, 'race', gender, training) and critically discuss how effective the policy has been in achieving its goals.

Summary

1 The main educational issues in the post-war period have been concerned with class, gender, 'race'/ethnicity and attainment, and more recently with educational standards and the relationship between education and industry. The main educational perspectives are functionalist, Marxist, liberal (reformist), 'free market', and interactionist.

2 One of the main functions of education is the socialisation of the young and thus the reproduction of a society's culture. Durkheim stresses the necessity of such socialisation for a society's effective continuation and Marxists emphasise that intentionally or not, working and middle class children are largely socialised differently within the educational system. Paul Willis describes how 'working class lads get working class jobs' and Christine Griffin describes how gender crucially affects class in the context of educational socialisation. Liberals recognise the importance of class in educational socialisation but stress that, partly as a result of education, a person's class of origin may not be their class of destination, i.e. education can enable social mobility to occur.

3 The perspectives on the relationship of education to the economy are in each case closely linked to what they say about socialisation. What occurs through educational socialisation greatly affects job prospects. Functionalists and hereditarian psychologists argue that the educational system is broadly effective in selecting people for appropriate roles. Marxists argue that, on the contrary, the educational system helps to reproduce and legitimate the class structure of capitalist society. Liberal, A H Halsey disagrees with both, arguing that the educational system has the potential to reach disadvantaged groups more effectively.

4 Two aspects of the role of schools are specifically considered. First is the process of labelling and stereotyping which can reinforce class (and gender and racial) disadvantage. Second is the issue of whether, regardless of the social origins of pupils, a 'good' school can significantly help them. The answer is that it can, but schools alone cannot wholly compensate for wider social inequality and disadvantage.

5 The terms ideology and discourse relate educational knowledge to power. Marxists are concerned with ideology and class power, Foucault was more concerned with the controlling and disciplining aspects of 'expert' knowledge.

6 The first major area of educational policy in the post-war period concerned class and equality of opportunity. Both the tripartite system and the comprehensive system were initially conceived as attempts to bring about greater equality of opportunity and to tap previously 'wasted' sources of talent and ability. Compensatory education was relatively a more socialist policy in that it attempted to reverse disadvantage in homes and communities. The existence of an independent

education sector alongside the state sector, sharply poses the issue of class inequality and education.

7   Gender is a second area of educational policy in which issues of equality arise. Average attainment of males and females is now roughly equal, but differential subject specialisation remains an issue. Actual reform such as that embodied in the Sex Discrimination Act largely reflected liberal views of equality of opportunity. Radical-feminists and socialist-feminists would go further. Both seek to challenge patriarchy in all its aspects within education, and by implication in society. This involves a variety of forms of 'consciousness raising'.

8   'Race'/ethnicity is a third area of educational policy in which issues of inequality arise. The education attainment level of children of given minority groups is highly varied. Although the attainment level of Afro-Caribbean children seems to be improving, there are a variety of factors which may still disadvantage them educationally.

9   There are a number of perspectives on 'race'/ethnicity in education. Assimilationists consider that the educational system should be used to enable minority groups to adapt to British culture. Multiculturalists believe that schools and the curriculum should reflect the variety of ethnic culture. Anti-racists argue that racism within education – individual and structural – should be opposed. The 'basic needs' approach is not incompatible with the other perspectives but stresses that the prime purpose of education for black and white children is the teaching of necessary skills.

10   The Conservatives' attempts to relate education more closely to industry and to create an 'entrepreneurial culture' are critically discussed.

11   The 1988 Educational Reform Act inaugurated a potential conservative revolution in education. Its key aspects are a centrally prescribed national curriculum and system of testing, and the creation of a 'free market' in schools, at the expense of local education authorities. The effects and possible contradictions of these two aspects are discussed.

Research and coursework

Gender and education is an area in which both a substantial amount of theoretical analysis and a good deal of practical reform has occurred. A piece of research which linked the two would be demanding but potentially rewarding. You could attempt to analyse the 'gender equality' reforms and activities in your own institution in terms of the leading feminist positions: liberal, radical and socialist – and perhaps also establish the basis of any opposition to them. You might well find differences in the views of 'leading players'. Thus, a Head Teacher may take a different view of matters than, let us say, a sociology teacher.

It would be essential precisely to define the focus of such a piece of research. Essentially, it is about the relationship between theories and practice. Does belief by certain individuals in a particular theory explain why particular changes have occurred in your institution? Or is there little apparent connection between theory and practice? You need to decide which issues you want to explore and how. You are likely to need copies of the institution's key policy statements on 'gender equality' and to require to interview leading policy-makers within the institution. There are easier subjects to research in this area – such as the relationships between gender and subject choice or performance or between ethnicity and educational performance, but these too would have to be adequately 'theorised'. Finally, if your school or college has changed substantially as a result of the 1988 Act, you could research the implications of these changes. Interviews with ex-students and teachers with long-service at the school/college might be appropriate.

Further reading

On education and gender, M Arnot and G Weiner *eds, Gender and the Politics of Schooling* (Hutchinson, 1987) is recommended. On education and race M Mac an Ghaill's *Young, Gifted and Black* (Open University Press, 1988) combines gender, race and class perspectives. A number of books written or edited by Stephen Ball cover post 1988 developments.

Readings

Reading 1
The correspondence principle

From Samuel Bowles & Herbert Gintis, *Schooling in Capitalist America* (Routledge and Kegan Paul, 1976), pp. 130-31

Our critique of education and other aspects of human development in the United States fully recognises the necessity of some form of socialisation. The critical question is: What for? In the United States the human development experience is dominated by an undemocratic, irrational, and exploitative economic structure. Young people have no recourse from the requirements of the system but a life of poverty, dependence, and economic insecurity. Our critique, not surprisingly, centres on the structure of jobs. In the US economy work has become a fact of life to which individuals must by and large submit and over which they have no control. Like the weather, work 'happens' to people. A liberated, participatory, democratic, and creative alternative can hardly be imagined, much less experienced. Work under capitalism is an alienated activity.

To reproduce the social relations of production, the educational system must try to teach people to be properly subordinate and render them sufficiently fragmented in consciousness to preclude their getting together to shape their own material existence. The forms of consciousness and behaviour fostered by the educational system must themselves be alienated, in the sense that they conform neither to the dictates of technology in the struggle with nature, nor to the inherent developmental capacities of individuals, but rather to the needs of the capitalist class. It is the prerogatives of capital and the imperatives of profit, not human capacities and technical realities, which render US schooling what it is. This is our charge.

The Correspondence Principle

In the social production which men carry on they enter into definite relations which are indispensable and independent to their will; ... The sum total of these relations of production constitutes ... the real foundation on which rise legal and political superstructures, and to which correspond definite forms of social consciousness.

(Karl Marx, *Contribution to a Critique of Political Economy*, 1987)

The educational system helps integrate youth into the economic system, we believe, through a structural correspondence between its social relations and those of production. The structure of social relations in education not only inures the student to discipline of the work place, but develops the types of personal demeanour, modes of self-presentation, self-image, and social-class identifications which are the crucial ingredients of job adequacy. Specifically, the social relationships of education – the relationships between administrators and teachers, teachers and students, students and students, and students and their work – replicate the hierarchical division of labour. Hierarchical relations are reflected in the vertical authority lines from administrators to teachers to students. Alienated labour is reflected in the student's lack of control over his or her education, the alienation of the student from the curriculum content, and the motivation of school work through a system of grades and other external rewards rather than the student's integration with either the process (learning) or the outcome (knowledge) of the educational 'production process'. Fragmentation in work is reflected in the institutionalised and often destructive competition among students through continual and ostensibly meritocratic ranking and evaluation. By attuning young people to a set of social relationships similar to those of the work place, schooling attempts to gear the development of personal needs to its requirements.

Questions

1 In your own words, what is the correspondence principle? Give some examples of it.
2 Bowles and Gintis published their theory of the correspondence principle over twenty years ago. To what extent do you think it now applies to the education system? To what extent and in what ways does the correspondence principle operate in your education institution?

Reading 2
The education market

From R Bowe and S Ball with A Gold, *Reforming Education and Changing Schools: Case Studies in Policy Sociology* (Routledge, 1992), pp.53-4

It is clear that the ideology and political rhetoric of the market, as directed towards the welfare state, celebrates the superiority of commercial planning and commercial purposes and forms of organisation against those of public service and social welfare.

The argument is that the ends of public service will be achieved more effectively and efficiently by market means; although effectiveness and efficiency are often conveniently confused. Part of this shift from public service to competitive provision and client choice is achieved by legislative means (like changing the basis for school funding) but part of it also requires a change in culture and a change of values within the newly competitive educational enterprises. Keat (1991) makes precisely this point:

During the course of the 1980s, the idea of an enterprise culture has emerged as a central motif in the political thought and practice of the Conservative government in Britain. Its radical programme of economic and institutional reform had earlier been couched primarily in the rediscovered language of economic liberalism, with its appeals to the efficiency of markets, the liberty of individuals and the non-interventionist state. But this programme has increasingly also come to be presented in 'cultural' terms, as concerned with the attitudes, values and forms of self-understanding embedded in both individual and institutional activities. Thus the project of economic reconstruction has apparently been supplemented by, or at least partly redefined as, one of cultural reconstruction – the attempt to transform Britain into an 'enterprise culture'.

In part this will come about via the 'forced' adaptation of individuals and institutions to the new methods and constraints of the quasi-market – adjust and survive. Some schools, some teachers clearly embrace the new culture wholeheartedly and, in addition, new actors are arriving on the scene; governors from industry, consultants and bursars, bringing with them the new values and sometimes advocating 'new ways of thinking', new forms of self-understanding. But … educational reform involves complex processes of adaptation, mediation and resistance. Reform does not eliminate historical cultures, it confronts them. Concerns about values and ethics have surfaced regularly as the case study schools began to come to grips with the education market. Certain aspects of marketing and competition were reacted against, caused discomfort, stimulated debate. But then again others were taken up unproblematically and incorporated into 'normal' practice and 'normal' ways of thinking.

Questions

1 How is it suggested that the government sought to use the education system 'to transform Britain into an 'enterprise culture'? Discuss *two* examples of this approach from government policy.
2 Indicate and briefly discuss some 'aspects of marketing and competition (which) were reacted against, caused discomfort, stimulated debate'.

5

Stratification and Differentiation: an Introduction

Class: It may not be as obvious as *that*, but that does *not* mean that class has disappeared. What is the reality of class today?

Aims of this chapter

1 To introduce and evaluate the major theories of stratification.

2 Critically to discuss certain relationships between

differentiation, stratification and community.

3 To introduce and evaluate four views on whether or not stratification is inevitable.

Definition and importance of stratification

Stratification is the division of a society or group into hierarchically ordered layers. Members of each layer are considered broadly equal but there is inequality between the layers. Among the main criteria by which people tend to be stratified are: class, gender, 'race'/ethnicity and age. However, the relevant criterion for stratification can vary greatly according to context: speed for sprinters, dexterity for conjurors, or (among other things) oratorical skills for politicians.

The division of society into layers, or strata (stratum – singular), as they are more frequently called, is often compared to geological formation. But to compare social stratification to layers of rocks, one on top of each other, suggests more rigidity in social structure than is usually found. If we remind ourselves that the relationship between geological strata can shift and change, the simile begins to tell us more about the dynamic relationship between social strata. Further, just as in certain cases, where there is extreme tension between geological strata, an earthquake can erupt and change the structure of the land, so too, extreme social conflict, in the form of revolution or invasion, can overturn a given social structure.

It would be a small-minded contemporary sociologist who failed to recognise wider units of stratification than those within the nation-state: most conspicuous is the division of the world into richer and poorer nations. As we will see in the Chapter 20, the wealthy nations have vied for influence in the poorer or 'Third' World, using as their means 'aid', and in some cases military intervention.

Stratification on the bases of the important criteria mentioned above – class, gender, 'race'/ethnicity, and age – should be analysed in an international as well as a national context. The capitalist class, whether seen in individual terms (e.g. Rupert Murdoch, the late Robert Maxwell) or institutional terms (e.g. International Publishing Corporation, Maxwell Communications) is increasingly international in scope. Different patterns of gender stratification throughout the world provide challenging comparisons with Western practice (see pp. 592-4). International migration has long meant that 'race'/ethnicity can only be properly understood in an international context. Age provides perhaps the most contrasting international comparison of all with Europe and the United States increasingly 'ageing', and most of the rest of the world struggling to maintain young, largely dependent populations.

The term 'social differentiation' is closely associated with that of stratification, although it has even broader application.

Differentiation refers to that which makes an individual or group separate and distinct: thus differentiation can provide a basis for categorisation and comparison. For instance, within class strata, occupation, income and education provide criteria for differentiation, classification and comparison. Where differences on the basis of a given criterion, say, class or age are ranked *hierarchically* (e.g. the old being regarded as more important than the young), stratification occurs. The extent to which differentiation inevitably leads to stratification is a matter of debate (see p. 154).

We will introduce the concept of social mobility only briefly here, as a full section will be devoted to it in Chapter 6. Social mobility refers to movement either up or down the social scale to a different social status or position. In industrial society this is usually brought about by occupational change.

Theories of social stratification

This section is mainly concerned with describing the theories of stratification put forward by Marx and Weber. Influential though these theories have been, neither has been fully adopted as the 'official' basis for presenting class in Britain. The Registrar General's social class scale is based on classification according to occupation and a rather simple division of all occupations into manual and non-manual. John Goldthorpe's class schema is also based on occupation but greatly reflects Weber's influence.

Feminists have found all the above theories and classificatory schemes deficient in their tendency to assume that the class position of women is derived from that of men: either husband or father. This issue is discussed at some length below. The relationships between 'race'/ethnicity and class, and age and class are analysed in later chapters.

Marx's theory of stratification (class conflict)

The origin and scope of class conflict

Marx argued that conflict between social classes is inevitable because of their different relationship to the means of production (see p. 139). There is always a dominant and a subordinate class: the former is the class which owns the means of production (e.g. land or machinery) and the latter sells its labour to survive. There are two exceptions to this: the primitive communism of hunting and gathering societies and the mature communism that Marx believed would eventually replace capitalist society. Marx's historical typology of societies is described later (see pp. 000-00) and is summarised schematically here:

Primitive Communism	Non-class Society (Simple Equality)
Asiatic Mode of Production	
Ancient Form of Society	Class societies
Feudalism	
Capitalism	
Communism	Non-class Society

Figure 5.1 Marx's typology of societies

Whereas Weber considered that in some societies stratification is based primarily on status (honour/prestige) rather than class differences, Marx considered that class is always the over-riding basis of social stratification. Thus, Weber considered that status differences embodied in the law and supported by military might have predominated in feudal or estate societies. Similarly, in caste societies, such as Hindu India, status differences, sanctified by religion, predominate. In contrast, Marx considered that it was the economic control and power of the feudal nobility and of the Hindu upper class/castes that was the basis of their dominant position in society. Marx viewed as mere ideological convenience the claim that such wealth and power was sanctioned by law or religion – whether or not this was recognised within these societies.

We now consider in detail Marx's analysis of class conflict in capitalist society, the two major antagonistic classes are the capitalist or bourgeoisie, and the industrial working class or proletariat. In the following quotation, Marx briefly reviews the history of class conflict up to the capitalist 'epoch':

> *The history of all hitherto existing society is the history of class struggles.*
>
> *Freeman and slave, patrician and plebeian, lord and serf, guild-master and journeyman, in a word, oppressor and oppressed, stood in constant opposition to one another, carried on an uninterrupted, now hidden, now open fight that each time ended, either in a revolutionary reconstitution of society at large, or in the common ruin of the contending classes.*
>
> *The modern bourgeois society that has sprouted from the ruins of feudal society has not done away with class antagonisms. It has but established new classes, new conditions of oppression, new forms of struggle in place of the old ones.*
>
> *Our epoch, the epoch of the bourgeoisie, possesses, however, this distinctive feature. It has simplified the class antagonisms. Society as a whole is more and more splitting up into two great hostile camps, into two great classes directly facing each other – bourgeoisie and proletariat.*
>
> *(Marx and Engels, 'The Communist Manifesto', 1979)*

In Marx's view, class conflict, rooted in the economic realities of differential relations to the means of production, flowed into every aspect of social life, including work, politics, education, family and religion. With particular reference to capitalist society, let us discuss what he meant by conflict in the economic context before describing how it operates in other areas. Marx contended that those who own the means of production always try to make a profit on the commodities (goods, services) produced by those who work for them. The lower the wages paid, the higher the profits made by the capitalist. The difference between the wages and the price of commodities (goods, services) produced by those who work for the capitalist class Marx called surplus value. The interest of the capitalist class is to maximise surplus value and thus increase profits. Marx's contention that the economic relations of production produce the framework for social relations, is aptly illustrated by the startling facts of economic inequality. Even in our own day, the richest one per cent own over seventeen per cent of personal wealth and the bottom 50 per cent about six per cent (1988). In Marx's time inequality was even greater. He and his friend Engels commented bitterly on the low wages, poor housing, insanitary living conditions, and lack of medical care of the working class (see Engels' *The Condition of the English Working Class*, 1844).

The base and superstructure

In order to explain how Marx considered class conflict operates, it will be helpful to introduce the simple, two-part classification of the social system which he put forward – the division of society into the base or infrastructure, and superstructure. We have already described what Marx meant by the base: it is the economic system and the bipolar (two-part) class system that economic relations produce. The superstructure refers to all other major aspects of society, such as politics, education, intellectual and religious life and so on. Marx argued that the base greatly influences and even determines the nature of the superstructure, although there is much argument about how complete he considered this determination to be. He certainly thought that class relations are lived out in all major areas of social activity. The superstructure can be roughly divided into the state (government, civil service, judiciary) and ideological institutions (e.g. the educational system, the church, the media). Marx's model of society can be presented in diagrammatic form (Figure 5.2).

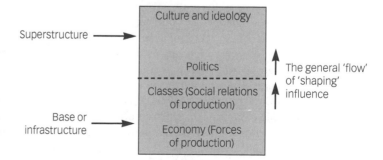

Figure 5.2 Marx's view of society: an outline

Marx considered that, in a capitalist society, control of the state is in the hands of the economically most powerful class, the bourgeoisie. The following quotation, again from *The Communist Manifesto* was meant for political rather than academic consumption but is a very clear statement of Marx's analysis:

> *Each step in the development of the bourgeoisie was accompanied by a corresponding political advance of that class ... the bourgeois has at last, since the establishment of modern industry and of the world market, conquered for itself, in the modern representative state, exclusive political sway. The executive of the modern state is but a committee for managing the common affairs of the whole bourgeoisie ...*
>
> *(From The Communist Manifesto:80)*

Marx and Engels' statement does not mean that they thought that capitalists and businessmen held all, or most, of the top positions in politics, civil service, or in the legal profession themselves. They meant that the power of the bourgeoisie as controllers of wealth and production is so great that it limits the power of other groups effectively to act against the capitalist system and the capitalist class. For Marx, therefore, economic power is the key to political power: the economically most powerful class is also the ruling class. We will examine in detail later, Marx's controversial analysis of the relationship between economic and political power (Chapter 11, pp. 312-6).

Marx is as clear and consistent, within the terms of his own analysis, about the relationship between class and ideology, as he is about that between class and state. He believed that, in any age, the ruling ideas (those predominant and most generally accepted) are those of the ruling class. For example, in the feudal period most people believed that the monarchy was, in some sense, divinely ordained. A Marxist would argue that this idea became widespread because it suited the practical interests of the monarchy that it should be. If people believed that the monarchy was 'hedged in with divinity' they would be more likely to respect and accept it. Today, when the monarchy is no longer powerful, few believe that it is a divinely inspired, rather than a purely human, institution. The same analysis is applicable to 'bourgeois' ideology. Marx described the ideology of the capitalist class as bourgeois liberalism or bourgeois individualism. As far as he was concerned, this meant little more than the liberty of the bourgeoisie to pursue private gain and wealth. Bourgeois ideology, like bourgeois society, emerged out of feudalism. In feudal society people were expected to keep to their station and there was legal restraint on individual initiative, particularly in the area where the bourgeoisie most resented it – the economic. The bourgeoisie achieved their aims through parliamentary pressure, refusing to pay certain taxes, and by civil war. Marx pointed to communism, which emphasised collective action and greater material equality, as an alternative to bourgeois liberalism. In his analysis of the spread of bourgeois ideology to other sections of the population besides the capitalist class, he was

particularly concerned to explain how some sections of the working class came to adopt a bourgeois liberal ideology rather than communism, which he considered to be more in their interests. How modern Marxists consider people are socialised to conform has already been referred to in Chapters 1 and 4, and we examine this issue further in Chapter 17.

Conflict and change

So far, our account has tended to stress Marx's analysis of how the ruling class establishes and maintains its position. We know, however, that he considered change and conflict to be at the heart of the social process. He argued that the position of the working class in the economic structure placed it in conflict with the capitalist class. Trade unions are the organisational means by which the working class seek higher wages and better working conditions. Marx also stressed the need to establish a revolutionary party of the working class, with socialist and communist ideals. He observed several contradictions and developments in the capitalist system which, he felt, would promote the rise of revolutionary class consciousness. He suggested that a major contradiction in the capitalist system was that, in order to make as much profit as they could, the bourgeoisie would pay as low wages as possible to the working class and thus immiserate them (make their situation miserable). The precise meaning of Marx's so-called immiseration hypothesis is the subject of scholarly debate, but we can take it that he expected the working class to suffer increasing economic exploitation, and that this would provide a stimulus to revolutionary discontent. Critics of Marx argue that, in fact, working people have become much better off under capitalism and that therefore this 'scenario' for revolution was wrong.

In retrospect, Marx's analysis of the contradiction that can develop between the relations of production (the formal and legal framework governing the relations of workers and capitalists) and the forces or means of production (machinery/technology), seems a more important and lasting contribution to sociological theory. He meant that technological developments can make obsolete, and so help change, the relationships of social classes to one another, even to the point where the established system breaks down. (A clear example of technological change producing profound, if not 'break-down' social effects, is apparent in our own time in the impact of the micro-chip 'revolution'.) Marx argued that the capitalist class itself rose to power because it controlled capital (money) and productive machinery, and that these became even more important than the old basis of wealth and power – land. A revolution in both the forces and relations of production constituted a change in the mode of production, a term encompassing both concepts. Marx believed that the development of large-scale production would eventually make it a reasonably simple matter for the working class to take over control of industry, if they were to consciously organise to do so.

Marx stressed the need for the working class to become conscious of its collective power as a pre-condition of revolution.

In this respect he distinguished between the working class as a *class in itself* (i.e. its members had a certain objective relationship to the means of production) and as a *class for itself* (i.e. a class conscious of its own power and potential, and therefore willing to act for itself). In the latter case there is a sense in which a class becomes a community.

A factor that facilitated the development of working class consciousness of its own power and interests was that its members were increasingly crowded together in urban areas and factories. This gave them the opportunity to react collectively to collective grievances and to organise against them. Marx expected that the factors promoting the creation of revolutionary consciousness among the working class would prove stronger than those persuading them to accept capitalist society. He did not, however, assume that this would happen without the conscious efforts of committed individuals and groups to bring about change and revolution.

Other social groups (petit-bourgeoisie, peasantry, lumpen proletariat)

So far, our analysis of Marx's account of social class in capitalist society has referred to only two social classes; the bourgeoisie and the proletariat. This fairly reflects Marx's own emphasis. Nevertheless, he recognised the existence of other groups which he envisaged would be transitional while polarisation into two classes became virtually complete. He referred to small businessmen and, sometimes, to professionals as petit-bourgeois. He considered that, as the conflict between the bourgeoisie and the proletariat developed, the petit-bourgeoisie would be forced into one side or the other of the class struggle. At the bottom of the social strata are two further groups: the peasantry and the so called 'lumpen' proletariat. Marx considered that, in an industrial and urban society, the peasantry would become smaller, less powerful and less relevant to the central class conflict of the capitalist order. The lumpen proletariat refers mainly to the unorganised working class: it includes those in low-paid and irregular employment and those who, for one reason or another, are virtually unemployable. Many of these are poor. Marx rightly considered that the lumpen proletariat was much less powerful than the industrial proletariat. (See Reading 1 for Marx's description of class polarisation.)

Marx and stratification: conclusion

We will deal with various criticisms and revisions of the above aspects of Marx's class analysis in the appropriate parts of this book. However, some major general criticisms of Marx's class analysis may be briefly referred to here.

First, Marx's class analysis is seen as too simplistic. Critics argue that even in Marx's own time the class structure of capitalist societies was becoming more complex rather than resolving itself into a bi-polar system. Second, Marx is criticised for exaggerating the importance of class and particularly class conflict. His historical analysis and prediction of future society ultimately depends on a total antagonism between classes that many find unlikely. Third, and relatedly, frequently the consciousness and behaviour of the working class has proved much more 'moderate' and open to compromise than Marx envisaged. Fourth, Marx's class analysis is sometimes seen as a mixture of political and ideological bias and quasi-religious wishful-thinking purporting to be scientific analysis. We will return to the view of Marxism as 'the God that failed' later.

Conveniently, Max Weber addressed himself fully to several important issues raised by Marx, and it is to Weber's analysis of stratification that we next turn.

Max Weber: power and stratification

Class, status and party

For Weber, as for Marx, the public life of a society is largely concerned with power conflict. Whereas Marx saw stratification and power conflict in terms of an exclusively class-model of society, Weber defined two additional dimensions of stratification – party and status. Weber used these terms to refer to three separately distinguishable but greatly overlapping areas of stratification: the economic (class), the political (party), and the social (status). It is much easier to differentiate these factors in theory than in practice, but Weber was keen to distance himself from Marx's view that party and status are merely functions of class. (Reading 2)

Class

Although Weber did not attach the absolute importance to class that Marx did, he still considered it to be a most important aspect of stratification. He differed from Marx, however, on the precise definition of class, making a distinction between economic class and social class. He defined economic class as a person's situation in the economic market; both the commodity market (buying/selling) and the employment market (providing or seeking jobs). Qualifications and experience largely determine a person's situation in the economic market, and the better qualified and experienced can usually command greater rewards. Social class includes economic class but, in addition, members of the same social class share similar chances of social mobility (thus people from a low social background would tend to have a poor chance of upward mobility). Members of a given social class, therefore, share a common socio-economic situation. This difference in the definition of class led to a fundamental disagreement between Weber and Marx about the class structure of capitalist society.

Depending on how finely an individual's market position is differentiated, Weber's definition allows for any number of class gradations. However, he indicated four main classes: upper, petit bourgeois, middle and working class. He agreed with Marx that the most powerful class in capitalist society is that of the owners of property and wealth – the upper class. Again, like Marx, he recognised that, in rare cases, education could provide entry to the upper class from lower down the stratification hierarchy. He also agreed with Marx that a second class, the petit bourgeoisie, was likely to become of less importance and that the growing strength of the third group, the manual working class, gave it great potential importance. Contrary to Marx, however, Weber gave great emphasis to what he considered was a distinct and numerically expanding class: propertyless white-collar employees. He referred to them as 'technicians, various kinds of white-collar employees, civil servants – possibly with considerable social differences depending on the cost of their training'. It is Weber's view of the role and importance in capitalist society of this class that fundamentally distinguishes his class analysis from that of Marx who was far more interested in the industrial proletariat. Weber regards white-collar employees as middle class. What distinguishes their market situation is that they sell mental or intellectual labour and skill rather than manual. In general, these skills are rarer than manual skills; thus the market situation of the middle class tends to be stronger than that of the working class. Obviously, this applies to some more than to others: it is more true of a top civil servant than of a clerk.

Status

Weber defined a 'status situation' as any aspect of social life 'determined by a specific, positive or negative, social estimation of honour'. He went on to state that any factor might be the basis of shared honour or status – religions, taste, ethnic group membership or whatever. The main expression of status group membership is style of life or lifestyle. Membership of a status group gives exclusive right to certain privileges and opportunities, as in the estate and caste systems discussed below. Ascribed status is the status a person is born with, and achieved status is acquired during the course of life. Weber argues that ascribed status has rapidly declined as a means of access to economic and political power in modern societies. In the political area, for example, the titles and functions of royalty and aristocracy have generally become of symbolic significance only – they are certainly no longer an automatic passport to national or local leadership. Similarly, he regards economic and career opportunities as increasingly open to competition in modern society.

Estate system

As mentioned above, according to Weber, estate and caste social systems are two main types of society, mainly determined by status. The former is a system of a reciprocal rights and duties sanctioned by law, and the latter is a social system reflecting a particular religious world-view. It is worth describing these further in Weberian terms. Estate systems date back to the Roman Empire, but the European feudal system is a more recent example of this form of stratification. In an estate system, the people of the various strata were identified by the rights they had and the duties they were expected to perform. These rights and duties were enforceable by law or by military might. At the top of the feudal hierarchy in medieval England were the king, nobility and clergy. The gentry, free tenants, and serfs followed in order of descent. Each of these groups was a separate status group within an overall status system. A most important right, from the king's point of view, was that of being able to summon the nobility to provide soldiers for him. This was established when they took their oath of allegiance to him. It was generally believed that the feudal system was 'sanctioned by Almighty God'.

In general, there were therefore strong legal barriers against social mobility in estate systems. Exceptions could occur, however. The king could ennoble a given individual. The church provided an avenue of social ascent for some able individuals – as, indeed, it was intended to do. The growth of a powerful commercial and industrial class, and with it the increasing demand for economic and political rights, contrary to feudal law and practice, eventually undermined the feudal system in Europe. Even so, its influence lingers on – perhaps most conspicuously in the survival of the House of Lords in Britain.

Caste system

Another form of stratification is the caste system. A pure caste system is a form of stratification rooted in religious belief, involving rigid ranking according to birth, and restrictions on occupation and marriage. The Hindu caste system of India comes closest to matching this definition. The term 'caste' has also come to be used more widely to refer to any hereditary and exclusive social group. In caste societies, social mobility is open to groups but not to individuals. this is because every individual, from the highest to the lowest, is considered to be divinely predestined to fulfil the role into which s/he has been born. In India, the caste system has been undermined, but by no means destroyed, by Western influence: caste and class exist uncomfortably side by side. An example of the deep-rooted nature of caste affiliation occurred in 1990. Indian Prime Minister Singh, announced his determination to pursue reforms which would enable India's tens of millions of untouchables (literally, 'out castes') to have access to the society's institutions on a basis of equality rather than continue to suffer the exclusion legitimated by the caste system. Among the widespread protests against this was the suicide of over 60 high-caste youths by self-immolation.

Weber argued that particularly extreme forms of status stratification can occur when different ethnic groups live in close proximity. When such stratification involves a dominant and subordinate ethnic group, a caste situation occurs. Weber gives the example of the Jews as an historically subordinate caste throughout Europe. Modern Weberians, such as John Rex, argue that the apartheid system in South Africa was a caste system, and it is possible it may remain so despite the formal abolition of apartheid.

Other examples of status stratification, status and class

Weber's concept of status is of especially interesting application in relation to generational stratification. Berger and Berger, for instance, considered that membership of the 1960s youth movement crossed class (but seldom age) lines, thus creating a form of status based on age stratification. The concept of status group or status sphere – whether membership be based on youthful lifestyle or some other criterion – does seem to have relevance to the late twentieth century when 'style groups' form and evaporate with apparent ease and regularity.

Weber's difference with Marx on the nature of status is worth stressing again. Marx regarded status distinctions primarily as a product of class stratification. Certainly, the overlap between the three dimensions of stratification – which Weber himself stressed is particularly obvious in the case of status. In modern societies, an individual's status is usually derived from his economic or class situation. The wealthy generally adopt the status symbols they can afford, as do other groups. Even though Weber accepted this, he also believed that the chain of causation can operate in the other direction: status group membership can give access to economic and political power and advantage, as he argued it did in the caste system. Later, we further examine Weber and Marx's disagreement about the importance of the concept of status in the context of our analysis of race and youth.

Finally, in a telling contrast between status group and class membership, Weber states that whereas status groups are 'communities', classes are usually not. By 'community', he meant that members 'know each other' and have a degree of common consciousness and identity and exclude those unlike themselves. On the other hand, class membership is determined by economic criteria and members of the same class will usually have no knowledge of each other, let alone belong to the same community. Marx dealt with this issue by distinguishing between class membership in simple economic terms – a class in itself – and a class that had become conscious of itself or developed into a 'class community ' – a class for itself. Whereas Weber argued that classes are 'not naturally' communities, it has been a central problem of Marxism that the working class as a whole has not become an active, ultimately political, community.

Party

According to Weber, parties 'live in a house of *power*'. Their 'actions are always directed towards a goal which is striven for in a planned manner'. Party membership may be based on a single social group or on many: Weber suggests that '(i)n most cases they are partly class parties and partly status parties, but sometimes they are neither'. Thus, to take contemporary examples, the Labour party is partly a working class party, the Ulster Unionists are largely a status (Protestant religious) party, and, according to its own members' claims, the Liberal Democrats appeal beyond the lines of class and group interest.

For Weber, then, parties are a further and distinct dimension of stratification adding to the complexity of the total picture. He did not regard political power as a function of economic factors as Marx did. In further contrast to Marx, Weber did not regard liberal political democracy as mere 'window dressing', designed to obscure the fact that the capitalist class had the real decision-making power and influence. He felt that once the working class had won the vote, it could be used as a powerful lever to achieve social change. He considered that policies such as nationalisation, redistributive taxation, expansion of the welfare state and public education, adopted by political parties supported by the working class, could help to provide new economic and social opportunities for the working class. For Marx, of course, these policies were no substitute for socialist revolution and 'real' change.

Weber insisted that, although economic factors could certainly affect political ones, the reverse was also true. For instance, the policy of nationalisation favoured, in some degree, by most European Socialist parties of Weber's own day, was likely to have profound economic consequences. In the chapter on political sociology (Chapter 11), we will look much more closely at the relationship between economic and political power. For the moment, it is enough to be aware of the major issues involved in Marx and Weber's 'great debate' on power.

Weber and stratification: conclusion

In conclusion, Weber's overall model of society – if, indeed, such a precise description is appropriate – is both more pluralistic and more voluntaristic than Marx's base/superstructure model described above. He considered that a variety of groups, based on class, status or whatever (pluralism) form and by their judgement and action genuinely influence (voluntarism) society. He also argued that the relationship between culture (Marx's 'superstructure') and class (part of Marx's 'base') is 'looser', more 'two-way', and less predictable than did Marx.

Although Weber is rightly seen as a conflict theorist, he deliberately set out to qualify Marx's extreme emphasis on conflict. He argued that party and status identities could cut across class lines and thus blur the edges of class conflict. In rejecting Marx's polarised analysis of the class structure and replacing it with a more finely graded version, he attempted to undermine further Marx's theory of stratification. Yet, the basis of Weber's perspective is power-conflict. He sees throughout society individuals and groups competing for power and control and the wealth and prestige that often accompanies them. On this fundamental point, he and Marx were in agreement.

The Registrar-General's class categories

Since 1921, social class in the United Kingdom has been officially described in terms of the Registrar General's social classes. These are the class categories used by the Office of Population Censuses and Surveys, and also widely used in sociology and public life. As Marshall *et al.* put it, the 'Registrar-General's class schema rests on the assumption that society is a graded hierarchy of occupations ranked according to skill' (18). Occupations are put into five social classes on the basis of how skilful they are considered to be.

Table 5.1 The Registrar-General's class categories

Class		Percentages
1	Professional, etc.,	3.7
2	Intermediate occupations	24.9
3N	Skilled occupations, nonmanual	22.4
3M	Skilled occupations, manual	27.2
4	Partly skilled occupations	16.1
5	Unskilled occupations	5.1
(6	Armed forces	0.7)
		100.0

Note: The percentages in each class are taken from the Essex Survey Findings

The schema has been extensively criticised. Firstly, the theoretical principle of the schema was changed in 1981 when the classificatory basis of occupations was changed from 'standing within the community' to occupational skill. However, the principles behind this reconceptualisation were not explained by the Office of Population Censuses and Surveys (OPCS). David Rose has suggested that a new system may need to take account of relative earnings, as well as skill levels.

Secondly, the occupations going into given social class categories have been changed so often as to cause doubt about the basis of the categorisation. Thirdly, feminists are critical of the Registrar-General's schema, as they are of other 'mainstream' or 'male-stream' approaches because it was designed with mainly 'male' occupations in mind and cannot be very effectively used for studying the class position of females as individuals, (i.e. as distinct from their husband's class position, see pp. 147-8).

A number of class schemas have been developed which attempt to be both theoretically more explicit and consistent and empirically more reliable than that of the Registrar General. In 1995 the OPCS accepted that a new way of determining class ought to be devised in time for the next census in 2001.

The Goldthorpe social class schema

John Goldthorpe's social class schema, devised for the Oxford Social Mobility Inquiry, is used widely by academics in studies of social mobility. Goldthorpe observes that all capitalist societies have a roughly similar social division of labour in which some employees enjoy better working conditions than others. A class is a group or, more precisely, an aggregate of individuals and their families who occupy similar locations in the social division of labour time. Goldthorpe defined these class locations on the basis of two criteria: 'market situation' and 'work situation'.

'Market situation' is defined in terms of how an individual earns income from a job (e.g. self-employment, selling labour); how much is earned from a job; and the prospects for promotion and wage increments. 'Work situation' describes the degree of control and autonomy (freedom) characteristic of a particular occupation and, thus, its place within the overall structure of authority. The influence of Weber on the Goldthorpe schema is obvious.

Table 5.2 presents the Goldthorpe social classes. The percentages in each social class given in the table are based on a sample of 10,000 adult males living in England and Wales. The larger class categories of service, intermediate and working, are used as short-hand referral points to describe the British class structure. The Goldthorpe schema is neither hierarchical nor static. Individuals are constantly upwardly and downwardly mobile.

Two main sources of criticism of Goldthorpe's class scheme are the Marxist and the feminist.

Marxist criticism of the Goldthorpe scheme

Marxists define class not on the basis of market position but on that of an individual's relationship to the means of production. Given this different starting point, it is not surprising that disagreement follows. In particular, Marxists argue that for Goldthorpe to classify major capitalists, such as Lord Hanson and Richard Branson in the same category as higher professionals and top managers greatly understates their wealth and power as a class. This categorisation occurs because large-scale capitalists record occupational statuses such as company director – though these do not indicate their great economic power and wealth. Goldthorpe defends his approach on the technical grounds that the sample of 10,000, who formed the basis of the Oxford Study, would have produced very few large-scale capitalists, and on the theoretical grounds that the Oxford Study is about mass rather than elite social mobility. However, Marxists continue to argue that a social class scheme which provides a separate category for the 'petit-bourgeoisie' (small business people) but not large-scale capitalists seriously misrepresents the class structure.

Table 5.2 Goldthorpe class categories, and distribution of respondents to Oxford Social Mobility Inquiry, 1972

Class			Percentages
SERVICE	I	Higher-grade professionals, self employed or salaried; higher-grade administrators and officials in central and local government and in public and private enterprises (including company directors); managers in large industrial establishments; and large proprietors.	13.6
	II	Lower-grade professionals and higher-grade technicians; lower-grade administrators and officials; managers in small business and industrial establishments and in services; and supervisors of nonmanual employees.	11.5
INTERMEDIATE	III	Routine nonmanual – largely clerical – employees in administration and commerce; sales personnel; and other rank-and-file employees in services.	9.2
	IV	Small proprietors, including farmers and smallholders; self-employed artisans; and all other 'own account' workers apart from professionals.	9.4
	V	Lower-grade technicians whose work is to some extent of a manual character; and supervisors of manual workers.	11.6
WORKING	VI	Skilled manual workers in all branches of industry, including all who have served apprenticeships and also those who have acquired a relatively high degree of skill through other forms of training.	21.2
	VII	All manual wage-workers in industry in semi- and unskilled grades; and agricultural workers.	23.5
Total			100.00

N = 9,434

(Source: *Social Mobility and Class Structure in Modern Britain*, Table 2.1)

Feminist criticism of the Goldthorpe scheme

Feminists such as Michelle Stanworth and Sarah Arber contend that Goldthorpe's class schema inadequately represents the class position of women. Goldthorpe's sample of 10,000 were all men and he argues that an all-male sample effectively demonstrates the class position of families because, in general, men earn substantially more than women, that wives, careers tend to reflect family convenience and so are regarded as secondary to those of

their husband's, and that roughly 40 per cent of women are not in paid employment at any given time. Goldthorpe further argues that contemporary marriages tend to be homogeneous in class terms, i.e. members of families share common experiences and attitudes. In support of this position he cites empirical evidence that married women tend to adopt class identities and voting behaviour derived from their husband's occupational position rather than their own separately considered. Further, on the question of social mobility, his particular concern, his analysis of data from the *British General Election Survey* of 1983, leads him to conclude that the relative rates of mobility within the sexes are virtually the same. This confirms him in his view that separate consideration of male and female class positions is not required. In doing so, he believes he is partly accepting feminist argument that women are disadvantaged in paid work because of being stereotyped into domestic-type roles.

Goldthorpe's initial position, then, was that the family is the appropriate unit for class analysis and that the class position of families is best determined by locating the occupation of the male breadwinner (which he later termed the 'dominance principle'). Importantly, however, he has been persuaded by Robert Erikson that in female-led single-parent families (the large majority), the occupation of the female head of household should be considered to define the class position of the family. This concession, however, has not been sufficient to satisfy critics who want a much fuller location and consideration of females in the class structure.

Alternatives to the Goldthorpe scheme

Two forms of classification have been put forward more adequately to deal with the class position of women (as their proponents see it). One is a system of joint classification of husband and wife and the other is a system of classification based entirely on individuals. Both are dealt with in the section 'Feminist classificatory schemas' (see pp. 147-8). Proponents of the system of joint classification, Anthony Heath and Nicky Britten, argue that many differences between families (e.g. in voting behaviour and fertility patterns) can be better explained if data about wives as well as husbands is used. In principle, this seems a modest and likely claim. A system of individual classification has been advocated by Michelle Stanworth, and by Sarah Arber and her colleagues at Surrey University (see p. 147).

Stanworth's position is that considered independently the majority of women are in a very different class position than the majority of men. Generally, they are in inferior class positions and she suggests that this is fundamentally because of the discriminatory way the class system itself operates, rather than because of negotiation between married couples about 'who would do what'. The class system is gendered to the disadvantage of women. In order therefore to understand the total structure of class the occupational position of women must be separately considered (see p. 147 and, in bar chart form p. 201). Marshall *et al.*, succinctly summarise the basis of Stanworth's radical opposition to Goldthorpe:

> *Stanworth in fact challenges all three of Goldthorpe's principal claims; namely that, within families, husbands have the major commitment to labour market participation; that wives' employment is conditioned by husbands' class positions; and that contemporary marriages are largely homogeneous in social class terms*
>
> *(66)*

The above debate leaves unresolved 'the unit of analysis' problem in class investigation. Even if a joint or individual classification schema is adopted, it is not clear how to 'average' or otherwise analyse two individual and often different class positions in a household. However, the complexities of how class and gender stratification may operate do appear to be emerging into better focus.

Perhaps Gordon Marshall is a little kind to Goldthorpe when he states, in his review of the latter's book, that Goldthorpe and his feminist critics are 'in large measure talking at cross purposes' – and, therefore, presumably both right in their own way (*In Praise of Sociology* Unwin Hyman, 1990). It is certainly true that Goldthorpe tells us much about patterns of social mobility and class formation within families. However, even within Goldthorpe's own terms, in not providing data about females within families, and, in particular, in excluding information about females, he seems to risk an incomplete account of class structure. The nub of the feminist criticism of Goldthorpe's class schema is that it is yet another patriarchal account of a patriarchal class structure and, as a result, fails even to address why the class system is patriarchal.

Modern Marxist class schemas

Modern Marxists continue to define the basic class division as that between those who own and those who do not own the means of production. The framework of Marxist analysis of class structure, therefore, continues to be the division between the bourgeoisie and the proletariat.

'The problem' for modern Marxists has been to locate in their analysis of the class structure the many new or greatly expanded occupations which are not traditional proletarian (manual employment) that have developed during the twentieth century. These range from managerial and professional jobs on the one hand to routine clerical on the other. In general, Marxists have pursued a two-fold solution to this issue. First, higher white-collar groups have usually been seen as 'intermediate' or 'contradictory' class locations. 'Intermediate' in the Marxist sense means that these class locations have features in common with both the bourgeoisie and the proletariat. Thus, as a group they enjoy higher wages and more freedom at work, but on the other hand they sell their labour for wages and are subject, to some extent, to the authority and control of others. Second, Marxists now widely regard routine white-collar employees as working class although they recognise that this group's involvement with the process of production is

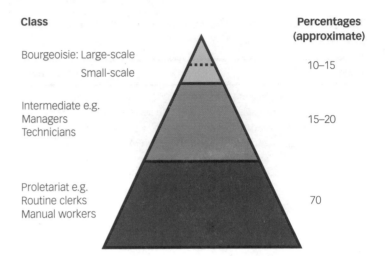

Fig 5.3 Braverman's class schema: a diagrammatic presentation

somewhat different from those involved in manual work.

Writing in the early 1970s, Harry Braverman employed the above framework of analysis to class in the United States. A schematic summary of his analysis of the class structure of that country is given in Figure 5.3.

Another American Marxist who has also written influentially in the area of class analysis is Eric Olin Wright. Wright has reformulated Marx's concept of capitalist economic control. He states that capitalist control includes: control over the physical means of production, mainly, land, factories and offices; control over investment capital; and control over labour-power. This conceptualisation of control brings into focus for Marxist analysis the financial and service sectors of the economy in addition to the industrial sector which so concerned Marx himself.

Recognising the importance of the financial and service sectors also enables Wright to reconceptualise the proletariat (see p. 147) and to develop a Marxist analysis of a range of higher non-manual employees whom he describes as being in contradictory class locations.

Wright argues that there are a range of contradictory class locations in capitalist society 'which are exploiting along one dimension of exploitation relations, while on another are exploited'. What enables certain non-members of the bourgeoisie to 'exploit' others (whilst themselves being exploited by the bourgeoisie) is that they have 'assets' of skill, credentials (qualifications) or organisational control, so, they benefit from subsidiary and lesser systems of exploitation within the overall exploitative capitalist system of production. Table 5.3 divides vertically into owners of the means of production (1, 2, and 3) and non-owners (4-12). Read horizontally, the figure divides into three groups with different degrees of organisational assets.

Critics of Wright argue that there is little difference between this analysis of contradictory class locations and Weber's analysis of the new white-collar classes. However, Wright argues that in locating contradictory class positions within an overall structure of exploitation he is distinctly Marxist rather than Weberian.

Table 5.3 Olin Wright's class model (Marxist)

Owners		Non-owners (wage labourers)						
1	Bourgeoisie 2.0%	4	Expert managers 5.6%	7	Semi-credentialled managers 7.9%	10	Uncredentialled managers 3.2%	+ Managers
2	Small employers 4.5%	5	Expert supervisors 2.2%	8	Semi-credentialled supervisors 3.8%	11	Uncredentialled supervisors	Organisation assets >0 Supervisors
3	Petit bourgeoisie 6.0%	6	Expert non-managers 4.1%	9	Semi-credentialled 14.4%	12	Proletarians 42.9%	– Non-management

	+	>0	
	Experts	Skilled	Non-skilled
		Skill/credential assets	

Note: The percentages are taken from the Essex Class project.

Table 5.4 Surrey Occupational Class by employment status and sex

Surrey Occupational Class	Men full-time	Women full-time	Women part-time	Women unwaged
		Percentages		
1 Higher professionals	6.1	1.2	0.4	0.6
2 Employers and Managers	13.4	5.3	1.7	2.5
3 Lower professionals	5.3	13.3	9.2	8.1
4 Secretarial and clerical	9.1	39.4	19.8	29.2
5 Foremen, self-employed manual	12.0	3.5	3.8	1.6
6 Sales and skilled manual	32.3	5.1	3.0	6.3
7 Semi-skilled	15.2	16.2	9.7	20.3
8 Unskilled	3.4	2.1	17.2	6.0
Total	100	100	100	100
N =	(7498)	(2967)	(2379)	(3418)

(Source: *The Measurement of Social Class* (Social Research Association, 1986), p. 84)

Feminist classificatory schemas

Two types of class schemas have been suggested by feminists: individual classification and joint classification.

Individual classification is more radical in that it discards the view that the head of household and family should be the basis of class analysis and replaces it with the individual as the basic unit. One of the most useful of such schemas has been produced by a group from Surrey University: S Arber, A Dale and G Gilbert. The Surrey Occupational Class Scale (Table 5.4) is devised to discriminate as precisely as possible between occupations in which

females are concentrated but can also be used for classifying males. In fact, such comparison is particularly instructive in that it confirms the dominance of males in higher occupational areas.

Arber *et al.* are not equally happy with the bases of classification for the four groups given in the table: men, full-time; women, full-time; women part-time; and women unwaged. They see little problem in respect to the first two categories, classifying them according to current full-time occupation. Although they classify women in part-time work on the same basis, the latter are more likely to change jobs frequently and their paid work may be an indifferent indicator of their overall socio-economic situation. For unwaged women, the best indicator of individual class position is the occupation held prior to their first child's birth, but unfortunately this information can be difficult to obtain. For this group, the most recent occupation is a poorer indicator of class position.

Despite the above classificatory problems, the Surrey Occupational Scale does successfully highlight occupational areas in which females (and males) are concentrated and it also shows up a significant difference in the areas of concentration between full-time and part-time female employees. As Arber *et al.* claim:

> *The two main advantages of SOC for women are, first, it provides a distinction, blurred in … RG class …, between employers and managers (SOC 2) and lower professionals (SOC 3). SOC 2 is predominantly male, containing thirteen per cent of full-time men compared to five per cent of full-time women and under two per cent of part-time working women, and SOC 3 is predominantly female, containing thirteen per cent of full-time women compared to only five per cent of men. Second, it separates shop work (SOC 6) from secretarial/clerical work and sales representatives (SOC 4), and separates personal service workers (SOC 6) from semi-skilled factory workers (SOC 8). These two changes highlight the concentration of part-time women in shop and personal service work, 35 per cent, compared to fourteen per cent of full-time women and a bare three per cent of men. They also show clearly the smaller proportion of part-time women in clerical and secretarial occupations, which is masked in other classifications. Under 20 per cent of part-time working women are in SOC 4, compared with 33 per cent in RG class IIIN and 44 per cent in collapsed SEG 3.*
>
> *(From 'The Measurement of Social Class', p. 68)*

Joint classification is based on the premises that the class position of household is derived from both partners' occupations. Only on this basis, can a fuller picture of a household's class position be established. This is especially so in the case of cross-class families i.e. families in which husband and wife are in different class positions. Thus, A Heath and N Britten argue in *Women's jobs do make a difference: a reply to Goldthorpe* (1984) that joint classification can produce useful data not afforded by simply classifying according to the husband's occupation. For example, families in which the wife is a white-collar employee and the husband a blue-collar employee tend to have different fertility and voting patterns from those families in which both partners are blue-collar.

Goldthorpe and Wright empirically applied: the Essex University class project

In 1988 G Marshall, H Newby, and D Rose of Essex University and C Vogler of Oxford University published *Social Class in Modern Britain* which reported a wide-ranging survey on that topic. Their data was produced from structured interviews with 1770 men and women.

A useful aspect of their work is that they analyse their data in terms of both Goldthorpe's and Wright's definitions of social classes and, within each, in terms of females as well as males. Understandably, the results are complex. In general, they judge that Goldthorpe's classificatory schema makes better sense of their data than Wright's. They do, indeed, point out some apparently odd 'anomalies' which result from using Wright's definitions. Thus, in Wright's schema the following, who are allocated service class status in Goldthorpe's schema, appear as proletarian: a lawyer, a chartered accountant, a couple of electrical engineers, one lecturer in higher education and others of similar occupation.

The Essex data will be used in Chapter 6 to help resolve some key issues of debate on social class, mainly between Marxists and Weberians. However, their data and conclusions require critical handling – not least, because the Essex team is strongly Weberian.

Marx and Weber combined: a new model of class: W G Runciman

It is arguable that all the models of class presented so far are incomplete. Marxist derived models of class are based on ownership or non-ownership of wealth and tend to say little in detail about class in terms of position in the job market. On the other hand, Weberian models are based mainly on personal marketability but lose sight of class differences produced by inequalities of wealth ownership. Class models based on ownership and those based on marketability tend not to be effectively combined. For instance 'Social Trends, 1996' states that little work has been done on the relationship between wealth and income (generated mainly in the job market) – a significant gap in sociological research. A third area of distinct concern has arisen in recent class theory, that of control. This has focused particularly on the rise of white-collar management (although Marxists still see capitalists as the ultimate controllers).

W G Runciman has developed an ambitious class scheme to integrate differences of ownership, marketability and control in a single model of class. His unifying concept is that of economic *role* which he considers to be the basis of class. He defines roles as 'positions embodying consistently recurring patterns of institutional behaviour informed by mutually shared beliefs about their incumbents' capacity directly or indirectly to influence the behaviour of each other' i.e. roles are socially structured and it is understood that different roles have different degrees of influence or power. The amount of power which characterised an economic role defines an individual's position within the class structure. Economic power is based on roles in relation to ownership, marketability and control.

Runciman defines these three terms as follows:

- 'Ownership' implies legal title to some part of the means of production, whether held directly or by way of equity or loan capital or in partnership or as a trust or other beneficiary. (i.e. business ownership).
- 'Marketability' implies institutionally recognised possession (whether by formal credentials or otherwise) of an attribute of capacity relevant to some part of the process of production (or distribution or exchange), i.e. some ability to sell in the job-market.
- 'Control' implies a contractual right to direct the application to the process of production of some part of the means of production, whether fixed or financial assets or labour, (i.e. the management function).

Assessing the power of economic roles on the basis of the above definitions, Runciman constructs a seven part class model. The percentage size of each class could only be established by empirical research and he describes the figures given in Table 5.5 as 'very rough approximations':

Table 5.5 Seven part class model

Class	Percentage size (1990)
Upper Class	0.2 to 0.1
Upper Middle Class	Less than 10
Middle Middle Class	15
Lower Middle Class	20
Skilled Working Class	20
Unskilled Working Class	30
Underclass	5

The most innovative and potentially useful aspect of Runciman's model is that unlike many, if not all, Weberian models of class, he locates an upper and an underclass. In contrast, some versions of a middle and working class (or classes) appear in all Weberian models of class. At a time when the rich appear to be getting richer – absolutely and relatively – and still to be exercising great economic power, it is particularly useful to have the upper class designated as a separate class. Uniquely – and here Runciman reflects Marx – its power is based significantly on ownership. Unfortunately, Runciman does not address the problem of the extent to which the upper class delegates operational control of big

business to the upper middle class. However, despite the brevity of Runciman's analysis, he at least removes the misimpression perpetrated by so many class schemas that the upper class does not require distinct representation and specific analysis. Reflecting Runciman's model, a more detailed analysis of the upper class is given in Chapter 6 (see pp. 165-8).

Similarly, by virtue of this definition of the diverse basis of economic power or lack of economic power, Runciman 'brings into play' a possible underclass. He defines this term to include those 'whose roles place them more or less permanently at the economic level where benefits are paid by the state 'to' those unable to participate in the labour market at all' i.e. those with virtually no economic power of the three types described above. Runciman claims that one such group are the long-term unemployed. However, as we shall see later there is evidence that this group should better be considered as part of the working class rather than as a distinct underclass.

Runciman's class model is broad in scope but not fully worked through. He does not even go into much detail on how much economic power in terms of ownership, marketability and control each class has, although in most cases this is fairly obvious. Nevertheless, the model suggests one way of integrating Marxist analysis of class inequality with Weberian attention to the complexity of class.

Questions

1 What are the main similarities and differences between Marx and Weber's theories of stratification?
2 Whose theories have been best supported by subsequent developments in the system of stratification, those of Marx or Weber?

Differentiation, stratification and community

Although the concepts of stratification and community are distinct, there is increasingly good reason for examining the relationship between them and the areas in which they overlap. Narrowly defined, class refers to the occupational or economic grouping to which the individual is allocated on the basis of some stated 'objective' criterion (be it that of Marx, Weber or Goldthorpe). Community refers to a common sense of identity or belonging – it is based on shared feeling rather than similarity of economic situation. Closely-knit neighbourhood or church groups are communities (see pp. 481-4). The first reason for explaining the link between stratification and community is that to a significant extent it is already present in classical sociology. Both Marx and Weber recognised that members of a given class may sometimes act as a community i.e. in a way that reflects a common sense of identity. Thus, upper class males who mutually identify themselves as part of 'the old boy network' are a class (and patriarchal) grouping acting as a community. Although much has been written about working class community (see pp.74-5), upper class community is arguably stronger and more durable (see p. 107).

Secondly, although it is frequently not recognised, communal groups usually divide the world into at least two strata – those entitled to belong to 'our' community and those not so entitled. Communities, therefore, are defined on the basis of those whom they exclude as well as include – and this is as true of class-based as well as, for example, religious or ethnic-based communities. Communities, therefore, certainly differentiate between each other and where one community considers itself superior to another (a frequent occurrence) and can enforce its view, stratification also occurs. One form of stratification of this type is ethnic stratification but in a rough and ready everyday fashion all sorts of gangs, peer groups and regional groupings attempt to stratify themselves in this way. Of course, in theory and sometimes also in practice, communities may accept each other as entirely equal. Democratic pluralism – the dominant form of Western democracy – is partly founded in the pursuit of the ideal of communal tolerance and equality – but it is not easily achieved.

Thirdly, much recent sociology, particularly that influenced by postmodernism implies a changing relationship between the concepts of class and community. Thus, the implication of the writings of Zygmunt Bauman, whose work is discussed below, is that community is a more fundamental and meaningful way than class of dividing the world. 'Us' and 'them' *begins* not with class but with family. Beyond family, individuals and groups differentiate between, and stratify themselves and others in many ways, of which class may be one, but is of declining importance. We now examine Bauman's controversial and provocative ideas in this area.

Self, stratification, community and identity: an interactionist perspective: Zygmunt Bauman

The perspectives on stratification so far described in this chapter are heavily structural in nature. Even Goldthorpe and Marshall, writing within a tradition which recognises the importance of subjective (personal) meaning, allocate individuals to 'objective' class frameworks. Zygmunt Bauman, in his *Thinking Sociologically* (1990), approaches the issue of social division in a quite different way. In fact he does not use the term 'stratification' at all to indicate this area of sociological concern (the word does not even appear in the book's index nor, in fact, does that of 'class'). The titles of the three chapters covering what would traditionally be considered as stratification and differentiation are: 'Us and Them', 'Strangers' and 'Together and Apart'. I suggested earlier (see p. 17) that the conceptual vocabulary of some (mainly postmodern-influenced) sociology is beginning to change, and this is a prime example.

Bauman's choice of language is highly significant. He is indicating the importance to social actors of individual and shared (collective) feelings and experience in defining social reality. He suggests that for 'ego' or self the issue of 'us and them', who do 'I' belong with/who does not belong with us, is fundamental or core to personal identity. Crucially, Bauman locates individual identity in a social context – that of others ('who are divided into us and them').

In-group and out-group

Bauman equates the terms 'us and them' with those of *in-group* and *out-group* which he regards as the most basic form of differentiation. He stresses that antagonism is inherent to the relationship between in- and out-groups. He goes on to state that this 'opposition is, first and foremost, a tool which I (i.e., the individual) employ to draw the chart of my world (my principle of classification, the frame assigning to others their places in my map of the divided universe)' (41). Bauman gives a wide range of examples of possible in-group/out-group classifications: neighbours/not neighbours; my team/not my team; decent taxpayers/'spongers' and so on …

Bauman contends that it is the family (in *idealised* form) which 'serves most often as a model for that mutual sympathy and assistance which we tend to ascribe to, or demand from or hope to obtain from an in-group'. Of course, real families are often shot-through with tension and conflict but the ideal of the family as 'a haven in a heartless world' still often exercises a powerful imaginative pull. As Bauman notes, members of larger in-groups – such as political or religious groups – sometimes refer to each other as 'one big family' or as 'brothers and sisters'. Again, there is a strong measure of positive idealisation in this process of identification.

In-groups as communities

For Bauman the ties that bond in-groups together are primarily emotional rather than rational. In explaining this, he virtually equates in-groups with communities or aspired-to communities:

> *What all this amounts to is the feeling which precedes all reflection and argument; the feeling of community, or an in-group, which is a pleasant place to be, which is truly one's home, and whose boundaries ought to be defended at any price, just as ones home tends to be.*
>
> (43)

Bauman distinguishes between small and large in-groups. In particular, the size of a group presents different problems in maintaining a sense of unity and community. Smaller groups are able to create their sense of identity *face-to-face*. Larger groups such as ethnic groups or nations have to be 'made' or constructed into communities by the efforts of politicians, ideologies or cultural visionaries. It is through their preaching or ideology that people who may not otherwise know or ever meet each other can imagine

Figure 5.4 Ethnicity as community: Chinese New Year in New York

themselves as communities. Thus, Martin Luther King's 'I have a dream' speech was an imaginative vision of both black community and of human community. Similarly, a sense of nation and national community requires articulate expression before it can be widely shared. Both ethnicity and nationality have become popular communal themes in recent years although it is possible that this is more out of a sense of threat rather than strength. Thus, Margaret Thatcher's reference to the people of Britain (i.e. 'the nation') being 'rather afraid' that 'this country might be swamped by people with a different culture' had a defensive ring about it. Moreover, the contrast between Margaret Thatcher's vision of community and Martin Luther King's illustrates just how differently community can be imagined.

As Bauman points out, genders and classes are among other large groups which can be imagined as communities. Thus, it used to be common among feminists to refer to other women as 'sisters' and to extol the virtues of 'sisterhood'. Marx, in effect, argued that a class conscious of its common interest and whose members acted in solidarity was a community (see pp. 381-4 for an extended example of a study of working class community). However, Weber argued that status groups which, by definition, share the same cultural values and symbolic order are far more likely than classes

to be communities. Thus, for him ethnic community is more likely to develop than class community.

Bauman does not mention age as a possible reference point for community identification but others have frequently done so. Peter Berger suggested that to some extent hippie-style youth groups in the 1960s were constituted as 'status spheres' – within and between which young people of various class and ethnic backgrounds moved and interacted (1971). More recently, John Förnas has argued that youth groups do, indeed, exercise informal closure (exclusion) broadly on the basis of age and, to that extent, age overrides class in defining their identity (1995).

The boundaries of community

Community, then, is about feelings, relationships and a sense of belonging. It has relatively little to do with place as such. Bauman is implying that the communities which ego or self belongs to – small and large – are the most important aspect of ego's social life (the assumption here is that family/kingship groups are types of community). The matter of membership of communities is, therefore, also of the highest importance. Gaining membership of communities of others which involve profound feeling, and express and symbolise a deep sense of identity is generally not easily achieved. The significance of 'marrying into' a family (and larger kinship network) involves ritual, rights and obligations. Even access to peer and friendship groups can involve an informal period of 'probation' and partial exclusion from the full range of activity and knowledge (e.g. 'secrets') of a group. Similarly membership of larger communities such as nations or religions is often not easily granted. Nationality in the sense of citizenship is refused to many applicants and even when granted cannot ensure personal acceptance by individual members of the established national community. Communities of faith invariably require applicants to undergo some preparation and ritual of initiation. In the cases of certain sects these processes can profoundly affect the individual's sense of identity as new values and priorities are imposed.

Bauman, then, considers that the process of establishing a dividing line between 'us' and 'them' in various communal contexts is fundamental to social activity:

> *Making the boundaries as exact and precise as possible, so that they can be easily noticed and once noticed understood unambiguously, seems to be a matter of supreme importance of human beings living and trained to live in a man-made world.*
>
> (55)

However, as Bauman observes, there are some people whose identity is ambiguous, who are neither us nor them. These people Bauman terms 'strangers'. They are 'strangers' not in the sense that they are entirely unknown but in the sense that they are present but not well known. Migrants and immigrants are categories of strangers. To an extent strangers can be ignored, separated or segregated. Often they are subject to prejudice and discrimination. Sometimes they cross the boundary of identification (or succeed in changing its line of demarcation) and become part of 'us'.

EGO (SELF) FAMILY COMMUNITIES (US) e.g. < Neighbours / Ethnic Groups / Nation

STRANGERS e.g. Immigrants or Migrant Workers

OTHERS (THEM) e.g. Other Communities, Other Nations

Figure 5.5 Bauman's 'model' of social identity and social division: a diagrammatic presentation

Community groups and purpose groups

Bauman distinguishes between communities and *purpose groups*. Whereas communities embrace the whole person, including the affective (emotional) side, purpose groups or organisations exist to fulfil given tasks. People are allocated to particular *roles* within organisations. Typically, these roles involve only a limited part of an individual's skills and feelings. The distinction between communities and organisations is fundamental to modern life. It represents another form of social division as perceived by Bauman. Communal relations and formal work relations tend to be very different in nature, the more so where the latter involve people occupying very different levels in an organisational hierarchy. Work relations tend to be highly instrumental (oriented towards practical productive goals) and serious expressions of personal emotion are regarded as disruptive to them.

Comment on Bauman's 'Theory of stratification'

Bauman's approach to social division is so different to that of the structural theorists that one hesitates to refer to it as a 'theory of stratification' at all. Not only is his approach different but the resulting description of the social world has a qualitatively different feel to it than that which emerges from the work of the structuralists. The key difference in approach is that Bauman's analysis starts *and stays with* the needs, emotions, and actions of the individual self as the latter are expressed in the context of social interaction – mainly through communal or purpose groups. Bauman's approach is just as sociological as that of the structuralists. However, because structuralists concentrate mainly on the effects of stratification on behaviour, they inevitably place themselves closer to the structuralist or positivist tradition of sociological research. Within the structural approach individuals appear more acted upon than acting, more effects than agents.

Neither the structuralist nor interpretist approach is necessarily better than the other. They are frequently regarded as complementary and increasingly attention is being given to combining them.

Nevertheless, the blend of symbolic interactionist and postmodernist-influenced theory developed by Bauman does produce particular insights and raises distinctive issues. As seen through Bauman's eyes, society is about individuals seeking expression and identity largely in the context of families and communities (e.g. ethnic, gender or class communities). It is also about their roles within purpose-groups or organisations. By implication, for him the important strata in society are those to which the individual 'belongs' or does not belong (i.e. in-groups/out-groups or communities). Put otherwise, individuals identify with some people but not with others and this produces a variety of social divisions.

In Bauman's approach, it is cultural rather than economic differences between groups that are emphasised. It is not economic base of gender, ethnic, religious or even class groups that he stresses but members' own definitions of their cultural identities. Thus, gender groups say, feminist; ethnic groups – say, British Indians; and class groups – say, the working class; are seen as creators of their own culture. Of course such cultural actors respond to external circumstances and challenges but they do so meaningfully.

'Self', 'Community', 'Identity', 'Culture' – these concepts focus the concern of an apparently growing number of sociologists, notably those influenced by interactionism and postmodernism.

They are less interested in class and stratification as conceived in predominantly economic or materialist terms. Differences of culture and identity, however, do interest them. Bauman's introductory text, *Thinking Sociologically*, impressively captures these significant trends.

Criticisms of Bauman's 'Theory of stratification'

In fairness, it must be said again that the material reviewed above is specifically about community rather than stratification *per se*. However, Bauman certainly presents a theory of social difference and division and as such his work invites comparison with the more traditional, structural theories of stratification presented earlier in this chapter.

The main weakness of Bauman's approach to social division is the 'flip-side' of its strength. Bauman leads us convincingly towards culture and meaning but has little to say about class or other kinds of inequality – or how these affect opportunity and quality of life. Following Weber, his analysis of purpose groups or organisations, including work organisations, concentrates on issues of inter-personal power and control and on the alienating effects of bureaucracy (rational organisation) rather than on how productive relations/occupation help to generate the class system with all its related inequalities. In what is often regarded as his great work, *Modernity and the Holocaust* (1985), Bauman focuses on the extent to which the 'ordinary' executioners of the Jews had allowed themselves to become machine-like extensions of the technology of genocide and thus to distance themselves from the moral promptings of their consciences. There are few more important issues than this one but those Weberians such as Goldthorpe and Marshall who continue to pursue another aspect of Weber's work – class analysis, including material inequality and inequality of opportunity – are also working within a vital tradition.

A second criticism of Bauman's in-group/out-group theory of stratification is the extent to which he stresses the antagonism between the two types of groups. Indeed, unusually for him, he is rather unsociological on this matter, seemingly assuming that such deep antagonism is inherent or 'natural'. While the survival instinct no doubt does prompt a degree of caution on the part of in-group members in relation to 'others' and 'strangers', by no means all interactions involving 'other' communities are deeply antagonistic. What often makes in-group/out-group relations antagonistic is concrete and social in nature such as competition for resources and even misunderstanding or poor communication. There is no fixed boundary between 'them' and 'us' – as Bauman himself recognises. The many efforts to achieve wider community demonstrate this. There are certain respects in which even the ideal of a global community appears realistic and necessary (see p. 224).

Social equality and freedom: four views. Is stratification inevitable?

What is the relationship between equality and freedom? What are the implications for the ideal of equality of the failure of Soviet and Eastern European communism. Is social inequality part of the 'nature of things' or is it possible greatly to diminish if not wholly to abolish it?

This section discusses four perspectives on the issue of equality and the relationship between equality and freedom. These are:

- Classical liberal: New Right
- Functionalist
- Marxist
- Social democratic (or 'reforming' liberal)

The classical liberal and functionalist perspectives on equality are broadly complementary, although they have distinct roots – the former in economics, the latter in sociology. The social democratic or modern liberal reformist perspective draws from both Marxism and the classical liberal tradition but is manifestly different from both.

Classical liberal perspective: New Right

Classical eighteenth and nineteenth century liberals emphasised economic liberty or freedom rather than material equality. Adam Smith (1723-1790) considered that a 'free' economy i.e. a capitalist economy, was the basis of a free society. The 'free market' was the basis of freedom to travel, to meet others of all kinds, and to make one's own individual wealth and happiness. Nineteenth century and modern free market thinkers also often argue that a free market is a pre-condition for democracy. In the early nineteenth century, the only equality that such freedom implied was the equal right in law to protection and to compete economically. However, limited equality under the law in no way implied that the state should help those with fewer resources. Rather, people were considered to have the right to succeed or fail on the basis of their own resources. In the late 1970s, when the first edition of this book was being written, it would have occurred to few people that nineteenth century liberalism would be revived – in the form of Thatcherism and Reaganism – and become the dominant political ideology of the 1980s. Contemporary free market theorists, such as Frederich Hayek and Milton Friedman, have reiterated the points made two centuries ago by Adam Smith. Already, their views have had considerable practical application although widespread criticism of them increased in the late 1980s and 1990s.

The implications of the classic liberal position for social equality have been well summarised by Peter Saunders, a sociologist who has some sympathy for this perspective. Saunders points out that writers such as Hayek:

> *... argue that inequality is the necessary price to be paid for economic growth in market societies. In this view, individuals pursuing their own self-interest indirectly benefit everybody else at the same time as they benefit themselves. This is because, in a capitalist society, some individuals will try to make money by innovating, setting up business, or investing in other people's business to enable them to expand ... thus, a few entrepreneurs become rich, some others fail and go bust, and meanwhile the rest of society grows more affluent as it gains by their efforts; Capitalism is dynamic because it is unequal, and any attempt to equalise wealth and income will succeed only at the expense of stifling initiative, innovation and social and economic development*
>
> *(Saunders, 1990:53)*

Saunders' arguments are admirably clear. Not only is capitalism an unequal system but it has to be in order to work effectively. However, as capitalism is a system devoted to the creation of wealth, 'the rest of society grows more affluent' as a result of the efforts of 'a few entrepreneurs'.

Functionalist perspective

Within sociology, the view that stratification is inevitable has always been associated with functionalist theory. The definitive functionalist presentation of this issue was by Davis and Moore (1956), but the roots of the functionalist position can be traced to Durkheim and Herbert Spencer. Both of them considered that as societies evolve and grow more complex a greater variety of social roles and functions develop. One of the first examples of role differentiation in the evolution of most societies is that of tribe or band 'leader' or 'priest', or perhaps a combination of both. Now differentiation need not lead to stratification if equal power, status and rewards are attached to all roles but, in practice, this rarely, if ever, occurs. Indeed, Durkheim and Spencer assumed the opposite – that key or particularly demanding roles, such as leader or chief, would be recognised as having more status than functionally less important and demanding ones. Since role differentiation, in a factory or bureaucracy, for instance, is so much a part of modern life, so must stratification be. A complex system of stratification is seen by functionalists as a necessary product of a complex society.

Davis and Moore extend some of the arguments of earlier functionalists and add a number of their own. they contend that some positions in the social system are more important than others for the functioning and stability of society. Thus, the position of 'chief' or managing director are both relatively crucial in these respects. Functionally important positions require talented people to fill them and there are only a limited number of such people in a given population. Even talented people must undergo long periods of training if they are to execute such key roles as surgeon, air pilot or research scientist. In return for undergoing lengthy training and for the qualifications and skills thus acquired,

they require more pay and 'perks' than less able and less well-trained people. In addition, they would also expect their occupations to carry high status. The existence of a group with greater access to material and status rewards than others means, in effect, that a system of stratification also exists. As such a group is necessary to all societies, it follows that stratification must be inevitable as well as functional.

Marxist scholars have been notably energetic in revealing and attacking the assumptions behind the arguments of Davis and Moore. Recently, Bowles and Gintis have pointed out that, in the United States, economic success (and thus career success) is less associated with intelligence than with the socio-economic status of a person's parents (see Chapter 4 for details of this argument).

Tom Bottomore, writing several years before Bowles and Gintis, firmly refutes the contention that the occupational hierarchy is a true reflection of innate 'talent' or ability:

> *The major inequalities in society are in the main social products, created and maintained by the institutions of property and inheritance, of political and military power, and supported by particular beliefs and doctrines, even though they are never entirely resistant to the ambitions of outstanding individuals*
>
> *(Bottomore, 1991)*

Bottomore has further argued that this state of affairs is only mitigated, not abolished, by increased educational opportunity and more open competition in the job market.

Davis and Moore have also been attacked by Tumin for failing to appreciate the great wastage of talent and potential amongst the lower classes that stratification can cause. Because of social background disadvantages there is not, in his view, equal opportunity. Tumin also stresses the human costs of stratification in terms of the frustration and sense of failure that quite able, but less privileged, members of society can feel.

Marxist perspective

Marxists argue that stratification exists because of the unequal ownership of private property. They consider that if private property is abolished and communism established, class stratification will cease to exist. Marx argued that capitalism is characterised by certain inherent contradictions which make it prone to self-destruction. In particular, he contended that capitalism creates increasing inequality and involves the 'immiseration' (increased impoverishment) of the proletariat. On this point, the evidence seems, to say the least, strongly to favour the classic liberal view – that capitalism has increased the wealth of the majority as well as the minority. However, this in itself by no means destroys the Marxist critique of capitalism or the argument for a different kind of society. Whether the working class has been becoming increasingly poor or not, many of its members have undoubtedly been 'exploited' in respect to their working conditions and pay. This is especially so, if capitalism is examined as a world system. To cite the extreme case, there are examples where capitalists have treated labour as little better than cattle, providing unhealthy and even dangerous working and living conditions, no job security, and wages at around subsistence level. Examples of this kind have been, and continue to be so numerous that it is entirely reasonable to pose the possibility of a less 'exploitative', more equal socio-economic system.

The difficulty for Marxism has not been in criticising capitalism but in producing theoretically and practically a convincing alternative. Marx's own descriptions of what communist society would be like are fairly skimpy. The main practical attempt to produce a communist society in Soviet Russia appears, at the time of writing (1997) effectively to have been abandoned. Similarly, the Soviet 'satellite' countries of Eastern Europe have, to a greater or lesser extent, adopted mixed (i.e. partly capitalist) economics. Former communist East Germany has capped all this by unifying with former West Germany – perhaps Europe's most successful post-war capitalist economy.

As a practical example of equality, then, communism has lost much credibility. First, the above societies did not even approximate to social equality and did not appear to be developing towards it before introducing capitalism. However, material equality was probably rather greater in these societies than in the capitalist West even though their general level of wealth was lower. Second, none of these societies achieved a high level of political, cultural and social freedom compared to Western European and North American societies. This provides some evidence for the view of Hayek and Friedman that communism and freedom do not mix. In summary, the record of these communist societies compared to the capitalist Western ones was slightly more material equality; substantially less wealth; and substantially less freedom. That this is perhaps a fair summary is supported by the abandonment of authoritarian communism by the Eastern European former communist countries.

Marxists seem able to cite enough evidence to demonstrate that stratification benefits some at the expense of others and that it persists, not merely because it is useful, but at least partly because the rich and powerful wish it to. However, they tend to overlook the possibility that as well as benefiting the rich and powerful at the expense of the less advantaged (as most systems of stratification certainly do), stratification may exist for other, more necessary reasons.

The essence of the functionalist position is precisely that somebody must do the more difficult and skilful tasks and will, as a result, expect higher rewards and status. This argument could still be true, whatever the social origins of those who came to occupy the top occupational positions. It would be sustainable even if children of lower class origins were disproportionately successful (instead of the opposite). The Marxist reply to this would be that, if people were rewarded according to need rather than on the basis of the nature of the work they performed, no material or status

inequality would result from differences in occupation. In a communist society, all property would be held in common and the product of all human labour would be shared on a rough basis of equality, with variations depending on individual circumstances and requirements. In addition, as far as possible, jobs would rotate so that more people had an opportunity to do interesting work and escape being permanently trapped in boring and unhealthy occupations.

In an ideal sense, Marx's vision – for it is a visionary's dream – of a classless society is 'better' (if we may speak for a moment in moral terms) than the stratified societies that we are more familiar with. But whether such a society is possible is another matter.

Social democratic (or 'reformist' liberal) perspective

The social democratic (or modern liberal reformist) tradition can be considered as an 'intermediate' position between classical liberalism and Marxism, although it has roots partly independent of both. Social democrats accept that the free enterprise system is the most effective means of producing, distributing and exchanging goods. Probably most now agree that political freedom largely depends on the existence of economic freedom. They accept, too, that a mainly capitalist economy produces great social inequality. It is at this point they differ from both classic liberals and Marxists. They differ from the former in that they consider the extent of the inequality typically produced by capitalism to be unacceptable. For instance, the general widening of the gap between rich and poor under Thatcherism is the reverse of what most social democrats regard as fair and just. This presents social democrats or modern liberals with the problem of achieving greater equality within a fundamentally capitalist economy.

There are at least three ways in which social democrats seek to bring about greater equality. They seek to ensure equality of opportunity: to redistribute wealth through taxation, the Welfare State and the provision of public services; and, where necessary, they are prepared to control or regulate the economy in the public interest. The concept of equality of opportunity is at the heart of modern liberalism and social democracy just as the equal right to individual protection under the law and free competition is central to classical liberalism. Throughout the 30 years following the end of the Second World War, a series of measures designed to reduce class, racial and, finally, gender disadvantage or discrimination and to increase equality of opportunity were passed (these are discussed in the relevant sections of this book).

The second great aim of social democracy in relation to equality is to reduce the 'excessive' inequality of outcome (i.e. income and wealth) that may occur despite, or even because of attempts to increase equality of opportunity. The main mechanism through which they have sought so do this has been the Welfare State. Social democrats can reasonably claim that the improvements in the material conditions of the mass of the people which classical liberals attribute to capitalism, are partly if not mainly, the result of the Welfare State. It is certainly a defensible reading of history to argue that capitalists do not significantly distribute wealth downwards unless required to do so by the state or pressured to do so by workers' organisations – usually, both. However, the arguable success of the Welfare State has been tarnished by waste, inefficiency and by the bureaucratic and undemocratic way in which welfare agencies have often operated. These rather large areas of weakness provided opportunity for the 'new broom' of Thatcherism to sweep in, although Thatcherite reforms, too, are now mature enough for criticism. In particular, massive unemployment; widespread low pay and the redevelopment of what has been termed a new underclass provides ample scope for social democrats to counterattack with reformulated ideas and policies.

The control and regulation of the economy (where deemed necessary) in the public interest, is the third aspect of social democracy chosen for discussion here. Opinion is fast-changing on how this might be best achieved and, in any case, different circumstances require different strategies. Nationalisation of an industry can be effective in ensuring supply of a particular commodity or service to the public and in maintaining necessary investment. However, some now consider nationalisation rather a blunt instrument of control and associate it with the bureaucratic and undemocratic aspects of welfarism referred to above. Regulatory bodies, inspectorates, and taxation are now more popular instruments of regulation. An example of the latter would be an environmental tax which would require polluters to repay the cost of pollution to the community.

Conclusion

The above interpretations of the relationship between equality and freedom offer very different visions of society. Classical liberalism offers an extreme commitment to economic freedom whereas Marxism aspires to socio-economic equality. Social democracy accepts that neither full economic freedom nor total social equality are possible but seeks an effective and humane balance between the two.

Questions

1 Does the formation of 'in-groups' and communities inevitably lead to stratification?
2 Critically discuss the social democratic view of social equality.

Summary

1 Stratification is the division of a society into hierarchically ordered layers. Members of each layer are considered broadly equal but there is inequality between the layers. Differentiation refers to that which makes an individual or group separate and distinct (e.g. income/wealth): thus, differentiation can provide a basis for categorisation and comparison.

2 The theoretical frameworks of Marx and Weber still inform current debates on stratification including attempts to categorise people on the basis of class.

3 Marx stated that class is determined by a person's relationship to the means of production (i.e. whether they own, say, agricultural implements/land or productive machinery) or, on the contrary, have to sell their labour to survive. The former is the dominant class and the latter, the subordinate class. The two major classes in any society are in conflict. In capitalist society, the two main antagonistic classes are the capitalist, or bourgeoisie, and the working class or proletariat.

4 Marx divided society into the base and the superstructure. The base is the economic system and the bi-polar (two part) class system that economic relations produce. The superstructure refers to all other major aspects of society, such as politics, education, intellectual and religious life and so on. Marx argued that the base greatly influences and even determines the nature of the superstructure. The relationship between the base and superstructure has been a matter of considerable debate among later Marxists.

5 Weber described stratification in terms of social divisions of class, status and party. Although these forms of stratification are distinct, they are also connected (e.g. a person's class affects their status (prestige) in society and, possibly, the party (political) they support). Importantly, Weber defined class differently to Marx, making a distinction between economic and social class. Economic class is a person's situation in the economic market and social class (which is related to economic class) refers to a person's chances of social mobility – members of the same social class share similar chances of social mobility. Qualifications and experience largely determine a person's situation in the economic market and the better-qualified and experienced can usually command greater rewards.

6 Weber's overall model of society – if, indeed, it can be called that – is both more pluralistic and more voluntaristic than Marx's base/superstructure model described above. He considers that a variety of groups (pluralism) form and by their action genuinely influence (voluntarism) society. He also argued that the relationship between culture (the superstructure) and class (the base) is 'looser', more 'two-way', and less predictable than did Marx. Both Weber and Marx are conflict theorists but Weber's group conflict approach implies generally less intense and concentrated conflict than Marx's class conflict approach.

7 The Registrar General's class categorisation of occupations is the most widely used official class schema but has been criticised for a variety of inadequacies.

8 John Goldthorpe's social class schema is widely used by academic sociologists. He defines a class as a group or, more precisely, an aggregate of individuals and their families who occupy similar locations in the social division of labour over time: these locations are determined by 'market situation' and 'work situation'. Goldthorpe's class schema has been criticised by both Marxists and feminists.

9 Contemporary Marxist class analysis has been faced with the central problem of where to locate in the class structure many new or greatly expanded service sector occupations. Generally, routine white-collar employees have been classified by Marxists as working class and higher white-collar groups as in 'intermediate' or 'contradictory' class locations.

10 Feminist classificatory schemas reject what they regard as the 'male-biased' view that the 'head' of household should be the basis of class categorisation. Two types of alternative classification are suggested: individual and joint. The former, in particular, results in a very different model of class structure than traditional schemas.

11 The Essex University Class Project analyses data on social class from a sample of 1770 men and women and in terms of both Goldthorpe and Wright's social class schemas and, in respect to some issues, the Registrar General's as well.

12 William Runciman suggests a model of class which is more comprehensive than others in that it combines key aspects of both Marx and Weber's class analyses.

13 Zygmunt Bauman offers a very different approach to social 'division'. He sees the concepts of 'us' and 'them' and 'in-group' and out-group', the subjective feelings of belonging or not belonging as fundamental to social division.

14 Is stratification inevitable? Or, put another way, how much social equality is possible? How can equality be best balanced with freedom. Four views are discussed in the text?

• Classical liberal perspective
• Functionalist perspective
• Marxist perspective
• Social democratic (or 'reformist liberal') perspective

Classical liberals regard inequality as the inevitable price of the freedom provided by 'the free market' system. Classic free market liberals are much less inclined than reformist liberals to 'interfere' with the free market to reduce its inegalitarian effects.

The functionalist perspective regards stratification as functional, inevitable and, therefore, as universal.

Marxists argue that stratification exists because of the unequal ownership of private property, the main example of which is unequal relations to the means of production.

Social democrats accept the economic advantages of the free market but seek in various ways to reduce the inequalities it creates.

See the end of Chapter 6 for 'Research and coursework' and 'Guide to further reading'.

Reading 1
Marx and Engels: class struggle and class structure

From K Mark and F Engels, *The Communist Manifesto* (Penguin, 1981), pp.79-80

The proletariat goes through various stages of development. With its birth begins its struggle with the bourgeoisie. At first the contents is carried on by individual labourers, then by the work people of a factory, then by the operatives of one trade, in one locality, against the individual bourgeois who directly exploits them. they direct their attacks not against the bourgeois conditions of production, but against the instruments of production themselves; they destroy imported wares that compete with their labour, they smash to pieces machinery, they set factories ablaze, they seek to restore by force the vanished status of the workman of the Middle Ages.

But with the development of industry the proletariat not only increases in number; it becomes concentrated in greater masses, its strength grows, and it feels that strength more. The various interests and conditions of life within the ranks of the proletariat are more and more equalised, in proportion as machinery obliterates all distinctions of labour, and nearly everywhere reduces wages to the same low level. The growing competition among the bourgeois, and the resulting commercial crises, make the wages of the workers ever more fluctuating. The unceasing improvement of machinery, ever more rapidly developing, makes their livelihood more and more precarious; the collisions between individual workmen and individual bourgeois take more and more the character of collisions between two classes. Thereupon the workers begin to form combinations (trade unions) against the bourgeois; they club together in order to keep up the rate of wages; they found permanent associations in order to make provisions beforehand for these occasional revolts. Here and there the contest breaks out into riots.

Now and then the workers are victorious, but only for a time. The real fruit of their battles lies, not in the immediate result, but in the ever expanding union of the workers. This union is helped on by the improved means of communication that are created by modern industry, and that place the workers of different localities in contact with one another. It was just this contact that was needed to centralise the numerous local struggles, all of the same character, into one national struggle between classes. But every class struggle is a political struggle. And that union, to attain which the burghers of the Middle Ages, with their miserable highways, required centuries, the modern proletarians, thanks to railways achieve in a few years.

This organisation of the proletarians into a class, and consequently into a political party, is continually being upset again by the competition between the workers themselves. But it ever rises up again, stronger, firmer, mightier. It compels legislative recognition of particular interests of the workers, by taking advantage of the divisions among the bourgeoisie itself …

Of all the classes that stand face-to-face with the bourgeoisie today, the proletariat alone is a really revolutionary class. The other classes decay and finally disappear in the face of modern industry; the proletariat is its special and essential product. The lower middle class, the small manufacturers, the shopkeeper, the artisan, the peasant, all these fight against the bourgeoisie, to save from extinction their existence as fractions of the middle class. They are therefore not revolutionary, but conservative. Nay more, they are reactionary, for they try to roll back the wheel of history. If by chance they are revolutionary, they are so only in view of their impending transfer into the proletariat; they thus defend not their present, but their future interests; they desert their own standpoint to place themselves at that of the proletariat.

The 'dangerous class,' the social scum, that passively rotting mass thrown off by the lowest layers of old society, may, here and there, be swept into the movement by a proletarian revolution; its conditions of life, however, prepare it far more for the part of a bribed tool of reactionary intrigue.

Questions

1 Describe Marx and Engels' outline of class structure and how and why they thought it would change.
2 In what ways do you consider Marx and Engels were accurate or inaccurate in their analysis of class change in the above extract?

Reading 2
Max Weber: class, status and party

From Max Weber, ed., C Wright Mills, *From Max Weber* (Oxford University Press, New York; 1970), pp. 181, 184, 185, 185-86, 187, 189

Determination of class-situation by market-situation

In our terminology, 'classes' are not communities; they merely represent possible, frequent, bases for communal action. We may speak of a 'class' when 1 a number of people have in common a specific causal component of their life chances, in so far as 2 this component is represented exclusively by economic interests in the possession of goods and opportunities for income, and 3 is represented under the conditions of the commodity or labour markets. (These points refer to 'class situation', which we may express more briefly as the typical chance for a supply of goods, external living conditions, and personal life experiences, in so far as this chance is determined by the amount and kind of power, or lack of such, to dispose of goods or skills for the sake of income in a given economic order. The term 'class' refers to any group of people that is found in the same class situation.) …

Status honour

In contrast to classes, *status groups* are normally communities. They are, however, often of an amorphous kind. In contrast to the purely economically determined 'class situation' we wish to designate as 'status situation' every typical component of the life fate of men that is determined by a specific, positive or negative, social estimation of *honour*. This honour may be connected with any quality shared by a plurality, and, of course, it can be knit to a class situation: class distinctions are linked in the most varied ways with status distinctions. Property as such is not always recognised as a status qualification, but in the long run it is, and with extraordinary regularity. In the subsistence economy of the organised neighbourhood, very often the richest man is simply the chieftain. However, this often means only an honorific preference. For example, in the so-called pure modern 'democracy', that is, one devoid of any expressly ordered status privileges for individuals, it may be that only the families coming under approximately the same tax class dance with one another. This example is reported of certain smaller Swiss cities. But status honour need not necessarily be linked with a 'class situation'. On the contrary, it normally stands in sharp opposition to the pretensions of sheer property …

Guarantees of status stratification

In content, status honour is normally expressed by the fact that above all else a specific *style of life* can be expected from all those who wish to belong to the circle. Linked with this expectation are restrictions on 'social' intercourse (that is, intercourse which is not subservient to economic or any other of business's 'functional' purposes). These restrictions may confine normal marriages to within the status circle and may lead to complete endogamous closure. As soon as there is not a mere individual and socially irrelevant imitation of another style of life, but an agreed-upon communal action of this closing character, the 'status' development is underway …

'Ethnic' segregation and 'caste'

Where the consequences have been realised to their full extent, the status group evolves into a closed 'caste'. Status distinctions are then guaranteed not merely by conventions and laws, but also by *rituals*. This occurs in such a way that every physical contact with a member of any caste that is considered to be 'lower' by the members of a 'higher' caste is considered as making for a ritualistic impurity and to be a stigma which must be expiated by a religious act. Individual castes develop quite distinct cults and gods.

In general, however, the status structure reaches such extreme consequences only where there are underlying differences which are held to be 'ethnic'. The 'caste' is, indeed, the normal form in which ethnic communities usually live side by side in a 'societalised' manner. These ethnic communities believe in blood relationship and exclude exogamous marriage and social intercourse. Such a caste situation is part of the phenomenon of 'pariah' peoples and is found all over the world. These people form communities, acquire specific occupational traditions of handicrafts or of other arts, and cultivate a belief in their ethnic community. They live in a 'diaspora' strictly segregated from all personal intercourse, except that of an unavoidable sort, and their situations is legally precarious. Yet, by virtue of their economic indispensability, they are tolerated, indeed, frequently privileged, and they live in interspersed political communities. The Jews are the most impressive historical example.

A 'status' segregation grown into a 'caste' differs in its structure from a mere 'ethnic' segregation: the caste structures transforms the horizontal and unconnected coexistences of ethnically segregated groups into a vertical social system of super- and subordination. Correctly formulated: a comprehensive societalisation integrates the ethnically divided communities into specific political and communal action. In their consequences they differ precisely in this way: ethnic coexistences condition a mutual repulsion and disdain but allow each ethnic community to consider its own honour as the highest one; the caste structure beings about a social subordination and an acknowledgement of 'more honour' in favour of the privileged caste and status groups. This is due to the fact that in the caste structure ethnic distinctions as such have become 'functional' distinctions within the political societalisation (warriors, priests, artisans that are politically important for war and for building, and so on). But even pariah people who are most despised are usually apt to continue cultivating in some manner that which is equally peculiar to ethnic and to status communities: the belief in their own specific 'honour'. This is the case with the Jews …

Status privileges

For all practical purposes, stratification by status goes hand-in-hand with a monopolisation of ideal and material goods or opportunities, in a manner we have come to know as typical. Besides the specific status honour, which always rests upon distance and exclusiveness, we find all sorts of material monopolies. Such honorific preferences may consist of the privilege of wearing special costumes, of eating special dishes taboo to others, of carrying arms …

The decisive role of a 'style of life' in status 'honour' means that status groups are the specific bearers of all 'conventions.' In whatever way it may be manifest, all 'stylisation' of life either originates in status groups or is at least conserved by them. Even if the principles of status conventions differ greatly, they reveal certain typical traits, especially among those strata which are most privileged. Quite generally, among privileged status groups there is a status disqualification that operates against the performance of common physical labour …

Parties

Whereas the genuine place of 'classes' is within the economic order, the place of 'status groups' is within the social order, that is, within the sphere of the distribution of 'honour'. From within these spheres, classes and status groups influence one another and they influence the legal order and are in turn influenced by it. But 'parties' live in a house of 'power'.

Their action is oriented toward the acquisition of social 'power,' that is to say, toward influencing a communal action no matter what its content may be. In principle, parties may exist in a social 'club' as well as in a 'state'. As over against the actions of classes and status groups, for which this is not necessarily the case, the communal actions of 'parties' always mean a societalisation. For party actions are always directed toward a goal which is striven for in a planned manner. This goal may be a 'cause' (the party may aim at realising a program for ideal or material purposes), or the goal may be 'personal' (sinecures, power, and from these, honour for the leader and the followers of the party). Usually the party action aims at all these simultaneously. Parties are, therefore, only possible within communities that are societalised, that is, which have some rational order and a staff of persons available who are ready to enforce it.

Question

1 With close reference to the above passage, how did Weber define class, status and party?
2 What are the main relationships between class, status and party?

6

CHAPTER

Class Stratification in Britain

The face of inequality today

Perspectives on the changing British class structure

The purpose of this section is to outline four perspectives on the mass of data about social class given later in this chapter. Their respective claims to provide the best account of the British class structure are discussed below. With the exception of the Marxist approach, there are obvious points of overlap between the perspectives. All of the perspectives apart from the Marxist are essentially 'liberal'. Here, it is class structure that is the primary focus. Class culture is discussed in Chapter 16. However, as structure and culture are in practice inseparable, there is considerable overlap.

A liberal perspective: and the 'embourgeoisement' thesis

A common view among certain sociologists of the post-war period is that social class has become less important both subjectively, in terms of its perceived significance to individuals and families, and, objectively, in terms of social structure. Thus, individuals are thought to have other preoccupations than class – often centred on consumption – and, objectively, the general increase in wealth is considered to have reduced the significance of remaining inequalities. American sociologist, Clark Kerr, saw these developments as part of the 'logic of industrialism' which would eventually make extreme industrial and social conflict redundant. Daniel Bell agreed with him, declaring an 'end of ideology' in the sense of radically conflicting social and political systems of belief. In the 1980s, there was a revival of the view that the importance of social class in Britain has declined.

Gordon Marshall *et al.* – although disagreeing with this view – have conveniently summarised the key themes which characterise the 'decline of class' interpretation in relation to Britain. These are briefly listed, then explained:

- The restructuring of capital and labour
- The growing complexity of class processes
- The emergence of instrumental collectivism and sectionalism
- The privatisation of individuals and families
- The fatalistic acceptance of structural inequality – allied to an inability to conceive of an alternative

The main factor in the 'restructuring of capital and labour' is the decline of manufacturing industry and the rise of service industries with the consequent numerical decline of the manual or traditional working class. Capitalists are considered to have used the changing economic situation to have reasserted control over labour. Second, greater variety and difference is considered to occur within the major class grouping than in the past (a view discussed separately below, p. 163). Third, instrumental collectivism describes the tendency of workers in a particular industry (sector) or members of a union to pursue their own advantage rather than that of the working class as a whole. Fourthly, a corollary to this is that individuals and families are seen as becoming increasingly home-centred and privatised and as often enjoying relatively affluent consumer lifestyles. Finally, against the background of these developments, 'remaining' issues of inequality are either obscured or seen as less pressing. It is important to add that liberals consider that, as a result of these developments, a more classless culture and less consciousness of class identity and difference are characteristic of modern Britain.

The 'embourgeoisement' thesis was associated with liberal thinking. It was applied to the affluent manual working class who were described by some as 'becoming more middle class' (embourgoisement, see pp. 172-4). Although specific to this group, the embourgoisement thesis reflects a more general belief in the decline of class. The thesis had wide currency in the 1950s and 1960s and was revived in somewhat different form during the 1980s (see pp. 180-1).

A Marxist perspective: proletarianisation

The main Marxist response to the 'embourgeoisement' thesis is the 'proletarianisation' thesis. This is the view that, far from better-off manual workers becoming middle class, service sector employees have been progressively 'deskilled' in their work and are becoming members of the working class i.e. proletarianised. The proletarianisation thesis is most notably associated with Harry Braverman who developed it in relation to class structure in the United States but others have argued its application to Britain.

In addition to their work on proletarianisation, Braverman and fellow American, Eric Oln Wright have each produced full and somewhat similar analyses of the total American class structure. Again, these approaches are applicable to the class structures of other advanced capitalist societies, including Britain. In addition, there has been substantial Marxist and radical analysis of the British class system by British sociologists.

The importance of culture and consciousness must be noted in relation to Marxist as well as liberal class interpretation. It is of limited usefulness for Marxists to demonstrate the continued 'objective' existence of a large proletariat if, in practice, its members do not live and think like members of the same class and community or, at least, show some signs of doing so.

Two Weberian views

1 A fragmentary class structure

It has already been suggested that, taken to its extreme, Weber's analysis of class implies that every individual has a more or less distinct position in the employment market and, therefore, a unique class position. Few Weberians find it constructive to push matters so far, but some greatly stress the increasing differentiation and even fragmentation of the British class structure. Fragmentation is said to be occurring not only between classes but within them. Thus, Ralf Dahrendorf uses the telling term 'decomposition' to describe the processes of change which he argues have affected both the capitalist and the working classes (see p. 167).

A specific study of the middle class argues that 'decomposition' or, to use the authors' term, 'fragmentation' is occurring to this group also. Roberts *et al.* examine the 'class images' (roughly, 'consciousness' of class) of a wide range of male white-collar employees. They conclude that a variety of class images occur and that this is indicative of the fragmentation of the middle class into various strata. Accordingly, it is no longer accurate to talk of *the* middle class.

There are considerable similarities between the above view and the liberal view. 'Fragmentation' and 'embourgeoisement' are compatible tendencies. However, there is less emphasis on generalised affluence and more on continued inequality in Dahrendorf's work. To this extent, he has more in common with the Weberians discussed next than with the liberals.

2 Continuing class inequality in the context of greater affluence

The authors of the Essex Class Project – Marshall, Newby, Rose and Vogler – produced results that largely support and extend those of John Goldthorpe. They readily agree that there has been an increase in wealth and mass consumption in the post-war period and considerable social mobility, especially upwards. However, they also find substantial relative inequalities in wealth and consumption, together with substantial cultural differences between the classes, including those of political orientation. They also reiterate Goldthorpe's observation that the relative chances of social mobility have remained remarkably constant between the classes over a period of about 50 years. For them, therefore, class structure, class attitudes, and class relations have changed less fundamentally than the 'embourgeoisement' liberals and Dahrendorf contend.

While Marshall *et al.* accept that instrumental collectivism (acting in group self-interest, see p. 179) is typical of all the classes, they refute the analysis that this is particularly new among the working class. On the other hand, they also reject the view that people, including working class people, act collectively exclusively on the basis of self-interest and suggest that an appeal to social justice might still be a powerful motivating force.

The economic context of class change: from a manufacturing to a service economy

The most striking change in the British economy in the post Second World War period has been the decline in the numbers employed in the manufacturing sector and the increase of those employed in the service sector. There has also been a big drop in the percentage employed in the tertiary sector - mainly agriculture and extraction – which in 1994 accounted for less than four per cent of the total labour force. The decline in manufacturing jobs during the recession of 1979-81 was particularly notable. In 1994, just over twenty per cent of the labour force was employed in manufacturing. Figure 6.1 graphically states the comparative trends in employment in the manufacturing and non-manufacturing sectors in 1948 and 1994 – with the former declining from 45.6 to 20.2 per cent of employees and the latter rising from 37.2 to a huge 73.4 per cent.

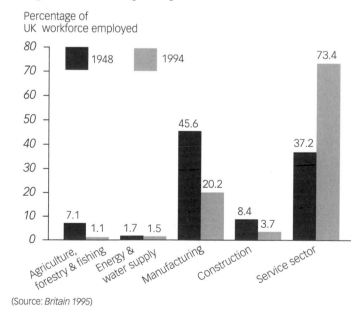

(Source: *Britain 1995*)

Figure 6.1 Employment by sector, 1948 and 1994, UK

Table 6.1 Civilian labour force economic activity rates[1]: by gender and age

	16-19	20-24	25-34	35-44	45-54	55-59	60-64	All aged 16 and over [2]
Great Britain				Percentages				
Males								
Estimates								
1971	69.4	87.7	94.6	96.2	95.7	93.0	82.9	80.5
1981	72.4	85.1	95.4	96.0	94.8	89.4	69.3	76.5
1991	70.4	85.6	94.0	94.7	91.0	80.3	54.1	73.7
1993	63.9	83.8	92.5	93.6	90.3	75.4	52.2	71.9
Projections								
2006	55.7	77.9	92.6	93.9	89.1	74.0	45.5	69.0
Females								
Estimates								
1971	65.0	60.2	45.5	59.7	62.0	50.9	28.8	43.9
1981	70.4	68.8	56.4	68.0	68.0	53.4	23.3	47.6
1991	69.1	72.7	69.7	76.7	72.7	54.5	24.1	52.4
1993	63.8	70.7	70.7	77.0	74.8	54.6	14.8	52.6
Projections								
2006	59.0	68.8	80.6	85.2	78.1	56.7	27.0	56.0

1 The percentage of the resident population, or any sub-group of the population who are in the civilian labour force.
2 Includes those aged 65 and over.

(Source: Employment Department; *Social Trends*, 1996:66)

Women in Great Britain have become increasingly economically active, and this is projected to continue. This increase is partly due to the increased availability of part-time jobs, and is associated with economic and social changes such as falling birth rates. The economic activity rate for women aged 25 to 34 years rose by 25 percentage points between 1971 and 1993. A part of the increase may be attributable to an increase in the average age at which women have children (see Chapter 4: pp. 52-3). The proportion of men who are economically active has decreased in every age group over the same period; this fall was particularly large for men aged 55 and over. The average economic activity rate for men is projected to continue falling but at a slower rate; for the 25 to 34 and 35 to 44 age groups it is actually projected to be higher in 2006 than in 1993. Overall, women are projected to make up 46 per cent of the civilian labour force in 2006, compared to 44 per cent in 1993 and 37 per cent in 1971.

Whether or not a woman is economically active is dependent, to some extent on the number and ages of her children. In Spring 1994 women whose youngest dependent child was over five years old were most likely to be working part-time; women with no dependent children were most likely to be working full-time. In addition, the more children a woman has, the more likely she is to be economically inactive (see Table 6.2). For example, in Spring 1994, 66 per cent of women with four or more dependent children were economically inactive, compared with only 32 per cent of women with one child.

Table 6.2 Economic activity status of women: by age of youngest dependent child, Spring 1994

	Age of youngest dependent child				
	0-4	5-10	11-15	No dependent children	All women aged 16-59
United Kingdom			Percentages		
Working full-time	16	20	34	46	36
Working part-time	30	45	40	23	29
Unemployed	6	6	4	5	5
Inactive	48	29	22	25	30
All women (= 100%) (thousands)	3,414	2,085	1,497	9,817	16,813

(Source: *Social Trends*, 1996:66 – adapted)

The most notable trend within employment in the service sector has been the numerical 'rise and rise' (i.e. steady increase) of female employment (see Table 6.3). Between 1960 and 1980 the numbers of women employed in the service sector increased by over two million. By 1986 the number of females employed in services outnumbered the number of males by almost 1.5 million (see Table 6.1). However, it is important to remember that a very much larger proportion of women than men are in part-time and/or temporary work although this proportion is steadily decreasing. Between 1987 and 1995 the number of women in full-time work increased by eight per cent whereas that of men fell by two per cent.

Table 6.3 A comparison of occupational class: including and excluding female employees.

		Men and women	Men
		Percentages	
Higher Grade Professionals etc.	I	9.4	13.1
Lower Grade Professionals etc.	II	17.9	17.1
Routine Non-manual – Clerical etc.	III	19.5	6.0
Small Proprietors etc.	IV	8.7	11.4
Lower-Grade Technicians etc.	V	8.1	11.4
Skilled Manual Workers etc.	VI	12.5	17.4
Other Manual Workers	VII	23.9	23.6
	Total	100.0	100.0

Note: The Goldthorpe class categories are used with data from the Essex Class Project Survey.

(Source: Marshall *et al.*, p. 86)

The effect on the occupational structure of the expansion of the service sector and the related increase in female employment has been large and significant. In terms of understanding occupational structure and social class in contemporary society, it has become increasingly necessary to record and consider female occupational status as distinct from that of male occupational status and to reject the view that it is adequate to locate females within their husband's occupational category. Table 6.3 shows clearly why this is so. It provides two descriptions of class structure – the first based on male and female occupations and the second based on male occupations only. As Marshall *et al.* comment:

> *A concentration on males only tends to inflate the proportions within classes I, IV, V and VI, while decreasing (rather spectacularly) the relative importance of class III. These differences are entirely what one would expect given the sexual segregation of occupations …*
>
> *(Marshall et al., 1988:1997)*

Any relevant discussion of class and work in contemporary Britain must, then, engage firmly with 'the gender question'.

British class structure and culture

The upper class and the managerial

The upper class consists of the few thousand wealthiest and most culturally privileged businessmen and property owners in the country. We also consider top managers and professionals in this section because they often work closely with the upper class and are highly privileged themselves. By this group is meant people like managing directors of large companies rather than middle level management; chiefs of staff rather than high ranking officers; top rather than middle level civil servants, and so on. The important issue is whether the wealth and opportunities of the upper class also give much greater power and control over industrial, political, and cultural life than other groups.

Upper class culture

A common culture is an essential aspect of a fully developed class. During the twentieth century, traditional landed, and newer commercial wealthy have, perhaps until recently, increasingly shared a similar background and cultural outlook. Their way of life is substantially different from that of most of the rest of the population. Writing about upper class culture, Anthony Giddens says:

> *The most striking characteristic of the British upper class in the latter half of the nineteenth century is the mutual penetration of aristocracy and those in commerce and industry … Certainly the dominant ethos [cultural tone] remained a 'gentlemanly' one, facilitated by the entitlement of industrialists, or at least of their offspring; but the very creation of the notion of the 'gentleman' was in substantial degree the product of the nineteenth century, and the rise of the public schools was the milieu [cultural context] for effecting this peculiar fusion of the old and the new. In this manner there came about that 'blend of a crude plutocratic [power based on money] reality with the sentimental aroma of an aristocratic legend' which R H Tawney described as the feature of the British upper class.*
>
> *(Giddens, 1979)*

David Carradine's *The Decline and Fall of The British Aristocracy* (1990) charts the gradual loss of 'senior-partner' status by land owners to industrialists in the aristocratic-business coalition. Other authors have argued that the 'Thatcher revolution' has accelerated the dominance of newer, business wealth within the upper class. The partial decline of the major public school both as a cultural status symbol and as a means to success in a top career seems to be at the heart of the apparent change. Thus, Jeremy Paxman cites as evidence of a 'change to the meritocrats' that seventeen out of nineteen of Margaret Thatcher's 1979 Cabinet had attended public schools, whereas the 1990 Cabinet contained several members who had been to grammar schools, only half the number of old Etonians as the 1979 Cabinet, and a preponderance of members who had been to 'second division' public schools rather than major ones. Paxman describes this as 'not quite the supremacy of the self-made man that the party (Conservative) likes to pretend, but a distinct shift none the less' (Paxman: 1990).

It may be that the 'Thatcher revolution' most notably occurred where one might expect – in business. The following extract from a newspaper report, which draws on academic research, certainly suggests there has been rapid change in this area with those of grammar, rather than public school background, gaining an increasing role in corporate leadership.

> *Educational Background and Corporate Leadership*
>
> *Executives spurring Britain's top companies to success in Europe are now more likely to have been educated by the state than by public schools.*
>
> *Britain provides 20 of the top 30 corporate performers in Europe. Yet only one has a chairman who went to a major public school.*
>
> *Eleven years after Margaret Thatcher, herself a product of Kesteven and Grantham Girls' grammar school, became prime minister, evidence is emerging that the grip of public schools on British life is being broken.*

The revolution has been bloodless, but rapid. In 1979 the old-boy network still opened boardroom doors. Now seven of the top 20 UK firms in Europe have chairmen who went to a grammar school ...

Separate research by the London School of Economics also shows a sudden shift away from public schools in Britain's top 50 industrial companies.

In 1979, nine chairmen of these companies went to Charterhouse, Eton, Rugby, Shrewsbury or Winchester, 20 to other public schools and only nine to grammar schools. Last year, however, only one of the chairmen surveyed attended a top public school. Lord Prior, chairman of GEC, is an old boy of Charterhouse. Of his fellow chairmen, 20 are now past pupils of grammar schools.

Sir Denys Henderson, chairman of ICI, went to Aberdeen grammar school; Sir Michael Angus, chairman of Unilever, was a pupil at Marling grammar school in Stroud; Sir Jeffrey Stirling, chairman of P & O, is from Reigate grammar school.

In all, 70 per cent went either to a grammar school or to other state-maintained schools.

Professor Leslie Hannah of the LSE has described the changes in the class and educational background of industrial leaders as 'astonishing'.

Sir Philip Harris, who left Streatham grammar school at fifteen with one O-level after the death of his father and now chairs the Harris Ventures chain of carpet and furniture shops, said: 'I think grammar school gives you more of a basic education and is more linked to the needs of industry. Eton is more for scholars.'

Lord Tombs, chairman of Rolls-Royce, said companies were no longer appointing chairmen from within the family ...

(From M Chittenden and A Davidson, The Sunday Times, 1990:1)

The above developments can be interpreted to support rather than undermine Marxist analysis of capitalist society. They can certainly be presented as showing the emergence of a bourgeois or pro-bourgeois group over the more traditional aristocracy – roughly what Marx foresaw. It may be that in a decade or so, increasing numbers of people from comprehensive school backgrounds will acquire top business positions. It is possible that what is occurring is not particularly the 'Thatcher revolution' but first, the effects of the tripartite educational reforms, and perhaps next, the effects of the comprehensive system. In both cases, the capitalist system is left intact. Indeed, Marxists see upward social mobility as strengthening capitalism. By contrast, reforming liberals favour the opening of opportunity suggested by the data cited above while remaining concerned at continuing inequality and poverty.

The above observations are to some extent speculative and need to be balanced against the evidence of the continuing influence of the public schools and Oxbridge cited Chapter 4 (see pp. 105-9 of which it would be useful to re-read). First, business has long been the most open entry point to the upper class (even though still not always seen as having the same status as landed wealth). In the areas of finance, the public services and the so-called great professions, the evidence of continuing public school dominance and hegemony is substantial.

Upper class weath and economic power

We now consider the wealth and economic, financial and industrial power of the upper class. The wealth of the upper class has diminished as a percentage of total wealth but remains formidably large. Wealth is much more unequally distributed than income, mainly because of the importance of inherited wealth. According to Lord Diamond's commission, in 1923 the top one per cent owned 61 per cent of all private wealth. In 1974, this had dropped to 22 per cent but, by 1976, had risen to 25 per cent. The increase between 1974 and 1976 was due mainly to the rises in share prices during that period. During the Thatcher administrations, the top ten per cent became relative wealthier and the bottom 50 per cent relatively slightly poorer – a trend which sharpened from 1983/4.

Not unexpectedly, the wealth of the very rich tends to be made up differently from that of other people. Despite the increase in share ownership in the 1980s they are disproportionately likely to own shares, often in large quantity. Frequently they own exclusive property, including land. They are also more than likely others to own art treasures, precious metals and jewels. The preservation and creation of substantial wealth gives the upper class a shared material basis for class identity and sets them apart from the majority. Upper class exclusiveness can be partly explained as an attempt to maintain and defend its common interest.

Few of the wealthy depend on earned income as a major source of their wealth. The share of all national incomes of the top one per cent of income earners in 1981/82 was 4.6 per cent – a small figure compared to the percentage of wealth owned by the most wealthy one per cent. Many major shareholders draw salaries as directors of the company or companies in which they have holdings. Usually, however, the day-to-day running of large companies is in the hands of paid managers who are now usually extremely wealthy people in their own right. This raises the crucial issue of where industrial power lies in contemporary capitalism – with owners (or, at least, large shareholders) as Marx argues, or with managers. It should be noted that the new managerial class is just as well-established in central and local government and in the remaining nationalised industries as in private enterprise.

Dahrendorf: the 'decomposition of capital'

The Weberian, Ralf Dahrendorf has made a significant contribution to the debate about where power lies in modern societies. He argues that with the development of large scale joint stock companies which enable the general public to buy shares in a company, much control is exercised by top salaried managers and less by capitalist owners. He refers to this process as the

Figure 6.2 Is the grammar school 'Type' replacing the public school 'Type' in business? If so, what difference will it make?

'decomposition of capital'. Following Weber rather than Marx, he goes on to argue that in advanced industrial societies, power operates through large organisations rather than through a few very rich individuals (those who make up the capitalist class). Managers of organisations, unlike old-style capitalists, cannot pursue their own interest alone, but must answer to shareholders, perhaps to government, and even to the general public. According to Dahrendorf, this applies especially to the managers of publicly owned companies and to top civil servants. Dahrendorf, therefore, sees modern societies as 'managed' societies. To understand modern societies, 'capitalist' or socialist, it is necessary, therefore, to come to terms with their institutional (organisational) nature (see Chapter 10 for the development of this point). He further contends that the rise of managers has produced considerable potential for conflict within the economic elite (that is, between owners and management). He considers that whereas owners tend to be interested in profit, managers are more concerned with the long-term productivity and security of the corporation which they see both as in their own interest, and in that of its shareholders, small and large. Again, managers are regarded as more constrained (controlled) by the rules of the large organisations of which they are a small part than the tycoons of early capitalism ever were. It is part of Dahrendorf's thesis that management is also constrained by the powerful organisations of the working class, mainly unions, as well as, to some extent, by government.

Giddens: it's *still* capitalism

Anthony Giddens criticises Dahrendorf sharply on two counts. First he points out that, even though the growth of joint stock companies has broadened the basis of ownership, profit remains the purpose of capitalist enterprise: thus, the system is still a capitalist one. In addition, only a minority still gains substantial profit from shareholdings. There is a huge difference between multi-millionaires, like Sir James Goldsmith, with majority holdings in several major companies and somebody who owns, perhaps, a few hundred pounds of shares. Giddens's second point is related to his first. He suggests that far from there being a conflict of interest between capitalists and top managers, there is more likely to be a close identity of interest. This is intensified by the fact that many managers are themselves large shareholders in the companies they work in. They are both primarily concerned with the success and profitability of the company. As far as companies having a public 'conscience' is concerned, there is no guarantee of this, although some do. We examine in Chapter 19 several examples in which companies put their own welfare before that of the general public, if the latter is considered to include workers (made redundant) and local communities (variously neglected or abused).

Scott: changing capitalism

John Scott also sees the economic structure of contemporary Western societies, including Britain, as no less capitalist than in the recent past. He considers that capitalist business methods are dominant throughout these societies – in agriculture as well as manufacture, commerce and finance. Scott divides capitalists into three groups: entrepreneurial capitalists; internal capitalists; and finance capitalists. Entrepreneurial capitalists tend substantially to own and control 'their own' business. They are closest to the nineteenth century model of individualistic and family capitalism but are now a less significant group (see the decline in individual ownership of share equities, Table 6.4). Internal capitalists are the top career managers discussed above, but whom Scott considers to be rather less important than a third group, finance capitalists. Finance capitalists are the representatives of banks, insurance companies, pension funds and similar institutions who, to a greater or lesser extent, own, manage and finance big business. Table 6.4 shows the extent to which such institutions have become the main owners of equities in British industry.

Table 6.4 Who owns UK equities?

Institutions	1963	1975	1981	1989
		Perce	ntages	
Pension funds	6.5	16.9	26.7	32.0
Insurance (life and general)	10.1	15.9	20.5	20.0
Unit and investment trusts	12.6	14.6`	10.3	8.0
Total	29.2	47.4	57.5	60.0
Personal sector		Perce	ntages	
Individuals	53.8	37.5	28.2	20.0
Government	1.5	3.6	3.0	3.0
Other UK	8.6	5.9	7.7	8.0
Overseas	6.9	5.6	3.6	9.0
Total	70.8	52.6	42.5	40.0

(Source: *The Observer*, 21.10.1990:00)

Although Scott particularly emphasises the rising power and control of finance capital, he contends that the three groups referred to above form a 'constellation of interests' and together run capitalism. In this respect, he is in broad agreement with Giddens. Scott argues that as far as Britain is concerned, the dominant interest is probably finance capital, although he concedes that in Japan and the United States internal or managerial capitalists may be more powerful. He describes the trend in Britain from individual and family control of the capitalist system to institutional control as the 'depersonalisation' of property.

Upper class socio-economic and political power

Giddens' contention that owners and top management – the economic elite – share common goals, leads to the important and wider question of whether the upper and middle class dominate the other major institutional elites, as well as the economic elite, of

the country. Drawing on a study of elites, carried out at Cambridge, he concludes that at least half the top positions in all major institutional sectors in Britain, including the economic, the military, the armed forces, the judiciary and the church, are filled by people from public school backgrounds (see Chapters 4 and 11 for details). In other words, a majority of those in top positions in this country come from a privileged and, more or less, wealthy upper or middle class background. Whether these people can be called a ruling class is also discussed in Chapter 11.

The importance of the Dahrendorf-Giddens disagreement needs emphasising. It is, after all, about who controls our society, how they do so and in whose interest. This must surely matter to all of us. Do capitalists manipulate our world in their own interest or is power mainly located in large organisations which, almost impersonally, run our lives? We can agree with Dahrendorf that we live in a society of large organisations run by 'experts', and with Giddens that there is still a rich and powerful upper class with a distinctive culture. How and to what extent these two points can be reconciled we leave for further consideration (see especially Chapter 11).

The 'middle' classes

The word 'middle' in the title of this section is put into inverted commas because the precise position of both managerial, administrative and professional groups and of routine white-collar employees is hotly debated. There is certainly no consensus among sociologists that they are middle class.

Managerial, administrative and professional

The Registrar General's and John Goldthorpe's class scales locate managerial, administrative and professional groups in high social class categories – which can be thought of as broadly upper middle class. However, although these groups form the basis of Goldthorpe top class category, the service class, he divides them into higher and lower grade – recognising, for instance, a difference in class location between lawyers and nurses, and between managers in large and small companies. Those allocated to the service class are considered to be in a better employment market position and to enjoy better work situations than those allocated to lower class categories.

A number of Weberians have examined the way in which professions operate, particularly in defending the power and rewards of their position. Frank Parkin has employed Weber's concept of social closure in this respect. Parkin distinguishes between two forms of social closure: exclusion, which is aimed at keeping social subordinates out of the profession, and usurpation, which is aimed at advancing a group's position at the expense of another dominant group. Exclusion is achieved mainly on the basis of credentialism: the use of qualifications to control and restrict entry to a profession. The hoped-for effect of exclusion is to secure or improve the market value of the services offered by a profession.

Parry and Parry take a similar approach to that of Weber and particularly examine the role of self-governing professional associations in effecting exclusion.

As has already been explained, the massive expansion of managerial, professional and administrative employment has presented Marxist class theorists with a problem. Does this group belong with the capitalist or working class, or should it be categorised in some other way (see p. 146)? In fact, most Marxists describe this as being in some way in a contradictory class location. Both Marxist and Weberian views on this issue are discussed at greater length later (see pp. 178-80).

White-collar employees: 'lower middle' or 'working class'?

There is lively debate over the class position of routine non-manual employees – mainly clerks and sales personnel. Most Weberians would describe this group as lower middle class but, in the view of Marxists, Wright and Braverman, they are mainly 'new' working class. The latter view is referred to as the 'proletarianisation' thesis. For Marxists, the importance of establishing that routine white-collar employees are working class is obvious. According to the Standard Occupational Classification, 17.9 per cent of all employees in 1988 were clerks, 7.6 per cent personal service and 6.8 per cent sales: a group of about the same size as manual employees. Further, whereas this white-collar group is increasing in size, the numerical decline of manual employees continues. It is only on the basis that routine non-manual employees can be considered working class that the Marxist model of capitalism, class conflict, and change can plausibly survive. However, there has been no shortage of work by Weberians, notably David Lockwood, to demonstrate that the class position of lower white-collar employees is distinct from that of manual employees.

Charles Wright Mills: white collar employees

C Wright Mills published *White Collar: The American Middle Classes*, the first major post-war analysis of the white-collar employee, in 1951. He draws almost exclusively on American data but the basic developments he comments on are also a feature of British society. His work reflects the influence of both Marx and Weber. The influence of Marx is apparent in Mills' distinction between the old, property owning and self-employed middle class and the new, salaried white-collar class. He includes in the latter group managers, paid professionals, sales people, and office workers (a wider but comparable definition to our own). Even in 1940, this group outnumbered the old middle class and now does so overwhelmingly. Thus, the United States has gone from a nation of small capitalists to a nation of hired employees. A similar process has occurred in most advanced industrial countries. In this sense, what Zweig calls debourgeoisement has certainly taken place. Whatever we call the 'new class' it is certainly not identical with the old bourgeoisie and petit-bourgeoisie.

Mills recognised that, in terms of their class situation, source and size of income (often relatively small), the white-collar group could be considered working class – but he hesitated to classify them as such. In fact, he tended to refer to them as the new middle class for reasons which recall Weberian stratification theory. He claimed that the white-collar group had higher status than manual workers among all sections of the public. Historically, this was largely because of the 'borrowed prestige' they acquired from working in close proximity to ownership and management. This 'reflected' status has become less common with the growth of separate, often relatively large-scale 'office areas', many of which seem closer to the factory floor than the boss's room. More recently, it is the better 'perks' associated with white-collar work and the continuing belief that non-manual work is more prestigious than manual work that gives the white-collar class a status edge over manual workers.

Mills observed that the white-collar class is uncertain of itself and insecure about its future position relative to that of well-paid manual workers. The high wages and comfortable standard of living of the affluent manual workers challenged the white-collar group's marginal superiority, sometimes causing what Mills referred to as 'status panic'. He saw several possible directions of development for the white-collar class. These were:

1 It might become part of the working class or proletariat.
2 It might establish itself more securely as part of the middle class.
3 As it increases in number and power, it might form a buffer between labour and capital and so blunt class conflict.
4 It might become a distinctive class, separate from others.

Thus, over 40 years ago, Mills sketched out the main possible directions of class development for white-collar employees. One possibility he does not mention is that it might itself become a fragmented sector. This view is actually proposed in relation to British white-collar employees by Roberts, Cook *et al.*

White-collar employees: David Lockwood; Howard Davis

In contrast to Mills, David Lockwood's 1958 study of clerical work in Britain, does come to a firm conclusion about their class position. He rejects the proletarianisation thesis and argues that in most respects they are in a better class situation than manual workers. Lockwood examined the social position of clerks broadly under the model of stratification presented by Weber. He analysed their market position, work situation and status situation. It will be remembered that, according to Weber, the major indicator of class is market position. Lockwood was in no doubt that the market situation of clerks is substantially better than that of manual workers, even though the average wage of skilled workers was higher than that of clerks. Clerks have more job security, better prospects of occupational mobility (into management) and, generally, better pension rights and fringe benefits, such as cleaner, more comfortable work conditions and longer holidays. More recent data come from Lord Diamond's *Commission on the Distribution of Income and Wealth*. In 1977, employee benefits added the equivalent of twenty per cent of the value of their pay for white-collar workers, compared to only fourteen per cent for the blue-collar workers. The value of these benefits is, however, increasing fast for both groups. Lockwood also emphasises the higher wages of clerks as compared to manual workers although this is now less true than at the time he wrote.

Lockwood extends Weber's conceptualisation of class to include the work situation of clerks. Again, he argues that, historically, clerks have tended to be closer to, and more influenced by, management than labour. He concedes, however, that in large, modern mechanised offices, separated from management, identification with 'the boss' is less apparent. Developments since Lockwood wrote show a continuation of this trend. In particular, a rapid unionisation among white-collar employees hardly suggests deferential attitudes to employers. In 1970, white collar union membership as a percentage of all white-collar employees was 38 per cent, an increase of one-third since 1964. Despite the overall sharp decline in union membership during the1980s, unionisation among white-collar employees has remained relatively higher (see p. 269).

Finally, Lockwood argues that although the status position of clerks has declined somewhat in the post-war period, it is still distinctly higher than that of manual workers. On the other hand it is lower than that of managers and professionals. On this basis, Lockwood describes the situation of clerks as characterised by 'status ambiguity'.

Most of Lockwood's observations and arguments about the class situation of clerks were supported by Goldthorpe *et al.*, in *Social Mobility and Class Structure in modern Britain* published in 1980. Goldthorpe locates routine non-manual employees at the top of an intermediate class grouping which is below the service class and above the working class. Generally, they have more job security and higher status – partly reflected from their association with the service class – than the working class. However, Goldthorpe does not consider that they have, or are likely to develop, a strong class consciousness, largely because their considerable horizontal and vertical occupational mobility militates against this developing.

Howard Davis's study of the 'class images' of nineteen senior clerks supports the view that this occupational group has not developed a strong, distinctive class consciousness. Although the clerks invariably call themselves 'middle class' they are, nevertheless, reluctant to define themselves as 'not working class' because many of them 'came up' from the working class and consider that opportunities of mobility still exist. To a much greater extent than the traditional working class, they believe in the effectiveness of individual action in career terms and also in making social relationships not necessarily bound by ties of class. The following quotation from one of the respondents makes the latter point quite eloquently:

> *I don't like to try and put people in compartments. I've always tended to take people as I find them … I don't think class is a valid way to describe … Someone from the poorest slum can be a hell of a nice person and a person from the top drawer can be a so and so.*
>
> *(Davis, 1979:168)*

Marxists would typically regard such sentiments as showing an extremely limited level of 'class consciousness'. However, affiliations based on individual preference or felt status rather than class commonly occur and present one of the biggest barriers to the development of 'mature' class consciousness as envisaged by Marx.

White-collar employees: The proletarianisation thesis

Marxist analysis of the class position of white-collar employees occurs within a different theoretical framework from neo-Weberian. Whereas the latter define class mainly in terms of market position, Marxists define it in terms of relations to the means of production. The French sociologist Serge Mallet in an influential article titled *The New Working Class* (1963) suggested a reconceptualisation of productive relations to accommodate the realities of modern capitalist industrial organisation. He argued that occupations which perform 'a productive function' even though they are separate from the physical process of production should be classified as working class. In particular, he contended that 'white-collar' technicians in large research units 'in which working conditions grow increasingly similar to those of a modern workshop, but devoid of physical strain, dirt and stink' should be categorised as working class along with traditional working class occupations.

Harry Braverman

Perhaps the best known application and development of the proletarianisation thesis is Harry Braverman's *Labor and Monopoly Capital* in which he analyses white-collar employment in the United States and the position of this group in the class structure. Braverman extends the view that a large number of non-manual employees are in a working class relationship to the means of production and applies it not only to routine non-manual employees such as clerks but to some professional and semi-professional groups such as teachers and nurses. Typically, these groups work either in large capitalist organisations or for the capitalist state. Importantly, Braverman emphasises the creation of millions of low-level service jobs which people used either to do for themselves (or their mothers/wives/sisters used to do) or, in the case of the wealthy, servants used to do. Thus, cleaning, washing, cooking (cheap, quick meals), and childcare are rapidly expanded occupational areas. Braverman argues that the genuine service element has virtually disappeared from these jobs and the relevant work is produced as a 'commodity' just as physical commodities are produced by the traditional working class. Most employees of this kind work for large capitalist or state organisations. These relatively unskilled occupations can, then, also be considered as working class, and Braverman emphasises the fact that in order for the jobs to be done, women have been increasingly drawn into the paid labour force.

Braverman controversially argues that, in general, 'working class' occupations, including some professional and most routine white-collar occupations, have been subject to a process of 'deskilling'. The main cause of this is that, largely to impose their own control, employers have divided up the process of work into specialised functions requiring little skill. For example, whereas in the late nineteenth century, clerks carried out a wide range of tasks, they now carry out only a limited, specialised number. Braverman argues that modern technology, notably office technology, has intensified rather than reduced specialisation. Lack of control over the work process and possible low levels of work-satisfaction could produce alienation. Braverman draws heavily on his deskilling argument to support the proletarianisation thesis:

Does the proletarianisation thesis apply to Britain? Not surprisingly, Braverman's wide-ranging hypotheses have sparked empirical work aimed at testing them as well as further theoretical elaboration. A Stewart, K Prandy and R M Blackburn (1980) studied a sample of male white-collar employees in large firms (i.e. with a minimum of 500 employees). They conclude that for their respondents the issue of proletarianisation is largely an irrelevance because 81 per cent are no longer clerks by the age of 30 and that of these, 51 per cent have been promoted. They support Goldthorpe in seeing the occupation of clerk as intermediate not only in the class structure but in the additional sense that it is transitional in the career of most males who hold it and, therefore, not conducive to the development of consciousness, working class or otherwise.

An obvious criticism of Stewart et al.'s study is that it ignores females – to whom Braverman's proletarianisation thesis particularly applies. This criticism was made by R Crompton and G Jones (1984) who themselves made a study of 887 white-collar employees from three institutions, one from the public sector and two from the private sector. 70 per cent of the clerks in their sample were female, of these 82 per cent were on clerical grades, compared to 30 per cent of males sampled, which suggests deskilling in relation to females in the sense that they experienced poorer promotional prospects. In examining the work done by the clerks they found that only a low level of skill was required and that computerisation seemed to accentuate this tendency. Further, they argue that the occupations into which some of their sample (mainly males) had been promoted had also been subject to deskilling. Overall, then, Crompton and Jones's findings tend to support the proletarianisation thesis.

The proletarianisation thesis: a critical examination: Marshall et al.

G Marshall et al. give extensive consideration to the proletarianisation thesis in *Social Class in Modern Britain*. Because their sample of 1770 contains both men and women, they are able to compare the relevance of the thesis to both sexes. They do not claim to make an exhaustive study of the issue but they examine the following important areas:

1 Skill as technique (the level of skill required in doing the job).
2 Skill as autonomy (the degree of freedom available in doing the job).
3 Rates of occupational mobility.
4 'Cultural' proletarianisation.

1 and 2 Skill as technique and autonomy

Even in respect to areas 1 and 2, Marshall et al., concede that more definitive conclusions would require direct observation over a long period of time. In fact, given that Braverman is arguing that deskilling has occurred during a period of over 100 years, historical data would seem to be necessary to examine the issue.

In true Weberian mode, Marshall et al. approach the questions of deskilling in respect to technique and autonomy by asking respondents to state their own view of what has happened: specifically, they were asked to report on whether their present jobs required more, less, or approximately the same skill as when they started them (technique). On the issue of autonomy, a range of questions was asked covering control and freedom in relation to the design, pace and routine of work. In relation to both areas, they feel able broadly to dismiss the proletarianisation thesis on the basis of their data. In particular, the responses of category III (a crucial group for the proletarianisation debate and which contains clerks), show that the perceptions of both females and males about skill and autonomy to be similar and not supportive of the proletarianisation thesis. However, Marshall et al. do produce considerable evidence in relation to the III N group – personal service workers such as receptionists, check-out operators, and shop assistants – which suggests that their perception of their work situation, particularly in relation to lack of autonomy, 'is similar to that of the manual working class' (117). Notwithstanding Marshall et al.'s tendency to dismiss the proletarianisation thesis, there is some support for it, albeit in relation to only one group. However, as this group contains a large majority of female employees – about whom the proletarianisation thesis is considered particularly to apply – this finding is clearly important.

3 Occupational mobility

Marshall et al.'s data on occupational mobility again do not lead them to support proletarianisation. In general, there has been more upward than downward social mobility in the post-war period even if personal service work is considered as a working class occupational category – which it is in Marshall *et al*.'s calculations. Although proportionately more women than men from the service-class are downwardly mobile into other forms of employment and fewer are upwardly mobile into the service-class from clerical or working class occupations, there is significant upward mobility among females from routine clerical work to professional occupations. Overall, Marshall *et al*. conclude that 'it is not the case that their relative mobility rates are different from those found among men'. However, as some Marxists consider that 'professions' such as teaching and nursing, into which women are typically mobile, are themselves being proletarianised, these findings can be subject to different interpretation.

4 'Cultural' Proletarianisation

We now turn to the issue of 'cultural' proletarianisation. Throughout our discussion of proletarianisation, the importance of subjective or self-assigned class consciousness has been emphasised. People tend to think and act on the basis of their own perception of their class identity, rather than on the basis of some 'objective' classification. In this respect, Marshall *et al*. corroborate the previous work of Lockwood and others in reporting that their 'evidence is that routine clerical employees will more probably describe themselves as 'middle class' than 'working class' if they are males, and are almost as likely to do so if they are females.' An examination of their data (Table 5.14) bears this out in respect to men in IIIa (clerks) but not in respect to women in the same category who are more likely to self-assign themselves to the working class. Again, those seeking evidence for proletarianisation could actually find some support in Marshall *et al*.'s figures. Matters are further complicated by the fact reported by Marshall *et al*. that the majority of married women self-classify themselves and vote according to their husband's occupation – whatever 'their own' class.

The manual working class

The most obvious fact about the British manual working class has been its decline in size. This parallels the increase in white-collar employment discussed above into which a sizeable minority of the manual working class moved. In the decade between 1961 and 1971, Britain employed 12.5 per cent fewer people in the manufacturing sector. By contrast, Japan employed 21 per cent more and Germany two per cent more.

Table 6.5 shows that the decline in percentage employment in manufacturing industry continued into the1980s.

Two features of the optimistic liberal view of industrial society should be noted. First, relatively high rates of social mobility, including mobility out of the working class, were seen as increasing prospects for affluence and success. Second, the more affluent sections of the working class were thought of, by some commentators as becoming, in a variety of ways, more 'middle class': the embourgeoisement thesis.

Table 6.5 The decline in employment in manufacturing industry

	1973	1979	1983
	Percentages		
Agriculture, forestry and fishing	2	2	2
Manufacturing	34	31	26
Coal, oil and gas extraction	2	2	2
Construction	6	5	5
Total industry	42	38	33
Wholesale, retail, hotel, catering	18	18	20
Transport, postal, telecommunications, electricity and gas	8	8	8
Banking and finance	5	7	9
Public administration	19	21	22
Other services	6	6	6
Total services	56	60	65

(Source: D N Ashton, *Unemployment under Capitalism*, Wheatsheaf Books, 1986)

The embourgeoisement thesis is described and criticised below. An equally strong area of criticism of liberal optimism about class development focuses on the emergence in the 1980s of what some have termed a new underclass (see pp. 387-92).

The affluent worker: embourgeoisement or white-collar convergence?

The 'embourgeoisement' hypothesis, first presented in the late 1950s, sparked off one of sociology's classic debates. The issue is about what is happening economically, socially, politically and culturally to the upper end of the working class. Are its members, as Zweig suggested, becoming more middle class – that is, experiencing 'embourgeoisement'? Or, is what is happening more complex than this term suggests?

The 'embourgeoisement' hypothesis seemed particularly persuasive in the aftermath of the decisive defeat of Labour in the 1959 general election. As with the 1979 election, twenty years later, there was a swing against Labour among the working class. D E Butler and R Rose suggested that Labour might be experiencing particular trouble in holding the affluent working class vote. The response of A R Crosland, a leading Labour politician, was to suggest that Labour should try to widen the basis of its political support to include as many middle class people as possible, rather than rely too exclusively on its traditional working class support.

In this atmosphere of rather speculative and politically charged debate, John Goldthorpe, David Lockwood and their collaborators decided to put the embourgeoisement hypothesis to empirical test. Their inquiry, which spanned several years in the early1960s, is considered something of a model of sociological research, but has also attracted criticism.

Their initial assessment was that the embourgeoisement thesis was probably an oversimplification. In order to avoid bias, however, they followed the scientific procedure advocated by Karl Popper and sought to disprove their own expectations. This meant choosing an area and sample as favourable as possible for the validation of the embourgeoisement thesis. (A selected sample of this kind is termed a purposive sample.) Luton, a prosperous and expanding town, qualified well as a suitable locale. It had the particular advantages of having a substantially migrant labour force – clearly willing to move to find better paid work – and of being without a strong Labour tradition. The research was based primarily on 229 manual workers and, for comparison, 54 clerks of various grades. The former were drawn from three high wage paying local manufacturing firms. The sample consisted of married men, as the researchers had a particular interest in examining family lifestyle, although this meant that the sample was not representative in terms of marital status and age.

Goldthorpe and Lockwood questioned their respondents within three broad areas: economic, relational (family/community relationships and social attitudes); and normative (mainly political orientation).

Economic

Goldthorpe and Lockwood did not consider that wages alone determined class – several other factors are also relevant. Nevertheless, they found that the high wages of the men in the sample did put a 'middle class' standard of living within their reach. They shared many of the consumer items enjoyed by the middle class, such as televisions, refrigerators and automatic washing machines. Apart from this, their economic situation was largely different from that of the middle class. Firstly, their high wages were usually gained only at the cost of overtime: the average working week was 40 to 50 hours. Moreover, 75 per cent of the sample were on shift work. A 'normal' background of overtime and shift work could put pressure on family and social life in a way rarely experienced by the lower middle class. Secondly, promotional prospects were appreciably worse than for non-manual workers and this was fully realised by the majority of both groups sampled. The manual workers appreciated that any economic advances they made were likely to be on the basis of their present economic role and through collective bargaining, with the help of their trade unions. The non-manual sample typically entertained more hope of personal progress. Thirdly, as already mentioned, white-collar employees generally benefit from greatly superior fringe benefits. Fourthly, and perhaps more importantly, most of the manual workers expressed much lower levels of intrinsic satisfaction (pleasure in the job for itself) than did the white-collar sample.

Relational

Goldthorpe and Lockwood's second category, relational aspects, may be thought of as cultural and community life. Not surprisingly, given the nature of the sample, few of the men studied shared the traditional pattern of community life often found among urban industrial workers and their families. Equally lacking, however, was any evidence that middle class company and lifestyle was sought, as might have been expected if 'embourgeoisement' had taken place. Kin still played a relatively prominent part in the social lives of the couples studied. This was particularly true of the (approximately) 50 per cent of the sample whose kin lived mainly within a 50 mile radius of London, but it still applied to many of the rest. 41 per cent of the former and 22 per cent of the latter named kin in response to the question 'who would you say are the three people that you spend most of your spare time with?' (apart from spouse and children). Otherwise, close neighbours, rather than selected individuals from within the larger community, provided most friends. Interestingly, white-collar couples had more contact with friends who were not neighbours, even though they also spent still more time with kin (probably because their kin were generally nearer).

Only seven per cent of the couples sampled deviated from the above relational pattern to the extent of having predominantly and unambiguously middle class friendship networks. Generally, affluent working class couples associated with those whose presence in their lives was largely 'given', such as kin, close neighbours and workmates. Relations were usually informal. They were, for instance, much less likely to have people round for dinner than the white-collar groups. They were also far less likely to belong to formal organisations and those they did participate in, such as working men's clubs, tended to be solidly working class.

The changes in relational patterns that did typify the sample were not in the direction of embourgeoisement. The difference between them and the traditional working class could be explained by reference to major objective factors of their existence, such as work and geographical and residential mobility. Their relatively high level of consumption was explicable in terms of their hard work and relatively high pay. Their family centredness of privatisation can partly be explained in terms of new leisure facilities in the home and lack of traditional community links. In these limited aspects the lifestyle of the affluent worker converges with that of the lower middle class.

Political

Goldthorpe and Lockwood's findings under their third heading, the political aspect, are dealt with in Chapter 11, and are summarised only briefly here. They concentrated particularly on the voting behaviour of the main sample. On the basis of what they admit is limited data, they found a negative correlation between working class affluence and Conservative voting. In other words, the affluent worker is less likely to vote Conservative than less affluent workers. Again, they explain this by reference to the social, and not merely economic, realities of the affluent worker's life. Employment in large-scale industry, high union membership (87 per cent) and frequent life-long membership of the working class are factors cited. It is interesting, however, that Goldthorpe and

Lockwood note a marginal trend away from Labour among affluent workers. This trend was apparent in their own data, assessed on the basis of the way members of the sample had voted in 1959 compared to their intended votes for 1964. Certainly, the long-term tendency since 1945 has been for the Labour vote to drop as a percentage of the total vote, and much more recent data than that available to Goldthorpe and Lockwood suggests that 'defections' among affluent workers have contributed to this trend. They themselves comment that the strong Labour vote among affluent workers was based on instrumental (practical self-interest) thinking rather than traditional emotional solidarity (identification) with the party. This important finding left open the possibility that they would change their vote if it seemed to suit their interests to do so.

In a separate article, Lockwood analyses the basis of 'the privatised workers criterion of class division'. This is money – what Lockwood refers to as the 'pecuniary model' of society. Money makes consumption possible. Beyond kin membership, what differentiates people is how much money they have got. Privatised, interested in money and consumption – Lockwood is describing a familiar type of 1980 and 1990s. This adds contemporary relevance to his perceptive analysis (Reading 1).

Middle and working class convergence?

In place of the 'embourgeoisement' hypothesis, Goldthorpe and Lockwood offered the observation that some convergence was occurring between the upper working and lower middle class. Instead of the upper working class becoming more like the middle class, both classes are in some respects developing a number of common characteristics. As we have seen, convergence is not much apparent in the political and social relational areas. It is, however, occurring in the field of economic consumption. Both groups seek a good standard of living, particularly in furnishing their homes with modern amenities. Given this, it is logical that home and family centredness should be a feature of members of both groups. Outside the family, their patterns of social life continue to be distinct. Money is the basis on which the consumer-family lifestyle exists and it is not surprising that, in pursuit of it, collectivisation in the form of unionisation has been increasingly adopted by the salaried middle class as well as by the working class. The areas of convergence are, then, economic consumption, *family centredness* and *privatisation*, and *instrumental collectivism*.

A H Halsey adds the observation that, in addition, status distinction between the middle and working classes has become less obvious and less important during this century and especially since the last war. He attributes this primarily to increased rates of social mobility. With so many more first generation middle class people about, spotting the 'right' accent or the 'right' dress becomes a more precarious way of identifying status. But Halsey is aware of the relative superficiality of this. Just as important for him in the making of a fairer and more equal society are the political and legal rights (mainly of association, such as the right to join a union) only acquired or consolidated by the majority during this

century and discussed elsewhere in this book (see, especially Chapter 14). Even so, he cannot be accused of underestimating the extent of continuing inequality. The middle sections of society may have converged but the vestiges of status no longer cover the continuing huge discrepancies of wealth and poverty at the social extremes (see Chapter 13).

Class culture and ideology

The concept of culture has already been introduced as meaning 'way of life'. A much fuller discussion of culture, including class culture is given in Chapter 18. However, it is important to indicate here how culture and ideology can either strengthen or change a given class structure. As Nicholas Abercrombie suggests, there are two broad Marxist interpretations of working class culture (1980). First is the approach which sees working class (and bourgeois) culture as based on class *membership* and *interest*. In this perspective, shared interest is seen as likely to produce shared culture and consciousness. Second, the working class is seen as sometimes misled by 'bourgeois ideology' and as a result some of its members develop 'false consciousness' and may break from working class cultural values. Abercrombie has described the latter interpretation as the 'dominant ideology thesis'. Many, probably the vast majority of Marxists draw on both interpretations, and regard the first situation as desirable and the second as undesirable.

In contrast to Marx, Weber considered culture to be much more loosely associated with class. He did not regard it as unlikely, still less as 'false', that members of different classes should have common cultural interests and perhaps belong to the same groups, such as religious or leisure groups. For Weber, the class dimensions of culture are just one aspect of cultural diversity.

Contemporary Marxism tends to give great emphasis to cultural and ideological analysis. In general, the tendency has been to conceptualise culture as a contested area between the working and capitalist classes. Gramsci's concept of *hegemony* has been highly influential. 'Hegemony' refers to the cultural ascendancy that a given class may achieve. Typically, this is 'won' through ideological power and influence, particularly through education and the media. Many Marxists argued that 'Thatcherism' attained a hegemonic influence in Britain during the1980s. Gramsci makes the central point that hegemony is a 'moving equilibrium', it can always be challenged.

French Marxist Louis Althusser divides the capitalist state into the *repressive state apparatus* and the *ideological state apparatus*. The former includes the army and police and the latter, the educational system (see p. 88) and the media. He stresses the power of the capitalist state in ideologically reproducing capitalism. However, his concept of 'the relative autonomy of the superstructure' embodies the notion that some cultural opposition to the dominant order is possible. Overall, though, he is less optimistic about the likely effectiveness of cultural challenge to capitalism than is Gramsci.

In Britain, E P Thompson, Raymond Williams, and more

recently Stuart Hall and Paul Willis have attempted to present working class culture as vital and resilient and as potentially alternative and socialist. *Common Culture* (1990), a recent contribution by Willis is discussed at length in Chapter 15. In this book, Willis appears to argue that cultural activity offers more immediate potential for progressive change than political action.

It is arguable that the trend among some Marxists to regard culture as a crucial (perhaps, as the central) area in which capitalism can be contested, brings them closer to Weber and liberal thought in general. We have already seen that class culture - flexibly conceived – plays a central part in the work of Goldthorpe and, more recently, Marshall.

Social mobility

Terminology and factors associated with social mobility

We have already defined the concept of social mobility as movement up or down the social class hierarchy. Mobility may be long-range (e.g. from manual working class to professional/higher managerial) or, much more commonly, short-range. Individual and stratum mobility can occur and the former is considered to be generally more possible in modern than in traditional societies. Ascribed status refers to social position which is predetermined by others and is usually acquired at birth on the basis of the social standing of the individual's parents. Achieved status refers to the social position individuals acquire in their own lifetime, whether higher or lower than the one they had at birth. Again, the possibility of achieving a change in social status is considered to be greater in modern than in traditional societies, although most people remain in the class of their birth. The word 'achieved' is slightly misleading in this context, because merit is not necessarily implied in a change of social status.

The terms class of origin and class of destination provide a more neutral alternative to describe the same phenomenon. Class of origin refers to the class into which a person is born and class of destination to the one s/he acquires. Intragenerational mobility describes the situation when an individual acquires a different social status from the one which s/he previously held. Intergenerational mobility describes social mobility between generations and it is our main concern here. Finally, the terms vertical and horizontal mobility are frequently used. Vertical mobility is simply another way of referring to upward or downward mobility, and horizontal mobility involves a change from one occupation to another of equal status. Strictly speaking, horizontal mobility refers to occupational rather than social mobility as it involves no change of social status.

Status and class differences usually coincide, but rapid social mobility can cause them to be 'out of joint'. For example, a public school 'type' who finds himself having to do, say, a manual job may find the symbols of middle class status, such as accent and dress, something of an embarrassment. The same can happen to the working class 'lad' who suddenly 'makes it': he may appear to lack the polish of the more established rich. 'Status dissonance' is the term used to describe this kind of occurrence.

It should be remembered that most people remain in the class into which they are born. This can be partly because their lifestyle effectively cuts them off from other groups. For example, the traditional working class were often culturally very 'inbred' i.e. its members had little cultural experience beyond their own class. Parker has referred to this as social closure.

We now give a list of the major factors associated with social mobility – simply as a checkpoint: they are explained later in the section. It is scarcely possible to separate the overlapping factors affecting group and individual mobility. Broadly speaking, however, those affecting groups come first:

1. Substantial change in occupational structure
2. Differential fertility
3. Educational opportunity (Qualifications)
4. Social and cultural factors
5. Intelligence and talent
6. Marriage

All these are explained and illustrated below in our detailed analysis of social mobility in England and Wales (Table 6.6).

Social mobility in England and Wales: a test of the liberal ideal of equality of opportunity

There have been few more important public issues in twentieth century Britain than that of equality of opportunity. For Britain to be the 'open society' of liberal ideals, a society in which equality of opportunity exists, a good deal of social mobility must take place. More precisely, people must be able to compete for occupational position, on equal terms, regardless of their social class background. Many liberals of various political persuasions have regarded equality of opportunity as a pre-condition of a fair society. Of course, equality of opportunity does not guarantee equality of outcome: it means that people will achieve jobs suitable to their intelligence and talents, regardless of social background. As we have seen, Marxists want a different kind of equality from this: they want resources to be distributed in terms of need rather than competition. Others, again, are influenced by both views. Here, however, we examine how far the classic liberal ideal of equal opportunity is achieved in Britain. To do this, we must analyse the extent of social mobility in this country.

Studies of social mobility in Britain

There have been two major studies of social mobility in England and Wales, the first led by David Glass in 1949 and the second conducted by a team of sociologists at Nuffield College in 1972. The latter is known as the Oxford Mobility Study. Like most mobility studies prior to the Essex one, these two argued that trends in female social mobility could be derived from data about males.

Ideally, the findings of the two surveys would be directly comparable, and it was certainly the intention of the Oxford group to achieve this as far as possible. In fact, they do not attempt precisely to replicate Glass's methodology partly because of a number of criticisms that have been convincingly made against it. The major effect of the flaws in Glass's methodology is that he may have underestimated the rate of social mobility, particularly long-range upward mobility. As one of his important findings was that there was little long-range mobility, either upwards or downwards, the methodological criticisms are significant. Glass also found that family and social background had a major effect on social status and that most people remained at a similar level to their fathers.

Our analysis of the 1972 study will be assisted by reference to Table 6.5 which presents the main findings. The top half of the table (a) gives data about the class origin of respondents in 'Outflow' terms, and the bottom half (b) in 'inflow' terms. Thus (reading across), in Table (a), 45 per cent of those with a class I father were themselves in class I, whereas only six per cent were in class VII. In Table (b), the total percentage inflow into the various classes is given. Thus (reading down), of the total percentage inflowing into class I, 24 per cent had a class I father, whereas thirteen per cent had a class VII father. It is notable that of the 'inflowing' into class VII only two per cent were from class I whereas 39 per cent were from class VII.

Broadly, the findings of the Oxford Study confirm two popular clichés. The first is that the chances of improving one's social status got better in the post-war period, and the second – perhaps more a sociologist's than a layman's cliché – is that it is still much easier to retain high social status once born to it than it is to achieve it in the first place. Let us take these points in order.

Because of the expansion of the middle or service class since the war, there has been more opportunity for the lower middle and working class to move upwards. John H Goldthorpe, a major contributor to the Oxford Study, rejects the thesis that a significant degree of 'closure' exists at the higher occupational levels of British society. Writing of the upper end of the middle class (the top seven per cent occupationally) he argues that the survey data shows 'a very wide basis of recruitment and a very low degree of homogeneity in its composition'. In other words, people from a great variety of social origins are members of this class (recruitment), and by that very fact its members are in many ways dissimilar (lack homogeneity). Another interesting illustration of lack of homogeneity is that in 1972, marginally more members of social class I originated in social class VI than in social class II. Generally, the data shows a very much higher rate of long-range

Table 6.6 Intergenerational class mobility among men in England and Wales

(a) Class distribution of respondents by class of father at respondent's age 14 (% by row)

Class of father		I	II	III	IV	V	VI	VII	(N)	Total %
		Class of respondent								
S	I	45	19	12	8	5	5	6	(688)	7
	II	29	23	12	7	10	11	9	(554)	6
	III	18	16	13	6	13	15	17	(694)	7
I	IV	13	11	8	24	9	14	21	(1329)	14
	V	14	14	10	8	16	21	18	(1082)	12
	VI	8	9	8	7	12	30	26	(2594)	28
W	VII	6	8	8	7	12	24	35	(24930)	25
	(N)	(1285)	(1087)	(870)	(887)	(1091)	(2000)	(2214)	(9434)	
Total	%	14	12	9	9	12	21	23		100

(b) Class composition by class of father at respondent's age 14 (% by column)

Class of father		I	II	III	IV	V	VI	VII	(N)	Total %
		Class of respondent								
S	I	24	12	9	6	3	2	2	(688)	7
	II	13	12	8	4	5	3	2	(554)	6
	III	10	10	10	6	7	5	5	(694)	14
I	IV	13	14	12	37	11	10	12	(1329)	14
	V	12	13	12	9	15	11	8	(1082)	12
	VI	15	21	25	19	29	39	30	(2594)	28
W	VII	13	18	24	19	29	29	39	(2493)	25
	(N)	(1285)	(1087)	(870)	(887)	(1091)	(2000)	(2214)	(9434)	
Total	%	14	12	9	9	12	21	23		100

Note: Percentages may not add up exactly because of rounding.

(Source: Adapted from Marshall, 1990: 19, from the Oxford Mobility Study)

upward mobility than Glass found. Perhaps most notable, however, is the large percentage of people of working class origin achieving intermediate occupations i.e. the large amount of short-range mobility.

Concluding this point, then, opportunity for upward mobility substantially increased in post-war Britain. There is, however, quite another way of looking at the findings of the Oxford Study and we must adopt this perspective now.

The chances of a class I son remaining in class I compared to the changes that a working class son has of reaching class I have changed little over recent generations. Again, summarising from the table, the proportion of sons of middle class origin who retained middle class status is more than one in two, whereas only about one in seven working class sons achieved this status. What has happened is that increased opportunities have been shared more or less equally between the classes: there have been rather more opportunities for all. But if the chances of upward mobility for working class sons have improved, the shrinkage of working class jobs and the expansion of middle class ones has protected the middle class against downward mobility. Overall, therefore, relative mobility rates or the odds ratio (7:1, class I/VII) have changed remarkably little. Goldthorpe concludes that the pattern of intergenerational mobility in recent decades has been one of stability or even marginally increasing relative inequality.

It needs to be said that the Oxford Study does not address itself directly to the Marxist concern with the upper class. Other data show that there is much more self-recruitment to this group than to the much larger class I as a whole. It is also quite probable that those of non-upper class origins who do become members of it tend to adopt the values and attitudes of that class. Marxists are also able to interpret what is happening to the working class in a way quite consistent with their perspective. The working class is the most closed class and despite the differences between them, its members remain relatively disadvantaged. These factors may provide a sound basis for solidarity and collective action.

Factors explaining the recent pattern of social mobility in Britain

We now turn to discuss the factors that account for the pattern of social mobility described above. First, the increase in upward mobility has been largely due to a substantial shift in employment from the industrial to the service sector. Men have particularly benefited because lower status white collar jobs have been filled mainly by women, and men have been able to fill most of the new professional, technical, administrative and managerial posts. The increase has had little, if anything, to do with government policy. Indeed, in so far as the relative class rates of mobility have not changed, government policy to achieve greater equality of opportunity can be said to have failed.

Historically, differential fertility rates between the middle and working classes (that is, middle class families have produced fewer children) has created 'space' into which some working class people could move. Quite simply, the middle class did not produce enough children to fill all the middle class jobs available. This has been especially true in the rapid expansion of the service sector in the post-war period. Since the mid 1960s, there has been a tendency for family size to fall throughout the social classes, and although differences remain, differential fertility is now less important in explaining upward social mobility. The slight general decrease in the birth rate in the mid 1990s, even if sustained, is not likely to change this.

We have already examined the effect of educational expansion on social mobility and there is no need to rehearse the contents of this lengthy section here (see Chapter 4). In summary, Halsey *et al.*'s research on the tripartite system and various less extensive studies of the comprehensive system show little relative change in the educational success and career achievements of children of different class origins in the post-war period. The middle class has taken as much, if not more, advantage of state education as the working class and has virtually sole access to the privileged private sector. Gamely, but not entirely convincingly, Halsey argues that a further expansion of educational opportunity must, by deduction, disproportionately benefit the working class. There may be no

liberal alternative than but to try this, but history warns against excessive optimism about the likely results.

The influence of social and cultural factors on both educational and career opportunities does not need to be laboured here. It has been a constant theme in earlier chapters. The material disadvantages of a lower working class background are obvious, but the cultural disadvantages, if any, remain open to debate despite Halsey's sophisticated statistically-based attempt to show that they are much less than Bernstein and Bourdieu have argued.

However much intelligence may be helped or hindered by social environment, there is no doubt that the possession of high intelligence can be of assistance in upward mobility, and that low intelligence is a near fatal bar to it. Obviously, this factor applies virtually exclusively to the lower classes. It requires no intelligence at all to be born into the upper classes (although it usually requires, at least, the intelligence to appoint a good accountant to stay there). Lipset and Bendix have suggested that high intelligence may help working class children to recognise middle class attitudes and norms and to see the advantage of imitating them.

Traditionally, exceptional talent in either entertainment or sport has been an avenue to the top for a few working class people and, particularly in the United States, for some black people. But for most, this possibility is just a dream. There are not many Madonnas or Paul Gascoignes. A further miscellaneous group of factors, such as character, looks and luck can no doubt play a part in mobility but they are too unpredictable and personal to require more than brief acknowledgement here.

Of more sociological importance is the fact that women achieve upward mobility by marriage more often than men. This is a result of their generally inferior economic position and earning power. 'She's a gold digger' can be understood more sympathetically in the context of a society in which women depend heavily on men for material comfort and social status. This dependency is not the fault of individual women but lies in the nature of our unequally gendered society (see Chapter 7).

If the recent past is a good guide, the prospects for upward mobility in Britain depend on the further expansion of the service sector. In the early 1990s, the medium term prospects are for more employment in this area. Clearly, expansion cannot go on for ever. If higher status and better paid jobs are not available, a better academically qualified population will go to waste at the dole queues.

Questions

1 Critically discuss the proletarianisation thesis.
2 Discuss the arguments and evidence for and against the view that Britain is a society of 'equal opportunity'.

How important is class in contemporary Britain: is class in decline?

However class is defined, only a few sociologists would argue that 'class does not exist' in contemporary Britain. Relations to the means of production, job market and work situations remain highly unequal. However, increasingly sociologists from various perspectives attach different degrees of importance to social class and some argue that it has greatly declined in importance in relation to gender, ethnicity and more personal aspects of differentiation/identity. In particular, sociologists influenced by postmodernism, such as Robin Murray (1988), tend to consider that the 'old' industrial class structure has irreversibly fragmented and is likely to continue to do so. In addition, a wide range of sociologists, including some neo-Marxists now imply that even in the past, the importance of class may have been exaggerated. This is mainly because of the apparent 'failure' of the Marxist 'working class project' i.e. the failure of the working class to become the dominant class.

The idea that the importance of class and class conflict is declining in Britain (and in the rest of the advanced capitalist world) is not new. As early as the 1950s, Ralf Dahrendorf argued that both the capitalist class and the working class were 'fragmenting' or 'decomposing' (see p. 167). It is especially in relation to the traditional working class that the case for the decline of class has been pursued. Crudely summarised, the embourgeoisement thesis of the 1950s/60s maintained that the affluent working class was becoming absorbed into an expanding middle class. Even Goldthorpe's revision of this thesis in terms of *convergence* left room for the view that class conflict and differences were blurring (see p. 174). The growth of consumerism (noted by Goldthorpe), the growing prosperity of all classes (until the 1980s), and the steady numerical decline of the manual working class were widely seen as having the potential to 'take the edge off' class conflict.

In reviewing the continuing debate about the importance of social class in Britain, it will help to keep three key aspects in mind. These are:

1   The material inequalities caused by class, i.e. by class understood broadly as Weber or Marx defined it.
2   The effects or influence of class e.g. it has been argued that these include an effect on educational attainment and voting behaviour.
3   Consciousness of class i.e. awareness of one's own and others' class identity. Although class consciousness cannot be separated from the material aspects of class or the effects of class, it will be useful to do so for the purpose of analysis.

These three points will occur to different degrees in the following discussion. These are Marxist, Weberian, New Right and Postmodernist.

Marxist

Problems and limits of class analysis

Contemporary Marxism is on the defensive. This is not surprising. First, the collapse of the Communist regimes of Eastern Europe in 1989 inevitably tainted Marxism in general. While it is true that may Western Marxists had long distanced themselves from the Soviet model of Marxism, some had continued to fellow-travel even after the repressive and sometimes brutal nature of Soviet Communism was clear.

Secondly, the working class has not behaved quite as Marx predicted and few now think it will. Scott Lash and John Urry, both of whom remain radical, left-thinking sociologists, put the point uncompromisingly:

> *It once appeared that a whole set of economic, spatial and social developments in organised capitalism were propelling the working class forwards: it was on the side of history, it represented the 'modern' … What our claim amounts to is that such a possibility has in a number of specific western societies disappeared. Time cannot be set in reverse, the moment has passed.*
>
> *(1987:310-11)*

Thirdly, however important some sociologists consider class to be, their opinion does not appear to be shared by the general public. Put otherwise, even though class may be an *objectively* powerful structuring force on people's lives, many do not seem *subjectively* to think so. Again, a neo-Marxist expresses the point Richard Scase states that:

> *… class is generally regarded by most people as being of little relevance for the understanding of the everyday lives. In describing themselves, people tend to refer to such characteristics as age, gender, ethnicity, place of residence, occupation, etc., rather than class membership … (I)t is only with the considerable assistance of interviewers that respondents participating in social surveys are likely to refer to themselves in class terms and to allocate themselves to one of a number of class categories presented to them.*
>
> *(1992:79)*

Table 6.7 Functions of capital and labour, class and occupational categories.

Social relations of production →	Class structure →	Occupational categories
Functions of capital relating to:		
(a) Ownership		(a) Shareholders and proprietors
(b) Control and co-ordination	Middle class	(b) Directors, managers, higher-grade professional employees
(c) Research and technological development		(c) Scientists, engineers and technologists
Functions of labour relating to:		
(d) Production of economic surplus	Working class	(d) Productive manual workers
(e) Execution of necessary but non-productive tasks		(e) Clerical, secretarial, routine 'non-manual', 'support' and maintenance workers

(Source: *SCASE*:25)

The continuing importance of class analysis: Richard Scase and John Westergaard

It might seem that Richard Scase is too emphatic in his comments on the subjective irrelevance of class to 'most people'. However, he is in no doubt that class remains 'a concept that is vital for understanding the structure of present-day capitalist society'; and that 'the capitalist mode of production cannot exist without class relations' (1992:80). Scase goes on to reiterate the Marxist orthodoxy that contrary to occupationally based models of class, it is still the relations of production which create class structure. He makes the point graphically in Table 6.7.

Other neo-Marxists, notably Frederick Jameson and David Harvey, continue to press Marxist analysis in relation to the global context. However, much as they dislike capitalism, they differ from Marxists of previous generations in offering little realistic prospect of any alternative.

John Westergaard also finds the Marxist approach to be useful in understanding capitalist society, notably in relation to class inequality. However, his *Who Gets What? The Hardening of Class Inequality in the late Twentieth century* is not a rigorously argued Marxist text. He considers that any well-grounded analysis of class would establish the existence of enormous inequalities of income,

wealth and opportunity in capitalist society (of the kind frequently referred to in this book). His book decries a whole range of extreme and growing inequalities in late twentieth century capitalist Britain which he sees as broadly class-based. Even if some inequalities are necessary, he asks, need they be so extreme? In his final chapter, he addresses the question 'Is class now dead – again?' The irony in the question implies Westergaard's answer – it is not. Indeed, class-based inequalities have been increasing.

Although Westergaard generally supports the redistributive mechanisms of social democracy – progressive taxation, an effective system of welfare – he offers no fundamental solution to how substantially greater equality could be achieved. In a review of Westergaard's book, Robert Blackburn, comments on the former's desire substantially to reduce inequality:

> (I)n a competitive world, where there are big differences of wealth between countries, and those in the higher-ranking positions (or simply highly-paid, like professional golfers) can move freely across national boundaries, it is difficult to see how narrow differentials could be maintained. To be fair, no one else has an answer but that does not invalidate his egalitarian logic.
>
> (In *Work, Employment and Society*, Vol. 9 No. 4, 1995)

The Weberian class project

Gordon Marshall and others

Writing at different times with different colleagues, Gordon Marshall has continued to argue the relevance of a Weberian-based model of social class of the kind he and his co-authors put forward in *Social Class in Modern Britain in 1988* (see pp. 171-2). In 1992, Marshall and Goldthorpe published an article titled *The Promising Future of Class Analysis: A Response to Recent Critiques* (*Sociology*, Vol. 26, No. 3). In it they thoroughly distance themselves from Marxist class analysis and deny that the criticisms made of the latter can be fairly applied to the class research programme which they are pursuing. In particular they reject the Marxist theory of class as the engine of historical change.

Marshall and Goldthorpe first clarify the nature and purpose of class analysis and then make the case for its continued relevance by reviewing findings from three key areas of current research. Citing Charles Wright Mills, they contend that class analysis can investigate connections 'between historically formed macro social structures … and … the everyday experience of individuals within their particular social milieux, together with the patterns of action that follows from this experience.' In other words, whether people are aware of it or not, social class profoundly affects their lives. They illustrate this with reference to social mobility, education and political partisanship. There is no need to rehearse here the details of the strong connections they refer to between class and these central areas of life (they are all dealt with elsewhere in this book).

If they are correct, then the continued relevance of class and class analysis would seem to be established although they acknowledge that the precise ways class 'operates' or 'the mechanisms of class' still require much further research.

Criticism of, and comments on Marshall

Peter Saunders (1989) criticises Marshall *et al.*'s 1988 study of social class partly on the grounds that because their interviews were highly structured around social class their respondents were led towards identifying themselves with aspects of social class and were not facilitated to talk about other aspects of their identity. Fiona Devine takes up this criticism in her own research on lifestyles and identity in 1986-87. She carried out in-depth interviews of 32 working class couples in the Luton area as part of the long-running 'Affluent Worker' series. She argues that 'qualitative interviews may overcome some of the limitations of using highly structured questionnaires; better enabling interviewees to 'speak freely and develop their own ideas, concepts and arguments'.

On the basis of her research, Devine concluded that people seem to 'hold a variety of social identities'. Important among these were:

1 **Regional:** 'a sense of belonging' to a particular place. People born and brought up in the same place (e.g. in Luton itself, or who had migrated from London to Luton) often tended to socialise with each other;

2 **National:** 'affiliation with a nation, and sometimes differing nations simultaneously, was a significant dimension of the interviewees' identity'.

Devine observes that the presence of Indian and Pakistani communities led 'almost all of the British Irish interviewees to assert their British identity, their Christianity and, of course, their whiteness'. She adds that 'Racist beliefs were prevalent'.

3 **Class:** along with other social identities, Devine found 'a high level of class awareness'. While the interviewees did not hold 'a clear and coherent picture of class … this did not inhibit them from invoking the importance of class on their political beliefs, attitudes and vote'.

Devine concludes that: 'The main finding to emerge from the qualitative data is that a high level of class awareness can co-exist with other significant social identities'. In fact, Marshall and his colleagues fully accept that such diverse identities exist (although it has not been their purpose fully to explore them). However, two main points remain unresolved in the 'importance of class' debate:

1 How do class and other aspects of identity such as ethnicity and a sense of place interact (an issue emphasised by Devine as still outstanding)?

2 What is the relative importance of class in comparison to other aspects of identity? Is it possible that class has now been superseded by other forms of identity?

New Right perspective: Peter Saunders

Peter Saunders has made a number of significant contributions to class analysis and in 'labelling' his position 'New Right', it is important not to oversimplify his work.

Saunders' book, *A Nation of Home Owners* (1990) argues that a new type of social division – sectoral division – is emerging and that as a consequence the importance of class is decreasing. Sectoral divisions are defined in terms of public or private ownership. Thus, those who own their own houses, use their own vehicles rather than public transport, or take out private health insurance are 'in' the private rather than the public sector in those respects. Saunders considers that these divisions of consumption are superseding those of class. The sectional 'cleavage' examined in detail by Saunders is housing. Saunders argues that home ownership is of major importance both materially and in terms of identity. Home ownership provides a base for personal wealth and for status and lifestyle. For many, owning their own home may mean more in terms of identity than the job they do. Further in terms of broader identification, home owners are likely to vote for the Conservatives – the party of privatisation – whereas council house tenants have a vested interest in voting Labour (see pp. 324-5). For Saunders, then, consumer divisions rather than occupation become the main aspect of stratification – an analysis which Ben Fine refers to as 'unwittingly a parody of the (crudest) Marxist theory of class based upon production (Miller ed. 1995).

It remains to be seen whether the extension of home-ownership under Thatcherism will have the long-term significance Saunders attributes to it. For millions, home ownership has meant a loss, not a gain of wealth, and it is not clear what the political consequences of this might be. Saunders' extension of his thesis about the importance of consumption and the decline of class identities to other 'cleavages' than housing seems to stretch the evidence. In fact, the correlation between private education and health insurance with social class is very strong. It could well be that class explains these patterns of consumption as effectively as any other variable.

Saunders' other major contribution to the 'decline of class' debate, is his proposition that there may be a virtual equation of the British class system with a natural meritocracy. He argues that research on intelligence and heredity suggests that to a remarkable extent people occupy the class positions they merit in contemporary Britain. If that is so, Saunders suggests, why so much left-wing concern about inequality? For him, as for Functionalists, the inequality of the British class system is fair and, by implication, we might better spend time on other things than imagined class injustice.

Saunders' arguments are recent and contradict much previous social scientific research. However, it is likely that he will require his opponents to address again the relationship between heredity, social environment and class position.

Postmodern perspective

There are many different streams within postmodernist thinking but virtually all give a central place to cultural consumption – usually at the expense of emphasising production and class. In the early 1970s, the then mainly Marxist researchers at the Centre for Contemporary Cultural Studies at Birmingham University began to publish a series of works which examined the cultural dimensions of class and, increasingly, of other aspects of stratification as well. Their earlier work located cultural activity clearly within social structural context, especially class. By the early 1990s, however, several of the most influential of these researchers were analysing culture on the basis that it is, or can be, a fairly free form of self or group expression. In a characteristically postmodern way, writers such as Angela McRobbie and Paul Willis were examining culture and consumption as fairly autonomous of social class.

There were other developments that led some radical sociologists away from a traditional emphasis on class and material matters of cultural analysis. In particular, post-Fordists argued that mass production/consumption no longer met the needs of an increasingly wealthy and differentiated consumer population. 'Niche' production and consumption increasingly developed (see pp. 252-5 for a critical account of post-Fordism). More complex interplay between producers (supply) and consumers (demand) enabled more people to express themselves through more complex and differentiated lifestyles. A person's class did not provide a reliable basis for predicting her or his consumption habits or lifestyle.

Colin Campbell has noted similarity between postmodernist and advertisers' approaches to consumption and class. In both cases identity is categorised on the basis of patterns of consumer choice (in Miller ed., 1995). However, it can be added on behalf of postmodernists that in distinction from advertisers, they are interested in collective consumer action as well as individual consumer action. Many social movements have a consumer consciousness and collective conscience element about them. Vegetarians, animal rights activists and environmentalists act, in part, as socially sensitive consumers. Their action may lack the power of traditional class action and may often be fragmented and of short duration but can also be more immediate and meaningful than conventional political action.

Conclusion

Taken together the various arguments that the importance of class has waned in the post-war period merit consideration. Not least, is the loss of belief in the working class project as outlined by Marx by many Marxists themselves. Further, sociologists of all perspectives recognise that the decline in the size of the industrial proletariat accompanied by a steady growth in average individual and family wealth is no basis for revolution. It is probably true that the populations of the advanced capitalist societies are more concerned to preserve their advantage in relation to the rest of the world than to risk the internal upheaval of a radical redistribution of wealth.

In such circumstances, it would not be surprising if many in the capitalist West have become increasingly preoccupied with consumption. Also, if class has declined, one would expect differences of lifestyle based on age, ethnicity and gender to emerge more strongly.

However, as Richard Scase points out, the socio-economic system of the West and the world is capitalist. It is characterised by increasing inequalities, can be highly destructive and raises moral issues that trouble many people. Capitalism may yet be radically challenged, though not necessarily as has been anticipated in the past.

Questions

1 How would you describe the class structure of contemporary British society?
2 Has the importance of class declined in post-war Britain?

Summary

1 In the welter of detail about the British class structure, it is helpful to bear in mind four perspectives/interpretations of Britain's changing class structure. These are:
   i Liberal Perspective: and Embourgoisement.
   ii Marxist Perspective: Proletarianisation
      Two Weberian Views:
   iii A fragmentary class structure.
   iv Continuing class inequality in the context of greater affluence.
2 A liberal perspective. The term liberal is a broad one but in this context it is intended to indicate the view that class has become less important in British life largely because of the general increase in wealth.
3 Marxist perspective on class requires some development to deal with the substantial numerical reduction in the size of the manual working class and the corresponding rise in numbers of non-manual workers. A large part of 'the answer' is Harry Braverman's 'proletarianisation thesis' which argues that most of the latter group are working class.
4 Two Weberian Views:
   i The view that the British class structure is fragmenting or 'decomposing' is basically as simple as it sounds – the British class structure is considered to be 'breaking up' partly due to the increasing complexity of the occupational system.

ii Continuing class inequality in the context of greater affluence is a view propounded by more 'hard-nosed' Weberians such as John Goldthorpe. They reject the progressive optimism of the liberal perspective described above in the light of substantial evidence of continuing and even increasing inequality.

5 The economic context of class change, particularly the rise of the service sector and the decline of manufacturing employment is relevant to class analysis both because of the relative increase in white-collar employees and in female employment.

6 The Upper Class. The key issue in relation to the upper class is whether its power and influence has declined or not. In Marxist terms, is the upper class (still) a 'ruling class'?

7 The 'Middle' Classes. The key issue in relation to lower white-collar employees is whether they are best categorised as middle class as David Lockwood argues in his study of clerks, or whether they are mainly working class as Braverman contends.

8 The Working Class. The key issue in relation to the working class is whether it is in some sense declining and losing its identity (or perhaps 'converging' with the middle class), or whether it remains a distinct, potentially powerful, social grouping.

9 The 'underclass' is not a class at all in the sense that its members share a common occupational location or relationship to the means of production. The term describes people who, for various reasons, are 'cut-off' from the relative affluence of the rest of society. The issue of the underclass is discussed in the context of poverty in Chapter 13.

10 Social mobility is movement up or down the social hierarchy. Although there has arguably been an increase in higher status jobs in post-war Britain, the relative chances of achieving high status jobs between middle and working class people has hardly changed.

11 Is the importance of class declining in contemporary Britain? A variety of arguments on this theme are reviewed. It is paradoxical that while capitalism has become objectively stronger, subjective class consciousness among the majority of people appears relatively weak. However, recruitment to the upper class has helped to revitalise its strength.

Research and coursework

Several of the studies of class cited in this chapter are large-scale social surveys such as the Oxford Study and the Essex Project. It would be quite impossible to attempt anything of this scope. However, some of the issues raised by these studies are open to exploration on a smaller scale. The Essex Project, for instance, opens up a number of class/gender matters. A hypothesis that could be tested is whether when a married couple are both in paid work, the female tends to derive her view of her own (and perhaps her family's) class position from her own occupation, her husband's or both. Another matter which could be explored in this piece of research is whether female married partners' political views are more likely to be influenced by their husband's occupational status than their own. If you include a question on whether or not female respondents would describe themselves as 'feminist' you might find that those answering 'yes' emerge as a sub-group with distinctive views. Again, however, be wary of allowing your research to get out of hand. A study of ten couples might require say, twenty in-depth interviews and even this might be too much in practical terms.

Further reading

For those who want to do project work on class or simply to study the questions relating to it more deeply, it is worth emphasising that methodological appendices - though they may look technical – can be the most useful part of a book. It is in appendices that you can sometimes learn how to conceptualise problems and formulate questions. Two examples occur in, respectively, G Marshall *et al.*, *Social Class in Modern Britain* (Hutchinson, 1988) and Howard H Davis, *Beyond Class Images* (Croom Helm, 1979).

Readings

Reading 1
The privatised worker's image of society

From David Lockwood, 'Sources of Variation in Working Class Images of Society', reprinted in Anthony Giddens and David Held eds., *Classes, Power and Conflict: Classical and Contemporary Debates* (Macmillan, 1982), pp.370-2

The social isolation of the privatised worker reflects itself in his ideology of a 'de-socialised' class structure. The single, overwhelmingly important, and the most spontaneously conceived criterion of class division is money, and the possessions, both material and immaterial, that money can buy. From this point of view, for example, education is not thought of as a status-conferring characteristic, but rather simply as a good (commodity) that money can buy and as a possession that enables one to earn more money. In general, power and status are not regarded as significant sources of class division or social hierarchy. Power is not understood as the power of one man over another, but rather as the power of a man to acquire things: a purchasing power. Status is not seen in terms of the association of status equals sharing a similar style of life. If status is thought of at all it is in terms of a standard of living, which all who have the means can readily acquire. It may not be easy to acquire the income requisite to a certain standard of living and hence qualify for membership in a more affluent class; but given the income there are no other barriers to mobility.

Within this pecuniary universe, the privatised worker tends to see himself as a member of a vast income class which contains virtually the great mass of the population. This class may be called 'the working class' or 'the middle class'. Whatever it is called, it is a collection of 'ordinary people' who 'work for a living' and those who belong to it include the majority of manual and non-manual employees. They are united with one another, not by having exactly the same incomes, but by not having so much or so little income that their standard of living places them completely beyond the upper or lower horizons. A minority of persons in the society have either so much wealth or such an impoverished existence that they lie outside the central class. They are the very rich and the very poor. Since the main criterion of class membership is money, the lower and, especially, the upper limits of the central class are hard to define, and are consequently defined arbitrarily or regarded as indeterminate. In general the 'upper' or 'higher' or 'rich' class is not perceived as wielding power or deserving of respect. It is simply a vague category of 'all those up there' who have incomes and possessions and a standard of life that are completely beyond the bounds of possibility as far as the ordinary worker is concerned. The rich, however, are different form the rest only in the sense of Hemingway's rejoinder to Scott Fitzgerald: that they have much more money.

Finally, the central class with which the privatised worker identifies himself is seen as a relatively new phenomenon, brought about by the incorporation of the old middle class into the new 'working class', or, alternatively, by the incorporation of the old working class into the new 'middle class'. Whether the end result of the change is seen as a 'working class' or a 'middle class', its identity is basically an economic one; people are assigned to this central class because they have roughly similar levels of income and possessions.

Questions

1 What is meant by a 'pecuniary model' of society? How might the privatised worker have built up this model?
2 How might a Marxist explain and account for the privatised worker's pecuniary model of society?

Reading 2
Not only class, but also regional and national identities

From Fiona Devine 'Social identities, class identity and political perspectives' in *The Sociological Review*, 1992, pp. 236-38

However, in one important respect, Luton and its residents were different to the town which the Luton team, and Zweig (1961) before them, visited in the early 1960s. In the late 1960s and 1970s, a new influx of people from India (via East Africa), Pakistan and Bangladesh moved to Luton. Like the migrants from other parts of Britain and Ireland, they invariably moved to Luton in search of a livelihood – a job and a home – although the circumstances in which they moved were far less favourable than those of earlier migrants to the town. Like them as well, they relied on kin and friends to find them jobs, temporary and then permanent accommodation and, as a consequence, re-grouped in the town (centre) as well. Again, kin and friends were an important source of companionship and support. Clearly, their identity with their country, its people and their hopes and plans, fears and aspirations, their way of life and their culture was significant. And, of course, being non-white was a particularly important dimension of this identity, heightened by racial conflict in the town. As one interviewee from Kenya, but of Indian origin, who had moved to Luton with his parents in the 1970s, recalled: 'When we first came here, there were a lot of racial attacks on people. There were a lot of National Front people, a lot of problems. Basically, we never used to get out of the house after 7 p.m. It was better to stay at home.'

He now felt that Luton had changed for the better, one reason being that 'a mosque has been built which is good for us being Muslims. It is somewhere for us to go and pray'. Even so, he also identified himself as British, referring to India, his parents' country of origin, as an ex-colony of Britain, and still a Commonwealth country.

Discussion on the influx of people of different origins into the town, and of the Indian or Pakistani communities in particular, led almost all of the British/Irish interviewees to assert their British identity, their Christianity and, of course, their whiteness. While the distinctions between people of different geographical origins from Britain and Ireland had been drawn light-heartedly, the divisions between them and 'coloured immigrants' were discussed in distinctly pejorative terms. Racist beliefs were prevalent. They spoke of the decline of the residential areas in which they lived with the proliferation of families living together in the same house. The 'immigrants'' poor house and the way in which they stayed so close to their family and friends indicated their failure to assimilate themselves into the town in particular, and into Britain in general, and to adopt the respectable lifestyles of the British. As one native Lutonian explained: 'Too many overseas people have congregated in the area. Of all the towns with jobs, they have congregated in small patches, spreading out, taking over all the shops and ruining the area. B … used to be a different area with nice houses, gardens, and trees but now it looks as if a bomb's been dropped. If I went to their country, we would have to abide by their rules. They have brought in their own rules, their own culture.'

Thus, affiliation with a nation, and sometimes different nations simultaneously, was a significant dimension of the interviewees' identity. While identities based on geographical origins within Britain and Ireland were typically latent, a national identity was extremely pronounced. Their national identity was heightened because it was the basis of different and seemingly conflicting beliefs and attitudes - at least amongst the white Irish and British interviewees. It was also the source of conflict over the distribution of resources such as council houses and jobs.

Given that the majority of the interviewees felt very strongly about immigration (concurring with Sarlvik and Crewe's (1983:242) finding that those who think they live in a 'high immigrant area' are more likely to feel very strongly about the issue than those who do not), it might have been expected that attitudes on the issue would shape political affiliations and party choice. After all, Luton's two MPs - John Carlisle and Graham Bright – are well known for their tough stands on immigration. However, this was not the case even though the interviewees were well aware of where the political parties stood on immigration. They knew that the Conservative Party wanted to restrict immigration while the Labour Party took a more liberal stand. It was mentioned only by the long-standing Conservative Party supporters in the sample as a

justification for their political allegiances and why they did not vote Labour. Referring to conflict over the distribution of resources, an interviewee who had always voted Conservative said: 'I agree that we shouldn't allow more immigrants in. The Labour Party would let more in. We have youngsters of our own who want jobs. It gets harder for those here.'

As we shall see, however, the majority of the interviewees were Labour Party Supporters or disillusioned Labour Party supporters who justified their present or past party choice on a class basis. The interviewees' national identity did not translate into party choice, remaining, instead, a 'dormant' frame of reference in the political arena.

In sum, the interviewees identified with a range of social groups as Saunders suggested. Moreover, as Emmison and Western also found, and affiliation with 'a sense of place' was particularly important social identity. It shaped the way in which the interviewees saw themselves and interacted with other people. The importance of social identities, other than class, therefore, cannot be denied. However, all of the interviewees also identified with a class. Indeed, their class identity brought them together whereas their regional/national identities differentiated them. Their regional/national identity, however, did not prohibit their class identity or vice versa. This implies that people identify with many different and sometimes contradictory social groups. In turn, this suggests, as Marshall's and Rose's position implies, that a high level of class awareness can co-exist with other social identities. Asserting that class is a common source of reference is not tantamount to denying the significance of other social identities as the critics claim. That said, it will be seen that the interviewees' awareness of class was not as clear and coherent as the Essex team suggested.

Questions

1 Describe what being British means to:
   a Indians and Pakistanis in Luton
   b Irish in Luton
2 Using the above and other sources:
   Discuss the view that class is the most important social identity.

7

Gender and Sexuality

```
HUMAN DEVELOPMENT REPORT 1995: GLOBAL STATISTICS
IN MOST RESPECTS, IT IS STILL AN UNEQUAL WORLD

♀                            WORK                            ♂
                    ECONOMICALLY ACTIVE POPULATION
WOMEN'S SHARE 1994 38%                    MEN'S SHARE 1994 62%

                        EARNED INCOME
26%                                                    74%

                            POWER
                      SEATS IN PARLIAMENT
10%                                                    90%

                      NATIONAL CABINET
6%                                                     94%
```

(Source: United Nations Development Programme in *The Times*, 18.8.1995:23)

There is a long way to go before gender equality is achieved. Why has progress been so slow?

Theories of sex and gender

First perspectives on sex and gender will be discussed below. These are the sex differences approach, the cultural (or sex roles) approach, an integrated approach and the social construction of sex/gender approach.

The sex differences perspectives

The sex differences approach is based on the theory that the main social differences between males and females are caused by, and are reflections of biological differences. Thus, in this view, 'biology is destiny', in the sense that women are considered biologically programmed for childrearing and related domestic work, whereas men are regarded as 'naturally' breadwinners. Tiger and Fox present a particular radical version of this thesis, arguing that the two sexes have different 'biogrammars' which determine their conduct. Several psychologists have posited a biologically-based maternal instinct matched by a mother-need in babies. This analysis is particularly associated with John Bowlby who, however, modified his position to the extent that he allowed that a 'mother substitute' could meet a child's need for love and affection.

Functionalist explanations of gender differences allow for greater cultural flexibility on the biological base. George Murdock sees the sexual division of labour with women bearing and rearing children and men doing tasks involving strength, as a matter of practicality and convenience. Each sex is *biologically* best suited to these respective tasks. Talcott Parsons is more culturally relative in his analysis of the sexual division of labour. He considers that it is functional in the context of capitalist society that women should fulfil the expressive (nurturing, caring) role and men the instrumental (competitive, acquisitive) role. In this way, a married couple complement rather than compete with each other. Parsons reflects something of Freud's view of the 'naturalness' of sex-gender differences. However, Parsons did recognise that women might not be entirely fulfilled as housewives and mothers. Writing in the late 1940s he suggested that 'any attempt to force or persuade an overwhelming majority of American women to accept a role of pure and virtuous domesticity alone is probably doomed to failure' (*The Social Structure of the Family*). In view of the avalanche of feminist criticism to come, he might be thought to have understated the case!

A cultural perspective

The cultural perspective explains gender differences – roles and related behaviour and attitudes – as the produce of cultural socialisation. Ann Oakley's explanation of the difference between sex and gender has been basic to the cultural approach. She states that sex differences are biological in nature, whereas gender differences are culturally produced. This distinction has the further implication that sex differences are more or less unchangeable, whereas gender differences are very much open to variation, change and adaptation. The definitive sex difference between males and females is based on the parts of the body concerned with sex, procreation and nurture: the genitals and breasts. An example of a difference in gender behaviour occurs in some Muslim societies. Frequently women veil their faces, whereas men do not. Clearly, there is nothing 'natural' about this. Due to the greater cultural influence of the West in Kuwait than in Saudi Arabia, this custom is somewhat less prevalent there.

Many cross-cultural studies show a wide range of gender behaviour. In particular, Margaret Mead's work seeks to demonstrate that there is no universal 'masculine' or 'feminine' personality. For example, in her fieldwork in the South Pacific she found that both sexes of the Arapesh conform roughly to our traditional stereotype of 'femininity', and both those of the Mundugumor to our 'masculine' stereotype.

A society which provides evidence to support the cultural approach is that of the Wahiba, a Bedouin tribe of central Oman in the Persian Gulf. Gender relations bear little similarity to what would be regarded as 'normal' in Western society:

> *The men live with their mothers, apart from their wives, whose huts may be as much as 50 miles away, and just visit them occasionally. Both men and women share the work of making the home but wives then have sole ownership.*
>
> *In general, work is equally divided, with goats and sheep being the responsibility of the women while the men tend the camels ...*
>
> *One of the traditional tasks of the men is the cooking ...*
>
> (The Observer, 19.11.1978)

The term 'gendered' is particularly associated with the cultural approach. Male and female roles learnt through socialisation are considered to be 'gendered'. Thus, for the Wahiba, domestic cooking is gendered as a male activity, whereas in Britain and the United States it still tends to be gendered as a female activity.

An integrated perspective

A third approach to understanding gender is increasingly adopted. For simplicity, I will refer to it here as an integrated perspective. It is integrated in that it draws on both biology and culture and thus avoids the 'either/or' approach of cruder versions of the other two perspectives. It is also an historical approach and, for the reasons below, this is sometimes identified as its main feature.

R C Lewontin and his co-authors argue in *Not in Our Genes: Biology, Ideology and Human Nature* (1984) for 'an integrated understanding of the relationship between the biological and social' rather than either biological or cultural determinism. Such an approach recognises that biological differences occur between individuals and between the two sexes but the interpretations of their significance and meaning can substantially vary. Emily Martin's *The Woman in the Body* (1987) illustrates the main aspects of the integrated approach. Martin examines three specifically female biological experiences – menstruation, childbirth, and the menopause (which have no precise male parallel). She compares the way women undergoing these experiences tend to be dealt with by scientific medicine, with the way the women respond to these experiences, and to medical management of them. She argues that male dominated medical science treats these female biological processes as a form of production: menstruation is 'failed' production; childbirth, a form of labour, 'managed' by the medical team; and the menopause is the end of productivity.

Martin finds more resentment and opposition to the practice of scientific and managed medicine among working class than middle class women. Here are some brief statements of 'resistance' (188):

> *He did an episiotomy without asking or telling me, he just did it. By that time I was his as far as he was concerned.*
>
> (Carol Gleason)
>
> *They didn't let me stay in labour too long. My doctor said he didn't want me to go through pain ... I wanted to go through it all, it wasn't hurting that bad.*
>
> (Juliet Cook)
>
> *I remember when I went to the hospital. Considering I'm not in a good financial position, not being married and having a baby, she said to me, 'Oh, you're going to put the baby up for adoption?' I really, really was angry ... I felt like saying, 'How dare you talk to me that way! I'm not some sleazo or some piece of shit or something!'*
>
> (Elizabeth Larson)

Martin is well aware that the above type of statement does not represent a developed feminist position or consciousness. But such statements could be interpreted as a step on the way to a wider understanding of oppression. The psychology of oppression and of liberation remain part of much current feminist analysis: the key questions being: 'How can the oppressed become aware of the source and nature of their oppression?' and 'What will prompt them to do something about it?'. By making use of frequent historical and cross-cultural references, Martin shows that females can take much greater control of these three basic biological processes and experience them much more positively and creatively than under 'modern' medicine. Martin also contends that in attempting to empower themselves in stereotypically female areas such as 'health and domestic', females may begin to draw parallels with their relative lack of power in paid employment. They may become aware that their roles in the latter area are similar to those they play in the domestic and child production/care areas.

A word of caution may be needed about the integrated approach to gender described above. It is certainly not a perspective which states that biology determines gender differences – indeed, it is radically opposed to such an approach. Those who adopt an integrated approach tend to stress how biological differences are differently interpreted historically and across cultures and to be highly conservative in drawing social consequences from biology. Finally, it needs to be said that the integrated approach is really not so new. In practice, much of the work of cultural socialisation theorists, including Ann Oakley, recognised the reality of biological differences between the sexes and took these into account in analysing the gendering process. Ann Oakley's own analysis of scientific medicine (see pp. 430-1) and Gaye Tuchman's study of the objectification of the female body in some media (see p. 513) stress the impact of patriarchal ideology on the way women are treated but each assumes that things could be very different.

A social constructionist perspective on sex, sexuality and gender

Useful through the sex (biology)/gender (culture) distinction has been in stimulating research in the latter area, it has come under increasing criticism. The main direction of this criticism is that the body itself, including its sexuality, is subject to social and personal definition and evaluation. For instance, some lesbians have deliberately changed their physical presentation, including posture, in order to move away, from conventional, 'emphasised femininity' (see p. 193). This makes sense in that they presumably want to avoid sending non-verbal messages of a kind that males might 'read' as encouraging a sexual approach. Similarly, some males – aware of the criticisms of 'macho' masculinity – now attempt to be less physically, verbally and spatially dominating although it is not easy to say how widespread or effective this new sensitivity is.

Sue Scott and David Morgan have made one of the clearest rejections of the sex/gender differences model in *Body Matters* (1993). In the first paragraph in the following quotation, they appear to accept that there are certain general differences between male and female bodies. However, in the second paragraph they make their central point that the body and biology in general are not fixed 'givens' but are subject to historical construction:

Clearly there are observable differences between most male and female bodies (although the existence of hermaphrodites and transsexuals calls even this assumption into question – see Foucault, 1980; Garfinkel, 1967) and it would seem that these differences have remained fairly constant over time (it is difficult to ascertain to what extent artistic representations are a result of actual variation rather than the result of cultural preferences and proscriptions). However, the modern period has seen changes in the interpretation of these differences which have undoubtedly had widespread repercussions. For example, there is evidence that, prior to the eighteenth century, males and females were understood as having basically the same genitalia, the major difference being that the female's were located inside and the male's outside the body …

If we are to develop a better understanding of the social place of the body and of the ways in which we experience ourselves as embodied, then we must begin to understand biology as historically and culturally located. The body is not simply a set of facts which are gradually being uncovered by biomedical science. Obviously the body is made up of parts, but the perceived relative importance of these parts and their relationship to the whole is culturally defined. Even Gray's Anatomy *needs to be understood as a cultural artefact (Armstrong, 1983), as a topic to be studied rather than more straightforwardly as a resource.*

What sociology must do is to open up the biological/natural package and insert history and culture, in order to develop an understanding of the relationship between the social and biological as one of practical relevance rather than causation (Connell, 1987) and to illustrate the ways in which this relationship varies with age, class, gender and ethnicity. Indeed, a sociology of the body may be a significant point of departure for transcending or blurring the conventional opposition between nature and culture.

(S Scott and D Morgan, 1993:6)

(The above should become clearer by attempting an application)

Question

What different conventions and limits 'govern' the presentation of the body in a classroom and at a disco – and why? Are these differences gendered?

R W Connell, on whose work Scott and Morgan draw, has strongly refuted biological or 'naturalistic' explanations of gender differences. In *Gender and Power* (1987), Connell particularly targets functionalist approaches for criticism but further observes that certain feminists have also adopted a 'naturalistic' analysis of sex and gender. According to Connell, Talcott Parsons argues that

the biological facts of sex and reproduction constrain or limit the sex (gender) roles available to males and females. In other words, females' social roles are primarily to reproduce and rear children while males provide the main means of survival (see p. 186). As we shall see, Connell rejects the view that any such constraints are inevitable (and certainly in Britain and Europe, the proportion of females to males in paid work has been increasing).

Connell particularly criticises what he calls the 'additive approach' (see p. 73) of functionalists and some others, to the relationship between sex and gender differences. In this approach, biology is seen as 'establishing a certain difference between human females and males but this is insufficient for the complexities of social life. It must be added to, built upon. Society therefore *culturally elaborates* the distinction between the sexes' (73).

Connell comments that while certain (radical and liberal) feminist sex-role theorists condemn the way, for instance, that gender socialisation through education and the media 'add on' to sex-role differences they nevertheless routinely accept that biological differences provide a predetermined framework of sex difference which then gets 'added to' by society. Connell's point is that sexuality as well as gender is formed by social influence and personal choice. By clear implication, therefore, Connell rejects the sex/gender distinction made by Oakley. He refers scathingly to the theoretical inadequacy 'of the very large body of literature on sex-role socialisation' some of which Ann Oakley helped to inspire. In its place, he offers a model which analyses sex, sexuality and gender in social and historical context i.e. as practices which can change. In short, Connell:

1 Rejects the sex (biology) and gender (culture) separation, and
2 Argues that both are formed by social context and personal choice i.e. are socially constructed.

Patriarchy; sexism; capitalism and stratification

Patriarchy is the system and practice by which males dominate and exploit females. The patriarchal system refers to the principles, regulations and structures of male domination (such as that men are 'naturally' superior to women, or that only men should have certain rights or hold given offices) and to the power and control of men over organisations, institutions and other practical areas of life. The practice of patriarchy refers to the everyday gender relationships which reflect and reproduce the system of patriarchy.

Sexism is discrimination against someone on the basis of their sex or gender. Women rather than men have been systematically discriminated against as a sex, although as individuals, men too may be victims of sexual discrimination. Patriarchy is a system based on sex/gender discrimination.

As we shall shortly see, Marxist feminists link patriarchy with capitalism. Class stratification is seen as the basic context in which patriarchal oppression is structured. Similarly, a number of black feminists have insisted that patriarchy as experienced by black women has been 'mediated' (or structured) by racism. They then attempt to explain the relationship between gender, class and racial stratification.

Perspectives on gender

Women have been the main subordinate group within patriarchy although men perceived as 'effeminate' have also often been victimised. Unsurprisingly, females have produced the main theories of, as well as the main, challenges to patriarchy. The following section briefly sketches these theories of female subordination and hoped for liberation. This section also includes R W Connell's description of the structure of gender including various types of masculinities.

In an essay entitled *What is feminism*, Rosalind Delmar helpfully constructs a 'base-line definition of feminism and the feminist' which most people, feminist or otherwise could probably agree on. She suggests that:

> At the very least a feminist is someone who holds that women suffer discrimination because of their sex, that they have specific needs which remain negated and unsatisfied, and that satisfaction of these needs would require a radical change (some would say a revolution even) in the social, economic and political order.
>
> (Delmar in J Mitchell and A Oakley eds., 1986:8)

There are three aspects to this definition:
A feminist is someone concerned with:

1 Discrimination against women.
2 Unsatisfied needs of women.
3 The necessity for radical change (or revolution) if these unsatisfied needs are to be met.

These points offer an outline agenda for describing and explaining the position and aspirations of feminists and women in general. However, they will not be pursued sequentially here but will be used as a reference point throughout the chapter. Thus, discrimination against women, their unsatisfied needs, and policy solutions (i.e. ways of meeting these needs) are all more or less explicitly discussed in the context of gender and the family, gender and education and gender and work. Delmar defines a feminist as 'someone' concerned with the above issues. You may wish to consider further whether 'someone' can include males as well as females (i.e. can males be feminists?).

Having provided a basic definition of feminism, Delmar goes on to remark – with good reason – that beyond this 'things immediately become more complicated'. They do so because while feminists can probably agree on a broad description of 'the

problem', they differ in their explanations of it and in the solutions they offer. The main feminist perspectives are now discussed in detail. Apart from some radical feminists, feminist approaches are broadly social constructionist (i.e. they stress the formative power of society) although many were developed before Connell applied social constructionist analysis to sex as well as gender.

Marxist-feminism: feminist-Marxism

In the 1970s, a number of feminists began to draw on Marxist theory in order to explain the oppression of women. There were frequent references in their writings to Engels' *The Origin of the Family, Private Property and the State* which attempted to explain how the legal status of a woman had evolved into that of the private property of her husband (see p. 55). In an article published in 1972 titled *The Role of the Family in the Oppression of Women*, Sue Sharpe analysed the function many women have in reproducing and sustaining the labour force – at great cost to their freedom, potential for development, and often mental health (New Edinburgh Review Seminar, 1972). She suggests that women are thoroughly taken for granted in both the home and the workplace:

> What are the consequences of ... work in the home? A woman frequently sinks her identity in that of her man, becoming a mirror image of his successes and failures and a receptacle for his joys, sorrows and angers ...
>
> Employers ... frequently regard women as mere temporary labour, and consider that they should be thought lucky to have the opportunity to earn some money for themselves. They can be used as a surplus labour force, to be employed or laid off at will.
>
> (Sharpe:1972)

Juliet Mitchell's *Women's Estate* (1971) is a Marxist-feminist attempt to analyse the nature of female oppression, particularly in capitalist society, and to explore how to combat it. She rejects a simple biological explanation of the sexual division of labour in the sense that women 'have to' bear and produce children. Instead, she points to the superior physical power and ability to coerce, of men. The point is that men have been able to make women do almost whatever they wanted. In her words 'Women have been forced to do women's work'. And 'women's work' can be almost anything. Thus, in many zones of tropical Africa women still perform many heavy 'customary' duties, such as carrying loads. The richness of Mitchell's analysis is, however, that she does not exclusively emphasise any one factor in explaining male domination. She considers that repression can operate in any of the three interconnected 'structures' of the family – the sexual, the reproductive, and through socialisation – and also in the sphere of economic production.

Accordingly, she urges that the 'fight' for liberation must be directed at all these structural levels, with particular reference to whichever is weakest at a given time.

Like other Marxist-feminists, Mitchell sees women's oppression within the family and in economic production as closely related: women's lack of power in the economic sphere is 'explained' in capitalist society by the supposed 'need' for them to be housewives. She is particularly interested in the psychological aspects of female oppression both in terms of how adult women come to accept their oppression as 'normal' and 'natural' and in terms of how young females are socialised into inferiority. Mitchell sees the oppressed mentality of women as a product of their structural position within the family and society.

> *What does our oppression within the family do to us women? It produces a tendency to small-mindedness, petty jealousy, irrational emotionality and random violence, dependency, competitive selfishness and possessiveness, passivity, a lack of vision and conservatism. These qualities are not the simple product of male chauvinism, nor are they falsely ascribed to women by a sexist society that uses 'old woman' as a dirty term. They are the result of the woman's objective conditions within the family – itself embedded in a sexist society. You cannot inhabit a small and backward world without it doing something to you.*
>
> *(Mitchell, 1971:162)*

Like a number of Marxists writing in the 1960s and early 1970s, Mitchell drew upon the work of Sigmund Freud in trying to explain the psychological aspects of oppression. In particular she cites Freud's interpretation of the Oedipal situation to explain why '[t]he girl will grow up like her mother but the boy will grow up to be another father'. The Oedipal situation is that a son loves his mother and sees his father as a rival for her, whereas a daughter loves her father and experiences her mother as a rival. In brief, the male rivalry is 'buried' rather than resolved whereas the female rivalry tends to settle down. The difference is that according to Freud, whereas the young male feels his penis to be dwarfed by his father's and so initially opts out of the contest, the young female compares herself more equally with her mother who, like her, has not got a penis at all. In puberty, the young male reasserts himself. All this appears to leave females in a passive role.

Nancy Chodorow offers a very different explanation of how young males and females learn gender identity and rules in which the latter play a more active role (1978). She argues that initially both females and males identify with their mother and that it is fairly straightforward for females to continue to do so. Males have the specific and often emotionally painful problem of detaching themselves from the identification and developing a male identity. Male anger and aggression can sometimes be related to this process. According to Chodorow, young females 'draw in' males later when they are needed as mates. As a model for explaining the reproduction of female identity this is simpler and perhaps more plausible than the Freudian one adopted by Mitchell. In any case, Mitchell's synthesis of Marx and Freud has been rejected by many Marxist-feminists and certainly does not seem necessary to explain the oppression of women.

Mary Maynard adopts a distinction between Marxist-feminists and feminist-Marxists. The former emphasise the economic subordination of women and the latter their ideological subordination. Thus, she classifies Veronica Beechey as a Marxist-feminist. Beechey argues that women are a source of cheap labour for capitalism both domestically and in paid work (Beechey, 1987). Michele Barrett is classified as a feminist-Marxist, as she contends that the explanation of why women accept social arrangements which clearly oppress and disadvantage them is that they are ideologically mystified into doing so. They come to believe that the way things are, including their own subordination, is the only way things can be (Barrett, 1980). The different emphasis of these two groups implies a different analysis of the route to women's liberation: Marxist-feminists stress the need to overthrow the capitalist economic system and feminist-Marxists argue that before this can happen, an ideological change must occur in the consciousness of both sexes, but particularly females which frees them from dependence on traditional gender roles. Juliet Mitchell's view is that the relationship between economic and ideological oppression can vary but that both have to be dealt with, partly reconciles the two approaches.

Radical-feminism

Radical-feminism is based on the analysis that patriarchy – the domination of females by males – is the central issue to be faced by feminists.

Two books that can be classified as early radical feminist are Kate Millett's *Sexual Politics* (1970) and Shulamith Firestone's *The Dialectic of Sex* (1972). Millett describes but does not account for the widespread nature of patriarchy. She concentrates particularly on the ideological reproduction of patriarchy by which many females become willing collaborators in their own oppression. Firestone argues that the core of male domination of females is their control of females' roles in reproduction and child-rearing, which has its origins in a biological 'inequality' between the two sexes and is expressed through the nuclear family. The result of bearing and rearing children is to make women dependent on men for the material necessities of life and protection. She, therefore, writes of 'sex class' as an additional category to 'economic class'. She argues that the liberation of women depends on the abolition of the family and the 'power' relationships and psychology that its unequal structure breeds. It is probably true to say that, as a result of Firestone's work, many feminists recognise more clearly the issues that can result for women from their reproductive roles. However, rather than the abolition of the family, they look for other solutions, including much more available and better child care facilities and a redefinition or even abolition of gender roles.

During the1970s, the focus of radical feminism moved to female-male relationships and, in particular, to the issue of male violence against females. The matters of female socialisation and their stereotyping as 'sex objects' or 'helpmates' to men are dealt with in later sections of this chapter. These have become common concerns not only within feminism but within the media, education and elsewhere. Here we will briefly concentrate on the issue of male violence against females.

Table 7.1 Offences involving violence reported to selected police departments in Edinburgh and Glasgow in 1974

Offence	Total number of offences	Percentage of offences
Violent: Family		
Wife assault	776	24.14
Alleged wife assault	32	1.00
Husband assault	13	0.40
Child assault	110	3.42
Parent assault	70	2.18
Sibling assault	50	1.56
	(1051)	(32.70)
Violent: Non family		
Male against male	1196	37.20
Male against female	292	9.08
Male against police	452	14.06
Female against female	142	4.42
Female against male	53	1.65
Female against police	29	0.90
	(2164)	(67.31)
Total	3215	100.00

(Source: Dobash and Dobash, 1980)

Official statistics on violent crime show men to be overwhelmingly the more violent sex. A study by Dobash and Dobash of offences involving violence in parts of Edinburgh and Glasgow showed that the largest category of such offences was 'male against male' with 'wife assault' being the second largest (see Table 7.1).

In analysing the above and related data, Jan Pahl adds that many women comment that 'the mental battering was worse than the physical battering'. She also points out that the more accurate presentation of the issue is as 'the problem of violent husbands' rather than as a problem of women.

Pahl interprets male battering of their spouses as 'the extension of the domination and control of husbands over wives' i.e. as a logical, if brutal, aspect of patriarchy. She suggests that part of a solution to the problem of violent husbands would be a general recognition that the problem is not a private or personal one but a major public issue. Dobash and Dobash estimated that only about two per cent of assaults against wives are reported to the police, which does suggest that society is far from adopting a frank and open perspective on the issue – let alone finding a solution to it.

Capitalism and patriarchy

The feminist perspectives so far considered have given the greatest emphasis either to class (Marxist/socialist feminist) or to patriarchy (radical-feminist). Another perspective is to argue that both capitalism and patriarchy must be taken into consideration when explaining the oppression of women. Some analysts, such as Zillah Eisenstein, see capitalism and patriarchy as highly interwoven, whereas others such as Magrit Eichler regard them as separate systems. Eichler's analysis is considered later (see pp. 204-5).

Sylvia Walby also considers patriarchy and capitalism to be distinct but related systems (see pp. 204-5).

Liberal-feminism

Whereas both Marxist and radical-feminists stress the need for structural change, liberal-feminism is a reformist and incrementalist ('brick by brick') approach. Its promise is that there should be equal opportunity for women and men. The Equal Pay Act (1970) and the Sex Discrimination Act (1975) are the fruits of a widely supported effort to achieve liberal equality between the sexes (see pp. 205-6). Although a leading member of the Labour party, and inclined robustly to describe herself as a socialist, Barbara Castle was a liberal feminist in this sense and an influential supporter of these measures. Liberal-feminism has been particularly effective in the sphere of education where the right of females to compete on equal terms with males has increasingly come to be accepted both in principle and practice (see pp. 110-5).

Marxist-feminists consider that the liberal approach merely encourages females to complete in an unequal and class-divided world. Radical-feminists find that liberalism does not sufficiently address the psychological, relational and institutional aspects of patriarchy. Nevertheless, most feminists supported liberal gender reforms as a modest step on the way to creating a society less oppressive to females.

R W Connell: the structure of gender relations

Since the publication of his book, *Gender and Power* in 1987, Bob Connell's attempt to outline a theory of gender has grown in influence. Like Anthony Giddens' theory of structuration it is increasingly used by others in the interpretation of their own empirical work.

Connell's analysis of the structure of gender uses two main concepts; structural model and structural inventory. Connell is uncomplicated in his definition of structure:

> *… I will assume that the concept of structure is more than another term for 'pattern' and refers to the intractability of the social world. It reflects the experience of being up against something, of limits on freedom … The concept of 'social' structure expresses the constraints that lie in a given form of social organisation (rather than, say, physical facts about the world). 'Constraints' may be as crude as the presence of an occupying army. But in most cases the constraints on social practice operate through a more complex interplay of powers and through an array of social institutions. Accordingly, attempts to decode a social structure generally begin by analysing institutions.*
>
> *(92)*

Structural model

First we need to be clear about what a structural model is. A structural model is an outlining of the main 'parts' or institutional areas of society and how they 'work' and change in relation to each other (see Chapter 1, pp. 6-9)

What, then, is the structural model adopted by Connell for analysing gender relations. Connell suggests that there are three major institutional areas to be considered in this context:

1 Labour
2 Power
3 Cathexis ('personal' particularly sexual, relations).

It is obvious that there is a labour – (domestic and paid) and occupational structure which shapes work and consumption. Much of this chapter deals with the gendering of work in British society – largely in a patriarchal way. Power is a more abstract concept than labour but the realities of gendered power permeate society from families to military hierarchies, from partner relations to rich/poor world relations. Connell states that:

> *If authority is defined as legitimate power, then we can say that the main axis of the power structure of gender is the general connection of authority with masculinity …*
>
> *(109)*

In examining cathexis, Connell concentrates almost exclusively on sexual relations. His starting point is that: 'to recognise a social structure in sexuality it is necessary first to see sexuality as social' (111). The social shaping of sex is apparent in many ways. For instance, in the laws relating to rape, the age of consent and homosexuality, and in the customs regulating the initiation of sexual relationships and in what circumstances. The social control and regulation of sex is comparable in importance to the control and regulation of violence although individuals and groups constantly challenge constraints and renegotiate the margin of acceptable behaviour. Again, sexuality is another area in which

males tend to dominate although this bold statement is elaborated and qualified elsewhere in this chapter.

Connell emphasises that the three institutional areas of his model are inter-related and that the relationship between them can change. Change occurs partly because individuals and groups strive to achieve it – sometimes successfully. Connell does not argue that change in one area is necessary before change in another area can take place although change is likely to be interconnected. For instance, greater equality between the sexes in the work place would also tend to equalise gender relations in the other two areas.

Structural inventory

The terms 'gender order' and 'gender regime' are key to Connell's analysis of the structure of gender relations. A gender order is 'a historically constructed pattern of power relations between men and women and definitions of femininity and masculinity prevalent throughout an entire society' (99). Thus, briefly to apply the concept of gender order to Britain: males, particularly upper and middle class ones, tend to dominate females in most, if not all the major institutional areas of British society, and to define masculinity and femininity in a way that legitimates their own values and behaviour and subordinates women.

The concept of gender regime 'describe(s) the state of play in sexual politics … on a smaller stage' and Connell uses it to describe the state of gender relations in a particular institution. In his own research, he used the term in the context of schools but it could equally be applied to a family, peer group or club. Thus, the gender hierarchy in a school and the way female and male pupils are taught and generally treated are aspects of the gender regime in a particular school. Mac an Ghaill's *The Making of Men* provides an example of an analysis of gender regimes (see pp. 196-8).

It should be noted that Connell defines both gender orders and gender regimes in dynamic terms i.e. as open to change. Here the second part of the phase 'the structure of gender relations' is significant. Gender is about relations and relationships and people make and can change the structures – the 'orders' and 'regimes' – that bind them.

Gender relations in contemporary capitalist society: masculinities and femininities (and beyond?)

There are many different ways of being what we refer to as masculine or feminine which is why these terms are frequently pluralised in sociological literature: masculinities/femininities. Connell has introduced a basic vocabulary which can be used in analysing gender relations. Despite significant challenges to it, patriarchal power still structures gender relations (see Figure 7.1).

Connell refers to 'hegemonic' and subordinate masculinities. 'Hegemonic' masculinity is the dominant form of masculinity in society as a whole. Connell cites Humphrey Bogart, John Wayne,

Sylvester Stallone and Mohammed Ali as examples of what is the hegemonic form of masculinity in Western societies (and, presumably, in so far as Western culture is globally dominant, throughout the world). More contemporary examples of contemporary Western hegemonic masculinity might include Tom Cruise, Prince Naseem and Will Carling. Connell argues that hegemonic masculinity always exists in relation to subordinate masculinities as well as through the domination of women (which is its main object). Most obviously homosexual masculinity – stereotyped as the opposite of being a 'real man' – is a subordinate form of masculinity. Even though the gay liberation movement has won greater acceptance of homosexuality, it remains a subordinate and stigmatised identity in society as a whole. Many still do not regard homosexuality as an equally acceptable gender identity as, say, hegemonic masculinity.

Connell states that femininities are formed in the context of 'the global subordination of women to men' (183). Perhaps the commonest form of *subordinated femininity* is still what Connell refers to as '*emphasised femininity*'. This form of femininity 'is oriented to accommodating the interests and desires of men' (183) and is still massively portrayed in the media. Many top female models and female stereotypes in advertisements and pornography provide examples of emphasised femininity.

Other forms of femininity may, to a greater or lesser extent,

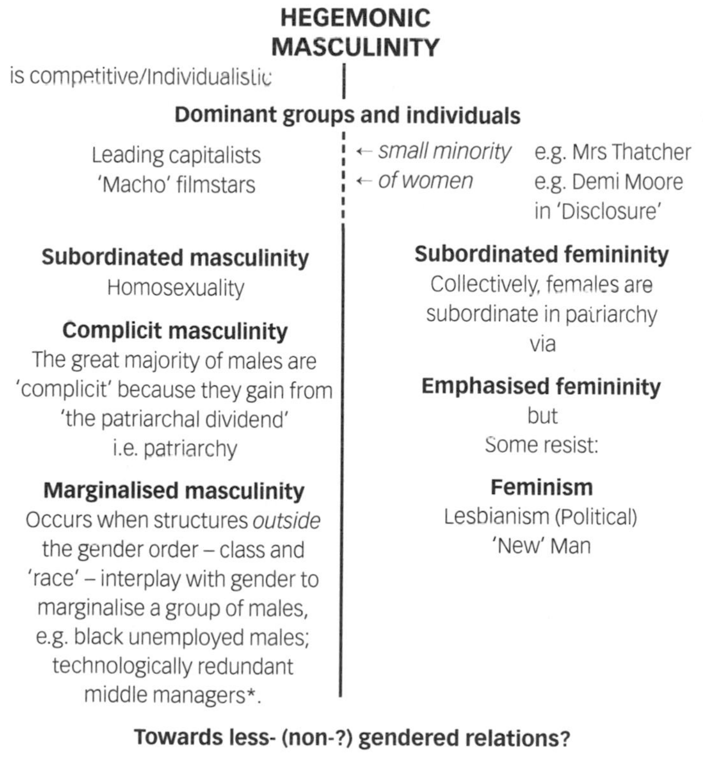

reject emphasised femininity and the subordination that goes with it. Women who have adopted various 'liberated' feminist attitudes and practices seek non-subordinated identities and lifestyles. One can add to Connell that, perhaps at a less conscious level, many women who might not think of themselves as 'feminist' have retreated from the ideal of 'emphasised femininity' and, in fact, images of such women are often now portrayed in mainstream films and drama. For instance, whatever the limitations of its format, the presenters of Channel 4's The Girlie Show adopt a much tougher, more egalitarian gender image than that of emphasised femininity. Connell strongly argues that gender stratification is not dependent on, or secondary to class or any other type of stratification. However, he is equally clear that the main types of stratification – class, ethnicity, age and gender – tend to act together and reinforce each other. As he puts it:

> *The sheer complexity of relationships involving millions of people guarantees that ethnic differences and generational differences as well as class patterns come into play.*
>
> *(183)*

Connell himself does not examine these interconnections in detail but many sociologists working in the field of gender have done so (see Mac an Ghaill, below, p. 195).

An essential part of Connell's analysis is that the behaviours and attitudes often associated with masculinity and femininity can characterise members of either sex. Given his argument that sex/gender is socially constructed, it follows that changes in social or personal circumstances may lead to changes in gender identity. In the contemporary world, the most common types of masculinity – hegemonic – is associated with males and perhaps the most common type of femininity – emphasised – with females. However, both individuals and groups can and do change their gender orientation. Thus, perhaps disillusioned with abusive experience of male power, some females decide for personal/political reasons to become lesbians, (although this is, of course, not the only basis of lesbian identity). To give another example, in the past 30 or so years, many heterosexual women have changed their perception, expectations and demands of males.

To some extent, therefore, tying the concept of masculine to males and feminine to females is probably becoming increasingly inaccurate. Nevertheless, we are an inestimably long way from a non-gendered world in which individuals and groups are treated equally whatever their character and identity.

Table 7.2 summarises the various perspectives on gender in this section.

HEGEMONIC MASCULINITY

is competitive/Individualistic

Dominant groups and individuals

| Leading capitalists | ← *small minority* | e.g. Mrs Thatcher |
| 'Macho' filmstars | ← *of women* | e.g. Demi Moore in 'Disclosure' |

Subordinated masculinity
Homosexuality

Complicit masculinity
The great majority of males are 'complicit' because they gain from 'the patriarchal dividend' i.e. patriarchy

Marginalised masculinity
Occurs when structures *outside* the gender order – class and 'race' – interplay with gender to marginalise a group of males, e.g. black unemployed males; technologically redundant middle managers*.

Subordinated femininity
Collectively, females are subordinate in patriarchy via

Emphasised femininity
but
Some resist:

Feminism
Lesbianism (Political)
'New' Man

Towards less- (non-?) gendered relations?

*See Reading 1

Figure 7.1 Gender relations in contemporary capitalist society (R W Connell)

Table 7.2 Summary of perspectives on gender

Perspective	Summary-definition
Marxist-feminism	Patriarchy in capitalist society reinforces and complements capitalism. The fundamental nature of female oppression is economic.
Feminist-marxism	Patriarchy in capitalist society reinforces and complements capitalism. The fundamental nature of female oppression is ideological.
Radical-feminism	The fundamental inequality and injustice faced by females is the domination of females by males.
Capitalism and patriarchy	This catch-all phrase describes feminist perspectives (distinct from the above) which regard capitalism and patriarchy as separate systems. Disagreement occurs on how far the two systems are interwoven.
Liberal-feminism	Liberal-feminists seek equal opportunity for women and men.
Biological-determinism	Males and females are 'naturally different' and this explains their traditionally different roles.
Functionist-perspective	Differentiated gender roles (traditional) are practical and functional for society.
Social-constructionist	Gender orders, including contemporary patriarchy are structured in domination/subordination.

Gender socialisation: the ideological reproduction of patriarchy

Family (education and media)

Gender behaviour is first learnt through primary or basic socialisation within the family and is reinforced later in practically every sphere of social life and particularly at school and work. Socialisation refers to the various ways in which a child learns to act in a manner acceptable to a given society. Gender socialisation is part of this process. Traditional patterns of socialisation in most Western countries distinguish sharply between male and female, although this has begun to change in the wake of the women's liberation movement. It is probably still true that by the time they are sixteen, the majority of young men and women have been socialised into an ideology of male supremacy even though the forces of resistance to this ideology are stronger than they were and patterns of socialisation based on gender equality occur more frequently.

Table 3.3 suggests that a substantial minority retain stereotypical attitudes to job roles and it is worth remembering that people's behaviour may be substantially less 'liberated' than their attitudes.

There is a considerable body of British and American research which claims to demonstrate substantial differences in the socialisation of baby and infant boys and girls. H Moss observed that in the early months of life boys received more attention than girls. Later boys were encouraged to display more active and exploratory behaviour whereas mothers interacted more closely with girl babies and were more likely to comfort them. Ann Oakley argues that the differences in the types of toy given to infant males and females can greatly affect their concept of gender appropriate roles. She suggests that differences in behaviour caused by differential gender socialisation are often cited to 'prove' that the sexes are 'naturally' different. Boys and girls are still routinely socialised towards future gender roles in a variety of ways. Boys are often given presents of batman and superman models, doctors' outfits and meccano sets, whereas girls are given Barbi-dolls, nurses' uniforms and cookery kits. The implied message could hardly be stronger. Jobs involving leadership and construction skills are for boys, whereas girls are expected to care for, assist and give service to others, either at home or at work. The basis of this division of labour is often clearly laid down in childhood. This is most obviously so in families in which the jobs children are given to do around the house are based on gender – say, cleaning and sewing for the girls, and mending broken plugs or furniture for the boys.

Children's literature often reinforces gender stereotypes. This is especially true of traditional fairy tales in which helpless damsels in distress are forever being rescued by handsome and dynamic princes. More recently written stories often reproduce gender stereotypes. Thus, in the 'Janet and John' series, John is frequently at the centre of the action while Janet hovers admiringly in the background only coming into her own when refreshments are served. Birthday cards and Christmas cards also frequently perpetuate gender stereotypes. Sue Sharpe quotes two classic examples of the gender stereotyping of males and females from birth congratulation messages:

> *Bet she's sugar and spice*
> *And everything nice.*
> *A pink and petite little treasure*
> *Your new little 'she'*
> *Who's certain to be*
> *A wonderful bundle of pleasure!*
>
> *A Son is Fun!*
> *He'll keep you busy*
> *With blankets an' pins*
> *and charm your hearts*
> *With his boyish grins!*
> *What's more he'll make you*
> *Proud and glad*
> *Congratulations mother and dad!*

Probably an increasing number of contemporary parents deliberately try to avoid socialising their children into traditional gender roles. One enterprising group of mothers in Liverpool, finding that the images of gender portrayed in available children's story books were too traditional, set about writing their own material. They rejected stereotypes in which the female is always weak and dependent and the male strong and dominant. Why shouldn't princesses sometimes rescue princes? If Little Red Riding Hood had been trained in basic self-defence, perhaps she could have dealt with the wolf on her own account. Such notions may strike many as odd, but recorded interviews with some of the children who heard or read the stories showed they understood the point behind them. In small ways like this, social change can perhaps take place.

Gender socialisation occurs in the educational system and via the media despite considerable attempts to mitigate the process, particularly within education. Partly because of the selling power of traditional sexual and romantic images, gender stereotyping has proved especially difficult to combat and reduce in the commercial media. There is, however, considerable consensus among feminists of all perspectives that such imagery should not dominate the portrayal of gender. (The sections in this book which deal with gender socialisation in education and in the media are on pp. 110-5 and p. 513 respectively.)

Gender roles: symmetry or continuing inequality?

There are two main areas in which inequality of gender roles occurs: in the family and in the economy. We have already extensively discussed the former in Chapter 3 so a brief treatment is appropriate here.

As we have seen, Young and Willmott interpret their survey into the matter to suggest that symmetrical gender roles are replacing segregated ones. By this they mean that there is more democracy, equality and sharing between partners, not necessarily that partners do similar amounts of given roles (such as household repair or cooking). This pattern initially developed among middle class couples, and particularly when both husband and wife worked as professionals. As Rhona and Robert Rapoport (a dual-career couple themselves) point out, it is still among dual-career families that symmetrical roles most frequently occur. With more women of all classes in paid work, however, role symmetry may be becoming rather more common among working class couples. One survey, by Hannah Gavron, actually found that working class husbands shared housework more than middle class husbands, though this goes against other findings. Ann Oakley is, in any case, sceptical about whether there has been a marked recent trend for couples to share housework and child rearing (see below). Mary Maynard has also robustly refuted the symmetry thesis (see pp. 65-6).

Most of the remainder of this chapter illustrates that different

and unequal gender roles persist throughout the economy. Indeed, women employees form a majority in each of the ten worst-paid occupations.

Table 3.3 (see p. 65) shows that the actual division of household tasks remains highly gender differentiated and much more so than people think should be the case. The percentage of men who wash the dishes has gradually increased over the years but in itself this is hardly a massive blow for gender equality. The division of labour in relation to other domestic tasks has changed little.

In assessing possible trends to gender role symmetry, it is important to remember that people's behaviour may be considerably different from, and more rigid than, their expressed attitudes.

Education and the making of masculinities ('race' and class)

Martin Mac an Ghaill's *The Making of Men* (1994) examines 'the processes involved in the interplay between schooling, masculinities and sexualities'. Most of the empirical material in the book is based on a three year ethnographic study of a cohort of male students at Parnell School between 1990 and 1992. The students were in year eleven during the 1990-91 school year. A main theoretical influence on the work is W R Connell's conceptualisation of different forms of masculinity referred to above (see pp. 191-3).

Mac an Ghaill states that his 'primary concern was with the question of how school processes helped shape male students' cultural investment in different versions of heterosexual masculinity'. He also discusses young female students' experiences of teacher and student masculinities. Additionally, using a different set of data, he explores a group of gay male students' experiences of schooling and sexuality. In examining the construction of various masculinities, Mac an Ghaill makes full reference to other agencies of socialisation, especially family socialisation, and to the influence of structural forces, such as the labour market. Mac an Ghaill distinguishes four main types of emergent heterosexual masculinity within the school each of which is structured partly in relation to class:

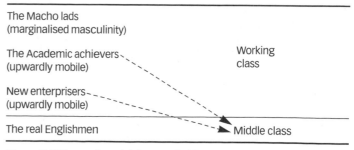

Figure 7.2 Types of youthful masculinities

The macho lads: a white working class crisis of masculinity

The culture of the macho lads, including their attitudes towards school and education has already been described earlier in this book (see pp. 89-90). All the macho lads were in the bottom two sets for all subjects and were hostile to school authority and learning. Mac an Ghaill likened the lads of Parnell School to the lads famously depicted in Paul Willis's *Learning to Labour: How Working Class Kids Get Working Class Jobs*, (1977):

> *Like Willis's Lads, the Macho lads at Parnell School made a similar/association of academic work with an inferior effeminacy, referring to those who conformed as 'dickhead achievers'.*
>
> (59)

However, almost twenty years on, the relevant phrase in Willis's title would be 'How Working Class Lads ***Don't*** Get Working Class Jobs' – at least, not easily.

Mac an Ghaill goes on to analyse what he sees as a crisis of white working class masculinity. Willis argued that work was essential to the lads' sense of status and identity. More specifically, physical work – well paid enough to finance pleasures such as watching football and going to the pub as well as to impress the girl-friend – was central to working class male self-image and self-presentation. By the mid 1980s much of this kind of work was gone. For the non-academic achieving working class male this presented practical and psychological problems. Youth training and temporary creation schemes of various kinds, often followed by a period of unemployment, did not remotely fill the gap for the lads. Unsurprisingly, the urban disorders of the early 1990s involved mainly white working class youth. Modest economic expansion from 1992 saw the creation of more part-time and temporary, usually low-paid jobs, in the routine service sector. There were signs that – slowly – growing numbers of young males as well as females were prepared to take these jobs. Understandably, others found such adjustment difficult to make.

The academic achievers

Mac an Ghaill describes the academic achievers as 'reminiscent of grammar school 'scholarship boys', adopting a more traditional upwardly socially mobile route via academic subject credentialism'. The group Mac an Ghaill researched had tended to study arts 'A' levels, especially drama. As a result a 'number of teachers and students positioned the academic achievers as 'effeminate'.

The academic achievers developed a number of strategies for coping with a stereotyping which they rejected. First as so-called 'dickhead achievers' they had learnt to live with macho bullying. Second, sometimes they would 'camp it up', wrong footing those

who insulted them. More fundamentally, however, their very success had given them the confidence to cope with jibes from 'low-set' kids. Mac an Ghaill argues that a 'central element of the academic achievers' masculine identity was their projected future of a professional career' (63). Against such expectation, they could afford to be dismissive of the 'no hope' macho lads.

The new enterprisers

Mac an Ghaill contextualises the students he refers to as 'New Enterprisers' within the high-status end of the new vocational curriculum developed during the 1980s. Such students would prefer business studies or computer science to traditional academic 'A' levels which they were inclined to see as a waste of time.

Mac an Ghaill observes that the new enterprise students 'were negotiating a new mode of school student masculinity with its values of rationality, instrumentalism, forward planning and careerism' (63). To that extent they were children of 'the enterprise culture' and market ethic so determinedly promoted in the school system during the Thatcher period. Mac an Ghaill also notes that a similarly oriented body of teachers – whom he refers to as the 'new entrepreneurs' – achieved hegemony and power in much of the educational system during the 1980s and 1990s. He stresses throughout his book the interaction of the social, school and individual/small group and the emergence of the enterprisers is a particularly notable example of this.

The real Englishmen

The 'real Englishmen' in Mac an Ghaill's study are 'a small group of students who displayed an ambivalent response to the academic curriculum and who consequently were the most problematic middle class peer group for many of the teachers'. Their parents' occupations tended to be in the liberal professions and the media.

Mac an Ghaill describes this group as having an 'ambiguous relationship' to certificated school knowledge and its potential value in the labour market. On the one hand, they considered themselves as 'arbiters of culture' and as such superior to teachers and what they had to offer. Their own values of individuality and autonomy did not fit easily with the demands of the formal curriculum. On the other hand, they envisaged entry into higher education and a professional career. In part, the solution to this dilemma was to appear to achieve academic success effortlessly.

A priority for this group is the 'control of time, space (and) systems of meaning'. They sought the freedom to structure their own lives in pursuit of what they saw as worthwhile. They saw the instrumental and materialist motivations of the academic achievers and new enterprisers as shallow.

Gay students in heterosexual education regimes

In addition to the male heterosexual students above, Mac an Ghaill also reports on a two-year ethnographic study of a group of sixteen to nineteen year old homosexual students from three institutions. He focuses on the students' perception and experience of 'the heterosexist and homophobic power relations that circumscribes their lives' (153).

The students claimed that the normative values underlying classroom discussion of relationships and sexuality were heterosexual, assumed the appropriateness of the two-parent nuclear family lifestyle, and took for granted 'traditional' role relationships between men and women. The students felt unable openly to disclose their own sexuality.

Significantly, Mac an Ghaill reports that eight out of ten of the gay students regarded sexuality as open to social constructionist rather than as an unchangeable biological given. Two were undecided. Plummer puts these two positions – the essentialist (biological) and constructionist – in clear, if arguably, somewhat polarised terms:

> *Briefly essentialists assume that homosexuality has an essence; is found across societies and history as a universal form; and exists as a condition within us at birth or certainly very early in life. By contrast, constructionists assume that erotic and emotional attachments between people of the same sex are potentials in everybody but come to exist in fundamentally different ways, in different times and places. There is no transhistorical, transcultural universal essence of gayness.*
>
> *(quoted in Mac an Ghaill:158)*

Mac an Ghaill goes on to state that the gay students were highly critical of the tendency to conflate sex and sexuality i.e. that males have a given sexual orientation and females another. *Their* world was more complex and not remotely addressed by schools or teachers. Rather, they had to cope with a mixture of being ignored and stereotyped in a way that was perhaps more crude than malicious. Whatever one's view of the nature of sexuality – essentialist or constructionist – it is easy to agree with Mac an Ghaill that homosexuality is not yet being responded to adequately, fairly or sensitively within the school system.

Young women's experiences of student and teacher masculinities

Mac an Ghaill discusses a wide range of areas of relevance to the gendered experience of female students at Parnell school and, by implication, to other young women. It is worth listing these areas simply to indicate how pervasive the effect of patriarchy still is on these young women's lives:

> *the sexual division of labour, the remasculinisation of the new vocationalist curriculum …, male teacher discourses, the use of public spaces, talk of boys and men, future waged and domestic labour and cultural contestations, disruptions and resistances.*

Here we will concentrate on how interaction and perception between the female students and male teachers and students is institutionally gendered and sometimes contested. Mac an Ghaill's evidence relates mainly to female students of working class background. These were mainly in the bottom two sets but a few were upwardly mobile and in the top set.

The remasculinisation of the new vocational curriculum refers to the tendency of males to predominate in high status vocational subjects such as business studies, technology and computing and for females on lower level courses to do stereotypical work experience e.g. work in retail. When asked why so few girls were doing IT, a male teacher replied: 'Well obviously the boys are naturally more interested' – but added – 'I personally think it's a shame because we have tried different things to get them in.' (116) No doubt the explanations for such regendering of the curriculum relate to deeply embedded social and school practices and assumptions (see pp. 110-1). Some of the female students observed that just as males seemed privileged in school, so their brothers were in the home context in relation to domestic work.

The heterosexual, working class, 'non-academic' young women of Mac an Ghaill's study often expressed discomfort or worse with male dominance yet also sought boyfriends. The latter was less true of Asian female students who felt 'less pressure' in this respect. The young women seemed to complain of stereotyping and occasional sexist comments on the part of male teachers more than of young males of their own age. Although they did not like the hyper-masculinity of the Macho lads, they saw it as a legitimate defence against teachers' authoritarianism. In any case a relationship with a young male was a key goal. In pursuit of it the female students were keen to avoid acquiring a 'loose' reputation. Even paid work tended to be seen by non-academic females as a potential 'marriage market' and they attached great importance to appearance when talking of jobs. However, the more upwardly mobile female students saw careers more in terms of independence and achievement.

In interpreting the tension and negotiation in the young women's relationship to males and masculinity – at once dominating and manipulative and attractive and desired – Mac an Ghaill draws on a considerable body of research in addition to that carried out for *The Making of Men*. Much of this is referred to elsewhere in this book (see pp. 90-1). In general, Mac an Ghaill rejects a simplistic 'resistance' framework of analysis – although manifestly many of the young women at Parnell do resist sexism and male domination with varying degrees of success. Instead, he adopts a more complex framework in which he describes various 'negotiations' and 'solutions' which may involve, 'cultural contestations, disruptions and resistances'.

Comment on W R Connell and M Mac an Ghaill: theorising masculinities

Connell's main contribution to gender theory is to locate – persuasively and in detail – masculinities and patriarchy itself within the wider concept of gender. Masculinities are aspects of 'a wider structure' – the gender order. Possibly without exception, every gender order in the world is to a greater or lesser extent patriarchal. In theorising gender fully to include masculinities and femininities, Connell arguably provides the most complete and developed theoretical account of gender so far achieved. However, he is at his best when theorising masculinities, and there are many better feminist accounts of female experience of patriarchy and the various attempts to challenge it.

Although Connell differentiates a number of types of masculinity, it perhaps needs to be stressed that he considers that hegemonic masculinity appears successfully to be rebutting the challenges to it. He sees militarism, environmental destruction, and growing global inequality as partly the product of hegemonic masculinity:

> *the successful maintenance of a competitive and dominance-oriented masculinity, in the central institutions of the world order, makes each of these trends more dangerous and more difficult to reverse.*
>
> *(Masculinities, 1995:216)*

Connell himself includes four sets of case studies of masculinities in his otherwise mainly theoretical work *Masculinities* (1995). These include a study of young Australian working class males discussed under the heading *Live Fast and Die Young* and a technically expert 'new' middle class group discussed under the heading, *Men of Reason*. As one would expect the first group resembles in many respects the slightly younger 'Macho Lads' of Mac an Ghaill's study discussed above. Both writers remark on a crisis of working class masculinity which appears to be occurring throughout the Western world. Mac an Ghaill's analysis of this and other types of youthful masculinity is perhaps the most insightful empirical analysis of this matter in Britain. He does not pretend to quantify the 'importance' of various masculinities but his subjective approach does provide a high level of empathetic understanding.

As Connell observes, the idea that men are rational and women emotional has long been a theme in patriarchal ideology. Recently, this stereotype has been explored by the British sociologist, Vic Seidler. It is a central thesis of Seidler's writings that historically males have been thought of as 'rational' and females as 'emotional'. He suggests that men need to explore their 'emotional side' and that females need them to (Seidler, 1991). Connell himself applies the concept of rationality to describe the masculinity based on technical knowledge and mastery of new middle class males as distinct from forms of masculinity organised around direct domination such as corporate capitalism and military command. He sees some tension between these two masculinities although it is not clear how this might develop to general benefit.

A number of feminists, including Sylvia Walby, have argued that masculinities need to be more fully theorised within gender theory. This is clearly now happening. Although very much within the feminist tradition, Walby's own recent work (discussed below) offers a flexible and dynamic conceptualisation of gender structures and relations and lends itself to a complementary reading to that of Connell and Mac an Ghaill (see pp. 206-7).

Questions

1 Describe a gender regime of your own experience. How do you account for its power structure?
2 With reference to one or more perspectives on gender, show how either masculinities or femininities are socially constructed.

Gender inequality and the sexual division of labour

Gender, the family and work

So far we have described how gender identity is culturally created in advanced Western societies through socialisation and role-allocation. The question must now be asked why gender differentiation occurs at all. Mitchell and Oakley argue that a division of labour has developed in capitalist society by which women tend to be primarily involved in child nurture and domestic work and men in acquiring the basic means of livelihood. Socialisation prepares girls and boys for their future roles in the socio-economic system. Now, the only biologically inevitable feature of this particular form of sexual division of labour is that women give birth to children. The rest is open to gender adaptation. What follows, therefore, more closely reflects the perspective adopted by Mitchell and Oakley, rather than that of Firestone, that the sexual division of labour in capitalist society has taken a 'severe' form because this has been convenient for the capitalist system. The fact that in the last hundred years women have become increasingly involved in paid employment illustrates rather than refutes the point – they have been needed in the expanding service sector. Nevertheless, the sexually based division of labour as described above is still powerfully entrenched in contemporary capitalist society, as was shown in the two recent recessions when female labour was widely treated as more expendable than male labour. The sexual division of labour in capitalist society has resulted in a large degree of female dependency on males. This dependency has resulted in lower social status for women and correspondingly higher social status for men. As well as having less economic power and social status than men, women have also tended to be politically less powerful, because they are isolated and less organised e.g. through trade unions. In short, although the social consequences of the sexual division of labour in capitalist society have tended to be disadvantageous to women and advantageous to men, this state of affairs is not inevitable. Both cross-cultural comparison and historical analysis of gender roles in Britain show that change is possible. We adopt the historical perspective next.

Changing gender relations within the family and economy: historical and contemporary perspective

Pre-industrial

One of the few generalisations supported by recent research into the pre-industrial family in Britain is that it was patriarchal at all social levels. Fathers had decisive power over their daughters and husbands over their wives. Young and Willmott suggest that brutalising their wives can rarely have been in the interests of husbands but wife-beating was an accepted way of asserting domination and, sometimes no doubt, mere ill temper. Most peasant families were units of agricultural production in which women took a full part. Women matched men in work if not in power. Ann Oakley states that 'in their role as agriculturists, women produced the bulk of the family's food supply'. They managed dairy production, grew flax and hemp, milled corn and cared for the poultry, pigs, orchards and gardens. Men were primarily responsible for planting, cultivating and harvesting crops and for maintenance. Women allocated tasks, including household ones, to daughters, and men to sons. Textile work was second in national importance to agriculture and was shared between men, women and children: men doing the weaving, and women the spinning and allocating minor tasks, such as picking and cleaning, to the children.

Many better-off households had servants. Laslett calculates that 40 per cent of children spent part of their lives as servants and twenty per cent were raised in households with servants. As Harris puts it, the majority of members of such households were 'the dependants of some senior or more powerful person, usually of the male gender'. Laslett's thesis, endorsed by Harris, is that industrialisation broke up not the extended family (which was not, anyway the dominant family form) but the patriarchal family/household. For many modern feminists, however, the patriarchal family is a long time in dying!

The nineteenth century

Industrialisation disrupted traditional patterns of gender behaviour as it disrupted so much else. For a time, working class men, women and children worked together in industrial production and mining. Between 1802 and 1898, however, a series of Acts abolished child labour and gradually reduced female labour in these areas. Though many women found other work, often in the low-paid domestic service sector, a woman's place was increasingly considered to be in the home. In some ways the position of the working class woman in industrial society was worse than that of the peasant wife. In pre-industrial society most families produced some of their own food and clothes – largely under the wife's organisation – whereas in industrial society the wife was often wholly dependent on what money her husband chose to give her to buy these things. This was a position of striking subordination. No doubt some of the above legislation was passed in a spirit of paternalistic protectiveness but it was also notably convenient to have the labour force adequately catered for domestically (for a specifically Marxist interpretation of this point see Chapter 3, p. 55). In this way, the workers were both healthier and more productive.

Although the economic situation of middle class women was much better than that of working class women, they were similarly dependent on their husbands for money. In a wealthy family, servants might free 'the mistress of the house' from domestic toil and childcare, but there were limits to what she could then do with her time. Most professions, apart from teaching, were barred to women. In practice, middle class women were likely to spend their often ample leisure time in socialising, improving the decor of their homes and sometimes in charitable works.

The law put the lid firmly on the trap of female subordination. As we have already observed, women were debarred from the best paying working class and middle class jobs. Worse than that, women had no legal existence at all in early nineteenth century Britain. Before marriage a woman was the responsibility of her father, and afterwards she and her possessions belonged to her husband.

By the end of the nineteenth century a series of Acts had partly improved this situation. One of these, the Married Women's Property Act of 1882, gave a wife the right to own property and to dispose of it to whom she wished.

The early twentieth century: the growth of feminist consciousness

The decline of the Victorian patriarchal family has been a major feature of twentieth century social history. Contraception (the control of fertility) undermined the Victorian family and the position of male as patriarch as much as anything else. Given the choice, most women preferred to have two or three children rather than six or seven. Traditional taboos against contraception did not die overnight, and in addition some socialist women were suspicious that population control might be used as an alternative to social reform. Even so, the practical advantages of birth control were too obvious to miss. 'Having a family' of six or seven was a lifetime's work for many women, and could be physically ruinous as well as intellectually severely limiting. In any case, the beginning of a steady fall in the birth rate occurred in the late 1870s and this correlates with an increase in propaganda in favour of birth control. Certainly, in the long run, women have overwhelmingly accepted that family planning is a pre-condition of their own independence. Decrease in family size, coupled with the development of efficient time-saving household technology, enabled many women to spend much longer as part of the paid labour force. In turn, experience of work widened women's horizons, boosted their confidence and whetted the appetite of some for more freedom and equality. The massive involvement of women in production, service industries and administration during the First World War strengthened this new mood.

The fight for female political and civil rights was substantially a middle class led movement, although as historian Sheila Rowbotham says, the tendency of accounts of the suffragette movement to concentrate on the Pankhursts as personalities has meant a lack of detailed work on the social composition of the movement. There were certainly many working class women participants, including the doughty Hannah Mitchell, who criticised the 'talk' of some of the middle class radicals whom she found better preachers than practitioners of sexual equality:

> *Even my Sunday leisure was gone for I soon found that a lot of the socialist talk about freedom was only talk and these socialist young men expected Sunday dinners and huge teas with home-made cakes, potted meat and pies, exactly like their reactionary fellows.*

It would be absurd to underestimate the importance of the acquisition of the vote for women. The vote is a basic right of modern citizenship. Nevertheless, merely having the vote in no way solved the problem of sexual inequality at work and domestically. More recent legislation has, with limited success, attempted to deal with the former but the latter, perhaps because it concerns the 'private area of life' has not been seriously dealt with by legislation and government policy in Britain. In Sweden and the major former communist societies, however, legislatively supported policies in this area have been both pursued and enforced more effectively (Chapter 3, p. 80).

Women in the contemporary labour market

So far, we have considered domestic and paid labour together because they are two sides of the same coin: one would not be possible without the other. It is necessary, however, to give a more detailed analysis of women's position in the employment market. Generally, increased job opportunities for women have been seen as part of their assumed 'liberation' and work has certainly often provided individual women with an escape from the tedium of domestic toil. Marxists and feminists point out, however, that there is considerable evidence of female 'exploitation' and accompanying under-achievement in employment, and that female employment and unemployment has varied with the economic need for it. Women have been the most expendable of workers. First, we will look at some of the main facts relating to female employment and then we will examine some theoretical explanations.

Even in the mid-Victorian era, when working class women were legally banned from working in heavy industry and mining, and middle class women were denied the right to qualify for most professions, women were by no means entirely excluded from the labour market. Working class women were 'needed' as domestic servants and a certain number of middle class women worked in lower status professions. Working class women often had to find work to supplement the wages of their husbands. They frequently did so as full- or part-time domestic servants of whom there were well over half a million at this time. Hundreds of thousands of others were employed in textile production, an area of traditionally high female employment and low wages. Middle class women who needed to work, perhaps because they were spinsters or widows, could earn a living as elementary school teachers. By the 1890s, there were almost 150,000 female teachers. Nursing was also a major area of female employment. The 'semi-professions' of teaching and nursing were of much lower status and pay than the major professions of law and medicine (for instance) from which women were excluded.

The situation of women at work began to change towards the end of the nineteenth century and even more so in the twentieth century. Even allowing for population expansion, the increase in the numbers of women in paid work has been massive. Between

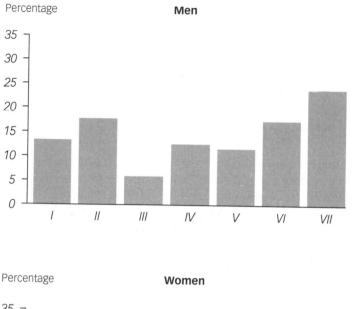

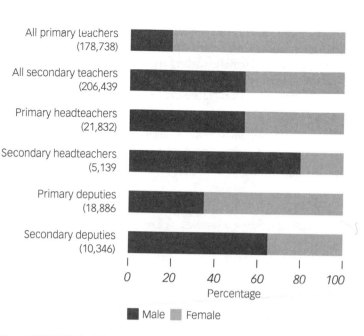

(Source: DES/NUT in the *TES*, 31.5.1994)

Figure 7.4 Male and female full-time teachers in primary and secondary schools, 1990

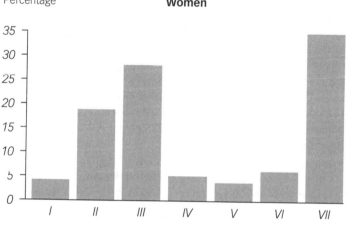

Note: See pp. 144-5 for details of class categories.

Figure 7.3 Goldthorpe class distribution for men and women

1911 and 1989 six million more women were added to the total labour force of about 28 million. Of the six million people in part time work, well over half are women.

Although most women who do paid work probably want to, it would be a mistake to assume that the increase in female labour has been an unmitigated boon for them. Women in full-time work have for a long time been paid less than men, even though the gap has narrowed substantially in recent years. Yet even though the Equal Pay Act of 1970 established the legal principle of equal pay for equal work, the average wage of women in manual jobs is about 72 per cent of men's pay and that of women in non-manual jobs only 63 per cent of the male wage. This is largely because, historically, women have been concentrated in low paid jobs. Clerical and secretarial work which became increasingly available to women from the latter half of the nineteenth century is often poorly paid (class category III).

A comparison of the occupational concentration of males and females amply illustrates the overall difference in status and rewards enjoyed by the two sexes (see Figure 7.3).

One of the most notable comparisons in the two figures is the much larger percentage of males than females in class I, top professional, administrative and managerial. Even in social class II where there is a much higher proportion of women, men are disproportionately likely to occupy senior positions. This is even true of school teaching – one of the most stereotypical of female professions (see Figure 7.4).

About two-thirds of all female employees do either routine non-manual work (III) or semi or unskilled manual work (VII). This a formidably large concentration of women in lower paid, lower status, and probably less intrinsically satisfying jobs. Women's work situation is often directly subordinate to men for whom they act as assistants. Even women in social class II – nearly twenty per cent – are often in what are thought of as 'the caring professions'. It is almost as if the domestic role of looking after others is transferred into the work situation. Like domestic labour itself, work in these areas is comparatively poorly paid. The fact that teaching is sometimes said to be 'not badly paid for women' is perhaps more a reflection on the historically low wages of women generally, than on the great financial rewards offered by that profession. In any case, in teaching as in all professions, women tend to occupy lower scale, less well-paid posts. Figures 7.3 and 7.5 (women only) give a clear and detailed picture of the paid work men and women do – and merits close study.

In addition to enjoying less authority, status and wages at work than men, women also tend to have less security. Although 29.5 (1995) per cent of female workers are unionised, the majority still lack the strength and protection union membership gives. Until recently, part-time workers are in an especially weak position in the labour market. Of Britain's six million part-time workers, three and a half million are women. Until recently, part-time workers employed for fewer than sixteen hours a week were not entitled to redundancy payment, nor most other benefits under the Employment Protection Act. Protection has now been extended to them under European law.

Percentage of employees that are women, by occupation and industry; Great Britain, winter 1994-1995

By occupation

By industry

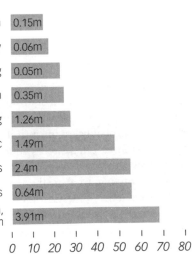

The figures given are the number of women employees in each occupation/industry, in millions.
*= mainly cleaners, domestics, kitchen porters and catering assistants. There are 10.3 million women employees (44% of women employees worked part-time compared with only 7% of men).

(Source: *Employment Gazette*, July 1995 in Fact File 1996, Carel Press, 1996)

Figure 7.5 Women's work

Homeworkers

Homeworkers or 'outworkers' are particularly disadvantaged in terms of pay and conditions. These workers are overwhelmingly women and disproportionately of Asian origin. Many work in the textile industry in the midlands and north. It is estimated that there are over a million of them in Britain (*Observer*, 5.6.1988). When classified as self-employed, homeworkers have no statutory rights to protection under the 1978 Employment Act. The requirement that employers should register them with the Local Authority seems widely ignored by the former and unenforced by the latter. Pay of around 50 pence an hour is not uncommon. A survey (1990) by the National Homeworking Unit found that homeworkers typically had virtually no guaranteed conditions of work at all either in relation to health, security of contract, let alone entitlement to maternity leave, redundancy pay or pension. Why, then, do they do it? Kabron Phillips of the NHU suggests, reasonably enough, that they need the money – little though it may be. She goes on to argue:

> *Homeworkers need basic employment rights, a decent wage, a contract of employment, a right to a payslip and holiday and sick pay.*
>
> (*The Guardian*)

Employers might reply that they could not afford this and would have to lay off homeworkers, and some of the latter might prefer even low-paid work in poor conditions to no work. Fundamentally, however, a rich society has to determine what are the minimum standards acceptable for its workforce and then allocate resources to ensure these are met. Employers, government, trade unions and public opinion need to reach a realistic and caring consensus on this matter.

The double burden

A fundamental weakness of most women as independent wage-earners lies in the fact that they also produce and are usually expected to bring up children. This means that they are not usually consistently involved in a career between the ages of approximately 25 to 35, which is a crucial period for gaining experience and promotion. Highly qualified as well as less qualified women are disadvantaged. Female recruitment to the professions is almost equal to male recruitment but as Figures 7.3 and 7.4 suggest, many leave professional work and few occupy high status positions. In practice, because of their dual commitments as housewives and workers, many women do not seriously attempt to compete effectively with men in the labour market. Many find 'tempting' or part-time work fits in best with their domestic responsibilities. In addition, it is well established that large numbers of women welcome an 'escape' from the home, even into work that does not seem particularly fulfilling. Further, women who start their careers at, say, 35 sometimes do not have quite the same expectations as a similarly qualified man of the same age. In time of high unemployment, they are frequently glad to be able to get a reasonably suitable job at all. Those who have families and try simultaneously to develop careers often put immense pressure on themselves – despite sometimes succeeding The result of this accumulation of disadvantage can be seen from Figure 7.6. Davies and Josh show that the lifetime earning of husbands are consistently much higher than that of their partners. On the basis that two living together produces economies, a full pooling of wages benefits the women – although often the male keeps substantial money for himself (average).

Lifetime income profile for medium-skilled couple with two children, £000 per annum (1994).

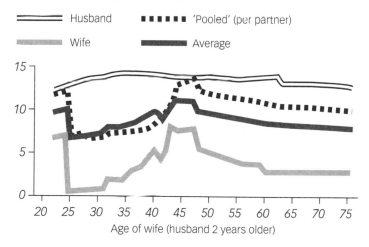

(Source: Davies and Joshi, EOC)

Figure 7.6 Family fortunes

Research by Catherine Hakin indicates that it is females who plan ahead for careers when young and who remain single that have career patterns comparable to males (1991).

A society which presents half its population with the above range of options seems deeply flawed. The basic problem is that, as Hannah Mitchell put it, women compete 'with one hand tied behind their back' - the hand that 'holds the baby' and does the housework. That problem can only be solved either by relieving women of much domestic work or by rewarding them more substantially and securely for it. We deal with this issue in the next section.

A genderquake? Not quite yet

In 1994 a book titled, *No turning Back: Generations and the Genderquake*, authored by Helen Wilkinson, was published. The following is the author's own summary of her central thesis that the current generation of young women, defined as eighteen to 35 year olds, has a distinct set of values and economic opportunities compared to older generations of women:

> *Evidence of values and attitudes suggests 'major generational differences', particularly amongst women. Younger women value autonomy, work and education more than family or parenting. In addition to culture and technology a key 'drive of change is economics': the large shift of women into work; the feminisation of the economy and jobs; companies becoming more aware of the need to develop policies that attract and retain women. This is being pushed further by women's greater success in education, itself in part a response to the changing labour market.*
>
> (58)

Wilkinson cites two sources of evidence to support her thesis of emerging gender change. First is the evidence on values. This comes from Synergy, a market research company which used representative samples of 2,500 people over a period of 25 years to analyse changing values. In general, both females and males seem to have moved away from more traditional or 'outdirected' values to 'more innerdirected ones, such as empathy, connectedness, autonomy, peace and green concerns. However, the data suggests that women have been at the forefront of these changes:

> *... there are clear signs of a movement away from rigid moral codes and puritanical values. As a group their values are becoming androgynous; they are much more willing than men to think flexibly about gender roles.*
>
> (7)

The second source of evidence of emerging gender change cited by Wilkinson concerns women's changing place in paid work. There are many sources of such evidence and it is widely quoted – usually to demonstrate that matters are changing to the benefit of women. The female/male gap in earnings has narrowed (although it remains substantial); there has been a steady rise in female employment (although employment has fallen among low income women); far more women are entering the professions (although they are still far more likely than males to 'break' their careers and still much less likely to occupy top positions in professional hierarchies). Wilkinson also points to women's power as consumers and although this is traditional, it is 'shifting away from utilitarian purchasing for the home to consumption that is more closely tied to identity' (11).

Comment on the 'genderquake' thesis

There is always a danger in approaching evidence with the intention of proving one's thesis rather than, as Popper suggests, attempting to disprove it (i.e. testing it 'to destruction'). Wilkinson obviously favours the developments which she sets out to chart. Clearly gender change is occurring but evidence that it may amount to less than a 'genderquake' merits consideration.

First, on the matter of attitudinal change, it is quite conceivable that as the younger generation of women grow older and the majority of them have children and acquire other commitments, their attitudes will change. There may at least be some shift away from prioritising paid work over children noted by Wilkinson. Even so, it does seem likely that women will continue to push for greater economic equality.

On the question of economic change, the trends seem open to less optimistic interpretation than offered by Wilkinson. Thus, for each positive trend she notes above, I bracketed a qualifying negative point (the 'althoughs'). In particular, the very flexibility that women (traditionally!) offer is open to exploitation in the context of new economic developments. The majority of service sector jobs for which they are preferred to men are low-pay/low-status. If women are prepared flexibly to offer part-time, temporary, or job-share work and *still* continue to suffer lower pay and less promotion than males, employers are likely to let them.

Gender inequality and patriarchy, is structured into British society. The organisation of domestic and paid work will continue to reproduce patriarchy for a long time yet, unless swift and radical change is introduced. Wilkinson's challenging thesis should be set against the feminist theories of patriarchy which are presented in the following section. Arguably, these theories give a more accurate measure of the 'gender problem'.

Explanations of the position of women in the labour market

A reserve army of labour? Neo-Marxist perspective

The term 'reserve army of labour' refers to a section of the labour force which can be easily and cheaply hired and easily fired and so can be used to facilitate the functioning of capitalism. Black minority workers and female workers are considered to be a disproportionate and, in the latter case, growing proportion of this reserve army. Clearly, if employers can use female labour in this way it would be profitable for them to do so. Further, Veronica Beechey has argued that because females' wages often represent a second source of family income, employers are therefore able to depress male wages.

Irene Breugel's 1982 review of the above thesis in relation to the experience of female labour from 1974–78, provides only mixed support for it. She did find that the rate of unemployment of women rose three times more quickly than that of men and that the decline in female employment in industries experiencing increased unemployment exceeded that of men. Part-time female employees were particularly hard hit. On the other hand, the rapid expansion of the service sector to some extent protected the market position and employment security of women. More recently, Marxist-feminist Juliet Mitchell has speculated that micro-chip technology and the demand for jobs of males displaced from manufacturing industry may weaken the position of women in the service sector. Pessimistically Breugel suggests that women's best protection is the low pay they receive.

Dual labour market theory

We will discuss in detail the concept of a 'dual labour market' when considering the Fordist/post-Fordist debate (Chapter 9, pp. 252-4). Barron and Norris argue that there are two distinct labour markets, the primary and secondary (1978). The former is characterised by well-paid, secure work with good promotion prospects and in a pleasant environment whereas the latter is characterised by the opposite. Women are considered overwhelmingly to be located in the secondary labour market.

Like the reserve army of labour theorists, dual labour market theorists emphasise the profitability for capital of having access to a pool of easily expendable labour. In terms of the Fordist/post-Fordist debate, the existence of such a group adds to business 'flexibility'. The mechanisms by which women remain in the secondary labour force include not putting them on promotion tracks and failing to plan institutionally to ensure women are not disadvantaged because their pattern of paid work may be disrupted by maternity. Indeed, it seems likely that until the issue of childcare is dealt with at a national level, the fact of maternity will continue to be used directly or indirectly as justification for disadvantaging women.

Radical feminist perspective

The basic radical-feminist position on the domination of women by men in the area of paid work is that it is another example of patriarchy. As we have seen, radical-feminists tend to stress male exploitation of women's biological functioning, particularly child-bearing. The logic of this analysis is that there should be much more adequate public funding of childcare facilities to off-set female disadvantage.

Patriarchy and capitalism

A number of feminists see patriarchy and capitalism as separate but interlocking and largely complementary structures. Thus, Eichler (1980) acknowledges that women are exploited in the economic sphere, but unlike Marxists she sees the source of their inequality within the family rather than in relations to the means of production (i.e. the economy). See sees the family not as a capitalist but as a 'quasi-feudal institution' within which women are virtually serfs, uncertain of what, if any, economic reward they may receive from their husbands. Married women as a group, across class lines, are in this position which as well as disadvantaging them within the family, radically reduces their chances of success in paid work and may even affect their control of their own wages. Eichler considers that single women in paid work are in a different structural position to married women. Their exploitation is essentially based on their position in paid work. However, she does see a basis for common cause between the two groups.

Women and the labour market: conclusion

There are a number of important comments that need to be made about the above theoretical explanations of female oppression in the labour market. In general, what these theories have in common is perhaps more significant then what divides them. First, they all offer a structural rather than an individualistic explanation of the position of women in the labour market and of their place in the occupational structure. Each theory avoids 'blaming' individual employers or politicians, men or women (blaming the victim!) to explain gender inequality, and instead concentrates on the structural relations between the family and the economy and the roles of females and males within them. Patriarchal ideology – belief in male supremacy by either or both men and women – is seen as the product of experience within patriarchal (and capitalist) structures rather than as the result of a male conspiracy.

Second, there are obvious similarities between the 'reserve army of labour' theory and 'dual labour market' theory. Indeed, the reserve army and the secondary labour force appear to be virtually synonymous (although the way they function within the capitalist system is open to different explanation).

Finally, however, it would be misleading totally to homogenise the theories of female exploitation in the labour market. It is clearly necessary for feminists to debate to what extent, and in what ways, female emancipation can occur in a capitalist society. A number of serious differences of perspective and policy among feminists are discussed elsewhere (see pp. 209-11).

Women's liberation: policy and continuing problems

We have seen the extent of gender inequality. We now ask what governments have tried to do about it. The main measures of the 'equality package', as Ann Oakley calls it, are as follows: the Equal Pay Act (operative from 1975); the Sex Discrimination Act (1975); and the Employment Protection and Social Security Pensions Acts (1975). The 1967 Abortion Act and the Divorce Law Reform Act (implemented in 1971) also have profound implications for women, though they are not specifically part of the 'package'. The first two focus largely on employment. None of this legislation has resulted in a reduction of the concentration of women in low paid occupations. A more interventionist policy might, for instance,

involve guaranteeing women a minimum quota of top and middle level positions in business companies and professional establishments. Sometimes, what is required is to achieve actual equality more than legal equality. After all, we are all legally entitled to eat the Savoy Grill … The terms of the Sex Discrimination Act are more easily enforceable in education, and there are more signs of greater quality of achievement in that area, though the gap remains wide in certain respects .

The Employment Protection Act contains the first legal entitlement to maternity leave for women in Britain. It bans dismissal on grounds of pregnancy and guarantees mothers their jobs for up to 29 weeks from childbirth. Circumstances (and there are potentially many: the death of the child is one) in which paternity leave rather than maternity leave might be desirable are not recognised by the Act, and to this extent, it has an element of chauvinistic protectionism about it. Still, 29 weeks 'grace' is better than nothing, although it could hardly have been much less. Further, the Social Security Pensions Act puts women's sickness and unemployment pay and pension rights on an equal basis to those of men.

Despite the above legislation and the seemingly not very effective Equal Opportunities Commission, women's status at work relative to that of men did not much improve during the 1980s and early1990s.

Relatively few cases are taken to the Employment Appeals Tribunals under the Equal Pay and Sex Discrimination Acts. Thus, in 1988/89 only 368 cases were heard under the former (of which complainants were successful in 14), and 300 under the latter (of which 78 were successful). Proof of discrimination can be difficult, but such a record is unlikely to encourage those who believe they have got a grievance even to attempt redress. In addition to the prospect of failure, there is also the cost (if this is not borne by the Equal Opportunities Commission), and the possibility of later victimisation by employers. Like the comparable legislation covering racial discrimination in employment (see p. 237), this legislation or, at least, its implementation is in danger of being impaired because of inadequate funding.

Little legislation was passed during the Thatcher administration specifically to improve the position of women in society. Indeed, the freezing between 1986 and 1990 of child benefit which is paid directly to women may be considered to have disadvantaged them. The exception was the new tax ruling by which, from 1990, the earnings of husband and wife were automatically taxed separately without the husband having to forfeit the married man's tax allowance (which had previously been the case if separate taxation had been opted for). As Martyn Denscombe puts it, the move allows women 'privacy and control over their own financial affairs for the first time since the income tax system was introduced some 200 years ago' (Denscombe, 1991). In 1996, it appeared fairly certain that women would be guaranteed a share in their husband's pension rights in the case of divorce.

The extent of women's participation in politics may be taken as one measure of their influence on national life. On this basis their influence is low – notwithstanding Margaret Thatcher. In 1996, only six per cent of MPs were women, two of whom were members of John Major's cabinet.

Education is often thought of as the key to the further advancement of women. As we have seen, in many ways females have already closed 'the achievement gap' between males and females. While differential subject choice persists, this may be further eroded by the implementation of the national curriculum. However, the education successes of women have not yet been substantially reflected in career success. Without again rehearsing why this is so, it is worth quoting Joanna Forster, Chairwoman of the Equal Opportunities Commission that it is the 'pitiful' lack of childcare facilities 'which confines most women to part-time, marginalised, low-paid work'. (EOC Report, 1990)

Sylvia Walby: 'Theorising Patriarchy' – an overview

So far in this chapter a variety of historical and contemporary detail about gender as well as much theory has been given. One of the strength's of Sylvia Walby's *Theorising Patriarchy* (1990) is that it imaginatively integrates historical and theoretical interpretation. As such it can partly serve to pull together the plethora of facts, developments and theories already referred to here – although the book merits an account in its own right.

Walby's own theoretical approach is to regard patriarchy and capitalism as distinct systems which may interact harmoniously or disharmoniously depending on particular historical circumstances. Thus, capitalism benefits from patriarchy in that female domestic labour is unpaid and sustains male labour – a situation which, broadly, was in place in the late Victorian period and benefited both patriarchy and capitalism. However, when capital needs female labour – as during the two world wars – conflict between patriarchy and capitalism can break out. Nevertheless, she sees it as mainly due to women's own efforts that in Britain they have partly broken out of private patriarchy and achieved a stronger position on paid work. This analysis has obvious application to the 1990s when the increasing numbers of females in paid work is widely considered an element in a 'crisis of masculinity'. Walby remarks that, in general, the 'main basis of tension between capitalism and patriarchy is over the exploitation of women's labour' (185) (see Reading 2).

Walby, then, presents six main structures within which patriarchy occurs. These are:

- Paid employment
- Household production
- Culture (including Religion, Media, Education)
- Sexuality
- Male violence
- The State

These six structures of patriarchal domination and control are linked to *two forms of patriarchy* distinguished by Walby: *private* and *public*. Private and public patriarchy are differentiated by the main strategies of patriarchal domination adopted in each: 'exclusionary in private patriarchy and segregationist in public patriarchy'. Thus, in private patriarchy, male domination occurs directly within the household structure and also by the exclusion of women from public life. In public patriarchy women play roles within paid employment and in other structures but their subordination is implemented by segregating them from the main areas of wealth, power and status (e.g. in clerical work – see Figure 7.3).

In addition to being differentiated by, respectively, exclusionary and segregationist strategies of control, private and public patriarchy are also differentiated by different relationships between the six structures (all of which occur in both forms of patriarchy). Walby summarises these shifting structural relationships in respect of British patriarchy from the Victorian period to the present which she argues has moved from private to public patriarchy:

> *Within paid work there was a shift from an exclusionary strategy to a segregationalist one, which was a movement from attempting to exclude women from paid work to accepting their presence but confining them to jobs which were segregated from and graded lower than those of men. In the household there was a reduction in the confinement of women to this sphere over a lifetime and a shift in the main locus of control over production. The major cultural institutions ceased to exclude women, while subordinating women within them. Sexual controls over women significantly shifted from the specific control of the husband to that of a broader public arena; women were no longer excluded from sexual relations to the same extent, but subordinated within them. Women's exclusion from the state was replaced by their subordination within it …*
>
> *(179)*

Walby observes that 'women are not passive victims of oppressive structures'. She comments that in some ways the early feminists won their goals, particularly in relation to political rights. However, she is strongly of the view that public patriarchy institutionalises and enforces continuing gender inequality:

> *Women are no longer restricted to the domestic hearth, but have the whole/society in which to roam and be exploited.*
>
> *(201)*

This comment leads naturally to consideration of what a gender equal order might be like. It is to this – still speculative – issue, that we will shortly turn. First, however, some critical evaluation of Walby's undeniably substantial contribution to gender theory is appropriate.

Comment on Walby

In writing *Theorising Patriarchy*, Walby aimed to avoid some of the rigidities or limitations she associated with established feminist perspectives. Radical feminism in conceptualising patriarchy and males as the universal problem lacks the necessary historical specificity to explain changes and variety in patriarchy, similarly, Marxist feminism and dual systems theory both stipulate a given relationship between patriarchy and capitalism of a reinforcing kind – whereas Walby observes possibilities of tension; and liberal-feminism lacks adequate structural analysis. It is arguable that Walby has largely achieved an account of patriarchy in nineteenth and twentieth century Britain, and to a lesser extent, the United States which is flexible in its analysis of structure and is historically dynamic.

Jackie Stacey has suggested that despite its strength, Walby's account of the six structures of patriarchy is unevenly theorised (1993). The exploitation and organisation of women in paid employment and their ideological representations in culture is clearly conceived. Other contemporary feminists, however, see the state as less a means of patriarchal power and privilege than Walby and argue that the use of state power to achieve further gender reform should be a main strategy of feminists (see p. 82).

Terry Lovell makes the comment that the 'explanatory pluralism' of Walby's approach, 'cannot, however, tackle the lack of plausibility that vastly different societies, across time and space, should all share in common oppressive hierarchical relationships between men and women, even though the form and content of this relationship may vary greatly, unless there is at least some rudimentary underlying predisposing factor' (1996: 316). Then, again, no one else has quite explained this matter either.

Afro-Caribbean identities: gender, class and ethnicity

Drawing on a wide range of literature, this section attempts to sketch in outline the main types or patterns of gender identities constructed by Afro-Caribbeans in the often difficult and oppressive circumstances in which they have found themselves. Three preliminary points need to be made:

1 Gender identities occur within wider gender orders. As R W Connell points out, masculine behaviour can only be adequately understood in relation to feminine behaviour and the overall structure of gender in a given society.
2 Gender occurs in interaction with other aspects of stratification. Gender, class and ethnicity – as well as sometimes racism – interact together and mediate each other's effects. Thus, just as class mediates the masculinity of white working class males, so it does that of black working class males.
3 'Masculinity' and 'Femininity' are not fixed 'essences' or 'entities'. In that sense 'essentialism' is rejected in what follows. Afro-Caribbean gender identities like other identities, can and do develop and change.

A dynamic model of Afro-Caribbean gender identities

Afro-Caribbeans have adopted or negotiated several discernable strategies of adaptation or resistance in the face of racial discrimination, class inequality and gender stereotyping. These can be summarised in Table 7.3 below. Of course, individuals and groups may mix strategies at any time or change them over time.

Table 7.3 Afro-Caribbean strategies of adaptation/resistance

Strategies of adaptation/ resistance	Explanation
Accommodation	To the Dominant System
Adoption (assimilation)	Of the Dominant System
Resistance/rebellion	Against the Dominant System
Retreatism/separatism	From the Dominant System
Mixed/changing strategies	To the Dominant System
[Equality/pluralism?	Within the System?] (see pp. 236-8)

Note: All the above strategies of adaptation have consequences for Afro-Caribbean gender identities and relations.

Accommodation

The majority of Afro-Caribbean immigrants into Britain in the 1950s – most of whom initially were males – were law-abiding, skilled or semi-skilled working class people who wanted a better life for themselves. Without surrendering the distinctively ethnic aspects of their identity, most were willing to accommodate to the culture and institutions of the 'mother country' which, to a large extent, they felt well disposed to. This positive but low-key approach (somewhat akin to what Goffman describes as 'playing it cool') had less appeal to second and subsequent generations. This was because of the high level of racism, discrimination and frustrated aspirations experienced by many Afro-Caribbean immigrants (see pp. 224-31).

Nevertheless, it has remained true that the majority of Afro-Caribbeans in Britain continue to seek work within the legitimate opportunity structure. O'Connell reports that even in inner-urban Toxteth where unemployment among Afro-Caribbean youth reaches 60 per cent, the majority still want to find work (1995). However, in the absence of work, some have developed alternative strategies of survival which to some extent differ along gender lines.

Whereas the adaptation to British society of most younger Afro-Caribbean females could be described as one of robust accommodation, a large but difficult to quantify minority of younger black males have pursued strategies involving 'resistance' (see below). There is now a large body of sociological literature – much of it written by Afro-Caribbean females – describing and explaining aspects of their own tough and usually effective coping strategies. Much of this literature has already been referred to in this book. Anne Phoenix has described the positive self-image many Afro-Caribbean girls acquire from their mothers. The latter are often effectively involved in both paid and domestic labour. Young Afro-Caribbean females – perhaps to a somewhat larger extent than white females – outperform their ethnic male peers both at primary and secondary school (Fuller, 1979; Tizzard, 1987). The decline of employment in the manufacturing sector and increase in service sector jobs, means that on 'leaving' school, the females are more likely to find work than the males.

What effect the above developments have on heterosexual gender relations within the Afro-Caribbean community will be discussed later in this section.

Adoption (Assimilation)

As Chapter 8 describes, in the early years of post-war immigration there was a widespread, if naive, assumption on the part of many white people that black people would simply 'assimilate' to 'the British way of life'. However, relatively few Afro-Caribbeans seem to have envisaged their identity in this way. Most British Afro-Caribbeans have retained a strong sense of their roots often adopting hyphenated or even double-hyphenated identity-descriptions (e.g. black British, British Afro-Caribbean).

It is perhaps inevitable that as some British Afro-Caribbeans become wealthier, a number would adopt lifestyles and mannerisms associated with the white middle class (although arguably this class is itself becoming increasingly differentiated). This does not necessarily mean that such upwardly mobile individuals lose touch with their ethnic roots. Thus, the newscaster, Trevor McDonald combines an advocacy of the merits of standard English with an interest in African and Caribbean culture. Perhaps a group which 'went over the top' in imitation were the mainly male BUPIES (black urban professionals) of the mid to late 1980s. Even the Bupies, however, owed something in the style and content of their culture to the Caribbean as well as Afro-America.

Resistance/Rebellion

The controversial but useful concept of resistance is discussed elsewhere in this book (see p. 232 and pp. 454-5). Here it used to describe one strategy used by Afro-Caribbeans for coping with (or adapting to) the inequalities and exclusions of British society. Resistance is an attempt to solve problems and express alternatives at the level of culture and lifestyle. Thus, entertainment – particularly, music and comedy – has provided both an 'alternative' source of money and career to Afro-Caribbeans *and* a means to express a wide variety of sentiments and feelings including anger and resentment against racism. Cultural resistance is particularly, although by no means exclusively, associated with Afro-Caribbean males. The reasons for this partial gendering of cultural resistance have already been largely explained. Whereas the energies and aspirations of Afro-Caribbean females are usually channelled into either or both domestic and paid work, this is relatively rather less the case with Afro-Caribbean males.

In a society, then, in which racial discrimination is quite likely to bar the full expression of talent and ability through conventional careers, Afro-Caribbean males often look elsewhere for fulfilment as well as for money. Although music, the arts and sports are far from free of discrimination, achievement in them is harder to deny or ignore than in mainstream careers. Inevitably, some young black males seek rewards in crime (see pp. 346-8). Overall, a real tension exists between many young Afro-Caribbean males and an economic and social system often reluctant to open opportunity to them.

Undoubtedly, the urban disorders of the 1980s reflected a degree of pent up frustration on the part of some young Afro-Caribbean as well as some young radicals. To that extent these events can be referred to as 'rebellions'. However, most participants probably had little, if any, developed political agenda other than a specific resentment of the police and a generalised anger against racism.

It is not difficult to see why masculinity comes into play in the resistance of black males. Class and racial oppression virtually provoke a reassertion of worth in gendered 'masculinist' terms. As slaves and then as cheap wage labour, black males were often deprived and humiliated in explicitly sexual terms. 'Their' women were often forcibly taken from them under the first system and variously abused or exploited by white males under the second. Both practically and psychologically, black masculinity was at stake and it is not surprising that Afro-Caribbean males have often sought to reassert their physical and psychological strength and courage.

In Connell's terms, it is the class system and racism that 'marginalise' black males. However, gender plays a part in this process. Black/white male relations have historically been characterised by sexual tension. The British Empire was a gendered enterprise – wrought mainly by upper class white males and suffered differently by black males and females. When oppression and exploitation continues to occur – there is an additional historical residue of collective anger and frustration to call on by black males.

Connell uses the term 'authorised' to describe the allowance dominant male groups may extend to marginalised masculine groups to gain some benefit from their masculinity (i.e. to obtain 'the patriarchal dividend'). Authorised areas such as sport and entertainment have tended to foster a physical version of black masculinity which has left unthreatened white masculinity in areas of commercial and intellectual competition. (Reading 1)

Retreatism/Separatism

The term retreatism can cover a wide range of activity. On the one hand, it can refer to subcultures of withdrawal in which the participants have drifted into a life of drug dependency and crime (the aim of which is often to support the drug habit (see p. 353). On the other hand, it can refer to a conscious and intentional retreat from a situation – sometimes to the point of separating from it.

Retreatism in the first sense is not greatly characteristic of Afro-Caribbean subculture. The use of drugs is seldom fatalistic and defeatist. Drugs more often function as a pleasure enhancer in the dynamic Afro-Caribbean leisure culture or as an aid to spiritual experience (ganja (*marijuana*) is a sacred drug within Rastafarianism). Selling drugs can also be a 'career' – a way of making a living. As such, it is another – albeit illegal – strategy of coping much closer to resistance than retreatism. Drug-pushers or hustlers are usually male and can achieve significant wealth and status through their activity. Hustlers are engaged in a high risk activity and often develop a 'hard edge' to their character. They are notoriously sexist and sometimes work as pimps as an additional source of income.

The strategy of separating from white society as a response to its incorrigible racism has recurred throughout recent black history. The Rastafarians aspire to 'return to Africa' as the only place where they will be free of white oppression. Within Rastafarianism, gender relations have tended to be patriarchal (Cashmere, 1981). Males are considered to be the natural authority and female roles to be traditional and supportive. A biblical basis for this relationship is sometimes cited but it can also be seen as a response to concern about 'the break-up of the black family'. The solution to this 'problem' is partly perceived in terms of reasserting the traditional male role.

Afro-Caribbean gender relations: equality/pluralism

Issues of gender dominance, oppression, equality and fairness are as relevant to British Afro-Caribbean as to others. There is some disagreement among researchers about how work – domestic, including childrearing, and paid – is shared among Afro-Caribbean adults. The writings of two Afro-Caribbean feminists, Ann Phoenix and Heidi Mirza, exemplify this. As discussed earlier, Phoenix accepts the data which strongly suggests that single-parent families are significantly more common among the Afro-Caribbean community than otherwise. Paradoxically, 'families without fathers' mean more work for Afro-Caribbean mothers but seems to have some real benefits for their female off-spring. Heidi Mirza's, *Young, Female and Black* gives a somewhat different account of family and gender relations in the Afro-Caribbean community. She acknowledges that single-parent families are more common in the Afro-Caribbean than the general population, although 79 per cent of the not necessarily typical Afro-Caribbean girls she interviewed came from two-parent households. Mirza uses the positive term 'relative autonomy' to describe relations between adult male and female partners. By this she means that adult partners often construct tolerant and flexible relationships. The basis of this is that both partners are likely to be involved (or seeking) paid work and that, while males are far from wholly egalitarian about domestic work, they will often get involved with their children.

Whatever the precise gender balance among Afro-Caribbean partners, it is appropriate to view matters historically and in terms of social context. Given that middle class, overwhelmingly white Surrey is the 'divorce capital of Europe', moralistic posturing about other communities on matters which are at once highly individual and socially complex, is inappropriate. A genuine pluralistic society combines a commitment to equality with an acceptance of difference (see pp. 236-8).

Questions

1 Describe and explain how the sexual division of labour has developed in Britain from the Victorian period to the present.
2 Describe and explain the sexual division of labour among the Afro-Caribbean ethnic group. How, and to what extent does it differ from the sexual division of labour among the majority ethnic group?

Gender liberation: directions, images and issues

It is fairly clear what feminism opposes. It opposes the oppression of women by men and the resulting inequality of the sexes. Despite the differences between various feminist perspectives, most feminists welcome the reforms of the 'equality legislation package' even if some would doubt its effectiveness in the absence of more radical change.

However, many feminists want more than merely an end to the oppression of females by males. They want a world in which gender relations are freer, more equal and more fulfilling. What do these fine phrases mean? In this section, we look at some interpretations – variously complementary and contradictory.

Re-evaluating the historical roles of women

Recently, an interesting strand of opinion has become more noticeable in the feminist movement. It cannot easily be labelled but it involves a re-assessment and upgrading of the historical roles of women, and a better appreciation of their variety and necessity. While insisting on policies of equal opportunity in the job market, those who share this emerging perspective reject the notion that the success of women should be judged merely or even mainly by their achievements in traditionally male dominated areas (such as warfare or banking). Instead, three things are stressed. Firstly, that some domestic and child-rearing work can be creative and humanly very rewarding – this carries the rider that men could beneficially involve themselves in it more. Secondly, historically, in any case, women have borne a heavy and necessary burden of labour. Of course, such labour has often been oppressive and it is worth repeating Sheila Rowbotham's warning that attempts to idealise 'women's work' are invariably 'reactionary'. Ideals of motherhood tend to collapse before the distasteful reality of

changing nappies and scouring toilets. Third, as feminist researchers increasingly examine the historic contribution of women to literature, science and ideas, they are finding it was much more substantial than (men) previously thought.

Feminists have constantly stressed the skill and caring that goes into much domestic work while also recognising the long hours, elements of drudgery, and typical thanklessness that characterise it. Ann Oakley virtually despairs that men will ever recognise that qualities traditionally associated with women but which can occur in either sex – such as caring, gentleness and sharing – might provide a better moral blueprint for human conduct and survival than such traditionally 'masculine' characteristics as ambition, aggression and competitiveness. Ann Oakley, in the article quoted from above, cites a variety of feminist science fiction which speculates on precisely this possibility. Men are sometimes missing from this hypothetical future – their destructiveness is implicitly seen as both undesirable and dangerous. In the spirit of this literature, perhaps the nuclear bomb can be seen as a symbol of the male contribution historically: an achievement heavy with destructive potential. If so, it is perhaps time that the 'other' sex had a turn at, or at least more involvement in, the creation of a new social reality based on more positive and life-enhancing principles.

Ann Oakley severely questions whether the way towards women's liberation is simply to compete with men in the employment market. Yet she despairs that men will ever recognise or allow proper reward for the work women do. As long as this is so, the prospects are that women will continue to depend materially and psychologically (for security and identity) on men. As she says:

> *Men and women cannot be equal outside the home if they are not equal partners inside it.*
>
> (Oakley, 1979: New Society, 22.8.79)

Paid housework, or a guaranteed right to a proportion of the main breadwinner's salary, are possible solutions to material dependency (although they do not appear to have much support). In reality, however, Oakley is thinking mainly of the need for a change, indeed, a revolution in attitudes – of both sexes – to the quality, dignity and humanity of child-rearing and domestic labour – whoever does it.

Second, the massive contribution of female labour – physical and mental – has typically been underestimated. Virginia Novarra's book *Women's Work, Men's Work* forcefully asserts that women's work has made a vital contribution to the survival of the race. It has done so in the following major ways:

1 Reproduction.
2 Agricultural production (globally, more women are involved in agricultural production than men).
3 Clothing the family (often making or mending clothes).
4 Tending the family and others.
5 Cultural transmission.
6 Caring for the home and home environment (unpaid or lowly-paid work).

Of course, a re-evaluation of work traditionally done by women does not guarantee them more of the power and resources largely monopolised by men.

The third point refers to the rediscovery, or perhaps, discovery - mainly by women – of a vast, disregarded body of creative and intellectual work done by women. Novels, diaries and contemporary accounts of 'forgotten' female writers have been published and there has also been an outpouring of work by current female writers.

Becoming like men: assimilation

In undermining patriarchy, it is possible that females may adopt traditional 'masculine' attitudes themselves. Aggression, personal ambitions, the desire for power and control are functional characteristics in 'a man's world' and in attempting to 'beat them', some women may have ended up 'joining them'. This approach to female progress may be referred to as the assimilationist model although those who adopt it may not always have formally thought it through. Margaret Thatcher is often cited as an example of this kind of approach. Demi Moore's portrayal of a hyper-aggressive business-women in the film 'Disclosure' provides a fictional example (see p. 193).

Uneasy about accepting a patriarchal world on its own terms, a number of feminists have stressed that to achieve equality on 'male' terms may be a 'hollow' victory.

Female alternatives: separation and pluralism

The previous section presents the argument that there is much of value and therefore much worth preserving in female practice and achievement – even though women have worked within oppressive structures. One feminist response to this perception has been that what has developed as distinctly female is so in need of nurture and so threatened by men that women need to adopt a separatist strategy of development. Some feminists have gone further and regarded separation from men as an ultimate goal. In particular some lesbian feminists feel that they can better develop their relationships and way of living by excluding males. Separatism has also been adopted in a much more limited way in specific

institutional contexts such as education and politics. Thus, Dale Spender has argued that females achieve more in sexually segregated, than in mixed schools (see pp. 112-3). Beyond education, however, Spender accepts that the sexes will mix freely.

Perhaps the best known example of separatism was the women's peace camp at Greenham Common. It was, in part, an experiment in what a society of liberated women might be like. The women organised the camp along participatory, egalitarian and organic lines, doing jobs because they needed to be done and not for power, status or reward. Specifically, the camp was a peace protest, and many feminists do feel an overriding commitment to preventing nuclear holocaust and have little confidence that men of power will do what is necessary to achieve this.

A gender pluralist world would be one in which, although different gender roles would be distinguishable, there would be equality between them. Thus, women might still make up the majority of housepersons but would have comparable independence, status and rewards to men. Simply to describe gender pluralism in the abstract is to indicate that it is probably not fully achievable. Historically, domestic work, including childcare and rearing, has been of such low status and power that it is likely to continue to be so as long as women do most of it. In any case, a growing majority of women want work in the main economy. They will, therefore, need more public, commercial or male-partner help with childcare and other domestic work. This leads to a final alternative.

A non-gendered society: an end to gender roles?

What practical progress there has been towards women's liberation has probably been mainly in the slow and partial breaking down of traditional gender stereotypes and roles. Economically, women appear to be more empowered than in the recent past both as a result of increased earnings and because legislation has partly established a more effective framework of financial independence and security. In terms of qualifications, females already match males up to and including 'A' levels and should reach parity at degree level around the year 2000. If and when equality of qualifications is ever reflected in equal occupational status and rewards, and equality of domestic effort between the sexes, then unequal gender roles would cease to exist. Figure 7.7a which illustrates the contemporary sexual division of labour and Figure 7.7b which illustrates what a non-gendered division of labour might look like suggest we are a long way from this point.

(a) The social process of the sexual division of labour as it *actually* is:

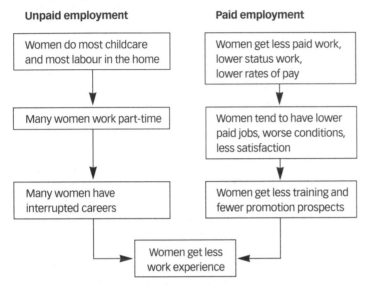

(b) A new (imagined) social process: a non-gendered society?

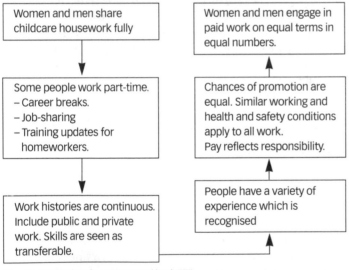

(Source: Open University, D103 SS Workbook:5(2))

Figure 7.7 Women's work

Activity

Try to construct what relations would be like if an institution with which you are familiar was non-gendered e.g. family, place of work.

Questions

1 What is it that various feminists have objected to about patriarchy?
2 What changes do you consider to have been brought about by the feminist movement? Critically discuss the direction of possible further changes in how society is gendered.

Summary

1 There are both biological and cultural explanations of gender differences. More recently attempts to understand the biological in relation to the cultural in a more integrated way have occurred. The most widely used approach to sexuality and gender is now the social constructionist.
2 Patriarchy is the system and practice by which males dominate and exploit females. Sexism is discrimination against someone on the basis of their sex.
3 There are a number of key perspectives on gender. The most important of these are feminist perspectives in that they reflect the prime concern of women for emancipation (i.e. freedom from domination and equality with males). A full summary of gender perspectives is given on p. 194.
4 The ideological reproduction of patriarchy occurs initially through family soicalisation and also through education and the media. Whether or not stereotypical gender roles are breaking down is debatable. Gender orders and regimes, particularly the formation of different types of masculinity are examined through the work of W R Connell and M Mac an Ghaill.
5 The sexual division of labour refers to how work, both domestic and non-domestic, is organised between the sexes. This has changed considerably through history with women by no means being involved only in 'housework'. Indeed worldwide they have probably carried out the majority of certain kinds of agricultural labour such as planting and harvesting crops. Most of the world's food (three-quarters) is grown by women!
6 Women increasingly returned to paid work during the twentieth century, having been excluded from large areas of the economy during the nineteenth century. This paralleled a growth in the political consciousness of many women and the rise of feminism.
7 The position of women in the contemporary labour market is one of sharp disadvantage in terms of status and rewards. Women tend to be concentrated in low status occupations and within these at the lower levels of the hierarchy. The fact that 'the qualification gap' between males and females has been greatly reduced has not yet produced an obvious 'pay-off' in women achieving higher status jobs.
8 There are a number of explantions of why females are occupationally disadvantaged. One theory is that, along with certain other groups, females constitute a reserve army of labour: easily hired and easily fired. Rather similarly, dual labour market theory argues that there is a well paid, secure labour force and less well paid, easily-shed labour – with women being predominantly in the latter. Radical-feminists stress that patriarchy structures work both within the family and the economy.
9 Mainly during the 1970s a number of reforms were implemented – the equality package – aimed at establishing

equality of opportunity and rights between men and women. Despite this, actual economic inequality stubbornly persists. Sylvia Walby integrates a range of feminist analysis in her theory of public/private patriarchy.

10 Afro-Caribbean gender relations are studied in the context of several types of adjustment made in the British context.

11 There are several possible outcomes of the women's movement. Assimilation would involve becoming like men in terms of attitudes and behaviour. Separatism would mean cutting off from men. Pluralism implies equal but different roles. A non-gendered society would not link roles with sexual differences.

Research and coursework

There are many areas of social life immediately accessible to students in which gender issues occur: the family, education, leisure, paid work and others. A more ambitious piece of coursework might try to find a relationship between two or more areas. Thus, an enquiry into the occupations and work patterns of a group of younger women (say, twenty to 30 years old) could include questions on their educational qualifications, experience, the domestic division of labour in their households and perhaps a question or two on their attitudes to their sons' and daughters' education and career prospects. The expected level of theoretical sophistication could come through probing the effect of class on the women's situations (Marxist-feminist perspective) and the ways in which patriarchy structured their lives (this would involve reference to radical-feminist perspective).

There is much scope for examining the basis of male power and control of people and resources in a number of contexts. Images related to and the experience of traditional 'masculinity' could be explored and explained as could that illusive phenomenon 'the new man' and/or 'new lad'.

Further reading

The updated second edition of Sue Sharpe's *Just Like a Girl* (Penguin, 1994) is accessible. There is not yet an easy introduction to 'masculinities' but W R Connell's *Masculinities* (Polity, 1995) is a key text.

Readings

Reading 1
Relations among masculinities: Hegemony, subordination, complicity, marginalisation

From W R Connell, *Masculinities* (Polity Press, 1995), pp.76-8

With growing recognition of the interplay between gender, race and class it has become common to recognise multiple masculinities; black as well as white, working-class as well as middle-class. This is welcome, but it risks another kind of oversimplification. It is easy in this framework to think that there is a black masculinity or a working-class masculinity.

To recognise more than one kind of masculinity is only a first step. We have to examine the relations between them. Further, we have to unpack the milieux of class and race and scrutinise the gender relations operating within them. There are, after all, gay black men and effeminate factory hands, not to mention middle-class rapists and cross dressing bourgeois ...

'Hegemonic masculinity' is not a fixed character type, always and everywhere the same. It is, rather, the masculinity that occupies the hegemonic position in a given pattern of gender relations, a position always contestable.

A focus on relations also offers a gain in realism. Recognising multiple masculinities, especially in an individualist culture such as the United States, risks taking them for alternative lifestyles, a matter of consumer choice. A relational approach makes it easier to recognise the hard compulsions under which gender configurations are formed, the bitterness as well as the pleasure in gendered experience.

With these guidelines, let us consider the practices and relations that construct the main patterns of masculinity in the current Western gender order.

Hegemony

The concept of 'hegemony', deriving from Antonio Gramsci's analysis of class relations, refers to the cultural dynamic by which a group claims and sustains a leading position in social life. At any given time, one form of masculinity rather than others is culturally exalted. Hegemonic masculinity can be defined as the configuration of gender practice which embodies the currently accepted answer to the problem of the legitimacy of patriarchy, which guarantees (or is taken to guarantee) the dominant position of men and the subordination of women.

This is not to say that the most visible bearers of hegemonic masculinity are always the most powerful people. They may be exemplars, such as film actors, or even fantasy figures, such as film characters. Individual holders of institutional power or great wealth may be far from the hegemonic pattern in their personal lives. (Thus a male member of a prominent business dynasty was a key figure in the gay/transvestite social scene in Sydney in the

1950s, because of his wealth and the protection this gave in the cold-war climate of political and police harassment.)

Nevertheless, hegemony is likely to be established only if there is some correspondence between cultural ideal and institutional power, collective if not individual. So the top levels of business, the military and government provide a fairly convincing *corporate* display of masculinity, still very little shaken by feminist women or dissenting men. It is the successful claim to authority, more than direct violence, that is the mark of hegemony (though violence often underpins or supports authority).

I stress that hegemonic masculinity embodies a 'currently accepted' strategy. When conditions for the defence of patriarchy change, the bases for the dominance of a particular masculinity are eroded. New groups may challenge old solutions and construct a new hegemony. The dominance of *any* group of men may be challenged by women. Hegemony, then, is a historically mobile relation. Its ebb and flow is a key element … of masculinity …

Subordination

Hegemony relates to cultural dominance in the society as a whole. Within that overall framework there are specific gender relations of dominance and subordination between groups of men.

The most important case in contemporary European/American society is the dominance of heterosexual men and the subordination of homosexual men. This is much more than a cultural stigmatisation of homosexuality or gay identity. Gay men are subordinated to straight men by an array of quite material practices …

Oppression positions homosexual masculinities at the bottom of a gender hierarchy among men. Gayness, in patriarchal ideology, is the repository of whatever is symbolically expelled from hegemonic masculinity, the items ranging from fastidious taste in home decoration to receptive and pleasure. Hence, from the point of view of hegemonic masculinity, gayness is easily assimilated to femininity. And hence – in the view of some gay theorists - the ferocity of homophobic attacks.

Gay masculinity is the most conspicuous, but it is not the only subordinated masculinity. Some heterosexual men and boys too are expelled from the circle of legitimacy. The process if marked by a rich vocabulary of abuse: wimp, milksop, nerd, turkey, sissy, lily liver, jellyfish, yellowbelly, candy ass, ladyfinger, pushover, cookie pusher, cream puff, motherfucker, pantywaist, mother's boy, four-eyes, ear-'ole, dweeb, geek, Milquetoast, Cedric, and so on. Here too the symbolic blurring with femininity is obvious.

Complicity

Normative definitions of masculinity, as I have noted, face the problem that not many men actually meet the normative standards. This point applies to hegemonic masculinity. The number of men rigorously practising the hegemonic pattern in its entirety may be quite small, yet the majority of men gain from its hegemony, since they benefit from the patriarchal dividend, the advantage men in general gain from the overall subordination of women.

As Chapter 1 showed, accounts of masculinity have generally concerned themselves with syndromes and types, not with numbers. Yet in thinking about the dynamics of society as a whole, numbers matter. Sexual politics is mass politics, and strategic thinking needs to be concerned with where the masses of people are. If a large number of men have some connection with the hegemonic project but do not embody hegemonic masculinity, we need a way of theorising their specific situation.

This can be done by recognising another relationship among groups of men, the relationship of complicity with the hegemonic project. Masculinities constructed in ways that realise the patriarchal dividend, without the tensions or risks of being the frontline troops of patriarchy, are complicit in this sense.

It is tempting to treat them simply as slacker versions of hegemonic masculinity – the difference between the men who cheer football matches on TV and those who run out in to the mud and the tackles themselves. But there is often something more definite and carefully crafted than that. Marriage, fatherhood and community life often involve extensive compromises with women rather than naked domination or an uncontested display of authority. A great many men who draw the patriarchal dividend also respect their wives and mothers, are never violent towards women, do their accustomed share of the housework, bring home the family wage, and can easily convince themselves that feminists must be bra-burning extremists.

Marginalisation

Hegemony, subordination and complicity, as just defined, are relations internal to the gender order. The interplay of gender with other structures such as class and race creates further relationships between masculinities.

In Chapter 2 I noted how new information technology became a vehicle for redefining middle-class masculinities at a time when the meaning of labour for working-class men was in contention. This is not a question of a fixed middle-class masculinity confronting a fixed working-class masculinity. Both are being reshaped, by a social dynamic in which class and gender relations are simultaneously in play.

Race relations may also become an integral part of the dynamic between masculinities. In a white-supremacist context, black masculinities play symbolic roles for white gender construction. For instance, black sporting stars become exemplars of masculine toughness, while the fantasy figure of the black rapist plays an important role in sexual politics among whites, a role much exploited by right-wing politics in the United States …

Though the term is not ideal, I cannot improve on 'marginalisation' to refer to the relations between the masculinities in dominant and subordinated classes or ethnic groups. Marginalisation is always relative to the *authorisation* of the hegemonic masculinity of the dominant group. Thus, in the United States, particular black athletes may be exemplars for hegemonic masculinity. But the fame and wealth of individual stars has no trickle-down effect; it does not yield social authority to black men generally …

These two types of relationship hegemony, domination/subordination and complicity on the one hand, marginalisation/authorisation on the other – provide a framework in which we can analyse specific masculinities. (This is a sparse framework, but social theory should be hardworking.) I emphasise that terms such as 'hegemonic masculinity' and 'marginalised masculinities' name not fixed character types but configurations of practice generated in particular situations in a changing structure of relationships. Any theory of masculinity worth having must give an account of this process of change.

Questions

1 What is hegemonic masculinity? Using the above text and other sources give some examples of current Western hegemonic masculinity.
2 Describe with an example what Connell means by the marginalisation/authorisation type of relationship.

Reading 2
The changing form of patriarchy in the twentieth century

From Sylvia Walby, *Theorising Patriarchy* (Basil Blackwell, 1990), pp. 185-6

The movement towards a more intense form of private patriarchy was dramatically reversed during the period at the turn of the century. The twentieth century has seen a shift in the form of patriarchy from private to public as well as a reduction in the degree of some specific forms of oppression of women.

This is not merely a statement that there were important changes, but, further, that the very direction of change was reversed. All six patriarchal structures are involved in these changes. There was a struggle by feminists against patriarchal social practices which met with resistance. Their campaigns took place in the context of, and were shaped by, the capitalist demand for labour. The outcome of these battles was a change from one form and a high degree of patriarchy to another form together with some lessening in the degree of patriarchy in specific areas. These had complex interconnected effects on other aspects of patriarchal relations. Capital's demand for increased supplies of labour was in conflict with the private patriarchal strategy of privatising women in the home. First-wave feminism's victories of political citizenship gave women not only the vote, but education, and hence access to the professions, property ownership and the right to leave marriages. In combination these meant that women eventually gained effective access to paid employment and the ability to leave marriages, which led to significant changes in the notions of appropriate sexual behaviour. To start with first-wave feminism achieved a victory principally at the political level of the state; the eventual changes at the economic level provided the material possibility of the mass of women taking advantage of their legal

independence. The two changes, political and economic, had their impact as a result of their specific combination. In the absence of the political victory the increase in women's wage labour would have been merely additional exploitation. It was only because of the citizenship rights that women were able to use the economic changes to broaden further their sphere of operation.

Capitalism and changes in the form of patriarchy

The main basis of the tension between capitalism and patriarchy is over the exploitation of women's labour. On the one hand, capitalists have interests in the recruitment and exploitation of female labour, which is cheaper than that of men because of patriarchal structures. On the other, there is resistance to this by that patriarchal strategy which seeks to maintain the exploitation of women in the household. The first forms of capitalist industrialisation saw the successful recruitment of women (and children) into the cotton textile factories in greater numbers than men. Prolonged patriarchal resistance through political pressure on the state to pass the Factory Acts and by the craft unions to bar women's entry to specific jobs was not able to do more than stabilise the situation in this industry. In other occupations which entered the capitalist factory later, such as skilled manual engineering work, the men's craft organisations were successful in excluding women. Indeed there was often a strong cross-class patriarchal alliance which supported the exclusion of women, even in the absence of strong male unions. However, this cross-class alliance had weaknesses when it cut across the interests of employers to recruit the cheaper labour of women. Conflict would break out, as it did over the question of women entering the munitions factories during the First World War.

An alternative patriarchal strategy developed of allowing women into paid employment, but segregating them from men and paying them less. Clerical work is a good example of this process, where the male workers' organisations were insufficiently strong to defeat employers' insistent attempts to recruit women. The problem was resolved by a compromise in which the employers ceased trying to substitute women directly for men and instead recruited women for new sub-occupations, which were segregated from those of the men, graded lower and paid less, while maintaining the men in the upper reaches of white-collar work (see Walby, 1986). Whether the exclusionary or the segregation strategy was followed depended upon the balance of capitalist and patriarchal forces in a particular industry in a particular locality. The former was based upon a private form of patriarchy in which women were controlled by excluding them from the public sphere, especially from paid work. The latter was based upon a public form of patriarchy in which women were controlled within all spheres. The power of capital precluded the successful maintenance of the exclusionary mode, except in certain small tight pockets of patriarchal power and resistance. (For instance, the typesetters were able to sustain this until the last decade, as Cockburn (1983) has shown.) The exclusionary form of patriarchy was also under attack by a large powerful feminist movement from the middle of the nineteenth century to the first quarter of the twentieth.

The development of the economical structures of capitalism was not sufficient by itself to cause the shift from private to public patriarchy. This could only occur in the context of a powerful feminist movement in Britain, and indeed most of the West. Where we find capitalism in the absence of a feminist movement, there is no such change in the form of patriarchy. For instance, in some parts of the contemporary Third World young women have been pulled into wage labour for the capitalist factories of foreigners, yet are still subject to the patriarchal control of their fathers (Jayawardena, 1986; Mies, 1986). Wage labour by itself does not provide freedom from patriarchal control. In the case of Western industrialisation first-wave feminism created a different balance of forces.

Questions

1 Describe the shift in the form of patriarchy which, according to Walby, occurred from the turn of the century.
2 What were the factors that contributed to this change?

'Race', Ethnicity and Nation

Shared humanity goes beyond race. Why is race so significant to some people?

Aims of this chapter

1 To discuss various theories of racism and racial discrimination and, in particular to discuss how racism has been constrcuted in post-Second World War Britain.

2 To describe and explain the situation of Britain's black ethnic minorities in the labour market and class system.

3 Critically to analyse British and English identities.

Terminology and perspectives

'Race' and ethnicity: minorities

'Race', in the sense of certain innate biological differences existing between given groups of people, has proved a vague and unconvincing basis for explaining differences of attitude and behaviour. Indeed, it has proved dangerous and destructive as demonstrated by Nazi theories of Jewish inborn moral corruption used to justify genocide and American and European theories of African inhumaness used to justify slavery. A Nazi reference to the great scientist Einstein as 'that immoral Jewish Scientist' illustrates the intellectual and human level to which this kind of deterministic biological theorising could sink. Following the Second World War, the United Nations commissioned a number of leading biologists and social scientists to analyse and define the meaning of race. The biologists concluded that the human species had a single origin and that so-called races were distinguishable by the greater statistical likelihood of individuals having certain physical characteristics such as hair type or skin colour but that these characteristics overlapped between groups. They did not consider that psychological and behavioural differences correlated with the physical differences.

A primary focus of the sociology of 'race' is why and how concepts of biological 'race' are frequently used so oppressively. Frequently, in the relations between groups, one group's 'theory of race' about the other is essentially a form of oppressive ideology (a body of interconnected sentiments and ideas) as the above theories about Jews and Africans indicate. It is 'race' as ideology that is of concern to sociologists, and for that reason the term is used in inverted commas here. Very often, contemporary sociologists indicate the extent to which 'race' is invented or imagined by referring to 'the social construction of race'. As Bob Carter succinctly puts it:

> It is the construction and reproduction of 'race' discourses that requires explanation.
>
> *(Social Science Teacher, 1992)*

Whereas 'race' refers to ideologies and discourses of superiority/inferiority based on (mis)interpretations of biology, ethnicity refers to cultural differences between groups. Duncan Mitchell defines ethnicity as denoting membership of a distinct group of people possessing their own customary ways or culture. He illustrates this as follows:

> *The Germans, the Jews, the Gypsies are all ethnic groups, so also are Congo pygmies and Trobrianders. It will be observed that the characteristics identifying an ethnic group or aggregate may include a common language, common customs and beliefs and certainly a cultural tradition …*
>
> *(Mitchell, 1979)*

It is important to note that aspects of ethnicity can change and develop (such as language) but that ethnicity also provides a sense of group continuity and identity as, for instance, in the area of religion and 'folk' mythology. Thus, cultural heroines and heroes (real or imagined) provide role models and foci of communal feeling and unity. Churchill is an example from British culture and perhaps Crocodile Dundee from Australian.

In everyday life the above distinction between 'race' and ethnicity is often disregarded. In particular, those discriminating against another group may do so on ground of 'race' or ethnicity or both. John Stone therefore suggests that rather than 'race' or ethnic group, 'the concept of *minority* is a better tool to use in the analysis of race and ethnic relations' (Stone, 1985:42). The term minority will be used here unless a specific reference to 'race' or ethnicity is required. For instance, we will refer to Afro-Caribbean, Jewish, and Greek and other minorities. A minority assumes a majority and this term will be used to describe the most numerous and usually most powerful 'racial'/ethnic group in a particular community or society.

Racism, racialisation and institutional racism

In defining racism it is helpful to distinguish between narrow and broad definitions. Narrow definitions limit the use of the term *racism* to describe belief systems based on the premise that there are certain biological or 'natural' differences between 'racial' groups on the basis of which cultural differences supposedly develop. The Marxist, Robert Miles, has robustly adopted such a definition:

We can ... define racism as any set of claims or arguments which signify some aspect of the physical features of an individual or group as a sign of permanent distinctiveness and which attribute additional, negative characteristics and for consequences to the individual's or group's presence.

(Miles, 1990:149)

Miles goes on to suggest the use of the term *racialisation* to describe the discriminatory categorisation of a given individual or group on the basis of supposed 'racial' criteria. He argues that British politics has been continually 'racialised' since the 1960s as black people have been 'scapegoated' for a variety of 'ills' such as unemployment and rising crime rates.

The rhetoric of racialisation? Enoch Powell, 1968

As I look ahead, I am filled with foreboding. Like the Roman, I seem to see 'the River Tiber foaming with much blood'. That tragic and intractable phenomenon which we watch with horror on the other side of the Atlantic but which there is interwoven with the history and existence of the States itself, is coming upon us here by our own volition and our own neglect. Indeed it has all but come. In numerical terms, it will be of American proportions long before the end of the century .... they found their wives unable to obtain hospital beds in childbirth, their children unable to obtain school places, their homes and neighbourhoods changed beyond recognition, their plans and prospects for the future defeated.

For the record – he was wrong about numbers which have never been more than a fraction of American proportions. (But is it racist to 'play the numbers game?')

The 1991 census was the first in Great Britain to include a question on ethnic group. Slightly over 3,000,000 people, 5.5% of the population, described themselves as belonging to an ethnic minority group (see Table 8.1).

Table 8.1 Ethnic population of Great Britain by ethnic group, 1991

Ethnic group	Population	Ethnic group as a percentage of total population
White	51,874,000	94.5
Indian/Pakistani/Bangladeshi	1,480,000	
Black	891,000	5.5
Other ethnic minority groups	645,000	
	54,889,000	100

(Source: *Social Trends*, 1994)

Broader definitions of racism include deterministic belief systems in which supposed 'superiority' and 'inferiority' may be based on cultural as well as biological criteria. John Rex, a leading Weberian, adopts this broader approach to racism. He states that racism can be understood 'in terms of some kind of deterministic theory, whether that theory be of a scientific, religious, cultural, historical, ideological or sociological kind' (Quoted in Solomos, 1989:8) Barker uses the term 'cultural racism' to describe what is more generally referred to as ethnic (cultural) prejudice. He considers this to be the most common form of contemporary racism.

Rex also employs the term 'institutional racism' to describe what he sees as a particular type of racism. It describes institutional rules and procedures which discriminate against one group but not another. Some use the term particularly to describe unintentional and indirect discrimination of this kind. Rex cites the procedures governing the way public rented accommodation was allocated in the 1960s as an example of institutional discrimination:

There were ... rules about overcrowding, which prevented the allocation of houses to large families. The first of these sets of rules, but the second to some extent, had the effect of preventing the allocation of houses to black families. The problem then was one of indirect discrimination. Quite essential to fighting institutional racism then was the task of combating such indirect discrimination.

(Rex, 1986:112)

Table 8.2 Definitions/measures of racism

	Attitudinal	**Behavioural**
Individual	Personal attributes, Opinions, Values	Personal acts Behaviours, Choices or
Institutional	Organisation/Societal Norms, Symbols, Fashions, Myths	Organisational/Societal Procedures, Programmes, Mechanisms

(Source: Adapted from Chester and Delgado, 1987:185)

Table 8.2 summarises some aspect of individual and institutional racism. The reader might find it useful to think of examples of the various factors indicated.

Finally, for the same reason that sociologists refer to the 'social construction of race', racism is seen as socially constructed rather than 'natural'. Because racism takes different forms in different contexts – from so-called 'scientific' racism (see Figure 8.2) to racist charting – sociologists often refer to racisms to indicate this.

Racial harassment

It is difficult to estimate the number of cases of racial harassment but there are many tens of thousands of incidents every year (the BCS Survey, 1991, estimates about 171,000). Of these, about half were threats, a quarter were assaults, and a quarter acts of vandalism. Racial harassment can be brutal and vary in its effects from creating inconvenience to disabling or murdering people. Here are some examples of 'routine' racism in Britain (see also Figure 8.1).

> *Mrs Zerbanoo Gifford, who is standing as a parliamentary candidate (1992) was warned by a national Front supporter that her home would be fire bombed if she stood. Her home was broken into and a death threat left there.*
>
> *Eugene Sutton, a building site worker, was subjected to a racist taunts which a member of the management contributed to. In the court case, his employees said that such language was 'common parlance' on building sites.*
>
> *A youth was slashed with a knife by an older white boy as he walked along a school corridor between classes.*
>
> *A family was burned out of their home and a pregnant woman and her three children killed.*
>
> *Note: The first two of the above cases were reported in The Times, 13.6.1991, and the others are cited by Paul Gordon in Citizenship for Some.*
>
> *(Runnymede Trust, 1989)*

It would be serious to misunderstand racism to imagine that it occurs only in areas of high immigrant population. Indeed, there is considerable evidence that racist attitudes can be more widespread among those who have had little experience of immigrants (Cashmore, 1987). The impact of racist attacks on victims in areas of low immigrant settlement may be greater because of their isolation. Often victims in these areas are Asian small business people. In Neath, in 1994, Moh Singh Kullar was murdered in a racist attack. According to Searchlight, the anti-Fascist monitoring group, Combat 18, the terrorist organisation has targeted Wales as an 'action' area. In 1995, in West Country Yeovil, the owners of a Bangladeshi restaurant were constantly and sometimes violently harassed. After speaking out on their behalf Paddy Ashdown, the local MP, had his car torched.

The historical and economic background of racism in Britain and the West

'Race' is a crucial contemporary issue both in Britain and internationally. South Africa remains a major focus of racial tension in the world, because until recently racial differentiation was openly proclaimed there as the very basis of stratification. That system was known as apartheid, although it was also presented as 'separate development'. Apartheid involved the legally enforceable separation of whites and blacks in a way that ensured far higher

Type of racial incidents on the Treviot estate

September 1990–June 1991

Police figures ▨   Housing Department ☐   Homeless Families Campaign, Tower Hamlets, Law-Centre ■

Categories: Racial abuse, Harassment, Damage to property, Serious assault, Assault, Serious violence, Robbery

Figure 8.1 Ten months of racial violence on an East London housing estate. Is a new law making specifically racial violence a criminal offence required?

'There is a gang who hang around, some are black boys and some white and when they see an Asian kid they chase him. The children want to go out. It's very painful to see them crying.'

'One day my husband went out shopping when they started banging on the door with a wooden stave. I just sit at home, I'm scared to let the children out and I can't go out and see people.'

An example of 'scientific racism'

| Irish Iberian | Anglo teutonic | Negro |

The Iberians are believed to have been originally an African race, who thousands of years ago spread themselves through Spain over Western Europe. Their remains are found in the barrows, or burying places, in sundry parts of these countries. The skulls are of low, prognathous type. They came to Ireland, and mixed with the natives of the south and west, who themselves are supposed to have been of low type and descendants of savages of the Stone Age, who, in consequence of isolation from the rest of the world, had never been out-competed in the healthy struggle of life, and thus made way, according to the laws of nature, for superior races.

Note: Attempts to establish a biological basis of radical difference between the 'races' was a part of the late nineteenth early twentieth century intellectual climate of evolution. The above is an example of 'scientific racism'. Today 'cultural racism' is perhaps more common. However, attempts to establish radical differences between the races continue – as Charles Murray's The Bell Curve *(1995) shows.*

Figure 8.2 Example of racial stereotyping in the nineteenth century from the American magazine *Harper's Weekly*. Such categorisations were the absurd product of so-called 'scientific racism'.

material and status rewards for the former. Due partly to the efforts of President Nelson Mandela of the African National Congress and of Vice President de Klerk, apartheid has been formally abolished, but its effects will last a long time. In certain other countries, the lines of racial stratification are less sharply drawn than in South Africa but are still quite clear. In Britain and the United States, black minorities tend to hold low paid, low status jobs, to live in poor housing and to be less well-educated than the white majority.

The historical background of race relations

The roots of contemporary racial division lie in the expansion of European empires, particularly during the eighteenth and nineteenth centuries when these empires straddled the world. The British Empire extended to the Far East, but more significant from our point of view was the occupation of India, Pakistan, large parts

of Africa, and several islands in the West Indies. A key factor in laying the foundations for later racial conflict in Britain, the United States, and parts of Africa was the exploitation of Africans, especially West Africans. The major element in this exploitation was the slave trade. Slave traders, mainly from Britain, France, Spain and Portugal, bought and kidnapped Africans, and transported them to the southern United States and the West Indies, where they were sold to work on plantations. In the southern states, a social structure based on slave labour developed, which left a legacy of bitterness, bigotry and exploitation, even after the formal abolition of slavery in the United States in 1863.

Between the two world wars, Britain and other European imperial powers sought to hold down discontent in conquered territories. By the early 1960s, most British colonies had acquired independence, and already immigration into Britain from the former colonies had begun. The focus of conflict shifted from the struggle for independence in the colonies to problems associated with the settlement of black immigrants in Britain itself. As early as 1958, 'race riots' occurred in the Notting Hill area of London. After 1980, when Zimbabwe (formerly Rhodesia) became independent under majority rule, the only African country in which a minority of European extraction (in this case a large one) continued directly to dominate the black majority was South Africa.

The desire for economic gain is certainly a major motive for imperial expansion. The hope of acquiring political power and prestige, and of converting the conquered to, for example, Christianity or Marxism, are others. Economic realities clearly underlie much twentieth century racial conflict, the spread of racial conflict, in the United States is an example. From the late nineteenth century, there was a strong demand from northern industrialists for cheap, black labour from the south. Later, this demand also occurred on the west coast. As well as being cheap, black labour could be used to undermine the power of trade unions and to divide black and white working class people along racial lines. For their part, many black people were glad to leave the south, still darkened by the shadow of slavery, even though they encountered resentment and sometimes violence from the white working class in the urban areas of the north and west. In the mid 1960s, the big cities of the north and west USA were as torn by racial conflict and riots as the south.

The economic background of race relations (with particular reference to Britain)

Economic factors also provide the major explanation for the pattern of black immigration in Britain and, to some extent, for the 'panic' about immigration in the late 1960s and 1970s.

Migration can be explained in terms of 'push' and 'pull' factors. The 'push' factors refer to conditions in the country of origin, such as unemployment and poverty, which persuade people to leave; the 'pull' factor is the demand for labour in the country of immigration. The economic motive is considered by Peach and others to be the dynamic influence behind British post-war immigration. A major personal motive for migration is sometimes to rejoin family and kin.

Immigrants to Britain went mainly into unskilled and semi-skilled jobs in industrial production. This enabled more of the indigenous population to move up into the expanding service sector – a fact which, at first, certainly sweetened acceptance of immigration. Not all immigrants, however, started at the bottom of the social hierarchy. Many thousands of doctors and nurses from India, Pakistan and the West Indies were needed to support Britain's overstrained health system: even so, they tended to get the toughest and least prestigious posts, often in large metropolitan hospitals.

In some areas where a shortage of labour existed, active recruitment occurred. London Transport recruited drivers directly in the West Indies and the Health Service also advertised widely. Official figures show that, in 1965 alone, Britain took 1,015 doctors from India, 529 from Pakistan and 182 from other Commonwealth countries. The Health Service is a striking, though not unique example of Britain's dependence on the work of immigrants. In 1975, 35 per cent of hospital doctors and eighteen per cent of family doctors came from outside Britain.

It is useful to draw a parallel between migrant workers in Europe and British immigrants. In the post-war period, the expanding economies of Western Europe needed foreign labour to increase production. Those countries which had colonies or former colonies, such as Britain or France, first recruited labour from these. Other countries which were without colonies, particularly West Germany, Luxembourg and Switzerland, had to recruit from elsewhere. They did so mainly from the poorer, less-industrialised countries of Eastern and Southern Europe – Greece, Turkey, Yugoslavia, Italy, Spain and Portugal. In 1974 it was estimated that 15 million immigrant or migrant workers and their families were living in Western Europe.

Table 8.3 Im/migrant labour in Western Europe: 1974

Countries	Im/migrant workers in the labour force Percentages
Luxembourg	35
Switzerland	25
France	11
Germany	10
UK	7
Belgium	7
Denmark	2
Netherlands	3

(Source: *EEC Report*, 1974)

These workers were overwhelmingly concentrated in low paid jobs with unpleasant and sometimes quite dangerous conditions (such as asbestos processing) and long hours (like the restaurant trade). They were also particularly vulnerable to redundancy during recession.

A vital difference, however, exists between Britain's immigrants and migrant workers in some other European countries. Immigrants to Britain who were Commonwealth citizens had a right to settle here with their families and to exercise full civil and political liberties, including voting. Most came believing that they would receive fair and equal treatment with white citizens. For many, these hopes have not been fulfilled.

The practice of using migrant labour has increased globally in recent years. The poorer countries of the far and middle east can gain valuable export income by exporting workers. In 1991 Bangladesh earned 71 per cent of its export earnings in this way. Britain itself receives thousands of such workers – especially from the Philippines and their rights and conditions of work have become a serious issue.

Ethnic nationalism and internationalism and the decline of communism

In modern history and contemporary society, ethnic groups concentrated in particular geographical areas often perceive themselves as 'nations' (see Figures 8.3 and 8.4). For instance, a strong sense of religious and cultural identity fed the development of nationhood in Ireland (Eire) as did centuries of subjugation to

Figure 8.3 Ethnic nationalism was a major force in breaking up the Soviet Union

England. To take another example, a widespread stirring of ethnic nationalism occurred throughout the Soviet Empire both before and after the collapse of Soviet communism (see Figures 8.3 and 8.4). Estonia, Latvia and Lithuania were the first Soviet republics to declare independent nationhood in 1991. The other republics of the Soviet Union became sovereign and independent following the failed communist 'coup'. Some joined a new voluntary federation but others remain reluctant. Tension exists between some of the states, including Christian Armenia and Muslim Azerbaijan. The area most affected by ethnic tension following the sharp decline of the Soviet Empire has been the former Yugoslavia, where Muslims, Serbs and Croats entered upon a bloody civil war.

The spread of liberal free market and democratic ideals within the former Soviet Empire has had a destabilising as well as an invigorating effect. Now that the grip of Soviet totalitarianism has been removed, regions and states are freer to express their sometimes substantial differences and disagreements. Ironically, Marxists have long argued that when the masses reject socialism, they frequently turn to nationalism. In the case of stronger states, nationalism can take the form of assertiveness internationally and/or imperialism.

Internationally, the most expansionist ethnic movement in the past two decades has been Islam. For many people in poorer parts of the world, Islam has replaced Marxism as a focus of identity and source of hope. However, Islam does not always coexist easily with Western liberalism – the other ideological success story of the post-war era. The Rushdie matter and the Gulf War have sharply and tragically demonstrated the massive potential for conflict between these two ideologies (see p. 542).

There are some signs that international solutions are being increasingly sought to ethnic conflict and national aggression. The Western European nations exercised a major role in the ethnic conflict in former Yugoslavia. Iraq was defeated by an alliance authorised by the United Nations albeit one dominated by the United States. Communism itself was touted by its adherents as an ideology of international solidarity which would transcend and make redundant 'petty' ethnic and national conflicts. It failed to do this. However, the collapse of communism has left a power vacuum which is likely to require a strong, benign and constructive internationalism to achieve greater global peace and justice. These issues are further discussed in Chapter 20.

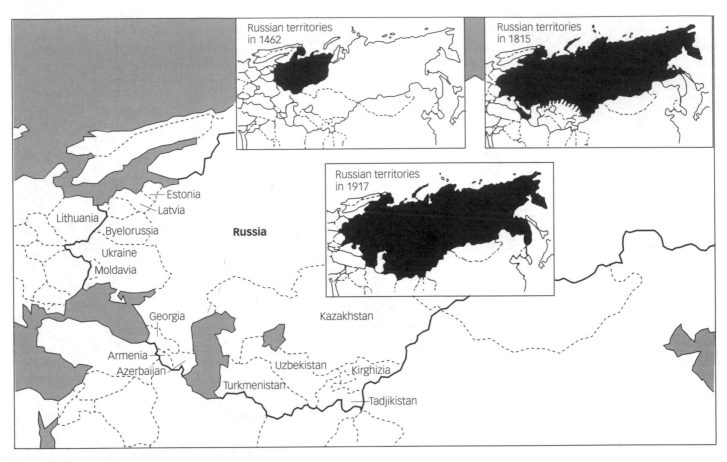

(Source: *The Times*)

Figure 8.4 The states of the former Soviet Union

'Race' and ethnicity in employment

This section will first present the facts – as provided by official surveys – about the occupational distribution of various groups, particularly black ones. It will then examine a number of explanations why minority ethnic people *tend* to occupy lower positions in the occupational hierarchy than white people. We will then briefly examine the distribution of housing in a similar context.

In general, different ethnic groups will be referred to by specific title in this section. However, in contexts in which racism and anti-racism is being discussed, the term black will occasionally be used to indicate people of both African and Asian descent and sometimes by extension all non-whites.

Self-employed as a percentage of all in employment and by ethnic origin

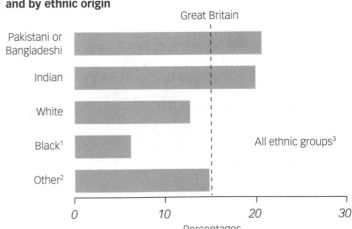

1 *Includes Caribbean, African and other black people of non-mixed origin.*
2 *Includes Chinese, other ethnic minority groups of non-mixed origin, and people of mixed origin.*
3 *Includes ethnic group not stated.*

(Source: Employment Department in *Social Trends,* 1994:59)

Figure 8.5 Broad occupation groups by ethnic origin

Table 8.4 Job levels of male employees by ethnic group, 1988-1990

	All origins	White	Total ethnic minority	Afro-Carib-bean	African Asian	Indian	Pakistani	Bangla-deshi	Chinese	African	Other mixed
					Column percentages						
Prof./Manager/ Employer	27	27	21	12	27	25	12	12	30	21	30
Employees & Managers – large establishments	13	13	7	5	6	9	4	1	7	9	11
Employees & Managers – small establishments	7	7	5	3	10	5	4	5	10	3	7
Professional workers – employees	7	7	8	4	11	10	4	6	14	9	12
Other non-manual	20	20	22	19	30	18	16	14	19	34	31
Skilled manual & Foremen	32	33	28	39	26	29	34	5	10	20	18
Semi-skilled manual	15	15	23	23	13	24	31	65	36	18	16
Unskilled manual	4	4	5	6	3	4	6	5	4	4	2
Armed Services/ inadequately described/not stated	1	1	1	1	0	0	1	0	1	3	3

(Source: Jones, 1995:99)

Data on employment by ethnic origin

The data provided in Figure 8.5 give the occupational pattern for different ethnic groups (based on employed people of sixteen and over).

Tables 8.4 and 8.5 separately show job levels of male and female employees by ethnic group. The data comes from Trevor Jones' re-analysis of the Labour Force Survey for 1988, 1989 and 1990 (1995). Jones' re-analysis shows up better than the original LFS data both the extent of inequalities between certain groups and the sometimes considerable occupational distribution differences between ethnic groups. Nevertheless, the occupational inequality between whites and others, especially males is greater than the raw data in Tables 8.4 and 8.5 indicate – for reasons discussed below. We will comment first on male job levels. First, certain minority groups are significantly under-represented in non-manual employment. Only about a third of Afro-Caribbean males are in non-manual occupations with the 'shortfall' being particularly marked in the area of professional and managerial employment.

Similarly, only about a third of Pakistani and Bangladeshi males are in non-manual employment. These two groupings together make up about 60 per cent of black minority males in employment and a large majority of them are in manual employment, much of it low paid and low status. A considerably larger percentage of black minority than white employees are concentrated in the retail and hotels and catering sectors. In contrast, a similar percentage of Indians as white employees are in non-manual employment.

Tariq Modood has attempted to explain the 'Indian economic success' (1991). According to Modood's figures (which are slightly different from Jones') 27 per cent of Indian men are in self-employment and fifteen per cent in other non-manual categories, whereas for white men, the proportion in self-employment is only fifteen per cent. Modood rejects the view that Indian self-employment is largely in 'dead-end shops', arguing 'a distribution of success at all levels'. Community and family self-help and commitment to education are factors Modood cites to explain Indian success. One can also add that the relatively large number of Indians of middle class origin may contribute (see p. 222).

Table 8.5 Job levels of female employees by ethnic group, 1988-1990

	All origins	White	Total ethnic minority	Afro-Carib-bean	African Asian	Indian	Pakistani	Bangla-deshi	Chinese	African	Other mixed
					Column percentages						
Prof./Manager/Employer	11	11	9	8	7	10	4	*	16	11	12
Employees & Managers – large establishments	6	6	4	5	3	4	1	*	4	5	4
Employees & Managers – small establishments	4	4	3	2	2	2	3	*	5	3	4
Professional workers – employees	2	2	2	1	2	4	0	*	7	2	3
Other non-manual	55	56	53	54	58	47	42	*	53	47	63
Skilled manual & Foremen	5	5	5	4	9	5	7	*	2	6	3
Semi-skilled manual	22	22	27	25	25	34	45	*	20	32	17
Unskilled manual	7	7	5	9	1	4	2	*	9	4	5
Armed Services/inadequately described/not stated	0	0	0	0	0	0	0	*	0	1	0

Sample size too small

(Source: Jones, 1995:99)

However, Modood acknowledges that Indians are under-represented in some professions and concedes that the 'success hypothesis' is not fully proven (Reading 1).

A second point to be borne in mind when interpreting minority employment patterns is that within occupations minority males (especially) and females tend to receive lower wages. Table 8.6 shows that members of foreign born minorities receive lower wages than whites, other things, such as qualifications, being equal (Labour Force Survey, 1996). The situation is little different for non-foreign born members of the same minorities (i.e. the second and third generations).

Table 8.6 White earnings advantage over foreign born minorities

	Males	Females
	Percentages	
Black Caribbean	15.3	17.8
Black African	34.9	17.8
Black Other	9.5	19.1
Indian	21.7	14.5
Pakistani	29.6	13.6
Bangladeshi	62.4	21.7
Chinese	20.1	6.8
Other Asian	25.9	18.7
Other	17.0	13.8

Note: Black Other refers mainly to people who describe themselves as British. Other refers mainly to North African, Arab, Iranian or of mixed origin.

(Source: D Leslie, *The Guardian*, 24.8.1996)

Thirdly, as Figure 8.6 shows, unemployment is higher among black minority males than among white males. Whereas white male unemployment is given at nine per cent, Pakistani/Bangladeshi male unemployment is 25 per cent, and West Indian/Guyanese eighteen per cent. These differences are substantial and represent one of the major areas of inequality between ethnic groups. It is particularly young males in the above groups that are likely to be unemployed – with potentially disastrous effects.

Around two-thirds of all employed women are in non-manual occupations in the case of both white and minority women. However, economic activity rates vary greatly among women of different ethnic groups. They are highest for women of West Indian origin at 76 per cent and lowest for those of Pakistani or Bangladeshi origin at 28.6 and 22.0 per cent respectively (although it is possible that the Labour Force Surveys under-represent the latter group by failing to reach many homeworkers – see p. 202). Although there are some differences in the pattern of employment between white and minority women – notably, more of the latter being employed in health services and parts of manufacturing, the Labour Force Survey finds that the overall pattern of employment between the two groups is very similar. Chinese women, however are somewhat over-represented in the professional etc. category and under-represented in the skilled manual..

Further, Indian, Pakistani and West Indian women's wages are a higher percentage of black men's wages than are white women's wages of white men's. Contrary also to stereotype the formal qualifications of women of West Indian origin (though not those of Pakistani/Bangladeshi origin) are on a par with those of white women.

Great Britain
Economically active persons of working age
Average: Spring 1987, 1988, 1989

Percentage

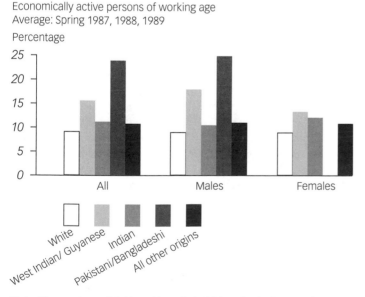

Note: The numbers of Pakistani/Bangladeshi females in the sample were too small to be considered significant.

(Source: LFS estimates, in *Employment Gazette*, February 1991:67)

Figure 8.6 Unemployment rates by ethnic origin and sex

Un/employment and black minorities: a summary

1 *Area of settlement*

Continuing concentration in industrial regions and in areas of original settlement.

2 *Unemployment*

Substantially higher unemployment for all ethnic minorities than for Whites in all regions and areas;

Substantial inter-ethnic difference: Indians best placed, followed by West Indians, the Pakistanis and Bangladeshis.

3 *Level of employment*

No clear, overall white:ethnic minority differences;

Indians and Whites more concentrated in higher level positions; West Indians, Pakistanis and Bangladeshis in lower level positions.

4 *Gender differences*

i Unemployment: Men better off among Indians, Pakistanis and Bangladeshis, women better off among West Indians.

ii Area of settlement: Indian women worst off in dispersed locations, no difference among Whites and West Indians.

iii Level of employment: Female employment levels more closely matched across ethnic minority groups; highest concentration of *male* higher level positions among Indians, of *female* higher level positions among Pakistanis and Bangladeshis; no substantial gender difference in employment level of Indians/Whites, but among West Indians and Pakistanis/Bangladeshis employment level of men is substantially lower than among women.

(Source: R Ward and M Cross in P Cohen; 1991:124)

Despite the above considerations, Irene Breugel has argued that 'in terms of the *total employment package*, minority women can be seen to be considerably worse off than white women' (Breugel, 1986). She points out that minority women work longer hours in both full-time and part-time work, that they are concentrated in London (where wages are higher but so is the cost of living); and that their younger 'and hence better qualified profile' has not yet fully resulted in the corresponding rewards. Black women earn less per hour on average than white women and black women graduates earn 71 per cent of what white women graduates earn. Both black women and men are much more likely than white people to be overqualified for the job they are doing: twenty per cent in both cases, compared to ten per cent of white women and one per cent of white men. Breugel suggests that the 'over qualification phenomenon' is probably due to racism. A Warwick University study based on answers given in the 1991 census supports Breugel's analysis. Experienced and skilled minority ethnic women were found to be twice as likely to be unemployed as comparable white women and to work longer hours when in work. It is to the issue of racial discrimination in the labour market that we now turn.

Explanations of the position of minority ethnic groups in the employment market

There are few, if any, more important preconditions of a racially harmonious and tolerant society than fairness and justice in employment. There are various explanations of the continuing substantial inequalities experienced by black minorities in the employment market and in employment. Some of these explanations overlap, but they are distinct enough to require separate analysis. The explanations examined below are:

- Ethnic Adjustment (Liberal Perspective);
- Racism and the Dual Labour Market: A Black Underclass;
- Marxist Perspectives
  i   Reserve Army of Labour: Castle and Kosack
  ii Class Fraction: Robert Miles
- Marxist feminist and Black feminist interpretations.

Before evaluating these explanation, however, it will be helpful to examine some empirical evidence of racism in the employment market.

Evidence of racism in the employment market

The most convincing evidence that extensive racial discrimination occurs in the employment market, comes from the research of the Policy Studies Institute (formerly Political and Economic Planning – PEP). There have been three major PSI studies of this issue – in 1973-74, 1977-79, and 1984-85. The method adopted by the PSI team was for black and white 'candidates' (some were actors) to apply for specific jobs. The candidates were precisely matched in qualifications, experience and other relevant criteria. A substantially larger percentage of white candidates received positive responses and roughly the same percentage of black people were discriminated against throughout the studies. In 1973-74, 27 per cent of West Indians and 28 per cent of Asians were discriminated against and in 1984-85, the percentages were 27 per cent and 27 per cent respectively. The 1984-85 report notes that a reason for the persistence of discrimination is the extreme unlikelihood of proving that it has occurred.

M Noon reports on a somewhat similar more recent piece of research (1993). Two fictitious job applicants – Evans and Patel – sent letters to the personnel managers of the top 100 British companies. The applicants were profiled as in the final year of their Masters in Business Administration and as having had relevant experience. Overall, white candidates received more help and

encouragement. Although companies with equal opportunities statements in their annual reports were somewhat more likely to treat candidates equally than those without, 48 of the former still failed to do so.

A very different and less formal piece of research – a piece of television journalism (*Black and White*) – also demonstrated high levels of discrimination in the employment market and other areas. Geoff Small, a black journalist, and Tim Marshall, a white journalist, tested the extent of racism in various situations by each approaching, in turn, for example, an employer or landlord as applicants for an advertised job or room. Small appeared to be discriminated against on numerous occasions including four out of ten occasions when applying for a job (the figure for bed and breakfast was five out of fifteen).

The following section presents more theoretical interpretation of the position of black minorities in the employment market each perspective addressing the issue of racism differently.

Ethnic adjustment (liberal perspective)

When the first post-war black immigrants came to Britain, it was a commonly expressed view, especially among more liberal politicians, that as the new immigrants adjusted to British life, increasing numbers would move up the occupational hierarchy. It was assumed that language, educational and cultural adjustment problems experienced by the first generation which affected their position in the labour market would less strongly affect their children and grandchildren. Even when it became clear that white racism might impede black advancement, optimists felt that a continuation of anti-discrimination legislation and immigration control would secure generally fair conditions for black Britons.

The ethnic adjustment perspective is derived partly from the experience of immigrant groups in the United States. Each wave of ethnic immigrants into the United States took its place in turn on the bottom of the ladder and began to clamber up – sometimes on the shoulders of the next incoming group. The British, Italians and Eastern Europeans have all done this. A version of the same process has happened to black Americans who have edged significantly beyond the Hispanic elements (those of mainly Mexican and Puerto Rican origin) in the population. A problem in applying this model to black Britons is that no further large wave of immigrants is likely to replace them on the bottom rung of society's ladder. Nevertheless, those who take the ethnic adjustment perspective are able to point to some black progress in employment and housing to support their view.

Racism and dual labour market theory: a black underclass?

We have already discussed dual labour market theory in relation to female labour and, more generally, in the context of 'post-Fordism'. The essence of the theory is that there are two labour markets, the primary and secondary. The first recruits to well-paid, secure and more crucial jobs and the latter to generally less well paid, less secure and perhaps occasional jobs. John Rex and Sally Tomlinson have argued that black employees are substantially more likely than white employees to be in the secondary labour market. The following is an extract from their mid 1970s study of Handsworth, Birmingham, *Colonial Immigrants in a British City: A Class Analysis*:

> *In Handsworth it is fair to say that about half of the non-white population are employed in semi-skilled and unskilled manual work and less than ten per cent in white-collar jobs, whereas only about a quarter of whites are in the low-skill groups and a third in white-collar jobs. That already suggests a considerable difference despite the overlap. If one then looks at industrial and occupational differences, one finds that the West Indian and Asian populations are more concentrated in labouring jobs and in hot and dirty industries, and are poorly represented in professional, scientific and administrative jobs. Both West Indian and Asian workers had to work extra hours to earn the same as white British workers, and were also more likely to be on shift work ...*
>
> *These figures may not confirm that there is a completely dual labour market situation with whites gaining internal appointments and promotions in protected jobs and the immigrants getting what jobs they can in the open market. But they are consistent with the notion of two kinds of job situations with whites predominant in one and blacks in the other. In fact, the degree of apparent overlap may be deceptive and case studies of actual employment might well show that in each industrial, occupational, skill and social class category, the actual job situation of the black is less desirable and secure than that of the white ...*
>
> *(Rex and Tomlinson, 1979:279)*

Rex has gone on to argue that due mainly to racism, black disadvantage and segregation in employment (and housing see p. 559) is such that a black underclass has been created in Britain. He felt strengthened in his analysis when often irregularly employed black youths prominently participated in the urban disorders of 1981 and 1985. Nevertheless, many commentators, both liberal and Marxist, have argued that Rex over-interprets the evidence in developing dual labour market/underclass theory. Indeed, in the above passage, there is some degree of tentativeness about whether black employees are fully in a dual labour market situation. If there were a degree of overlap between the situation of black and white employees in the late 1970s, the Labour Force Surveys of the late 1980s suggest considerably more (see pp. 225-6). More recently, Rex has accommodated his analysis of 'race' and class better to express the upward social mobility of some black people. Upward mobility does occur but is limited in scale and extent by racism. Figure 8.7 attempts to illustrate this in diagrammatic form. (For a fuller account of black underclass theory, see pp. 388-93).

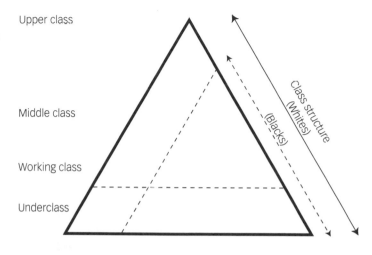

Note: The model indicates class hierarchy but it is not to numerical scale.

Figure 8.7 A model of John Rex's analysis of the effect of racism on the class structure

Marxist perspectives on the employment of minorities

Castles and Kosack give an analysis of black immigrants into Britain in which their situation is seen as essentially similar to that of migrant workers in Western Europe (*Immigrant Workers and Class Structure in Western Europe* (Oxford University Press, 1973)). Both immigrant and migrant workers are seen as part of the working class but as a particularly disadvantaged group or 'bottom stratum' within it. They function as 'a reserve army' of labour which can be drawn on during periods of capitalist expansion and relatively easily laid off during periods of contraction.

Castles and Kosack argue that the use of black immigrant labour provides a further advantage to the capitalist class in addition to flexibility – its presence divides the working class by allowing indigenous workers to move into employment with better pay and conditions from which they typically seek to exclude the 'newcomers'. They stress the deep and stubborn nature of this division and argue that:

> *it can only disappear when it is supplanted not merely by a correct understanding of the position of immigrant workers, but by a class consciousness which reflects the true position of all workers in society.*
>
> *(Castles and Kosack, 1973:482)*

Robert Miles also regards class stratification as more fundamental than 'racial' or ethnic division but recognises that due partly to racism, the British working class is 'fractionalised' i.e. divided within and, in his view, against itself. Miles further makes the point that black people are by no means all in the working class or, as he puts it, they occupy 'all the main economic sites in the relations of production' (Miles, 1989: 121). He points out that there is 'a small, but increasing, Asian and Caribbean petit bourgeoisie'; that they represent a significant part of the 'surplus population' (i.e. unemployed); and that there are significant differences between black workers, not least, according to sex and nationality'.

On the basis of the above observations, Miles specifically discusses underclass theory:

> The view that Asian and Caribbean people in Britain collectively constitute a 'black' underclass, a collectivity homogenous in its poverty and economic disadvantage relative to 'white' people as a result of racism and systematic exclusionary practices, is therefore mistaken.
>
> (Miles, 1989:123)

However, he does recognise that 'the economic position occupied by a large proportion of Asian and Caribbean people is inferior to that of the indigenous population'. Racism plays a part in producing an inferior class situation for many black people but it does not, as Rex contends, create a black underclass.

A new phase in migrant labour exploitation

Sivanandan (1988) and Cohen (1991) see a new phase in racism in capitalist Western Europe. The issue of colour has partly subsided as migrants, refugees and asylum seekers from as far afield as Chile and Iran find their way into Western Europe. Often they work in the hotel or catering trades or as contract cleaners in hospitals and airports etc. Cohen argues that there are now three categories of immigrant and migrant workers: citizens – who are now relatively advantaged (e.g. second generation black immigrants); denizens (of recognised but insecure status); and helots (largely illegal (see Reading 2)). Asylum seekers are a significant and recently growing proportion of the third group – helots. They are virtually unemployable while they are waiting for their status to be decided and in certain cases their access to social security was made more difficult in 1996.

Marxist-feminist and black-feminist interpretations

Marxist-feminists tend to argue that the position of white and black women in the labour market is much more similar than that of white and black men. For instance, there is less difference between white and black women in terms of earnings and job levels. Sheila Allen suggests that this is because the exploitation both white and black women experience as women leaves limited scope for black women to be still further exploited as black:

> The position of black women in the labour market can be understood only by relating it to women more generally. Briefly the sexual division of labour segregates women into very few industrial sectors and within these they are usually in the lower segments of occupational hierarchies. They are in the main found in service industries, in jobs designated as semi-skilled, and they earn less than men. In the professions, they either constitute a very small percentage relative to men, for instance in law, medicine or university teaching, or where they are a higher percentage, such as in school-teaching, they are found disproportionately in the lower grades. A suggested explanation of the similarity between the wages of black and white women which was reported in 1974, was 'that the enormous disparity between men and women ... left little scope for racial disadvantage to have a further, additive effect'.
>
> (Brown, 1984:169. From Allen, in C Husband, 1987:182)

As we have already seen, Irene Breugel illustrates a degree of inequality in employment between black and white women (see p. 227). Hazel Carby puts the matter in broader historical context by arguing that British employers have been inclined to view black women as more 'normally' in paid work than white women. While black and white women are part of a reserve army of labour, black women are more routinely and frequently exploited.

Black minorities, the employment market and stratification

Table 8.7 links explanations of the position of black people in the employment market with parallel theories of how they are stratified in the social structure. Table 8.7 is intended to clarify the stratificational aspects of the particular perspectives.

Table 8.7 Perspectives on the relationship between occupation and stratification

Source	Labour market theory	Main causal factor	Type of stratification
Liberal/ Social Democrat	Equal opportunity – but initial difficulties	Adjustment problems	Pluralist
Weber John Rex	Dual labour market	Racism	Black underclass
Marxist	(Part of) reserve army of labour	Class exploitation	Class-fractionalised by racism. Emergent black middle class

It can be debated whether the differences between John Rex and Robert Miles are as sharp as Miles himself presents. Putting it simply Rex is saying that due to racism the situation of black people within the class structure tends to be worse than that of white people to the extent that the majority of black people form an underclass in danger of becoming separated from the rest of the working class. Miles argues that while black people are increasingly distributed throughout the class structure, the majority are working class and their situation is further disadvantaged by racism. Both Rex and Miles are much more pessimistic about the effects of racism than liberals who incline to the view that ultimately the class profile of black minorities will not be greatly different from the national class profile.

Perhaps the main point on which Rex and American underclass theorist, Douglas Glasgow (1981), differ from Miles is the extent to which they consider black people, particularly young black people, to be cut off from upward social mobility by racism. This tends to make the black underclass intergenerational. Although a higher percentage of black workers are members of trade unions than white workers, Rex argues that the trade union movement has done little to promote the cause of black people or black workers within it. He finds it unsurprising, then, that given little assistance from dominant 'white' institutions and often victimised by racism, a number of black people, including younger ones, have turned inwards toward their own ethnic communities. This process can take many forms, including family self-help in business, ethnic politics, and a less organised 'dropping out of the system'.

Questions

1 With particular application to Britain, critically discuss major theories of racism and 'racial' stratification.
2 What evidence is there of racial discrimination in employment?
3 Account for the positions of various ethnic groups in the occupational and stratification structures.

Minority and majority culture and class

The debate about the relative effect of class and racial/ethnic factors on forming the lives of black minorities will now be briefly examined in the context of majority and minority cultures. This will prepare the way for a later discussion on politics, class and ethnicity. First, however, it is necessary to describe the possible range of adaptation/rejection that a minority group might experience in relation to the majority culture. This process is a two-way one involving members of both a given minority and of the majority. In this sense, it is a negotiated process, although power and coercion may be involved.

The possible relationships between a minority and majority can be presented in the form of the following model which should be regarded as indicating points in a continuum.

A much fuller use of a similar model was made in Chapter 7 in the analysis of Afro-Caribbean gender relations (see pp. 207-9). Here only an abbreviated version is given.

Possible Relationships between Minority Ethnic and Majority Cultures:
Accommodation   Assimilation   Resistance
Pluralism   Separatism

Accommodation is simply trying to work with the institutions and culture of the majority without surrendering one's own ethnic identity.

The assimilation of a minority occurs when it becomes fully absorbed into a majority culture. Thus, the descendants of French Huguenots (who fled from persecution to Britain) now appear to have little or no distinct ethnic identity. Ethnic pluralism occurs when a minority group retains its own customs and identity but also fully participates in the 'mainstream' life of a society. For instance, Jews frequently maintain their own religious and cultural practices while playing a full part in 'mainstream' society's economic, political and social life. Resistance to the majority or dominant culture and its institutions can occur when the majority and a minority fail to accommodate each other. Resistance theorists argue that resistance can occur at the level of culture or lifestyle as well as through political action. Total minority separatism is virtually impossible in highly inter-connected modern societies. Certain groups of Asian origin, particularly Bangladeshis, appear to fall between pluralism and separatism, on the model. Whole groups may have few English speakers and participate relatively little in life outside their own families and ethnic community.

There are some problems with the above model, as applying it to Britain makes clear. Can we usefully use the concept of 'British culture' (or 'English culture') as a basis for analysis. What is it? Does it change over time? If so, are there parts that remain stable and perhaps fundamental and parts that change? It would take too long a detour adequately to answer these questions here. What can be said is that culture as a sociological concept refers to 'a way of life' and that this is expressed in a group's norms, customs and values, and in its language and shared experience (history). In this way, and obviously at a high level of generality, it may be possible to refer to British or German or other national cultures in which the majority of members of these societies participate. Minority groups emigrating or migrating to a society interact with it both adapting to and, to a greater or lesser extent, changing the majority culture. It is not only ethnic groups that form subcultures within a majority culture but also regional, class and other subgroups.

Perspectives on minority/majority relations

The following perspectives on minority/majority group relations are as much ideological as sociological. Issues of 'race', ethnicity and nationality can be highly fraught with emotion and subjectivity.

Assimilationist

The assimilationist view is that incoming ethnic minorities should fully conform in major public areas to what they take to be the established British way of life. This approach is particularly associated with the New Right (i.e. the right-wing of what used to be referred to as 'Thatcherism'). Thus, Roger Scruton argues that the prime purpose of education in Britain is to facilitate the participation of the individual in British culture and that 'there can be no real argument for a *multi-cultural* curriculum' (Scruton, 1986). Similarly, assimilationists do not consider that other institutional areas of British society should adapt to minority groups but contend that the latter should do the adapting. However, perhaps few would insist on assimilation in the area of private life and personal taste. Norman Tebbitt is an exception. His 'cricket test' was that a true 'English' person would support the English cricket team rather than, say, the West Indies.

Liberal-pluralist

The pluralist or liberal-pluralist view is that a variety of cultural groups can and do exist in Britain within a common legal and democratic framework. Again, this approach can be illustrated in the area of education where liberal-pluralists argue that the curriculum ought fully to reflect the multicultural nature of contemporary Britain while also educating in basic skills and fundamental values. Pluralists also consider that in other institutional areas of British life, such as the welfare state and social services, accommodation to and awareness of specific cultural needs is desirable.

Marxist (resistance theory)

Marxists argue that ethnic culture is of secondary importance to class culture. They use the concepts of dominant and subordinate class cultures rather than those of majority and minority cultures. Writing about the notion of a majority culture, Charles Husband has argued that 'there is no single monolithic ideology' of nation 'shared by all Britons' but the people have varying 'images' of Britain which do 'not necessarily have the same range of meaning' (Husband, 1982). Thus, for some, British Imperial history embodies the essence of British 'greatness' whereas for others it may seem a national disgrace. Further, Marxists contend that ethnic and nationalistic identification tends to be reactionary and to create a false unity among groups who, at a deeper level, are divided by social class.

Marxists and neo-Marxists are primarily responsible for developing the concept of resistance and applying it to black youth.

Anti-racist

The anti-racist perspective has already been explained in the context of education (see pp. 119-20). It is based on the analysis that people of Asian and African descent have been the victims of common economic and, relatedly, 'racial' exploitation. The term 'black' is used of both groups to describe this common experience. As the linking of economic/class and 'racial' issues suggests, anti-racist perspective is particularly associated with Marxists and socialists but the term is adopted by many others as well.

New ethnicities?

While remaining steadfastly anti-racist, a number of social scientists, some of minority ethnic background, have begun to question the appropriateness of the term 'black' to describe so different and various a range of peoples as those of African and Asian extraction. We will shortly discuss this matter and the lively debate that has surrounded it.

Underclass

John Rex's analysis that a black underclass may have emerged in Britain, has an application to culture. A group that is racially and economically oppressed is likely to have a common awareness and resentment of its oppression and to develop a culture that reflects this. This is particularly true of young unemployed or irregularly employed Afro-Caribbeans whose music, religion (i.e. in the case of Rastafarians), and politics often express an opposition to racism. As Rex has noted, during the 1980s (and early 1990s) there was also evidence of increased militancy against racism among young Asians.

A full analysis of 'black' underclass theory, including conservative interpretations of it, is given later.

Identity, culture and class: a black and white issue?

Labels and identity

People are frequently prepared to die for the right to define their own identity – to label themselves. Millions have died rather than surrender their religious, political or cultural identities. Christianity, liberalism, Judaism and Islam – all have their martyrs.

The term 'black' arose as a sign of identity – particularly of solidarity among 'black' people. To understand its meaning and the fact that its use has become somewhat controversial, requires a brief historical excursion.

Five phases of Afro-Caribbean/American identity

Identity	Period
Self-Defined (Traditional in Western Terms)	Pre-Western contact
Negro/Slave/Coloured (Imposed by the West) Serious discussion among white intellectuals about whether black people are human …	Mid sixteenth to mid nineteenth
'Freed Slaves'/Wage Labourers	Mid nineteenth to mid twentieth
Black People – Self Defined by American and British people of African descent. Applied to/Accepted by some people of Asian descent.	Mid 1960s to 1990s
Hyphenated Identities? Multiple Identities? New Ethnicities? Beyond Black?/As well as Black? What Identities?	Late 1980s/ 1990s

Fig 8.8 An early demonstration of black power: the USA 4 x 400m gold medal-winning team at the 1968 Olympic Games in Mexico City

The above figure is self-explanatory but two key points of tension in the change and development of 'black' identity need to be noted as far as this discussion is concerned. The first is the radical break in 1960s when a large number of people of African descent asserted their own positive description of themselves. Increasingly, the description 'black' became applied to and accepted by people of

Asian as well as African descent and other non-whites. Undoubtedly, much damage was done to black people's self-esteem in the slavery/colonial period and after, but from the 1960s there has been no shortage of confidence and assertion. It is important to note that use of the word 'black' derives its meaning not from the colour black in itself. The colour black was a symbol adopted to challenge 'white' assumptions of superiority and power. Of course, in so far as one reference for black is 'black' skin, the word also had an obvious physical relevance. Similarly, the use of the word 'white' did not imply that black people necessarily opposed or blamed all white people. Much of the ideology of the black liberation movement focused on capitalist exploitation and differentiated, for instance, between upper and working class racism.

The Meaning of 'Black'

Why Black?

1 It challenges and reverses the white defined/dominated symbolic order.

White definitions of black	Black definitions of black
Black is stereotyped/labelled	
Ugly	is beautiful
Inferior *becomes*	is power(ful)
Stupid	is gifted

2 It provides a simple and unifying slogan.

3 It plays an ideological role in an emerging political/social movement – black liberation movement.

Question

Why then? i.e. why did 'black' emerge as the preferred description in the 1960s?

The second point of tension to note in the development of the identity (or identities) of people of African and Asian descent is the questioning from the late 1980s of the appropriateness of the use of the term black to describe people of Asian as well as of African descent and even whether the term was the best description of the latter.

Of course, the use of the term black to describe a wide range of groups has never precluded using more specific terms – such as British-Indian, British Asian Muslim, British Barbadian – to describe other aspects of minority identity. However, some critics now want to scrap the use of the word 'black' altogether to describe certain groups (T Modood). Others, while retaining the use of the term black in the context of anti-racism, seem to be *substantially* moving toward a much more differentiated analysis of minority ethnic groups – which some see as a threat to black solidarity.

The next section examines a strong challenge by a British-Indian academic to the use of the term black to describe British Indians and the following section examines its appropriateness in relation to British people of African descent.

Tariq Modood: why Asians should not be called 'black'

In his article, *Political Blackness and British Asians*, Tariq Modood makes seven distinct points arguing that the term 'black' is not an appropriate description of British Asians (*Sociology*, 1994). These are summarised in the following:

Seven reasons why Asians should not be called black: Tariq Modood

1 *Doublespeak*

The term is used inconsistently – sometimes meaning 'blacks' (i.e. people of African descent)/sometimes 'blacks and Asians'.

2 *Too narrow a view of racial discrimination*

Racial discrimination occurs on other grounds than colour, e.g. culture. Asians and Africans can be racist against each other.

3 *A false essentialism*

Non-whites do not have an essential commonality.

4 *'Black' obscures Asian needs and distorts analysis*

'Black' is powerfully evocative of people of African origins'.

5 *A too politicised identity*

The term has 'historical depth' and 'cultural texture' for African-Caribbean's but not for Asians … who, anyway, have diverse identities.

6 *Not conducive to ethnic pride*

Based on 'how *others* treat oneself' Asian group *pride* is needed.

7 *The coerciveness of the advocates of 'black'*

Evidence suggests most Asians don't accept the term …

Some of the summarised points require further comment. Modood's second point that racism occurs on other grounds than colour would be accepted by most anti-racists and others who use the term black. As explained above, and as Modood is otherwise aware, the use of the term black is primarily symbolic.

Modood's third point that non-whites do not have an essential commonality is crucial. Much of his writings have illustrated the many differences between British Indians, other minorities and British whites. Undoubtedly, difference matters and its importance is increasingly being acknowledged by others as well as Modood. However, there is one central experience which, collectively, 'black' people have suffered. That is white racism – on an historical and structural scale that dwarfs perhaps any other manifestation of racism except Nazism. For many, that still constitutes an argument for using the term 'black' in the context of racism/anti-racism.

Modood's fourth to sixth points inclusive develop his view that while the term 'black' has real historical meaning and serves as a power identifier for people of African origin, it does not have the same resonance for Asians. His argument is that the source of Asian group pride lies elsewhere – within Asian cultural, communal and economic achievement

Finally, Modood makes what is really a double argument: that 'most' Asians do not accept the term 'black'; and that sometimes they are unduly pressured ('coerced') to accept it. On the latter point, to the extent that coercion occurs, it should stop. In an open society 'coercing' people to accept given positions or identities is unacceptable although legitimate persuasion is of course, acceptable. Modood cites only limited evidence that 'most' Asians do not accept the term 'black' (perhaps about 70%). It may be the more politically aware and active that do accept it but the extent of their influence among the majority of British Asians may be limited.

Modood's arguments indicate the extent of difference between ethnic groups of Asian and African descent. However, there are also great differences within these two large groupings. For instance, a degree of rivalry occurs between some British Africans and some British Afro-Caribbeans. There are also immense differences within those two groups as there are within various Asian ethnic groups. It is to a classic study of British Afro-Caribbeans, mainly of Jamaican extraction that we now turn in order to illustrate the latter point.

Why has the term 'black' become questioned?

The limits/decline? of black collective identity: Summary

1 Differences *between* black ethnic groups became more apparent … religious/cultural/economic.
2 Differences *within* ethnic groups became more apparent and some increased.
3 The radical climate of the 1960s has passed.
4 The growing cultural emphasis (postmodern) on choice and individuality may have weakened collective frames of identity.

'Postmodern' identities tend to be more hybrid complex, fluctuating …

But 'black' still remains a broad description and referent …

Ken Pryce: difference and variety in a British-Jamaican community.

The late Ken Pryce's *Endless Pressure* (1979) reflects the variety of Afro-Caribbean culture in Britain. Pryce carried out a participant observational study the Afro-Caribbean community in Bristol, which is largely of Jamaican origin, in which he focused particularly on lifestyle. Nevertheless, as some of his terminology indicates, there is a significant class as well as lifestyle dimension to Pryce's analyses. He designated the following terms to describe the six 'lifestyles' crystallised from his data: hustlers, teenyboppers, proletarian respectables, saints mainliners, and in-betweeners. He further grouped these according to two major 'life-orientations': the 'expressive-disreputable' orientation and the stable law-abiding orientation. These groupings can be presented in diagrammatic form as follows:

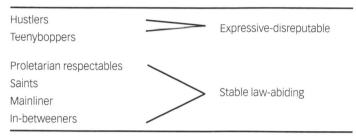

Hustlers
Teenyboppers ⟶ Expressive-disreputable

Proletarian respectables
Saints
Mainliner ⟶ Stable law-abiding
In-betweeners

Pryce's terminology is perhaps idiosyncratic and in some respects dated but it takes us straight into the variety and contrast of Afro-Caribbean lifestyles in Bristol. 'Hustlers' are male, hate 'slave labour', tend to be socially marginal, and are hedonistically inclined. 'Teenyboppers' are second generation male refusers of slave labour and may get involved in delinquency or black consciousness movement such as Rastafarianism (in the 1986 edition of his book, Pryce made it clear that he did not wish to imply that Rastafarianism itself is delinquent). It needs to be added that because of the major recessions of the 1980s and 1990s, young black males were often not even offered low level work and this further swelled the ranks of the black urban unemployed. The 1990s Yardies, can be regarded as a particularly tough and violent example of 'hustlers'. In contrast to hustlers, 'proletarian respectables' tend to be in regular employment or to be seeking it and to be conventional in their lifestyle. 'Saints' are Pentecostalists who have made a peaceful orientation to British society. The term 'mainliners' refers to a small minority of white-collar black people of generally liberal or conservative-moderate inclination. 'In-betweeners' are 'young, law-abiding West Indians in the eighteen to 25 age-group who would normally be mainliners but who, in keeping with their 'race-consciousness' and Afrocentric outlook, have assimilated into their lifestyle certain 'black culture' or Shanty town norms which cause them to lead an existence derived from the two opposing orientations' (241).

Cashmore and Troyna criticise Pryce for consigning black people to 'specific cultural categories known as lifestyles'. They go on to say:

> *Our investigations indicate that black youth did not and does not adopt one cultural lifestyle, but mix of many. So it would be feasible to expect the ostensibly docile bakery worker to be a hostile critic of white society, a part-time pimp, a pentecostal church mentor and the organiser of a black self help group. He does not have to belong to one culture; he may belong to many.*
>
> *(1982:27)*

Notwithstanding this criticism, Pryce does, at least, begin to describe in a systematic, empirical and theoretical way the complexities, varieties and tensions which occur within the Afro-

Caribbean community. It is a picture which gives space both to the ultra-conventional 'saints' and ordinary 'respectables' as well as to the more dramatic 'hustlers' so beloved of the popular press. Pryce suggests that his description would be broadly applicable to Afro-Caribbean communities in other urban areas of Britain. Whether acknowledged or not, Pryce's work seems to foreshadow the new multi-ethnic approach or new ethnicities approach.

Stuart Hall: 'new ethnicities'?

Stuart Hall has used the term 'new ethnicities' to describe what he sees as a 'new phase' in the development and emergence in Britain of minority ethnic groups. Hall observes a new awareness of and confidence in difference. Those who adopt this approach are generally keen to distance themselves from what they see as the simplicities and naivities of multiculturalism.

Although Hall is sympathetic to the emerging emphasis on what is ethnically distinctive and unique, he stresses the need to avoid the narrowness, jingoism and exclusivity which not infrequently characterises ethnic ideology. In particular, he is critical of the aspirations to cultural and political dominance of Thatcherism, as illustrated in the following notorious statement:

> *People are really rather afraid that this country might be rather swamped by people of a different culture ... the British character has done so much for democracy, for law, and done so much throughout the world, that if there is any fear that it might be swamped, people are going to react and be rather hostile to those coming in. So, if you want good race relations, you have to allay people's fears on numbers.*
>
> *(Margaret Thatcher, 1978)*

Hall's response to this type of sentiment is:

> *We are beginning to think about how to represent a non-coercive and more diverse concept of ethnicity, to set against the embattled, hegemonic concept of 'Englishness' which under Thatcherism, stabilises so much of the dominant political and cultural discourses and which because it is hegemonic does not represent itself as an ethnicity at all.*
>
> *(In Donald and Rattansi, 1992:217)*

In part then, the development and confident assertion of various ethnicities is defensive, it combats a 'white' hegemonic (ideologically dominant) ethnicity which does not recognise itself as such. But, as we shall see throughout this book, ethnic diversity is also an exploration and celebration of identities.

Conclusion: changing ethnic identities

The term 'black' is likely to continue as a general point of reference and solidarity. On the other hand, evidence accumulates on the difference and variety between not only ethnic groups but within them. In *Changing Ethnic Identities* (1994), Modood, Beishon and Virdee compare two generations of Afro-Caribbeans and four South Asian groups (74 interviews in total). They found both ethnic and generational differences. For South Asians, the two main variables indicating ethnic identity were national/regional origins and religion, whereas for Caribbeans they were regional original and African descent. Both Caribbean and Asian first generations were more traditional in terms of religion and in attitudes to marriage and family. Although the second generation are more likely to see being British as a part of their identity, this is not occurring unproblematically – not least, because some whites do not accept them as such. The authors call for 'a new vision of Britishness which allows minorities to make a claim upon it, to be accepted as British regardless of their colour and origins and without having to conform to a narrow cultural norm' (120).

Ethnic and/or class politics

In the 1970s and 1980s, John Rex frequently argued that it was likely that black minority groups would organise on a communal basis to confront issues such as black unemployment, the educational under-attainment of black youth, and racial victimisation by the police and other authorities. He thought that such action was likely to be locally based but he did not preclude the possibility of national action. In contrast to Rex, the major political parties have tended to assume that the bulk of black political action would occur within the party system. In practice, as we shall see, the black vote is strongly for Labour (although there are some signs on the development of an Asian middle class Conservative constituency). Marxists argue that black people should organise on the basis of class politics but of a much more radical kind than is likely to occur within the Labour party.

Ethnic politics

John Rex suggested that three types of black political movements occur: issue-oriented, personality-oriented and ideologically-oriented. A major example of an issue-oriented movement was the protest against the number of black youths arrested on suspicion ('SUS'). This was a charge under the 1824 Vagrancy Act which allows the police to arrest, without warrant, a person whom they reasonably suspect to be 'loitering with intent to commit a felonious offence'. Police evidence alone could be sufficient to convict. Estimates of the percentage of black people making up 'SUS' arrests vary from 44 per cent (Home Office) to 80 per cent for certain inner urban areas (Law Centres Working Group). The

'SUS' law and the manner of its application caused widespread concern within, and beyond the black community. The 'SUS' law has now been abolished but police relations with parts of the black community have remained fragile. Urban disorders in Brixton in 1981 and in Handsworth and Tottenham in 1985 were triggered by incidents involving black people and the police, although deeper socio-economic causes lay behind the conflict. Given these precedents, the targeting of 'mugging' by the London police in 1995, and the Chief Commissioner linking of the offence with young Afro-Caribbeans was a high risk policy – although in fact responses to it were orderly. The replacement of SUS by SAS (stop and search provision) has refuelled the accusation that the police tend to target young blacks.

Education is another quite different issue, which has provoked black action. In Redbridge and elsewhere, black parents and teachers have very positively involved themselves in supporting the school curriculum, with additional schooling in the evenings or at weekends.

We now consider Rex's second type of movement, the personality-oriented. An example of a nationally-known (though sparsely supported personality-oriented movement in Britain was the Black Power Group led by Michael X during the 1960s. He was a mere shadow of the much better known Malcolm X who led the Black Muslim movement in the United States. Rex has in mind, however, local personalities who can manipulate incidents sometimes to further a cause but often for maximum personal publicity.

A more reliable basis for a political movement than the merely personal is ideological belief – Rex's third category. The founding of an Islamic party in Bradford in 1990 is an example of this kind of movement. Within the British Afro-Caribbean community, there are a number of groups which are as much cultural as political, and which have distinctive ideologies. One example is the Rastafarian movement. Members of the group are disciples of the late former Emperor of Ethiopia, Haile Selassie, whom they believe to be divine. With varying degrees of conviction, Rastafarians subscribe to black separatism and some wed socialism to their religious beliefs. It has been said of this, and of other 'back to Africa' movements, that they represent an extreme defensive reaction by blacks against a white society which has already rejected them. A return to Africa is not, however, a realistic option, particularly as the majority of black immigrants have never been there in the first place. But the identity, confidence and expression that such movements provide should not be dismissed or underestimated. We develop this point further when discussing black youth (see pp. 454-5).

Class politics

Community politics alone are unlikely ever to be enough radically to change the position of Britain's black population. John Rex may virtually despair of an effective black and white working class alliance but he still recognises its ultimate desirability, if the massive governmental resources needed by inner city ethnic groups are ever to materialise. Community politics are necessary both to 'defend' and develop the community, but only government (arguably in combination with industry) can provide the means to lift 'ghetto' conditions – economic, housing and educational – much nearer to the acceptable national norm. In getting political support for such a programme, blacks are not without some political muscle. At the lowest level, political parties need black votes just as unions require members.

However, as Solomos and Back's recent study of local politics in Birmingham shows, black people, including black politicians do not simply gain full acceptance by joining a mainstream party. They are likely to be treated with suspicion in a generally racialised political content. Nevertheless, the trend is to mainstream political participation among black people.

Historically, black people who vote have overwhelmingly supported Labour although this is now somewhat less true of the Indian community. Surveys show that the issues which most concern black voters are generally those that most concern white voters: unemployment, the cost of living, and education. However, black people, particularly those of Asian origin additionally express great concern over immigration control. The number of black local and national political candidates has increased in recent years. For instance, in the 1979 general election, five black candidates stood unsuccessfully, whereas in the 1987 general election 27 stood, four successfully (all Labour). In all four cases, the Labour candidates were helped by a large black vote in their constituencies. It still remains to be seen whether black candidates will be able to run for office across the whole country without experiencing a racist backlash. The difficulties the black barrister John Taylor met in Cheltenham in 1990-91 after he had been adopted as prospective Conservative parliamentary candidate suggest others may face problems of this kind. However, Marion Fitzgerald's analysis of the result of black candidates in the 1983 general election suggests that they lost few votes because of their colour (Fitzgerald, 1983).

Politics, policy, racialisation and the law

Has the support of the large majority of black voters for the Labour party been justified by that party's policies when in office? On the credit side, it can be said that the three major Race Relations Acts aimed at preventing racial discrimination in key areas of public life were all passed under Labour governments and that only one of the Immigration/Nationality Acts (that of 1968) aimed at controlling immigration was passed by a Labour government (see right).

Immigration/nationality and race relations legislation: the 'liberal compromise'

(N.B. The letters 'L' and 'C' given in brackets after the title of an Act indicate whether it was passed under a Labour or Conservative administration.)

1948 British Nationality Act (L)

Commonwealth citizens allowed freely to enter and settle in Britain.

Immigration/nationality laws

1962 Commonwealth Immigrants Act (C)

Removed the rights of the 1948 Act for most new (black) Commonwealth citizens. Instead a limited number of *employment vouchers* were issued.

1968 Commonwealth Immigrants Act (L)

Restricted the entry to East African Asians who held UK passports issued by the British Government.

1971 Immigrant Act (C)

Made a distinction between patrials (those born in Britain or with a parent/grandparent born in Britain) who kept full British citizens' rights, and non-patrials (mainly black, new Commonwealth) who were required to obtain work permits prior to entry.

1981 British Nationality Act (C)

Restricted forms of British nationality provided for those whose entry rights had been removed by previous laws – by this time the entry of blacks for settlement is highly controlled and virtually limited to close relatives.

1988 Immigration Act (C)

An immigrant husband who wants his wife and children to join him in Britain has to prove he can house and support them.

1993 Asylum Act (C)

Asylum seekers and children to be fingerprinted.

1996 Asylum and Immigration Act (C)

Removed right to welfare benefits and public housing from refugees who do not immediately claim asylum

Race relations laws

1965 Race Relations Act (L)

i   Made discrimination illegal in certain places – *but* the means of enforcing the Act were very weak.

ii Made incitement to racial hatred illegal.

1968 Race Relations Act (L)

Enlarged the scope of the 1965 Act (discrimination being made illegal in employment and housing, for the first time) *but* enforcement still weak – relying on the new *Community Relations Council* to take up *individual complaints*.

1976 Race Relations Act (L)

Extended the anti-discrimination laws to *UNINTENDED* as well as intended discrimination – a very important principle.

This record provides a basis for the Labour party's claim that it has long had an active commitment to the creation of a society characterised by equality of racial opportunity. Anne Page of the London Research Centre defines the passage of the 1976 Act as a crucial moment in that the capital now 'enjoys a rich mix of people and culture unparalleled in Europe, and an atmosphere of racial harmony compared to its own recent past'. There is certainly great ethnic variety and therefore cultural choice in London and many other urban areas in Britain but this chapter has also given ample evidence of persistent racism as well. Critics, particularly from the left, argue that the Race Relations legislation and the institutions it established have lacked 'the teeth' to enforce anti-discrimination and, indeed, evidence can be cited to support the view that there has been little, if any reduction in racism and racial discrimination in Britain since the 1950s (see, for instance, p. 220). Ironically, such evidence can also be used to support the view of some Conservatives that legislative tinkering in race relations is unlikely greatly to affect actual behaviour. However, it must be said, that on the issue of immigration, Conservatives have been the opposite of non-interventionist and have passed legislation which has had the effect of tightly controlling black immigration but much less so white immigration. The implicitly racist nature of the 1971 Immigration Act and the 1981 Nationality Act is partly the product of what Solomos and Back refer to as the racialisation of British politics in the post-war period. However, in their recent book they are not wholly pessimistic. They suggest:

> ... that the contemporary politics of race and ethnicity in societies such as Britain are in flux ... we do not see a simple process of exclusion or inclusion as being the likely outcome of the current situation.
>
> *(1995:213)*

Those who continue to believe that the law can be used as an effective instrument in the creation of a racially equal society have generally shifted their emphasis from anti-discrimination to the setting of more positive goals, the attainment of which would clearly indicate the achievement of fairness and equality. Two examples of this occur commonly in the United States but not in Britain: establishing quotas and contract compliance. Quotas refer to specific numbers of black people required to be employed in a given organisation, say, a local police force, frequently by a target date. Contract compliance involves the granting of a contract, usually by central or local government, to a business provided that it employs a given number of black people – possibly at specified job levels and again sometimes subject to timing. Such techniques are considered by their supporters to have more 'teeth' than generalised anti-discriminatory legislation and to be particularly effective in combating institutional racism (see p. 219). However, it is arguable that, at the very least, anti-discriminatory legislation remains valid as a statement of a society's commitment and intent in the area of racial equality.

Questions

1 What are the various strategies – cultural and political – of coping with British society, adopted by black minority ethnic groups?
2 Critically present the various reponses (including political/legislative) to black immigration.
3 What is meant by 'black identity'? How useful do you consider the term to be?

Nation and 'race': Europe, the 'globe'

Definitions

What is a nation? The following elements are common, if not universal, in definitions of a 'nation':

1 Settlement of a territory which is
2 Organised under a self-contained political system and whose members
3 Believe they share a common identity.

(see Smith, 1983)

A nation, therefore, involves geo-political and cultural (identity) aspects. A stable nation-state is likely to be one in which these three elements fit together in a complementary way. Where they do not, there can be problems. Thus, Gibraltar is politically part of Britain, but geographically closer to Spain; Northern Ireland is politically part of Britain, but a large minority of its inhabitants feel themselves not to be; Formosa is geographically close to China but not politically. So, although nations can provoke the most intense emotions and feelings of identity, they are often rather awkward constructions. All three elements under discussion are missing or weak in the case of many African states. This is because their boundaries were created n the process of competition between European imperial powers.

One of the reasons for the awkward construction of many nation states is that – as Smith's definition implies – their boundaries are often the product of conflict with other nation states. Thus, the British province of Northern Ireland is the product of a peace settlement between Britain and what is now the Republic of Ireland. However much nations may yearn to achieve what they perceive as their 'natural' geographical and/or cultural boundaries, they often fail to do so because another nation – with a different perception stops them. As we shall see below, British identity is formed as much by limits and rejections as by possessed territory and shared culture.

Yet, the nation is one of the most powerful of modern foci of identity. Patriotism – love of one's country/nation – is widely seen as a basic value. Nationalism, one definition of which is 'the valuation of the nation state above all else' (i.e. all other political entities) (*Oxford Dictionary of Sociology*) is also a powerful force in the modern world although its cruder and more violent expressions attract condemnation.

What are the origins of the national state? Four elements are frequently suggested for the rise of the nation state:

1 The break-up of the feudal order.

Territorial competition and expansionist ambitions led to the unification of less powerful usually smaller, feudal states under single, powerful monarchs. Germany was formed in this way and so was 'greater' Russia. The unification of the British nation occurred over several centuries. Southern Ireland was never effectively integrated into Britain.

2 The rise of capitalism and the bourgeoisie.

The rise of the bourgeoisie broadened the basis of those who identified with the 'nation' and gave a new class possible access to state power. International competition between new national bourgeoisies stimulated both nationalism and imperialism.

3 The growth of democracy.

The growth of democracy progressively gave more social groups both a sense of ownership and of belonging to or identity with the nation – first the bourgeois, then, the working class and, finally women. Nineteenth and twentieth century nationalism – of which imperialism was, in part, an extension involved widespread popular participation.

However, nationalism is possible without democracy. Both Nazi Germany and Communist Russia were aggressively nationalist regimes.

4 The centralisation of government and development of modern communications.

The centralisation of government potentially increased the power of government over people and its ability to provide services. The development of modern communications enabled government and the media – sometimes acting together – to create a sense of community or, at least, shared communicated experience among 'the people'. Demagogues like Hitler and Mussolini were masters in manipulating the media and 'the masses'. So, more benignly, was Winston Churchill.

Nationalism and racism

Robert Miles argues that it is important to distinguish between 'nationalism' and 'racism' although he stresses that in contemporary societies the two often 'articulate' closely i.e. occur together and reinforce each other. Other commentators are content to describe highly intolerant and exclusionary manifestations of nationalism as 'racist' even though in the case of nationalism the ideological justification is cultural rather than biological (see Barker, 1981 and Modood, 1992 (later in this section). 'Nation',

then refers to 'our country and people' rather than 'our race'. Equally, it cannot refer to ethnicity as most nations contain groups of widely differing cultural origins.

Miles's point about the often close 'articulation' of nationalism and racism is easily illustrated. Late nineteenth and early twentieth century European imperialism was ideologically sustained by 'scientific' racism. Certainly many leading imperialists believed in the 'superiority of the white race' as the poet of Empire, Kipling's famous reference 'to lesser breeds without the law' illustrates. Such combinations of nationalistic and racist sentiment were widely echoed among the populace. Fascism – National Socialism – was the evil flowering of this ideological trend.

Imagined nations

Benedict Anderson has been influential in popularising the concept of nations as 'imagined communities' among sociologists (1988). Thus, he states that 'a nation is an imagined political community – and imagined as both inherently limited and sovereign'. Unlike communities whose members are immediately physically present, members of a nation have to be imagined. Though the power of imagination and feeling, membership of the same state becomes an experience of political community. Membership is defined by those who do not belong as well as those who do i.e. the community is 'limited'. 'Sovereignty' refers to the independence and integrity (wholeness) of a nation – and is widely perceived as a central aspect of national power and identity.

Some see the twin processes of 'Europeanisation' and 'globalisation' as challenges to British national identity (see pp. 241-2). However while not denying the significance of national identity, Stuart Hall suggests that a feature of modernity is that people are members of multiple 'overlapping' identities – class, ethnic (perhaps multi-ethnic), national and perhaps European and global.

The British nation-state

The point was made earlier that the boundaries of nation-states are often the product of conflict and competition with other nation-states. David Held usefully expands this observation to suggest that the nature and form of the nation-state system is:

> crystallised at the intersection of 'international' and 'national' conditions and processes ... In fact, it is at this intersection that the 'shape' of the state was largely determined – its size, external configuration, organisational structure, ethnic composition, material infrastructure and so on.
>
> (1992:90)

Held's comments require some explanation. The 'intersection' to which Held refers is the boundary between one nation-state and another or others. In Britain, the English have been able to establish a boundary that has so far included Scotland, Wales and Northern Ireland but were not able to retain Southern Ireland. There a separate national identity has formed. Held points to the role of war in carving out national or potentially national boundaries and this is particularly obvious in the case of the British state. We will now briefly examine how the aspects of the 'shape' of the British state referred to by Held were formed by historical circumstances.

The size and shape ('external configuration' in Held's terms) of the British nation-state might be different if certain conflicts had been resolved differently. Thus, Scotland could, conceivably, have seceded from Britain, or Southern Ireland might have been forced to 'remain' British. The 'organisational structure' of the British nation-state has several distinctive characteristics, including a constitutional monarchy (reflecting a feudal past) and a Parliament which is sovereign rather than the people (as is the case in the United States). As far as ethnic composition is concerned, the imperial and post-imperial history of Britain has resulted in a much more multi-ethnic nation than would otherwise have been the case. The multi-ethnic nature of contemporary Britain worries some white people who may, mistakenly think of themselves as 'true Brit'. In fact, they are likely to be as culturally and biologically 'mixed' as the groups they wish to reject as 'not British'. Finally, the class system cuts across any cosy notion of national community – appealing though the latter may be to some.

British and English identities

England is the largest component of the British nation-state. Indeed, in his radio series on 'the British', Billy Bragg found that whereas the Scots and Welsh were generally clear about the difference between Scottish or Welsh identity and Britishness, many English people tended to confuse Englishness with Britishness (R.4, 1994). The sense of superiority that this confusion suggests, no doubt reflects the long history of imperial and post-imperial dominance of England in Britain.

Robin Cohen examines the complexities of English and British identities in *Frontiers of Identity: The British and the Others* (1994). These complexities derive in part from the fact that the British have travelled and settled in their millions throughout the world and others, likewise, have settled in Britain in their millions. Whatever else, the British are a mixed and various people with connections and influences flowing both ways across the globe. Yet, as inhabitants of an island or group of islands, the British have been able to see themselves as somewhat apart from 'others' and perhaps as somewhat protected, different, and special.

Cohen suggests six 'frontiers' of British identity but it is obvious that these 'frontiers' and what lies beyond them partly define as well as limit British identity or identities. Cohen refers to 'a series of blurred, opaque or 'fuzzy' frontiers surrounding … the core identity' (which also changes constantly) (1994:7). These proposed 'fuzzy frontiers' are:

- The Celtic Fringe
- Class and Gender Dimensions
- The Dominions
- Empire and Commonwealth
- The Atlantic and Anglophone (English Language) connection
- Britain in Europe

It is possible only to comment briefly on these points of identity here although the second, class and gender dimensions, have been referred to elsewhere in this chapter.

The Celtic fringe

As Cohen implies, the Celtic fringe, represents a potential fault-line on the margin of the body politic in Britain. It is an 'internal' frontier and possible line of division. It is unlikely that the Welsh will pursue an identity which will separate them from Britain but it is quite conceivable that Scotland might seek independent national status. For reasons already indicated Northern Ireland's membership of Britain cannot be assumed secure. There is a sense in which these territories can be regarded as the first and last possessions of Empire …

Class and gender

The second of two internal frontiers to which Cohen refers is class and gender. Cohen succinctly explains how British imperialism could variously unite or differentiate and divide the classes:

> (T)he expansion of the British abroad in the form of colonies of settlement and Empire often had a differential impact on different classes. It is true that all classes were drawn into expressions of patriotism or jingoism at particular moments … But the Empire was often an upper and middle class quest. Even the colonies of settlement were, for many working class people, outposts that they were condemned to by poverty, unemployment, orphanhood, homelessness or a vicious judge, rather than being 'undiscovered' frontiers for the brave and patriotic spirits among them.
>
> (13)

It is relevant to add some comment on contemporary British nationalism and class. Just as some of the most strident support for imperialism in the late nineteenth and first half of the twentieth century came from sections of the working class, so in the post-imperial second half of the century, some of the shrillest expressions of nationalism came from the low-paid or unemployed – sometimes responding to the urgings of self-styled patriots such as Enoch Powell and Norman Tebbitt. Nationalism of this kind seems to provide a sense of status and superiority for those who perhaps otherwise lack them, as well as for some, an outlet for aggression. It is also true that the living standard of the British working class as a whole was raised by the exploitation of the resources and labour of empire. Even so, the middle classes, particularly commercial and financial, benefited most. Despite all this, it needs to be stressed that many working class people have retained a scepticism about the wilder excesses of nationalism and that both the socialist and social democratic traditions of thought also express reservations about it. In particular, the view is expressed that the sense of unity or 'community' created by nationalistic sentiment can obscure deep and serious social inequality and division.

On the matter of gender, women generally shared a similar range of attitudes to empire as men. Today, the same appears true of nationalism, post-empire. However, Cohen makes the useful observation that attitudes and behaviour are gendered in this area, as in others. To illustrate the point, males overwhelmingly fight the wars – from the Crimea to the Falklands – and females do much of the resultant caring and grieving (as well as some of the exultation and celebration). No doubt the differently gendered experience by females of war and domination partly motivated the setting up of the Women's Peace Camp at Greenham Common of the 1970s and 1980s.

The Dominions, Empire and Commonwealth

On the whole, Britain has moved away from what used to be the Dominions and the still existing Commonwealth as a major focus of its own identity. The Empire, of course, is gone although the attitudes of superiority and racism associated with it persist among some. The Dominions were New Zealand, Canada, Australia, Rhodesia and South Africa. Cohen comments that what linked these countries was that they were powerful enough to assert, or try to assert, their independence from Britain. Today, they have more or less gone their separate ways and, significantly, it is very possible that Australia will become a republic in the near future. Although never formally a Dominion, the United States to some extent represents a prototype for the (ex)Dominions and its influence has partly replaced that of Britain among them (see below).

The ex-Dominions remain part of a highly multi-ethnic Commonwealth to which most other countries which were previously part of the Empire also belong. The Commonwealth continues mainly as a moral talking shop but even in that area Britain's leadership was profoundly undermined when, in Margaret Thatcher's premiership, Britain, almost alone among the countries of the Commonwealth, opposed trade sanctions against the apartheid regime of South Africa. There is also a view in some parts of the Commonwealth that Britain's handling of its own ethnic relations has been less than exemplary. Economically and politically, Britain's main interests have been defined as lying with Europe and the United States, not the Commonwealth.

The Atlantic and Anglophone (English language) connection

In the case of the Untied States and Britain, the child has greatly outgrown the parent in power and influence. Under President Clinton, it is clear that the United States' government wants Britain to take a committed place in a strong Europe rather than to provide Britain with an Anglo-American axis that could function as a serious alternative. The various spats between Clinton and John Major may be personal and temporary, on the other hand, they may well indicate a longer term disenchantment between the two nations. In the past, Britain and the United States have tended to assist each other in times of major or acute crisis. Whether or not this mutuality will survive as a 'fall-back' position remains to be seen. However, the United States is likely to retreat as a 'frontier' of British identity. It may be that the greatest long term contribution of the Americans to the British will be the international boost they have given to the use of the English language. However, it does seem to be the American rather than the English version that most of the world has adopted …

Britain in Europe: 'little England', 'fortress Europe' and the wider world

Britain, especially under recent Conservative governments, has found it difficult to shift its identity decisively towards Europe. When there were twelve members of the Community, a common joke among other members was that the Community was made up of '11 + 1' – so often was Britain an exception to Community thinking and policy. In the 1990s, Britain has opted out of both a commitment to a timetable for monetary union (a single European currency) and to the social chapter which guarantees employees certain minimum rights. Although these actions have been taken in the name of Britain, it is quite possible that a majority of Scots and Welsh disagree with them. The term 'little England' refers to an identification with a narrow, old-fashioned idea of England which is suspicious of Europeans and others seen as 'different from us' or as 'not English'.

However, as well as Britain, other better off European countries besides Britain have restricted immigration and experienced increased racism in the last fifteen or twenty years. Among these are Germany, France, Holland and Italy. The term 'fortress Europe' was coined to describe this beleaguered mentality. Three reasons can be given for these developments:

1 Increased population, especially, labour *mobility* (governments often want cheap 'foreign' labour but do not wish to grant citizenship).
2 *Instability*, especially in Eastern Europe has resulted in an increase in political refugees.
3 Economic *insecurity*, including high unemployment, and Western Europe itself has stimulated less generous, more self-centred attitudes.

(Reading 2)

While, therefore, Britain vacillates toward Europe, Europe as a whole, including Britain threatens to turn away from the outside, poorer territories on its fringe – Africa and Eastern Asia. There is a possibility that three wealthy and powerful blocs will develop centred on Europe, the United States and Japan whose attitudes to the rest of the world will be motivated more by defensive self-interest than by desire to assist development. The fact that there are outposts of wealth in the poor world (often controlled by the West or Japan) and concentrations of serious poverty in the rich world complicates but does not invalidate this description.

Britain: one or many national identities? – The debate

Robin Cohen's useful exploration of the 'frontiers' of British identity leaves the question of what is the 'core' British (or English) identity, largely unanswered. In fact, Cohen's analysis of the two 'internal frontiers' – class/gender differences and the 'Celtic fringe' strongly implies that he considers that there is no single British national identity. The core itself is multi-layered. Different people and groups interpret British history in different and sometimes contradictory ways and create their own preferred images and meanings about national identity and direction. Thus, to pick a dramatic example, some undoubtedly see the Falklands war as an illustration of much that is best about Britain while others regard it as a dated and dangerous exercise in neo-imperialism. Neither 'side' is necessarily more patriotic – both are likely to care about their country. However, the same 'fact' or event means different things to different people. As Charles Husband summaries: 'there is no single monolithic ideology' of nation 'shared by all Britains' (1987).

Competing identities: right-wing nationalism and liberal pluralism (and new ethnicities)

Concepts of what it is to be English or British, then, vary greatly. Two important perspectives can be mentioned here: conservative or right-wing nationalism and liberal pluralism or multi-culturalism. Both have been referred to earlier in this chapter and in the chapter on education where what is termed in the present section 'right-wing nationalism' is analysed as the 'assimilationist approach'. Right-wing nationalism tends to be assimilationist in that they argue that minorities should learn and practise the cultural norms of the majority in public (though not necessarily private) life.

Right-wing nationalism

The conservative philosopher, Roger Scruton, argues that Britain does have an established common culture and that the education system should teach this rather than multi-culturalism to all

children. Scruton takes an extensive view of the scope of British culture which is presented below in itemised form:

> 'There is
> a common language,
> a dominant religion,
> a settled pattern of social expectations,
> a shared network of entertainment and sport,
> a common morality
> and a common law.'
>
> (1986)

Most commentators would agree that members of ethnic minorities should have full access to the English language in order to enjoy equal opportunity and that they should obey British law (an issue which came up during the Rushdie affair). Scruton, however, wants to go much further than this in framing a common culture. He implies that all the aspects in his list should be prioritised in 'British' education. Thus, consistent with his ideas, it is now compulsory for all state schools to carry out a daily act of *Christian* worship (1988 Education Act). He similarly seems to suggest that the 'entertainment and sport' occurring in schools should prioritise (exclusively?) 'British' varieties although this could both restrict the preferences of minority groups and cause cultural/moral conflict (for instance, in relation to dress and exercise routines in physical education).

Scruton's views reflect two underlying concerns. First, is his concern that culture should 'bind people together in a common enterprise'. In other words, the majority culture should reinforce social solidarity and identity. Second, Scruton distinguishes between 'high' and 'low' culture, the former being superior to the latter. 'High culture' contains 'universal values' and is exemplified in much of British literature, art and scholarship. Controversially – almost provocatively – Scruton does not include any of the South Asian cultures (e.g. Islam, Hindu) or Afro-Caribbean cultures in his list of 'high' cultures (in addition to their vibrant popular cultures, Afro-Caribbean societies do increasingly produce examples of what Scruton calls 'high' culture). In this second point, Scruton goes beyond saying that it is functional and useful deliberately to reproduce a common culture to asserting that British culture – at least, in its 'high' aspects – is better than certain other cultures (Islam?) which need not then be included in the 'national' curriculum.

Many expressions of right-wing nationalism are made less precisely than Scruton's. Indeed, they seem typically to be crude and offensive, and sometimes threatening and violent. Expressions vary from the heavy-handed wit of European sceptic, Norman Tebbitt, who suggested that pro-European, Kenneth Clarke's budget could be 'faxed from Frankfurt' to the apparently increasingly pre-planned destructiveness of English soccer thugs, a hard core of whom seem to have links with the fascist group, Combat 18. Robert Miles points out that nationalism and racism 'articulate' closely and this is certainly the case with the last

(Source: *The Observer Review*, 2.6.1996)

Figure 8.9 Blind loyalty?

mentioned groups. However, it is also the case that black people and anti-racist whites are increasingly organised against racism, including growing violent racism, both through stronger and more confident community and political representation and through bodies such as the Anti-Nazi League and the Anti-Racist Alliance.

Liberal-pluralist (multicultural) perspective

The liberal-pluralist or multiculturalist view of the British nation accepts and promotes diversity and difference within a framework of law, democracy, and, ideally, equal opportunity. This does not imply a less caring attitude to the nation than that of right-wing nationalists, rather, the caring and the view of the nation are different. There is no need for further basic introduction to multiculturalism here (see pp. 119-20). However, it is worth briefly examining what can be regarded as a newer variety of liberal-pluralism in a perspective sometimes referred to a 'new ethnicities'.

New ethnicities and liberal-pluralism

Stuart Hall published an article titled *New Ethnicities* in 1992. In it, he suggested that the period when black people might think of themselves primarily *as* black rather than, say, as Afro-Caribbean or as Muslim, appeared to be coming to a close. What seems to be

emerging is a recognition that there are many, often profound, differences between black people and that from these differences, they fashion different identities. Hall sees a trend 'which engages rather than suppresses *difference* and which depends, in part, on the cultural production of new ethnic identities' (257). Hall illustrates the exploration of different ethnic identities with reference to film. (For further analysis of this article see pp. 491-2).

An article published in the same volume as the one by Hall explores a more everyday aspect of ethnic identity but also reflects a concern with 'new ethnicities'. Tariq Modood's *British Asian Muslims and the Rushdie Affair* can be read as a challenge to liberal-pluralists to extend their capacity of tolerance and full recognition to groups that are very different and even alien to themselves – such as British Asian Muslims. In general, predominantly secular, pragmatic – pluralism is, at best, uneasy with religious, ideologically-oriented Islam. More specifically, liberals opposed the fatwa against Salman Rushdie and any acceptance it may have found in the Muslim community. In effect, Modood asks British liberals to embrace a concept of 'racial equality' based not always on treating people the same but which recognises that in some respects people are different and need to be respected and treated as such:

> *Britain now encompasses communities with different norms, cultures and religions. Hence racial equality cannot always mean that our public institutions and the law itself must treat everybody as if they were the same – for that will usually mean treating everybody by the norms and convenience of the majority.*
>
> *(1992:273)*

These comments from Modood contrast sharply with those of conservative, Roger Scruton, quoted earlier in this section. Whereas Scruton wants the majority culture to be given strong precedence, Modood discusses the possibility that the Muslim minority might be allowed to run its communal affairs, including presumably education, with considerable autonomy. Modood concludes with the question:

> *Is the Enlightenment (i.e. liberalism) big enough to legitimise the existence of pre-Enlightenment religious enthusiasm or can it only exist by suffocating all who fail to be overawed by its intellectual brilliance and vision of Man.*
>
> *(1992: 274 – Author's brackets)*

Clearly, there are different answers to the question 'what is British identity?'. It would be some achievement to maintain a reasonably peaceable society alongside the greater difference and variety that has developed in the post-war years. Such a society is still not yet secured.

Conclusion

Two constant and related themes of this chapter merit reflection. First, is the extent to which deeply felt ideologies such as racism, nationalism or ethnic pride are socially constructed or, in a sense, 'imagined'. People imagine differently what it is to be a member of the British nation. 'Black' means many different things to different people. It is a fact – a reality – that there is a political entity termed Britain and that there are people with black – or nearly black skins. But beyond those sparse facts much is interpretation and construction of meaning. Of course, this does not occur in a social vacuum. Social context greatly affects individuals and groups including in the formation of thought and opinion – thus, sociologists refer to the social construction of reality.

Second, modern global communications, have increased the number of images and the range of information available to people. There is a constant flow and flux of apparent possibilities from many different parts of the globe. This offers images and ideas for changing and developing identities. It also threatens established and previously stable ones. (For further discussion of British and English nationality, including, membership of Europe and the significance of the royal family.)

Questions

Read again the quotes on p. 240, p. 242 and p. 243.
1　To what extent do you consider that there was a shared view of empire and, in contemporary Britain, of 'nation' across the social classes?
2　Critically compare Roger Scruton and Tariq Modood's views of the place of culture in British society.
3　What does the concept/term 'black Briton' mean?

Summary

1　The term 'race' in sociology refers to people's often imprecise notions or theories of 'race' rather than any precisely established biological reality. Ethnicity denotes the membership of a distinct people possessing their own culture. Racism narrowly defined, refers to prejudice and discrimination based on a view of a group's supposed biological inferiority. Or broadly defined, it includes views based on a group's supposed cultural inferiority.
2　Contemporary racism in Britain has important roots in British imperial and economic expansions, particularly slavery. In present-day Europe inequality between people is largely based on international flows of labour.
3　Data on ethnic employment and unemployment for the 1980s and 1990s generally continues to show inequalities between whites and others, especially Afro-Caribbeans and Pakistani/Bangladeshis. The position of black and white women appears more similar but Breugel cites data to suggest that significantly greater inequalities are still experienced by black women.
4　Several explanations are offered for the position of black minorities in the employment market. The ethnic adjustment perspective argues that black minorities like other ethnic groups can progress in Britain. The underclass perspective contends that racism may well cut large numbers of black people off from advancement, thus creating an underclass. Marxist analysis presents black people primarily in class terms with the majority of them being seen as working class but particularly disadvantaged by racism. Feminist analysis stresses the additional gender disadvantage experienced by women in the labour market with different emphases occurring in respect of the relative importance of the links between class inequality and gender and racial inequality and gender.
5　Several perspectives occur on the relations between black minorities and the majority group. Assimilationists take the view that black people should wholly or largely forsake their own cultures and 'become British' (despite problems in defining precisely what 'British culture' is). Marxists argue that the concepts of dominant and subordinate class cultures have more explanatory value than those of minority and majority cultures, although they recognise that ethnic and national cultural identities cut across and complicate class culture. Anti-racist perspective is associated with Marxism but also has wider support. The cultural dimensions that some young black people, marginalised from occupational success, create their own alternative sub-culture.
6　The origin, nature and appropriateness of the term 'black' to describe various group identities is discussed. The use of the term in relation to Asians is challenged by Tariq Modood. Other approaches to ethnicity which also stress differentiation are discussed.
7　John Rex's underclass analysis leads him towards the view that the politics of ethnic self-defence and self-interest (ethnic politics) is likely to be a major feature of black minority political behaviour. Marxists argue that ultimately class is a sounder basis of action than ethnicity. The political parties appear to assume that black minorities will act within the party political system although the Labour party has made some adaptations to meet requirements of black groups.
8　The Conservatives have been mainly responsible for introducing the immigration control of black people and the Labour party for the Race Relations Acts.
9　The basis of 'nation' and nationality is discussed, particularly in relation to Britain. Competing perspectives on national identity are considered.

Research and coursework

The two main themes of this chapter have been about ethnic culture and racism. Obviously, it will be easier to research into ethnic culture if you live in an area in which there is a sizeable minority group or groups. In studying an ethnic group it would not be sufficient to be merely descriptive. It would be necessary to concentrate on some specifically sociological aspect of cultural processes such as how and to what extent a given group adapts to the majority culture. The Pakistani Muslim community in Bradford would provide an interesting case of both cultural continuity and change, and of examples of both harmony and conflict with aspects of the majority culture. Possible research might include observation (participant, if appropriate), social surveys, and use of the local press.

Racism needs to be treated as the sensitive subject for research that it clearly is. Attempts to observe racial harassment could involve risk and should be avoided. Content analysis of the presentation of racial issues in the press or in broadcasting (possibly using tapes) should generate useful data (see p. 525 for a description of how to go about content analysis in relation to gender bias in the media – this could be adapted for race). A comparison between certain types of publications or programmes would add point and interest.

Concealment in the study of racism: a brief discussion

One of the main practical problems concerning research into racism is that many are reluctant to admit to it. There is widespread disapproval of racist beliefs and attitudes (at least, formally) and much racist behaviour is illegal and so is hidden or denied.

Miles and Phizaklea (1979) adopted an indirect approach to researching racist beliefs among white working class people in Willesden, London. They asked no specific questions on race at all! However, they noted such references to race that respondents did make which were *assumed to be* genuine because they were not prompted (75 per cent did make negative comments about black people). Another study of racist attitudes and behaviour which contained an element of concealment was carried out by P A Green (1982) (see p. 118). Green wanted to establish whether teachers with more prejudiced racial attitudes also behaved in a less tolerant way towards black pupils. Part of the research involved the 70 participating teachers in completing an attitude inventory in which a 25-item prejudice scale had been 'buried' (he did find that teachers with less tolerant attitudes behaved less tolerantly).

The justification for concealment in studying racism is similar to that given for using a 'covert' or 'hidden' approach to participant observation Other things being equal, and if the concealment is successful, the subject of study should behave as normal. The ethical objection against concealment in the study of racism is perhaps less strong than in the case of most covert

participant observational studies. The ethical objection is to deceiving people about what is actually happening, specifically what is happening to them. Do they not have a right to know (and perhaps to decide whether or not they wish to be involved in the research)? Against this, in the case of racist behaviour, it can be argued that they should not be behaving in a racist way and would be unlikely openly to admit to their behaviour. Further, it is arguable that it is in the public interest, as well as in the interest of black people, that an accurate measure and account of discrimination should be available.

Further reading

There is now a wide range of material in this area. John Rex's *Race and Ethnicity* (Open University Press, 1986) written from a Neo-Weberian perspective, and Robert Miles *Racism* (Routledge, 1989) written from a Marxist perspective are introductory but quite demanding. More 'grassroots' is Ken Pryce's *Endless Pressure* republished in a revised edition 1986 by the Bristol Writer's Press. Like Rex's book, J Solomos and L Back's *Race, Politics and Social Change* (Routledge, 1995) is syllabus-relevant but somewhat difficult.

Readings

Reading 1
Indian economic success

From Tariq Modood 'The Indian Economic Success' in *Policy and Politics*, Vol.19, No. 3, 1991, p.188

As far as the Indian success is concerned it is important to recognise it as a genuine achievement but also not to overlook the cost. For it is paid for by a high degree of self-denial and loss of self-development by family discipline and the long hours of dull and often menial work on the part of parents, and the pressures on the young consequent on high parental expectation on academic success. All this in a context of racial prejudice and harassment, cultural adaptation and the inevitable fears on the part of the parents that they will 'lose' their children; while the young have to cope with cultural influences and attractions, family obligations and desire to seek acceptance in British society that do not always lend themselves to easy or painless syntheses. Some of the psychic tensions are beginning to show and Bhikhu Parekh has said he believes that the 'bubble of Asian success' is about to burst as the family and kinship mutual help, the foundations of this success, breaks down (Parekh, 1990, pp.1-2). For my part, I think this prognosis assumes a rate of 'assimilation', the triumphs of British ideas of self and family and happiness over Indian, that may be greater than is actually the case even among the young (Modood, 1990a, pp.147-8). My own speculation is that the Indian family and community structure will function long enough for Indians to reach and consolidate the above-average socio-economic positioning; its fate, thereafter, may primarily depend upon the extent to which the English allow Indians to be integrated into the class structure of this country or make them a marginal, if prosperous, caste. Like the Jews before them, the Indian family and kinship networks will last as long as Indians are not able to flourish without them.

Questions

1 What are the factors that have contributed to the suggested 'Indian Economic Success'?
2 What problems have had to be overcome in achieving the 'success'?

Reading 2
Immigrant labour: citizens, denizens and helots

From R Cohen, *Contested Domains: Debates in International Labour Studies* (Zed Books, 1991), pp.120-23

What's in a name?

Immigrants, guestworkers, illegals, refugees, asylum-seekers, expatriates, settlers – do these labels signify anything of importance? My argument here turns on a belief that although there are considerable similarities between international migrants of all types, the modern state has sought to differentiate the various people under its sway by including some in the body politic and according them full civic and social rights, while seeking to exclude others from entering this charmed circle.

The important role of citizenship as a means of integrating dissatisfied members of the lower orders and including them in the core society was first explicitly recognised by Marshall (1950). For him, access to citizenship allowed everyone so favoured to be given some stake in the society, at least in respect of periodic elections, protection, and access to some social benefits. With the rise of welfare and distributive states in the post-war world, the social wage – unemployment benefits, social security, housing allowances, tax credits, pensions, subsidised health care – has become a much more important symbolic and economic good. By the same token, states have sought to restrict access to the social wage by deploying workers with limited entitlements. The different statuses reflected in immigrant or guestworker categories reflect the differential access of such groups to the social wage and to the protection afforded by the agencies of law and order.

If we consider the various categories mentioned, three broad categories appear – citizens whose rights are extensive, an intermediate group (the denizens) and a group which remains a subject population akin to the ancient helots who hewed wood and toiled for the Spartans without access to democratic rights, property or protection.

Some of the typical sub-groups within the different status groups mentioned are listed below.

Sub-groups of citizens, denizens and helots

Citizens

Nationals by birth or naturalisation

Established Immigrants

Convention Refugees

Denizens

Holders of one or more citizenships

Recognised asylum applicants

Special entrants (e.g. ex-Hong Kong)

Expatriates

Helots

Illegal Entrants

Undocumented workers

Asylum-seekers

Overstayers

Project-tied unskilled workers

A few remarks on each of the three major categories will perhaps help to lend greater specificity to the labels.

Citizens

This group appears as an increasingly privileged one. Many states have moved from inclusive to exclusive definitions of citizenship, abandoning the principle of *jus soli* (citizenship by being born in a territory) to *jus sanguinis* (citizenship according to the parents' nationality). In the case of the European countries that once had empires (Belgium, France, Britain, Holland), binding guarantees of citizenship to colonial subjects have frequently been ignored or circumvented by subsequent legislation. While the Dutch on the whole respected the citizenship conferred on subjects of the Netherlands, the French maintained recognition only for a small number of people in the *départements* (French Guinea, Réunion. Guadeloupe and Martinique). The British, for their part, in the Nationality Act of 1982 stripped away the rights of residents of the colony of Hong Kong (and a few other places) and created a new citizenship of 'dependent territories' which conferred no right to live or work in the UK. Under the impact of the destablising events in China in 1989, however, and its consequent effects on the colony of Hong Kong, Britain has been forced to guarantee the admission of up to 50,000 Hong Kong families. The intention of this guarantee is to stabilise the last years of British rule in the colony (it reverts to Chinese rule in 1997) by buying the loyalty of key officials and entrepreneurs with the offer of settlement and full citizenship in Britain. This will require amendment of the 1983 British Nationality Act …

Denizens

I conceive of this group as comprising privileged aliens often holding multiple citizenship, but not having the citizenship or the right to vote in the country of their residence or domicile. Hammar (forthcoming) has produced a remarkable calculation that resident non-citizens living and working in European countries include 180,000 in Belgium, 2,800,000 in France, 2,620,000 in West Germany, 400,000 in the Netherlands, 390,000 in Sweden and 100,000 in Switzerland. Many of these alien residents may be well-paid expatriates (see above) who are not particularly concerned with exercising the franchise and have compensating employment benefits – a group, in short, that can be seen as transcending the limits of the nation-state. However, the numbers involved in Hammar's calculations suggest that many residents have been systematically excluded from citizenship and its accompanying rights without any compensating benefits deriving from their employment. These form part of the helot category.

Helots

I have used the category 'helots' in a somewhat more inclusive way in Cohen (1987). Here I refer more narrowly to people who have illegally entered the country, people who have overstayed the period granted on their entry visas, asylum-seekers who have not been recognised under the international Conventions, those who are working illegally, and those who have been granted only limited rights. A good example (cited in Castles *et al.*, 1984:77) appears in a statement given to officials as to how to operate the 1965 West German Foreigners Law:

'Foreigners enjoy all basic rights, except the basic rights of freedom of assembly, freedom of association, freedom of movement and free choice of occupation, place of work and place of education and protection from extradition abroad.'

Statements such as this reveal the powerful attempt to try to exclude, detain or deport foreigners who are regarded as disposable units of labour-power to whom the advantages of citizenship, the franchise and social welfare are denied.

Conclusion

As Marshall (1950) argues, conferring citizenship is the key indicator of integration and acceptance within a nation state. This basic symbol of inclusion is signified by the right to elect periodically a new government. But the exercise of the vote has become of rather lesser significance than the other attendant benefits of citizenship – access to national insurance systems, unemployment benefits, housing support, health care and social security. In addition to these undoubted advantages, citizens of the European nations within the European Community will soon have untrammelled rights to live, work, own property and travel within a wider Europe.

Helots and denizens are, by the same token, symbolically excluded and practically denied all the advantages just listed. In the case of the denizens, this may not be particularly burdensome – denizen may be an employee of a multinational company with access to private medical insurance. But for a helot, the denial of citizenship is usually a traumatic and life-threatening decision. Given their vulnerability, the helots have become the key means for inducing labour flexibility and provide a target for nationalist and racist outrages.

Our trichotomy leads one to speculate that a new form of stratification has emerged which in origin has little to do with income, occupation, racial or ethnic background, gender, or a particular relationship to the means of production. Of course, there are likely to be coincidences between the different patterns of stratification. A helot is likely to be a Third World migrant, a member of a stigmatised minority, with low income, holding an unskilled occupation and having limited access to housing, education and other social benefits. Similarly, a professionally-educated, urban, middle-class salary-earner, who happens to be a foreigner, is likely to be a denizen.

Migration after the 1970s to a new country will not necessarily carry the optimistic possibilities characteristic of migration at the turn of the century. Then the 'huddled masses', that time from Europe as well as from Asia, threw off their poverty and feudal bondage to enter the American dream as equal citizens. Equally it was perfectly possible for English and Irish convicts to become landowners and gentlemen farmers in Australia. Nowadays, one's legal or national status – whether, in my terms, a citizen, helot or denizen – will increasingly operate as indelible stigmata, determining a set of life chances, access to a particular kind of employment or any employment and other indicators of privilege and good fortune.

Questions

1 Describe the main differences in the status of 'citizens, denizens and helots'.
2 Describe and illustrate from the above passage neo-Marxist interpretation of labour im/migration.

Work, Unemployment and Non-work

Yesterday's working class. Today's …?

Aims of this chapter

1 To establish that work in Britain is influenced by the international context.

2 To introduce and critically review the Fordism/Post-Fordism debate.

3 To discuss the effects of changes in the labour market on major social groups.

4 Critically to present some classic sociological perspectives on the experience of work, including alienation.

5 To present and explain developments in industrial relations, including the roles of trade unions and professions.

6 To discuss the varied and changing relationships between work and non-work (mainly leisure).

Introduction

Developments in the economy and the workplace greatly affect the rest of society. On the other hand, the impact of Thatcherism – first economically then more widely – lends support to those who argue that ideas and ideology can influence society. This chapter starts with the changing structure and organisation of work. In particular, the so-called 'flexibility' of the contemporary labour market and capitalist-managerial strategies are discussed in terms of insecurity and anxiety. The chapter then briefly deals with how this affects people in terms of gender, 'race' and age. The following section deals with unemployment which is seen as a varying experience, though devastating for some. There follows a long section on the experience of work, which along with family, remains central to the life of most people. The sections on industrial interest groups and the professions cover the 'nitty gritty' of industrial organisations and relations. The final section on work and non-work explores the question of whether the relationship of work to leisure has radically changed.

However, we begin with the global context, the importance of which is perhaps still not fully grasped by Britain's notoriously insular population. It is well understood by Britain's big business community, however – 45% of the labour force of Britain's top 100 companies is based abroad and almost half of their profits are made abroad.

The changing international, national and regional context of work

Economic internationalisation means that in certain crucial respects, national economies are increasingly becoming part of a global or world economy. A key feature of economic globalisation is that more money is transferred more easily across national boundaries. Money is transferred in this way for the purpose of investment, i.e. to make more money. Much of this money is simply invested in foreign currencies – which may strengthen (increase in value) – and government bonds or bank accounts which pay interest. However, money is also invested more directly in business either through buying shares in a foreign company or by wholesale takeover of a foreign company (i.e. by purchasing enough shares to control it). This process has increased greatly over the past decade. It was made easier by the so-called financial 'big bang' of 1986 which 'deregulated' or reduced government regulation of the financial functions of the City of London. It is notable that in the period following 'big bang' European takeovers in Britain increased in total value by several hundred per cent (see Table 9.1a). According to one estimate, half of the British workforce will be employed by foreign owned companies by the year 2000. However, in the fast changing world of global investments such figures are mere guestimates. Thus, in 1996, there was some evidence that Britain was slipping relative to some other European countries as a site of inward investment. It is the very uncertainties of the global economy that can make national economies vulnerable.

Table 9.1 British industry and trade in global context

(a) Britain's looming takeover gap

Year	UK deals in Europe, £m	European deals in Britain, £m	Balance, £m
1984	348	145	203
1986	477	1,343	-866
1988	2,788	5,821	-3,033
1989*	2,382	4,038	-1,656

First 11 months

(b) Foreign firms' acquisitions in Britain 1988–9

Target	Bidder	Nationality	Value, £m
Rowntree	Nestlé	Swiss	2,622
Jaguar	Ford Motor	American	1,560
Inter-Continental Hotels	Seibu Saison	Japanese	1,350
Pearl Group	AMP	Australian	1,243
Morgan Grenfell	Deutsche Bank	West German	950

Note: table includes deals that are still pending 29.35%.

(Source: Acquisitions Monthly in *The Sunday Times*, 3.12.1989: D11)

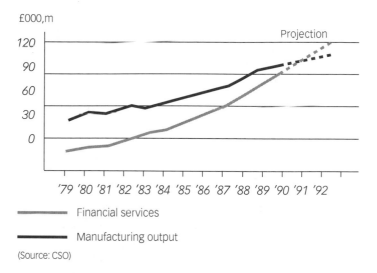

£000,m

Financial services

Manufacturing output

(Source: CSO)

Figure 9.1 A nation of bankers. The changing relative value of manufacturing and financial services.

Britain is a major focal point of global economic change. It is not possible to understand work in contemporary Britain without having at least a basic appreciation of how and why this is so. A preliminary distinction must be made between financial and industrial capitalism. Financial capitalism refers to the management of money by banks, investment houses, firms of stockbrokers and other financial companies. Nick Leeson was a currency trader for Barings bank. The fact that he was able to lose the bank almost one billion pounds without his fraudulent trading practices being discovered indicates the massive scale of this trade. Industrial capitalism refers to the production of goods and services for the market. Clearly, industrial capitalism requires investment loans from the financial sector.

London has been and remains a major world financial centre and although now relatively declining, Britain remains a major industrial power (see Figure 9.1). The role of London as a world financial centre can be readily appreciated by the fact that the annual worth of European, Japanese and United States financial business done in London (often involving companies, banks, and governments from all three – and elsewhere) dwarfs the value of exclusively British financial business. The financial services sector generates a large number of high status and well-paid jobs as does the fact that London is the location of central government and much of the civil service. Professional, administrative and business people are supported by a vast army of lower white-collar employees which tends to keep employment relatively buoyant in the capital and the south east.

The tendency for business investment and ownership to become more international is well exemplified by Britain. The flow of capital investment both into and out of Britain has greatly increased since the mid 1980s. As Table 9.1 shows, between 1986 and 1989 European companies invested much more in takeovers in Britain than British companies invested in takeovers in continental Europe, a trend which has tended to continue. Figure 9.3 gives details of the foreign takeover of Britain's car industry.

The gap with Europe has been somewhat offset by massive

takeover action by British companies in the United States, where in the second half of the 1980s, they took over £30 billion worth of corporate America. Further, British international companies generally enjoy powerful if not dominant positions in relation to less developed economies (see Chapter 20). What we are witnessing, therefore, is a genuine internationalisation of the economy, not simply an increase in 'foreign' investment in British industry – although it may sometimes appear like the latter within Britain. Figure 9.2 shows that in 1993, British foreign investment grew to 10 billion. Two-thirds was in Europe where investment grew fastest and one-third was in the rest of the world.

The internationalisation of the British economy has affected different regions differently. As described above, London as a world financial centre (and as the seat of central government) has been the main beneficiary from internationalisation. The south east and much of the rest of the south has enjoyed a 'knock-on' effect from the wealth and prosperity of London. The north (and west) have been more peripheral to international wealth and investment. In addition, the decline of manufacturing industry has adversely affected the north much more than the south. The result of these factors are that the north, by most measures, is at a substantial economic and social disadvantage to the south. Figure 19.2 (see p. 557) gives two bases of comparison although many more could have been selected. They show the south at an advantage, respectively, in average income and in its lower unemployment rate. Even the 1991-2 recession which 'bit' first in the south has not greatly affected this pattern.

It is possible to exaggerate the differences between south and north. The average differences between the two areas such as those given above are far less than the extent of the differences that occur within each. There has been Japanese investment in the north east and Wales as well as the south; there is poverty in London as well as Liverpool and millionaires in both cities. Nevertheless, there are substantial regional differences reflecting the uneven development of the British capitalist economy. However, there are signs that job

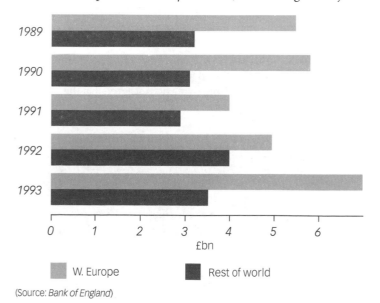

W. Europe   Rest of world

(Source: *Bank of England*)

Figure 9.2 UK foreign direct investment, outflow by region

A possible capacity scenario for 1997?

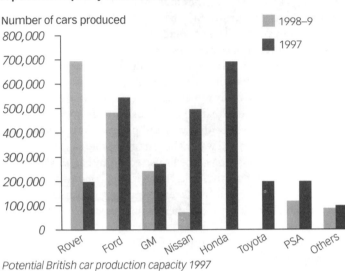

Potential British car production capacity 1997
(overwhelmingly Japanese and American owned)

Note: The 1997 figures for Rover proved pessimistic – only because Rover
was taken over by BMW.

(Source: Adapted from D G Rhys (Cardiff Business School, 1990) reprinted in Running The
Country, Open University, 1992, Unit 12:133)

Figure 9.3 Britain is part of the global capitalist system

cuts in the service sector in the1990s, along with other factors, may
have affected the south more than the north, thus, reducing
regional inequalities.

The Fordism and post-Fordism debate

The analysis that capitalist production is moving from a 'Fordist' to
a 'post-Fordist' era is an interesting but much challenged one. The
analysis was popularised by M J Piore and C F Sabel *The Second
Industrial Divide: Possibilities for Prosperity* (1984). They argue that
capitalism is undergoing a process of 'restructuring' and becoming
in a number of ways less rigid and more 'flexible'. As we shall see,
although most commentators on technological and economic
change recognise that some fundamental developments in
capitalism have been occurring, many do not agree that the
Fordism/post-Fordism polarisation is the best way of describing
them.

Philip Cooke gives a useful description of Fordism:

> *Fordism was associated with large-scale, mass production
> methods as pioneered by Henry Ford in Detroit and extended
> even to the factory building of mass housing in the 1960s.
> 'Fordism' is a shorthand for the method of social, political and
> economic regulation which linked, by making interdependent,
> mass production and mass consumption.*
>
> *(1989:8–9)*

The prototype of Fordist production is, of course, the original
Ford car itself – coming off the production line as it did in
standardised millions. The organisation and experience of mass
assembly-line production at a much later date was well described
in Huw Beynon's *Working for Ford* (1973): 'they [management]
decide on their measured day how fast we will work. They seem to
forget that we're not machines'.

Such highly controlled and precisely measured work is
associated with the management techniques developed by
Frederick Taylor (see below, p. 288) which complemented mass
production methods.

Fordist mass production depends upon, and helps to foster
mass consumption. Without the mass consumption of mass-
produced products, companies would quickly go bankrupt.
Indeed, thousands of Ford cars remained unsold when the mass
car market collapsed following the 1929 Wall Street Crash.
Governmental support for large-scale Fordist-type industries takes
the form of grants, tax concessions, government-industry
partnership schemes, and planning and development co-operation
and assistance. More important perhaps, governments also
undertook to stabilise demand for products through 'full'
employment and income support schemes i.e. to ensure people
could buy products.

The key concept of post-Fordist analysis is 'flexibility'. Piore and
Sabel argue that 'flexible specialisation' is a growing feature of
capitalist production. As a result, greater variety and variation of
products occurs (Table 9.2).

Specialisation can occur in several ways but commonly involves
higher skilled, more co-operative work to produce small,
sometimes customised batches. One example of specialised
production is the emergence of smaller, specialised firms which
may adopt quasi-craft production processes, aided by high-tech
equipment to produce individualised, high quality, and sometimes
customised products. According to Piore and Sabel, the causal
driving force behind these developments is the increased demand
from the consumer market for more varied and different products.

J Atkinson: the flexible firm

J Atkinson, in a series of publications, has discussed the
management of labour in terms broadly complementary to post-
Fordist theory. He has developed a model of the flexible firm which
contrasts strongly with the Fordist mass production monolith.
According to Atkinson, the flexible firm concentrates chiefly on
ensuring a flexible labour force. There are two main aspects to this:

1 Numerical flexibility
2 Functional flexibility

Numerical flexibility involves having a somewhat smaller core
of permanent full-time workers than in the traditional industrial
firm and the use of more temporary, part-time, and sub-
contracted workers. Functional flexibility involves employing and
often training a labour force that is more multi-skilled and using it

in a variety of work which might well cross the demarcations traditionally insisted on by unions. Implicit, therefore, in the development of the flexible firm is the decline of traditional unionism and the individualisation of the work force and/or the emergence of unions willing to negotiate more 'flexible' working conditions. Not surprisingly, some have seen this as a threat to the strength of unions and to job security. Certainly, in Britain it is a process that has been facilitated by the 'Thatcherite' legislation on the unions (see p. 270).

Atkinson's flexibility model substantially draws from the longer established dual labour force theory. This theory argues that due largely to the strategy of capitalists, the labour force has become increasingly divided into a core (or primary) groups and a peripheral (of secondary) group (see Figure 9.4). The core labour force is appointed to give reliable, full-time service in meeting the essential and predictable needs of a firm, for which it is relatively highly rewarded in terms of pay and job security. It tends to be overwhelmingly male and disproportionately white. The peripheral labour force is employed, as far as possible, when and how a firm's management requires. It tends to be largely female and disproportionately black. This latter group is sometimes referred to as a 'reserve army of labour' – easily hired in a time of economic expansion and redundant during contraction.

By no means all occupational groups indicated by Atkinson fit into the core/periphery model. Indeed, as Figure 9.4 indicates, a growing number of self-employed (e.g. business consultants) and sub-contractors, usually enjoying high pay and status are outside the primary labour market. However, employers expect quality and reliability of service from such groups.

Table 9.2 Fordist and post-Fordist production summarised

	Fordist	**Post-Fordist**
Technology	Dedicated, fixed machinery	Micro-electronically controlled, flexible, multi-purpose machinery
	Economies of scale	Economies of scope
	Vertical integration	Sub-contracting
	Mass production	Batch production
Product	Mass-consumption	Varied and 'niche' products
	Relatively cheap	Varied/High price Varied/High quality
Labour process	Highly fragmented	More integrated
	Few tasks	Many tasks
	Little autonomy	Greater autonomy
	Hierarchical authority and technical control	Group (e.g. 'task-group') control
Contract	Collectively negotiated	Varied (Individually) Negotiated
	Rate for the job	Performance related pay
	Secure	Varied dual labour force

Note: The points under 'Technology' and 'Product' roughly summarise Piore's analysis and those under 'Labour Process' and 'Contract' Atkinson's.

Extending post-Fordist analysis

The application of the Fordist/post-Fordist framework to economics, industrial organisation and relations, and, by implication, to class is highly significant in itself. However, this theoretical model has been extended to apply to developments in politics, education and culture as well. These applications are taken up at the appropriate points in this book. However, it is relevant to give here M Rustin's ideal type summary model of Fordism/Post-Fordism along with brief, necessary explanations in order to demonstrate the scope of this theoretical approach.

The ideal types of Fordist and post-Fordist modes of production and regulation can be summarised (with some sectoral applications) as shown in Table 9.3 on the next page.

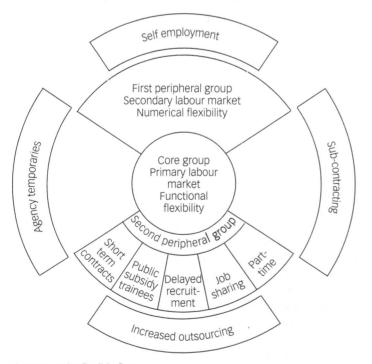

Figure 9.4 The flexible firm

Table 9.3 Fordist and post-Fordist modes of production

Area of society	Fordism	Post-Fordism
Industry	low technological innovation, fixed product lines, long runs, mass marketing	accelerated innovation, high variety of product, shorter runs, market diversification and niche-ing
	steep hierarchy, vertical chains of command, mechanistic organisation vertical and horizontal integration, central planning	flat hierarchy, more lateral communications, organismic organisation autonomous profit centres, network systems, internal markers within firm, out-sourcing
	bureaucracy	professionalism, entre-preneurialism
	mass unions, generalised wage-bargaining	localised bargaining: core and periphery; workforce divided
Class/politics	unified class formations, dualistic political systems	class politics, pluralised class formations, multi-party systems, social movements
	institutionalised class compromises, nationwide parties	fragmented political markets, regional diversification
Welfare state/ education	standardised forms of welfare prescribed 'courses' in education	consumer choice in welfare, credit transfer, modularity, self-guided instruction; 'independent' study
Private consumption/style	standardised consumption (cars, houses, dress)/styles	more varied consumption and personalised styles

(Source: Rustin, *The Politics of Post-Fordism* in *New Left Review*, No. 175, 1989 – adapted and extended)

Most of the content of Rustin's summary should be clear from what has already been said. However, the model does highlight an aspect of post-Fordist analysis not so far specifically emphasised: the less hierarchical, decentralised modes of management supposedly characteristic of the post-Fordist 'era'. Again, this is to allow more flexibility for local managers, or managers within large firms dealing with particular work teams to deal with problems specific to their own situation. The section of the summary model on management is from 'steep hierarchy … flat hierarchy' to 'bureaucracy/professionalism'. The model also suggests that the traditional 'dualistic' mould (middle versus working class) of politics is fragmenting and that the welfare state, too, is being remoulded to respond to the different demands of various consumer groups. The model further presents education as becoming increasingly flexible in terms of skills and courses taught,

methods of access and delivery, and of assessment. Finally, the model suggests that the basis of politics is becoming significantly more decentralised and regionally based and focused around issues which give rise to social movements distinct from the traditional class parties (e.g. the feminist movement, see Chapter 7).

Even Rustin's broad summary model does not give the full scope of the Fordist/post-Fordist analysis. The analysis of post-Fordist production links easily with the postmodern emphasis on consumption and style. Thus, consumption, like production, is seen as more individualised, less 'massified' and less predictable. The importance of consumption in the analysis of post-Fordism continues to gain ever greater emphasis. It is central, however, to Robin Murray's relatively early and highly influential article 'Fordism and Post-Fordism'. Murray argues that both retailing and manufacturing have become more flexible but that, on balance, retailing – the market – drives manufacturing. He describes in detail how computerised retailing enables retailers to respond quickly to consumer demand by feeding the relevant information to manufacturers and suppliers. The analysis that consumption has replaced production as the central feature of late capitalist society is highly controversial but – overblown or not – it addresses a genuine phenomenon (see Reading 1).

Criticisms of post-Fordism analysis

It is not uncommon for proponents of a new theory to exaggerate the possible extent of its application. Stephen Wood (1989) suggests as much in respect to Piore and Sable and their Fordist/post-Fordist analysis. He argues that in some cases, they consider what, in his view, are relatively minor changes in the organisation of production to be examples of flexible specialisation. Thus, he contends that the modifications to traditional Fordist production adopted by Japanese firms such as the introduction of quality circles, flatter management structures (and, more recently, project managers), do not amount to a radical transformation of work. Indeed, he dubs such approaches 'neo-Fordist' – emphasising that they are incorporated within Fordism. Further, the success of Japanese firms has not been based mainly on production for 'niche' markets (although there have been some recent moves in the latter direction).

A number of commentators have been highly critical of the limited empirical basis of claims that a full transition to post-Fordism has occurred in Britain. Bryn Jones' examination of the British engineering industry failed to establish a systematic trend towards flexible specialisation (1988). As a technologically advanced industry, such a trend might have been expected in engineering if it is, in fact, occurring in Britain. Christabe Lane's comparison of the extent of flexible specialisation in Britain and Germany finds substantial evidence in the case of the latter but little in the case of the former. Jones further observes that labour market segmentation appears to have occurred more in the public than in the private sector (e.g. the creation of more part-time and temporary posts in education) where Conservative governments have been able to enforce Thatcherite policies.

Anna Pollert (1988) has strongly criticised post-Fordist theory, and particularly the work of Atkinson. In general, her arguments and interpretation of empirical data lead her to emphasise variety and complexity rather than any single overarching trend such as post-Fordism. Thus, she argues that Fordism was never so overwhelmingly dominant a method of production nor have new methods replaced Fordism to the extent that some analysis suggests. For instance, batch production continued alongside Fordist production and currently many smaller firms cannot afford to invest in flexible, computerised technology. Second, she rejects the implication that flexibility generally requires a more skilled workforce. Actual practice again suggests a complex picture with both skilling and deskilling occurring in different situations. Third, Pollert is also unconvinced that there has been an increase in the numbers of 'peripheral' workers. She points to a decline in proportion to full-time workers in manufacturing although there is no doubt that there has been a sharp increase in part-time female workers in the service sector.

Marxists differ in the extent to which they consider that neo-Fordism has taken over from Fordism. However, they are agreed that – where it occurs – neo-Fordism is an adaptation within capitalism and, therefore, offers at best only limited gains for workers. Workers are still managed – perhaps, even more managed – and 'exploited' by capitalism for profit. Further, it has become clear in the 1990s, that middle level employees thought of as 'core' may also be subject to 'down-sizing' and redundancy. In terms of salaries and security, it is those at the *very* top that are the main beneficiaries of recent changes in managerial strategies and techniques. In Braverman's theoretical framework, capitalists use management to implement ruthless policies to make more profits. Nor do Marxists consider that under neo-Fordism workers regain significant power and control over their own work, the workplace or what they produce. For this, the kind of changes discussed later in this and the next chapter would be required (see pp. 267-8 and pp. 293-7).

In *The Nature of Work* (1989), Paul Thompson refutes some of the key elements of post-Fordism as presented by Murray. He argues that Fordist production methods were themselves being developed more flexibly; that Fordist methods – far from being moribund – were in some cases being adopted in 1980s Britain; and that the age of mass production is far from over. An extract from Thompson develops these points (Reading 2).

Finally, Thompson and Acroyd warn against mistaking the current period of capitalist-managerial ascendancy as a necessarily permanent state of affairs. In their article *All Quiet on the Workplace Front: A Critique of Recent Trends in British Industrial Sociology* (1995), they comment that '(t)he essential conditions for resistance and misbehaviour are still present'. Indeed as Marxists, they go further and assert that 'as industrial sociologists, we have to put labour back in by doing theory and research in such a way that it is possible to 'see' resistance'.

Post-Fordism: for and against – a summary

Areas of general agreement:

1 Advanced technology (especially micro-chip) has increased flexibility – more machine than labour intensive, greater product variety.
2 The globalisation of capital (though Marxists refute the notion of a *fundamentally* changed and different capitalism and free-market theorists note the complementary rise of small-business).
3 Changes in the organisation of the work force e.g. removal of job demarcation lines more individualised contracts (post-Fordists see this as flexibility, Marxists as a potential strategy for capitalists better to exploit labour).
4 The production of a greater variety of consumer products.

Areas of general disagreement:

Economic

1 No consensus that the labour force is organised in a fundamentally different way than in the 'Fordist' phrase of capitalism or that labour militancy is 'dead' (Marxists disagree on both counts).
2 Empirical data on some key aspects of post-Fordism is inconclusive e.g. the relationship between full-time and part-time employees.

Political and cultural

3 There is not agreement that the class basis of politics is over or even greatly diminished.
4 'Consumerism' is seen as a sign of progress by some but as a form of capitalistic control and manipulation by others.

The changing context and conditions of work: insecurity and opportunity

At the height of Thatcherism in 1987-88, there was a widespread feeling of economic optimism and opportunity. The recession of 1989-92 reversed that feeling and a new climate of insecurity has lingered into the late 1990s. The optimism of the late 1980s was certainly excessive and it is possible that the gloomier mood of the 1990s will also prove exaggerated. However, there are substantial underlying developments which indicate that for many, the level of security enjoyed in work and life may not be as high again for the foreseeable future.

First, the managerial approaches and techniques described above – whatever name one gives them – mean relatively more power for management and less for other employees. Management policies described by such terms as 'restructuring', 'down-sizing' or 're-engineering' often imply redundancies, job-reassignment or invitations to employees to reapply for their jobs. Second, managerial monitoring and surveillance of employees' activities is greatly facilitated by new technology. Marsden argues that electronic technology can assist those responsible for 'human resources' and organisational behaviour to 'observe, examine and normalise performance and behaviour' (1993:118). Third, and perhaps most importantly, the push for 'efficiency' savings and increased profits comes from capitalists themselves – whether they be major individual or institutional owners (shareholders).

Fourth, government policy generally supported capital and management at the expense of labour during the Conservative period in office. The Thatcher-Major years saw a stream of legislation which reduced controls on economic activity (deregulation), removed much employment protection and reduced trade union power. The latter is significant enough to be regarded as a major factor in the growth of economic insecurity in its own right.

Percentage of all adults 16–59/64

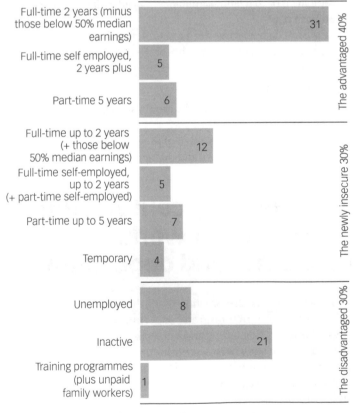

(Source: Hutton in *The Guardian*, 30.10.1995:2)

Figure 9.5 The 30/30/40 society

Who has been affected by labour market change?

In order to achieve a clear approach to this question, it will help to employ the economist Will Hutton's concept of the '30/30/40 society'. Although Hutton is politically left of centre, the factual basis of his analysis appears neutral. Figure 9.5 describes the subgroups which make up his three main categories of the disadvantaged (30%), the newly insecure (30%), and the advantaged (40%). Obviously, Hutton's framework is not static and the precise percentages in each grouping will change over time. However, his model does seem to capture the general impact of the labour market and managerial changes discussed above.

The disadvantaged (30%) (the unemployed and economically inactive)

Table 9.4 gives the numbers unemployed by region since 1992. The unemployed are among those whose disadvantage is obvious and established. However, there are significantly different degrees of disadvantage among the unemployed as is discussed later in this chapter (see pp. 260-2).

Hutton comments that the 21 per cent of the working population who are now economically inactive is a particularly worrying figure because of its changing membership and because it is an expanding group. In the relatively full-employment period of the early 1970s, this segment was mainly comprised of women bringing up children, who had voluntarily withdrawn from the labour market. Now it is made up largely of men of working age and of single parents.

Britain has the lowest percentage of its single parents in paid work in the European Community. There are two reasons for this. First, is Britain's inadequate provision of pre-school childcare. Second, is the poverty-trap – pay in the low pay sector is so poor that many single parents would gain little from taking a paid job. Both these points are discussed elsewhere (see pp. 78-80).

One in four men in Britain of working age is now unemployed or economically inactive. The main cause of the latter is early retirement – frequently due to redundancy. Hutton goes on to cite an even more remarkable statistic – that nearly one in two men between the ages of 55 and 65 are economically inactive compared to ten per cent in 1977. People – of whatever age – with non-transferable or only limited skills, have the least chance of re-employment. Thus, according to the Coalfield Communities Campaign, the unemployment rate among miners a year after losing their jobs was about 46 per cent. Many of these were young men. Those who found employment, experienced an average wage drop of 30 per cent.

The fear of redundancy is a major cause of insecurity, if not anxiety, among many employees. This is not surprising in view of the findings of the report on the Future of Social Protection in the European Union (1995), that the unemployed in Britain are relatively worse of them in any of the other major industrial states of the Union.

Table 9.4 Misery league

The number of people made unemployed at least once since the 1992 election

Region	Total
Greater London	1,400,260
South-east	1,397,200
East Anglia	289,060
South-west	709,080
West Midlands	814,680
East Midlands	582,140
Yorks and Humberside	775,900
North-west	1,018,020
North	498,880
Wales	419,640
Scotland	821,240
Great Britain	8,726,100

(Source: *JUVOS Cohort database*, CSO in *The Independent* 4.3.1996:2)

The newly insecure (30%) (low-pay; part-time work, redundancy)

A much larger proportion of those in paid work are vulnerable to fairly easy dismissal or, for the self-employed uncompensated job loss compared to the 'job for life' society of 30 years ago. Part-time, temporary, and full-time either self-employed or employed by others of less than two years standing, fall into this growing category. Even in post-recession 1996, it was estimated that redundancies would run at 800,000 per year for the foreseeable future.

Why has this category of potentially insecure employees mushroomed? Hutton gives two reasons: successive Employment Acts have reduced employee protection and as companies have come under intense and growing pressure from institutional shareholders, they have often 'down-sized' to increase profitability and dividends. A third reason, is the growth in part-time and temporary work which has affected mainly women. One estimate is that the percentage of jobs which are part-time will increase from 25% to almost 50% between 1994 and 2004 (Low Pay Network). This is almost certainly an exaggeration based on an atypical time-period – but the trend to part-time work is clear.

Hutton stresses the negative factors of the new insecurity. These certainly seem to outweigh any positive ones as far as most employees are concerned although some no doubt gain something from labour market 'flexibility'. Writing in *The Observer*, Neasa MacErlean finds that for those with marketable skills, redundancy need not be a disaster.

> *But people with a wide range of skills can find redundancy liberating. Chartered accountant Paul Le Druillence works in the media industry. He has been made redundant three times and has himself given the chop to about 30 people over the last seven years. He has just added lecturing his usual activities of advising businesses and individuals on tax and finance.*
>
> *Every time I have been made redundant I have always gone on to more work. It's more perilous but more fun and more satisfying working for yourself.*
>
> *(Down and Out Britain, The Observer, Business Section, 17.3.1996:1)*

Frankly, Paul Le Druillence is likely to be the exception even among the better qualified and more highly skilled. However, MacErlean does cite figures in pit-closures which indicate that one year after being made redundant ten times as many senior and middle managers as miners had become self-employed. For Hutton, the doubling of self-employment between 1985 and 1995 to fifteen per cent illustrates growing job insecurity rather than the success of the entrepreneurial culture. No doubt self-employment is a different experience for different people but 40 per cent who start up in small businesses will have gone out of business within three years.

There is a strongly gendered aspect to the newly 'flexible' (or insecure) labour market just as there is to the poverty trap. This is discussed separately below (see pp. 259-60).

The advantaged (40%) (full-time (two years) and part-time (five years) in employment)

It is important to stress that the advantages are, as Hutton's label suggests, in a more advantageous position in terms of job security and wages than others. Their jobs are covered by union or professional association negotiated agreements. They have enjoyed a relatively large share of the increase in national wealth (see p. 376).

Yet, there is evidence that many of the advantaged, too, have begun to feel economically vulnerable and insecure. Hutton observes that full-time, tenured employment is decreasing at the rate of one per cent per year – a trend which builds up cumulative significance over a number of years. By the year 2000, Hutton estimates, this type of employment will be in the minority.

Figure 9.6 The nervous nineties. Shadows of their former selves: middle managers stripped of power and security

Stuck in the nervous nineties

Another factor that has unsettled this mainly middle class category is that, increasingly they have been losing their jobs. Between 1990 and 1995, 100,000 jobs were lost in banking. Credit agency, Standard and Poor's, estimates that the life insurance industry will lose 45,000 of its 140,000 jobs between 1996 and 1998. After the culling of the manual worker, comes the culling of the clerks! Already, tens of thousands of middle class jobs have been cut as the privatised utilities such as British Gas have sought efficiency gains.

Unsurprisingly, a Gallup poll survey published in early 1995 showed that the white-collar middle classes were expressing feelings of economic insecurity and job anxiety almost on a par with the working classes (Table 9.5).

One apparent symptom of anxiety in the workplace is the fact that the British work the longest hours in the European Union (Figure 9.7). While this is not a new phenomenon, it is notable that the length of the usual working week in Britain increased during a period when it was generally decreasing in other EU countries.

Seumas Milne, a labour correspondent, comments:

> *The shift towards longer hours in Britain is partly the result of the exceptionally high level of overtime worked. But it also reflects the trend towards longer hours – often unpaid – being worked by managerial and professional employees to ensure successful career development.*
>
> *(The Guardian, 14.2.1995:1)*

Anthony Sampson: interpreting middle class anxiety

In his article *Stuck in the Nervous Nineties* (*The Observer*) based on his book, *Company Man: The Rise and Fall of Corporate Life* (1995), Anthony Sampson draws together some useful insights on the middle class. He cites United States politician and author, Robert Reich's distinction between the 'anxious class' – professionals, bureaucrats and middle managers – and the 'over-class' of the competitive middle classes. This broad distinction is between those who fear the developments under discussion and those who think they will thrive on them. Unsociological as Reich's comment may be as an approach to class, it pin-points a significant split in the middle class between the enthusiasts and prime beneficiaries of recent change – often towards the top of big business – and those less comfortable with change, more often at middle level positions. As Sampson puts it the corporations 'are replacing lifetime employees with short-term consultants and temporary managers. And they have more powerful, richer men at the top'.

Reich suggests that the 'coming political battle' will be fought for the vote of 'the anxious class'. Reich is writing primarily of the United States but his comments are equally relevant to Britain. Tony Blair seems to share Reich's perception in claiming that 'the central question of modern democratic policies is how to provide security during revolutionary change' (*The Financial Times* 20.3.1996:18).

Table 9.5 Unemployment in the middle and working classes

Middle class fear spectre of unemployment

By Anthony King

Gallup's interviewers asked: *There is a lot of talk at the moment about 'economic security' – the feeling that people don't know whether their jobs, earnings or homes are safe or not.*

From your own personal experience, do you think a lot of people are feeling economically insecure or not?'

Respondents were than asked: *'Do you yourself feel economically insecure?'*

Feelings of insecurity are still more widespread among manual workers but more than half of all middle class people now admit to feeling threatened:

	Middle classes	Working classes
Think a lot of people feel economically insecure	92	94
Feel economically insecure themselves	52	68

More than one-fifth of middle class families, 21 per cent, say they are already affected by unemployment and nearly three times that number, 60 per cent, may have jobless friends or acquaintances.

Gallup asked those in work in both classes: *'Do you think that your present job is safe or do you think there is any chance you may become unemployed?'*

As the replies show, middle class people are now almost as likely to be anxious about their job as manual workers:

	Middle classes	Working classes
Chance of unemployment	31	40
Job safe	66	53
Don't know	3	6

Respondents were asked: *'How confident are you that the amount of money you and your family have to spend will remain as high as it is now during the coming year?'*

Nearly half the middle classes, 45 per cent, are either *'not very confident'* or *'not at all confident'*:

	Middle classes	Working classes
Very confident	14	6
Fairly confident	38	28
Not very confident	30	37
Not at all confidence	15	23
Don't know	3	6

(Source: Gallup poll interview for *The Daily Telegraph* 9.1.1995:5. The author is Professor of Sociology, Essex University)

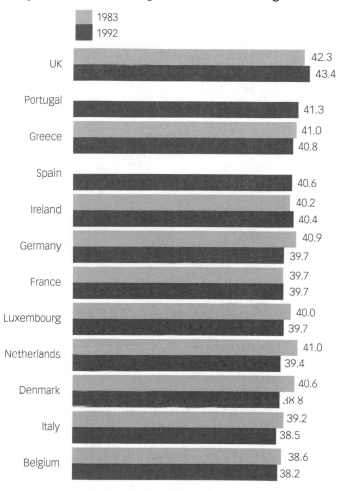

Changes in the usual working week, hours. EU average: 40.3

- 1983
- 1992

	1983	1992
UK	42.3	43.4
Portugal		41.3
Greece	41.0	40.8
Spain		40.6
Ireland	40.2	40.4
Germany	40.9	39.7
France	39.7	39.7
Luxembourg	40.0	39.7
Netherlands	41.0	39.4
Denmark	40.6	38.8
Italy	39.2	38.5
Belgium	38.6	38.2

(Source: *Eurostat* in *The Guardian*, 24.1.1995:1)

Figure 9.7 Working late

The changing labour market: gender, race and age

The economic developments and changes in the workplace and working practices so far described in this chapter have resulted in changes in the labour market. The particular effect of these changes on women, black people and youth are discussed in the relevant chapters but a brief overview is appropriate here. Although job insecurity has become widespread in the 1990s, these groups are especially vulnerable.

By no means all, but a disproportionate number of women, black people and youth are disadvantaged in the labour market. It can be argued that in each case there is an element of discrimination in the disadvantage. Women have tended to fill the

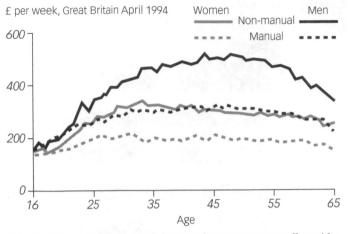

£ per week, Great Britain April 1994

Note: Full-time employees on adult rates whose pay was not affected for this survey period by absence.

(Source: *Social Focus on Women: 1996*)

Figure 9.8 Average gross weekly earnings

more routine office jobs and many positions (usually lower status) in the educational and welfare professions that the massive expansion of the service sector has provided. The crux of disadvantage in the case of women lies in the fact that the time and work they put into childcare and the household frequently damages their career prospects. Patriarchy is the system that tolerates and fosters gender inequality, i.e. it is a system which discriminates against women. Figure 9.8 show the effects of patriarchy in hard cash terms over a working life.

Black people tended to do low paid jobs in manufacturing or other manual work during the 1950s and 1960s. There is ample evidence that racial discrimination has been a major factor barring their progress up the occupational hierarchy (see pp. 228-9). The labour market position of many black people has been made acutely worse by the fact that it is in the areas on which the employment of black people has been concentrated – manufacturing and manual work generally – that large-scale job losses have occurred. During the recession of the early 1980s job losses in these areas were massive as was unemployment among black people. Black youth was particularly severely affected. A similar pattern developed in the recession of the early 1990s.

The position of contemporary young people – particularly the poorly qualified – became more difficult during the 1980s and 1990s. The majority of young people move into work, training or further education at sixteen. However, during the 1980s and early1990s, unemployment has varied in a range from about 1.5 to three million, which is extremely high compared to the rest of the post-war period. Quite simply, this has weakened the bargaining power of young people in the employment market and for a substantial number made getting a job more difficult – particularly

for the less well qualified in areas of high unemployment. The average wage of young people as a proportion of the national wage has declined. Some young people have had to take places on training schemes or face unemployment without access to social security. However, both the quantity and quality of training schemes in Britain have been criticised compared to those of several other European countries (see Table 4.10, p. 121). According to the Department for Education and Employment, 7.1 per cent of modern apprentices were in hairdressing and 0.1 in telecommunications. Overall, the position of young people relative to other age groups has weakened, particularly when compared to that of '1960s youth' although this is less true of the south than the north. The position of young people in the labour market should improve somewhat during the late 1990s due to demographic factors.

It is debatable whether there is a single theoretical approach which fully and satisfactorily explains the labour market position of women, black people and youth. Both women and black people have been variously seen as a 'reserve army of labour' or as peripheral workers (see pp. 252-3). The problem with the latter approaches is that they fail to explain why significant numbers of women and increasing numbers of black people, especially of Asian origin, do achieve occupations of middle class status. Marxists argue that it is particularly working class women, black people and youth that experience problems both in obtaining work and when they are in work. They do not deny that gender, 'race' and age play a part in disadvantage and discrimination but argue that this should be contextualised in the broader context of class conflict and exploitation.

Unemployment

Unemployment is an issue that has never been far from national concern from the late 1970s into the1990s. This is because it has twice increased and then twice declined during this period more or less rapidly. In the early 1970s unemployment was somewhat less than one million, by 1985 it was three million, by early 1990 it was 1.6 million, and by 1993 it was close to three million again (see Figure 9.9). However, by 1997 official unemployment was once more under two million. In the first four post-war decades, it was the conventional political wisdom that no government could survive unemployment at over one million, yet the Conservatives have three times won elections when the figure was well over two million. Was the conventional wisdom wrong, or has the nature of unemployment changed, or perhaps people's perception of it?

Thousands

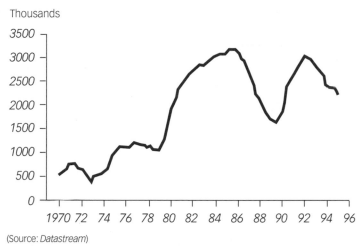

(Source: *Datastream*)

Figure 9.9 Unemployment

Measuring unemployment

The official definition of unemployment is a tight one:

> *People claiming benefit – that is, Unemployment Benefit, Income Support or National Insurance Credits – at Unemployment Benefit Offices on the day of the monthly count, who say on that day they are unemployed and that they satisfy the conditions for claiming benefit.*
>
> *(Department of Employment, cited Employment Gazette, Jan. 1991)*

During the period that the Conservatives have been in office, there have been 32 changes in the way unemployment is measured which together have substantially reduced the official total (see Table 9.6). Thus unemployed men over 60 have been re-classified as retired. Other groups not included in the official figures are those out of work who do not claim benefit, and those on government training schemes. In 1996, the introduction of the Job Seekers Allowance had the immediate effect of removing an officially estimated 15,000 from the unemployment statistics. The Unemployment Unit argues that compared to the old basis of calculation, the official figures underestimate unemployment by about one million (1991). Others claim that overall official figures probably overestimate unemployment. Thus, the voluntarily early retired, who may have no intention of taking employment, can appear in the figures.

Table 9.6 Changes in unemployment counting methods between 1986–89

Change	Estimated alteration
1986	
*Two week delay introduced into announcement of statistics	−50,000
New method of calculating unemployment percentage	−1.4%
Abolition of part-rate unemployment benefit	−30,000
Voluntary unemployment disqualification extended to 13 weeks	−9,000
Restart and availability for work tests toughened	−300,000
1988	
Voluntary unemployment disqualification extended to 26 weeks	−12,000
Definition of part-time work toughened	No estimate
New denominator used to calculate five per cent unemployment	No estimate
*Sixteen and seventeen year olds barred from benefit	−120,000 (−90,000)
Unemployment benefit contributions tests toughened	−38,000
Some 55-60 year olds paid pensions instead of benefits	−30,000
1989	
*Ex-miners not required to register	−26,000 (−15,500)
Claimants required to prove they are looking for work	−25,000
Low wage levels no longer good reason for refusing a job	−25,000
Tightening of regulations to requalify for benefit	−350
Change to the way earnings affect right to benefit	−30,000

*Employment Department agree change in counting methods alter unemployment figures. Department figures in brackets.

(Source: The Unemployment Unit in *The Times*, 19.4.1991:2)

Experiencing unemployment

Probably all commentators on unemployment recognise that it is a complex phenomenon. Crudely, it is not the same for everyone. However, there is still a difference, at least in emphasis, between those who generally see unemployment as a social evil and those who consider that its impact may vary greatly from group to group and from individual to individual. We will refer to the former as 'universalists' and the latter as 'relativists'.

Andrew Sinfield may be counted among the universalists in that he points out that historically, unemployment has tended to hit hardest those least able to cope with it:

> *It is important to emphasise that the most likely to be unemployed are people in low-paying and insecure jobs, the very young and the oldest in the labour force, people from ethnic or racial minorities, people from among the disabled and the handicapped, and generally those with the least skills and living in the most depressed areas. Unemployment strikes, and strikes most harshly and frequently those who are among the poorest and least powerful in the labour force and in society as a whole.*
>
> *(Sinfield, 1981)*

More relativistic approaches to unemployment stress that a variety of individuals in a variety of situations become unemployed. Thus, the type of job a person does, marital status (including whether there are dependants), and age may affect the experience of unemployment. Ken Roberts highlights the age and dependants factors in the following quotation:

> ... spells on the dole appear far less devastating for school-leavers than working class adults with family responsibilities, like life-long steelmen and dockers, who have anchored their identities in the occupations.
>
> (Roberts, 1982)

Long term unemployment correlates strongly with age. In the case of males the percentage of the unemployed who have been out of work over 104 and up to 156 weeks rises with each age group until that of 60 and over. The pattern is similar, if slightly less consistent for women. In particular, generally fewer are unemployed between the ages of 25 and 34 because they are more likely to be out of the employment market. A recent factor which will undoubtedly greatly affect the experience of unemployment is the introduction of 'workfare' programmes. These highly controversial programmes were introduced first in the United States and then in Britain. Like the replacing of unemployment benefit with the Job Seekers Allowance, these programmes embody the philosophy that the able unemployed should orientate their lives to finding work. If they do not do so, benefit can be withdrawn. Critics see this as illiberal and even coercive.

In general, unemployment becomes progressively more likely from the 'top' to the 'bottom' of the occupational scale (see Table 9.7). However, there are variations within and between each sex. Male professionals/employers and managers are a slightly smaller percentage of the unemployed than intermediate/junior non-manual, and skilled and semi-skilled/unskilled manual also make up roughly the same percentage.

In contrast, in the case of females, 85 per cent of unemployment (1988), is concentrated on the intermediate/junior non-manual (48 per cent) and semi-skilled/unskilled manual (36 per cent). These figures vividly reflect the concentration of women in jobs of lower socio-economic status.

As employment becomes increasingly concentrated in the service sector, it is inevitable that relatively more employees in the service sector than in the manufacturing sector will be unemployed. This trend was particularly apparent in the recession of the early 1990s. One indicator of this was that in early 1991 over half the reduction in vacancies at Job Centres was in managerial, clerical and service sector jobs – indicating a sharp contraction in these areas.

Table 9.7 The unemployed: by sex and socio-economic group, 1984 and 1988

Great Britain	Male		Female		All	
	1984	1988	1984	1988	1984	1988
	Percentages		Percentages		Percentages	
Socio-economic group[1] Professional/employers and managers	9	10	6	6	8	8
Intermediate/junior non-manual	10	13	47	48	24	27
Skilled manual	41	39	8	9	29	27
Semi skilled/unskilled manual	39	39	39	36	39	38

1 *Those who did not know or inadequately explained their status prior to unemployment; armed forces; those who have never been in employment or have been unemployed for 3 years or more are excluded from the percentage.*

(Source: *Labour Force Survey*, Department of Employment)

Questions

1 What have been the main changes in the organisation of work in the post-war period?
2 What effect on various groups have the above changes had?
3 Critically discuss the various explanations and theories which seek to account for the broad pattern of unemployment since its rapid rise in the late 1970s/early 1980s.

The experience of work

Broadly, there are three possible responses to work: alienation, neutrality and satisfaction, and we study these below. Beyond mere satisfaction lies the prospect of genuine fulfilment at work and we also consider what this might mean.

Alienation

Marx and Weber

Two accounts of alienation must be distinguished. First is that of Marx: he considered that workers in capitalist society are alienated from work because they own neither what they produce nor the means by which they produce it.

He is quite clear about this:

> *Finally, the alienated character of work for the worker appears in the fact that it is not his work but work for someone else, that in work he does not belong to himself but to another person.*

A further aspect of alienation is apparent in the quotation. Because of the need to sell 'his' labour, the worker loses his independence in work; he becomes alienated from his own activity and thus from himself. The contemporary Marxists, Bowles and Gintis, have attempted to relate the nature of the division of labour in capitalist society to the need of the ruling class to maintain control over the workforce. By daily repeating the same limited task(s), workers are prevented from understanding the whole of the process of production. What they do not understand they can hardly aspire to control. Bowles and Gintis do not, of course, regard the capitalist mode of production and the resultant alienation and mystification of the workforce as inevitable.

A second analysis of alienation is widely adopted. To understand it we must first briefly describe what bureaucracy is. Bureaucracy is a form of organisational structure characterised by a variety of roles, some of which have more authority and status than others. Nearly all large-scale organisations in modern societies are organised in this way and we are so familiar with this form of organisational structure that we tend to think (wrongly) that it is the only type possible (for alternatives see Chapter 10). This approach to understanding alienation rests on the work of Weber, although he himself did not employ the term. In this approach, alienation is seen as caused by the effect on the work situation of the bureaucratic division of labour. Weber considered that working particularly at the lower levels of bureaucracy, such as in a factory or an office, is alienating for two basic reasons. Firstly, doing the same thing over and over again, say, filing invoices, is boring to most people. Secondly, bureaucratic employees have little control over their work situation, and this is unsatisfying. Woodward, Touraine and Blauner have applied Weberian-type analysis specifically to industrial work and we examine their conclusions below. Weber himself was probably the first sociologist to appreciate that lack of identity and control, and a sense of meaninglessness – in short alienation – can equally affect the clerk, the typist, the soldier or anyone who fulfils a small role in a large, bureaucratic organisation. He stressed that alienation can occur as easily in state bureaucracies as in privately owned ones. Indeed, he anticipated that alienation would be a particular problem in socialist societies because of their inevitably (in his view) bureaucratic nature.

Despite the above major differences, Marx and Weber described the psychological consequences of alienation very similarly. The phrase 'feelings of alienation' refers to the same human experience for both. Writing of the industrial labourer, Marx says:

> *He does not fulfil himself in his work but denies himself, has a feeling of misery, not of well-being, does not develop freely a physical and mental energy, but is physically exhausted and mentally debased.*

Etzioni summarises Weber's view and usefully links it with that of Marx:

> *… the worker, soldier, and researcher – and by implication all employees of all organisations – are frustrated, unhappy … When asked, 'all said and done, how satisfied are you with your work?' about 80 per cent of American blue-collar workers answered 'not satisfied'. Alienation is a concept that stands for this sentiment and the analysis of its source in Marxian-Weberian terms.*
>
> *(Etzioni, 1964)*

Despite their common understanding of what it means 'to feel alienated'. Marx and Weber's difference over the origin of alienation is highly significant. Differing diagnoses lead to differing prescriptions. For Marx, the ultimate solution to inequality and alienation to work is to abolish capitalism and establish a communist system in which the means of production and what is produced are the common property. What is produced is then distributed on the basis of need, not purchasing power. This is a road down which Weber had no wish to travel – as we have noted, he anticipated that, whatever the theoretical ideal, communist societies would be very bureaucratic. He offered no solution to bureaucratic alienation, but regarded the march of 'rationality' as inevitable in all modern societies whether capitalist or socialist. He saw practical advantages in bureaucracy but feared its potential to alienate. Perhaps this accounts for the occasional pessimism and faint sense of regret for more romantic and less 'rational' times past in Weber's work.

Blauner, Touraine, Woodward and their critics

About the early 1990s, a succession of books appeared which examined the relationship between technology and work satisfaction. Notable among these were works by Touraine, Blauner and Woodward. The findings they presented were very much in accord. The French sociologist, Touraine, summarised three recent historical stages in production technology and worker involvement: *flexible machines/craftworkers; standard machines/unskilled workers; automation/superintendents*. He associated the first and third of these with relatively higher levels of satisfaction. Blauner's typology is similar though slightly more complex.

Blauner's model is virtually self-explanatory. Machine-minding is usually required in *batch production* which is technically less efficient than *assembly-line mass production*, but usually involves the worker in a slightly more varied way. Although the empirical basis of his work has been criticised as not very adequate, his conclusions find support not only from other sociologists but from common experience. Many artists have preferred the creativity and fulfilment of *craftwork* to the humdrum security and financial rewards of a safe but boring job. At the other end of the satisfaction-alienation spectrum is assembly-line work. Of course, as we shall see, workers find ways of surviving and coping, but the phantoms of monotony, repetition and sheer tedium are never are away. In *process work*, by contrast, the worker is 'freed' from the machine. S/he oversees much, if not all, of the process of production and therefore has a closer involvement and identity with the whole. The brutal fracturing of the division of labour is partly healed.

Woodward's terms – *unit, batch, mass* and *process* production – cover the same area as Blauner's typology – craft, machine, assembly-line and process production. Like Blauner, she sees mechanisation as causing an increase in alienation until the onset of process production, which would show on a graph as the upside-down 'U curve' of alienation, takes a steep plunge. She also notes that in unit and process production, the dividing line between workers and technical and supervisory staff tends to be more blurred than in the case of batch and mass production. The situation was closer to what Burns and Stalker call the organic model of organisation involving more communication and democratic decision making. Thus, less alienation occurred through powerlessness.

Blauner's optimistic view of the effect of automation on work satisfaction has been sharply criticised by Duncan Gallie. He notes pointedly that the size of Blauner's sample of process workers was only 99, of which 78 were sampled in 1947 and 21 in 1961. Gallie himself, however, did not choose a sample survey method. Instead he made four detailed case studies of workers in automated oil refineries, two in France and two in Britain. The point of this was to supply a comparative cultural frame of reference which he felt was missing in Blauner's work. In both cases Gallie found that indifference, not satisfaction, was the most frequently expressed attitude to work. On a whole range of other matters mainly affecting industrial relations, however, he found substantial differences between the French and British workers. He concluded that broad generalisations about workers' attitudes and about industrial relations, should consider variables relative to given cultures and not simply technological change. We can accept this basic point of Gallie's but it should be said that other work, including that of Wedderburn and Crompton, tends to support Blauner, Woodward and Touraine's conclusions that automated labour is in itself relatively more satisfying than other forms of mechanised labour.

We earlier made an important distinction between Marx's and Weber's understanding of the major cause of alienation. Blauner, Woodward and Touraine are closer to Weber in that they analyse alienation in terms of the technical organisation of production rather than in terms of the private ownership of the means of production. Blauner suggests four dimensions of alienation, which he contrasts with four non-alienated states:

Alienated states

- Powerlessness
- Meaninglessness
- Isolation
- Self-estrangement

Non-alienated states

- Control
- Purpose
- Social integration
- Self-involvement.

There is no need to explain the use of these terms at length. A little thought will make it clear why a fragmented, partial relationship to production tends to lead to alienation, and a fuller one to a more satisfied set of responses. 'Self-estrangement' can be regarded as the final stage of alienation in which the individual begins to lose self-respect and motivation. Blauner's list is a useful summary of what has already been said or implied about the psychology of alienation (see Table 9.8).

Table 9.8 Technology and alienation

Type of work	→ Craft	Machine minding	Assembly line	Process
Type of Production/ Product	→ No Standardised Product	Mechanisation and Standardisation	Rationalisation Standardised product	Rationalisation Uniform product
Level of Skill	→ High	Low	Low	Responsibility and understanding needed
Level of Alienation	→ Low	High	Highest	Low

One point of Blauner's can usefully be taken further here. It is the contrasting conceptual pair of self-estrangement and self-involvement. The notion that work can alienate people from themselves is common to both Marxist and Weberian inspired literature on alienation. The idea presupposes that there does exist a self to be alienated from. The humanist psychologist Abraham Maslow has attempted to define broadly what the fundamental, common properties of human nature are. He argues that whereas practically all jobs provide the means to satisfy basic social needs (food, shelter), fewer satisfy egoistic needs (status), and fewer still allow for relatively full self-actualisation (self-fulfilment, creativity). Others have elaborated on Maslow's simple scheme, but as a clear statement of the root social-psychological cause of alienation it is difficult to improve. Alienation is the frustration of human potential as a result of unfulfilling work.

Marx revisited. The 'deskilling' debate: Harry Braverman and his critics

Harry Braverman's *Labour and Monopoly Capital: The Degradation of Work in the Twentieth Century* (Monthly Review Press, 1974) has perhaps been the most influential book on the nature and experience of the labour process in the last quarter of a century. Braverman argues that in capitalist society the organisation and experience of work is the product of managerial control rather than of 'rationalisation' required by technology in itself. To the extent that Braverman sees alienation as the product of social relations (i.e. between capitalist-management and workers), he is in the tradition of Marx himself.

As the title of his book suggests, Braverman considers that the quality of work has been 'degraded' during this century. He argues that degradation has taken place because management has sought increasingly to control workers partly by deskilling the labour process. The bulk of his analysis is of manufacturing industry but he applies his thesis equally to clerical workers and personal service and retail trade workers. As he puts it:

> The giant mass of workers who are relatively homogeneous as to lack of developed skills, low pay, and interchangeability of person and function (although heterogeneous in such particulars as the site and nature of the work they perform) is not limited to offices and factories. Another high concentration is to be found in the so-called service occupations and in retail trade.
>
> (Braverman, 1974:359)

According to Braverman, the main organisational strategy adopted by management to control and exploit labour is labour specialisation. Braverman's particular target is F W Taylor's theory of scientific management (see p. 288). Briefly, Taylor argued that if management divided the labour prices up into small functions both increased efficiency and greater control over the labour force would result. Organising labour in this way would lessen the chance of workers understanding the whole process of production and enable the appointment of less intelligent workers. Taylor is quite frank on the last point, stating that the full possibilities of his system:

> will not have been realised until almost all of the machines ... are run by men who are of smaller calibre and attainments, and who are therefore cheaper than those required under the old system.

Conveniently, in view of our previous analysis of the Fordist/post-Fordist debate, Braverman gives the mass production of the model T Ford as an early example of the degradation and deskilling of manufacturing work. It is worth quoting his description and comment at some length:

> The key element of the new organisation of labour was the endless conveyor chain upon which car assemblies were carried past fixed stations where men performed simple operations as they passed. This system was first put into operation for various subassemblies, beginning around the same time that the Model T was launched, and developed through the next half-dozen years until it culminated in January 1914 with the inauguration of the first endless-chain conveyor for final assembly at Ford's Highland Park plant. Within three months, the assembly time for the Model T had been reduced to one-tenth the time formerly needed, and by 1925 an organisation had been created which produced almost as many cars in a single day as had been produced, early in the history of the model T, in an entire year.
>
> The quickening rate of production in this case depended not only upon the change in the organisation of labour, but upon the control which management, at a single stroke, attained over the pace of assembly, so that it could now double and triple the rate at which operations had to be performed and thus subject its workers to an extraordinary intensity of labour.
>
> (Braverman, 1974: 147-8)

Braverman also amply illustrates how – as he sees it, the labour process has become increasingly controlled through timing, simplification and routinisation in office work. Indeed, he claims that 'management experts of the second and third generations after Taylor erased the distinction between work in factories and work in offices' (319). He cites the time standards for various clerical activities suggested in a handbook widely used in American companies. The examples given here are 'drawer' and 'chair' activities:

Open and close	Minutes
File drawer, open and close, no selection	.04
Folder, open or close flaps	.04
Desk drawer, open side drawer of standard desk	.014
Open centre drawer	.026
Close side	.015
Close centre	.027
Chair activity	
Get up from chair	.033
Sit down in chair	.033
Turn in swivel chair	.009
Move in chair to adjoining desk or file (4 ft. maximum)	.050

(*Cited Braverman, 321*)

Braverman goes on to mention that the handbook gives the time value for 'Cut with scissors' as .44, with '.30 for each additional snip'.

Braverman is aware that other approaches to the organisation of capitalist labour than Taylorism occur. However, he dismisses them as of relatively little importance. Thus, he considers human relations theory – which pays specific attention to the human needs of workers – as merely concerned with the adjustment of the worker to the ongoing production 'as that process was designed by the industrial engineer' i.e. 'Taylorites' (87).

Critics of Braverman

A number of commentators on Braverman – both Marxist and liberal – have contended that he underestimates the extent of class conflict in general and specifically industrial conflict resulting from workers' struggle. They further argue that control strategies have been affected by worker power and resistance. Richard Edwards, himself sympathetic to Marxism, and Andy Friedman have both made these points. Edwards argues that not one but several types of control have been adopted by capitalists over workers. Initially, in the nineteenth century, 'simple control' (direct and personal control) was typically used by capitalists (or their foremen or managers) whereas later 'technical control' (i.e. control by machinery) and then 'bureaucratic control' (i.e. control by hierarchical organisational systems) became dominant. Like Edwards, Andy Friedman distinguishes between the types of control adopted by management What he refers to as 'direct control' involves the explicit exercise of managerial authority whereas 'responsible autonomy' allows workers some freedom in the work process provided they operate within the framework of company goals. Stephen Wood succinctly describes Friedman's view that workers' efforts have forced management to adopt more 'liberal' (or, what Paul Thompson refers to elsewhere as, more 'consensual' managerial strategies)':

> Both Friedman (1977) and Edwards (1979) who emphasise the importance of resistance by workers, for example to Taylorism, in relation to managerial behaviour illustrate … arguments. In the twentieth century, management share had to come to terms with resistance, especially in times of full employment. As a result, they have had to adopt more liberal methods than Taylorism: what Friedman terms 'responsible autonomy' strategies. Methods such as the gang system, human relations, job re-design, are all treated by Friedman as genuine alternatives to Taylorist methods, or 'direct control' strategies, as he prefers to call them. In certain circumstances management has to come to terms with human needs and potential recalcitrance of workers, by building real autonomy and discretion into jobs or by allowing groups of workers to run themselves. This contrasts with Braverman's position, according to which such methods merely represent an alternative style of management rather than a genuine change in the position of the worker. For Friedman, the collective organised strength of work groups can force management to adopt strategies other than direct control, or Taylorism.
>
> (Stephen Wood, in R Deem and G Salaman eds., 1985: 81-2)

Feminist perspective has provided a second standard of criticism of Braverman. It is suggested that Braverman underestimates the level of skill involved in much of the work done mainly by women in capitalist society. In this way, he himself reflects the patriarchal assumptions of capitalist society. Thus, as Veronica Beechey argues, the skill involved in a wide range of occupations, such as sewing, cooking and apparently routine office work may be much greater than the low status and rewards associated with them. Further, work in which females tend to be concentrated has frequently been classified as less skilled than male-dominated occupations in order legally to maintain the sex pay differential. This strategy was sometimes adopted to avoid the consequences of the Equal Pay Act (1975).

A research project funded by the Economic and Social Research Council, throws some empirical light on the deskilling issue. A survey of employees was conducted to find out what their own subjective views on their skill range might be. Over half of the respondents felt that they had acquired more skills over the previous five years. This was true of respondents in both the manufacturing and service sectors which, of course, runs counter to Braverman's degradation thesis. However, this data does not comprehensively disprove Braverman's case – though it does damage it. First, what people think has happened and what has happened on the basis of more objective criteria may be very different. To find out the latter would require a different kind of survey. Second, the survey does suggest that whereas the skills of those who already possessed high level skills tend to increase, those with lower level skills – notably part-time female workers – tended to experience a decrease in their skill levels.

A social action approach to the experience of work: Goldthorpe and Lockwood

Both Marxist and technological theories of alienation have been rejected by Goldthorpe and Lockwood who adopt a social action approach to this issue in which they give prime consideration to workers' own meanings. They point out that many of the workers in their sample did not have high expectations of work and were not therefore disappointed by their experience of it. They worked not for satisfaction, still less for fulfilment, but for money. Goldthorpe and Lockwood call this an 'instrumental' orientation to work (the term orientation is preferred to attitude): it is used as a means or instrument to get something else – money. Their sample was mainly of young married workers who, mindful of family commitments, may have been particularly 'money conscious', but other research bears out and extends this finding. Dubin shows that, for many industrial and white-collar employees, work is not a major area of interest and self-expression. In a generally more representative sample of the male manual workforce than Goldthorpe and Lockwood's, Wedderburn and Crompton nevertheless confirm the latter's findings. The cumulative implication of these findings. is that the workers are neither consciously alienated from, nor satisfied with, work but accept it neutrally as a means to an end. They work largely to finance their family and leisure life which does have personal meaning to them.

Another way of explaining this is to distinguish between *intrinsic* and *extrinsic* orientations to work. A person who works for intrinsic reasons does so for the satisfaction the job gives. Such people include craftsmen or vocationally motivated nurses. In this context, extrinsic means the same as instrumental. Most people appear to work for predominantly extrinsic reasons, and to have low expectations of what the job offers in itself. If dissatisfaction is the difference between expectation and experience, then, most are not dissatisfied, because they expect little in the first place. Thus surveys suggest that women in routine office work are more satisfied than men doing work of a similar level of skill. A possible reason for this is that work is less of a central life interest for them than for men and so they are more easily 'satisfied' with it.

We seem then to have two almost contradictory perspectives on work experience: on the one hand, certain kinds of work are considered alienating and, on the other, the people who do these kinds of work may regard them as a neutral but not alienating experience. We can easily reconcile the two views if we extend our understanding of alienation. Alienation is not just a description of subjective (personally experienced) feelings of many workers; it is also a more objective (more widely generalisable) statement about the waste of human potential that certain kinds of routine work, both manual and white-collar, involve. In this sense, alienation is about lack of fulfilment, not just actual feelings of misery. It is quite possible to have many unfulfilled capacities without knowing it. Such a grossly unfulfilled person is alienated from her or his true

potential. Marx argued that fulfilment at work is generally possible in socialist, but not in capitalist society. Weber thought fulfilment at work for the majority was incompatible with the extreme division of labour of large scale organisation, whether in capitalist or socialist societies. We need to look at the concept of fulfilment in greater detail because its use does imply the value judgement that some kinds of activity, including varieties of work, are more or less better (in the sense of more fulfilling) than others.

Fulfilment in work

Abraham Maslow's theory of human needs can be usefully applied to the concept of fulfilment at work. Nearly everybody will expect to meet their basic needs of food and shelter through work, and most will hope for some pleasant social interaction while at work. Fewer will acquire substantial esteem or prestige for the work they do though only the most humble will be outside the positive status hierarchy altogether. Only a tiny minority achieve self-actualisation or self-fulfilment through work. Very few are allowed to perform at a level of personal excellence that brings their best creative skills and abilities into play. Examples of some who can, are people at the very top of our occupational elites, such as managing directors of large companies, stars of sport and entertainment, and creative academics. Many others are perhaps haunted by what Gouldner calls 'the unemployed self' – a sense of potential underdeveloped and a life wasted in senseless work.

We have noted that Marx did not consider fulfilling, non-alienating work to be generally possible in capitalist society. Some Marxists regard with suspicion the limited industrial participation or power-sharing schemes involving workers, which have been adopted in Germany and Sweden, but others consider them a step on the road to a more socialist and less alienating society. Those who, unlike Marx, see alienation primarily as the result of technological and/or organisational factors, naturally look for solutions within these terms (we exclude of course, those who ignore the problem or believe it to be insoluble). We examine a variety of attempts to achieve relatively more 'human' systems of organisation and technology both later in this chapter and in Chapter 10.

Informal attempts to deal with alienation: an interactionist perspective

Reform and revolution aside, those who have to work in boring jobs are faced with the day-to-day need of 'getting by'. Here are some of the ways they use to do so.

The interactionist concept of managing self and others provides a helpful perspective on the many people who 'survive' monotony at work (and school). Apart from snatched conversational exchanges, day-dreaming is perhaps the most universal 'strategy'. As Jason Ditton remarks in his participant study of work in a factory bakery:

> *Although the workers looked as if they were doing the work automatically, one man who had worked for twelve hours a day for two years in the 'dough' ... pointed out that, underneath this, the mind never stops. though giving the impression of working without thinking, he said that 'you think of a hundred subjects a day' ...*
>
> *(Ditton, 1972)*

Doubtless his 'hundred subjects a day' cover a similar range of musings as those in which you and I indulge.

Next to 'escaping into your head', the most common way of dealing with stress and monotony is probably by humour – 'having a laff'. In this authentic description of 1950s working class life in Nottingham, *Saturday Night and Sunday Morning*, Alan Sillitoe gives us more than a few examples of 'laffs' through the actions of the novel's anti-hero, Arthur. Here is one:

> *At a piecework rate of four-and-six a hundred you could make your money if you knocked-up fourteen hundred a day – possible without grabbing too much – and if you went all out for a thousand in the morning you could dawdle through the afternoon and lark about with the women and talk to your mates now and again. Such leisure often brought him near to trouble, for some weeks ago he stunned a mouse – that the overfed factory cats had missed – and laid it beneath a woman's drill, and Robboe the gaffer ran out of his office when he heard her screaming blue-murder, thinking that some bloody silly woman had gone and got her hair caught in a belt (big notices said that women must wear hair-nets, but who could tell with women?) and Robboe was glad that it was nothing more than a dead mouse she was kicking up such a fuss about. But he paced up and down the gangways asking who was responsible for the stunned mouse, and when he came to Arthur, who denied having anything to do with it, he said: 'I'll bet you did it, you young bogger!' 'Me, Mr Robboe?' Arthur said, the picture of innocence, standing up tall with offended pride. 'I've got so much work to do I can't move from my lathe.*
>
> *(Sillitoe, 1958)*

A tough sense of the ridiculous is at the heart of traditional working class life. In part, it is a way of coping with the absurdity and tyranny of work. We discussed working class humour and other cultural attitudes earlier (Chapter 6).

The ultimate escape at work is going to sleep. Quite often, night-shift workers are 'allowed' an informal 'kip' after they have finished their quota, but the former British Leyland worker who was dismissed after bringing a bed to work was obviously considered to be taking things too much for granted. Apart from such arrangements, many workers have some recollection of occasionally going to sleep while working, either through monotony or fatigue – just as most students do.

An experienced and sympathetic floor manager will usually not attempt to stop harmless attempts by workers to 'kill time' or, at least, make it pass more quickly. S/he may even extend a tea-break or stop to chat with an obviously tired, sick or stressed worker when the occasion seems to demand it.

All the daydreams, 'laffs', 'kips', and 'tea and sympathy', however, cannot make fundamentally boring work interesting. As we shall see, alienation is arguably the underlying cause of much industrial conflict and discontent as well as the milder, improvised 'escape attempts' described above.

The real escape, though, is leisure time. It is then that workers, starved of meaning and expression at work, can hope to 'do their own things'. If, to use C Wright Mills' image, people sell little pieces of themselves for money during week-days, they attempt to reclaim themselves in the evenings and at weekends with the coin of fun. Mills' tart irony rightly suggests that the problems of personal freedom, pleasure and leisure are more complicated than this simple division of time into 'work and fun' suggests. We examine these issues after the following section on industrial interest groups and conflict.

Industrial interest groups and conflict

Industrial interest groups are formal organisations concerned with the interests of their members. There are two broad types, employers' associations and, for employees, trade unions and professional associations. Historically employees made more use of formal interest group organisations than employers. This is partly because employers are supposed to be in competition with each other, and indeed the law discourages co-operation that might restrain trade or raise prices artificially. It is also because it is often easier and more convenient for employers to consult informally and in private. Both employers and trade unions are represented by national bodies, the Confederation of British Industry (CBI) and Trades Union Congress (TUC) respectively.

The growth and 'retreat' of unionism

Union membership grew from about seven million in 1945 to a peak of over twelve million in 1980. It was back at around seven million in 1995. The number of unions had declined from 186 unions affiliated to the TUC in 1951, to less than 80 in 1991. As Jenkins and Sherman point out, this trend to 'concentration and enlargement' matches the same process in industry itself.

The traditional and still the main purpose of trade unions is to protect and improve the pay and working conditions of their members. Hyman states that:

> *A trade union is first and foremost, an agency and medium of power. Its central purpose is to permit workers to exert, collectively, the control over the conditions of employment which they cannot hope to possess as individuals.*
>
> *(1975:64)*

What Hyman's robust definition of the purpose of unionism does not tell us is that between 1975 and 1995, the number of workers having their pay determined collectively has dropped from nine out of ten to four out of ten. In addition to pay, issues of job security, participation in management and even environmental and social policy issues can also fall within the range of union's concern.

The growth of unionism to 1979

Apart from the recessionary 1920s and early1930s, union membership grew steadily throughout the twentieth century from two million in 1900 to over six times that figure in 1979. The reasons for this were straightforward enough: unions provided a means of negotiating and protecting pay and conditions for workers and the legislative framework was favourable to their growth.

Henry and Kelly present a typology which they argue broadly indicates the historical development of union official/member relations in the post-war period:

1 1940s-mid 1960s. Professional servicing relationship. Union negotiators serviced a largely passive membership.
2 1960s-late 1970s. A participative relationship. Membership was much more actively involved.
3 1980s Managerial servicing relationship. Union members seen as reactive consumers by the leadership.

Although this periodisation is seen as over-simple, it is recognisable against the facts. What it does not do is capture the continuous ebb and flow of accommodation and resistance to capital that ran throughout the whole period.

In retrospect, the 1960s and 1970s appear to have been the heyday of union power (though matters could change again). In the corporate economy of Harold Wilson, top union officials often worked alongside government and business leaders in the decision making process, particularly in economic and industrial policy but also in social policy. The social contract between the TUC and the Callaghan government (1976-1979) involved an agreement by unions to exercise industrial restraint in return for improved social programmes. Its breakup presaged a long period of Conservative government.

For most of the 1960s and 1970s business seemed quite ready to accept and co-operate with a powerful union movement. No doubt some saw this as simply an unfortunate necessity but others considered that a degree of partnership and shared responsibility was a sound basis on which to run British industry. It was often

easier to deal with established union leaders than more directly with the sometimes more radical demands of shopfloor workers. In particular, employers sought to by-pass the powerful grassroots shop-stewards movement by negotiating with higher level officials. Nevertheless, it was often shop-stewards who gave immediate direction and leadership to local industrial section in this period. Generally, larger employers readily accepted the closed shop (i.e. where union membership is made compulsory for all employees) – again, because this seemed to facilitate management and especially the negotiating process.

The shift in the British economy from the manufacturing to the service sector would have brought about a decline in overall union membership much earlier than 1980 had it not been for the rise of white-collar unionism in the 1960s and 1970s. For instance, during these decades membership of the mainly white-collar National Union of Public Employees and Civil and Public Services Association rapidly increased while that of the National Union of Miners and National Union of Railwaymen rapidly declined. However, between 1979 and 1987, the period of the first two Thatcher administrations, membership of all these four unions rapidly declined although some white-collar unions did manage to continue membership expansion during the1980s.

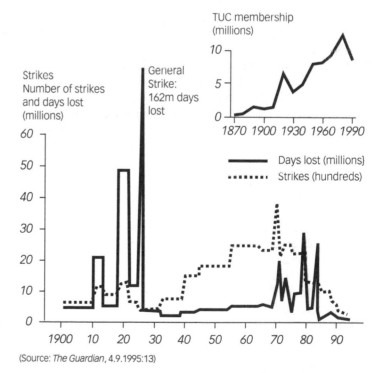

(Source: *The Guardian*, 4.9.1995:13)

Figure 9.10 The state of the unions

The 'Retreat' of Unionism, 1979-?

There was just over a three million drop in union members between 1979 and 1988. Union density (the percentage of the workforce unionised) also dropped from over 50 per cent in 1979 to 30 per cent in 1996 (see Figure 9.10).

Managerial Unionism? Quotes from the TUC's General Secretary

On the TUC: 'We are changing boldly and decisively.'

'The TUC is not aligned to any political party.'

On unions: 'The tide was turned decisively towards trade unionism.'

'Trade unionism has always been more than the AA for the workplace. We have richer traditions.'

On strikes: 'The job of unions is to avoid strikes, particularly ones of any duration.'

'There is going to be a smaller chance of avoiding industrial conflict in the future.'

On the future: 'Our task is to replace 1970s-style corporatism and today's economic jungle with social partnership.'

On class: 'We are all working class now.'

On his job: 'I will put myself behind those who are unemployed, and all those who feel exploited, vulnerable and scared.'

(Source: *The Guardian*, 4.9.1995:13)

Is the 'retreat' of unionism during he 1980s and first half of the 1990s likely to continue or can it be reversed? The opinions of commentators vary on this issue. J Kelly argues that the unions coped well with the recession of the early 1980s (1988). Union membership declined over a period of about fifteen years during the 1920s and early 1930s and then revived sharply. Against Kelly, it has to be pointed out that no such revival occurred during the boom of the late1980s. Moreover, the recession of the early 1990s had the effect of further reducing union membership. In 1990, more company collapses occurred than in any previous year and according to a union survey 33,000 jobs in manufacturing were lost in the first six weeks of 1991. There were also heavy jobs losses in the service sector during this period. This seems more like a recipe for a further setback for the trade union movement rather than a revival, though Kelly, of course, could not have been aware of it.

Ken Coates and Tony Tophan argue that there has not only been a numerical decline in union membership but a substantial reduction in their power, influence and functions (1986). This has occurred both within the context of industrial relations in which they are now much more constrained by law and in the wider context of government policy and decision making in which, as far as Conservative governments are concerned, they are largely ignored.

It is arguable that Thatcherite employment legislation has introduced a new system of industrial relations into Britain (see p. 274). Four Employment Acts and a Trade Union Act (1984) were aimed at achieving three broad goals:

1 The closed shop was undermined and then abolished (1990) – the closed shop is a requirement at a given place of work that an employee be a union member.

2 Strike activity was restricted in a number of ways. Secondary (or supportive strike action by those not directly involved in an industrial dispute) was first restricted and then made illegal (1990). Unions became required to hold secret ballots before strike action could be taken (1984).

3 Union power has been reduced and in certain respects unions have been democratised. The 1990 Employment Act made it possible to sue unions if they fail quickly and formally to repudiate unofficial calls for strike action.

It cannot be assumed that changes in the law – even major changes such as those discussed above – can inevitably or alone cause a fundamental change in a society's system of industrial relations. It is too early to say whether the reduction in strike activity of the 1980s (apart from 1984) and early 1990s will prove the beginning of a new era. However, the 'retreat of the unions does appear to be linked with long term structural changes in the economy and employment such as post-Fordist 'flexible' labour processes and 'Japanisation' of management technique (see pp. 252-3). John Monks, the TUC's general secretary believes that the job insecurity (described above) will drive white-collar and professional people increasingly to union membership. Monks believes that the new emphasis on managerial competence will appeal to this constituency. This approach is a long way from the confrontationalism of the 1960s:

> *Union members have the right to expect their organisations to be managed in a modern and effective way. The world has changed and we have to look forward rather than back. The adversarial approach hasn't delivered great benefits. We need to increase employment by developing world class skills.*
>
> *(The Observer, 24.3.1996:136)*

Richard Hyman points out that a variety of circumstances coincided with the Thatcher reforms to change the balance of power in industrial relations ('What is Happening to the Unions', *Social Studies Review*, March 1989). Most of these such as the decline in manufacturing industry, we have already discussed above. Hyman also mentions as relevant that 'the attitudes of employers have also been altering'. There has been a shift away from quasi-partnership concepts of industrial relations to notions of 'human resource management' in which employees are viewed in terms of the skills they can offer. This approach tends to be more hierarchical and directive in nature.

A shift in public opinion against the unions in the late 1970s also smoothed the way for the employment legislation of the1980s. However, public opinion and socio-economic circumstances could change again. It is always dangerous to declare that a new historical epoch has commenced in any area!

The pent-up frustrations of the Thatcher years may yet result in greater 'adverserialism' – despite the aspirations of John Monks.

Types of industrial conflict

There are numerous types of industrial conflict, of varying degrees of severity. The most important is the strike. Associated with striking is picketing – trying, within the limits of law, to persuade other workers to join a strike. Another form of action often used as an alternative to the strike weapon in industrial conflict is 'working to rule'. The sit-in involves the occupation or take-over of a factory by workers and is often a reaction to large-scale redundancies or closure. It usually occurs as a last resort but sometimes leads to a positive attempt by the workers to save the factory themselves.

Another type of conflict, industrial sabotage, can occur for a variety of reasons, from personal boredom or malice to opposition to management policies or even the capitalist system in general. Minor acts of sabotage sometimes have a comical aspect which helps to release tedium and frustration, as when a distinguished foreign client was delivered a new Mercedes complete with six Coca-Cola bottles clanking deep within its bonnet. Huw Beynon tells of the response of a line worker, who was prone to absenteeism, to the question of what it felt like to come into work on a fine, bright Monday morning. The answer was that he didn't know! The implication is, of course, that the worker found better things to do than work on fine, bright Monday mornings. Certainly, children 'bunk off' school because they find it 'boring' and 'a drag'. (see Chapter 4) Presumably some of 'the dads of the lads' indulge in similar practices for much the same reasons. Beynon also gives a number of examples of industrial sabotage which contain a serious message to perhaps otherwise inattentive management. Thus, workers who felt they were undermined or expected to work too quickly sometimes sabotaged cars to make their objections known. As Taylor and Walton imply, sabotage is a somewhat primitive method of communication, and it has been largely, though not entirely, superseded by trade union negotiation. Absenteeism is a form of escapism or even of rejection, rather than conflict. It mostly occurs in industries which take a severe physical and mental toll.

Strikes

The damage that strikes do or do not do to the economy of Britain is a matter of recurrent controversy in this country. This often bitter debate is frequently conducted with only scant attention to relevant facts. Figure 9.10 (see p. 269) presents some data on strikes which we can use as a basis of our own discussion.

The graph shows that the general level of strike activity in the 1970s was much higher than in any period since the last war. Between the wars only the short period between 1919–22 produced a higher average level. It was the length, not the number of strikes that had increased. However, the graph also puts the 'turbulent 1970s' into perspective. Apart from the 1970s and 1984 – the year of the miner's strike – the number of working days lost through strikes has tended to be fairly modest. The reduction both

in working days lost through strikes and in work stoppages in the Thatcher years compared to the1970s, looks typical rather than exceptional in the longer perspective. However, the continuing decline of strike activity into the 1990s does raise the possibility of a longer term decline.

Compared with other industrialised Western societies, Britain's recent strike record is moderate rather than exceptional. Between 1968–77 the average number of working days lost in Britain was 452 per 1000 workers, compared with 1887 per 1000 in Australia, 1893 in Canada and 1500 in the United States. Some of Britain's more immediate competitors did lose markedly less: West Germany, 24; Sweden, 18 and Holland, 36. In the 1990s Britain itself was much closer to these figures.

Why, then, were the1970s such a relatively strike-prone period? W W Daniel and N Millward's *Workplace and Industrial Relations in Britain* (Heinemann, 1983), gives several indications. They report the findings of a survey of about 2000 workplaces of all sizes which enquired into the frequency and type of industrial action (not just strikes) in each one between mid 1979 and mid 1980. Their findings seem particularly revealing given what we now know of trends in industrial conflict, particularly strike activity, during the1980s. They found that workplaces that were unionised were more likely to take strike action than those that were not. Among unionised establishments, several factors were associated with greater strike activity: a higher proportion of union membership; a higher proportion of manual workers; a greater proportion of male workers; a greater proportion of full-time employees; and, finally, strikes were more likely to occur in establishments which were the main place of collective bargaining.

A 'stereotype' picture of the late 1970s striker is, therefore, a unionised, male, full-time, manual worker. In the 1980s this stereotype was in numerical decline (Figure 9.11). Union membership substantially declined, female workers increased in proportion to male workers, part-time workers increased in proportion to full-time workers, and service sector workers

Percentages of male and female workers who are union members   ■ Men ■ Women

	1989	1990	1991	1992	1993	1994	1995
Men	43.9%	43.0%	41.8%	39.2%	38.1%	36.1%	34.6%
Women	32.3%	32.0%	32.3%	31.7%	31.5%	30.5%	29.5%

(Source: Labour Force Survey)

Figure 9.11 The decline and fall of union membership

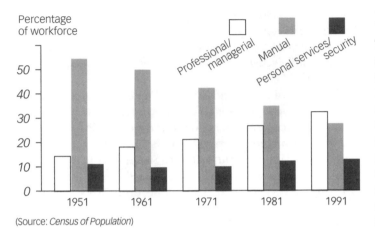

Percentage of workforce

Professional/managerial

Manual

Personal services/security

(Source: *Census of Population*)

Figure 9.12 The changing occupational structure has tended to weaken trade unionism

increased in proportion to manual workers. Given, therefore, that the type of people more likely to strike were becoming a smaller proportion of the labour-force, logically fewer strikes might be expected (see Figure 9.12). This was, in fact, the tendency during the 1980s and the first half of the1990s. The link between strike activity and the main site of collective bargaining weakened during the 1980s as wage negotiations became more decentralised. Localised collective bargaining became more, not less, common but it did so in the context of a weaker union movement, higher unemployment and with the support of the Conservative government and much of management. In general, as Richard Hyman argues, the extent to which the decline in the factors associated with strikes was the conscious result of government policy and Thatcherite ideology should not be underestimated.

In a work published in 1984 (*Strikes* third edition, Fontana), Richard Hyman divides the period from 1974 to 1983 into three 'phases' in terms of industrial relations. The first was 1974-76 – the phase of the 'Social Contract' between the Labour government and the unions – which was a time of relative co-operation and lower industrial conflict. The second was 1977-79 – a phase of increased industrial conflict ending in the notorious, strike-riven, 'winter of discontent' of 1979. The third phase 1979-?, has been what Hyman calls one of 'coercive pacification' in which the law (including its physical enforcement) and other means were used to weaken and control the unions.

Factors associated with strikes

The previous section will have made it clear that the factors associated with industrial conflict vary in impact and relative importance over time. At a surface level, it may seem that the economic motive – the first factor discussed below – is likely to be dominant in the majority of cases but Marxists and other conflict theorists argue that tension about control and independence (and, to that extent, alienation) at work often underlie conflict about pay and conditions.

The economic motive

The most commonly stated motive for striking is to improve pay and this is often linked with demands to improve working conditions and reduce hours – broadly material factors. Between 1965-74, 56.1 per cent of disputes and over 80 per cent of working days lost were the result of conflicts over pay. Most of the strikes during the so-called 'winter of discontent' of 1978-79 were mainly about pay, and were all the more intense as a result of the previous period of voluntary wage restraint. Between 1965-74, 80 per cent of stoppages were about economic issues, and these involved 90 per cent of the days lost. Even the steelworkers strike of 1980 was superficially about pay; relatively little was said about the British Steel Corporation's plan to reduce its workforce by approximately a third over a period of years – a strategy that might have been expected to result in industrial action. Sometimes strikes also concern working conditions or other matters affecting workers' welfare. The miners threatened to strike in early 1977 if the National Coal Board refused to implement early retirement plans for them.

Two key strikes of the mid 1980s – the miners' strike of 1984 and the teachers' strike of 1985 – were partly about pay but illustrate the frequent complexity of major strikes. Some of the leadership in both cases was motivated by political opposition to the government and again in both occupations there was widespread concern that government plans involved a decrease in security and autonomy at work.

Structural conflict between capital and labour

Conflict theorists argue that there is an 'in-built' conflict between capital and labour. Hyman makes the general point: the confrontation within the workplace of two bases of control provides a constant source of instability and conflict.

Given that owners and management on the one hand and the labour force on the other want as large a share as possible of the profit of their mutual toil, disagreement and friction is virtually inevitable. Even the most optimistic personnel manager would hardly expect to do more than 'regulate' it in the context of modern large-scale industry. It is because they too see a day-to-day conflict of interest between capital and labour, that Lane and Roberts claim that strikes should be seen as 'normal' rather than labelled a 'problem' (once the public is presented with a 'problem' the next stage is often to look for the 'culprit' – not the most fruitful approach in industrial relations).

Marxists see a final solution to class conflict in industry only in the introduction of a socialist society. Others see a functional need to make the capitalist system operate more effectively. Thus, human relations theorists, Scott and Homans, argue that better communications between management and workers – for instance, through trained personnel managers – can provide a more constructive atmosphere and reduce disruption. Marxists consider this approach to be biased towards management and manipulative of workers. At worst it passes off deep problems of structural conflict and exploitation as personal or even psychological difficulties.

Underlying issues of control and independence: economic globalisation

Alvin Gouldner's *Wildcat Strike* (1957) finds that a strike for higher wages was just one event in a long chain of conflict between workers and management. The conflict stemmed from a change in management at the plant. Traditionally, worker-management relations were informal, friendly and based on trust. The new manager, an outsider, introduced new machinery and attempted to 'rationalise' the administration of the plant. This limited the independence and offended the pride of the workers, particularly the miners. The relationship between workers and management was redefined in terms of conflicting interests, rather than a sense of mutual understanding and interest. It was in this context that the wildcat strike 'for higher wages' occurred, but to see it simply in terms of money would be sociologically unsubtle.

The argument that some strikes are about control and independence in the workplace is compatible with the Marxist view that there is a fundamental conflict between capital and labour in which labour is alienated – whether it knows it or not. However, relatively few strikes are overtly political (to some extent the first half of the 1980s was an exception – see below). It is possible to accept Gouldner's point without agreeing with broader Marxist analysis. More recently Marxists and others have observed that the ability of multinational companies to switch production around the world has severely weakened the collective power of labour to resist exploitation.

Multiple motivations for strikes: workers' meanings

The major stated motive for strikes is the economic one. We have also suggested a range of other important contributory factors. As Hyman points out, however, it is a false dichotomy to assume that the causes of a given dispute must be either economic or non-economic. He adds that the relative importance of the various causes that contribute to the start of a strike may change as it goes on, and new reasons for continuing it may appear. The sheer determination 'not to lose' may increase as a strike goes on. Lane and Roberts point out that strikes can snowball. New grievances may become apparent as the strike continues and support may come from the previously uncommitted, at the prospect of a good settlement. As the interactionist Silverman succinctly puts it, industrial relations must be seen as a changing process and not merely in structural terms. We must also reiterate that the broad social, political and legal structure within which a strike occurs (or is prevented from occurring) is of fundamental importance in comparing the strike profiles of different countries.

Hyman is emphatic that there is no single, over-arching explanation for strikes in general. He points out that the strike records of firms in the same industry using the same technology can vary greatly. This is true of the steel industry which has a militant history in south Wales and a harmonious one in north-east England. He refers ultimately to historical accident, cultural variation and the particular meanings different employees attach to similar circumstances to 'explain' the varied and impredictable pattern of strike activity.

Causes related to specific industries: heavy industry; technology; community

So far, we have talked about the general causes of strikes. The extent to which strikes occur, however, varies between industries (as well as between societies). We now attempt to account for variations within different industries. James Cronin found that highly unionised workers in industries crucial to the national economy, which tend to use incentive schemes to increase production, and which are subject to economic fluctuation, tend to be prone to strike. His 1970s study showed that, on average, miners, dockers, car workers, shipbuilders and iron and steel workers accounted for a quarter of strikes and a third of working days lost, even though they only cover about six per cent of employees. However, these industries now represent a much smaller proportion of the labour force and in the second half of the 1980s white-collar employees such as teachers and nurses were relatively more likely to be involved in strike activity.

On the basis of her study of a variety of production systems, Woodward has argued that 'the face of industrial relations ... seemed to be closely related to ... technology' (*Management and Technology*, HMSO, 1958). Again, this relates particularly to heavy industry such as car manufacture and steel production. However, Hyman and, more recently Woodward herself, have argued that technology is only one factor of varying relevance in explaining strike activity (Hyman, 1984). There is considerable international variation in strike activity in both the car and steel industries.

Large-scale industries in areas with strong working class communities are, or were particularly associated with strike activity. Union strength and militancy and class solidarity are often the norm in such occupational communities. In some respects, however, this picture of the typical strike-prone industry is out of date. Firstly, these kinds of communities are now in decline, and some of the workers involved in these industries conform more closely to the 'privatised' pattern of living observed by Goldthorpe and Lockwood, rather than the more open community lifestyle of the traditional working class. Secondly, as we have already discussed, strike activity now occurs more widely across a variety of occupational groups although overall activity is currently at a lower rate than in the 1970s.

Strikes as 'normal'

Roberts and Lane argue that strike activity is a normal part of industrial relations – even where those relations are generally good (1971). In their own case study of a strike at Pilkington's glassworks, they found that a strike occurred at the end of a period of quite good industrial relations in which most workers expressed no major grievances about pay or other matters. A strike also occurred in similar circumstances at the Vauxhall car assembly-line plant at Luton shortly after Goldthorpe and Lockwood completed their 'affluent worker' study. Lane and Roberts conclude that strikes should be regarded as 'normal', in the sense that they are an accepted 'weapon' in the bargaining process between management and labour.

Tom Keenoy adopts and extends the argument that strikes are a normal part of the bargaining process in his *Invitation to Industrial Relations* (Blackwell, 1985). In doing so, he seeks to refute 'the myth' of trade unionists as industrial spoilers and points out that management itself can sometimes be responsible for a strike.

Comparative industrial relations systems analysis: the 'Thatcher' system

We will conclude this consideration of the causes of strikes with a comparison of the British system of industrial relations under Margaret Thatcher with that of some other European countries. Although industrial relations system analysis particularly reflects the sociological perspective of Talcott Parsons, its basic principles are more generally applicable, and need not embody his own conservative values. This approach links the particular workplace or industry to the wider society. Strikes are seen in the context of the total national system of industrial relations, including workers and unions; management and government agencies especially concerned with the workplace; the work community and, finally, the tradition of industrial relations in a given society. Industrial law is an important part of the 'environment' of industrial relations in most advanced countries and has often been a cause of dispute between labour and government in Britain. In the space of two years, between 1969 and 1971, both major parties attempted to introduce substantial legal changes in the position of the unions. Both failed, mainly because of the strength and effectiveness of union opposition.

Between 1980 and 1990, the legal framework of industrial relations in Britain was radically changed. Margaret Thatcher came to government in 1979, following a period of substantial strike activity and with the clear intention of curbing union power (see p. 270 for development of this issue). Whether Britain's previously largely collectivist system of industrial relations has been replaced by a largely individualistic one remains to be seen. One indicator that a more individualistic approach to workplace grievances might be developing is the sharp increase in cases going to industrial relations tribunals between 1990 and 1995 (see Figure 9.13).

On balance, Germany's extensive legal framework of co-determined (i.e. between capital and employees) industrial relations appears to have contributed to the greater industrial harmony experienced there in the post-war period than in Britain. Germany's system is both more participatory and more protective in relation to workers. In the old Soviet Union, despite some economic liberalisation, industrial 'harmony' was mainly achieved

Justice at work

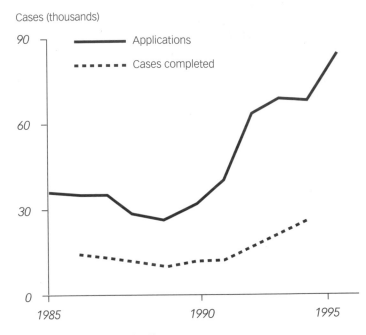

(Source: *The Observer*, 16.6.1996:10)

Figure 9.13 Are industrial relations tribunals now taking the strain of industrial conflict?

by legal compulsion – a generally unpopular means in the West. Theirs was a system of industrial relations in which power was concentrated in the Government's hands. The opposite approach would be to adopt a system of real industrial democracy, that is, union participation or control. We consider this option in Chapter 10 (see pp. 293-7), and that section can be regarded as a continuation of this discussion.

The professions

The expansion of professions is a further feature of the growth of the service sector characteristic of modern societies. In addition to managers and administrators, professionals make up a large proportion of what Halsey refers to as the 'service class'. Higher professionals include lawyers, scientists, engineers, doctors and dentists. Their market position is significantly stronger than that of lower professionals such as teachers, social workers and nurses and this shows in the much higher salaries they tend to command. Most lower professionals work for the government. Among higher professionals, private practice is becoming more rare and employment in the service of industry or the government increasingly common. This change in the market position of professionals has increased the possibility of conflict with other groups.

Until quite recently, sociological writings on the professions tended to assume both their high social status and that the contribution or 'service' of professionals to the community was qualitatively superior to that of 'lower' status workers. Marxists are an exception to this, as they have always placed the highest value on manual labour. Current analysis of the professions is much more inclined to use the concept of conflict in interpreting their relationship to society. This is apparent in two main ways. First, no necessary 'community of interest' is assumed between client and professional. On the contrary, their interests tend to be seen to be in structural conflict, regardless of the 'goodwill' of individual professionals. Secondly, because most professionals are now paid employees, their relationship to their employers is also regarded as a potential source of conflict similar to that experienced by other employees. Both are part of the general process by which work has become increasingly bureaucratised.

The functionalist approach and 'trait' analysis approach

The work of functionalists such as Bernard Barber and Talcott Parsons, typifies traditional sociological analysis of the professions. Quite simply, this perspective sees the professions as fulfilling useful social functions. They provide necessary medical, legal, architectural or religious advice and service based on specialised knowledge and competence. The key attribute of professions is considered to be a primary commitment to community rather than self-interest. Terence Johnson distinguishes between 'functionalist' analysis of professions and 'trait' analysis though the two approaches are highly compatible. 'Trait' analysis has proved to be something of a blind alley. On the basis of his own survey of the relevant literature, Millerson points out that no two authorities agree precisely on what the basic traits of a profession are. The following, however, are frequently mentioned: professional authority (over the 'layman'); the sanction by the community of the power and privilege of professionals; the confidential nature of the professional client relationship; a code of ethics (rules) regulating the profession; a theory of knowledge underlying the practice of the profession (such as medical research/theory); and the existence of a professional culture. A professional culture involves broad consensus about how to behave as a professional, and is said to be passed on to new recruits. Even today, barristers can still participate in a quite ritualised common culture.

The 'trait' approach is so uncritical of official professional ideology (the views professionals hold of themselves) that it is almost 'pre-sociological'. Client response is assumed automatically to 'fit in' with the expert's view and the possibility of conflict between professionals and other individuals and groups is unexplored. The functionalist approach is hardly more sophisticated. Johnson charges that they do not examine the historical development of professions and so fail to appreciate that professional practice is deeply involved with power relations in society, including those based mainly on money. Consistently

enough, he illustrates his argument by reference to various historical stages in the development of professions, and in particular stresses changes in the professional-client relationship. In the sixteenth and seventeenth centuries, professionals were typically answerable to wealthy patrons. The professional's freedom was limited by this dependence and s/he certainly did not serve the majority of the community. Industrialisation changed the status of the professions. Their members and independence increased. The technical expertise of, for instance, engineers and specialist lawyers, was formidable and professionals achieved new status and power. Leading professions were able to persuade the general public of their own ideology – their own assessment of their skill and importance. It was at this time that professions developed into self-regulating organisations which were able to control their specialist areas of work, including the standard of entry to them. Control of entry enabled them to regulate the supply and therefore the price of professional services. Obviously, this was a very desirable position for professionals to be in. Medieval craftsmen similarly attempted to regulate occupational entry and the supply and price of services. No doubt members of most occupations would wish to do the same. The difference between professions and other occupations is that they have succeeded in convincing the public of their special skills and importance and of their need for corresponding privileges, whereas others have not.

Neo-Weberian perspective on the professions

The common theme of much recent neo-Weberian analysis of the professions is that they organise and operate primarily on the basis of self-interest largely by controlling their own market position. Thus, professions are seen as seeking to control entry, public access to services, and, especially, the price of services. Frank Parkin (1979) and Parry and Parry (1977) exemplify this approach. More recently, Keith MacDonald has dubbed the attempt of professionals to achieve and maintain a monopoly of their particular practice, 'the professional project' (1996).

Parkin employs the concept of 'closure' to describe how professional group self-interest operates. There are two main types of closure: usurpation and exclusion. Usurpation involves taking power from a dominant group and exclusion involves preventing lower status groups from accessing one's own position. It is the concept of exclusion that Parkin applies to professions. They achieve exclusion mainly by 'credentialism' which controls entry. Credentialism is the requirement of a period of training and assessment which, if successful, results in certification. Interestingly, in 1990, the government made a limited attempt to by-pass the usual qualificatory route for teachers by introducing a licensed teachers scheme which allowed certain candidates for teaching to train in schools rather than in higher education.

Noel and José Parry regard a profession as an occupational

group which has successfully established control in the market for the services it produces. It is characterised by a self-governing association of formally equal colleagues which controls recruitment, regulates professional conduct, and determines who can practise. On this basis, they regard medicine as a profession, but not teaching. Teachers are seen both as having less occupational autonomy and as less able to command a high level of reward than doctors. In the twenty or so years since the Parrys published, substantial differences in power (of self-regulation), status and rewards between doctors and teachers have remained. However, the National Health Service, including doctors as well as the teaching 'profession' has been subject to considerable change by government including a new, centrally prescribed managerial regime. It can be argued that in certain respects, NHS doctors have lost some autonomy and this is even more the case with hospital consultants (see p. 441).

Some neo-Weberians specifically relate the ability to maintain exclusive professional control to the knowledge and technical base of professional work. Thus, Johnson argues that, for instance, lawyers and doctors are in a better position than clients to define what clients 'need' and how best their needs can be met. Unsurprisingly, professional closure both in terms of other groups and other knowledge does not go unchallenged.

Keith MacDonald's *The Sociology of the Professions* (1996) puts the 'professional project' of closure in a wider context. The conservative protectionism of the professions has made it difficult for females and black people to 'break in'. It has also meant that 'professional knowledge' tended to be defined in hard, scientific, 'masculinist' terms rather than more openly and humanistically.

Comment on neo-Weberian perspective

Neo-Weberians fully recognise that professional control is open to challenge. However, they may somewhat exaggerate the extent to which the higher professions have achieved independence. The main sources of pressure and alternative bases of control are the public, including clients, management, government and business.

Ivan Illich is a celebrated champion of the client and critic of 'professionalised knowledge'. He considers that often professional ideology functions primarily in the interests of professionals despite its supposed concern with standards and quality of service. He reacts against the wrapping up of knowledge in parcels labelled 'expert' because this produces a passive and even timid attitude to learning and makes the client unnecessarily dependent on the professional. He believes in as much open access to information as possible whether it be about medicine, the law or whatever. Underlying his suggestions is a belief that education, formal and informal, should be an active process in which the teacher or expert advises rather than dictates, participates rather than controls.

There has been an increase in public interest in finding alternative routes to meeting needs than those supplied by professionals. Thus, there are 'simple' kits available to do one's own conveyancing and a range of alternative approaches to medicine

(see p. 417). Stewart Clegg and David Dunkerly suggest that organisational and technical developments have reduced the authority and exclusivity of professionals:

> *Increasing standardisation has taken place in the legal and accounting professions. The popularity of 'do-it-yourself' house purchase and divorce is evidence of such routinisation; accountancy, largely through the effects of computers, has become more and more codified, standardised and routinised. In other words, not only clerical work but professional activities as well appear to be subject to an increasing division of labour characterised by routinisation.*
>
> *(Clegg and Dunkerly, 1980:363)*

Weber left relatively unexplored the relationship between professionals and managers. This relationship frequently occurs when professionals are employed either by the state, such as teachers, or by business, such as lawyers, solicitors, accountants, and engineers. Table 9.9 gives a broad outline of how several professions fared in their attempts to maintain autonomy and control against the counter-claims of government, managers and the public.

The professional in this situation loses the freedom associated with independent practice and, sometimes, the opportunity to employ a broad range of expertise. S/he tends to do highly specialised work (in a sub-branch of law or accountancy) and, although professional judgement is usually accepted within a limited area, has to submit to the overall authority of management. In general, professionals are better qualified than management but have less authority within organisations. As Burns and Stalker point out, some managers deal with this situation by adopting more flexible, open-ended and democratic modes of decision-making. They use the term 'organic' to describe this tendency. A large-scale empirical study of the same issue led Peter Blau to conclude that this is, indeed, often the approach taken by management who have well qualified professionals on their staff. As Etzioni points out, however, professional and management functions are different, and the possibility of conflict cannot be entirely removed. In ideal-type terms, professionals make recommendations on the basis of what seems 'right' by professional principles, whereas managers look for solutions that 'work' in terms of the rules and goals of the organisation.

A body of legislation passed during the 1980s changed the relationship between management and professionals in education, including higher education. For instance, the collegiate (collective professional) power of academies in the running of higher educational institutions tended to be reduced while that of managers, reflecting government legislation and goals, increased. Thus, management was required to ensure the introduction of plans for appraisal and performance-related pay – subject to the government withholding part of the annual salary award to academics.

Table 9.9 The changing state of the professions: 1979 and 1995 compared

	Doctors	Teachers	Academics	Accountants	Solicitors
Pay	Proportionally higher than in 1979 than other public sector workers, but lower compared with other professions.	Up compared with inflation rate, but down in comparison with other white-collar workers. Can no longer negotiate pay.	Down since 1979 in comparison to other white-collar workers.	Rose in the 1980s, fell off in the 1990s. Proportionally higher than in 1979.	Rose steeply in 1980s boom, then fell off. Most firms proportionately better off than in 1979.
Entry qualifications	No change. Medical degree needed.	No change. B.Ed degree or Post Graduate Certificate of Education needed.	Generally harder. PhDs more difficult to obtain, and many new academic jobs are short-term.	Vary depending on type of accountancy. Most accept only graduates.	No change. Degree, solicitors' exams and training course needed.
Disciplinary/ complaints procedures	General Medical Council is self-regulatory body. New Government regulations include complaints procedures in NHS hospitals.	School governors can dismiss incompetent or negligent teachers. Government keeps a list of struck-off teachers.	Determined by individual institutions.	Largely self-regulated – major complaints go to the Joint Disciplinary Scheme. Auditors must be registered with government.	Solicitors Complaints Bureau is a self-regulatory body. Legal Services ombudsman set up by government in 1990.
Exclusivity	Increased blurring of edges between nurses' and junior doctors' duties. Nurses can now make limited prescriptions.	Government attempts to introduce a 'mums' army' of non-graduate infant school teachers thwarted in 1993.	No change.	Accountancy qualifications are needed to join a firm of accountants or audit public companies.	Lost their monopoly on conveyancing in 1986, but gained rights of advocacy in High Court in 1990.
Unionisation	80% of doctors are members of the BMA, as against 70% in 1979.	Most teachers are union members now, as in 1979.	About 50% of long-term academics are union members. Little change since 1979.	All accountants must join one of the accountants' associations, which set the exams.	All solicitors must be members of the Law Society.
Government legislation	1984 – NHS general management introduced. Doctors made more answerable to managers 1990 – introduced GP fundholders and NHS Trusts.	1988 – Education Reform Act. Introduced National Curriculum. 1991 – Teachers' Pay and Conditions Act. Introduced pay review body. 1993 – Education Act. Introduced Ofsted.	1988 – Education Reform Act. Abolition of academic tenure, which gave academics jobs-for-life. Higher Education Funding Council set up and inspection system created.	Various Companies Acts since the 1980s have tightened up regulations on auditing large companies.	1985 – Administration of Justice Act removes monopoly on conveyancing. 1990 – Courts and Legal Services Act introduces 'no win, no fee' principle for personal injury cases.
Power	Less than 1979. Many powers removed by NHS reforms.	Influence reduced, despite government compromise over testing.	Academics disparate as a body. Decline in status since 1979.	Little influence as a body, now as in 1979.	Feel threatened about future position.

(From Perm 6, Demos, *The Independent,* 9.8.1995:11 – adapted)

Marxist perspective on the professions

Whereas Weberians commence analysis with the market position of professionals, Marxists start with their relation to the means of production. It is the relationship to, and functioning within, the total class structure of the professions that Marxists are primarily interested in.

Marxists analysis of managerial, administrative and professional groups, unlike Weberian, does not present these groups as rather independent, would-be self-determining groups. On the contrary, they are typically seen as occupying an ambiguous class position. This perspective is partly the product of the general Marxist framework of class analysis which presents all classes in relation to the capitalist/working class polarity. We have already seen that the very top individuals in these groups – roughly, those wealthy enough to make substantial independent investments in the companies with which they are associated – are generally considered by Marxists as part of the (ruling) upper class. Otherwise, both Eric Olin Wright and Harry Braverman locate these occupational groups within a contradictory class location between the bourgeoisie and the proletariat. This means that they have certain characteristics in common with capitalists and others in common with the working class. Examples of the former are greater independence and status at work and, often, authority over others. Examples of the latter are that many have to 'sell' their labour either to capitalists or the 'capitalist state' and, in Marxists terms, are therefore in an alienating situation.

It is particularly in respect to the functions they perform for the capitalist system that Marxists see managerial, administrative and professional employees as close to the capitalist class. These include legal and financial functions, and also managerial and administrative functions in relation to the work force. Thus, Vicente Navarro considers that the National Health Service in advanced capitalist societies is a ruling class dominated sector within which management and professionals carry out the task of servicing working class people who have been physically and mentally undermined by life in capitalist society (see p. 424). Similarly, Marxists such as Althusser argue that teachers function largely as agents of social control and as reproducers of the class system. In contradiction to Parkin's neo-Weberian view of the professions as quasi-autonomous, Marxists tend to see them as agencies of capitalism functioning with the overall structure of the capitalist system.

Braverman's 'deskilling' and 'proletarianisation' thesis, discussed earlier (see pp. 264-6), is relevant to our consideration of the functioning of professions and their place within the class structure. Braverman argues that as professionals are increasingly brought into the service of the capitalist state and business, so their work is increasingly organised and routinised by capitalist management. The need of capitalism for efficient professional service both through the state (e.g. education and training) and within business corporations (e.g. efficient accounting and legal advice) means that professionals are in a working context in which the demands of capital dominate. Professional independence tends to be eroded in the face of targets, deadlines and delivery pattern stipulated by management. Thus, scientific research in industry is routinely driven by a company's practical and competitive needs and within education, courses are increasingly assessed on the basis of 'skills' (some of which are suggested or even stipulated by industry) rather than on the basis of subject content.

Barbara and John Ehrenreich (1979) also consider that professionals contribute to the functioning of capitalism, but argue that they occupy a distinct upper middle class position rather than a 'contradictory' position between capital and labour. The Ehrenreichs classify professionals alongside management in a professional-managerial class whose main function is to reproduce capitalist culture and facilitate (or manage) class relations. This

analysis of the functioning of professionals is not dissimilar to that of other Marxists, such as Althusser, but the Ehrenreichs are unusual in allocating a specific class location to them.

Increasingly, Marxist analyses of international capitalism include the very top professionals in multinational companies – for instance, lawyers and accountants – as members of the capitalist class. Such individuals often have large shareholdings and managerial as well as professional influence .

Questions

1 'Managers and professionals are merely better paid workers.' Discuss.
2 Describe and account for the changing pattern of British industrial relations since the 'winter of discontent' of 1979.

Work and non-work: consumption

The division of existence into work and non-work time is very basic. However, these are better categories than work and leisure because much non-work time may be devoted to activities other than leisure. A number of attempts to develop the work/non-work categorisation have been made. Stanley Parker (1976) makes the following divisions: work; work obligations; existence time; non-work obligations; and leisure.

Parker defines work as earning a living – broadly, employment. Work obligations include activities done outside normal working hours which are associated with the job but beyond what is necessary to achieve a minimum level of performance; voluntary overtime and second jobs. The remaining three categories are, to a progressive extent, leisure categories. The third category, existence time, is the satisfaction of physiological needs such as 'sleep, eating, washing, elimination'. Non-work obligations refers mainly to domestic duties. Finally, leisure is 'time free from obligations either to self or to others – time to do as one chooses'.

Elias and Dunning's categorisation of work/non-work can be matched fairly closely with Parker's scheme: private work and family management; rest; catering for biological needs; sociability; and 'mimetic' or play activities.

These types of categorisations are useful when considering the lives of males in full-time employment. They give a fair sense of the daily experience of necessity and pleasure. However, they are inadequate for understanding the work/non-work experience of those mainly involved in domestic labour, still overwhelmingly women. Sue McIntosh and her colleagues have criticised Parker sharply on this point. She takes each of Parker's categories in turn and shows their inadequacy when applied to housewives. First, she points out that in defining work as 'activity involved in earning a living', women in full-time housework are automatically excluded from Parker's framework. She observes that the work (domestic) activities of the housewife tend to overlap with, and undermine the quality of their leisure. She gives a contemporary, feminist's slant to the old saying 'A woman's work is never done'. Again, she describes the distinction Parker makes in his categories of work and work obligation as 'fairly meaningless' for housewives. McIntosh's comment on the functions of existence time – eating, excretion, etc. – is that housewives often help others meet them, – work, indeed! On the fourth category, 'the domestic part of work obligations', she observes that this is a large part of her total work in the home. She asks, 'Is women's work therefore to be equated with male 'semi-leisure?' About leisure itself, she states, 'Women have very little of this time'. Even the time a woman has may be defined by the choices her husband makes and she may be deterred from doing things on her own because of his possessiveness.

McIntosh, then, presents a typical work-leisure model of the housewife. The central feature of it is that domestic activity or concern virtually never ceases: there are few total 'escapes' into leisure, little real 'free time'. She pointedly raises the question of how women can gain more genuine leisure time and we will return to this later.

There are other variables besides gender which Parker's model does not adequately encompass. These include age, unemployment and 'race'/ethnicity. Parker's view that work is the major influence on leisure is also of limited usefulness when applied to groups not in full-time work. In fairness, however, we ought to consider the group to which Parker's model best applies. people in full-time employment (mainly males).

Before presenting his own theory of work and leisure, Parker reviews existing work in the field. He classifies this into two schools of thought, segmentalists and holists. The former believe that work is separated from leisure, and the latter that there is a tendency towards a fusion of work and leisure. Parker suggests that both approaches are too generalised and selective in their use of evidence. His own survey data found that both perspectives were relevant in relation to different, specific occupations. Consequently elements of these approaches appear in his own categorisation of the typical ways in which people relate their work and leisure:

1 The extension (holist) pattern.
2 The neutrality pattern.
3 The opposition(segmentalist) pattern.

1 *The extension pattern* consists of having leisure activities that are often similar in content to one's working activities, making no distinction between what is considered work and what is considered leisure, and having one's central life interest in work rather than in family or leisure spheres.

He gives as examples of occupations in which this pattern is most likely to occur: 'successful businessmen, doctors, teachers, some skilled manual workers and social workers'.

Parker's observation about successful businessmen finds support from Young and Willmott's data on the work and family life of 190 managing directors. Work tended to dominate their

lives, and even leisure activities were shared with (usually) male business associates rather than with their families. Given the mainly instrumental attitude of many middle and lower level employees to their work, it is doubtful whether this pattern will diffuse down through the occupational system as Young and Willmott thought it might. However, it is worth speculating that as a result of the increase in high income earners in both Britain and the United States in the first half of the1980s, the extension pattern may become more common among higher social groups. Against this is the trend for more high income families to depend on a double income (indeed, particularly in the United States, children at school or college also often work part-time and thus add to the total income). Where women contribute substantially to the family income, they may be less willing to take total responsibility for the domestic side or to 'lose' their husbands to work and work-oriented pursuits to the same extent.

2 Parker describes *the neutrality pattern* as having leisure activities that are somewhat different from work, making a distinction between work and leisure, and having one's central life interest in family or leisure rather than in the work sphere.

He gives the following occupations as typically associated with this pattern: 'clerical workers, semi-skilled manual workers, and minor professionals other than social workers'. These occupations offer only low or medium autonomy at work, limited intrinsic satisfaction, but provide substantial leisure time for relaxation

3 *Opposition pattern* leisure activities involve a sharp demarcation between work and leisure, and central life interest in the non-work sphere.

This pattern is 'to some extent exhibited by routine clerical workers' but 'seems more typical of unskilled manual workers, and those occupations such as mining and distant-water fishing'. The associated work factors are instrumental motivation, low autonomy in the work situation, limited opportunities for expression of abilities, and alienative attitudes.

Parker's analysis of the opposition pattern is based largely on two studies of extreme occupations: Denis, Henriques and Slaughter's *Coal is our life* (1956) and Jeremy Tunstall's *The Fishermen* (1962). For workers in these occupations, leisure is recuperative and even escapist. Heavy drinking helps obliterate memories of harsh work and lowers inhibitions. Pleasure takes the form of release of pent-up energy in fun and macho fooling about the fantasy.

It is interesting to apply Abraham Maslow's model of human needs (see p. 267) to Parker's analysis. Only those working in occupations associated with the extension pattern appear to have jobs which will greatly engage them in the process of self-actualisation (the achievement and expression of their highest needs). The neutrality and opposition patterns are associated with jobs unlikely to meet more than certain deficit needs. Some might provide such low status and public recognition that they might not even fully meet the need for self-esteem. Further, some work appears either so exhausting or intellectually blunting as to make the achievement of high levels of self-expression in leisure unlikely.

This trend of thought easily reconciles with Marxist analysis of the alienating nature of wage labour in capitalist society. Marx argued that the worker in capitalist society is alienated from her/himself and her/his species (human) being. In Maslow's terms her/his human potential is frustrated. However, Parker does not link his analysis of work and leisure to a critique of capitalism and Marxists would regard this as a criticism of his work. For them, both the production and consumption of leisure goods and services are alienated under capitalism. In particular, Bero Rigauer argues that the professional production of sport, fragments and bureaucratises the experience of participants, just as industrial production does that of workers. Similarly, the audience for commercialised sport may be distracted both from their exploitation and from a more active expression and development of their own talents – including, sometimes, sporting.

There have been other critics of Parker's model in addition to Marxist and feminist. The Rapoports show there are strong associations between age/the life course and types of leisure activity (although, as we have seen, these links can be open to change, see p. 71). Kenneth Roberts emphasises that people as participants and consumers make their own leisure choice – albeit within social limits – an issue presented in more detail through a discussion of the work of Lunt and Livingstone in a later chapter (see pp. 496-7).

The future of work and leisure: postmodernity (see also Chapter 16, pp. 493-8)

Technological progress has not yet 'liberated' people from work and introduced the 'new age of leisure' some had predicted. Of course, most people do have much more leisure time than they did 150 years ago but not very much more than they did 50 years ago. Work, paid and/or domestic still dominates the weekdays of the majority of adults age 16-65 and still provides most of them with their core identity. It is as though we have looked at the possibility of a world defined by leisure and turned back from it. At times it seems as though technology – household, office, business – drives us rather than we, it. Perhaps we like it that way – preferring the familiar and secure rhythm of work to vistas of leisure time. Filling that time might require creativity, imagination and effort. At a practical level, as long as money is distributed primarily through work, people will be highly motivated to compete against each other economically. Yet, the wealth to provide a basis for human fulfilment, as Marx and Maslow envisaged it, is increasingly available.

The postmodern argument that identity is formed more in consumption – and by implication – in leisure, than through one's place in production and the occupational hierarchy is discussed elsewhere in this book (see pp. 493-8 and pp. 635-6). It is certainly significant that people spend more of their time 'on leisure' than 'in work' compared to earlier periods but the relationship between production and consumption remains strong. Most obviously, the

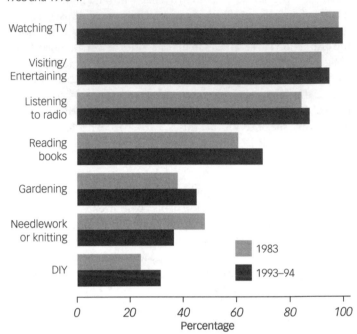

Participation in home-based leisure activities, 1983 and 1993-4.

(Source: Office of Population Censuses and Surveys in *The Guardian*, 9.8.1995)

Figure 9.14 Participation in home-based leisure activities, 1983 and 1993-94

size of one's earnings largely determines what one can consume but work is also related to leisure taste – as Parker argues.

As Figure 9.14 shows, the pattern of home-based leisure activities has, in recent years, been a fairly stable mix of new media and traditional pursuits and hobbies. Almost as many participate in visiting and entertaining as watch TV. Taken together more participate in reading books and in gardening than listen to the radio – and both the former activities are increasing at a faster rate than the latter. No doubt the level of creativity and awareness that goes into these activities varies but this hardly seems to be the zombiefied world of the more pessimistic postmodernists such as Baudrillard (see pp. 518-20).

Question

To what extent has the relationship between work and leisure changed in recent years (approximately since the 1960s)?

Summary

1 The British economy is increasingly influenced by global factors. The flow of investment, already becoming more international, became rapidly more so after the deregulation of the stock market in 1986. Increasingly, the fate of British firms and employees is affected by wider factors.

2 Piore and Sabel (1984) argue that capitalist firms have moved from a Fordist to post-Fordist model of production in which labour and technology are used more flexibly. Among the many comments on this analysis is the Marxist observation that whether or not this adaptation has occurred, the relationship between capital and labour remains basically the same.

3 The flexible labour market and tougher strategies of capital and top management created greater job insecurity in the 1990s – among the middle as well as the working classes.

4 Economic and employment market changes have impacted strongly on women, ethnic minorities and the young. Details about each group are given in relevant chapters – respectively 7, 8 and 15.

5 Various attempts to theorise the experience of work are presented. Several theories of alienation are discussed and these are contrasted with Goldthorpe and Lockwood's social action approach who find that their sample of manual workers works for instrument (money) motives and that alienation does not greatly figure in their considerations. A discussion of the concept of fulfilment in work concludes this section.

6 Unemployment resurfaced as a major issue of the 1980s and 1990s. The universalist approach – that unemployment is invariably and almost equally a disaster – is contrasted with the relativist approach which sees it as a more variable experience.

7 The growth of unionism in the 1950s, 1960s and 1970s is explained largely in terms of the representation and protection offered to members by unions and by the positive acceptance of them by government and employers. The 'retreat' of unionism in the 1980s is explained largely by recession and government policy.

8 There are a variety of types of industrial conflict of which strikes are the main one. Factors associated with strikes vary from explanations arguing an 'in-built' conflict between capital and labour to causes related to specific industries such as those experiencing difficult and dirty working conditions. Some strike activity may be regarded as 'normal'.

9 There are three main approaches to analysing the professions. 'Trait' analysis presents supposed key characteristics of the professions such as service to the community and self-regulation. Neo-Weberian analysis sees the professions as motivated mainly by group-interest including a desire to 'close' others out of their rewards and status. Marxists variously place the professions within the class structure although their precise position tends to be seen as 'ambiguous'.

10 Work is contrasted to non-work because much of non-work time is not, in fact, leisure. This is especially true of people primarily involved in domestic work who rarely experience a 'five o'clock release'.

11 Stanley Parker's model of work-leisure assumes that a person's work greatly influences the nature of his/her leisure. Marxists tend to see capitalism as dominating the structure of both work and leisure time.

Research and coursework

Many students have part-time jobs and 'doing research' into a place of work is a convenient possibility. However, there is a danger that such a study will be over-descriptive and anecdotal ('gossipy') and lack theoretical perspective and objective analysis. It would be better to do a well-planned study of an unfamiliar place of work than, say, a participant observational study of a familiar one that is highly participant and poorly observed.

The following are some research issues:

1 Alienation (the operationalisation/measurement of the concept is a key problem).

2 The extent to which a particular organisation is 'post-Fordist' in character (this would require establishing criteria for assessing the extent of post-Fordism and perhaps comparing two occupational groups in the organisation to determine whether they fitted the primary/secondary labour force model).

3 An unusual project would be an examination of the industrial relations record of a particular organisation (probably over a brief historical period). It would be important to provide sociological explanations for the findings.

4 A replication of Parker's study into the relationship between work and leisure could be highly interesting. A close preliminary examination of his methodology would be required.

Further reading

There is a need for collections of readings which cover current debates such as 'post-Fordism' and 'deskilling'. Two are Stephen Wood ed., *The Transformation of Work* (Unwin Hyman, 1989) and Kenneth Thompson ed., *Work: Past, Present and Future* (Open University Press, 1984). Two 'topic books' written specifically for 'A' level students are John Horne, *Work and Unemployment* (Longman, 1987) and Rosemary Deem *Work, Unemployment and Leisure* (Routledge, 1988).

Readings

Reading 1
The break-up of Fordism: the culture of consumption

From Robin Murray, 'Fordism and Post-Fordism' in S Hall and M Jacques eds., *New Times and the Changing Face of Politics in the 1990s* (Lawrence and Wishart, 1989), pp.41-3

Fordism as a vision – both left and right – had always been challenged, on the shopfloor, in the political party, the seminar room and the studio. In 1968 this challenge exploded in Europe and the USA. It was a cultural as much as an industrial revolt, attacking the central principles of Fordism, its definitions of work and consumption, its shaping of towns and its overriding of nature.

From that time we can see a fracturing of the foundations of predictability on which Fordism was based. Demand became more volatile and fragmented. Productivity growth fell as the result of workplace resistance. The decline in profit drove down investment. Exchange rates were fluctuating, oil prices rose and in 1974 came the greatest slump the West had had since the 1930s.

The consensus response was Keynesian one, to restore profitability through a managed increase in demand and an incomes policy. For monetarism the route to profitability went through the weakening of labour, a cut in state spending and a reclaiming of the public sector of private accumulation. Economists and politicians were re-fighting the battles of the last slump. Private capital on the other hand was dealing with the present one. It was using new technology and new production principles to make Fordism flexible, and in doing so stood much of the old culture on its head.

Post-Fordism

In Britain, the groundwork for the new system was laid not in manufacturing but in retailing. Since the 1950s, retailers had been using computers to transform the distribution system. All mass producers have the problem of forecasting demand. If they produce too little they lose market share. If they produce too much, they are left with stocks, which are costly to hold, or have to be sold at a discount. Retailers face this problem not just for a few products, but for thousands. Their answer has been to develop information and supply systems which allow them to order supplies to coincide with demand. Every evening Sainsbury's receives details of the sales of all 12,000 lines from each of its shops; these are tuned into order for warehouse deliveries for the coming night, and replacement production for the following day. With computerised control of stocks in the shop, transport networks, automatic loading and unloading, Sainsbury's flow-line make-to-order system has conquered the Fordist problem of stocks.

They have also overcome the limits of the mass product. For, in

contrast to the discount stores which are confined to a few, fast-selling items, Sainsbury's, like the new wave of high street shops, can handle ranges of products geared to segments of the market. Market niching has become the slogan of the high street. Market researchers break down market by age (youth, young adults, 'grey power'), by household types (dinkies, single-gender couples, one-parent families), by income, occupation, housing and, increasingly, by locality. They analyse 'lifestyles', correlating consumption patterns across commodities, from food to clothing, and health to holidays.

The point of this new anthropology of consumption is to target both product and shops to particular segments. Burton's – once a mass producer with generalised retail outlets – has changed in the 1980s to being a niche market retailer with a team of anthropologists, a group of segmented stores – Top Shop, Top Man, Dorothy Perkins, Principles and Burton's itself – and now has no manufacturing plants of its own. Conran's Storehouse group – Habitat, Heals, Mothercare, Richards and BHS – all geared to different groups, offers not only clothes, but furniture and furnishings, in other words entire lifestyles. At the heart of Conran's organisation in London is what amounts to a factory of 150 designers, with collages of different lifestyles on the wall, Bold Primary, Orchid, mid-Atlantic and the Cottage Garden.

In all these shops the emphasis has shifted from the manufacturer's economies of scale to the retailer's economies of scope. The economies come from offering an integrated range from which customers choose their own basket of products. There is also an economy of innovation, for the modern retail systems allow new product ideas to be tested in practice, through shop sales, and the successful ones then to be ordered for wider distribution. Innovation has become a leading edge of the new competition. Product life has become shorter, for fashion goods and consumer durable.

A centrepiece of this new retailing is design. Designers produce the innovations. They shape the lifestyles. They design the shops, which are described as 'stages' for the act of shopping. There are now 29,000 people working in design consultancies in the UK, which have sales of £1,600 million per annum. They are the engineers of designer capitalism. With market researchers they have steered the high street from being retailers of goods to retailers of style.

These changes are a response to, and a means of shaping, the shift from mass consumption. Instead of keeping up with the Joneses there has been a move to be different from the Joneses. Many of these differences are vertical, intended to confirm status and class. But some are horizontal centred around group identities, linked to age, or region of ethnicity. In spite of the fact that basic needs are still unmet, the high street does offer a new variety and creativity in consumption which the Left's puritan tradition should also address. Whatever our responses, the revolution in retailing reflects new principles of production, a new pluralism of products and new importance for innovation. As such it marks a shift to a post-Fordist age.

There have been parallel shifts in manufacturing, not least in response to the retailers' just-in-time system of ordering. In some sectors where the manufacturers are a little more than subcontractors to the retailers, their flexibility has been achieved at the expense of labour. In others, capital itself has suffered, as furniture retailers like MFI squeeze their suppliers, driving down prices, limiting design, and thereby destroying much of the mass-production furniture industry during the downturns.

Questions

1 Outline the main changes in the organisation of retailing as described by Murray and describe 'the point of' what he calls 'this new anthropology of consumption'.
2 What are the main changes in consumption indicated in the passage?

Reading 2
Criticisms of the post-Fordist thesis

From Paul Thompson, *The Nature of Work: An Introduction to Debates on the Labour Process* (Macmillan, 1989), pp.224-5 (adapted)

A powerful case has been made that changes in work organisation necessitate a major theoretical shift. But how valid is the analysis? Unfortunately there is every indication that it is based on very shaky foundations. The basic dichotomy between mass production and flexible specialisation is seen by many commentators as crude and ill-considered ... It neglects the significance of process and batch variations and repeats the myth of the dominance of the assembly line. Mass production itself is defined in a very narrow way, when in practice it is not necessarily inflexible and limited to using dedicated equipment to produce in a standardised way. Flow lines can now cater for considerable diversification and multi-model lines. Indeed, many of the Japanese advances have been made within such a framework. Even the standard version of Fordism 'still represents a powerful model of transfer, specialisation and work integration at the level of the factory'... Hyman (1988) notes the irony that sectors of the British economy were shifting to a Fordist model of product planning and labour control just as flexible specialisation was supposed to be taking root as a global trend in the 1970s.

Caution should also be used in discussion of flexible technology. Advanced programmable machinery remains an extremely expensive investment, especially for the small firms who are to be at the leading edge of customised production. It is necessary to break the idea of any necessary link between flexibility and advanced manufacturing technology. The latter is not always flexible or used for this purpose. Emphasis is as likely to be on co-ordination of the labour process, quality and routeing ...

Again, many Japanese companies have achieved flexibility through methods of organising production such as JIT[1], without always having the most sophisticated technology.

Finally, the idea that mass markets are saturated is also vastly overstated ... Many industries, including those covering most consumer goods, continue to sell to mass markets, while products such as colour televisions and videos are commonly produced on the basis of families of interrelated models. If we turn to the concept of flexible specialisation itself, we find it is 'very elusive' beyond reference to shorter production runs and less rigid technologies ...

Williams *et al.* (1987) ... show clearly the standard of evidence used by Piore and Sabel to be often poor or non-existent. Of course, there are the regions such as those of the 'Third Italy'[2] mentioned earlier. However, their analysis also highlights some sectors of the engineering industry at the expense of the more Fordist ones ... Nor is it correct to generalise about the existence of craft labour. Such work is undertaken by a minority, mainly men, and coexists with semi-skilled assembly work carried out by women and heavy forging and foundry tasks done by southern Italian and North African workers.

1 *JIT – just in time – a flexible production technique pioneered by the Japanese.*
2 *These are areas in Italy in which production organised on 'post-Fordist' lines allegedly occurs.*

Questions

1 Briefly summarise the points Braverman makes against the post-Fordist thesis.
2 On balance do you think the importance of post-Fordism has been exaggerated? Give reasons for your answer.

10 Organisations and Co-ordination

Are modern communications changing modern organisations? If so, how?

Aims of this chapter

1 To describe and analyse a wide range of theories of organisations and co-ordination.

2 To explore the extent to which organisations and co-ordination can be democratic.

3 To discuss and explain organisational change under Thatcherism, including the 'new managerialism'.

Introduction: organisations and modernity

Organisations are a person issue as well as a public reality. The problem is, people often fail to see the personal importance of organisations. Organisations are a pervasive feature of modern life and there is renewed debate about how they affect us or – put more positively – how people organise and co-ordinate their lives. Most of us will spend our working lives with large or medium-size organisations and if we do not learn to 'manage' them, they will certainly manage us. Perhaps the feelings of alienation that many students experience at the very thought of studying organisations is a symptom of the fact that they can only conceive of being controlled and manipulated by them, and not vice versa. This quiet desperation was given a voice by the 1960s student radical, Mario Savio, when he urged fellow rebels at Berkeley, California, to stop the bureaucratic machine of the university by 'laying' their bodies on it. Partly to combat this pessimism, we will examine not only the structure and functioning of organisations but who has power and control within them, and also whether more democratic organisational systems are possible.

Both Weber and Marx were fully aware of the importance of the concepts of power and control in analysing organisations. They agreed that organisations are the instruments which 'run' modern life but disagreed about which groups had real control of them. Weber's organisational theory is linked closely to his analysis of the 'new class'. He had no doubt that top organisational officials had great power both in private industry and government departments. He anticipated the dictatorship not of the proletariat, but of the official. He compared bureaucracy to 'an iron cage' which incarcerates individuals. He felt that as bureaucracies expanded they would develop vested interests, and argued that even a democratically elected parliament would have problems in controlling top civil servants and their departments (although he believed it should try). Marx, however, contended that in capitalist society the capitalist class controls the bureaucrats and uses them for its own ends. He argued that this was true not only of the salaried officials of private industry but, ultimately, of state bureaucrats as well, because he considered that the capitalist class also controlled the state.

Durkheim was not primarily interested in class control of organisations. He was more concerned with how a society, made up of complex organisations and characterised by an advanced division of labour, could *hold together*. As we have seen, he believed that this was possible because of organic solidarity – the interdependence of people and organisations in modern societies (see Chapter 19). Durkheim's point was a general one: later sociologists have had much more specific interests in the field of the sociology of organisations than he did.

Today – in what some term late modern society, there is need to look at organisations in a wider context and as subject to changing and different forces. Increasingly, the context and forces are global or international in scope. As a result, organisational boundaries are often more porous and their structures less stable.

Formal and informal organisations: a preliminary distinction

David Silverman attributes three features to formal organisations: they arise at an identifiable point in time; social relations are more bounded by rules than in informal organisations like the family; and consequently much attention is focused on the planning and development of those relations.

Formal organisations are operated on the basis of established rules by appointed personnel, to achieve specific goals. Practically all the large organisations of modern society such as factories, office complexes, supermarkets and schools, are formal structures. Their respective officials, rules and goals are familiar to us all. Although formal organisations are a particular feature of urban, industrial societies, certain examples such as armies and monasteries have existed for centuries. To an extent, formal organisations in modern societies have taken over or supplemented functions previously performed by family, kinship and community groups (see Chapter 3, pp. 63-4). Thus, state welfare as well as family help is available to the sick and needy through various organisational channels.

Informal organisations develop within all formal organisations. Informal organisations are freely created social group relationships outside or inside formal organisations. It is difficult to imagine that even the most rigidly run prison or concentration camp does not have some form of 'underground' system of communication. The achievement of formal goals may depend on whether informal groups operate 'for' or 'against' the formal organisation. To put it in functionalist terms, they may be functional or dysfunctional. Thus, anti-school peer-groups are an example of informal organisations which are dysfunctional to the achievement of formal educational goals.

It would be misleading to leave the impression that informal organisations exist only within formal structures: friendship groups of peers and gangs occur outside them. Typically, perhaps, people find more meaning in their informal relationships than in their formal ones. The reservation sometimes felt about the 'over-organised' quality of modern life is partly based on the feeling that formal organisations seem to be intruding more and more into the private area of life. Even though more leisure time exists, it is largely 'organised' for us by the mass media rather than used imaginatively and intelligently. Obviously, this view is controversial and we assess it critically in Chapter 17.

Theoretical perspectives on organisations

Although there are many organisational theories that the student might come across, we can conveniently divide them into four main groups. These are the bureaucratic or mechanistic; systems theories – particularly organic systems theory; theories based on the concept of interaction; and conflict theory. Although these perspectives are frequently contrasted they are by no means wholly exclusive in all respects. Indeed, we will consider the bureaucratic and organic approaches together as much to show their complementary as their contradictory aspects.

We make no analytical distinction between industrial and other kinds of formal organisations in this section. The types of organisational structures described below can occur in both the industrial and non-industrial sectors such as central and local government departments.

1 Bureaucratic and systems theories

Bureaucratic or mechanistic theory

Max Weber laid down the classical or bureaucratic model of organisational theory. His model is a functionalist one. He maintained that bureaucracy is the most functionally efficient form of organisation, even though it can sometimes operate in a rather 'inhuman' way. Bureaucracies are formal organisations generally recognisable by certain characteristics. He constructed an ideal type of bureaucracy to show what these characteristics are. We can summarise them as follows:

1 Specialisation:
  The existence of different offices (or positions) governed by rules, the purpose of which is to fulfil a *specific* function or functions.
2 Hierarchy:
  The *hierarchical* organisation of offices – that is, some positions have more *authority* and *status* than others.
3 Rules:
  Officials are required to observe established, usually written, rules and procedures.
4 Records:
  Management based on files and records used with the assistance of office staff.
5 Officials:
  The appointment of trained personnel to occupy roles in the bureaucracy.
6 Impersonality:
  Officials and clients are subject to the same rules of procedure.
7 Public/Private Division:
  Organisational matters are governed by publicly stated rules, not by private preference or favour.

Weber saw the growth of bureaucratic organisation as a major example of the application of rational thought to practical problems. He regarded the triumph of rationality as a characteristic feature of the modern world. Another of its manifestations was the massive development of science and technology. Weber also described the nature of an official bureaucratic position. Above all, it involves a commitment to performing the functions the official is appointed to do, and not to any powerful person or patron who might wish to interfere with the official's course of duty. It was necessary for Weber to make this point because, in the middle ages, this principle did not apply. When a king or lord appointed someone to a high position of service within his household, he expected his appointee to be loyal to him personally rather than merely to perform pre-determined and agreed functions. By contrast, a modern bureaucratic official is expected to do the job described in the terms of his contract. The contract defines the duties, establishes the salary scale and gives security of tenure subject to an agreed period of notice and good conduct. However, this predictable and secure situation is gradually becoming less common as 'flexibility' and 'market principles' have become more pervasive.

A classic example of a modern bureaucracy is the civil service. A pupil leaving school with a clutch of GCSEs may begin as a clerical officer. In time, s/he becomes an Executive Officer and then, perhaps, a Senior Executive Officer: more remotely, the office of Principal beckons. Each office has its own functions and the further one progresses up the hierarchy, the more power and status accrue. Even the civil service, however, has been subject to the application of market principles in the Thatcher-Major period (see pp. 302-3).

Criticisms of Weber's bureaucratic model will become apparent as we examine alternative organisational theories and some dysfunctions of bureaucracy. One point is worth making immediately, however. There is an implicit contradiction in Weber's bureaucratic functionalism, and his more usual emphasis on conflict. Oddly, Weber did not fully develop the perspective that as well as fulfilling useful functions, organisations are also frequently the focus of conflict between groups. We develop this issue later in this chapter.

Organic systems theory

The organisational type that most obviously contrasts with the bureaucratic is what Burns and Stalker (1961) termed the organic system. They contrast organic systems with what they call mechanistic systems but, as the latter are in no way distinguishable from bureaucracies, this need not detain us.

Organic systems are characterised by a less rigid division of labour than mechanistic ones; they are less rule-bound, less hierarchical and more open to the influence of the informal group. The last point is crucial. The skill and experience of the individual can be communicated laterally (sideways) across the network of those involved in the task. The team as a whole shares power and responsibility. Overall, the organic approach shows a more subtle awareness of the complex nature and effects of interaction, formal and informal, than does the bureaucratic. Such an approach is often considered appropriate for relatively high level technical or scientific employees in, say, the electronics industry – for example, a team of computer programmers. Nevertheless, it has also been successfully tried with manual workers. At their Kalmar plant, Volvo broke down assembly work into twenty sets of functions. Each set is performed by a team of fifteen or twenty workers. The cars pass from team to team on trolleys, allowing the workers considerable freedom of movement. The teams are not hierarchically organised, and solutions to problems are supposed to be reached through co-operation and not by authoritarianism.

Although the bureaucratic or mechanistic, and the organic systems models of organisations are, to some extent, in competition with each other, there are circumstances in which one model may be more appropriate that the other. Burns and Stalker suggest that bureaucracy is often suitable for the pursuit of clear goals in stable conditions, such as producing a commodity for a safe and established market, and that an organic system is appropriate to less stable conditions in which precise goals may still be developing, such as electronics research.

Scientific management theory

Frederick W Taylor's theory of scientific management reflects the same principles as Weber's bureaucratic theory, and, to a lesser extent, human relations theory and socio-technical theory bear comparison with organic systems theory.

Taylor, an American contemporary of Weber, reached his conclusions independently of the Austrian social scientist. Taylor was specifically interested in industrial organisations and particularly in developing ways to improve production. What he said about the role and function of the industrial worker was comparable with Weber's comments on the lower level white-collar employee. Further, both recognised that higher level bureaucrats and managers had relatively more power. Like Weber, Taylor decided that efficiency was best obtained by task specialisation and standardisation, and the centralisation of decision-making power at the top of the hierarchy. He argued that all mental work should be removed from the workshop, and put in the hands of management. He presented his ideas in a book entitled *Scientific Management*. An explicit guiding principle was actually to treat the worker as an extension of the machine or organisation and, indeed, this notion is, more or less, implicit in all bureaucratic structures. Among the advice he offered was that 'the two hands should begin and complete their motions simultaneously' and that 'proper illumination increases production'. In addition, he recommended that pay levels be closely tied to productivity. It seems appropriate that Taylor's approach is often referred to as mechanical or mechanistic theory.

Human relations theory

Human relations theory originated as a reaction against Taylor's scientific management theory. From 1927 to 1932, a series of studies was mounted into worker productivity at the Hawthorne Works of the Western Electricity Company in Chicago. Initially, the researchers, led by Elton Mayo, were positively influenced by Taylor and their area of enquiry was actually suggested by his work. They wanted to find out the optimum level of illumination and other environmental factors to maximise production. There is more than a touch of comedy about the way they arrived at the 'results' of their research. They 'found' that the relation between the variables of illumination and production was virtually non-existent. In one of the studies in which the workers were placed in a control room in lighting conditions equivalent to moonlight, they still maintained a reasonable level of production: it fell off only when illumination was so reduced that they could not see properly!

Ultimately, the Hawthorne experiments were of outstanding importance both because of the new theory of industrial relations they suggested, and by virtue of their contribution to a better understanding of social scientific method, specifically that of observation. We have already discussed the second of these, the effect of the researcher on the behaviour of the subject of research, in Chapter 2. We concentrate now on the first, the content of their findings. To put it simply, they found that the productive performance of the workers was affected by social factors, as well as material ones, such as the level of illumination. The social factor at work in this case was the interest of the research team in the workers. Unexpectedly, this seemed to stimulate them to greater efforts than otherwise. The presence of researchers in a factory is, however, rare.

Follow-up studies by the Mayo team showed that the informal relationships of the workers themselves constitute the most important social variable affecting production. The role of informal groups was established by the notable Western Electric Company Bank wiring room experiment involving the wiring of switchboards. A group of fourteen workers was set up separately and observed for six months. It was found that, although they were paid on the basis of a productivity bonus scheme, the men did not respond to this by individually trying to maximise their production, but established their own production norms as a group. Group disapproval was equally the fate of those who produced either more or less than the agreed norm.

Underlying the human relations approach is a more complex and more humanistic theory of human needs than that implied by classical theory. The latter assumes that individuals will work harder in improved material conditions and if they are given higher material rewards for more work. Human relations theory argues that people also need the security, companionship, identity and guidance of the informal peer group. These psychological needs are only capable of fulfilment with others. Taylor's attempt to treat the work force as isolated individuals was based on the misleading fiction that workers are, in fact, isolated. In modern, large-scale organisations, work is a collective experience.

Socio-technical systems theory

The socio-technical systems theory attempts to combine both the technical and social factors affecting work so as to bring about the most effective overall performance. Mary Weir summarises three major points suggested by socio-technical system theorists to achieve this end: the individual must have some power to control and regulate her or his work; s/he should be able to adapt her or his own standards of work both to the expectations and demands of others and to the changing work situation generally; and the job should be both varied and have a coherent pattern. Finally, it should be linked meaningfully to the rest of the production process. It should also provide the worker with status in the community.

Both the human relations and socio-technical systems approaches have been criticised as merely 'making exploitation more bearable'. In a challenging critique of management theories the Marxist, Harry Braverman, attacks both Taylor's theory, and human relations and similar schools. He suggests that Taylorism did not last because it was too obviously crude and insensitive. The 'softer' theories provided the necessary ideological fig leaves to cover the still basically exploitative nature of capitalist production. But they fail to confront the private ownership and control of industry which Marxists traditionally regard as the root of alienation. Even given Braverman's premise, however, there remains the argument that it is better to be exploited in comfort than discomfort! (Aspects of Braverman's analysis are discussed in greater detail on pp. 264-6.)

The dysfunctions of bureaucratic organisation

The arguments in favour of bureaucracy are considerable. Firstly, the bureaucratic division of labour combined with technological innovation has greatly increased the production of goods and services: to that extent it is efficient. Secondly, a bureaucracy usually ensures a degree of predictability: production quotas are pre-determined, people know how they are likely to be treated. Thirdly, partly because of its very impersonality, bureaucracy is often a condition of fairness. People are appointed to offices on the basis of qualifications and merit rather than patronage. Further, clients are dealt with by bureaucrats on the basis of equality and need, not favouritism. That, at any rate, is the theory, although

several sociologists have criticised and modified it.

Arguing within a functionalist framework, Robert Merton points to several dysfunctions of bureaucracy which can lead to inefficiency. First, rigid adherence to bureaucratic rules may prevent an official from improvising a necessary response to unexpected circumstances. Thus, to offer our own example, a secretary in a production company, in the absence of superiors, may happen one day to find herself having to deal with an important client. Conceivably, by retreating behind her official role – 'I'm sorry, I'm only the secretary. I don't have the authority to deal with business matters' – vital orders may be jeopardised or, at a minimum the client may feel s/he has not been well treated. In such a case, initiative, confidence and some imagination are needed. Bureaucracy does not always teach these qualities and can actually smother them. The results can be 'passing the buck'. Secondly, there is a danger that those rigidly trained to obey rules rather than to consciously achieve goals will become what Merton calls ritualistic. This means that they attach more importance to observing rules and procedures than to achieving the purpose for which they exist: this is referred to as goal displacement. As lower level bureaucrats are often not kept informed about general organisational goals, ritualism must be considered a potential fault of bureaucracy, rather than an individual failing. Merton classifies ritualism as a form of anomie (see p. 352). Finally, Merton argues that the sometimes alienating effect of bureaucracy on both bureaucrats and the public with whom they deal can be dysfunctional. Bureaucratic or ritualistic characters are not the most adaptable and efficient of people, and clients who have to submit to long bureaucratic procedure before, say, they can receive needed social security are unlikely to be very co-operative.

Merton argues within functionalist assumptions but, as we have seen, Burns and Stalker suggest that in certain circumstances it is more efficient to break with the bureaucratic method of organisation altogether. Broadly, this is when co-operative and organic rather than competitive and hierarchical structures are more suitable to organisation goal attainment. Arguing along similar lines, Peter Blau gives a number of examples in which formal bureaucracy proved inappropriate. One such instance occurred in an isolated American navy island base. Virtually cut off from external control, the formal organisation of the base broke down and natural leaders, who worked effectively but within an informal framework emerged. A better known study by Blau is of an American state employment agency. He compared two groups of job placement interviewers who operated on different organisational principles, the one highly bureaucratic, the other much more informal and co-operative. On balance, the second approach proved more effective in placing clients in jobs. Blau did not over-generalise from this casestudy to the point of concluding that informal organisation is more efficient. Indeed, he found evidence to suggest that it sometimes operated in a biased manner as there were fewer bureaucratic checks to prevent officials favouring some clients at the expense of others. Rather, he suggested that what is often needed is balance, varying with circumstances, between formal and informal methods.

It is worth recalling two studies that we have already met which point to the limits of a rigidly bureaucratic approach. First is the pioneering Hawthorne study presented earlier in this chapter which established the importance of the informal social group in production. Second is Alvin Gouldner's casestudy of a wildcat strike which showed that unrest can occur when workers, used to informality, responsibility and independence, have a bureaucratic regime imposed upon them.

Finally, there can be no clearer demonstration of the limited effectiveness of rigid rule-following in achieving goals than the fact that workers use the strategy of 'working to rule' (doing all tasks by the book) in the industrial bargaining process.

Refusing to work overtime is a common example. The result is often inconvenience to the public. Thus, transport workers can make chaos out of timetable schedules merely by working a 'normal' day. Strict and time-consuming adherence to safety check rules or a rigid refusal to allow more people on a bus than is officially stipulated can also be used as pinpricks in industrial campaigning. Put negatively, working to rule can be presented as a 'withdrawal of goodwill'. The National Union of Teachers (NUT) adopted this approach in their industrial action of 1979. In particular, lunchtime supervision of children was suspended. This was hardly lethal in its effect but it did result in a number of 'mad hatter's dinner parties' here and there. Clearly, then, relationships and goodwill, as well as rules are a part of organisation.

Talcott Parsons' functional-systems theory

Parsons' organisational theory is interesting in that it combines elements of Weberian functionalism with those of systems theory. He retains the notion that organisations have goals, but describes them as potentially much more flexible and capable of adaptation than does Weber.

Parsons treats organisations virtually as though they were small-scale societies, and his organisational analysis strongly recalls his social systems theory (see Chapter 21, pp. 626-7). The various parts of organisations are seen as interdependent; they have certain needs that have to be met for survival; they have goals; the whole is something more than the sum of all the individuals who are members of the organisation. The organic analogy is clearly apparent in all this; even so, there is nothing so far mentioned that adds substantially to Weber's analysis of bureaucracy. Parsons, however, goes beyond Weber in two important ways. Firstly, he pays more attention to the capacity of organisations to interact with one another and with the environment in general. The notion that, in order to function effectively, organisations must adapt their structure and goals to changes in the environment has certainly been of influence in modern management. In a fast-changing age the possibility of 'being left behind' is ever-present. An organisation that cannot adapt is not likely to survive. An example of an organisation that has adapted to change is the House of Commons, a very different body now from that of several hundred years ago. British Leyland was an example of an organisation that

found adaptation – particularly in its response to foreign competition and new technology – a struggle, to which it eventually succumbed.

Secondly, Parsons recognises that organisations must, in some way, meet people's expressive as well as their instrumental needs. Even so, it is clear that he considers these needs are to be accommodated within the terms of the organisation's pre-set goals and certainly not as ends in themselves. This seems a deterministic and unconvincing way of reconciling personal needs with rational organisational goals. In reality, the individuals and groups that make up organisations often disagree much more than Parsons is willing to concede.

A well known application of functionalist systems theory is Peter Selznick's analysis of the Tennessee Valley Authority, set up in 1933 by President Roosevelt to help the region combat the effects of the depression. The Authority was set up with the intention of involving local people in policy making. In practice, this did not happen and instead powerful local farmers were the major effective interest group consulted by the Authority's officials. Selznick suggests that the reason why this occurred was that for the organisation to 'survive' and its officials to retain their jobs, compromise had to be made with the major local power group. This may have been so but it is just as easy to see these developments in terms of interest group or class conflict as organisational survival.

2 Social action and interactionist theories

Social action theory

David Silverman describes the meanings that individuals attach to, and find in, organisations, to be the major concern of action theory. People, not organisations, have goals. He is, however, appreciative of Parsons' attempt to conceive of organisations in terms of change and development, and he himself contextualises action within a wider institutional and social environment. He cites the previously mentioned study of Gouldner as an excellent example of an analysis that combines a sense of historical and institutional context with an understanding of the meaning actors attach to their behaviour.

Another excellent example of the importance of understanding how human behaviour, particularly in its emotional rather than its rational aspects, can affect organisations, is given by Ralph Glasser. In a television documentary (1980), Glasser tells how the olive producers of the Italian rural village of San Georgio refused to use a co-operative olive press – even though there existed good 'rational' economic arguments for doing so. Instead, they preferred to take their olives for pressing to the owners of private presses who were usually wealthy. Glasser suggests that the olive farmers acted in this way because they had a traditional relationship, based on established expectation and *fiducia* (trust) with the private press operators. By contrast, as Glasser points out, 'You can't have a relationship with a co-operaive'. In fairness, it should be said that co-operatives do sometimes work well, and people do have relationships within them. Nevertheless, it is obvious that the producers did not feel that they could relate to the new situation. This feeling became the major operative factor in the above situation and accounts for the failure of the co-operative. Glasser indulges in some conservative romanticism, but underlying this is a wise awareness of the texture of relationships and feelings woven over time, and a fear of what the brutal blade of technology and bureaucracy might do to them in the name of progress and rationality.

A better known example of a piece of research utilising action perspective, is Goldthorpe and Lockwood's affluent worker study. It will be recalled that they studiously avoided attributing motives to the workers but took the trouble to ask them what their motives were. It turned out that a majority had an instrumental orientation to work, or, simply, they worked for money, not satisfaction (Chapter 4, pp. 171-4).

Total institutions: interactionist analysis of the 'ultimate' in bureaucracy

Social action theory and symbolic interactionism are compatible theoretical approaches, but whereas the former has been developed mainly in Europe, the latter was founded in the USA, and has its own characteristic concepts and vocabulary.

We may live in an increasingly bureaucratic world, but most of us can escape from it into our private lives and personal relationships. Most of us think of these 'escapes' as necessary to a balanced life and even to sanity itself. There are, however, some who live all the time, and for a long period, in highly bureaucratic organisations, in total institutions. How does the self – to use the interactionist term – adjust to omnipresent and 'permanent' bureaucracy? Before answering this question, we must briefly examine some different types of total organisations.

A major distinction between different types of total organisations is whether membership is voluntary or compulsory. Monasteries are an example of the former, prisons of the latter. Whether members belong to an organisation by choice or not, will tend greatly to affect the quality of life within it – as a brief consideration of the difference between a monastery and prison should show. The voluntary-compulsory membership distinction does not, however, apply in every case: the members of some institutions, old people's homes and mental hospitals, for instance, may contain both types. A further way of categorising total institutions is simply in terms of the purposes they serve. Thus, goals may be custodial (prisons), protective (mental hospitals), retreatist (monasteries), or task-oriented (armies, boarding schools). Often a total institution may serve several purposes, for example, prisons protect the public and, sometimes, seek to reform their inmates.

Total institutions and modes of adjustment

Erving Goffman's *Asylums*, based on a field study carried out in a hospital in Washington in 1955-56, remains the best known study of a total institutions. In order to see at first hand the personal and psychological effects on the patients of life in an asylum, Goffman undertook a participant observational study, playing the role of an assistant to the athletic director. We can divide what Goffman refers to as the career of the mental patient into two stages, the breaking down of the old self and the construction of a new self. Part of the second stage is the adoption of modes of adjustment which enable the individual to 'get by' on a day-to-day basis and perhaps to salvage some of his sense of individuality.

The first blow to a person's old or established sense of identity is when someone – often a close relative – complains of 'abnormality'. Identity is further broken down during the in-patient phase. Not all mental hospitals are equally bureaucratic, but the admission procedures Goffman mentions include photographing, finger-printing, number assigning, listing personal possessions for storage, and undressing. Not surprisingly, he refers to this as the process of 'mortification' of the self. In the second stage referred to above, the inmate attempts to build a new self centred on the institution. The system of privileges and rewards operated by the institution in return for obedience or, perhaps, for doing work around the hospital, focus the individual's attention and energy, and may give a sense of meaning and purpose and so help to reintegrate the personality. Despite the fact that total institutions are geared to standardise behaviour, inmates manage to adopt individual modes of adjustment. Withdrawal or retreatism is an extreme and often irreversible adjustment. Two forms of adjustment in which the institution tends to 'take over' the inmate are conversion and colonisation. Conversion is when the inmate accepts the institution's definition of himself as, say, 'emotionally immature' and tries to conform to the pattern of 'perfect inmate'. Colonisation occurs when the institutional regime so engulfs the individual that it comes to seem preferable to the world outside. Prisoners, as well as mental patients, who prefer to have their lives 'run for them' sometimes adopt this mode of adjustment. Goffman uses the term, playing it cool, to describe a general posture of strategic adjustment. The mental patient may adjust to the bureaucratic power structure, and to other inmates largely as an attempt to improve his chances of discharge. In prisons, a similar adjustment is often rewarded with a remission of sentence. Goffman considers playing it cool to be the most common form of adjustment.

Some inmates rebel or, to use Goffman's precise term, take an 'intransigent line' rather than genuinely adjust, although he says relatively little of this possibility. The film *One Flew Over The Cuckoo's Nest*, based on a novel by Ken Kesey, was a dramatised version of the rebellion of McMurphy, a patient in a mental hospital. McMurphy simply refused to accept the total planning and routinisation of his life. For him, the officially pre-programmed and controlled timetable – meal times, basket-ball games, television watching, lights out and, above all, day trips –

provide opportunities for anarchic self-assertion. One episode in the film in which a bus-load of mental patients, led by McMurphy, take over a ship is a classic of comic absurdity. Finally, McMurphy ends up subdued by a brain lobotomy – the ultimate form of control. Lobotomies may be rare but electric shock treatment, the use of drugs, and manipulation of privileges, rewards and punishments to achieve conformity are common. The film does not moralise but, in the end, McMurphy's madness compares well with official thought and personality control. We are reminded that when 'society' defines someone as deviant, the consequent loss of that individual's freedom, and the tools used in reforging acceptable behaviour are formidable. Still, the film ends optimistically with McMurphy's friend, a previously subdued Indian, breaking out of the hospital in a bid for freedom.

Surviving long-term imprisonment: modes of resistance

A book very much in Goffman's style (although not uncritical of him) is *Psychological Survival: The Experience of Long-Term Imprisonment*, by Stanley Cohen and Laurie Taylor (1972). The authors frankly proclaim that one of their purposes is to provide a 'manual of survival' for long-term prisoners. Accordingly, they devote one chapter to 'making out and fighting back'. They find much more evidence of resistance in Durham prison – where they did their research – than Goffman did among patients in the Washington hospital. Accordingly, they write of modes of resistance rather than adjustment. They list five types of resistance: *self-protection, campaigning, escaping, striking* and *confronting*. Self-protection and campaigning are individual types of resistance. Cohen and Taylor spend little time on the material side of self-protection, for example getting more and better food. They concentrate on the protecting of self-image. They stress how prisoners reject the most damning 'labels' – 'killer', 'thug', 'brutal psychopath' – sometimes humorously and sometimes in anger. Campaigning, the most popular form of which was sending letters to MPs, was more often done as a way of 'getting back' at authority, rather than in any real hope of progress on given issues. Escaping, striking and confronting, all involve a high degree of collective effort or connivance. The term 'confronting' needs to be explained. It describes any major collective effort to force the prison authorities, and sometimes a wider audience, to listen to the prisoners' complaints and opinions. There could hardly be a more conspicuous example of trying to draw public attention to grievances than, for instance, occupying a prison roof for a period – as has sometimes happened.

Cohen and Taylor show typical interactionist awareness that the differences between 'normals' and 'deviants' is generally one of degree rather than of kind. In a later book, *Escape Attempts: The Theory and Practice of Resistance to Everyday Life* (1976), they extend their concept of resistance to more everyday, as distinct from totally bureaucratic, situations. We have already seen how, at work and in schools, people attempt to 'manage' their own

situations, despite the constraints imposed by the organised environment. Chapters 12 and 16 examine further the tension between the demands of society for order and conformity, and the frequent tendency of individuals not to 'fit in'.

3 Conflict theories

This section should be regarded as a direct continuation of the opening part of this chapter, in which the conflict perspectives on organisations of Marx and Weber were introduced. Whereas Parsons tends to see power as being used for 'necessary' purposes in the common interest, for example, in maintaining law and order. Marx and, to some extent Weber, sees it as being used by groups or classes mainly in their own interests. Thus, Weber feared the abuse of power by bureaucrats on their own behalf, and Marx on behalf of the capitalist class.

Marxist conflict theory

Clegg and Dunkerly reminded us of what should really be obvious – that the reason for existence of most organisations is the need to organise the labour process, and that this involves the control of workers by employers. Like Bowles and Gintis, they regard the extreme fragmentation of the labour process in industrial and office work as one means of controlling the workforce, because it prevents them from understanding the nature of the whole production process. They differentiate not only between buyers and sellers of labour but also between working groups of different power in the market. Thus, they explain at length the reasons for the particular exploitation of female labour, as we also did in Chapter 7. Their discussion leads naturally to the question of different forms of organisational control (see next section), and to whom the product of labour rightly belongs, and how it should be shared. As they point out, their perspective is pertinent to organisations in both communist and capitalist societies. The most obvious difference between organisations today and in Marx's time is that many are now operated by the state. They show that a 'them and us' feeling in the workforce can occur in undemocratically run state enterprises such as those in the former Soviet Union, as well as in capitalist ones. A state that simply gathers in profit or surplus value and redistributes it unequally is hardly likely to be perceived as any improvement on a capitalist entrepreneur.

Wallerstein's comments on organisations are comparable with those of Clegg and Dunkerley. He gives the broadest dimension possible to organisational analysis. He suggests that national societies are inadequate units for economic and social analysis and that they should be seen as only one organisational level within the capitalist world economy. Specific organisations, like the nation-state or multi-national corporations, operate within the capitalist world system.

One matter on which Clegg and Dunkerley say relatively little is how private troubles arising in organisations can be related to 'public issues'. An obvious example is how a corporation's policy of plant closures or cut-backs – perhaps the result of recession – can cause the personal misery of unemployment. There is need for much more analysis of how individual and, indeed, national experience is formed by organisations operating in an unpredictable world system.

Liberal conflict theory

A number of liberal structural sociologists have applied Weber's concepts in a way that emphasises the functional aspect of organisations but shows an awareness of conflict. We have already seen that Weber considered that socialist societies were likely to become as bureaucratic, if not more so, than capitalist ones. More recently, this view has been presented as part of the broader, more controversial convergence thesis. In this context, convergence means that the economic and organisational structure of advanced societies, whether capitalist of socialist, are becoming increasingly similar. The view that such societies need some central economic planning and large governmental bureaucracies to implement decisions is crucial to this idea. Another aspect of this thesis appears in the work of Daniel Bell and Ralf Dahrendorf. They argue that the complex problems of advanced societies require advanced management techniques. Political argument will not solve essentially technical problems, and may make them worse. Thus, national investment in energy may need to be planned years ahead, regardless of which government is in power. In their view, top managers and their technical advisers are vital in giving long-term continuity in both advanced capitalist and socialist societies. Dahrendorf, and, particularly, Bell, consider this new class of experts to be a highly influential elite (see Chapter 6 p. 167 and this chapter).

They see potential for conflict between this high status and well paid elite and the less privileged and less well-off. Nevertheless, they consider this inequality to be inevitable and a feature of communist as of capitalist societies.

As we have seen, Marxists do not consider that managers have as much power as Bell and Dahrendorf suggest. In the West there is also the power of capital to consider and, we must add, in the Soviet Union, that of leading politicians and possibly, military leaders. Nevertheless, the massive extent of bureaucracy and the power of top management to use bureaucracy as their instrument are noteworthy and quite recent features of modern society.

Integrating Marxist and Weberian conflict theory

Marxists can certainly learn from Weberian-inspired organisational analysis. Two points are apparent. Firstly, the 'new managerial class' is both highly paid and relatively powerful. In their eagerness to establish the primacy of capitalist power, Marxists tend to disregard this even though it is a fact that can be easily accommodated to Marxist theory and policy. Arguably, managerial power increased substantially during the 1980s (see pp. 299-300). Secondly, as Weber realised, the power of large organisations to control and alienate is immense because of their very size and of the remoteness of those who control them. The novelist, Kafka, caught the sense of how in modern societies organisations seem to 'run people's lives' almost without personal direction – especially, in his view in the (then) communist societies of Eastern Europe. Clegg and Dunkerley appear to have integrated this important insight into a substantially Marxist framework. They recognise that bureaucratically run organisations tend to produce alienation not only among lower level workers but even among professional employees as well. Crucially, however, they insist that it is still necessary to locate and analyse the major source of control behind organisations, whether it be capital or a political elite. Only then does it become possible adequately to relate organisational analysis to the issues of inequality of power and wealth. The basic question remains 'in whose interest is this organisation run?'.

Control and involvement, oligarchy and democracy in organisations

We have already seen that Weber considered that modern organisations are best run along bureaucratic lines. For him, bureaucracy meant hierarchy and hierarchy meant oligarchy, that is, that power and control are concentrated at the top. More recent theorists have examined the issues of control and involvement in organisations and, as we shall see, have produced a more complex picture. The organic systems theory, mentioned above, has already introduced the notion that organisations can be run on somewhat more democratic lines than the bureaucratic model suggests. We now examine this matter more directly.

Etzioni takes three of Weber's major concepts, power, authority and legitimation, and applies them to the understanding of the way organisations work. Etzioni starts with the basic problem of how the majority of people, workers and employees, can be persuaded or forced to do what they might not freely choose to do – work for others. To understand Etzioni's answer, we must first know what Weber's three terms mean: power is the ability to impose one's will (for example by brute force); legitimation is the acceptance of power because it is considered to be rightly exercised (for example that of a king); and authority is legitimate power. Weber offered a three-part ideal-type model of authority: traditional, charismatic, and rational-legal. Traditional authority is 'hallowed with time', like that of a king, an established dynasty or a pope. Charismatic authority is generated by the personality of the individual, like that of Hitler or Martin Luther King. Rational-legal authority is established in law or written regulations. We have already said that it is this latter type of authority that characterises modern bureaucratic organisations.

Why is it that individuals accept the control and power of organisations and, specifically, of top organisational officials over their lives? Etzioni presents in turn, an explanatory typology of control: coercive, utilitarian and normative or social. Coercive power is control based on physical means, such as brute force.

Utilitarian power is based on the use of material means, such as money payments: it embodies an element of positive incentive to conform, in the form of a reward. Normative power is based on morality and social conscience. When people conform for normative reasons they do so because they believe they ought to. Normative power and conformity are associated with legitimation because they occur when people accept that a given power is legitimate. Thus, a Roman Catholic who accepts the authority of the Pope does so out of normative conviction. A citizen may obey the law from normative conviction although, for others, the threat of coercion may be necessary. Likewise, employees in an organisation, say a commercial one, may feel normatively disposed to accept its authority even though they originally joined it for utilitarian reasons (to make a living). Bureaucracies are largely based on rules and often create an atmosphere of normative conformity. A little thought will make it clear that in many types of organisations, such as schools, two or even three kinds of control operate.

Etzioni matches three types of involvement with his typology of control. Coercion tends to produce alienation, utilitarian control is based on calculative commitment, and normative control on moral commitment. Calculative and moral commitment have, in effect, already been explained. Alienation is the opposite of commitment: it is the rejection by the spirit of what the body has to do, such as to serve a life-sentence in prison or to do endlessly repetitive and boring work. In part, Etzioni sees it as a leadership problem to decide what kinds of incentives are necessary to involve members in the organisation's goals. He also recognises, however, that workers and employees are likely to have their own ideas about the nature of their involvement, and that these will affect the running of the organisation. As we shall see, there is perhaps more to this issue than Etzioni himself allows.

Question

To what extent do you consider the main perspectives on organisations to be complementary?

Is democracy in organisations possible? Michels and Gouldner

The most uncompromising statement of the inevitability of managerial elites is the so-called 'iron law of oligarchy' of Robert Michels (1949). With the German Socialist party chiefly in mind, he argues that popularly representative parties and unions, whose aim is to replace autocracy with democracy, are forced by necessity to develop a 'vast and solid' bureaucratic organisational structure themselves. In due course, the party bureaucracy itself becomes centralised and undemocratic. The vested interest of the organisation's elite rather than the needs of the people at large effectively becomes the most important consideration, despite professed democratic and socialist ideals. Ordinary people acquire no more power or control as a result of these movements. One set of masters replaces another. In that sense, Michels' 'law' is similar to Pareto's theory of circulating elites.

Alvin Gouldner criticises Michels' account as unbalanced. Michels emphasises only the ways in which organisational needs work against democratic possibilities. Tellingly, Gouldner suggests another need – ignored by Michels – that of the consent of the governed (or employees), to their governors. He sees a certain recurrent tension between the need for central leadership and authority and the desire of many people for more power, satisfaction and involvement at work than a rigid bureaucratic regime might allow. He says, with some poetic finesse:

> *if oligarchical waves repeatedly wash away the bridge of democracy, this eternal recurrence can happen only because men doggedly rebuild them after each inundation.*
>
> *(1971)*

The recent 'democratic revolution' in the Soviet Union seems to provide a particular instance of the resilience of democracy referred to by Gouldner.

Gouldner's thoughts conveniently bring us to the nub of the debate about organisational oligarchy and democracy. Both democracy and oligarchy are possible in organisations and, for that matter, in political systems. What people get depends on what they want, and their power to obtain it balanced against that of others. Power-conflict is a process not an outcome. Thomas Jefferson, the second American President, counselled the people to be ever vigilant in the protection of their democratic rights, lest they be whittled away by central government. 'God forbid' he said 'that we should be twenty years without a rebellion'.

Gouldner has rough words for Selznick as well as Michels. He refers to Selznick's 'dismal' catalogue of organisational needs. These are 'needs' for security; stable lines of authority; stable relationships, and homogeneity (similarity of parts). Gouldner, maintaining his emphasis on democracy, juxtaposes what he sees as an equally important set of needs: needs for challenge, for lateral communication, for creative tension, for heterogeneity (diversity) and the consent of the led. We return to the oligarchy-democracy debate shortly in the context of union organisation.

Control and involvement: Likert

Gouldner, therefore, sees neither oligarchy nor democracy as 'inevitable' but as alternatives to be championed and contested. Similarly, Rensis Likert offers a model of control-involvement which is more representative of the full range of possible management-worker structures than is Etzioni's. He identifies four important systems of organisation: exploitative/authoritative; benevolent/authoritative; consultative; and participative group management. We can add a fifth: the democratic/egalitarian system of management favoured by some contemporary socialists but probably not fully achieved in any socialist regime.

In exploitative/authoritative systems, power and control are centralised and workers are treated exclusively in terms of their productive capacity. In the early stages of industrialisation in both

Britain and America, powerful industrial moguls, such as Ford and Rockefeller, ran their industrial empires in this way. Frequently, this pattern became modified to the extent that the entrepreneur did begin to develop an interest in the general welfare of his workforce – the benevolent/authoritative pattern. Often this was for ulterior motives: a healthy workforce was a better workforce and, in any case, entrepreneurs often wanted to 'spike the guns' of unions which built up on the basis of working class discontent. Frederick Taylor was the theoretical philosopher of authoritative or, perhaps more accurately, authoritarian style of management.

The consultative approach recognises that the workforce may have something to offer the management, at least in certain areas, in the way of experience and advice. Even where regular consultative meetings are established, however, ultimate decisions remain in the hands of ownership or management. Again, this system can become little more than decorative diplomacy. The concept of participative group management has had considerable support and success in parts of Europe in the post-war period. In Germany, workers have the legal right to 50 per cent representation on the supervisory boards of companies with more than 2,000 employees. Management is responsible to these boards. An employer is quoted as commenting that: 'Codetermination has really forced both sides to understand the other side better' (*The Guardian*, 9.10.1990). Similar systems of representation operate in Scandinavian countries. In Britain, the Bullock report of the late 1970s recommended that the nationalised industries should implement a similar system of participation. The report's recommendations were rather complicated and their partial application to British Leyland and the Post Office petered out. The participation 'debate' continues, however, and the Social Charter proposed for adoption across the European Economic Community would harmonise workers' rights, including those of industrial representation.

Both the CBI and the Thatcher-Major governments have opposed the adoption in Britain of Works Councils along the lines of the rest of the EU. The 1991 British opt-out of the social chapter of the Maastricht treaty secured this exemption. Nevertheless, some British Companies, particularly with strong European links have set up works councils voluntarily. United Biscuits is a case in point (see Figure 10.1). Their human resources director states:

> *Consultation for us has proved to be effective in improving performance ... If people understand what we want to achieve, they are better able to see what they have to do.*
>
> *(The Financial Times, 17.1.1995:18)*

Research by Fernie and Mekalt based on a sample of 1,500 joint consultative committees (weak works councils) supports this positive view. The latter are associated with high productivity job generation, and a good industrial relations climate. (Reported in *The Guardian*, 22.5.1995:13)

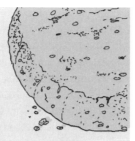

The new United Biscuits works council

- UB operates in 28 countries, with 40,000 employees worldwide; 55 per cent of its sales are outside the UK.

- The works council will cover its 26,000 employees in Europe of which 20,000 are in the UK.

- The council will cover overall group commercial strategy. Under union insistence UB agreed its employment strategy should also be included on the agenda.

- The council will consist of twenty employee representatives chaired by UB's human resources director, plus further company representation with a senior executive, normally the chief executive.

- There will be seven worker representatives from UB's mainland European operations and thirteen representing UK plants, ten nominated by the trade unions with the other three representing white-collar staff.

- Four full-time trade union officials will accompany the employee representatives to the council's meeting once a year.

- Council proceedings will be 'communicated as widely as possible to all employees'.

(Source: *The Financial Times,* 17.1.1996:18)

Figure 10.1 The new United Biscuits works council

The democratic-egalitarian model goes beyond the concept of the participation of 'both sides of industry' to that of abolishing the notion of 'sides' altogether. For a Marxist, this would first involve the abolition of class inequality. This does not, of course, mean that separate roles, such as manager or production worker, will cease to exist; rather, it is a question of making management democratic. Perhaps managers could be elected for a term of some years, as MPs are now, and positions on the board could rotate (as the American presidency does in the sense that it can only be held for two four-year terms – for good democratic reasons!). To be genuinely egalitarian, this system would also involve a reduction, if not the abolition, of the differences in reward and status between management and workers. Obviously, this model would be barely acceptable within the limits of capitalist economic and social belief. The implementation of a democratic-egalitarian system would probably require socialism. We discussed this matter in some detail in Chapter 5, pp. 154-5.

It is appropriate at this point briefly to discuss whether, regardless of their capacity to participate in industrial democracy, unions can be successfully democratic themselves. This returns us to Michels' thesis. Lipset, Trow and Coleman (1956), on the basis of a study of a printers' union in the United States, found that in certain circumstances democracy is possible. The printers' union had a thriving two party system. They put this down to the fact that the long and odd hours worked by the printers produced work-connected leisure organisations which, in turn, provided a basis of communication for, and involvement in, union politics, But Lipset's broader conclusion is more pessimistic. In most industries, the majority of workers quickly leave work for home, and it is only a minority which actively involves itself in union politics. This is so in Britain, where, prior to postal ballots, seldom more than a third of workers voted when given the opportunity. Allen, however, points out that the formal machinery of union democracy is time-consuming and cumbersome to operate. In practice, the way union leaders are kept in check is more simple. If the workers disapprove of what they are doing, membership declines. Allen's argument is not entirely convincing, As early as 1949, C Wright Mills pointed to the communication gap between national union officials and branch officials and between both these groups and the mass membership. These problems are by no means resolved today.

Hierarchical ◄────	Power Concentration	────►	Egalitarian
Type Authoritative Exploitative/ Benevolent	Consultative	Participatory	Democratic
Example Fordist (USA, UK, 1950s/60s)	Japanese ◄──► Swedish Industry (1970s/80s onward)		Co-operatives

Figure 10.2 Power and types of organisations

Gouldner perceives oligarchy and democracy as matters of preference and belief rather than 'inevitabilities'. This is not to deny that certain circumstances tend to promote oligarchy and others democracy. Professor Schumacher's book, *Small is Beautiful* (1974), made the point that large organisations tend to require centralised power and that smaller ones can be democratically run. Nevertheless, given the intent, a measure of democracy is possible even in large organisations. At root, preference for organisational oligarchy or democracy depends on a view of human nature. Those who consider that people work best in a highly regulated structure will prefer classical or bureaucratic models: those who consider that people best express themselves in freer contexts will tend to support more democratic organisational structures. Even where democratic systems may be more time-consuming and less efficient, they may still be preferred, for human and moral reasons. But to leave the matter thus would be to mislead. Might, not right or need, usually determines the way organisations operate. Historically, there are almost no examples of democracy being achieved without struggle. Figure 10.2 summarises the way power is distributed in different types of organisations.

Organisations in the 'post-Fordist' era: does more flexibility mean more democracy?

Post-Fordism has been critically presented in the previous chapter (see pp. 252-5). the key concept of post-Fordism is flexibility. Industrial organisations are seen as needing to be flexibly organised so as to be able effectively to respond to and even mould market conditions. Thus, the 'core' labour force is required to adapt and innovate quickly and the 'peripheral' labour force can be easily employed, re-deployed or laid-off as necessary (this is especially true in Britain where part-time employees have fewer rights than in most other European countries). Similarly, productive technology is designed to be easily and swiftly reprogrammed and otherwise adapted to meet the variety and extent of market demand. How far the post-Fordist model is actually being implemented is debated (see pp. 254-5 and 283).

Employees: economic democracy

Granted that post-Fordist methods of employee organisation are more flexible than Fordist ones, how far are they also more democratic? In other words has the distribution of power changed in organisations which adopt post-Fordist organisational methods. On the issue of prime importance – that of ownership – the answer is 'no'. Ownership remains out of the hands of employees – a reality which employee share ownership schemes barely affect. The tendency for top management to hold shares in the company for which they are employed was established prior to post-Fordism and is distinct from it.

There is more room for debate about whether post-Fordist organisational approaches promote more democracy in *the process of production*. However, as we shall see, democracy is probably too strong a term to describe the degrees of responsibility and involvement allowed to employees in the productive process. In dealing with this issue, it is essential to differentiate between at least three groups: first, management, professional scientific and research staff; second, skilled manual or white-collar employees; third, 'peripheral' employees. At the first level, there is evidence from companies such as ICI and IBM that 'networking' or working in teams in a fairly autonomous way in order to 'problem solve' has become more common. In rapidly changing, highly competitive economic conditions, autonomous teams working within a given framework can often reach solutions more quickly, efficiently and inexpensively than the same number of individuals working more or less in isolation. At the second level – skilled employees – similar principles have also been applied, initially by the Japanese and more recently by their imitators, including some British companies. 'Quality circles' provide an example of this. These are meetings of employees, usually directly involved in production, the purpose of which is to improve production and the product by pooling and discussing ideas. The meetings are attended by or report back to management. Other means of achieving employee feedback – some as simple as providing a 'suggestions' sheet or 'post-box' – have also been widely adopted in industry during the 1980s and 1990s.

Figure 10.3 A quality circle meets. How meaningful is this level of involvement? Or is it more a matter of further control?

It can, then, be argued that flexibility has or, certainly, can involve full-time, 'permanent', employees at all levels in more consultation and even participation in the process of production. In general, the higher status the employee has, the stronger this tendency is likely to be. Clearly, part-time and/or temporary employees are likely only to be marginally affected by these tendencies even in employment contexts in which they are well established. Limited experience of and commitment to 'the firm' is likely to limit any effective feedback. For many in their situation, the sharper realities are the need to make money conveniently and the possibility of losing their jobs. As Robert Reich is reported to have said: 'when you hear the word 'flexibility', reach for your wallet!'

It must be stressed that even for the 'core' labour force, flexibility may involve greater democracy only in the process of production and not in ownership. The power, resources and security that come from ownership are not extended to employees. Indeed, during the recession of the late 1980s/early1990s, tens of thousands of highly qualified employees were 'flexibly' removed from industry, particularly such service industries as banking and finance (see pp. 257-9). Although flexibility may increase satisfaction and involvement in the workplace, it is ultimately a strategy for making production more efficient. As such, it implies a more flexible hiring and firing of the workforce. 'Democracy' in the context of flexibility is a secondary and perhaps even incidental issue.

Another group that experienced a 'boom' in the middle 1980s but struggled during recession was small business. The 'autonomy' and 'freedom' many small businesses enjoy in fact depends increasingly on supplying big business. When big business contracted, so did sub-contracting which demonstrates that the apparent independence of the small business sector can mask structural dependency.

The strengthening of managerial power during the 1980s to some extent ran counter to the potential employee involvement brought about by 'flexibility'. This trend is discussed in detail below, but needs to be mentioned here in the context of organisational democracy. It is particularly in the public sector – notably in health, education and social work – that the power of management has been increased by government at the expense of that of professionals – doctors, teachers, and social workers. Led more or less directly by government, management is required to set targets, specify and limit costs, and often to stipulate how a service should be 'delivered' to the 'customer' (no longer referred to, in the traditional professional jargon, as the 'client'). This organisational framework is hierarchical and probably even less democratic than the more professionally controlled system which preceded it. In its extreme but typical form, the new managerialism seeks to by-pass both professional and bureaucratic power. In fairness, however, the new managerialism is also related to a new (or revived) concept of customer power and it is to this issue we now turn.

Consumers and citizens

The concept of customer or consumer power has been central to notions of broadening economic democracy in contemporary society. In recent debate, consumer power has usefully been linked with the goal of 'quality' in the production and delivery of goods and services. Recently also consumer theory has been linked to citizenship theory by the three major political parties.

Two views of the relationship between consumption and quality can be distinguished here. First, is the *laissez-faire* liberal approach now associated in its more uncompromising versions with the political right. In this view, the choice of the consumer in the market place forces the producer to meet the consumer's requirements – or risk losing business. This approach can be referred to as consumerism. A second approach to consumer power has been developed particularly in relation to the consumption of public services. In this view, the consumer has a democratic right as a citizen to influence the quality of the goods or service s/he consumes. This approach can be referred to as participatory democracy or, simply, the democratic approach.

The consumerist approach was 'repackaged' in the 1980s by linking it to a new managerialist emphasis on quality control. One of the 'gurus' of management theory, Philip Crossby, defined quality as 'meeting the customer's requirements' (a very different definition from traditional ones which define quality in terms of characteristics of inherent excellence). A means of achieving the goal of 'total quality' is for employees in the same firm to treat each other as 'internal customers'. Critics of the consumerist approach suggest that it is as much motivated by the desire to persuade employees to work harder as by any real concern for the consumer. The competitions, prizes and awards associated with the 'total quality' movement are seen as ways of obtaining cheap publicity. However, the existence of such motives does not necessarily preclude the achievement of greater product quality.

Following the logic of 1980s consumer rhetoric, John Major's Conservative government has attempted to extend the concept of consumer rights to the public services in the forms of a 'Citizens' Charter'. By 1992, this approach had received its fullest application to education in the form of the document *The Parent's Charter: You and Your Child's Education* (DES, 1991). The heavily consumerist emphasis of the charter is underlined on the second page where five key documents which parents are entitled to receive are listed:

- *A report about your child*
- *Regular reports from independent inspectors*
- *Performance tables for all your local schools*
- *A prospectus or brochure about individual schools*
- *An annual report from your school's governors*

The main purpose of the charter appears to be to ensure that parents (consumers) have enough information effectively to pressure schools to raise standards (quality).

A critique of the consumer model in relation to the public services

Naomi Pfeffer and Anna Coote explore what they refer to as the 'democratic' approach to quality in *Is Quality Good For You? A Critical Review of Quality Assurance in Welfare Services* (1991). As Labour party policy experts, they are at pains to stress the difference between their 'democratic' approach and a purely consumerist one. They contend that the right merely to be a competitive individual consumer is insufficient in relation to the public services. In the context of education, welfare and social security, it is in the general interest that everybody's needs are equally met and that services are universally maintained at a high standard (as far as resources allow). The right to information about and representation within public services is to achieve more effective co-operation rather than competition. Citizenship is linked to and underpinned by both a commitment to meeting basic needs and to the right to a substantial democratic involvement in how needs are met. Both these principles are well-expressed in a checklist for action to combat poverty presented by Peter Beresford and Ruth Lister:

- It's best to build from a local level, although local campaigns aren't always the easiest.
- It's important to start where people are.
- Involving people takes time, support and resources.
- It works best by word of mouth.
- Education and training have an important part to play in gaining confidence and skills.
- Much can be learnt from disability and other self-advocacy movements.
- Poor people have allies in professional agencies who will help.

(*The Guardian*, 17.7.1991:23)

They stress, however, that the right to democratic participations is complemented by 'the human and civil rights' to housing, income and education.

It is possible that the political debate for the 1990s will substantially focus on defining and delivering some version of consumer and/or citizens' rights. The way these rights are implemented organisationally – democratically or otherwise – will be crucial to their effective attainment.

Question

Describe, with examples, how different types of organisations differ in terms of power control and involvement.

Organisational change under Thatcherism

Thatcherism demonstrated that government can play a significant role in setting the ideological and political conditions within which organisations operate. The impact of government policy on public sector institutions was partly decentralising but in other respects centralising.

Two main complementary motives behind Thatcherism were the desire to extend the free market and to reverse what were seen as the bureaucratic tendencies of socialism. In pursuit of these goals, Thatcherism had a major impact on the organisational structure of much of Britain's institutional life. The impact was most direct and obvious in the public sector for which the government had immediate authority. In education, for example, the free market element was strongly apparent in the open enrolment and opting out policies (see p. 128). These policies considerably reduced the power of local education authorities. On the other hand, a centralised national curriculum was established and local educational inspectorates strengthened partly in order to oversee its enforcement. Within schools and other teaching institutions the power, pay and status of senior management was increased relative to that of teachers.

A similar policy pattern occurred in relation to health. Hospitals and general medical practitioners were able to apply to 'opt out' of the control of district health authorities (see pp. 437-8). On the other hand, throughout the NHS, the power of management was increased at the expense of professionals and particularly within hospitals, at the expense of consultants. There was a shift from management by committee and consensus towards management by individual managers. As Clarke *et al.*, have ironically noted, senior managers were the 'heroes' who were to implement the 'Thatcher' revolution (1994) (See Reading 1). Management itself became more responsible to central government for the achievement of prescribed 'goals' and 'targets' (points on the way to goals). While, therefore, there was considerable institutional decentralisation under Thatcherism, crucial aspects of control remained with central government and were even strengthened at the expense of local control. Further, within particular organisations, management often tended to become more, not less hierarchical.

Two key characteristics of management trends under Thatcherism require specifying. First, more power, responsibility and control was put into the hands of management, particularly senior management. While the power and control of senior management tended to be strengthened, direct lines of responsibility through senior, middle and junior management were streamlined and clarified. Middle and junior management tended to lose decision-making power to senior managers. In the late 1980s and 1990s, many middle and junior managers were seen as dispensable and lost their jobs. Thus, the overall effect has been to intensify hierarchy. Once strengthened, management was

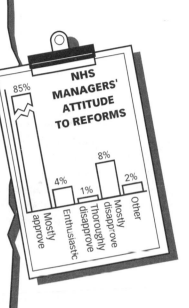

Managers 'put care second'

TRUST managers are putting business before patient care and failing to consult doctors on the running of an internal market, consultants said yesterday (Jill Sherman writes).

At a meeting of the British Medical Association's consultants committee, doctors complained that managers were seen as 'an alien occupying force'. Although ministers had made clear that NHS reforms would work only if doctors were fully consulted, members of the 80-strong committee said their views had been largely ignored.

Dr Jim Johnson, a consultant in Merseyside, said managers at Broadgreen Hospital Trust, Liverpool, refused to provide x-ray facilities when its own x-ray department ran into difficulties.

Whiston Hospital, which is directly managed, put together a package to assist Broadgreen, but Dr Johnson claimed that the chief executive refused it. 'Looking after sick people is about co-operation not competition,' Dr Johnson said.

(Source: *The Times*)

Figure 10.4 A Manager's Charter? Conservative reforms were popular among managers if not among NHS professionals ...

expected to achieve greater productive and cost efficiency i.e. more and better education, health or broadcasting at an economic rate. Whether or not this has happened is, of course, one of the key issues on which Thatcherism will be judged (see Reading 1).

A second and related characteristic of managerial change under Thatcherism, was the requirement that organisations more clearly establish goals and targets and that individuals be held accountable for their part in achieving these goals. Thus, within education, five year plans became the order of the day (ironically reflecting the Bolshevik model!). Senior management was primarily responsible for ensuring that goals were achieved.

In education and health, considerable new tension developed between management and professionals. The latter felt that power, control, prestige (and sometimes, rewards) had shifted away from them towards management. Indeed, they themselves felt more controlled within the above 'managerial' frameworks and, particularly, by techniques such as appraisal which could take the form of a detailed self-account of performance by a professional to a manager. Underlying this tension were two different models of organisational control. One is the centralised and hierarchical model described above and the other is a more consensual model of professional control described elsewhere.

Comment on organisational change under Thatcherism

There are two levels on which comment on the Thatcher organisational reforms of the public services can be made. First, has it been successful in its own terms? Second, probing more deeply, how worthwhile are the more fundamental purposes of the above reforms and who are their prime beneficiaries? To address the first point, then, are the public services in Britain more efficient as a result of Thatcherism? The only fair answer to this question at the time of writing (1997), is that the jury is still out – although there is no shortage of provisional judgements. A reasonable comment might be, however, that these reforms would have to be quite clearly successful in achieving efficiency gains to convince critics that the anxiety and disruption they provoked was worthwhile.

The second issue, concerning the fundamental purposes of Thatcherism is one on which people legitimately take different views. The Thatcher governments were strongly, almost militantly, pro-capitalist and made no secret of their intention of reducing the relative cost of the public sector to the private, capitalist sector. Marxists such as Claus Offe argue that Thatcherism was precisely about creating an institutional context and cultural climate favourable to capital and, in particular, rescuing British capitalism from a crisis of profitability, i.e. regulating capitalism. Indeed, Offe has argued that the social democratic Labour government of James Callaghan was attempting to do exactly this prior to the 1979 general election defeat. However, most Labour and other politicians of the centre left, while agreeing on the need for a successful private sector would also want greatly to distance themselves from Thatcherism. In particular, they argue that they would allocate relatively more resources to public services and implement policy in a different way and through different means than did Margaret Thatcher.

'Ways and means' relate to the issue of 'organisation'. Any serious aspiration to implement 'democratic socialism' – the professed aim of the Labour party – would promote more democracy in organisations in both the private and public sector. As described earlier in this chapter a number of Britain's European partners have implemented more industrial democracy than Britain and this is a policy favoured by Labour. On the issue of professional involvement and responsibility, it is Labour's policy to establish a Teachers' Council which may initiate a greater share of power and prestige for teachers. To many, however, Labour's commitment to extending organisational democracy still appears lukewarm. The extension of democracy has long been the neglected part of the agenda of social democracy, yet the history of socialism suggests that the achievement of greater material equality

without achieving greater democracy fails ultimately to satisfy the people.

Finally, although this section concentrates on organisational issues within the public sector, the interplay between Thatcherism and organisational ideology and practice within capitalist enterprise is important. It will be clear from reading the sections on post-Fordism (see pp. 252-5) and Thatcherite industrial policy (see p. 274) that Margaret Thatcher introduced elements of post-Fordism into the public sector with perhaps more robustness and determination than occurred in the private sector. John Major broadly pursued similar policies following the Conservative general election victory of 1992.

The wider context of organisations in late modernity

Organisations exist for a purpose. If not, they have outlived their time. Saying this points out the fact that the study of organisations cannot be self-contained – it must always relate to the wider realities of power and purpose.

In the modern or, arguably, late-modern era organisations are constantly being reshaped in the context of technological development and aggressive management in the light of market competition, often international in scope. This is most obviously true of larger business organisations. In the week during which I am writing this paragraph in mid-1996, the Royal Insurance and Sun Alliance, a British and an American company have merged. Over 5,000 jobs will be lost. In the same week, National Westminster Bank has announced that it will be replacing thousands of employees with a variety of computer-automated service systems. The bank states that is has fallen behind competitors in terms of adopting cost-saving mechanisms – for example, banking by telephone.

In this often global, technology and market-driven context, the notion of business organisations as solid, let alone unchanging, structures is as redundant as many of the roles in them have become. Equally, the bureaucracies of government have been reshaped ('down-sized', 'flattened', rendered 'flexible' or whatever). We have already looked at how this has affected work and leisure life and will examine the latter further (see pp. 493-8). Here emphasis is on equally radical change in the way many organisations operate.

Scenarios for new organisational theory

With the above developments in mind, some organisational theorists are beginning to question the established framework of their discipline. Michael Reed does so in *Scripting Scenarios for New Organisational Theory and Practice* (1991). He comments that organisations are not a single coherent category of entities but vary greatly and often change rapidly. It might be closer to present reality if instead of seeing organisations as structures, they were envisaged as processes created by people in consensus or in conflict which they construct or deconstruct continuously.

Such a conceptualisation seems partly inspired by the theorising of the French poststructuralist, Michel Foucault (see pp. 98-100 for an introduction to his key ideas). Foucault discards the notion that organisations have fixed normative structures and sees them instead as the outcome of power and ideas in practice. If this seems abstract, Foucault's descriptions of nineteenth century prison and asylums are anything but (see pp. 366-7). These institutions of correction and treatment were generated by the powerful ideas of modern reforming movements. More recently – Cohen suggests from the 1960s – liberal 'power-knowledge' and the 'regimes of truth' (i.e. its own truth) which it helped to generate have been challenged by decentralising movements from the Left and Right, including Thatcherism (see Table 12.4, p. 349).

Had Foucault lived long enough fully to see it, he might well have found the revival of free market thinking an apt example of a rampant form of power-knowledge. Margaret Thatcher and her close supporters imposed market reforms on the public sector and facilitated a freer market in the private sector. The civil service, education, health, social services were radically changed. In the private sector, industrial legislation empowered senior management and rendered labour largely impotent. Thatcherism or free market liberalism was a classic case of an idea whose time (of power) had come. Yet ironically, to achieve these market reforms, Thatcherism also increased the power of the central state.

Organisations and co-ordination

Thatcherism and, indeed, reforming liberalism illustrate that organisations can be bent or shaped to the will of the powerful. In order to capture the effect of power on organisations, it is useful to employ the concept of *co-ordination*. Co-ordination literally means to order things together, or, to make things work. In the Open University course, *Running The Country*, the concept of co-ordination is used to analyse how Britain is run.

Three models of co-ordination were used to analyse how the country is run. Everyday public activity – work, voluntary work and leisure – was considered part of the running of the country as well as the activities of politicians, business people and other public figures. The three models of co-ordination are: hierarchy, market and network. Figure 10.5 illustrates that these types of models of co-ordination refer to general types of collective purposeful activity. Co-ordination can be achieved without organisations. Thus, if two people exchange or swop commodities, a market activity has occurred but no organisation in an institutional sense is involved. Similarly, people network constantly to achieve goals. Thus, people in a given locality frequently network to put on money raising or leisure activities. Nevertheless, Figure 10.5 gives examples of organisations which embody each type of co-ordination: a government department – hierarchy; the stock exchange – market; and neighbourhood watch – network. Reading 2 further explains these three models of co-ordination.

Basic concepts	Area of application	Example
Hierarchy Authority/rules	Administration/ Large scale organisation	Government department
Market Contract/ Exchange/Price	Economic activity	Stock Exchange
Network Solidarity/ Agreement	Small group	Neighbourhood watch

(Source: *Running the Country*, Open University, D212, Unit 1-7:73)

Figure 10.5 Three models of co-ordination

Although co-ordination is a more generalised or higher level concept than the established sociological usage of the concept of organisation, there are obvious links between the two. Bureaucracy is a type of hierarchy; organic systems are a type of network. Until recently, the sociology of organisations has not greatly considered the role of the market. This is perhaps because the main point about market activity is the exchange of goods and services for which the organisational framework is often very incidental (many markets are physically very transient only really existing in the activities of buyers and sellers). Even Marxist-oriented organisational sociology has concentrated more on institutionalised relationships of 'domination and subordination' within capitalism rather than how market activity precisely impacts on organisations and society.

Globally, the trend to deregulating economic markets i.e. unharnessing the free market has forced commentators to think through their effects on organisational activity and on society generally. In Britain, Thatcherism has required analysis of the effect of markets or quasi-markets within the public services. Some of the effects – on education and health, for instance – have been huge and are discussed in the relevant parts of this book.

The point, then, is that organisations can only be understood in the wider context of ideology and power, and in terms of the application of technological change. It is an odd pairing but in their very different ways both Foucault and Margaret Thatcher have illustrated the central importance of these observations.

Question

To what extent do you consider that the mainly market-oriented changes in organisation and co-ordination of the Thatcher-Major period made Britain more or less democratic?

Summary

1   A preliminary distinction is made between formal and informal organisations. Formal organisations are operated on the basis of established rules by appointed personnel to achieve specific goals. Informal organisations are freely created social group relationships outside or inside formal organisations. The impact of wider forces on organisations is indicated.

2   Bureaucratic organisations are operated hierarchically by trained personnel on the basis of specified rules and with the help of formal records.

3   Organic systems are organisations which operate on less formal, less bureaucratic lines in which members 'network' (communicate quite freely) with each other.

4   Several organisational theories tend to reflect either bureaucratic or organic theories. However, social action/interactionist theories and conflict theories do offer distinctive alternative perspective although they are not necessarily or wholly incompatible with the previous two approaches.

5   Traditional organisational theory can be contrasted as follows:
Bureaucratic
(Mechanistic)
Scientific management
Functional systems theory
Organic
Human relations theory
Socio-technical systems theory

6   Social action and interactionist theories argue that within organisations people seek to make their roles and activities meaningful. Erving Goffman's classic study illustrates this in relation to an asylum.

7   Conflict theories raise issues of power, control, domination, exploitation and legitimation and various forms of conflict including interest group and class conflict as these affect organisations. They also explore how organisations may be made more democratic.

8   Thatcherism attempted to introduce elements of the free market into the public sector, and strengthened management at the expense of professionals. Arguably, there is some tension between these two policy aspects.

9   Organisational theory must consider the wider context which shapes their purposes. Political and economic ideology and power – sometimes global in reach – routinely impacts on organisations.

Research and coursework

You have probably realised by now that the term organisation can be applied to a vast variety of contexts, formal or informal, in which people relate in a more or less structured way over time. This gives wide choice for research of types of organisation and situations of co-operation, conflict or negotiation within organisations. Whatever organisation or organisational situation you may choose to research, it is essential to retain an overall theoretical perspective.

Theoretical questions asked about organisations are:

• What are the functions/purposes of the organisation and how are these achieved?

• Do informal groups within the organisation contribute positively or negatively to the achievement of its goals?

• How meaningful/alienating are the organisation's purposes and processes to its members?

• Is the organisation characterised by consensus or conflict?

• Does the organisation operate on behalf of one group or class at the expense of another?

If you find your research is not addressing questions of the above scope, it is probably weighted too much towards description and too little towards theoretical enquiry and analysis.

Further reading

A useful general introduction to the area is Glenn Morgan's *Organisations in Society* (Macmillan, 1990). Erving Goffman's *Asylums* (Penguin, 1968) is an interactionist classic. The Reader for the Open University Course, *Running the Country* has many useful contributions – Grahame Thompson *et al.*, eds., *Markets, Hierarchies and Networks: The Co-ordination of Social Life* (Sage Publications, 1991).

Readings

Reading 1
The new managerialism

From J Clarke, A Cochrane and E McLaughlin eds., *Managing Social Policy* (Sage, 1994), pp. 14-5

Pollitt has argued that there are at least two varieties of managerialism currently circulating which have significance for the restructuring of public services. The first, and most influential, in the 1980s is what he terms 'neo-Taylorism', … This refers to a model of management primarily devoted to the rational analysis of organisational inputs and outputs, and committed to the creation of efficiency and increased productivity as its over-riding objectives. As such, it provided the managerial analogue for wider political concerns with the financial 'burden' of public sector spending: the drive to impose the 'three Es' (economy, efficiency and effectiveness), to create 'value for money' services, and to deliver 'more for less' by driving down the labour costs of public services. Neo-Taylorist beliefs and practices manifested themselves in all public sector organisations, framed by the prolonged 'fiscal squeeze' from central government. Put crudely, most organisations found themselves trying to deliver 'more for less', simply because they were given less and asked to do more.

Overlapping with neo-Taylorism was a rather different version of managerialism, sometimes referred to as the 'new managerialism', sometimes as the 'Excellence School' and sometimes as 'new wave management' (Wood, 1989). Where neo-Taylorism focuses on intensifying the systems of control (of resources and effort), the new managerialism offers a model of the organisation which is 'people centred' and views bureaucratic control systems as unwieldy, counterproductive and repressive of the 'enterprising spirit' of all employees. Its notion of the route to competitive success is to loosen formal systems of control (within what was tellingly termed a 'loose-tight structure') and to stress instead the value of motivating people to produce 'quality' and strive for 'excellence' themselves. Managers become leaders rather than controllers, providing the visions and inspirations which generate a collective or corporate commitment to 'being the best'. This managerialism stresses quality, being close to the customer and the value of innovation.

This 'new managerialism' overlaps with neo-Taylorism both in time and in its objectives, since it too stresses getting 'more for less' and providing 'value for money'. But it differs in its view of organisations and management role within them as to how such objectives are to be achieved. Pollitt has argued that, although this new managerialism played a rhetorical part in the changes of the 1980s (with statements about quality, staff development and the like), it was neo-Taylorism which shaped most of the practice of public sector management. We would differ from this assessment in two ways. The first is that, by the end of the 1980s, the new managerialism had come to take on a greater significance in practical terms as more emphasis came to be placed on the necessity of transforming the 'culture' of public services such as the police, civil service agencies and social services, especially in the context of moves towards greater devolution and decentralisation. The second is that public service organisations have been increasingly marked by the coexistence of these two models of management, rather than a succession between one and the other. Organisations have been trying simultaneously to carry out neo-Taylorist models of productivity improvement through resource and effort controls and new managerialist models of inspirational leadership, corporate culture formation and excellence/quality commitments …

Such a coexistence is not a theoretical problem, although it may cause many practical ones for those involved in the processes. Ideologies are not singular, coherent or homogeneous entities – indeed they are often characterised by an ability to carry conflicting or contradictory messages. In this context, conflicts between different models of management are harmonised by their being subject to a higher level of integration. Both models of management fall within the wider ideology of managerialism – the commitment of 'management' as the solution to social and economic problems, particularly those of the public sector; the belief in management as an overarching system of authority; and the view of management as founded on an inalienable 'right to manage'.

It is precisely these characteristics of management which were deployed in the neo-conservative political project of restructuring the state. Management provided a new system of authority, a new mode of control, which could be drawn on to unlock the bastions of bureaucratic and professional power.

Questions

1 Summarise the differences and similarities between 'neo-Taylorism' and the 'new managerialism'.
2 To what extent, if at all, do you consider either approach to be democratic?

Reading 2
Forms of co-ordination

From Walter W Powell, *Research in Organisational Behaviour* (1990), adapted and reprinted in Grahame Thompson *et al.*, eds., *Markets, Hierarchies and Networks: The Co-ordination of Social Life* (Sage Publications, 1991), pp. 268-70

My aim is to identify a coherent set of factors that make it meaningful to talk about networks as a distinctive form of co-ordinating economic activity. We can then employ these ideas to generate arguments about the frequency, durability and limitations of networks.

When the items exchanged between buyers and sellers possess

qualities that are not easily measured, and the relations are so long-term and recurrent that it is difficult to speak of the parties as separate entities, can we still regard this as a market exchange? When the entangling of obligation and reputation reaches a point that the actions of the parties are interdependent, but there is no common ownership or legal framework, do we not need a new conceptual tool kit to describe and analyse this relationship?

Surely this patterned exchange looks more like a marriage than a one-night stand, but there is no marriage licence, no common household, no pooling of assets. In the language I employ below, such an arrangement is neither a market transaction nor a hierarchical governance structure, but a separate, different mode of exchange, one with its own logic, a network.

In practice, most organisations are of 'mixed' form rather than of one 'pure' type. Here an indication is given of likely mixes.

Many firms are no longer structured like medieval kingdoms, walled off and protected from hostile forces. Instead, we find companies involved in an intricate latticework of collaborative ventures with other firms, most of whom are ostensibly competitors. The dense ties that bind the auto and biotechnology industries cannot be easily explained by saying these firms are engaged in market transactions for some factors of production, or by suggesting that the biotechnology business is embedded in the international community of science. At what point is it more accurate to characterise these alliances as networks rather than as joint ventures among hierarchical firms?

Stylised comparison of forms of economic organisation

Key features	Forms		
	Market	Hierarchy	Network
Normative basis	Contract – Property rights	Employment relationship	Complementary strengths
Means of communication	Prices	Routines	Relational
Methods of conflict resolution	Haggling – resort to courts for enforcement	Administrative fiat – supervision	Norm of reciprocity – reputational concerns
Degree of flexibility	High	Low	Medium
Amount of commitment among the parties	Low	Medium to high	Medium to high
Tone or climate	Precision and/or suspicion	Formal, bureaucratic	Open-ended, mutual benefits
Actor preferences or choices	Independent	Dependent	Interdependent
Mixing of forms	Repeat transactions (Geertz, 1978)	Informal organisation (Dalton, 1957)	Status hierarchies
	Contracts as hierarchical Documents (Stinchcombe, 1985)	Market-like features: profit centres transfer pricing (Eccles, 1985)	Multiple partners

Formal rules |

Questions

1 (Linking with Chapter 9). What model of co-ordination was dominant in the 'Fordist' period and what in the 'post-Fordist' period? Illustrate your answer.
2 Give a critical description of an organisation with which you are familiar.

Power, Politics and People

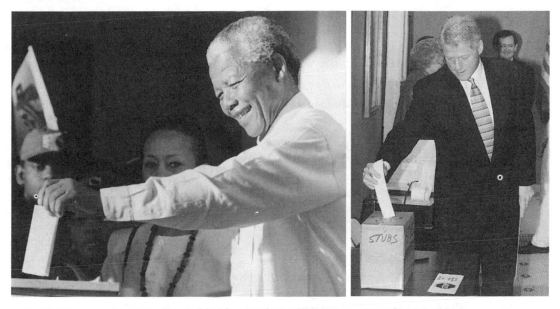

Representative democracy is basic to political freedom in the West. However, people are seeking new ways to make their opinions count.

Aims of this chapter

1 To compare Marx and Weber's analyses of power and to examine the relationship of power to systems of government.

2 Critically to compare Liberal and Marxist theory of the state and democracy.

3 To discuss several interpretations of New Social Movements – one of the most interesting contemporary social developments.

4 To discuss the merits of three theories of voting behaviour.

5 To explain the rise of the New Right and the 'triumph' of its ideology – using this as a case study of the potential influence of ideas.

6 To apply sociological perspective to key contemporary political issues and to discuss the issue of British nationality in detail.

Power and systems of government

Power, authority and politics: Weber and Marx

Politically, to be 'in power' is to have control of certain resources with which to 'get things done'. Weber and Marx's analyses of political power differed in important respects and in this, as in other matters, they have bequeathed distinct traditions.

Weber: power and authority

According to Max Weber, power is 'the probability that one actor within a social relationship will be in a position to carry out his own will despite resistance, regardless of the basis on which this probability rests'. In more ordinary language, power is the ability to get one's way – even if it is based on bluff.

Although we think of power as being associated particularly with politics it is, in fact, an aspect of all, or nearly all, social relationships. As Weber writes, positions of power can 'emerge from social relations in a drawing room as well as in the market, from the rostrum of a lecture hall as well as the command post of a regiment, from an erotic or charitable relationship as well as from scholarly discussion or athletics'. We can add that power plays a part in family and school relationships also. If Weber's sociology has a single central concept, it is that of power. He considered that economic and social goals as well as political ones are achieved through power-conflict. People compete for limited resources and status: for every one who achieves fortune and fame, there are thousands who do not. Nevertheless, it was characteristic of Weber that he stressed the importance of the political sphere. Political decisions, such as changes in taxation or educational policy, could be taken, and these could have great effect on the economic and social life of a country.

Weber distinguished authority from power. Authority may be thought of as *legitimate power* (power that is accepted as being rightfully exercised). He divided authority into three broad types: *traditional, charismatic* and *rational-legal*. We have already examined authority in the context of organisations. Here, our interest in it is as a form of political power: accordingly, we choose our examples from the political sphere. The sense of the inevitability of traditional political authority is well illustrated by an established dynasty, such as the centuries old Hapsburgs of Austria. By contrast, charismatic authority is generated by personality and the myths that surround it. Hitler, Martin Luther King and the Cuban revolutionary leader, Ché Guevara, are all examples of charismatic leaders. The fact that they are all recent figures shows that charismatic authority is still a feature of modern politics. In advanced industrial countries, however, rational-legal authority tends to be the predominant type and has, in particular, replaced traditional authority. Rational-legal political authority is established in law. The American system of government provides the best example of it because, unlike Britain, it has a written constitution (articles of government). This establishes the relationship between the legislature (which passes laws), the judiciary (which can determine if these laws are constitutionally allowable), and the executive (which, under the law, runs day-to-day government). Britain is often considered to have an 'unwritten' constitution but this has never been codified in a single, rational-legal document.

Weber's commitment to 'liberal democracy' was largely on the basis that he considered it to be based on rational-legal principles. Power is obtained and used within a framework of rules and part of the rules are that power can be 'lost'. Thus, democracy ensures against the 'raw' and easily abused power of dictatorship – it is safer if not always more efficient.

Marx: power and class

Marx emphasised the origin as much as the use of power and this led him to a different view than Weber on the nature of liberal democracy. For Marx, the basis of power lies in the relations of a group (or class) to the means of production. In any age, the ruling class – the class 'in power' – is the class that owns the means of production. He did not consider that liberal democracy – which he sometimes referred to as 'bourgeois democracy' – changed the basis of power in capitalist society. He argued that the economic power of the capitalist class gives them a political power greater than 'the vote' gives the rest of the people.

This fundamental difference between Weber and Marx provides a central theme of this chapter although many others 'cross' the debate with a variety of contributions and developments.

Systems of government

Politics is about power and purposes. It is the struggle to achieve the means to do certain things or, more precisely, to implement policies. Sometimes, what politicians want to do becomes obscured in the struggle to get the power to do it, but we must recognise, at least analytically, both these aspects of political activity.

Firstly, we deal with the means of power. The major means of political power is government and we can conveniently discuss the chief types of government here: democracy, oligarchy and dictatorship. We will consider each in turn.

Democracy: representative, participatory and delegatory

Democratic systems can be divided into three broad types: representative or indirect democracy; participatory or direct democracy, and delegatory democracy.

Representative democracy

In representative or indirect democracy, the people do not rule directly but elect representatives to rule for them. Representative democracy is associated with parliamentary institutions to such an extent that it is often referred to simply as parliamentary democracy: Britain and USA are major examples. In addition, representative democracies tend to be characterised by what are termed civil liberties. These include freedom to organise politically, freedom of speech and of the press, and the equal status of citizens under the law. In practice, these freedoms – except arguably the last – are not absolute. They are established in, and limited by law. Thus, freedom of the press in Britain is limited by the laws of libel and contempt (which cover what can legally be written about other people), and the Official Secrets Act. In the USA the comparable legislation is less strict and, to that extent, it has a freer press than Britain. The principle that freedom, like anything else, has to be balanced against other values, applies in both countries.

The crux of our concern with democracy is the debate between liberals and Marxists about the nature of democracy in advanced capitalist countries. Liberals consider that, for instance, Britain, West Germany, Italy, Australia and the United States are genuinely democratic. Marxists disagree: they argue that, at best, these countries are 'bourgeois democracies' which deny 'real' freedom to the majority of their population. For Marxists 'real' freedom depends on greater equality. For instance, freedom under the law may not seem very meaningful to someone who cannot afford a lawyer. This liberal-Marxist debate is a major recurrent theme of this chapter.

Participatory democracy

Participatory or direct democracy strictly means that people represent themselves and take their own decisions. The term 'participatory', however, is often used to mean some degree of personal involvement in decision making, short of direct democratic control. It has been in small communities, such as ancient Athens and medieval Geneva, that something approaching direct democratic self-government has proved most feasible. Nevertheless, in modern Tanzania, popular involvement in day-to-day affairs has been found possible at the local or village level. However, this has not replaced central government and bureaucracy (such as the civil service), often of a rather authoritarian kind, at the national level. The Russian revolutionary Lenin hoped and believed that a socialist revolution would replace the capitalist state with a proletarian state largely run by, or at least answerable to, direct democratic institutions called soviets or communes. At first, there were some signs that this might happen during and after the revolution of 1917. The fact that it did not, and that an authoritarian government developed instead, poses problems for modern socialists, who continue to seek more direct forms of democracy than are common in parliamentary democracies.

Delegatory democracy

Delegatory democracy is a form of 'half way house' between direct and indirect democracy. Delegates are *mandated* (told) by those who elect them to carry out specific orders and are, therefore, much more 'tied' to the wishes of their constituents than are undelegated representatives. In the late 1970s and early 1980s there was a fierce debate in the Labour party which focused on the extent to which MPs should be representatives or delegates.

Oligarchy

Oligarchy is government by the few: the term is usually used to describe government by an unrepresentative few. Frequently, the basis of oligarchical power is military. Thus Greece, the ancient home of democracy, was ruled by a junta (group) of colonels for several years. Although it is theoretically possible to talk of representative oligarchy, different terms are usually preferred. Liberal political theorists use the terms 'representative elite' or 'democratic elite'. Marxists deny that what liberals call democratic elites are, in fact, genuinely democratic; instead, they use the term 'ruling class'.

Dictatorship

Dictatorship is government by a single individual responsible only to himself or herself. Hitler and Stalin were dictators, each man professing different political ideologies, Fascism and Communism respectively. Yet it is for the similar way in which they both concentrated total power in their own hands, and the great inhumanity with which they exercised it, that they are remembered, rather than for their ideological differences. The term 'totalitarianism' is often associated with dictatorship, but has a rather wider usage. Totalitarian regimes are those in which power is wholly concentrated in the hands of a few people or of a single person.

The modern state and people

Central to any analysis of political sociology must be an understanding of the modern state. According to the *Oxford Dictionary of Sociology*: 'The State is a distinct set of institutions that has the authority to make the rules which govern society. It has in the words of Max Weber, a 'monopoly' of legitimate violence 'within a specific territory'. (506)

Governments, whether democratic, oligarchical or dictatorial, generally exercise power through the state. The state includes the government itself – of whatever kind – both in its capacity as the maker of law and of policy. It also includes the civil service – a vast bureaucracy of many thousands of people. The judiciary and magistracy are also part of the state. Local government is, by definition, not part of the central state apparatus but is often greatly influenced and, in some respects controlled, by central government. Local government can, therefore, sometimes be a powerful arm of central government. (The Labour governments of 1960s and 1970s persuaded most local authorities to accept and implement some form of comprehensive education.) In addition, local governments have their own bureaucracies. As we shall shortly see, Marxists tend to see the state as an instrument of class rule. In their view, the violence it exercises may not be 'legitimate'.

The modern state: a description

Dunleavy and O'Leary suggest that the modern state has five characteristics. Aspects of their description are open to debate but are presented as neutrally as possible. The five characteristics are:

1   The state is a recognisably separate institution or set of institutions, so differentiated from the rest of its society as to create identifiable public and private spheres.
2   The state is sovereign, or the supreme power, within its territory, and by definition the ultimate authority for all law, i.e. binding rules supported by coercive sanctions. Public law is made by state officials and backed by a formal monopoly of force.
3   The state's sovereignty extends to all the individuals within a given territory, and applies equally, even to those in formal positions of government or rule-making. Thus sovereignty is distinct from the personnel who at any given time occupy a particular role within the state.
4   The modern state's personnel are mostly recruited and trained for management in a bureaucratic manner.
5   The state has the capacity to extract monetary revenues (taxation) to finance its activities from its subject population.

(Dunleavy and O'Leary, 1987:2)

The first point describes how the modern state has created a distinct sphere within which the struggle for and exercise of (public) power and authority occurs. Other matters such as family and leisure life remain apart from the state (although they may be affected by its decisions). Secondly, within modern societies, the state is the supreme authority (not, for instance, a religious figure or outside political body – although on the latter point, membership of the European community raises important issues of sovereignty). The authority of the state can be enforced by a variety of sanctions. Thirdly, in a modern society no individual is outside the sovereignty of the state. The fourth point emphasises the bureaucratic way in which modern states are run and the fifth states that they have the crucial power to raise revenue.

The modern liberal democratic state is claimed to represent the people. The extent to which it does so is now discussed.

Liberal model of the democratic society

Those who contend that liberal democracy 'works' argue that parties and pressure groups effectively represent people and influence government. Further, they believe that political government, reflecting the will of the people, is the supreme state power. The civil service is seen as the 'servant' of government: the judiciary is regarded as independent of government, but is not expected to concern itself with political matters. The liberal model of democracy is examined below. In addition to the term 'liberal democracy', that of 'liberal pluralist' or, simply, 'pluralist' is often used. Pluralist refers to the many groups – notably parties and pressure groups – that liberals believe participate meaningfully in democratic politics.

Parties, political elites and the state

Parties and classes

Political parties existed in Britain well before universal suffrage (that is, the right of all people to vote). Parties, therefore, pre-date democracy. Nevertheless, the party system has adapted well to the demands of liberal democracy. The major parties attempt to appeal consistently to certain broad groups of people. The Labour party seeks support mainly from the working class and certain sections of the middle class, such as members of the new professions. The Conservative party is traditionally the party of the middle and upper classes. There is, however, much overlap in the class basis of party support, in particular, among the upper working and lower middle classes. Even so, a major party seems to require a solid base of class support to achieve power. The Liberal party rapidly declined as a major party when it ceased to appeal to an identifiable section of society. The compatibility of the two party system with liberal democracy is further suggested by the American example. Two competing parties quickly established themselves after the Americans had won their independence from Britain. In time, these developed into the present day Democratic and Republican parties. Like the main British parties, these also tend to represent particular major social groups although not to the same extent. As we shall see below, some hold the view that the class basis of party support in Britain is weakening.

Party ideologies

Although first Thatcherism and, then, Blairism have shifted the ideological bases of the two main parties, somewhat, the parties still tend to adhere to certain ideological principles and beliefs which reflect quite closely the values and material interests of those groups and classes from which they draw most of their support. The British Conservative party is strongly committed to capitalism and market solutions. The Labour party is no longer socialist in the sense of seeking nationalisation but remains more willing to intervene in the economy for social ends (see p. 405). It is still probably true that the Conservative party is the party of tradition, whereas the Labour party identifies with progressive change and reform (see pp. 309-10). For liberal-democratic theorists these are significantly different ideological positions, but Marxists argue that, rhetoric aside, the two major parties actually behave rather similarly when in government.

By contrast, liberal-democratic theorists consider that philosophical differences can lead to practical policy differences. Thus, various measures of the Labour government of 1945-50 would be considered distinctly socialist, and in sharp contrast to the clearly free-enterprise policies of the Thatcher government elected in 1979. In fairness, this example is selected to suit the argument and most Labour and Conservative governments have been more similar to one another than this. In any case, it is a tacit assumption of liberalism that no major party will seek to overthrow the basic social and political 'consensus' – although Thatcherism perhaps came fairly close.

Liberal representative elite theory

Liberal democracy is, in part, a theory about the relationship between the majority of the people and their leaders, the political elite. This relationship has balancing elements, the elite is representative, and yet it also leads. We will deal with these two aspects separately.

Historically, elite theory has tended to be undemocratic. Of the two major early twentieth century elite theorists, Pareto and Mosca, it was the latter who argued that the political elite could be generally representative of the people or 'masses', to use the term preferred by elite theorists. The party system, free elections and pressure group activity were means to ensure representatives.

An important related issue to the representative nature of elites is the extent to which, once elected, they remain under democratic control. Is democracy 'real' only once every five years when people cast their vote? Robert Dahl believes that elections play an important part in controlling government and he also cites a second major means by which leaders are made answerable to the people:

The election process is one of two fundamental methods of social control which, operating together, make governmental leaders so responsive to non-leaders that the distinction between democracy and dictatorship still makes sense. The other method of social control is continuous political competition among individuals, parties or both. Elections and political competition … vastly increase the size, number and variety of minorities whose preferences must be taken into account by leaders in making policy choices.

(1968:18)

Above all, elections, or the certainty that an election must come, mean that a governing party must always conduct itself in a way that will ultimately appeal to the majority of the electorate. There is evidence that widespread retrospective voting does occur: many voters do remember major features in the overall performance of administration and this acts as a check upon it. As Dahl points out, however, many particular policies may be concerned with the interest only of a minority, such as farm subsidies for the agricultural interests, though this does not necessarily mean that they therefore alienate the rest of the electorate. Many policies which please a minority are non-contentious of the majority. When the election comes, nevertheless, the government knows that, to win, it must have the backing of a 'majority of minorities'. This, according to Dahl, keeps it in check. For him power is widely diffused throughout liberal society – it is not the possession of one group or class.

Liberal elite theorists have stressed the necessity of leadership by the political elite almost as much as its representative nature. In large societies, only a minority can be involved in leadership. Further, competitive political selection should ensure that the elite leads on merit. The prime general function of leadership is to create social consensus and establish social order. Edward Shils believes that, in doing this, the elite protects its own interests, as well as those of the majority. Whilst agreeing that the process of consensus production does occur, Marxists deny that in capitalist society it works for the common good. On the contrary, it merely misleads the working class. Class conflict tends not to be stressed by democratic elite theorists. The alternative term to classes, 'masses' – which obscures classes and class conflict – sounds too contemptuous to modern ears to be used by liberal theorists. Instead, they stress the need for the political elite to lead the public towards a workable consensus.

We can link Dahl's democratic theory with the functionalist view put forward by Talcott Parsons of how power operates in a democracy. Parsons argues that leaders use power for the general good or, more precisely, for collective goals. Leaders are 'brokers' in power. Defence of the country and maintenance of law and order are two examples of the necessary use of power for the general good. It is crucial to Parsons' theory that how much power political leaders use ultimately depends on the will of the people. In war-time, the representative of the people in Congress or Parliament may sanction the use of greater powers by the government. Emergencies aside, the use of power is controlled by the processes described by Dahl. Parsons, therefore, conceives of power rather as some economists think of money: more or less can be created as the situation demands.

The liberal view of the state

Liberal theorists tend to regard the relationship between government and the rest of the state as relatively unproblematic. The government rules and the civil service implements its policies. The Marxist idea that the capitalist class is the 'real' controller of the state is simply not taken seriously. Weber, however, raised an important question in relation to the civil service. He considered that, like all bureaucracies it created its own vested interests and tended to be slow-moving. Civil servants, for reasons of their own, may give partial advice to ministers or take too long in producing it. Weber regarded a powerful Parliament as the best protector against an oppressive civil service bureaucracy.

Pressure groups

Pressure groups, as well as parties, are parts of the liberal-democratic model. If parties are the bulwarks of democracy, pressure groups are the supports and buttresses. They are an essential part of the pluralist vision in which power is seen as widely shared and exercised. Like parties, pressure groups pre-date democracy but like them they have become part of liberal democracy. Jean Blondel, who shares the pluralist perspective, sees parties and pressure groups as equally involved in the democratic process, although in different ways:

> *Interest groups differ from political parties by their aim, which is not to take power but only to exert pressure. They differ from parties by their objects, which are usually limited in scope. They differ from parties by the nature of their membership, which is often limited to one section in society.*
>
> *(1969:160)*

There have always been groups sharing a common interest which have collectively pressed their case to the powerful. The Wolfenden Report states that in the period since the war, the number of pressure groups has increased considerably. From the liberal point of view, pressure groups provide a necessary means of limited conflict on specific issues but this takes place within a context of fundamental consensus.

Protective and promotional pressure groups

We can classify pressure groups into two broad types: sectional (or protective) and promotional. Sectional groups are those whose membership has some common factor, such as occupation. It is to defend the common interest of their membership that such groups

exist. Trade Unions and professional associations provide the best known examples of sectional pressure groups. A large union is the Transport and General Worker's Union (TGWU), and a well known professional association is the British Medical Association (BMA). Sectional groups are usually economic but can also reflect for instance, religious or ethnic interests. The Islamic Society for Racial Tolerance and the Indian Workers' Association are examples.

Table 11.1 Pressure groups

	Sectional Groups	Promotional Groups
Permanent	Trades Union Congress	Child Poverty Action Group
Ad hoc	Archway Road Campaign	Band Aid

Promotional groups seek to promote a cause. One example is Amnesty International which seeks to aid and assist political prisoners throughout the world. Political prisoners are prisoners of conscience as opposed to criminals. Amnesty International is an organisation for which there is likely to be a long-term need. By contrast, other promotional groups achieve their aim, and can then disband. For example, a variety of anti-Vietnam War groups sprang up in the 1960s but dissolved when the war came to an end.

We need to distinguish between pressure groups in terms of the time-span of their existence, as well as on the basis of their interests or the causes they champion. The anti-Vietnam War groups were examples of *ad hoc* groups, formed to contest a specific issue, whereas Amnesty International and, still more obviously, the Trades Union Congress (TUC) are permanent groups (see Table 11.1 for further examples). Blondel also makes the important point that certain organisations which are not strictly speaking interest groups may occasionally use their influence in the political process. Thus, the Catholic Church makes its official (though not necessarily representative), opinion felt on such matters as divorce and abortion legislation.

The effectiveness of pressure groups

Pressure groups use a variety of means to influence public opinion, such as advertisements, demonstrations and meetings. Sometimes they focus more directly on Parliament or the executive government. Often this means lobbying a powerful or influential individual such as an MP. Our interest, however, is less in the detail of the methods of pressure group activity than in whether or not the results of this pressure are effective. Pluralists would say that they are, Marxists that they are not. At least, that is the essence of the argument, although both positions require some qualification. Christopher Hewitt has attempted to test which of these two cases is more correct by reference to empirical data. He examined the roles of a variety of interest groups in relation to 24 major post-war crisis issues which cover the area of foreign, economic, welfare and social policy. The issues he analysed include the debate and struggles over the Suez crisis, the nationalisation of steel, the National Health Service Act and the Commonwealth Immigration Act of 1962. He includes interest groups from all major sections of national life in his study, including trade unions (blue- and white-collar); business organisations; religious organisations; local government bodies; research organisations; and various promotional groups. He concludes that policy-making in Britain is not elitist in the sense that any single elite or interest is dominant, but that different interests succeed at different times. Statistically, the unions were particularly successful in that issues were most frequently resolved as they wished (something that happened much less under Thatcherism). The Marxists response to this argument is that issues dealt with in national politics are within the national consensus and that genuinely alternative (Marxist) principles and policies are not discussed. This view is examined in the next section.

Further liberal arguments for pressure groups

There are other arguments put forward by liberal democrats in support of the pressure group system. Pressure groups provide an accessible, day-to-day means by which popular opinion and influence can be expressed. They act upon political parties but are not necessarily part of the party system. In practice, however, the two major industrial interest groups tend to be tied into the party system. The unions and the TUC, and business and the CBI tend overwhelmingly to support, respectively, the Labour party and the Conservative party. It is significant, although seldom stressed by pluralists, that in a society noted for its class system, the two major parties and the two major interest groups should divide along class lines. Nevertheless, the major groups which support and, in part, finance the political parties exact a 'price' for loyalty: in return, they expect their interests to be protected and advanced. If, in their opinion, this does not occur, then, on a given issue, they may oppose the party they normally favour. Thus, the proposals to change the legal position of the unions, put forward by the Labour government of 1966-1970, were opposed with great determination by the union movement.

Criticism: pressure groups and the less powerful

A further criticism of interest group politics, in addition to that put forward by Marxists referred to above, is that it tends to leave out, or at least to leave behind, those who are least able to organise themselves: these people are found in the overlapping categories of the poor, the old, and the chronically sick and disabled. Immigrant groups also have tended to be less organised than their needs require. This is partly because they are financially and materially disadvantaged, and therefore have difficulty in affording the cost of organisation, and partly because it takes time for a group to accumulate the knowledge and experience to deal with the complex structure of institutionalised power in this country. It was a feature of British and American politics that, in the 1960s and 1970s, the disadvantaged became increasingly organised and vociferous. Instead of assuming that the welfare state would 'take care of them', the disadvantaged formed groups such as Claimants Unions (concerned with supplementary benefits) and Tenants Associations aimed at obtaining what they saw as their rights. Even pensioners were seen to converge on Parliament Square to lobby MPs.

Often the disadvantaged were assisted in pursuing their interests by community social workers or radical professional people and, occasionally, students. Sometimes this link took an institutional form. Des Wilson and Frank Field, the former directors of Shelter (the pressure group concerned with housing) and The Child Poverty Action Group, respectively, exemplify this kind of alliance. Of course, the involvement and concern of radical intellectuals with the poor is by no means new, but it did receive fresh stimulus in the 1960s, and there was also a revival in concern in the 1980s as people from a wide social spectrum combined in the anti-poll-tax movement. The large number of pressure groups, particularly involved with the disadvantaged, may suggest that pluralism works; equally, however, the continuing need for these pressure groups may indicate that the way liberal capitalism functions fails to satisfy the wants of large numbers of people. Arguably, the emergence of a so-called 'underclass' indicates the failure of pressure group politics as far as the poor are concerned.

Stephen Lukes: power – the limits of the liberal perspective

Stephen Lukes has argued that there are three dimensions of power only one of which the liberal perspective fully takes into account. Thus, Robert Dahl and those who adopt his approach look at those who are 'successful in decision making'. Like Hewitt (above) they conclude that a real process of competitive, though regulated, decision making occurs in liberal society. Lukes notes a second dimension of power explored by Bachrach and Baratz – the power to control 'what does or does not reach the agenda' for debate. Thus, it is arguable that the big sugar processing interests manage to keep the issue of the damage excess sugar does to health off the agenda of political action and discussion. Thirdly, Lukes suggests that 'the shaping of the beliefs and desires of others is an important dimension of power' – the more so because it can operate at a subtle, even unconscious level in the case of both the powerful and the less powerful.

Conclusion: 'The least worse system'?

It would be foolish to undervalue the freedom that does exist in liberal societies. Within broadly defined limits, people can speak their minds, even if some have far easier access to a public audience than others. People are able to organise for a cause even though some, by virtue of greater knowledge, wealth or influence, can do so more easily than others. Private lives are largely left private by the State – in their own homes, at least, people can 'be themselves'. These freedoms might not seem so substantial or so precious if we did not have before us the bloody alternatives of totalitarianism practised in Germany and the Soviet Union in the1930s. Perhaps the major argument in favour of liberal democracy is that attempts to improve on it have usually resulted in something much worse and in the reduction of political, civil and personal freedom. Perhaps Churchill was right when he described liberal democracy as 'the least worse system'.

Marxist/liberal debate: ruling class or representative political elite

Marxist perspectives on the 'capitalist state'

Most Marxists would deny that the model of democracy described in the previous section represents 'real' democracy. For them, it is merely 'bourgeois democracy', a smoke-screen behind which the capitalist class pursues its own interests. Parliament and political government are not considered to be the major source of power. Capitalists make the important decisions and control politicians. Although many contemporary Marxists would modify this view, some also retain a firm commitment to it in its classic form.

We have discussed in sufficient detail already Marx's view of society as fundamentally divided by class conflict. Of more relevance here is the issue of how Marxists consider that the ruling class rules. Tom Bottomore makes the point that, if capitalists do rule, they do so indirectly. They cannot do so directly as they are in a minority, both in the legislature and the executive in most capitalist countries. In feudal society, there was a much more precise correspondence between economic and political power. The feudal lords were the ruling class in the sense that they occupied the major political as well as economic positions. The landed nobility fulfilled the most important positions in central and local government. That is not true of capitalists today, although they are well represented in politics. If capitalists rule at all, therefore, they do so indirectly. Because of this, Marxist attempts to 'prove' the existence of a ruling class have often tended to be either circumstantial (relying on suggestive rather than conclusive evidence), or rather abstract and theoretical. Ralph Miliband's book, *The State in Capitalist Society* (1969), appears to fall into the first group. As the title of his book suggests, he is concerned with the control and operation of the state in capitalist society. He considers the state to be made up of the following institutions: the government, the administration (the civil service), the judiciary and parliamentary assemblies. State power lies in these institutions. In addition to what Miliband says, it is useful to bear in mind Althusser's concept of state apparatuses. The capacity

of the state to control the armed forces and police (the repressive state apparatus) as well as the major means of communication, notably the media, (the ideological state apparatus) is crucial to its power. This control is open to challenge and, in any case, it is fiercely argued between liberals and Marxists precisely how much power the state in capitalist societies has over the ideological state apparatus. Obviously, the relationship between the government and media differs somewhat in different capitalist countries but, generally, Marxists argue that there is relatively limited freedom of expression, whereas liberals take the opposite view.

The upper class background of occupational elites

A major part of Miliband's book examines two related questions whose answers, taken together, in his view determine whether or not there is a ruling class in British and other European capitalist societies. Firstly, is the state actually operated by people from the same upper class social background? Secondly, if so, do these people run the state in their own interest and at the expense of other classes? Miliband's answer to both questions is 'yes', although he has an easier time answering the first than the second. On the common social background and experience of those who dominate the command positions of the state, Miliband is unequivocal:

> *What the evidence conclusively suggests is that in terms of social origin, education and class situation, the men who have manned all command positions in the state system have largely, and in many cases, overwhelmingly, been drawn from the world of business or property, or from the professional middle classes. Here, as in every other field, men and women born into the subordinate classes, which form of course the vast majority of the population, have fared very poorly ...*
>
> *(Miliband, 1969:61)*

Although Miliband is primarily concerned with Britain, he cites considerable empirical evidence to show that the same situation prevails in other Western European 'democracies'.

Miliband's book was published in 1969, but substantially the same argument was presented in 1979 by the non-Marxist Anthony Giddens who, in fact, makes a broader claim than Miliband – that there is no major institutional sector in Britain where less than half of those in top positions are of public school background, and, by implication, also of upper or upper middle class background (for details, see Chapter 6). Drawing on a study of elites carried out at Cambridge, Giddens concludes that over 80 per cent of Anglican bishops, of principal judges and of army officers over the rank of major-general were from public schools, as were 60 per cent of chief secretaries in the civil service, and 76 per cent of Conservative MPs (1951-70). In contrast, only 26 per cent of Labour MPs had a public school background. (For a summary of data on the social original of Britain's elites – some of it more recent than Giddens and Miliband, see pp. 105-8.)

Giddens emphasises especially the upper class dominance of industry, which, from the Marxist point of view, is particularly important because the economy is seen as the ultimate basis of power. In a sample taken from the Cambridge survey, 73 per cent of the directors of the industrial corporations and 80 per cent of the directors of financial firms proved to be of public school background. While the Thatcher 'revolution' appears to have significantly opened up industrial leadership to mainly men from non-public school backgrounds, this is less true of finance.

Giddens cites other work which shows that directors of industrial and, especially, financial companies very often have kin in the same occupation. The phenomenon of interlocking directorships is a point emphasised in both British and American literature on industrial elites. The term 'industrial elites' refers to the way in which various individuals hold directorships in more than one company so that the same individuals may sit together on several different boards. Accordingly, they may influence and even co-ordinate the policy of two or more companies: indeed, this is often precisely the intention of interlocking directorships. The Cambridge study showed an increase in directorial connection between large companies. At the beginning of the century, fewer than half of the 85 corporations studied were linked by shared directorships, whereas in 1970, 73 out of 85 organisations studied appeared in the network of connections. Potentially, this provides an impressive basis for control of industry.

Is the upper class also a ruling class?

We come now to Miliband's second area of enquiry. Does the upper class rule in its own interest, and at the expense of others? As Miliband is well aware, to demonstrate upper class dominance of major elites does not prove either that the upper class is the 'real source of political power' or, still less, that it rules in its own interest. In particular, the powerful position of the upper class in industry does not automatically mean that it can control the political process or that, 'in the last resort', its economic power is more decisive than the political power of government. These issues require further examination.

In attempting to determine whether the upper class is also a ruling class, Miliband seeks to establish what links exist between business and politics. If these are considerable, we can conclude that there is at least the potential for business to influence the political process and, perhaps even to control it in its own interest. A study by Roth and Kerbey shows that, between 1960 and 1966, MPs held, in total, 770 directorships and 324 positions as chairmen, vice-chairmen or managing directors. It is highly significant that 90 per cent of these positions were held by Conservative MPs. In so far as the economic-political flow of influence does express itself through personal links of this kind, it is, therefore, far more likely to be found in the Conservative party than in the Labour party. The upper class is well represented in

both industry and the Conservative party. As we have seen 76 per cent of Conservative MPs over the period 1951-70 went to public school, a major purveyor of upper class culture, compared with only 26 per cent of Labour MPs. Few Marxists, however, regard the Labour party as the likely means by which capitalism will be abolished and socialism established. Why is this so?

Marxism and the Labour party

Marx himself held out little hope that socialism could be successfully introduced through Parliament, although there is evidence that he thought that the arrival of universal male suffrage (voting rights) might make the system more responsive to socialist demands. In the event, Marxists are able to point out that, despite seventeen years of Labour government since 1945, the fundamental facts of inequality have not changed very much. Everybody has become better off, but the relativities have not changed significantly. Marxists tend to consider that the welfare state has partly 'humanised' but not fundamentally changed the position of the working class and the poor. Writing in the late 1960s, but expressing a perennial mood among Marxists, Miliband says:

> Social-democratic parties [Labour parties] or rather social-democratic leaders, have long ceased to suggest to anyone but their most credulous followers [and the more stupid among their opponents] that they were concerned in any sense whatever with the business of bringing about a socialist society.
>
> (Miliband, 1968:244)

In qualification of Miliband's remark, it should be said that there is still a sizeable socialist group within the Labour party, which continues to work for radical change through the parliamentary system, despite its dissatisfaction with the performances of the Labour government of the 1960s and 1970s. It will be interesting to see if such a group comes to the fore, should Labour win the 1997 general election.

Nicos Poulantzas: a structural interpretation

Further analysis of the role of the ruling class in capitalist society is presented by Nicos Poulantzas, a French Marxist. In a celebrated exchange with Miliband, Poulantzas criticises him for concentrating too much on details about the social background of various occupational elites and of the ruling class as a whole. For Poulantzas, these factors are not particularly crucial. In his view, it would be possible for large numbers, even a majority, of people of quite humble social background to administer capitalist society – but it would still be capitalist society and therefore run in the interests of the capitalist class and not the proletariat. This brings us to Poulantzas's central point and the one on which he considers that he differs, at least in emphasis, from Miliband. Poulantzas contends that it is the structure of the capitalist system and not the social background of the various elites which is the major factor for Marxists to consider when analysing the state. According to him, what matters is the relationship of the parts, including the state, to the social totality (the whole of society). Thus, it comes as no surprise to Poulantzas that socialist parties with a wide basis of popular support and even, perhaps, with leaders of working class origins, should find it difficult to implement socialism when, supposedly, 'in power'. The British Labour party might be elected 'to power' but what it can actually do is limited by the rest of the system. It would almost certainly be afraid to introduce policies that would lose the confidence of international financiers and stock exchange investors. To do so would probably cause a major economic crisis. There might even be the possibility that radical policies would turn the military against the government. This threat, however, is most easily demonstrated in relation to underdeveloped countries. Thus, the popularly elected (although not with an absolute majority) president Allende of Chile, a Marxist, was overthrown by a conspiracy involving some of the parliamentary opposition, members of the armed forces and the American Central Intelligence Agency. The implication is that when legality fails to protect the interests of capital, then illegal means may be used.

The above does not mean that Poulantzas dismisses the state as unimportant – far from it! Some years after his debate with Miliband, he wrote: 'The state plays a decisive role in the relations of production and the class struggle'. But Poulantzas warns that what a socialist party could actually do with state power, if it were to obtain it, would be conditioned by the relationship of the state to the rest of the system at that time. This would include such matters as the strength of capital and the extent of socialist support among the working class.

There is an element of 'shadow boxing' about Miliband's and Poulantzas's disagreement, because the former insists that his work is a structural critique of the state in capitalist society and not just a collection of loosely interpreted empirical data. In any case, Poulantzas's point, that an adequate theory of the state must be related coherently to the rest of the social system, is valid.

Miliband and Poulantzas: evaluation

It is worth briefly exploring the wider implications of Poulantzas's remark that 'the state plays a decisive role in the relations of production and the class struggle'. In saying this, he is rejecting deterministic interpretations of Marx's base-superstructure model of society. He denies that capitalism will inevitably collapse as a result of its inherent economic 'contradictions' as some Marxists still believe. (Whether Marx himself ever believed this, in any simplistic sense, is debatable.) For Poulantzas, the capitalist nature of society and class relations arising from relations to the means of production do structure class conflict – both in the economic and political context – but they do not pre-determine its outcome: socialism has to be achieved through political struggle. With some reservations, the American Marxist sociologist Erik Wright

supports this position in his book, *Class, Crisis and the State*. In particular, he offers a sensitive discussion of the issue of whether socialism can be achieved through the 'bourgeois' democratic system or whether it requires violent revolution. We have already referred to some of the problems of the former approach: the difficulties in relation to the second are perhaps greater. Firstly, the human cost of violent revolution needs to be profoundly considered. Can it be justified? Secondly, modern government have at their disposal such powerful and centrally controlled arsenals of destruction that they seem virtually unassailable (although several communist regimes were overthrown from below during the1980s).

Ideology and power

A crucial question that Marxists need to explain is why the majority, who are not the prime beneficiaries of capitalism, do not oppose the system more vehemently. Miliband and Poulantzas are agreed that the dominant ideology plays a vital role in securing the compliance of the majority to the power and position of the ruling class. We have already discussed how the educational system can teach people to conform – even to a society in which they have relatively little material stake – and the role of the mass media in this respect is worthy of much more space than we can give it here. For the moment, a single quotation from Miliband will serve to represent the Marxist perspective:

> *Given the economic and political context in which the mass media functions, they cannot fail to be, predominantly, agencies for the dissemination of ideas and values which affirm rather than challenge existing patterns of power and privilege, and thus be weapons in the arsenal of class domination.*
>
> (Miliband, 1969:211)

Ideological control involves power over people's minds. As Bachrach and Baratz point out, an aspect of this is the ability to decide which issues should be allowed to become publicly debated and which should not be, for instance, control of the press. As we saw, Steven Lukes takes this point further by frankly recognising that the values, attitudes, and even wants of the majority can be moulded by the power of a few. Marxists are unimpressed by exercises such as those carried out by Hewitt (discussed earlier) which seem to support a pluralist model of power, because they argue that the issues that really matter are seldom discussed publicly, anyway. For Marxists, such issues would include whether a society based on private property (including that of the ruling class) can be socially just, whether violence is necessary to destroy the capitalist system and what a 'liberated' socialist culture might be like. The limits of the political debate are reflected in decisions taken and not taken (for example, issues of pollution and poverty may be disregarded and defence, law and order and immigration policy vigorously pursued).

Althusser and Gramsci

Like his colleague, Poulantzas, Althusser was a Marxist structuralist. He gave great emphasis to the role of capitalist ideology in bringing about the conformity of the working class. He considered the capitalist state to be far more extensive than just the central institutions of government. He referred to the former as the Repressive State Apparatus and to the media, education, family and other areas of ideological reproduction as the Ideological State Apparatus. Ideology 'interpolates' (or summons) individuals who become 'subjects' of the system.

Gramsci's concept of hegemony also offers a Marxist explanation of why the working class 'consent' to their subordination. They do so because the ideological forces of the system produce ways of thinking and seeing which reinforce capitalism and exclude alternative conceptions. However, in describing hegemony as shifting and potentially open to challenge, he is generally regarded as less deterministic than Althusser.

Power elite versus ruling class theory: a radical disagreement: Charles Wright Mills

Before summarising the merits of the pluralist and Marxist views of democracy, we must briefly analyse the power elite theory of the American radical sociologist, C Wright Mills. Mills was a conflict theorist but was much less of a Marxist than the other authors so far discussed in this section. He probably owed more to Weber than to Marx. He was a severe critic of post-Second World War American society. His fierce but measured language broke across the bland face of functionalist orthodoxy like a fire-cracker. A startled Talcott Parsons compared him to a gun-happy outlaw, free with the trigger but not very accurate in his aim. It is true that Mills began more than he was able to finish, but by the time of his death in 1962, he had sown the seeds of a radical revival in American sociological scholarship, and provided an intellectual starting point for the emerging political radicalism of the American New Left. His best known and most influential work is *The Power Elite*, first published in 1956. It is typical of Mills's intellectual inventiveness that he reworked traditionally conservative elite theory within a radical perspective. He argued that there are three unrepresentative elites at the top of American society: the political elite, the military elite and the industrial elite. Together, these made up the power elite. The relative power of the three elites could vary. He disagreed with Marxists that capitalists necessarily 'rule' directly or indirectly – viewing this perspective as economic determinism (see Reading 1). In his own time, when the Cold War was at its height, he believed that the military was the most powerful of the three. He insisted, however, that members of the elites shared common material interests as well as, frequently, a common upper class background. Individuals such as President Eisenhower moved easily between the elites, and thus helped to fuse more closely

Figure 11.1 Mills popularised the idea that in democracies powerful groups ruled 'above' the people

identity of ideology and interest. Mills was in no doubt that the power elite 'ran' America to its own benefit and against that of the majority of people.

Mills considered that the American Congress operated only at the middle level of power and was unable to check the power elite. It was influential mainly on those issues that did not fundamentally affect the structure of society or the essential interests of the power elite. Thus, it might legislate for a little more or a little less welfare aid but not for a fundamental redistribution of wealth. Below the power elite was what Mills did not hesitate to describe as 'the masses'. They comprised the middle and working classes and the poor. He regarded the middle class as fragmented and generally concerned with its own various sectional interests, and the working class as sufficiently 'well-fed' to be thoroughly de-radicalised and uninterested in change. Mills's comments on the working class had plausibility in relation to the relatively unorganised and non-socialist American labour force but they were rejected by European Marxists as much less applicable to that continent. The poor consisted of such groups as the unemployed, the old and disproportionate numbers of black minorities. Mills saw little prospect that this group would become an effective agency for change, but he did refer, in passing, to the 'moral idea of a counter-elite' and to 'images of the poor, the exploited, and the oppressed as the truly virtuous, the wise and the blessed'.

As we shall shortly describe, this notion had considerable appeal to the young American radicals of the 1960s to whom Mills became something of a folk hero and intellectual father figure. In turn, Mills regarded young, radical intellectuals as the best, if still unlikely, chance for radical change in America.

Liberal pluralist and Marxist theory: summary

Pluralist theorists take liberal democracy more or less 'at face value'. They believe it works, and consider that political parties and interest groups adequately represent the people. Marxists present a variety of arguments to demonstrate that pluralist claims are incorrect and that power in capitalist societies is, in reality, in the hands of the ruling class. They point to the dominance of the upper class in various major elites and, in particular, to the overlap between Parliament and industry. Even Labour governments have been seen to pose only a minimal threat to the ruling class and to have made no fundamental change in inequalities of power, wealth and prestige. The power of the ruling class in the area of ideological control helps to explain, for Marxists, the acquiescence of large sections of the working class in their own 'exploitation'. Mills's mixed legacy defies categorisation, but he caught the ascendant mood of the emerging American and European New Left of the1960s. The popular slogan of that decade 'power to the people' is not so distant an echo of Mills's inspirational rhetoric. It is an echo that has been heard again in the 1980s and 1990s in the new social movements.

Questions

1 Which theory best explains the distribution of power in Western capitalist societies? Give reasons for your answer.
2 Compare and contrast Marxist ruling class theory with Mills's theory of the power elite.

New social movements (NSMs)

The term social movements 'is used most commonly with reference to groups and organisations outside the mainstream of the political system' (*Oxford Dictionary of Sociology*:489). Roughly in historical order, the classic social movements are the working class movement, the women's liberation movement and the black liberation movement.

Although it has not achieved all the aims, the working class movement is now incorporated into the system in the form of the Labour party and the Trade Unions. This is not true of the women's liberation and black liberation movements but both have achieved some of their goals and are institutionalised in, for instance, the

Equal Opportunities Commission and the Commission for Racial Equality. However, gender politics and ethnic politics remain very relevant in the 1990s and play a part in contemporary or new social movements.

Simon Hallsworth gives a good indication of the variety and scope of the post-war social movements:

> (T)he term (social movements) is usually applied to cover the feminist movement; anti-racists groups such as Black Power: the radical students' movements of the 1960s; anti-war groups such as CND; environmental movements such as Greenpeace and Friends of the Earth; animal rights groups such as the Animal Liberation Front; and Gay Rights organisations such as Outrage and more recently Queer Nation
>
> (1994:7)

The student, black and feminist movements of the 1960s to some extent provided a rough model for later social movements. Their criticism of 'mainstream' politics, willingness to practise direct action and civil disobedience, and their attempt to marry personal lifestyle with political action have all been echoed by social movements in the 1980s and 1990s. The view that decisive change could be affected in the cultural area more easily than in the political also occurs commonly among radicals in both decades.

Theoretical Interpretations of New Social Movements

Alberto Melucci: individual autonomy/collective identity

In Melucci's view new social movements do not have as their primary object the achievement of reforms through the means of the state – although this is likely to be one of their goals. The title of his book suggests his focus on personal autonomy: *Nomads of the Present: Social Movements and Individual Needs in Contemporary Society* (1989).

Melucci considers new social movements to be *new* or unique in four respects:

1 They are not concerned over the production and distribution of material goods.
2 Actors' participation in the movements is not primarily to achieve an external object (e.g. reform) but is adopted as an alternative lifestyle and as such operates as a 'sign' or 'message' to society. Lifestyle ecologists are one example.
3 NSMs are seeking new continuities between the 'private' and 'invisible' networks that are their main expression, and the public world of employment and politics in which they may only appear irregularly or 'part-time'.
4 NSMs have an acute awareness of the interdependence of the planet e.g. ecologically.

Given that Melucci does not consider that the object of NSMs is

(Source: *The Guardian*, 6.5.1996)

Figure 11.2 Signalling alternatives: environmental protestors at Twyford Down

to redistribute resources, what is the focus of their social concern? They are concerned about large-scale organisations – the state, industry, the media – which seek to regulate and control people's lives. They express their concern by adopting alternative ways of life while still accessing some of the resources of modern organisations, especially the media. Recognising that commercial and political interests use the symbolic power of the media, they use it, too. Engagements with system of control is largely symbolic – through lifestyle alternatives and through media subversion (see Reading 2).

Melucci's perspective is postindustrial in that he observes (and reflects) a shift in focus from material to cultural, symbolic and lifestyle issues. It is postmodern in that it is precisely his concern with individual and collective meanings and identity that characterises postmodernism.

Alain Touraine: identity orientation

Touraine sees social movements as central to social conflict and social change. He considers that for a social movement to be effective in bringing about change its members must develop a collective identity and identify what they want to change. He considers that the working class movement failed to do this. Its 'members' did not develop a shared consciousness.

Touraine argues that to achieve change, a social movement needs both to develop an alternative lifestyle and to take over the state. In the first respect Melucci would agree but not in the second. Touraine considers that the French ecology movement did develop alternative lifestyles but in failing to confront the state, lapsed into utopianism. The Solidarity movement in Poland was successful in both key respects.

Touraine takes very seriously the importance of continuity between personal lifestyle and public or political position. He argues that sociologists should join social movements critically oriented towards the capitalist state. He agrees with Melucci that a cultural lifestyle orientation is appropriate to postindustrial society.

Jurgen Habermas: privacy and participation

Habermas explains the rise of NSMs in the context of the functioning of the state in late capitalism. In the classical – late nineteenth/early twentieth century – stage of capitalism, the working class movement sought material redistribution. The mechanism that was established to achieve this was the welfare state.

In late capitalism, the state has come to operate in a way that can threaten individual privacy and lifestyles:

1 The state struggles to regulate capitalism and afford the welfare state (see pp. 407-8). In a situation of scarcity, it risks favouring one group – usually capital – at the expense of another.

2 Partly in order to achieve its (difficult) objectives, the state frequently invades the private realm. Or put otherwise, political power is extended at the expense of civil rights. Thus, in Britain during the 1980 and 1990s it could be argued that the thrust of family and education legislation has reduced individual liberty.

Habermas sees the NSMs as a *rational* response to the above developments. Habermas's own 'project' could be described as 'a more rational society'. For this to be achieved, truthful dialogue is necessary and he sees the NSMs as able to participate in, and perhaps enhance this process. Although like Melucci and Touraine, Habermas emphasises the lifestyle aspect of the NSMs he considers issues of material redistribution still to be highly important.

Mayer Zald and John McCarthy: resource mobilisation

Writing in the 1970s, Zald and McCarthy present a more traditional approach to social movements. In contrast to Melucci, they concentrate on *how* rather than *why* social movements develop. Thus, money, professional expertise, and links with existing organisations might be sought . However, 'resources' also refers to ideologies, symbols and rhetoric.

There is also less emphasis in Zald and McCarthy on the distinctive, arguably postindustrial and postmodern nature of NSMs. This is a reminder that for many people in Western Europe and even more in the global context, material issues are still of prime importance.

Alan Scott: continuity between 'old' and 'new'

Alan Scott does not deny that there are differences between the old and new social movements but argues that there are also important continuities. He argues that no categorical distinction can be made between social movements and that they can best be viewed as a continuum from highly decentralised networks to much more formal organisations. There is often overlap between the two poles within a single movement. Thus, the women's movement is densely networked but also produces formal organisation. Scott also takes the view that all social movements have some orientation towards the state.

Mark Kirby, in his own useful review of social movements, adapts Scott's schematised contrast between old and new social movements (Table 11.2). Helpful as this is, it is important to remember Scott's own emphasis on overlap between old and new social movements.

Table 11.2 Contrasts between the old and new social movements

	Workers movement	New social movements
Location	Increasingly within the state	Civil society
Aim	Political integration/ Economic rights	Changes in values and lifestyles/Defence of civil society
Social Base	Economic class/ Industrial society	Post-industrial society
Theme	Citizenship	Autonomy
Organisation	Formal/hierarchical	Network/grassroots
Medium of action	Political mobilisation	Direct action/cultural innovation

(Source: Adapted from Scott (1990, p.19) and Scott (1992, p.142) in M Kirkby, *Investigating Political Sociology*, Collins Educational, 1995:71)

Criticisms of new social movement theory: Ralph Miliband, a Marxist view

While highly sympathetic to many of the NSMs, Miliband argues that they do not have the power and resources to replace capitalist society with a more just system. Nor have they developed the necessary theoretical framework with which to understand and confront capitalism. For Miliband, the labour movement continues to have 'primary' importance. Only labour is positioned at the 'core' of capitalism – in productive relations – and has the potential to overturn capitalism. To do this, however, it requires a theoretical and practical alternative system to capitalism which, in his view, is socialism. He urges members of NSMs to work as part of a wider socialist movement in which they can achieve most effect. (For a Marxist interpretation of urban social movements see p. 558.)

Paul Hirst: a liberal-pluralist view

Hirst agrees with Miliband that the NSMs have tended to underestimate the 'opposition'. However, as he observes, most of the NSMs have targeted the corporate state rather than capitalism itself as the main problem. Hirst raises three problems in this respect:

1 Movements in the West attempting to operate exclusively (or mainly) in civil society cannot hope to by-pass and supplant the state. The civil and political arenas are profoundly interconnected in Western democracies – especially through the media. To achieve change, the issue of state power requires to be addressed directly.

2 Unlike in Eastern Europe, the Western European states have sufficient democratic and popular legitimacy to avoid a people's revolution. The NSMs are, in the end, in the minority.

3 In addition, the Western European states have the strength – in terms of co-ordination and force – to cope with any likely level of insurgency.

Questions

1 Explain with examples what is a social movement.
2 How effective in achieving change do you consider social movements to be?

Voting behaviour: three models

Until the mid 1970s one model explaining voting behaviour was overwhelmingly dominant: the class model. In general elections between 1931 and 1970 the percentage of the total vote of the Labour and Conservative vote added together was between 84.2 (1945) and 96.8 (1951). It seemed to be a fact of political life that the vast majority voted for either the Labour or the Conservative parties and, generally, it was the working class who voted for the former and the middle class who voted for the latter. In the two general elections of 1974, however, the share of the vote of the two main parties was almost precisely 75 per cent on each occasion – a substantial drop on what had been the norm. In contrast, the Liberal vote had leapt from 7.5 per cent in 1970 to 19.3 per cent in the first election of 1974. These trends did not reverse. Something appeared to have changed (see Figures 11.3 and 11.4).

The picture painted by the facts given above is misleadingly simple. The trends underlying the shifts in voting behaviour since 1970 are a matter of dispute as are the explanations of them. Two models of voting behaviour have emerged to challenge the class model – the rational choice or consumer model and the radical model. The three models will be discussed under the following headings:

1 The party identification and social class model.
2 The rational choice model.
3 The radical model.

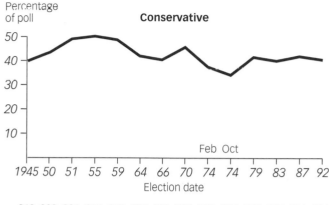

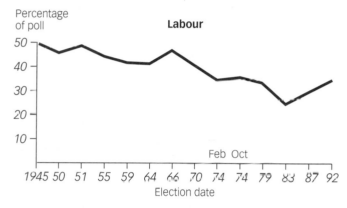

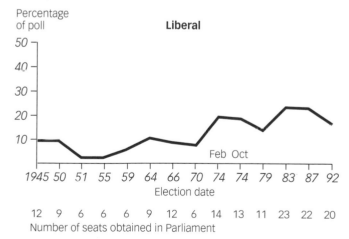

Figure 11.3 Voting trends 1945-92: the fate of the parties

The party identification and social class model

David Butler and Donald Stokes were influential in putting forward this interpretation, particularly during the 1960s. They argue that social class factors resulted in a large majority of voters developing a long-term attachment and loyalty to a particular political party (party identification). In interviews, they found that over 90 per cent of respondents expressed such an attachment (*Political Change in Britain*, 1969). In general elections the majority of middle class voters voted Conservative 70 per cent in 1955) and the majority of working class voters voted Labour (69 per cent in 1966). Data from Tapper and Bowles comparing the class percentages voting Labour and Conservative between 1945-58 do show a very strong link between class and voting behaviour during this period (see Table 11.3).

Table 11.3 Class percentages voting Labour and Conservative 1945-58

	AB	C1	C2	DE
Conservative	85	70	35	30
Labour	10	25	60	65

(Source: Tapper and Bowles in L Robins *ed.*, 1982:175)

Theorists adopting the class model of voting behaviour invariably distinguish between objective and subjective class. Objective class is based on a generally accepted definition of class, such as the Registrar General's used in Table 11.3. Subjective class is the class to which a person thinks s/he belongs.

The relationship between subjective class and voting behaviour is even stronger than that between objective class and voting behaviour. Evidence from a number of sources, including Butler and Stokes, has shown that about 80 per cent of those who are both objectively and subjectively working class vote Labour, whereas the objective working class vote as a whole never rose above 69 per cent between 1952 and 1962. The strength of subjective class image and voting patterns is further illustrated by the behaviour of the minority of unskilled workers who think of themselves as middle class. According to Butler and Stoke's data, 55 per cent of this group voted Conservative in 1959. The tendency for those at the top of the occupational hierarchy who see themselves as working class to vote Labour is not quite as marked, but is still statistically very significant.

Class voting and socialisation

Socialisation is the 'mechanism' by which most people come to identify with a particular party. Working class homes 'breed' Labour voters and middle class homes Conservative voters. Socialisation is stronger if both parents support a given party. Neighbourhood schools tend to reflect the class of the children who attend them and this reinforces class/party identification. Similarly, children of middle class origins are more likely to get middle class jobs than working class children and vice versa – again reinforcing class experience and identification. Where continuity of class experience is broken – say, by social mobility, there is an increased chance of a change of party allegiance. Otherwise, the class model

of voting behaviour, presents party preference and, therefore, attitudes on a range of political matters, as well established from a young age and likely to 'become more set as a person gets older'.

Frank Parkin: dominant and class ideology

Frank Parkin offers an interesting explanation of the strength of traditional working class identification with Labour during the 1950s and 1960s (1972). He suggests that, given the generally conservative nature of British society, what is surprising is that a majority of the working class consistently voted Labour. He contends that the traditionally dominant institutions of society – the established church, the monarchy, the military, legal and civil service elites, the public schools and ancient universities, the institutions of private property and the media – embody values which are both middle class and closely in accord with conservatism. Conservatives have for a long time appealed to communal values, such as nationalism, monarchy, religion and imperialism to 'unify' the country. It would seem almost inevitable that this powerful and pervasive conservative influence would encompass all classes. How is it, then, that a majority of the working class resist its full import? Simply, various 'shields' or 'barriers' exist against it, which allow socialist values to be fostered. These protective barriers are formed by working class subcultures which generate different values from the dominant culture. The major source of these values is the work-place. There, working people may experience both the collective strength of their peers, and possible conflict with employers. Thus, the work-place is the cradle of socialist values. Parkin also sees the traditional working class community as an additional basis of working class and socialist solidarity. Where occupational communities such as mining towns and dock areas exist, solidarity is likely to be especially strong. These areas, however, have greatly declined (see Chapter 9, p. 273).

Goldthorpe and Lockwood: affluence, class and voting

Goldthorpe and Lockwood in their *Affluent Worker* study (1968) recognised the influence of class socialisation but also, importantly, observed that more individualistic attitudes to social and, potentially, political life may have been developing among some workers. They divide the working class into three groups:

1 'Proletarian' traditionalist.
2 'Deferential' traditionalist.
3 'Privatised' worker/Instrumental collectivist.

The proletarian traditionalists are those who have internalised the traditional and historic values of the working class community such as collectivism and solidarity. Deferential traditionalists are those who have succumbed to the powerful conservative influences in society (indicated by Parkin) and accept 'their place in the hierarchy'.

The privatised workers/instrumental collectivists (see p. 174) are, however, of immediate interest. These are workers who are committed to a collective approach to unions and the Labour party, not out of loyalty or solidarity, but because of what they can get out of them. In a quota survey that is now almost 30 years old, Goldthorpe and Lockwood found that affluent workers tended to support Labour to an even greater extent than the working class as a whole, for precisely these instrumental reasons. This analysis does, however, allow for the possibility that instrumentally motivated workers will switch their vote if it seems in their interest to do so. More recent evidence argues that this may, indeed, be what some of them do.

'Conformist' and 'deviant' voting in the class model

In the class model of voting behaviour, those who vote according to their class status are considered 'conformist' voters, and those who do not, 'deviant'. We will in turn look at explanations of middle and working class 'deviant' voters.

Middle class 'deviant' voters

Consistently in general elections there are fewer middle than working class 'deviant' voters. Three types of middle class 'deviant' voters are described in the literature. These can be termed:

1 The 'intellectual' left.
2 The 'status deprived' left.
3 The 'recently upwardly mobile' middle class.

The first group tends to contain many with considerable experience of higher education: these can be referred to as the 'intellectual left'. They include, particularly, some academics, journalists and 'media people' and members of vocational or 'helping' professions, such as social work or teaching. Slightly controversially perhaps, it can be argued that the wide education and knowledge of these people enables them to see beyond their own interest and to sympathise with the disadvantaged. They vote Labour because they see it as the party which better represents the disadvantaged.

The second group is those with low status within the middle class. Unlike the first group, they do not vote Labour for idealistic reasons, but more out of pique and insecurity. Typically, they rank higher in education and qualifications than in social status: they find outlets for the resulting resentment in radical politics. (It is worth noting that the analysis of radicalism in terms of status deprivation has been influential in recent American sociology and history, where it has been criticised as both conservative and speculative.) Certainly, this approach employs a highly cynical interpretation of motive. In refuting it, Frank Parkin argues that low status jobs are a result of radical ideals and not vice versa. He suggests that the political attitudes of middle class radicals are formed before they start work, and that they choose work which is most compatible with their radical values. This tends to be vocational and of relatively low pay and status. However, Parkin's analysis could equally apply to higher status middle class radicals.

What both have in common is a concern for the welfare of others as well as themselves.

The third group for consideration are numbers of first generation white-collar employees, or 'the sons of affluent workers' as John Goldthorpe calls them. It seems that some of these continue to support the Labour party even after their rise in socio-economic status. No doubt this partly reflects loyalty to their 'roots' but it also suggests that, as the traditional working class shrinks, the Labour party may have succeeded in presenting policies that potentially widen its basis of support.

Working class 'deviant' voters: 'deference' and 'secular' voters

The most convincing explanation of the large working class Tory vote, and one which is echoed in most writings on the subject, is that the dominant institutions of British society embody conservative and middle class values. As a result, the working class as well as the middle class becomes socialised into conservative values unless more radical socialisation cuts across this central flow of influence (see Parkin, above). In functionalist terms, this simply means that a 'consensus around the central value system' is created by institutions such as the monarchy and the church, which exist partly for that purpose. Marxists agree, but consider that this process misleads or 'mystifies' the working class into conforming, sometimes enthusiastically, to a social system that exploits them.

Detailed study of the working class Conservative vote supports the above analysis. As we have seen, Goldthorpe and Lockwood have given the term deferential traditionalists to one group of working class Tories. Referring to the same group, McKenzie and Silver use the term 'deference voters'. These are people who prefer ascribed 'socially superior' leaders to those who have risen by their own efforts. McKenzie and Silver found these attitudes among some of the urban proletariat, although they are more usually associated with farm labourers. Often it seems that isolated, individual workers, such as caretakers of prestige, private establishments, or personal and domestic employees of the wealthy, adopt deferential attitudes.

McKenzie and Silver suggested that what they term 'secular voters' may be superseding deferential voters as the major working class basis of Conservative support. Compared to deference voters, secular voters are young and well-paid. In general secular voters seems to describe the group referred to by Goldthorpe and Lockwood as instrumentalists. The latter, of course, deny that this group is tending to become more Conservative and, in doing so, refute the embourgeoisement hypothesis. Nevertheless, the strong swing (11.5 per cent) of affluent workers from Labour to the Conservatives in the 1979 election suggested that the embourgeoisement hypothesis or something like it might have more long-term mileage in it than Goldthorpe and Lockwood suspected. In any case, they themselves pointed out that instrumentalists are more likely than traditionalists to change their voting habits to suit their perceived interests – a point also made by McKenzie and Silver. The latter also pointed out that instrumentalists tend to be less attracted to Labour by socialist values than by the benefits of practical policies. If such benefits are not apparent they might decide to vote for another party (see also p.174).

Has there been a decline in the class basis of voting since 1974? Crewe versus Heath *et al.*

Ivor Crewe has argued that both party or partisan de-alignment and class de-alignment have been occurring in Britain since around the early to mid1970s. Party de-alignment refers to a tendency for fewer voters to feel attached to the Labour and Conservative parties. Class de-alignment refers to the tendency for class-based voting to decline.

The evidence in favour of party de-alignment is quite strong and is related to the rise of the Liberals, now Liberal Democrats. From the 1950s to the 1980s the third party vote increased by about fifteen per cent and the total vote for the two largest parties decreased by a similar percentage although up to and including the 1987 general election, the decrease was greater in the Labour vote. Further, party membership of both major parties decreased steadily from the 1950s. Conservative membership more than halved during that period (to 1.2 million) and Labour membership dropped five-fold (to 300,000). Similarly, party identification has weakened. In 1964, 81 per cent identified with the two main parties, 40 per cent very strongly, whereas in 1987, 67 per cent and 24 per cent were the respective figures: a substantial drop.

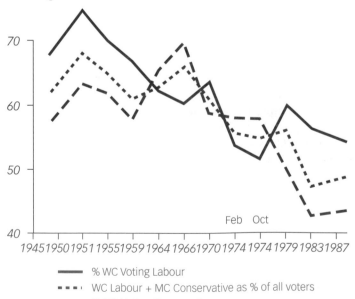

Percentage

Feb Oct

1945 1950 1951 1955 1959 1964 1966 1970 1974 1974 1979 1983 1987

—— % WC Voting Labour

---- WC Labour + MC Conservative as % of all voters

– – % MC Voting Conservative

(Source: Dearlove and Saunders, 1991:93)

Figure 11.4 Share of votes

The evidence for class de-alignment is more disputed. It is clear that in absolute terms Labour's share of the total working class vote has fallen and the Conservative's share of the total middle class vote has fallen. Figure 11.4 shows these trends very clearly.

It is particularly notable that in 1983 and 1987, the working class Labour and middle class Conservative votes added together were less than 50 per cent of all votes. This was largely due to the strength of the third party during these elections which attracted both middle and working class votes as well as the working class 'Tory' and middle class Labour votes.

Ivor Crewe argues that the 1987 election showed a politically divided middle and working class. In the election, the university educated and those working in the public sector swung away from the Conservatives compared to 1983, whereas those working in the private sector voted overwhelmingly for them in both elections (64 per cent in 1983 and 65 per cent in 1987). Crewe contends that the 'Conservatives' vote only held steady because they made further inroads into the affluent working class'. They gained 36 per cent of the manual workers' vote, the largest percentage for any post-war election. However, the gains were exclusively among the skilled manual; the Conservatives lost support slightly among semi-skilled and unskilled manual workers and substantially among the unemployed. Whereas 43 per cent of skilled manual workers voted Conservative, only 34 per cent voted Labour. Crewe noted a modest swing in the direction of class-aligned voting in 1992 but not on a scale to cause him to modify his position.

Criticism of Crewe

Heath, Jowell and Curtice (1985) oppose the view that the class basis of voting is weakening. In their analysis of the 1983 general election, they argue that the Labour vote declined among both the middle and working classes and that relatively the decline was much the same in both groups. They point out that such an overall decline is normal for the party which loses a general election. If and when the fortunes of Labour substantially revived, then a relative increase in both its working and middle class support could be anticipated. In fact, briefly in April 1990, an opinion poll taken when the Conservative government was extremely unpopular gave Labour a lead of 62 per cent to 20 per cent among skilled manual workers over the Conservatives which does suggest that trends can spectacularly change in direction.

Comment on the social class model of voting behaviour

It is common to suggest that the social class model of party identification 'works well' up to and including the 1970 general election but less well and perhaps increasingly less well after that. However, as we shall see, others do not consider that a sharp shift from 'old' to 'new' explanations of voting behaviour is justified. The class model already accommodates considerable variation from the 'norm' of voting according to social class – particularly if Parkin and Goldthorpe and Lockwood's analyses are considered as constructive amendments to it. It contains a recognition that various cross-currents of socialisation can disrupt party identification built-up through early class socialisation. Thus, deferential working class voters may be particularly strongly exposed to conservative social and economic influences, and Parkin, in any case, sees these are generally a strong counter-influence to radicalism.

Nevertheless, there was a substantial change in voting patterns from 1974, however it is interpreted. Figure 11.3 illustrates this in terms of the percentage of votes cast for the three main parties. It is to the economic and social developments that underlie this and other changes in political behaviour that we now turn.

Influences on voting behaviour other than class: regional, gender, age, ethnic and religious

A problem with discussing several of the factors other than class which may affect voting behaviour is that, on closer examination, they tend to 'dissolve' into class. This is particularly true of the geographical-spatial factor. Here we briefly examine the geographical-spatial, gender, age, ethnic and religious factors.

In recent elections up to and including that of 1987, there has been an increasing tendency for 'the South' to vote Conservative and 'the North' to vote Labour. Clearly, it is unlikely that there is

anything about the geography or climate of these regions that turn people one or other political direction! Underlying the spatial factor, then, must be something more fundamental. The deeper factor is probably the economic. The greater development of manufacturing industry in the north and service industry in the south means that the spatial distribution of classes is skewed accordingly. Further, economic expansion has favoured the 'middle class' south, whereas recession has tended to hit hardest in the 'working class' north. This appears to have had the effect of intensifying regional support for the two largest parties. In 1990, the 20 constituencies with highest unemployment were all Labour held and the 30 constituencies with the lowest unemployment were all Conservative held. The former were overwhelmingly in the north and the latter in the south. Table 11.4 gives details of the five constituencies with the highest and lowest unemployment respectively.

Support for a party in a particular region, if well established, can be cumulative. Party policy comes to reflect a region's needs, and local socialisation tends to reinforce existing political attitudes.

There used to be a greater tendency for women than men to vote Conservative but this has been reduced to negligible proportions since the 1979 election. The slightly higher percentage vote among women for the Conservatives in 1987 (see Table 11.5) is better explained by the age than the gender factor. Women tend to live longer than men and the elderly are slightly more likely than other age groups to vote Conservative. However, the age factor, too appears to be of diminishing effect. In the 1987 general election, the Conservative vote was slightly less among the under 21 than among other age groups, but even in this case ran ahead of Labour.

There is a strong tendency for members of black ethnic minorities to vote Labour. This is partly due to Labour's policies on immigration and race relations which are perceived as more sympathetic. However, again, the class factor may be the most influential one as most members of black minorities are working class. There are some signs of a slightly greater tendency to vote Conservative among upwardly mobile Asian-Britains.

It used to be said that the Church of England is 'the Tory Party at prayer'. However, with few people participating in formal prayer at all, this epigram has lost its relevance. In a secular society, religion appears less and less significant in explaining voting behaviour but as a general factor in politics there are signs of a modest revival in its importance (see pp. 534-6).

Table 11.4 Comparison of constituencies

a) Constituencies with highest unemployment

Constituency	of men	of women Percentages	Total
Liverpool Riverside (Lab)	31.7	12.2	23.4
Manchester Central (Lab)	27.6	9.2	19.9
Glasgow Provan (Lab)	25.8	10.5	19.5
Glasgow Springburn (Lab)	24.5	9.9	18.2
Birmingham Smallheath (Lab)	23.5	9.9	18.2

b) Constituencies with lowest unemployment

Constituency	of men	of women Percentages	Total
Henley (Con)	1.5	1.0	1.3
Mole Valley (Con)	1.7	0.8	1.3
Wokingham (Con)	1.6	1.1	1.4
Surrey North West (Con)	1.7	1.1	1.4
Mid-Sussex (Con)	1.8	0.9	1.4

Table 11.5 Gender and voting behaviour

	Con	Lab	Lib/SDP	Others
ALL	43.3 (–0.2)	31.5 (+3.3)	23.1 (–2.9)	2.0 (0.2)
MEN	41 (0)	33 (+3)	23 (–3)	3 (–1)
WOMEN	43 (–1)	31 (+3)	23 (–3)	3 (+1)

Note: Figures in percentages; changes since 1983 in brackets.

(Source: ITN/Harris exit poll)

The rational-choice model of voting behaviour

The rational-choice model of voting behaviour sees the voter as a thinking individual who is able to take a view on political issues and vote accordingly. It rejects the notion that voting behaviour is largely determined by class socialisation. Rather, this logic is reversed and those who vote for 'the party of their class' – a diminishing number – are regarded as doing so because it serves their interests and meets their views on particular issues.

At a theoretical level, the rational-choice model of voting behaviour neatly dovetails with Thatcherite notions of economic rationality in which rational behaviour is seen as the pursuit of self-interest in the market. Anthony Downs develops this parallel in *An Economic Theory of Democracy* (1957) in which political parties are compared to firms supplying products (policies) to individual consumers (voters). Voters do not 'belong' to parties but may change if it suits them to do so.

The main piece of empirical research reflecting the rational-choice model approach is Himmelweit *et al.* is *How voters decide* (1987). A small sample of men from the Greater London area were repeatedly interviewed between 1959-74. They found that the strongest influence on voting behaviour was the individual's own response to the issues of a particular election which, of course, change to a greater or lesser extent from election to election. Two 'weaker' influences are also observed to affect voting behaviour. These are the habit of voting for a particular party and the example of significant others. Again, the comparison with market activity is made, party loyalty being compared to brand loyalty, and the influence of spouses, friends and others on voting behaviour is compared to the influence such people may have on an individual making a purchase.

Himmelweit *et al.* recognise limits in the parallel between the economic and political:

While the analogy between purchasing a party and purchasing goods is a useful one, there are aspects which make choosing a party that much harder. In the case of voting, options are few and the policies on offer are those generated by the parties, not the voter. The timetable too is fixed by government. De facto, there are few opportunities for the ordinary voter, only moderately interested in politics, to hear the parties' claims seriously challenged, except by the other parties' counter claims. There is also no Trade Description Act to limit the claims of the parties, nor is there a consumer guide like 'Which?' to assess their realism. Relative costs and incompatibility of policies are rarely mentioned; for example, that it would be difficult to reduce government expenditure while improving the lot of the needy, health and education services, as well as provide help for the developing countries. Yet all parties claim these as their objectives.

Is it any wonder that there are wide fluctuations in the opinion polls and that the voter is particularly critical of the party for which he had voted last time or the one he tried 'for size' in the pre-election period?

(Himmelweit et al.,1987:210)

As the concluding sentence of the above extract indicates, Himmelweit *et al.* see the world of political support and voting behaviour as one of considerable and perhaps increasing flux.

Comment on the rational-choice model of voting behaviour

Two main criticisms of Himmelweit *et al.*'s research can be offered. First, the interview sample was small and unrepresentative and became more so as the research continued. Of the original sample of 600, only 178 took part in every stage of the interviews and of those who did, the large majority were upper middle or middle class. This almost certainly skewed the findings in the individualistic direction that, as it happens, coincided with the authors' bias. Second, whereas the Butler and Stokes model is structural and almost anti-individualistic, Himmelweit *et al.* make the reverse emphasis. As Dearlove and Saunders succinctly express it:

(t)his individualistic perspective on voting behaviour fails to provide an account of the origins of the political attitudes of those interviewed.

(199:101)

What, then, appears still to be needed is detailed work on the links between the political attitudes of individuals and the social background variables that must influence them.

The radical approach to voting behaviour

In *British Democracy at the Crossroads*, P Dunleavy and C Husbands argue a third and radical interpretation of voting behaviour. They regard the class-based model as outdated and insufficiently complex to explain contemporary developments and consider that the rational choice model inadequately addresses the new social structural issues that influence voting.

Dunleavy and Husbands argue that two main sources of influence structure political alignments in contemporary Britain:

1 Sectoral cleavages which separate people into groups with different interests and priorities – e.g. public sector employees; private sector employees; those dependent on public services; those dependent on the private sector. Dunleavy and Husbands particularly emphasise the importance of public/private sector cleavages which result

from the involvement of the state in production and consumption (see below).

2 Dominant ideological messages which are conveyed mainly through the media and which form 'political consciousness'. In Dunleavy and Husbands' view, consciousness is directed away from more fundamental issues of class cleavage towards more superficial but immediate issues such as the management and delivery of education or health.

The political parties compete, and people's political attitudes are formed within the context of the above two influences. Again, it needs to be emphasised that this is at the expense of the presentation, appreciation and debate of deeper class issues.

Dunleavy and Husbands present the two main aspects of their analysis as part of a total framework of explanation. It is because voters are ideologically confused about their deeper class interests and identities that they become so focused on more limited sectoral issues. However, it is their analysis of sectoral cleavages that has had the widest influence. For instance, Ivor Crewe's views on the divided middle and working class votes draws directly from data on sectoral cleavage within both classes. Both Table 11.6 and Figure 11.5 explore elements of sector cleavage in relation to the working and middle classes and in the case of the former geographical data on voting patterns is also given.

Table 11.6 shows cleavages formed in the workplace (i.e. at the point of production) and household status which is a *consumption cleavage*. It is quite clear that working class people who work or live in the private sector are more likely to vote Conservative than those who work or live in the public sector. However, it is worth noting that even in the 1987 election, the tendency for the latter groups to vote Labour was still considerably stronger than for the former groups to vote Conservative. A revival of Labour's fortunes would probably see big changes in these figures.

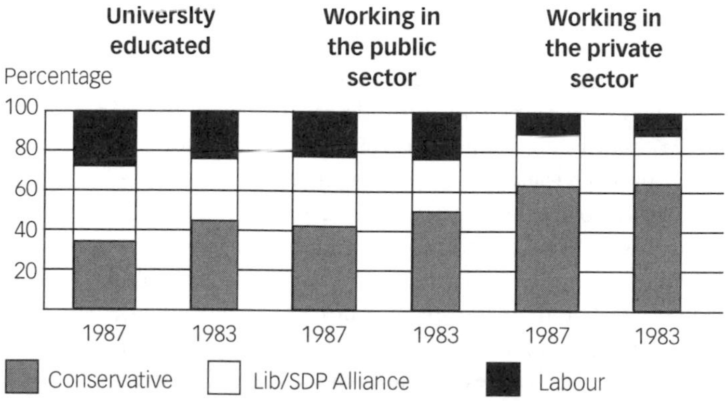

Note: The figures show the parties' shares of the three-party vote: the columns do not always add up to 100% as the figures have been rounded to the nearest whole number.

(Source: *Social Studies Review*, September 1987:5)

Figure 11.5 The new division in the middle classes (percentage)

The middle class vote in 1983 and 1987 showed a greater tendency for those working in the public than the private sector to vote Labour. Similarly, the university educated were more likely to vote Labour than the non-university educated middle class. However, there was a greater swing towards the Liberal/SDP Alliance than to Labour among both middle class public sector employees and the university educated in 1987. It may be that both other parties will benefit, if groups such as teachers and, more latterly doctors, perhaps begin to feel disenchanted with the Conservative policies towards public education and health respectively. Again, it is necessary to put these still quite short term trends in context. The Conservatives' support among the 'self-made' in the private sector slightly strengthened in 1987 to 65 per cent and even among public sector employees it was 44 per cent.

Table 11.6 The working class vote, 1987: sectoral and geographical cleavages

| Party | Geography | Consumption | Production | Production | Geography | Consumption | Production | Production |
	Lives in South	Owner Occupier	Non-union member	Works in private sector	Lives in Scotland or North	Council tenant	Union member	Works in public sector
Conservative	46	44	40	38	29	25	30	32
Labour	28	32	38	39	57	57	48	49
Lib/SDP Alliance	26	24	22	23	15	18	22	19
Conservative or Labour majority in 1987	Con +18	Con +12	Con +2	Lab +1	Lab +28	Lab +32	Lab +18	Lab +17
Conservative or Labour majority in 1983	Con +16	Con +22	Con +6	Lab +1	Lab +10	Lab +38	Lab +21	Lab +17
Category as percentage of all manual workers	40	57	66	68	37	31	34	1
Changes since 1983	+4	+3	+7	+2	−1	−4	−7	−

Note: Figures have been rounded to the nearest whole number, so totals do not always add up to 100%.

(Source:Adapted from *Social Studies Review*, Vol.3, No.1, September 1987)

Comment on the radical model of voting behaviour

Dunleavy and Husbands convincingly present what had often previously been referred to as the 'deviant' working and middle class votes in a significantly new context: that of sectoral cleavages. Their approach is likely to influence other models although it is unlikely to replace them. They themselves contend that there are deeper divisions than sectoral ones and in their view, these are class divisions – a familiar and traditional view. The aspect of their analysis which remains relatively untested and the point on which many disagree with them is that much of the working class fails to appreciate its true interests because of the strength of the dominant capitalist ideology.

A possible 'solution' to the problem of competing models of voting behaviour would be to try to construct a composite model from the three. In fact, commentators do acknowledge and use elements in each other's models. Few adopt an unreconstructed class-based model of voting but whereas some still work within such as model, others find it increasingly inadequate to explain recent voting patterns in general elections. However, although the rational-choice model has restored the importance of political issues and personalities to consideration, it is widely seen as part of, rather than the total explanation of voting behaviour. The radical model of sectoral cleavage might appear to explain the more fragmented pattern of contemporary voting but Dunleavy and Husbands themselves are residual class model theorists! Class is

Table 11.7 How Britain voted in 1992 by gender, class, housing and region

Percentage	Con	Lab	Lib Dem	Other
All voters	43	35	18	5
Men	42	37	17	5
Women	43	37	19	3
Aged 18-24	36	37	21	6
Aged 25-34	40	38	17	5
Aged 35-54	44	34	18	4
Aged 55+	45	35	17	2
AB	59	20	19	2
C1	52	24	20	5
C2	41	38	17	5
DE	29	50	17	4
Owner-occupied	53	27	18	2
Council rented	22	53	18	6
Scotland	25	39	11	24
North	38	44	16	1
Midlands	42	41	15	2
South	50	26	23	2

Figures rounded up; therefore, do not always add up to 100%.

(Source: NOP)

not out of the picture. It may be significant, however, that the Liberal Democrats seem to have survived the chaos of the centre parties in the late 1980s and again have support comparable to that of the Alliance in the mid-1980s. If the relative strength of the centre party or parties (if the Greens regain their 1989 form), is the incontrovertible new factor since the mid 1970s, then, the least that can be said is that more voters are opting out of the Conservative/Labour option than in the previous period. Whether the introduction of proportional representation in place of the present 'first past the post' system would further break the mould of traditional voting patterns is an hypothesis not yet tested.

The general election of 1992

The general election of 1992 confirmed most of the trends referred to above (see Table 11.7). Labour decisively lost the middle class vote but gained a larger percentage of the AB vote than historically. Labour failed even to reverse the fact that since 1979 more skilled manual workers (C2s) have voted for the Conservatives. The Labour vote among the partly skilled and unskilled (DEs) was strong but those groups are numerically declining and do not provide an adequate basis for electoral victory. The gender, age and regional voting trends were broadly in line with those of recent elections as was voting according to the type of housing occupied. Although the Liberal Democrats did not do as well as the Alliance in 1983 or 1987, they did well enough to suggest that third party politics and the issue of proportional representation are here to stay.

Conclusion: middle class New Labour?

Arguably, Labour did just well enough in the 1992 election to suggest that it can still win an election. Ironically – considering the long running debate about Labour and the working class vote – Labour's apparent revival under Tony Blair seemed based on an increased appeal to the middle class (*Sunday Times:* 7.4.1996:1). Official full membership figures for the two main parties were:

	Household's (£10,000+)	Earnings (£30,000 +)
Labour	57%	30%
Conservative	45%	25%

Professor Patrick Seyd commented that 'New Labour is recruiting the crucial group of young and affluent voters to its ranks'.

Opinion poll evidence – although liable to much fluctuation – gave some support for the above trend in comparison with recent general elections:

	Classes A, B, C1 vote	
	Conservative	Labour
Election 1987	54%	18%
Election 1992	54%	23%
Opinion Poll 1996 (approx)	29%	40%

The opinion poll figures are unlikely to be repeated in a general election. However, if they indicate a consistent trend, the key question on voting behaviour may be about the middle class Labour voter rather than the working class Tory!

The 1980s and 1990s: politics and policies

The 1980s were the decade of Thatcherism or the New Right. The next section seeks to understand why this was so from a sociological point of view. Several factors were at work: the economic difficulties experienced by the previous Labour government; the development of a 'New Right' solution; its presentation by an increasingly charismatic Margaret Thatcher; the declining size of Labour's traditional working class support.

Although the New Right might rise again, it is fairly clear that its period of national hegemony dating from the early 1980s is over. It is much less clear what has replaced Thatcherism. If there is an ideological content to Majorism, it lacks the substance, clarity and dynamism of Thatcherism. Arguably, John Major was elected leader of the Conservative party because he is neither Margaret Thatcher nor Michael Heseltine i.e. he was just about acceptable to the right and liberal wings of the Conservative party. In practice, Major has continued with Thatcherite policies. His various attempts to stamp his own identity on policy – such as 'back to basics' (i.e. basic values) – have not been successful.

In the absence of a convincing Tory renewal, what caught media and public attention in the early to mid 1990s was Tony Blair's attempt to define and direct New Labour. First, however, the 1980s.

The New Right: forward to the past – 1980s and 1990s

However defined, the New Right was the dominant influence in British politics during the 1980s. This is certainly true in terms of ideas and probably true in terms of policies – although in the latter case the need to compromise frequently resulted in a dilution of ideological purity. One of the big questions of domestic politics is whether the removal of Margaret Thatcher from a position of political dominance also means that the ideas she stood for will decline in influence. It may be that in the long term, 'the Thatcher revolution' will be more significant in the areas of ideas than in the precise policies introduced between 1979 and 1990.

The ideology of the new right

Ideology is used here in two senses. First, it is used simply to describe the ideas and values – roughly, the philosophy – of the New Right. Secondly, and more briefly, it is used in the specifically Marxist sense of self-interested or class-interested ideas, i.e. ideas which may be presented as fair and objective but which, on closer analysis, can be shown to reflect personal or class interests.

In Britain, for a time, the New Right became equated with 'Thatcherism' and in the United States with 'Reaganism'. However, there is an underlying body of ideas associated with the New Right which transcends the comings and goings of Margaret Thatcher and Ronald Reagan. These ideas will be described in detail in the broader context of world development/under-development (see pp. 589-91) and several practical applications of them are given in this book (see pp. 122-3 and pp. 396-401). As Dunleavy and O'Leary state, the 'core value' of the New Right is 'freedom, concerned as an argument that individuals should be free from the inappropriate coercion of others' (1979:93). For the New Right, then, freedom is virtually synonymous with radical individualism. There are economic, political and moral aspects to New Right ideology. The fundamental context in which freedom occurs is the economic market. According to both the European Hayek and the American Friedman, individuals must be allowed to buy and sell in the market. Friedman considers that this freedom is a precondition of democracy (see p. 590). Hayek particularly stresses the role of the market as a source of information about what people want, and do not want and therefore of the value of goods and services and of what should be made and provided.

Both Hayek and Friedman wish to see political power limited. They recognise that the state has certain specific functions but they also regard it as the potential enemy of economic freedom. In particular, they oppose socialist economic planning, attempts to redistribute wealth and to provide (social) services to the general public, i.e. on a universalistic basis (see pp. 394-5). Friedman describes the legitimate areas of government concern as defence, law and order, the provision of necessary public works not provided by the market and the protection of those who cannot protect themselves.

The moral aspect of New Right philosophy is largely based on the perception of economic activity as productive and useful, and attempts to control and exploit it (e.g. through taxation) as parasitical and destructive of the 'engine of wealth'. As will become clear below, many other moral overtones became attached to New Right ideology during the 1970s and 1980s.

New Right ideology has the same legitimate status as other political and social ideologies. In the1980s, it appeared to be an ideology 'whose time had come' and it remains dynamic and developing in the1990s. But whose interests does New Right ideology most represent? Undoubtedly, it is a capitalist ideology and has had great appeal to business people and the wealthy. However, New Right ideas have reached far beyond the upper class, not only to the middle but also to large sections of the working class. What has been the basis of this appeal?

The rise of the New Right

So far I have described what the New Right stands for. However, it is largely because what the New Right opposed to was in such disarray in the late1970s, that Margaret Thatcher was elected in 1979. This was true in both an immediate and longer term sense. Immediately, the Labour government of Jim Callaghan (1976-79) had become somewhat discredited. The government was partly blamed for the strike-torn 'winter of discontent' of 1978-79 and there was also a feeling that after a long period in power from 1964, broken only by the Heath administration of 1970-74, Labour was beginning to 'lose its way'. Before the 1979 election, Callaghan rather fatalistically observed what he thought was a 'sea change' in the political climate – destined to bring Margaret Thatcher to power. More profoundly, what was changing ran deeper than politics and had begun to gather momentum at least several years earlier. It was a growing reaction against the progressive and 'permissive' culture associated with the1960s. Politically, this progressive period was represented by a series of reforms including in the areas of divorce, abortion, and 'race' and gender. Culturally, it was reflected in less formal lifestyle and apparently freer sexual morality.

Thatcherism and reaction: a boundary crisis

The concept of 'boundary crisis', introduced by Durkheim, is useful in understanding the rise of Thatcherism. Margaret Thatcher was able to exploit a feeling – which she no doubt sympathised with – that 'things had gone too far'. Thatcherism was, in part, an ideology of reaction. The country could plausibly be presented as economically and socially in disarray, and, generally, in decline. Both personally and ideologically Margaret Thatcher appealed greatly to those who felt this supposed decline most – the 'respectable' middle class. To varying degrees they felt uneasy or appalled by the developments of the 1960s and1970s. To that extent, the progressive and permissive epoch had left them dispossessed. They were almost without a spokesperson – except Mrs Whitehouse who could easily be presented as a joke. 'Cometh the hour, cometh the woman'. Margaret Thatcher articulated the sentiments and won the affection of much of 'middle class' England who helped to return her to power on an unprecedented three consecutive occasions.

Tory nationalism

Thatcherism appeared to offer the hope of a return to traditional standards and even to national greatness. The economic and increasingly the political reality had been one of steady relative national decline in the post-war period. The facts suggest that

Thatcherism did not reverse this decline but for some, the illusion of national revival was created. Margaret Thatcher's style of leadership grew in confidence and robustness as the decade progressed. Her popularity soared after the Falklands war of 1982 – although in retrospect the war looks like a last venture of imperialist irrelevance (whatever its specific rights and wrongs). She became a genuinely charismatic leader, embodying the energy and enterprise she insisted the nation needed. Stuart Hall has used the term 'authoritarian populism' to describe her political style. She offered strength and direction (Hall would say, the wrong direction) to the 'masses' (her appeal to 'the nation' crossed class lines) where previously there had been a sense of muddle and drift.

The 'enemy' within

Frequently, national revivalism is associated with a tendency to locate a scapegoat or scapegoats who bear the blame for national decline. Margaret Thatcher found a number of groups 'in need' of this kind of castigation and correction. In the 1979 election she highlighted two: black immigrants and the trade unions. She referred to the former as people of 'a different culture' who might 'swamp' Britain if allowed to do so. Most of the popular press endorsed this negative attitude to black people blaming them for a variety of ills, including 'mugging', taking 'white people's' jobs, and being social security 'scroungers'. It is perhaps not surprising that a sinister backdrop to Thatcherism was a high level of racism, including brutal street violence. The trade unions were blamed (along with 'socialism' and the Labour party) for Britain's economic decline. By the end of her period as Prime Minister their powers had been greatly reduced.

The policies and values of the New Right

Although there was considerable continuity of values and objectives throughout the Thatcher governments, there were substantial developments and changes in how these were to be achieved, i.e. in policy.

The main themes in domestic policies during the first two Thatcher administrations (1979-87) were 'clearing away' the apparatus of 'socialism'; privatisation; and creating a 'vibrant', free enterprise economy (which required controlling inflation and making tax cuts). The dismantling of aspects of socialist planning such as the abolition of the Prices Commission and the National Enterprise Board (i.e. government funded, not private enterprises) and the steady trimming of union power were pushed through with little lasting objection. Nevertheless, the deep recession of the early 1980s resulted in equally deep government unpopularity from which it might never have recovered had it not been for the Falklands war. Even in the traditional mid-term dips in government electoral support of the next two administrations, such depths of unpopularity were never plumbed again.

The second Thatcher administration was the main period of

privatisation and apparently the beginning of the promised long term economic recovery. Privatisation involved selling publicly owned industries such as British Airways, British Telecom, and British Gas by inviting offers for shares both from institutions (e.g. insurance companies) and individuals. Privatisation was appreciated – at least by participants – as something of a bonanza as shares in privatised companies invariably increased substantially in value as soon as they were quoted on the stock exchange. However, the beneficiaries of privatisation were generally Conservative supporters. A shrewder move in terms of potentially gaining new support for the Conservative Party was the sale of hundreds of thousands of council housing units throughout the Thatcher years. Again, this was appreciated by those who benefited from the policy but this clearly did not include those on the waiting list for council accommodation who suffered from the diminishing stock of houses and flats. Critics of privatisation argued that public assets were being sold cheaply – 'selling-off the family silver-ware' in the words of former Conservative Prime Minister, Harold Macmillan. The reduction in public housing and the growth in homelessness became a major issue in the emerging debate about 'uncaring' Thatcherism.

Economic 'boom and bust'

Crucial to the Conservative election victory of 1987, was apparent economic recovery and growing prosperity for the majority – but not for a 'new underclass' of about twenty per cent of the population (see pp. 387-93). Economic optimism almost became euphoria following the Nigel Lawson 'give away' budget of 1988 when he reduced the top rate of income tax from 60 to 40 per cent and basic rate from 27 to 25 per cent. However, even before the 'miracle' evaporated into a 'mirage' and the second severe recession in a decade developed, the seeds of possible disaffection from Thatcherism were apparent. Indeed, in retrospect, the hard basis of support for Thatcherite values and policies may have been a good deal less than the powerful performance and unwavering confidence of the lady made it seem.

Unpopular policies?

In June 1988, *The Sunday Times* published the details of a Mori poll into the political values and opinions of the electorate. With the benefit of hindsight, the answers to the following questions are particularly revealing (see Table 11.8).

A decisive majority opposed the privatisation of electricity and water (7 and 9 above). Yet the government went ahead and privatised these industries despite clear signs that public support for such measures was beginning to fade. Responses to question 6 are perhaps the most telling of all. A two to one majority opposed the introduction of what became widely known as the poll tax. Again, Margaret Thatcher went ahead with this measure and perhaps more than anything it brought about her downfall. Significantly, whereas the privatisation measures of the previous Thatcher administrations had benefited substantial minorities and superficially appeared not directly to damage the majority, the

Table 11.8 The shape of things to come? 1988

Do you support or oppose the government adopting the following policies?

		Support	Oppose
		Percentage	
1	Giving legal protection to trade union members who refuse to join a strike, even if a majority of members have voted in favour.	64	27
2	Selling British Rail to private shareholders.	40	52
3	Withdrawing state benefit from anybody who is unemployed and refuses to take a low paid job.	39	52
4	Giving people who contribute towards private health insurance a tax allowance because they are less likely to use the NHS.	38	57
5	Replacing student grants with loans.	30	60
6	Replacing the system of domestic rates with a fixed charge paid by people in each household aged over 18 (the 'poll tax').	31	61
7	Selling the electricity industry to private shareholders.	30	63
8	Introducing a system in the National Health Service whereby people could pay extra to get treatment more quickly.	30	66
9	Selling the water authorities to private shareholders.	25	66

(Source: Mori)

policies she introduced after the 1987 election victory immediately confronted the material interests of the majority. The poll-tax was the single major domestic issue which 'broke' Margaret Thatcher. Perhaps even more important in the long run were the areas of education and health. Privatisation and even cuts in welfare directly affected only a minority, but these two public services are at the core of the welfare state and both are used by well over 90 per cent of the population. Education and health emerged as even more important issues in the post-Thatcher era but they began to loom larger on the agenda prior to her downfall.

Market mechanisms

The Conservatives wanted to bring 'the disciplines of the market' to education and health as they had done with the nationalised industries. However, there was little public support for privatising these basic public services. To have done so would have been political suicide. Aided by a battery of think-tanks and advisors, Margaret Thatcher came up with alternative solutions. The 1988

Educational Reform Act introduced a free market package of local management of schools, open enrolment and opting out – in addition to the National Curriculum (see p. 128-30). For health, the market mechanism was to allow General Practitioners to opt out and administer their own budgets, and to allow hospitals to opt out and to sell their services to the highest bidders (among GPs) (see pp. 437-9). In both cases, the main criticism has been that a two tier system will be created. In education, opted out schools have been presented as likely havens of privilege – generously funded by central government – whereas schools remaining within local authorities are seen as likely to have to educate the less privileged with less funds. In health, the two tiers are seen as created by the ability of GPs with budgets to bid ahead and, therefore, jump the queue in front of GPs without their own budgets whose patients are then disadvantaged and whose health may suffer.

'Proceed with caution …

The Thatcher agenda developed in such a way that the simpler and more popular measures were introduced early or relatively so in her period of office and the more difficult and controversial measures came later. It was in these deeper, choppier waters that she floundered. The determination and confrontationalism that had apparently helped to carry her policies through before 1987, rebounded against her later. The headline in the 1988 *Sunday Times* piece referred to above was perceptive: 'So far so good, but now proceed with caution'. Caution was not Margaret Thatcher's way and she paid the price. With the additional problem of an emerging second recession, the three-time winner began to look like a probable fourth-time loser, and she was unceremoniously ditched by her leading party colleagues.

The Thatcher legacy?

Many of the key issues for Britain in the 1990s have been posed by Margaret Thatcher even if she herself will not personally resolve them. Will education and health be primarily concerned with equality of public access or will they be 'driven' by competitive internal markets? Will there be a return to greater planning and partnership in industrial policy, perhaps involving some participation by the trade unions as well as more formal consultation between government and industrial leaders? In foreign policy, will a 'little England' nationalism prevail or will a mood of internationalism embracing Europe and the 'new' emerging world prevail?

Tony Blair or John Major or another may seek other answers to these questions than would Margaret Thatcher, but in fairness, their answers are likely to be different simply because of the fact that Margaret Thatcher was around.

The sociology of Thatcherism

The above analysis of the New Right, particularly in its Thatcherite version, weaves sociological concepts into a broad historical backcloth. Here, we stand back somewhat and examine what light the larger theoretical perspective of sociology throws onto Thatcherism and vice versa.

The 'Thatcher phenomenon' raises interesting problems in relation to personality and social structure. Was Thatcherism a product of circumstances or a product of Margaret Thatcher? Or, put another way, was the reaction against the 1960s and 1970s so 'inevitable' that someone else would have played the role Margaret Thatcher played, if she had not played it – as, indeed, Ronald Reagan played a similar role in the United States. Was the stage set and the script written so that who played the main part was almost incidental?

The above view is a deterministic one – that 'events are in the saddle and ride humankind'. Max Weber's concept of 'congruence' offers a more qualified alternative analysis. He suggests that sometimes circumstances are 'ripe for' or 'congruent with' particular ideas (and ideologies). By 1979, British social democracy had, for the time being, completed its agenda and had become associated with certain problems, such as industrial unrest, welfare bureaucracy and even, in a vague way, cultural permissiveness. Margaret Thatcher offered an alternative to social democracy and an antidote to some of the problems for which it was blamed. However, there is no basis for seeing the details of her policies as pre-determined. In fact, some of these seemed rather improvised.

Marxists frequently explain Thatcherism in terms of a structural crisis of capitalism. With the support of capitalists, Margaret Thatcher attempted to restore conditions of greater profitability for the capitalist system. In this perspective, she and her ideology are seen more as symptoms than causes of the revival of capitalism that occurred during her period of office. Thus, she is seen as part of a wider capitalistic movement rather than as a uniquely innovative individual.

In the end, Margaret Thatcher perhaps did overestimate her own uniqueness and power. Circumstances had moved against her and she had changed circumstances rather less than she thought. Certain charismatic leaders develop an almost symbiotic relationship with their 'times' and with 'the people' but if they lose their 'touch', the fall from grace can be swift and complete.

Question

What explanations can you offer for the electoral failure of the Labour party between 1979 and 1992?

The big issues in the 1990s: what is the British nation?

The policy positions of the two main parties and, to a lesser extent, those of the Liberal Democrats have been dealt with in the appropriate sections of this book. Crucial areas of debate are:

1 Job Security: Employment/Unemployment (see pp. 252-62 and pp. 387-93).
2 Social Welfare (see pp. 393-407)
3 Education (see pp. 100-33)

In these and other areas, there are significant differences as well as some similarities between the positions of the parties.

However, government policies in the above area – crucial as they are – may fall short of radically shifting the country's pattern of development. What is already a big issue and may be the big issue of the late 1990s is the idea and meaning of 'nation' itself.

Nation, royals and constitution

One of the sub-themes of this book is that ideas can contribute to social change. The ideology covered by such terms as Thatcherism, New Right perspective and free market liberalism had enormous impact in the 1980s. This impact has been worldwide and continues to reverberate. In Britain, however, the thrust of market reform seems to be weakening. Much market reform has now been implemented and it is not easy to keep coming up with fresh applications. Positive effects for the market reforms can be claimed but they also seem to have had negative, perhaps unintended consequences; and, finally, there is the long-delayed but threatening swing of the political pendulum.

It may well be that after two economic recessions and one boom during the 1980s and early 1990s, many people want security. However, security is a need or desire, not an idea. Labour's 'stakeholder' idea is designed partly to meet the desire for greater security. In addition, it is an idea which resonates with belonging and with social solidarity, rather than with competitive individualism of Thatcherism. Yet, this idea will only take root in the popular imagination if it comes to mean something practical – such as a minimum standard of living or a better pension. Only time will tell on that score.

Surprisingly, perhaps, what promises to be the big idea in the second half of the 1990s is, again, a revived one and, again, it is most vociferously sponsored by the political Right. It is the idea of 'nation'.

The British nation

Despite or perhaps even because of peoples' awareness of larger frames of reference such as Europe and 'the globe', the 'nation' remains for many a valued source of identity. A good illustration of a nationalism occurred during the 1997 'mad cow disease' episode which gradually shifted in the media and public consciousness from being primarily a health issue to one of 'them (Europeans) versus us'. The image of members of the British beef industry sporting placards bearing the slogan 'British Beef is Best' shows how compelling chauvinistic sentiment can be in the face of dauntingly contradictory evidence.

The importance of national identity is such that no political party can afford to present itself as less than fully patriotic and wholly committed to national welfare. In 1997, the leaders of both the Conservative and Labour parties claimed that theirs was the party of 'one nation'. Conceivably, both could be right although each was implying that the other was wrong. For Major, Labour has sold out to Europe and is irresponsible towards Britain's national interests. For Blair, the Conservatives are a party of sectional rather than national interest, incapable of uniting the nation for the common good.

Yet, for all the attempts by the party leaders to claim the national high ground, it is Conservative Eurosceptics such as Norman Tebbitt and Kenneth Baker who have most persistently 'played the national card'.

Different parties and groups, then, interpret the concept of a nation to fit their own ideology and interest. Does that mean there is no such 'thing' or, better, referent (point of reference) as 'the nation'?

Let us examine a definition of national identity by an author who is strongly supportive of the concept and who considers that a shared sense of a national identity can provide the basis for building other identities and relationships (for a more critical view see pp. 238-44). David Miller's *On Nationality* (1995) provides a summary-definition of what he considers to be the five key elements of national identity. My explanations (in brackets) on quotes from Miller. National identity is based on:

'(A) community is

1	constituted by shared belief and mutual commitment	(members accept each other as belonging to the same nation)
2	extended in history	(the existence of the nation 'stretches backwards into the past')
3	active in character	(are communities that do things together, take decisions, achieve results ...)
4	connected to a particular territory, and	(it (national identity) connects a group of people to a particular geographical place)
5	marked off from other communities by a distinct public culture.'	(a set of understandings about how a group of people is to conduct its life together).

Miller concludes that the above five elements 'serve to distinguish nationality from other collective sources of personal identity' (27).

As in the case of Bauman's general discussion of community, (see pp. 150-3) and Cohen's discussion of specifically national community (see pp. 240-2), Miller stresses that national identity is defined to exclude as well as include. With Cohen, the enquiry, is rather on the exclusion – on boundaries or 'frontiers' – whereas Miller emphasises what is held in common.

In summary, Miller is stating that national identity is shared by those who accept each other as belonging to the same community (1), which has a past (2), who interact (3), in a given place (4), and have in common a distinct public culture (5).

Elements 1 to 4 are as close to matters of uncontroversial fact as one can get and are acknowledged as aspects of national identity in other relevant literature. This moves us a good way to defining what nations are but it does not deal with the issue of a 'distinct public culture' (5). As Miller states: 'It is not so easy ... to pin down precisely what this entails'. This is true. What Miller is clear about is that a distinct public culture need not exclude various 'races' and subcultures. In the end, Miller seems to accept a relative definition of the public culture as that broadly accepted by a given national community at a given time. In doing so, he again, confirms what is now established thinking on national identity i.e. it does not have an essential content but is socially constructed by those who adhere to it:

> *National identities are not cast in stone ... they are above all 'imagined' identities, where the content of the imagining changes with time. So although at any moment there will be something substantial that we call our national identity, and we will acknowledge customs and institutions that correspond to this, there is no good reason to regard this as authoritative in the sense that excludes critical assessment.*
>
> *(127)*

He goes on to refer to 'common membership in a nation where the meaning of membership changes with time'. (127) In practice, therefore, Miller's concept of a 'distinct public culture' virtually dissolves into nothing more substantial or permanent than the shifting and constantly debated ideas of nation as presented by Giddens (see p. 41) and Hall and Cohen (see pp. 238-44).

(Source: *The Guardian*, 10.10.1995:25)

Figure 11.6 Whose nation? How would *you* express *your* nationalism/patriotism, if at all?

Britain in the 1990s. A question of identity?

What insight do the above considerations provide in understanding British national identity in the 1990s? Miller makes a general observation which is helpful on the 'not so easy' issue of Britain's 'distinct public culture'. He argues that *modern* nationality and democracy *are* part of the same movement of liberation. The modern nation provides a framework in which democratic rights can be established and protected. Thus, modern democracy is a liberal ideal. Crucially, then, Britain's public culture is that of a liberal democracy. Even this, however, is not uniquely distinctive. First, there are other liberal democracies. Second, there have been and still are in Britain those who challenge liberal democracy, notably Fascists of one kind or another.

Beyond a wide acceptance of liberal democracy, it is very difficult to find what Miller refers to as 'something substantial that we call our national identity'. It can no longer be found in support for the monarchy (still less the national football or cricket teams!). 'English' ('British'?) literature and music and also religious values are all contested areas. Perhaps, we are in a period, of the kind to which Miller refers, when national identity is changing. In any case, as Hall and Cohen more clearly state, the meanings of national identity are always a matter of interpretation. One person's national symbol is another's symbol of subordination and division. Even the union jack itself does not mean the same to a Cornish separatist at to, say, Tory Eurosceptic MP, Teresa Gorman.

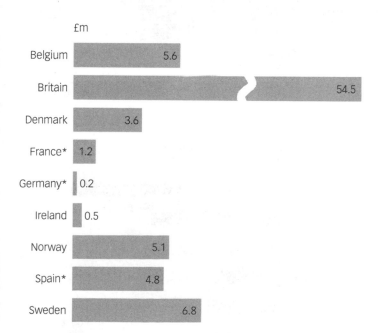

£m

Belgium	5.6
Britain	54.5
Denmark	3.6
France*	1.2
Germany*	0.2
Ireland	0.5
Norway	5.1
Spain*	4.8
Sweden	6.8

*Excludes some costs

(Source: *The Economist* reprinted in *The Guardian*, 10.1.1995:G2)

Figure 11.7 European heads of state public subsidy 1993

Interpretation of national identity: a conservative nation?

It is arguable that Britain is a relatively conservative nation in that much of its feudal past still remains of significance. For instance, the British monarch is much higher profile and receives a vastly larger state public subsidy (see Figure 11.7) than any other European head of state.

Such wealth and status is no longer justified as in feudal times as a matter of right – although it remains hereditary. Instead, the present Queen has dedicated herself to the 'service' of the people of Britain and the Commonwealth. Although 'service' itself can be seen as a traditional concept, it can also be presented in modern terms as work for money invested (see Figure 11.7).

The wider royal family and, therefore, the institution of monarchy itself has run into trouble partly because some of its members have appeared to take public money and offer little in return at a time of some hardship for many citizens. More importantly, perhaps, the young adult generation has forfeited the mystique of monarchy. This is partly because the media now reports matters that even a generation ago it tended discreetly to ignore.

As a result of these developments, republicanism has become a much more popular, albeit still a minority option in Britain. At a

THE SUBJECT	THE CITIZEN
Someone in chains	Men and women marching
Crouching in the dark	Invariably handsome and fit
Old-fashioned fop	Staring straight ahead
Doffing his feathered cap	Incredibly big pectorals
Uriah Heep	A bit frightening
Ever so 'umble	But proud
Sweating and	Always bathed in light
Unctious	With very piercing eyes

Source: *The Guardian*, 10.1.1995:7; Words by Sue Townsend; Cartoons by Martin Rowson)

Figure 11.8 An idealised contrast: subject and citizen

time when both left and right stress individual achievement, ascribed status seems an anachronism to some. A television poll of 1997 voted 66 to 34 per cent in favour of retaining the monarchy – a big majority but probably one shifting away from supporting the monarchy in recent years.

The House of Lords is also an institution with roots in the distant past. Hereditary peerages are a feudal institution. Even life peers are the product of party – mainly prime ministerial – patronage, although some are appointed on the basis of public service. In other words, the House of Lords is an updated feudal rather than a democratic institution. The case in nearly all other democracies is that the second chamber is elected on some basis. Further, the power and influence of the aristocracy in business, agriculture, the voluntary sector, and social life persists more than is often appreciated. Although the aristocracy has been challenged by new wealth it often, shrewdly, allies with it (see pp. 379–80).

What is the effect of this feudal network – partly strengthened by new blood – on British citizens in general. Despite the robustness of the British working class movement, it is arguable that the persistently traditional and hierarchical nature of British society has fostered attitudes of deference and conformity and slowed the achievement of full citizens' rights by the majority (Figure 11.8). Bryan Turner contrasts the early history of British citizenship with that of French and American (1990). In the latter case, citizenship was achieved by popular movements from 'below' and the people established themselves as the 'sovereign' body of the nation. In contrast:

> (T)he constitutional settlement of 1688 created the British citizen as the British subject, that is a legal personality where indelible social rights are constituted by a monarch sitting in parliament. The notion of citizen-as-subject indicates clearly the relatively extensive notion of social rights also the passive character of British constitutions. The defeat of absolutism in the settlement of 1688 left behind a core of institutions (the Crown, the Church, the House of Lords and traditional attitudes about the family and private life) which continued to dominate British life …

Turner implies that in comparative terms, the development of British citizenship may not be complete. The people are not even sovereign in their own country but, in law and partly in fact, are ruled by a set of institutions redolent of another age.

The Conservative party and nation

For reasons already previously discussed the British or, at least, the English have tended to be ambivalent towards the European Community. This ambivalence runs across the two main parties although the leadership and apparently a majority of MPs in both parties still support European membership.

In these circumstances the Eurosceptic wing of the Conservative party – those who oppose or who have grave reservations about British membership of the Community – have raised the banner of nationalism in their cause. In part, their nationalism seems simply

(a) Attitudes to EU membership (1994)

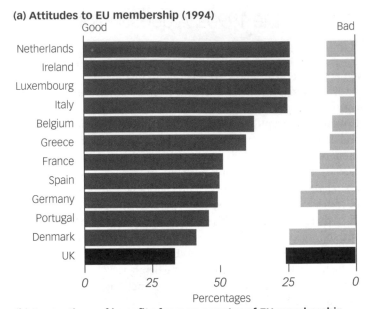

(b) Perceptions of benefits for own country of EU membership (1994)

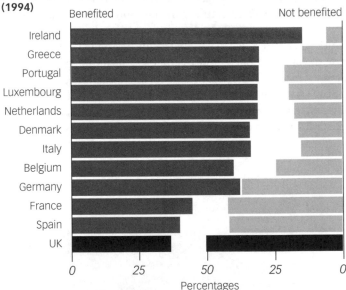

(c) Support for EU policies and institutions (EU average and UK, % in favour 1994)

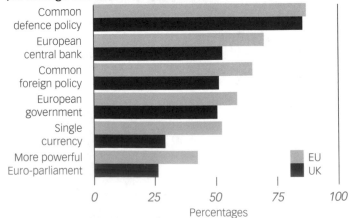

(Source: Eurobarometer, Eurostat reprinted in *The Financial Times*, 30.10.1995:9)

Figure 11.9 How UK compares

to be in the tradition of right-wing chauvinism that reached its height at the time of Empire. Accordingly, virtually any Community policy that can be interpreted as diminishing British sovereignty is anathema. Moves to European inter-governmental co-operation on defence, towards a single European currency, and towards a (qualified) majority system of voting on the European Commission are all opposed by the Eurosceptics.

The above kind of 'gut nationalism' was expressed by Michael Portillo at the Conservative Party Conference in 1995. Among other nationalistic utterances he remarked apparently, in response to a European Court finding against the SAS:

> *Around the world three letters send a chill down the spine of the enemy: SAS. And those letters spell out one clear message: don't mess with Britain.*
>
> *(The Independent, 11.10.1995:1)*

The President of the European Commission was officially said to have found the barrage of anti-European sentiment expressed at the conference 'deplorable' and 'grotesque'.

Nationalism is a powerful ideology in itself but it can also serve as a cover to quite concrete interests. Conservative opposition to the Social Chapter, including the minimum wage, is sometimes presented as being in the national interest but would equally be seen as in the interest of low paying businesses and against that of low paid workers. Similarly, the government's poor record at the European Court of Justice could perhaps be seen as frustrating national political and judicial independence but equally it could be interpreted as a clash between authoritarian and liberal values.

It should not be assumed that the Eurosceptic view is without substantial support in Britain, especially England. The opposite may well be true. The extent to which Britain is conservative and traditionalist has already been emphasised. In 1995, the Policy Studies Institute published a report, *The Future of Britain in Europe* (1995), which described Britain as the least enthusiastic member of the Community and as prone to 'chauvinism and nostalgia for the glories of the past'. Britain comes bottom or nearer the bottom on a wide range of measures of enthusiasm and commitment to Europe. The three charts of Figure 11.9 illustrate this.

The report does not assume that all moves to European integration and centralisation are necessarily a good thing and argues that national and local autonomy will be preferable in some areas. However, it warns that outside of Europe, Britain may struggle to find a dynamic identity.

The left: citizenship, constitution and nation

Whereas it is possible to review the Conservative party's record in government on 'national' issues, the Labour party has been for long confined merely to statements. These change. What follows is a discussion of views expressed on the Left in and around the Labour and Liberal Democrat Parties.

Ideas of nation of the Left are predictably more egalitarian than those of the Right. Membership of the European Community is seen as a way of making Britain a fairer society rather than as a threat to nationality. Europe also provides examples of constitutional reform.

There is substantial support for constitutional reform and a Bill of Rights on the Left. Abolishing the House of Lords and replacing it with an elected chamber is seen as a modernising as well as a democratic measure. Support for a republic is more muted in the Labour party, particularly because the party leader appears to oppose the idea. Nevertheless, the possibility of a republic has been put on the agenda mainly as a result of media discussion. In early 1996, *The Independent* came out in favour of a republic and *The Guardian* ran a series of articles on the issue – most of them supportive of republicanism. Sue Townsend, the author of the popular satire, *The Queen and I*, argues that a republic would push people towards responsible and aware citizenship rather than passively leaving matters to 'them'.

> *People accept their lot … But we cannot afford to put our trust in bodies that, if not actively corrupt, are outmoded or self-serving.*
>
> *A republican constitution would have the virtue of opening doors that will allow us to know our rights …*
>
> *(The Guardian, 10.1.1995:G97)*

A republic would certainly require a Bill of Rights. Regardless of republicanism, there is considerable support for a Bill of Rights, notably the Charter 88 group which was founded for that purpose. Britain has never had a written constitution but there is a disparate body of legislation which collectively secures a wide range of rights generally considered fundamental to modern citizenship. However, the Charter 88 group argues that these rights are not always clear or complete and that, in the absence of a Bill of Rights, they can more easily be curtailed. The Criminal Justice Act which limits the right to public protest is cited as an example of curtailment. A first step towards a written constitution might be the incorporation of the European Convention of Human Rights into British law. This would enable British citizens who wanted to make a human rights case to do so within the British Courts rather than have to go to the European Court of Justice.

Civic nationalism

A D Smith (1991) and Michael Ignatieff (1994) have used the term 'civil nationalism' to describe the egalitarian, multicultural commitment to common citizenship described in the previous section. Nation defined in terms of common rights cuts out unresolvable debates about what the 'true', 'essential' historical and cultural nature of the nation is. As Ignatieff points out in his evocatively titled *Blood and Belonging* insistence on the 'right' definition (one's own) of nation can lead from debate, to argument, to bloodshed. A Bill of Rights does not end debate but it does channel it into the courts and frames it in terms of the people versus the government (should the latter contravene rights) rather than the people versus the people.

David Miller considers that civil nationalism and the constitutional patriotism he associates with it is too abstract and ahistorical a basis for national identity:

> *In particular, it does not explain why the boundaries of the political community should fall here rather than there; nor does it give you any sense of the historical identity of the community...*
>
> *(163)*

Two points can be made in reply to Miller. First, he is right that the human rights which are likely to be the basis of any national Bill of Rights are extendible beyond nation to Europe and to the world. However, this is seen by supporters of a Bill of Rights as a strength. Second, he is also right that civic nationalism removes the issue of national citizenship from historical debate. Again, though, this is intentional. British history is viewed by the Left as not simply a matter for polite debate. It has formed the unequal society or 'community' and the only partially democratic political system of today. It is these inequalities that the Left seek to change and so they can hardly form the basis of nationalism. Miller himself notes that:

> *At the core of conservative nationalism stands the idea that national identity integrally involves allegiance to authority. To think of oneself as British is ipso facto to acknowledge the authority of institutions such as the monarchy which form the substance of national life.*
>
> *(124)*

While Miller himself rejects conservative nationalism, he perhaps does not fully acknowledge that any nationalism based on historical interpretation is likely to divide rather than unite. In contrast, the approach to a nationality of the Left puts more emphasis on constitutional rights and government observance of them. In Will Hutton's view 'Notions of community, of membership, of belonging and of participation are established here or not at all' (*The State We're in*, 1995:186).

My country and the world

David Miller argues that like family, peer group, or locality, the nation is an established and often fruitful basis of identity. He links modern nationalism with the rise of liberal democracy and democratic citizenship in the West but does not want what he sees as distinct national public cultures dissolved into a wider internationalism. On the other hand, the nationalism of the Left, including civil nationalism, clearly does have one foot in the wider world – European and global. Perhaps this is with good reason. There are still parts of the world where material survival as well as human rights are not established. In this global perspective,

nationalism takes a smaller place. Bryan Turner comments that in the contemporary world 'there is a stronger notion of globalism and global political responsibilities. The concept of citizenship is therefore still in a process of change and development. We do not possess the conceptual apparatus to express the idea of global membership.' (1990:211)

Questions

1 Compare and contrast Robin Cohen's (see pp. 238-44) and David Miller's perspectives on British nationality.
2 To what extent do you consider that the rights of citzenship rather than a shared national culture are the basis of membership of the British nation?

Summary

1 A distinction must be made between power and authority. Power is the ability to achieve one's own will. Authority is legitimate power. Weber considered that liberal democracies exercise legitimate power on a rational-legal basis but Marx challenged the legitimacy of liberal democracy arguing that, in reality, capitalists 'rule'.
2 The liberal model of democratic society argues that in a liberal society, the state is, and should be answerable to the people who organise mainly through political parties and pressure groups. Liberal theorists state that democratic political elites are representative of the people and are ultimately accountable to them at general elections.
3 Marx considered that in liberal capitalist democracies, the capitalist class rules, not the people (the majority of whom are working class). There is a debate within Marxism between Miliband and Poulantzas about how capitalist power is exercised. Miliband argues that class power operates partly through personal contact and shared experience among capitalists, whereas Poulantzas contends that the institutional structure of capitalism would function in favour of the capitalist system whoever 'operates' it.
4 Elite theorists offer another model of modern government. Elites may be either representative (democratic) or unrepresentative (undemocratic). C Wright Mills argued that the United States is ruled by a power elite made up of three subsidiary elites – the military, business, and political. Representative democracy functions at a level of power below that of the power elite.
5 Social movements operate outside of the mainstream of British politics but can have an effect on it. 'Old' and new social movements (NSMs) are discussed and criticised.
6 There are three main models of voting behaviour:
   i   The party identification and social class model.
   ii The rational-choice model.
   iii The radical model.

7 The party identification and social class model argues that both historically and in contemporary Britain, the main factor explaining voting behaviour is social class. The mechanism through which this occurs is class socialisation. 'Conformist' voters are considered to be those who vote according to their class and 'deviant' voters are those who do not.

8 The rational-choice model argues that people vote mainly on the basis of self-interest in relation to the issues presented to them by the political parties. The notion of the voter as 'consumer' has a parallel in free market economics.

9 The radical model argues that sectoral cleavages (e.g. whether people work in or consume in mainly the private or public sector) explain some major trends in contemporary voting behaviour. These distract people from the deeper cleavages of class which still remain.

10 New Right ideology is founded on the view that the free market provides a basis for freedom in other aspects of life. The New Right has never satisfactorily dealt with the inequalities that the free market also creates. It was this ideology which characterised 'Thatcherism'.

11 National identity is emerging as one of the big issues of the 1990s. Various interpretations of national identity are discussed and put in historical context.

Research and coursework

It is unlikely that a project focusing on national politics could involve much original research. What this topic does provide is the opportunity to address some interesting issues relating to the theory and practice of political power. What is the evidence for the Marxist view that Britain is (still) governed by a 'ruling class'? Or is Mills' power elite theory applicable to Britain as he attempted to apply it to the United States? A demanding area of enquiry would be the role that ideology played in the rise and 'reign' of Thatcherism – does a detailed examination of the history of 'the Thatcher decade' tend to support the view that her success depended on the appeal of her ideas? An examination of these quite theoretical areas would require a careful review of the relevant literature and perhaps analysing press and/or periodicals.

A more concrete topic would be to examine the functioning and effect of a pressure group. National pressure groups such as 'Friends of the Earth' have regional offices and/or representatives which provide the opportunity for interviews and material.

Further reading

A demanding but useful book is Ralph Miliband's *Divided Societies Class Struggle in Contemporary Capitalism* (Oxford Paperbacks, 1991). For 'A' level, Mark Kirkby's *Investigating Political Sociology* (Collins Educational, 1995) fills a gap.

Readings

Reading 1
Mills' criticism of the concept of ruling class

From Charles Wright Mills, *The Power Elite* (Oxford University Press, 1956), p.277.

'Ruling class' is a badly loaded phrase. 'Class' is an economic term; 'rule' a political one. The phrase, 'ruling class', thus contains the theory that an economic class rules politically. That short-cut theory may or may not at times be true, but we do not want to carry that one rather simple theory about in the terms that we use to define our problems; we wish to state the theories explicitly, using terms of more precise and unilateral meaning. Specifically, the phrase 'ruling class', in its common political connotations, does not allow enough autonomy to the political order and its agents, and it says nothing about the military as such. It should be clear to the reader by now that we do not accept as adequate the simple view that high economic men unilaterally make all decisions of National consequence. We hold that such a simple view of 'economic determinism' must be elaborated by 'political determinism' and 'military determinism' that the higher agents of each of these three domains now often have a noticeable degree of autonomy; and that only in the often intricate ways of coalition do they make up and carry through the most important decisions. Those are the major reasons we prefer 'power elite' to 'ruling class' as a characterising phrase for the higher circles when we consider them in terms of power.

Questions

1 What is Mills' criticism of the term 'ruling class'? Do you agree with it? Say why or why not.
2 (Read pp. 312-6 as well as the above passage). Do you consider that Mills' power elite analysis to be applicable to contemporary Britain? If not what model of power do you consider best applies? Justify your selection.

Reading 2
The characteristics of social movements

From John Dean, Introduction to Alberto Melucci, *Nomads of the Present. Social Movements and Individual Needs in Contemporary Society* (Hutchinson Radius, 1989), pp.5-6.

While Melucci is uncomfortable with the term 'new social movements', he parts company with most other contemporary commentators by specifying at least four unique features of today's movements.

First, unlike their nineteenth-century counterparts, contemporary social movements are not preoccupied with struggles over the production and distribution of material goods and resources. They challenge the administrative logic of complex systems primarily on symbolic grounds. Today's movements are more concerned with the ways in which complex societies generate information and communicate meanings to their members. This emphasis on the central role of information extends from demands for the right of citizens' access to 'factual information' (such as missile testing plans and the extent of ecological damage caused by industrial spills) to debates over symbolic resources, such as the challenge of the women's movement to sexist advertising.

Second, the constituent organisations of today's movements consider themselves more than instrumental for attaining political and social goals. Actors' participation within movements is no longer a means to an end. Drawing upon Marshall McLuhan, Melucci argues that the very forms of the movements – their patterns of interpersonal relationships and decision-making mechanisms – operate as a 'sign' or 'message' for the rest of society. The organisations of the women's movement, for instance, not only raise important questions about equality and rights. They also, at the same time, deliberately signal to the rest of society the importance of recognising differences within complex societies. Participation within movements is considered a goal in itself because, paradoxically, actors self-consciously practise in the present the future social changes they seek. Collective actors are 'nomads of the present'. They are no longer driven by an all-embracing vision of some future order. They focus on the present, and consequently their goals are temporary and replaceable, and their organisational means are valued as ends in themselves.

Third, present-day social movements also rely on a new relationship between the latent and visible dimensions of their collective action. Social movements normally consist – here Melucci's work is at its most original – of 'invisible' networks of small groups submerged in everyday life. These 'submerged' networks, noted for their stress on individual needs, collective identity and part-time membership, constitute the laboratories in which new experiences are invented. Within these invisible laboratories, movements question and challenge the dominant codes of everyday life. These laboratories are places in which the elements of everyday life are mixed, developed and tested, a site in which reality is given new names and citizens can develop alternative experiences of time, space and interpersonal relations. For Melucci there is a complementarity between these 'private', submerged networks and their publicly visible dimension. Movements appear relatively infrequently as publicly visible phenomena – for instance, during public demonstrations in favour of abortion or against nuclear power – and yet their involvement in observable political action is only temporary. Movements are only part-time participants in the public domain, precisely because they practise new forms of everyday life.

Finally, contemporary movements are acutely aware of the planetary dimension of life in complex societies. Their emphasis upon the interdependence of the world system helps stimulate a new consciousness of ourselves as members of a human species which is situated in a natural environment. Melucci places considerable emphasis on the peace and ecological movements, precisely because they are testaments to the fragile and potentially self-destructive connections between humanity and the wider universe. These movements publicise the fact that local events have global ramifications – that nuclear war would bring with it the end of civilisation, and that every Chernobyl and chemical spill ultimately affects all individuals and their environment.

Throughout this book, Melucci's reconsideration of social movements is twinned with a deep concern about individual needs and experiences. His interest in the 'subterranean' dimensions of contemporary social life provides a succinct account of changing patterns of individual experience in such matters as time and space, birth and death, health and illness, sexuality and our relations with natural environment.

Questions

1 In what ways and to what extent would you say social movements differ from mainstream politics?
2 Summarise the strengths and weaknesses of social movements.

Deviance and Difference

The changing face of crime in the late twentieth century: Nick Leeson and Ernest Saunders

Aims of this chapter

1 To adapt a critical approach to criminal statistics and how they are constructed.

2 To analyse the various perspectives on social order, control and deviance, including their different and complementary aspects.

3 To appreciate the sociology of suicide as an example of

sociological theory and method.

4 To analyse and explain how corporate and white-collar crime differs in its construction and characteristics from other types of crime.

5 To explain how theoretical approaches to deviancy, crime and 'reform' are changing from the modern to the 'late' modern era.

Introduction

This chapter begins by considering issues concerning the data on which theories of deviance are based, particularly in relation to official criminal statistics. Problems concerning official statistics and class, gender, 'race' and age are considered.

There follows a major theoretical section on social order, control and deviance. In the recently published book, *The Problem of Crime* (1996), the editors John Muncie and Eugene McLaughlin stress that those who define and control social order i.e. make the rules, determine what is deviant more than those who are regarded as deviant. The following quotation from them on crime could equally apply to deviance as a whole:

> *Asking how ... social order is structured, and how its economic moral and political interests are protected, will tell us more about what constitutes 'crime' than any sample examination of the characteristics of 'known offenders'.*
>
> *(4).*

Thus, this chapter discusses 'deviance' in relation to social order, power and control. Of the theories discussed in this chapter only functionalism and Marxism and to a lesser extent interactionism offer developed theories of order and control as well as of deviance. However, other theories of deviance are also presented. In particular, an analysis is made of Colin Sumner's view that the concept of deviance is now dead and that the focus should be on why some forms of *difference* are *socially censured* whereas others are not. The chapter also includes a discussion of suicide – a topic which raises again some of the problems in relation to official statistics and sociological theory and method analysed in the first section of this chapter.

Official statistics and their limitations

The data on crime and suicide given in official statistics represent only one measure. The most widely used measure of crime is based on crimes known to the police and officially recorded. Similarly, the official measure of suicide is based on verdicts of coroners. The

analyses of criminal and suicide statistics in this chapter raise important questions about how these are compiled as well as key issues of sociological theory and method.

Table 12.1 gives the number of notifiable offences recorded by the police for the years 1981 and 1994 for England and Wales, Scotland, and Northern Ireland respectively. There are minor differences in the way the statistics were compiled in the three areas. The trend in all categories in England and Wales is up – in most cases sharply. Burglary was down in both Scotland and Northern Ireland and some other categories also saw reductions for the latter country.

Figure 12.1 shows the trend in a number of criminal offences in England and Wales for 1993-95 (reported, 1994-96). It is included because of an apparently significant downward trend in most categories although the sharp rise in theft from the person and robbery continue to cause much public concern. Predictably, the Home Secretary claimed that the government's tough strategy in

Table 12.1 Notifiable offences recorded by the police: by type of offence

	England & Wales		Scotland		Northern Ireland	
	1981	1995	1981	1995	1981	1995
	Thousands					
Theft and handling stolen goods, of which:	1,603	2,452	201	222	25	33
Theft of vehicles	333	508	33	38	5	8
Theft from vehicles	380	813		71	7	7
Burglary	718	1,239	96	74	20	16
Fraud and forgery	107	133	21	22	3	5
Violence against the person	100	213	8	16	3	5
Criminal damage	387	914	62	87	5	4
Robbery	20	68	4	5	3	2
Sexual offences,	19	30	2	3		2
of which: rape	1	5		1		
Drug trafficking		21	2	8		
Other notifiable offences	9	29	12	65	3	2
All notifiable offences	2,964	5,100	408	503	62	69

Notifiable offences recorded by the police: by type of offence, 1981 and 1994

(Source: *Social Trends*, 1997)

relation to crime was having an effect. However, other factors are likely to have been at work. First, crime and the economy are now known to be related (see p. 359) and emergence from recession probably contributed to the reduction. A relatively smaller generation of teenagers – the age group relatively most responsible for crime – and the fact that more had continued in education were probably also relevant factors. According to the British Crime Survey (BCS), the recent apparent drop in the crime rate is due to a greater tendency among the police not to record certain behaviours as crime. Ian Burrell and David Leppard give some interesting examples below:

> *Fall in crime a myth as police chiefs massage the figures.*
>
> *The government's much heralded fall in crime is a myth. Hundreds of thousands of serious crimes have been quietly dropped from police records as senior officers massage their statistics to meet new Home Office efficiency targets. Crime experts say that at least 220,000 crimes, including burglary, assault, theft and car crimes, vanished from official statistics last year as a result of police manipulation of the figures. The disclosure undermines claims by Michael Howard, the Home Secretary, that the government's controversial law and order policies are finally winning the war on crime. Last month Howard announced a 5.5% fall in recorded crime – the biggest drop for 40 years. However, police and crime experts revealed that most of last year's fall of 311,000 crimes could be accounted for by officers 'cooking the books'. They said the dishonest practice of not recording crimes known in police circles as 'cuffing' – was becoming increasingly common. Their views are backed by the British Crime Survey, which recently reported that actual crime rose faster over the past two years than during the 1980s. This weekend chief constables revealed a range of 'Spanish practices' which allowed them to conceal the full extent of crime. These included cases where, victims of violent attacks, previously classed as actual bodily harm, are having the crimes described by police as common assault, a civil offence which does not feature in official crime statistics. Attempted burglaries are logged as criminal damage to windows and doors and not put down as crimes. Thieves caught breaking into cars are being charged with tampering rather than theft.*
>
> *(Ian Burrell and David Leppard, The Sunday Times, 16.10.1994)*

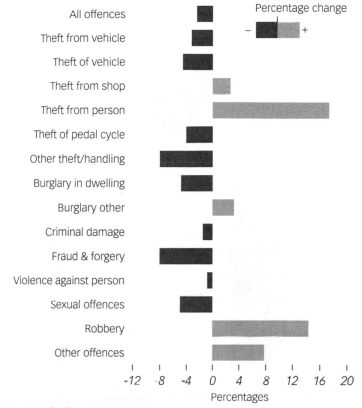

(Source: *The Times*, 27.3.1996:7)

Figure 12.1 Percentage changes in crime 1993-95. official figures

How to measure crime. 'Statistical cons'?

According to criminologist David Rose:

> *Most crime figures, mainly collated by the police, are extremely unreliable; they can easily be distorted by different counting methods and means of classification. But there is one kind of crime figure which can be relied on absolutely: the numbers of people convicted for each offence.*
>
> *(The Observer, 21.1.1996:16)*

It is in the falling rate of convictions that Rose finds evidence of government failure in the last ten to twelve years (see Figure 12.2). Since 1980, convictions as a percentage of recorded crime have plummeted (see Figure 12.3). For example:

> *Take rape. The total of offences reported to police has risen fivefold, from 1,200 in 1980 to 5,039 in 1994. Some of this increase is due to the changes in the way the police handle victims, and the reporting of more so-called 'date rapes'.*
>
> *Yet in 1980, nearly half of those who did report a rape saw their assailant convicted in court. Now this ratio has fallen to just one in 12. In 1994, there were actually fewer rape convictions – 441 – than the 459 in 1980.*

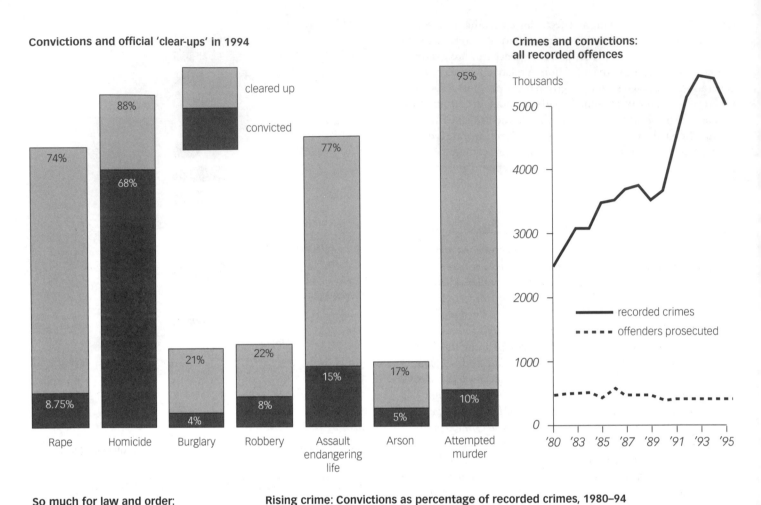

Convictions and official 'clear-ups' in 1994

cleared up

convicted

- Rape: 74%, 8.75%
- Homicide: 88%, 68%
- Burglary: 21%, 4%
- Robbery: 22%, 8%
- Assault endangering life: 77%, 15%
- Arson: 17%, 5%
- Attempted murder: 95%, 10%

Crimes and convictions: all recorded offences

Thousands

— recorded crimes
····· offenders prosecuted

'80 '83 '85 '87 '89 '91 '93 '95

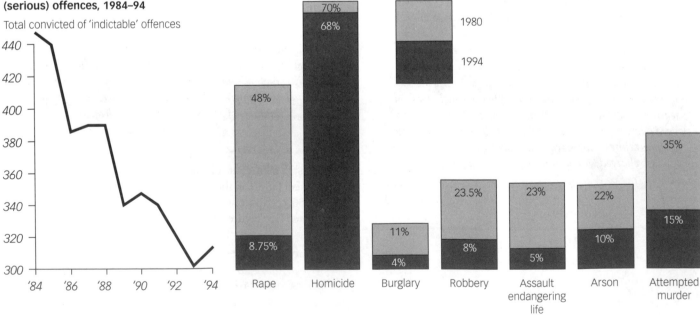

So much for law and order: Plummeting convictions for indictable (serious) offences, 1984–94

Total convicted of 'indictable' offences

'84 '86 '88 '90 '92 '94

Rising crime: Convictions as percentage of recorded crimes, 1980–94

1980

1994

- Rape: 48%, 8.75%
- Homicide: 70%, 68%
- Burglary: 11%, 4%
- Robbery: 23.5%, 8%
- Assault endangering life: 23%, 5%
- Arson: 22%, 10%
- Attempted murder: 35%, 15%

(Source: *The Observer*, 21.1.1996: 16)

Figure 12.2 Rising crime – falling convictions

As Rose points out, the Home Secretary has tended to avoid citing conviction rates and instead relies on 'the clear up' rate for public consumption. Thus, in 1994, 74 per cent of rapes were cleared up but convictions were only obtained in 8.75 percent of cases. Low conviction rates suggest that either the wrong people are being accused of crimes or that 'guilty' parties are being found 'not guilty' – a highly unsatisfactory and even dangerous state of affairs for the general public. 'Cleared up' means solved or sorted out but it is far from a 'clear' category. Crimes are considered to be cleared up if witnesses disappear thus stopping proceedings; if an offender dies; or if a prisoner admits to crimes for which s/he will not be prosecuted or for which the police or Crown Prosecution Service think they 'know who did it'. These are known as 'secondary clear ups'. Rose comments that: 'clear up rates have been maintained only by being fiddled'.

This is somewhat unfair on the police as they are applying prescribed criteria for secondary clear ups. However, the point is that statistics can be both constructed and presented misleadingly.

Other measures of crime

There is no doubt that figures based on crimes notified to the police substantially underestimate the amount of crime committed.

One source of such evidence is the Home Office's *British Crime Survey*. Its findings are based on interviews with a representative sample of 10,000 people about their knowledge of, and feelings about, crime, including experience of being a victim. In all categories of crime shown in Figure 12.3 there is a massive difference – in most cases of several hundred per cent – between recorded crime and the aggregated figure of the three categories – recorded, reported but not recorded, and unreported crime (the so-called 'dark figure'). If these figures are even approximately accurate, the number of notifiable offences recorded by the police grossly underestimates the amount of crime.

The *British Crime Survey* provides a range of other data which can be used to clarify the understanding of crime of both criminologists and the public. Thus, it may surprise some that as well as being the most likely perpetrators of crime, young males are by far the most likely of any age/sex group to be victims of it. The BCS showed that young males were seven times more likely to become victims of violent street crime than women over 61, yet the latter group was much more fearful of such crime (but see below).

The *Islington Crime Survey* (No.2, 1990) also provides information on the amount, nature and experience of crime unavailable in official police statistics. The survey is based on detailed interviews of a demographically representative sample of

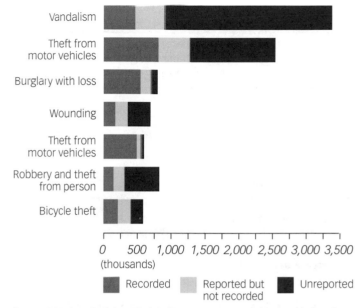

(Source: P Mayhew, C Mirrlees-Black and N Aye Maung, *Trends in Crime: Findings from the 1994 British Crime Survey*, Home Office Research Findings No.14)

Figure 12.3 Levels of recorded and unrecorded crime 1993

1,600 people living in Islington, London. Many of its findings are generalisable to other inner urban neighbourhoods. In order to provide a further rough measure of the amount of crime, respondents were asked if they knew people who had committed given crimes: 38 per cent knew someone who had stolen from a shop, 53.5 per cent knew a cannabis smoker, and 13.5 per cent knew a burglar.

The Islington Crime Survey gives a different and perhaps more sympathetic analysis of public fear of crime, particularly among females. The survey found that 30 per cent of respondents had been victims or knew victims of street robbery in the previous year. Fear of crime greatly affects the behaviour of many women in inner urban areas: 26 per cent of women aged between 16-24, 27 per cent aged between 25-54, and 68 per cent aged over 55 never go out alone at night. Further, 74 per cent of women compared to 40 per cent of men stay in very or fairly often, and when they do go out are more likely to restrict their movements as a precaution against crime. This can include avoiding certain streets or public transport. The survey states that 'It is not an exaggeration to conclude that many women in inner city areas live in a state of virtual curfew'. Thus, crime appears to be a further area in which mainly male behaviour largely controls female behaviour. However, as Table 12.2 shows, it is younger men who are most likely to be victims. Older people, especially males, were least likely to be victims.

Table 12.2 Fear and risk of street crime

		Percentage feeling very 'unsafe'	Percentage of victims of 'street crime'
Men	16–30	1	7.7
	31–60	4	1.6
	61+	7	0.6
Women	16–30	16	2.8
	31–60	35	1.4
	61+	37	1.2

Note: percentages represent responses to the question: 'How safe do you feel walking alone in this area after dark?'. Weighted data; unweighted n = 10,905.

(Source: Hough and Mayhew, 1983:25, Table 5)

Methods of acquiring crime data other than official statistics: victim surveys; self-report; experiment

As was indicated above, the British Crime Survey and the Islington Crime Survey employed a variety of questions to establish more information about crime and its impact. These included asking respondents if they had been victims rather than perpetrators of crime (the latter question invariably produces a lower figure than the former – as you can probably discover by putting both to any group of people). A victim survey, then, involves researchers asking respondents if they have been victims of given crimes. The difference between recorded crime and crime claimed by victims to have occurred is high in some categories – such as vandalism – and much less in others – such as bicycle theft and motor vehicle theft. It is generally true that more serious offences are reported to the police and appear in their statistics.

It would be a mistake to assume that the results of victim surveys provide the 'real' measure of crime. Victims do not always realise when a crime has been committed against them. In fact, such a large proportion of white-collar crimes – such as offences against the Trade Descriptions Act – may go unnoticed that victim surveys are probably an inadequate instrument for measuring such crime. Indeed, white-collar crime is, in general, particularly difficult to measure.

Another technique for measuring crime rates is the self-report study. A self-report study seeks voluntary information from respondents about whether or not they have committed crime. In general, such studies show that a large majority have committed criminal acts at some point in their lives, although only a minority have acquired a criminal record. In a number of self-report studies of young people, the ratio of working class to middle class delinquent activity drops from the 5/6:1 of official statistics to

about 1.5:1. Indeed, Kinsey (1992), using the self-report technique found little difference in the crime rate of middle and working class children. Again, typical images of criminals partly depend on how particular sets of criminal statistics are compiled.

Experimentation offers a third means by which the information and stereotypes purveyed in official criminal statistics can be tested. Farrington and Kidd (1980) left apparently genuine letters enclosing money in various public places. The letters varied in the amount of money they contained and in certain other key respects. The individuals who picked up the letters were observed and a check was effected on whether they kept them or posted them on. Women proved as likely to steal as men except where larger sums were involved, when about a quarter of the women and half the men stole. Despite the latter finding, the experiment as a whole suggests that, contrary to what might be argued from official statistics, females are scarcely less 'naturally' prone to theft than males when given the opportunity. Unlike the other two techniques of enquiry, however, this one refers not to crime committed in 'natural' social circumstances but in 'unnatural' experimental conditions.

Crime statistics and stereotyping: class; sex; age and racial stereotypes

Official statistics influence popular stereotypes of 'the typical criminal'. The classic criminal stereotype is working class, male, young, and more recently black. Of course, not all of these stereotypes always occur together. For instance, organised, large-scale crime is associated with older rather than younger males. Nevertheless, there is a tendency for these stereotypes to reinforce each other. Figure 12.4 represents the likelihood of going to prison dependent on class, gender, 'race' and age (the figure is based on American data but the trends are similar throughout the Western world). The data in the figure appear to support popular stereotypes of criminals but how far are these data and data which appear to show similar trends, the result of the existence of stereotypes in the first place? To what extent do the police and courts look for what they expect to find, and so create self-fulfilling prophecies in relation to 'the typical' criminal? We will briefly examine the class, sex, age and 'race' stereotypes in turn. Much evidence in relation to these stereotypes will shortly be discussed in other sections of this chapter and will, therefore, be only summarily referred to here.

Class and crime

Is the stereotype that working class people commit more crime than middle class people correct? Broadly, it is only accurate in relation to certain types of crime, particularly, 'street crime' and burglary. These types of crime tend to be obvious and likely to be recorded whereas white-collar crime is more likely to be both

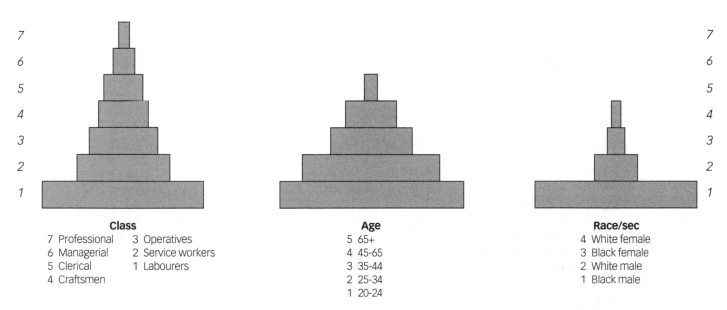

Class		Age	Race/sec
7 Professional	3 Operatives	5 65+	4 White female
6 Managerial	2 Service workers	4 45-65	3 Black female
5 Clerical	1 Labourers	3 35-44	2 White male
4 Craftsmen		2 25-34	1 Black male
		1 20-24	

(Source: Adapted from J Lea and J Young *What is to be done about law and order?* Penguin, 1984: 98)

Figure 12.4 Likelihood of going to prison: broad patterns according to class, age and 'race'/sex

under-detected, under-recorded and, arguably, under-punished. We have already cited a range of studies by both interactionists and Marxists which seek to demonstrate an in-built (though not necessarily always conscious) bias of the social and legal systems in favour of the upper and middle classes and against the working class. As early as the 1940s, Edwin Sutherland produced evidence that white-collar crime might be substantially under-estimated in official statistics. He found that often the petty crimes of pilfering or major crimes of bribery passed unnoticed or were dealt with 'within the firm'. Even the flouting of commercial and industrial law was more likely to be the subject of governmental reprimand than legal action. A study by W S Carson of 200 firms in south east England some 25 years later, similarly found that only 1.5 per cent of officially detected breaches of factory legislation were

Table 12.3 Government departmental thefts and losses 1991/2–1995/6

Department	1991-2	1995-6	1991-2 – 1995-6		1991 – 1996
			Increase	Percentage rise	Total
	(£)	(£)	(£)		(£)
Attorney General	8,700	21,812	13,112	150.7	99,350
Treasury	12,789	68,662	55,893	437.7	236,146
Education	0	31,400	31,400	–	60,100
Employment	52,291	487,041	434,750	831.41	1,421,683
Defence	104,000	n/a	n/a	n/a	122,0000
Home Office	10,885	139,435	128,550	1,180.9	235,101
Foreign Office	865	21,106	20,241	1,340	82,968
Social Security	89,799	851,020	761,221	847.7	1,320,016
Environment	n/a	45,285	n/a	n/a	87,768
Cabinet Office	2,250	29,252	27,002	1,200	110,815
Scotland	n/a	13,000	n/a	n/a	21,00
Wales	5,067	32,496	27,429	541	65,804
Health	10.800	232,020	221,220	2,048	514,700
Transport	n/a	n/a	n/a	n/a	186,389
N Ireland	23,011	n/a	n/a	n/a	111,056
National Heritage	0	513	513	–	513
DTI	96,000	n/a	n/a	n/a	266,000
Total	416,437	1,973,042	1,556, 605	373	4,941,409

prosecuted. To these we must add the more far-reaching allegations, made by Marxists, of crime involving local ruling elites and, internationally, large corporations (see p. 355).

It should be stressed, however, that as Britain becomes more a service society and less a manufacturing society, and there is a corresponding decrease in the size of the traditional working class and increase in the number of white-collar employees, the types of crime committed and the perception of crime are beginning to change. Computer crime and business and financial fraud have increased alongside burglary and car-related theft. In turn, more attention has been given to white-collar crime both by government and law enforcement agencies, which affects statistics and perception in relation to this type of crime. Indeed, government departments themselves have been recent major victims of theft (see Table 12.3). Between 1991-2 and 1995-6, thefts from government departments – particularly computer equipment – increased by a massive 373 per cent. Although the thefts were linked to organised gangs, using contractors' passes to gain access, an increase in inside theft also seems likely. In the late 1980s and early 1990s, there was a spate of major fraud trials in both Britain and the United States including the Guinness share price fixing case and the multi-billion dollar swindles of Ivan Boesky and Donald Milken. Both the potential for this type of crime and the surveillance of it has increased. However, in all these cases the penalties appeared comparatively lenient.

Ethnomethodoligist Aaron Cicourel's *The Social Organisation of Juvenile Justice* (1976) indicates how misleading statistics might be compiled about crime among young, middle and working class males. He examines how two towns, with almost identical populations, experience quite different rates of juvenile crime as recorded in official statistics. He gives two explanations: the different organisational policies pursued by the police in the two towns, and the different way police policy towards delinquency was interpreted 'via the background expectancies' of officers dealing directly with juveniles. In the first town, a loose attitude to recording delinquent acts and an informal approach to dealing with delinquents made the problem appear small, and vice versa in the other town where much 'tighter' practices and stricter assumptions prevailed. In the first case what came to be regarded as a small problem seemed to require progressively fewer officers to deal with it, whereas in the second case the problem became amplified and so more manpower and resources were deployed to 'solve' it. All this, of course, affected that statistics of delinquency in the two towns in opposite ways, decreasing them in the first instance, and increasing them in the second. Cicourel's general conclusion for sociological research is:

> *A researcher utilising official materials cannot interpret them unless he possesses or invents a theory that includes how background expectancies render everyday activities recognisable and intelligible.*
>
> (Cicourel, 1976)

Offenders aged under 21 found guilty of, or cautioned for, indictable offences: by sex and age

Great Britain

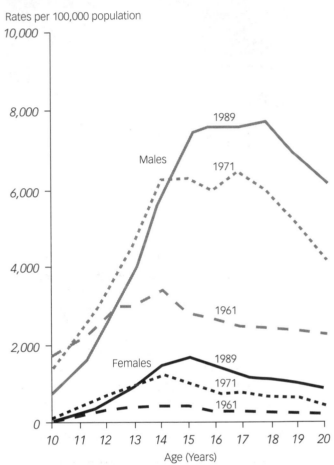

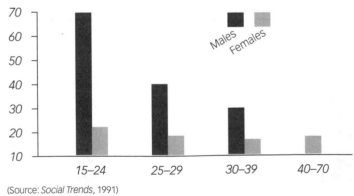

(Source: *Social Trends*, 1991)

Figure 12.5 Gender, age and crime

Gender, age and crime

Figure 12.5 gives the comparative number of cautions and convictions for indictable offences for males and females under 21 for three years: 1961, 1971 and 1989. While the rate of increase of crime for young females has been slightly greater, the total amount of crime committed by young males was still recorded as about six times greater than that committed by young females in 1989. Similar differences between the sexes occur at other age stages but the fourteen to 21 age stage is the peak period in the life-cycle for criminal activity. One third of all crimes known to the police are committed by people of seventeen years of age or under. Given that a large majority of youthful offenders are not convicted of crime as adults, it is difficult to avoid the view that their crimes are transitional learning experiences – which most decide not to repeat. The research of (1992) Richard Kinsey *et al.* in which they interviewed 4,000 children aged eleven to fifteen in Edinburgh appears to support this view: Two-thirds had committed a crime in the previous nine months with middle class children almost as involved as working class children. However, the level of arrests of the latter was higher.

The work of Anne Campbell on female juvenile delinquency goes some way towards undermining the statistical basis for the view that far more males commit crimes than females. Official statistics put the ratio of male to female crime at about 6:1 – the precise ratio varying with age groups. In a self-report study of 105 adolescent girls, Campbell found that in an overall average of offences, the male to female self-admission rate was 1.12:1. She attributes this to paternalism on the part of the police who favour what they consider to be 'the gentle sex' in matters of law enforcement. As a result, they issue far more informal and unrecorded cautions to females than males. Campbell's research cannot be considered conclusive, although Farrington and Kidd's evidence (see p. 344) also suggests that female crime is under-represented in official statistics. A further consideration is that crimes of violence against the person and property – which males are more likely to commit – are difficult for the police to ignore, whereas it is easier to disregard a crime such as publicly soliciting for sexual purposes – which females are more likely to commit. Certainly, the view that men are 'naturally more aggressive' than women and, consequently, more prone to crime needs to be treated with caution. As more women have moved into the labour force and have received 'tougher' socialisation, the ratio of female to male crime has tended slightly to narrow – even as measured by official statistics.

In 1993 a national sample of 1,721 young males and females aged fourteen to 25 (plus a booster sample of young people from ethnic minority groups) provided self-reported data on the extent, frequency and nature of offending in this age group. Figure 12.6 shows that overall, the extent of crime among young males is somewhat less than twice as much as among young females – reasonably close to the findings of other self-report studies. Males are almost three times as likely to commit violent offences than females but whereas both sexes commit fewer violent offences as they get older, males are more likely to commit property offences and females much less (Figure 12.7). Figure 12.9 summaries key points from the survey.

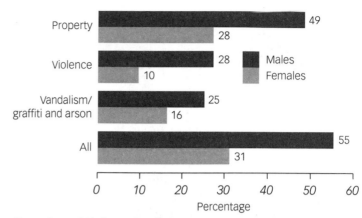

(Source: *Research Findings*, Home Office, No. 24, 1995:2)

Figure 12.6 Percentage of males and females who said they had offended at sometime

Offence group	14–17	18–21	22–25	14–17	18–21	22–25
	Percentage males			Percentage females		
Property offences	17	25	27	13	9	3
Violent offences	12	9	4	7	4	<1
Vandalism, graffiti and arson	8	8	0	8	1	<1
Drug use	17	47	31	17	17	22
All offences (excluding drug use)	24	31	31	19	11	4

(Source: *Research Findings*, Home Office, No.24, 1995:3)

Figure 12.7 Participation in offending and drug use by age-group and sex in 1992

'Race' and crime

Both official crime statistics and most scholarly studies tend to show a comparatively high rate of 'street crime' among Afro-Caribbeans, especially among the fifteen to 24 year old age group. There are various interpretations of why this is so but the two extreme opposing positions are:

1 Young inner-urban blacks actually do have a higher rate of street crime and

2 Police activity (broadly, 'labelling' blacks as criminal) results in the difference in the general crime rate, although there is little or no real difference.

The police themselves tend to take the first position. For instance, the London Metropolitan Police have used victim surveys giving evidence on the colour of attackers as well as criminal statistics broken down by ethnicity to support their case that the rate of 'street crime' (e.g. assault, robbery, drug-selling) – among young blacks is particularly high. While many police accept that some racism exists among them, racist labelling is seldom cited as a significant factor explaining black crime statistics. Yet, self-report studies *suggest* young whites are slightly more prone to certain crimes than young black (see Figure 12.8).

Stuart Hall *et al.* present a complex analysis of black crime in *Policing the Crisis* (1979) in which they see the oppressive role of the police as part of an oppressive society. They describe inner-urban areas with large concentrated Afro-Caribbean populations as 'colonies' which respond to exploitation by developing their own alternative consciousness and way of life. Hall and his co-authors see crime of 'hustling' as part of this way of life or subculture. For many it offers a better life than drifting between unemployment and dead-end jobs – with 'mainstream' opportunity closed by racism. Even so, it is only the most successful hustler who can avoid paid work altogether. Hall refers to the activities of these subcultures as 'cultural resistance' because their members generally reject racial and economic exploitation.

Hall does not consider that the 'high crime rate' of Afro-Caribbean youth is simply a result of police labelling. Rather, society's racism has 'marginalised' many young blacks and it falls to the police to deal with the resulting 'problem' of social control. As a result of these processes, a significant number of young blacks become 'criminalised'. Hall argues that in the early and mid 1970s blacks were scapegoated for, among other things, the cause of white unemployment and of the 'rise in crime'. In particular, young blacks were often seen as potential 'muggers' – a perception certainly shared by numerous police, according to Hall.

John Solomos's observations on crime and the Afro-Caribbean community in *Race and Racism in Contemporary Britain* are compatible with those of Hall. Solomos considers that the way in which young blacks have been presented by much of the media and some agencies of social control as a 'problem' and even as 'the

enemy within' (Solomos's phrase) is part of the racialisation of British public life in the 1970s and 1980s. They, rather than the difficult social and economic conditions they experience, become the object of blame.

John Lea and Jock Young offer an alternative explanation of the role of Afro-Caribbean crime to what they term as the 'colonial' approach of Hall and others. They describe their own perspective as 'a subcultural approach to race and crime'. They consider that young 'Afro-Caribbean people are more likely to be involved in certain types of crime but also that police stereotyping occurs. These two factors create a vicious circle which has the effect of worsening relations between the police and the black community – a major factor in several urban disorders. Among some young black people an alienated subculture has developed within which crime plays a significant part.

It does need to be emphasised, however, that it is only in relation to certain types of crime that Young and Lea's analysis might apply. On the basis of the 1993 self-report survey referred to above, young whites commit slightly more offences in most categories than Afro-Caribbeans – and both commit more than young Asians (Figure 12.8). Again, there is a clear need to be wary of stereotypes.

Questions

1 How accurate a picture of crime is presented by official statistics?
2 Critically discuss the construction of official crime statistics, including possible sterotyping, in relation to two of the following: class, 'race' and age.

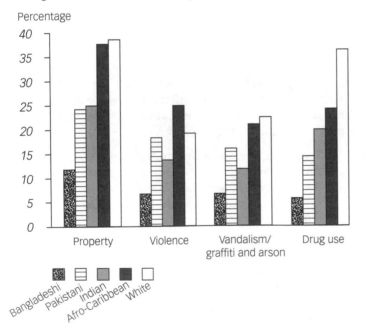

Percentage

(Source: *Research Findings*, Home Office, No.24, 1995:3)

Figure 12.8 Percentages of ethnic minorities who said they had offended/used drugs at some time (under age 25)

Social order, control and deviance

Terminology and basic concepts

The concepts of order, deviance and control describe some of the most basic realities of social life. Order is a state in which social life – actions and interactions – can be conducted without major disruption. The basis of social order is conformity to social norms or rules. Norms may be formal – such as laws – or informal, such as who 'normally' sits where in a common room.

When a society is functioning in an orderly way, most people will generally be observing most norms. Deviance occurs when norms are broken. Deviance can vary from political terrorism (a challenge to social order itself) to failing to observe accepted eating habits. The control of deviant behaviour may be formal or informal. The main formal means of control include the police, the courts, the prison and probation systems and ultimately, the army. Informal control often takes the form of a look, nudge or frown which says 'behave yourself' or 'get into line'.

Although order is necessary for social life, it is not in itself

---

Young people and crime
John Graham and Ben Bowling

Little is known about why some young people who commit offences stop whilst others go on to commit crimes as adults. This study provides an estimate of the extent, frequency and nature of self-reported offending among fourteen to 25-year-olds in England and Wales, establishes why some young people start to commit offences and why some stop offending whilst others do not.

KEY POINTS

- Involvement in offending and drug use amongst young people is widespread – every other male and every third female admitted to committing offences and the same numbers admitted using drugs at some time – but most offending is infrequent and minor and most drug use is confined to using cannabis.

- About three per cent of offenders are responsible for a disproportionate amount of crime (about a quarter of all offences).

- Young Asians are less likely to commit offences and/or use drugs than whites and Afro-Caribbeans.

- The peak age of self-reported offending is 21 for males and sixteen for females.

- Females aged fourteen to seventeen are nearly as likely as males to be involved in offending but as they get older, this offending drops off sharply in comparison with males.

- The rate of participation in property crime by males increases with age, whereas for females it declines; the seriousness and frequency of all offending by males and females declines with age.

- The strongest influences on starting to offend are low parental supervision, persistent truancy and associating with others involved in offending, all of which are strongly related to the quality of relationships with parents.

- Female offenders who become socially mature adults are significantly more likely to stop offending than those who do not, whereas this development process makes little difference for male offenders. However, males who continue to live at home into their mid-20s, avoid heavy drinking, drug use and association with other offenders, are more likely to stop offending.

(Source: *Research Findings*, Home Office, No.24, 1995)

Figure 12.9 Young people and crime

morally 'good' or 'bad'. How order is achieved in a given regime is a key issue. This can vary from dictatorship to democracy. The purposes to which order is put is also important. Hitler achieved a high degree of order but some of the purposes to which he put it prompted Churchill to refer to Nazism as 'the most wicked and monstrous tyranny that has ever corroded the human breast'.

Concern with the issue of social order long pre-dates the emergence of sociology as a distinct discipline. The political philosophers Hobbes (1588–1679) and Locke (1632–1704) produced work on the themes of power, order and control which is still relevant. Broadly, Hobbes believed that the only way to ensure order was for people to agree to the existence of a single sovereign and absolute governing power – preferably, in his view, monarchy. In contrast, Locke believed that people have natural rights which they cannot sign away and that government must therefore be by consent – this implies that governments which grossly abuse natural rights can be removed (which Hobbes did not accept). The tension between the need for order and the liberties and rights of human beings is expressed widely within sociology and political science.

Historical phases in deviancy control

The control of deviant behaviour varies considerably between historical periods. Stanley Cohen has examined both the philosophy and practice of deviancy control in three periods: the pre-eighteenth century; the nineteenth and first half of the twentieth century; and the contemporary period from the mid twentieth century (*Visions of Social Control: Crime, Punishment and Classification* (Polity Press, 1985) (Table 12.4)).

Cohen's historical analysis is very useful to set against the more static picture of deviance presented by the various perspectives discussed below. Cohen describes the control and definitions of deviant behaviour as culturally dynamic and shifting, reflecting

Table 12.4 Two contrasting approaches to deviancy control

	Nineteenth-Century Transformation	1960s: Counter Ideologies/Deconstructing Movements
Trends away from the State	1 Centralised state control	Decentralisation, deformalisation, decriminalisation, diversion, divestment, information, non-intervention
The Expert	2 Categorisation, separate knowledge systems, expertise, professionalisation – e.g. social workers, probation officers	Deprofessionalisation, demedicalisation, delegalisation, anti-psychiatry, self-help, removal of stigma and labels
The Institution	3 Segregation: victory of the asylum/prison	Decarceration, deinstitutionalisation, community control
'The Mind' (i.e. 'Mind Control')	4 Positivist theory: move from body to mind – treatment, cure of 'causes'	Back to justice, neo-classicism, behaviourism

(Source: Adapted from S Cohen, 1985:17)

changes in the economic, social and political areas. Table 12.4 deals only with the 'transformation' from nineteenth century principles and practice in relation to deviance to contemporary ones – but it is very illuminating. Cohen sees a movement away from state control of deviance, from unquestioned acceptance of 'expert' opinion, from segregating deviants from the rest of the community, and from a simplistic belief that the causes of deviance could be established by research and treated by science. (For a fuller discussion of these points, see pp. 366.)

Theories of social order, control and deviance

Of the perspectives discussed below, only functionalism, Marxism and, perhaps, interactionism give full theoretical accounts of social order and control as well as of deviance. Two of the perspectives discussed – the psychological and the ecological – concentrate mainly on deviance. The concluding perspective, the 'rational choice' approach, does consider the issue of control but within too narrow a framework to qualify as a fully evolved social theory.

Psychological perspectives

The view that some individuals are psychologically predisposed to crime as a result of their biological inheritance is not, of course, sociological, although sociologists must consider its validity against sociological explanations. The recent origins of this view are traceable, in crude form, to Cesare Lombroso, an Italian doctor whose ideas were influential around the turn of the last century. Lombroso believed that certain 'primitive' physical characteristics, including large jaws, acute sight and a love of orgies(!) indicated a criminal type, but empirical research by Charles Goring established no such correlations. More recently, it has been suggested that men possessing an extra male sex chromosome (Y) are more likely to commit violent crime than others. This is so, but such men still account for a very small proportion of all violent crime.

Hans Eysenck is the champion of the hereditarian argument in this as in other fields. He claims to have established a link between certain genetically based personality traits, such as extroversion, and criminal behaviour, although he prudently describes this as a predisposition, not a necessarily causal factor. Sociologists tend to react sceptically to such arguments. It can never be finally proved that a given action is primarily the 'result' of genetic predisposition rather than either the influence of social environment or individual choice. Sociologists are, however, more favourably inclined to psychological arguments which explain behaviour as a response to social or, for that matter, physical environment, rather than heredity. Thus, the Chicago school of sociologists, whose work we discuss later, appreciated that the material deprivation, physical decay and tough cultural environment of the inner city influenced children in such areas towards delinquency. Sociologists also accept

that extreme conditions of this kind might produce mental illness, including criminal pathology (acute material or psychological deprivation, or both, could make someone criminally insane). Nevertheless, few sociologists, if any, see such unusual circumstances as the basis of a general explanation of crime. What they do accept is that certain social conditions might produce a given kind of response, such as delinquency, but such resultant activity is certainly not regarded as mentally abnormal. Some sociologists are occasionally accused of being sympathetic to deviants. If true, this is perhaps less dangerous than regarding them as mentally aberrant, for what solutions to crime does this explanation lead to? Drug treatment? Brain surgery? A course of behaviourist psychotherapy? To some, these treatments seem more insane or, to be consistent, more 'criminal' than the behaviour they seek to control.

Functionalism: the need for order and control

Functionalists stress that order is necessary for effective social life. The complex functioning of what Parsons describes as the four sub-systems – the economy, politics, kinship and community, and cultural organisations – requires social order.

Order is achieved partly through socialising members of society into the accepted values and norms. Socialisation is the means by which value consensus (agreement) is brought about. In other words, the basic values members learn in a given society will generally lead them to conform and therefore behave in an orderly way. Those who are not successfully socialised and become 'deviant' may be controlled by more coercive means – such as the police.

Durkheim emphasised the importance of values (though he used the term 'morals') in controlling disruptive individual passions:

> *The totality of moral rules truly forms about each person an imaginary wall, at the foot of which the flood of human passions dies without being able to go further ... if at any point this barrier weakens, (these) previously restrained human forces pour tumultuously through the open breach; once loosened they find no limits where they can stop.*
>
> (E Durkheim quoted in Giddens, 1972)

Durkheim also stressed the positive as well as the controlling aspects of moral values in that they can enable individuals to feel that they are part of something bigger than themselves (in this case, society). The following quotation from a more recent functionalist, Edward Shils, makes the same point. The second part of the quotation moves on from describing the unifying effect of values to that of symbols which are representations of something 'larger' (thus, the reverence which may be inspired by a national flag occurs because it symbolises a nation).

> *The existence of a central value system rests, in a fundamental way, on the need which human beings have for incorporation into something which transcends and transfigures their concrete individual existence. They have a need to be in contact with symbols of an order which is larger than their own bodies and more central in the 'ultimate' structure of reality than is their routine everyday life.*
>
> (E Shils quoted in Worsley, 1972)

The main values of a society – what Shils calls 'the central value system' – are, then, seen as essential in creating conformity and order.

Two familiar criticisms of functionalism in general can be applied to the above analysis of social order. These are that it overstates the degree of value consensus in many societies, and underestimates the amount of conflict. In fairness, the functionalist model of society does allow for considerable conflict within the system and also acknowledges that systems can break down. However, functionalists disagree with Marxists that conflict is at the very heart of society, neither do they accept that order operates primarily in the interests of 'the ruling class'.

Functionalist theory of deviance

Durkheim: the characteristics of deviance

Durkheim was perhaps the first to analyse deviance, or 'social pathology' as he called it, in terms of broad sociological theory. He argued that deviance is universal (and normal), relative, and functional. We will discuss these characteristics in turn.

Deviance: universal (and normal)

Durkheim argued that in every society some people deviate from the norms and that deviance is therefore universal. However, he stressed that although certain types of deviance may occur normally in a given society, levels can reach abnormal proportions.

Sociologists agree about the universality and normality of deviance in the above limited sense. While the idea of a normal 'level' of deviance is now little used, sociologists certainly do seek to explain major changes in the rate (or level) of particularly types of deviance – such as child abuse or theft.

Deviance: relative

In saying deviance is relative, Durkheim meant that what is defined as deviant varies, because different cultural groups have different norms (although there may be some overlap between groups). Thus, to consume alcohol would be deviant in an orthodox Muslim community, but not in most Christian ones. A further illustration of the relative nature of deviance is that what is considered deviant can change historically within a given culture.

Thus, divorce used to be generally considered deviant in British society but is now commonly accepted as within the bounds of normal behaviour.

Because of the relative nature of deviance, Durkheim argued that people should completely abandon the still-too-widespread habit of judging an institution, a practice or a moral standard as if it were good or bad in itself, for all social types indiscriminately.

Deviance: functional

Durkheim argued that deviance can be functional to society providing it does not reach excessive proportions (for that society). Thus, he wrote that 'crime is, then necessary' because it contributes 'to the normal evolution (development) of morality and law'. Deviance makes this contribution by stimulating social disapproval and thus causing normally acceptable behaviour to be affirmed. Durkheim referred to this as a 'boundary-maintaining' function – by drawing the line between 'them' (deviants) and 'us' (normals), and by punishing the former, 'society' emphasises what is and is not acceptable conduct.

Durkheim also believed that occasionally deviant behaviour can be functional by contributing to social change. Although he did not use the example, the illegal actions of the suffragettes in their campaign for voting rights for women would be regarded as an illustration of this point.

There is clearly some truth in Durkheim's arguments about the functional nature of deviance. However, it is equally arguable that most deviance is generally more damaging (or dysfunctional) to society (and individuals) than functional. Thus, the functions of murder and theft hardly seem to outweigh the damage they do.

Deviance: as 'social pathology'

While probably all sociologists would agree with Durkheim that deviance is both relative and universal, and the majority would accept that it is, in some sense, functional, many query his characterisation of deviance as 'social pathology'. In making this equation, Durkheim seems influenced by his analogy of society with a biological organism – the organic analogy. He was in no doubt that social pathology tended to increase during times of great social change. In such times people are often left without clear rules or normative guidelines, and so become more prone to deviance. In particular, the decline of religious certainties could undermine security and confidence in traditional morality. Durkheim referred to this state of 'normlessness' as 'anomie'. We analyse his detailed application of this concept to suicide later in this chapter. He considered that the rapid changes of the late nineteenth century generated a climate of anomie characterised by increasing rates of suicide, homicide, drunkenness and other signs of pathological desperation. He believed that the major problem in modern society is to find a new basis of moral solidarity. He did not believe that mutual self-interest, the basis of organic solidarity, was quite enough.

Durkheim: conclusion

Durkheim was not content merely to theorise about deviance. His empirical study, *Suicide* (1897), was a deliberate attempt to test some of his main ideas through research and we examine this work later (see pp. 361-3). His influence on the sociology of order and deviance has been immense and even those who have disagreed with him have generally fallen into dialogue with his ideas.

Urban ecology and crime

The inner city is the major location of crime associated with deprivation, and the Chicago school attempted to establish links between environment, deprivation and crime, both theoretically and empirically. Mainly by the use of official statistics, they attempted to demonstrate empirical correlation between high rates of crime, numerous other forms of deviancy, such as alcoholism, mental illness, prostitution and suicide, and the conditions of life prevailing in what Burgess called the 'zone of transition' of the urban area. Both the transience of the inner urban population (that is, its unsettled, mobile nature) and the physical decay of the environment were conditions conducive to deviance. The Chicago sociologists, when referring specifically to the physical environment, tended to use the terms 'zone of deterioration' or 'twilight zone' and when referring to population mobility, 'zone of transition'. Decaying conditions helped to create stress on the family, to weaken community relationships, and to isolate the individual, thus giving rise to anomie. Such circumstances could predispose individuals towards deviant behaviour. The fact that these areas were already generously populated by more than their share of assorted crooks, pimps and conmen made the possibility of 'picking up' a criminal 'trade' all the more likely.

The Chicago theorists, like Durkheim before them, contrasted the high crime rates of the inner city with the much lower crime rates of rural and suburban areas. They found an explanation for this, to some extent, in the thinking of Durkheim and Tönnies on the break up of traditional community and the growth of anomie. Small, rural communities can 'police and protect' their own, but in cities, both property and people become impersonal. Cars and luggage, for example, can be stolen in full view of the public who may have no idea of what is going on. Related to this is the vast growth in the amount of property, both personal and public, during this century and particularly since the war. When 'nobody' seems to own, say, a lamp-post or a telephone kiosk, it becomes, psychologically, easier to hurl a brick at it. A further point is that the sheer mass and variety of conflicting interests in the city makes community control difficult, and generates friction conducive to crime.

Robert Merton: social structure, anomie and nonconformity

Functionalist, Robert Merton, greatly modified Durkheim's analysis of deviance. He dropped any notion of deviance as social 'pathology' (illness) and instead conceptualised it as the product of 'strain' between individual goals and the means provided by society for achieving these goals. Where such strain existed, individuals would be more likely to adopt deviant means to achieve their goals. In developing this theory, Merton modified Durkheim's concept of anomie. Durkheim had argued that deviance is likely to increase in circumstances of anomie, i.e. circumstances in which social norms are no longer clear and people are morally adrift. Merton used the term anomie to describe the strain which occurs when individuals experience conflict between their pursuit of society's goals and the means society provides to achieve them (see Table 12.5). Merton's theory is sometimes referred to as 'structural' because like Durkheim's, it contextualises deviance or nonconformity within the total social structure.

Merton contrasted conformity with four types of non-conformity (deviance) – see Table 12.5. Non-conformity occurs as a result of strain due to anomie.

For him, conformity lies in accepting the 'culture goals' of society – material success is such a 'culture goal' in the USA – and in pursuing them by legitimate 'institutionalised means' – that is, within the limits of normative and legal acceptability. Correspondingly, three of the four forms of adjustment lie in rejecting either or both culture goals and the institutionalised means by which they can be pursued. The fifth, rebellion, involves both a rejection of the goals and means of the old order (-) and an attempt to assert new ones (+).

Table 12.5 Merton: conformity and non-conformity

	Culture goals	Institutionalised means
1 Conformity	+	+
2 Innovation	+	−
3 Ritualism	−	+
4 Retreatism	−	−
5 Rebellion*	±	±

*This fifth alternative is on a plane clearly different for that of the others. It represents a transitional response which seeks to institutionalise new procedure orientated toward revamped culture goals shared by members of the society. It thus involves efforts to change the existing structure rather than to perform accommodative actions within this structure, and introduces additional problems with which we are not at the moment concerned.

(Source: Taken from Peter Worlsey, *ed., Modern Sociology*, 1978:619)

There is much to question in Merton's model, as we shall see when we examine his analysis of 'innovation' (his major concern) as applied to criminal deviancy, but he does map out the chief areas of deviancy in a way that is interesting and suggestive of possibilities for further research. Merton himself has developed the concept of ritualism as applied to bureaucratic work. He points out that people involved in such work can become so dominated by rules of procedure and routine that they lose sight of the purpose of their work. Thus, to suggest a contemporary example, a social security official who delays urgently needed assistance until every bureaucratic check has been made on a client is indulging in ritualistic behaviour. Merton feared that such 'bureaucratic characters' might become something of a plague in large-scale, highly organised modern societies.

Merton describes retreatists as those who can succeed neither by legitimate nor deviant means. These 'drop-outs' include 'psychotics, autists, pariahs, outcasts, vagrants, vagabonds, tramps, chronic drunkards and drug addicts'. However, there is a wide range of explanations as to why such people might become retreatist or otherwise nonconformist, which Merton's rather schematic model does not even hint at. Generally, his plus and minus signs tend to oversimplify the complexity of real life, although his model has some value as a starting point for classifying types of deviance.

Subcultural explanations of deviance

The work of Albert Cohen (1955) and Cloward and Ohlin (1961) moves the focus of analysis to the nature of deviant subcultures. A key concept in Cohen's explanation of young working class male delinquency is 'reaction formation'. He describes these delinquents as reacting in a hostile way to middle class or 'college boy' values but at the same time recognising the status and legitimacy that these values bring. The reactive nature of their delinquency maintains the link with middle class values. Part of the reason why a minority of working class boys become delinquent is that they find it hard to cope with the 'middle class world' – including schools. Delinquency is an adjustment to this problem – though not the only possible one. It is partly anger and frustration which drive the delinquent to pursue values which are in opposition to, or to use Cohen's phrase, 'the very antithesis of', middle class values. The delinquent way of life, then, provides alternative ways of achieving status. Cohen stresses that the most convenient and supportive context in which to pursue delinquency is to join a group or gang. Despite this, Cohen suggests that most delinquents still feel a lingering attachment to the more respectable world they have 'lost'.

Cloward and Ohlin offer a useful typology of deviant subcultures (which clearly owes something to Merton's typology of nonconformity). Whereas Merton highlights that access to legitimate opportunity is unequal, they point out that the same applies to illegitimate opportunity. As a result, the forms deviant subcultures take vary.

They describe three types:

1 **Criminal subcultures.** These are fairly well organised and hierarchical criminal groups in stable lower class areas. They are run by adults who keep control over potentially erratic younger criminals partly by offering a criminal career structure of possible advancement.
2 **Conflict subcultures.** These occur in more disorganised, less stable neighbourhoods. Crime is not controlled by an adult hierarchy and street violence, including gang warfare, among young males typically occurs.
3 **Retreatist subcultures.** These occur among lower class youths who have failed to enter either criminal or conflict subcultures. These members typically withdraw into drugs.

Walter Miller (1962), unlike Cohen, does not see lower class delinquency as a reaction against middle class values. Instead, he presents the behaviour as part of the 'distinctive' culture of the lower class as a whole. The lower class way of life is characterised by certain 'focal concerns', among which are a liking for trouble, toughness and masculinity, smartness, excitement, a belief in luck, and a liking for freedom coupled with a dislike of authority.

Two further aspects of Miller's analysis are worth stressing. First, delinquent boys learn their delinquent behaviour within their own subculture. In principle, therefore, learning delinquent behaviour is the same as learning to conform. If delinquency is learnt, then it is not biological or psychological in origin. Second, lower class 'focal concerns' become magnified among adolescents because of the importance of peer group conformity and particularly the need for peer group status among adolescents.

Comment and criticism: structural and subcultural theory (David Matza)

Both Merton's structural theory of nonconformity and the various subcultural theories explain deviance in terms of a sharp difference between the mainstream and the deviant. In the former case, criminal behaviour is seen as due to difference in legitimate opportunity (i.e. lack of it on the part of the criminal) and in the latter, cultural differences between the mainstream and deviant subcultures are stressed. Both these explanations have achieved wide, if qualified, acceptance in deviancy theory. Further, the views that lack of opportunity and/or cultural environment can 'push people' towards crime have considerable popular credibility.

David Matza (1964) finds structural and subcultural theory mechanistic and deterministic. First, he argues that there is less difference between conformists and deviants than subcultural theorists propose. Most deviants want what most people want. They also share with other people conventional moral values as well as what Matza refers to as 'subterranean' or hidden values of excitement, pleasure and gratification (see p. 458). Unlike others, however, deviants express the latter values illegitimately, i.e. in a deviant way. They are able to do this by 'neutralising' or suspending moral controls. Often this involves a justification of the deviant act. Thus, victimising a member of a minority group may be seen as a contribution to 'cleaning up' society. Matza considers that once moral neutralisation has occurred a person may more easily 'drift' into crime. His second point is complementary.

Despite the complex circumstances that may contribute to the committing of a crime, he still allows for an element of individual choice. He regards structural and subcultural theory as over-deterministic in their emphasis on 'external' social factors in explaining crime.

Subcultural perspective and British deviancy theory

As might be expected, the concepts of social structure (including norms and values) and subculture figure prominently in British deviancy theory. Thus, we saw that the concept of pupil subculture was widely used in the context of education (see pp. 96-7) and earlier in this chapter in relation to youth (see pp. 347-8). However, the concepts tend to be used somewhat differently than in American theory.

First, the highly structured gang is regarded as less typically a British phenomenon. Both Downes (1966) and Corrigan (1981) present descriptions of delinquent 'lads' in which the latter kick against authority in a fairly disorganised way. Downes sees delinquency as providing the most exciting leisure opportunities available to the boys and similarly, Corrigan sees them as mainly motivated by the search for 'kicks' and 'fun'. Second, class cultural analysis tends to take a different form in British deviancy theory. This is because it is mainly influenced by Marxist and interactionist theory rather than functionalist/subcultural theory. Thus, Paul Willis does not see a rigid contrast between 'the lads' and 'dominant society' so much as a highly complex relationship within which the lads are ensnared. Willis conveys the subtleties of this relationship by use of such originally interactionist concepts as labelling (see pp. 96-7). To a considerable extent, Willis and others echo some of the qualifications made by Matza in analysing cultural aspects of deviancy.

Granted the above comments, there is a broad similarity between American subcultural theory and the British theory referred to above. Stanley Cohen, sees relatively little fundamental difference between the two. Both groups of theorists describe structural 'strain' between the 'deviant' minority and the majority which comes to be expressed in cultural and behavioural terms (Preface to *Folk Devils and Moral Panics*, (Robertson, 1980).

Marxism: power, order and class rule

Marxists recognise that for a society to function efficiently, social order is necessary. However, apart from communist societies, they consider that in all societies one class – the ruling class – gains far more from society than other classes. Because of the benefits, the ruling class seeks to maintain or impose social order – by a variety of means.

Marxists agree with functionalists that socialisation plays a crucial part in promoting conformity and order. However, unlike the latter, they are highly critical of the ideas, values and norms of capitalist society which they term 'capitalist ideology'. Modern Marxists particularly point to education and the media as socialising agencies which delude or 'mystify' the working class into conforming to a social order which works against its 'real' interests. Althusser refers to these agencies as the 'ideological state apparatus'. Nevertheless, most Marxists believe that the working class may come to question dominant ideas and challenge social order which enforces their own inequality. N Abercrombie, N Hill, and B Turner argue that the working class's own collective experience of oppression at work and elsewhere provides them with a possible alternative basis of values and ideology (1980).

If ideology is the 'soft edge' of social control, the hard edge is the army, police, courts and custodial system – what Althusser calls the 'repressive state apparatus'. Marxists suggest that these come increasingly into play when the capitalist system is seriously challenged.

Despite attempts by the ruling class to maintain order in class-divided society, Marxists argue that conflict not consensus is the fundamental social reality. However, they believe that the effective way of combating oppression and inequality is through political organisation and action rather than through acts of deviance. Some Marxists see high rates of crime and other forms of deviance as signs of the weakness of the capitalist system but few consider that such behaviour contributes significantly to the achievement of a new social order.

Marxist theory of deviance

Marxist theory makes two main points about deviance. First, deviance is partly the product of unequal power relations and inequality in general. For example, in a capitalist society the rules (e.g. laws) operate broadly in favour of capitalism and the capitalist class and to the disadvantage of the working class. Because of this 'bias', working class people are more likely to become classified as deviant. This is especially true of the poor who may be driven by necessity into crime. Second, despite the fact that 'the rules' operate broadly in favour of the dominant class, some of its members often break and 'bend' the rules for their own gain.

Let us look at these two points in more detail. Marxists' analysis of power relations in capitalist society leads them to take the view that the basic legal framework of capitalist society and the way the law is enforced tend to support capitalist society. On the question of the content of the law, they see individual property rights as much more securely established in law than the collective rights of, for instance, trade unions. The latter are seen as insecurely established and likely to be whittled down as they were during the Thatcher administrations of the 1980s. For instance, the closed shop has been abolished and union membership has been left entirely to the individual.

Marxists argue that not only does the law protect inequality but that, depending on class, people have unequal access to the law. Having money to hire a good lawyer can mean the difference between being found innocent or guilty. At a more subtle level, the ability to present a respectable image in court might appeal favourably to the sentiments of predominantly middle class magistrates, judges and jurors. These points may well explain why there is some evidence to suggest that working class people are more likely to be found guilty than middle class people for the same offence (see p. 345 for evidence supporting these arguments).

By citing such examples, Marxists are able to throw back the ideals of liberal justice at those who profess them. Does freedom under law simply mean freedom to be unequal? Can freedom exist without a much greater degree of equality? Does equality under the law really exist when the content and operation of the law seem to favour the middle class? Of course, these are Marxist questions based on controversial Marxist assumptions, but they merit consideration.

We now turn to the second main aspect of Marxist theory of deviance – the crimes committed by the rich and powerful.

Crimes of the powerful

In *Crimes of the Powerful* (1976), Frank Pearce offers a critique of upper class crime. He outlines and in part empirically illustrates a full Marxist theory of the law, crime and power of what Marxists call the ruling class. Central to his argument is the concept of 'ideology' which he treats, in traditional Marxist terms, as the ideas of the ruling class (which are sometimes also believed in by sections of the working class). To a large extent, the idea of 'law and order' in capitalist society is regarded by Marxists as simply an ideological tool of the ruling class, intended to make sure that the working class conform. Public moral concern with lower class crime and the money, time and energy spent on controlling it diverts attention for the exploitative activities of the ruling capitalist class, whose leading representatives would not creditably survive close legal scrutiny of their own business or professional lives. Generally, they have the wealth and power to ensure that such examination seldom occurs, but gradually a body of research on upper class crime is being produced. Pearce himself quotes an American Federal Trade Commission estimate that detectable business frauds in that country accounted for over fifteen times as much money as robbery.

William Chambliss' detailed study (1976) of organised crime in Seattle, Washington, reaches the conclusion that leading figures in the business, political and law enforcement fields made up the city's major crime syndicate and worked together for massive criminal gain in gambling, prostitution and drug trafficking. Much illegally made profit was then ploughed back into legitimate business. Chambliss contends that crime occurs among all classes, but that the types of crime committed and the extent to which the law is enforced varies between classes. The crimes of the powerful are likely to be more lucrative and to escape prosecution. It is important to get Chambliss' work in perspective. He does not show that the majority of the local upper class in Seattle is criminally corrupt, and still less that the majority of the upper class in the United States is corrupt. Nor does he or any Marxist have to do so to prove that capitalists control the capitalist system. They do

this, according to Marxists, whether they break the law or not. If the 'rules of the game' are weighted in their favour, they may not need to break them. Perhaps the point of Pearce's and Chambliss' research is that if the needs or convenience of the upper class require them to commit crime, some of them do. Robert Maxwell is a spectacular case in point and it cannot be *assumed* he is *wholly* exceptional.

Marxists believe that there is a need for the general public to be more precisely informed about the 'crimes of the powerful' and particularly about the relationship between powerful economic interests, the law and political power. The Watergate scandal and aspects of the Westland affair, concerning the relationship between business and politics, hardly fill the public with confidence. Similarly, the large sums shown to have been illegally paid by many international companies to help create favourable trading relations with given countries make petty theft look very petty indeed. To what extent do these cases, however extreme, throw light on what is typical? Here is a tangled but fascinating web for researchers to trace and explain (see pp. 263-5).

Just as Marxists do not accept the law in capitalist society at face value, neither do they accept the categories of crime and deviance as fair or objective. On the contrary, many so-called criminals and deviants in capitalist society are seen as 'victims of the system'. Yet the plight of the lower class criminal and deviant has never concerned Marxists to the extent that it has liberals. This is because Marxists see the hope for social change in a revolutionary movement of the 'solid' working class, certainly not in the criminal fraternity.

Comment on Marxist theory of deviance: 'idealism' and 'realism'

Although there is considerable empirical data to support some aspects of Marxist analysis of deviance described above (particularly in relation to the 'crimes of the powerful'), the sheer scope of the overall theoretical framework is perhaps so broad as to be impossible to prove or disprove conclusively. This seems especially true of the central Marxist point that in capitalist society the law and its enforcement basically favours the capitalist class rather than the majority of the public.

Recently some Marxist and Marxist-influenced criminologists have argued that legal justice is more complex than 'idealistic' Marxism suggests. Notable among these is Jock Young whose more recent work we referred to above (see p. 348). Young, John Lea and others describe themselves as 'left realists' and distinguish themselves from 'left idealists' whom they see as tending to romanticise working class crime. First, they have begun to pay more attention to the victims of crime – and have acknowledged that often – probably most often – the main victims of 'working class' criminals are working class people. Second, and relatedly, Marxist-influenced criminologists have, in practice, accepted that democracy and the law in capitalist society can be used to improve the protection of working people against crime and criminals. Thus, former 1960s radicals such as Young have joined other criminologists in seeking adequately to survey and more effectively to control crime (however they sharply distinguish themselves for those they see as 'right realists' (see pp. 358-60). An extract from Young's *The failure of criminology: the need for a reduced realism*, is provided at the end of this chapter.(Reading 1)

Interactionism: imposed and negotiated order

Interactionism does not provide a 'grand theory' of order in society but focuses on small or medium scale social interaction. Groups and individuals are presented as trying to impose their will on others or, more democratically, to negotiate with them.

Howard Becker, perhaps the most influential interactionist theorist of deviance, frequently stresses the extent to which people use power to get their own way:

> *People are in fact always forcing their rules on others, applying them more or less against the will and without the consent of those others.*
>
> *(1966:9)*

In various studies, Becker presents groups and individuals as seeking to impose their order – indeed, their view of 'reality' – on others. Thus, he argues that the law banning the use of marijuana for social purposes in the United States was largely the result of a publicity campaign by the Federal Bureau of Investigation which manipulated the media and Congress. At a smaller scale level, Becker cites evidence that teachers are able to affect the attainment levels of pupils by the force of their own expectations – which can function as 'self-fulfilling prophecies'.

Interactionists consider that in most situations total power is not in the hands of one group or individual. They employ the term 'negotiation' to describe the bargaining process by which order is 'worked out' in contexts as varied as the courts, the classroom and the home. Aaron Cicourel gives an example of negotiation in his book, *The Social Organisation of Juvenile Justice* (1976) in which he researches responses to juvenile delinquency in two Californian cities. One finding was that after arrest, middle class juveniles were less likely than working class juveniles to be charged with an offence. Ultimately, this affects both criminal statistics – in which working class juveniles 'appear' more prone to crime – and the public's 'image' of the kind of person who is most likely to threaten 'law and order'. The power to 'negotiate', therefore, can have substantial social consequences.

Interactionist theory of deviance

Labelling: Howard Becker

Becker argues that the 'central fact about deviance' is that 'it is created by society'. This seems to return the 'commonsense' notion of deviance on its head. Society, not the deviant, is being held responsible for deviance. What does Becker means by this?

> *I mean … that social groups create deviance by making the rules where infraction constitutes deviance, and by applying those rules to particular people and labelling them as outsiders.*
>
> *(1966:8)*

Becker goes on to give his famous definition of deviance: 'deviant behaviour is behaviour that people so label'. Much of Becker's analysis of deviance concentrates on how and why some people are labelled as deviant and the effect this can have on them. Once a label such as 'troublemaker' or 'criminal' has been given, it can be difficult to get rid of.

Becker does not present the deviant as merely passive. He stresses that much deviant activity is learnt and that learning often has an active aspect to it. The idea that deviant behaviour is learnt is implied in the title of Becker's key essay *Becoming a Marijuana User*, and is consistent with Mead's theory of socialisation. Becker points out that to smoke marijuana and find it enjoyable, the technique has first to be learnt; then it is necessary to learn how to perceive the drug's effects and, finally, the user has to learn to enjoy them. It perhaps needs to be explained that, without this learning process, taking the drug can be both unpleasant and seemingly without effect. (We give a fuller account of the meaning of psychedelic drug use in pleasure-seeking sub-cultures in Chapter 15.) Learning and meaning are linked in Becker's analysis. People only voluntarily learn what seems meaningful to them. Like Mead, Becker fully allows for the influence of 'significant others' (in this case dance musicians who use marijuana) on the individual. Using it is part of their way of life; it fits in with their style and they naturally offer 'established newcomers' the opportunity to try it. Becker notes that the individual is likely to drop or cut back on marijuana smoking when he or she leaves this environment, and the habit ceases to have much cultural meaning.

There is some tension between the concepts that society 'creates' deviance and that individuals act in ways that are meaningful to them. Several concepts used by Becker embody both notions. Thus, the concept of negotiation implies that the individual has some power over his or her situation, including perhaps whether a deviant label is successfully applied in the first place. On the other hand, the concepts of deviant career and career contingencies tend to stress the influence of factors outside the power of the individual. Like any 'career', that of a deviant is affected by a variety of unpredictable factors which Becker refers to as career contingencies. For instance, happening to come into contact with a deviant individual or group may be crucial in turning a person's 'career' in a given direction.

Primary and secondary deviance: Edwin Lemert

Whereas functionalists stress normative consensus, interactionists argue that modern societies are characterised by a great variety or plurality of values and norms. This diversity of attitude exists in most areas of human activity, including religion, sex, politics and 'race'. Conformity to the law is seen not as a product of moral consensus but either as the ability of some groups to impose rules, or as a matter of practical necessity.

Interactionists do not, then, analyse deviance simply as rule breaking, but equally in terms of how and to whom the rules are applied. This is the basis of Lemert's distinction between primary and secondary deviance. According to him, primary deviance is the initial commission of a deviant act. Secondary deviance is the effect that 'societal reaction' has on the conduct of the deviant subsequent to the commission of the initial deviant act. 'Societal reaction' means the reaction of society, or specifically of any group within society, such as the police, the courts, the family and acquaintances of the deviant, the media and, through the media, the public. Lemert's relative silence on primary deviance is a matter we will return to, critically, later.

Lemert and other interactionists have overwhelmingly given their attention to secondary deviance. If, as Howard Becker claims, 'an act is deviant when it is so defined', (an act is deviant when societal reaction declares it to be), then it is what happens in the life of the deviant after the social definition has been made that is the focus of interactionist analysis. We can illustrate the distinction between primary and secondary deviance in schematic form (see Table 12.6).

Table 12.6 Primary and secondary deviance

Primary deviance	Label	Secondary deviance
(Rule Breaking) for example, Speeding →	(Societal Reaction) → Charge, Conviction *or* No Label for example Ignored, Not Noticed Rationalised (Seen as a 'Mistake')	That is, Deviant Status In this case, 'Traffic Offender' (Minor Criminal)

Stanley Cohen: deviancy amplification, moral panics and boundary crises

The insight that deviance is 'constructed' by a combination of individual action and societal reaction is central to interactionism. We use Stanley Cohen's book, *Folk Devils and Moral Panics* to provide a detailed analysis of this process which rests squarely on Lemert's concept of secondary deviance.

Interactionists frequently argue that societal reaction can actually increase or 'amplify' the deviant behaviour of the labelled individual or group. Stanley Cohen has used the example of the rival 'Mod' and 'Rocker' youth factions of the mid 1960s to illustrate the point. The dramatic pre-publicity given to their expected confrontations almost certainly attracted many more young people than might otherwise have been present. In this way, the media helped to create the events it anticipated, or as Cohen says, 'these predictions played the role of the classic self-fulfilling prophecy'. Similarly, over-reporting of what did (or did not) happen at a confrontation could help attract more people on another occasion (don't we all like 'being in the papers'?) In turn, over-reporting could provoke excessive public reaction. Once a 'spiral of amplification' of this kind is generated, it can acquire an artificial momentum of its own: when this happens, what is 'real' and what is imagined is not easy to disentangle (see pp. 513-6).

Given that the media does not consciously seek to popularise deviant activity, why does this over-reporting take place? There is, of course, the sound commercial reason that deviancy stories make good copy and sell newspapers. A more sociological explanation is offered by Cohen. It is suggested in the title of the book itself: *Folk Devils and Moral Panics: The Creation of the Mods and Rockers*. In what sense, then, were the Mods and Rockers 'devils' and what was the nature of the 'moral panic' they precipitated? To answer this question, Cohen uses the concept of 'boundary crisis'. Post-war Britain was relatively affluent, but the majority had not yet adjusted psychologically to the new prosperity. The frank pleasure-seeking and instrumental attitude to work of some groups of young people seemed to undermine the work ethic in a dangerous and uncomfortable way. Although most people had experienced a shift in the balance between work and leisure in their own lives, commitment to the values of hard work and self-discipline prevented them from entering the newly-discovered pleasure gardens with the abandon of the Mods and Rockers. The activities of the latter could be tolerated to a greater degree than would have been imaginable in the1930s, but even so, morality dictated that 'there had to be limits'. The press presented 'the need for limits' as 'self-evident' and a matter for 'common sense', but such terms should not be taken at face value by the sociologist. Whatever their moral validity, their effect is to tend to close down a debate in favour of the dominant consensus. No doubt this is partly because an open discussion on some of the issues raised by the behaviour of the Mods and Rockers, including attitudes towards drugs and sex, would by definition bring into question majority consensus on such matters.

Courts and 'commonsense': Pat Carlen; Harold Garfinkel

Pat Carlen examines the labelling process in relation to the judicial system (1976). Carlen's study, like a number of other interactionist and ethnomethodological ones, concentrates on the actors in the courtroom drama itself, usually with due attention to what happens 'behind the scenes'. The variety of accidental contingencies that can affect the outcome of a trial is striking. The kind of support a defendant gets from key figures, such as probation officers and social workers, can often greatly influence and even determine the nature of a sentence. If, for instance, a probation officer decides that a client has finally 'gone too far' (admittedly an unprofessional response) and makes this clear in the report to the court, a harsher judgement may be likely. The 'plea-bargaining' system, prevalent both in Britain and the United States, is a practice which would seem to lend itself to abuse. Plea-bargaining involves the accused obtaining more favourable treatment in return for an admission of guilt. Firstly the interrogation of suspects in police custody can involve 'deals' in which, say, a lesser charge is 'traded-off' for a statement admitting an offence. Secondly, judicial officials sometimes give more lenient sentences in return for guilty pleas. When justice is put in the market place like this, the possibility of a 'bad deal' for the poor and less well-informed seems correspondingly greater. Needless to say, this trade-off process can facilitate police and court business and sometimes gains prestige for the police and prosecution: that is, presumably, the justification for it.

The kind of detailed, closely observed study we have been describing is frequently favoured by the ethnomethodologists, although such an approach is by no means their monopoly. Harold Garfinkel (1967), one of their chief exponents, was led to his conclusions partly by his attempts to analyse the deliberations of a group of jurors. In the following taped comment, he appears to be saying that the jurors used their own commonsense knowledge of society to arrive at what seemed to them a fair verdict:

> *What I mean is that it was for them a matter that somehow or other in their dealings with each other they managed, if you will permit me now to use it [i.e. commonsense], to see.*

Garfinkel further suggests that it is the job of sociologists to describe and understand what this commonsense knowledge is and how it is applied in a particular context. The application of this view to control theory is that jurors arrive at verdicts not merely on the basis of legal considerations but by calling upon a much wider fund of general knowledge, including an acquired idea of justice. Functionalists tend to consider that the process of legal enforcement is relatively unbiased. Ethnomethodologists make the point that even though people are, to some extent, guided by mutually accepted standards of conduct, behaviour is diverse, different and not wholly predictable. This includes the process of normative and legal enforcement. To put the matter extremely, in a given case justice can be what jurors and judges decide it is, rather than something more objective.

Comment on interactionist theory of deviance

Two major criticisms of the interactionist approach can be made. Firstly, it does not offer an explanation of primary deviance. Secondly, it is said, particularly by Marxists, that it fails to explain adequately the relationship between power, especially class power, and deviance. We take these points in order. Even Lemert hurries past primary deviance on his way to analysing secondary deviance, which is clearly his main interest. Becker, with engaging frankness, agrees that 'stick-up men' do not 'stick people up' simply because somebody has labelled them 'stick-up men', but he still leaves unexplained why some men and women behave in this way whilst others do not. It is true that interactionists do not claim fully to explain why deviance occurs in the first place, but this does result in certain weaknesses in their general theory. In particular, the notion that certain social environments – perhaps those which are in some way 'deprived' – may be associated with certain sorts of deviant behaviour is, apparently, of little interest to them. Yet this view is not necessarily incompatible with the interactionist perspective and, if it were explored by interactionists, might even be found complementary to it.

We now turn to the second criticism commonly made – that it deals inadequately with the relationship between power and deviance. More precisely, this is a specifically Marxist criticism that most interactionists do not sufficiently link their analysis of law and deviance to class theory. In the Marxist view, the law and the state ultimately operate in favour of the ruling class. Marxist sociology of deviance is, therefore, concerned with showing how this is so. Many interactionists do not subscribe to a Marxist class conflict theory of society. Rather, they see the power structure in terms of a contest between all sorts of groups – including ethnic, religious, feminist – as well as classes which seek to establish their own interests and moral values. Becker's own case study of the interests behind The Marijuana Tax Act of 1937 (aimed at stamping out use of the drug) does not mention class at all, but concludes that the Federal Bureau of Narcotics was the major influence or 'entrepreneur' in getting the Act passed.

The above Marxist-interactionist disagreement in no way invalidates basic interactionist labelling theory nor its associated concepts. Indeed, many Marxists freely use interactionist concepts and notably so in the area of subcultural analysis. We have already come across examples of this in the work of Paul Willis. Further, when interactionists deal with class and power, they often reach conclusions compatible with Marxism. Thus, the proposition that white-collar crime might be under-recorded in official statistics because of police and judicial bias in favour of the middle class is commonly found in Marxist and interactionist literature.

Rational choice and situational explanations of deviance: control theory; right realism

Rational choice and situational explanations of crime and the current emphasis on making it more difficult to commit crime (control) are closely related developments in the field of criminology. Rational choice interpretation is based on the simple premise that people choose to commit crime or not by weighing the possible benefits against the risks. Clearly, possible benefits and risks depend largely on the situation in which a crime may be committed. Thus, forcing the door of a wealthy house may offer more 'benefits' than that of a poor house – though if the door of the latter is actually open, the risks may be so reduced that a criminal will choose to rob it rather than the less accessible wealthy house. On the basis of such logic – supported by research – some criminologists have suggested that the best way to reduce crime is not to try to change the criminal but to take practical measures of prevention, i.e. to control it.

Writing in the late 1960s in, respectively, the United States and Britain, Travis Hirschi and Steven Box have suggested the situations in which people are more or less likely to choose to commit crime. Hirschi gives four elements which make the choice of crime less likely – all of which relate to the strength of the bond between the individual and society:

- Attachment
- Commitment
- Involvement
- Belief

Thus, people in regular work or school attendance, with busy home lives who believe they should obey the law are less likely to commit crime than those less involved with mainstream society. The latter have more opportunity and 'reason' to deviate. For example, several studies show that when school truancy is reduced the day-time crime rate in the relevant area tends to drop. Steven Box further develops the idea that it is those in situations of less commitment to society and therefore of less social restraint that are more likely to commit crime and deviance. The following factors can be conducive to crime:

- Secrecy (chances of concealing deviance).
- Skills (having the ability to commit the deviant act).
- Supply (of the means to commit the act).
- Social support (peer approval).
- Symbolic support (e.g. behaviour indicative of high status).

Control theories have tended to develop in a policy-orientated context. It was at the Home Office Research and Planning Unit that Clarke, Cornish and Mayhew developed this approach. On the basis of situational theory, they devised policies which would create situations in which potential criminals would be less likely to choose to commit crime. Thus, crime might be able to be controlled by making it situationally more difficult to commit. Two examples of this approach are target hardening (such as strengthening telephone coin-boxes) and surveillance (such as designing built environments so that people can see what happens within them – including criminal activity). Alcohol consumption can create situations in which deviance is more likely to occur (see Figure 12.10).

Clarke, Cornish and Mayhew saw situational theory as an approach to crime which might lead to practical ways of combating it. They were disillusioned with highly theoretical

The percentage of incidents in which alcohol is involved

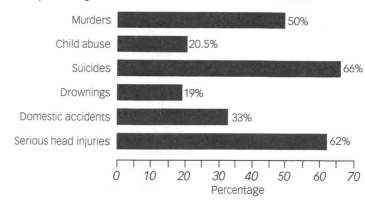

(Source: *The Guardian*, 21.6.1988:20)

Figure 12.10 Alcohol can contribute to the creation of situations resulting in injury, including criminal injury

explanations of crime – of the kind discussed in previous sections of this chapter – which saw the causes of crime either within the individual's psychology, biology or within the social environment. They were scathing that these theories had not produced any effective solutions to crime during a period when the crime rate was rapidly rising. They pursued their work, therefore, with a highly practical intent.

Jock Young has characterised control theorists as 'right realists' and has been highly critical of what he sees as punitive, 'law and order' types of solution to crime. However, his own 'left realism' is pragmatic enough to support more technical aspects of crime control such as improving police deployment and 'target hardening'.

Comment on rational choice theory of deviance

Rational choice and situational explanations of crime and control theory have undoubtedly made a contribution to understanding and controlling crime. However, their long term effectiveness in controlling and reducing crime remains to be proven. If, in fact, potential criminals are often merely diverted from more to less well defended 'targets' or if, in time, they develop more effective means of dealing with them, criminologists may again be forced to prioritise the question of why certain people tend to commit certain sorts of crime.

Two further comments can be offered about these theories. First, control methods may have unintended consequences that may be problematic in themselves. It may be that the cost of controlling crime will result in an 'armoured society' or, at least, a society in which the richer social groups feel the need to 'armour' their possessions against criminals. This has, perhaps, already occurred in certain areas in the United States, particularly in wealthy, urban districts adjacent to much poorer ones. In such areas, houses, hotels and business premises are often fortified with locks and chains, burglar alarms, bars, walls, guards, dogs and double-doors. There is more than a touch of Orwellian 1984 about all this!

The second comment is that in societies in which the social extremes are growing more unequal (e.g. in the United States and Britain), expensive investment in protecting the life 'situations' of the wealthy may separate them even further for the lives of the less well off. This may or may not be considered to matter, but it is an observation of some sociological interest.

The discussion in the previous paragraph leads back to wider theoretical considerations about the causes of crime, notwithstanding the reluctance of some control theorists to probe them. In fact, the earlier rational choice theories of Hirschi and Box do recognise that the wider social experience of individuals affects the likelihood of their becoming deviant. In effect, both suggest that those with less of a material or psychological stake in society are more likely to commit certain kinds of crime. If so, it remains necessary to consider the social context of the deviant in explaining deviance and, perhaps, to direct policy towards it. For instance, if it is true that the poor are more likely to rob the rich than vice versa, then policies to improve the situation of the poor may yet reduce crime. Of course, 'throwing money' at so-called 'social problems' is now a discredited way of dealing with them but ignoring their wider social causes may, in the end, prove even less effective.

Indeed, recent research from the Home Office establishes a long-term correlation between increases in personal spending power and decreases in the growth of property crime and vice versa (*Trends in Crime and Their Interpretation*, Home Office Research Study 119). The study was completed before the large increase in property crime in 1990 occurred. However, the fact that the increase coincided with the beginnings of a recession provides further evidence for the link between spending power and crime. Thus, this research gives a sounder basis for the old adage: 'poverty breeds crime'.

Complementary aspects of structural and interactionist deviancy theory

The above theoretical approaches to social order and deviance are often presented as mutually exclusive. Certainly, it would be ludicrous to imagine that 'sticking them all together' would somehow result in a complete theory satisfactory to all parties. Nevertheless, in some ways the major theories can be seen as complementary rather than contradictory. Further, in some instances, differences in terminology obscure a larger measure of agreement than might at first be apparent.

Even on the subject of social order, control and integration, it is possible to uncover elements of agreement between the two major structural theories about how society functions. Functionalists argue that conformity and consensus are necessary for the orderly functioning of society, but Marxists, too, need to explain why, in many capitalist societies, the majority accept the system, and

appear to have no taste for revolution. Marxists believe that the many working class people who accept and even support the capitalist system have been deluded by 'bourgeois ideology' into a state of 'false consciousness'. Both theories are describing the same phenomenon: what differs is the terminology and the underlying political values: functionalists tend to support and want to conserve capitalist, liberal society, whereas Marxists do not. Not surprisingly, these preferences often seep into their theoretical analyses.

There is also a considerable measure of unstated agreement between Marxism and functionalism about social deviance. Merton thought of criminal behaviour as a result of exclusion from the legitimate opportunity structure of society, and strain theorists examined what this meant in terms of economic and status deprivation. There is a clear implication in all this that 'society' bears at least some responsibility for crime simply because the gateways to legitimate achievement are wide open for some and almost closed for others. Marxists observe the same unequal access to material and status reward hierarchies but condemn it more comprehensively. To them, theft is just the distorted mirror image of capitalism's already ugly face. The convergence between the two perspectives is even apparent sometimes at the level of moral evaluation. The Marxist 'what can you expect?' response to the high crime rate in Western Europe and the USA expresses a sentiment comparable with that of the liberal Daniel Bell, when he refers to crime as 'part of the American way of life'.

The major achievement of interactionism has been to rediscover for sociology the notion that the central social reality is individual meaning and experience. In view of the tendencies towards determinism within both structural theories, this is a crucial contribution. As an account of how people behave in everyday life in relation to the legal and normative order, interactionism seems closer to what actually happens than the functionalist conformity-deviance model. Life is more complex than the functionalists allow. Marxists argue, however, that interactionism is inadequate in its analysis of how the power of institutions and the class interests behind them affect and even control individual lives. The laws, rules of norms of institutions are powerful means of regulating behaviour, and this is notably true of the institutions that constitute the 'bourgeois' state. Moreover, institutional frameworks often survive the coming and going of individuals. In their different ways, Marxists and functionalists appreciate better than interactionists that it is the institutional structure of society that both limits and provides opportunities for individual and group action.

Perhaps interactionism would be more effective if, as well as concerning itself with individual meaning, its protagonists also attempted to develop it more vigorously as a 'linking theory' between the concept of the 'creative' individual, and the 'formative' institutional structure of society. We have already noted some efforts in this direction, though these have been more a matter of Marxists using the interactionist perspective than the other way around. Despite the limits of the interactionist approach, many would feel that amidst such abstract concepts as order, social control and deviance, individual meaning and reality should be retained.

This chapter concludes with a discussion of a number of theoretical approaches which directly or indirectly question the concept of deviance itself. Foucault is associated with the postmodern notion that 'deviance' can be subsumed into 'difference'; somewhat similarly, Jock Young now considers that the 'norm/deviant' dualism has become very blurred; and Colin Sumner has attempted to write the 'obituary' to the concept of deviance and replace it with that of 'ideological censure' (see p. 366).

see pp. 551-2

> ## Questions
>
> 1 Critically discuss the contribution to deviancy theory of one of the main theories of deviance.
> 2 How true do you consider it to be that when individuals commit crime, they are making a 'rational choice'?

Suicide

The study of suicide has become a sociological classic. This is because major studies of suicide so well illustrate theoretical and related methodological debate within sociology. In particular, they illustrate the main differences between positivism/quantitative methods and interpretism/qualitative methods.

Durkheim and positivism

Durkheim argued that even in the case of apparently so individual an act as suicide, the suicide rate or 'social suicide rate' as he termed it, is the product of social 'forces' external to the individual:

> *There is, therefore, for each people a collective force of a definite amount of energy, impelling men to self-destruction. The victim's acts which at first seem to express only his personal temperament are really the supplement and prolongation of a social condition which they express externally.*
>
> *(Durkheim, 1970:299)*

Durkheim presents a model of four types of suicide – altruistic, fatalistic, anomic and egoistic – and relates each one to the degree of 'integration' (connectedness) of the suicide with society.

Altruistic suicide is the result of the over-integration of the individual into the social group. The individual sacrifices herself or himself to the 'greater good' of society. A spectacular example of altruistic suicide was the action of Japanese pilots who dived their planes into enemy shipping, thus committing *kamikaze*. Durkheim associated altruistic suicide and traditional societies which are characterised by mechanical solidarity (see pp. 551-2). He considered individuality to be less developed in such societies and that members would observe even self-destructive norms. Another example was the ritual self-immolation on their husband's funeral pyres of widows in certain parts of India.

Fatalistic suicide is also the product of the over-regulation of the individual by society. In this case, the individual feels powerless before 'society' or 'fate' – and simply 'gives up'. Durkheim did not much refer to this category. Many prison suicides have a fatalistic element about them (see Figure 12.11).

Anomic suicide occurs when lack of social regulation causes low social integration. Thus, Durkheim considered that 'anomic' social conditions (i.e. conditions of great and rapid change in which people tend to become morally and normatively confused) produced an increase in 'anomic suicide'. Anomie, then, is part of the 'collective force' in society 'impelling' people to suicide. We can illustrate the point by taking an example which, again, occurred after Durkheim's own death in 1917. The Wall Street crash of 1929 caused an outbreak of suicide among the American rich or, more precisely, the previously rich. It can be argued that they were driven to suicide not only by material loss but also because of stress in the face of the psychological and normative adjustment to the different lifestyle that loss demanded. Durkheim's own nineteenth century research substantiated the view that economic change, whether for better or worse, tended to increase the suicide rate.

Egoistic suicide arises because an individual's links to the social group become weakened or broken. Durkheim argued that the greater personal and moral freedom allowed by Protestant countries explained why they tended to have a higher suicide rate than Catholic ones which were more likely to be morally integrated communities.

Durkheim found that although the social suicide rate varies between societies, it tends to be 'regular' over time in a given society. He considered that this demonstrated that there are indeed consistent social forces which determine the suicide rate within a given society. Perhaps few sociologists would now make such a

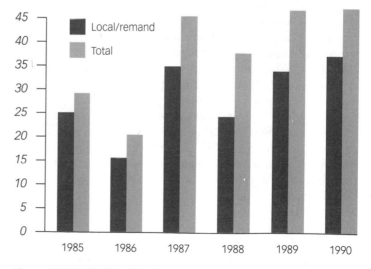

Figure 12.11 Self inflicted deaths in prison

claim – without considerable qualification – and probably fewer still would set out to prove it. Durkheim's great work is a reminder of the original aim of sociology to establish correlations and, if possible, causal relationships between 'social facts' – usually by use of statistics. Although this enterprise has been made more complex by advances in statistical techniques and sociological theory, for many it remains a central aim of the discipline.

A number of criticisms have been made of Durkheim's study from those who share his broadly positivist approach (see p. 362). M Halbwachs was an early commentator (1930), suggesting that the key variable explaining the difference in the suicide rate between Protestants and Catholics was probably their respectively predominantly urban and rural locations, rather than their religions. More recently, Gibbs and Martin (1964), have argued that Durkheim did not define the concept of social integration in a way that could be adequately operationalised (see p. 31 for an explanation of this term). Inevitably this would adversely affect the quality of his empirical analysis.

The interpretist critiques of Durkheim

Durkheim's study, *Suicide*, has been extensively criticised by two interpretists, J D Douglas (1967) and J M Atkinson (1978). As is indicated by the title of Douglas's book, the core of their criticism is Durkheim's failure to consider the different meanings given to suicide by different people and within different cultures. This results in two major mistakes. First, the statistical basis of Durkheim's study is inaccurate. Second, in assuming all suicides to be 'the same', he fails adequately to categorise the phenomenon. Let us take these two related points separately.

Both Douglas and Atkinson give many examples of potential statistical problems resulting from Durkheim's failure to address the issue of meaning. They both criticise Durkheim for apparently assuming that all coroners used the same criteria in deciding what was or was not suicide. They are easily able to give evidence to the contrary. Douglas points out the example of one coroner who would decide that suicide had occurred only if the evidence of a suicide note could be produced. Other coroners accepted less conclusive evidence. Ultimately, this meant that different coroners were contributing a different range of 'facts' to the 'same' statistical category, with the result that 'statistical reality' could be imprecise and misleading. Let us take a further example of this point: the issue of the statistical basis supporting Durkheim's claims about the distribution of egoistic suicide. Durkheim explains the relatively 'low' rate of suicide in Catholic societies as compared to Protestant ones, in terms of the greater integration of the former. But another explanation can be given for the differences in the recorded rates of suicide between the two types of society. The Catholic religion condemns suicide as a mortal sin, something which merits eternal damnation. In many cases this cultural attitude towards suicide might very well influence coroners to return a verdict other than suicide. Pressure of this kind would not generally be put on coroners in Protestant societies where moral condemnation of suicide tended to be less. In view of this,

uncritical acceptance of official suicide statistics for the purposes of comparative social analysis would be poor methodology.

Douglas forcefully argues that despite dismissing the stated intentions and commonsense interpretations of others, Durkheim himself used his own version of commonsense.

Both Douglas and Atkinson argue that a more precise and valid approach to the study of suicide should involve the study of particular cases. However, whereas Douglas argues that different types of suicide can be usefully categorised and compared according to social meaning, Atkinson considers that each case of suicide is unique and must be considered as such. Thus, Douglas suggests that in Western societies one classificatory category might be 'revenge' suicides (i.e. on a person or people who have hurt the suicide) and in some traditional societies religious categorisations such as 'transformation of the soul' might be appropriate. For Atkinson the purpose of sociology is to study the unique meaning of the individual case.

In his commentary on interpretist critiques of the use of official statistics, Barry Hindess is sharply critical of the 'strong' position adopted by Atkinson but finds the 'weak' position, such as that adopted by Douglas, uncontroversial. In refuting the 'strong' position, he suggests that a standard of certainty is implicitly being demanded which is unavailable in any walk of life. Sociologists, like the practitioners of other disciplines, must simply make sure that, as far as possible, their data, including statistical data, are representative and internally consistent (that is, that each unit that is supposed to refer to a given phenomenon actually does so). Admittedly, this is more easily said than done, but it must be done if sociology is to be practised at all. The second or 'weak' version of the interactionist position as construed by Hindess is that because the 'everyday understandings' of police, magistrates and others help to 'create' official statistics, these must be taken into consideration when evaluating and interpreting a given set of statistics. Hindess agrees with this but considers it to be a statement of the obvious. In effect, it is the position he himself takes in refuting the first, and in his view more typical version of the interactionist position. In putting forward the view that the 'everyday misunderstandings' of those who create statistics must be considered in this way, Hindess also refutes the simplistic positivistic position: that official statistics can be used unquestioningly to 'prove' a given case.

Steve Taylor: an integrated theory of suicide

Steve Taylor has attempted a theoretical analysis of suicide which seeks to include both personal meaning and the underlying causal structures of suicide. On the basis of his own research he agrees that official statistics do not give the 'real' picture in relation to suicide.

Figure 12.12 Taylor's typology of suicide

Taylor's own typology of suicide is straightforward although expressed in an unfamiliar vocabulary. He identifies two broad categories of suicide:

1 Ectopic suicide is prompted by a person's view of themselves – submissive when they are certain they want to be dead or thanatation when they are uncertain whether they want to live or die and so gamble with death.
2 Symphysic suicide is directed towards others. Sacrifice suicide is a response to hurt and an attempt to provoke guilt. Appeal suicide reflects uncertainty about how others feel and implies a need for communication. Appeal suicide suggests that life could be worth living in improved circumstances.

Taylor succeeds in illuminating a range of possible motives underlying suicide. However, his approach is far closer to symbolic interactionism than to the structuralism of Durkheim. He does not achieve a genuine integration of the two perspectives. His search for the underlying causes of individual action leads him to the influence of significant others rather than to the large-scale structural realities that were Durkheim's central concern.

Question

Critically discuss Durkheim's theory of suicide. Assess its contribution to the development of sociological theory and method.

Corporate crime

Corporate crime in the 1980s and 1990s

About 50 years ago, Edwin Sutherland defined white-collar crime as follows:

> *White-collar crime may be defined approximately as a crime committed by a person of respectability and high social status in the course of his occupation.*
>
> *(1949:9)*

As Mary Langan observes in her excellent overview of corporate and other white-collar crime, the term has since been extended to include offences committed lower down the occupational hierarchy (1996). She herself identifies five categories of white-collar crime:

- Large corporate crime.
- Large-scale criminal corporations.
- Small-scale criminal firms.
- Occupational crime.
- Other white-collar crime (i.e. committed outside employment).

We will look at each of these individually sometimes using other data than that provided by Langan. As Langan points out, it is particularly true of white-collar crime that it is not always clear whether it is a crime or an accident that has occurred.

Large corporate crime

Otherwise legitimate corporations sometimes violate the civil or criminal law or other regulatory codes. These violations can involve offences against employees (see p. 345), against consumers, the public, other firms and the state. Currently, offences against consumers – particularly where unhygienic or unsafe food production may be involved – is of particular public concern. A different type of consumer case was the capsizing of the ferry, *The Herald of Free Enterprise*, resulting in 192 deaths. The Sheen enquiry blamed the ferry owners, P. & O for failing to provide a safe operating system, and the boatswain for falling asleep while on duty. A charge of corporate manslaughter was not able to be sustained.

Large-scale criminal corporations

Unlike the corporations previously discussed, there are some which set out to make money or otherwise profit through criminal means. Such companies may have a legitimate front but fraud is their main business.

The classic example of modern 'megafraud' is the Bank of Credit and Commerce International. The bank speculated with clients' assets. At the time it was closed down in 1991, the bank had debts of 10 billion and 200,000 creditors, 30,000 of them in Britain. The bank concealed its losses of creditors' funds by taking out fictitious loans and investing deposits.

The world banking system is routinely used to launder profits from the biggest of all illicit international trades – drugs, mainly cannabis, heroin and cocaine. UN experts have warned that unless action is taken against this trafficking these 'crime multinationals' may corrupt and 'criminalise' the key institutions of the global economy (Reading 2).

Small-scale criminal firms

All kinds of business people and professionals commit a vast variety of frauds – from the builder who uses cheap, perhaps unsafe materials to boost profits, to the solicitor who wacks up fees well beyond the value of services rendered. The rapid expansion of the small business sector during the Thatcher-Major period, notwithstanding its positive features, has probably added substantially to this type of crime.

Occupational crime

Employees in both the public and private sector perpetrate a wide range of crimes. These vary in nature and scale depending on the level in the hierarchy of the offender. Thus, some Chief Executives have made grossly excessive expenses claims whereas at the middle level petty theft of, say, office equipment is more typical. Employers vary in their attitude to this widespread phenomenon – some 'live with it' whereas others crack down on it and pursue prosecution and dismissal.

Table 12.7 gives data for a Mori survey of Britain's top 1000 companies. Job insecurity, loss of loyalty due to organisational down-sizing, and personal gain were relevant factors in a growing area of crime.

Table 12.7 Employee fraud

The main perpetrators	Percentage
Senior management	4
Middle management	34
Junior management	22
Clerical staff	16

(Source: Mori in *The Guardian*, 5.6.1995:15)

Other white-collar crime

Middle class individuals also commit crime outside of their corporate or occupational situation. Tax evasion is the classic example. Yet, tax evasion is often rarely fully constructed as a crime in that the tax inspectorate often negotiate an agreement rather than seek prosecution of an apparent offender. D Cook (1989) gives figures running at fewer than 500 a year compared with 8,000 prosecutions for social security fraud. This seems to be an example of the social construction of (officially labelled) crime on the basis of class. A recent boom area of white-collar crime is insurance fraud. By the late 1980s the insurance industry and police had begun accelerated additional moves to reduce this crime.

Deconstructing corporate crime: its character and regulation

What is constructed can be 'deconstructed'. Sociological deconstruction of crime simply means analysing its characteristics. Langan suggests four main characteristics of corporate crime:

- low visibility
- complexity
- diffusion of responsibility
- diffusion of victimisation

The low visibility of corporate crime is partly due to the fact that much of it is carried out under normal occupational routines. In contrast, crimes of violence or robberies are often highly visible. Corporate crime can often be of great complexity. For instance, Robert Maxwell fraudulently moved money around his international business empire in a way that took months to untangle after his death. The increasing use or misuse of computers in crime excludes probably the majority of the population from fully understanding the technicalities of this type of crime.

The diffusion of responsibility for corporate crime occurs

largely because it is often difficult to establish individual blame. Despite several attempts to prosecute individuals in relation to *The Herald of Free Enterprise* disaster, none succeeded. Diffusion of victimisation can occur to the extent that individuals may not even know they have been victimised or may only find out later. Damage due to pollution such as radiation-related malignancies or asbestosis fall into this category.

There may, then, be other factors accounting for the relatively lenient regulation of corporate crime in addition to possible class bias on the part of enforcement authorities. These are the low visibility, complexity and diffuseness of this type of crime discussed above.

Despite recent attempts to pursue and prosecute corporate and white-collar crime, regulation continues to be relatively relaxed in comparison with other crime. The City of London still enjoys a high degree of self-regulation despite recent scandals. Although major corporate crimes are criminal offences, many offences in relation to safety and health, including environmental health are *regulatory offences*. They are often dealt with informally or in the civil courts. In addition, a combination of low detection rates, low prosecution rates and, despite a recent tightening up, more lenient sanctions give white-collar crime the appearance of being more officially 'condoned' than other crime.

Explanations of corporate and white-collar crime

Although the character of white-collar crime and official response to it may differ from those of other crime, it does not follow that the reasons for its occurrence are different than for those of other sorts of crime. We will now look at some suggested explanations of corporate and white-collar crime.

1   Individual pathology

Marshall Clinard associated certain pathological personality characteristics with the black marketeers he studied in post-war America (1946). These characteristics included greed, ruthlessness and a willingness to take risks.

More typically, however, sociologists reject individualistic explanations for crime (see pp. 349-50). In particular, Sutherland argued that as middle class crime, like lower class crime occurred quite widely, there was no need to search for explanations of individual pathology in either case.

2   Rational choice theory

The application of rational choice theory (discussed above) to white-collar crime is clear. Individuals commit it, not because they are usually pathological, but because they calculate that it is in their interests to do so. Thus, Robert Maxwell stole millions of pounds from pension funds to use in his own businesses.

3   Differential association

Sutherland argued that people commit crime not usually because they are 'sick' but because they have learned criminal behaviour:

> *... in association with those who define such behaviour favourably and in isolation from those who define it unfavourably, and that a person in an appropriate situation engages in such criminal behaviour if, and only if, the weight of favourable definitions exceeds the weight of unfavourable definitions.*
>
> (234)

In short, people are influenced to commit crime by those around them and, again, this applies as much to middle as to lower class crime. Mary Langan extends this analysis to apply to companies such as BCCI which are essentially criminal and therefore present employees with criminal associations. She cites the Governor of the Bank of England's comment that the company was 'rotten right through'.

What can be added in qualification of Sutherland's theory of differential association is that not everyone who associates with criminals becomes a criminal. This may be because they choose not to.

4   Social disorganisation (and strain on individuals)

We looked at Merton's theory of conformity/non-conformity earlier in this chapter. Merton argued that social disorganisation can generate tendencies to non-conformity, including criminal behaviour. He states that social disorganisation 'refers to inadequacies in a social system that keeps people's collective and individual purposes from being as fully realised as they could be'. Thus, crime, including white-collar crime, can be seen as an innovatory response to lack of legitimate opportunity due to social disorganisation. The precise source of the pressure on the individual can vary – it could be pressure to 'perform' from the firm, or from developments in the national economy, say, a rise in unemployment.

Sutherland himself, thought that the development of bureaucratic corporate capitalism in the United States at the expense of small scale family businesses had caused a decline in civilised behaviour and an increase in social disorganisation resulting in an increase in crime. Although this view is somewhat traditionalist, like the radical views discussed next, it suggests that capitalism itself or, at least, large scale capitalism can be conducive to crime.

5   Marxist and radical theories

Marxist and radical criminologists argue that modern capitalist enterprises exist to make profits and that if they cannot do so legally, they will very possibly adopt criminal means (see pp. 354-5).

A common view among radical sociologists is that there is a cognisance between 'the spirit of capitalism and corporate criminality' (Langan 250). Mary Langan cites Mars' comment that 'there is only a blurred line between entrepreneurality and flair on the one hand and sharp practices on the other'. The succession of prosecutions brought by the Serious Fraud Office against leading corporate executives in the 1980s and 1990s lends some support to this observation.

Conclusion

The decline of the working class and rise of the white-collar class, the increase in computers as both tools of crime as well as objects of theft, the appeal of the relatively low visibility and low detection risk of much white-collar crime, may lead to a change in what is perceived as typical crime. People may begin to think of themselves as more likely to be the victims of credit card or other financial fraud rather than of a 'mugging' in the street. Similarly, stereotypes of those who commit crime may change. What was once regarded as a minority activity may come to be the main object of criminological study.

The social construction of deviance

The section on corporate and white-collar crime demonstrates how differently that type of crime is socially constructed in comparison, say, to crimes involving immediate and intended violence to people or property. In these cases class assumptions partly underlie perceptions and responses. In the case of domestic crimes of violence a different construction is at work again – typically involving assumptions about family privacy and patriarchy.

Although the term *social construction* is relatively new to sociology, in fact, the sociological perspective is inherently social constructionist. Functionalist and Marxist analysis of deviance each reflect the theoretical view that the behaviour of individuals and groups is influenced by social structure. Some proponents of these perspectives underplay the role of individuals and small groups in the process of construction. In this respect, symbolic interactionism has provided a rich range of concepts despite its own shortcomings in terms of wider structural analysis. Muncie and McLaughlin give an excellent summary of the social constructionist approach to crime and the contribution of interactionism to this approach:

A vast array of behaviours have been (or can be) deemed 'deviant' or 'criminal' because they violate legal, normative or human rights prescriptions. But there is no common behavioural denominator which ties all of these acts together. Propositions, such as society is based upon a moral consensus or that the criminal law is merely a reflection of that consensus, also remain contentious. An interactionist school of sociology, for example, argues that there is no underlying or enduring consensus in society. Rather, the social order consists of a plurality of social groups each acting in accordance with its own interpretations of reality. Such diversity is as likely to produce conflict as much as consensus. Interpretations of reality are learnt through the ways in which people perceive and react, either positively or negatively, to the various behaviours of others. Thus, with respect to crime, an interactionist position would argue that defining crime with reference to legal or norm-violating actions is seriously limited. Rather, crime is viewed as a consequence of social interaction: that is, as a result of a negotiated process that involves the rule-violator, the police, the courts, lawyers and the law-makers who define a person's behaviour as criminal. Behaviour may be labelled criminal, but it is not this behaviour in itself that constitutes crime.

(Munzie and McLaughton: 13)

Deviance as ideological censure: Colin Sumner

There is an obvious reason why sociologists should – as Colin Sumner contends – bury the term 'deviance'. Given that all sociological, if not psychological and biological, perspectives are agreed that deviance is constructed quite differently in different societies and at different times, then, there is no such 'thing' as deviance or no essential deviance. This simple but powerful point underlies Sumner's *The Sociology of Deviance: An Obituary* (1995). Of course, Sumner's argument is more specific and detailed than that and we will return to it shortly.

Firstly, however, what does Sumner mean by ideological censure? Sumner's use of the concept of ideological censure gives emphasis to the power and self-interest of those who primarily make the rules and the particular system of social order that the rules underpin. The concept would appear to dovetail nicely with Althusser's concept of the *state ideological apparatus*: it is the powerful – in Althusser's terms the ruling class – that is best positioned to shape dominant notions of 'normality and deviance' through the media and educational system. Once Sumner's concept of ideological censure is understood as located within an analysis of power, order and control (or, put otherwise, political economy) it can clearly be seen to be different from labelling theory with which it nevertheless shares an appreciation of the

relative nature of both norms and deviance. Sumner is closer to Chambliss (see p. 355) than Becker although he does not see the criminal law merely as a product of class power – the process of law and rule making is complex and contested as is the process of negotiating them. Muncie and McLaughlin explain this emphasis:

He (Sumner) prefers to treat crime and deviance as matters of moral and political judgement – as social censures rooted in particular ideologies. The concept of crime, then, is neither a behavioural nor a legal category, nor an expression of particularly cultural and political configurations. Neither is 'crime' simply a label, but a general term to describe a series of 'negative' ideological categories with specific historical applications ... categories of denunciation or abuse lodged within very complex, historically loaded practical conflicts and moral debates ... these negative categories of moral ideology are social censures.

(16)

If Sumner's use of ideology owes something to Althusser, there is something of Gramsci's concept of hegemony in the sense of challenge, flux and potential change which is part of the process of social censure.

Foucault: the (changing) order of things

The influence of Foucault is now significant in many areas of social science, including the one under discussion. In Chapter 4, Foucault's approach to understanding society and some of its key concepts were presented.

Of the authors referred to in this chapter, Foucault's influence is perhaps most apparent in Stanley Cohen's *Visions of Social Control* (1986). Cohen's description of the change in the nineteenth century to highly rationalised and institutionally ordered systems of discipline, punishment and treatment is directly influenced by Foucault. Foucault's work certainly reinforces the consensus that has emerged in sociology that it is particular social orders – 'regimes of truth' in Foucault's terms – that generate particular categories of deviance. Thus, according to Foucault, in the nineteenth century, the category of mental illness, and its various subcategories were defined as a specific type of behaviour rather than merely as part of a wider range of anti-social or socially awkward behaviour as it had previously been seen. The category of mental illness was allocated causes and symptoms and particular forms of treatment. Those who could not be 'normalised' were consigned to asylums away for the 'rational' majority. A similar process of rationalisation occurred in relation to crime and other forms of deviance. Cohen argues that the climate of liberal, rational reform which generated these innovations was challenged in the 1960s and continues to be challenged.

The subject matter of much of Foucault's work as indicated by the title of his books would appear to fall within what is traditionally thought of as the area of social control and deviance. These include: *Discipline and Punish, Madness and Civilisation, Mental Illness* and *Psychology*, and *The Birth of the Clinic*. Further, his *The History of Sexuality* deals with cultural definitions of sexuality and the endorsement by government of certain forms of sexual behaviour rather than others. Foucault's earlier work develops his theoretical and methodological approach, notably the concepts of discourse and power-knowledge (see pp. 98-100). The list of titles just given can be read as case studies or empirical examples of his approach. One of Foucault's major themes is how societies arrive at their definitions of 'normal' and 'abnormal' in various spheres of activity. For example, how, in a given society, is the line between 'sanity' and 'madness', the 'criminal' and the 'non-criminal' or the sexually 'acceptable' or 'deviant' drawn? In more sociological terms, how are such definitions constructed and enforced? His later work concentrates less on the creation of 'expert-knowledge' and more on how power-knowledge is linked with certain technologies of surveillance, enforcement and control. He gives Jeremy Bentham's Panopticon as an example. This was a suggested prison design which would enable the warden to oversee any prisoner at any given time.

Foucault brings into consideration how the body is socially disciplined – a matter which is obviously of great importance but often ignored. Barry Smart states that:

> *Discipline is a technique of power which provides procedure for training or for coercing bodies (individual and collective). The instruments through which disciplinary power achieves the hold are hierarchical observations, normalising judgement and the examination.*
>
> (Smart, 1985:84)

Bentham's Panopticon is an excellent example of bodies organised for observation. The video camera is also frequently used as a means of observation in contemporary society. Barry Smart quotes Foucault to illustrate how power can be exercised through judgements aimed at normalising body (and other behaviour):

> *The workshop, the school, the army were subject to a whole micro-penalty of time (lateness, absences, interruptions of tasks), of activity (inattention, negligence, lack of zeal) ... of the body (incorrect attitudes, irregular gestures, lack of cleanliness. (Figure 12.13 illustrates that even military discipline can be breached.)*

Figure 12.13 A body breaks discipline: a soldier makes his point

The third instrument of discipline, the examination, combines the other two in the form of a 'normalising gaze' which puts people into given categories. Experts frequently keep detailed records of people in the process of normalising them within a given category of behaviour e.g. mental health. However, the process of pressurising individuals to conform is not confined to experts.

Although Foucault had no intention of prescribing a grand theory of society, he did develop a methodology of social enquiry and a battery of concepts that has provided a non-Marxist reference point for a generation of radical sociologists. Yet, arguably, Foucault's world is one of shadows rather than people. Agency and imagination never seem to move social 'subjects'. In fact, Foucault was explicitly anti-humanist and did not consider that individuals have these 'human attributes'. For him subjectivity, often thought of by others as the relatively autonomous, thinking, feeling self, is 'constituted' by forces external to the individual – by discourse and regimes of truth. He stated that the actor is erased 'like a face drawn in sand on the edge of the sea'. Of himself, he wrote: 'I am no doubt not the only one who writes in order to have no face' (*The Sunday Times* 6.6.1996:10). At least, he was consistent!

Figure 12.14 Michel Foucault

Concepts of crime in late modernity: Jock Young

Stanley Cohen's *Visions of Social Control* illustrates how well-intentioned, modern, liberal attempts to reform a wide range of 'deviant' behaviours began to fall apart. Attempts to reform criminals did not stem a steady rise in crime, attempts to 'cure' the mentally 'ill' simply filled the asylums. Jock Young takes further the argument that conceptions of crime (and deviance) are in the

Table 12.8 The shift into late modernity: changing conceptions of crime and its control

		Modern	Late modern
1	Definition of crime	Obvious	Problematic
2	Prevalence of offender	Minority	Extensive
3	Incidence of victimisation	Exceptional	Normal
4	Causes of crime	Distant, determined, exceptional	Present, rationally chosen, widespread
5	Relationship to 'normality'	Separate	Normal/continuum
6	Relationship to wider society	Leakage	Integral
7	Locus of offence	Public	Public/private
8	Relationship of offender to victim	Stranger, outsider outside/in-group	Stranger/intimate,
9	Locus of social control	Criminal justice system	Informal/ multi-agency
10	Effectiveness of social intervention	Taken for granted	Problematic: 'Nothing works'
11	Public reaction	Obvious and rational	Problematic: irrational 'fear of crime' and moral panics
12	Spatial dimension	Segregated	Contested space

(Source: L.S.E. Lecture, 1995)

process of radical change. In doing so, he adopts a description of the earlier period as 'modern' and the later or present one as 'late modern'. However one refers to the two periods, the list of contrasting conceptions of crime in the 'modern and late modern' periods captures many of the points made by other authors referred to in the later part of this chapter. It will be used here partly for the purpose of general summary (Table 12.8).

Young's first contrasting pair reflect the fact that definitions of crime constantly shift and the law is less and less seen as a reflection of 'right and wrong'. In any case, much of the law is now concerned with the bureaucratic regulation of society rather than with the implementation of moral principles. Because of these developments crime is not merely the activity of a criminal class but a widespread, if for many, only an occasional activity – Young's second point. Thirdly, therefore, the experience of crime has become a relatively normal part of everyday life. Fourthly, if crime is such a widespread activity, then, it seems likely that often it is rationally chosen – not requiring of any profound explanation (although different types of crime will occur in different types of environment). Fifth, on the same basis, most crime is part of 'normality' rather than a separate, unusual or atypical occurrence. Sixth, crime is so often entwined with economic, social and political activity that it seems integral to rather than separate from them.

Seventh, contemporary research constantly shows that crime is not an activity exclusive to public life – a great deal occurs within personal relationships and families. Eighth, by the same token the perpetrator of, for instance, sexual offences and violence against the person, is quite likely to be an intimate. Ninth, much crime, especially of a personal kind, may require the expertise of a social worker, counsellor or probation officer. Tenth, with the line between crime and legality, the deviant and the normal, seemingly blurred, and with the proliferation of crime, the issue of appropriate intervention becomes a complex problem. Eleventh, because people feel vulnerable to crime and because of press manipulation, public response can be panicky and irrational. Finally, crime is no longer an activity occurring 'somewhere else' as far as most people are concerned – from pushers and vagrants in public spaces to transnational financial fraud – it is all about.

Questions

1 What are the main characteristics and causes of white-collar crime? To what extent does it differ from 'working' or 'lower' class crime?

2 Critically discuss the view that deviance is socially constructed.

Summary

1 There was a substantial and steady increase in most categories of recorded offences between 1971 and 1996. However, recorded offences underestimate the extent of crime by several hundred per cent in most categories. Victim surveys, self-report studies and even experiment suggest a much higher rate of crime.

2 Both the general public and agencies of law enforcement are affected by stereotypes of criminals. Class (working class), sex (male), age (young) and 'race' (black) are stereotypical characteristics frequently associated with criminals. There is a substantial body of detailed research which suggests that stereotyping of criminals tends to be misleading. More qualified and measured statements are more accurate.

3 Of the theories discussed in the remainder of the chapter, only the functionalist, Marxist and interactionist can be considered to offer fully developed perspectives on social order, control and deviance.

4 Early psychological explanations of criminal behaviour are now generally discredited. Sociologists tend to be sceptical of attempts to demonstrate a genetic basis of criminal behaviour and rather explain it as behaviour, learnt within the context of a particular social environment.

5 Much of Durkheim's analysis of deviance remains fundamental and, even when opposed, of continuing influence. Durkheim stated that deviance is universal (it occurs in all societies), relative (it takes different forms in different societies), and functional (it focuses and reinforces communal morality). Abnormally high rates of deviance indicate that social solidarity (order/cohesion) is under strain – thus, Durkheim's analysis of deviance is part of a total understanding of social functioning.

6 Merton, like Durkheim, explains deviance or 'nonconformity' as he calls it, in terms of the total social structure. In his case, he explains crime as the pursuit of society's 'goals' by illegal 'means'.

7 As the term implies the subcultural theorists explain deviance in group or subcultural rather than in individual terms. There is some disagreement among subcultural theorists about the origin of the values and behaviour of members of deviant subcultures: Albert Cohen considers that they imitate mainstream culture – albeit in deviant ways – whereas Miller thinks they are indigenous to working class culture. In describing deviant subcultures in terms of hierarchies which broadly mirror those in mainstream society, Cloward and Ohlin are closer to Cohen. British subcultural theories of deviance variously reflect Marxist and interactionist influence and overall appear more complex than American theories.

8 Marxist theories explain deviance firmly within the context of capitalist society. Emphasis is put on the frequently 'hidden' crimes of the powerful and on the disadvantaged and 'oppressive' conditions which may promote deviancy among the working class.

9 Interactionists define deviance as behaviour which is labelled as such. Secondary deviance occurs once a deviant label has effectively been attached to someone. Stereotyping by agencies of social control can greatly affect who is labelled 'deviant'. Class, sex, age and 'race' can be the basis of stereotyping.

10 Rational choice and situational theories of deviance explain criminal behaviour as deliberate action in pursuit of self-interest which takes circumstances (situations) into consideration. Despite the appealing 'commonsense' of this approach, it has recently come under criticism from researchers who demonstrate an apparent link between economic recession and the crime rate.

11 It is possible to find many complementary aspects between the major structural theories of deviance – functionalism and Marxism – and the major interpretist theory – interactionism. In particular, Marxism and interactionism have frequently been blended to create a more complete approach.

12 Durkheim's *Suicide* and Atkinson's and Douglas's reply now have the status of a classic set-piece illustration of the contrast between positivism and interpretism. Steve Taylor offers an alternative approach.

13 The shift from an industrial to a service society has also shifted the nature of crime. A full section is therefore devoted to corporate and white-collar crime.

14 A number of more theoretical contributions on the theme of the social construction of deviance are discussed.

Research and coursework

A problem with doing first-hand research into deviance is that it could take you into places and situations you should not sensibly be in. This topic could provide an opportunity for a piece of coursework based on existing literature.

Students often find the interactionist perspective on deviance particularly interesting. An intensive and critical study of a single book – such as Goffman's *Asylum* (Penguin, 1968) or Cohen's *Folk Devils and Moral Panics* (Martin Robertson, 1981) could be made. Such a study might concentrate on the use and development of a number of key interactionist concepts such as 'labelling' and 'stigma' in Goffman's book or 'amplification' and 'moral panic' in Cohen's. Reference is likely to be made to the use of these concepts in other works – although in less detail. Critical perspectives could be achieved by using other theoretical approaches to assess the effectiveness of the concepts used.

A piece of original work that could be attempted is the analysis of a deviant youth subcultural group. You will need to develop a theoretical perspective and to do this reading relevant studies such as S Hall and T Jefferson eds., *Resistance through Rituals* (Hutchinsan, 1979) or, again Cohen's classic would be helpful. However, on analysis of some aspect of contemporary youth would also require reference to more contemporary literature (see pp. 455-6 and pp. 463-7). A key decision for the fieldwork is likely to be whether to research covertly or overtly. Another study could be a comparison of official crime statistics with crime as reported on the media. More locally oriented research could explore a local 'moral panic' or a victim survey could provide the basis of a piece of research.

Further reading

For teachers Colin Sumner's *The Sociology of Deviance: An Obituary* (Open University Press, 1994) is a stimulating overview of the 'life and death' of the concept. Students will find J Muncie and E McLaughlin eds., *The Problem of Crime* (Open University Press, 1996) up-to-date and accessible.

Readings

Reading 1
The case for left realism

From Jock Young (1986) 'The Future of Criminology: the need for radical realism', in R Matthews and J Young eds., *Confronting Crime* (London: Sage, 1986) pp. 23-4

Crime is not an activity of latter day Robin Hoods – the vast majority of working-class crime is directed within the working class. It is intra-class not inter-class in its nature. Similarly, despite the mass media predilection for focusing on inter-racial crime, it is overwhelmingly intra-racial. Crimes of violence, for example, are by and large one poor person hitting another poor person – and in almost half of these instances it is a man hitting his wife or lover.

This is not to deny the impact of crimes of the powerful or indeed of the social problems created by capitalism which are perfectly legal. Rather, left realism notes that the working class is a victim of crime from all directions. It notes that the more vulnerable a person is economically and socially the more likely it is that both working-class and white-collar crime will occur against them; that one sort of crime tends to compound another, as does one social problem another. Furthermore, it notes that crime is a potent symbol of the anti-social nature of capitalism and is the most immediate way in which people experience other problems, such as unemployment or competitive individualism.

Realism starts from problems as people experience them. It takes seriously the complaints of women with regards the dangers of being in public places at night, it takes note of the fears of the elderly with regard to burglary, it acknowledges the widespread occurrence of domestic violence and racist attacks. It does not ignore the fears of the vulnerable nor recontextualise them out of existence by putting them into a perspective which abounds with abstractions such as the 'average citizen' bereft of class or gender. It is only too aware of the systematic concealment and ignorance of crimes against the least powerful. Yet it does not take these fears at face value – it pinpoints their rational kernel but it is also aware of the forces towards irrationality.

Realism is not empiricism. Crime and deviance are prime sites of moral anxiety and tension in a society which is fraught with real inequalities and injustices. Criminals can quite easily become folk devils onto which are projected such feelings of unfairness. But there is a rational core to the fear of crime just as there is a rational core to the anxieties which distort it. Realism argues with popular consciousness in its attempts to separate out reality from fantasy. But it does not deny that crime is a problem. Indeed, if there were no rational core the media would have no power of leverage to the public consciousness. Crime becomes a metaphor but it is a metaphor rooted in reality.

Reading 2
Transnational crime

'Crime, Inc.', *The Times*, 21.11.1994:19

Not for nothing are Italy's magistrates its popular heroes. Their courage in bringing Mafia and Camorra godfathers to justice started a process of national regeneration. Brave men, including Giovanni Falcone, paid with their lives. Those deaths shocked Italians into revolt against the endemic corruption which had given organised crime its protective core. Italy has secured convictions against more leading Mafiosi in the past two years than in the previous four decades. But the increasingly transnational character of the syndicates' operations means that no country can hope to defeat them with purely national means.

The first United Nations conference at ministerial level on transnational crime opens today in the appropriate setting of Naples. Its aim is to encourage governments to catch up with the organised crime fraternity, which has modernised its operations more rapidly and skilfully than have the institutions for crime prevention, detection and law enforcement. Groups may recruit in one country, obtain supplies in another, sell in several others and launder the proceeds through a string of tax havens and electronic transfers. As the established Western financial centres adopt more stringent controls to prevent money-laundering, they are turning to the fast-growing and ill-regulated markets in Asia or Latin America.

Gangs which once fought over territory now think of global markets. Their combined annual sales are estimated at £500 billion, larger than the gross domestic product of many countries; the Cali cartel in Colombia has three times the turnover of General Motors. Traditionally insular, they are now making deals with each other. The Colombian cartels linked up with Nigerian drug-runners in the 1980s; Chinese triads have networks the length of the Silk Route; the Mafia is advising Russian gangs on money-laundering. If they are to out-manoeuvre 'Crime Inc.', governments need to link up as effectively as the criminals.

The only way is to deprive them of 'safe havens' by closing loopholes in national legislation. A start was made in 1988, with a UN convention on drug-trafficking which binds states to share intelligence, facilitate extradition, criminalise money-laundering and supply training to countries that need it. But the gangs have diversified; up to half the traffic is now in other areas, ranging from white slavery and the smuggling of illegal immigrants to trafficking in arms, nuclear material, body parts and endangered species. They are moving rapidly into computer-related crime.

Every step towards better co-ordination of the fight against crime runs, however, into concerns about sovereignty. Interpol is an information exchange network, with no powers of investigation. An OECD Financial Action Task Force has come up with 40 sound rules to prevent money-laundering, but only half the OECD's 26 members abide by them. The fledgling Europol is not Europe's equivalent of the FBI. The UN's tiny crime branch can act only as a catalyst for decisions by governments.

Italy strongly supports the UN's case for a new convention to define what constitutes transnational crime, improve exchanges of information and make it easier to investigate, arrest and prosecute criminals and seize their assets. Britain is sceptical, preferring unspecified 'practical measures' to a new convention. Were the existing rules adequate, this stance would be reasonable, but they are not. A coherent global crime policy cannot be assured by treaty, but by setting out rules within which to work, a treaty would increase the pressure on governments to work together. A start can and should be made in Naples this week.

13

Wealth, Inequality, Poverty and Welfare

Beveridge: chief architect of the welfare state. Is his legacy now in danger? How well has his heritage lasted?

Aims of this chapter

1 To describe the distribution of income and wealth in Britain.

2 To discuss the measurement, extent and causes of poverty.

3 Critically to discuss definitions and interpretations of the 'underclass'.

4 To discuss the historical development of social and welfare policy and to evaluate a variety of approaches to it.

5 Critically to comment on the so-called 'crisis' of the welfare state.

Introduction

The issues of wealth, poverty and welfare are of first rank importance. The very high rate of popular participation in the National Lottery and the emotions it generates indicates how enticing the dream of wealth is to many. It is a dream that crosses class lines (see Figure 13.1). Equally, in the 1980s and 1990s images of poverty have confronted people through the frequent sight of begging on the streets, and on television screens through, for instance, news coverage of housing repossessions. Fundamental issues lie behind these powerful images. For instance, what is an acceptable poverty line in a society where wealth is high and still increasing? What ought to be the top rate of tax (at present it is 40 per cent (1997))? How much of the nation's wealth and income should be devoted to public services and projects? What is the role of welfare? – should it be a minimal safety net for the poor or a comprehensive system of security and service for all? Much political debate and conflict occurs over the relevant answers and policies.

Who plays the game?
The social class of lottery players, percentage playing.

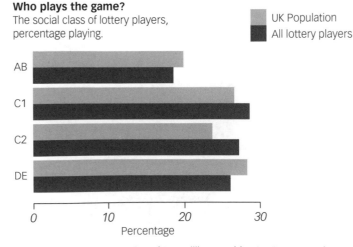

Note: Even a top lottery prize of £15 million would not get you anywhere near entry to the richest 500 in Britain.

(Source: *The Guardian*, 4.11.1995:7)

Figure 13.1 'The dream of wealth'

The sheer scope of the topics of wealth, poverty and welfare is daunting. In practice, much of the ground is covered elsewhere in this book, including in a separate chapter on health problems and policy (see Chapter 14). Two earlier chapters dealt with social class

and laid the groundwork for a more detailed examination of the distribution of wealth, income and poverty. Class and wealth are closely related (see pp. 166-8). The broad structure of social inequality is as much the result of wealth inherited or accumulated over the years as of differential income distribution. The particular aim of this chapter is broadly to describe and explain inequalities of wealth and income but to leave detailed issues for discussion elsewhere. The exception is poverty and the related matter of the 'underclass' which are fully analysed here. Inequality and poverty are not the same. A person with one million pounds is not equal in wealth to a person with ten million pounds. Neither are in poverty. Whereas most people, including politicians, view poverty as a matter of concern, there is much less agreement about inequality. Some would like to see less, others see no reason why there should be limits.

Income and wealth: definitions and an outline of inequalities

A distinction is generally made between income as the *flow* of economic resources (Table 13.1) and wealth as the total *stock* of economic resources (Table 13.2). For instance, wages and dividends are regarded as income, dwellings and pension funds as wealth. Here it is personal wealth that is under consideration – as listed in Table 13.2. Total household income rather than individual income is the definition of income adopted – except where otherwise indicated.

As John Scott notes there are a number of different, often technical, ways of defining income and wealth but most indicate similar distributions and trends. This chapter shares his focus on the advantage or disadvantage that wealth and income can generate. It is necessary to consider wealth and income to understand inequality and poverty.

A problem in adopting household income rather than individual income as the focus, is that gender issues in relation to the distribution of income are less easy to perceive and analyse. However, Chapter 6 provides much data relevant to this matter and there is some further discussion here.

In 1995 total disposable household income was £493 billion (i.e. after tax and National Insurance deductions) and £599 billion

Table 13.1 Household income

Source of income United Kingdom	1971	1976	1981	1986	1991	1995
				Percentages		
Wages and salaries	68	67	63	58	58	56
Income from self-employment	9	9	8	10	10	10
Rent, dividends, interest	6	6	7	8	9	7
Private pensions, annuities, etc.	5	5	6	8	10	11
Social security benefits	10	11	13	13	11	13
Other current transfers	2	2	2	3	2	3
Total household income (= 100%) (£ billion at 1994 prices)	305	354	386	458	556	599 (493 after tax)

(Source. *Social Trends*, 1997:90 – slightly adapted))

Table 13.2 Composition of the net wealth of the personal sector

United Kingdom	1971	1981	1991	1995
		Percentages		
Life assurance and pension funds	15	16	27	34
Dwellings (net of mortgage debt)	26	36	37	26
Stocks, shares and unit trusts	23	8	8	15
National Savings, notes and coin and bank deposits	13	10	9	10
Shares and deposits with building societies	7	8	8	7
Non-marketable tenancy rights	12	12	8	5
Other fixed assets	10	10	5	5
Other financial assets net of liabilities	−6	−	−2	−2
Total (= 100%) (£ billion at 194 prices)	1,172	1,416	2,529	2,830

(Source: *Social Trends*, 1997:102 – slightly adapted)

gross. Net personal sector wealth was £2,830 billion in the same year. The ratio of wealth to disposable household income was, therefore, about 6:1. These figures hide a myriad of individual differences of wealth and income, many of them spectacular in scale. As Tables 13.1 and 13.2 show, there was a substantial increase in both real income and wealth between 1971 and 1995. By official measure, at least, Britain became richer during that period as it has done so steadily throughout the twentieth century. A H Halsey interprets official figures to tell us that 'since 1900 the United Kingdom has at least tripled and possible quadrupled its gross national product in real terms. (1995:39)

Income

As Table 13.1 shows, the importance of the various different sources of income changed significantly during the 1971 to 1995 period. Wages and salaries declined from 68 to 56 per cent of income. This was balanced by a rise in private pensions and annuities (a single sum payment on the maturity of a pension) on the one hand, and in state benefits on the other. The former applied mainly to the older middle class who both increased in numbers and among whom there was a trend to earlier retirement (see pp. 257-8). However, redundancy payments also financed the early retirement of many manual workers.

The increased social security bill was mainly a result of the large increase in the unemployed and in single parents and married couples with children on state benefit which occurred over this period. Whereas the number of old people living on social security fell by 25 per cent between 1974 and 1991 the number of children dependent on benefits quadrupled (see pp. 381-3). Dependency in

the sense of an increase in non-wage earners, increased greatly between 1971 and 1995 and was partly paid for by the state (or, more precisely, the tax payer) and partly by private savings, mainly pensions. The increase in the numbers of wealthy or comfortably-off older people and in the numbers of families with young children who were dependent on the state for income indicates the growing inequality that characterised this period of almost a quarter of a century.

Who received most of the increased income referred to above? Figure 13.2 refers specifically to the Thatcher period in office of 1979-1990. It shows the percentage change in income of the bottom half of the population by decile group (tenths). The bar on

Change in real income of bottom half of British populations 1979–1990/1

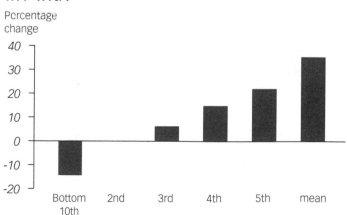

(Source: *Old and New Poverty: The Challenge for Reform*, Rivers Oram Press, 1995)

Figure 13.2 Growing income inequality in Britain

the right hand side of the table also shows the mean (or average) percentage rise in income of all groups and as this is much larger than that for any groups in the bottom 50 per cent, then, the percentage income increase of the top 50 per cent was also much greater than that of the bottom 50 per cent. The richest tenth experienced a 50 per cent increase.

The bottom tenth of the population is the only group that had its income reduced in absolute terms during this period – by the large factor of 14 per cent. This happened mainly because of increased unemployment and welfare cuts and because of the growth of the low pay sector (see p. 357).

Comparative studies by both the Joint Centre for Political and Economic Studies (Washington) and by the European Commission show that Britain experienced the sharpest increase in poverty and inequality in the European Community in the 1980s. One measure of income inequality is the percentage of households with less than 40% of median (typical) *household income* (i.e. income into households after all central and local government tax). By this measure, inequality increased more sharply in Britain than anywhere in Europe or North America, although the United States and Canada are still more unequal than Britain in this respect (Figure 13.3).

The less sharp rise in income inequality by this measure in France and Germany partly reflects their commitment to the European Community's social chapter (which Britain opted out of under the Conservatives). Among other things this guarantees a minimum wage and social security levels. This issue is one of keen political debate not least because it has such important human consequences.

The Institute for Fiscal Studies uses real household disposable income to measure the pattern of income inequality over a longer period, 1971-1993 (Figure 13.4). By its calculations, the richest ten per cent increased income from £275 a week to £450. The average household disposable income increased by 45 per cent. The income of the poorest ten per cent of households was fairly stable at just under £100 in 1971 and just over in 1993. This is a slightly

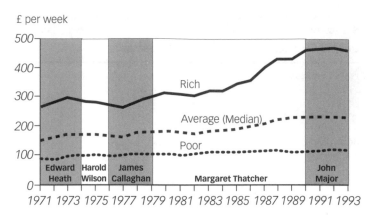

(Source: Institute for Fiscal Studies)

Figure 13.4 Real household disposable income

better situation for this group than for the shorter, mid 1970s to mid 1980s period, and is probably accounted for by the relatively more egalitarian policies of the 1974-79 Labour governments. However, it does appear that the ballooning inequality in household incomes stabilised in the early part of the Major years. This was probably due to a business recession rather than government policies. The sharp increase in top salaries compared to wages between 1994-96 suggests that the trend to inequality was resumed.

Salary differences

Another source of evidence of growing income inequality during the Conservatives' period in office is provided by a salary comparison published by Hay Management Consultants (1994). Their research shows an over 600 per cent net salary increase for chief executives between 1979 and 1994 against a net increase of 400 per cent for the average earner (figures not adjusted for

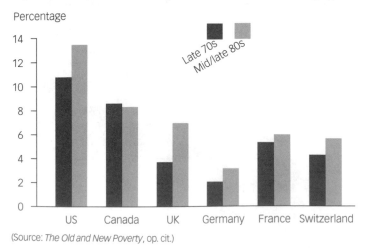

(Source: *The Old and New Poverty*, op. cit.)

Figure 13.3 Households with less than 40% of median household income

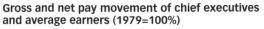
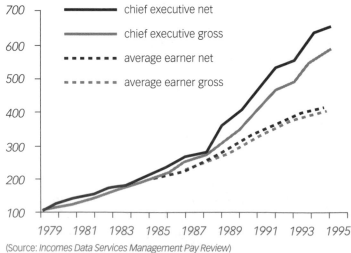

(Source: *Incomes Data Services Management Pay Review*)

Figure 13.5 Average gross salary rises: July 1992-93

Figure 13.6 Former chief executive of British Gas, Cedric Brown. His controversial pay and perks award came to symbolise 1990s inequality

inflation). Clerical salaries increased by only 333 per cent during the period. (see Figure 13.5) This disparity of pay awards continued into 1995-96 although there was a general increase in wages in the run-in to the 1997 election.

In the mid 1990s, the large salary increases of many top executives caught public attention partly because these privatised companies were often simultaneously enforcing wage-restraint on their employees and reducing their numbers. One of the most celebrated cases was that of Sir Cedric Brown chief executive of British Gas. In 1994 he gained a salary increase of £205,000 bringing his total salary to £475,000.

This was at a time when the pay of showroom staff was to be reduced and thousands of British Gas employees were being offered redundancy. The 'perks' of chief executives – such as cheap share options, generous pensions, and 'golden goodbyes' was also a matter of much concern. In Cedric Brown's case, he faced the prospect of retirement in 1996 on a pension worth up to £4 million over 5 years and a free chauffeur driven car. A number of members of the gas workers union paraded a pig – called Cedric – at the 1995

British shareholders' meeting and this came to symbolise their view of these matters.

Reasons for increased income inequality in Britain 1971-90

1 Government policy

The Thatcher administrations set in place policies that were bound to increase inequality and were intended to. The top band of income tax was reduced from 60% to 40%; tax policy shifted from the progressive (taxing the rich relatively more) to the regressive (taxing the less well off relatively more – mainly through extending and increasing Value Added Tax). The nationalised industries were privatised – among smaller investors, it was the upper and middle classes who could afford most shares; and various non-taxable saving schemes were introduced. In the words of Nigel Lawson, philosophically the Conservatives had 'no problem with inequality' but were, he said, concerned about poverty. However, Keith Joseph stated that the country needed more millionaires and more paupers. If this was the goal, it was arguably achieved with some success. Between the mid 1980s and mid 1990s the number of millionaires approximately doubled from 20,000 to 40,000.

2 The workings of the capitalist market

Extreme inequality in the United States – the leading capitalist society – and growing inequality in Britain strongly suggests that a relatively free market increases inequality overall. The use of government power to counterbalance this inequality would have contradicted the essential thrust of Thatcherism. However, it had to be used, at least to provide a safety net given the extent of poverty and social disintegration that developed during the 1980s.

3 Management/capitalist policy and the restructuring of the economy

From the 1970s into the 1990s, Britain moved further and rapidly from industrial to service sector employment. In the late 1980s and 1990s, the service sector, too, experienced massive job losses. Given the competitive capitalist and technological nature of the global economy, this restructuring was no doubt seen as necessary by capitalists and senior managers. On the other hand, it can be argued that the process was used in excess in order to control labour (see pp. 254-5). It increased unemployment, insecurity and inequality.

4 The decline of the trade unions and the reduction in employment rights

Increasingly, employees had fewer rights and more lost union protection during this period (see pp. 268-70).

5 A growing number of the very rich in Britain are of foreign origin

Many of the new entries into the 'Sunday Times: Britain's Richest 500: 1996' list were of international background. This reflects the Conservative government economic 'deregulation' (free market) policies.

6 There is a mathematical reason for growing inequality

Even if the higher paid only averaged the same *percentage* salary increase as the less well paid they would get more in *absolute* terms. Year by year this difference would be cumulative. In fact, the higher paid tend to average higher percentage salary increases than the less well paid. Redistribution through the taxation system only reduces this trend, it does not reverse it. The only way income inequality could be reduced is by policies much more radical than so far adopted by any recent government.

Wealth

In the section that follows, it will be useful to be aware of the distinction between marketable and non-marketable wealth (see Table 13.3). The former refers to any saleable asset e.g. land, most savings. The latter refers to non-saleable assets such as state and occupation pension rights, the latter being non-marketable.

Changes in the basis of personal wealth

Table 13.2 indicates that in real terms, Britain's people were over twice as wealthy in 1995 as in 1971. There had been some change in the basis of personal wealth between those two dates. The percentage of personal sector wealth made up by life assurance (often linked to house purchase) and pension funds increased from fifteen to 34 per cent – a massive jump of eighteen per cent. The relative decrease occurred across a number of areas but most notable in other forms of savings, especially individually held stocks, shares and unit trusts.

What happened was that savings were channelled into making house ownership and old age more secure – predominantly to the benefit of the middle and upper class. Over the full period the big pension and insurance companies soaked up contributions which they invested mainly in the stock market whereas direct personal holdings in stocks, shares and unit trusts declined as a percentage of personal wealth from 23 to fifteen per cent. Although there was an increase in the number of small shareholders during the Thatcher privatisation period of the second half of the 1980s, this tailed off during the 1990s. According to one of its academic supporters, Peter Saunders, the experiment in shareholder

Table 13.3 Distribution of wealth

United Kingdom	1976	1981	1986	1991	1993
			Percentages		
Marketable wealth					
Percentage of wealth owned by:					
Most wealthy 1%	21	18	18	17	17
Most wealthy 5%	38	36	36	35	36
Most wealthy 10%	50	50	50	47	48
Most wealthy 25%	71	73	73	71	72
Most wealthy 50%	92	92	90	92	92
Total marketable wealth (£ billion)	280	565	955	1,711	1,809
Marketable wealth plus occupational and state pension rights					
Percentage of wealth owned by:					
Most wealthy 1%	13	11	10	10	10
Most wealthy 5%	26	24	24	23	23
Most wealthy 10%	36	34	35	33	33
Most wealthy 25%	57	56	58	57	56
Most wealthy 50%	80	79	82	83	82
Total marketable wealth £ billion)	472	1,036	1,784	3,014	3,383

(Source: *Social Trends*, 1996:111 – slightly adapted)

democracy was a comprehensive failure. The private sector of the economy continued to be dominated by international companies, major capitalists, and the insurance and pension funds.

The distribution of personal wealth

Around 1900, Britain was a society of extreme inequality. In 1911, the top one per cent owned 69 per cent of aggregate personal wealth and the top five per cent owned 87 per cent. By 1981 this was down to 18 per cent and 38 per cent, respectively, since when it has only dropped a further one per cent. This historic pattern of redistribution (largely through inheritance tax) has stalled in recent years. As Social Trends, 1996 puts it: 'Wealth is much more unequally distributed than income and this has not changed much over the years.' (see Table 13.3).

Top ten most wealthy: 1996

Philip Beresford's list of 'Britain's Richest 500: 1996' gives a useful indication of change and continuity in the make-up of Britain's wealthy. There is clearly a shift from aristocratic wealth to wealth made in business (see Figure 13.7). Four out of the top five wealthiest individuals in 1996 were businessmen and there was just one aristocrat, the Duke of Westminster. Yet, inherited wealth of one kind or another, accounts for 177 of the 1996 entries – 35.4 per cent. Of the 1989 list of 200, 57 per cent had inherited their wealth.

By far the biggest sector of wealth creation was retailing and commerce which had 148 entries or 30 per cent. Industry accounted for 100 entries or 20 per cent, a revival from 1989 when it accounted for only 7.5 per cent. Retailers such as the Sainsbury family and financiers such as James Goldsmith and George Soros are more typical of the super-rich than industrialists (see p. 380).

The number of women in the 500 most wealthy dropped from 40 to 38 in 1996. Overwhelmingly, these are towards the bottom end of the list. Although Beresford states that women 'continue to make their mark' these are the statistics of substantial gender inequality. The impact of women has been greater at the lower and middle levels of business and the professions but even there progress has been difficult and uneven (see pp. 203-4). No separate figures for black British ethnic minorities are given but they do not seem prominent on the list (with the exception of some Indian names).

The glamour names of sport – better known to the general public than the super-rich – scarcely appear on the list. Nigel Mansell is the only sports star to have accumulated (just) the £35 million pounds that is the entry threshold to the 'top 500'. Entertainment stars do better, although typically the fortunes of the 32 individuals on the list are a small fraction of those of the businessmen in the top ten. Andrew Lloyd Weber does best with a fortune of £550 million.

Variation in the wealth of the rich

Much of the wealth of the very rich lies in assets which can change greatly in value over a very short period. The average worth of the top 500 increased by over £30 million in 1995 to £140 million. This

---

Aristocrats on the slide (but slowly …)

The list of the richest names in the country is no longer dominated by aristocrats. Although classifications of this kind are notoriously easy to pick holes in, the latest top 500 rankings published by the *Sunday Times* – which has become the official 'bible' on the subject – shows a clear trend: only 75 families are 'old' money, while just 35 per cent of entries inherited their wealth, compared with 57 per cent in 1989, when the first rankings were published.

Comparison with a *Money Magazine* survey of 10 years ago makes the point more dramatically. In 1986, the 10 richest aristocrats were all among the 40 richest names in Britain. Today, the tenth-richest aristo, the Duke of Northumberland, comes in at a lowly 55th on the overall list (the Royal Family has been excluded from the rankings)

1996 (overall rankings in brackets)

The Duke of Westminster	£1,650m	(4th)
Viscount Rothermere	£1,000m	(8th)
The Vestey family	£650m	(14th)
The Earl of Iveagh	£600m	(17th)
Earl Cadogan	£450m	(26th)
Viscount Cowdray	£400m	(32nd)
The Duke of Devonshire	£375m	(36th)
Lord Cayzer	£325m	(39th)
Lord Howard de Walden	£275m	(49th)
The Duke of Northumberland	£250m	(55th)

1986

The Duke of Westminster	£1,400m	(4th)
The Vestey family	£1,000m	(7th)
The Cayzer family	£600m	(9th)
Viscount Chelsea	£410m	(12th)
Duke of Buccleuch	£309m	(15th)
Viscount Portman	£300m	(20th)
Lord Howard de Walden	£250m	(24th)
Marquis of Bath	£198m	(32nd)
Duke of Northumberland	£166m	(36th)
The Keswick family	£147m	(39th)

(Sources: *The Sunday Times 'Richest 500'*, 21.4.1996; Money Magazine, 1986)

Figure 13.7 Hereditary wealth

---

was because in 1995 there was a record stock market performance, a rise in art values, a sharp increase in land values and a lively market in the sale of companies. Another year this could be reversed, but in the long run the value of these assets tends to increase ahead of 'ordinary savings' in banks and building societies. The richest 500 are only a tiny fraction of the top one per cent most wealthy but it would not be surprising if the figure for the total percentage wealth of this larger group does not increase for 1995 and 1996. (17 per cent of total wealth before tax in 1993).

Corporate and individual wealth: the crucial connection

The fundamental power of capital is institutional rather than individual. Shell and Glaxo are two of Britain's three biggest companies and contribute substantially to the development of local and even national economies and create or lose thousands of jobs. In presenting wealth in such an individualised, league table fashion, the 'Sunday Times Richest 500' can easily mislead about the way power and opportunity function within the capitalist system. Insurance and pension funds are far bigger shareholders than the wealthiest individuals. The institutional nature of capitalist economic power and its links with political power are discussed elsewhere (see pp. 313-16).

Many of the wealthiest 500 individuals are significant players within British capitalism and a few are within global capitalism. Both George Soros and Sir James Goldsmith have significantly affected British government policy in the 1990s. However, it is largely international capital of which the larger British companies are a part, which creates wealth and jobs and to which government policy orientates itself. Individuals can succeed on a massive scale and rather more seem to be doing so but there are only a few of them relative to the total population. To 'swallow' an ideology of economic individualism would be to risk missing the point.

Wealth and well-being

Wealth does not determine how fit you can be, how long you can live, how much food you can eat, how much love you can make and how many songs you can sing. Wealth and well-being are not the

Table 13.4 Human Development Index 1992

Country index		Rank
High 0.886		
1	Canada	0.932
2	Switzerland	0.931
3	Japan	0.929
4	Sweden	0.928
5	Norway	0.928
6	France	0.927
7	Australia	0.926
8	USA	0.925
9	Netherlands	0.923
10	United Kingdom	0.919

same thing. The United Nations Development Programme (UNDP) has come up with a new measure of 'wealth' it calls the Human Development Index (HDI) (see Table 13.4).

This index measures levels of education and health while discounting the value of incomes beyond a certain point. So some countries that seem to have a lot of money, like Saudi Arabia and Luxembourg, do relatively badly on the HDI because they neglect general welfare in favour of the rich and super-rich.

Others that don't have a lot of money, like China and Costa Rica, do relatively well on the HDI because they have been more willing to use what they do have for human development. The countries that did best on this index between 1960 and 1992 are Japan, Spain, Hong Kong, Singapore, Cyprus, Greece, Barbados, Malaysia, Jamaica and Portugal – although some, like Malaysia, might fare less well if human rights were included on the HDI, which they are not.

The HDI does not show wealth differentials within countries: black South Africans taken separately would rank 123 on the Index, just above Congo, while whites would rank 24, just below Spain. Also the North/South divide persists – almost all the countries that are high on the HDI are in the North.

> ### Question
>
> With close reference to the data provided above, describe and explain the distribution of income and wealth in Britain between 1971 and the early 1990s.

Definition and extent of poverty and inequality

Poverty

Poverty and inequality are not the same things. A wealthy businessperson and a 'comfortably-off' teacher are materially unequal but the teacher is not poor. Social inequality means that certain individuals or groups have more material or cultural resources than others.

Poverty implies some *insufficiency* in the material or, arguably, cultural resources of an individual or group. There is considerable disagreement about what constitutes poverty in modern societies. Is not being able to afford a colour television set poverty? Or not being able to afford a family holiday away from home? Some have defined poverty to include such situations. Others consider that these situations involve inequality rather than poverty. Taking this view, former Chancellor of the Exchequer Nigel Lawson stated that he saw no reason to limit inequality but that he was concerned about poverty. Critics of this view argue that poverty is more likely to occur in a society which accepts extreme inequality.

Absolute poverty

Poverty may be defined as either absolute or relative. Absolute poverty is insufficiency in the basic necessities of existence: in practical terms, this usually means being without adequate food, clothing or shelter. In 1899, Seebohm Rowntree carried out a survey into poverty in York and attempted to define poverty in absolute or subsistence terms in order to establish eligibility for state help. He stated that in order to qualify for such help 'nothing must be bought but that which is absolutely necessary for the maintenance of physical health and what is bought must be of the plainest and most economical description'. Thus, Rowntree introduced the notion of a 'poverty line' which in its first conception was thought of as minimal. In practice, Rowntree himself revised his definition of a subsistence standard upwards in later surveys of poverty in York in 1936 and 1950.

More recent attempts to establish what absolute poverty means in practice have also met problems in defining and operationalising the concept. Drewnowski and Scott attempted to operationalise the concept of absolute poverty by suggesting measures of both basic physical and cultural needs (e.g. security, education). The admitted fact that such needs, especially cultural ones, vary between individuals, between societies, and within the same society over time, ironically means that absolute standards of poverty are unlikely to be other than approximate and tentative. It would appear unwise to put much reliance on them except in cases of extreme scarcity and necessity.

Although Britain became an increasingly unequal society in the late 1980s and early 1990s, *absolute* poverty remains rare and exceptional. In parts of the so-called 'Third World', however, it is commonplace. The relationship between the West and the 'Third World' is itself one of great inequality and, some would argue, exploitation. Chapter 20 examines inequality and poverty in the 'Third World', broadly in an international context (see especially pp. 576-7).

Relative poverty

A second type of poverty is *relative* poverty. Peter Townsend has argued that those who have 'resources so seriously below those commanded by the average individual or family that they are, in effect, excluded from ordinary living patterns, customs and activities' are relatively poor. Similarly, Joanna Mack and Stewart Lansley consider that relative poverty exists in the absence of 'a minimum standard of living on socially established criteria and not just the criteria of survival or subsistence'.

Critics of relative definitions of poverty argue that those who adopt this approach tend consistently to move the poverty line upwards – thus obscuring the fact that in Britain, as in other wealthier countries, those at the bottom of society have tended to become better off – as have other groups. In 1988, the Department

of Health and Social Security stated that measuring poverty on the basis of the numbers receiving means tested benefits, as is commonly done, can make it appear that more become poor when benefits are increased – because more become eligible for them. Speaking on the same theme, the then Social Security Secretary, John Moore argued that in advanced societies such as Britain, some people were 'less equal' but not in poverty.

Measuring poverty

Official measures

Although there has never been an official poverty line in Britain, figures based on those receiving benefits have provided a gauge for measuring poverty. Thus, until 1985, the numbers receiving supplementary benefit (replaced in 1988 by income support) provided a quasi-official measure. However, the government stopped producing this calculation from 1987 and instead introduced a new statistical series based on the number of households with below average or half average income. In order to maintain the two-yearly comparison of the numbers (of families) on supplementary benefit, the Institute for Fiscal Studies calculated the relevant figures for 1987. In practice, both the calculations based on supplementary benefit and those based on household income showed a sharp increase in poverty between 1979-1987 (i.e. relative poverty – given the real increase in the value of supplementary benefit and of average income).

In addition to the 4.3 million families living on supplementary benefit in 1987, another 1.9 million families were living on income lower than the safety net level of social security and of these over 800,000 failed to claim the state benefits to which they were entitled (Table 13.5). Between 1985 and 1987, there was a four per cent increase in families not receiving benefit but having an income on or below benefit level. According to the House of Commons Social Security Committee, lack of take-up of benefits increased after the implementation of the 1988 Social Security Act.

Table 13.5 Number of low-income families

	Supp. benefit	Equivalent or less	Total
1979	2,590	1,420	4,010
1981	3,010	1,610	4,620
1983	3,640	1,880	5,520
1985	4,110	1,830	5,940
1987	4,330	1,910	6,240

(Source: Department of Social Security, 1981-83; IFS, 1985-87)

Official statistics on both households with below half average earnings and on supplementary benefit/income support as a percentage of average earnings show a clear increase in relative poverty (Table 13.6).

Table 13.6 Households with below half average earnings (figures in thousands)

	1979	1987
Before allowance for housing costs	3.7	7.7
After allowance for housing costs	4.9	10.5

(Source: Department of Social Security)

The Department of Social Security argued that the continuing decrease in the benefit rates as a percentage of average earnings demonstrated that work incentives – a main aspect of government policy – were increasingly effective. (see Table 13.7). Others might see them as further evidence that an underclass has developed in Britain, significantly adrift from the majority in terms of its standard of living.

Table 13.7 Supplementary benefit/Income support as a percentage of average earnings

	July 1986	April 1987	April 1988
Single person	20.8	19.5	19.1
Couple	32.1	30.3	28.3
Couple + 1 child	38.5	36.4	32.9
Couple + 2 children	43.1	40.8	37.1
Couple + 3 children	47.2	44.8	41.1
Couple + 4 children	51.0	48.5	44.8

(Source: Department of Social Security)

Peter Townsend

The numbers of those on supplementary benefit/income support (whether measured individually or as families) show a sharp increase in relative poverty over the decade of the1980s – an increase that accelerated during the economic recession of 1990-2. However, there have long been those who argue that the 'official' measure of those in poverty is inadequate. Peter Townsend has argued this case for over three decades. In 1979, he published his huge empirical survey *Poverty in the United Kingdom*, in which, on an admittedly much 'higher poverty line' than the government's, he found fourteen million people (or 22.9 per cent of the population) in poverty.

More recently, Townsend has led a research team from Bristol University which concluded that government rates for income support were about 50 per cent too low. The team reached this conclusion on the basis of both subjective and objective measures. The research is based on surveys in Greater London and separate studies in Islington, Hackney and Bromley but, possibly with minor qualifications, its conclusion should be nationally applicable.

The subjective measure of poverty was obtained by asking people, in Townsend's words 'their opinions on the meaning of poverty, its presumed causes, how the household managed on its income and how much was needed in weekly income to stay out of poverty' and 'whether household income was much above or below this level' (*The Guardian*). The survey covered ten different types of households, and nearly all respondents put the basic income needed much higher than that payable under social security rules, with the average at 61 per cent higher.

The objective evidence supporting the above perceived need, was obtained by giving the same respondents 'a long list of questions about their diet, clothing, housing, home facilities, environment, location, work, rights in employment, family activity, community integration, participation in social institutions, recreation and education … The intention was to cover every possible major aspect of material and social life.' The research team established that there was a level of income below which multiple-deprivation almost certainly occurred. This level was 57 per cent above government rates of means-tested assistance for couples under pensionable age; 51 per cent for couples with two children; and 68 per cent for single-parent families.

Townsend comments on the closeness of the subjective and objective measures of poverty produced by the research team: both indicating that Government rates for income support fall short of need by over 50 per cent. Townsend concludes this article by asking whether these rates are so low that they are 'simply perpetuating … poverty'.

Breadline Britain: 1983 and 1990 compared: J Mack and S Lansley

In their book, *Poor Britain* (1985, 1993) Joanna Mack and Stewart Lansley attempted to establish a relative definition of poverty by questioning members of the public on what they considered were 'necessities' for an 'acceptable' standard of living and, on that basis, attempted to measure degrees of poverty in the country. They carried out two surveys, one in 1983 and a follow-up in 1990.

They established that there was a considerable degree of consensus among the British public on the necessities required to maintain 'a minimum standard of living on socially established criteria and not just the criteria of survival or subsistence'. In 1985, over 90 per cent of people (from a representative quota sample of 1174 respondents) agreed on the importance of the following for basic living in the home: heating, an indoor toilet (not shared), a damp-free home, a bath (not shared), and beds for everyone. A further 21 items – from having enough money for public transport to possessing a warm waterproof coat – were regarded as necessities by more than one-half of respondents. This list of 26 necessities, established by the majority of respondents, is the basis on which Mack and Lansley measured poverty in 1985 (a slightly different list was established in 1990 (see Table 13.8). They find that 'all those with an enforced lack of three or more necessities are in poverty. … All fall below the minimum way of life laid down by society as a whole'. On this measure, 7.5 million people were in poverty in 1983 and 11 million in 1990. Severe or intense poverty was measured by the lack of seven or more necessities. The increase between 1983 and 1990 was from 2.6 to 3.5 million. The authors comment on those in intense poverty: 'their lives are diminished and demeaned in every way, so far do they fall below the minimum standards of society today'.

Mack and Lansley find five main groups whose living standards are too low: the unemployed, single parents, the sick and disabled, pensioners and the low paid. In 1983 there were roughly as many in poverty who were in low paid work as there were unemployed, but the unemployed were almost twice as likely to suffer intense poverty. The authors argue that the impact of the 1981 and 1990

Table 13.8 Lack of necessities: 'the top ten'

1983	
Necessity	Percentage of households unable to afford
1 Holiday	21
2 Two pairs of shoes	9
3 Meal or fish every other day	8
4 Hobby	7
4 Damp-free house	7
4 Warm coat	7
4 Weekly roast	7
8 Leisure equipment for children	6
8 New clothes	6
8 Washing machines	6
1990	
1 Regular savings	30
2 Holiday	20
3 Decent decoration	15
4 Outing for children	14
5 Insurance	10
6 Out-of-school activities	10
7 Separate bedrooms	7
7 Hobby	7
7 Telephone	7
10 Best outfit	8
10 Entertaining of children's friends	8

(Source: Frayman, 1991:6, reprinted in Scott, 1994)

recessions – particularly the very high level of unemployment – and government social policy which has resulted in an increase in income for the super-rich and a decrease for the poor, are the main causes of current renewed concern about poverty. In the 1985 edition *Poor Britain* they note a waning in the backlash against 'welfarism' which partly swept Margaret Thatcher to power and they found a majority (57 per cent) who thought the government was doing too little to help those lacking necessities. However, public opinion did not have the effect of preventing further cuts in welfare during the Thatcher-Major period.

Question

What are the main *general* differences between the two lists?

Poverty in the 1990s: its character and extent

It is the accumulation of missing 'necessities' – three or more – which Mack and Lansley regard as building up 'a way of life' which can be termed 'poor'. There were more people and, notably, more children in such a position in 1990 than in 1983. Public perception of what constituted an 'acceptable way of life' changed somewhat between the two dates. In 1990, over 50 per cent now saw a telephone, a weekly outing for children, being able to afford to have children's friends round once a fortnight, and a best outfit as necessities. Further, several new items were now perceived as necessities by over 50 per cent: fresh fruit and vegetables, a decent standard of decoration in the home, savings of at least £10 per week, participating in out-of-school activities for children, and home contents insurance. Six of these nine items were actually in the 1990 top ten items perceived as necessities.

What appear to be the differences in the way poverty is perceived in the two lists of necessities? In both cases, respondents are thinking within a framework of relative, not absolute poverty. Yet, the 1983 top ten list is predominantly concerned with food, basic clothing and shelter (six out of ten items or seven, if a washing machine is included). There are no such items of near *basic* necessity in 1990 – decent decoration, separate bedrooms and best outfit are one level of need above this but now generally considered 'normal' requirements. Certainly, individuals and families might suffer in their absence.

So, despite the increase in the numbers in poverty and continuing concern about the diet and in housing of many poor, the public seems to be edging to a broader concept of lifestyle poverty (in addition to that of basic poverty). While there is a danger in this attitude that an assumption will be widely made that 'real' poverty is no longer a serious issue, it also raises the possibility of a much fuller and dynamic notion of what an acceptable quality of life for all citizens might be.

Theoretical perspectives on the causes of poverty

Four theoretical perspectives on poverty are discussed below. The controversial concept of the underclass is considered by some to be a further perspective on contemporary poverty (see pp. 387-93).

Individual inadequacy: conservative perspective 1

Nineteenth and early twentieth century writers on social problems, including poverty, in both Britain and the United States commonly sought their causes in individual pathology or weakness of either a physical, mental or moral kind. Belief in self-help and the survival of the fittest gave support to the view that the deserving succeed and the weak and worthless fail. This philosophy is indicated in the title of Charles Henderson's textbook on social problems published in 1906: *An Introduction to the Study of Defective, Dependent and Delinquent Classes*. Religious and moralistic motives were common among those who helped the poor and the urge to uplift them spiritually was as strong or stronger than the desire to assist them materially. At this time few envisaged that the state would largely take over 'charitable' activities from the churches.

Individualist explanations of social problems flourished again in the 1970s and 1980s. Such approaches have always had some popular currency but in this period they gained substantial political and academic support. Both Ronald Reagan, the former American President and Republican party leader, and Margaret Thatcher, the former British Prime Minister and Conservative party leader, vigorously adopted philosophies of individual enterprise and reward, and cut back on many welfare programmes. Thus, Thatcher stated 'Let our children grow tall, and some grow taller than others'. More down to earth was her then Minister of Employment, Norman Tebbitt's advice to the unemployed to 'get on your bike'.

To those who argue that poverty in modern capitalist society is largely social structural in nature, such comments misleadingly individualise poverty and inequality. In their view welfare dependants are more likely to be the 'victims' rather than the 'villains' of capitalism – typically offered jobs so lowly paid that some might find there is little incentive. Their solution lies in a higher wage economy and, generally, a more equal distribution of wealth.

The culture of poverty thesis: conservative perspective 2

Another explanation of poverty popular among conservative thinkers is that it is generated and regenerated by the cultural attitudes and lifestyle of the poor. This is the 'culture of poverty'

theory. It often involves 'trait analysis' of the lifestyle of the poor. These traits, or characteristics, are said to include present-centredness, a sense of resignation and fatalism, and a strong predisposition to authoritarianism. At its most extreme, this interpretation sees the poor as inadequate and pathological. Edward Banfield describes the 'lower class individual' as follows:

> *Although he has more 'leisure' than almost anyone, the indifference ('apathy' if one prefers) of the lower class person is such that he seldom makes even the simplest repairs to the place that he lives in. He is not troubled by dirt and dilapidation and he does not mind the inadequacy of public facilities such as schools, parks, hospitals and libraries; indeed, where such things exist he may destroy them by carelessness or even by vandalism. Conditions that make the slum repellent to others are serviceable to him.*
>
> *(Cited in Raynor and Harris eds., 1977:234)*

Given that Banfield regards the cause of poverty as rooted in psychological attitudes, he is dubious about easy solutions aimed at changing the way in which people live. Cultural attitudes tend to undermine imposed reform.

An earlier study by Oscar Lewis puts the concept of the culture of poverty in a wider context. The conditions in which it flourishes include a low-wage, profit-oriented economy and inadequate government assistance for the poor. These are frequently to be found in Third World areas which are undergoing 'development' by foreign capital and, more locally, in inner-city areas almost anywhere in the world. Given this wider context, the culture of poverty thesis loses its conservatism and becomes, generally, more useful.

Keith Joseph's concept of the 'cycle of deprivation' has some similarity to the 'class culture' approach but it lays greater stress on the effect of material factors, such as poor housing and low income, in undermining prospects for self-improvement from generation to generation. Among cultural factors, he particularly emphasises the inadequacy of parental upbringing and the home background. The logical answer to this is to help and strengthen the family. Whether this can be done on a piecemeal basis is highly debatable. In any case, research led by Michael Rutter has shown that most poverty is not intergenerational.

Dependency culture

The notion of 'the dependency culture', popular among Conservative politicians and ideologies in the late 1980s, is essentially a version of the culture of poverty thesis. According to Charles Murray, there are broadly two types of poverty, that of the 'deserving' and 'undeserving' poor. It is the latter who have created for themselves a 'culture of dependency' and they have been able to do this by living off welfare. A one-time adviser to President Reagan, Murray attempts in his book *Losing Ground, American Social Policy 1950-1980* to provide intellectual and empirical support for the above philosophy and related policies. Murray argues that in the post-war period in the United States, the most marked improvement in the condition of the poor occurred throughout the 1950s and early 1960s before the War on Poverty of the Johnson administration and the continued massive welfare programmes of his successors prior to Reagan. Ironically, after two decades of relatively steady progress, improvements in the condition of the poor, as measured by a number of indicators, slowed in the late 1960s and stopped altogether in the late 1970s. In other words, poverty got relatively worse as programmes to reduce it increased. According to Murray, this is because many found it preferable to be 'on welfare' (i.e. in poverty) than to work: they took advantage of what he calls 'the generous (welfare) revolution'. This view, of course, has also frequently been voiced on this side of the Atlantic. In fact, Murray himself, had access to leading British Conservative politicians in 1989 and, as we have seen, applied his ideas to the British context (see pp. 390-1).

It may not be coincidence that two of the three most important measures of the Conservative government for the 1989-90 session related to issues identified by Murray as central to the dependent underclass: single-parent families and rising crime. The government set up the child support agency to trace absent fathers and secure maintenance payments from them. Among its legislation on crime were measures to make parents take greater responsibility for offences committed by their children, and to achieve tougher penalties.

In practice, notions of individual irresponsibility and cultural deficiency easily blend together. It is the 'inadequate' individuals who are considered to create 'inadequate' and 'dependent' culture. Murray also referred to this supposed group as 'the underclass' (see pp. 390-1).

Critique of the 'myth' of dependency

Dean and Taylor-Gooby (1992) have argued that the notion of the dependent culture is a Thatcherite 'discourse' and essentially a 'myth':

> *Politicians of the right condemned the 'dependency culture' ... contrasting it with the 'enterprise culture' ... At a level of political discourse, Thatcherism sought to blame its victims by constructing the pejorative notion of 'dependency culture' ... The essence of our argument is that notions such as 'dependency culture' and 'underclass' are discursive rather than objective phenomena.*
>
> (27)

These and other criticisms of underclass and dependency theory are taken up later.

Poverty as situational: liberal reformist perspective

An analysis of poverty developed in Britain and in the United States is that it is frequently the result of the situation an individual or group experiences. Thus, illness; unemployment, low pay and loss of income in old age can be immediate causes of poverty yet these are rarely the 'fault' of the people concerned. This approach tends to stop short of 'blaming capitalism' for poverty but seeks to help people to cope with the particular misfortune that has afflicted them. Nevertheless, many non-Marxists who adopt this approach are well aware that the capitalist system can operate in a way that can cause or exacerbate poverty.

This perspective on poverty is associated with progressive liberal or social democratic political ideas, and it inspired much of the reforming legislation that set up the framework of the twentieth century Welfare State. First, contributory old age pensions and then insurance for employees against sickness and unemployment were introduced by government. The Welfare State was consolidated and extended by the first post-Second World War Labour government. Two important measures were the setting up of the National Health Service, and of the National Assistance Board. The purpose of the latter was to provide help for those who remained unemployed after their unemployment benefit had been exhausted, or who were otherwise without income. The role of the NAB has since been taken over by the Supplementary Benefits Commission.

The reformer's view that poverty 'hits' certain identifiable groups, who must therefore be helped, is enticingly simple, yet poverty stubbornly persists despite the Welfare State. It is a severe disappointment to the many politicians and intellectuals, who hoped that the Welfare State would virtually abolish poverty, that millions are in receipt of social security in the mid 1990s. Such was certainly not the intention of Lord Beveridge whose official report was largely responsible for the structure of the NAB. He hoped that a low unemployment and high wage economy, coupled with a better system of unemployment insurance, would mean that the supplementary function of the NAB would substantially decrease rather than increase. There are other concerns about the way the Welfare State operates. One is that it fails significantly to redistribute wealth from the better off to the poor. This is because the middle class make more use of the Welfare State than the poor. Thus, they keep their children in education for longer, and, often, use the health service more. Further, as middle class people, from clerks to Principal Secretaries (top civil services), run the Welfare State, it is in a sense, an employment subsidy for them. Often, the bureaucratic way in which welfare is administered confuses of 'mystifies' those who need help. Long waits, form-filling and questioning may or may not be the norm, but they happen frequently enough – particularly in the administration of social security – to intimidate some.

Despite the above reservations, the extent of poverty in the middle of the 1990s ensured both widespread public support for the Welfare State and heavy demand for its services. An ageing population, high long-term unemployment, and increasing numbers of one parent families requires massive expenditure on social welfare.

'The capitalist system' as the cause of poverty: radical structural and Marxist perspectives

As understood here, radical structural and Marxist perspectives agree on one central point: that capitalism produces fundamental social problems. The classic free enterprise system, so praised by conservative individualists, is seen as inherently incapable of producing social justice and stability. The pursuit of profit and the exploitation of labour results in severe inequality. Radical structural and Marxist theorists tend to regard inequality not so much as a social problem but as the core social issue of capitalism, out of which other problems and issues are generated. Thus, Marxists in particular consider that problems relating to freedom of expression cannot be solved adequately unless the issue of inequality is first dealt with. People cannot enjoy freedom if their fundamental needs are not first met. J C Kincaid puts the Marxist point of view particularly strongly:

> *Poverty cannot be abolished within capitalist society, but only in socialist society under workers' control, in which human needs, and not profits, determine the allocation of resources.*

The above approach is, of course, more than a perspective on poverty, it is an analysis of a system – the capitalist system. Though theorists adopting this broad analysis agree on the basic cause of social problems in capitalist society, they do not necessarily agree on the solution. Some argue that social justice, equality and freedom can be achieved by the reform of capitalism whereas others consider that these goals cannot be attained unless the system is abolished. I refer to the former as radical structural theorists and the latter as Marxists. The disagreements between the two groups become more apparent in the section on policy later in this chapter.

The Marxists, John Westergaard and Henrietta Resler adopt a structural analysis of inequality in *Class in Capitalist Society: A Study of Contemporary Britain* (1976). They prefer the term inequality to poverty because the latter can so easily be (mis-)explained as an individual or group problem. They wish to focus on inequality as a product of the capitalist system. Inequality cannot be dealt with simply by making efforts to get certain groups above the poverty line. Reforms gained in times of expansion may be lost during a recession, or economic and technological developments may put new groups into poverty. For them, poverty or rather inequality is a class rather than an individual or group issue. All wage-workers, employed or unemployed, are potential victims of the capitalist system. Like Kincaid, their solution lies in collective action to change the system, not in supporting piece-meal 'remedies' which are not designed to produce wholesale change in the general structure of inequality'.

Marxists argue that capitalist politicians and the media typically obscure the real cause of poverty and inequality in capitalist society, sometimes by scapegoating the poor or other minority groups. Thus, Stuart Hall and his co-authors argue in *Policing the Crisis, Mugging the State and Law and Order* (1979), that black people in Britain have frequently been made the scapegoats of economic crisis, particularly rising unemployment. Political and media attention on the 'race' issue whipped up a series of moral panics which distracted attention from the failure of capital to generate economic growth and high employment. The 'mugger' was a particularly negative stereotype of young, black urban males which aggravated racial tension and hampered the development of class solidarity across racial lines.

Poverty in the West and global capitalism

Michael Harrington's *The New American Poverty* (1984) makes a structural analysis of poverty in that country which is almost equally applicable to poverty in Britain. A reforming socialist rather than a Marxist, Harrington nevertheless offers an analysis that would be broadly acceptable to many Marxists. He begins by locating 'a deep structural source of a new poverty that could persist into the indefinite future' – the 'internationalisation of the economy (and) of poverty' by the multinational corporations. The power of the multinationals to switch investment and production around the globe has weakened the bargaining power of labour in developed capitalist societies and has tended to lower wages and increase unemployment. Labour itself has become internationalised and far more disorganised and weak as a result. He refers to the millions of undocumented migrant labourers in the United States who are very low-paid and who may also depress the wages of indigenous workers by their willingness to work for so little. We examine the same process in relation to European migrant and many black workers in Britain in Chapter 9. As Harrington puts it, '(t)he third World is … not simply out there, it is within and at the gates'. He points out that most of the service jobs that are replacing those in heavy manufacture in both Britain and America are relatively low paid. He also dispels the myth that there will be many 'high-tech' jobs available. In fact, far more routine 'low-tech' than high-tech jobs are being produced and far more non-technical jobs in the low paid sector, such as fast-food and janitoring, than either.

Partly as a result of the above trends, Harrington sees a new 'underclass' developing, largely cut off from the materially good life available in various degrees to other Americans. The use of the term underclass will not recommend Harrington's analysis to Marxists, most of whom prefer that of lower working class, but there is little doubt that he has located an empirically real phenomenon however we conceptualise it. He uses the term underclass primarily to indicate those in long-term structural poverty among whom are disproportionate numbers of the unemployed, the low paid, ethnic minorities, the 'rootless' mentally ill or retarded, the less educated young, and one-parent families. The rise in the number of one-parent families – most of whom are headed by women – living in or at the margin of poverty, and of low-paid working women leads Harrington to refer to the 'feminisation' of poverty. In 1960, 65 per cent of poor families were headed by men under 65 years of age, and 21 per cent by women, whereas in 1979 the respective figures were 42.4 per cent and 43.7 per cent – a profound change and an ironic commentary on the position of women in the supposed age of female emancipation. Recent figures for child poverty in Britain show a remarkably similar pattern to that which has developed in the United States (see Figure 13.8).

Britain is even more vulnerable to international economic trends than the United States. Indeed, André Gunder Frank has suggested that Britain may be the first advanced capitalist country to 'underdevelop' (see p. 586). This would happen if, in the context of the international division of labour, Britain were to become a mainly low wage rather than mainly high wage economy. This might happen if, for instance, large sections of the labour force were engaged in assembling and manufacturing goods developed and designed in, say, Japan or Germany.

It will be clear that radicals see the causes of most poverty as structural rather than individual in nature. However, they do appreciate that there are cultural as well as material consequences of economic change of 'restructuring'. Thus, in an earlier book, *The Other America* (1963), Harrington wrote of the 'low levels of aspiration and high levels of mental stress' among the poor. Similarly, Coates and Silburn wrote of 'the hopelessness and despair of slum life in Nottingham' (*Poverty, the Forgotten Englishmen* 1970). For them, the main solutions as well as causes of

poverty are structural and their implementation requires a social system based on greater equality.

Conclusion: the causes of poverty

One way of developing your own judgement on the causes of poverty is to examine a breakdown of groups in poverty (Figure 13.8) and to attempt to determine the causes. You may also find that different causes apply to different groups. For information, major causes for family poverty are low pay and lone parenthood.

Poverty and the 'underclass'

The 'underclass': is the underclass a class?

The term 'underclass' has become an awkward and controversial one in sociology. It is awkward because there are so many different definitions of it and ways of explaining it – as we shall see below. Awkwardness is compounded by the fact the term has entered widespread popular usage while many sociologists do not wish to use the concept at all! All this is messy enough but matters are made worse in that the term has become controversially politicised as well. One interpretation of the underclass is individualistic and emphasises its supposedly dependent and work-shy culture. This approach can be termed *conservative*. A second approach stresses structural causes – such as the decline of industrial employment – and also government policy. This approach can be termed *radical*. A third approach cites a variety of causes behind the development of the underclass but is mainly concerned with the outcome – near *exclusion* from active citizenship. This approach is termed *liberal* although concern with exclusion is a general feature of the underclass debate.

This ideological categorisation of writings on the underclass is achieved by adapting and extending Duncan Gallie's division of the two main types of interpretations of the underclass categories of 'radical' and 'conservative'. Gallie specifically applies this categorisation to writings which take the 'view that the long-term unemployed constitute part of the growing underclass in British society'. However, this categorisation equally applies to interpretations of the underclass which include other groups within it as well as the long-term unemployed. Oversimplifying somewhat, conservative interpretations tend to 'blame the victim' i.e. members of the underclass themselves for their position in society, and radical interpretations 'blame the system', which can include the government. Gallie attempts empirically to test both of these hypotheses in relation to the long-term unemployed and we will return to his findings later. The point to note here is that I am adopting his categorisation of writings about the long-term unemployed and the underclass into 'radical' and 'conservative' to apply to most writings on the underclass.

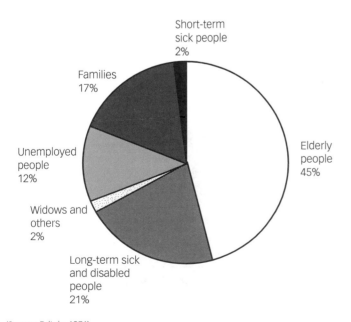

(Source: *Britain*, 1951)

Figure 13.8 Percentage of welfare expenditure by broad groups of beneficiaries

Radical theories of the underclass

A number of writers have used the term underclass to describe the position of the majority of black people in the system of stratification.

A black underclass?

1 John Rex: a black underclass in Britain?

John Rex referred to an 'immigrant underclass' or a 'black underclass' as developing in Britain as early as the 1970s (Rex and Tomlinson, 1979). His research was carried out in the Handsworth area of Birmingham but he considered that it was probably generalisable to other inner urban areas. He argues that primarily as a result of racial discrimination 'two kinds of job situations, with whites predominant in one, and blacks in the other' had developed (279). He felt that this was at least close to a 'dual labour market situation' with most whites in the 'primary' sector and most blacks in the secondary sector. The latter is characterised by low pay, less security and poorer working conditions. Rex also noted that immigrants were much more likely to be unemployed. Accordingly, he argued that black immigrants were in a fundamentally more disadvantaged position than the white working class:

> (The Immigrant underclass) is that class which is cut off from the main class structure of the society not merely in quantitative but in structural or qualitative terms and for the moment at least cannot be construed as merely an underprivileged part of the British labour movement.
>
> (In Miles and Phizacklea, 1979:86)

In the context of the wider underclass debate pursued here, there are two points to pick out of Rex's analysis. First, although the use of the term underclass was later greatly extended (some would say 'inflated') to include a variety of groups of mainly white people, the concept has never entirely become detached from overtones of 'race'. More than that, some sociologists, such as Julius Wilson and Robert Moore, have found some uses of the term at least implicitly racist. None of this is Rex's fault and, of course, sociologists need to employ concepts which describe the stratification effects of discrimination – which brings me to the second point. Although Rex insists on the broad class nature of his analysis of the position of black people in the labour market, he also gives great emphasis to the role of prejudice and discrimination – independently of class factors – in explaining their stratification position. In effect, he is using Weber's concept of status differentiation. Caste as distinct from class, is an extreme form of status distinction (see pp. 142-3) and, in fact, Rex does see a caste-like element in the way black people are stratified. Some later conceptualisations of a wider underclass also describe it in status as much as economic class terms. In these descriptions the underclass is seen as a low status group, lacking social honour and respect.

2 Douglas Glasgow: a young black male underclass

For Douglas Glasgow, the members of the American black underclass are specifically young, black males. In *The Black Underclass* (1981) he argues that mainly due to racism they lack job opportunities and prospects for upward social mobility. Such jobs as are available to them tend to be in the secondary (low pay, low status, less secure) labour market. 'Entrapment' becomes intergenerational fostering 'anger and despair'.

Unlike the Conservative Charles Murray who was influential in the late 1980s, Glasgow does not imply 'moral or ethical unworthiness' in employing the term underclass nor does he consider that it is 'necessarily culturally deprived, lacking in aspirations, or unmotivated to achieve'. However, Glasgow's work did contribute to making black male youth a focus of public concern which it continues to be in both the United States and Britain.

3 William Julius Wilson: from a 'black underclass' to the 'ghetto poor'

In his *The Truly Disadvantaged* (1987), William Julius Wilson adopts a broad definition of the term underclass to describe black and Hispanic people initially caught in urban poverty after migrating from respectively rural areas of the United States and from Latin America.

Wilson comments on the low skills of many of these migrants but like Rex sees racial discrimination as a major factor in consigning most of them to the secondary labour market. The more successful tend to leave for the suburbs while an intergenerational underclass is reproduced in the inner cities.

In 1990 Wilson renounced the use of the term underclass, suggesting instead that of *ghetto poor*. This is because he considered that by then the term underclass had become used and distorted to connote that its members were responsible for, indeed, to blame for their own social position. Wilson believes that it is structural factors – mainly economic – and discrimination which explain the development of 'the underclass'.

The black underclass:
Rex, Glasgow, Wilson: summary

Causes: 1 Racism
          2 Operation of the dual labour market

Effects: 1 Social entrapment of many black people – especially young black males
          2 Further stigmatisation of black people

Sociological Approach: Radical/Structural

Political Attitude: Sympathetic to black people

Figure 13.9 The black underclass: a summary of theories

A wider underclass?

4 Anthony Giddens: the dual labour market and a wider underclass

Like the three theorists of a black underclass discussed above, Anthony Giddens uses the concept of a dual labour market to explain the emergence of an underclass. However, his analysis also includes certain disadvantaged white people. Giddens recognises that black people and migrant workers are particularly likely to be within the secondary sector of the dual labour market. However, so also in his view are the low paid, long-term unemployed, and some single parents, many of whom may also be part of the underclass.

Giddens particularly emphasises how increasing economic globalisation allied to the use of new technology changes patterns of production and employment. Instead of highly unionised and expensive labour, employment markets have been destabilised and restructured to establish a highly skilled, highly rewarded core and a secondary labour market which offers cheap, often part-time temporary work, increasingly to women as well as other minority (in the sense of less powerful) groups.

Criticising Giddens, Kirk Mann observes that in capitalist society many jobs in the so-called primary labour market are as insecure as those in the so-called secondary labour market – raising questions about the basis on which the dual labour market is said to exist. Mann also criticises Giddens for not explaining why some groups, particularly women and black people, are especially prone to enter the secondary labour market but Giddens may well assume that the vulnerability of these two groups to discrimination is empirically well established.

5 Frank Field: structural change and government policy

The Labour MP, Frank Field, takes a different perspective in defining membership of the underclass. His emphasis in defining underclass status is long-term and enforced dependency on welfare benefits rather than the operation of the dual labour market. He states that:

> *The underclass is drawn from the long-term unemployed, single mothers on welfare with no hope of escaping and very frail old pensioners.*
>
> *(1989)*

With Field, therefore, it is the combination of exclusion or virtual exclusion from the labour market coupled with dependency on what Field considers are inadequate welfare benefits that creates an underclass. Field also comments on the vulnerability of part-time workers to dropping into the underclass because they have fewer employment and fewer welfare rights than full-time workers.

Field gives the following explanations for the development of the British underclass

i High unemployment.

ii Increasing inequality partly due to Conservative government policy and partly due to socio-economic change (e.g. pay settlements favouring the better off more of whom then spend on private health/education).

iii The exclusion of the poor from rising living standards.

iv A loss of public sympathy towards the poor, fostering the development of a culturally isolated and distinct underclass. In particular, the successful working class has largely disassociated itself from the underclass.

Field's focus on long-term welfare dependency as the defining feature of the underclass is typical of both radical and conservative definitions of the underclass from the late 1980s. Field recognises the role of the economy, including de-industrialisation and the increase in part-time work, in creating the conditions for the development of the underclass but does not give central emphasis to the dual labour market in the way that earlier radical theorists, including Giddens do. His analysis is not incompatible with dual labour market theory but it moves into other areas, particularly that of government social policy. It is precisely in this area that Charles Murray, the best known conservative theorist of the underclass, sees the cause of the development of the underclass (see below).

In comment on Field's analysis, its political flavour is clear. Field wants improved welfare benefits but also the provision of more opportunities to 'escape' from dependency for those who possibly can. Thus, he has stressed the importance of education and job training for such groups as the long-term unemployed and single parents who are able to do paid, in addition to domestic work.

6 W G Runciman: trapped at benefit level

Like Frank Field, W G Runciman regards those more or less *excluded* from the labour market and permanently living at the level at which state benefit is paid as the underclass. Prominent among this group is the long-term unemployed. In the context of his overall model of the British class structure, Runciman is specifically arguing that the underclass do not occupy secure occupational roles and that they are therefore not part of the working class. On the contrary, their roles are defined by their need for state welfare and they are therefore an underclass of – Runciman estimates – about 5% of the population.

In defining the underclass as generally outside the operation of the labour market, Runciman flatly refutes Giddens's dual labour market-based analysis of the underclass. For him, the underclass has little or nothing to offer in the labour market – and is below or 'under' the majority that have. In terms of the three economic criteria that Runciman considers determine class identity – ownership, control and marketability – the underclass is in a deficit situation.

7 Criticism of Runciman

Runciman's definition of the underclass is clear and logically consistent but considerable empirical criticism to it exists. Drawing on survey data from six British local labour markets, collected as part of the Social Change and Economic Life Initiative, Duncan Gallie argues that the long-term unemployed – the key group in Runciman's definition – are not part of an underclass. On the basis of their work histories (total experience in the labour market) and in terms of their political attitudes there is little basis to consider the long-term unemployed as a distinct, isolated group. The long-term unemployed in the survey had the same (average) number of jobs as the employed (6.0) and had tended to stay in jobs for a very similar duration of time as the employed (74 months against 76 months). The survey data on political attitudes does not suggest that the long-term unemployed are either unusually apathetic or so radicalised that they reject party politics in favour of direct action. In fact the unemployed were more likely than the employed to support the Labour party – a tendency that the experience of unemployment strengthened. Gallie acknowledges the increased poverty and frequently social isolation of the long-term unemployed but cites evidence that these experiences, especially the former, confirm rather than weaken traditional working class identification.

Runciman has also been criticised by Hartley Dean and Peter Taylor-Gooby for exaggerating the extent to which single parents are entrapped in the underclass. On average, single parents remain single for only 35 months – suggesting quite a high rate of mobility out of the underclass. It is worth adding in this context, that given that Runciman defines the underclass status of (many) single parents, in terms of their dependency on state benefits, then, state policy should be able to contribute to removing that status. In particular, it is notable that the relatively low labour force participation of single parents in the United Kingdom correlates with the even lower provision (comparatively speaking) of pre-school nursery places. Improved provision would be likely to enable increased labour force participation of single parents. However, in fact, between 1980 and 1990, labour force participation of single parents in the United Kingdom was the only example of steady decline in the eight countries compared in Figure 13.10. By 1990 it was the lowest of the eight.

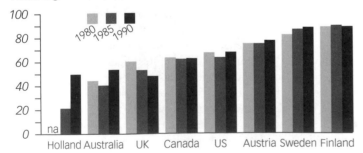

(Source: *Cabinet Office Document*)

Figure 13.10 Labour force participation of lone mothers

Conservative theories of the underclass

Charles Murray

Writing in *The Sunday Times* in late 1989, Charles Murray the American right-wing policy advisor, stated that:

> *There are many ways to identify an underclass. I will concentrate on three phenomena that have turned out to be early-warning signals in the United States: illegitimacy, violent crime, and drop-out from the labour force.*
>
> *(26.11.1989)*

Murray sees these three phenomena as connected and as produced by the same cause – over-generous welfare benefits resulting in female-headed single-parent families. According to Murray, prior to the welfare reforms of the 1960s, the single-parent family had scarcely been a viable economic unit. More generous welfare payments made it much more attractive for single females to have children outside of a stable relationship with a male. The result was that children in this situation lacked a male role model and the discipline of an older male. Young males ran wild. Unable to get work or rejecting routine and low paid jobs; they frequently turned to crime and drugs. Murray describes their behaviour as 'deplorable' and their values as 'contaminating the life of entire neighbourhoods'. These cultural traits get passed on to younger males.

Although Murray's thesis was developed in relation to the United States where he applied them particularly, though not exclusively, to blacks, in his lectures and interviews in the UK, it became clear that he considered that his analysis had substantial application here. He also had talks with Conservative politicians and seems to have been an influence behind Secretary of State for Social Security, Peter Lilley's measures to reduce the benefits of unmarried single parents in the early 1990s.

Murray wants to go much further in reducing welfare to this group of single parents than would be politically possible in England. In a word, he would take welfare away from them. In answer to the suggestion that some mothers would not be able to survive in these circumstances, he replied in a way that revealed the roots of his nineteenth century survival of the fittest philosophy.

> *You're gong to have a self-selection process. It will no longer be the case, as it is now, that if you take a baby home, you'll have an apartment, food and medical care. The young women who take their babies home will be the ones who have either managed to enlist the support of their own relatives or that of the father of the baby, and are therefore likely to be the best mothers.*
>
> *(BBC Interview 18.3.1995)*

For those who cannot afford their babies, Murray suggests adoption or that 'the private sector can take care of it'. Although neither the American nor British governments systematically applied Murray's recommendations, they were influential in the policy debate on 'the family' in the early-to-mid 1990s which still continues.

In 1995, Murray followed up his earlier work on the underclass with a work on ethnicity and intelligence, *The Bell Curve: Intelligence and Class Structure in American Life*. Murray claims that intelligence is unevenly distributed by ethnic group with, on average, blacks being fifteen points below whites and 'East Asians' ten to fifteen points higher. Although he stresses the link between heredity and IQ, Murray accepts that these ethnic differences in IQ may or may not be genetically determined. Nevertheless, he still argues that if the less intelligent – among whom black people are disproportionately represented – produce more children than the intelligent, this will create 'downward pressure' on the average intelligence in the United States – a process he refers to as 'dysgenesis'. This, then, becomes another argument for removing welfare from the 'underclass'.

Criticisms of Murray

Both Murray's theoretical analysis of the underclass and his policy recommendations are extremely controversial. Not surprisingly, he has attracted criticism.

On the crucial matter of the cultural attitudes of the so-called underclass, Murray appears to be empirically wrong in so far as his comments apply to Britain's long-term unemployed. Again, Duncan Gallie supplies the evidence. In order to measure the commitment to work of the long-term unemployed Gallie uses the measure developed by the Social and Applied Psychology Unit at Sheffield. He defines the long-term unemployed as those unemployed for 12 months or more and, as distinct from the non-active, still actively looking for work. As Table 13.9 shows 'the unemployed as a whole were actually more committed to employment than those in work' (743). It is important to note Gallie's definition of employment commitment.

Rather evidently the above data 'provides little support for the view that the unemployed have particularly low levels of work commitment'.

Another area in which Murray has come in for much criticism is his analysis of the role of single parenthood in contributing to the emergence of the underclass. Nicholas Deacon points out that many so-called illegitimate children share a household with cohabiting parents and suggests that Murray should be more careful in utilising official statistics. In addition, the points made in relation to Runciman in this context also apply to Murray (see p. 390). Further, it is not the case that the structure of the black family has been created by the welfare system but has a long history in which patterns of traditional African kinship and the effects of slavery require consideration (see pp. 59-60). In any case, as Joan Brown points out, single parenthood is hardly a lower class monopoly. Indeed, stockbroker belt Surrey is 'the divorce capital' of Europe.

Table 13.9 Employment commitment

	All	Men	Women
	Committed percentage		
Self-employed	72	75	66
Employed	64	66	61
U/E 6 months	76	78	75
U/E 12 months	75	78	70
U/E 12 months +	72	74	69
Non-Active	68	86	66
N	5258	2542	2716

Note: Respondents were defined as committed to employment if they reported they would wish to work even if they were 'to get enough money to live as comfortably as you would like for the rest of your life'.

(Source: D Gallie, *Are the Unemployed an Underclass*, in *Sociology*, Vol. 28, No.3, 1994:743)

Finally, a question often raised in relation to Murray's underclass theory is whether or not it is racist. Racism is a most serious charge but then Murray's own comments on the underclass have often been severe and judgmental. What is particularly interesting and perhaps revealing about his thinking is that he commences from an extreme individualistic position in which state welfare policy is castigated and concludes by advocating measures to deal with the 'illegitimate' children of young parents which smack of authoritarianism – adoption and placement in orphanages. Although he accepts that the average IQ level of ethnic groups may not be a function of biology he uses the highly biological term 'dysgenesis' to describe the effects of a high birthrate among the underclass. Whether all this amounts to racism or not is a matter of judgement as well as definition but it is perhaps not surprising that many radical, including some black, sociologists stopped using the term underclass as Murray began to popularise it.

Peter Saunders: an underclass by 'merit'?

Although Peter Saunders has not written extensively on the underclass, his perspective is worth presenting on two counts. First, as a leading right-wing sociologist, he is a thinker of considerable influence. Second, although a notably independent thinker, his analysis of the underclass, reflects a similar line of logic to that of Murray (without, however, repeating the latter's comments on ethnicity and genetics). Saunders dismisses the notion that either all black people or all women are part of an underclass but considers that it is probably useful to 'talk of the existence of an underclass' if we mean by it:

> *... a stratum of people who are generally poor, unqualified and irregularly or never employed. This underclass is disproportionately recruited today from among Afro-Caribbeans, people living in the north, those who are trapped in run-down council estates or in decaying inner cities, and young single people and single-parent families.*
>
> *(Saunders, 1990:121)*

Saunders goes on to enumerate what he considers are 'four key features' of the underclass:

1 Multiple deprivation.
2 Social marginality.
3 Almost entire dependence on state welfare provisions.
4 A culture of fatalism.

As a summary statement, the first three features of the underclass suggested by Saunders would probably be agreed to by most radical and conservative commentators (although some welfare recipients alleviate dependency by activity in the informal economy). Most radical commentators, however, reject the notion that the underclass is 'fatalistic' and earlier evidence to support a much less negative view of the long-term unemployed was cited from Duncan Gallie.

Saunder's suggested solution to the problem of welfare dependency is a negative income tax, supplemented by voucher schemes e.g. for health and education. Instead of being dependent on the judgement of middle class professionals, members of the underclass would be *empowered* to make choices and determine their own priorities. Thus, they might re-establish 'a sense of self-worth and dignity'.

In his more recent writings (1995), Saunders has put forward the view that Britain may already be a 'meritocracy' i.e. the class positions people hold are roughly what they merit in terms of their ability and effort. Presumably this observation applies to the underclass. He argues that the much greater educational and career success of middle class compared to working class children is a result of intelligence (which he regards as largely inherited) rather than environment. His key evidence for this is that working class children of high measured intelligence and level of commitment to school at the age of eleven have almost as good life chances as middle class children. Two points can be made in reply to this. First, most psychologists regard the first eleven years of a person's life as crucially important in the development of their intelligence and attitudes. The low scores of many working class children at eleven may be no more than an indication of undeveloped potential. If so, a rational response would be to try to enrich their early social and educational environment. Second, if most working class children are tending to score worse than most middle class children on the above measures at eleven and to go on to less successful careers, that, again, can be viewed as a challenge to improve their education from eleven onwards and so perhaps their life-chances. To regard the current situation as unchangeable is rather 'fatalistic'.

Saunders' individualistic values do not lead him to the authoritarian treatment of 'losers' that Murray can be accused of. However, Polly Toynbee suggests of his research that 'to follow its dreadful logic, we would simply abandon the poor to their 'genetic' fate ...' (*The Independent*, 17.12.1995:20)

A liberal approach to the underclass: Ralf Dahrendorf

In an article published in 1992, Dahrendorf presents four 'aspects' which he considers characterise the underclass:

1 Its members are 'not able, or perhaps not willing, or both to participate fully in the economic, the political and the social life of the communities in which they live'.
2 Its members are largely those who have 'dropped out' of the working class, such as the long-term unemployed'.
3 The underclass is strictly not a class – it makes no significant economic contribution and is not necessary to the rest of society.
4 Extending the entitlements of citizenship to the underclass might re-engage its members with the rest of society.

Given Gallie's research already referred to, it seems likely that Dahrendorf exaggerates the extent to which the underclass is cut-off and excluded from the rest of society. In particular, many of the long-term unemployed do eventually find jobs and presumably re-engage with their civic rights and responsibilities – assuming that disengagement did, in fact, occur. However, it is generally true that the civic and political participation of lower socio-economic groups is less than others, and in raising the issue of citizenship, Dahrendorf is in tune with what has become a major theme of the 1990s. The matter can be seen partly in terms of rights and responsibilities. In relation to the former, Dahrendorf discusses the policy of basic income guarantees but he also implies that as well as benefiting from society, individuals have a responsibility to put something back. The reciprocal nature of citizenship is a theme that has become increasingly central to political debate.

The underclass and poverty: conclusion

Dahrendorf makes the further point that as a variety of groups make up the underclass, no single policy will lift them all out of the underclass. Given the disparate nature of the so-called underclass and the lack of a common solution to its members' situations, it may be better simply not to use the term at all – as some have decided. The term gets stretched – differently by different authorities – to the point where it is in danger of losing any precise and effective meaning. The advantage of using the term 'poor' to describe those referred to as 'the underclass' is that it is already well established that 'the poor' are a highly varied group, that their poverty can be due to different causes and may require different and various solutions. As we have seen, there is much sociological theory devoted to poverty and the poor but the terms themselves, unlike that of underclass, do not carry any implication of a single theoretical conceptualisation. It is worth considering whether the term underclass and the discussion it has sparked adds very much insight to the area that the various theories of poverty do not already provide.

Questions
1 Which of the various explanations of poverty do you consider best applies to poverty in contemporary Britain?
2 Does the concept of the underclass add anything to our understanding of poverty and inequality?

Social policy

Definition of social policy

As Michael Hill suggests at the beginning of his book *Understanding Social Policy*, one way to answer the question 'What is social policy?' is to list the areas of public policy included under the heading. The areas that Hill himself deals with are social security, the personal social services, the health service, education, employment services and housing. Together these constitute the substance of the British Welfare State. However, as Hill emphasises, this simple definition of social policy will not suffice. Nor, any longer, will T H Marshall's classic statement that 'the avowed objective of twentieth century social policy is welfare'. Marxists and others argue that the objective of certain social policy measures is to control disaffected groups in the population rather than to act out of concern for their welfare. Indeed, the whole subject of social policy has been 'blown open' in that it is now widely accepted that social policy is generated through political conflict and debate and that its study must encompass this. Social policy analysis, therefore, must consider political ideology and the effect on social policy of other policy areas, especially economic (since economic factors greatly influence social policy). Hill suggests three points for consideration in defining social policy: first, that social policy may not only be concerned with welfare; second, that other policies (such as economic) may affect welfare more than social policy; third, that public policy should be seen as a whole and that social policy is related to other policies.

Finally, Hill does not give a single, brief definition of social policy. However, the following statement by Peter Townsend summarises the broad view of social policy now widely adopted:

> *If social policy is conceived of as the institutional control of services, agencies and organisations to maintain or change social structure or values, then what is at stake is not just the social division of welfare or the management of public, fiscal and private welfare, but the allocation of wealth, the organisation of employment, the management of the wage system and the creation of styles of living.*
>
> (Townsend, 1981:26)

In short, social policy is about the kind of society people want to create and what they do to create it.

Social administration refers to the means by which social policy is implemented. Given that analysis of policy goals involves political issues, then so must analysis of administrative means. Naturally social policy makers seek to shape their administrative machinery – say the social or education services – to their purposes. There are, of course, a variety of administrative skills but in so far as we are directly concerned with administration, it is a tool of policy. Administrators may intentionally or unintentionally hamper the goals of policy makers and this is a relevant point to study in policy outcome analysis. Indeed, the civil service is often criticised in this respect not least in the celebrated television series ironically titled *Yes, Minister*.

The welfare state and voluntary sector

Although the emphasis is now changing somewhat, much modern social policy analysis has focused on the Welfare State. Debates have ranged from fundamental matters of ideology to practical issues of costs and efficiency. Asa Briggs defines a welfare state as one which modifies the effects of market forces to provide citizens with a minimum income, to protect them against a range of problems such as sickness and homelessness, and to ensure equal access to a range of services such as education. Of course, what this comes down to in practice is a matter of public intent and political decision. As A N Rees points out, it can be far more difficult and humiliating to be 'on welfare' when the consensus is moving against welfare than when it is more favourable. A welfare state securing the citizen's accepted right to certain minimum provisions cannot be assumed.

Private charity was the main 'solution' to need and poverty prior to the development of the welfare state. A vast array of privately funded charitable organisations have continued throughout the post-war period and many individuals make tax-deductible contributions to them. Some are secular in orientation – such as the marriage guidance organisation, Relate. Others, like the Salvation Army are religious in inspiration.

As Paul Wilding says:

> *Welfare is, and has always been a mixed economy of formal and informal public and private, voluntary and family provision.*
>
> *(1992: 208)*

The Beveridge ideal: universal basic welfare

The British Welfare State was largely established by the Labour government of 1945 to 1950. The major exception was Butler's 1944 Education Act. The mood in support of social reform to achieve greater security and opportunity for the majority developed strongly as a result of wartime experience. Many felt that they had earned a fairer society by virtue of their efforts and deprivation over the war years. In addition, war often has a somewhat egalitarian effect by throwing the social classes together in a common cause. Personal value, including one's own, can become more important than status and wealth. Politicians recognised the new climate of opinion and a variety of government reports on a number of social issues were carried out during the war. The most important of these was the Beveridge Report (1942) often thought of as the blueprint for the Welfare State. The key point to note about the Beveridge-inspired reforms is that they were an attempt to institutionalise welfare for all – a genuine *welfare* state.

The five evils

Beveridge proposed an attack on the five giant evils of want, disease, ignorance, squalor and idleness. It helps to group these five evils into a triad: (1) ignorance; (2) disease; and (3) want, idleness and squalor. Ignorance was attacked by the Education Act (1944) and disease by the National Health Act (1946) although it was the Conservative, Butler, and the Socialist, Bevan, rather than the Liberal Beveridge, who were respectively most responsible for them. Beveridge's name is associated with the National Insurance Act (1946) which (along with the National Insurance Act of 1944) established a compulsory flat-rate system of contributions covering basic social needs, primarily sickness, injury, unemployment and old age pensions. Beveridge, then, led the attack on want. A N Rees refers to the above three pieces of legislation as the 'three pillars of the British Welfare State'. A fourth could be added in the form of the National Assistance Act of 1948 which was also inspired by Beveridge. This Act was the fruit of Beveridge's growing realisation that even in a welfare state intended to be universal – some would slip into poverty. However, he would have been astonished at the ten million plus on benefit in 1996. This provided assistance for special cases who slipped through the National Insurance safety net. Both the National Insurance Act and the National Assistance Act have been superseded by later legislation. Insurance contributions and major benefits now have an earnings related element and national assistance has been replaced by income support and family credit (1988).

Idleness was seen mainly as unemployment, and squalor mainly as inadequate housing. It was part of Beveridge's thinking that the government would take economic planning measures to ensure a very high (if not full) level of employment. This view reflected the Keynesian consensus of the period which followed John Keynes' view that the government could 'fine-tune' the economy to achieve a buoyant labour market. In part, the government used its control of the nationalised industries to do this. The Thatcher administrations from 1979 broke with the Keynesian consensus, believing that job creation occurs as a result of the expansion of the private sector. In reality, however, it intervened with a series of schemes and subsidies to stimulate the private sector comparable to those adopted by previous governments to assist both the public and private sectors. Beveridge's fifth evil 'squalor' is usually taken to refer to housing and, more recently, to the environment. Squalor was attacked by both the Labour and Conservative parties with substantial programmes of house building, programmes which were severely cut back during the 1970s and 1980s, particularly by the Thatcher governments. The New Towns Act (1946) was aimed at providing new and thriving environments for the inhabitants of deprived and decaying inner city areas (see p. 555). The Act is characterised by the sensitivity to environmental issues perhaps ahead of its time.

Criticisms of Beveridge

Beveridge was a man of his time and this showed in the limitations as well of the strengths of his ideas. First, following his contemporary, Keynes, he tended to assume full or almost full employment. As a result, his concept of national assistance was not thought through in terms of the millions of unemployed that occurred in the 1980s and 1990s. In fairness, this matter remains unresolved. Second, his notion of welfare was based on what came to seem a rather idealised and perhaps outmoded notion of the 'happy patriarchal family' – with most benefits coming to the male breadwinner who it was assumed would pass them on. Again, this is a matter which has been engaged with more recently. Third, the welfare state as built by Beveridge was not capable of coping with the development of relative definitions of poverty. As Richard Thomas says, when these were applied 'the Welfare State was found wanting'.

Beveridge in context: past and present

Beveridge was no revolutionary and the welfare measures of the war coalition and post-war Labour government did not amount to revolution. Rather, they represented the height of a long evolution of liberal or social democratic reform. Each of the major areas of reform – education, health and welfare – was characterised by a long period of increasing government involvement. The nature of capitalist industrial society stimulated this concern, raising as it does problems of inequality and insecurity, and of social order and control. Education to the age of ten years was made compulsory in 1880 although a national infrastructure of elementary education had been established ten years previously. The Public Health Act of 1875 was a legislative landmark, establishing a national system of local health authorities, yet, typically of the British reformist tradition, it codified and developed existing tendencies rather than established an entirely new system. Lloyd George's National Insurance Act of 1911 first established a contributory system of National Insurance against unemployment and sickness. Prior to this the poor had been variously treated as objects of charity or control, depending on whether humanitarian or punitive sentiments were uppermost. The Victorian workhouse reflected a tough, almost penal attitude to the poor, who, in the individualistic ideology of the period, were often blamed for their own condition. More recently, something of the same attitude was widely expressed in sections of the media and public opinion in the anti-'social security scrounger' campaign of the first Thatcher administration (see pp. 327-8). The National Insurance Acts of 1944 and 1946 greatly expanded the application of insurance which Beveridge envisaged as a citizen's right. Similarly, the liberal policy analyst, Thomas H Marshall wrote of the three rights of modern citizenship: legal, political and welfare. Within the liberal/social democratic tradition, Beveridge is considered to have made a major contribution to establishing welfare rights.

So far, the immediate post-war years have been the most productive period of welfare reform. However, many developments have since been introduced including some quite radical and controversial ones in the 1980s. Changes in the national health and education systems are described elsewhere (Chapters 4 and 14). Perhaps the most significant change in National Insurance has been the introduction of an earnings related element, initially by the Conservatives (1959) and extended by Labour (1966). In itself, this is less egalitarian than Beveridge's original scheme, involving only an equal contribution and equal benefits dependent upon need, but for many it removed the incentive to join private insurance schemes. By the 1990s, there was a widespread view – across the parties – that the Beveridge framework was no longer fully adequate or appropriate to British society. This view will be explained and, in part, questioned below.

Welfare: perspectives and policies

The policy perspectives discussed below are: liberal/social democratic – associated primarily with Labour and the Liberal Democrats; Conservative, including New Right, Marxist and Feminist. Conservative perspectives are discussed along with actual policies – as the Conservatives were the only party to be in power between 1979 and 1997. In addition to the introductory section on liberal/social democratic approaches, further coverage is given in the form of a 1997 'snapshot' of the welfare policies of the three main parties. Marxist and feminist perspective are presented separately as they represent radically different views of what genuine social welfare might be.

First, however, a basic distinction between two approaches to welfare must be made.

Universal and selective benefits: a key distinction

A key distinction is that between *universal* and *selective* benefits. Universalism is based on the principle of providing a service to all citizens as a matter of right. Selectivity involves establishing criteria of acceptability for a given welfare service and means-testing applicants accordingly. A parallel distinction is that between *institutional* and *residual* concepts of welfare. In the words of Harold Wilensky and Charles Lebeaux: 'a residual system provides that social welfare institutions should come into play only when the normal structures of supply, the family and the market, break down', whereas an institutional system sees 'the welfare services as normal, 'first line' functions of modern industrial society'. Beveridge recommended a system of national security that was universal and compulsory. Aneurin Bevan set up a national health service free to all. Yet, the principle of universalism has been eroded in both cases and by both parties, in the former case by introducing a two tier system of payments, and in the latter by introducing now quite substantial prescription charges.

We now consider the arguments put forward in favour of a universal/institutional system. First, it provides services on the basis of right and equality and therefore fosters a sense of common community. This amounts to a considerable social vision. Second, social democrats typically considered that a more socially secure society would be a more orderly one – a belief that parallels Smelser's functionalist argument that the development of welfare has promoted social integration. Similarly, a healthier labour force was widely perceived as likely to be more productive. The major argument against universalism is cost – the more comprehensive the system of free services, the higher the taxation. In addition, the related charges of abuse of services, dependency and loss of work incentive are made, mainly from the political right. More broadly supported was the view that emerged of the welfare bureaucracy as too large, inefficient and alienating. Richard Titmuss was committed to a basic 'infrastructure of universalist services' but tried to meet the above criticisms by suggesting that other services might be available only to certain 'categories, groups and territorial areas' on the basis of specific need. In this way, he hoped to avoid the means-testing of individuals which had caused great bitterness in the 1930s. In fact, in the post-war period, the drift of the British Welfare State has been away from universalism towards selective means-testing. After Margaret Thatcher came to power in 1979, this drift was given a sharper sense of direction.

The main argument in favour of the selective/residual model is that it is cheaper and resources go to those who 'really need' them. It is also seen by its supporters as less likely to spawn bureaucracy. Against this is the increase in humiliating means-testing and the possibility that once a service is no longer regarded as a universal right it can be qualified and reduced indefinitely. We will return to the universalism versus selectivity debate when dealing with the new right (Conservative) social policy perspective.

Liberal/social democratic perspective

As we have seen, the liberal/social democratic view dominated political and public opinion for the 30 years following the war. A 'corporate' approach to economic and social planning developed in which government, business and the trade unions co-operated for 'progress'. By the 1970s corporatism was coming under challenge.

The ideological and institutional crisis of the social democratic welfare state

The crisis in the British Welfare State preceded by several years the coming to power of Margaret Thatcher in 1979. Underlying the crisis of welfare was (and is) the long relative decline of the country's economy. This endemic problem was intensified in 1973 by the quadrupling of the price of oil following the action of the OPEC cartel. Against a background of world economic recession, the Labour governments of Harold Wilson (1974-76) and James Callaghan (1976-79) struggled to maintain intact the Welfare State and a policy of near full employment. However, the crisis was to test the post-war social democratic compromise between capitalism and socialism – basically accepted by all parties – almost to the limit.

Ten years previously, there was little appreciation of the crisis to come. In his professional inaugural lecture of 1962, F Lafitte expressed the optimistic orthodoxy that a well-managed mixed economy would supply the wherewithal for a gradual expansion of the Welfare State – particularly its 'communal services'. As late as the mid-1970s, Ramesh Mishra was still commenting unproblematically on the need for a balance between the values of 'fraternity and collectivity' of the welfare ideal, and of 'liberty and individuality' of the free market. In reality, however, the 'balance' or compromise was already under severe stress. This was because the free market itself failed to produce a reliably expanding surplus with which to finance the Welfare State. Social democrats of all parties were therefore faced with an unpleasant choice which few of them had foreseen: should government policy be directed mainly at taking pressure off the free market by trying to reduce taxation and expenditure, primarily welfare expenditure, or should it continue to support and even expand the Welfare State by squeezing the private sector? On the horns of the dilemma, social democracy split, letting in the Thatcherite New Right which, without a qualm or ambiguity, opted for the first solution.

A new corporatism?

No doubt in response to the ideological and policy turmoil of the late 1970s and 1980s, Ramesh Mishra has critically reviewed his own social democratic perspective. In *The Welfare State in Crisis* (1984), he presents a qualified case in favour of a particular form of social democratic Welfare State – the corporatist Welfare State. He believes that this model – relatively successfully practised by Austria

and Sweden – more effectively integrates economic and social policy than any other. The corporatist Welfare State retains the mixed economy, with a strong private sector, but is managed by a mixture of Keynesian demand stimulation and supply side economics (often associated with the New Right) to encourage production and labour mobility. On the social side, a 'social partnership' of capital and labour is encouraged by government, in which high levels of social welfare and of industrial productivity are pursued as mutually beneficial and compatible goals. As Mishra himself points out, such an approach can only deal with social problems at a national level whereas, in fact, many are now caused at the international level.

In retrospect (i.e. from 1997), Mishra's vision of welfare seems to belong more to the 1970s than to the period ahead. Even in 1997, Tony Blair is not 'talking corporatism'. However, some influential figures on the political left do see a constructive purpose in closer government and trade union co-operation.

The New Right: Thatcherism and after, 1979-97

In both Britain and the United States, it was the political right which primarily benefited from the problems of social democracy. In 1979 Margaret Thatcher became Prime Minister for the first time and in 1980 Ronald Reagan was elected President. Both were returned for a second period of office in 1983 and 1984 respectively and they left office within two years of each other in 1990 and 1988 respectively. The ideology of the New Right has been described earlier in this chapter (see p. 384) and, in detail in Chapter 11.

As far as social policy is concerned, it is relevant to divide the Conservative period in office into two parts, 1979-87 and 1987 onwards. The change is less one of rhetoric than of substance – not always the way in politics. What remained consistent throughout the Conservatives' time in office was the overall aim of creating a successful, free market economy. This was seen as requiring both cuts in public expenditure and a reduction in income tax. Cuts in public expenditure were more likely to be made in welfare than in, say, law and order or defence programmes.

Conservative social policy, 1979-87

The 1979-87 period covers the first two Thatcher administrations. Related to the overall goal of reducing expenditure and increasing efficiency in the area of social welfare, three aspects of Conservative policy are noteworthy during this period:

1 A move towards residual and away from universalistic welfare policies.
2 The privatisation of certain aspects of welfare and the development of the voluntary sector.
3 De-institutionalisation (using 'the community' as a resource).

Taking a broad definition of 'the community', the government's increased emphasis on the voluntary or charitable sector can be regarded as an aspect of this policy.

The move to residualism

Public housing policy illustrates both the move from a universalistic to a more selective/residual model and privatisation. In 1979 government policy was to keep council house rents generally low by means of a general subsidy. In fact, in 1979 council rents were at their lowest post-war level. The 1980 Housing Act gave the Secretary of State strong powers to push up rents in areas receiving the central subsidy. Between 1979 and 1982 rents more than doubled. However, for those who met the means-test criteria, protection was provided by increased rent rebate and supplementary benefit payments. A problem with such schemes is low take-up, particularly amongst the most needy. Only 50 per cent of eligible one parent families and 46 per cent of two parent families took up rebates compared to 82 per cent of childless households. To what extent this was due to inadequate publicity of the scheme, too little time on the part of harassed parents, or repugnance at the stigma of means-testing, is a matter for speculation. Further, those just above the eligibility line would have been particularly hard hit by the doubling of rents. The above and other aspects of Conservative housing policy lead Alan Murie (from whom the above data is taken) to term it 'a thoroughly residual policy'.

By forcing up council house rents, central government created a climate favourable to the sale of council houses. The impact of this policy was massive both in terms of raising revenue and in extending owner occupation. The 27 billion pounds raised was more than the rest of the privatisations put together up to 1990. Up to the same year, it created about 1.5 million more owner occupiers (see Figure 13.11a). Some authorities have suggested that this group has provided a new source of Conservative support but others argue that the evidence is they were inclined to Conservatism prior to buying their properties. As we have seen, critics of council house privatisation, see it as a squandering of a key public asset and as partly responsible for the growth in homelessness in the late 1980s and early 1990s (see Figure 13.11b). Critics of Conservative government housing policy, such as Peter Ambrose, argue that the mix of 'market' and 'social' (welfare) criteria in housing allocation has become too skewed to the former when compared to more effective policies in some other European counties (*The Times Higher Educational Supplement*, 31.6.1991).

There are other examples of the move towards residualism.

In the many cases where means-tested schemes already existed in 1979, the Conservatives frequently reduced benefits and/or eligibility. Thus, between 1979 and 1980, about 174,000 children lost entitlement to free school meals for which the government, in any case, gave up responsibility for nutritional quality. However, the number eligible tends to increase during times of high unemployment. It is not easy to quantify the reduction in social

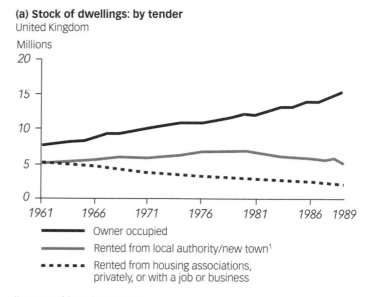

(a) Stock of dwellings: by tender
United Kingdom

(Source: Social Trends, 1991:135)

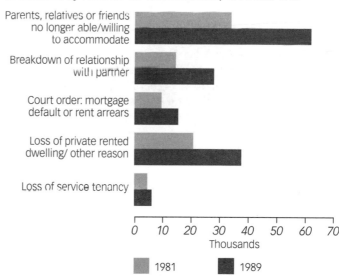

(b) Homeless households found accommodation by local authorities: by reasons² for homelessness, 1981 and 1989

1 Households found accommodation under the Housing Act 1985, which defines priority need
2 Categories in Wales differ slightly from those in England so cases have been allocated to the closest English category. Data for Wales include cases given advice and assistance.

(Source: *Social Trends*, 1991: 141)

Figure 13.11 The emerging housing problem for non-owner occupiers

security benefits under Thatcherism, let alone to trace their human cost. However, writing of the first administration, Ruth Lister and Paul Wilding referred to the 'cuts, nicks and slices which have in three and a half years taken some £2000 million away from those dependent on social security'.

The privatisation of aspects of welfare and the development of the voluntary sector

The privatisation of welfare was another aspect of the social policy of Reaganism and Thatcherism. Le Grand and Robinson indicate that it applies in three areas: the *provision, subsidy and regulation of services*. Examples of a reduction in state provision are the closing of local authority residential homes (some of which are now privately run) and the sale of council houses. Examples of state subsidy reduction are the reduction of the general subsidy to council house tenants and the increase in NHS prescription charges. On the other hand, subsidies were given to private businesses to carry out job training (see pp. 122-7). An example of decreasing regulation is the lifting of restrictions on competition between private and public bus companies.

A policy that covers so many situations is not easy to generalise about but the main issues are clear and vital. Those in favour of privatisation argue that it is more efficient than the public provision of services. Research on this point varies from case to case but, on balance, does not sustain this generalisation. Thus, Millwards' review of the evidence found that the private collection of refuse tended to be more efficient, but that this was not the case with the provision of water or electricity. By now, the privatisation of several major utilities should give most readers a chance to make their own judgement on this issue. Second, supporters of privatisation tend to argue that it increases liberty both by releasing initiative and increasing choice. However, it is as logical to argue that the Welfare State increases the liberty of the disadvantaged by providing them with the basic means of life, without which they could not make significant choices (whereas private enterprise does not seek to guarantee this). Third, critics of the Welfare State argue that it has failed to produce equality and that a combination of privatisation and income subsidies for the 'truly needy' would be more effective. The key issue here is how big the redistribution of income would be. In the absence of public services, it would have to be very substantial to increase equality. In any case, to do so is not a goal of Conservatives.

As well as privatising aspects of welfare, the Thatcher governments also promoted the voluntary sector. Ironically – for a government claiming to be non-interventionist – large sums of public money were diverted into the voluntary sector while the Welfare State suffered cuts. Some agencies, such as 'Shelter' clearly had a commitment in a fundamental area of welfare. Individual 'carers' were funded to carry out a wide range of services – with mixed results.

A voluntary sector so dependent on government runs the risk of vulnerability in terms of funding, decision making and policy direction (Reading 1 – in which Paul Wilding gives a review and assessment of the role of the voluntary sector in welfare.

De-institutionalisation (using the community as a resource)

The policy of de-institutionalisation, pursued by both the Reagan and Thatcher governments, provides an interesting example of the dovetailing of economic expediency with ideology. It simultaneously reduced public expenditure and large-scale welfare bureaucracy. De-institutionalisation means directing certain dependent groups out of public institutions and into the family and community. It has been practised mainly in relation to the mentally ill and handicapped but also in relation to the old. The policy has potential advantages, but for it to work, substantial support for the concerned families and communities (however that term may be defined) must be provided. Without this, two groups tend to suffer – as has been apparent in the de-institutionalisation of many of the mentally ill. First, are those who traditionally carry the burden of care – overwhelmingly women, often with many other commitments. Second, are members of the dependent groups – as was seen by the apparently increased numbers of mentally ill people wandering the streets in the mid 1980s. In a review of community care policy the Audit Commission estimated that over 40,000 inmates of mental hospitals had 'disappeared' from the records of health and welfare agencies. To attempt to save money at the risk of 'dumping', say, a middle-aged, long-institutionalised psychotic on his elderly mother is the kind of sad consequence that can result from under-financing de-institutionalisation. Yet, it is in these 'small' corners of human misery that the cost of cuts must be sought. In fairness, by the mid 1990s greater efforts were being made to monitor this policy.

The 1988 Social Security Act

Although the 1988 Social Security Act only came into force early during the third Thatcher administration, it was fashioned during the second. It illustrates that there was substantial continuity between the Conservative administrations before and after 1987 as well as the major differences referred to shortly. Although trumpeted by some as the most radical restructuring of social welfare since Beveridge, in retrospect the Fowler Act appears to have nothing like the vision and scope that inspired Beveridge's reforms. Indeed, critics see the 1988 Act as little more than a grandiose exercise in cutting public expenditure – at the expense of the poor. The main measures introduced by the Act are as follows:

Income Support is the main means-tested benefit for the unemployed. Calculation of it varies according to certain commitments of the claimants.

Family Credit supplements or 'tops up' the income of low paid workers with children.

Figure 13.12 A victim of 'community care' policy?

The Social Fund replaces grants formerly available through social security with loans (although a very limited number of grants are still made).

Housing Benefit: claimants have to be responsible for paying rent and rates to be eligible and have a low income.

Comment on the Social Security Act

At the time the Act was introduced there was widespread debate about which groups would gain or lose under the Act and the extent to which this would be so. Broadly, the government claimed there would be more gainers than losers and its critics vice versa. In June 1990, *The Guardian* published research by the Child Poverty Action Group into the first two years of the Act's operation. Even if the figures given below somewhat overestimate the degree to which groups have lost income, it still seems highly likely that the government reduced per capita spending on the poor as a result of its Social Security Act.

Changes in social security
In real terms (1990 prices) since 1987

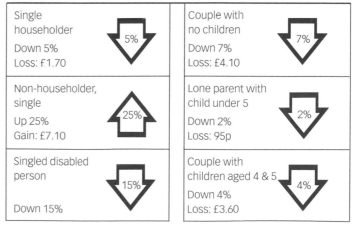

Single householder Down 5% Loss: £1.70 ▼5%	Couple with no children Down 7% Loss: £4.10 ▼7%
Non-householder, single Up 25% Gain: £7.10 ▲25%	Lone parent with child under 5 Down 2% Loss: 95p ▼2%
Singled disabled person Down 15% ▼15%	Couple with children aged 4 & 5 Down 4% Loss: £3.60 ▼4%

(Source: *The Guardian*, 4.6.1990)

Figure 13.13 Poverty and the 1988 Social Security Act

Perhaps one reform in particular illustrates the cost-cutting spirit of the Act: the change from a grants-based system through social security to a loans-based Social Fund as a means of last resort for the poor. This involved two important changes of principle. First, the social security grants were intended as a 'safety net' – people would get them if (subject to means-testing) they needed them. In contrast, the Social Fund budget is relatively small and limited and sometimes 'needy' applicants do not receive a loan. Second, the principle that those in most extreme or urgent need should pay back what they received from public assistance, was introduced. In conclusion, this 'reform' did achieve considerable savings which have been more precisely accounted than their human cost.

The cost of social policy: 1979-87

Figure 13.14a shows the cost of social welfare in Britain between 1959 and 1984 according to the main areas of expenditure. Figure 13.14b puts Britain's expenditure in comparative perspective and shows that the percentage of gross domestic product spent on welfare in Britain is much closer to that of the United States – the bastion of private enterprise – than social democratic Sweden.

The most notable point that emerges from Figure 13.14a is that no marked changes in trends emerge after 1979. Perhaps the clearest change is the increase in social security expenditure caused by the rapid and large rise in unemployment during the early 1980s (a similar rise has occurred as a result of the recession of the early 1990s). Even the very sharp drop in expenditure on housing began in the mid 1970s although many would argue that it has continued too long and been too steep. Only in the area of education is it clear that the Conservatives even slowed the rate of increase in expenditure.

Yet, government expenditure as a percentage of gross domestic product (GDP) did fall steadily between 1981 and 1984 (and continued to do so until 1989). The main reasons for this were that privatisation revenue is subtracted from government expenditure thus significantly 'reducing' it, oil revenue greatly increased during these years, and economic recovery boosted GDP in the years between the two recessions. However, as we have seen, expenditure on the major public services increased in real terms. In this respect, government policy failed during the early 1980s.

Given the high rate of expenditure on the public services in the early 1980s, it is arguable that the first and second Thatcher administrations made no radical break with the recent past on social policy. The Welfare State was maintained albeit trimmed in places. However, Thatcherites still criticised the Welfare State as costly and inefficient while acknowledging that the first two Thatcher administrations had not succeeded in solving these problems. After 1987, they set about dealing with these issues in a different way and in doing so found means which matched their radical rhetoric.

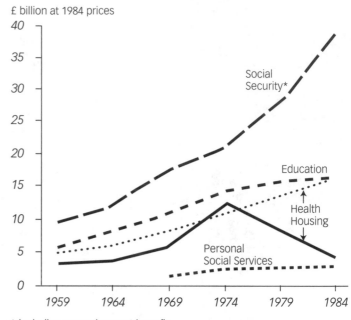

(a) How UK spending on social welfare divides up

£ billion at 1984 prices

* including unemployment benefit

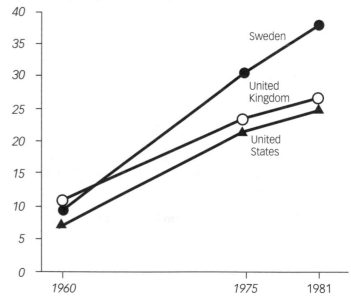

(b) How spending on social welfare programmes grew 1960–81

As percentage of gross domestic product

Figure 13.14 Social welfare in Britain

The Welfare State and 'quasi-markets' 1988-1997

Something of a watershed in Conservative social policy occurred in 1988-89. The goal of increasing efficiency and cutting costs (i.e. of improving productivity) remained, but a new 'mechanism' was introduced to achieve it. This 'mechanism' – a term used by the then Minister of State for Health, William Waldegrave – is the 'quasi-market' or 'internal market' as Ministers tended to call it.

A 'quasi-market' is a partial approximation in the public sector to the free market situation that supposedly exists 'normally' in the private sector. This requires that means be found to ensure that the public sector is operated on the basis of supply and demand, competition, and the resulting success or failure of institutions (i.e. schools or hospitals would be subject to the same market disciplines as businesses). The assumption of advocates of this view is that this would increase the efficiency of public services by requiring them to respond to the demands of the 'consumer'.

Prior to the attempt to introduce quasi-markets, the public services operated on the principle of meeting public need on the basis of equal access among individuals. Increases in demand for, say, education or health provision would be met (mainly) out of the public purse (taxation) and efficiencies would be achieved by management and professionals operating on behalf of the public (members of which sat as school governors or on health boards). We will leave aside, for the moment, criticism both of the quasi-market and public needs driven systems, and instead describe some examples of the former.

Major examples of quasi-markets occur within the education and health services and both of these are discussed in detail elsewhere. Only a brief description is needed here. In primary and secondary education, the two systems of open enrolment/local management of schools and opting out effectively puts schools in competition with each other. If parents/pupils do not like what they are getting, they can go elsewhere (see pp. 128-9). Funding follows pupil numbers. Similarly, in higher education there are built-in financial incentives to encourage institutions to expand. Those that expand are rewarded and those that do not, are less well funded and risk 'going under'. A more radical system would be the introduction of student vouchers which students could 'spend' at the institution of their choice – subject to their qualifications. The National Health Service increasingly operates in a similar way with nearly all major hospitals opted out of local authority control and others increasingly subject to competitive pressures (see pp. 437-41).

Attempts have also been made to introduce quasi-market elements into housing and personal social services. Thus, council tenants now have the right to choose a landlord other than the local authority. In the area of residential accommodation for the elderly, local authorities have increasingly used private residential homes. Case-managers operate on behalf of elderly clients in this context, rather as parents do for pupils in education and General Practitioners who have their own budgets do for patients – at least, this is the theory.

Comment

Assessments vary on how effective quasi-markets might be, or on the other hand how much damage they do. Arguments on both sides of the question are vociferous – understandably, given what is at stake. Those who support the quasi-market mechanism contend that it increases 'consumer' choice, improves efficiency, and will ultimately be fairer by improving the quality of welfare services. Those who oppose quasi-markets argue that the cost-cutting is likely to reduce the quality and scale of services. A second criticism has been that the managements and inspectorates which, respectively, control and police the new welfare systems, may become oppressive and expensive. There has been tension between teachers and management in education, and between hospital doctors and management in the NHS. A third criticism is made strongly by the Labour party. It contends that the changes discussed above are having the effect of creating a two tier system in both health and education, thus contradicting the principle of an equal service for all. Fourthly, and most fundamentally, it is argued that access to basic needs such as health and education is the equal right of all citizens and should be equally provided through public services rather than through the inevitably unequal mechanism of the market.

The notion that markets enhance consumer or client choice has had considerable appeal across political lines. Suggestions from the political left include childcare vouchers and health vouchers (to be 'spent' with a doctor of one's own choice). Julian Le Grand has pointed out that such vouchers will increase inequality, unless the less well off get vouchers of greater value than the rich. He refers to these as positive discrimination vouchers. Whether such schemes to increase consumer freedom are compatible with producing a fair and efficient welfare service may fall to a future Labour government to discover.

Parties, ideologies and welfare policies: a 1996-97 snapshot

1996: welfare still 'in crisis'

Commentators and politicians alike seemed agreed that the Welfare State remains in crisis into the 1990s. So strong was this view that both Labour and the Liberal Democrats set up commissions to report on welfare and the Conservative Secretary of State for Social Security published his own overview of matters. Reading across the party literature, the following two points were frequently perceived as problems:

1 The escalating cost of welfare.
2 The high numbers on welfare.

1   The escalating cost of welfare

According to *Social Trends*, 1996 'expenditure on social protection benefits increased by about two-thirds in real terms between 1980-81 and 1993-94, to nearly £170 billion' (143).

United Kingdom

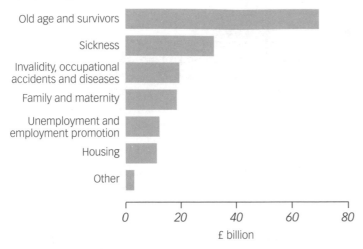

(Source: Central Statistical Office in *Social Trends*, 1996:143)

Figure 13.15 Expenditure on social protection benefits: by function, 1993-94

There is an abundance of evidence of widespread political concern at the cost of welfare but the issue has been a particular refrain of Peter Lilley. In a *Times* article he expressed an impeccably New Right approach to welfare:

> *I remain determined to control the growth of social security spending. Controlling that growth is important to keep taxes low, and so allow people to spend for themselves as much as possible of the money they earn.*
>
> *(23.9.1995:12)*

Labour MP and Chairman of the House Select Committee on Social Security, Frank Field also indicates his concern – in a *Guardian* article:

> *The social security bill grows like Topsy. Thirty years ago it cornered 17 per cent of all taxpayers' expenditure. Now it tops one-third.*
>
> *(7.11.1995:17)*

However, Field faces a dilemma. He believes more needs to be spent on welfare but that the taxpayer does not want to provide the wherewithal. His suggested solution is discussed below.

2 The high numbers on welfare

The cost of welfare and the numbers on it are obviously related. Reducing the numbers would reduce the cost. However, nearly 70 per cent of expenditure on social protection benefits is on the elderly (45 per cent) and the sick and disabled (24 per cent in total) (see Figure 13.15). Their numbers are very inelastic although in changing eligibility for incapacity benefit the Conservative government made financial savings.

Reducing expenditure

It is in the area of means-tested benefits that there is most margin for cost cutting. However, given that people in receipt of means-tested benefits are generally in the greatest need, such cuts are inevitably controversial.

In 1995, the government revealed that almost one in three households was in receipt of means-tested benefits (see Figure 13.16).

Numbers of recipients of means-tested benefits*, millions

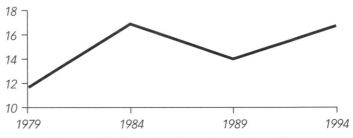

* *Some claimants will be in receipt of more than one benefit.*

(Source: *The Independent*, 9.8.1996:1)

Figure 13.16 The growth of dependency

Leaving aside for later consideration the issue of reducing benefits to save money, there are two issues which are often discussed in the context of reducing social security expenditure: the poverty trap and social security fraud.

The poverty trap occurs when an individual could work but it is not worth doing so because s/he gets more or less as much as the offered wage on social security. This can easily happen given the large low wage sector of the British economy. Ironically, government policy recently worsened this situation in relation to lone parents in paid work. When the government abolished one parent benefit to new claimants in 1995, it reduced the prospective income of certain low paid lone parents in work but not those on income support – the latter simply had their income increased to a minimum level. Figure 13.17 shows how this works:

Effects of scrapping one parent benefit on family with one child

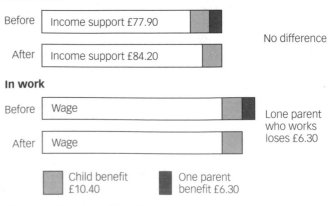

Figure 13.17 Worse off working

Social security fraud is universally condemned by the political parties. To what extent fraud is an important issue in comparison to other welfare issues is a matter of debate and depends largely on how much fraud there is. In 1995 Peter Lilley announced that his department's investigations had saved £717.6 million in 1994. This figure was arrived at by multiplying the fraudulent claim by 32 on the assumption that the claim would have gone on for an average of 32 weeks (*The Guardian*, 11.7.1995:5)

There are many other criticisms made of the welfare system but the issues of cost and numbers are the only one on which there is widespread agreement. Even so, there is no consensus on what might be done to decrease cost and numbers. Other criticisms of the Welfare State variously put forward include the way resources and services are administered and delivered, the extent of means-testing and the lack of co-ordination between economic and social welfare policy. We now consider the perspectives and policies on welfare of the main political parties.

The political parties and welfare policy

The above summary of three key documents on welfare provide one basis – and only one – for comparing the approaches to welfare of the three main parties. It is not at all certain that the party leaderships fully accept or, if returned to office, would implement these policies.

Differences between the parties on social policy

1 Universal versus selective benefits (again!)

Despite the claimed crisis of the Welfare State and the search of the three parties for fresh and effective solutions, the main difference that emerges between them is a very established one: Labour and the Liberals prefer universal benefits and the Conservatives means-tested or, at least, targeted benefits. This is apparent on the questions of pension reform and the minimum wage which the former support and the latter opposes. The Labour party is committed to dealing with the problem of the long-term decline in the value of the state old age pension. This decline has resulted in a major economic divide between those who have private pensions and/or other substantial resources and those who depend primarily on the state pension. The latter usually need other means-tested benefits as the state pension alone is now insufficient to live on.

Welfare is one of the hottest political potatoes. With the social security budget running at over £85 billion, all the major parties agree that radical reform is needed. But is there any policy? And where are the political divides?

LABOUR

Borrie Commission
set up by John Smith (1994)

- Basic state pension superseded by income-related universal Minimum Pension Guarantee

- National minimum wage of £3.50 an hour

- A Learning Bank with compulsory employer contributions

- National voluntary community service for young people

- Part-time unemployment benefit to encourage people into the labour market

- A national Housing Bank to support social housing projects

- Universal nursery education

LIBERAL DEMOCRAT

Dahrendorf Report
commissioned by Paddy Ashdown (1995)

- Compulsory earning-related second tier pensions plus increase in value of basic state pension

- Minimum wage, but level unspecified after internal disagreement

- Compulsory employee and employer contributions to Individual Learning Accounts

- Reform of the financial system to discourage short-termism

- Tax incentives to encourage people to invest in small companies, plus local network of investment agencies to channel funds specifically to smaller enterprises

CONSERVATIVE

Winning the Welfare Debate
by Peter Lilley, Secretary of State for Social Security (1995)

- People encouraged to provide for retirement through tax system while value of state pension diminishes

- Greater incentives for lone parents to work through tax breaks for childcare

- More local variation in provision of welfare e.g. housing and community care

- Minimal employer obligations – no minimum wage – to increase demand for labour

- Improvements in education and training in the state system, through provision National Curriculum and technology colleges

(Source: *The Guardian*, 26.7.1995.6 – slightly adapted)

Figure 13.18 Options for welfare

Both Labour and the Liberals want to add a compulsory universal and earnings-related element to the state pension. Where necessary, individuals will be assisted with contributions. Labour's response to the constant Conservative questions – 'how much will this cost?' – will be discussed shortly. In contrast, the Conservatives have offered tax cuts to those who contribute to a personal pension. For higher earners these can amount to 40 per cent. Of course, many cannot afford a private pension, and in the absence of other savings, become dependent on means-tested benefits.

Labour and the Liberals' commitment to a minimum wage and the Conservatives' opposition to it is also a substantial difference along the universalist/selectivist divide. The difference also reflects the former's commitment to the European Social Chapter and the latter's commitment to the free or deregulated labour market. The inevitable logic of the free market appears to be that those who can only command low or no wages in the free market must apply for benefits. In contrast, a minimum wage seems to imply some increased payment on the part of employers who would otherwise pay below it.

Labour and the Liberals, therefore, seek in these key matters to achieve a universal minimum standard for which either the taxpayer or industry must pay (although the second tier pension will have a sizeable individual contributory element).

Peter Lilley on means-testing

The Conservatives, in principle, do not want to raise taxes further or 'penalise' industry through introducing a minimum wage. In practice, this has meant a means-tested approach, making cuts where they could be 'justified', and pushing back responsibility to the individual. The Child Support Agency and the fostering of private health are examples of the latter. Peter Lilley expresses most of these Conservative attitudes in the following remarks:

> 'The Government does not accept that means-tested benefits are destructive'. In common with all statutory benefits 'they have disincentive effects,' he conceded, which was why his reforms 'focused not on extending means-testing, but on changing the conditions of entitlement to benefit' (examples here might be changing the basis of entitlement to disability benefit or, again, the CSA).
>
> Means-tests, however, were a long-standing feature of social security, and in the short run there were only two alternatives. 'One is to remove means-tested benefits', which 'would destroy the state safety net'. The other would be to give benefits that are currently means-tested to everyone. 'This would be immensely costly and not a good use of taxpayer's money.'
>
> The real issue was 'not means-tested benefits versus contributory benefits' but 'how to reduce benefit dependency'. The Government was encouraging self-reliance, with a revised family credit helping people support themselves in work and with employers being offered National Insurance rebates for taking on the long-term unemployed, he said.
>
> (The Independent, 9.8.1995:1)

Joan Brown, in a critical review of social policy under the Conservatives points out that not only have costs been cut but rights have been cut too. She suggests that there is evidence that public grievance turned against this approach in the 1990s. If she is correct, then Lilley may have been out of tune with public opinion (Reading 2).

Frank Field on means-testing – and an alternative

Labour MP, Frank Field's clear abhorrence of the means-tested approach to welfare is apparent in the following extract from his article New Welfare State. Here he turns the tables on right-wing critics of 'the dependency culture' by suggesting that it is the burgeoning of means-testing that has fostered dependency:

> But means-tests are the enemy within the welfare state. They actively support and reward aspects of human behaviour which are deeply dangerous to the health of the nation. Means-tests:
>
> • penalise effort: as income rises, means-tested help is withdrawn;
>
> • discourage savings: those who save know that they will be making themselves ineligible for help;
>
> • tax honesty: those who tell the truth about their income and savings risk being disqualified for benefit.
>
> By operating the means-test strategy, the Government acts as the recruiting sergeant to the dependency culture. It is this very dependency culture which it then turns around to attack. It now pays people to work the system rather than work to get off benefit.
>
> (The Guardian, 7.11.1995:17)

Field's own alternative, moves again in the direction of universalism. He proposes a revamped and extended system of National Insurance. This would deal more adequately with unemployment and care needs, it would be administered by a National Insurance Corporation run by employers and employees. Interestingly, Field links his ideas to the new 'flexible labour market'.

> The new unemployment insurance must be tailor-made to fit the emerging flexible labour market. It must aim to encourage people to take risks in getting back to work and reward risk-taking by ensuring an easier re-entry into unemployment-insurance cover. This reform would then counter Britain's emerging two-wage, no-wage economy. It would thereby do more than any other measure in a Labour Chancellor's power to equalise household incomes.
>
> The second insurance reform is to introduce a new care pension. At the moment help is given in residential and nursing care providing the person has almost no capital, or has used up his or her capital in meeting fees. It therefore actively operates against people acquiring second pensions,

> *saving during their working lives and acquiring their own home. A new care pension would be paid on the basis of medical need, not of income. It would therefore reinforce those values which are crucial to a free society.*
>
> *(The Guardian, 7.11.1995:17)*

A little coyly, perhaps, Field acknowledges that like his pension scheme, this programme, too, will cost more.

2   The economy and social policy

Although Labour has retreated from the policy that government should control the commanding heights of the economy – largely to achieve social objectives – the party remains more committed to linking economic and social policy than are the Conservatives. Indeed in recent years the latter have consistently stressed that, as far as possible, government should leave the private sector alone to get on with the job of wealth creation. On this matter, the Liberal Democrats are again closer to Labour.

The clearest example in the Barrie and Dahrendorf Commission of linking economic and social policy is the minimum wage. This policy strongly reasserts the principle that independence and self-sufficiency comes first through work and wage, and only secondly through social welfare. Two relatively small-scale Labour policy suggestions also make the economy/social policy link. Bringing part-time workers into the National Insurance system harmonises well with the steady increase in part-time work and would reduce benefit demand. A proposal to provide a programme of work or training for single parents has also been discussed both by Frank Field and by Chris Smith, the shadow Social Security Secretary.

Other than referring to the need for linking economic regeneration with social policy and with the exception of the minimum wage, Labour offers no 'big idea' in this area. Arguably, the Liberal Democrats do. Reforming the financial system to discourage 'short-termism' means, among other things, requiring industry to pay less in dividends to shareholders and to invest more year by year in the development of British industry. Financial reform would also direct the banks to finance and support business on a longer-term basis. What all parties agree on is that social welfare cannot be generously funded in the absence of a strong economy.

Similarities between the parties on social policy

Commitment to free market capitalism

In the past, Labour has been widely perceived as less friendly to business and as having less understanding of the free market than the Conservatives. Neil Kinnock and, especially, Tony Blair have gone to great lengths to reassure business and the City that, in government, Labour's policies will not be highly interventionist,

still less, anti-business. It is largely in this area that New Labour is seen by some as 'not much different from the Tories'.

Reluctance to raise taxes

Both of the major parties now present themselves as highly reluctant to raise taxes. For Labour this is partly an aspect of its business-friendly approach. Labour also judges that the tax payer (who is also the voter) is disinclined to pay any more in tax. However, the 'price to pay' for this is that Labour cannot plan social welfare reform on the basis of increased taxation. Plans to 'close tax loopholes' are unlikely to make a substantial difference.

The possible Labour reforms referred to above will be funded mainly by earnings related contributions. National Insurance, not taxes, will be the mechanism. This has been presented as enabling people to 'build a stake' in society but it is essentially an extension of an old idea. Similarly, Frank Field has suggested that a universal nursery system be funded through a tax on graduates (in return for state funded student loans) – thus, making the reform 'neutral' in tax terms.

In 1997, the Conservatives face the embarrassment that the British population is taxed as highly as when the last Labour government left office in 1979 (albeit more regressively). In the run-in to the 1997 election, its rhetoric was very much about reducing income tax. There seems to be a consensus between the two major parties that the maximum taxation burden has been reached.

This consensus is not unchallenged. The Liberal Democratic party has committed itself to increasing income tax by one penny in the pound to finance improvement in education and training. Will Hutton, the editor of the *Observer* has strongly questioned the basis of the assumption that Britain should not be taxed any more heavily. On the contrary, Britain's public services need greatly strengthening – and this will cost money (see below).

Welfare for self-improvement, individualism

Both Frank Field and Peter Lilley seem agreed that there is a problem of dependency in relation to the British welfare system. Field is inclined to blame the system itself, particularly means-testing and the poverty trap. His policy of earnings related benefits, including a second pension and unemployment pay, have a built-in incentive to work. A committed Christian, Field's writings are full of references to the need for welfare reform to encourage self-improvement. He goes so far as to describe 'the principle of self-improvement as the central objective of any reform' (*The Guardian*, 19.10.1994:3). On another occasion, he writes:

> *State welfare is dying. Long live the new forms of collective provision run by the punters themselves, which value honesty, work, savings and self-improvement.*
>
> *(The Guardian, 7.11.1995:17)*

This statement seeks to combine what are often thought of as the conflicting principles of individualism and participatory socialism.

Peter Lilley appears to blame certain individuals for becoming dependent on welfare. As Hartley and Taylor-Gooby suggest the ideal New Right alternative to dependency is for people to participate in some way in the enterprise culture. One of his policies has been to chisel off welfare some of the 'less deserving' poor. Lilley opposes Field's approach for both ideological reasons – abhorrence of collectivism – and for what he regards as practical reasons of cost.

Nevertheless, there is a common thread of individualism in both politicians' approaches which reflects the highly individualistic character of the time. Field's stress on self is softened by a larger collectivist vision, whereas Lilley's welfare state is cautious and residual.

Will Hutton: Britain can afford more welfare

Will Hutton established himself as perhaps the major independent thinker on the political left with the publication of *The State We're In* in 1995. In that book and elsewhere he has developed an overall argument for economic, political and social reform which, while it impinges on official Labour party thinking, it is generally to the left of it. In addition to his political credentials as a scourge of Conservatism, Hutton brings to the debate on welfare and poverty a passionate concern for the poor.

First, Hutton is a strong exponent of the view, adopted by the Liberal Democrats more than Labour, that British industry needs to invest more for growth and development rather than seeking shorter term profits for shareholders. In the long run this could provide the wealth to finance a more adequate welfare state. Hutton also supports the EU practice of involving employees in the running of firms and in profit sharing. He is (one of several people) credited with the 'stakeholder' idea adopted by Tony Blair.

Second, Hutton argues that by international standards, Britain's social spending as a percentage of national output is low (see Figure 13.19). Of the seven OECD's leading industrial countries, Britain is second from the bottom in percentage terms, with only Japan below. The European average percentage of 18.7 is almost five percentage points more than Britain's expenditure.

Hutton further argues that for a variety of reasons Britain is likely to be in a relatively favourable financial position over the forthcoming years. One reason for this is demographic. As a result partly of Britain's population structure pensions payments are likely to be fairly consistently covered by contributions. This is far from the case in relation to Germany, France and, to a lesser extent, the United States.

In Hutton's view there is no good reason why in the course of a generation, Britain has slipped from being a model welfare society to running with the exception of Iceland, 'the meanest, tightest, lowest-cost social security system in the world' (*The Guardian*, 16.10.1995:15). He illustrates his view extensively. Here his comments on Conservative housing policy will suffice (see also

Percentage GDP, 1994

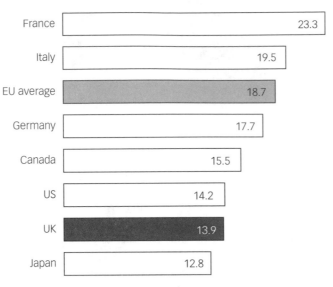

(Source: OECD in *The Guardian*, 16.10.1995:15)

Figure 13.19 Social Security spending

Homeless per thousand people, 1991/92

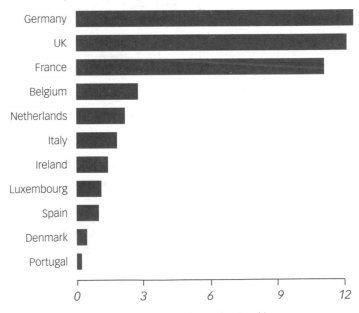

(Source: M Daly, *Abandoned: Profile of Europe's Homeless People*)

Figure 13.20 Homelessness

Figure 13.20). This he considers compares unfavourably with post-Beveridge achievements. His remarks demonstrate his opposition to the rigorous application of market principles especially to those in real need who cannot fully compete:

> *Under Treasury pressure the Department of Environment has raised rents on the public sector's housing stock to 'market levels', while the continual withdrawal of grants from housing associations has compelled them to follow suit. Rarely can an act of policy have been so self-defeating, for as rents have risen, so has state support for low income rent payers. Three-quarters of local authority tenants live on less than average earnings, and housing association tenants are even poorer. The Joseph Rowntree Foundation estimates that as a result, the DSS finds itself paying at least two-thirds of any rent increase as housing benefit. More than half the 'out of control' social security budget – on pensions, unemployment and housing benefit – is easily explained.*
>
> *Here reality starts to crowd in. For what is driving the rest of social security spending as in the case of housing benefit, is real need.*
>
> (The Guardian, 18.9.1996:(2)2)

Question

What are the strengths and weaknesses of the universalist and selectivist approaches to welfare? Illustrate your answer with reference to the policies of the main political parties.

Marxist perspectives on social policy

Welfare and fiscal crisis

Marxists have always faced a dilemma in relation to the liberal Welfare State. On the one hand, elements of the Welfare State benefit the working class and have been won partly by the efforts of the trade union movement, the Labour party and other predominantly working class organisations. On the other, Marxists commonly view the Welfare State as a means developed by the ruling class of reducing working class militancy and demand for socialism. This conflict has produced some ambivalence in Marxist perspectives on the Welfare State.

One of the most influential recent Marxist works is James O'Connor's *The Fiscal Crisis of the State* (1973). The crisis to which he refers lies in a contradiction between what he describes as the two main functions of the state: accumulation (of wealth through capitalist enterprise) and legitimisation (partly through the pacificatory effects of the welfare state referred to above). The crisis is that the cost of legitimisation is becoming more than private enterprise is willing to support – hence the budget deficit.

O'Connor further argues that the 'regulation' of capitalism including the control of labour is shifting to business and the market and away from the state and welfare. In concentrating on the different 'modes' of regulating capitalism, O'Connor is an exponent of 'regulation theory'. In commenting on O'Connor's work, Ramesh Mishra concedes that he focuses on a potentially contradictory tendency in liberal capitalism. However, Mishra argues that it is only a tendency and that, in general, the Welfare State supports rather than weakens capitalism. Whatever the general merits of Mishra's observation, there is no doubt of the current relevance of O'Connor's analysis when most social democracies do appear to be struggling with the contradiction he indicates.

Reforming and reactionary policy

Whereas O'Connor concentrates on the fiscal crisis of capitalism, Ian Gough and other Marxists analyse in addition the broader aspects of the economic crisis of the 1970s and particularly its consequences for the working class. These writings agree that capital would try to make labour pay the price of this crisis in lower wages and reduced welfare. Nevertheless, Ian Gough in *The Political Economy of the Welfare State* (1979) argues that working class organisations should continue to press for reform. The state of the political left in the 1980s and 1990s was one of much greater disarray than Gough anticipated but his contention that socialists must distinguish between reforms that promote 'welfare capitalism' and those that promote 'welfare socialism' continues to be of use.

Ramesh Mishra's response is that, in practice, such a distinction is not possible: the aim of many social reforms is both to improve conditions (socialist-inclined) and to adjust beneficiaries to 'the system' (capitalist-inclined). My own view favours Gough because any political movement must struggle to bend change in its own preferred direction. In fact, several Thatcherite and post-Thatcherite initiatives require carefully discriminating responses: examples are community versus institutional care, and the various attempts to empower the consumer and render the professional accountable in education, health and the social services (see p. 277). More broadly, Gough sees potential for such groups as the Claimants' Union and Women's Aid, supported by the trade union movement, to defend and ultimately extend the more socialist aspects of the Welfare State.

There was never a 'Golden Age' of welfare

Whatever the room for manoeuvre of the kind Gough indicates, Marxists consider that no major party has yet attempted to introduce a genuinely socialist Welfare State in Britain. Similarly, they point out that the Labour government preceding the first Thatcher administration had already begun to make cuts in welfare – largely to defend the capitalist economy. Accordingly, in *Public Opinion, Ideology and State Welfare* (1985), Peter Taylor-Gooby, argues that 'the view that the Welfare State is currently the victim of a sudden attack by the New Right is somewhat misleading'. In support of Taylor-Gooby, it is arguable that even before 1979, the British Welfare State was barely better than minimal, certainly when compared to those of the Scandinavian countries. In practice, Thatcher found it difficult to cut 'fat' without flesh and has made most of her savings through privatising nationalised industries rather than reducing welfare expenditure. Even so, whatever the long-term estimates of the Thatcherite cuts, it is worth recalling Harold Wilson's comment on unemployment, and applying it to social welfare reductions: 'If it happens to you, it's a hundred per cent'. Taylor-Gooby goes on to state:

> *The vision of the history of the Welfare State as a decline from the golden age tends to mask the conflicts and continuities that have always existed in policy. The contemporary problems of the Welfare State arise from the failures of policy to meet the demands of changing circumstances – from inertia rather than the radical development of policy.*
>
> (Taylor-Gooby, 1985)

Socialism and welfare

The 'radical development of policy' Taylor-Gooby considers necessary is socialist. However, publishing in 1985, he was well aware that few, even of the working class, are Marxist (indeed, in recent general elections the majority of them did not even vote Labour!). Norman Ginsburg in *Class, Capital and Social Policy* (1983) examines the wider problem of why the consciousness of the working class is not more socialist. He considers that it is seduced by capitalist commodities into obsessive consumption (commodity fetishism) – a behaviour which is strongly expressed and regenerated within the family. Partly as a result, class solidarity is fragmented. Patriarchy is also obscured by commodity fetishism and by the individualisation of the collective family concerns into 'accepted' roles. The Welfare State is widely presented and perceived as another mechanism for distributing commodities rather than as a potential instrument of socialism. Interestingly, the social democrat, Ramesh Mishra, argues that Marxists uselessly lament the consumer tendencies, or applying O'Connor's term to workers as well as capitalists, accumulative tendencies of the working class. Its members merely share these desires with other classes and Marxism must provide for them if it is to have political appeal. Whilst Mishra's point may be valid, it is worth commenting that socialism is not merely concerned with material consumption, but with the quality of human relations and culture. Thus, in theory, consumption as well as production would be organised and experienced differently under socialism than capitalism.

While Gough cautiously draws attention to the socialist potential of the Welfare State, Taylor-Gooby and Ginsburg tend to stress its limits and, indeed, its services to capitalism. One conclusion from this is that any Marxist or socialist party needs to be quite clear on what it can realistically expect to achieve through the Welfare State, given a situation of influence or power. Clarity of vision would be especially necessary in a situation of transition towards socialism.

Feminist perspectives on social policy (with particular reference to family)

The Marxist/socialist 'wing' of the contemporary feminist movement appears to have reached a generally clear analysis of female oppression within capitalism and a clear programme of change. The purposes of this section is critically to present the latter, but it will help first to recall how they conceptualise women's oppression. Mary McIntosh's article *The State and the Oppression of Women* (1978) argues that in capitalist society the family household has two basic functions – 'it serves (though inadequately) for the reproduction of the working class and for the maintenance of women as a reserve army of labour, low paid when they are in jobs and often unemployed'. The point is that women's labour is made cheap in capitalist society: domestic labour is unpaid except by grace of the husband and their paid work is more poorly rewarded and more easily expended with than men's.

Structural oppression

McIntosh argues that within capitalism the family household has been 'importantly structured and constrained by state policies' to ensure that it achieves its functions. The form of marriage encouraged by the state has involved a 'dependent-breadwinner' structure. This family structure provides unpaid maintenance of male labour (the reproduction of labour) and systematises biological reproduction. Family policy in particular, and welfare policy in general, reinforce this situation though less so than when McIntosh wrote (see pp. 394 and 403). Women who do not fit into the system may suffer as a result. Women living with their husbands or lovers, and school leavers cannot claim certain benefit and can only claim unemployment benefit if they have paid full contributions. McIntosh suggests that policy towards one parent families has provided the means to survive, whilst seeking to avoid encouraging the practice. McIntosh is aware of the 'Marxist functionalist' nature of the argument but strongly differentiates it from classical functionalist perspective by insisting on the 'contradictions' between the family and state within capitalist society and within the family itself. A central contradiction is that the role of women as cheap reproducers of (male) labour and as a reserve army of labour themselves can conflict – thus forcing substantial direct state intervention in the supposedly 'private sphere' of the family, as notably occurred, for instance, during the Second World War (see also Chapter 3, Reading 1, p. 82).

C C Harris sharply criticises the kind of Marxist functionalist arguments used by McIntosh on the grounds that they may explain how but not why institutions function in a given way. Thus, no historical explanation is offered as to why women rather than men perform domestic labour (though see p. 55). Harris also seems to regard the focus on oppression as emotive and unscientific. However, it is hardly surprising that women should focus on this matter and suggest policies to relieve it.

A socialist reform package: Anna Coote

Anna Coote's article *Labour: The Feminist Touch* assumes that women have been domestically oppressed and that the main strategy for dealing with this is for them increasingly to penetrate the labour market and to achieve equality within it as a basis for full equality. Publishing in 1985, seven years after McIntosh, she argues that the number of women in paid work (60 per cent) 'suggest that we are no longer a 'reserve army of labour' we are regulars'. What remains to be done, however, is for women to gain equality at work whilst the needs of children and people (men or women) doing domestic work are met. The programme she offers is bold but perhaps no bolder than is necessary to achieve the end she seeks:

> The strategy focuses on the spheres of reproduction and production, but starts with the former, on the grounds that this is the primary sphere, from which production springs.
>
> The strategy would give priority to breaking down the traditional division of paid and unpaid labour, so that responsibility for children would be shared equally among men and women, and between home-based parental care and community-based collective care. It would mean a much shorter working week for men and women, vastly improved child-care provision outside the home, and a restructuring of family income, by increasing female earning power and child benefit, and improving the 'social wage'.
>
> (Coote, 1985:14)

The shorter working week Coote refers to is to provide more jobs for women and more time for men to do domestic work (including caring for their children). She also suggests extended parental leave, on an equal basis for men and women. To protect low paid workers, a disproportionate number of whom are women, she emphasises the need for a statutory minimum wage.

How does the socialist feminism of McIntosh and Coote relate to other strands in the feminist movement. Neither appear to want to be at odds with the libertarian wing of the movement as represented by, for instance, the Americans, Leghorn and Parker (see pp. 592-4). However, they clearly consider that the localised, network-based activities of feminists must be complemented and supported by central government action. Neither McIntosh nor Coote seek to improve the situation of women by attacking only patriarchy. Coote's programme blends an attack on patriarchy with an attack on certain aspects of capitalism. While recognising that men are unlikely voluntarily to relinquish power, she nevertheless attempts to make a feminist-sensitive programme of social reform appealing to them (e.g. in its job creation and leisure aspects). Nothing as specific or coherent as this has emerged from those feminists who regard patriarchy as the sole source of female oppression (referred to as radical feminists). Indeed, arguably the equality package of the mid 1970s has largely established the framework that they want for fair and open competition between the sexes (see pp. 205-6). McIntosh and Coote seek a framework of equality and co-operation founded on mutual independence between the sexes, rather than competition.

To summarise, the socialist feminist programme seeks to restructure the family household both in terms of functions and roles. Families will continue to reproduce children but the rearing of them will be shared more equally between the sexes and much better public childcare facilities will be established. All modern movements to release women from domestic bondage – from the kibbutz to Soviet socialism – have attempted to find means other than the mother to rear children. Britain has not seriously done so. Even progressive local authorities such as Camden in London have only a small number of publicly provided nursery places relative to need. For instance, the children of many single-parent families are not provided with places – virtually making it impossible for their mothers to work. Coote argues that better nursery and pre-school facilities and more male involvement in child-rearing would better enable women to achieve the equality that decently paid work brings. Thus, the era in which women are 'second bested' at home and in paid work could begin to draw to a close.

The Welfare State and equality

The universal services

To what extent has the Welfare State brought about greater equality in Britain? Again, this point is discussed in relation to education and health elsewhere (see Chapters 4 and 14). In brief, in respect to education, formal equality of opportunity does not compensate for class, gender or ethnic disadvantage and the result is that cumulative inequality of outcome occurs from primary to higher education. As far as the NHS is concerned, a relatively high degree of equality of class access has not resulted in the outcome of equal health across the classes (see pp. 424-9). This is largely because members of the middle class use the NHS more effectively and adopt healthier lifestyles – partly because they can afford to.

The contribution of the rest of welfare to social equality is a complex matter. Most commentators agree that the relatively small component of the Welfare State involving cash transfers – such as rent rebates and one parent family allowances are broadly redistributive. The charge that the Welfare State is inegalitarian is generally aimed at the universal services, i.e. those subsidies and services available to all. These include public transport, public libraries, tax relief to owner-occupiers (as well as most of the NHS and educational systems). Summarising his own work on the matter, Julian Le Grand states that 'the better off almost invariably used such services to a greater extent than the poor, and … such services have failed to achieve equality, however defined'. In the 1990s, this has probably become less true of the NHS as increasing numbers of the middle class have taken out private health insurance.

Housing

Arguably, the attack on housing squalor and inadequacy has been one of the more successful aspects of Welfare State policy since the war. Since the mid 1980s major problems have again developed. However, as Donnison and Ungerson point out, compared to the 1940s and 1950s there is now greater equality of housing access by most basic standards of measurement. Thus, there are more houses per number of households, more rooms per person, and a higher proportion of baths and toilets per person than in 1945. The basic housing of the majority has greatly improved. Ironically, however, for a significant minority of people one of the great areas of welfare progress – better housing – is now under threat. First, the relative position of those in rented council and private property in relation to owner-occupiers has worsened since the early 1980s. The Conservatives' taxation and 'economic' rent policies have reduced housing benefit whilst significant, if now reduced, tax concessions for mortgage holders remain in place. Alan Murie argues that a highly polarised and segregated housing market is the most likely consequence of continuing failure to develop housing policies other than to encourage owner-occupation. Second, the policy of selling council houses has reduced both the number and quality of public housing stock. Third, and related to the last point, the number of homeless families and families on council waiting lists has been increasing. This may be another indication of the development of a growing 'underclass' or, in Marxist terms, lower working class, substantially worse off than the rest of the working class. However, in qualification of the above, some owner occupiers also experienced major housing problems in the early 1990s – victims of a house price boom and slump.

Employment

If the attack on squalor (housing problems) is now a tarnished success story of the British Welfare State, the ideal of full employment has become its Cinderella. The widespread belief that the levels of unemployment seen in the 1930s would never be approached again has proved an illusion. In 1985 the number of unemployed (as conservatively measured by the government) exceeded the peak of the 1930s although the percentage figure (thirteen per cent) was still lower. International economic factors certainly played a part in this, and throughout Europe governments of a variety of political complexions struggled to stem the rising tide of unemployment. However, in Britain what was new in 1979 was a government which disclaimed primary responsibility for reducing unemployment, and which by its monetarist policies, was widely considered to have exacerbated it. In any case, the British unemployment rate became the second highest in Europe. In 1991 unemployment again rose towards three million apparently confirming that such high figures may be part of a new economic 'reality'. By 1997, unemployment had dropped below two million but there were questions to be asked. Would unemployment be stabilised at a lower figure or rise again? What is the quality and level of pay of the new jobs. Is the lower unemployment figure partly the result of the increase in redundancies and retirements of the first half of the 1990s?

Who pays? Class and taxation

In assessing how egalitarian is the Welfare State, we need to consider who pays for it as well as who benefits. This involves a brief review of the British taxation system and particularly the extent to which it is progressive, i.e. taxes the rich more, or regressive, i.e. taxes the poor relatively more. Two recent developments have made the British tax system more regressive. First, the proportion of income on which tax is paid has been increasing for most of the post-war period. In other words, the tax threshold – the point at which people start paying income tax – has got much lower and non-taxable earnings allowances much less (in percentage terms). As a result, quite low paid employees are taxed on more of their income than previously. This tendency was only partially reversed by Kenneth Clarke in the mid 1990s. Second, the introduction of Value Added Tax, and particularly the raising of this to 17.5 per cent in 1991, has proved regressive. A higher percentage of the incomes of the poor than the rich goes in VAT, though, of course, in absolute terms a rich person pays more than a poor person. In addition, there are a great variety of ways in which the better off, and the corporations from which they derive much of their wealth, can avoid taxation. Overall, Westergaard and Resler conclude that, apart from the lowest paid who are taxed relatively less, the British taxation system is barely progressive. So whilst the burden of paying for the Welfare State is relatively evenly shared across the classes, the middle class is, in many respects, the prime beneficiary. Further, government figures show that between 1981-87 the average income (after housing costs) rose by almost twenty per cent whereas that of the bottom tenth of the pay scale rose only two per cent. To put it mildly, this does not amount to a situation remotely suggesting social equality.

Gender, equality and welfare

The question of whether the Welfare State has increased equality can be applied to gender, particularly to whether it has improved the situation of women. Beveridge's support for family allowances which were adopted during the war had been widely campaigned for by feminists in the inter-war years. However, reflecting the general view of his time, Beveridge did not question the sexual division of labour and by channelling family and other welfare benefits mainly through the male, probably strengthened patriarchy (see p. 394). With Beveridge's traditional family ideals partly in mind, feminist Elizabeth Wilson suggests that his plan 'now reads as deeply conservative'. Many contemporary feminists seek a system – supported by the state – which will secure the individual welfare of women and children, i.e. income and benefits without dependency on males. The right of divorced partners to a fair pooling of the pension rights that each may (or may not) have built up was passed into law in 1996. This was a significant move towards financial equality and therefore social equality.

Conclusion

The above review clearly indicates that the Welfare State has not achieved full equality of access (availability) or equality of outcome (use) in relation to key services, though the situation varies greatly between them. Neither is the financing of the Welfare State very egalitarian. Since 1979, Britain has become a more unequal not a more equal society. In fairness, many Conservatives do not consider that this matters greatly – as long as people are not in real poverty. Few, if any politicians, want complete material equality. New Labour has emphasised equality of opportunity and a more effective Welfare State.

Questions

1 Critically discuss one of the following perspectives on welfare:
   • Social Democratic
   • Conservative/New Right
   • Marxist
   • Feminist
2 To what extent do you consider that the development of the British Welfare State has helped or hindered the liberation of women? (See also Chapter 3, Reading 1, p. 82)

Summary

1 The distribution of income and wealth is discussed. The increase in income inequality in the Thatcher period is explained.
2 Wealth is discussed largely in terms of the significant advance of 'new' in relation to 'old' wealth.
3 A distinction must be made between social inequality and poverty. Social inequality means that certain individuals or groups have more material or cultural resources than others. Poverty means that an individual or group has insufficient of some material (or cultural) necessities.
4 Absolute poverty is insufficiency in the basic necessities of existence e.g. in food or shelter. Relative poverty is existence below a minimum standard of living on socially established criteria.
5 There is considerable debate about how best to measure poverty. In particular, Peter Townsend argues that government rates for income support are about 50 per cent below what is required to achieve a decent standard of life.
6 There are four main theories of the causes of poverty:
   i   Individual inadequacy: conservative perspective I.
   ii The culture of poverty thesis: conservative perspective II.
   iii Radical structural and marxist perceptive.
   iv Poverty as situational: liberal reformist perspective.

7 Poverty is sometimes seen as caused by individual pathology or weakness of either a physical, mental or moral kind.
8 Poverty is sometimes seen, usually by more conservative thinkers, as generated and regenerated by the cultural attitudes and lifestyle of the poor.
9 Radical structural and Marxist perspectives agree that, whatever its benefits, capitalism also produces fundamental social problems. The pursuit of profit and the exploitation of labour results in severe inequality and poverty.
10 The 'underclass' is presented primarily in the context of poverty rather than stratification. Radical, conservative and liberal perspectives are discussed.
11 Social policy is introduced in relation to political ideology. The key axis of universalism/selection is discussed.
12 Welfare policy and ideology from Beveridge to Major is analysed. The extent of agreement and disagreement between the major parties is explored.
13 Marxist and feminist perspectives are presented as critiques of, and alternatives to more mainstream welfare policies/ideologies.

Research and coursework

The areas covered in this chapter are vast and the scope of any project would have to be carefully defined and limited. There is a strong case for doing a project based on secondary rather than primary research. One possibility would be to carry out a critical review of one of the major poverty surveys – such as one of the Breadline Britain surveys. It would be appropriate to give attention to methodology as well as findings. Another research area might be a socio-historical study of some aspect of welfare ideology or policy. This could be quite wide, such as changing government and public attitudes to the poor in the post-war period or quite specific such as family or pensions policy.

A practically feasible piece of primary research would be to study the effects of different degrees of wealth on, say, six people – two at each selected level (high, medium, and low income). The foci of study would have to be specified, e.g. political behaviour, lifestyle and probably a preliminary hypothesis formulated. As always, methodology would have to be thought through and appropriate.

Further reading

John Scott, *Poverty and Wealth: Citizenship, deprivation and privilege* (Longman, 1994) covers most aspects raised in this chapter. The references to the two extracted readings – from Paul Wilding and Joan Brown are worth chasing up and are accessible to students.

Readings

Reading 1
The Mixed Economy of Welfare: Welfare Privatisation: The Voluntary Sector

Paul Wilding, 'The British Welfare State: Thatcherism's Enduring Legacy' in *Policy and Politics*, Vol. 20, No.3, 1992, pp. 205-7 (slightly adapted)

Welfare is, and has always been, a mixed economy of formal and informal, public and private, voluntary and family provision.

What Thatcherism did was to take this fact, give it a particular ideological twist, and promote this interpretation as aspiration and policy. Welfare pluralism as ideology can mean very different things. For some, it expresses the aspiration to develop non-statutory services which complement public provision because there are certain things which the non-statutory sector can do better than the statutory. For other people, it means supplementing public services because they always fall short of what is required. For others, welfare pluralism is the idea, and the fact, which makes it both possible and legitimate to work towards the replacement of state welfare as the dominant mode of provision. Thatcherism used welfare pluralism in this latter way as a stick with which to beat state provision, and as the reality which gave legitimacy to such an assault.

Webb and Wistow describe one of the important developments of the decade beginning in the mid-1970s as being 'the collapse of the pure doctrine of state welfare'. It is a good example of how to reveal truth by exaggeration – there never was a pure doctrine of state welfare but it did collapse in the 1970s and 1980s.

Thatcherism abhorred public monopoly. Hence it sought to encourage alternative sources of welfare. It promoted the private sector through public subsidies, tax breaks, the opening up of services to private contractors, the vigorous encouragement of commercial sponsorship and by incorporating it in public policy – for example, Norman Fowler's twin pillars' approach in the reform of social security in the mid-1980s which sought a new partnership between the state and private sectors.

The voluntary sector was similarly favoured. A considerable expansion of direct financial support from central and local government followed.

The government's aim was both to assert and promote the significance of private and voluntary welfare provision, even if that meant substantial injections of public money at a time of tight restraint on expenditure on traditional services.

The Thatcher governments also discovered and eulogised the informal sector and particularly the carer – those individuals, largely women, who devoted themselves to caring for frail and dependent elderly people. They were the pillars of family care – though the government preferred to describe it as 'community care'. Their labours saved the long-suffering taxpayers many billions of pounds. They were living embodiments of the great virtues and value (particularly to others!) of individual and family responsibility. They illustrated – when the respective contributions were compared – how relatively trivial was the contribution of state-provided services to human well-being. It was easy to shift the emphasis from 'relatively trivial' to 'essentially unimportant'.

That welfare is a mixed economy is a statement of simple reality. Recognition of that reality should clearly inform policy. In the 1980s it did much more than that. It was used to justify and legitimate a reduced role for public provision and an expanded role for the non-statutory sector – private, voluntary and family. Private and voluntary welfare have become more firmly embedded in government policies. They are central to the development, for example, of the enabling local authority. Emphasis on the actual, and socially desirable, key role of the family helps to give legitimacy to the reduction of public services.

Thatcherism took up and used the fact of the mixed economy for ideological and political purposes. The private sector has grown and it has become more important in overall policy. Similarly, the voluntary sector has expanded – sometimes in a gadarene-like rush. Some elements have become dangerously dependent on government funds – and have suffered and perished as government priorities changed. It has become more important to government – and the converse is equally true.

Private and voluntary welfare have both become key elements in government policy. There are three reasons why this new stress on the mixed economy of welfare is likely to be lasting – welfare is a mixed economy, public opinion is supportive of a mixed economy, and the intricacy and complexity of the relationship which has been created and the practical difficulties involved in unpicking it.

Questions

1 Why did the Thatcher governments favour the private and voluntary 'side' of the 'mixed economy of welfare'?
2 What are the advantages and disadvantages of the public and private approaches to welfare?

Reading 2
Conservative policy on social security and public opinion.

From Joan Brown, 'Poverty in Post-war Britain' in J Obelkevich and P Catterall eds., *Understanding Post-war British Society* (Routledge, 1994), pp. 124, 125, 126

During the 1980s the rights of poor people have been diminished. This loss of rights has not occurred through the large-scale repeal of social security and other programmes. Instead, there have been small and repeated changes, which cumulatively have added up to a steady loss of entitlements. To give some examples: rights under the Employment Protection Act, particularly for women, have been whittled away; and changes in the contributions rules for National Insurance have made it harder to qualify for benefit by right and reliance on means-tested benefits has increased accordingly. Rights that people believed they had acquired through contributions have gone, as a number of benefits have been abolished or converted to means-tested benefits. Benefit rights for 16 and 17 year-olds have been withdrawn. More generally, the policy emphasis has been shifted from benefits by right to a far greater stress on 'targeting' money on the poor, through means-tested benefits.

It is true that some other rights have been acquired. There are new rights for women in social security, though it has to be said that many of these have been forced upon a reluctant government through the operation of EC Directives and the European Court.

At the beginning of the 1980s, government attitudes seemed matched by public opinion – both hostile to the unemployed and dismissive of the poor. But at the beginning of the 1990s, there are signs that public attitudes have changed. There is serious public concern about the numbers of homeless people sleeping in our city streets. Policies that disadvantage the elderly arouse hostility. Any further damage to the NHS and what it is seen to stand for is unpopular. A new EC public opinion survey published in 1990 showed that only 21 per cent of those questioned thought that poverty was caused by laziness (Commission of the European Communities 1990), down from 43 per cent in 1977. It may be that there is now a sense that we have drifted too far from the goals of the 1940s.

I shall end with two quotations that illustrate the difference between the goal of governments in the 1940s and the 1980s//90s. The first is from John Moore in 1987, when he was the Secretary of State for Social Security, speaking of what he called a culture of dependency on the state:

'This kind of climate can in time corrupt the human spirit. Everyone knows the sullen apathy of dependence and can compare it with the sheer delight of personal achievement ... The indiscriminate handing out of benefits not only spreads limited resources too thinly, it can also undermine the will to self help and build up pools of resentment among taxpayers who are footing the bill.' (Moore 1987)

The second is from James Griffiths, Minister for National Insurance, introducing the 1946 National Insurance Bill. He said:

'To those who profess to fear that security will weaken the moral fibre and destroy self respect let me say this. It is not security that destroys, it is insecurity. It is the fear of tomorrow that paralyses the will, it is the frustration of human hopes that corrodes the soul. Security in adversity will, I believe, release our people from the haunting fears of yesterday and make tomorrow not a day to dread but a day to welcome.' (House of Commons, 1946:1758)

Questions

1 Give reasons why public opinion may have been more supportive of Conservative policy on social security in the early 1980s than in the 1990s?
2 To what extent do you consider government policy was the main cause of growing insecurity in the 1980s/90s?

The Sociology of Health and Health Policy

'Safe in our hands'? Does the Welfare State still provide universal and comprehensive security from 'the cradle to the grave'?

Aims of this chapter

1 To present and explain the social construction of health.

2 To describe and explain the relevance of class, gender and ethnicity to health.

3 Critically to examine various health policy approaches, including those of recent Conservative governments.

Themes and definitions

There are two main and recurrent themes in this chapter. The first is that there are different paradigms or frameworks for perceiving and organising health. Cultural anthropology is the discipline best suited to exploring these different frameworks. Accordingly, the chapter begins with a survey of cultural paradigms of health and illness: magical, religious (briefly), modern scientific, and holistic medicine. A particularly narrow form of scientific medicine - 'mechanistic' or positivistic – is subject to criticism from a more humanistic medical perspective (of which holistic medicine is an example). Mechanistic and humanistic approaches to medicine are also contrasted in the sections on mental health and illness and on gender and health. The sociology of knowledge examines the relationship between paradigms and social context and, along with the section on the sociology of educational knowledge (see pp. 98-100), the examination of health paradigms is a main example of the sociology of knowledge in this book.

The second major theme is the unequal distribution of health, and it explicitly or implicitly occupies most of the chapter. It includes and analysis of health inequalities in relation to gender and the poorer countries as well as social class. The chapter concludes with a review of sociological perspectives on health and relates these to social policy perspectives.

Webster's Dictionary gives a commonly accepted definition of health: it is 'the condition of being sound in body, mind or soul; esp: freedom from physical disease or pain' (1965). The constitution of the World Health Organisation presents health as more than freedom from disease but in addition as 'a state of complete physical, mental and social well-being': a quality of life as well as a material issue. Such generalities aside, understanding of health and illness, perhaps especially mental illness, varies significantly from culture to culture and even within cultures. The terms illness and disease will be used interchangeably here although a useful distinction is sometimes made between them.

L G Moore *et al.* (1980) present disease as 'a reflection of failure to adapt to the environment ... usually manifested by abnormalities in the structure and function of body, organs and systems'. Illness, however, relates to the 'experience' of such abnormal conditions and 'thus includes those social psychological aspects of disease that not only affect the ill person, but may also affect the person's family and friends'. How we experience disease is an important aspect of being ill. Figure 14.1 is intended to stimulate consideration of the relationships between illness and disease. Disease reads down and illness reads across.

Cultural paradigms of health: the social construction of health

A paradigm is 'the entire constellation of beliefs, values, techniques, and so on shared by members of a given community' (Kuhn, 1970). Without using the term, James Frazer, in effect, presented the evolution of human knowledge in terms of the paradigms of magic, religion and science (*The Golden Bough*, 1922). More recent research has shown Frazer's scheme to be over-simple, but he does usefully indicate the major cultural paradigms of explanation and belief.

Magical and religious paradigms of health and illness

Health and illness can usefully be understood within wider cultural paradigms or belief systems, particularly those of magic, religion and science. Magic involves the manipulation and control of the natural world by certain individuals such as witches, sorcerers and shamans. These powerful figures were considered able to cause or alleviate much misfortune, including illness. Two forms of magic are witchcraft and sorcery. Witchcraft is generally regarded as an in-born ability to generate misfortune, whereas sorcery requires conscious effort and often involves the ritual manipulation of items belonging to the object of the sorcery.

Edward Evans-Pritchard carried out an anthropological study of the African Azande, including their understanding of death and illness as a result of witchcraft and sorcery (1937). Whereas disease is generally regarded as a materialistic phenomenon in the West, for the Azande it is generated psychically and spiritually. The Azande believe that witchcraft is a substance in the bodies of witches, the 'soul' of which may leave the witch and take possession of the victim at any time but especially at night. The 'resulting'

		Disease	
		Yes	No
Illness	Yes	Influenza	Mental illness
	No	Undiagnosed cancer	Good 'health'

Figure 14.1 Dimensions of illness and disease

illness is seen as the product of witchcraft and often a witch hunt follows.

Accusation plays a key role in the response to witchcraft. From the perspective of the Azande and cultural groups with similar beliefs, accusation is part of the process of explanation and reparation. From a more detached sociological perspective, we can see that the practical affirmation of the belief system strengthens social solidarity. Accusation is the vehicle for this as it labels and stigmatises deviant behaviour. In Durkheim's terms, accusation helps to redraw normative boundaries. Conflict theorists point out, however, that certain groups may benefit more than others from ritual reaffirmation of the social status quo. Andre Singer and Brian V Street adopt this approach in Zande themes. They note that the beneficiaries of witchcraft are invariably the wealthy and powerful. Members of the princely class are not accused of witchcraft but by successfully accusing others they can acquire forfeits and thus extend their wealth and power.

Not all examples of witchcraft and sorcery lend themselves so easily to explanations of self-interest or social systems maintenance (solidarity). In any case, respect is due to magical belief systems simply because they may in certain ways be true and powerful. This is the impression left by Carlos Castaneda's long and continuing study of the magico-religious beliefs of the Yacqui Indians and of M J Harner's research on the Jivaro Indians of the Ecuadorian Amazon. Even the anthropological detachment of Evans-Pritchard seemed on one occasion to falter into affirmation of magic when he became a 'witness' himself: 'I have only once seen witchcraft on its path …'

I will deal very briefly with the relationship between religion and health and illness because what has been said about magic applies equally to religion. Frazer's key and still useful distinction between magic and religion is that the former is said to be controlled by human beings and the latter by God or spirits. In practice, this distinction is not always so clear. For example, powerful religious intermediaries have something in common with shamans or benevolent sorcerers, especially in their roles as healers and interceders with the divine. More fundamentally, despite the fact that they are different systems of knowledge, both magic and religion are non-scientific (though not illogical in their own terms). Just as magic explains illness in terms of witchcraft and sorcery, so many religions explain it at least partly in terms of 'God's will'. Like magic, religion is sometimes used as ideology to justify self or group interest (see pp. 531-2). There is a potential, but not inevitable conflict between the religious and scientific explanation of illness.

Modern scientific medicine: the biomedical model

Lorna G Moore *et al.* present two major defining assumptions of modern scientific medicine: first is the germ theory of disease and the need to cure infection to restore health; second, is the efficacy of preventive medicine. The two arms of modern scientific medicine are, then, the *curative* and the *preventive*. Scientific theory depends on the empirical demonstration of causal relationships and it was the work of Louis Pasteur on germ theory, particularly germ contagion, in the mid to late nineteenth century that established the basis of modern medicine. Criticisms of modern scientific medicine tend to focus on:

1 A limited approach to curative medicine that has developed, based on drugs and surgery,
2 A corresponding failure adequately to emphasise the role of prevention .
3 A tendency to undervalue subjective feeling states. Few, however, would oppose the use of science in medicine, it is the abuse that is more usually criticised.

Allopathy, homeopathy and naturopathy

The advantage of Moores' broad definition is that it highlights the common assumptions underlying certain traditions of treatment within scientific medicine. Moore states that allopathy, homeopathy and naturopathy share the two core assumptions mentioned above. There are also significant differences between them. Allopathic medicine is based on the principle of finding a means to counteract disease. Drugs are the main counteractive agents used. Because of the successful use of drugs in combating germs, Western medicine is often identified with allopathic medicine to the neglect of other systems of treatment. Homeopathic medicine is based on the principle that a particular sickness can be treated by administering minute doses of a remedy that produces the same symptoms as the disease. The homeopath regards symptoms of disease as an attempt by the body to restore homeostasis (balance), a process which treatment seeks to stimulate. Reactions to disease vary and individuals rather than diseases are treated. In so far as homeopathy reaches out to the whole person, it shares the principles of holistic medicine (see pp. 419-20). Naturopathy is based on the principle that a natural, mainly fruit and vegetable diet, provides the body with the ingredients it needs to avoid disease. Similarly, herbal remedies are used when disease does occur. Naturopathy can also include regular exercise, a healthy environment, avoidance of and techniques to deal with stress.

Characteristics of the bio-medical model

Although allopathic medicine remains dominant in the West (see Table 14.1 for one example) and is increasing in influence elsewhere, serious criticisms of the way it is practised are now widely made. The essence of these criticisms is that a machine-like, dehumanising model of health and illness has come to dominate allopathic medicine and there is, in addition, too much dependence on surgery and 'high-tech' medicine. Elliot Mishler refers to this approach as the *biomedical model* and he identifies four assumptions which underlie it.

1 Disease is seen as deviation from normal biological functioning. A criticism of this assumption is that effective biological functioning varies somewhat from person to person.

Table 14.1 Percentage lacking their own teeth (UK, by age group) – one measure of the effectiveness of scientific medicine

	1978	1988
	Percentage	
25–34	4	1
35–44	13	4
45–54	32	17
55–64	56	37
65–74	79*	57
75+	79*	80

*1978 figure is average for both age groups

2   There is the doctrine of specific aetiology or causation, i.e. a specific germ causes a given disease. A problem here is that individuals do not respond to germs in the same way so that other factors in disease causation must exist presumably related to the individual's health and ability to maintain health.

3   There is the assumption of generic diseases which means that the same kinds of diseases occur in all human societies. Despite its analytical usefulness, this perspective tends to ignore the variety of cultural interpretation given to disease.

4   There is the assumption that medicine is scientifically neutral. In fact, as we shall see, the practice of medicine has profound personal and social implications which the attitude of scientific 'objectivity' can obscure.

Criticisms of the biomedical model

1   Samuel Osherson and L Amara Singham

In essence, the above criticism of the biomedical paradigm is that it is too mechanistic (sometimes it is referred to as the bio-mechanical model) and fails to take account of either individual variety and need, or of cultural diversity. A particularly sharp critique of the biomedical model is given in *The Machine Metaphor in Medicine* by Samuel Osherson and Loran Amara Singham which appears in Elliot Mishler's edited volume *Social Contexts of Health, Illness and Patient Care*. I shall use their discussion of the influence of the mechanical metaphor on the management of death to illustrate their main points. They present three dimensions of a machine metaphor which they find expressed in contemporary medicine.

As a result of mechanistic thinking, hospitals rarely provide the atmosphere and rituals in which the individual's spiritual and emotional feelings about death can be freely and fully expressed and discussed. Medics and paramedics do not see this as their 'job': they are not trained and sensitised to help deal with this 'side' of death. Thus, this is one nurse's idea of role-appropriate behaviour

at the impending death of a patient, quoted by Glaser and Strauss (1981):

> *A stern face, you don't have to communicate very much verbally, you put things short and formal. … Yes, very much the nurse.*
>
> (Mishler, 1981:241)

Osherson and Amara Singham's primary message is that 'to understand medicine truly, we must look beyond it'. Personal and cultural meaning and context are relevant to the consideration of health, illness and death. They are certainly not opposed to scientific medicine or even to all applications of mechanistic medicine, but they see a need for a broader perspective. There are, of course, others who are opposed in principle to the major forms of treatment of 'mechanistic' medicine, drugs and surgery. However, complete rejection of the biomedical paradigm is not the only response to the critique of it presented in this section. (For feminist criticism of the biomedical model, see pp. 430-1.)

2   Ivan Illich: Iatrogenesis

The brunt of Illich's critique against modern medicine is clear enough. Based in Mexico, the immediate object of his attack in *Limits to Medicine* (1975) is the medical establishment of the industrialised countries. He argues that there are three kinds of iatrogenesis or damage caused by modern scientific medicine. First, is *medical iatrogenesis* (illness caused by medicine itself) such as the ill-advised use of drugs or unnecessary surgery.

Second, *social iatrogenesis* refers to the injury – much of it psychological – caused by the bureaucratic and impersonal way in which modern medicine is organised: it occurs when the language in which people could experience their bodies is turned into bureaucratic gobbledgook; or 'when suffering, mourning, and healing outside the patient role are labelled a form of deviance'.

Third, *cultural iatrogenesis* describes the wide-spread acceptance of 'managed health' and failure to accept personal responsibility for one's own health. Illich also adopts the concept of 'medicalisation'. This term describes how even minor problems such as a headache or a depressive mood which individuals could often cope with, alone or with friends' help, have been 'taken over' by medical professionals.

Marxist, Vicente Navarro argues (1976) that Illich's critique of modern bureaucracy in *Limits to Medicine* and other works is based on a disillusionment with industrial society. Illich echoes the scepticism of Tönnies and Simmel about the 'bigness' and impersonality of modern society which they saw as undermining individual and local power and involvement in many aspects of life. These populist sentiments were revived in the 1960s and early 1970s when Illich became something of a cult figure among radical activists. From his own socialist perspective, Navarro suggests that Illich offers no real alternative principle of social organisation to capitalism. Illich's reply might well be that most socialist systems are as open to his criticisms as capitalism: democracy and participation are readily found in socialist theory and authoritarianism and bureaucracy more easily in practice.

3 Kenneth Pelletier: an holistic alternative

Holistic medicine understands health and illness not merely in biomedical terms but in total personal and cultural terms as well. Moore *et al.* refer to holistic medicine as a biocultural approach (which embraces personal/social factors) rather than simply a biomedical approach. There is wide agreement in the literature about the nature and goals of holistic medicine. The following comments by Kenneth R Pelletier define holistic attitudes to health and illness and express the humanistic emphasis of holistic medicine. By emphasising the integration of mind and body, he rejects the dualism of the biomedical model:

> *Holistic medicine recognises the inextricable interaction between the person and his psychosocial environment. Mind and body function as an integrated unit, and health exists when they are in harmony, while illness results when stress and conflict disrupt this process. These approaches are essentially humanistic and re-establish an emphasis on the patient rather than upon medical technology. Modern medicine has tended to view man as a machine with interchangeable parts, and has developed sophisticated procedures for repairing, removing, or artificially constructing these parts. ... Consideration of the whole person emphasises the healing process, the maintenance of health, and the prevention of illness rather than the treatment of established disorders.*
>
> *(Pelletier, 1979:8)*

The title of Pelletier's book is *Mind as Healer. Mind as Slayer: A Holistic Approach to Preventing Stress Disorders.* He contends that stress-induced disorders have substantially replaced infectious disease as the major medical problem of developed industrial nations. In Western Europe, the United States and Japan, cardiovascular disorders, cancer, arthritis, and respiratory diseases are prime causes of ill-health and death. Pelletier argues that mental processes play a part in the contraction and management of these diseases. In making his case, he conducts an interesting incidental 'dialogue' with the language of scientific medicine in which he attempts to 'rehumanise' it. Thus, he rejects the dominant definition of 'psychosomatic' as a disorder which persists in the absence of clearly diagnosed organic pathology (and which is sometimes thought of by practitioners as 'imaginary'). Instead, he uses the concept 'to convey ... a fundamental interaction between mind and body which is involved in all diseases and all processes affecting health maintenance'.

Pelletier describes a number of techniques for controlling stress,

including meditation and biofeedback. An important aspect of both is the active involvement of the individual in maintaining her/his own health. Yet, Pelletier emphasises that it is possible to measure scientifically the effectiveness of this subjective involvement. He refers to '(n)umerous research projects (which) have demonstrated that medication is psychologically and physiologically more refreshing and energy restoring than deep sleep'. Among the measurable indications of this in an experiment with Indian Yogis are the extreme slowing of respiration to four to six breaths per minute and a predominance of alpha brain-wave activity (associated with the absence of stress). Biofeedback is the monitoring of bodily functions to establish the effect of given factors on them. Pelletier refers to research and clinical practice which show that a large range of bodily functions normally thought to be involuntary can be brought under conscious control. These include heart rate, muscle tension, body temperature, and more experimentally, stomach acidity and white blood cells. The potential here for taking personal responsibility and action for one's own health is obvious.

A lay challenge to medical hegemony?

There is today a wider awareness than say 30 years ago of the importance of a range of factors in health and illness among people, many of whom have barely heard of holistic medicine. This awareness gained impetus from the humanistic and naturalistic movements of the 1960s. There is now greater understanding of the importance of exercise, as illustrated by the popularity of jogging, aerobics and various other workouts. The same is true of diet and stress-control. There is also more willingness to challenge alleged medical malpractice, negligence or even misjudgement through the Courts. One case in the United States concerned unsightly scar-tissue left after a breast in-plant. An important outcome of second wave feminism has been the emergence of the feminist health movement. The basic philosophy is for women to take ownership of their own health and certainly to reject any tendency among medical practitioners to assume the role of moral entrepreneurs, e.g. in contraception and family planning (see p. 187 and pp. 430-1).

Pelletier, writing soon after the 1960s, speculated that a 'profound transformation of human consciousness' was fuelling these developments. In the tough, 'realistic' 1990s, it is not easy to feel that this is still so, but there has certainly emerged a lively health movement that looks beyond 'mechanistic' medicine to a more independent and holistic approach to health.

However, such movements tend to be much more strongly rooted in the middle than in the working class. In a survey of the predominantly middle class readership of its own 'Health Page', *The Guardian* found that a majority of 386 interviewees had experienced one or more complementary therapies (see Figure 14.2).

Choice of therapies

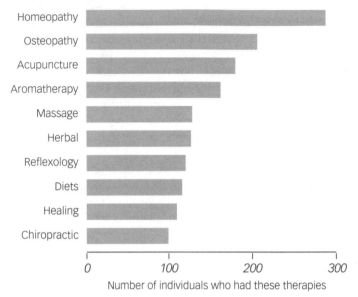

Number of individuals who had these therapies

How was it for you?

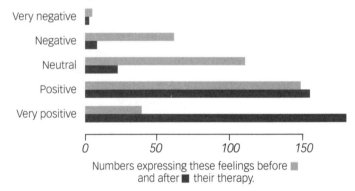

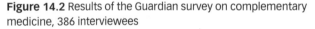

Numbers expressing these feelings before ▓
and after ■ their therapy.

Figure 14.2 Results of the Guardian survey on complementary medicine, 386 interviewees

Sociological and social policy perspectives on health

The established sociological perspectives will be employed to different degrees in the remainder of this chapter. Marxism may have faltered politically but it still offers a powerful critique of capitalism and notably so in the area of health. Interactionism is distinctively useful at relating the personal and the structural and is used to do this (see below). Functionalist perspective is not employed other than to describe Parsons' concept of the sick role. To a degree New Right or market liberal analysis has replaced functionalism as the main expression of more conservative

sociological thinking. As well as free market liberalism, social democratic liberalism is relevant for consideration in this chapter as a perspective on health policy.

Marxism

In the case of Marxism, political and sociological perspective are closely related: The analysis of what 'ought to be' is implicit in the analysis of what 'is'. Marxist analysis of health begins, as with other matters, with the economic system and particularly relations to the means of production. Thus, Lesley Doyal explains the poorer health of the working class in historical and contemporary capitalist society by reference to the exploitation of their labour. Both she and Vivienne Walters then analyse the whole complex of working class health and ill-health – including the workplace, housing, the environment, commodity consumption, use of and access to health facilities – in terms of social class inequality. In her analysis of British colonial Africa, Doyal shows how the exploitation of labour and resources led to a disruption of local cultural and environmental stability, leading to widespread ill-health. In the post-colonial period, the multinational company is seen by both Doyal and Vicente Navarro as the main agent of Western domination of the Third World. Navarro, in particular, argues that the structure of health inequality in the Third World (Latin America is his example) is a product of underdevelopment. Foreign and domestic capitalists and the upper middle class consume quality health care whereas the peasantry and the poorest elements in the urban population suffer scarcity. Neither foreign nor domestic capitalists are primarily committed to development which would benefit the majority. The former seek resources and cheap labour but their products are sold mainly in the advanced countries whereas the latter are more concerned with their own wealth than developing mass domestic production and markets. Thus, underdevelopment, including health underdevelopment, occurs. According to Navarro, Rostow's 'take-off' stage of development which requires mass domestic consumption and would improve the general quality of life, including the level of health, is hampered by the economic domination of the multinationals (see Chapter 20).

Navarros' disagreement with modernisation theory extends even to a sharp critique of the radical populist, Ivan Illich. Problems that the latter attributes to modern science and organisation, Navarro attributes to capitalist control of these areas.

Functionalism

Functionalist perspective on social welfare indicates that the 'mass' health policies of modern societies represent 'adjustments' to popular pressure for an improved environment and health facilities, and also serve the function of maintaining a healthy labour force. However, it is Talcott Parsons' analysis of the sick role that has been the seminal functionalist work of the post-war period in this field.

He defines sickness as a form of deviant behaviour which, like crime, requires a social response (1951). He presents four cultural expectations which he felt the sick person typically understands and accepts when adopting the sick role:

1 Relief from normal duties.
2 Non-responsibility for own condition and cure.
3 That the condition is undesirable and the patient must want to get well.
4 Medical help should be sought.

By structuring the sick role in this way, society asserts control over and copes with sickness. Left to themselves, the sick might be a considerable source of havoc and hamper the well functioning of society. Acceptance of the sick role contains the problem and implies an intent to 'get back to normal'.

Parsons' concept of the sick role has generated much research and comment. He himself observed that not all sick people accept that they *are* sick. Some 'fight it', literally until they drop, and such behaviour can cause problems. Various studies have examined whether all 'sick' people do, in fact, accept the four exceptions. Thus, the notion that the sick person must want to get better (3) does not appear to be accepted in the case of those with chronic afflictions. Similarly, reliance on others for cure (2 and 4) has limited applicability to those seeking psychoanalysis because most analysts require clients to participate in their own recovery. Arguably, this expectation is becoming more widespread in most branches of medicine and to that extent Parsons' model of the sick role is beginning to date.

Two further criticisms can be made of Parsons' model. First, his tendency to describe the sick role as rather helpless and dependent on the medical 'expert' lays him open to the now familiar criticisms of over-scientific medicine. Second, in presenting the social structuring of the sick role primarily in terms of society's need for maintaining order and stability, he fails to explore the links between capitalism and ill-health. Rather, he assumes that the relationship between (capitalist) development and health is generally positive. As we have seen conflict theorists provide contrary analysis and evidence.

Interactionism

The premise of interactionism is that people create meaning through symbolic communication. This perspective is helpful in understanding the various paradigms of health presented in the first section of this chapter. Thus, the magical and scientific paradigms of health describe two very different, but internally consistent, frameworks of thinking and action. Interactionists explore the idea that people create their own reality at the micro level of interaction as well as the macro-cultural level. As this chapter will illustrate, concepts such as negotiation, labelling and self-fulfilling prophecy illuminate the doctor-patient relationship as much as, for instance, the teacher-student one. Analysis of negotiational dynamics is most effective when important variables

such as the class, gender and ethnicity of the participants are considered.

Despite the insight interactionism provides into cultural processes it is not a fully developed theory of social structure. This is because it does not adequately address the issue of power. Often, interactionists are a little vague about who has power and how it is used or, they adopt liberal-pluralist, functionalist or Marxist theories of power. In the area of health and health policy, as in others, interactionism can supplement (and sometimes humanise) the major structural perspectives.

Liberal reformism and free market liberalism

Much of this chapter will be devoted to discussing these two forms of liberal perspective in relation to health. Liberal reformism or social democratic reformism was the dominant philosophy underlying the NHS from its founding in 1948 to the late 1970s. Few doubted that a driving motivation behind the NHS was to provide equal access to equal health services on the basis of need.

The New Right policy of quasi- or internal markets has introduced into the NHS a principle of competition which appears to have an inherent aspect of inequality – 'winners' and 'losers' are produced, i.e. some patients systematically get quicker and/or better health care than others (see pp. 437-41). The purpose of introducing competition is to achieve greater efficiency in terms of costs and more effective delivery (although the NHS was already relatively efficient in cost terms prior to the introduction of the reforms).

> **Question**
>
> What criticisms and insight does sociology offer into the biomedical model of health and institutionalised health?

The British system of health care

Historical

Important improvements in the health of the British people had occurred well before the setting up of the National Health Service following the 1946 Act. Indeed, some of these developments can be traced back to and probably beyond the mid eighteenth century. Progress in prevention rather than cure accounts for the gradual improvement of the health of Britons up to the time when the use of new curative drugs, (notably antibiotics) became widespread in the mid twentieth century. All the major infectious diseases – tuberculosis, typhus, measles etc. – were well in decline before antibiotics and immunisation were introduced (see Figure 14.3). This was due to improvements in public and private hygiene.

First, improvements in the quality and cleanliness of the environment contributed substantially to health improvement. This was (and remains) a fundamental matter as Disraeli's reference to the need for good 'air, light and water' when speaking for what became the 1872 Public Health Act indicates. This act codified over a century of fragmented central and local government initiative in the health field and required all local authorities to appoint medical officers of health, and sanitary inspectors. Sewage, drainage, the construction of pavements, roads and housing, street-lighting, and the quality of food production, storage and distribution, all continued to improve.

A second factor, improvement in personal and family nutrition and hygiene, is complementary to the first. Clearly the availability of running water and the existence of adequate sewage and drainage helped people to a more hygienic lifestyle. Better quality and availability of cleansing agents and utensils was also a factor as was the contribution of health education in schools, attendance at which became compulsory to the age of ten in 1880.

Third, the government took steps to improve the quality of professional health care. Thus, in 1858 the Medical Act established a Medical Register administered by the Medical Council with the

purpose of establishing and monitoring professional standards among doctors. The Certification of Midwives Act of 1902 did the same for that group and improving standards of midwifery and this is no doubt contributed to the fall in child mortality in the immediately ensuing period.

Fourth, the role of government, obvious in points one and three, deserves separate mention. Both Tory and Liberal governments, often against their preferred laissez-faire principles, had repeatedly passed reforming legislation to reduce the rigours and ill-health of industrial, urban life. In the early twentieth century, the (then) major parties were further stimulated in this direction by the rise of the Labour party. The Liberal government elected in 1905 passed a series of measures which foreshadowed the post-Second World War Welfare State. Acts were passed which used the school system to improve the nutrition (school meals) and health (medical inspections) of children. The National Insurance Act of 1911 was highly significant in the history of popular health provision. It provided financial benefits and free doctor's services for the poor. Government, employers and employees made weekly contributions to pay for the scheme which was run by private insurance companies. The Liberal package made a fundamental contribution to the basic security of the lives of millions of working people but was partly motivated by the hope of buying off socialist revolution and gaining the party working class support.

The decline in the death rate and general improvement in the population's health occurred before the invention and widespread availability of most modern 'wonder' drugs. However, these further improved matters. The infectious diseases that were the main killers before the nineteenth century, such as the 'plague', smallpox and typhus, are now, in the main, curable. Instead, diseases of physical and mental degeneration such as cancer, which modern medicine has been less successful in treating, increasingly take their toll. Even so, the spread of AIDS in the 1980s and 1990s reminds us that new types of infectious diseases which are difficult to cure can still develop. Again, this emphasises the key role of personal hygiene and the limitations of scientific medicine.

Finally, it is worth noting that the steep decline in infant mortality lagged behind that of adults and older children. This decrease did not occur until the birthrate itself began to drop sharply. The lesson seems to be that fewer children generally get more and better resources and attention. In addition, services for mothers and children expanded rapidly during the first quarter of the twentieth century.

The National Health Service

That National Health Service was established in 1948. It was organised into three separate parts, a 'tripartite' structure: *the hospital sector, the executive council sector,* and *the local health authorities.* Hospitals were not run by local authorities but by regional hospital boards on which consultants were strongly represented. Consultants retained the right to do some private as

(Source: T McKeown, *The Modern Rise of Population,* 1976)

Figure 14.3 Measles death rates of children under fifteen in England and Wales. The decline in deaths through measles before immunisation began was typical of what happened in the case of most infectious diseases.

well as National Health Service work. Primary services to individuals and families were to be the responsibility of general practitioners, dentists, opticians and pharmacists who were answerable to the executive council. The local authorities were to take care of a range of remaining health concerns including environmental health, maternity services, home helps and school services. All health services were to be free. In 1974, the tripartite structure was unified into a single hierarchical system: Secretary of State for Social Services: Department of Health and Social Security, Regional Health Authorities and Districts. Unfortunately, the level at which a (rather weak) degree of popular participation was built in – the area level – proved ineffective and was dropped in 1982. In 1989 the Department of Health and Social Security was divided into two separate Departments.

The National Health Service was introduced to the accompaniment of much idealistic rhetoric. The setting up of the service had been one of the major recommendations of the Beveridge Report of 1942 which had been enthusiastically received by a wide public. Considerable national support for and pride in the NHS remains – making a cool assessment of its achievements difficult. Even many critics of the service's limitations and failures make it clear that they support it in principle. In any case, the achievements of the NHS are substantial. These include a much fairer distribution of General Practitioners and certain other medical services to women on a comparable basis with men – which the 1911 Act had conspicuously failed to implement, and notable comparative cost effectiveness. However, there remain substantial inequalities of health care and the NHS continues in certain respects to be a centralised and undemocratically administered service. Whether the reforms implemented in the early 1990s are improving or worsening these problems is discussed below.

Two issues – the dominance of the hospital sector of the NHS and the continuing role of private medicine – were apparent in the negotiations leading to the setting up of the system. The consultants effectively established their claim to a substantial share of resources, for research as well as practice, and to the right to practise a limited but highly lucrative amount of private medicine within NHS premises. Many consultants, therefore, seem to get the best of both worlds. More broadly, the power and prestige of the hospital sector is a prime example of the triumph of curative rather than preventive medicine in the NHS. The allocation of a large share of resources to high-level, 'scientific' medicine occurs at the expense of preventive medicine and the delivery of mass services. Another important penetration of the NHS by private profit is the operation of the drug companies. Their return on capital has typically been twice as much as that for manufacturing industry as a whole. Doctors are often bombarded with advertising for new products which are in many cases little different from existing lines. Recently, the government has promoted the of buying generic drugs (as opposed to 'brand' names) to cut costs. As we shall see, measures have also been taken to reduce the power of hospital consultants.

Vivienne Walters: a critique of the early NHS

After a detailed review of opinion and debate leading to the setting up of the NHS was, Vivienne Walters concludes that 'the NHS was not so much a response to the difficulties working class patients experienced in obtaining care, as an attempt to rationalise an inefficient health care system and provide it with a stable financial base'. Before 1948 many people were not covered by insurance and frequently could not afford treatment. This, of course, affected the earning potential of doctors and other medical practitioners. The NHS extended their clientele and guaranteed their income. A second point is that though the NHS functioned to improve the quality of the existing and future labour force, it certainly did not deliver control or extensive participation in the health service to working people. Government, professional, managerial and commercial interests remained dominant. These comments do not seek to detract from the immense personal benefit many, especially women and children, obtained in gaining access to free primary and hospital care for the first time.

Walters does not suggest any elite conspiracy about the way the NHS was set up. Indeed, she emphasises that neither the TUC nor the Labour party pressed for a genuinely democratic socialist health service but broadly supported the NHS as it was set up. Lesley Doyal who, like Walters, writes from a Marxist perspective, argues that British medicine is best thought of as 'nationalised' rather than 'socialised'. She suggests that the NHS represents a definition of health by the state largely in terms of access to care. This approach has been at the expense of a more thorough exploration of 'the links between health, the organisation and delivery of health care and the nature of class relations in British society'. Echoing Althusser, she goes on to say that '(t)his suggests that the state has served an ideological function in so far as it has legitimised medical definition of health and failed to address class inequalities in health and the political bases of these'.

Doyal argues that a socialist system of health care will not be achieved in the absence of powerful working class demand and organisation for it. As it stands, the NHS is a social democratic compromise in which the state mediates the interaction of classes and interest groups in the health field within the framework of a mixed economy.

Inequalities in British health care: sectorial, regional and social class

In the past, three areas of inequality have frequently been noted in relation to the NHS: inequalities of resources between different sectors of the NHS; inequalities of resources between different regions; and an unequal distribution of health between higher and lower classes. These will now be considered in turn although the second two are clearly related.

Sectorial

As was mentioned above, the hospital sector was the dominant one within the NHS. In 1948 it accounted for 55 per cent of total NHS expenditure and in 1974, 65 per cent. This inequality was increased in the case of those teaching hospitals with private endorsements. Resource allocation between different medical specialities shows a complementary pattern. More resources were available for the acute sick, the major client population of such hospitals, and less for the chronic sick, particularly the mentally ill and handicapped, who are typically treated in non-teaching hospitals (which also received relatively fewer resources for acute patients).

Chris Ham claims that the Conservative health reforms of the 1990s have brought about a 'shift in the balance of power within the NHS. He states that now the GPs and health authorities are 'in a much better position to shape the direction of' hospital service development (1995).

Regional

As far as geographical differences in resource allocation are concerned, the south fares better than the north and the richer areas better than the poorer. Despite this, matters have somewhat equalised since 1948 and, according to the *Inequalities in Health Report* (1979), England has a more even regional distribution of doctors than other industrialised Western countries. Even so, in 1995 it was estimated that about 700 doctors would have to be moved from the south to the north for provision to be equalised. Of the twenty districts in England with the smallest proportion of doctors, seven are in the north, two in the midlands and one in inner London – all in areas with relatively poor public health records (North West Surveys and Research, 1995).

Other resources are also unequally distributed. Sunderland has 38 per cent fewer practice nurses than average and Brent and Harrow 27 per cent more.

That resource provision does correlate with positive and negative health outcomes is shown in respect to perimortality (Figure 14.4) and mortality due to heart disease (Figure 14.5).

The average rate of mortality per 100,000

Figure 14.5 Heart disease: the north-south divide 1995

Perinatal mortality rates

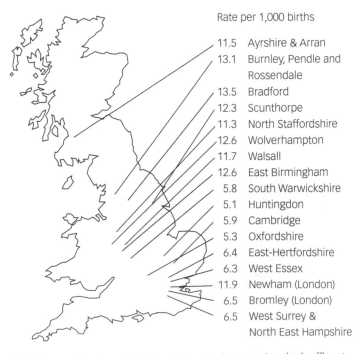

Rate per 1,000 births	
11.5	Ayrshire & Arran
13.1	Burnley, Pendle and Rossendale
13.5	Bradford
12.3	Scunthorpe
11.3	North Staffordshire
12.6	Wolverhampton
11.7	Walsall
12.6	East Birmingham
5.8	South Warwickshire
5.1	Huntingdon
5.9	Cambridge
5.3	Oxfordshire
6.4	East-Hertfordshire
6.3	West Essex
11.9	Newham (London)
6.5	Bromley (London)
6.5	West Surrey & North East Hampshire

Note: The variation in perinatal mortality rates between London's affluent Bromley and less well off Newham indicate that social factors are more important then regional ones in explaining inequalities.

(Source: *The Times*, 23.3.1990)

Figure 14.4 Regional variations in perimortality

The rough correspondence between the unequal geographical distribution of health resources and social inequality generally, leads Julian Tudor Hart to suggest the 'inverse care law'; the more a social group has need for medical resources, the less likely it is to find them locally available.

While there is a correlation between regions and inequalities in health, it will become clear that other factors – including relative poverty – are almost certainly more significant in explaining those inequalities.

Social class and health inequality

The facts of health inequality between the social classes are well-documented. Mortality and morbidity rates are higher among the working class, especially social class V, than among the middle class. As Vivienne Walters points out, infant mortality rates 'are among the more sensitive indicators of class inequalities in health' and '(s)tatistics published since the turn of the century have consistently shown higher death rates for lower social classes and though the rates for all classes have declined, the differences between them have not narrowed'. Figure 14.6 illustrates the inequality and it is also typical of the pattern of class morbidity and mortality inequality of adults of both sexes.

As Lesley Doyal remarks, these continuing differences in mortality arise both from the greater incidence of 'new' diseases such as lung cancer and of 'older' diseases such as TB and bronchitis which are 'traditionally associated with poverty'. Not surprisingly, class patterns of sickness or morbidity follow the same trend as the mortality rate.

Lesley Doyal's comment after analysing much of the relevant data on morbidity and mortality has fundamental, indeed, revolutionary implications for health care:

> *These class differences in morbidity and mortality, ... provide strong evidence to support the argument that social and economic factors remain extremely important in determining the ways in which people live and die.*
>
> *(Doyal, 1979:65)*

According to Doyal, then, relative ill-health, is largely the product of socio-economic inequality and could be reduced with the reduction of inequality.

With the exception of east London and the City the ten areas worst affected by heart disease are in the north and the ten least affected are in the south. Even within some regions there is a wide disparity partly because of well-focused preventive treatment and care.

The Audit Commission recently reported that better measures to prevent and treat the disease could save up to 8,000 more lives annually by the year 2000.

Stillbirths, 1984*

Stillbirths/1,000 total births

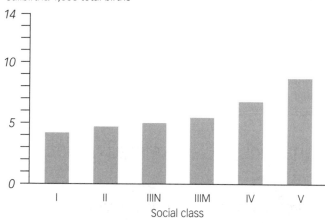

Infant (less than 1 year), 1984*

Infant deaths/1,000 live births

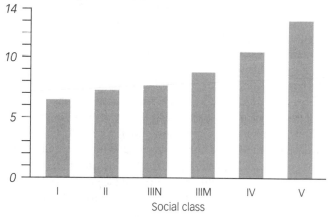

*England and Wales

(Source: OPCS in *Inequalities in Health Report*, 1988:229)

Figure 14.6 Occupational class and mortality in babies

Social class and labelling/negotiation

As Doyal notes, ever since the inception of the NHS, there has been a continuing debate about whether working or middle class patients use it most. Simplifying somewhat, it seems that the working class use curative services more than the middle class but not to the extent that their need implies, given their higher morbidity and mortality rates. However, the middle class use a broader range of services particularly of a preventive kind such as mass miniature radiography, cervical cytology, and antenatal and postnatal care. On the issue of quality as distinct from quantity of service, the middle class appear to be at an advantage. This is largely because facilities and availability of services tend to be better in middle class areas.

The quality of social relationships requires analysis as well as the material and technical quality of health care. Interactionist as well as structural perspective is helpful here. Structural perspective suggests that middle class patients may come to medical practitioners with a number of cultural advantages such as language skills and greater self-assurance. As David Tuckett puts it, the absence of these in working class patients 'may hinder a relationship of mutual participation', leaving power and decision-making entirely in the practitioner's hands. Interactionist perspective is helpful in understanding the detail of the doctor-patient relationship, particularly in the matter of negotiation or lack of it.

Explanations of class-related health inequalities

1 Material poverty: social democratic perspective

What is it about social class that seems to generate the health inequalities presented above? The *Inequalities in Health Report* (1979) identifies poverty and the relatively poor access of lower social-economic groups to the knowledge and resources which help to maintain health. So both the cultural and material disadvantages of the working class are indicated as causal factors, with the latter considered to be the more fundamental. Health inequality is simply a function of structured social inequality. The health of the working class, particularly the lower working class, would improve if it had 'sufficient household income, a safe, uncrowded and unpolluted home, warmth and hygiene, and means of rapid communication with the outside world'. In proffering a solution to health inequality, the *Inequalities in Health Report* itself takes a radical social democratic line, arguing that the poor need a significant increase in income, resources and services, especially health services.

The incoming Conservative government shelved the *Inequalities in Health Report*. Faced with evidence of growing health inequalities among the poor, the Major government set up a Nutrition Task Force in 1991 which came up with the conclusion that 'people on limited incomes may experience particular difficulties in obtaining a healthy and varied diet'. Accordingly, a second task force, the Low Income Project Team sought evidence on the links between diet, low-income and ill-health. However, a condition of the enquiry was that members were banned from discussing income support levels. Nevertheless, the team's report took what can reasonably be called a reforming social democratic approach. It noted that – due largely to the development of supermarkets – there were 'whole communities with inadequate access to the constituents of a healthy diet'. The team urged the government to plan and cost a national strategy – involving five key departments – to reverse the trend to ill-health among the poor (see Reading 1).

2 The capitalist system: class and inequality, Marxist perspective

Marxists, such as Doyal, consider that health inequality is reproduced throughout the major institutional areas of capitalist society. The system of private profit generates this inequality and she traces health inequality through the processes of production and consumption.

Production

Doyal's research in this area was carried out in the 1970s, before the sharp decline in the numbers of traditional working class jobs. However, it is equally possible to apply the Marxist principles of her analysis to contemporary industry. She shows that health inequality begins at the point of production. Industrial accidents and disease tended to occur more often in traditional working class occupational areas such as mining, construction and railways. In part, this is due to the nature of heavy manual work but more could have been done to secure a safer working environment. For instance, in 1975-76, 59 miners were killed at work, 538 seriously injured, and 52,946 injured and off work for more than three days. The toll of industrial disease among miners was particularly high. Today, there is perhaps more concern about work-related stress than physical injury. There have also been attempts to raise public and government concern about the long hours some home-workers are known to work. However, the Conservative government favours a de-regulated labour market and has made no significant intervention in these matters. Publishing in 1979, Doyal argues that the traditional defenders of the working class – trade unions and the state – have not been very effective in achieving adequate enforcement of industrial health and safety legal regulations. She would have little reason to change her judgement in the 1990s. For example, there are still very few factory inspectors in relation to the number of workplaces to be visited and even when successful prosecutions do occur, penalties are often very light.

Doyal states the problem of the production/consumption of unhealthy items sharply:

> *Commodities are being produced for sale and consumed at an ever-increasing rate, and a great many of these products are not 'useful' according to any commonsense definition of the term. More than this, they may actually damage the health of consumers.*
>
> (Doyal, 1979:80)

Consumption

For discussion of the issue of consumption I will adopt Doyal's examples of tobacco and certain processed foods, though I am responsible for the detailed commentary.

Tough tobacco curbs 'vital'

Chris Mlhill
Medical Correspondent

TOUGHER controls on smoking are needed to halt the lung cancer epidemic as government targets to cut cigarette consumption look increasingly unlikely to be met, the Cancer Research Campaign warns today. A report by the CRC points out that lung cancer is the commonest cancer, and most cases are caused by cigarette smoking. In the UK it accounts for some 42,400 new patients annually.

The CRC warns that there are continuing and widening differences in smoking rates between socio-economic groups, with manual workers being more than twice as likely to smoke as those in the professional classes.

It warns that progress towards meeting the Health of the Nation targets on smoking is not being made, especially in young people.

The targets are aimed at reducing the death rate from lung cancer by 30 per cent in men and fifteen per cent in women by 2010, to reduce the prevalence of smoking to no more than twenty per cent by 2000, to reduce consumption of cigarettes by 40 per cent by 2000, and to reduce smoking among eleven to fifteen year olds by 33 per cent.

The Department of Health conceded in a report last July that the target on young people was not going to be met. It said overall smoking rates among eleven to fifteen year olds rose from ten per cent in 1993 to twelve per cent in 1994.

The CRC says more needs to be spent on tobacco prevention campaigns, cigarette advertising should be banned, and the tax on cigarettes sharply increased.

Lung cancer is the commonest cancer in men, responsible for 22 per cent of all new cancers. In women across the UK as whole, it ranks third, behind breast and skin cancer. In Scotland and parts of the north of England lung cancer is the number one killer of women.

The report explains that despite much research and a number of experimental therapies, lung cancer remains one of the hardest to treat. About 75 per cent of people will be dead within one year of diagnosis – and 95 per cent within five years.

The CRC is highlighting the fact that by the age of fifteen, one in four children is a regular smoker.

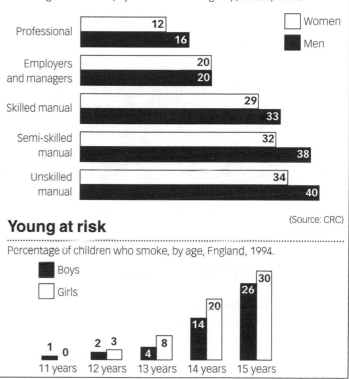

Smoking at work

Percentage who smoke, by socio-economic group, Britain, 1994.

	Women	Men
Professional	12	16
Employers and managers	20	20
Skilled manual	29	33
Semi-skilled manual	32	38
Unskilled manual	34	40

(Source: CRC)

Young at risk

Percentage of children who smoke, by age, England, 1994.

	Boys	Girls
11 years	1	0
12 years	2	3
13 years	4	8
14 years	14	20
15 years	26	30

(Source: *The Guardian*, 6.5.1996:6)

Figure 14.7 Smoking: class, gender and age

1 Tobacco

Despite the known correlation between tobacco smoking and lung cancer, government allows a situation in which the public is overwhelmingly encouraged rather than discouraged to smoke (for instance, in 1975 between £50-70 million was spent on the former, and £1 million on the latter). It is not only the massive quantity of tobacco, particularly cigarette advertising, but the insidious nature of it that seems to be effective. Appeals are variously made to status, masculinity, femininity, and 'coolness' depending on the brand and the 'bright ideas' of the 'creative' (advertising) department. Members of the public sometimes claim that they are 'not affected' by such advertising beyond being amused or entertained in passing. One wonders, however, whether if the proportion spent on encouraging and discouraging tobacco smoking were reversed tobacco consumption would remain stable.

There are social class and gender dimensions to tobacco consumption. As information has spread to the public about the unhealthy effects of tobacco, rates of consumption have fallen among higher socio-economic groups but not among lower.

Speculatively, it may be that working class people are more aware of and affected by pro-tobacco advertising than by scientific evidence on its harmful effects. It may also be that 'having a smoke' or 'a fag' is more deeply embedded in the culture of working class relaxation. Smoking may be felt as a necessary release from the stress of hard, physical work (even though, in fact, it increases stress in the long run). The rapid growth in tobacco consumption among working class women may also be related to the increasing number who work in the occupational as well as the domestic economy. Smoking may be experienced as a crutch against the pressures of dual roles.

Questions

1 What explanations can you offer for the class differences in smoking shown in the smoking at work chart (Figure 14.7)?
2 Describe and attempt to explain the pattern in which smoking is gendered.

A variety of reasons are cited for the government's tolerance of the above situation. First, the government relies for a significant part of its tax revenue on the sale of tobacco – about five per cent of total tax revenue. Second, the tobacco industry is a powerful and well organised lobby. It has presented an appearance of compromise such as developing 'safer' cigarettes and acquiescing in the banning of cigarette advertising in cinemas and on radio and television whilst managing to retain the bulk of its commercial 'freedom'. Third, Britain is predominantly a capitalist society and to control an established area of free enterprise may be ideologically repugnant to some and seem to set an undesirable precedent. Finally, perhaps a society as well as an individual can become addicted to a bad habit. Apparently, the collective will to 'kick it' is not yet here.

2 Diet

There have been several significant changes in dietary patterns in Britain over the last 150 years. Whilst food is more abundant and usually more sanitary, there is often cause for concern about its content – or lack of certain content. Between 1860 and 1960, it is estimated that the average annual consumption of refined sugar doubled, while that of fat increased by 50 per cent whereas the consumption of fibre decreased by 90 per cent. Increasingly, dietary experts regard these developments as unhealthy especially where there is little balancing intake of fresh vegetables and fruit which is more likely to be the case among the working class. The processing of food is a significant feature in the above trends. Processing creates homogenous (consistent) and long-lasting products, i.e. the product always tastes the same and has a long shelf-life. Processing also forms and even stimulates taste and consumption by, for instance, adding sugar or other sweeteners. There is obvious commercial advantage in all this. This is achieved mainly by chemical and other additives but what is taken out of many natural products must also be considered. Thus, refined sugar and processed bread lose many natural nutrients (which may or may not be artificially replaced). Sometimes, what is removed is sold as a separate product to increase profit.

Criticisms of Marxist perspectives: Nicky Hart

Nicky Hart uses the comparative method to criticise Doyal's linkage of ill-health to the capitalist system of production and consumption. She cites data which show that the rates for death caused by industrial accidents were somewhat higher in the (then) socialist societies of Czechoslovakia and Hungary than in Britain, and that whilst lung cancer caused a higher proportion of deaths in Britain the rate for circulatory disease was rather lower. Hart argues that the 'drive for industrialisation' and the lack of workers' freedom to protect themselves may account for these rather higher rates. She also observes that a substantial improvement in the general level of health has occurred in Britain under capitalism. Recent figures on the percentages of people in various age groups now keeping their own teeth provide an effective, if mundane, illustration of Hart's point (see Table 14.1, p. 418).

3   Culture of poverty (including ill-health): the New Right

The concept of the culture of poverty came up in Chapter 13. The emphasis in this approach is that the poor fundamentally create their own culture and lifestyles. This concept was somewhat reshaped by New Right thinkers such as Charles Murray. Murray adopted the view that those who lived the culture of dependency should be held fully responsible for the consequences of their behaviour. If they 'chose' poverty, they should experience poverty – not welfare.

This perspective has been applied specifically to health. Thus, the high incidence of smoking and poor diet among working class people illustrated above is regarded as a matter of their own voluntary choice. MacIntyre points out that four behavioural habits are associated with levels of health: smoking tobacco, consuming alcohol, diet and exercise. She cites evidence to demonstrate that the first two occur more heavily among the working class (more clearly so in the case of tobacco than alcohol) and that the diet and exercise regimes of the middle class tend to be healthier. Of course, all this is more or less well known and what is distinctive about MacIntyre is her interpretation. For her the lifestyle/health behaviour of working class people is voluntary rather than the production of circumstances.

Similarly, the working class are seen as 'choosing' to use certain key health services less often than the middle class although MacIntyre regards this as less important in explaining the class pattern of health than the lifestyle factors mentioned above.

A first criticism of MacIntyre's interpretation is that it is equally arguable that the poor behave as they do because of the circumstances they are in rather than out of pure choice. As far as diet is concerned, the irony is that food tends to be more expensive in poorer inner-urban areas. Supermarkets tend not to locate in the inner city whose residents often lack the transport to travel to them and which is necessary to make cheaper bulk purchases. Reading 1 by Judy Jones develops these points but does so with examples that indicate that people need not be defeated by difficult circumstances.

4   Labelling/negotiation

The point has already been made that there is evidence that members of the middle class may be less likely to be negatively labelled by medical professionals and in any case are more likely to have effective negotiating skills (see p. 421).

It is most useful to view labelling theory as a micro or middle level theory which links the personal and the cultural/structural. Thus, the level of interaction between say, doctor and patient is one important context in which cultural advantage or disadvantage comes into play.

5   Social constructionist perspective

Social constructionist perspective is increasingly being adopted as a theoretical approach which overcomes extreme social determinism and extreme voluntarism. Without specifically adopting the term social constructionist, Rob Mears puts the case for a more integrated theoretical and policy approach to health:

> *The debate about the origins of health inequalities has tended to polarise. There are those who favour materialistic explanations, which leads them to focus on the need for structural change, and those who prefer cultural explanations, which leads them to concentrate on changing individual behaviour. What is the way out of this dilemma? Maybe it is mistaken to assume that a choice must be made between these alternatives. The problem lies partly in the terminology and concepts used by the protagonists. A false dichotomy is erected by counterpoising 'structure' and 'culture' … Ultimately decisions about how to respond to data on health inequalities depends on ideological, moral and political allegiances. Explanations at the level of the 'individual' or 'society' are not necessarily mutually exclusive. Similarly, advocating policy initiatives at the level of the 'individual' does not preclude action at a structural level. For example, Government Ministers may lecture the elderly about the benefits of wearing woolly hats indoors as a preventive measure against hypothermia in winter. However, advice of this sort is not necessarily an alternative to providing more generous state retirement pensions or subsidising fuel costs.*
>
> (R Mears in O'Donnell, 1993:369)

After the rampant individualism of the 1980s, there are some signs that the political parties are looking at social policy, including health policy, with fuller consideration of a range of factors not merely those they are predisposed to favour.

A case study: taking action against malnutrition

In Reading 1 (see p. 442), journalist Judy Jones focuses in a concrete way many of the more theoretical points made above. The price and quality of food in Tipton in the Black country is a feature of a generally deprived existence. However, Jones describes a response to it that is not one of cultural passivity but of enterprising co-operation. There are 80 co-operatives throughout the country set up to provide better food for the poor and while these may not change 'the system', they clearly have a significant effect on the lives of those involved.

Gender and health

This section examines gender and health in the context of the power and status of women within the health professions; the relative health of females and males; and in relation to the 'medicalisation of childbirth'. Further, discussion of the issue of fertility occurs in Chapter 20, pp. 606-7. The important work which women do as informal and largely unpaid providers of health care was discussed in Chapter 13, pp. 408-9.

Medicine: a gendered occupational area

The dimension of gender cuts through health as it does through other aspects of life. In general, health services are still managed by men and 'manned' at the lower levels by women. Although nearly 80 per cent of employees in medical and other health and veterinary services are female (1983) only about 25 per cent of doctors are female – well reflecting the 'doctors and nurses' stereotyping of childhood. Yet there is nothing 'natural' in these figures as comparative data show. In the USA women make up eight per cent of doctors., in Finland 24 per cent, in Poland 46 per cent and in the former USSR 74 per cent. In the Eastern European societies childcare and health are associated areas, heavily supported by the state, which present women with a wide range of career choices Even though women are much less well represented at the policy-making level in these societies, the general pattern in the health professions remains less patriarchal than in Britain and the United States.

The relative health of females and males

Although, as the next section suggests, the *experience* of health services of females and males may often be different, the main explanation for the general pattern of health inequality relates to class rather than gender. However, in general, adult males smoke and drink more than adult females and this must have some bearing on the fact that the average female lifespan is longer than that of males. Men reaching pensionable age can expect to live to 79 whereas females can expect to live until 83. However, the steady increase in life expectancy has not been matched by an increase in the period of healthy expectancy. This remained almost constant for men between 1976 and 1992 at seven years and has increased for females from nine to just ten years (see Figure 14.8).

Due partly to their greater tendency to smoke, men are still more likely to die of coronary heart disease and lung cancer than women – although the gap is closing as relatively more women start smoking. In any case, British women already have the highest death rate due to heart disease among women in the world (see Figure 14.9). British men are second in their league. Imogen Sharo, director of the National Forum for Coronary Health Disease Prevention attributes these figures to 'high fat diets and appalling levels of physical activity', as well as to smoking. These figures have

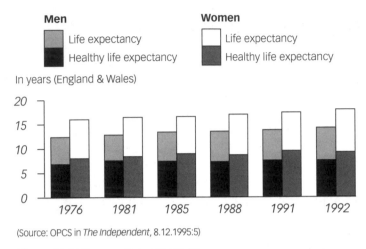

Men
■ Life expectancy (grey)
■ Healthy life expectancy (black)

Women
□ Life expectancy
■ Healthy life expectancy (dark grey)

In years (England & Wales)

(Source: OPCS in *The Independent*, 8.12.1995:5)

Figure 14.8 Life expectancy at age 65

made government health targets in these areas appear optimistic (see p. 439).

Although men are more likely to succumb to certain diseases than women, the latter are more likely to suffer from a range of less fatal diseases and ailments, including varicose veins and rheumatoid arthritis. They are also over 50 per cent more likely to be diagnosed than men as having a mental disorder. There may be an element of gender labelling (by doctors) or self-definition (by patients) in this. However, the still gendered pattern of work and leisure may also play a role. Women are more likely to be isolated in the home and suffer related emotional and mental stress, whereas traditionally male sociability – and disease – is associated with tobacco and alcohol. It is significant that as more females gravitate

Heart attack rate per 100,000, in 1985-87, age standardised

Finland
UK Glasgow
UK Belfast
Canada
Poland
US
Russia
Sweden
Germany
France
Italy
Spain
China

□ Men
■ Women

0   200   400   600   800   1000

(Source: WHO in *The Guardian*, 12.7.1994:3)

Figure 14.9 High and low extremes

towards lifestyles previously associated with males, the patterns of morbidity of the sexes is converging in some areas.

The experience of childbirth: the medical model

We now consider the quality of care provided by the health services and, in particular, what Ann Oakley refers to as the 'medicalisation' of childbirth. Health care can intrude into what is normally regarded as core personal space – the body (and, in the case of mental health, the mind). Quite obviously, sex differences can play a major part in the dispensing and experience of health care. Female fertility is the key differentiating factor. A pregnant female, whether she gives birth or terminates, embarks upon a series of experiences unavailable to the male. Yet, it is usually males who attempt to manage these experiences. Let us take the case of childbirth. In *Women Confined: Towards a Sociology of Childbirth* (1980), Ann Oakley identifies five features of what she refers to as the 'medical frame of reference' which she describes as 'a qualitatively different way of looking at the nature, context and management of reproduction' from that of mothers. These are the five features:

1 The definition of reproduction as a specialist subject in which only doctors are experts in the entire symptomatology of childbearing.
2 The associated definition of reproduction as a medical subject, as exactly analogous to other pathological processes as topics of medical knowledge and intervention.
3 The selection of limited criteria of reproductive success, i.e. perinatal and maternal mortality rates.
4 The divorce of reproduction from its social context, pregnant parenthood being seen as women's only relevant status.
5 The restriction of women to maternity – their derived typification as 'by nature' maternal, domesticated, family-oriented people.

After an extensive critique of the above 'medicalised' model of childbirth, Oakley tries to establish the subjective reality of childbirth. It is a complex human experience, involving losses and gains and often unmet expectations. Her proposals for changes in the management of birth indicate the direction of her argument: an end to unnecessary medical intervention in childbirth, the re-domestication of birth, a return to female-controlled childbirth and the provision of therapeutic support for women after childbirth. (It will be clear from the above that as well as attacking the medical framework of childbirth, she also seeks to demolish popular romantic conceptualisations of childbirth and motherhood.)

Oakley's arguments are applicable to the general paradigm of 'mechanistic' medicine as well as to the particular case of medicalised childbirth. (see also Chapter 7, p. 187 for further analysis of scientific medicine and gender, including childbirth). Male domination and scientific domination (though not science itself) are presented as twin partners in the repression of not only womankind, but of humankind. Accordingly, her proposals for change extend beyond birth to the bringing up of children and to the wider social context. These proposals have much in common with those offered in Anna Coote's social policy package described in the previous Chapter 13 (see p. 409).

Ethnicity and health

As one would expect in such a diverse ethnic population as the British, there is considerable variation in the pattern of health and ill-health. Certain patterns require very specific explanations. Thus, sickle cell disease is an inherited trait which affects one in four from West Africa and about one in ten people of Afro-Caribbean origin. Other patterns of diagnosis and ill-health are much more controversial and require more complex explanation. An example is the much higher rate of diagnosis for schizophrenia among Britain's Afro-Caribbean and Asian population than among whites.

Marmot gives examples of differing mortality rates for given causes of death in respect of people born outside of but resident in Britain over twenty years of age (1987). Africans were more likely to die from strokes, violence/accidents, in child-birth, and tuberculosis. Those from the Indian sub-continent experienced higher rates for diabetes, tuberculosis, liver cancer, heart disease, maternal deaths, and accidents/violence. Afro-Caribbeans were more likely to die from strokes, violence/accidents and diabetes. These three groups were less likely to die from lung disease than white Britons. As will be obvious from the above, morbidity as well as mortality patterns also vary across ethnic groups. Rickets is relatively more common among the Asian population.

Infant mortality also shows some variation in relation to ethnicity. Rates are relatively high among mothers born in Pakistan or Bangladesh but are falling quite rapidly among later generations. The infant mortality rate is also almost 50 per cent higher among mothers born in the Caribbean Commonwealth than among those born in the United Kingdom.

The above data on morbidity and mortality are merely a selection but they indicate a wide range of difference – not all of which is obvious or predictable. Accordingly, explanations need to be carefully considered.

Explanations for differential patterns of ethnic health

The explanations already given for class related health inequalities overlap considerably with those of ethnic health inequalities. However, ethnic culture, cultural stereotyping and other aspects of racism add to the complexity. The following five explanations will be considered and it needs to be borne in mind that although, to a degree, they are competing explanations, they are probably all appropriate in some situations:

1 Genetic
2 Material poverty
3 Cultural/individual
4 Immigrant adjustment
5 Racism discrimination, Racial stereo-typing, Institutional racism

Genetic

Some populations are more prone to certain genetic disorders than others. Sickle cell trait has already been mentioned. Another example is thalassaemia which affects various groups of Asian, Middle and Far Eastern and Mediterranean origin and can cause still-birth and severe anaemia in early childhood. A main issue in such cases is how well the National Health Service adjusts and responds.

Material poverty

Immigrant groups tend to occupy poorer quality housing, be in lower paying jobs, and suffer higher unemployment than the indigenous population. In part, these problems are socio-economic or class-based and they are all associated with poorer health.

Rickets is an illness associated with poverty and there was a high incidence of it among the British working class of the 1930s. This disorder is now most common among British Asians. As a disproportionate number of Bangladeshis and Pakistanis are poor, it is likely that the main cause of rickets among them is poverty. However, as Donovan (1986) has noted, there has been a persistent tendency among researchers to 'blame' Asian diet for the illness. This would seem to be a rather ethnocentric view given that Asian diet tends to be healthy if sometimes basic. As in this case, material or class disadvantage can be complicated and sometimes intensified by cultural misunderstanding.

Cultural/individual

Cultural explanations seek to interpret ethnic health inequalities in terms of the culture or lifestyle of the affected group. The example of rickets, raised above, can be continued as an illustration of a dubious application of this approach. In addition to diet, the following two aspects of Asian culture have been suggested as contributing to the high incidence of rickets: Asian women's failure to take antenatal advice; insufficient exposure to sunlight due to cultural taboos against body exposure. As David Mason (1995), points out, such observations imply that minority groups will simply *assimilate* to majority cultural practices. In fact, the process of minority/majority cultural interaction is much more complex than this and often minority groups do not wish to give up cultural practices and associated meanings.

It is because individuals form their identities within cultures that 'commonsense' advice exhorting individuals to adopt healthier habits can have limited effects. Health policy and medical and social work practice needs to be culturally informed and open to negotiation with cultural minorities, as well as medically sound.

Nevertheless, it is the case that some cultural practices are unhealthy. Tobacco smoking is an obvious example. It may be that the relatively high rate of certain cancers among first generation Indian immigrants is partly due to consuming beetle nut and chewing tobacco. In such cases, health authorities and experts need to strike a balance between cultural habit and freedom and the benefits of good health to the individual and to the community.

Immigrant adjustment

Apart from cultural issues, immigrants, especially poorer ones, can face a variety of practical problems which may adversely affect their health. The main ones relate to housing and employment referred to above (see pp. 224-8). Finding work and accommodation – and then perhaps trying to improve both – can be stressful. Rory Williams' study *The Health of the Irish in Britain* (1992) suggests that females fare better than males both in health terms and in terms of achieving upward social mobility. It may be that the two are connected.

Again, it is clear that minority ethnic health issues are complex – not only do class and cultural factors interweave, but the gendering of health varies between ethnic groups (see below).

Racial discrimination/racial stereotyping/institutional racism

Intentional and conscious racial discrimination in the public services is illegal and assertions that it is occurring should not be lightly made. It is not easy to know how much intentional discrimination occurs in the health services. However, the concepts of racial stereotyping and institutional racism both allow for the possibility that people can be discriminated against without those who discriminate being fully aware of what they are doing or of the effects of their behaviour.

Thus, Isobel Bowler found a range of stereotypes among a group of midwives. She interviewed 25 midwives and made observations in maternity wards over a three month period. Most of the patients were Moslems of Pakistani or Bangladeshi origin. One stereotype was that the patients were rude and unintelligent. This stereotype was largely constructed on the basis that the women could not understand English – even though the midwives often used professional jargon (e.g., 'waterworks'). A second stereotype, was that the women were abusing the system by having too many children. A suggested solution by some was that the Asian mothers needed to use contraception. A third stereotype was that the women made a lot of fuss. Some midwives held the view that the patients had low pain thresholds.

Bowler comments that such stereotyping can lead to a poor midwife-patient relationship and therefore affect the quality of care.

One of the most frequently discussed areas in relation to racial stereotyping and ill-health, is the high rate of diagnosis of schizophrenia of Afro-Caribbeans and Asians (but also of other ethnic minorities). Aspects of this matter are discussed later (see p. 433). Here the issue of institutional racism and health can be introduced by briefly examining the forms of treatment received by non-white minorities following diagnosis. According to Bhat, they are likely to receive different treatments in three ways: they are more likely to be compulsorily hospitalised under the Mental Health Act; they are more likely to experience severe forms of treatment such as electro-convulsive therapy and intra-muscular medication; and Afro-Caribbeans, in particular, are more likely to be placed in secure units. Institutional racism occurs when procedures appropriate for one group are applied without consideration or adjustment to another, different group. There must be at least a strong possibility that something of this kind is happening in relation to the diagnosis and treatment of schizophrenia in relation to ethnic minorities. Reading 2 illustrates that matters can be very different in other cultural and institutional contexts.

Questions

1 Why is health in Britain not equally 'distributed' across the population?
2 Present and explain one of the following areas of health inequality:
 • Class
 • Gender
 • Ethnicity.

Mental health and illness

Psychiatry

The biomedical model of medicine is perhaps most sternly tested in its application to mental illness. The classic example of this model in mental health is the psychiatric hospital which commonly relies on drug-based treatments. First, the organic basis, if any, of a mental illness is much harder to establish than in physical illness. Thus, chemical changes in the brain seem to accompany schizophrenia, but precisely what relationship these have to the values, attitudes and behaviours of schizophrenia is quite unclear. Second, partly because the etiology (causes) of mental illness are so unclear, effective scientific treatments of mental illnesses have proved particularly difficult to develop. Third, the very label mental illness has been called into question in a way that reference to physical illness could hardly be questioned (see below). Fourth, there is evidence that sometimes those who claim to be able to recognise scientifically (diagnose) the symptoms of mental illness cannot do so reliably.

Rosenhan: questioning labels

The previous point requires substantiation as it implies scepticism of a body of 'expert' opinion which is widely, though far from universally, accepted. D L Rosenhan's *On Being Sane in Insane Places* (1978) reports two experiments which test the claims of scientific psychiatry on its own traditional territory, the psychiatric hospital. The first experiment describes how eight sane people gained secret admission to twelve different hospitals. Apart from alleging certain symptoms, the falsifying name, vocation and employment, no further alterations were made. After admission – which was gained in every case – the pseudopatient ceased simulating any symptoms of abnormality. Despite their normal behaviour following admission, none of the pseudopatients were detected. All, apart from one, were admitted with the diagnosis of schizophrenia, and each was discharged, not as wrongly diagnosed, but with a diagnosis of schizophrenia 'in remission'. Length of hospitalisations ranged from seven to 52 days, with an average of nineteen. Rosenhan comments:

> The label 'in remission' should in no way be dismissed as a formality, for at no time during any hospitalisation had any question been raised about any pseudopatient's simulation. Nor are there any indications in the hospital records that the pseudopatient's status was suspect. Rather, the evidence is strong that, once labelled schizophrenic, the pseudopatient was stuck with that label.
>
> (Rosenhan, 1978)

As Rosenhan observes, whereas labels of physical illness are not commonly pejorative, psychiatric labels are. The failure of the psychiatrists to change their diagnosis contrasts vividly with the observations of many ward patients that the pseudopatients were normal (35 out of 118 patients made comments to this effect on the first three cases, when accurate counts were kept).

The reports of the pseudopatients also provide data on the experience of being in a psychiatric hospital. The fact that patients appear to have made more accurate observations than psychiatrists on the conditions of the pseudopatients indicates that their experience in relation to the hospital power structure was profoundly de-personalising. In this respect, the findings complement those of Erving Goffman's study *Asylum* to which Rosenhan sympathetically refers (see pp. 291-2).

In critically scrutinising his own findings, Rosenhan raises the possibility that there may be a tendency in psychiatry, as in medicine, to diagnose illness rather than health – 'to be on the safe side' (referred to by statisticians as the type two error – a false positive). An experiment was therefore arranged to test the reverse tendency – to diagnose the (supposedly) insane as sane. The staff at a research and teaching hospital were told that in the course of the next three months, one or more pseudopatients would attempt to gain admittance. Staff were asked to rate each patient according to likelihood of pseudopatient status on a scale of one to ten, with one and two reflecting high confidence that the person was a pseudopatient. Judgements were obtained on 193 patients from all staff with whom they had contact – attendants, nurses, psychiatrists, physicians and psychologists. 41 were considered with high confidence to be pseudopatients by at least one member of staff, 23 judged suspect by at least one psychiatrist, and nineteen suspected by one psychiatrist and one member of staff. In fact, no pseudopatients from Rosenhan's group presented themselves during this period. Rosenhan comments:

> The experiment is instructive. It indicates that the tendency to designate sane people as insane, can be reversed when the stakes (in this case, prestige and diagnostic acumen) are high. But what can be said of the nineteen people who were suspected of being 'sane' by one psychiatrist and another staff member? Were these people truly 'sane', or was it rather the case that in the course of avoiding the type two error the staff tended to make more errors of the first sort – calling the crazy 'sane'? There is no way of knowing. But one thing is certain: any diagnostic process that lends itself so readily to massive errors of this sort cannot be a very reliable one.
>
> (Rosenhan, 1978)

Schizophrenia, ethnic minorities and labelling

It is now well established that in Britain people of Afro-Caribbean and Asian origin are much more likely to be diagnosed as schizophrenic than white Britons. Estimates vary greatly on the extent, but the difference may be around five times more for Afro-Caribbeans and three times more for Asians (Bhat, 1988). How can such a degree of difference be accounted for?

One possibility is that many of the diagnoses are wrong and occur because of cultural misunderstanding or racism (i.e. labelling). However, in evidence to the House of Commons Health Committee, Professor Roger Sims argued that the diagnoses are correct:

> There is very solid research evidence to show schizophrenia has a very much increased prevalence among second generation Afro-Caribbean people. I mean prevalence, not diagnosis. Most sound opinion would suggest the diagnosis is correct.

A policy paper from MIND, the mental health charity puts an alternative view:

> The accuracy of such diagnoses is questionable. The medical basis of psychiatry allows little room for racism. Stereotypical assumptions about black people and lack of understanding about different cultures further affect accuracy of diagnosis.
>
> (reported in The Guardian, 8.6.1993).

Matters are further complicated by the fact that the incidence of schizophrenia is higher among all ethnic minorities, not just Afro-Caribbean. This suggests that a variety of social pressures may play a part in precipitating schizophrenia.

Reading 2 explores the relevance of cultural context in recovery from schizophrenia. It reports the research of Professor Julian Leff who points out that the cultural context for recovery in the West is often less favourable than that in poorer societies.

Psychoanalysis

Szasz: the 'myth of mental illness'

In his two books, *The Myth of Mental Illness* (1960) and *The Myth of Psychotherapy* (1985), Thomas Szasz rejects altogether the labels mental illness (and the accompanying stigma) and psychotherapy (and the accompanying mystery of cure). He replaces them with the proposition that people have problems in living about which they may have conversations (i.e. seek solutions). In rejecting the biomedical model of mental illness, he insists that complexities of behaviour and communication should not be reduced to the organic level. He argues that the label mental illness obscures what in fact is a normative judgement: people call others mad when they do not like them or when they disagree with their behaviour. In his view, normative disagreements should be stated and resolved not in medical terms but in social, legal and ethical ones. Thus chronic hostility should not be seen as a mental problem but as an ethical and social one. In surveying the vast and various range of 'psychotherapies' in his more recent book, Szasz argues that most of them are of no more than some help in solving problems, rather than the comprehensive cure-alls some claim to be. At worst, some of these therapies are bogus 'rip-offs' as well as confusing and confused 'mumbo-jumbo'.

In comment, Szasz's work leaves more than a doubt that there are certain conditions and related behaviours for which the term mental illness may still be appropriate, viz. those for which no apparent rational explanation exists. Thus, the notion of mental illness could be relevant in the case of the 'schizophrenic' who murders his mother for no apparently 'rational' motive, whereas it would not apply to an otherwise 'normal' person who murders his mother for a comprehensible motive such as to speed his inheritance. Of course, to take this view, is to make judgement about what is rational, which Szasz would consider subjective. Szasz's own argument attempts to restore to normality a huge range of problems frequently regarded as instances of mental illness – depression, chronic hostility and repression. He attacks the almost religious mystique that has developed around therapy, at the centre of which is the psychotherapist as priest or guru – the only one with sacred access to the temple of psychic mysteries. Instead, he suggests that people talk about their problems – to friends or to others who may help, including, sometimes, psychotherapists.

Foucault: madness and civilisation

Michel Foucault's 'archaeological' approach to the 'history of madness' in *Madness and Civilisation* also treats mental illness in a non-judgemental way. Foucault's method is to ignore current and recent writings on madness in the past and to immerse himself in primary sources. Just as an archaeologist reassembles artefacts from the past, so Foucault reassembles cultural attitudes and ideas. He deliberately avoids defining madness because what is regarded as mad, and reactions to madness, vary from period to period. Thus, the medieval world maintained an uncertain but persistent dialogue with madness. Madness was not without meaning as the influential figure of the court 'fool' indicates. The 'Age of Reason' incarcerated the mad and madness as the unwanted opposite of its own rationality. Foucault extended his scepticism to what he takes to be a positivist approach to mental illness in our own time. Madness becomes the alienated object of science with which there is no meaningful discourse.

The social construction of mental handicap

The discussion so far in this section has repeatedly illustrated that how others think about and act towards those they perceive as mentally ill or handicapped crucially constructs the social experience and meaning of those labelled as such. The labelling and the experience can be positive or negative. This applies equally to physical as to mental handicap. The community can construct itself so that the handicapped can participate or it can, to various degrees, stigmatise and exclude them. In this respect, it is an unfortunate fact that one of the most widely disregarded of all laws is the one requiring larger firms to employ a minimum number of handicapped people.

This does not deny that the basis of some handicap is physical or biological. This is rather obviously the case where someone is blind or paralysed but equally, physical damage to the brain can cause mental handicap. Even so, there is currently a debate in the deaf community which makes one reconsider even the previous 'obvious' observation. The debate is about whether deafness should be regarded primarily as an affliction requiring cure or whether it should be regarded as part of the framework which defines the community of the deaf – and accepted as such. In any case, sociologists who deny a physical aspect of certain conditions risk alienating themselves from the wider public who – with some reason – are likely to see this position as extreme.

Four models or constructions of mental handicap

Four models or constructions of mental handicap or impairment are apparent in the last century. These fall into approximate but overlapping historical periods and each one had the endorsement of 'experts' and also became part of popular, 'commonsense' thinking. In Foucault's terms these constructions were expert discourses which became popular discourses.

Table 14.2 Social construction of mental handicap

Mental handicap as:	Key defining moment:
Threat to society (genetic model)	1913 Mental Deficiency Act
Sick people (medical model)	1946 National Health Service Act
Subnormality	1959 Mental Health Act
Special needs	1978 The Warnock Report
	1981 Education Act

(Source: Derived from D103 SS, Module 5, *Sources of Identity*)

Model 1 (genetic model)

The construction of mental illness as a threat to society reflected the influence of evolutionary interpretations of humanity dominant in the late nineteenth and early twentieth century. There was a belief that mental handicap was passed on genetically. As a result, the prime need was seen to be the segregation of the mentally handicapped from 'normal' society. This was done on a large scale in hospitals and institutions throughout the country. There is no doubt that by today's criteria many were diagnosed wrongly and had their lives wrecked as a result. In 1907 the Eugenics Society was founded aimed at improving the quality of the population. In 1911 a number of leading churchmen, politicians, academics and intellectuals called for 'the genetic control of the subnormal'.

Model 2 (medical model)

Hitler's genocidal policies towards the Jews had the effect of discrediting eugenics. In post-war Britain, a more sympathetic medical approach to mental handicap became dominant. The NHS took over existing institutions for the mentally handicapped. The full repertoire of scientific medicine – administered under professional control – in theory became available to the mentally handicapped. However, some regimes changed little and there is no shortage of grim accounts of lives lost in 'mental hospitals' in the first 30 or 40 post-war years. Further, as we have seen, powerful critiques of the use of some, or all, applications of scientific medicine to the mentally impaired were developed (see pp. 291-2 and pp. 433-4).

Model 3 (subnormality)

The 1959 Mental Health Act shifted the definition of mental disability from sickness to subnormality. In other words, the mentally impaired were seen not as sick but as not fully normal. One category of subnormality was considered to be low intelligence (i.e. an intelligence test score of below '70' where the average 'normal' score or IQ is '100').

A problem with this approach is that once an individual was measured and categorised, s/he tended to be labelled in a static way. This happened with 'normal range' children in the eleven plus which included an IQ test component. Children 'became' what their test scores 'showed' they were – winners or losers, 'bright' or 'dull'.

Model 4 (special needs)

The Warnock Report and the subsequent Education Act (1981) developed the concept that 'subnormal' people were educable and that their 'special needs' should be met. Currently, a child with special needs has the right to a *statement* saying what those needs are and what the child is entitled to. This is negotiated between, and signed by the parent(s) and local authority. The latter is then legally bound to deliver on the entitlement. However, the quality of special needs services varies between local authorities.

Special needs policy has not 'solved' the issue of how best the community should respond to handicap. The policy structures handicap in a highly individualistic way leaving the handicapped person or parents to cope with the complexities of local authority bureaucracy. Len Barton argues that in practice 'special educational needs' has become an euphemism for failure – as long as society allows the handicapped to be disabled by their learning or other difficulties, they will not enjoy equal citizenship.

Conclusion

The Union of the Physically Impaired Against Segregation (UPIAS) state that people have impairment but that *disability* is socially imposed. According to Sutherland, disabilities are imposed by society which discriminates against people with impairments by denying them the means to exercise their capabilities (1981).

Like other movements of liberation, UPIAS seeks equality. It demands that society should so construct itself that the handicapped can express themselves on an equal basis with others.

The continuing battle of the handicapped and their supporters for equality does not mean that no progress has been made in responding to their difficulties. The concept of special needs is surely better than that of genetic degeneracy. However, because the handicapped are less able than others to achieve power, their gains, such as they are, may be more precarious.

Health in poorer countries

For far more people in the poor world than in the West, health is an urgent matter of life and death. As we will see, the people most at risk are children (see pp. 611-2). It was probably the death and threat of death to children particularly, that sparked the worldwide response to famine in Ethiopia in 1985. I have attempted to cover the main policy issues concerning the health of Third World children in Chapter 20: here the emphasis is on the broader theories linking development or underdevelopment with health.

Free market approach (New Right)

Modernisation theory provides limited insight into this matter and a better starting point is the free market theory of Peter Bauer and the new Conservatism. His comments on birth control and population are pertinent to health. He criticises internationally-funded birth control programmes in the same terms that he criticises international aid – they interfere with the processes of choice and with the real limitations of circumstances which for him define socio-economic life. A first criticism of Bauer is that many (probably millions) of preventable deaths will occur if what he regards as natural forces are left to work themselves out. The chances of low wage and subsistence economies sustaining the population of poorer 'developing' countries, particularly in sub-Saharan Africa, are remote. Second, there is nothing essentially natural in the economic and social relations of the West and the rest of the world. The contrary is equally arguable. The impact of the West on many traditional societies has been chaotic and often destructive, as well as sometimes beneficial (see below). Third, it is entirely subjective (though germane to his theory) to regard help organised by governments and international agencies as somehow unnatural and interfering (see pp. 589-91 and pp. 607-8 for a more detailed account of Bauer's approach).

Social democratic approach

What differentiates liberal social democrats from Bauer and his ilk is the acceptance of the last three points. The Brandt Report (1981), for instance, takes a broadly capitalist world economy for granted but seeks to modify the negative effects of its distortions and failings. Thus, it advocates help for those exploited by, or struggling within the capitalist world economy – ultimately as a matter of 'mutual interest' (see pp. 591-2). Clearly these arguments apply more urgently to health than many other matters. On the matter of hunger and food, Brandt says simply: 'there must be an end to mass hunger and malnutrition' mainly by a combination of improving the food producing capacity of developing countries and by increasing food aid. To some extent both these policies have been implemented since the report was published.

Marxist approach

Marxist scholars argue that historical and contemporary capitalism has grossly exploited the health as well as the labour of the peoples of the Third World. Authors such as Teresa Hayter and Lesley Doyal amply illustrate that the spread of disease, slaughter and massive social and psychological disruption were typical products of European expansion. The slave trade is perhaps the most vivid example, although it was not only the enslaved whose lives and health were threatened through contact with Europeans. In the nineteenth and early twentieth century, the migrant labour system in sub-Saharan Africa resulted, in Lesley Doyal's assessment, in a deterioration in the health of the workers involved. Contact with Europeans and European diseases, the unhealthy living and working conditions imposed on the labour force, and the disruption of the traditional rural economy undermined the health of men, women and children. The argument that the economic interest of employers favoured a healthy labour force hardly applied – a common pattern was to send unhealthy workers back to their villages and simply recruit more. The break-up of families and communities, the isolation of males in labour compounds and the frequent poverty of women and children, resulted in an increase in alcoholism and prostitution. Ironically, some colonialists saw the poor and unhealthy life they had created for Africans as proof of black inferiority.

Although Marxists welcome the achievement of political independence by colonial nations, they stress that in the 'post-colonial era', the economic dependency of much of the Third World continues. Vicente Navarro's *Medicine Under Capitalism* (1976) is a study of health inequality in the Third World which complements Gunder Frank's broader theory of underdevelopment. Like Frank, he takes Latin America as his area for detailed study. In countries such as Colombia, Peru and El Salvador, he typically finds urban enclaves of privileged bourgeois consumption and largely poor and exploited rural areas. In health terms, this translates into the consumption of largely private, curative medicine for the urban rich and a lack of investment in preventive measures, such as water and sewage projects that would benefit the rural majority. Nor is the wider development that might ultimately benefit the standard of living and health of the majority occurring:

> *The industrial sector ... is controlled by and functions for the lumpen-bourgeoisie and its foreign counterparts, not for the benefit of the development of the whole of the individual country.*
>
> (Navarro, 1976:41)

Communist China provides an interesting example of a socialist solution to the health problems of a developing nation. When the communists came to power in 1949, they were faced with widespread famine and disease and a broken-down and inadequate system of medical care. Emphasis was put on sanitation and other forms of prevention such as inoculation and the Chinese also developed a tiered medical system which has been an influential model to other developing socialist societies. The base of the system is made up of the tens of thousands of 'barefoot' doctors who provide a basic medical service designed to reach all the peasantry. They receive a maximum of eighteen months training which combines Western medicine with traditional Chinese medicine, particularly herbal treatment and acupuncture. In addition, the doctors stress the role of personal and communal responsibility for health. A similar system of grassroots medical care operates in urban areas, but here more developed and professional facilities are usually available. Medical problems that cannot be treated by a 'barefoot' doctor can be referred to more fully trained doctors and nurses. Hospitalisation is also possible where necessary. Part of the cost of the Chinese health system is financed by individual payments or insurance, nevertheless, it seems broadly egalitarian and effective.

Conservative health policy, 1979-96

Great controversy surrounded the Conservative government's health reforms introduced in the 1980s and implemented in the 1990s. These reforms made radical changes in the NHS but the aims behind them were consistent with those of the first two Thatcher governments in relation to health policy.

In the early 1980s, government ministers frequently emphasised the need for efficiency and value for money in the public services, including health. This was a change from previous prime concern with inequalities of health. The government was acutely conscious of the increased demands an ageing population would continue to put on the NHS. Several policies had a major cost-cutting element about them including a sharp reduction in the amount of time patients spent in hospital, a reduction of 25 per cent in the number of hospital beds between 1977 and 1989, and the community care policy (see p. 398). Nevertheless, overall spending on the NHS more or less kept pace with the rise in gross domestic product during the 1980s (see Figure 14.10). This was partly because short-stay hospital visits greatly increased in numbers.

By the late 1980s, the government was looking for new ways to increase efficiency (or productivity) and keep costs down in the NHS. As described Chapter 13, it was during this period that the strategy of introducing quasi-markets into the public services was adopted (see pp. 297-8). A quasi-market is an attempt to introduce the conditions of the free market into the public sector, including public services. Quasi-markets in the public sector are often referred to as internal markets. Before examining how this strategy has been applied to health, it is necessary to be clear about the organisational structure of the NHS (see Figure 14.11).

In outline, the structure of the NHS in 1990 was not

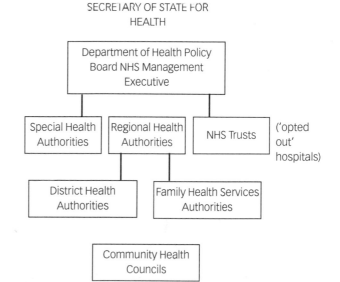

Figure 14.11 Health markets within the NHS

fundamentally different from what it had been since it was set up in 1948 (see p. 422-3): The Secretary of State for Health is at the top of the managerial chain and is responsible to Parliament. The fourteen Regional Authorities are responsible for planning the development of services within national guidelines. They allocate resources to, and monitor the performance of District Health Authorities and Family Health Services Authorities. The District Health Authorities are responsible for purchasing hospital and community health services for their residents. The DHAs work closely with Family Health Services Authorities which manage the 'grassroots' services of general medical practitioners, general dental practitioners, retail pharmacists, and opticians. Hospitals which have opted for the new trust status (see Figure 14.12) are not contractually tied to DHAs to deliver hospital services to the local area, as other hospitals are. They can deliver their services 'in the market' – to any DHA, fundholding GP (see below) or private individual (in the latter case they cannot use NHS funds although some access to NHS facilities and equipment is allowed). Briefly, Special Health Authorities have very particular purposes, such as overseeing medical training. The Community Health Councils are advisory bodies representing the public interest which are outside the NHS management chain.

Some further description is required in order to clarify how a quasi-market has been introduced into the NHS. The quasi-market operates mainly through NHS Hospital Trusts, described above, and through those General Medical Practitioners (local doctors) who have been given their own budgets to administer (51 per cent of the total by 1996). In both cases, funding comes from central government. Unlike other doctors, budget holding doctors are not managed by DHAs but can buy hospital services for their patients wherever they choose – from trusts, private hospitals, or the few remaining directly managed units (hospitals) of the District Health Authorities. Figure 14.12 compares and contrasts

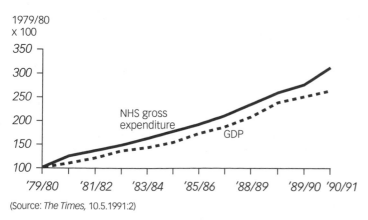

1979/80 x 100

(Source: *The Times,* 10.5.1991:2)

Figure 14.10 NHS spending compared to GDP

the situation of non-budget and budget holding GPs. A new system of purchasers and providers was thus created – to fuel the new NHS market. Both fund holding GPs and District Health Authorities were able to 'shop around' the hospitals to buy services for their patients.

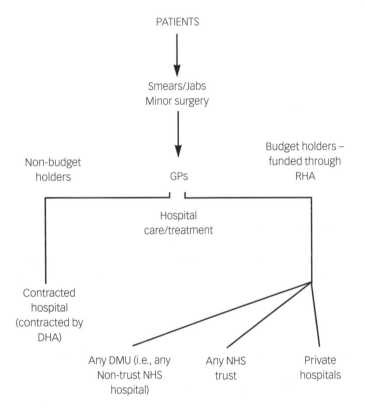

Figure 14.12 Organisation of the NHS in England, 1990

Table 14.3 Public and private health spending: a comparison

Spending on Health as a Percentage of GDP, 1989		Total Health Spending, 1987	
		Public	Private
8.7	France	74.7	25.3
8.2	Germany	78.4	21.6
6.7	Japan	72.9	27.1
8.3	Netherlands	73.8	26.2
6.3	Spain	71	29
8.8	Sweden	90	9.28
5.8	UK	86.4	13.6
11.8	US	41.4	58.6

(Source: OECD)

The Conservative health reforms: for and against

The aim of the above reforms is to limit the cost of health services without cutting patient care or, put simply, to increase productivity in the provision of health services. The mechanism for doing this is to introduce an element of competition by creating a limited medical marketplace. Only time will establish whether effectiveness and fairness is achieved by the reforms.

Was there need for the above changes or are they more the product of a stubborn commitment to right-wing ideology? The Conservative government has not been able to claim that the National Health Service has been expensive compared to the cost of 'delivering' health in other advanced countries. As Table 14.3 shows, spending on health as a percentage of the gross national product is exceptionally low. Moreover, it is clear that this economy has been achieved overwhelmingly within the public sector as the private health sector in Britain, although steadily expanding, is still relatively small.

Such seemingly impressive figures of the NHS do not mean that greater improvement is impossible. The Conservatives have pointed to the fact that considerable differences between districts in the length of waiting lists and, more controversially, success in specific treatments existed prior to their reforms. Table 14.4 illustrates the more extreme differences in relation to waiting lists for general surgery.

The assumption behind the reforms is that under the new competitive regime within the NHS there will be an all-round improvement in the performance of hospitals and particularly of the less efficient ones.

A common criticism of the reforms made by opposing politicians is that they have created a 'two tier health service'. GP budget holders are able to buy 'the best' whereas non-budget holders are contracted to a specific hospital. This criticism has been heard less often as more and more GPs have become budget holders. However, the new health market remains an issue (see below).

Chris Ham: a review of the Conservative health reforms

In a review of the Conservative reforms, Chris Ham argues three aspects are worth keeping. They are:

1 Maintaining the closer connections between GPs and Health authorities.
2 Maintaining health targets (introduced in 1992).
3 Maintaining a separation between the roles of purchasers and providers.

These will be discussed in turn, with appropriate elaboration and comment.

Table 14.4 Health districts with some of the longest and shortest waiting lists for general surgery (March 1989) – showing inequalities and inconsistencies in the pre-reformed NHS

District	Patients on list	Waiting over a year (Percentage)
East Cumbria	1,262	42
Hull	1,515	51
North Herts	1,415	46
West Essex	2,332	45
Brentwood	2,363	44
West Lambeth	872	72
NE Hants	903	52
Salisbury	969	51
Bristol	2,296	52
Oldham	1,661	45
St Helens	237	0
Halton	115	1
NW Durham	113	1
East Yorks	293	0
Bassetlaw	82	0
Cambridge	361	3
SW Herts	267	0
West Dorset	471	7
Southmead	58	19
Bromsgrove	263	0

(Source: *The Guardian*, 2.8.1990:2)

1 GPs and Health Authorities

GPs have more power and resources to provide primary care. More nurses, physiotherapists and counsellors are now employed by GPs. Ham also notes an increase in health promotion in general practice and an increase in the number of special clinics. He sees a crucial and welcome 'shift (in) the balance of power' in the provision of services from hospitals to GPs.

2 Health targets

Ham supports the policy of establishing Health of the Nation Targets. He sees this as a shift away from cure to prevention. Most would agree with this in principle and it is obvious that if targets

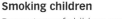
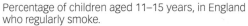

Smoking children

Percentage of children aged 11–15 years, in England who regularly smoke.

Target by 1994 (less than 5%)

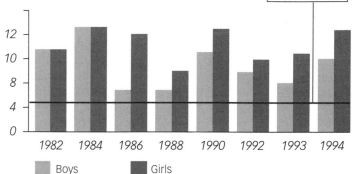

Boys Girls

Weight of the nation

Percentage overweight

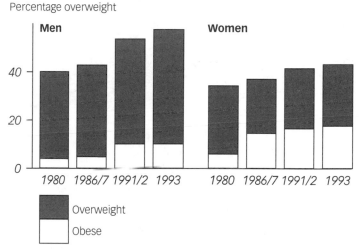

Overweight
Obese

(Source: Department of Health in *The Guardian*, 20.7.1995:6)

Figure 14.13 British way of health

are not met or are insufficiently demanding then questions should be asked. So far (1996), the government's record in this area has been mixed. The targets for the year 2000 in smoking, excessive drinking and obesity seem likely to be missed (see Figure 14.13).

Figures from the 1994 General Household Survey provide data for assessing progress towards health targets. After dropping between 1990 and 1993, smoking among eleven to fifteen year olds, both male and female, increased 1993 and 1994. More optimistically, the prevalence of cigarette smoking among adults continues to fall but recently at a reduced rate among males for whom there has been a recent slight increase in lung cancer. Also on the positive side is a downward trend on the suicide rate and in sexually transmitted diseases.

The target to reduce obesity by 2005 is a reduction of about one third: from twelve per cent to eight per cent of women and for seven per cent to six per cent of men. In 1993 obesity among women had increased to sixteen per cent with overweight also an expanding problem. However, heart disease, to which both obesity and smoking can contribute, dropped by eleven per cent between 1993 and 1994.

Percentage drinking more than the then recommended sensible limit: England

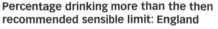

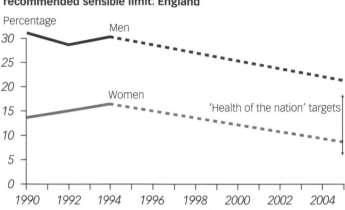

Prevalence of cigarette smoking in England

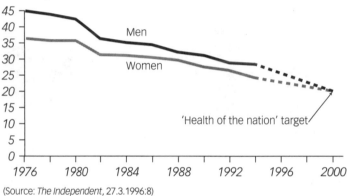

(Source: *The Independent*, 27.3.1996:8)

Figure 14.14 Targets and trends in drink and smoking

In 1994, the steady rise continued in the numbers for both sexes drinking above what were then described as sensible limits. The unbroken lines in Figure 14.14 show actual trends and the broken line shows the target line. Nikki Bennette, the head of the General Household Survey from which the data for Figure 14.14 are taken, commented in reference to women:

> *Alcohol is more readily available, but women also have increased independence and wider social lives now that more are working. More women have moved to college and away from home at an earlier age.*
>
> *(Quoted in The Independent: 27.3.1996:8)*

In 1996, the government adjusted upwards its targets for alcohol consumption.

In part, the government's approach to improving the health of the nation has been an individualist one. Information has been provided, advice indicated and it then becomes up to the individual to act 'sensibly'.

Critics say that this approach is insufficient. One suggestion is to ban cigarette advertising altogether but this has been specifically rejected by the Conservative government which prefers to pursue a strategy of deterrence through increasing the rate of tax on tobacco.

In the long run, diet is a more fundamental issue than smoking. It is not difficult to argue a social as well as an individual aspect to this matter. First, we have already seen that good quality food is often more difficult to access in poorer areas (just as cash points are). Further, the poor can less afford to travel to buy food and often do not have any means of carrying bulk purchases. Urban planning and transport policy could help with this problem. Second, legislation already exists to ensure the quality of food products in certain respects. Given the damage that excess sugar intake can do, might there not be a case to legislate to reduce the sugar content in a range of basic items, not least products favoured by children such as baked beans and 'hula-hoops'. Finally, is the argument about advertising. Advertising is primarily about creating images to sell the products of capitalism. It is at the heart of capitalism and of many critiques of capitalism. Arguably, the balance of advertising is far too heavily skewed towards image rather than information – albeit that advertisements are required to be 'legal, decent, honest and truthful'. Still, the best advice in relation to many products is – read the small print.

3 The separation of the purchaser/provider roles (i.e. the health market)

Chris Ham supports the purchaser/provider system introduced by the Conservatives. He states that:

> *It is this that lies behind the shift in the balance of power within the NHS and which has enabled weaknesses in service delivery to be addressed. To propose the return of the NHS trusts to management by health authorities would be to run the risk of providers recapturing control over resource allocation. This must be avoided if there is to be capacity within the NHS to strengthen health services still further.*

In effect, Ham welcomes the new NHS market. He considers that power in hospitals is better in the hands of managers than consultants (whose power has been a long standing issue in the NHS). As already stated, he also welcomes the new independence of budget-holding GPs. We will examine the views of John Gray who does not (see below). However, Ham does have some reservations about the sharp increase in *managerial* costs in the reformed NHS. Without being specific, he calls for 'a much greater measure of local democracy' in terms of managerial accountability.

John Gray: abolish the NHS market structure

The potential tension and conflict between managers and professionals has been discussed previously in this book (see pp. 299-300 and pp. 302-3). Following the Conservative education reforms of 1988 and health reforms of 1990, these two areas have experienced major conflict between these two groups. Just as Chris Ham gives decisive, if qualified, support to the new management system in the NHS, John Gray decisively opposes it.

Gray opposes the 'Tory managerial revolution' in the NHS (and elsewhere) essentially on traditional grounds (*The Guardian*, 5.1.1995:6). First, he considers that the NHS worked well 'on a basis of professional ethos and a sense of public service'. Second, he finds the new managerial system to be self-seeking and bureaucratic. Evidence to support his case is available in that, like education managers, the new NHS managers tended to award themselves very high salary increases, and in 1992 the number of managers in the NHS increased by 25 per cent against virtually no growth in medical staff.

The term Gray uses to describe the organisational principle on which the new NHS is operated is 'market corporation'. It is a term which conveys the irony and contempt he feels for what has occurred. He argues that Thatcherism sought to put an end to the corporation of the 1960s and 1970s and yet has replaced this with its own version of the managed society.

In comment, Gray does not deal with the problems of the NHS when it was – at hospital level – largely dominated by consultants. They, too, were and are well paid. It was also in their interests to allow long waiting lists to build up so that wealthy patients could be creamed off for private treatment. Rudolph Klein has said, consultants and managers are now forced 'to get into bed together' – although it is not yet clear that this will benefit the public.

Conclusion: markets, equity and resources

The new managerial jargon of targets and efficiency should not allow us to forget that the aim of the NHS is (or was?) equitable or fair treatment for all. John Gray's strongest point is that the public seemed to trust the old NHS and much less so the reformed NHS. The reality is that both systems harbour inefficiencies and inequities. Ideology aside, what is likely to satisfy the public is a system that is fair and seen to be fair in delivering health services and, second, is as efficient as possible. It will be the job of the government elected in 1997 to establish an organisational structure – perhaps of a hybrid kind – which achieves these goals. By definition, such a system will clarify where resources need to be directed and, given the rather average health of the nation, increased.

Questions

1 Discuss with illustrations the application of the concept of social construction to 'mental handicap'.
2 'The National Health Service did not provide equal access to health services before the Conservative market reforms and it still does not do so.' Discuss.

Summary

1 A distinction is made between illness and disease. Illness is a subjectively felt state of ill-health whereas disease is socially defined, usually by experts such as doctors.
2 There are several broad cultural paradigms or perspectives of health in addition to established sociological and social policy perspectives. The following cultural perspectives are discussed:
   • Magical and religious;
   • Modern scientific;
   • Holistic.
3 Magical explanations of ill-health explain it in terms of witchcraft or sorcery. Purely religious explanations do so in terms of divine intervention. Modern scientific theory of health and disease is based on the premise that the latter is caused by an outside agency (usually a germ). Holistic medicine understands health and illness not merely in biomedical terms but in a total personal and cultural context.
4 Among the main sociological approaches to health are:
   • Marxist;
   • Functionalist;
   • Interactionist;
   • Liberal reformist and free market.

The Marxist approach is summarised in point 9. Functionalist perspective sees 'mass' health policies as functional in maintaining the labour force and as adaptation to popular pressure. Interactionist perspective stresses that outcomes in treatment and health are partly the product of negotiation between medical personnel and patients. Liberal reformist and free market liberal approaches differ in the way in which they consider health resources should be distributed.

5 The National Health Service was established to improve the health of the British people. However inequalities of health remain reflecting the following factors:
   1 Sectoral differences within the NHS.
   2 Regional differences in resourcing and in standards of health.
   3 Class.
   4 Gender.
   5 Ethnic differences.
6 There is overwhelming evidence of a correlation between class factors and ill health. Marxists argue that the inequalities and exploitation of the capitalist system cause ill-health. Others point out that certain inequalities were not being reduced in former communist societies.
7 The important issue of women as providers of informal and largely unpaid (health) care and the price they pay for doing this work is dealt with in other sections of this book (see pp. 408-9). In this chapter, the relative health of males and females, the medicalisation of childbirth and, briefly, the lack of power of women within the medical profession are dealt with.

8 The debates within mental health and illness echo those within the area of health as a whole. The traditional psychiatric model of mental illness seeks physical causes and solutions to 'the problem'. Within psychoanalysis more social and humanistic approaches occur.

9 The important issue of mortality rates in undeveloped countries is dealt with in Chapter 20. In this chapter free market, social democratic and Marxist perspectives on the relationship between development and health are discussed. One free market view is that attempts to 'help' the undeveloped world simply hinder the 'natural' processes by which people flourish or not. It is precisely the processes of the capitalist world market that Marxists see as injurious to people in the undeveloped world. Social democrats argue that a combination of aid and market adjustment can contribute to improvements in health.

10 The health policy of the Conservative governments was less concerned with inequalities in health than with achieving cost efficient delivery of health care. The attempt to do this was based on the introduction of elements of the free market within the NHS and by strengthening management. Views for and against this and other aspects of Conservative policy are discussed.

Research and coursework

This topic offers possibilities for both micro and macro level research – and for linking the two. At a micro level a comparison could be made between the informal caring done by an appropriately matched middle aged woman and man (possibly two or three pairs). The research could be carried out by interview, perhaps observation, and some element of quantification of care might be introduced. Another area appropriate to small-scale research is the interaction/negotiation between doctor/patient or nurse/patient.

At a macro level, the 'politics of health' offer possibilities for theoretical-historical analysis. Particularly interesting is the relationship between the health ideologies of various political parties and their policies when in office.

Further reading

Peter Aggleton's *The Sociology of Health* (Tavistock, 1990) is a standard introduction to the area. A simple non-sociological introduction to recent (1980s/90s) changes in the NHS is Chris Ham's *The New National Health Service* (Radcliffe Medical Press, 1991).

Readings

Reading 1
Why the Poor Eat Badly

From Judy Jones, 'The Bad Food Trap', in *The Observer*, 21.12.1995:23 (slightly adapted)

It was a revelation when Graham Haines first brought cut-price fruit and vegetables to the council estates of Tipton. People would peer into his van, point at the celery and ask: 'What on earth's *that*?'

Deprivation in this part of the Black Country was, and remains, deeply ingrained. In many of its streets, car ownership and a working head of household are the exception rather than the rule. But there's a much more fundamental problem, largely hidden behind closed doors and in high-rise towers. The time-bomb ticking away in Tipton – and in thousands of other urban communities, impoverished by a decade and more of industrial decline – is malnutrition.

It's a word we associate with the bloated bellies of people starving in the Third World. But a group of top nutritionists, food scientists and civil servants, brought together by the Government, has concluded it is happening here, and that 'whole communities' are suffering from it. No one knows how many this means, but it is likely to run into millions.

The healthy-eating boom that swept muesli-belt Middle England through the 1980s by-passed Tipton. Money was too tight. Like thousands of other communities across Britain, it had been transformed by the exodus of the big supermarkets to out-of-town greenfield sites into what the experts call a 'fresh food desert'.

Tipton is part of Sandwell, in the heart of the Black Country, the third most deprived English borough outside London. Dereliction and decay is never far from one's gaze. Car ownership is the exception in many streets, where large numbers of unemployed, elderly, lone parents, disabled and long-term sick people live.

Alarmed at the grinding poverty, ill-health and the appalling diets of thousands of its people, a group of residents got together and decided to do something. Two years ago, they formed the Sandwell Food Co-operative. They decided that if the people couldn't get to the fresh food, the only sensible solution was to bring it to them. The result was Graham and his van.

Thanks to the promise of funding over five yeas, an annual £38,000, from the local health authority, more than 500 low-income families are now benefiting from taking matters into their own hands – by growing their own food on unused land. The Salford and Sandwell schemes are among more than 80 food co-ops around the country set up to bring fresh food to poor people. They have taken root as the number of food shops in Britain decreased by 35 per cent between 1980 and 1992, and the number of superstores on the outskirts of towns increased four-fold.

Much of this grassroots action is directed at schools in areas where cooking skills and food education have virtually disappeared. Children commonly emerge into independent adult life totally ignorant of the rudiments of cooking and eating healthily. The income of the poorest ten per cent fell from £73 a week to £61 in real terms (after housing costs) between 1979 and 1991, according to an Institute of Fiscal Studies report in 1994. Put another way, the number living on less than half average earnings – the EU definition of poverty – was five million in 1979, compared with thirteen million in 1990. The Government has never accepted that UK poverty exists, preferring instead to refer coyly to 'health inequalities' and 'low-income families'.

Some blame the poor for not feeding themselves properly. A model diet, so the argument goes, is that of the average Mediterranean peasant – lots of pasta, fresh vegetables, bread and cheese. It is easy to eat well on a modest income, the theory goes. So why is it that millions don't?

Some, of course, choose to ignore the message, and not just among the ranks of the poor. But for millions there is no choice – in short, they cannot afford what goes hand in hand with getting a good diet.

'A family without a car or access to public transport is much more dependent on small local shops where the range of fresh produce is smaller and the prices higher than in an out-of-town supermarket,' said Suzi Leather, nutrition consultant to the National Consumer Council. 'They often have less storage, fridge and freezer facilities, and may be concerned to save money on power for cooking.'

In Britain, the average household spends about seventeen per cent of its income on food. Surveys suggest that the poorest need to spend between a quarter and a half. In September 1994, Sainsburys compiled a low-income shopping basket for a family of four costing £11.66 a week per person. In the same year, the average two-child family was living on benefits of £113.05 a week so the Sainsbury's basket would take a 40 per cent chunk of income.

Poor parents routinely go without proper meals, snacking instead on a 'tea and toast' diet, so that their children may eat, surveys have repeatedly shown. Nearly half of parents using family centres run by NCH Action for Children regularly do so, according to research by the charity.

Maureen is bringing up her eight-year-old son alone in her former council flat in Devon on £77.95 state benefits a week. Her fixed outgoings, including debt repayments, top £65.54 which leaves per precisely £12.41 to feed herself and her boy. 'I might go two days without a main meal – I just eat, like, a sandwich at lunchtime and at supper if we have enough bread. Thursday is my best day. I collect my Giro cheque then. I usually buy something like mince and we'll have spaghetti or something. I might have one banana a week. That's the only fruit.' Her son has learned not to ask for biscuits or sweets. 'Sometimes when he has said to me he's hungry, I just feel very desperate and alone … and a bit of a failure, really.'

Questions

1 What explanations can you give for why the poor eat badly?
2 Describe and assess the effectiveness of the 'Tipton' response.

Reading 2
Schizophrenia and labelling

From Glenda Cooper, 'Mentally ill do better in Third World than in West', in *The Independent*, 22.2.1996:9

People who suffer from schizophrenia in the Third World are twice as likely to recover as sufferers in the West, according to a report by the World Health Organisation.

Stigma and lack of strong family networks mean that only fifteen per cent of schizophrenics in the West are likely to have made a good recovery from the first attack of their illness compared with 37 per cent of those in underdeveloped countries, Professor Julian Leff told the Royal College of Psychiatrists yesterday.

The college, in collaboration with the National Schizophrenia Fellowship (NSF), was launching a leaflet, *Help is at Hand*, which aims to educate the public about the disease. Some 250,000 people suffer from the illness in the United kingdom.

No one knows what causes schizophrenia, a group of psychotic illnesses characterised by disturbed thinking, emotional reactions and behaviours. But there is a genetic link, with a child of a schizophrenic having a twelve per cent chance of also suffering.

Professor Leff, of the Institute of Psychiatry in London, told the RCP that whereas fourteen per cent of schizophrenics in Dublin and 29 per cent of those in Nottingham would have a good outcome after two years, 51 per cent of those in Ibadan, Nigeria, and 54 per cent of those in Agra, north India, would recover. The worst affected places were Honolulu (3.5 per cent), Nagasaki (5.7 per cent) and Moscow (7.9 per cent).

'In the West, about one in four people recover very well from a first attack of the illness and remain well for many years. In non-Western countries the outcome is conspicuously better; about one in two people do well,' Professor Leff said.

He said the outcome was better in the latter because of strong support networks, the opportunity to work and lack of stigma in areas where beliefs in witchcraft and karma mean the condition is accepted more easily.

'The large number of people in households (in developing countries) means that there is a network of people who can share the responsibility for the patient's care and recovery. There is a strong sense of duty and they all share the burden. In the West you are more likely to find a middle aged person with schizophrenia being cared for by one carer and the burden of emotional and physical care falls on one person.'

Cultures that avoid confrontation also worked in

schizophrenics' favour. Other advantages were the lack of competitiveness and more opportunities for unskilled labour in agrarian economies. 'Sufferers feel they are contributing to the economy and they feel valued.'

Professor Leff called for more resources, particularly more community psychiatric nurses who could work with families and sufferers.

A schizophrenic who has attempted suicide and spent two and a half years of the last decade in hospital, called for a culture change among Britain's' psychiatrists.

Janey Antonious, 38, a molecular biologist, said, 'I've found police and social workers will listen to me. But I believe there needs to be a culture change among psychiatrists and nurses, who are much harder to talk to'.

Questions

1 Describe and assess the evidence that diagnoses of schizophrenia may sometimes involve cultural labelling.
2 Why do certain cultural contexts seem more conducive to recovery from schizophrenia than others?

Note: Further material on the organisational aspects of Conservative health policy, including a reading and questions partly relating to health occurs in Chapter 10, pp. 299-300 and pp. 302-3.

The Life Course: Age and Generation (with particular reference to youth culture)

Youth, like all age stages, can be very different in different societies: traditional warriors and modern protestors

Aims of this chapter

1 To introduce and explain the concept of the life course and related concepts.

2 To review post-war youth culture and subcultures in the light of various theoretical approaches.

3 Specifically to compare the continuities and differences between 1960s and 1990s youth.

Terminology: the social construction of the life course and age stages

The term 'life course' has become the over-arching concept within sociology for the consideration of matters relating to age and generation. Life course refers to the whole span of a person's life whether it be long or short. Gaynor Cohen explains why the term life course is now generally preferred to that of 'life cycle':

> The term 'life course' is used here rather than the more familiar 'life cycle' as the latter implies fixed categories in the life of the individual and assumes a stable social system, whereas the former allows of more flexible biographical patterns within a continually changing social system.
>
> (Social Change and the Life Course 1987:1)

So, a life course approach takes into consideration the variety of personal history and action (biography) and allows for the likelihood that the relationship between age groups such as youth or the old, and society, will change constantly. The life course is roughly structured into *age stages* which vary over time and across cultures. Therefore, when references are made below to the 'age stages' such as childhood, youth, young adulthood, middle age and old age, it should be remembered that each individual experiences and 'negotiates' these stages differently and that the stages themselves change over time ('childhood', according to Ariès 'did not exist' as a social category in the middle ages – see below). Sociologists, then, are interested in age stages primarily as social, not as biological or chronological categories, i.e. they study the *social construction of age*. Again, Cohen presents these points clearly:

> The life course is like a bus journey punctuated by stages, with boarding and embarkation points ... (T)hese stages are not fixed, have changed in length in response to wider social change, and ... new stages have emerged. The boarding and embarkation points for childhood, youth, and mid life have either lengthened or shortened over time and vary according to region or culture.
>
> (3)

Figure 15.1 illustrates how social circumstances affected the life of a poorer person at given points in the late Victorian period – a pattern modified but not eradicated by the Welfare State.

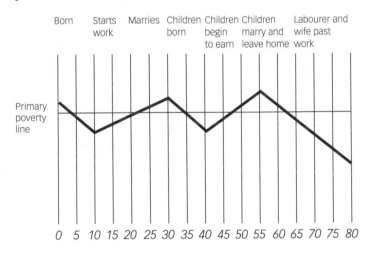

The variety of age stages will become clear with reference to the historical and comparative material examined in this chapter.

(Source: Adapted from Rowntree, 1901; in Abrams 1978:9)

Figure 15.1 Poverty and the life course

Perspectives on age stages and the life course with particular reference to youth

In general, contemporary sociologists approach the study of the life course and of particular age stages within it broadly along the lines indicated above by Gaynor Cohen. They adopt a perspective which recognises that the experience of age groups is socially constructed by, for instance, the state of the economy, including availability of work, but also consider more than was common in the past how individuals and groups cope and make sense of the situations which confront them. For instance, such an integrated perspective underpins a largescale longitudinal study of 5000 young people growing up in four labour markets which was funded by the Economic and Social Research Council (M Banks *et al.*, *Careers: Identities*, 1993). The authors' description of their approach is typical of contemporary sociological perspective on the life course and on youth in particular. They state that they want to study 'the ways young people approach adulthood and the kinds of adults they become' and that they 'wanted to discover how young people find their niche in the economic and occupational structure and how they form political judgements and make political choices' (ix). Thus, young people (and members of other age groups) are perceived as agents acting within and potentially changing structures.

If contemporary approaches to the life course seem so promising, why bother with others. First, previously popular approaches, such as Functionalist and Marxist, do still provide useful insights. Second, it is possible to combine the latter approaches with contemporary ones – and some sociologists do. Third – a more general point – the way sociologists saw matters in the past often says as much about them as about what they were commenting on. Thus, the 'gender blind', neo-Marxist sociology of youth of the 1960s and 1970s which concentrated almost exclusively on young males can now clearly be seen as patriarchal in a patriarchal society.

Biological and psychological perspectives

Almost one hundred years ago, G Stanley Hall suggested that 'adolescence' is 'naturally' a period of psychological 'storm and stress'. Sociologists tend to be highly cautious about assertions that behaviour is biologically pre-programmed and offer alternative sociological evidence and explanation. In fact, the emotional experience of youth varies greatly between individuals and across cultures. Where youthful turmoil does occur an alternative sociological hypothesis to Hall's psychological one is that conflict occurs because young people often lack power and status in relation to adults. Growing up sometimes involves a struggle to acquire these.

Erik Erikson's 'conception of the life cycle' attempts to integrate biological, psychological and sociological perspective (Table 15.1). He charts eight 'psycho-social crises', the successful or less successful resolution of which form individual character and development. Table 15.1 shows a slightly modified version of Erikson's scheme.

Erikson goes further than would most sociologists in emphasising psychological drives and innate developmental processes. However, he also observes that how development occurs is dependent on social factors and, as his model makes clear, outcomes 'unfavourable' to the individual and society are quite possible.

Nevertheless, Erikson's 'life cycle' model is open to sociological criticism. First, the data on which Erikson bases his model are very limited, especially in relation to older 'life cycle' stages. He draws largely on his own, necessarily few, in depth case studies. Second, the data problem is compounded because Erikson over-universalises his model. Judith Stevens-Long suggests that his

Table 15.1 Eight stages of psycho-social development

Stages	Psycho-social crises	Significant social relations	Favourable outcome
1 First year of life	Trust versus mistrust	Mother or mother substitute	Trust and optimism
2 Second year	Autonomy versus doubt	Parents	Sense of self-control and adequacy
3 Third through fifth years	Initiative versus guilt	Basic family	Purpose and direction ability to initiate one's own activities
4 Sixth year to puberty	Industry versus inferiority	Neighbourhood; school	Competence in intellectual, social and physical skills
5 Adolescence	Identity versus confusion	Peer groups and outgroups; models of leadership	An integrated image of oneself as a unique person
6 Early adulthood	Intimacy versus isolation	Partners in friendship; sex, competition, co-operation	Ability to form close and lasting relationships; to make career commitments
7 Middle adulthood	Generativity versus self-absorption	Divided labour and shared household	Concern for family, society, and future generations
8 The ageing years	Integrity versus despair	'Mankind'; 'my kind'	A sense of fulfilment and satisfaction with one's life; willingness to face death

(Source: Erik Erikson, *Childhood and Society*, W W Norton, 1963, as modified in S R Hilgard *et al.*, *Introduction to Psychology*, Harcourt Brace Jovanovitch, 1979)

enthusiasm for monogamy and the nuclear family is somewhat ethnocentric, reflecting then dominant Western values rather than any truly universal ones. Further, writing before the resurgence of feminism, Erikson has what many would now regard as a stereotypical view of gender roles (see stage 7 in Table 15.1). Third, sociologists tend to be much more relativistic in their analysis of the life course. It is by no means clear that everybody experiences 'crises' that are particularly linked to stages in the 'life cycle'. Thus, the supposed crises of 'integrity versus despair' of the ageing years does not seem to occur in the lives of many apparently functional individuals.

Perhaps what is most useful in Erikson's model from a sociological perspective is his emphasis on the complex and sometimes difficult relationship between individuals, at a given age

Table 15.2 The social structuring of age in contemporary Britain

Age Stage issues	Structure	Contemporary
Childhood	Parents State (law)	Neglect Pre-schooling Abuse Poverty
Youth	Parents School Peers relationships sex Work training	(Dis)order Authority Control Commitment 'Resource'
Young adulthood	Committed relationship or not Children? Career	Stability/Divorce Responsibility Equality (Gender)
Middle age	Continued parental role, but commitments/ responsibilities reducing Key theme: Achievement/ failure	
Early old age	Retirement 'Leisure'	Marginality Wealth (or not)
Late old age	Retirement Single living	Gender Community Care Cost

stage, and society – in the form of significant individuals and social institutions and structures. In Table 15.2, I have attempted to indicate a more culturally specific framework for understanding how, in contemporary Britain, people at different age stages engage with, and negotiate socially structured issues and challenges. The table is neither complete nor incontrovertible and you may wish to 'play around' with it.

Psychology and 'problems' of youth

In the Western world, crime and suicide rates are relatively high among the young. A variety of mental disorders shows a sharp upwards incline during the teenage years. According to data assembled by Michael Rutter, these include alcoholism, schizophrenia, anorexia nervosa and depression – although only a minority actually suffer from these illnesses. No single sociological explanation would precisely cover all these phenomena but, in general, the sociological perspective is that the complexities and pressures of modern adolescence are such that signs of difficulty and instability are to be expected. Poverty and joblessness can make matters worse.

A contrary argument, put forward by Anna Freud and others, is that adolescence is naturally and universally a period of rebellion. Margaret Mead's *Coming of Age in Samoa* was an attempt to refute such theories by demonstrating that in Samoa 'adolescence represented no period of crisis or stress, but was instead an orderly developing of a set of slowly maturing interests and activities'. However Derek Freeman's formidable critique of Mead's methodology in this study undermines her claim to have found a crucial 'negative instance' of the universalist view. Mead believed that her study of 50 Samoan adolescent girls showed that in general their adolescence was orderly and constructive thus providing a 'negative instance' to invalidate the proposition that adolescence is universally problematic. However, Freeman finds that of the 25 girls Mead studied in greatest detail, four were delinquent and three at odds with their kin: a percentage total of 28. His point that this suggests quite a high level of stress and conflict seems well taken.

While, therefore, it is certainly the case that the behaviour of young people varies greatly with historical and social circumstances – certain general behavioural trends also seem to occur. Psychology can be especially useful in interpreting the latter.

Structural perspectives: functionalist, Marxist and radical

Functionalist, Marxist and radical perspectives on the life course cover a vast range and they are clustered here purely for introductory purposes. Each is referred to in more detail below. Radical perspectives on youth include an emphasis on the relationship of youth to either 'race' and/or gender as well as class and, increasingly, on all three.

Functionalist

Each of these perspectives stress the role of wider social factors in structuring the position of age groups. Functionalists are particularly concerned with the issue of how age groups, particularly youth, integrate with 'the social system'. In this respect, anthropologist, A Radcliffe-Brown introduced the concepts of 'age grade' and 'age set' in his 'Structure and Function in Primitive Society' (1952). He defines an age grade as 'the recognised division of the life of the individual as he (sic) passes from infancy to old age' and age sets are groups of individuals of similar age who proceed together through life undertaking a specific role for a given period of time. Age grades occur only in certain traditional (generally pre-literate) societies in which they function as a means of organising aspects of life – mainly work – not organised by family or kin. Thus, male aborigines pass through the age grades of hunter, warrior and elder. Entry into each age grade is accompanied by a group or collective ritual.

Such formally constituted age grades do not occur in modern

society but less formal age groups do occur, especially among youth. American functionalist, Eisenstadt has argued that in modern societies, age groups of the young facilitate the often demanding transition from the particularistic (personal) values of family to the universal (rule-bound) values of work (1956). Age groups, then, help to integrate their members into society by providing support and identity and are also oriented towards adult work roles.

Marxist

For Marxists and others who emphasise the effects of class, the central focus of social structure is not integration but class division. The life course is deeply affected by class factors such as occupation and income and is, therefore, broadly different for members of different classes. Many non-Marxists also stress the role of class in structuring the life cycle. As early as 1901, Seebohm Rowntree sketched an outline of the likely life course of a poor person (see p. 446). In relative terms, the life course for the poor is probably little different today. For the wealthy, however, the pattern was and is different. Apart from being generally better off, the precipitous loss of income in old age is much less likely to occur – because of higher savings and private pensions.

The main application of Marxist analysis considered below is to youth subcultures. As far as the latter is concerned, most of the research was published in the 1960s and 1970s by male sociologists about young, white males. This imbalance has since been righted by a growing body of work published on young females and ethnic minority youth. By the late 1980s, larger scale studies of youth tended routinely to factor in a consideration of class, gender and ethnicity.

Radical social constructionist

Government policy and the changing state of the labour market came increasingly into consideration in relation to the life course in the 1980s and 1990s. A smooth transition from education to work could no longer be assumed for most young people; many of the middle aged became less certain of their jobs and their future; older people experienced a relative decline in the value of the state pension. This framework of change and insecurity has become the context in which much recent sociology of the life course has been undertaken. For the purposes of identification, such an approach can be referred to as a modified social constructionist perspective. The 'modification' is that most contemporary approaches allow for more individual and group agency and negotiation than narrowly defined social construction approaches. I adopt a modified social constructionist approach in the next section – while drawing on sources reflecting a variety of perspectives – and this approach informs the rest of the chapter. While it is possible to imagine a conservative application of social constructionist perspective, all the authors referred to below are radical in the sense that they employ gender, ethnic/'race' as well as class perspective (see p. 13).

Youth

The social context of the rise of modern youth

1 General context: universal education – the collective condition

Youth as a distinct social category is largely a modern phenomenon. It is the long – seemingly ever expanding – period between childhood and work that has created this stage in the life course. The early modern industrial economy first required a basically literate, numerate and disciplined labour supply and, more recently, one more differentiated in skills and work orientation (see pp. 121-2). Mass or universal education was established to meet this demand and modern youth is largely a by-product of it. Just as the modern proleteriat was a product of the factory system, so modern youth was partly the product of the education system.

Universal education helps to shape the experience of modern youth as it does childhood. At first, education was mainly an upper and middle class male privilege – as described fictionally in *Tom Brown's Schooldays* – but it is now a universal right and legal requirement. Although the purpose of universal education was mainly to control and socialise youth, in sharing a common structural situation, young people easily develop a sense of shared interest.

It is in the informal peer groups that intra-generational interaction is most free to flourish. S N Eisenstadt observes that the peer group provides a means for experimentation and experience in roles, status and romance, and is a vehicle for transition between childhood and the complex demands of modern adulthood. Phillipe Ariès states that in much the same way as universal education, though to a lesser extent, national service also provided a basis of collective experience and identity for many young men. Sometimes, generational peer groups turn against dominant norms and adopt delinquent and/or culturally deviant lifestyles. Geoffrey Pearson points out that riotous behaviour by young people not constrained and motivated by either education or work, long predates the 1980s. Peer groups can form and operate on the streets – sometimes in a disorderly and criminal way. Finally, peer groups generated largely within the educational context or on neighbourhood streets reflect the influence of class, 'race', gender and individuality.

2 Specific context: post-Second World War: affluence and America

Before the 1950s, there were groups of young people – gangs even – who sometimes clashed with authority and drew opprobrium from older generations. But there was nothing of a scale or of a kind comparable to the youth culture (and subcultures) that emerged in the post-Second World War period. Between the late 1950s to the early 1970s, the media and much of the public seemed obsessed with youth. They had good reason. In 1968, youth-led political and cultural movements seriously threatened the French government and caused serious concern to those of Britain and the United States and elsewhere.

What were the conditions that enabled youth – not all, but substantial groupings – to achieve such effects? Very different factors were of relevance depending on the class, ethnic or gender identity of the young people concerned – and these will be addressed later. However, certain general factors re-positioned youth in relation to other generations and society in general. These can be indicated here and will be discussed in detail in specific contexts below.

Factors underlying the rise of youth culture/subcultures (in Britain):

- Greater affluence.
- Increased leisure.
- Mass production/consumption of electronically-powered entertainment.
- The influence of American culture.

Modern youth culture and subcultures

The developments referred to above provided the conditions for the emergence of what can be termed 'youth culture'. Increased leisure provided time for young people to do things, affluence provided purchasing power, and electronic consumer goods provided the means for them to create a 'culture' or 'way of life' distinctive of youth. From the 1950s to the present day, few young people seem untouched by youth culture. This is partly because youth is seen as a 'consumer market' and targeted for specific fashion items and particular music and entertainment.

Because youth culture is mediated by class, ethnicity and gender, sociologists often use terms such as working class youth culture, Afro-Caribbean youth culture, and working class, female youth culture to indicate more specific areas of analysis.

The terms youth subculture is used for a youth group whose members share a lifestyle which is clearly and visibly different and distinct from that of other young people. Examples discussed below are the 'Teds' and the 'Rude Boys'. Such groups often have strong class (the Teds) or ethnic (Rude Boys) roots but develop their own characteristic style of dress and, often, argot (language, 'slang'). Frequently, they also develop ideologies (such as the Rastas) or, at least, a rough framework of shared beliefs (e.g. the Punks).

Figure 15.2 describes the various levels of influence and frames of reference on youth. Youth culture is the broadest; at a more specific level, class, gender and ethnicity invariably affect a young persons life. A minority of youth 'belong' to some specific subculture or movement but most 'ordinary' youth do not. Virtually all, however, relate to a peer group or own-age group either for friendship or, at least, as a general point for self-comparison and reference.

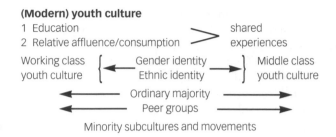

Figure 15.2 Youth culture: shared experiences and differentation

Working class youth culture (1950s to 1970s): 'lads' and work

Working class youth culture tends to be concentrated in areas such as the inner city and, more recently, public housing estates. It is a field of research that has been well studied both in Britain and the United States. The Chicago School of urban sociologists began the serious sociological study of this topic (see Chapter 19), but much interesting material has been published in Britain. It will be helpful to list some of the main values underlying working class male youth culture as a reference point for what follows. These are: anti-authoritarianism; pleasure-seeking ('fun'); a strong sense of territory; masculinity and an admiration of physical strength and skill. Although the traditional manual working class decreased in size between the 1950s and 1990s, these values persist even though they are sometimes expressed with what seems a desperate sense of their growing irrelevance to changes in society (see pp. 89-90). Feminist critiques both of the 'macho lad' dominance of working class youth culture and of male sociologists' celebration of it appeared from the mid 1970s onwards.

Annoying 'authority' is often seen as a good way of 'having fun'. The baiting of authority is a constant theme in the now vast literature on the activities of working class youth. Teachers, the police and youth club leaders are the frequent butt of their ridicule and, less often, of their practical jokes. In an observational survey of a group of working class youths, Paul Corrigan found that a large number thought of teachers as 'big-heads'. We saw similar antagonism reported by Hargreaves and Willis (Chapter 4). Social workers and probation officers possibly escape more lightly because they usually work on a one to one basis with 'clients' rather than as obvious representatives of large and dominant institutions such as schools or the police force. At school, fun often takes the form of a rearguard action against being bored. The ultimate resort is to 'bunk off'. In all inner city areas, there are always some working class 'kids' on the streets or at home during school time. They might be playing football, listening to music or just 'waiting for something to turn up'. In more official jargon, they might be referred to as 'at risk'. The increase in exclusions from schools in the 1990s has probably increased the number of young people in this situation.

It would be misleading to suggest that working class youth culture is exclusively or even mainly concerned with mocking authority. Much of it is positively motivated and energetically pursued. Mending, painting and decorating motor-bikes and cars, playing football and being a football supporter, 'chatting up girls' can all involve great commitment and skill. There are many middle class teenagers relatively deficient in these areas compared with the working class. A minority of working class 'kids' play music and write songs, and many more take an intelligent interest in music, although the research of Murdoch and Phelps suggest that, for the boys, music is largely a matter of background noise or 'aural wallpaper'.

Working class 'lad' culture was not, then, inherently deviant although it had great potential for friction with middle class culture (see pp. 89–90). Peter Willmott's *Adolescent Boys in East London*, published in 1966, roughly quantifies the range of attitudes among his sample of boys:

1   Those with middle class aspirations 20%.
2   Satisfied 'solid' working class 70%.
3   Delinquent 10%.

A major social issue in the 1990s is the relative collapse of 'solid' working class jobs and the difficulties for the lads in getting middle class jobs.

Working class youth subcultures case study I: the Teds

After an initial few years of post-war scarcity and readjustment, by the early 1950s the British people were generally much better off than ever previously – and feeling it. This was especially true of young people in work – and virtually all school-leavers were apart from the small minority in higher education. The average youth wage was a higher percentage of the average adult wage than at any previous time and much higher than in the 1990s. The MacMillan 'you've never had it so good' years were still half a decade away but a sense of affluence and material progress was already present in the early 1950s.

Affluence

The Teds – the first post-war subcultural group – were partly the product of and also flamboyantly expressed this affluence. In explaining the rise of post-war youth subcultures, then, affluence is as much the all-pervading context as first cause. Mark Abrams' book of the period, *The Teenage Consumer* pointed to the increased income, leisure and consumer opportunities of 'modern youth' as young people were then often referred to. Among the items and entertainments on the 'new' consumer market were portable record players and '45' speed records, transistor radios ('tranies')

and American 'youth culture' films starring such icons as Elvis Presley (*Jailhouse Rock*), Marlon Brando (*The Wild One*) and James Dean (*Rebel Without a Cause*).

Style

Along with music, dress, including make-up and self-ornamentation (jewellery does not seem an adequate description of what was to develop) have been the salient forms of expression of post-war youth, particularly subcultural youth. The Teds certainly set an impressive precedent in this respect.

Although typically from manual working class backgrounds, the Teds showed a sharp sense of status in the dress styles they adopted. The name 'Ted' is derived from the Edwardian style dress that was initially revived and tailored for the upper class 'toffs' of the early 1950s but which the Teds stole from them (the 'toffs' dropped the style once it ceased to be distinctive of *their* status). According to Tony Jefferson (1975) originally 'the dress consisted of a long, narrow-lapelled, waisted jacket, narrow trousers (but without being 'drainpipes' (- a later development -)), ordinary toe-capped shoes (later to be replaced by the celebrated 'winkle -pickers), and a fancy waistcoat.'

Jefferson's interpretation of the meaning of the Teddy boys style is that it expressed both new found affluence and an assertion of status. Their sense of status was somewhat uncertain and Jefferson comments on the Teddy boys' sensibility to slights which sometimes led to violence. Jefferson also argues that, like the skinheads later, the Teddy boys were concerned to assert their territorial and job claims which they perceived as threatened by black immigrants. Teddy boy aggression against black people was a major factor in precipitating the Nottinghill 'race riots' of 1958.

American influence

American popular youth culture has had a massive impact on British youth culture during the post-war period (even though the flow of influence has by no means been only one-way). In the 1950s the music, style and hero-figures came across the Atlantic in a deluge. Two such heroes were Marlon Brando (*The Wild One*) and the archetypal hero who died young, James Dean (*Rebel Without a Cause*) (see Figure 15.3). But it was rock and roll that above all initiated an era of youth culture. The combination of music and film had a powerful impact. The film *Rock Around the Clock* with its hit record of the same title played across Britain to packed youth audiences causing some consternation in the press and more 'respectable' public.

If the early Teds copied English upper class 'toffs' the later influence was American. Dick Hebdige comments 'the quiffs, the drapes, the Brylcream and the 'flicks' … came to mean America, a fantasy continent of Westerns and gangsters, luxury, glamour and 'automobiles'.

In retrospect, the British 'answers' to Elvis Presley – Cliff Richard – and Buddy Holly – Adam Faith – seem pale, synthetic imitations. But they stirred the pot and in the 1960s a much more

Figure 15.3 Youth icon: James Dean

authentically British 'pop' music developed – although its leading exponents, the Stones and Beatles, also looked partly to America for inspiration. The underlying influence for both American and British 'white' pop music was black American music. Chuck Berry 'met' Buddy Holly as black rhythm and blues picked up speed and emerged as multi-racial rock.

Class

The Teddy boys were working class. In interpreting them in class terms, Jefferson draws on the American subcultural theorist, Albert Cohen (see pp. 352-3). The latter suggested that the toughness and aggressive display of American 'lower class' males was due to status frustration. Other American subcultural theorists such as Miller, took a different view. Miller argued that the tough but loyal culture of working class boys was rooted in their own class and not merely the product of frustrated reaction. This is the interpretation that

came to be adopted at the Centre of Contemporary Cultural Studies (although Jefferson's analysis of the Teds was influenced by Cohen). It is the approach adopted in John Clarke's analysis of the skinheads presented below.

Between the Teds and the skinheads, were the mods and rockers. They represented, respectively, the 'smart' and the 'tough' sides of working class youth culture. Even more than the Teds, the mods are regarded as the classic conspicuous consumers of post-war youth subcultures – 'dedicated followers of fashion'. Stan Cohen's classic study of the mods and rockers – *Folk Devils and Moral Panics* (1973) – particularly examines the interplay between the two subcultures and the media and the resulting 'moral panic'. For that reason, the mods and rockers are analysed in Chapter 17 (see pp. 514-5).

Working class youth subcultures case study 2: the skinheads and resistance

Like other groups of young lads, no doubt the aggressive and occasionally violent behaviour of the skinheads can be explained in terms of a pursuit of excitement, but John Clarke, in a contribution to the collection of writings, *Resistance Through Rituals* (edited by Hall and Jefferson, 1976), offers additionally a more thought-provoking explanation. He suggests that the behaviour and style of the skinheads, far from being random and irrational, closely reflects the realities of their lives. He points out that many features of the skinhead style – the short haircut, the wearing of braces over shirts, turning trousers up inches above the ankles, the wearing of cheap, heavy boots – were only slightly exaggerated and dramatised versions of traditional working class dress. Clarke suggests that, by dressing in this way, the skinheads were, perhaps unconsciously, reasserting traditional class and community identity.

This interpretation gains credibility when we remember that East End working class communities have been damaged and destroyed in the post-war period. Decline in employment opportunities, housing clearance programmes, near-chaos in parts of the London educational service must have caused disorientation, anger and despair in many lives, not least in those of the young. It is perhaps not surprising – although deplorable in itself – that the skinheads sometimes turned their aggression against immigrants rather than on the investors, developers and planners who were more responsible for their grievances and fears. Clarke, therefore, sees skinhead aggression and violence as largely defensive. He explains their behaviour as 'a symbolic defence of (threatened) territory' and as 'a magical attempt to recover community'. There was a later resurgence of racism among 'skinhead types', loosely associated with the British National party, during the recession of the early 1990s.

Clarke and his co-contributors to *Resistance Through Rituals* see the aggressive/defensive behaviour of the Teds, skinheads and other working class youth subcultural groups as 'cultural resistance'. There is no suggestion that the lads are making a conscious political statement – except, perhaps, to the extent that their frequent racism is neo-fascist. In so far as the lads are, in wider social terms, relatively powerless and vulnerable to the power and authority of others, the theory of resistance is plausible. However, it is not a complete explanation – tending to offer little comment either on the majority of working class youth or on working class females. In fairness, however, the editors of *Resistance Through Rituals* – Stuart Hall and Tony Jefferson – argue that the problems faced by the lads are commonly experienced by working class people, young and adult.

Working class youth subcultures case study 3: the punks and the problem of incorporation

Arguably, the punks were the last of the spectacular subcultures which could claim both strong roots in working class experience (in this case, unemployment) and to be as much concerned with protest/resistance as style and fun. Beyond punk lay 'glam rock' and even the yuppies. Punk itself was subject to considerable commercial pressure.

Even in the 1960s and 1970s, sociologists could not locate all youth subcultures so convincingly in a class context as Clarke did the skinheads. This is partly because big business and the media tend quickly to take up and popularise stylistic and creative subcultural aspects – a process referred to by Dick Hebdige as 'incorporation'.

Hebdige describes two forms of incorporation: the commodity form and the ideological form:

1 The commodity form is the conversion of subcultural signs (dress, music, etc.,) into mass-produced objects for sale.
2 The ideological form is the labelling and redefinition of subcultural activity by dominant groups (e.g. media, police) in order to dismiss and/or trivialise it. Hebdige acknowledges that Stan Cohen's interactionist approach explains much of the process of incorporation but argues that Marxist perspective contributes a sharper analysis of the economic motives underlying incorporation.

It may be that punk music and style of dress was originally the product of unemployed, working class youth but, within a few months, the movement was being commercially exploited in the youth market generally The punk clothes worth hundreds of pounds which were advertised in *Vogue* magazine illustrate the point. In adopting subcultural forms such as punk music for mass consumption, the commercial enterprises involved, and the media, attempt to adapt the product for maximum acceptability and consumption. Thus the attempt to 'devulgarise' the Sex Pistols was seen by the group as an attack on their freedom to produce and perform the material they wanted. When a subcultural symbol, like punk rock music, is commercialised, instead of providing a long-term focus on which the movement can coalesce and identify, the

symbol is 'stolen' by the pop industry, reprocessed and presented to a wider audience which does not seriously associate it with the protest and rebellion it may have originally represented. In contrast to the punks, the skinheads produced little that was saleable on the mass market, although some London and fashionable provincial boutiques attempted to market skinhead style clothes. (Note: For further analysis of the punks, see pp. 487-8.)

'Invisible' girls

In the hard world of working class youth subcultures, the position of the female was very much that of pillion-passenger. Motor-bike 'burn-ups' and gang fights (real or mock) are forms of display, and all the better if girls are there to observe closely. As a Sunday Times newspaper analysis of a gang fight wryly states: 'excitement is heightened if police, press, TV – and girls – are in attendance'.

However, it would be a mistake to see the girls – even in the 1960s – as mere status symbols and prizes in the status game-playing of the boys: the female friendship group has a distinct and important existence within the larger teenage peer group itself. Girls share much leisure activity. They are more likely than the boys to know details of the top twenty, to read teenage magazines, and to be familiar with the latest dance routines – which they perform, usually in protective togetherness, at discos. A serious relationship with a male may temporarily detach working class girls from the single-sex friendship group. If they can, they tend to marry earlier and have lower career aspirations than middle class girls. This can easily lead to domestic entrapment and very limited job opportunities (see pp. 90-1).

As was discussed in Chapter 4, the above patterns changed somewhat in the 1990s. Working class girls seem less likely to be 'taken in' by romantic ideology and to be better aware that they may need to be able to cope with economic insecurity (Sharp, 1994). The power and position of working class boys relative to girls has also declined somewhat since the 1970s. However, it is decidedly premature to declare patriarchy 'dead' in this or other areas of social life.

Public and academic reaction to working class youth culture

Although, as we have seen, there was considerable continuity between traditional working class culture and 'modern' working class youth culture/subcultures, this was not clear at the time. There was widespread media and public concern and condemnation of what was perceived as youth's new disruptiveness. There were, as well, more sympathetic voices. Stanley Cohen has charted the widespread public 'moral panic' about the activities of the mods and rockers (see pp. 514). Cohen usefully adopts the term boundary crisis to describe the apparent threat to conventional norms and standards made by youthful 'folk devils'.

Prior to the mods and rockers, panic had already occurred in response to the Teds as this extract from a letter to the Evening Standard (1954) illustrates:

> *Teddy boys are ... are all of unsound mind in the sense they are all suffering from a form of psychosis, Apart from the birch or the rope, depending on the gravity of their crimes, what they need is rehabilitation in a psychopathic institution ... it is the desire to do evil, not lack of comprehension which forces them in to crime.*
>
> *(Family Doctor, Evening Standard, 12.5.1954)*

The closer one reads the above extract, the more contradictory and irrational it seems. Yet, it was not untypical of much reaction at the time. Very similar language was used of the Teds by an *Any Questions* panel whose members seemed to regard the film *Rock Around the Clock* and the youthful response to it as a threat to 'civilised' standards and behaviour.

Civilisation or, at least, British culture was scarcely threatened, but it was in the process of significant and rapid change. Cultural critic, Richard Hoggart had a more informed and measured sense of what was happening although he was none too enthusiastic about it. Hoggart considered the American influenced youth culture was a threat to what he considered the much more authentic and worthwhile traditional working class culture. For him, superficial mass culture was threatening solid class culture. Dominic Strinati (1995) introduces the following quote from Hoggart's *The Uses of Literacy* (1957). Some of Hoggart's most extended condemnations of the impact of Americanisation are reserved for working-class youth. The 'juke-box boys', who frequented what were known in the 1950s and early 1960s as 'milk bars', get special attention. ...

> *The milk-bars indicate at once, in the nastiness of their modernistic knick-knacks, their glaring showiness, an aesthetic breakdown so complete that, in comparison with them, the layout of the living-rooms in some of the poor homes from which the customers come seems to speak of a tradition as balanced and civilised as an eighteenth-century town house ... most of the customers are boys aged between fifteen and twenty, with drape-suits, picture ties, and an American slouch. Most of them cannot afford a succession of milkshakes, and make cups of tea serve for an hour or two whilst – and this is their main reason for coming – they put copper after copper into the mechanical record-player. About a dozen records are available at any one time; a numbered button is pressed for the one wanted, which is selected from a key to titles. The records seem to be changed about once a fortnight by the hiring firm; almost all are American. ...*
>
> *(R Hoggart in Strinati:29)*

As Strinati observes Hoggart's view of the influence of American imagery and consumerism is deeply negative. On the positive side, Hoggart then and since has sought to articulate what are fundamental cultural and aesthetic values in an epoch when, as he foresaw, the reality of such values has appeared increasingly in question.

Afro-Caribbean and Asian youth: 1960s and 1970s

Although most Afro-Caribbean and Asian youth are working class as measured by parental occupation, it is not appropriate to treat them exclusively under the heading of working class youth because of the importance of racism and cultural (ethnic) factors. As we saw in Chapter 8, the same argument applies to minority adults. All young people have the problem of forging a workable identity, but for black youth it can be particularly acute. They are presented with two potentially conflicting adult models. First is that of the British citizen, sharing equal rights and duties with whites; second is that of a person, with a cultural heritage that goes back to the Punjab, Nigeria, Barbados or Hong Kong. Achieving a workable balance between these identities is possible but often difficult. There are two major reasons for this. Firstly, as we have just mentioned, it is bound to be difficult to bring into focus two separate national, historical identities. Secondly, the problem is made much worse by the experience of prejudice – since self-identity partly depends on what others think of you. Black immigrants and their children cannot avoid seeing themselves in the mirror of white people's eyes. What they often see there is suspicion and resentment, and sometimes hatred. (We studied this more empirically in Chapter 8). The cultural life of immigrant groups, and particularly of the young, cannot be properly understood without bearing in mind the hurt and anger that racism can provoke. Equally, it must be remembered that Britain's minorities, including second and third generation 'immigrants' are proud of, and attached to, their ethnic cultural heritage. This is obvious in many areas such as literature, language, dress, food, religion, family tradition and so on. The phrase 'black is beautiful' captures both the pride and defensive self-assertion that has notably characterised ethnic groups in America and Britain since the 1960s.

Afro-Caribbean youth

We will take Afro-Caribbean youth subculture for more detailed analysis here. Love of music, religion and a liking for a street based social activity are well known aspects of West Indian culture. Unemployment, or irregular employment is also part of the familiar background of life, and young black people, both here and in the Caribbean, are accustomed to dealing with it. The Afro-Caribbean hustler in Britain has his parallel in the Jamaican 'rude boy' or 'rudie'. Between about 1963 and 1971 a rude boy subculture flourished in some of Britain's inner urban areas. Despite the racism of the skinheads, the latter held the rudies in some respect and were influenced by their style and music. Rudies cope with the indifference of the job market by 'hustling' a living out of dealing in drugs, gambling, pimping or stealing. As a last resort, some hustlers may 'play the welfare system', but they have little taste for the bureaucratic 'hassle' this can involve. Often they live in some style, sporting smart cars and well-cut clothes. Not altogether surprisingly, some prefer this lifestyle to the lower-level manual work that might occasionally be offered them. Ellis Cashmore (1983) and Dick Hebdige (1979) evaluate the rudies very differently – suggesting that subcultural interpretation can be highly subjective. Cashmore writes that 'like the skinheads … (they) were aggressive in that they seemed to derive satisfaction from non-instrumental violence, racists in that they hated Asians, and sexist …' (42). In contrast, Hebdige, in describing the decline of the rudies and rise of the Rastas in the early 1970s, strikes a romantic note:

> *Thus the rude boy was immortalised in skas and rock steady – the lone delinquent pitched hopelessly against an implacable authority – was supplanted in the central focus of identity by the Rastafarian who broke the law in more profound and subtle ways.*
>
> (37)

We must be careful not to suggest that the hustler is the typical figure of Afro-Caribbean youth subculture. Many young blacks look hard for work and are demoralised and embittered if they do not find it. All that we are doing here is describing some options available to West Indian youth.

The cool, worldly image of the hustler contrasts sharply with the religious conviction of another major West Indian youth sub-cultural figure, the Rastafarian. The 'Rasta' movement illustrates the defensive, retreatist trend which is often a part of the cultural tradition of a group actually or potentially oppressed. Rastafarians trace their spiritual roots back to Africa; their plaited hair and sometimes their style of dress imitate African originals. They believe that the late Emperor Haile Selassie of Ethiopia will be reincarnated and will lead them out of 'Babylon' a biblical reference to capitalist society. From Kingston to Brixton, Reggae is the music of Rastafarianism. Reggae lyrics are heavy with biblical references, and the music's slow, moody rhythms reflect the influence of the 'sacred' drug, ganja (a type of marijuana).

Stuart Hall has described the ways of life of many young black people, which brings them into conflict with 'white' power structures as 'cultural resistance' (*The Empire Strikes Back*, Hutchinson, 1981). Thus, the term is one he applies generally to 'subordinate' youth – both working class and black. Certainly, the simmering resentment of many young black people helped to fuel the urban disorders of 1981 and 1985 as well as more routine conflict with the police. However, Hall points out that the conditions of cultural resistance lie in racism and class inequality.

Did the 'resistance' theorists get it wrong? Neo-tribe?

Two criticisms of the resistance theory developed at the Centre for Contemporary Cultural Studies can be summarised here. First, Steve Redhead argues in *The End of the Century Party. Youth and Pop Towards 2000* that the concept of resistance is more the product of the theorists of subcultures than of the actual participants (1990). As he puts it, 'authentic' subcultures were produced by subcultural theories, not the other way round.'

Redhead's comments provoke the question of what the 'subcultures' were about if they were not about resistance. This leads to a second criticism of resistance theory. David Muggleton (1995) argues that the youthful activity mistakenly, in his view, referred to by CCCS theorists as 'subcultural resistance', is much more about asserting *individual autonomy* than collective resistance. Muggleton's own interviews with young people provide numerous examples of assertions of individual autonomy and rejections of labelling, including sometimes subcultural labels, and the youthful conformity this implies. Thus, he quotes one punk's reply to the question of what is the meaning of punk:

> *Punk is basically being yourself, freedom, doing what you wanna do, looking like you wanna look, and then if you look like a punk, well, you don't even have to look like a punk cos there's a lot that don't have mohicans or nothing.*
>
> (*'From Subculture to 'Neo-tribe': Identity, Paradox and Postmodernism in Alternative Style'* 3).

Muggleton rejects the term 'subculture' with its strongly collective connotations but does consider that many young people do associate with others in loose alliance mainly in order to facilitate 'the social expression of individual autonomy' (14). Accordingly, he proposes 'that this movement towards affinity based on heterogeneity (variety/difference) may be better encapsulated through the concept of 'neo-tribe' (14).

Undoubtedly, Muggleton makes a strong point. In tracking back what is often thought of as postmodern youthful individualism to the so-called subcultural era, he almost certainly rebalances the historical record. On the other hand, it is arguable that the Teds, Skins, and, not least, Punks were often collectively involved in verbal, stylistic and sometimes physical battles with public authorities – educational, police and others. There is also plenty of cited evidence that they saw themselves as 'in it together', as 'mates' i.e. collectively. The CCCS research papers are full of references of this kind. Given that the 1960s and 1970s was a much more collectivist era than the 1980s and 1990s, it is not surprising that a collectivist orientation should have manifested itself in the subcultures. Relatedly, their members often expressed quite a strong sense of group identity. My own view, then, is that Redhead and Muggleton considerably shift the 'resistance' paradigm but do not overturn it. Table 15.3 briefly summarises the previous section.

Table 15.3 Perspectives or youth culture

Theoretical points and perspectives on working class and black youth: a summary
1 Mass culture perspective: Richard Hoggart
2 Cultural resistance/incorporation: Stuart Hall, Dick Hebdige
3 Boundary crisis/moral panic: Stanley Cohen
4 Feminist: Angela McRobbie, Sue Sharp
5 Criticism of resistance theory: Steve Redhead, David Muggleton

Questions

1 Account for the rise of working class and ethnic youth subcultures in the post-war period.
2 What evidence is there of 'resistance' among working class and ethnic youth subcultures between 1950 and 1985? What, if anything, were they 'resisting'?

Middle class youth culture and subcultures: 1950s to 1970s

Middle class youth as a whole attracted far less attention from sociologists than working class youth from the 1950s to the 1970s. Educational research showed the obvious – that generally middle class youth benefited from their relatively privileged position and went on to further capitalise occupationally and economically. The observation that younger members of the middle class largely conformed to middle class values and behaviour patterns did not have the romantic appeal to sociologists of the 'resistance' of working class youth subcultures.

Sociological interest in middle class youth accelerated with the development of the partly university campus-based political and cultural radical movements of the 1960s. Even at the height of these movements in 1968, it is doubtful whether a majority of (mainly middle class) students in Britain and the United States would have described themselves as radical. Nevertheless, a whole campus generation was affected by these movements. In *Radical Man*, Charles Hampden-Turner has suggested in relation to American youth of the 1960s that many experienced a contradiction between the liberal and humanistic values of their upbringing and the monetary and instrumental values of the organisations and corporations they were expected eventually to work in (1971). I would suggest that this tension was and perhaps still is felt by many young people in British as well as American higher education who find the reality of the world of work can fall a long way short of the best values learnt in their families and at school.

The radical youth movements of the 1960s: a movement rather than just a subculture

The widespread generational upheaval of the 1960s was more than just the product of the activity of one or several subcultures. A better term to describe the radical political and cultural activity that occurred is *youth movement*. Karl Mannheim's concepts of a generation of *location* and a generation of actuality are also useful in grasping the scale and nature of this phenomenon. The former term refers simply to those born at or located in roughly the same point in time. A generation as an actuality shares a community of feeling and experience. The nostalgia that many of the 'sixties generation' feel for 'their decade' perhaps indicates that something was shared on a large scale. However, there were many splits of class, ethnicity and gender through this generation – as with others – and many individuals who might claim 'not to have been part of it at all'.

A romantic movement

What was 'it'? One witticism has it that 'if you remember what you were doing in the sixties, then you weren't really there'. Obviously this reference to the drug-taking habits of some of sixties youth will not substitute for an analysis but it gives some indication of the cultural experimentation that many at least dabbled with. In order to understand the movement it is necessary to distinguish between its political and cultural radicalism – although the two is overlap, particularly in second wave feminism which tried to bridge the political and the personal-cultural. Figure 15.4 summarises in a compare/contrast format, the main political and cultural trends and issues of the 1960s youth movement.

My own preferred description of the 1960s radical youth movement is that it was a *romantic* or *idealistic* youth movement. What is meant by this will be explained below. First, however, it will help to describe the conditions which helped to stimulate the 1960s youth movement.

The Issues

BRITAIN		UNITED STATES	
Political	**Cultural**	**Cultural**	**Political**
1 New Left Review (Marxist Journal)	Marxists focus on culture	Protest Music (Bob Dylan, Joan Baez)	Civil Rights
2 Campaign for Nuclear Disarmament (CND) Beatniks	Beatniks	Beatniks	Anti-Bomb Protests
3 Continuing Revival of Marxist Thought		Anti-University Bureaucracy	'Free Speech Movement'
4 Feminism	Feminism	Feminism	Feminism
5 Anti-Vietnam War Critique of Military-Industry Complex	'Pop' Music more political (e.g. Stones! 'Street Fighting Man')	'Pop' Music more political (e.g. Grateful Dead: 'Working Man's Dead')	Anti-Vietnam War Critique of Military Industrial Complex
6 'Paris 68', Bader Meinhoff Angry Brigade	Hyde Park 'Stones Concert' Seventies Reaction/Backlash	Counter-Culture Hippies	Weathermen

Figure 15.4 The sixties political and cultural radicalism

The social context of the 1960s youth movement

The general social context which stimulated the rise of working class youth culture and subcultures was, of course, the same one which gave rise to the more middle class radical youth movement. Figure 15.5 summarises these factors. Factors 1, 2, 3 and 5 in the summary below broadly apply to the rise of modern youth culture generally. However, 'broadly' is an operative word. Within the new environment of affluence, consumerism and growing permissiveness, middle class, educated youth developed (indeed, partly, learnt from their parents) a rather different range of values and cultural practice from working class youth. These differences are briefly indicated in the key summary (Figure 15.5).

Points 4 and 6 apply virtually exclusively to young middle class radicals. Their shared collective experience and education helped to create a community of concern about a wide range of issues which were either inaccessible to or of little interest to most working class youth. There were exceptions to this generalisation in both directions.

Sixties youthful romanticism and mainstream realism

Describing the sixties youth movement as romantic and idealistic requires substantiation. First, it helps to locate the sixties movement within a given tradition. A comparable example is the politico-cultural movement of early nineteenth century British romantic poets. Wordsworth, Southey, Coleridge and others were, in their youth, enthused by the French and American revolutions,

---

Why did the 1960's radical youth movement happen?

1 **Affluence**:
A 'feeling' of affluence. Basic necessities had been dealt with – more emphasis was possible on quality, creativity, pleasure and ideals.

2 **Post-war baby boom**
'Pig in the Python' i.e. the large sixties generation threatens to dominate others throughout its own life course.

3 **New 'youth market'**
'Pop' Music – Cinema – Disco. However, the music and style of middle class, often campus based youth culture differed considerably from working class youth culture.

4 **Higher education expansion**
Students – a new 'collectivity' (group)

5 **Economic expansion/political liberalism**
Cultural optimism and experimental action

6 **The issues** (see Figure 15.4)
Crucially, the sixties movement was about certain events, trends and issues which motivated the participants but not necessarily other young people.

'1960s' – a rare example of a romantic movement.

Like the revolutionary 1820s.

'Bliss was it then to be alive, but to be young was very heaven'

(William Wordsworth)

Figure 15.5 Causes of 1960s radical youth movement

were culturally somewhat bohemian, planned to set up a commune (on the banks of the Susquehanna river in the United States) and Coleridge, at least, took drugs. They were also much concerned about inequality and with industrial damage to nature – what today we would call the environment.

Second, what is meant by the term romantic needs to be conceptualised in more detail. This can be done with reference to Freud's concept of the pleasure and reality principles (as re-worked by Marcuse and further elaborated by Jock Young). The values designated by Marcuse as central to the pleasure principle may also be regarded as characteristic of romantic movements and those designated under the reality principle characteristic of mainstream or dominant society (Table 15.4).

Table 15.4 Marcuse: the pleasure and the reality principles

Romantic	Mainstream (Institutions)
Pleasure principle values	Reality principle values
Immediate satisfaction	Delayed satisfaction
Pleasure	Restraint of pleasure
Joy (play)	Toil (work)
Receptiveness (to stimuli and experience)	Productiveness (in work)
Absence of repression	Security (in return for self-repression/control)

Note: The terms 'Romantic' and 'Mainstream' are the author's.

(Source: *Marcuse*, 1956:12)

Table 15.5 Formal and subterranean values

Formal work values	Subterranean values
Reality principle	A New reality principle
1 Deferred gratification	Short-term hedonism
2 Planning future action	Spontaneity
3 Conformity to bureaucratic rules	Ego-expressivity
4 Fatalism, high control over detail, little Over direction	Autonomy, control of behaviour in detail and direction
5 Routine, predictability	New experience, excitement
6 Instrumental attitudes to work	Activities performed as an end-in-themselves
7 Hard productive work, seen as a virtue	Disdain for work

(Source: From J Young, *The Drugtakers: The Social Meaning of Drug Use*, Paladin, 1971:126)

Following Matza, Young describes the pleasure-seeking, bohemian lifestyle in terms of subterranean values, although he is careful to point out that the use of psychedelic drugs is only one aspect of this way of life. Other subterranean values are short-term hedonism, spontaneity, excitement, and dislike of conventionally organised work. These contrast with formal values such as deferred gratification, planning future action, predictability and acceptance of productive work as virtuous. Broadly, subterranean values are concerned with pleasure and self-fulfilment for its own sake, and formal values with work and the necessary control that goes with it. The contrast between subterranean values and formal work values reflects Freud's pleasure and reality principles Young expresses this as shown in Table 15.5.

Sixties cultural radicals or romantics sometimes took psychedelic drugs, such as cannabis and LSD, because they believed that these would improve their moods, and even enhance their perception of the world. Cannabis is a relatively mild psychedelic and is taken for its relaxing 'mellowing' effect. LSD is stronger, and some claim that under its influence new insights may be realised and joyful and profound states of awareness achieved. It must be added that any psychedelic drug may also produce the opposite effect, especially amongst inexperienced or 'naive' users. Young suggests, however that experienced users can often exercise considerable control over the effects of psychedelics, and the drug then becomes part of the whole way of life of the subculture rather than its main dominating influence. Psychedelic drug-taking may fit in with the kind of music, literature, leisure style and even personal relations preferred by this type of group. To get a 'feel' for bohemian subculture, it helps to read the novels of, say, the American 'beat' of the 1950s, Jack Kerouac, or to listen to the 'sixties' music of the Grateful Dead or Jefferson Airplane. Of course, these artists belong to different 'moments' in the history of 'bohemia', or cultural romanticism, but they are, nevertheless, part of the same broad tradition. It is likely that the drug 'ecstasy' has similar cultural associations.

Youth in the 1980s and 1990s

It is always interesting to compare different generations of youth. There is now just about a generation between the 1960s/early 1970s generation and the generation of the late 1980s/1990s who are largely their offspring. However, interesting though this exercise is, it is fraught with the danger of unfounded generalisation. Given this, it is helpful that the Economic and Social Research Council (ESRC), carried out a large social survey of sixteen to nineteen year olds between 1987 and 1989.

The ESRC study is particularly useful in providing detailed information on young people's experience in the labour market although data on their beliefs, attitudes and values on a wide range of matters are also presented. Two studies which focus specifically on youth and cultural issues are Paul Willis's *Common Culture: Symbolic Work at Play in the Everyday Cultures of the Young* (1990) and Förnas and Bolm's *Youth Culture in Late Modernity* (1995). Each of these two studies will be separately examined prior to making some comparative generalisations about 1960s and 1990s youth.

The ESRC 16–19 initiative: structure and identity

The Economic and Social Research Council's 16-19 initiative is a study of how young people approach adulthood – their choices, constraints and dilemmas – and about the kind of adults they become. At the heart of the initiative was a longitudinal study of 5000 young people growing up in four labour markets (Swindon, Sheffield, Liverpool and Kirkcaldy) in which two groups aged fifteen to sixteen and seventeen to eighteen, respectively, were followed up for two years between 1987 to 1989, with data collected in each year. An integrated theoretical and methodological approach was adopted with no repetition among the various authors of the kind of 'perspectives battles' common in 1960s and 1970s.

The main publication reporting the findings of the 16-19 initiative is Banks *et al.* eds., *Careers and Identities* (Open University Press, 1992). Additionally, I Bates and G Riseborough *eds., Youth and Inequality* (Open University, 1993) provides a rich source of qualitative and ethnographic material from the study. The study as a whole represents a concern with all young people – ordinary and extraordinary alike – and with their central life concerns – jobs, relationships and identity – which had become partly obscured by the sharp focus of 1970s sociology of youth on 'the spectacular subcultures'.

Structure: stratification and jobs, changing transitions

However, despite the difference in emphasis, the ESRC 16-19 initiative largely confirmed the basic findings of 1970s work on youth. Social structural factors – class, gender and racial – were again found to be crucial in affecting the opportunities of young people. These factors, of course, are themselves affected by changes in the economy, particularly the job market. Ken Roberts shows how this was so in the 1980s with particular reference to social class:

> *The 1980s did create more opportunities for working-class young people to ascend. These opportunities were mostly constructed not from the enterprise initiatives … but by the expansion of high-level employment and the academic mainstream. However, from a working class perspective, an equally significant change during the 1980s was the increased risk of descent. Young people who failed to enter short careers and reasonably secure jobs stood real risks of unemployment and survival on poverty incomes with no escapes in sight … For middle-class youth, the expansion of professional and management jobs meant that their positions were less vulnerable than before. Their typical problem was to choose between the widening range of occupations at, and routes towards, this level.*
>
> *(Youth and Inequality: 244-5)*

The differences Roberts points to can be clarified with reference to a typology of education/work transitions which he refers to in another publication (*Youth and Unemployment*, 1995). Roberts refers to three types of transitions: extended, short and careerless. The key measure of each is the time between entering the career and reaching top earnings and the pay and status at this point. This would usually be a long time for those embarking on extended careers. Such people would normally be well qualified and take up careers in business or the professions. Roberts observes that the expansion of, for instance, 'high tech' jobs and of banking and finance provided opportunities for such students. Their problem might be whether to proceed via traditional academic routes or by one of the various new higher status vocational routes (see pp. 124-5). However, even this group is no longer likely to be entering 'a career for life'. Such is the rate of change in work roles (see pp. 459-60). Further, the chances of experiencing graduate unemployment are now greater.

'Short' careers lead to earlier maximisation of earning and status than extended ones. Apprenticeships lead to these kind of careers. Craft skills of this kind, however, have been in decreasing demand. In the mid 1990s there were fewer than half the apprenticeships of a quarter of a century previously. This has caused real difficulty for millions of young people who would ideally have aspired to this type of career.

'Careerless' transitions from school to work are characterised by very early maximisation of status and, low pay. Unskilled and semi-skilled manual work used to provide jobs of this kind but, like short careers, there are now millions fewer. However, the expansion of a 'restructured' low pay sector is generating jobs (see pp. 256-7).

Roberts comments that 'by the end of the 1980s young people's routes into the work-force had become more numerous and complicated' and one can add, often more uncertain than in the 1960s.

Roberts also gives data indicating the substantial impact of racism on the career opportunities of young blacks. At age eighteen to nineteen, 50 per cent of young blacks in Liverpool were

Figure 15.6 Reality for some. Finding a job could be difficult for young people in the 1980s and 1990s

unemployed, twice as many as had full-time jobs and most of the latter were at the lower end of the labour market. An earlier study by Clough *et al.*, (1984) in Sheffield and Bradford found that among young people with four or more 'O' levels, young blacks were three times as likely to be unemployed as whites and among the unqualified, 1.5 times as likely. These data indicate a situation of severe 'racial' inequality.

Status transitions

In Youth and Social Policy (1995), Bob Coles further develops the concept of 'transition' to describe the move from youthful to adult status. His analysis of the transitions from education to work, from family of origin to family of destination, and from parents' home to own home is the subject of Reading 1. Coles sees 'achieving the status of adulthood' as 'dependent upon successfully making at least some of these transitions'. He uses the term 'career' to describe individual transitions or non-transitions.

Gender (class and jobs)

The ESRC study confirms that gender continues to structure the aspirations and opportunities of young people. Although the academic attainment of females is broadly comparable to that of

males and there is some similarity in early career patterns, the tendency of many – probably still most – females to 'revert to the domestic' and, in particular, society's failure to accommodate this tendency by the provision of adequate childcare and other support – ensures a widening gap in career status and income between males and females from the late teens/early twenties onwards. Inge Bates' study of a group of trainee 'Care Girls' (in retirement homes) concludes that the impact of class-gender socialisation on these girls is such that they 'have come to the conclusion that there are no real alternatives to this job' (*Youth and Inequality*, 29).

Rather similarly, George Riseborough's observational study, *GBH – The Gobbo Barmy Harmy: One day in the life of 'the YTS boys'* describes a group of young males apparently resigned to the strong possibility, if not the probability, of unemployment. In their attitudes and behaviour – sexist, racist, viciously defensive and loyal to each other – they seem to live in a timewarp, behaving little differently from the 'lads' of Paul Willis's *Learning to Labour* (1976). However, one difference in their lives is crucial – the lads were pretty sure of getting jobs. The 'Barmy Harmy' is marginal in terms of purpose and power and redundant, culturally as well as economically. Their labour-power is underused and poorly rewarded and their attitudes and lifestyle apparently adrift from mainstream change (see pp. 89-90).

Identity

The concern of contemporary social scientists to balance social structural factors with a consideration of subjective factors or personal agency and meaning is very apparent in the ESRC 16-19 study. The authors describe identity as follows:

> Identity, as we conceive it, embraces the individual's own perception of himself or herself generally and in specific domains – for example, occupational identity, political identity, domestic identity … its development is fundamental in relationships with others and, consequently, the ability to function in the social world, including the world of work. Its evaluative aspect, self-esteem is also central to social action …
> The idea, which we endorse, of the individual as an active 'agent' implies purposive choices and actions following them …
>
> *(Careers and Identities:12)*

Identity is about who the individual thinks s/he is, how s/he evaluates herself or himself and how s/he sees her or his relationship to the world. Identity involves a negotiation between self and society in the course of which an individual's sense of self can change and develop.

Self-efficacy and estrangement

Self-efficacy (effectiveness) and estrangement (alienation) are two key areas explored in the ESRC study. The young respondents completed self-evaluation questionnaires aimed to assess these aspects of their identities, which were administered in 1987, 1988 and 1989. The questions and responses to them are summarised in Table 15.6.

It will be obvious from examining the table that the great majority of respondents felt themselves to be self-efficacious or not to be estranged. The small number who had a less confident and satisfied view of themselves were found in roughly the same numbers across the four geographical areas in which the survey was conducted. They were more likely to be males than females – a finding which is perhaps slightly counter-intuitive (although the suicide rate among young males is much higher than that among young females). More of the less satisfied were found among disadvantaged groups, particularly those who had not got a job on leaving school. Those on YTS courses were more likely to feel negatively than those who got jobs or stayed on at school. The minority with negative self-image decreases through the three years of the survey. This does confirm the view that youth is, in part, a period of transition on the other side of which lies the probability of a more confident and integrated identity. Indeed,

Table 15.6 Self-evaluations in 1987, 1988 and 1989 (percentages)

	1987		1988		1989	
	Agree	Disagree	Agree	Disagree	Agree	Disagree
*If I can't do a job the first time, I keep trying until I can	91	2	90	2	93	2
*I avoid trying to learn new things when they look too difficult for me	11	89	11	88	10	80
*I give up easily	9	82	9	83	8	83
*I seem to be capable of dealing with most problems that come up in life	79	6	82	5	5	87
*I find it easy to make new friends	77	9	76	10	77	10
*I do not know how to handle social gatherings	13	63	13	65	10	71
**I feel unsure about most things in life	15	67	13	70	12	73
***I find it easy to adapt to new rules and regulations	69	14	68	13	74	11
**If I could, I would be a very different person from the one I am now	22	61	19	61	16	66
**I find it difficult to know what is going on in the world	16	67	12	72	11	75
**I am happy to be the person I am	79	9	77	9	78	9
**I sometimes cannot help but wonder if anything is worthwhile	35	44	32	48	26	57
**I am often troubled by emptiness in my life	22	62	21	63	19	68
**I feel that I am as worthwhile as anybody else	82	5	81	6	84	5

* = self-efficacy item
** = estrangement item
*** = not included in either scale

(Source: *Careers and Identities*, 114)

even as mid-teenagers most young people, judging by those respondents, have a robust sense of identity although one still open to further development and experience.

Beliefs, attitudes and values (on gender, 'race' and politics)

Table 15.7 shows the issues about which the young respondents in the survey expressed strong feelings.

Table 15.7 Issues about which young people have strong feelings

Mean percentages agreeing or disagreeing strongly with statements about:

Race	37
Roles of men and women	34
Sex	30
Environment	26
Youth training	23
Education	22
Taxation, government services and spending	21
Police, rules, law authority	19
Family	18
Regional contrasts	17
Political parties, processes, and politicians	16

(Source: *Careers and Identities*, 129)

Young people felt most strongly about areas of sexual and racial equality, opportunity and discrimination. Almost all female respondents and over 80 per cent of males supported equality of opportunity and obligation between the sexes in relation to training, the workplace and the home. Similarly, over 80 per cent expressed no objection to having a boss of another race, did not mind working with people of another race, believed that people of different races should be free to intermarry and that the different races should be able to live together. This appears to be a strong endorsement for a tolerant, broadly liberal, open society (see Reading 2). Another major area of concern for young people in the survey was the environment. This concern tended to cut across any support for particular political parties and was particularly strong among high educational attainers and those who stayed on in education after sixteen.

Conventional politics was an area of low concern to survey respondents. The issues of power and authority that concern them are much closer to home. As the authors put it:

> *The political terrain for young people is defined more in terms of the issues of immediate concern to them in their daily lives than in terms of the policies of the political parties. Thus the exercise of authority at home, at school or outside is a salient 'political issue' for a teenager living at home, as is everything to do with sex and relations between the sexes and different races.*
>
> (*Careers and Identities*, 148)

Nevertheless, the researchers were able to discern three broad ideological groups among the young respondents – Conservative, Socialist, and Environmentalist. Allegiance to these ideologies correlated with father's occupation and region, but also with the young peoples own attitudes.

From subcultures to common (but differentiated) youth culture: Paul Willis

Paul Willis and his co-authors of *Common Culture: Symbolic Work at Play in the Everyday Cultures of the Young* (1990) suggest that cultural variety and individualism has superseded subcultural conspicuousness. Willis *et al.* now find that the symbolic creativity they once associated particularly with subcultural types is characteristic of many young people. Most – perhaps all – young people create meaning in one way or another – if they cannot make music, they can make their own interpretations of it; if they cannot buy an expensive wardrobe of clothes, they might make their own.

Willis sees evidence of cultural democracy and power in this hive of cultural busyness. He argues that the commercial market in fashion and culture does not necessarily control how individuals actually use, for example, tapes, records, posters, clothes etc. Consumption can itself be a productive activity, if done with a degree of individuality. Moreover grass roots cultural activity can influence commercial production as well as vice versa. For instance, reggae and rap started 'on the street' before being commercially mass-produced. Willis goes so far as to suggest that cultural activity, not only of the young but also of other age groups, is the main dynamo for change in contemporary society. He would prefer that the direction of change be towards socialism but does not assume that this will be so. Controversially, however, he does find evidence of incipient socialism in what he refers to as the 'proto-communities' which people create in responding to certain widely and deeply felt issues. He gives as examples Live-Aid, Comic Relief, and the public response to the Hillsborough tragedy in which 95 Liverpool football club fans died. He sees these events as a merging of cultural style and social concern, although whether this can be thought of as nascent socialism is highly debatable.

Comment

Common Culture is a challenging book which provokes comment. First, it is suffused with a kind of cultural populism which, despite

Willis's Marxist pedigree, curiously echoes Thatcherism. Both Willis and Thatcher invest their 'faith' in the thinking consumer (or consumer-producer), although for Willis the communal and social aspects of consumption are substantially more pronounced. Willis's thinking consumer is certainly potentially more subversive than Thatcher's. Second, compared to *Learning to Labour*, *Common Culture* is relatively atheoretical. Again, this is partly the result of Willis's determination not to attribute meanings to people's activities that they do not attribute themselves. Third, and relatedly, this book verges on being apolitical. Willis implies that 'the people', not Paul Willis, will define socialism by their own activity (or perhaps they will not define it at all). All this rather begs the larger question of whether or not the direction of modern culture, youth or otherwise, is towards a greater degree of personal and communal liberation. Willis seems to be suggesting that it is but he does not really address this key issue.

Finally, the matter of whether the 'age of youth subcultures' is over can be briefly addressed. Willis seems to imply that stylistic creativity is now so widespread that particular subcultures are unlikely to stand out as quite so spectacular or bizarre. While this may be so, it is also true that considerable scope for peer group subcultures reflecting specific aspects of, for example, ethnicity or class remains.

Willis's analysis seems broadly compatible with David Muggleton's (see pp. 455-6) except that Willis still hankers for an interpretation that sees some radical direction (incipient socialism) into youthful activity. Both note characteristics of individualism, diversity and creativity (productivity in Willis's terms) among youth which occur much more widely than just within specific subcultures.

Youth: postmodern, or what? Bo Reimer

Bo Reimer's contribution to the collection *Youth Culture in Late Modernity* is titled *Youth and Modern Lifestyles* (1995). It is the most useful piece in the collection in terms of locating youth in relation to the rest of society and particularly in exploring what may be distinctive about contemporary youth culture.

Like most contemporary sociological work on youth, Reimer does not pursue a distinction between spectacular subcultural youth and 'the rest' or supposedly 'ordinary' youth. There are certainly differences among young people but this is not a major one, if, indeed, it ever was. Reimer does seek to explore whether or not youth can in some meaningful way be considered postmodern. His empirical data is largely on Swedish youth but he also draws on British and other European sources. Cautiously, it seems his analysis is likely to have application to late modern societies in general.

To determine whether or not youth culture is significantly postmodern, requires a definition of what the postmodern is. Two features which Reimer picks out as key in relation to youth are:

1   Popular culture is mixed with high culture.

2   The individual (or personal) is mixed with the social – a reorganisation and blending of elements previously often treated as distinct occurs. Thus, structural factors, such as class, are not seen as determining leisure and lifestyle options but the choice becomes ever more personal. A related supposed feature of postmodernity is the heightened importance of culture, particularly of the media. According to Reimer, the media plays a central and 'binding' role in most young people's lives.

Out of the above understanding of postmodernity has emerged what Reimer refers to as 'the hypothesis of the individualisation of lifestyles'. It is precisely this hypothesis – that personal choice and taste are becoming relatively more important than structural factors in influencing youthful lifestyles – which Reimer sets out to explore.

The central concept Reimer uses to explore youth culture is that of lifestyle which, as he notes, is currently in vogue in the social sciences. He defines lifestyle as 'the specific pattern of everyday activities that characterises an individual' (124). He goes on to say:

> *Each individual's lifestyle is unique: it is not identical to anyone else's. But at the same time, lifestyles orient themselves towards the common and the social. We choose lifestyles in relation to other people.*
>
> *(124)*

The thrust of his analysis is, then, about what lifestyles are more typical among youth and why particular lifestyles are chosen and changed.

Reimer links three concepts in attempting to understand youthful lifestyles: these are; lifestyle fields, modernity and subjectivity. By modernity he means the major processes typical of modern society in which young people's identities are formed e.g. industrialisation, urbanisation, secularisation, 'mediaisation' etc. By subjectivity he means the various (often contradictory and changing) identities experienced by an individual (for a discussion of the concept of multiple identities, see pp. 489-90). By lifestyle fields, Reimer means the range of cultural and socialising influences, including class and gender, in the social background of an individual which form cultural outlook and choices. This conceptual triad can be summarised as follows:

MACRO	INTERMEDIATE	MICRO
Modernity	Lifestyle fields	Subjectivity
e.g. Media	e.g. gender models, Class background	(identities)

Reimer elaborates the empirical detail of his analysis within this model. He reports that the typical lifestyle orientation of youth is the *entertainment orientation*. As he puts it, 'most young people want to have fun'. He goes on to state that: 'This orientation *unites* youth: it exists almost independent of socio-economic background' (135).

Young people, in general, then, of whatever class, are more likely than other age-groups to seek entertainment – pubs, films, discos and sport.

As Reimer says, 'this may seem trivial' but it leads to a significant conclusion: if a single pattern of explanation is to be found in this leisure activity, it is not class or gender, it is 'actually age'.

Conclusion

To return to the issue of whether youth culture is now postmodern, Reimer concludes that although there appear to be some changes in this direction, the case is not proven. First, let us look at his findings on the supposedly narrowing of the high/popular culture gap. The biggest change is that the low and highly educated and working and middle class youth watch a more similar range of TV programmes. The high/popular culture gap has been partially bridged in this respect.

In other respects, the gap persists albeit somewhat unpredictably. Young people coming from the middle class are much more likely than working class youth to be culturally active in both high and popular cultural areas. They are more likely to go to both the theatre and to the cinema. Gender differences in leisure patterns also exist, stemming mainly from a more outgoing orientation among young males and a home/family orientation among females. Reimer comments that two categories of youth 'differ quite radically in lifestyle orientation'. These are working class boys and middle class girls who for instance, use the media quite differently. 'The former watch more TV and music videos and the latter spend more time listening to music' (136). Drawing on his own empirical research between the admittedly short period of 1986-91, Reimer finds changes in these areas to be 'not particularly great'.

On the second and related point of the mixing of the personal and the social, Reimer is somewhat more supportive of the postmodern position. The 1980s was the decade of the yuppies but it was also the decade of Greenpeace and other movements which argued for moral consistency between personal lifestyle and political ideology and policy. Reimer, particularly, detects a perspective among many youth that 'personal pleasure and a more equal society' are 'equally important'. In Britain, it is perhaps the 'New Age' movement that implements this philosophy most consistently.

Finally, Reimer notes increased *differentiation* and *heterogeneity* among the lifestyles of the young. There are more different and varied alternatives than ever. He illustrates the point from music from which more and more genres emerge: 'If rock was previously marked off from pop, death metal is now separated from speed metal' (139). The same process would be as easily illustrated in clothes and fashion. This trend reflects an increase in the technical means of producing leisure items and the creative involvement of young people in the producer-consumer process (see Willis, pp. 462-3). Whether or not this development is seen as postmodern is largely a question of definition.

So, is 1990s youth postmodern? Reimer's conclusion is cautious and balanced. Despite giving the individualisation hypothesis every chance in his enquiry he finds that the formative effect of class and gender persist. Free floating individuals young people are not. However, it is possible that young people both have the means and inclination to pursue difference and individuality more effectively than previous generations. They may also be edging towards a view of public life which demands more consistency with personal morality. However, some of these features were also said to be typical of the 1960s youth movement.

'Ordinary' youth: the survey evidence

The subcultural theorists are often accused of ignoring the 'ordinary' majority of 1960s and 1970s youth. However, when one examines survey evidence representative of youth in either the 1960s/1970s or 1980s/1990s the results invariably seem unrevealing and even trivial. Surveys of teenagers tend to find that many experience some degree of conflict with their parents over dress and leisure habits, and do not have very strong or developed political views. Despite minor conflicts, parental and other authority is generally respected. So unremarkable are such findings, that the journalistic angle reporting these surveys is often that – surprise! surprise! – teenagers are not particularly rebellious. Thus, in 1996, the *Independent* reported a large survey of twelve to nineteen year olds under the headline 'Sober teens shun rebellion' (9.2.1996:1). The report went on to state:

> *In one of the most comprehensive surveys ever of young people's attitudes, it emerges that rather than rebelling against their parents, teenagers respect adults' points of view. More than nine out of ten young people believe that parents should have a say in what is taught at school… More than 60 per cent think that the courts should be able to sentence murderers to death.*

Despite the relative banality of such findings such surveys do sometimes throw up interesting data. Further analysis follows the presentation of some of these data.

Survey data on youth and young adults, 1974–1996

Youth

In 1974, the National Children's Bureau conducted a survey of more than 13,000 sixteen year olds (members of an age cohort not quite old enough to be the parents of current readers of this book). Respondents were all those still able to be contacted who were born in a single week of March 1958. Questions were asked on a wide variety of aspects of behaviour and attitude, but sex and drugs were excluded as topics, because answers were considered likely to be evasive. On questions relating to marriage and the family, mid 1970s teenagers emerged as thoroughly traditional in their attitudes and values. Only three per cent rejected the idea of marriage and most wanted to have children. Four out of five respondents said that they got on well with both their parents. The main areas of conflict with them were over dress and hair, although in only eleven per cent of homes was this a frequent source of friction.

In the early 1990s, several surveys of teenagers and, usefully from the point of view of comparison, of parents of teenagers, were conducted. These surveys concentrated mainly on *matters of behaviour* rather than attitudes and values, and particularly on behaviour in relation to sex, alcohol and drugs. They clearly showed a difference between parental demands and expectations of teenagers and the actual behaviour of teenagers. Thus, a nationwide survey of people born in 1970 carried out in 1990 found that 32 per cent of young men and 46 per cent of young women said that they had had sexual intercourse before their sixteenth birthday. In contrast, the National Opinion Poll survey (1991) of parents of eleven to sixteen year olds found that only five per cent expected that their own children would lose their virginity before the age of sixteen. As far as alcohol consumption is concerned, there is also a substantial gap between teenage reality and parental aspiration. over half of sixteen to seventeen year olds claim to go to pubs to drink alcohol at least once a week, yet the NOP survey found that only fourteen per cent of parents intended to allow their offspring to drink alcohol regularly before the age of eighteen. Similarly, parents mostly seemed unaware that many of their children took drugs (see below).

The findings of the above surveys are not surprising. It is hardly news that many teenagers, including some under-age, indulge in sex and alcohol and that their parents worry about this and tell them not to. It was ever thus! It may be that the AIDS epidemic and the injury contemporary teenagers can inflict on themselves and others through drunken-driving has added an edge of anxiety to parental warnings. Parents may also feel ineffectual given the relative affluence and freedom of many young people.

Young adults

While some teenagers behave contrary to their parents wishes on matters of lifestyle, there is little evidence to suggest significant political radicalism or cultural alienation among school-age teenagers. If anything, young adults are even more likely fundamentally to conform in these areas. A *Reader's Digest* (1991) survey of a rather older age group – eighteen to 34 year olds suggested little radicalism. The three main figures of influence cited were teachers, Members of Parliament and managing directors of large companies (see Figure 15.7). The majority said they were satisfied with and committed to their work and as many as three-quarters had turned up to work when feeling unwell. Although respondents did not appear radical, their view of 'important issues

facing Britain' perhaps has what Margaret Mead would call a 'prefigurative' flavour about it. Thus, 46 per cent saw pollution/environment emerging as a most important issue. Further, as many as 55 per cent expected that Britain would become part of a United States of Europe by the year 2000.

Drug consumption and youth culture

The evidence of greatly increased illicit drug consumption in the fourteen to 30 year old age-group in the past ten or fifteen years is substantial. A report (1995) from the Institute for the Study of Drug Dependence covers the fourteen to sixteen age group and one carried out by the Home Office research and planning unit based on the 1992 British Crime Survey covers the sixteen to 29 age group. We will deal with these separately.

(a) Important issues facing Britain

Q. What do you see as the most important/other important issues facing Britain today?

Q. What do you see as important issues facing Britain over the next ten years or so?

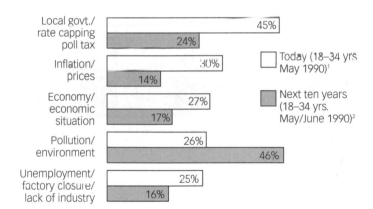

(b) Figures of influence[3]

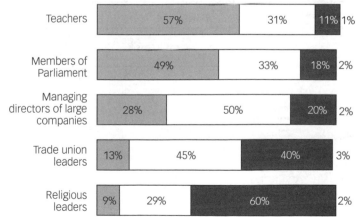

(Source: 1 Mori, *Reader's Digest*; 2 Mori, *The Sunday Times*; 3 Mori, *The Guardian*)

Figure 15.7 Who and what matters to younger adults (18-34)

'Drug futures': fourteen to sixteen year olds

The title of the report on fourteen to sixteen year old drug use is *Drug Futures: changing patterns of drug consumption amongst English youth* authored by Howard Parker, Fiona Measham and Judith Aldridge. The authors surveyed over 700 fourteen to sixteen year olds in north-west England over a period of three years between 1992-4. 51 per cent had tried drugs and half the remainder expected to do so. Among more regular users, cannabis was easily the most popular drug with 'hard' drugs a relative rarity.

According to the authors of the report, drug-taking has become an integral part of youth culture (see Figure 15.8). It is linked in with music, dance, youth magazines and the culture has generated its own covert vocabulary which partly serves to cut adults out of communication. According to the report, advertising has tapped into youth culture by, for instance, using 'thin, unhealthy, junkie lookalikes' to model grunge fashion.

School daze

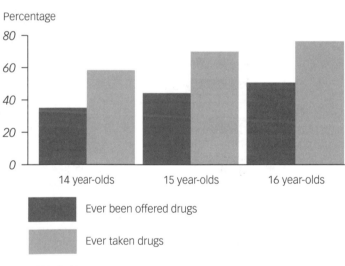

(Source: ISDD study)

Who uses what

	Age 14	Age 15	Age 16
		Percentages	
Cannabis (Spliffs, Puff)	32	42	45
Nitrites (Poppers, Rush)	14	22	23
LSD (Acid, Trips)	13	25	24
Solvents (Glue, Butane)	12	13	10
Magic Mushrooms	10	12	10
Amphetamine (Speed, Whizz)	10	16	18
MDMA (Ecstasy)	6	7	5
Cocaine (Coke, Crack)	1	4	3
Tranquillisers (Valium, Tranx)	1	4	2
Heroin (Smack, Skag)	0	3	1

Figure 15.8 'Just like having a cup of tea' – for some (14-16 year olds)

Although the report does not make the comparison, all this is reminiscent, in certain respects, of the 1960s counterculture at its height. Both 1960s, psychedelic music and house music titles make thinly veiled references to drugs. 1960s examples are *Sunshine Superman, Lucy in the Sky with Diamonds* and *Hey, Mr Tambourine Man*. 1990s examples are *Ellis Dee, Pure XTC* and *Easy E*. The 1960s psychedelic culture generated a language – partly drawn from black jazz culture – which described the states of mind and perceptions associated with psychedelic drugs. Examples are 'hang ups', 'far out', 'spaced out', 'turn on' and 'drop out'. The following are 1990s references to LSD 'trips' – Batmans, Penguins and Bart Simpsons.

The report suggests that drug-taking should be seen not merely as a problem of social control but as a type of consumption which has meaning within youth culture. A range of psychedelic drugs were popular among youth in the 1990s and it seems likely that they are consumed to produce similar pleasurable or psychological/religious effects as in the 1960s. Jock Young's use of Freud's concepts of the pleasure/reality principles as a way of illuminating these experiences seems as applicable in the 1990s as it was then.

Parker *et al.* stress the extent of the 'generational gap' between the requirements and expectations of adult authorities and the drug-consumption habits of many young people. This observation complements the findings of earlier surveys that parents are often unaware of the extent of their offspring's drinking of alcohol and experience of sex. Parker comments that young people are 'terrified of adults finding out' that they consume drugs and he suggests an approach based on open communication rather than punishment.

Report on drug consumption based on the 1992 British crime survey

The Home Office report on drug-taking states that there has been a rapid increase in drug use from the mid 1980s, especially cannabis, among sixteen to 29 year olds. It cites minimum consumption figures for the age group for 1991 as follows: one million had used cannabis, 400,000 amphetamines, 200,000 LSD, and 300,000 Ecstasy. In the population between sixteen and 59, twice as many people had used drugs as in 1982 – a doubling of use in nine years, the greatest increase being among sixteen to 29 year olds.

The report provides evidence that the observation of Parker *et al.*, that drug consumption is now an integral part of youth culture can be applied as much to the sixteen to 29 age groups as the fourteen to sixteen age groups. As one would expect, the evidence suggests greater use of more powerful drugs among the older age group. The Home Office analysis comments on the 'pick and mix' use of drugs for recreational purposes. They are almost as much a part of 'the scene' as alcohol and in some clubs, more so. To quote Parker *et al.* again: availability of drugs 'is a normal part of the leisure-pleasure landscape'.

A newspaper report by Cole Moreton titled *Goa Dance and LSD*

Craze Sweeps Clubs gives some idea of the role of drugs in 1990s youth culture (*The Independent*, 29.10.1995:6). Moreton begins:

> *Ecstasy, the rave drug of the Eighties is out. Goa Trance, the latest dance-music craze to seep the club world, a hypnotic blend of hard electronic rhythms and Eastern ideals, is fuelled by the archetypal Sixties hallucinogen, LSD.*

Allowing for possible journalistic excess (ecstasy 'out', LSD 'in'), Moreton does convey both the sense of fashionable faddishness and serious idealism which youth culture often combines. Moreton elaborates further on the idealism:

> *Goa Trance borrows more than ethnic imagery from its birthplace (India): Eastern spirituality is also being imported, as it was during LSD's heyday in the sixties. 'You can find Buddhism, Hinduism, and hundreds of ancient wisdoms and faiths which are thousands of years old there,' says Youth in this month's edition of the style magazine I-D. These beliefs attract British young people who are disillusioned by mainstream religion.*

The Home Office team provide interesting data on ethnic involvement in drug consumption. About a third of white and Afro-Caribbean respondents said they had taken drugs but only ten per cent of Asians. So, despite the association of certain drugs with 'Eastern spirituality', it seems that British Indians are substantially less involved in drug use than whites and Afro-Caribbeans. The report also comments that the most rapid increase in drug taking had been among females and Parker *et al.* also comment that girls are as likely to take drugs as boys. Parker *et al.* also claim that drug use is evenly distributed across social class and the Home Office report states that of sixteen to 29 year olds, 25 per cent who completed their education at sixteen had taken drugs, compared to 31 per cent who had completed it later.

Comment

The data referred to above confirm Reimer's contention that the basic lifestyle orientation of youth culture is towards entertainment. In Parker's terms it is a leisure-pleasure culture. This fundamental orientation cuts across class, gender and to a large extent ethnicity although detailed examination also shows important differences along these lines. These generalisations are as true of drug consumption as of other aspects of youth culture. The culture is to a considerable extent an integrated lifestyle – with music, dance, youth literature, fashion and style complementing each other.

Youth culture is also often somewhat cut-off from the adult mainstream. This is partly because certain activities (some of them like alcohol consumption and sexual intercourse) are forbidden to young people of a given age or in certain circumstances (alcohol) and therefore get driven 'underground'. This is even more the case

with drug consumption. The other aspect which partly explains the somewhat closed character of youth culture is the extent to which it is in fact, largely age-based. It provides an opportunity for young people to meet and associate with each other, to discuss life, and to have fun.

1960s and 1990s youth compared: differences and continuities

Given the detail already provided on youth in this chapter and in Chapter 4, this comparison of 1960s and 1990s youth will be of a summary nature. Each generation faces to some degree a different set of circumstances and makes its own response to them. The list of differences, then, will indicate how the experience of the two generations was distinctly socially constructed for and by them. The list of continuities will indicate what the two generations have experienced and created in common – there may be clues to more fundamental on-going changes in society here, a glimpse of the future.

Differences

1 Education/work transitions

These are much longer and often more complex and less certain for the 1990s generation and even if employment opportunities improve for youth are likely to remain so. (see pp. 459-60).

2 Social/control

Government reaction to the perceived 'permissiveness' and rebelliousness of 1960s youth and the urban disorders of the first half of the 1980s was an attempt to structure and control youth more. This was mainly done through education and training policy (see Chapter 4, pp. 120-34).

3 Political involvement

Whereas 1960s (middle class) youth was openly political, 1980s and 1990s youth has been more apparently quiescent. However, as Reimer's discussion of this issue makes clear, matters are somewhat more complicated than this generalisation indicates (see pp. 463-4).

4 Youth culture not subcultures

The youth subcultures of the 1960s and 1970s have, for the moment anyway, largely disappeared and their significance may, in any case, have been exaggerated by the media. Now, within youth culture, difference and variety occurs on a sufficiently general scale as not to be seen as 'spectacular'.

5 Realism replaces romanticism/idealism?

The much harsher economic climate from the second half of the 1970s reduced the idealistic aspirations of youthful radicals for fundamental change to a fairer and freer (i.e. morally better *and* more pleasurable) society. Thatcherism – Majorism was a philosophy of economic and social realism – competition, unequal shares and the need to fend for oneself were stressed. Anxiety affected youth as it did other social groups (see pp. 255-60). Nevertheless, under the eagle's eye, some idealism as well as hedonism still stirred.

Continuities

1 Individualism

Although an individualistic, even self-absorbed, character is often associated especially with the 1990s generation, an emphasis on 'doing your own thing' was very much a part of 1960s youth philosophy. It may be that 1990s youthful individualism is more fragmented in that youth relate less readily to collectivities, formal or informal, but the peer group remains strong (see p. 449) and social movements thrive (see pp. 316-8).

2 Structural influences

Reimer's work and that of others suggests that the influence of class, gender and ethnicity remain strong in the formation of youth cultural activities. If there has been a shift from structural influence to individual autonomy from the 1960s to the 1990s, it has been a change of degree or balance not a fundamental break (see p. 464).

3 Environmental concern

In the 1960s the concern of young radicals with environmental destruction was often regarded as rather cranky. The ESRC study of 1987-89 showed that support for environmental issues among the young rivalled their commitment to the two main political parties. Again, this is an indication that some characteristics of 1960s youth are taken up and carried forward by the later generation. What was once a novel concern becomes taken for granted.

4 Concern with gender identity and inequality

Second wave feminism and the gay liberation movement made gender and sexual equality and rights a major public issue in the 1960s. Both remain matters of concern but issues of gender identity have been widened to include 'masculinities' and more 'flexible', less rigid or stereotyped identities. The ESRC study further shows young people to be widely concerned with racial justice and equality.

5 Entertainment orientation (leisure-pleasure)

Pleasure seeking is virtually the logo of post-war 'modern youth'. Youth has developed a strong consumer or, perhaps better, consumer-producer orientation. Whether or not this particular lifestyle orientation has any wider significance for the rest of society as we approach the millennium is briefly discussed below.

6 An 'ordinary' majority: then and now

The assertion that most youth is ordinarily concerned with education, leisure, relationships and getting a job was partly a reaction to the concentration on the 'spectacular subcultures' of the 1960s and 1970s. Even so, youth is not ordinary in quite the same way that adults might be. There is a different structure and content to youth culture.

Youth and the future

Does contemporary youth hold the key to the future? In one sense, it clearly does. Those presently young will mostly be alive when the elderly and middle aged mostly will not. However, more searchingly, is there something in the lifestyle orientation of *modern* youth that may become more general when, say, they are middle aged? Margaret Mead offers a cultural model which enables this speculation to be more precisely structured.

In her essay *Culture and Commitment: a Study of the Generation Gap*, Margaret Mead focuses on the problems of youth by distinguishing between three kinds of culture: postfigurative, configurative and prefigurative. A postfigurative culture gains its authority from the past and little change occurs. The young learn and apply traditional wisdom. A configurative culture is one in which change is occurring and the model of behaviour is that of contemporaries rather than elders. A prefigurative culture is one in which the speed of change is so rapid that culture must become anticipatory; the future of the child, rather than the knowledge of the parent or wisdom of the elder must become its guiding light.

It is, at least, arguable that Western contemporary culture and society is changing so rapidly that it could be termed prefigurative and that youth is at the cutting edge of this change. Mead herself thought that the 1960s generation of romantic radicals – with their concern for the environment, for racial and gender equality and justice, for peace, and for leisure-pleasure – were in the process of creating a prefigurative culture. Their disillusionment with conventional politics and with corporate and government bureaucracy also augered radical change. Similarly, Charles Reich's *The Greening of America* (1970) and Theodore Roszac's *The Making of the Counterculture* (1973) argued that the concerns and lifestyles of radical youth would become more general.

What Mead, Reich and Roszac did not predict was the backlash of the New Right. Preaching the realism of self-interest, Thatcher and Reagan set out to crush the romanticism and permissivism of the 1960s generation. However, the above discussion of 1980s and 1990s youth shows that there are important continuities between the two youthful generations. All the concerns of 1960s youth listed in the previous paragraph remain of concern to the youth of the

1990s, some perhaps more so. Given the attempts to rediscipline and control contemporary youth, it is not surprising that they tend to express their concerns less publicly. Krishan Kumar (1995) has discerned a thread of romanticism and grounded idealism running from 1960s radicalism through to 1990s postmodernism. If postmodernity is a time of change and difference, then youth can be expected to be in the thick of it. But nothing is inevitable as the following brief consideration of middle and old age will show.

The middle aged and elderly: an ironic footnote

The middle aged and elderly are considered in a variety of contexts in various parts of this book (see p. 298 and pp. 402-5, for the elderly). Clearly they merit more than an ironic footnote. The purpose of this section is to comment on the ironic nature of the relationship between contemporary youth and the middle aged and on the probable consequences of the current age structure for younger people (see Figure 15.9).

The sheer size of the post-war baby-boom generation, otherwise known as the 1960s generation, creates a long term problem for the relatively much smaller current generation of 'teens and twenties'. The 1960s generation, including ex-radicals, is now 'in power' – in business, politics and most other areas of British and European society. There is every sign that they wish to hang on to what they have. High youth unemployment suggests that young people are at a relative employment disadvantage although redundancies among the middle aged partly clears a way for them (see pp. 257-8).

It is also likely that in terms of consumer power, the 45 to 59 year olds will outstrip that of the young. Many of them are at or about peak earning power. However, their expenditure and consumption shows a much more conservative pattern than that of young people described above. Indeed, Figure 15.10 suggests that their expenditure is just as conservative as that of adults as a whole. Diane Coyle comments that:

> 'those 50 year-olds still rocking along to the Rolling Stones have become, it seems, financially prudent home-bodies. Their cultural adventurousness is limited to a foray on the Internet from their home computer, and their social conscience is manifested in buying free-range chickens.
> (The Independent, 10.1.1996:13).

Relative percentage change in these three age groups between 1995 and 2025.

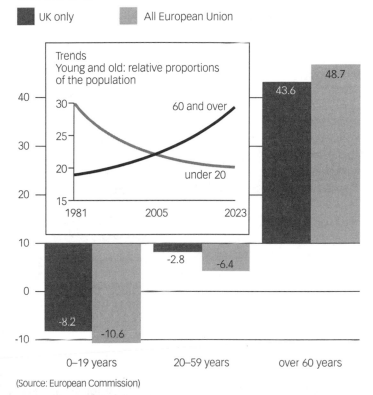

(Source: European Commission)

Figure 15.9 Generation gap

The mind boggles at the thought of what those 50 year olds not rocking along to the Rolling Stones do for fun!!

The fact that the baby-boomers will remain a relatively large generation throughout their collective life course – the 'pig in the python' factor – means that even when the present younger generation reaches middle age, they may still be somewhat smothered by their parents. Of course, by then, they may not mind.

Questions

1 Compare and contrast 1960s and 1990s youth culture and subcultures.
2 What are the problems and issues which have structured the experience of 1980s and 1990s youth? How have young people responded?

Top spending priorities if financially secure

August 1994. Base: 977 adults

- Save in bank/building society
- Buy something for home
- Decorate/minor home improvement
- Major home improvement
- Buy new car
- Long-term investment
- Medium-term investment
- Pay off some of mortgage
- Buy clothes/shoes
- Spend more on having a good time

0   10   20   30   40   50

(Source: *BMRB/Mintel*)   ■ Males   ■ Females

Edwina Currie

Trevor McDonald

Change in population

1996-2006

Age	
0-29	-554,000
30-44	+252,00
45-59	+1,315,000
60-77	+147,000
75+	+442,000
Total	**+1,780,000**

(Source: OPCS)

Figure 15.10 The middle aged – now as conservative as other generations?

Summary

1 The concept of the life course is a key one in studying age stages and generation. Within the life course, age stages are not fixed categories – society and the individual structure the life course.

2 The tendency to determinism of certain biological and psychological approaches to youth (or 'adolescence') is indicated. Of the various structural approaches discussed, a radical social constructionist approach (i.e. one supported by class, gender and ethnic analysis) is preferred.

3 The social context of modern youth. The general collective experience of education and a number of factors specific to post-war society are the context in which post-war youth emerged.

4 Class greatly affects youth culture and particularly subcultures. A classic example of a working class youth subculture is the skinheads. Their tough, 'macho', territorial, and anti-authoritarian attitudes reflect similar strains in male working class culture. Working class youth subcultures have tended to be male-dominated.

5 Race-ethnicity is a distinctive 'ingredient' in youth subcultures. Two examples of Afro-Caribbean youth subcultures are the Rudies of the 1960s and the Rastafarians. As with other youth subcultures, semiology (the interpretation of signs, including dress and music styles) is useful in understanding Afro-Caribbean youth subcultures. The hustler and Rastafarian lifestyles are more associated with adult as well as youth roles than is the case with other youth subcultural lifestyles.

6 Middle class youth culture also reflects the norms and values of its class. This is true of the partly campus-based movement which nevertheless also revolted against conventional values, exploring a subterranean world of pleasure and 'alternative', idealistic values.

7 A wide range of material on 1980s and 1990s youth is presented and discussed. Much of this is 'hard' structural material on job opportunity/unemployment and on ethnic/racial and gender inequality. There is also a sustained probing of the content of contemporary youth culture particularly whether or not it is 'postmodern' in some aspects.

8 A summary of the differences and continuities between 1960s and 1990s youth is provided (see p. 468).

9 The progress of contemporary youth is partly blocked by the currently middle aged and elderly.

Research and coursework

This area offers many research possibilities both relative to a single age stage or cross-generational. Childhood lends itself to cross-generational analysis, particularly in relation to the role of adult males and females since child care and socialisation (there is substantial relevant material in Chapter 3 on this topic).

Contemporary material such as newspaper reports and analysis can be useful in studying cultural attitudes and behaviour towards children. Children are not easy to interview successfully but observation can be effective.

For obvious reasons youth is an interesting area for many students to study but it is important to avoid simplistic and subjective judgements and analysis. An element of contrast within a study should lead to it being adequately theoretical and sophisticated. Thus, a comparison of the experience of males and females, black youth and white youth, working and middle class youth, should involve consideration of respectively, gender, 'race'/ethnicity, and class theory. In fact, it is likely that any project on youth will involve some consideration of all these theoretical areas although the amount and 'blend' will vary according to the topic. Similarly, a comparison of the 'ordinary' majority of young people in a given class with an 'extraordinary' or spectacular subculture (e.g. conformist working class youth with skinheads) should encourage theoretical development (including the use of some semiology). A particularly wide range of secondary sources and contemporary data is available on this topic and a rich variety of methods is appropriate for original research. What must be avoided is the merely descriptive and anecdotal.

Given that the habits of older people may partly be designed to avoid frequent contact with young people, there may be problems producing a well selected sample of this age group. It is never sufficient merely to interview one's own or a friend's 'granny' unless such an interview is part of a properly designed quota sample or merely a minor piece of biographical illustration in a larger study. Again, an in-built comparative element – middle compared to working class old, older males compared to older females – should move the research away from the merely descriptive towards the explanatory and theoretical.

Further reading

Ken Roberts, *Youth and Employment in Modern Britain* (Oxford University Press, 1995) summarises much current research. Stuart Hall and Tony Jefferson eds. *Resistance Through Rituals*, has become a classic of the subcultural approach although not all the articles in it are easily accessible to students.

Readings

(NOTE: These two readings are closely related and reflect two areas of concern in the recent sociology of youth. First, is the concept of youth as a series of transitions. Bob Coles describes three main areas of transition. Second, is the balance between social structure and individual choice and attitudes in explaining the experience of any particular young person. Choice – in relation to education and career – and attitudes in relation to gender and race are the subject of Reading 2.)

Reading 1
Youth as a series of status transitions

From Bob Coles, *Youth and Social Policy. Youth Citizenship and Young Careers* (UCL Press, 1995), pp. 8-11

Rather than seek a complex and often unsatisfactory age definition for youth, many academic writers have defined it as a series of transitions (Banks *et al.* 1992, Jones and Wallace 1992). Achieving the status of adulthood is thus dependent upon successfully making at least some of these transitions, rather than reaching some arbitrary chronological age. The main transitions of youth which are of critical importance are as follows:

– the transition from full-time education and training to a full-time job in the labour market (the school-to-work transition)
– the transition from family of origin (mainly the biological family) to family of destination (the domestic transition)
– the transition from residence with parents (or surrogate parents) to living away from them (the house transition).

One of the main concepts used within this book to theorise these transitions is the concept of 'career'. By career is meant the sequence of statuses through which young people pass as they move from childhood dependency to adulthood. Some of the these statuses may be prescribed by law, some will be the result of the intervention of an 'agency' of the state, while others will be 'chosen' by young people themselves, although often under the strong influence of their parents. But whatever the basis on which a particular status is allocated, this status sets in train a series of social processes which has the potentiality to 'determine' the likely course of a young person's future status sequence. Under the age of 16, all young people within the United Kingdom are required to be in full-time education. The particular school they attend and the type of education they experience are the result of a series of decisions made by education authorities about the provision of educational establishments and what the authorities and/or their parents deem to be appropriate for the educational development of each child. Parents are often involved in a key role in determining what they think is appropriate for their children, but in the case of children and young people being considered 'vulnerable' or 'at risk', social workers and social service departments may also be involved in the decision-making process. Partly on the basis of an assessment of a

young person's need, and partly based upon the wishes of parents, a young person may experience full-time education in a variety of different institutions, from neighbourhood comprehensive schools, to private (boarding or non-boarding) schools, to special schools (designed to educate those with special educational needs), to children's homes (with or without special educational provision), to Youth Treatment Centres designed to cope with highly disturbed young people in a secure setting. In later chapters of this book we will outline the ways in which the decisions to allocate this 'status' to young people at this early stage in their career carry with them long-term consequences for future career development.

The concept of 'career' as a series of staged status sequences is important in that each step in the sequence can be shown to determine future steps. It should be emphasised straight away that the notion of 'determination' is not being used here in a strong, precise or mathematical sense. It is not being argued that one stage automatically leads to the next but, rather, that the attainment of each status position, in turn, has the capacity both to open up and close down future opportunities. Thus, for instance, attaining educational qualifications at the age of 16 may open up the possibility of further full-time tertiary education between the ages of 16 and 18, and further qualifications gained at 18 may, in turn, open up the possibility of full-time higher education for three or more years. Good academic qualifications may thus enhance the possibility of a longer career in education. They may also serve to delay entry into the labour market until many young people reach their early 20s. This status sequence of an extended post-16 educational career does not, of course, follow automatically from attaining good qualifications at the age of 16. Some young people with equally good qualifications may 'choose' to enter the labour market at the age of 16 or 18. But without attaining the requisite number of qualifications, a young person may have little alternative but to leave school at 16 and seek work in the labour market. On the other hand ... should the decision be made that a young person should receive pre-16 education at a special school, in a children's home, or in a Youth Treatment Centre, this often has grave consequences for the likelihood of their attaining the requisite levels of qualifications at the age of 16 which would allow them to pursue either an advanced course of education after that age or a training place with good employment prospects. For these young people, the decision to allocate a particular educational status before the age of 16 sets severe limits to the post-16 careers likely to be open to them.

For those who are successful in gaining good qualifications at the ages of 16 and 18, obtaining a place in higher education may also offer further opportunities for them to move away from their parental home and so develop a 'housing career' (Jones 1987). Alternatively, getting a (good) job and earning a wage may give people the financial means to leave home and/or set up a new home with a partner or spouse. Young people who enter the labour market before the age of 20 are much more likely to marry earlier than those who go on to higher education, so decisions made about a career in education are likely to have an impact upon their domestic careers. Those who develop 'extended transitions' through education are more likely to delay their 'domestic careers' (Jones 1987). Those who experience 'fractured transitions', through being unemployed for extended periods, are also likely to suspend decision to marry or start a family (Wallace 1987). Each of the three main transitions do, therefore, interrelate and the status gained in one may both 'determine' and 'be determined by' the status sequences which are likely to be attained in another.

The three main transition lines described above contain structures of opportunities for young people. So far, they have been presented only as a series of structured choices which, before the age of 16, are made either by young people and their parents, or by other agencies responsible for young people's welfare. At the age of 16+ a young person may 'choose' whether to stay on at school, go on to sixth-form studies or take courses in colleges of further education, take part in youth training or seek employment. Yet these main structures of choice are themselves determined by social and economic conditions and these, in turn, are largely shaped by social and economic policies.

Questions

1 With reference to the text, choose two of the main status transitions of youth and illustrate how they may be experienced differently by young people of different social backgrounds.
2 Describe with examples what is meant by 'structures of opportunities for young people'.

Reading 2
Self concept and career trajectory: attitudes to gender and race

From Michael Banks et al., Careers and Identities (Open University Press, 1992), pp. 109, 116, 133-5.

But where does individual agency fit into this picture? Does the young person merely respond blindly to structural and situational influences or does he or she do anything actively to control them? Are there choices to be made or merely directives from cultural roots to reproduce the same lifestyles, values and aspirations that have gone before? How are competing pressures accommodated or resisted and the dilemmas they present resolved? 'Identities are negotiated, created wilfully out of the raw material provided by social relations and social circumstances' (Breakwell, 1987).

(W)e try to uncover something of this personal component in identity: what individuals perceive their attributes to be, what characterises their 'self-concept'. ...

Self-evaluation and career trajectory

There has been considerable debate about the effects of experiences in the education system and in the labour market upon aspects of

self-concept. Self-esteem has been found to be positively correlated with educational attainment (Rosenberg, 1989) but the causal direction is unclear. Is self-esteem a by-product of success at school or one of its determinants? There is probably a complex chain of interactions between the two over time and especially during the early school years. Later experiences in the labour market are also known to be associated with changes in self-evaluation. For instance, unemployment changes (lowers) self-esteem, but its impact is moderated by situational variables, its length, and the availability of a social support network. Its effect is also moderated by how committed the unemployed person is to employment. ...

Attitude Dimension

Beliefs about the roles of the sexes, sexual behaviour and race

As we have seen, 16-20-year-olds in Britain in the late 1980s were predominantly egalitarian in their views about the roles of males and females. The six questions we asked about aspects of male and female roles did nevertheless produce variations in opinion and these variations formed two clusters concerned with equality at home and in the workplace, and about women's maternal role, which proved to be interrelated. In effect, there were grounds for concluding not just that young people had differing views on various aspects of the roles of the sexes but that they had a position on sexual equality in general.

Females, not surprisingly, were more egalitarian than males, and sex-role egalitarianism was moderately related to educational attainment. However, this latter relationship diminished in strength between the first and third waves of the survey (i.e. as respondents got older). Egalitarianism was also related to labour market position at 18, but principally among the males; boys who had left school and gone directly into employment were the least egalitarian, those remaining in full-time education pursuing an academic track were the most egalitarian. As we have seen, in one area of equality, at home and in the workplace, both sexes were overwhelmingly in favour; in another, relating to women's role as mothers, they were much more divided.

Another attitude dimension, sexual conservatism, representing opinions for and against caution about sexual behaviour, was similarly endorsed by *more* females than males, but showed the reverse pattern with respect to career trajectory. Sexual conservatism was *lowest* in the academic and no-career groups and *highest* in the school-to-job groups.

It seems that girls' greater endorsement than boys of gender equality is distinct from their views about sexual behaviour, where they take the more conservative position. Yet at the same time the more highly educated among both sexes were the most likely to endorse both equalitarianism and sexual liberalism, and those who had gone straight into jobs at 16 were the most likely to reject both.

Attitudes to race equality, which were assessed in the second wave of the survey, showed the same pattern as for sex role. Although both sexes endorsed 'antiracist' sentiments, the girls again were ahead of the boys. Those staying on in education were again the most in favour of race equality and those leaving the least in favour of it.

All the sex role attitudes were also relatively stable over time. That is to say, those young people who were most egalitarian at 16 were also likely to be among the most egalitarian at 17 and 18. At the same time, there was little indication of any overall changes with age or between cohorts' attitudes.

Questions

1 What general differences in self-esteem and in attitudes on gender/sex issues and 'race' are reported between early and later school leavers? Make some suggestions to account for these differences.

2 What differences in beliefs about the roles of the sexes, sexual behaviour and 'race' are reported between males and females? Make some suggestions to account for these differences.

Culture and Identity: Community and Consumption

It's all culture. But what does it *mean*? The sociology of culture is about meaning

Aims of this chapter

1 To provide a working knowledge of the concepts of culture and identity and related issues and debates.

2 To introduce the following perspectives on culture and identity: Psychoanalytic, Interactionist, Functionalist, Marxist and various radical perspectives.

3 Critically to examine the work of the Centre for Contemporary Cultural Studies (CCCS), Birmingham.

4 Critically to examine the influence of Structuralism, Poststructuralism/Postmodernism, and Semiology on cultural theory in Britain, particularly at the CCCS.

5 To examine, in the context of the above class, ethnic and gendered culture (and to reference where else in this book these matters are presented).

Culture, identity and community

The definition of culture so far used in this book has been 'way of life' and this has included minority as well as majority cultures. This definition has its origins in structural sociology which stresses the formative influence on individuals of beliefs, values, norms and ideologies. In contemporary cultural studies and social science, the term culture is increasingly employed with a more specific, though not contradictory, emphasis than in the established usage. Particularly in the study of the media, culture describes sign systems, including linguistic and visual. Thus, youth subcultures created sign systems through language (slang/argot) and style which convey meanings distinct from those of the majority culture. Cultural analysis can, therefore, be used as a means of interpreting or decoding signs and the signification process (i.e. the process of constructing signs). Cultural analysis of this kind is virtually synonymous with semiology – the interpretation of signs (see below).

This second aspect of cultural studies was introduced into England in the early 1970s mainly by Stuart Hall at the Contemporary Centre for Cultural Studies (CCCS).

Cultural analysis as sign interpretation has been influenced by symbolic interactionism as well as semiotics. Symbolic interactionism focuses on the use of language and other meaningful systems of communication. Within the interactionist tradition, cultural communication is frequently presented as involving creative action or agency. This balances the structural emphasis of functionalism and Marxism. Semiotics or the analysis of cultural signs was popularised mainly by French structural social scientists. They tend to present sign systems, including language, as frameworks which constrain and even determine (or over-determine) individual and group meaning (a point further explained below).

Identity is formed within culture. A survey of the literature suggests three overlapping but clearly distinguishable uses of the concept of identity within sociology: personal or self identity, social identity and collective identity (see Figure 16.1). The definitions of these concepts given below are preliminary and are developed and criticised throughout this chapter. The first usage of identity emerges from the theory of the self as developed by interactionists William James and George Mead (see p. 9). As the

Oxford Dictionary of Sociology puts it, for interactionists, 'the self is a distinctively human capacity which enables people to reflect' both on themselves and on the social world through communication and language (1994:232). This view of the self allows for the possibility that the individual can participate in the formation of her or his own identity. Such an approach to personal identity as relatively autonomous chimes well with the view of some who adopt a postmodernist or late modernist perspective that contemporary Western society offers more options for self presentation and identity than in the early modern period. Among those who disagree with this view are French structuralists and poststructuralists, including Foucault who see subjectivity (personal identity) as 'constituted' by social forces (see pp. 98-100).

Social identity is ascribed by others to the individual whereas personal identity is self-defined. An individual may be socially identified according to occupation, religion, ethnicity or by other social categories. Social identity is close in meaning to social status but as Goffman helpfully observes, social identity can involve an evaluation of an individual's personal characteristics within the context of a given social position (1963:12). Thus, an individual may be socially identified as a 'good' or 'bad' plumber or Catholic or whatever. The trend of postmodern analysis is to suggest that traditional social identities such as class are 'breaking down'.

Collective identity is a shared identity which is consciously sought by an individual. Collective identity involves both the action of self and others and to that extent has aspects of both personal and social identity. Usually collective identity is voluntary but also involves acceptance by the relevant group. Collective

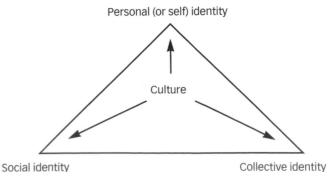

Figure 16.1 Aspects of identity

identities include trade unionist, feminist, membership of the Rotary Club and membership of Green Peace. Modern social movements such as the black liberation movement and the feminist movement have been major examples of collective identities. In so far as such collective identities involve shared values, emotions, symbols and goals, they constitute communities (see pp. 149-53). A church congregation or football supporters club are examples.

To a greater or lesser extent, cultural context influences each of the three above categories of identity. As we saw earlier, personal identity is formed partly through the influence of cultural environment (see pp. 459-64). What an individual 'wants to be' reflects possibilities and limits within a culture. Social identity is, in the end, a cultural categorisation whatever efforts the individual may have made to achieve a given position. Collective identity involves, by definition, a sharing of cultural meanings and purpose albeit usually on a voluntary basis.

Key issues and debates

Cultural 'levels' – elite/mass, high/popular: quality and inequality

Much of the terminology used in the sociology of culture and cultural studies is ideologically loaded. In other words, the terminology is not neutral but contains values and judgements. This is especially true of the following pairs of terms: 'elite/mass' culture and 'high/popular' culture.

The term 'elite' is a more specifically sociological one than 'high'. Elite culture simply refers to the culture of a socially dominant (i.e. elite) group. Thus, the medieval aristocracy had a way of life that was in many respects quite different from that of the peasantry. The aristocracy had access to careers, entertainment and lifestyle generally closed to the rest of the population. So, although the term 'elite' is sometimes used to imply 'better', within social science it is used simply to indicate a particular social stratum without implying that this stratum or its culture are better than others. On the other hand, the origin of the term 'high culture' lies within literary and art criticism. It is used to refer to classical music, 'serious' poetry and literature, ballet and 'fine' art.

As employed by critics such as F R Leavis, the term had clear connotations of excellence and superiority. Today, there is a tendency to avoid the term 'high culture' because of its judgmental and, some would say, snobbish overtones. However, not using the adjective 'high' does not itself help in deciding which kinds of cultural activity are 'superior' and why.

The term 'mass culture' is usually paired with 'elite culture'. The mass is 'the rest' – those who are not the elite. This was used widely in the 1930s, partly as an alternative to class(es). It referred to the ordinary majority of industrial society often seen as faintly threatening or obdurately ignorant by cultural and political elitists. Mass culture has often been described as the product of commercial manipulation. Although still in current usage, the term 'mass culture' clearly carries overtones that may seem insulting.

The term 'popular culture' is now frequently preferred as a less judgmental alternative to 'mass culture'. It was regularly used in the 1970s and 1980s by radical, including Marxist, commentators, before becoming more widely employed. Studies of popular culture frequently focus on the consciousness and pleasures of the public. In the last quarter century, studies of popular culture have included research into youth subcultures, media audience participation patterns, and holidays in 'popular' resorts such as Blackpool. The concept of popular culture does not supersede that of class culture. Much research into popular culture strongly reflects the structural and cultural aspects of social class, particularly the tension between working class cultural creativity and solidarity and the cultural products of corporate capitalism which often reinforce an individualistic consumer ideology.

Culture, identity and ideology

Much of this chapter will be about the ideological content of culture and about resistance to ideology. This is not the place to present the concept of ideology in detail (see pp. 98-100 and pp. 139-40) but it is important to clarify here the relationship of ideology to culture and identity. Marx argued that in capitalist society, the dominant class attempts to use cultural means – religion, the media, education – in an ideological way i.e. to legitimise its own position. It seeks to persuade the working class that the inequalities of capitalist society are in the best interest of everybody, including the working class. This implies a particular identity for working class people as subordinate and governed by those who, for whatever reason, deserve their superior position.

Marx suggested a different identity for the working class and believed its members would achieve it. This is a liberated identity involving greater material equality, greater cultural access and more decision making power. During this chapter we will be examining signs of resistance to dominant ideology and culture among the working class and other groups and exploring what cultural alternatives, if any, have emerged to capitalist consumer culture.

Perspectives on culture and identity

Biological: Eysenck and Glover

The relationship between the biologically inherited and socially structured aspects of identity is a sensitive and controversial area. Some biologists such as Hans Eysenck claim that genetic inheritance is largely responsible for personality type whereas sociologists tend to stress cultural factors in character and identity formation. Dogmatic statements from either discipline are unhelpful: the interplay of heredity and environment is complex and the balance of influence between the two factors may be different in the case of each individual. Further, it is likely to be the interaction of both influences rather than the effect of one or other separately that best explains personality and behaviour.

Hans Eysenck has classified personality along two related dimensions: introversion/extroversion (E Scale – Extroversion measure) and stable/unstable (N Scale – Emotionality measure). Eysenck relates certain personality types with particular patterns of behaviour. Thus, he cites evidence to suggest that prisoners score significantly higher than a control group on both E and N. A criticism of this and similar studies is that it may be that other groups would record similar measures – pop stars? sports stars? politicians? psychiatrists?

Glover stresses that the more obvious bodily aspects of identity should not be overlooked. He states that:

> *To see someone is to see a body. And bodies tell us a lot about people. We learn about their age, their sex, and perhaps their race, something about their strength, their state of health and their weight …*
>
> *(1988:70)*

However, all these matters are viewed or constructed differently in different societies or by different groups. Further, individuals present themselves very differently in relation to these matters. The chronology of age may be immutable but practically everything else is open to some change and greatly differing presentation. Some people are 'old' at 40 others 'young' at 50. Body carriage and 'language' is subject to personal and social influence – as observation of the military, prisons and schools will confirm. We even speak of sexual identity as open to change.

Psychoanalytic: Freud and Erikson

The psychoanalytic or psychodynamic tradition established by Freud 'stresses the inner core of a psychic structure as having a continuous (though often conflicting) identity' (*Oxford Dictionary of Sociology*, 1994:232). The capacity to develop an identity is considered to be innate and this is initially stimulated when the child assimilates aspects of external persons or objects, usually the beliefs and morals of the parent. From the beginning and throughout life, identity reflects the interaction of the individual with society (others).

Erik Erikson, a student of Freud continued to explore the concept of identity in terms of connections between the individual and society or, as he more elegantly put it, in psycho-social terms. We examined Erikson's theory of psycho-social development earlier (see pp. 447-8). Here it is enough to say that he regarded each of eight stages of life as presenting a psycho-social crisis or what could be termed a specific crisis of identity. The psycho-social crisis or challenge of adolescence is that of achieving a stable adult identity itself – identity versus confusion. Erikson stressed that the psycho-social crisis varies depending on social circumstances.

In Freudian based models, identity involves two main aspects. One is a continuous sense of being the same person, of having a personal history. The second is having a viable relationship with others – crudely, a role or roles in society. Some critics find Freudian-based approaches to identity and development too schematic and pre-determined. However, the Freudian model does provide a dynamic conceptualisation of the struggle of the individual to achieve purpose and affirmation in society and of how this process can run into difficulties.

Interactionist: Mead and Goffman

There is no need to repeat here the material on self and society given in the introduction to the interactionist perspective (see pp. 9-10). Goffman greatly extended Mead's sociology of interaction. Goffman compares the relationship of self and society to that of an actor in a play – his famous 'dramaturgical metaphor'. This metaphor effectively captures the double-sided nature of interaction: the individual or self is described as seeking to *manage* the impressions others receive of her or him- to 'put on a show' for others – while, at the same time being constrained by the rules of performance (their expectations which, in turn, reflect wider cultural expectations). Self is capable of presenting a certain image or identity to others but is normally limited by framework of expectation. There are then, two related 'sides' to what Goffman terms 'the interaction order'. The view that identity is formed through the interaction of the 'inner' or personal world and the 'outer' or social world is shared by Goffman with Mead and is characteristic of interactionism.

Goffman developed a conceptual vocabulary to describe the various aspects and complexities of the interaction order. Individuals are described as giving performances in which they enact 'routines' (e.g. indulge in eccentric manners) in which they use a 'setting' (e.g. a dinner party) and perhaps 'props' (e.g. perhaps making a stooge of some unfortunate fellow guest). By acting individually but within culturally acceptable limits, self achieves a socially recognisable identity. In Chapter 10 a detailed description is given of how, as Goffman presents it, patients consigned to an asylum manage to develop strategies of adjustment which enable them to win back some freedom and identity in the face of institutional control and definitions. Goffman does recognise that institutions have the power to label and control although generally he prefers to describe institutions in terms of the actions of groups and individuals rather than in terms of organisational norms and functioning.

In his book *Stigma: Notes on the Management of Spoiled Identity*, (1963), Goffman deals mainly with social definitions of identity. Goffman prefers the term social identity to that of social status as the former includes personal characteristics (e.g. whether or not a person is honest affects his or her social identity) as well as structural ones such as a person's occupation. Goffman distinguished between *virtual social identity* and *actual social identity*. Virtual social identity is the initial identity others give to a person on the basis of appearances and social setting. Actual social identity refers to the 'category (position) and attributes' the individual does in fact prove to possess (1963:12 – author's brackets). As we have seen, self plays a role in the process by which others establish her or his social identity but the power of others can override personal definitions of identity. This is especially so when an individual is *stigmatised*. Goffman uses this term to 'refer to an attribute that is deeply discrediting' which results in the individual being 'disqualified from full social acceptance' (1963:13, 9). There are three types of stigma: bodily (e.g. physical handicap may be stigmatised), moral (e.g. the stigmatisation of a child abuser) and tribal (e.g. the stigmatising of another 'race' or religion). The stigmatisation of the Jews provides an example of Goffman's use of the term. The Jews were for centuries disqualified from full social acceptance and citizenship throughout Europe. More recently, the dominance of whites over blacks enabled them to stigmatise black skin and those who possessed it. Despite the resistance to stigmatisation of both Jews and black people, it still persists.

Postmodern perspective

Postmodern perspective is dealt with briefly here in order to make a brief comparison with the interactionist approach and because both have a larger psychological component than any of the three structural theories examined below. Postmodern approaches are given a full section later.

Stuart Hall contrasts the way interactionism attempts to balance individual agency with cultural influence, with the greater emphasis postmodernism gives to the latter:

> *The subject previously experienced as having a unified and stable identity, is becoming fragmented: composed not of a single, but of several, sometimes contradictory or unresolved identities … This produces the postmodern subject, conceptualised as having no fixed, essential or permanent identity. Identity becomes a 'moveable feast': formed and transformed continuously in relation to the ways we are represented or addressed in the cultural systems which surround us.*
>
> *(1992:276)*

Hall favours the postmodern approach as he describes it. Recently he has referred to identity as follows:

> *Identities are … points of temporary attachment to the subject positions which discursive practices (ideologically influenced behaviour) construct for us. They are the result of a successful articulation or 'chaining' of the subject into the flow of discourse …*
>
> *(1996:6) (author's brackets)*

Figure 16.2 'I haven't even got dressed yet. I can't decide which me I want to be.'

To liberal humanists, such as Ernest Gellner, this approach substitutes cultural determinism for crude Marxist economic determinism. Many social scientists who employ the concept of post or late modernity take a different view to Hall. Anthony Giddens argues that late modernity is characterised by greater demand for and potential for personal autonomy (1992) (see pp. 492-3).

Social action: status and lifestyle

Weber's concepts of status groups and lifestyle foreshadowed aspects of the sociology of identity that have become a central concern of contemporary sociology. Weber certainly did not believe that individuals freely create their own identities regardless of social context and constraints but he did consider that membership of cultural, leisure and religious groups reflected an element of choice and preference which could easily cut across class lines. Thus, he anticipated the view of many postmodernists that individuals express taste and meanings through consumption which may have little to do with their class position. This analysis has been made particularly in relation to youth groups (see pp. 463-4).

In the late nineteenth century, Thorstern Veblen noted the role of consumption in the efforts of America's newly rich to establish their refined taste and high social status. In his *The Theory of the Leisure Class*, (1899), he coined the term 'conspicuous consumption' to describe their attempts at social display. Although more of a satirist than theoretician, Veblen did foreshadow the decoding of style and identity of later sociologists.

George Simmel focused on how people sustained a sense of identity in the stresses of the modern city (*The Metropolis and Mental Life*, 1903). He suggests that people tend to adopt rather superficial images and styles in order to get by: 'Our only outlet … is to cultivate a sham individualism through the pursuit of signs of status, fashion, or marks of individual eccentricity' (quoted in Harvey, 1989:26).

Functionalist: Durkheim and Parsons

Durkheim and especially Parsons saw culture largely in terms of its contribution to social order, identity and control. If individuals successfully internalise society's norms, beliefs and values, they are likely to conform, thus maintaining and benefiting from social order.

Despite the similarity of Durkheim and Parsons' approach to culture, the former conceived of culture more in terms of *symbolic* systems than the latter. He argued that religious symbolism such as sacred objects and ritual bound communities together by providing opportunity for collectively expressed emotion as well as ideological belief (see p. 530). In traditional societies in which everyone shared the same religious and social beliefs, there was very limited opportunity for the development of individual identity. Such universal belief systems provide the basis for what Durkheim referred to as mechanical solidarity – a type of social order and functioning based on shared values. Durkheim considered that in comparison to traditional societies, modern societies lack a shared moral basis for solidarity. Although Durkheim observed that modern societies are characterised by a new form of solidarity – organic solidarity – based on complex interdependence he was considerably perturbed by the difficulties of achieving order without shared morality. He was as much aware of the dangers as of the advantages of 'modern individualism'.

Durkheim's concern with social order and identity, and his highly structural definition of sociology led him away from issues focusing on specifically individual identity (see p. 47). Indeed, he considered such issues to be within the remit of psychology. Durkheim was only interested in individual behaviour in so far as it is socially conformist or deviant. He was not at all concerned with the motives and meanings individuals attach to their own actions.

Parsons also came down heavily on the side of culture rather than individual agency in his theoretical analysis of the relationship between the two. The following quotation from Parsons represents a very strong statement of the power of culture to *integrate* individuals into society. He proposed:

> … first, that culture is 'transmitted', it constitutes a heritage or a social tradition; secondly, that it is 'learned', it is not a manifestation, in particular the content of man's genetic constitution; and third, that it is 'shared'.
>
> *(1951:15)*

Although it was Parsons stated intention to incorporate social action within his theoretical framework, compared to the symbolic interactionists, he did not develop concepts which accommodated a vital notion of agency. In Parsons' work, identity invariably seems to take the from of a socially given role with little creative contribution from the individual actor. As Chris Jenks observes, for Parsons 'culture patterns … are, in turn, realities within individual consciousness and the collective world' (1994:61). The individual is a kind of cultural dope rather than somebody who may be intentionally and meaningfully different.

Marxist: social relations

There is a broad tradition of Marxist cultural studies which, although often seeming to pull away from Marx, nevertheless, is always framed within some kind of dialogue with Marx's own concern with collective identity and action.

The relationship between social structure and culture is relatively clearly presented in the case in Marx's writings. For Marx, the base (economy and social classes) is essentially social structure and everything else – for instance, politics, media, education – is culture or, what he terms, the superstructure (see pp. 139-40). Marx describes a *dialectical* relationship between structure and culture/superstructure. By this it is meant that the two affect and interplay with each other. Thus, the culture of the working class is formed by its members position in economic production (structure → culture) but Marx argued that in time the working class would develop the desire to change this relationship (culture → structure). There has been great debate within Marxism about the relative influence on each other of the base and superstructure. However, Chris Jenks expresses a majority view when he suggests that the key quotation from Marx given below points 'overall, to a greater weight being given to the significance and efficiency of the material factors (base) as the primary realities, and belief systems (superstructure/culture) as being both secondary, and emergent from them.' (1993:72)

> *The ideas of the ruling class are in every epoch the ruling ideas, i.e. the class which is the ruling natural force of society, is at the same time its ruling intellectual force. The class which has the means of material production at its disposal, has control at the same time over the means of mental production, so that thereby, generally speaking, the ideas of those who lack the means of mental production are subject to it … the individuals composing the ruling class possess among other things consciousness, and therefore think.*
>
> *(Quoted Jenks:72)*

Two key sources of influence in the forming of working class culture can be distinguished in Marx's analysis. These are:

1 The power and control of the ruling class repressing the working class and creating false consciousness among it.
2 The shared everyday experience of working class people which lead to feelings of solidarity and community (see pp. 174-5).

Marx argued that in the nineteenth century institutions such as the church, monarchy and (most of) the press tended to promote ideology favourable to the ruling class and, therefore conformity among the working class. The press purveyed capitalistic and nationalistic ideology in a 'taken for granted' way whereas 'dangerous, new, radical' ideas got short shrift. The libel laws and Stamp Act dogged what would otherwise have been a vibrant alternative press. With such considerations in mind, Marx stated that the ruling class 'rule also as thinkers, as producers of ideas, and regulate the production and the distribution of the ideas of their age: thus their ideas are the ruling ideas of their epoch.' (quoted Jenks:72)

Yet, Marx also strongly believed that the working class *could* reject ruling class ideology and achieve a new collective identity. His explanation of how it *would* do this involved both cultural, particularly political, activity and economic factors. He argued that economically capitalism was in the process of destroying itself (see pp. 180-1) but that the conscious involvement of the working class was necessary in forwarding this process.

Marx's concern with working class culture was mainly with its political activity. He did not attempt to describe the details of the working class way of life except in its alienated and impoverished aspects. He argued that great cultural opportunities would be available 'after the revolution' but was not very specific about what these might be.

Questions

1 Define and distinguish between:
   • Personal identity
   • Social identity
   • Collective identity.
2 Compare and contrast two of the main sociological perspectives on culture and identity.

The development of cultural studies: mid 1950s – early 1970s

Marx's own lack of interest in the detail of working class life was certainly not typical of the many Marxist influenced cultural critics, sociologists and historians of the first quarter century of post-Second World War Britain. Among these were the highly influential trio of Richard Hoggart, Raymond Williams and E P Thompson. The first two were literary critics and Thompson was an historian but they all contributed greatly to our understanding of the social and cultural aspects of working class life in the nineteenth and twentieth century. Collectively, they were among the founders of what came to be known as 'cultural studies' – the interdisciplinary study of the ways of life of social groups. The main source of what follows is Richard Hoggart's *Uses of Literacy* (1957). Hoggart's extensive analysis of post-war working class culture and community provides a case study which exemplifies the Marxist influenced cultural analysis of this time. In addition to drawing on Hoggart's work, the research of Willmott and Young and other left-wing inclined sociologists will also be referred to.

Working class culture and community in the 1950s and 1960s: a case study

Working class community

Working class communities grew up around places of work and this was still the case in the years after the Second World War. Occupational communities developed in mining, shipping and heavy industry areas. Working and living closely together created strong bonds between working class people, a sense of *solidarity*.

As well as enjoying everyday leisure pursuits, all cultural groups celebrate rituals and festivals. Many of the celebrations of working class people were rooted in their shared experience of work. To get a sense of the vitality of working people at play, it is worth quoting Michael Foot's description of a Durham Miners' gala at which he was a guest speaker:

I started there in 1947. that's when I shared the platform with Arthur Horner ... The Durham Miners' Gala is a fine occasion today, taking place as it does in that beautiful city; but in those days it was absolutely sensational. There were so many lodges, you see, and they had to start bringing them in at half past eight in the morning. The whole city absolutely throbbed with the thing from early in the morning, right through until you left. And you left absolutely drunk with it ... the music, the banners and all in that beautiful city. It overwhelmed you really. In those days it was, far and away, the best working class festival that there was in this country. Far and away the best. It was just marvellous.

(Quoted in Huw Beynon, 'The End of the Industrial Worker?' in N Abercrombie and A Warde eds., Social Change in Contemporary Britain (Polity Press, 1992:169))

Foot describes the best of it but it is worth recalling that in the early post-war years, everyday life in working class communities generally took place against a mundane, not to say, bleak background.

Community, family, 'us' and 'others'

There is debate within sociology about how precisely to define the term community or whether it should continue to be used at all. Preferred alternatives include social network, locale or locality (see pp. 548-9). Whatever the various merits of these debates, it is clear that a specific term is needed to refer to degrees of sociability and informal interdependence in a given locality. Where such interaction is relatively strong and recurrent it seems appropriate to use the term community. In this sense, working class community did exist and has declined as the traditional working class has itself declined.

The classic accounts of working class 'community' in the post-Second World War period, seldom over-romanticise their subject. There is nothing cosy or comfortable about the physical characteristics of the 'typical' working class neighbourhood of Richard Hoggart's description:

To a visitor they are understandably depressing, these massed proletarian areas; street after regular street of shoddily uniform houses intersected by a dark pattern of ginnels and snickets (alley-ways) and courts; mean, squalid, and in a permanent half-fog; a study in shades of dirty-grey, without greenness or the blueness of sky; degrees darker than the north or west of the town, than 'the better end'. The brickwork and the woodwork are cheap; the wood goes too long between repaintings – landlords are not as anxious to keep up the value of the property as are owner-occupiers.

(Hoggart:58-9)

However, though the neighbourhood may look bleak, it is familiar and mapped territory for residents:

But to the insider, these are small worlds, each as homogeneous and well-defined as a village. Down below, on the main road running straight into town, the bosses' cars whirr away at five o'clock to converted farm-houses ten miles out in the hills; the men stream up into their district. They know it, as do all its inhabitants, in intimate details – automatically slipping up a snicker here or through a shared lavatory block there; they know it as a group of tribal areas. Pitt Street is certainly one of ours; just as certainly as Prince Consort Street next to it is not, is over the boundary in another parish. In my own part of Leeds I knew at ten years old, as did all my contemporaries, both the relative status of all the streets around us and where one part shaded into another. Our gang fights were tribal fights, between streets or groups of streets.

(Hoggart:59-60)

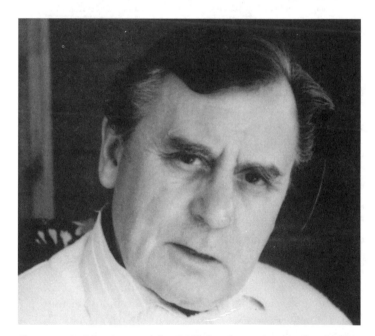

Figure 16.3 Richard Hoggart (b. 1919). A major post-war cultural critic

Young and Willmott observed in *Family and Kinship in East London* (1957) that whereas kin move easily in and out of each others homes, acquaintances and even friends meet more routinely on the streets. Philip Cohen explains the dynamics of street-based community very much in the terms of Young and Willmott. Cohen's comments about the self-policing of the streets is particularly interesting in the light of current more apprehensive perceptions. As he describes it adult-child interaction on the streets of the 1950s and 1960s East End was generally positive and supportive (Reading 1).

A gender stratified community

The culture and community of the traditional working class was heavily gendered – perhaps even more so than is generally appreciated. Married women and their infants 'occupied' the homes and streets during the day and men, young adults and youth took them over during the evening and night. However, only the youngsters used them specifically as leisure space – for the men and young couples, they were merely the means to get to where they were going, in the former case, usually the pub or Working Men's Club.

The term segregated conjugal roles has sometimes been used to describe the sharp separation of functions between married couples among the traditional working class. Females who married would typically do paid work during particular phases of their lives but for the majority the role of housewife was their prime function and identity. Few housewives with young children ventured out during weekday evenings, and almost none went alone to the pub.

Visits to the 'pictures' with a spouse were an occasional treat. In their description of the sex-segregated club and pub life in the north east, published in 1956, Dennis, Henriques and Slaughter, add po-faced, the following footnote: 'Only *old women* go to the public house during the week unaccompanied'. The following description of a typical weekend by Mr Aves, one of Young and Willmott's East Enders, is intended to stress the closeness of family life rather than its sex-segregated nature but it is perhaps the latter that seems most striking now:

> I see one of my brothers every Saturday at football, and then every Sunday the whole family comes down for a drink on Sunday morning. They've always done it. The men, my brothers and brother-in-law, go round to the pub and then the women get the dinner cooked and come round for the last half hour for a chat and a drink. Oh, it's a regular thing in our family.
>
> (Young and Willmott:103)

'Us' and others

The closely-knit world of working class community of the immediate post-war years was largely unaware of 'the dark stranger' – the black immigrant. One searches in vain the table of contents and indexes of Hoggart's *Uses of Literacy*, Young and Willmott's *Family and Kinship in East London* and Dennis, Henriques and Slaughter's *Coal is our Life* for mention of such words as 'immigrant', 'racism', 'black' or even the now dated 'negro'. Although mass black immigration into Britain had begun by the early 1950s it had not yet become constructed as a 'social problem'. However, in one way or another, all the above authors indicate the strong sense of collective self-identity characteristic of working class community. This identity was made up of a sense of belonging

and of exclusion in terms of both place and people. Put otherwise, there were elements of territoriality and of group membership in working class identity summoned up, perhaps, in the phase 'us and them'. Manifestly, the communal, solidaristic and collective aspects of working class life were elements in this sense of identity. It was an identity strengthened by the socially intense and physically localised nature of traditional working class life. In contrast, middle class social networks are more extended. The occupational communities – mining, docking, heavy industry – were the strongest of all. Here the 'in-group', 'us', were highly homogenous and 'them' could be virtually anybody else – although for many working class people, socialist ideals of proletarian brotherhood and sisterhood as well as other wider bases of identity, such as nation or church, were also real enough.

Richard Hoggart's famous description of the 'them' and 'us' attitude characteristic of the working class is worth quoting again for its insight:

> Presumably most groups gain some of their strength from their exclusiveness, from a sense of people outside who are not 'us'. How does this express itself in working-class people? I have emphasised the strength of home and neighbourhood, and have suggested that this strength arises partly from a feeling that the world outside is strange and often unhelpful, that it has most of the counters stacked on it side, that to meet it on its own terms is difficult. One may call this, making use of a word commonly used by the working classes, the world of 'them' …
>
> 'They' are 'the people at the top', 'the higher-ups', the people who give you your dole, call you up, tell you to go to war, fine you, made you split the family in the thirties to avoid a reduction in the Means Test allowance, 'get yer in the end', 'aren't really to be trusted', 'talk posh', 'are all twisters really', 'never tell yer owt' (e.g. about a relative in hospital), 'clap yer in clink', 'will do y' down if they can', 'summons yer', 'are all in a click [clique] together', 'treat y' like muck'.
>
> (Hoggart: 72,72-3)

What is startling about the above is the sense of powerlessness as well as exploitation conveyed. Powerlessness is felt not only in relation to the bosses but to 'the higher-ups' in general – including officials of the welfare state, medical officials, and apparently anybody concerned with law and order enforcement. This lack of empowerment within and even alienation from the institutional systems of welfare corporatism introduced by the Atlee governments is now widely seen as a fundamental failure of post-war Labour reform. An appreciation of why a sense of possession, ownership and involvement in the nationalised industries and welfare state did not significantly develop among the working class is central to understanding the decline of the socialist movement in post-war Britain. Dennis, Henriques and Slaughter's *Coal is our Life*, published in 1956 only a few years after the nationalisation of the mines, states what was a wider problem in relation to that industry:

> *What of the other characteristics of wage-working, particularly in the mining industry? Joint consultation, meant to be a method of drawing workers into the management of the collieries, is a failure, if only because the vast majority of the men are not drawn into it, so that their relation to the direction of work has not changed one iota. In the working situation the deputy, who has often been working in the same pit for forty years, still has an identical position vis-à-vis the men; to get an improvement in wages the contract-workers must contest views with the deputy. If a miner wants to question his wage-packet he still must go through the tiresome and often humiliating procedure of chasing the manager or the other officials outside of working hours.*
>
> *(77-8)*

Working class culture: aspidistras and 'sex in shiny packets'

It is difficult to read Richard Hoggart's description of working class life without concluding that in many ways, and perhaps fundamentally, the post-war working class was a culturally conservative class. The gender roles around which much of work and community life was structured and attitudes to others – whether authority or strangers – were often traditional to the point of rigidity and prejudice. Nevertheless, perhaps Jenks overstates it when he says that Hoggart's 'model of culture is 'passive, receptive and tending towards complacency', although 'vibrant and valuable in its own right' (154).

Leisure activity is a key area of cultural analysis. People are usually able to express themselves more in, say, their choice of decor, flower-arrangements and ornaments for their house or in their choice of sports to watch or participate in than at work. For males, the pubs, Men's Clubs – in the north, and playing or watching football or rugby (sometimes with 'the family') provided the backbone of outdoors leisure activity. Many males kept and sometimes raced pets, such as pigeons or whippets. Predictably, female leisure pursuits were more home-bound. Hoggart describes a robust tradition of home ornamentation some remnants of which are still visible in the homes of older working class people in the 1990s. However, newer leisure pursuits were beginning to appear. Indoors, listening to the radio or, increasingly, watching 'tele' already gave leisure activity a modern edge which had the potential to slice families into separate audiences (see pp. 517-8).

Hoggart was uneasy at the increasingly powerful commercial influences impacting on working class life. He considered that these influences were conveyed mainly through the export of American culture, particularly 'pop' music. His worries over early post-war youth culture – 'the juke-box, boys' – were described in Chapter 15, p. 454). Another aspect of the 'newer mass art' as he referred to it were 'spicey magazines' and 'sex-and-violence' novels. Never one to shrink from a moral or aesthetic judgement, Hoggart found these 'coarse' and 'garish'. Of the magazines he wrote:

> *'In general' these magazines belong to the world of the dirtier picture postcards; they have a similar vulgarity and a similarly circumscribed view of the possible situations for humour – backsides 'jerries', knickers, 'belly-buttons', breasts (and now 'falsies', the most popular new feature in all the sex-joke magazines).*

On reflection, he concludes:

> *They may be a little cruder than the post-cards.*
>
> *(256)*

Comment on Hoggart (Williams and Thompson)

Some 40 years on, Hoggart considers that the erosion of working class culture he detected in the 1950s has gone further. He has become less sure of the common-sense capacity of working class people to detect and reject 'tripe' – of which there is, in his view, a lot about. He is unimpressed by postmodernists' attempts to embrace popular culture – the less so because they do so in incomprehensible language. He is also none too impressed by comfortable middle class as his book on Farnham in Surrey – the home town of his later years – amply illustrates. Rude middle class women, acquisitive stock-brokers and bankers, vacuous shop-assistants, people his *Townscape with Figures – Portrait of an English Town* (1994).

John Carey in *The Intellectuals and the Masses* accuses Hoggart of 'elitism'. Hoggart is only too ready to agree. But for him elitism is not snobbishness but a commitment to the highest moral, intellectual, and artistic standards.

The other accusation commonly levelled at Hoggart is that he 'romanticised' working class culture – Jenks suggests to the point of sentimentality. It is true that Hoggart had an affection and respect for working class culture but he was realistic about its prospects – in fact, almost to the point of pessimism. In this respect, he foreshadows the disillusion of many 1990s Marxists and ex-Marxists much more so than did Williams and Thompson. Much of the work of these two scholars was framed within the traditional Marxist assumption that the working class is the historical agency of change – even though they explored this assumption from voluntarist rather than determinist perspective.

The Centre for Contemporary Cultural Studies 1970s–1980s: enter young males, females and black youth

Stuart Hall succeeded Richard Hoggart as Director of the Birmingham Centre for Contemporary Cultural Studies (CCCS) in the early 1970s. There followed a period during which the Centre achieved a high degree of creativity and influence which I will now outline. From 1976, a stream of books flowed from the Centre. The titles included: *Resistance through Rituals: Youth subcultures in post-war Britain* (1976); *On Ideology* (1977); *Women Take Issue; Aspects of women's subordination* (1978); *Working Class Culture: Studies in history and theory* (1979); *Culture, Media, Language* (1980); *The Empire Strikes Back* (1982).

Chris Jenks (1993) gives a fair description of the scope and dynamism of the Centre:

> *The CCCS generated a shared problematic (the Gramscian sense of ideology), a set of, albeit loose methods and strategies for research (such as ethnography), a particular range or perhaps strata of substantive topics (like 'subcultures') and a group of young, ambitious and multi-disciplinary theorists sprouting out of an imaginative postgraduate programme into film, media, cultural and communication departments and providing a momentum of enthusiasm, research and publication that has not waned up to the present.*
>
> *(Jenks, 1993:155)*

The wide scope of the Centre's concerns will be obvious from the partial list of its publications given above. The interest in working class culture was maintained. However, it was in the then 'newer' areas of youth, gender, and 'race' that the Centre made its biggest impact and it is to its work in these areas that we now turn. This book has already drawn extensively on empirical material produced by the CCCS, particularly in the sections on youth and education. Here, I will concentrate on some of the key concepts of cultural analysis popularised by the Centre's work. In addition, a further reference to Dick Hebdige's analysis of punk subculture will be given as an example of the Centre's work during this period.

The influence of European Marxism on the CCCS: hegemony, relative autonomy and semiotics

A key achievement of the Centre was to weave together by a series of linking concepts the areas of 'culture' and 'structure' or, what in Marx's terms, would have been referred to as 'superstructure' and 'base'. This was done largely by borrowing a number of concepts from European Marxism which expressed the relationship between culture and structure as more flexible than in cruder Marxist models.

Hegemony

The concept of 'hegemony', borrowed from the Italian Marxist, Antonio Gramsci (1891-1937) has perhaps influenced the collective thinking of the Centre more than any other. Gramsci defined hegemony as 'moral and philosophical leadership, leadership which manages to win the active consent of those over whom it rules' (quoted Slattery, 1991:126). Hegemonic leadership can operate alongside force or as an alternative to it when the latter is deemed either impossible or inappropriate. However, hegemony can be just as effective as force, indeed, perhaps more so when the subordinate group is successfully persuaded that the dominant group is legitimate. In *Resistance through Rituals*, Hall and his co-writers make clear the subtly embracing nature of hegemony:

> *... Gramsci used the term 'hegemony' to refer to the moment when a ruling class is able, not only to coerce a subordinate class to conform to its (the ruling class's) interests, but to exert a 'hegemony' or 'total social authority' over subordinate classes. This involves the exercise of a special kind of power – the power to frame alternatives and contain opportunities, 'to win and shape consent', so that the granting of legitimacy to the dominant classes appears not only 'spontaneous' but natural and normal ... the terrain on which this hegemony is won or lost is the terrain of the superstructure.*
>
> *(Hall et al., 1976:38)*

In later writings, Hall was frequently to refer to Thatcherism as having achieved, in effect, an hegemonic relationship with enough of the British people to gain widespread consent for her free market ideas and programme:

> *Thatcherism discovered a powerful means of translating the clichés of 'freedom of the marketplace' into the language of experience, moral imperative and common sense, providing an alternative ethic to that of 'the caring society'. 'Being British' became once again identified with the restoration of competition and profitability ...*
>
> *(Hall, 1984:25)*

How, then, is hegemony achieved? As Hall *et al.* state, 'hegemony works through ideology' (1976:39). Margaret Thatcher employed Saatchi and Saatchi to polish up the presentation of herself and her policies and she also gained the support of much of the press, particularly that of the media tycoon, Rupert Murdoch. Gradually, she was able to shift the 'common-sense' consensus of the time in the direction of Thatcherism which is, of course, a reassertion of capitalist principles, including those of competition and inequality.

In linking hegemony and ideology, Hall *et al.* distanced themselves from Karl Marx's own analysis of ideology (the term 'hegemony' postdates Marx). They reject the idea that hegemonic relations involve 'false consciousness' on the part of subordinate groups. Rather, hegemonic relations usually involve subordinate groups in a practical as well as in an ideological relationship with the dominant order. A couple of examples may help here. Thus, powerful right-wing leaders frequently adopt imperialistic or nationalistic postures which can make 'the people' feel superior in relation to other groups and perhaps offer them some benefit from war and conquest. At a more prosaic level, Mrs Thatcher 'tied' many working class people into the dominant system by offering cheap shares and housing through her privatisation programme. Such ideologically inspired policies build up mass support and therefore undermine class based opposition to the dominant group. However, as we shall see, the CCCS theorists argued that the potential for opposition and resistance by the working class had been reduced because of its subordinate and exploited structural position. More recently, however, some former scholars at the CCCS have retreated from even this residual or minimalist Marxist position. This has been partly due to the impact of poststructuralism and postmodernism on their thinking (see pp. 488-92).

Relative autonomy

Louis Althusser's concept of the 'relative autonomy' was only marginally less influential at the CCCS in the 1970s and early 1980s, than Gramsci's concept of hegemony.

Althusser addressed the issue of the relationship between culture/agency and structure which was of central concern at the CCCS. Althusser identified three universal 'social formations' the economic, the political and the ideological. Althusser wanted to 'free up' the areas of ideology and politics from the notion – associated with crude Marxism – that they are determined by the economy. To do this he introduced the concept of 'relative autonomy' by which he meant that each social formation had a degree of independence (relative autonomy) from the other two although the three formations constantly interact. Thus, Althusser felt able to encourage socialists to take political action and develop ideology on the basis that – yes – it could make a difference. However, Althusser qualifies the relative autonomy of the ideological and political formations by stating that 'the economic is determinant in the last instance'. Here, Althusser seems to be pulling back towards Marx's stress on the centrality of the economic and to that extent undermining his own concept of 'relative autonomy'.

Althusser lurches even more sharply towards determinism with his controversial but highly influential concept of the 'death of the subject' (borrowed from the French psychoanalyst, Jacques Lacan). By the death of the subject, Althusser means that individual will and consciousness are illusions and that the ideas and motives that people draw on (or *believe* they draw on) are, in fact, ideological in nature. Thus, most people *think* they are free under capitalism but in reality their ideas, taste and style are created by capitalism. Even socialism is an ideology, and structures people socialised into it in the same deterministic way. Unsurprisingly, Althusser was a committed opponent of humanism, a philosophy which is committed to the emancipation of human potential by human will, imagination and effort. This he considered to be romantic nonsense. Althusser was also severely critical of Gramsci on much the same grounds. He considered that the concept of hegemony allowed far too much scope for human agency both in resisting domination and exploitation and in creating alternatives.

My own view of Althusser's work is that he reneges on the promise of qualified 'freedom' implicit in the concept of relative autonomy. In the end, he creates a dungeon of determinism and despair beyond anything Marx himself suggested. Indeed, there is in Marx's writing the basis of a humanistic tradition which burns brightly in the writings of Williams, Thompson and Hoggart, and even flickers in the work of the CCCS under Stuart Hall albeit often dampened by weighty Euro-theorising. In so far as humanism is of any influence at the 1970-80s Centre, it emerges through the use of the term 'resistance', discussed next. However, the break with Hoggart was sharp. The 20 years between the publication of Hoggart's *The Uses of Literacy* in 1957 and Paul Willis's *Learning to Labour* (1977) marked off two generations of theory.

Of all the concepts popularised by the CCCS, that of *cultural resistance* was perhaps the most influential. The origins of the concept seem to lie as much within the Anglo-American interactionist tradition as within European social theory (although Gramsci's notion of the *struggle* for hegemony implies a capacity for effective resistance by the proletariate). As early as 1972, Laurie Taylor and Stan Cohen used the term resistance to describe the various strategies of 'making out and fighting back' adopted by certain inmates of Durham prison (see p. 292). They wanted a stronger term than Erving Goffman's 'secondary adjustments' which he used to describe the various strategies developed by inmates in a mental asylum to achieve some autonomy.

In the conceptual lexicon of the CCCS, the terms *subordination*, *negotiation* and *resistance* represent three possibilities along a spectrum of relations between the dominant and subordinate groups. An example of political resistance is a revolutionary working class political party. Such resistance is conscious and organised. Cultural resistance may be conscious and deliberate but not necessarily. For its more aware members, the hippie movement of the 1960s was a conscious cultural alternative to the mainstream. However, for the various working class youth subcultures analysed in *Resistance Through Rituals*, resistance is described as expressed through emotionally oriented behaviour – such as contempt for authority – and through leisure pursuits, language, dress and other aspects of style – such as loud, aggressive music. One of the best known analyses of a youth subculture produced at the Centre is John Clarke's 'decoding' of the style of the 1960s skinheads. Clarke's article has been referred to previously in this book (see pp. 452-3). Here it is enough to reiterate that Clarke convincingly presents a youthful working class peer culture decked out in defence against 'outsiders' of what its members refer to as *their* territory and *their* jobs.

In its attempt to find meanings in the everyday aspects of culture, the CCCS was influenced by the French structuralist literary critic, Roland Barthes who in turn had drawn on that of Swiss linguist, Saussure. Barthes developed semiology or semiotics which 'is the study of signs or sign systems' (*Oxford Dictionary of Sociology*, 1994). The main concept borrowed from Saussure and widely employed by Barthes in his studies of French popular culture was that of 'sign'. A *sign* is a combination of *signifier* and *signified*. The key characteristic of a signifier is that it can be perceived, such as a sound or object. The signified is what the signifier is associated with (or, simply, means). Thus, the 'bovver' boots (signifiers) of the skinheads could be taken to signify or mean 'bovver' or aggression. Together, the signifier and signified are a sign, in this case a sign of aggression. A *sign system* is a series of related signs which make up a *code*. Together, the 'skins' cropped hair, crude tattoos and bovver boots signalled their subcultural *messages*. The meaning of an object can be changed. Thus, in the early 1990s a boot-style very like the skinheads' 'bovver' boots became widely popular among the young but the style did not seem to signify aggression. If anything, the 1990s style seemed to suggest a certain ordinary, unpretentious classlessness which chimed well with their hardwearing functionality (although, predictably, up-market-styles of these boots were produced).

The meaning of punk – a case study

Dick Hebdige's *Subculture: The Meaning of Style* (1979) was the main work from the Centre focusing primarily on interpreting youth subcultural style – largely in terms of resistance to the dominant order. From 'the teds' to 'the punks' Hebdige charts a roar of (mainly working class) youthful discontent. One of the objects of the teds ill-feeling was black immigrants. The punks, by their own testimony, were prepared to express ill-feeling about anything and anybody.

Hebdige is far-reaching in the claims he makes for the subcultures. He concludes his book by stating:

> *Throughout this book, I have interpreted subculture as a form of resistance in which experienced contradictions and objections to this ruling ideology are obliquely represented in style. Specifically, I have used the term 'noise' to describe the challenge to symbolic order that such styles are seen to constitute.*
>
> *(1979:133)*

To paraphrase: capitalist ideology (particularly consumerism) is indirectly (obliquely) challenged (resisted) by subcultural activity ('noise'). The points of resistance are likely to be where capitalism is inconsistent (contradictory) and provokes opposition (objection). Thus, in the example of the punks given below, they explore and test the contradiction between the control of pop culture by capital and the rhetoric of individual 'freedom' in much pop music by inviting everybody to join in their music as equals. Similarly they express their objection to the glamorisation of popular music by making their music and themselves as unglamorous as possible. Hebdige does not claim that the targets of subcultural anger are always consistent, or in his view well chosen. It is in the nature of subcultural resistance that its cultural barrage sometimes gets scattered wildly. Thus, sometimes black people have been the objects of resentment and violence from teds and skinheads.

The case of the punks is a good one on which to examine Hebdige's claims of subcultural resistance. He has no problem in illustrating the cultural nihilism of the punks but his claim of cultural resistance requires more demanding substantiation. It does not take much semiological expertise to venture an interpretation of the examples of punk style offered by Hebdige (although Hebdige gives one):

> *(T)he most unremarkable and inappropriate things – a pin, a plastic clothes peg, a television component, a razor blade, a tampon – could be brought within the province of punk (un)fashion. Anything within or without reason could be turned into part of what Vivien Westwood called 'confrontation dressing' so long as the rupture between 'natural' and constructed context was clearly visible (i.e. the rule would seem to be: if the cap doesn't fit, wear it).*
>
> *Objects borrowed from the most sordid of contexts found a place in the punks ensembles: lavatory chains were draped in graceful arcs across chests encased in plastic bin-liners. Safety pins were taken out of their domestic 'utility' context and worn as gruesome ornaments through the cheek ear or lip …*
>
> *(107)*

Stylistic iconoclasm was not confined to dress:

> *Faces became abstract portraits; sharply observed and meticulously executed studies in alienation. Hair was obviously dyed (hay yellow, jet black, or bright orange with tufts of green or bleached in question marks) … Of course, punk did more than upset the wardrobe. It undermined every relevant discourse. Thus dancing … was turned into a dumbshow of blank robotics. Punk dances bore absolutely no relation to the desultory hugs and clinches … intrinsic to the respectable working-class ritual of Saturday night at the Top Rank or Mecca. (of the kind typical in Hoggart's 1950s Leeds – author's brackets)*
>
> (107-8)

Figure 16.4 Resistance through style?

Hebdige sees a gut egalitarianism and gritty resistance to commercialised pop culture in these rituals and styles but he also claims that a more conscious level of resistance occurred within punk. He cites the existence of an alternative critical space within the subculture itself to counteract the hostile or at least ideologically inflected coverage which punk was receiving in the media (1979:111). The various fanzines such as *Sniffin Glue* and *Ripped and Torn* were often published with manically incorrect spelling and page numbering and other features indicative of semi-intentional anarchic chaos. The constant tweaking of authority and challenge to established or 'correct' procedure was balanced by a rough democracy constantly reasserted. Hebdige states that examples abounded 'of 'ordinary fans' … who had made the symbolic crossing from the floor to the stage' (1979:111). Symbolic presumably of the fact that anybody could do it.

According to Hebdige subcultures express 'a fundamental tension between those in power and those condemned to subordinate positions and second-class lives' (1979:32). He suggests that there are two ways in which spectacular subcultures can be 'incorporated' or absorbed by the capitalist system: the commodity form and the ideological form. Commodificaiton occurs once the activity/product (e.g., music, dress, style) of a subculture becomes taken up by commercial enterprise and sold for profit. Ideological incorporation refers to the ways in which the media undermines the subcultures by presenting them to the public in a way that undermines the subcultures' own meanings and imposes a negative ideological interpretation on them (e.g. 'drug-crazed youth', 'violent youth', 'slippery slope to chaos'). The particular way the media often negatively characterised punks was as 'a threat to the family'. However, on other occasions, punks would be 'normalised' or claimed back into the fold by being shown in conventional family settings.

Conclusion

Dick Hebdige is well aware that the 'resistance through rituals and style' of youth subcultural groups does not amount to conscious political rebellion. He and other researchers from the CCCS were not claiming that their members were budding socialists. Far from it! In many cases, the sexism and racism of members of certain subcultures such as the teds and skins, twisted them towards the far Right of politics. This tendency reasserted itself in the 1990s when the overlap between skinheads, football hooliganism and Fascism became marked. The more measured interpretation of the CCCS that youthful subcultural activities represented an attempt to achieve some space, expression and freedom seems a viable one.

There is no need to repeat here the criticisms of subcultural theory and particularly the concept of resistance referred to in the previous chapter. In fact, by the mid to late 1980s, some of the most influential figures at the Centre in the previous decade had begun to move on both physically and theoretically.

Questions

1   Critically discuss studies of traditional working class community as exemplified by Richard Hoggart.
2   Describe and illustrate some of the main theories and concepts used by the Centre for Contemporary Cultural Studies in the analysis of cultural meaning.

The postmodern break: fragmenting collectivities

Conveniently, we can continue to use here the intellectual careers of a number of scholars who have at some time worked at the Centre for Contemporary Cultural Studies to illustrate a further phase in cultural theory as it has developed both in Britain and internationally. These include Paul Willis, Angela McRobbie, Paul Gilroy and Stuart Hall. However, other relevant contributors to the debate about postmodernism (and poststructuralism) will also be referred to.

Postmodernist and poststructuralist theory began to impact on British sociology and cultural studies from the early 1980s and poststructuralism perhaps half a decade earlier. Jean-Francois Lyotard's seminal *The Postmodern Condition: A Report on Knowledge* was first published in English in 1984. Foucault's poststructuralist perspective was beginning to exercise an influence on British scholarship as early as the second half of the 1970s though not noticeably at the CCCS. For our purposes, poststructuralism will be subsumed under the term postmodernism.

Postmodernism: declining metanarratives and decentred subjects

Two main aspects of postmodernist cultural criticism will be emphasised here. First, as Lyotard famously declared, there has been a loss of faith in great 'metanarratives' or philosophies which aspire to total explanation. This process began in earlier modernity with a decline of belief in religious metanarratives and was recently most powerfully expressed in the collapse of totalitarian Communism. To give another example of scepticism towards 'big ideas', postmodernists have suggested that social class is no longer as important a basis of identity as many on the left argued and that class conflict is no longer the main motor of historical change if, indeed, it ever was. 'Race'/ethnicity and gender were often seen as identities – both collective and individual – which were coming to rival social class in importance. More recently, however, and especially since the early 1990s, it has been increasingly suggested that gender, sex (see below) 'race'/ethnicity are themselves too broad as identity categories to capture the variety and difference between people. Thus, if gender identity is polarised as 'masculine or feminine' and 'race'/ethnicity as 'black or white' then, many may feel that their identities do not fit into the categories on offer (see pp. 192-3). Individuals may not even want to name their identity or aspects of their identity at all. Dominic Strinati gives a clear account of postmodernist perspective on the decline of metanarratives in which he describes its application to personal as well as public life (Reading 2 – in which other aspects of postmodernism are also described).

The second point about postmodernism to be examined here is concerned with individuality. On this matter, there are two somewhat conflicting emphases within postmodern thinking. First, it is suggested that the decline of large, collective identity categories such as class has paved the way for individuality to flourish. With all the variety of consumer possibilities before them, individuals can pick and mix their own identities. Second, not all postmodern theory of cultural identity is individualistic. More typically, structuralist and poststructuralist theory de-emphasises the autonomous individual or, to use the preferred terminology, the subject (individual) is seen as decentred. The decentring of the subject is easily explained by contrasting the modern and postmodern subject as described in postmodern theory. With the so-called 'death of God', modern man (and man it invariably was) increasingly made himself the centre of his own universe and vision of progress. His rationality was seen as the key to understanding and using the natural world. What postmodernism suggests is that the rationality of the subject (individual) is open to powerful influences which prevent it from operating in the 'free' way often assumed. The basic idea here is a familiar one to sociologists. We know that ideas and sentiments which we like to think are our own are partly the product of socialisation. In the writings of Althusser and Foucault individual subjects do not so much form ideas as ideas form them (i.e. create subjectivity). Thus, the subject is considered to be decentred – no longer the rational, controlling force in the world.

Stuart Hall: 'the final decentring' of the modern subject

In explaining what is meant by the de-centring of the subject, Stuart Hall usefully suggests five 'great advances in social theory' whose main effect 'it is argued has been the final de-centring' of the modern subject (1992:285). Taken together, these five perspectives show the individual subject controlled rather than in control. The five theoretical developments are:

1 Althusser's re-reading (reinterpretation) of Marx which sought to discredit notions of an essential human nature and to present instead human beings as formed in and by society.

2 Freud attempted to demonstrate that motives that often seem rational are driven by unconscious desire.

3 Saussure, the linguist, argued that words do not have fixed meanings and therefore statements are always open to different interpretations. For instance, it is quite possible to use words without being aware of the various meanings they can carry and which others might read into them (Saussure's ideas were influential in the development of semiotics referred to above p. 487).

4 Foucault argued that a new type of power – disciplinary power – evolved during the nineteenth century. As Hall says, '(d)isciplinary power is concerned with the regulation, surveillance and government of, first, the human species of whole populations and, secondly, the individual and the

body' (1992:289). For instance, disciplinary power is exercised in prisons, schools and places of work. Disciplinary power operates at the expense of individual freedom and choice.

5 Feminism both as a body of theory and as a social movement dislodged or de-centred the aggressive and dominating 'masculine' form of rationality. Feminism and other social movements originating in the 1960s questioned the thought and behaviour pattern of white heterosexual males.

Comment

This impressive list of 'subject de-centring' influences can be read in two ways. On the one hand, Hall takes comfort from the de-centring of certain dominant and dominating subjects – the racist, the sexist, the imperialist – and the prospect of liberation this seems to offer. On the other hand, if subjects are simply constituted by cultural discourses as Hall seems to believe where does the imagination and will to achieve greater freedom come from? The more positive vision of Gramsci seems to have been lost in favour of the opaque nightmare of Foucault.

The tension between freedom and determinism is very apparent in the work of Hall's students – now established academics – discussed below. Partly to balance this, there follows on a brief discussion of Anthony Giddens' recent work on culture in what he prefers to call 'late modernity' – before, finally, returning to Hall again.

Paul Willis: common culture

Reference has already been made to Paul Willis's work, including *Common Culture: Symbolic Work at Play in the Everyday Cultures of the Young* (see pp. 89-90 and pp. 462-3). The intention here is to locate him in relation to the trends in cultural analysis which emerged from the Centre for Contemporary Cultural Studies and in relation to postmodernism. The title of his book gives clues in both directions.

The phrase 'common culture' indicates a change in Willis's focus from working class youth subcultures to youth subculture in general which, in contrast to his earlier work, he describes as now much less differentiated by class. Implicitly, Willis seems to accept that all young people (and, he says, people in general) have to work out their creativity in relation to capitalism and that this now gives them much in common despite class differences. He even suggests that the term 'common' can replace that of 'mass' – shorn of the latter's offensive overtones:

> *The coming dominance of common culture marks, if you like, a decisive stage in cultural modernisation ... where the 'mass' has become properly and popularly culturally differentiated through the active and creative use of widely available cultural commodities and cultural media.*
>
> *(1990:129)*

In this vision of common culture people seem to be acting as individuals and groups – characterised by style, taste and creativity – rather than as classes. Although Willis refers to this development as a 'decisive stage in cultural modernisation', others have seen it as characteristic of what they term postmodernism. Like Willis, some other graduates of the CCCS have drifted away from class-based cultural analysis. They have certainly moved a distance from the concerns of Hoggart, Williams and Thompson.

Willis directly adopts a central idea of postmodernism in his explanation of the term 'common culture'. Postmodernists typically reject any fundament distinction between 'high' and popular or common culture. Willis appears to do this in the following passage. In any case, he is certain that such a distinction is of no interest to most young people along with much else besides:

> *It will certainly seem heretical for many to find the main seeds for everyday cultural development in the commercial provision of cultural commodities rather than in the finer practices of art, politics or public institutions. But we must start from unpalatable truths or no truths at all. The time for good lies is gone. We need worse truths, not better lies. The 'arts' are a dead letter for the majority of young people. Politics bore them. Institutions are too often associated with coercing and exclusion and seem, by and large, irrelevant to what really energises them. 'Official culture' has hardly recognised informal everyday culture ...*
>
> *(1990:129)*

The narrowing of the distance between 'high' and 'pop' as observed by theoreticians such as Willis reflects a real phenomenon of recent years. When opera tops the best selling CD charts and Vivaldi played by an exuberantly exhibitionist Aston Villa supporter threatens to do the same, then boundaries are beginning to be breached. If money – 'the provision of the market' – is at work in all this, then Willis seems willing to go along with it. That is one of the 'worse truths' he has come to accept.

Dominic Strinati gives a succinct account of the postmodernist perspective on 'the breakdown of the distinction between art and popular culture' in Reading 2.

Angela McRobbie: 'No real me'?

Angela McRobbie was one of the first British sociologists to 'rescue' young females from the oblivion that male oriented youth subcultural analysis had consigned them to (see p. 91 and p. 512). In 1976 in an article written with Jenny Garber in *Resistance Through Rituals*, she tweaks Paul Willis for failing to understand the passivity of the girls in the motorbike subculture he had studied. She and Garber argued that the relationship of the girls to the boys' activity was one of *structured secondariness* and that they had learnt to think of their primary identity as romantic and domestic.

In *Postmodernism and Popular Culture* (1994) McRobbie published a number of pieces written between 1985 and 1993. Like

Willis in *Common Culture*, McRobbie retains an interest in youth in this publication but also engages with wider themes, particularly relating to postmodernism. She is perhaps even more up-beat than Willis about the possibilities of postmodern culture:

> *Postmodernism has entered into a more diverse number of vocabularies more quickly than most other intellectual vocabularies. It has spread outwards from the realms of art history into political theory and on to the pages of youth culture magazines, record sleeves and the fashion spread of Vogue!*
>
> *(1994:15)*

McRobbie regards postmodernism as a way of breaking loose from, in her view, largely redundant, orthodoxies such as Marxism and liberalism and of allowing scope for new enquiry and questions. She disagrees sharply with Marxists, Jameson and Harvey, who see postmodern culture as the superficial product of the capitalist media and consumer production. She also takes issue with Dick Hebdige who is far less positive about the way postmodernism is expressed in youth culture than he was about the meanings he found in the youth subcultural styles of the 1960s and 1970s. Hebdige finds an excess of style in postmodernism, a slick, surface jokiness – the meaninglessness of style. In contrast, McRobbie is closer to Willis in continuing to find individuality, inventiveness assertiveness – 'small defiant pleasure' in youth subculture. Thus, she regards the pastiche and extravagant presentation of much young gay culture as a way of testing identity-limits, of rejecting convention with a smile.

In one of the later essays in her book, titled *A Cultural Sociology of Youth*, McRobbie finds particular vitality in black youth subculture and cites considerable evidence of inter-ethnic friendship and romance among the younger generation (a point on which more statistical evidence supports her). She suggests a research agenda in which 'it would be necessary to pay greater attention to the space of inter-racial, interactive experience and to explore the processes of hostility, fascination and desire which penetrate and shape the nature of these encounters' (188). Whatever the limits of postmodernist cultural analysis, this does seem an imaginative and challenging agenda and one which might do justice to the postmodern notion that identities are fluid and open to re-creation – a matter of becoming rather than being.

In conceiving of identities as dynamic and partly self-created, McRobbie does not suggest that they exist outside of social context. Again, in one of the later essays (1993), she refers to the 'multiplicity of texts, images and representations' with which 'individuals, groups and populations' interact. Such multiplicity is a further reason why she rejects the notion of fixed identities, particularly overarching collective identities. This includes feminism in the sense that she has no wish to prescribe feminism to all young females. There is no absolute or fixed identity – or 'real me' – of a feminist or any other kind.

In going with the tide of popular culture McRobbie and Willis jettison a lot of heavy baggage. Marxism goes because, despite Althusser and even Gramsci, its class analysis remains oppressively totalistic. Liberalism is rejected because of its record of savagery in relation to the poor world and because the promise of science and reason has not been delivered. High culture elides with popular culture or is simply ignored. 'The kids', it seems, 'are all right'.

Stuart Hall and Paul Gilroy: beyond black and white

Stuart Hall's departure from the Centre for Cultural Studies in 1980 just about coincided with Paul Gilroy's arrival. Hall's last article for the CCCS and Gilroy's first appeared in the collection, *The Empire Strikes Back* (1982). Two black males of West Indian extraction, almost a generation apart, they shared a common concern about the relationship between black minority and the dominant white culture. During the decade from the early 1980s to the early 1990s, the interest of both of them shifted from white racism and black response to it, to the complexities of 'race'/ethnic identities. It seems a little crude to describe that shift as one in the direction of postmodernism but, at least, that term is elastic enough to indicate the flexibility and subtlety of their thought.

In *There ain't no Black in the Union Jack* (1987), Gilroy attacked the insularity of British culture which he argued had failed to respond positively to the challenge of black immigration. Gilroy also emphasises in this publication the great variety and vitality of black cultures formed as they have been in so many different contexts as a result of the diaspora precipitated by slavery. Black culture in Britain reflects the richness of these roots and is powerful enough to impact strongly on and change existing British culture:

> *Black Britain defines itself crucially as part of a diaspora. Its unique cultures draw inspiration from those developed by black populations elsewhere. In particular, the culture and politics of black America and the Caribbean have become raw materials for creative processes which redefine what it means to be black, adapting it to distinctively British experiences and meanings. Black culture is actively made and remade …*
>
> *(1987:154)*

Black music is an obvious example of what Gilroy is referring to and he frequently draws on it to illustrate his argument. Black gospel developed in slavery, urban blues and jazz, Jamaican reggae, and even early rock and roll – all have their roots in the black experience. Resignation, suffering, protest, anger and anti-racism are sentiments that occur in different genres of black music – which perhaps more than any other popular music has an appeal far beyond its culture of origin. If, by comparison, the black literary tradition seems, until recently, weaker, it is worth remembering that under slavery black people were not taught to read and write. Those few that were, often clerics, frequently achieved impressive levels of learning and eloquence.

Gilroy's book *The Black Atlantic: Modernity and Double*

Consciousness (1993) is a richly illustrated account of the openness of black culture to multiple influences – African, European and American – and a powerful inditement of these 'cultural insiders' who cherish a narrow and closed view of 'their own' culture. He shows how a number of black American intellectuals including W E B DuBois and Richard Wright had a transnational vision of black culture encompassing a concern for the expression of black people in the United States and in the colonies of the European powers. Gilroy also observes that 'racial slavery was integral to Western civilisation' – a fact, the enormity of which the collective white psyche seems not yet to have absorbed. Given that he shares the black victims' view of the triumph of Western reason and power, it is not surprising that Gilroy takes some postmodern distance from the principles of modernity.

So, for much the same reasons, does Stuart Hall. Like Gilroy, he considers that the rationality of the liberal, Western powers has been exercised at the expense of others. As he has moved further away from Marxism, Hall has not found himself much tempted by a liberalism which he considers has still not faced its contradictions and failures. Instead, he suggests that people search for and construct their own answers and identities. He advocates that in doing so, people should adopt a positive attitude to ethnic rather than a narrow, inward-looking one. Hall finds such a positive cultural practice at work in such films as *Passion* and *Handsworth Songs*.

'The Crying Game': postmodern identities?

The film, *The Crying Game* was released after Hall gave the talk from which the above views are taken. However, it seems to illustrate his ideas about the process of identity formation in minority subcultures (youth and sexual, as well as, ethnic). A brief outline of the story will make the point. The film opens with a scene in Northern Ireland in which a black British soldier is kidnapped by an IRA unit. Eventually the unit decides to execute the soldier. In the course of carrying out his guard duty one of the IRA group – played by Stephen Rea – becomes friendly with the soldier who shows him a photograph of his girlfriend, a beautiful black woman. The condemned soldier asks the IRA man to deliver a message to his girlfriend in London. In fact, the soldier is not executed but does die through an accident. In a visit to London, the IRA man, now disillusioned with paramilitary politics, looks up the girl. He becomes romantically involved but curiously the girl keeps delaying the expected bedroom encounter. When it finally comes, it does so as a shock – to the IRA man and to, at least, this member of the audience. The girl presents irrefutable evidence that s/he is a man. What does the IRA man – who is quietly macho – do now? Immediately, he is sick. In the longer term, the relationship between the two men continues, though how it develops and changes is left to the imagination of the audience. The final scene of the film has the black man – in full transvestite gear – visiting the IRA man in prison, after the latter had been sent down for several years on an arms charge. Both seem to be counting the days…

The mixing of ethnic and sexual identities in *The Crying Game* challenges taken for granted assumptions about both ethnicity and sexuality and about how the two can combine. A black (?) British Soldier? A *white* man and a *black* woman or rather, man? What kind of relationship could a heterosexual white man and a homosexual black man have once they knew each other's 'real' identities? 'Real' identities?

Clearly, boundaries are being tested in this film but people will decode and interpret it in their own way. For some, it may present no problems, particularly for those who set few limits on self-expression and identity exploration. Others will certainly find that *The Crying Game* raises moral and emotional issues. Catholicism still bans active homosexuality and the Church of England hierarchy seem ambivalent on the issue. Schools often ignore it. (see p. 196). Film and other art forms can sometimes address issues that are otherwise difficult to explore.

Anthony Giddens: autonomy in late modernity: 'life politics'

If Stuart Hall tends to dwell on the formative power of culture, Anthony Giddens is more inclined to stress the capacity of human beings to reflect, develop and push out the boundaries of freedom – given the conditions. In *The Transformation of Intimacy: Sexuality, Love and Eroticism in Modern Societies* (1992), he draws some illuminating parallels between political democracy and democracy in personal relationships. In both cases, he argues that democracy is the best condition for autonomy. He refers to the everyday negotiating for autonomy – for democracy on personal relationships – as '*life politics*'.

He defines autonomy as follows:

> *Autonomy means the capacity of individuals to be self-reflective and self-determining: to deliberate, judge, choose and act upon different possible courses of action.*
>
> *(185)*

He summarises the conditions for political autonomy as follows:

> *One is that there must be equality in influencing outcomes in decision-making – in the political sphere this is usually sought after by the 'one person one vote' rule …*
>
> *Public accountability is a further basic characteristic of a democratic policy. In any political system decisions must often be taken on behalf of others …*
>
> *Institutionalising the principle of autonomy means specifying rights and obligations, which have to be substantive …*
>
> *(867)*

Transferred to the personal sphere, these three qualities involve:

1 Equal decision-making power within a relationship.
2 Openness and trust.
3 An equal and fair balance of rights and duties.

All this might seem obvious except that in the past – in traditional societies – the conditions for autonomy for women and sometimes – as a developmental value – for children have seldom existed at all. Often in contemporary societies, abuse of women and children occurs. However, Giddens considers that in late modern societies 'changes that have helped transform personal environments of action are already well advanced, and they tend towards the realisation of democratic qualities.'

So, although Giddens sees early modern notions of progress as flawed and traditional societies as limiting of autonomy, he retains an optimism about greater possibilities for autonomy in late modernity. More than that, he sees signs that such autonomy is emerging.

The culture/structure duality: culture to the fore

At the British Sociological Association's annual conference in 1996, Stuart Hall argued that of the two necessary concepts of structure and culture, it is the latter that has currently shifted towards the front in contemporary social science. Why is this?

Hall suggests that it is partly the failure of attempts to prescribe or predict how groups – pre-eminently the working class – should think and act, that has persuaded intellectuals to be more sensitive to the complexities, subtleties and variety of actual cultures. In practice, analysing a group's structural position has only been of limited use in predicting how its members will behave or even whether they will regard themselves as members of their 'assigned' group. Secondly, individuals seem increasingly to define and assert their own identities. Hall is not naive enough to imagine that they do so within a vacuum. On the contrary, identities are formed within a swirl of cultural imagery, ideology and discourse (see pp. 489-90).

Critics argue that cultural analysis of this sort offers little hope to the impoverished and powerless. Liberalism and Marxism in different ways offered the prospect of progress. Hall agrees that he has few solutions to offer, little to say – for instance – to black people who shoot each other in Chicago (or, presumably, Manchester). That, he says, is his 'tragedy'. Perhaps this is the price he pays for recognising and working with what Paul Willis refers to as 'unpalatable truths … worse truths, not better lies.'

Culture: sport and football
Sport and the civilising process

In addition to the Centre for Contemporary Cultural Studies, other academic centres and individuals have made influential studies of various aspects of culture. A rather different approach to the study of culture was developed at Leicester University by Norbert Elias (1897-1990). It is sometimes said the Elias did not found a school of sociology, however, he did establish a tradition of cultural studies that still flourishes at Leicester University.

Elias's key cultural concept is 'the civilising process'. Chris Rojek presents the concept well – and with a helpful warning;

> (T)he civilising process refers to long-term changes in the social organisation of deep emotions. Standards of restraint and thresholds of physical repugnance at the public display of naked physical aggression have risen. Similarly, in private life, most people feel embarrassed and self-conscious if their emotions get the better of them …
>
> Few theories in modern sociology have been so widely misunderstood as Elias's theory of the civilising process. The theory does not argue that intense and violent emotions have disappeared from society. What it does submit is that, in adult life, the face of physical aggression has become more calculating and discreet …
>
> (1985:23)

Following Elias, Dunning and Sheard make two points. They argue that their study of the development of rugby football shows that a reduction in aggressive outbursts occurred as the game became more regulated and professional. They suggest that a similar trend has occurred in relation to other legal and regulated sporting activities. Second, that organised sport has ritualised the expression of violence and aggression – allowing for it to occur without becoming 'for real' (although the line can be crossed).

A criticism of Elias's theory is that modern supposedly 'civilised' societies are often characterised by a high degree of non-regulated aggression and violence. The very high level of homicide in the United States is perhaps an outstanding example. However, while it *is* difficult to demonstrate empirically that violence is expressed in relatively more controlled ways in modern societies, in general, basic human functions and expression do appear to be framed in a less 'rude' and open way than in the middle ages. Even so, many think that more recently the modern veneer of manners and restraint has been shredded by commercial and egocentric values. If sex, vulgarity and exhibitionism sells – that is what the public will get.

In Rojek's view, Elias's concept of 'the civilising process' has continuing relevance. Ironically, what Rojek draws out is not any slow progress towards civilisation but the continued reassertion – through sport and other forms of public ritual – of powerful human emotions. Whether these emotions are innate or generated by society is debatable, the point is that they keep on coming – and in bucket-fulls. Competitiveness, aggression, triumphalism, nationalism, racism and, on the other hand, co-operation, mutual joy and pleasure, sporting behaviour, internationalism, and a sense of basic equality are all part of the sporting chameleon. It would be *some* society and (and *some* theory) that could order all this in some predictable fashion but equally, these strong feelings and how they are expressed cannot be left entirely to individuals.

Football hooliganism

Recent research at Leicester on football hooliganism far from adopting any grand historical theory, has been grounded in the analysis of specific and changing historical circumstances. Thus, Williams and Wagg summarise changing crowd behaviour at British football matches as follows:

> If the early years of the game were notable for the gambling, drinking and sometimes threatening and violent behaviour of local 'roughs', the inter-war years at football seem, by comparison to have been considerably more orderly … It seems fairly clear, however, that out of the fairly routine but in the main, by modern standards, relatively small-scale disturbances of the pre-First World War period, the game in England – and its audience – gradually, between the wars, became more 'respectable' and less tolerant and expectant of spectator violence … Whatever the reasons, 'crowd control' at football for the decade after the war seems to have been largely a case of dealing with the occasional pub fight, or with individual offenders …
>
> The picture of large, and largely orderly, football crowds began slowly to change in England from around the mid-1950s onwards. As some older fans drifted away and amidst a more generalised panic about rising rates of juvenile delinquency … young football fans … began to attract publicity for their train-wrecking exploits.
>
> (1991:160-1, 163)

Research at Leicester and elsewhere charts a close connection between working class culture, particularly youth culture and football hooliganism from the 1950s to 1980s. The values associated with 'the lads' presented earlier – territoriality, being macho, loyal to your 'mates' – were noted prominently in the behaviour of the 'hoolies'. The appearance of a stylistically much smarter type of hooligan in the 1980s led to a debate about whether now these soccer casuals were drawn from the ranks of that section of working class youth that had done well out of Thatcherism or whether middle class youth was also participating. In the latter case, hooliganism would seem to be becoming partly detached from its working class roots.

Hooliganism remained a concern into the 1990s but other issues came to the fore as the financing and organisation of soccer – and some other sports – changed quite rapidly. First, was the massive further commercialisation of soccer (and more recently, rugby, of both codes, and boxing), through the intervention of media moguls such as Rupert Murdoch. Media entrepreneurs such as Murdoch and Kerry Packer bought up individual sports events or sport series in order to capitalise on them through pay TV and advertising. In their own terms, they have done this with remarkable success – although a cost to the majority of others is that they have not seen the events concerned.

Second, linked with the commercialisation of sport has been the weakening or, perhaps changing, of the links between everyday or 'street' sport and professional sport. There are several factors involved here. Leading sports personalities are now 'superstars' on a par with pop stars. Whereas the wages of the likes of early post-war players such as Stanley Matthews and Tom Finny were perhaps three or four times the average annual wage, contemporary 'superstars' like Ryan Giggs earn more than the average annual wage in a week. The better players now tend to transfer more often and not to have roots in the local community of the teams they play for. On the other hand international sports stars move around more and are more visible as sports become Europeanised and even globalised. The professionalisation of much sport – the acquiring of agents, training in media self-presentation, and the highly managed nature of commercial sport – has also widened the gap between stars and the public in terms of everyday contact and community although, again, the media offers a different kind of access and visibility.

A third change is becoming apparent in sport and that is the nature of its audience. The total audience for big sporting evens (i.e. including the media audience) has increased in size and contains proportionately more females. Again, this is almost certainly due mainly to the 'mediaisation' (to invent a term) of sport. In a context in which 'half' the public seem highly engaged in the progress of national teams in big competitions, in which some of the tabloids are as xenophobic and even as racist as the 'hoolies', and in which young sports stars are expected or, at least, forgiven for behaving like 'lads' (or 'ladettes'?) – the hooligan becomes not so much irrelevant as superseded.

Sport and the media – and the two in combination – illustrate the importance and pervasiveness of consumption in late modernity. We now turn to this issue.

Culture, consumption and identity

The phrase 'consumer culture' closely links the concepts of culture and consumption in modern capitalist societies. However, these terms are intentionally separated in the title of this section because important as patterns of consumption are in defining a culture, consumption is not the only nor necessarily the most important aspect of culture (see below).

Consumption is a recurrent theme in this book in the same way that, say, alienation and differentiation are. However, the concept

Figure 16.5 Modern sport does not always support Elias's thesis of the 'civilising process': Gazza's civilised side?

Table 16.1 The rise of consumerism

Households with the following:

	1964	1992
	Percentages	
Refrigerator	34	99
Television	80	99
Telephone	22	89
Washing machine	53	88
Deep freeze/fridge-freezer	*	85
Video	0	72
Car	37	68
Microwave oven	0	59
Tumble dryer	neg	49
CD player	0	33
Home computer	0	23
Dishwasher	neg	16

* = the earliest available figure, published in Regional Trends 28, is 47% in 1980-81.
neg – negligible.

(Sources: Central Statistical Office (1993) *A report on the 1992 Family Expenditure Survey*, London: HMSO; Central Statistical Office (1994). *Social Trends 24*, London: HMSO; NEF estimates)

of consumption has become so important and current that it will be helpful to draw together the main points made elsewhere and extend them as appropriate.

A further preliminary point to make is that sociological concern with culture is not new. We saw earlier that Veblen and Weber associated consumption with lifestyle and membership to status groups (see p. 480). Marxists have invariably analysed popular consumption in capitalist society in terms of control and manipulation. Thus, Adorno and the Frankfurt school developed mass society theory in which they argued that popular consumption of the 'mass media' tended to deaden the capacity to make political and artistic criticism (see p. 515). In contrast, in liberal thinking, consumption has generally been regarded positively.

Consumption: the facts

There are a range of trends which together make an impressive case that modern society is shifting significantly towards consumption. In general, people are much wealthier than 50 or even twenty years ago, they buy or consume more and they have more leisure time in which to consume. The explosion in the consumption of household durables is well illustrated in Table 16.1.

A crucial aspect in the creation of so-called consumer society, is that the ability to consume quite a sizeable range of modern household consumer durables includes nearly all the poor (although they are deprived in other respects pp. 282-4). For instance, single-person households have a lower percentage of all consumer durables than do lone-parent family households with the predictable exception of the telephone.

If there is a rough egalitarianism in basic household consumption it is a picture which needs to be heavily qualified. First, the less wealthy are less likely to own even some quite basic household consumer durables than the better off. This is, of course, far more the case with semi-luxuries and luxuries. Second, there is no escaping the fact that for most people what they are able to consume depends on what they earn – and earnings differentials increased in the late 1980s and in the first half of the 1990s. There is no escaping the link between relations to the means production (Marx) and consumption, or, as Weber preferred to express it, between market position and consumption.

The meaning of consumption

Two recent theoretical approaches to understanding consumption in modern society have been described earlier in this book (see pp. 180-1). The first is associated particularly with Peter Saunders. He argues that cleavages in consumption such as ownership or not of a home can greatly affect outlook and behaviour, notably political. He finds evidence to support the Thatcherite thesis that personal ownership fostered values of individualism.

The second recent theoretical approach to consumption is to interpret consumer behaviour as *signifying* particular meanings. This approach was described at length in relation to youth in the previous chapter. Interpretations of the meaning of style and of consumption differ in their emphasis on the extent to which consumers are seen as making their own choices and meanings or are dupes of capitalist consumerism. In principle, both cases are possible and no doubt occur in various degrees.

Stripped of its theoretical baggage, the second approach is fundamentally that of Max Weber. The latter saw lifestyle as an important indicator of status and cultural identity. Undoubtedly, however, the semiology of Barthes, the poststructuralism of Foucault and the postmodernism of Baudrillard (see pp. 518-20) has added further insight to our understanding of the relationship between individual and collective consumption and culture, particularly the media which was considerably less technologically developed in Weber's day.

Consumer 'classes' and advertising

Traditionally, social class has been defined in relation to occupation and work. Occupational classes have typically been based on differences in qualifications, wages and status in the community (see pp. 144-6). However, as capitalism shifts more to consumption, concern focuses increasingly on people's spending habits. Advertisers and media entrepreneurs have attempted to construct their own consumer classes in order to target particular groups for advertising. Thus, in 1996, Carat, a media buying group, published a guide to advertisers which re-classified occupations mainly on the basis of consumer habits rather than occupation. University lecturers dropped from 'A' to 'B' and monks and nuns 'without special responsibilities' only made C1. Also in 1996 another consumer oriented classification – this time exclusively of males – was produced by EMAP Consumer Magazines. On the basis of survey data on their chief interests and relationships with the media, 'nineties men' were classified as follows:

New lads
Traditionalists
Ambitious modernists
New nineties men
Hedonists
'Meat and two veg' men.

Many radical critics tend to have great reservations about such

classificatory schemes. First, class schemes based on occupation have a built-in emphasis on inequality whereas those based on consumer habits do not. For Marxist and other conflict theorists, inequality and the potential conflict arising from it is centred on the dynamic of class. Second, such schemes have the potential to be highly manipulative. They do not merely reflect attitudes and behaviour but are directly intended to exploit them – through the advertising and selling of commodities. However, aware that such commercially oriented surveys will continue, a growing number of sociologists are researching consumption in an empirical way themselves. We will now examine such a piece of work.

Two discourses of consumerism: Peter Lunt and Sonia Livingstone

In *Mass Consumption and Personal Identity* (1992), Peter Lunt and Sonia Livingstone examine the role consumption in the lives of 279 respondents between the age of eighteen and 82, 62 per cent of whom were females and 38 per cent male. They found two main discourses or explanatory frameworks of consumerism among their respondents (many of whom expressed both views). These were the *regressive* and *progressive* discourse. The regressive discourse expressed concern at the threat to traditional morality, established institutions and local community that consumerism seemed to pose. Aggressive advertising, easier credit and other changes in the financial system caused insecurity. The progressive discourse reflected the desire to take advantage of the opportunities of modern consumer society.

As Lunt and Livingstone note, the debate people have about consumption in daily life is also one that occurs in the public arena. It has certainly been a long-running debate in sociology. On balance, sociologists have tended more to pessimism than optimism about the effects of consumer culture (the regressive discourse). For instance, Simmel foresaw profound consequences for the quality of human relations in the growing tendency to quantify everything in monetary terms. Marx coined the term 'commodification' to describe the same phenomenon. Much more recently, New Right sociologists such as Peter Saunders have been more enthusiastic about the choices and opportunities consumerism offers to ordinary people. There is also now more acknowledgement among radical sociologists of the significance of consumption, particularly on the postmodern left. Thus, in a contribution to the 'New Times' debate, Stuart Hall pointed to the continuing importance of collective consumption – in relation, for instance, to health and the environment.

What is particularly notable about Lunt and Livingstone's research is that they find the two discourses about consumption – negative and positive – among the mass of consumers as well as among sociologists. They do not find consumers to be empty-headed dupes. On the contrary, consumption plays a major role in the construction of self-identity:

> *The people we have talked to during our research for this book are engaged in a debate concerning the nature of identity in consumer culture. The dynamic of the debate is a natural milieu for them, there is no resolution offered, merely layers of discourse which play with a series of oppositions concerning tradition and modernity, freedom and determinism, opportunity and danger. Big issues played out in domestic settings.*
>
> (171)

They suggest that these daily domestic debates and decisions on consumption and identity can be considered as an example of what Giddens describes as 'life politics' (see pp. 492-3). They argue that it is not only members of new social movements but individuals who are constructively engaged in issues of consumption. Nor is their engagement purely economic or selfish in motivation: 'People are continually guided by moral and social issues in their economic choices' (166).

Alan Warde (1994) is one critic who has reservations about what he sees as 'far too individualistic a model of the consumer' apparent in the work of Giddens and Lunt and Livingstone. He reiterates the influences of the social (i.e. social factors) on what may appear to be individual 'choice'. These factors include: advertisements and consumer magazines; social contacts including family, peers and friends); the delegation of choice, e.g. to a partner; the persistence of convention, e.g. class culture; and sheer complacency. He argues that 'freedom' should not be imputed 'to an activity that is not in any important sense free'.

'Acknowledging consumption': Daniel Miller's conclusions

Daniel Miller is among the most optimistic of those sociologists who see consumption as a potentially liberating rather than as a repressive force. The title of his essay – 'Consumption as the Vanguard of History' – in *Acknowledging Consumption* (1995) expresses his view that the consumer is beginning to challenge the producer for the initiative in global capitalism. In the global market-place consumer demand can be met almost regardless of distance and season. For the Western consumer even cost has been cut by the cheapness of bulk transport and the low wages in poorer producer countries. It is such considerations that prompt Miller to argue that consumers and politicians must rethink the meaning, scope and effects of consumption.

He argues that consumption must be seen in terms of rights and responsibilities. He contends that consumption involves collective rights as well as the individual right of choice. Like Hall he strongly supports the collective organisation of education, health and welfare. Only collectively can universal standards be secure. But the consumer also has responsibilities. Consumption that damages the

environment or exploits poor people in other countries is irresponsible. Miller does not cite the example, but there has been considerable publicity about some of the less appealing aspects of the availability of cheap flowers in Britain in recent years. Some of them are cheap because they are picked by very cheap child labour . They are also genetically cultivated to survive the rigours of transportation from countries as far afield as Columbia. Sold in bulk in supermarkets, they threaten to put local florists out of business. All this could take the pleasure out of giving and receiving that most symbolic of gifts, flowers. As Miller says, consumer *citizenship* is complex – but necessary.

As the title of the edited collection – *Acknowledging Consumption* – indicates, Miller is more concerned to assert the centrality of the consumption than to detail the rights and responsibilities it entails. He takes issue with four 'myths' about consumption:

1 Mass consumption causes global homogenisation or global heterogenisation.
2 Consumption is opposed to sociality.
3 Consumption is opposed to authenticity.
4 Consumption creates particular kinds of social being.

The first 'myth' is really two opposing myths: mass consumption causes large numbers of the same product to be produced and consumed or, on the contrary, many different varieties of products are now produced and consumed. As Miller comments there is much evidence in both directions and, in fact both tendencies are occurring. Miller does not equate either tendency as the spread of 'consumer culture'. He considers that, in general, local cultures are capable of engaging with consumer products without being swamped. The second myth – that consumption is opposed to sociality – asserts that consumption makes people more interested in commodities than people. Miller regards this view as a sanctimonious hangover from medieval religiosity and, again, virtually impossible to prove. The third myth – that consumption lacks authenticity asserts that compared to production, consumption is a rather trivial and superficial activity. Miller strongly takes the view, referred to previously in this chapter, that consumption can be highly expressive and creative.

The final myth about consumption is that it creates a particular kind of social being. As summarised by Miller, the critics of consumption characterise this being as highly unpleasant, if not worse. The characteristics of the consumer include competitiveness over status, excessive individualism and conspicuous consumption and display – all in the context of great inequality. Miller argues that these characteristics may be associated with consumption – perhaps commonly in particular societies – but that they need not be. Consumers may consume for a wide range of positive motives. However, Miller argues that consumption itself is not *intrinsically* good or bad, it has different meanings for different individuals and in different social circumstances.

Miller's provocative essay throws down the gauntlet to those who regard consumption as highly secondary to production. His perspective prompts him to reframe positively the consuming activities of housewives and black minorities who, for different reasons, were not fully drawn into and defined by the discipline and routine of production. But his biggest challenge is to reconceptualise consumption in terms of the rights and responsibilities of global citizenship. It is likely that this debate has some way to run.

Questions

1 To what extent is it true that contemporary society provides more numerous and varied opportunities for the development and expression of identities than in the industrial age?
2 Give a critical account (with examples) of postmodern analyses of culture.

Summary

1 Culture and identity are defined as complementary concepts. Culture refers to 'ways of life' and to sign systems which convey meaning.
2 Biological, psychoanalytic and several sociological approaches to culture and identity are presented. The balance between self-expression and cultural influence is struck differently in different perspectives.
3 Cultural studies in the 1950s were greatly influenced by Marxist historical writing and literary criticism. Although not a sociological work, Richard Hoggart's, *The Uses of Literacy* was a classic community study of the period.
4 In the 1970s Stuart Hall led cultural studies in a different direction from that of Hoggart in the 1960s. The latter's emphasis on culture as a way of life was replaced by the former's analysis of the meanings of cultural codes – particularly in relation to youth.
5 Hall continued to be the dominant influence in British cultural studies as a mediator of the influence of postmodernism in the late 1980s and 1990s.
6 Anthony Giddens' *The Transformation of Intimacy* (1992) offers a view of the potential of individuals, relationships and culture that is more autonomous than is apparent in Hall's work.
7 A growing body of contemporary writings argues that 'consumerism' is of growing importance in late modern society.

Research and coursework

See the end of Chapters 15 and 17.

Further reading

Dominic Strinati's *An Introduction to Theories of Popular Culture* (Routledge, 1995) does precisely what its title suggests. Chris Jenks' *Culture* (Routledge, 1993) is more demanding.

Readings

Reading 1
Streets as communal space

Philip Cohen, in E Butterworth and H Weir, *The Sociology of Modern Britain* (Fontana, 1979), p. 111.

But how does the ecology of the neighbourhood work in practice? Let's take the street as an example. In these neighbourhoods the street forms a kind of 'communal space', a mediation between the totally private space of the family, with its intimate involvements, and the totally public space, e.g. parks, thoroughfares, etc., where people relate to each other as strangers, and with indifference. The street, then, is a space where people can relate as neighbours, can express a degree of involvement with others, who are outside the family, but yet not as strangers; it maintains an intricate social balance between rights and obligations, distance and relation in the community. It also serves to generate an informal system of social controls. For where the street is played in, talked in, sat out in, constantly spectated as a source of neighbourly interest, it is also policed, and by the people themselves. Nothing much can happen, however trivial (a child falling, a woman struggling with heavy parcels, etc.), without it becoming a focus of interest and intervention. The presence of corner shops and pubs in their turn also serves to generate social interaction at street level, as well as providing natural settings for 'gossip cliques', which if they do nothing else constantly reaffirm the reality of neighbourhood ties!

The net result is that neighbours as well as relatives are available to help cope with the day to day problems that arise in the constant struggle to survive under the conditions of the working class community. And in many areas, including the East End, institutions such as loans clubs, holiday clubs and the like developed to supplement family mutual aid, and formalise the practice of 'neighbouring'.

Questions

1 State, with examples, the advantages and disadvantages of the communal street life described in the above passage.
2 What main changes in working class community life as described in the above passage and in the text (see pp. 481-4) have occurred since the 1960s?

Reading 2
What is postmodernism?

What is Postmodernism? from Dominic Strinati, *An Introduction to Theories of Popular Culture* (Routledge, 1995), pp. 223-8

In order to identify postmodernism, the following – by no means exhaustive – set of points summarises some of the most salient features which writers about the phenomenon have chosen to emphasise ...

The breakdown of the distinction between culture and society

First, postmodernism is said to describe the emergence of a social order in which the importance and power of the mass media and popular culture means that they govern and shape all other forms of social relationships. The idea is that popular cultural signs and media images increasingly dominate our sense of reality, and the way we define ourselves and the world around us. It tries to come to terms with, and understand, a media-saturated society. The mass media, for example, were once thought of as holding up a mirror to, and thereby reflecting, a wider social reality. Now reality can only be defined by the surface reflections of this mirror. Society has become subsumed within the mass media. It is no longer even a question of distortion, since the term implies that there is a reality, outside the surface simulations of the media, which can be distorted, and this is precisely what is at issue according to postmodern theory.

This idea, in part, seems to emerge out of one of the directions taken by media and cultural theory. To put it simply, the liberal view argued that the media held up a mirror to, and thereby reflected in a fairly accurate manner, a wider social reality. The radical rejoinder to this insisted that this mirror distorted rather than reflected reality. Subsequently, a more abstract and conceptual media and cultural theory suggested that the media played some part in constructing our sense of social reality, and our sense of being a part of this reality (Curran *et al.*, 1982; Bennett, 1982). It is a relatively short step from this (and one which need not be taken) to the proposition that only the media can constitute our sense of reality. To return to the original metaphor, it is claimed that this mirror is now the only reality we have.

Moreover, linked to this is the notion that in the postmodern condition it becomes more difficult to distinguish the economy from popular culture. The realm of consumption – what we buy and what determines what we buy – is increasingly influenced by popular culture. Consumption is increasingly bound up with popular culture because popular culture increasingly determines consumption. For example, we watch more films because of the extended ownership of VCRs, while advertising, which makes increasing use of popular cultural references, plays a more important role in deciding what we will buy.

An emphasis on style at the expense of substance

A crucial implication of the first point is that in a postmodern world, surfaces and style become more important, and evoke in their turn a kind of 'designer ideology'. Or as Harvey puts it: 'images dominate narrative' (1989, pp.347-348). The argument is that we increasingly consume images and signs for their own sake rather than for their 'usefulness' or for the deeper values they may symbolise. We consume images and signs precisely because they are images and signs, and disregard questions of utility and value. This is evident in popular culture itself where surface and style, what things look like, and playfulness and jokes, are said to predominate at the expense of content, substance and meaning. As a result, qualities like artistic merit, integrity, seriousness, authenticity, realism, intellectual depth and strong narratives tend to be undermined. Moreover, virtual reality computer graphics can allow people to experience various forms of reality at second hand. These surface simulations can therefore potentially replace their real-life counterparts.

The breakdown of the distinction between art and popular culture

If the first two points are accepted it follows that for postmodern culture anything can be turned into a joke, reference or quotation in its eclectic play of styles, simulations and surfaces. If popular cultural signs and media images are taking over in defining our sense of reality for us, and if this means that style takes precedence over content, then it becomes more difficult to maintain a meaningful distinction between art and popular culture. There are no longer any agreed and inviolable criteria which can serve to differentiate art from popular culture. Compare this with the fears of the mass culture critics that mass culture would eventually subvert high culture. The only difference seems to be that these critics were pessimistic about these developments, whereas some, but not all, postmodern theorists are by contrast optimistic.

A good example of what postmodernist theory is getting at is provided by Andy Warhol's multi-imaged print of Leonardo Da Vinci's famous painting *The Mona Lisa*. The print shows that the uniqueness, the artistic aura, of the Mona Lisa is destroyed by its infinite reproducibility through the silk-screen printing technique employed by Warhol. Instead, it is turned into a joke – the print's title is *Thirty are better than One*. This point is underlined by the fact that Warhol was renowned for his prints of famous popular cultural icons like Marilyn Monroe and Elvis Presley as well as of everyday consumer items like tins of Campbell's soup, Coca-Cola bottles and dollar bills.

One aspect of this process is that art becomes increasingly integrated into the economy both because it is used to encourage people to consume through the expanded role it plays in advertising, and because it becomes a commercial good in its own right. Another aspect is that postmodern popular culture refuses to respect the pretensions and distinctiveness of art. Therefore, the breakdown of the distinction between art and popular culture, as well as crossovers between the two, become more prevalent.

Confusions over time and space

It is argued here that contemporary and future compressions and focusing of time and space have led to increasing confusion and incoherence in our sense of space and time, in our maps of the places where we live, and our ideas about the times in terms of which we organise our lives. The title and the narratives of the *Back to the Future* films capture this point fairly well. The growing immediacy of global space and time resulting from the dominance of the mass media means that our previously unified and coherent ideas about space and time begin to be undermined, and become distorted and confused. Rapid international flows of capital, money, information and culture disrupt the linear unities of time,

and the established distances of geographical space. Because of the speed and scope of modern mass communications, and the relative ease and rapidity with which people and information can travel, time and space become less stable and comprehensible, and more confused and incoherent (Harvey, 1989, part 3).

Postmodern popular culture is seen to express these confusions and distortions. As such, it is less likely to reflect coherent senses of space or time. Some idea of this argument can be obtained by trying to identify the locations used in some pop videos, the linear narratives of some recent films or the times and spaces crossed in a typical evening of television viewing. In short, postmodern popular culture is a culture *sans frontières*, outside history.

The decline of metanarratives

The loss of a sense of history as a continuous, linear 'narrative', a clear sequence of events, is indicative of the argument that, in the postmodern world, metanarratives are in decline. This point about the decline of metanarratives arises out of the previous arguments we have noted. Metanarratives, examples of which include religion, science, art, modernism and Marxism, make absolute, universal and all-embracing claims to knowledge and truth. Postmodernist theory is highly sceptical about these metanarratives, and argues that they are increasingly open to criticism. In the postmodern world they are disintegrating, their validity and legitimacy are in decline. It is becoming increasingly difficult for people to organise and interpret their lives in the light of metanarratives of whatever kind. This argument would therefore include, for example, the declining significance of religion as a metanarrative in postmodern societies. Postmodernism has been particularly critical of the metanarrative of Marxism and its claim to absolute truth, as it has been of any theory which tries to read a pattern of progress into history.

The consequence of this is that postmodernism rejects the claims of any theory to absolute knowledge, or of any social practice to universal validity. So, for example, on the one hand there are movements in the natural or hard sciences away from deterministic and absolute metanarratives towards more contingent and probabilistic claims to the truth, while on the other hand people appear to be moving away from the metanarrative of life-long, monogamous marriage towards a series of discrete if still monogamous 'relationships' (Harvey, 1989: p.9; Lash and Urry, 1987, p.298). The diverse, iconoclastic, referential and collage-like character of postmodern popular culture clearly draws inspiration from the decline of metanarratives.

Questions

1 In relation especially to youth, discuss the postmodern view that 'popular culture increasingly determines consumption'.
2 Do you agree that there has been a decline of metanarratives? If so, why?

Note: Reading 2, p. 473 provides an extract on the development of youthful identity.

Media (and Globalisation)

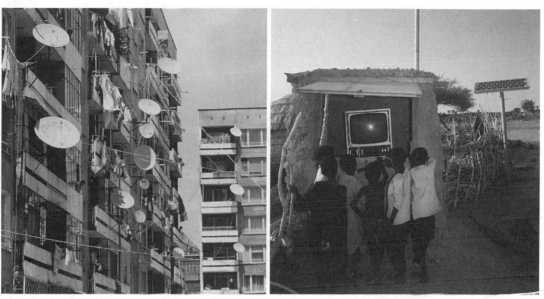

What social activities have the media replaced? What is the gain and loss of a media-soaked world?

Aims of this chapter

1 To describe the structure of the public and private sector media and to discuss the principles on which each is based.

2 To consider the social consequences of changing media technology and organisation.

3 Critically to present a number of perspectives on the influence of the media.

4 Sceptically to explore Jean Baudrillard's postmodern analysis of the media.

5 To discuss the impact of media globalisation on various levels of identity.

Structure and ownership

The media in Britain are divided into a public and a private sector. The public sector is concerned only with broadcasting, whereas the private sector covers the whole range of media.

Public sector media

The British Broadcasting Corporation was set up as a public company in 1926. It is currently financed by a licence fee, and run, not for profit, but in the public interest. It was responsible for all radio broadcasting and, from 1932, television broadcasting as well. The BBC is run by a Board of Governors which is constituted as independent of the government. However, there is a continuing lively debate about whether the BBC is, in practice, fully independent of government (see pp. 510-11). In the era of privatisation, the rumour that the BBC might be 'broken up' and largely privatised has occasionally surfaced.

Private sector media

The press is wholly commercially owned in Britain and there is also a strong trend towards greater commercialisation in relation to broadcasting. Commercial television started in 1955 and commercial radio in 1973. They are financed mainly through advertising revenue. The Broadcasting Act of 1990 greatly extended the potential scope of commercial television. In addition to the two existing commercial channels, three and four, provisions were made to set up several more. The Independent Television Commission was set up with the intention that it would regulate television with a 'lighter touch' than its predecessor, the Independent Broadcasting Authority.

The international satellite companies, SKY and British Satellite Broadcasting (BSB) company offered multiple channel viewing – at a price – and came on the air in 1989 and 1990 respectively. The two satellite companies planned to finance themselves from advertising revenue but also through subscription fees for access to various channels. However, in early 1990, SKY was losing two million pounds per week, and BSB also ran at a loss. It was little surprise when the two companies merged. Cable television, though not yet widespread in Britain, offers potential for commercial development.

Media ownership: concentration and conglomeration

Two main trends characterise media ownership in Britain: concentration and conglomeration. Concentration refers to business in a given area – in this case in the media – merging so that ownership becomes concentrated in fewer hands. This has notably occurred in relation to the national press. In 1948, the three biggest press groups commanded 48 per cent of total circulation whereas the figure for 1985 was 74.8 per cent. The tendency to concentration has affected local newspapers, many of which are owned by national media companies. Conglomerates form when one company takes over another (or others) in the same or a different line of business. Rupert Murdoch's News International is a massive global multi-media conglomerate and Murdoch also has interests in software, energy and transport. Whether these trends in ownership result in less free media, influence media content, and have an effect on audiences is discussed later. Broadly, liberals argue that, despite these developments, the media in capitalist democracies remain fundamentally free. Socialists and Marxists vary in the extent to which they consider business interests limit media 'freedom' but generally see these interests as purveyors of capitalist ideology whether intentionally or not. (Reading 1 explores key issues in relation to those developments.)

The effects of technological change on the media

The modern media are highly dependent on technology. Technological innovation has always 'driven' the development of the communications media, and businesses unable to afford or adapt to it have usually perished. This has been true from the printing press to satellite broadcasting.

Two consequences of technological change in the media should be noted. First, the cost of the technology and the competitive importance of early but sometimes high-risk investment in it, means that large, rich companies tend to control investment. This tends to promote media concentration. Thus Rupert Murdoch was able to invest in high-technology printing at Wapping and eventually recoup his investment through reduced labour costs and greater efficiency. As far as SKY is concerned, he was prepared and able to afford to lose about half a billion pounds before

Murdoch's new world

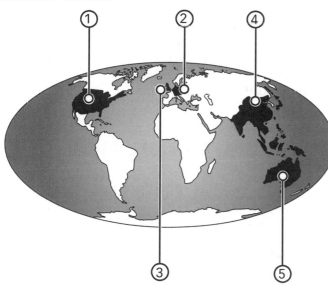

1 **US:** Twentieth Century Fox, including Fox TV, creators of mega-hits The Simpsons and NYPD Blue.
The New York Post, the TV Guide, and publishing house HarperCollins.
2 **Germany:** Vox satellite and terrestrial TV channel – 49.9 per cent owned by Murdoch.
3 **United Kingdom:** BSkyB satellite – 40 per cent owned by Murdoch.
Newspapers – Times, Sunday Times, Sun, News of the World, Today.
4 **Asia (India, China, Japan, Philippines, Thailand and Hong Kong):**
Star TV – 63.6 per cent owned by Murdoch.
5 **Australia:** Channel 7 – 15 per cent owned by Murdoch.
Numerous print groups and newspapers, including The Australian and Sunday Telegraph.

Also: Delphi ON-Line Internet Service.

Figure 17.1 An example of a media-based conglomerate

achieving profitability. Few are able to play a 'game' with such high stakes but there must be concern about how those that can, influence others (see Figure 17.1).

The second trend in media technology is towards greater access by the general public. This has different and possibly contradictory consequences to the first trend. A large range of media hardware (videos, tape-recorders, computers, including those with desk-top publishing facilities) and software (tapes, computer software) are readily and cheaply available. Undoubtedly, this increases potential choice and creativity (e.g. producing videos, newsheets etc.) both for individuals and groups. Of course, for those who do wish to create their own material for an audience, problems relating to the cost and quality of production and distribution still have to be overcome. In these matters, Rupert Murdoch has something of a start!

In this respect the internet *may* prove a democratic development. So far (1997) access is uncontrolled and content more or less uncensored. For instance, both business and radical pressure groups can and do by-pass the usual news channels and put their views directly to the 'net's' estimated 30 million users.

Forecast growth in dish and cable households, millions

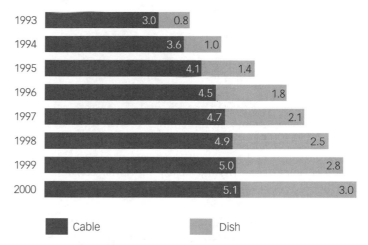

(Source: *Continental Research*, April 1994 in *The Guardian*, 30.8.1994:6)

Figure 17.2 Dish and cable growth

The expansion of satellite and cable: pay TV

The growth of satellite disc and cable television is expected almost to double between 1994 and 2000 (see Figure 17.2). In 1995, about a quarter of households linked up with satellite or cable. In total, satellite and cable offer more than 40 channels and the potential for providing more radio stations – with much better reception than existing radio – exists.

Superhighways of communication – in the near future?

The cable networks currently being constructed by the (mainly American) cable companies are expected to play a central role in Britain's information superhighway. They are able to offer a telephone service along with access to television channels (unlike British Telecom which is banned from broadcasting until 2001). Telephone access will facilitate interactive broadcasting. This means that the active 'consumer' (rather than the passive 'viewer') will be able to access a vast store of information in many areas (for instance, some daily newspapers are already available on the 'internet') including, local advertising and data about entertainment, consumer goods, official events, etc. This is in addition to the scores of television channels which could potentially be available. However, whereas the BBC is financed through the licence fee and ITV through advertising, these newer developments will be paid for directly by the consumer – more or less as SKY is now.

The BBC and ITV: the influence of competitive and commercial pressures

As has already been described, the BBC and ITV operate within a framework laid down by government. The Broadcasting Act of 1990 changed this framework by opening up both of them to more competition. However, certain measures were also introduced to try and safeguard standards and quality – as can be seen from the terms of the Act summarised below:

The Broadcasting Act, 1990: main terms

1 Organisation/Competition
   i The BBC to continue to be funded by a licence fee, but other sources of income also to be permitted, including subscription and sponsorship.
   ii The BBC to hand over some transmission time to other groups.
   iii The IBA to be replaced by a Commission with fewer powers of regulation.
   iv Channel 4 to keep existing programme instructions.
   v A fifth channel by 1993, and possibly a sixth, seventh and eighth later.
     (However, a fifth channel had still not been established by 1997 and with so many other new 'media' developments occurring, may never be.)
2 Standards/Quality
   vi ITV companies were made more open to competition, but quality thresholds (controls) were imposed.
   vii The (1988) Broadcasting Standards Authority was given more powers to monitor sex and violence.

In line with the expectations of the Conservative government, the BBC overhauled its 'business' practices between 1990 and 1994. This process was intensified when John Birt became Director General of the Corporation in 1992. His cost-cutting, market-focused management approach has been referred to as 'the Birting of the Beeb'. Among other things, he reduced the BBC staff from 25,000 to 20,000 in five years, greatly increased the number of programmes produced by non-BBC, independent producers, and increased the numbers of BBC programme 'spin-off' products such as audio and video cassettes and books.

In 1994, Birt's BBC was rewarded by the government with the renewal of its charter for ten years from 1997 and urged to develop further its market activities, particularly exporting from its vast programme library. But many inside and outside the BBC had doubts about, or frankly opposed Birt's management-led revolution. Mark Tully, a veteran professional broadcaster, spoke of Mr Birt's 'fear and sycophancy regime' and decried what he saw as the undermining of the BBC's traditional values of public service.

It is appropriate to consider now what are the larger issues of value and culture raised by the current 'media revolution' and not least, by the position of the BBC within it. Morley and Robins give a succinct summary of that shift from national to global controlled media (Reading 1). Their stimulating work *Spaces of Identity* provides the basis of the final section in this chapter.

The media: the big issues

Public and commercial (private) media

It is very likely that in the foreseeable future, the major development of the media will be by business and that the consumer will pay for what s/he accesses. Although the medium term future of the BBC is secure, this is only because its management has been prepared to enter the world of competition and markets. Nevertheless, it is possible that a future government – perhaps a Labour government – will revive the public service function of the BBC even though this seems to go against current trends.

What might the basis of a national, public service broadcasting corporation be as we approach the end of the twentieth century? Clearly, the BBC can no longer have the powerful influence on the nation's culture and morality that Lord Reith, the first Director General, believed it should (see p. 507). There are simply too many other media outlets.

What the BBC might do – with government approval – is to become the main or even exclusive outlet for national cultural, sporting and entertainment events such as a major drama series or the cup finals of various sports. This would ensure that such events could not be bought up by a commercial media company and shown only to a small minority of the population. In this way, the BBC would be providing a genuine public service and acting as a means to national shared experience. Currently protected status applies to:

PROTECTED EVENTS

Olympic Games
Football: World Cup. FA and Scottish FA Cup Finals.
Cricket: Test matches.
Tennis: Wimbledon finals.
Racing: Grand National and Derby.

Question

Do you agree with this list? Labour might add the Five Nations Rugby Internationals, and the Ryder Cup and British Open Golf tournaments.

Standards, quality and choice

The main justification for the expansion of satellite and cable broadcasting has been that they would provide something different or, in some respects, better and so increase consumer choice. The

(a) Social class

Households who have subscribed to cable/satelliteTV by social class

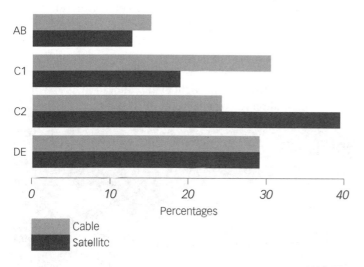

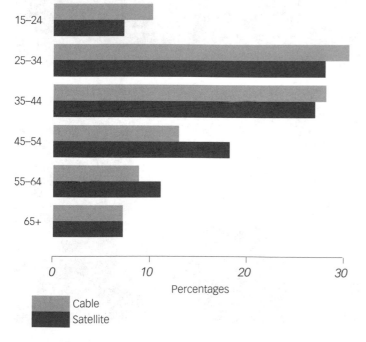

Figure 17.3 Cable and satellite subscriptions – by class and age

main criticism of their early period of development, especially of SKY, is that they have largely produced more of the same and often of lower quality than the established media. SKY has sometimes been referred to, perhaps rather snobbishly, as 'council house television'. Figure 17.3 certainly suggests that households in higher socio-economic brackets have been less inclined to buy SKY and, to some extent, cable than lower middle (CI) and upper working (C2) class households. This could change, however, when planned channels with specialities of greater interest to higher socio-economic groups come on-stream.

The newer broadcasting companies, especially SKY, have also been accused of lowering the standard of the media generally, including the BBC and ITV. In this view, competition is seen as reducing media output to the lowest common denominator in the scramble for good audience ratings. Successful competition from the newer companies also tends to undermine the financial position of the BBC and ITV. For both reasons, the latter rely more on cheap programmes such as repeats and old (often American) films than they did.

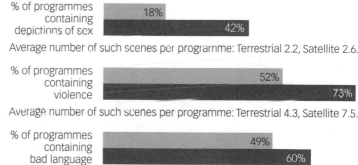

Average number of such scenes per programme: Terrestrial 2.2, Satellite 2.6.

Average number of such scenes per programme: Terrestrial 4.3, Satellite 7.5.

% containing serious bad language: Terrestrial 2%, Satellite 12%.

(Source: BSC in *The Guardian*, 27.1.1994:1)

Figure 17.4 Television standards: terrestrial and satellite compared

Figure 17.4 might seem to provide data to support a case of censorship. But how does this balance with freedom of choice? In any case, it is becoming increasingly difficult for governments to 'block' satellite broadcasts. Such is the speed of change in the media that government response is often uncertain, provisional and not wholly adequate.

Questions

1 Describe recent developments in the structure, ownership and control of the British media.
2 What issues of quality and choice do these changes raise?

Perspectives on the influence of the media

The title 'perspectives on the influence of the media' provides a broad umbrella for a variety of approaches to analysing the relationship between the media and society. In fact, these approaches are somewhat different in kind.

Liberal and Marxist perspectives are comprehensive paradigms of how societies operate and should operate. They function at such a broad level of generalisation that it is difficult, if not impossible, finally to prove one or the other 'right' or 'wrong'. However, specific propositions in liberal and Marxist theory are susceptible to empirical proof or disproof. Thus, the Marxist proposition that ownership of the media is concentrated in relatively few hands can be factually examined. Feminist and anti-racist perspectives are more limited in scope than liberal and Marxist ones. They are concerned, respectively, with sexism and racism and either can be integrated into broader perspectives such as liberalism and Marxism (in fact, anti-racist perspective is strongly associated with Marxism) or can stand alone as critical perspectives. The ideological values behind feminist and anti-racist perspectives are obvious – indeed, the perspectives only exist because of opposition to sexism and racism.

Interactionist perspective is less ideological than the others so far mentioned. This is partly because it is a 'middle range' perspective concerned mainly with how people perceive and construct everyday 'reality'. In particular, Marxists have drawn extensively on interactionism in explaining media processes at a more detailed level.

The material presented under the heading 'Effects research' (see p. 515) is largely positivist in nature. Most of it is based on the behaviourist view that when stimulated by something (e.g. television) people's behaviour will change (effect) and that this effect can be measured and quantified.

Liberal perspectives

Liberal pluralism

Liberalism – in one or another of its forms – is probably the most widely used perspective in understanding the media in Britain and other liberal-capitalist societies. In so far as most people, including journalists, 'believe in' this approach, it is the 'dominant ideology' or, simply, most popular understanding of the media. There are several main varieties of liberal ideology but all share certain fundamental principles. The basic form of liberalism is liberal pluralism. It is based on the view that for a society to be democratic, individuals and groups must be free to compete for political power and influence. It follows from this, that people must also be free to express themselves through the media – otherwise, they would not be able to compete politically. So, political freedom requires free media. Generally, liberal pluralists also believe that for political and

media freedom to be achieved, a society's economy must also be 'free' or largely 'free', by which they mean capitalist or mixed.

Liberal pluralists argue that the free market is the main enabling mechanism for a free media. Freedom to own and produce media and freedom to 'consume' media output means that audiences can feed back their opinions on media content to owners and producers who can then respond. In the pluralist model, consumers – the people – ultimately 'rule' because by exercising their right of choice in consumption they can influence and, sometimes determine media content.

There are other significant aspects to liberal pluralist media theory. Traditionally, liberals have taken the view that the potential power of individual media owners is limited by the convention of editorial independence, i.e. the right of the editor to shape, say, a newspaper's opinion stance and to control its day-to-day

Figure 17.5 The Sun edited by Kelvin Mackenzie (bottom) paid £1 million (later reduced) in damages for libelling Elton John (top). Invasion of privacy and misleading reporting became a major issue in relation to the popular press in the late 1980s and 1990s

operation. This convention has perhaps been tarnished by the willingness of owners, not least, Murdoch and Maxwell, to sack editors and by the fact that it has not been generally extended into commercial broadcasting. Finally, most media are open to some direct public access such as letter columns or 'open space' facilities.

Journalists themselves often hold a liberal (or *laissez-faire*) view of their own activities. They see themselves as trying to provide the public with objective facts to which it makes its own response(s). When journalistic opinion is expressed, the convention is that it is clearly indicated as such.

John Whale is a well-known advocate of the liberal pluralist view of the media. In the following extract he unambiguously concludes that readers rather than proprietors (owners) 'ultimately determine' the 'broad shape and nature of the press'.

> *It is readers who determine the character of newspapers. The Sun illustrates the point in its simplest and saddest form. Until 1964 the Daily Herald, and between 1964 and 1969 the broadsheet Sun, had struggled to interest working people principally through their intellect. The paper had declined inexorably. Murdoch gave up the attempt and went for the baser instincts. Sales soared. By May 1978, selling just under four million copies, the Sun was reckoned to have overtaken the Mirror – which had held the lead since winning it from the Express in 1949 – as the biggest selling national daily paper. At the Express, the message was received. The year before, after a struggle between assorted financiers, the Beaverbrook empire had passed to a shipping and property concern named Trafalgar House. The new chairman was Victor Matthews; and in November 1978 Matthews launched, from Manchester, a paper called the Daily Star which extended the Sun formula even further downmarket. At the London Evening Standard (another Beaverbrook paper) Matthew's dismissal of a cultivated editor, Simon Jenkins, in the same month presaged a similar approach there. These were owners' decisions, certainly; but they would have meant nothing without the ratification of readers.*
>
> *That, in the end, is the answer to the riddle of proprietorial influence. Where it survives at all, it must still defer to the influence of readers. The policy of the Daily Telegraph, its selection and opinion of the news it reports, is decided by the editor and his senior colleagues. But there is a regulatory force which keeps the paper's policy from straying too widely or suddenly from pre-ordained paths; and that force is not the proprietor but the readers. They chose the paper for qualities they expect to see continued.*
>
> (Whale, 1987:84)

There are two main criticisms of the liberal pluralist approach. The first is that the theory of the free market does not fully work in practice. In particular, capitalism can produce large conglomerates – including media conglomerates – which may dominate the market, stifling competition and variety (see pp. 508-11). Second, the criticism is frequently made that where the media is used exclusively or even primarily to make profit, quality can seriously suffer. For example, the highly profitable newspaper *The Sun* is often accused of tasteless, inaccurate and sometimes cruel 'cheque-book journalism'.

Liberal paternalism

The term liberal paternalism is used here to describe liberals who accept the basic principles of liberal pluralism but who also believe that, in part, the media should reflect high cultural goals and that systematic check, if not control, must be kept on the media to ensure certain general standards and quality. Liberal paternalists are prepared to accept a greater degree of state intervention in the media than pure *laissez-faire* liberals. Many liberal paternalists are strong supporters of public broadcasting, and believe that the BBC has achieved perhaps unequalled high standards.

The first Director General of the BBC, Lord Reith, was a prototype liberal paternalist. He believed in high quality broadcasting which would inform and educate as well as entertain. Reith had the personal charisma and power to impose his beliefs for many years, and the Reithian tradition has survived in the BBC, particularly in respect of its commitment to quality broadcasting.

By the early 1990s, the issue of media quality concerned many others besides liberal paternalists. There was widespread public revulsion against what were seen as the worst excesses of cheque-book journalism referred to above. Regularly, long-range photography and payment of large fees to ex-wives, lovers and 'friends' to elicit 'revelations' resulted in humiliation and invasion of privacy for the famous and, sometimes, not so famous. Successful libel actions by celebrities such as Elton John (see Figure 17.5) and Tessa Sanderson put pressure on the popular press. If anything, the establishment was more incensed than the general public – not least because some of its members were prime victims of tabloid journalism. Judges imposed high fines on publications which broke the libel laws and increasingly politicians began to threaten controlling legislation unless the press quickly 'put its house in order'.

The debate about both moral and cultural standards in the media was given urgency by the rapid expansion of the commercial broadcasting media during the late 1980s and 1990s, including SKY corporation which started broadcasting in 1989. The possibility presented itself of low-grade programmes beamed in by international satellite some of which might offend against existing norms and laws in Britain governing the portrayal of sex and violence. In 1988 the Broadcasting Standards Authority was set up to monitor sex and violence in broadcasting. Although it has powers to recommend rather than enforce, the possibility that its powers might be strengthened remains. The Broadcasting Act of 1990 was intended to enable the further commercialisation of British Broadcasting but it, too, reflected concern about quality. Companies granted broadcasting franchises had to guarantee to achieve certain quality thresholds (levels). The 1990 Broadcasting Act went some way to satisfying the aspirations of the freemarket lobby in respect to commercial television. Companies which sought franchises were required to bid against each other but any plan accepted by the ITC had to pass a quality threshold. However, critics argued that the auction system would force companies to bid beyond their means and leave them insufficiently funded to achieve high quality production. Some felt justified in their concern when the well-respected Thames Television was outbid in the first auction of 1991.

Concern about media standards, then, extends far beyond liberal paternalists. Groups ranging from Marxists to traditional religions expressed similar opinions – though, of course, they put it in different ideological context. Nevertheless, it is significant that a highly pro free-market government should have been sufficiently concerned about a threatened decline in broadcasting standards to implement even the limited measures outlined above. The Labour party favoured rather more guarantees of quality. The tradition of protective liberal paternalism has by no means been destroyed by free market liberalism.

Free market liberalism: the New Right

The free market liberals of the New Right have a particularly strong commitment to the free market and a corresponding objection to 'unnecessary' state interference in its operation. Ideologically, they are close to pre-welfare state nineteenth century liberalism. Norman Tebbitt and Rupert Murdoch are powerful exponents of this ideology.

Like the populist, Tebbitt, Murdoch is scathingly critical of those intellectuals whom he sees as interfering with audience freedom of choice by trying to impose so-called 'quality' media. In 1989 he made a rare formal statement of his views at the Edinburgh Television Festival. In his lecture, he attacked the BBC as elitist and slow to adapt, and held up American broadcasting as the model for the future. He contended that the BBC typically produces dull programmes, is obsessed with class and the past, is wary of the commercial spirit and wealth, and allows itself to be brow-beaten by government.

John Birt, then Deputy Director-General of the BBC responded by claiming that the BBC had shown itself capable of achieving both quality and popularity. He cited Ben Elton's comedy and Tony Harrison's celebrated drama-documentary of the Salman Rushdie issue, *Blasphemers' Banquet*, as then current examples. He was perhaps implying that, though Murdoch's output usually achieved 'popularity' as measured by sales, its quality was open to criticism. By 1991, it had become arguable that, even popularity might not be achieved, as SKY and BSB merged, for financial reasons, into BSKYB.

The main criticism of the New Right's media populism (attempt to appeal to a wide popular audience), is that it threatens the quality of the media by seeking the lowest – and most profitable – common denominator among the public. This criticism has two main aspects to it: a concern with journalistic quality and a concern with the moral standards expressed in the media. A wide section of public and political opinion has expressed worry on both counts, including the churches and sections of the Conservative party, especially the more traditional.

Marxist and socialist perspectives

Marxists argue that the continued existence of capitalist society requires that ideas and values favourable to it are the dominant ones expressed through the media. Liberals largely agree with this, but whereas they believe capitalist ideology is dominant because it has 'won out' in 'the market place of ideas', Marxists believe that the dominance of capitalist ideology reflects capitalist control of the media.

In *The German Ideology*, Marx wrote that: 'The class which has the material means of production at its disposal has control at the same time over the production and distribution of the ideas of their age'. Marx contended that the owners of the media (mainly newspapers in his day) were able to control content. Where owners appointed managers he believed them not to be independent but answerable to the owners. Nor did Marx consider that the spread of share ownership significantly affected the control of major shareholders. Liberal pluralists contradict Marx's analysis. They argue that a 'managerial revolution' has taken place (Burnham, 1943), with the result that the operational control of major industrial (and state) organisations, including media companies, is in the hands of management. Managers are answerable not only to shareholders but to the public – as consumers of their product.

Contemporary Marxists, Murdock and Golding have attempted to refute the managerial argument. First, they argue that the processes of media concentration and conglomeration have increased the control of owners. In *Capitalism, Communication and Class Relations* (1977), they point out that in the early 1970s the top five firms in the following sectors of the media accounted for:

- 71 per cent daily newspaper circulation
- 74 per cent homes with commercial television
- 78 per cent admissions to cinemas
- 70 per cent paperback sales
- 76 per cent record sales

The information in Figure 17.6 on newspaper market share suggests perhaps slightly greater market concentration in 1994.

In their more recent work they observe that concentration of ownership is as pronounced in new media fields as in established ones. For instance Robert Maxwell had major holdings in electronic data service companies, was the sole owner of Britain's largest cable TV network, and had a twenty per cent share in a French broadcasting satellite company, TDF-1. As previously noted, Rupert Murdoch's interests in media fields, established and new, are very extensive. A further point to which Murdock and

UK media groups: market share

GROUP	DAILY PAPER	MARKET SHARE*	SUNDAY PAPER	MARKET SHARE*	TV CHANNELS & RADIO
News International (UK subsidiary of News Corporation)	Sun Times Today	35.6%	News of the World Sunday Times	38.2%	40% of BSkyB
Mirror Group	Mirror/Record 43% of Independent	23.8%	Sunday Mirror 43% of Indep. on Sunday People	31.1%	20% of Scottish TV Wire TV and Live TV (cable)
United Newspapers	Express Star	13.8%	Sunday Express	9.2%	
Daily Mail & Group Trust	Mail Evening Standard	14.8%	Mail on Sunday	12.2%	20% of West Country TV 100% Channel One (cable) Portfolio of radio stakes
Hollinger	59% of Telegraph	7.3%	59% of Sunday Telegraph	4.2%	
Guardian Media Group	Guardian	2.7%	Observer	3.1%	15% of GMTV
Pearson	Financial Times	2.0%			14% of BSkyB
Carlton					Central TV, Carlton TV 20% of GMTV, 36% of ITN 20% of Meridian TV
Granada					Granada TV, LWT 11% BSkyB, 36% of ITN 14% of Yorkshire-Tyne Tees TV 20% of GMTV

*Titles' share of total national circulations July-Dec 1994

(Source: ABC, James Capel in *The Financial Times*, 23.5.1995:17)

Figure 17.6 The UK media: concentration of ownership

Golding attach great importance to is the interconnections between major shareholders of different companies who may appear to be in competition but can actually collude in their mutual interest.

Murdock and Golding's second point is that even those media organisations which may be operated by relatively independent management are also constrained by the need to maximise profits. In the drive for profit they function in a typically capitalist fashion. Thus, newspaper and television seek profitability by running advertisements and in trying to increase audience size. The BBC, too, is forced to compete for audience ratings and, despite public services ideals, is drawn into the ethos of capitalism which typifies its commercial rivals. Here, Murdock and Golding are almost tautological: capitalist society produces a capitalist media which partly reproduces a capitalist society. In fairness, however, they also stress that the accessibility and variety of much of the new media technology provides the possibility of alternative, radical media:

> *The possibility of using video as a cheap and flexible campaigning tool and means of expression is already widely accepted. Alternative computer applications are less well developed but potentially even more far-reaching. The scope for radical software is enormous. The possibilities of radical databases are even greater. Picture a continuously updated information store that contained and developed the kinds of materials that Labour Research now publishes monthly. Databases can also help to develop contact networks. In the USA for example, the National Women's Mailing List keeps a file with the names and interests of over 60,000 feminists who have agreed to be listed, making it very much easier for individuals and groups to contact people with similar interests or useful expertise. The word-processing facilities of many micro-computers can also be used to develop collective writing, since text can be added to, deleted or moved without having to retype. Computer networks can also be a valuable campaign tool. In the spring of 1985, for example, there were large demonstrations on campuses across America to urge university authorities to pull their investments out of companies operating in South Africa. Computer messaging was used extensively to exchange information and co-ordinate protests ...*
>
> (Golding and Murdock, 1986:183)

The Glasgow University Media Group: 'Bad News'

Bad News, the first major publication of the Glasgow Media group, concentrated on industrial relations. The group's method involved detailed content analysis of news programmes, with interpretations informed by interactionist and Marxist theories. Interactionist approach is apparent in the close analysis of the way media content is selected and framed, and Marxism in the broad class-based framework of analysis adopted. However, the Glasgow group's contention of media bias basically rests on their quantitative analysis of relevant data, i.e. news reports.

The Glasgow group demonstrates its findings on the existence of hidden 'codes' or patterns of assumption tending to favour dominant groups in several ways. First, they point out in *Bad News* that in reporting industrial disputes, the media tended to rely on official management sources. Second, they find that the language used to describe disputes favoured employers and disfavoured employees. Thus, initiatives of the former tended to be termed 'offers' or 'pleas' whereas those of the latter were described as 'demands' or 'threats'. Third, the non-verbal context of reporting similarly tends to favour employers. For instance, employers were more likely to be interviewed in orderly, dignified surroundings than employees' representatives. Fourth, the Glasgow group finds examples where the editing (and re-editing) of reports of disputes focuses on the negative role of striking employees (e.g. on the economy) whilst management is less critically treated. They give us an example of how a speech by then Prime Minister Wilson, warning both management and unions of the possible consequences of a strike at the Cowley car production plant, was edited down over a series of news bulletins by BBC1 to read as a warning given specifically to the unions. ITN embraced this view from the outset but BBC2 did represent the speech as critical of both management and workers. Cumulatively, the Glasgow Media group considers that the findings referred to above support their case of hidden ideological bias in television news journalism which sees industrial action primarily in terms of it being disruptive both to the economy and to the public. Such negative assumptions structure the 'agenda' – questions asked – by journalists when reporting in this area. The Glasgow group argues that in making these assumptions, journalists tend to believe that they are reflecting the consensus of public concern about industrial conflict.

In a later publication, *War and Peace*, the Glasgow group argue that the news about the Falklands War was more severely censured than required by the demands of military security (see Figure 17.7). In analysing news coverage of the Women's Peace Camp at Greenham Common, they find a similar bias in favour of 'official' interpretations as apparently demonstrated by their earlier work.

There has been considerable criticism of the Glasgow group's conclusions, especially from within the media. Both BBC and ITN have asserted that there is a more objective basis to their news coverage in which they do try to present all relevant parties fairly rather than favour establishment groups such as government or employers. They have received academic support from Martin Harrison whose own analysis of the relevant broadcasts concludes that the Glasgow group itself may be characterised by a bias in selection which favours their own Marxist interpretation.

In their analysis of news production, the Glasgow group frequently refer to Stuart Hall, who reaches similar conclusions to themselves. They quote Hall as follows:

> *News values appear as a set of neutral, routine practices; but we need also to see formal news values as an ideological structure – to examine these rules as the formalisation and operationalisation of an ideology of news.*
>
> (Glasgow University Media Group, 1976:11)

Radical alternatives (a regulated market economy)

However, both Hall and the Glasgow group believe that such 'official' ideology can be challenged both through the 'main-stream' and 'alternative' media. Hall prefers to use the concept of ideological hegemony rather than dominance (see p. 485). Hegemony, in the context of culture, means a broad power and influence to structure the cultural 'agenda' – but not the power to

Table 17.1 Alternative perspectives of the media

	Liberal	Marxist critique	Communist	Radical democratic
Public sphere	Public space	Class domination	–	Public arena of contest
Political role of media	Check on government	Agency of class control	Further societal objectives	Representation/counterpoise
Media system	Free market	Capitalist	Public ownership	Controlled market
Journalistic norm	Disinterested	Subaltern	Didactic	Adversarial
Entertainment	Distraction/gratification	Opiate	Enlightenment	Society communing with itself
Reform	Self-regulation	Unreformable	Liberalisation	Public interventions

(Source: Curran, 1991:461)

Falklands War (1982)

Twenty-nine carefully selected British reporters were kept under strict Ministry of Defence control. Reporters, who had to agree to censorship, were told what was happening after the event.
Some reports had to pass through three stages of vetting before they could be released.

(Source: *The Guardian*)

Figure 17.7 State censorship in war

dictate people's beliefs and values. Alternative ideas can be effectively, if seldom easily, expressed through the media – 'the balance of cultural power' is always in flux. Indeed, Hall's own work, including his televised history of the Caribbean, is a case in point.

In a wide ranging comparative review of media regulation. James Curran argues that national governments have other options than simply 'rolling over' before the technological and commercial power of global media corporations. In his summary of perspectives on the media (Table 17.1) Curran includes a column on two radical approaches as well as the Marxist and Communist (state controlled). The less radical approach is based on the principle of a *regulated market economy* i.e. government intervention to ensure that the market works fairly. The less radical of the two approaches aims to achieve a representative media in terms of existing structures of power and is exemplified by the Swedish press. The more radical seeks to provide countervailing power by means of a regulated mixed economy of the media composed of market, public, and civil sectors (see Reading 2).

Anti-racist perspective

Anti-racist perspective is opposed to racism in the media. It is a structural perspective which links racism in the media and culture generally to racism in the main institutional areas of society including the economy. Of course, much cultural activity occurs within organisational structures which, like other institutional areas, tend to be dominated by white middle class males. However, it is ideological rather than institutional racism that this section mainly explores although in reality the two areas reinforce each other. It is useful to conceptualise anti-racism in terms of Gramsci's concept of hegemony (see pp. 485-6). Anti-racism can be thought of as a challenge to the cultural 'grip' (hegemony) of racism although in suggesting this, it is essential to bear in mind that anti-racists regard their attack on racist ideology as part of a wider challenge to institutional racism. The latter is the 'ultimate' target because it is institutions which in a practical way bring about ethnic inequalities of power and resources.

Anti-racists see racism in British culture as bound up with the history and development of the British empire and capitalism. From the late sixteenth century, British explorers regarded blacks as inferior and this supposed inferiority became part of the ideological legitimisation for conquering and enslaving them. Racist beliefs, then, legitimised commercial exploitation, including trade in human beings. James Walvin charts how black people have been caricatured in British culture as indolent, stupid, sexually immoral, and much else over several hundred years. It is important not to conceptualise such stereotypes merely in individual terms but to link the choice of stereotype with its usefulness to those making it. Walvin suggests that the nature of the stereotype varied according to the convenience of those making it at a given time:

> *Between the English settlement of the New World and the fumbling attempts to reconstruct the colonial government of the former slave societies, successive generations had to cope with the intricate problems of colonial economics and government. Central to all these problems was the person of the imported Black. To justify his importation, his slavery, his freedom and finally his position as a free man, Englishmen conjured up a variety of stereotype images of the Negro best suited to each particular purpose. Almost without exception these images, which made such an impression on the public at large, bore little resemblance to fact. Caricature rather than truth was the hallmark of the English impression of the Negro.*
>
> (in Husbands ed., 1982)

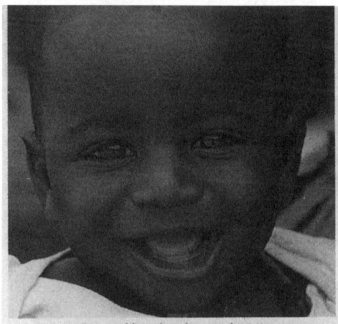

TB, measles, polio, whooping cough, tetanus or diphtheria could strike Musa down tomorrow.

Your £3 will immunise him for life.

Figure 17.8 A more positive image of a child in need?

Uncomplimentary stereotypes of blacks were purveyed by leading nineteenth century authors, for example Carlyle and Trollope, and continued to be widespread in literature during the twentieth century. Enid Blyton, the best-selling children's writer, created a character called Sambo who, in one story, is turned white (or 'pink') as a reward for doing a good deed: 'He was a nice looking doll now as good as any other … No wonder he's happy

little pink Sambo'. It is rarer today to find such absurd stereotypes in children's literature and many mainstream publishers now offer children's books which are broadly and positively multicultural. Even so, many children's books still appear to be written and illustrated in the belief that Britain is a wholly white society. Given the importance of childhood socialisation in attitude formation this remains a serious issue.

In contemporary Britain, perhaps the most extreme stereotypes occur in the popular press. Bhikhu Parekh reviewed one such case in *New Society* (7.11.1986). In 1986 the government had imposed visa requirements on visitors from five Commonwealth countries. A relatively small number of those to whom the new requirements were to apply decided to try to 'beat the deadline' Parekh takes up the story:

> *When around 2500 Asians arrived, the tabloid newspapers were awash with denigratory headlines. 'Asian flood swamps airport', screamed The Express. '3000 Asians flood Britain', shouted The Sun. 'Migrants flood in', echoed The Mail. The Sun, in a six-inch headline, called them 'liars'. Only The Independent and The Guardian agreed that the scenes at Heathrow were a 'disgrace' to Britain.*

Shortly after Parekh's article was published, The Sun weighed in with another headline: 'Cheating Asians Cost Us £5000 a Week' (27.11.1986).

It is, of course, not possible precisely to quantify the effect that such journalism has on readers. Current models of the media-audience relationship tend to be interactive rather than simple cause/effect. First, individuals select media material which interests them, and second, their attitudes are more likely to be reinforced than changed. Nevertheless, reinforcement of racism makes it more entrenched.

In addition, the media have a more general influence on society than reinforcing individual attitudes. Hartmann and Husbands (1974) suggest that the media 'provide people with a picture of the world' which may influence attitude development, particularly when people have no 'situationally based knowledge' (i.e. first-hand experience) of a given phenomenon. In a survey on the media and race, they found that respondents with little or no experience of blacks had broadly more negative impressions than those who had first-hand experience of them. They explained this in terms of the tendency of the media, especially the popular press, to present blacks negatively and in circumstances involving conflict.

Anti-racist perspective, like Marxist class perspective, contextualises the media in the wider society. Thus, racism in the media is seen as ideological reinforcement of structural racial inequalities. Many anti-racists are also Marxist and racism is seen by them as functional to capitalism (see earlier in this section). Thus, John Solomos (1989) argues that in the post-war period new stereotypes were found as needed which had the effect of 'keeping blacks in their place'. Broadly, he argues that initially much of the press (and some politicians) played on the popular fear of whites of being 'swamped' by blacks whereas since the 1970s blacks have more often been presented as the threat from within, and especially as the cause of 'social problems'. Racism can function to create inequality in subtle as well as the crudely obvious ways illustrated above. Thus, Adrian Hart in *Images of the Third World* (1989) points out how even well-meaning whites, such as those who run 'aid' organisations, often present blacks in a state of dependency on whites. Repeated portrayals of blacks as 'in need' and disempowered is arguably another form of negative stereotyping, however well intentioned. Yet, there is little difficulty in presenting positive images of black people (see Figure 17.8).

Feminist perspective: gender stereotyping

Research into representations of women in the media has shifted in emphasis from content analysis to semiotic interpretation (i.e. the 'decoding' of signs/images/language/style. In relation to gender and the media, content analysis simply counts or quantifies the number of a given sex portrayed in a particular category, such as domestic or 'boss'. It was the most widely adopted technique in the 1950s and 1960s. More recently, qualitative analysis in the form of semiotics (defined above) has become increasingly popular.

In 1978, Gaye Tuchman reviewed gender content analysis across a range of media in *Hearth and Home. Images of Women in the Media.* Her survey of the literature showed that women were portrayed in only two significant roles: the domestic and the sexual (including the romantic). In contrast, males appeared prominently in spheres of employment, family, politics and other areas of social life. Clearly, the media were presenting men as dominant and women as subordinate (and usually as accepting this situation submissively and passively). Tuchman describes this as a 'symbolic annihilation' of women. Strong though this phrase is, many feminists would feel that the 'symbolic annihilation' of women in the media reflects something akin to the real undermining of women in society.

Tuchman argues that the 'symbolic annihilation' of women in the media occurs through their absence, condemnation or trivialisation. They tend to be absent from positions of power, authority and status. They are condemned by such damning stereotypes as 'bitchy', 'catty', 'gossipy' and 'not interested in 'important' (i.e. male dominated things'. They are trivialised by being presented as mainly interested in romance or by appearing as sex objects or domestic workers. Whilst some media, including the main television channels, now seem less sexist in the way women are presented, in other areas, such as tabloid newspapers and 'teen' magazines, there appears to have been less change.

Angela McRobbie's *Teenage Girls: Jackie, and the Ideology of Adolescent Femininity* is an example of the more qualitative research mentioned earlier by Ross Gill. McRobbie finds that *Jackie*

is characterised by a recurrent 'code of romance' in which the ultimate object of a girl is a boy. Frame after frame reiterates this simple message:

> *Each frame represents a selection from the development of the plot, and is credited with an importance which those intervening moments are not. Thus the train, supermarket, and office have meaning, to the extent that they represent potential meeting-places where the girl could well bump into the prospective boyfriend, who lurks round every corner. It is this which determines their inclusion in the plot; the possibility that everyday life could be transformed into social life.*
>
> *Within these frames themselves the way the figures look, act, and pose contributes also to the ideology of romance …*
>
> *(Angela McRobbie, in Bernard Waites et al., 1983:272)*

According to McRobbie, there are two central features of the ideology of adolescent femininity as presented by *Jackie*. First, it sets up 'the personal' as of prime importance to the teenage girl. Secondly, *Jackie* 'presents 'romantic individualism', as the ethos … for the teenage girl'. So, individualism is not contextualised in terms of, say, the pursuit of career or academic excellence but in terms of 'romance' or 'falling in love'. 'In the end' (i.e. according to the 'code' or 'myth' or 'story'), romance overrides everything, including friendship with other girls (who may be both supporters and competitors in 'the search for romance').

What effect does reading material such as *Jackie* have on teenage girls? As McRobbie acknowledges, we do not know and research does not tell us. Perhaps, many girls 'read' it for relaxation or even to laugh at. On the other hand, perhaps the heroines of *Jackie* do offer a role model which is consciously or unconsciously imitated. In general, research at the Centre for Cultural Studies where McRobbie worked indicated a strong link between ideology and social structure. In this case, the romantic and individualistic ideology of adolescent femininity might socialise many girls for life – situations subordinate to males both domestically and in paid work and in society generally. In so far as females do tend to occupy such subordinate positions, there is a 'complementary fit' between ideology and structure.

In contemporary Britain, there are many attempts to counter traditional patterns of gender socialisation in the media by presenting females positively, with a capacity for independence, co-operation, and having varied and demanding goals and the ability to achieve them.

Interactionist perspective

Interactionist perspective on the media differs from liberal and Marxist in that it is less specifically political. The latter perspectives are based, in part, on theories of how society should be, whereas symbolic interactionism offers middle-range analysis of certain social psychological processes. Thus, 'labelling' and 'stereotyping' were originally interactionist concepts although they are now absorbed into sociology generally, particularly radical sociology.

Three specific applications of interactionist media analysis will be discussed here:

1 The production of media content by media professionals.
2 Audience interaction with the media.
3 The tendency of the media to reinforce consensus.

The first point – the production of media content – has largely been researched in relation to 'the news'. The news is first selected and then 'framed' within the context of assumptions about what is important (Hall, 1973) and within certain organisational routines and constraints. Howard Becker argues that news reporters tend to seek the opinions of those with power and status rather than those without them. He refers to this as 'the hierarchy of credibility'. Further, the powerful are able to use their knowledge of the routine of news production by, for instance, exploiting news deadlines in relation to press releases and speeches. So whilst the news media play 'gate-keeping' (decide what is or is not news) and 'agenda-setting' (decide the order of importance of news) roles in relation to the news, they do so under the influence of powerful people and institutions. It will be obvious that this analysis lends itself to Marxist interpretation and, in fact, Stuart Hall has argued that 'news values' reflect much more the interests of capital than of the working class.

It is in the area of audience interaction that interactionists have done some of their most imaginative work. Stan Cohen's *Folk Devils and Moral Panics: The Creation of the Mods and Rockers* remains a classic study of the relationship between the media and deviance. Cohen employs several concepts (as previously used by Howard Becker), which have become standard in media analysis. He argues that the media have the ability to 'amplify' certain forms of behaviour such as youth gang confrontations and soccer hooliganism. Amplification occurs in two forms: first, the media may make an event seem 'bigger' than it was; secondly, media coverage of an event may have 'the effect of triggering off events of a similar order'. Cohen refers to a 'spiral of amplification' by which the Mods' and Rockers' confrontations of the mid 1960s appeared to escalate as they fed off the media (see Figure 17.9).

Cohen's work can also be used to illustrate the consensus-reinforcing role the media can play. He gives a very useful ideal type model of how the process of deviancy selection, condemnation, and consensus-affirmation can occur. He titles the model, the Signification Spiral (that is, the labelling of deviance) and it is only slightly adapted here:

The signification spiral

1 Identification of specific issue: e.g. student political 'extremism'.
2 Identification of culprits: e.g. 'subversive minority', 'lunatic fringe'.
3 Convergence: Linking of issue to other problems: e.g. lack of discipline and control of the young.

4 Notion of thresholds: once they are crossed, further escalation must result – 'slippery slope to anarchy'.
5 Explaining, warning and prophesying: 'Look what happened elsewhere'.
6 Call for firm steps: clamping down hard leads to the effect of reinforcing consensus.

A key part in the process of consensus reinforcement is played by what Cohen refers to as 'moral entrepreneurs' or 'moral crusaders'. These people set themselves up as the conscience of society and orchestrate the 'moral panic' that is often the result of deviancy and/or deviancy amplification by the media. Mrs Mary Whitehouse of the National Viewers' and Listeners' Association is one of the best known of these.

In Britain, interactionist analysis of the media has frequently been integrated into broader structural analysis, particularly Marxist, which argues that inequalities present in the media reflect those in society. However, as Jock Young points out, people's social experience by no means always leads them to conform to the consensus and similarly there is scope in the media for the expression of divergent and alternative ideas and values.

Table 17.2 is largely based on a similar diagram by John Muncie (*Social Studies Review*, November 1987). Muncie suggest that the panics fall roughly into three phases: 'discrete' (1950s/early 1960s); more 'diffuse' (1964-70); and 'generalised' (1970s-early 1980s). In other words, the tendency to link specific examples ('outbreaks') with a supposed wider social 'crisis' has increased. Certainly, this fits in with the view that Thatcherism (Reaganism) was a response to a 'boundary crisis' in which the limits (boundary) of 'civilised' moral values were thought to be 'threatened' (see pp. 327-8).

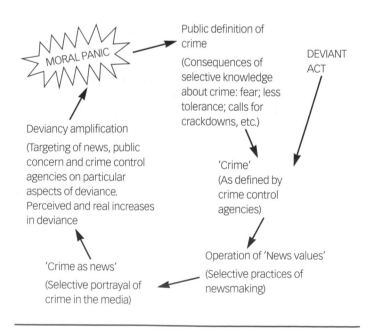

(Source: *Social Studies Review*, Nov. 1987)

Figure 17.9 Deviancy amplification and the role of the media

Who watches most?

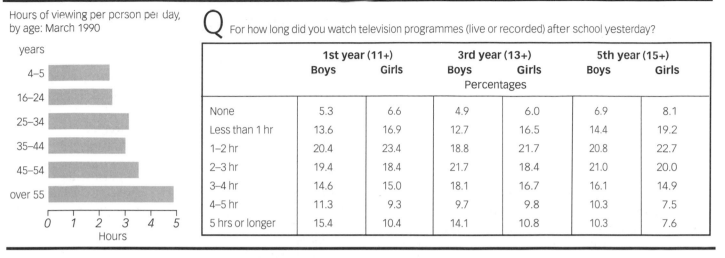

Hours of viewing per person per day, by age: March 1990

years

(Source: Barr)

Q For how long did you watch television programmes (live or recorded) after school yesterday?

| | 1st year (11+) | | 3rd year (13+) | | 5th year (15+) | |
| | Boys | Girls | Boys | Girls | Boys | Girls |
			Percentages			
None	5.3	6.6	4.9	6.0	6.9	8.1
Less than 1 hr	13.6	16.9	12.7	16.5	14.4	19.2
1–2 hr	20.4	23.4	18.8	21.7	20.8	22.7
2–3 hr	19.4	18.4	21.7	18.4	21.0	20.0
3–4 hr	14.6	15.0	18.1	16.7	16.1	14.9
4–5 hr	11.3	9.3	9.7	9.8	10.3	7.5
5 hrs or longer	15.4	10.4	14.1	10.8	10.3	7.6

(Source: Exeter University)

Figure 17.10 Some commentators express concern about the effects of television on the young, although older age groups watch more. However, a minority of the young watch almost to saturation point.

Table 17.2 Examples of moral panics

		Phases of media reaction
1950s	Teddy Boys	Discrete
Early 1960s	Mods and Rockers	
Late 1960s	Permissiveness – Drugs, Sexual 'freedom' Youth violence – skinheads, football hooliganism Radical trade unionism	Diffuse
1970s	'Muggings' (Racial overtones to 'the panic') Social Security 'Scroungers' Youth subcultures, e.g. Punks	Gener-alised
1980s	Feminist, e.g. Greenham Common protest Urban Disorder (again, with racial overtones), AIDS (Some scapegoating of homosexuals) Child abuse Drugs – especially 'crack'	

Effects research

To a greater or lesser extent, all the theories so far discussed are concerned with the effects of the media. However, liberal, Marxist and interactionist theory are all, to varying extents, interactive: they assume active involvement on the part of audiences in selecting and, generally, evaluating media content. The following theories have tended to present the audience as acted *upon* by the media.

1 The media and the masses

An early example of this type of approach – still occasionally adopted today – was mass society theory, sometimes referred to in its application to the media as 'hypodermic needle' theory, in which the masses are seen as 'doped' by the media. Mass society theory was most fully developed by the Frankfurt school. In general, it agreed that the development of industrial and urban society had deprived people of their individuality. People had been fragmented and atomised – living in the words of the song 'in little boxes' that 'all look just the same'. The role of the mass media – as seen by mass society theory – is to lull people into docile conformity. The theory is a neo-Marxist one in origin.

Katz and Lazarsfeld's *two-step flow* model was intended to present a more sophisticated model of the effects of the media on audiences. It suggested that *opinion leaders* or influential members of society form the response of audience members to media content. However, even in this model, the audience in general still appears passive. Further the research measured only short-term effects whereas it is the longer term effects of the media that are more significant (see 'cultural effects theory' below).

2 Survey work

Work by Dr William Belson 1980, and by psychologists H J Eysenck and D K Nias 1978 is far more empirical than mass society theory, but resembles the latter in its tendency to see the individual as the rather passive object upon whom the media 'produces effects'. Belson compared the behaviour and viewing habits of 1,565 London boys aged between thirteen and sixteen, between 1959 and 1971. Markedly less violence was admitted by those who watched less television. Of those who had watched a lot of violence on television, 7.5 per cent confessed to having engaged in serious violence themselves. Belson's findings clearly need to be taken seriously, but they are certainly open to criticism. It cannot be proved that watching more violence on television was the factor that 'caused' more violence. Other variables may have been operative. Watching a lot of television is itself associated with lower socio-economic status. Perhaps it is some other factor or factors associated with lower class culture that produces violent behaviour. It is almost impossible to separate the effect of television from other variables affecting behaviour.

3 Experimental work

Eysenck and Nias, in their own laboratory research into violence and the media, attempt to isolate the effect of violent films on behaviour from that of other factors. Groups – both adult and children – exposed to televised violence consistently behave more aggressively than control groups. If – and they do not show this – these effects were duplicated in real life then they would have proved their case. But before rushing to conclusions, some critical comments on Eysenck and Nias' work must be mentioned. As Anthony Smith points out, comparative cultural data complicates these findings. Japan, for example, has a very substantial degree of violence on its television, but a very low level of social violence. It seems that the Japanese emphasise the suffering caused by violence, rather than the aggression that caused it. This observation leads Smith on to a wider point. He suggests, in effect, that society gets the media it deserves. A violent society will tend to produce violence on the media – no doubt many will even want violence on the media. Though Smith does not say this, he seems to imply that what first needs reducing is real violence, then, perhaps, people will want less violent make-believe. This was not at all the conclusion of Eysenck and Nias, who asked for a degree of censorship of media violence and pornography. In so doing, they had the support of the National Viewers' and Listeners' Association, the 'brainchild' of Mrs Mary Whitehouse. Liberals and radicals alike tend to resist this. If entertainment, even art, can be censored today, who knows how far censorship may go tomorrow? The issue is important enough in itself but, for our more immediate academic purposes, it is worth noting how social scientific research can easily become a part of political and social policy debate. So much for the ivory tower!

4 Cultural effects theory

Cultural effects theory has, under different headings, been presented elsewhere in this chapter and its fundamental principle is much more important than the brevity of this section might suggest. The basic principle of this approach is that the important effects of the media on values, attitudes, beliefs and behaviour are long term. All the theories considered prior to this section would subscribe to this view although they differ in the way they consider audiences respond to media output. Thus, anti-racists, feminists and Marxists argue that the media present a picture of society which, on balance is exploitative of respectively, black people, women, and the working class. The Glasgow Media Group has attempted empirically to demonstrate that such cultural bias does occur in relation to, for instance, strike activity but also more generally (see pp. 510-13).

Audience response theories (micro level)

Since the mid 1980s, micro-level approaches to understanding how the audience relates to the media have developed. Far from presenting the audience as 'cultural dopes', this research stresses that its members can be actively involved with the media. Since there have been few observational studies of how people actually use the media in their own homes, sociologists lack information on everyday audience involvement. The new research seeks to provide this.

There are two areas relevant to audience response. First, there is media technology itself. Developments in media technology already described in this chapter show that people have access to far more media output than, say, 50 or even fifteen years ago – always provided they can pay for choice and always assuming that there is a genuinely different choice between most of the channels. If four channels are all showing old Hollywood 'movies' – is there one choice or four?

We should not assume that everybody has equal access to media technology. Every member of a wealthy family may possess his or her own television set or radio cassette CD unit but this is not likely to be the case in less wealthy families. If so, who controls the channel-switch or the remote-control when there is disagreement about what to watch or listen to? Some studies suggest that 'patriarchy rules' when 'the men' want sport on but this is surely not the case in every family (see the Activity on p. 517).

The second area relevant to audience response, is about what meanings members of the audience 'get out of' media programmes. We all know from discussions with others that people often 'see' or interpret the same programmes differently. Cilla Black's *Blind Date* is harmless fun to some but a tasteless trivialisation of personal emotions to others. Still others may just watch it because it happens to be what's on.

John Fiske (1992) has made a study of what the mainly female participants and audience 'get out of' some of the hundreds of game and quiz shows on United State's television. We will briefly summarise his comments on two of these here: *Perfect Match* and *The Price is Right*. *Perfect Match* is a sort of American version of *Blind Date*. Each show has two games. In one the woman chooses from three men and in the other, the roles are reversed. Fiske suggests that part of the popularity of the show among women is that they have equal power to chose as men. The show also assumes that women enjoy their sexuality as much as men do theirs. Women are not expected to feel guilty about their sexuality or 'wait for men to make the first move'. This kind of social equality may be taken for granted by many young women today but about 40 or 50 years ago, it certainly wasn't.

Fiske also looks at why some women find the American quiz show *The New Price is Right* appealing. The show consists of various games and competitions in which the winner is the one who best judges the price and value of given goods i.e. 'the best shopper'. Fiske suggests that the attraction of this game to the female participants and audience is partly that it recognises the everyday but often taken for granted knowledge and skill as consumers.

The newer approach to audience response gives recognition to the motives and intelligence of members of the audience. Unlike in some traditional Marxist media theory, the audience is not seen merely as a passive mass brainwashed by the forces of capitalist commercialism. Even so, Fiske himself does consider that the knowledge and skills shown by audience members usually operate only within a narrow range of understanding. There is nothing in the programmes which encourages critical consideration of the positive and negative points about capitalism or the 'cattle market' approach to romance. In fact, these matters are simply presented as part of the way things are. So, audience response theories can complement but do not replace larger theories about the capitalist media.

Activity

This activity is about who controls media access in your house.
1 Write down from recall (not very reliable) or observation (more reliable) who most often decides what is put on television (or other media) in your house.
2 What does your record suggest about who has power and control more generally in your house. Are you patriarchal, matriarchal, democratic or what?

Roger Silverstone: ethnography and audience response

Roger Silverstone has suggested a demanding research agenda which might fill in some of the details lacking about audience response. In his article *Television and Everyday Life: Towards an Anthropology of the Television Audience*, he argues that an ethnographic approach to family and household use of television is required: 'a laboratory for the naturalistic investigation of the consumption and production of meaning' (187). Like Fiske, however, he is emphatic that the empirical detail produced by such research will need to be interpreted in relation to the 'wider social and cultural environment.'

Silverstone suggests three key sets of issues that such an empirical programme of research raises. First, and most obviously, is the issue of *description* itself. Difficult though they may be in domestic context, 'observation and detailed and specific interviewing ... must ground any attempt to understand the embedded practices of the audience in the domestic setting'. Second, is the question of *dynamics* – the social dynamics within families which structure how the media are used, particularly who controls access where it is limited. Gender, age and class differences

are relevant in this context (see Figure 17.3). Another aspect of dynamics is what Silverstone refers to as 'techno-cultures' – differing attitudes and facility with media technology. This will vary between individuals and families and households. Third, is the issue of the *consequences* for individuals and families of the way they are involved with television. These are manifold and cover how individual and family viewing patterns influence family relations, and integration or separation from the local community and national society.

Other audience response oriented research: the displacement effect

There follows a discussion of a number of disparate pieces of research and analysis of television audiences which while they do not conform to Silverstone's rigorous methodological stipulations are broadly interpretist in nature and reflect the concerns so far raised in this section.

In *The Plug-in-Drug* (1984), Marie Winn reports on an interesting line in audience research which usefully indicates the considerable displacement of other activities that the media appears to have brought about. She refers to three experiments in which families voluntarily deprived themselves of television viewing for up to a month. They reported the following changes during this period:

More interaction between parents and children.
A more peaceful atmosphere in the home.
A greater feeling of closeness in the family.
More help by children in the household.
More outdoor play.

These findings suggest that the 'old chestnut' that television has changed (if not undermined) the quality of family and perhaps community life may not, after all, be far from the truth (see also pp. 569-70). A radical version of this analysis is presented by the cultural critic, Neil Postman in his controversial *The Disappearance of Childhood. How TV is Changing Children's Lives* (1985). According to Postman, what is causing childhood to 'disappear' is the promiscuously available and unfiltered nature of the television medium. Television 'messages' – news, views, sex, violence – do not differentiate among their audience but are equally available to all.

In their book *Uninvited Guests. The Intimate Secrets of Television and Radio*, Laurie Taylor and Bob Mullan found that for many watchers, TV serves as a kind of 'friend'. Taylor and Cohen do not go so far as to suggest that there is a trend towards television replacing 'real friends' but linked with the above research on the displacement effect of television, this might be a reasonable hypothesis to test. Given that the majority of households in Britain now contain only one or two residents, 'relationships' with the media are probably correspondingly more important. This aspect of contemporary life has been recognised in a growing body of research which analyses the viewing of 'soaps' and some other mass audience programmes such as game programmes as a form of participation in a 'make-believe community.'

However, the notion that television replaces human relationships in any straightforwardly quantitative or qualitative way is almost certainly far too simplistic. First, it is well documented that individuals often do other things while watching television, including talking to each other (sometimes, breaking physical isolation by using another modern electronic invention, the telephone). Second, what people watch on television provides a shared stock of experience and information which form the basis of many a conversation in daily life. Indeed, Cardiff and Scannell (1988) argue that British Broadcasting has linked together widely dispersed and otherwise different individuals and so fostered a sense of national communal identity. Interestingly, England's then coach, Terry Venables, claimed that England's successful run in the European championships of 1996 brought the nation together as a community. In suggesting that the media can foster community, Cardiff and Scannell include news, political and documentary as well as entertainment programmes. However, the proliferation of channels and increased audience segmentation may reduce this 'function' of the broadcasting media.

Questions

1 To what extent do you consider that the media presents a fair and balanced picture of society and fairly represents the interests of the main groups in society?
2 Does the media control people or do poeple control the media?

Postmodernism: Jean Baudrillard, consuming signs

Hyperreality and media

Baudrillard believes that we live in a media-dominated world. This 'world' is at one remove from reality. It is a world of *hyperreality*. It is hyperreal because the signs which constitute the messages or codes of the media are detached from whatever they may have originally referred to. Thus, Baudrillard contends that (what most believe to be) the 1991 Gulf War did not take place. By this, he can be taken to mean that what the media presented or 'hyped' as 'the Gulf War' was a code in itself – pro-Western, xenophobic, technocratic, visually and verbally selective – a media event. As John Lechte points out, those critics of Baudrillard who tried to 'prove' that the Gulf War was 'really' happening were missing Baudrillard's point (1994). They were talking the language of science mend modernity, he was talking in postmodern terms about media codes.

Baudrillard argued that Marx concentrated excessively on production at the expense of consumption. Baudrillard views consumption as not merely an economic and material activity but as a symbolic (meaningful) and status differentiating activity. Thus, gifts can symbolise friendship and consuming quality clothes can be a sign of high status. The media is drenched with sign-codes – not only advertisements but also news and popular drama programmes are replete with coded, often hidden messages (or *secondary* level meanings).

To give an example: coke advertisements at a conscious level are recommending a drink; at a secondary level they may be saying that the drink will bring acceptance, fun, romance or whatever; and at a more generalisable, third level, they reinforce the belief that such consumption is 'good'. The whole package is the 'real thing' (or is that Pepsi?). This is the world of hype that people live in and generally believe to be real. In fact, coke is mainly coloured and sweetened water and the 'values' associated with it are created largely by market researchers

The 'collapse' of 'reality' into hyperreality

In his earlier work, Baudrillard took the view that it is possible to resist media messages and make one's own interpretation of them. Subversion was seen as possible. Latterly, he has emphasised the *seductive* power of the media which for the great majority is overwhelming. The world of hyperreality becomes their real world. As a result, argues Baudrillard, it is pointless to criticise popular media consumption on the basis of artificial or manipulated versus real needs as the Frankfurt school do. Baudrillard's own example of hyperreality – Disneyland – superbly illustrates his view that 'reality' has collapsed into hyperreality:

> *Disneyland is there to conceal the fact that it is the 'real' country, all of 'real' America, which is Disneyland (just as prisons are there to conceal the fact that it is the social in its entirety, in all its banal omnipresence, which is carceral). Disneyland is presented as imaginary in order to make us believe that the rest is real, when in fact all of Los Angeles and the America surrounding it are no longer real, but of the order of the hyperreal and of simulation. It is no longer a question of a false representation of reality (ideology), but of concealing the fact that the real is no longer real, and thus of saving the reality principle*
>
> *(1981)*

Aspects of postmodernity

Other examples may help to illustrate what it is that Baudrillard means by hyperreality and the collapse of reality within it – his version of the postmodern condition. The film *Blade Runner* is set

Figure 17.11 Disneyworld, Florida: as 'real' as America – says Jean Baudrillard

in the kind of 'unreal', timeless city indicated in the above quotation. The leading 'female' character is a replicant, an artificial model of a human being, one of a number seeking to penetrate human society. Harrison Ford plays the male lead (a human) who's job it is to search out replicants. Somehow, replicants and humans get confused in the film. It is not just that – predictably – the two lead characters 'fall in love'. The background parade of blank human faces in the neon-lit jumble of the city suggests the question not so much of 'who's the replicant?' as 'what's the difference?' One replicant summarises the replicant and the human predicament rather well – 'Where did we come from, where are we going, how long have we got?' A world in which the real and the unreal rub shoulders together is – in Baudrillard's terms – the world we live in.

Andy Warhol is the artist who has most famously explored the boundary between art and reality and apparently found there isn't one. He paints perfect images of cans of Campbell's tomato soup and of the Mona Lisa, Marilyn Monroe and Elvis Presley. Which is the 'real' work of art? 'Thirty is better than one' is his helpful comment on the Mona Lisa reproductions.

The above examples illustrate some aspects of postmodernity as perceived by Baudrillard. First, is the importance of the image and style. It is often in the play between the stylish image and 'the reality' – replicant/human, Mona Lisa reproduction/Mona Lisa – that the characteristic irony and jokiness of postmodernism finds its play. Second, postmodernism celebrates or, at least embraces the technological. It is the smooth and clever world of high tech and instant information flows that postmodern heroines and heroes move in. Those who cannot cope or are excluded fall into a twilight zone of the underclass – vaguely and disturbingly present in the urban streets depicted in *Blade Runner*.

Thirdly, postmodernity and postmodernist art mixes or confuses time and space (see Chapter 16, Reading 2, pp. 499-500). The media and imaginative art are able to scan from one historical period to another, from one place to another – and to mix together historical periods and different places. This was first done consciously in architecture and art when the classical, modern (functional), and styles critical of the modern (e.g. surrealism) began to be presented *together* or in close proximity i.e. in a postmodern style. Figure 17.12 indicates how the traditional, modern and postmodern exist together in late or postmodern society.

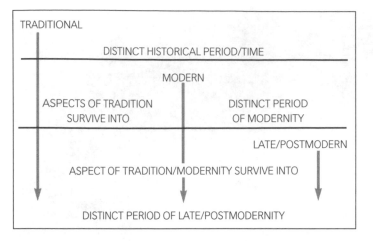

Figure 17.12 The mix of historical periods in late/postmodernity

The urban scenes in *Blade Runner* illustrate the mix of styles in the late modern city. The final struggle between Harrison Ford and replicant takes place on the roof of what looks like a particularly ornate American-Victorian building.

Finally, the collapse of reality into hyperreality, and the collapse of time and space into the fast moving present, have been accompanied – so the postmodern story goes – with a collapse of both traditional and modern values. Warhol seems to imply this by giving equal status to prints and originals and to prints derived from photographs of Marilyn Monroe with prints of Mona Lisa derived from Michelangelo's masterpiece.

Fighting back?

Given that Baudrillard argues that established critical values are redundant in relation to postmodernity, how does he envisage that 'the system' can be criticised or opposed. Again, he suggests that the system cannot be unbalanced by subjective value systems developed outside it. It can only be unbalanced from within. The unreality of the system's objects – Disneyland, the media Gulf War – generates extreme reactions of delight or horror which cannot be satisfied with the fantasy on offer. The paradox is that it is only by pursuing the objects of hyperreality that the limits of hyperreality can be tested. As John Lechte puts it:

> *Ecstasy, fascination, risk and vertigo before the object which seduces, takes precedence over the sober reflexivity of banal theory.*
>
> *(236)*

It may be impossible to explode hyperreality from outside but it may implode through failure to deliver on its own fantasies.

Criticism of Baudrillard

John Lechte makes the point that hyperreality may not be so all-embracing as Baudrillard believes. He suggests that the judgmental standards of the modern period – based on science and reason – are still significantly in place. Despite what Baudrillard contends, humanistic values can still be exercised effectively – perhaps. So, one might add, can more traditional, conservative values although those who uphold them may struggle to apply them in the turmoil of late modern technological and social change. It seems to be a radically disrupted and technologically mediated rather than a conservative and stable world.

Baudrillard, then, may be exaggerating the extent to which hyperreality is a closed-system. However, the lesson from Spielberg's fable of late modernity, *Jurassic Park*, seems to be that such exaggeration may not be that great. If we regard the hyperreal dinosaurs, which turned frighteningly real, as a symbol of the humanly created dangers of hyperreality – then the humans only just escaped and, even so, only some of them.

Technology, space and identity

Communications technology is opening up new forms and perhaps qualitatively different types of communication. Telephone, telegrams, fax, two-way radio, computer networks, video-conferencing and the internet have provided new opportunities for communication and, therefore, social intercourse. In short, they have created new social 'space'. They have done this by reducing the limitations previously placed on communication by physical space. Today it is possible – indeed, fairly easy, given the money – to conduct a global relationship in preference to a local one. A hundred years ago this would have been virtually impossible. Thus, it is now feasible to keep 'close contact' with someone 10,000 miles away and ignore someone who lives 10 yards away.

The new means of communication have, then, provided a basis for new patterns of sociability and, at the same time, have helped to erode more established patterns. Undoubtedly, the new media has changed both family and community/local life and patterns of global communication, exchange and sociability (see pp. 499-500 for a more empirically worked example of this). Part of the current interest in the sociology of identity is based on a realisation that the ever increasing means and variety of communication and the reduced significance of physical limitation on it, has the potential to affect human relations and the objects and images with which people identify. Just to give one example, there must now be millions of marriages and relationships facilitated by various forms of telephone datelines and, in some cases, video-dating. 1995 saw the first marriage spawned through the internet. So far, there is relatively little study of these relationships compared to those with more traditional origins. It may be that motives and behaviour of people involved in these relationships are significantly and interestingly different.

The media and levels of identity: some key points

Before discussing each of the above levels of social identity, it will help to make some general points that apply to them all:

1 *The various levels with which people identify interact with each other.* Thus, global products, such as Big Macs are globally advertised and marketed but can become part of local economies and culture. Conversely, local or individual phenomena, such as the Beatles or Tammy Wynette can become global without necessarily losing their local distinctiveness – which may be part of the global appeal.

2 *Relationships between the various levels can involve, sometimes acute, tension.* Thus, there is severe tension and sharp debate in Britain, especially England, on the relationship between national and European identity (a debate which is framed rather differently in Scotland).

3 *The identifications which people make at various levels e.g. 'human rights activist' (global), 'English patriot' (national), are 'imaginary' or imagined in the sense that they are constructred through media signs (including language), symbols and images.* Thus, it might be an Amnesty International advertisement that motivates a human rights activist or the televised feats of British sports people that stirs national feeling rather than any direct face-to-face experience. Even direct personal experience involves the interpretation of verbal and non-verbal sign systems and to that extent must be interpreted or imagined (for instance, is the person you see wearing a pair of shorts imprinted with the union-jack mocking or honouring Britian? And who decides this, you or s/he?

4 *Many commentators consider that capitalism is the prime force and influence underlying the globalisation of the media.* However, this view is not without its critics and is fully discussed below.

5 *Implicit in the previous point are the issues of power and purpose.* Are audiences puppets controlled by capital or is media power and control much more fluid as Foucault's approach might suggest?

The global level

In their book *Spaces of Identity* (1995), David Morley and Kevin Robins argue that a 'decisive shift' has occurred in the media from national bases of regulation purportedly in the national public interest to an increasingly globally deregulated system 'driven by economic and entrepreneurial imperatives' and aimed at consumer markets. Morley and Roberts then go on to discuss two perspectives on this crucial development: the free market liberal perspective – which they refer to scathingly as 'the mythology of global media' and the radical left perspective, often expressed in neo-Marxist terms, that the new world media system is fundamentally capitalist and is operated and controlled by transnational corporations. (see Reading 1)

Morley and Robins provide several quotations from a speech by Steven Ross, the former head of Time Warner, the world's largest media corporation, which illustrate in rather idealised terms the free market liberal perspective on the global media. The following snippets are examples of pure capitalist ideology and require no comment:

> *Time Warner stands for 'complete freedom of information' and the 'free flow of ideas, products and technologies in the spirit of fair competition'.*
>
> *The new reality of international media is driven more by market opportunity than by national identity.*
>
> *We are 'on the path to a truly free and open competition that will be dictated by consumers' tastes and desires'.*
>
> *With new technologies, we can bring services and ideas that will help draw even the most remote areas of the world into the international media community.*
>
> *Ross sees modern media inventions as 'tools of democratic revolution'.*
>
> *(1995:11-12)*

Although these are the remarks of a rich and powerful businessman, they make the link between the free market, freedom of expression and communication and democracy also put forward by perhaps more dispassionate liberal political scientists.

Radical, particularly Marxist, theorists, have never accepted these liberal arguments at face value. Rather, they regard such views as ideology which obscures a far less harmonious situation than that described by Ross. What Wallerstein describes as the world capitalist system is represented in the area of media/communications by what Herbert Schiller terms 'transnational corporate cultural domination'. Schiller argues that 'private giant economic enterprises pursue – sometimes competitively, sometimes co-operatively – historical capitalist objectives of profit making and capital accumulation, in continuously changing market and capitalist conditions' (quoted Morley and Robins:13). The 'transnational' corporations are seen as producing culture for consumption as 'commodities' with profit rather than quality in mind.

Radical and Marxist commentators on the media argue that there is too much inequality of power and resources to enable the kind of freedom that Steven Ross associates with media globalisation to develop. A comparatively small number of global players compete to supply global markets which are still largely *mass* markets rather than personalised and individualised (though the latter is a stated aim and may occur – see below).

Theodore Levitt argues that: 'The global corporation, looks to the nations of the world not for how they are different but for how they are alike ... it seeks constantly in every way to standardise everything into a common global mode' (quoted Morley and Robins:15). Thus, the criticism is often levelled at Rupert Murdoch's 'News Corporation' that it repeatedly shows old Hollywood films (available because it bought Twentieth Century Fox) throughout its global media empire with little consideration for how such programming might integrate with local cultures. Critics see this as offering very limited 'freedom' and choice, particularly when other media corporations are pressured to show a similar 'range' of programmes by the need to retain or build audiences.

Radical critics associate what they see as lack of significant choice in the current stage of media globalisation with lack of quality. Thus, Richard Hoggart suggests that those who market culture for profit 'can't help' but 'seek the lowest common denominator' because, for the moment, it is with mass markets/audiences that mega-profits still lie (Radio 4, 20.10.1995). Hoggart, a leading cultural critic over 40 years, believes 'things are getting worse'. However, Hoggart's judgement is ultimately a matter of opinion as all judgements are. What differentiates Hoggart from some other critics is his willingness to make judgements and to try to persuade others that he is right. A policy consequence of Hoggart's critical analysis is that there should be more public sector involvement in monitoring and maintaining the quality of the media. The data given in Figure 17.4 *may* be taken to support the case for such an approach in that it shows that in areas of established public concern, new satellite television does 'worse' than terrestrial television (see p. 505)

The global media is American

Critics of commercial media, particularly in its global form, are not merely concerned with its capitalist character – although this does tend to be the fundamental focus of concern. It is also overwhelmingly the case that the globalised media is American in ownership and programme content. In practical terms, therefore, it is the American, capitalist media that attracts most criticism.

American capitalism is uniquely dominant in the area of cultural production and distribution. The United States has been effectively challenged in many other areas from the automobile industry to computer hardware but it retains its ascendancy in the control of the production and distribution of media culture for global audiences (of course, what audiences make of the programmes when they receive them may be another matter – see below). Jeremy Tunstall noted that *The Media are American* in his book of that title in 1977 and since then dominance has extended beyond film and television to telecommunications. The books ('novelised' film scripts), T-shirts and general hype that often accompany a cinema or television film export adds to the cultural flow. 'World news' – a key opinion-forming area – is largely supplied by a very small number of Anglo-American press and news agencies.

In addition to exports, the franchising or copying of American TV formats is another major source of the Americanisation of global culture. This is particularly true of programmes with a strong personal interest flavour such as *The Oprah Winfrey Show* and *Blind Date*. The proliferation of programmes purporting to help in solving emotional and relationship problems is particularly controversial. Do they intelligently involve or manipulate audiences? Are problems solved or worsened? How do we assess the cultural quality and consequences of such programmes and, indeed, does it matter? Such programmes are often immensely profitable – isn't that their 'true' purpose?

Comment on criticisms of the global media

While the unease of radical critics about the Americanisation of global culture runs deep, it needs to be qualified and put in context. First – as we shall explore later – audiences are not made up of 'cultural dopes'. In fact, audiences differ, some exercising great discrimination in their viewing habits. Current evidence indicates that people with satellite television are watching rather less television than previously – perhaps because they are targeting programmes for viewing more precisely (Cited, *Evening Standard*, 18.10.1995). Second, as Morley and Robins point out, given the choice between nationally produced and American programmes of comparable quality, home audiences overwhelmingly prefer 'their own' cultural product. National preference is alive and vital in the area of media choice as otherwise (see p. 524). Third, while it remains true that the big American media corporations tend to seek out global mass rather than niche markets, the continuing development of technology and diminishing cost factors should slowly change this situation.

A fourth problem for critics of an American market-led media is that in many cases their own faith in the alternative – a public sector led broadcasting media is diminished. This is partly because they share a general disillusionment with big government – particularly in the role of big brother or guardian of cultural and moral standards – and partly because private capital and initiative is so dominant in global media development that the only realistic option appears to be to come to terms with it. However, radical critics do suggest various ways in which public sector involvement could increase (see for instance pp. 510-11).

The European bloc level

Europe impinges upon Britain as an economic and political entity more than as a cultural one. The British or, at least, the English generally seem to place their national identity well ahead of their European identity in order of importance. The main exceptions are probably centre left intellectuals who see a European cultural identity as an antidote to narrow-minded nationalism. Whether or not further European integration will weaken the predominance of national culture or cultures in the British Isles is a key question.

European culture has deep roots going back to early Christianity and classical civilisation. The latter has left a common imprint on most European languages. Shared tradition and geographical proximity do generate a sense of European identity but more at the level of background than in any immediate and urgent way. On a day-to-day basis, members of the European nations are probably more aware of what differentiates them than what unites them. 'Being European' comes into play as a basis of identity and potential collective action mainly in relation to still more remote others – who at different times have been 'infidels', Soviets and, more recently 'illegal immigrants'.

Where does the media fit into this somewhat disjointed scenario? The European Community has with varying emphasis pursued a policy of cultural 'unity in diversity'. The constituent nations have been too protective of what they see as their national cultures to allow for any centrally imposed European cultural homogenisation either through the media or otherwise. However, the Commission of the European Communities maintains that:

> *Television will play an important part in developing and nurturing awareness of the rich variety of Europe's common cultural and historical heritage.*
>
> *(quoted Morley and Robins:77)*

This statement was made in 1984, since when, despite a slight rise in Euro-awareness, television has remained basically national and American in content. In particular, British television remains strongly Anglo-American in content and cultural orientation. Currently, it seems unlikely that this will be remotely challenged, let alone replaced by either a 'gung ho' European 'nationalism' or by a more subtle and deeply rooted trans-European cultural influence. The latter seems scarcely even to be on the public agenda.

The national level

Much of the rest of this chapter focuses on the 'British' media – in so far as it can be separately considered from wider developments. Here it will help simply to indicate the various tensions and forces which are reshaping the media in Britain at the national level:

1 The relative decline of British public broadcasting

The audience share of BBC radio and television has been in long-term decline. This began with the onset of commercial television in 1955 and accelerated with the recent deregulation of broadcasting. One of the most important consequences of this shift has been the sharp decline in the power of the British establishment or elite – as represented by the Director General and Board of Governors – to mould public taste and morality (see pp. 507-8). It is a serious question whether or not the levels of taste and morality manifested in the contemporary largely commercial media are poorer than when the BBC dominated national broadcasting. What is indisputable is the relative decline of the BBC, as a focus and source of national identity.

2 The commercial/consumer culture of the British media

The commercial media has always raised revenue by selling consumer products and, with the rise of satellite, cable and pay-TV, by charging for viewing as well. Essentially, this means that the cultural content of the commercial media is treated as a commodity i.e. commodified (which does not mean that some content is not of high quality).

Together the loosening of public control and the commercialisation of the media has resulted in a much less respectful attitude to the country's elite and to royalty and a willingness to publish any kind of 'news' that sells providing that it is not likely to be expensively libellous. Along with royalty, the private lives of politicians, have been a particular focus of the media, especially the press. This trend applies somewhat less to the broadsheets than to the tabloids. However, Rupert Murdoch's *Sunday Times* has pursued 'royal' stories – with as much vigour as his mass market publications. The so-called 'rat-pack' of scandal mongers was not solely made up of tabloid journalists.

The contemporary commercial media has, then, contributed significantly to changing the cultural climate of Britain. British culture is more commercialised and consumption oriented partly as a result of the media – which is a major vehicle for selling commodities, including itself. British culture is also less deferential to the nevertheless still powerful establishment, including royalty. This development may well have been unintentional on the part of most owners, editors and journalists but, in fairness, Rupert Murdoch, and a some-time editor of his, Andrew Neill, probably did intend to open up what they regard as a rather hide-bound and unenterprising British establishment.

Notwithstanding its undermining of royalty and the national elite, much of the tabloid press, particularly the majority right-wing section, tended to be anti-European and often stridently nationalistic in the 1980s and 1990s. The tone was of a nation insecure and even threatened in its identity, not of the self-conscious, if often equally crude, superiority of the imperial epoch.

The local/regional level

Although national radio stations command relatively higher listening figures, the success of many local radio stations indicates a continuing demand for local/regional flavour material. Local news and some feature programmes are also routine in the regions of the national television channels.

However, the interest in these programmes is steady and not particularly resurgent. Viewing figures indicate it is generally the high cost, professionally produced, nationally networked programmes that achieve the highest audience ratings.

The development of cable television may stimulate somewhat further the demand for local/regionalised television content. However, the real competition and tension in the media is not between the local and the national but between the various national and international distributors of programmes who because of the proliferation of channels can provide for a growing number of niche interests as well as shared, large-audience interests.

Individual level

There never has been agreement among media theorists about the position of the individual in relation to the media. For years, mass society and liberal theorists put forward more or less contradictory views. More recently, audience response theory offers a model of the audience member as active and discriminating but open to influence from other audience members and from the media itself. The arguments continue as the media goes increasingly global and yet can be accessed and used in more individual ways. If the mass society theorists saw the individual audience member as a cultural dope, Baudrillard sees the individual now as entirely detached from reality. Others see great potential for entertainment, information access and communication in the still rapidly developing media. Among these is John Birt, Director General of the BBC perhaps more often noted for the opprobrium his managerial policies attract from creative media people:

> *Last September, the BBC launched digital audio. Digital satellite is already a reality in the United States. In Britain, it is pencilled in for 1998. But this is only the start. In the digital age, broadcasting itself can break out of its cage, as the distinctions between two-way telephone talk, one-way television reception and the brain power in your personal computer begin to break down. All three kinds of kit will be able to think and chew gum at the same time.*
>
> *So via your 'tel-com' of the future, you will be able to tune to a rock station in San Francisco, download research form Harvard, have a video-chat with your sister in Sydney, clinch a contract in Tokyo, e-mail an eco-group in Frankfurt or shop till your keyboard drops. You will be able to call up BBC news on demand – See-fax in place of Ceefax – access the BBC's Shakespeare library, vote with the studio audience or change the plot of the latest soap.*
>
> *(John Birt, 'Broadcasting Breaks Out of its Cage', The Observer, 5.5.1996:16)*

Questions

1 What role does the contemporary media play in creating people's sense of identity and reality?
2 To what extent and in what ways is the media 'global'?

Summary

1 Media ownership in Britain is characterised by concentration and conglomeration. Concentration refers to the merger of media businesses so that control becomes concentrated in fewer hands. Conglomerates form when one company takes over another (or others) either in the same or in a different line of business.

2 The expansion of satellite and cable TV has underlined a number of key issues. The commercialisation of the media affects public as well as privately financed media, the issue of quality and standards has also come to the fore.

3 There are a number of perspectives on the influence and effects of the media, including three types of liberal perspective:
- Liberal pluralism considers that many influences and opinions are expressed through and exerted upon the media. The media are perceived as democratic.
- Liberal paternalism modifies a commitment to a democratic media with a concern that the media is required to maintain high cultural standards.
- Free market liberalism wants a wholly private media responsive to competition and to consumer demand.

4 Marxist and socialist perspectives argue that private control of the media threatens media freedom. To a greater or lesser extent, the media is seen as reproducing and reinforcing capitalist ideology.

5 Feminist perspective is opposed to representations of women in the media which continually reinforce negative stereotypes, e.g. women as decorative or compliant. Positively, feminists want women to be presented in the media as creative, assertive and as the equals of men.

6 Anti-racist perspective is opposed to representations of black people in the media which continually reinforce negative stereotypes, e.g. as subordinate to white people or as 'clowns' or 'entertainers'. Positively, anti-racists want black people to be presented in the media as capable of exercising power and authority.

7 Interactionism is mainly a middle-range perspective which explores the two-way flow of influence between the media and audiences (who can sometimes almost 'take over' the media).

8 Effects research reflects the positivist model that the influence of the media on behaviour can be isolated and measured. Effects research particularly concentrated on the effects of media images of sex and violence.

9 In contrast, audience response theories emphasise the active involvement of audience members – but within a framework of social influences.

10 Baudrillard argues that reality is now defined by the media. His analysis provides an interesting if extreme version of postmodernism.

11 This analysis of the global influence of the media and responses to it, links up with the earlier sections on media structure, control and technology.

Research and coursework

The media is the graveyard of many a well-intentioned student project or assignment. This is because many media projects attempt to establish what the effects of the media are on behaviour. It is very difficult to establish such effects in any circumstances and particularly so given the limitations of student research. Rather than make generalised research suggestions here, it may be better briefly to explore a particular research technique – content analysis. Content analysis can be either purely quantitative or, better, involve both a quantitative and qualitative aspect. Ros Gill suggests five stages in the content analysis of a daily paper but these could apply to other publications, including 'teen' magazines. (It needs to be stressed, however, that content analysis in itself is simply a research technique and would only be part of an adequately theorised piece of work.)

Using sexism as an example, Gill's five stages are:

1 Having *familiarised* yourself with the newspaper, count how many articles feature a woman or women as the main subject. (You may wish to do a comparison with the number featuring men.)

2 *Measure* up how many column inches the articles on women take up as a proportion of the total paper.

3 Decide how to *categorise* or label the articles according to type, e.g. about sportswomen, businesswomen, etc.

4 Analyse more thoroughly two or three articles about women. If you wish to maintain the *quantitative* nature of your research, you could count the number of words or references to, for instance, a woman's physical appearance or to her domestic or family role.

5 Stage four takes the research perhaps as far as it can go in a quantitative direction. From there you could move into a more *qualitative interpretation* of the words, images and any other 'code carriers' in your material. You may or may not find themes of female subordination (romantic? sexual?) and male dominance. If you do find positive images of females, it may be worth analysing in what context these occur. Do they still appear positive, even after you have examined their context?

Further reading

Most of the familiar introductory volumes to media sociology were published well before 1990 and do not cover recent major developments. D Morley and K Robins, *Spaces of Identity: Global Media, Electronic Landscapes and Cultural Boundaries* (Routledge, 1995) is H.E. level but excellent. Simon Cottle's *Behind the Headlines: The Sociology of News* in the third edition of my *New Introductory Reader in Sociology* (Nelson, 1993) is very useful.

Reading 1
From national to global media

From D Morley and K Robins, *Spaces of Identity* (Routledge, 1995), pp.10-11

'For business purposes … the boundaries that separate one nation from another are no more real than the equator. They are merely convenient demarcations of ethnic, linguistic and cultural entities. They do not define business requirements or consumer trends.'

(IBM, 1990)

Until very recently, what has prevailed in Britain, as elsewhere in Europe, has been the system of public service broadcasting, involving the provision of mixed programming – with strict controls on the amount of foreign material shown – on national channels available to all. The principle that governed the regulation of broadcasting was that of 'public interest'. Broadcasting should contribute to the public and political life of the nation; in the words of the BBC's first Director General, John Reith, it should serve as 'the integrator of democracy' (quoted in Cardiff and Scannell, 1987:159). Broadcasting should also help to construct a sense of national unity. In the earliest days of the BBC, the medium of radio was consciously employed 'to forge a link between the dispersed and disparate listeners and the symbolic heartland of national life' (ibid.:157). In the post-war years, it was television that became the central mechanism for constructing this collective life and culture of the nation. In succession, radio and television have 'brought into being a culture in common to whole populations and a shared public life of a quite new kind' (Scannell, 1989:138). Historically, then, broadcasting has assumed a dual role, serving as the political public sphere of the nation state, and as the focus for national cultural identification. (Even in the very different context of the United States, where commercial broadcasting was the norm from the beginning, national concerns were paramount; the 'national networks' of CBS, NBC and ABC served as the focus for national life, interests and activities.) We can say that, on either side of the Atlantic, broadcasting has been one of the key institutions through which listeners and viewers have come to imagine themselves as members of the national community.

Now, however, things are changing, and changing decisively. During the 1980s, as a consequence of the complex interplay of regulatory, economic and technological change, dramatic upheavals took place in the media industries, laying the basis for what must be seen as a new media order. What was most significant was the decisive shift in regulatory principles: from regulation in the public interest to a new regulatory regime – sometimes erroneously described as 'deregulation' – driven by economic and entrepreneurial imperatives. Within this changed context, viewers are no longer addressed in political terms, that is as the citizens of a national community, but rather as economic entities, as parts of a consumer market (Robins and Webster, 1990). The political and social concerns of the public service era – with democracy and public life, with national culture and identity – have come to be regarded as factors inhibiting the development of new media markets. In the new media order, the overriding objective is to dismantle such 'barriers to trade'. No longer constrained by, or responsible to, a public philosophy, media corporations and businesses are now simply required to respond to consumer demand and to maximise consumer choice.

Driven now by the logic of profit and competition, the overriding objective of the new media corporations is to get their product to the largest number of consumers. There is, then an expansionist tendency at work, pushing ceaselessly towards the construction of enlarged audiovisual spaces and markets. The imperative is to break down the old boundaries and frontiers of national communities, which now present themselves as arbitrary and irrational obstacles to this reorganisation of business strategies. Audiovisual geographies are thus becoming detached from the symbolic spaces of national culture, and realigned on the basis of the more 'universal' principles of international consumer culture. The free and unimpeded circulation of programmes – television without frontiers – is the great ideal in the new order. It is an ideal whose logic is driving ultimately towards the creation of global programming and global markets and already we are seeing the rise to power of global corporations intent on turning ideal into reality. The new media order is set to become a global order.

Questions

1 What are the main changes in control in the shift from 'national to global media'?
2 What might be the main consequences of these changes for the 'citizen-consumer'?

Reading 2
Radical approaches to media organisation

James Curran, 'Rethinking the media as public sphere', in P Dahlgren and C Sparks eds., *Communication and Citizenship* (Routledge, 1991), pp. 49-52

Problems with the liberal approach

In short, the free-market approach has three central flaws. It excludes broad social interests from participating in the control of the main media. It leads to concentration of media ownership. And it promotes cultural uniformity, particularly in TV output. These shortcomings should be viewed in terms of what a democratic society should require of its media. At the very least, an adequate media system should enable the full range of political and economic interests to be represented in the public domain, and find expression in popular fiction. A market-based media system, in modern conditions, is incapable of delivering this.

The advantage of the collectivist approach is that it can enable interests with limited financial resource – which are excluded in a market-driven system – to have a share in the control of the media. It can also prevent control of the media from falling into the hands of an unrepresentative, capitalist elite. And through collective arrangements, it can also ensure that media output is pluralistic and diverse.

Problems with the collectivist approach

But the potential promise of collective provision has often been contradicted by its actual practice. This is partly because collective provision through the state can result in state control, as is illustrated notoriously by the stalinist experience. A multi-tiered system of control was evolved in the Soviet Union – based on formal legal censorship, control over the material production and distribution of communications, control over senior appointments, indoctrination in journalism schools and, more indirectly, control over the flow of information – which turned the media into an instrument of the state and the Communist party.

The collectivist approach proved more successful in European countries with a tradition of liberal democracy. Even so, a number of problems recurred. State pressure was sometimes brought to bear on broadcasters, through control over appointments, public funding and the allocation of franchises. Even when the direct abuse of state power was minimised, effective control over broadcasting was exercised, to a lesser or greater extent, by a professional elite integrated into the hierarchy of power. Their domination was legitimised in some countries by a paternalistic definition of public-service broadcasting which emphasised the leadership role of cultural bureaucrats in educating and informing the masses. This led to insensitivity and lack of responsiveness to the diversity of public taste, particularly in situations where there was no effective competition.

Radical approaches

1   A radical approach is the *regulated market economy*, represented by the Swedish press system. The thinking behind this is that the market should be reformed so that it functions in practice in the way it is supposed to in theory. Its most important feature is that it lowers barriers to market entry. The Press Subsidies Board provides cheap loans to under-resourced groups enabling them to launch new papers if they come up with a viable project. The Board has acted as a midwife to seventeen new newspapers between 1976 and 1984, most of which have survived. The second important feature of the system is that it tries to reconstitute the competitive market as a level playing field in which all participants have an equal prospect of success. Since market leaders have the dual advantage of greater economies of scale and, usually, a disproportionately large share of advertising, low-circulation papers receive compensation in the form of selective aid. The

introduction of this subsidy scheme has reversed the trend towards local press monopoly.

A number of safeguards are built into the system in order to prevent political favouritism in the allocation of grants. The Press Subsidies Board is composed of representatives from all the political parties. The bulk of its subsidies – over 70 per cent in 1986 – is allocated to low-circulation papers, with less than 50 per cent penetration of households in their area, according to automatically functioning criteria fixed in relation to circulation and volume of newsprint, irrespective of editorial policy. Beneficiaries from the subsidy scheme include publications from the Marxist left to the radical right: the paper which has the largest subsidy is the independent Conservative *Svenska Dagbladet*, which has been a consistent critic of successive Social Democratic governments. The subsidy scheme is funded by a tax on media advertising.

The twin precepts on which the Swedish press system is based – the facilitation of market entry and the equalisation of competitive relationships – could be extended to broadcasting, even though spectrum scarcity prevents the creation of a full broadcasting market. Indeed, this is already in the wind. In 1989 the European Commission issued a directive calling for member countries to introduce a system whereby broadcasting organisations are required to commission a proportion of programmes from independent companies. Although the directive set no date, this policy has already been adopted in some countries. Market entry could be further facilitated, it has been argued, by establishing the broadcasting equivalent of the Swedish Press Subsidies Board, which would assist the funding of under-resourced groups, with viable projects, to compete in the radio or sectors.

A policy of market equalisation is also being considered in a European context. The ability of national agencies to shape the ecology of broadcast systems so that they are a democratic expression of the societies they serve is threatened, it is maintained, by economies of scale in the global TV market. US programmes are sold for foreign transmission at a fraction of their original cost, and at a price that is much lower than the cost of making original programmes in Europe. The threat posed by cheap US syndication to national broadcast systems has been blocked hitherto by official and unofficial quotas limiting the import of American programmes. But this protectionism is being breached by the emergence of satellite TV enterprises which transmit quota-breaking US programmes across national borders. This has prompted the call for satellite TV to be brought within the ambit of a regulated market economy through the auspices of the Council of Europe and European Commission. So far, both bodies have proposed an undefined limitation on non-European imported programmes to be policed by national agencies at the point of up-link to satellite TV delivery systems. This lack of definition ensures, however, that it will have no practical effect.

2 A further radical approach arises from the current debate in Poland about how broadcasting should be reorganised, with similar discussions occurring elsewhere within social democratic parties. It takes the form of a proposal for a regulated mixed economy, composed of public, civic and market sectors. One version of this proposal entails having a major, publicly owned sector committed to public-service goals, including the provision of mixed, quality programmes and politically balanced reporting. The market sector would be subject to minimum controls, and would be established through the sale of franchises to commercial companies which would also pay an annual spectrum fee. This would help fund, in turn, a civic sector whose role would be to extend the ideological range and cultural diversity of the system. The civic sector would have assigned frequencies and an Enterprise Board which would help fund new and innovatory forms of ownership and control, including employee ownership, subscribers with voting rights, consumer co-ops and stations linked to organised groups. The Enterprise Board would function not as a traditional regulatory body, policing programme content, but as an enabling agency assisting financially the emergence of new voices in the broadcasting system.

Questions

1 Discuss and illustrate the disadvantages of the free-market and collectivist (government/public) approaches to media regulation (as suggested in the Reading).
2 How far do you consider the two radical approaches effectively deal with the problems discussed in question 1?

18 Religion, Tradition and Modernity

A sign of religious decline? Or has religion gone somewhere else? Churches converted to secular uses

Aims of this chapter

1 To analyse the classic sociological writings on the sociology of religion and relate them to the context in which they emerged.

2 To gain a critical knowledge of arguments for and against secularisation.

3 To appreciate and understand the differences between liberal ideology and Islam.

4 To locate contemporary religion within the context of modernity/postmodernity.

Introduction: the social relevance of religion

Sociologists cannot decide between the competing claims of religions nor should they try to do so. Religious belief is based on the view that there is a spiritual reality in addition to material reality. Sociologists have no access to 'divinely revealed truth' but must seek to reveal their own 'truth'. This is concerned with the relationships between social phenomena, including the meanings people have and the consequences of these meanings for themselves and others.

Religious and other beliefs have social consequences and it is these that sociology studies. The following are the kind of questions addressed by sociologists of religion. Is it true that Protestants are more likely to commit suicide than Catholics and, if so, why? Why are a disproportionate number of young people attracted to religious sects and cults? What is the effect on a person's way of life of being an 'untouchable'? Is there something in the belief-systems of Muslims and Western liberals which means that tension and conflict between them is likely or even inevitable?

This last question brings into focus the possibility of a clash between tradition and modernity in the contemporary world. To some extent this issue is challenging the 'secularisation hypothesis' as the central concern of the sociology of religion (see pp. 539-42).

The social effects of religion: the classic theorists

Religion and social solidarity: Emile Durkheim

Durkheim argues that religion functions to reinforce the collective unity or social solidarity of a group:

> There can be no society which does not feel the need of upholding and reaffirming at regular intervals the collective sentiment and the collective ideals which make its unity and its personality.
>
> (Durkheim extracted in Bocock and Thompson, 1985:54)

One way in which a society can express its shared identity and unity is through religious worship and ritual.

Durkheim stated that traditionally people divide phenomena into the sacred and the profane or the religious and the secular. The category of the sacred is concerned with those matters and forces which seem beyond everyday experience and explanation. Durkheim compares religious sentiment to the feelings of awe which people may have towards royalty or the famous. For believers, the profane is subject to the greater authority of the sacred: 'Sacred things are those which the interdictions (religious rules/prohibitions) protect and isolate; profane things are those to which these interdictions are applied and which must remain at a distance from the first' (quoted *Concise Oxford Dictionary of Sociology* 457).

Symbol and ritual are crucial to Durkheim's analysis of the social function of religion. Symbols – such as the ancient totem or Christian cross – provide a focus of emotion and belief. Rituals – such as animal sacrifice or the Catholic mass – bring people together and bind them in shared experience. In social terms, Durkheim is clear that what people are 'worshipping' is society. In reference to clan worship, Durkheim says that it awakens 'within its members the idea that outside of them there exist forces which dominate them and at the same time sustain them …' He considers that public rituals – whether religious or secular – in modern societies function in the same way:

> Moral remaking cannot be achieved except by the means of reunions, assemblies and meetings where the individuals, being closely united to one another, reaffirm in common their common sentiments; hence come ceremonies which do not differ from regular religious ceremonies, either in their object, the results which they produce, or the processes employed to attain these results. What essential difference is there between an assembly of Christians celebrating the principal dates of the life of Christ, or the Jews remembering the exodus from Egypt or the promulgation of the decalogue, and a reunion of citizens commemorating the promulgation of a new moral or legal system or some great event in the national life?
>
> (Durkheim extracted in Bocock and Thompson 1985:54-5)

Religion and ideology: Karl Marx

Marx considered religion to be a form of alienation – both emotional and intellectual. Religion serves as a poor substitute for social justice and happiness in the present world, and offers even poorer explanations as to why these are 'unobtainable'. Marx considered that religion stood in the way of the emotional and intellectual development of the working class and prevented them from developing a non-alienated society in the 'real' world. He referred to religion as the 'opiate of the masses' and some latterday Marxists have pilloried it as 'pie in the sky when you die'. Marx believed that once the working class had thrown off the 'illusion' of religion, its creative potential might express itself in work, art, and intellectual life.

Marx regarded religion as a form of ideology. It both developed 'false consciousness' and conformity among the oppressed (an aspect of alienation) and justified the behaviour of the powerful to themselves and others. Marx's analysis of tribal religion goes straight to the heart of what he regarded as its ideologically exploitative nature. Priests and witch-doctors conspired to relieve ordinary tribal members of their surplus wealth by claiming that they needed to be supported in order to practise magic and to communicate with the gods. Often contributions were such that they were able to do so in some style. He considered that working people in nineteenth century Britain were equally the victims of religion. He urged them to shake off the 'chain' of religion and 'cultivate the living flower' of social justice in the 'real' world:

> The task of history, therefore, once the world beyond the truth has disappeared, is to establish the truth of this world. The immediate task of philosophy, which is at the service of history, once the saintly form of human self-alienation has been unmasked, is to unmask self-alienation in its unholy forms. Thus the criticism of heaven turns into the criticism of the earth, the criticism of religion into the criticism of right and the criticism of theology into the criticism of politics.
>
> (Marx and Engels, extracted in Bocock and Thompson, 185:10-11)

Marx also considered that religion could be used as ideological justification by dominant groups and cited the role of Protestantism in justifying capitalism.

He argued that merchants and industrialists of the sixteenth century and later, were drawn to the Protestant rather than to the Catholic religion because the former satisfied their commercial requirements more than the latter. Whereas Catholicism forbade usury (lending money at exorbitant rates), it was acceptable under Protestantism. Whereas Catholic theologians regarded great interest in acquiring wealth as greedy, Protestants, and particularly Calvinists (members of a Protestant sect) looked upon material success as a sign of God's grace and favour. Protestant philosophy offered a further bonus to practical minded capitalists. Hard work and industry were at the core of Protestant moral practice and these virtues applied as much to the working class as to the bourgeoisie. Credit in the heavenly bank account rather than a hefty wage-packet was to be the reward of labour. This view had much to commend it to industrialists concerned with profit, accumulation and investment rather than the standard of living of the working class.

Freud and Marcuse

Freud considered that human beings are driven by powerful instincts of aggression (thanatos) and love (eros). 'Love' includes sexual needs as Freud understood it. He believed that in order to achieve 'civilisation', society had to control these instincts – otherwise they would wreak havoc. He argued that historically religion had played a major role in directing surplus and unexpressed instinctual energy, particularly 'erotic'. He referred to the displacement of love from people to spirits, saints or God as sublimation. In this way, he believed that religion functions as a form of social control. However, like the other major 'turn-of-the-century' social scientists to whom we have referred, he was inclined to think that religion would lose its credibility in the face of the rise of science and rational explanation.

Marcuse attempted a neo-Marxist blend of the thought of Marx and Freud. He argued that historically some members of the working class had been misled into misplacing their intelligence, creativity and much of their capacity for pleasure and fun. He borrowed the concept of ideological (intellectual) repression from Marx and that of emotional repression from Freud. He argued that a thoroughly repressed working class offered little threat to the capitalist system. However, Marcuse did not consider that the rise of science and reason would necessarily liberate working people. Rather, he believed that capitalism had created a new 'god' of consumerism through the media and advertising.

Max Weber

Religion and social change

In one of the most celebrated of historical-sociological encounters, Max Weber took issue with Marx on his analysis of religion as ideology. Superficially, the debate is about a question of empirical fact, but at a deeper level it concerns the cause and nature of historical change. The factual issue is itself profound enough: was Protestantism primarily the product of capitalism, or did it on the contrary help to produce capitalism? Marx takes the former view, Weber the latter. Marx's position has, in effect, already been explained. He argued that, like other forms of religious ideology, Protestantism helped to justify certain social relations – in this case the exploitation of the proletariat by the bourgeoisie. For Weber, the matter was less simple. He argued that Calvinism, a particular form of Protestantism, had played a major role in creating a cultural climate in which the capitalistic spirit could thrive. It would be too crude to say that Weber thought that Calvinism 'caused' capitalism, but he did consider that there was a certain correspondence between Calvinist ideas and the qualities required to be a successful capitalist. Calvinism provided favourable conditions for the development of capitalism. For instance, Calvinism preached hard work and frugality, the Protestant ethic – very useful virtues to a businessman. Weber cited many examples of Calvinists who became businessmen while, however, fully recognising that factors other than the spiritual content of Calvinism contributed to the rise of capitalism. An important one was the development of new machine technology which massively increased production potential.

Weber's major theoretical point is that ideas can change history, and in so doing can contribute to changes in the material context of life. It will be remembered that the whole trend of Marx's analysis of religious ideas is in the opposite direction. He sees them primarily as justifying existing social and economic circumstances, and certainly not as providing a major source of historical change. On the contrary, religion was an ideological pall intended to obscure new and different ideas. But Marx did recognise that new ideas could be developed. Human consciousness is able to react thoughtfully and creatively to experience, particularly everyday work experience. Socialism itself had to be 'thought of' before it could become a reality. However, for Marx, ideas are formed within, and structured by, socio-economic material reality. Socialism only becomes possible or practically 'thinkable' when society is economically and socially developed to the point where socialist ideas are seen to be realistic.

Weber's studies of religion are also important from the methodological point of view. As an exercise in comparative sociology, they rank alongside Durkheim's study of suicide. Weber drew his examples of the relationship of religion and society from worldwide. His conclusion was that the relationship is one of variety. Religion can help to cause change or impede it; it might be used to support the status quo or against it.

Secularisation: de-sacrilisation, 'disenchantment' and rationalisation

Like Durkheim, Weber considered that it is a feature of modern life that the supernatural is little used to explain events and behaviour. A process of 'de-sacrilisation' has occurred.

The medieval world in which God was Creator, 'His' mother a virgin, and in which spirits, good or evil, were believed to intervene in everyday life must have been perceived in a qualitatively different way from that in which most westerners see the world today. Belief in mystery and miracle has receded, although by no means entirely. 'Disenchantment', to use Weber's term for this, has set in. The triumph of science and reason has been at the cost of myth, fable and spiritual romanticism. This is part of the process of secularisation which is defined and discussed in the next main section.

For Weber, secularisation was an aspect of the wider process of rationalisation. He considered that the underlying principle

behind modernisation is rational, scientific thought – the use of the most effective means to achieve given ends. Applied to technology and to organisation, rational thought has restructured the social world. Equally to the point, applied to the human race's understanding of itself and its place in the universe, rational thought has undermined religion and replaced it with various secular and, largely, materialistic explanations of our existence and relationship to nature. Darwin, Freud and Marx were also major contributors to the replacement of religious explanations of human behaviour by scientific ones. Loss of intellectual authority and status helped to erode the moral authority of the church.

Religion, pluralism and modernity

Peter Berger has taken further Max Weber's arguments about the effect of modernity on religion. Not only is rational explanation different from, and *potentially* conflicting with religious explanation, the rational, scientific approach has produced a world which tends to undermine the possibility of a single dominant religious truth being established. Increased social and geographical mobility and the development of modern communications have exposed individuals to a great variety or plurality of religious influences. Pluralism, whether religious or otherwise, feeds off itself in the sense that once a new religion has been experienced, it can be passed on without fear of repression.

Steve Bruce cites some further aspects of modernisation which tend to undermine a single, shared or communal religion of the kind Durkheim described in relation to tribal societies. Industrialisation fragments society into a variety of cultural groups. In Britain, for instance, the class and ethnic divisions of labour are reflected in different religious beliefs. Among Afro-Caribbean immigrants, Pentecostalism is popular, whereas among the nineteenth century working class, Methodism gained a strong hold. Political conquest or annexation can result in people of different religions having to learn to tolerate each others beliefs. Finally, Bruce comments that religious 'innovation may also arise from within a stable population when the once-dominant culture has become so weakened that people feel free to search the global supermarket of cultures for new ideas and new perspectives'. (1995:95) This applies to Britain in so far as the cultural grip of formal Christianity has been loosened.

Bruce's last point reflects Berger's comments on the effect of modern communications and mobility on religious belief but also the analysis of Thomas Luckmann, Berger's frequent colleague. Luckmann argues that, in contrast to traditional society, in modern society no public 'truth' is imposed on the individual. Modernity has fostered a process of *individualisation* in which, in principle, people can chose what to believe. The root of this freedom, Luckmann sees as tying in with the modern separation of the public (or communal) and private (or personal) spheres:

> *In comparison to traditional social order ... personal identity becomes, essentially, a private phenomenon. This is perhaps the most revolutionary trait of modern society. Institutional segmentation left wide areas in the life of the individual unstructured ...*
>
> *(Quoted, Giddens, 1992:226)*

As co-authors of *The Social Construction of Reality* Berger and Luckmann argue that people routinely try to construct meaning out of their experience. Religion is one type of meaning system. Religion is a particularly effective type of explanation because it encompasses the whole of 'reality' – spiritual as well as temporal.

There are, however, a wide variety of non-religious philosophies by which their adherents seek to construct a meaningful interpretation of existence. Thus, secular humanists argue that their concern for the welfare of fellow human beings needs no added religious motive to be effective and vital. Marxism is another belief system. It has frequently been argued that Marxism emerged as an alternative belief system to religion and, in fact, has many religious characteristics.

Secularisation and modern intellectuals

The work of four great modern intellectuals – Marx, Freud, Darwin and Nietzsche – had an impact which in itself helped to generate the process of secularisation. Collectively, they appeared to many to have removed the need for religion, to have explained it away.

Marx and Freud we have already discussed. The first saw religion as ideological mystification and the second saw it as the projection of emotional need. Darwin was widely taken to have explained 'the origin of the species' without reference to God. Nietzsche took the next apparently logical step of announcing 'the death of God'. In God's place, Nietzsche urged the emergence of 'overman' or superman. Overman would surpass the achievements of man so far:

> *I teach you the overman. Man is something that shall be overcome (surpassed). What have you done to overcome him. All beings so far have created something beyond themselves ... Behold, I teach you the overman. The overman is the meaning of the Earth.*
>
> *(Quoted Jencks, 1993:139-40)*

Nietzsche perhaps had in excess the belief in human progress that the others shared. These four and many lesser intellectuals helped to spread a pervasive optimism about human improvement which had its earlier roots in the eighteenth century enlightenment. Despite his belief in science, Freud was the most cautious. After the carnage of the First World War he concluded

that the death instinct – the psychological equivalent of original sin – would continue to mar human development.

The rest of this chapter puts up for question two aspects of modern thought: a tendency to accept that secularisation is occurring and a belief in progressive human improvement (humanism).

The secularisation debate

The thesis that British society has become more secular – the secularisation thesis – is easy to grasp in outline but complex to define and demonstrate in detail. Broadly, the secularisation thesis proposes that religious belief and practice have declined and that science and rationality have increased in importance. Duncan Mitchell emphasises the former in the following definition:

> *Secularisation (or the secularisation process) is the term popularly used to depict a situation in which the beliefs and sanctions of religion become – or are in the process of becoming – increasingly discounted in society as guides to conduct or to decision-making.*
>
> *(Dictionary of Sociology, 1979)*

This proposition is of obvious importance. If correct, the secularisation thesis describes a radical and fundamental change in the cultural and institutional foundation of society. If 'God is dead' or generally believed to be, then, the life of human beings is likely to be very different as a result.

Despite its apparent importance, the very notion of the secularisation thesis has received severe criticism. David Martin contends that the concept is 'an intellectual hold-all' made up of a variety of unconnected arguments (1979). More recently, Michael Prowse has suggested that the secularisation thesis is 'out of date' – so great, in his view, is the evidence of the continuing vitality of religion ('Changing Patterns in the Search for Faith', *The Financial Times*, 1.4.1990).

Given the importance of the secularisation debate, it is no doubt better to define secularisation precisely rather than dispose of the concept altogether. Various aspects of possible secularisation have been identified. Both leading proponents of secularisation, such as Bryan Wilson, and leading opponents, such as David Martin, commonly accept three areas as relevant: formal religious practice; the influence of the church as an institution on other areas of society; and individual 'consciousness' of religion. Glock and Stark (1970) tease out several dimensions of what they term 'religiousness'. In addition to religious practice, they define belief, experience, knowledge and the consequences on daily life of these aspects as 'core dimensions' of religion. It is easier to measure formal religious practice than the other dimensions and it is to this issue we first turn.

Secularisation: formal religious practice

There is fairly widespread agreement among students of secularisation that there has been a steady general decline in formal religious observance among the Trinitarian churches during the post-war period (the Trinitarian churches are those that believe in the union of the Blessed Trinity in one God). Bryan Wilson has particularly cited statistical evidence in arguing for the secularisation hypothesis. Table 18.1 gives details of the decline in adult membership of the major Trinitarian religions between 1970 and 1994 which is estimated at over 25 per cent overall. Active church membership is quite a vigorous definition of membership and many who are not actively religious would claim membership of some religion. A comparable decline occurred in participation in the rites of passage – baptism, confirmation, and church marriage. Table 18.2 shows that the number of civil as opposed to church marriages in Great Britain rose from 40 per cent in 1971 to 48 per cent in 1988 although this is still a majority in the latter category.

Table 18.1 Church membership (Adult active members)

United Kingdom	1970	1980	1992	1995
		Millions		
Trinitarian churches				
Roman Catholic	2.7	2.4	2.1	2.0
Anglican	2.6	2.2	1.8	1.7
Presbyterian	1.8	1.4	1.2	1.1
Methodist	0.7	0.5	0.4	0.4
Baptist	0.3	0.2	0.2	0.2
Other free churches	0.5	0.5	0.6	0.7
Orthodox	0.2	0.2	0.3	0.3
All Trinitarian churches	8.8	7.4	6.6	6.4

(Source: *Social Trends*, 1997)

Table 18.2 Civil marriages as a percentage of all marriages

Great Britain	1971			1988
	All marriages	First marriages[1]	Second or subsequent[2]	All marriages
		Percentages		
England and Wales	41	31	78	48
Scotland	31	29	70	42
Great Britain	40	31	77	48

1 First marriage for both partners.
2 Remarriage for one or both partners.

(Source: *Office of Population Censuses and Surveys: General Register Office (Scotland)* in *Social Trends*, 1991)

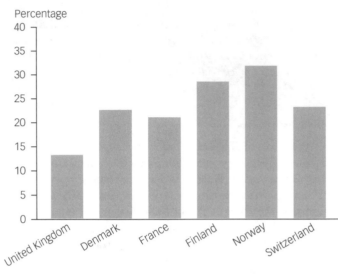

(Source: *Social Trends*, 1991)

Figure 18.1 Active church membership in selected European countries

Britain's reputation as 'the most secular nation in Europe' is supported by Figure 18.1 which shows active church membership in Britain clearly lower than that of five other European countries.

Even among Roman Catholics, among whom church attendance has historically been high, there has been a recent sharp drop in the numbers attending Sunday mass (see Figure 18.2). Between 1988 and 1995, numbers fell by 200,000 or over fifteen per cent.

David Martin does not disagree that a decline in formal religious practice occurred during the post-war period. However, he does question whether certain previous periods were such 'golden' eras of religion as is sometimes assumed. There is evidence of considerable religious scepticism and non-observance in the middle ages. Martin also suggests that the high church attendance rate of the Victorian middle class may have reflected their concern with respectability rather than religious commitment! In addition to Martin's comments, the relative flourishing of major non-Trinitarian churches and the recent growth of world religions such as Islam, in Britain (discussed below) must also be considered to qualify the argument that formal religious observance has generally declined.

Secularisation, the institutional influence of the church: disengagement?

Writing in 1977, Bryan Wilson argued that the 'content of the message that the churches seek to promote and the attitudes and values that it tries to encourage, no longer inform much of our national life' ('How Religious Are We?' in *New Society*, 17.10.1977).

A *disengagement* of church and state into separate domains has replaced their near unity in the middle ages. He sees the role of religion in school and at the workplace as now almost negligible. Although religion has a more secure place in the National

Estimated Catholic mass attendance in England and Wales

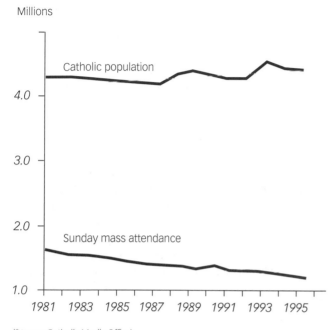

(Source: *Catholic Media Office*)

Figure 18.2 Falling attendance

Curriculum, it is unlikely that Wilson would see this, as radically changing its low subject status. He suggests that the workplace is perhaps the environment 'most alien' to religious values. Bureaucratic principles of organisation, whether in factory or office, seem almost the antithesis of religious myth and values. The remoteness of contemporary religion from political life has tended to progress from the middle ages. In the reign of Henry II, the major political opponent of the King was the Archbishop of Canterbury. It is difficult to imagine the contemporary church ever being more than an irritant to its political 'masters'.

Nevertheless, there was certainly an increase in political and social comment during the 1980s and 1990s on the part of the church, both as a body and by individuals. Most famously there was the report, *Faith in the City* (1985) published by a commission set up by the Archbishop of Canterbury. The report criticised the effect of government policies in the inner city for 'making the plight of some classes of citizens actually worse'. This was strong and specific comment and may even have had some effect. In 1987 Margaret Thatcher declared that a main goal of her new administration was to revive the inner cities. Arguably, however, the moral agenda and tone of the 1980s was set by Margaret Thatcher and her supporters rather than by her critics. After her election victory of 1979, she quoted St Francis of Assisi on the steps of 10 Downing Street and subsequently frequently stated or implied a moral basis for her policies. Philosophically, Thatcherism represented a moral backlash against the 'permissivism' and social reformism of the 1960s and 1970s in favour of traditional morality and individual effort. Undoubtedly,

this meant 'losers' as well as 'winners' economically. The bishops' report was mainly concerned with the 'losers' but it was responding to the dictates of Thatcherism.

Even the radical Bishop of Durham, David Jenkins, opposed Thatcherism from a largely defensive posture. In particularly, he was concerned with the closure of coal pits and the resulting effect on mining communities. However, in his book written with Rebecca Jenkins, *Free to Believe* (1991), he reached beyond reaction politics to outline the basis of a new political consensus in which national and global problems – poverty, the environment, war – might be dealt with in a renewed spirit of international collective understanding and co-operation. This coincided with a post Gulf War, reinvigorated United Nations – the most likely practical agency for such a movement.

In opposing the secularisation thesis, David Martin does not deny that there has been a long term decline in the influence of the church on national life. However, he turns the argument on its head and suggests that the church may be more effective and retain more integrity by concentrating on its own chief concerns, the spiritual and moral. To others this might seem like condemning the church to practical irrelevance – rendering to 'Caesar what is Caesar's and to God what is God's' could leave the latter in danger of seeming irrelevant to modern society! In any case, church leaders have continued to comment on political and social matters. In 1991, the recently appointed Archbishop of Canterbury, Dr Carey, argued that urban disorder, specifically that in Tyneside, was 'inextricably linked to social and economic conditions'.

A survey of church leaders' opinion published in early 1996 precisely illustrates this difference of opinion between those who take either David Martin or Dr Carey's view about how the church should respond to contemporary issues. The survey was carried out on the 547 members of the Church of England Synod. The Synod is divided into three houses – the bishops, clergy and laity. 443 responded to the survey including 38 out of 50 bishops.

In general, the bishops' responses were more liberal and 'progressive' than those of the laity. Table 18.3 lists the moral issues considered most important by the bishops. Economic and social issues are clearly thought to outweigh more personal issues of morality such as euthanasia, extra marital affairs and homosexuality. A lower proportion of bishops than laity were concerned about adultery (although both laity and clergy agreed with the bishops about what were the top three issues).

The survey shows the leadership of the Church of England to be highly focused on the moral aspects of secular public issues. In contrast, two-fifths of the bishops and two-thirds of the laity said the churches did not give adequate answers on more personal matters such as the family and spiritual needs.

In Martin's terms, then, the issue is whether or not the church's attempt to be relevant to society – what may be termed its secular agenda – deprives it of its unique purpose to address personal moral and spiritual issues. Within the Church of England, traditionalists would tend to take this view whereas liberals insist the church must address the problems of society.

Table 18.3 Morality

Issues of morality chosen by bishops as the most important:

Unemployment	25	(19.4%)
Environmental Issues	25	(19.4%)
Third World Problems	23	(17.8%)
Government/Politics	17	(13.2%)
Racial Disharmony	15	(11.6%)
Euthanasia	9	(7%)
Disarmament issues	7	(5.4%)
Abortion	4	(3.1%)
Extra-Marital Affairs	4	(3.1%)
Homosexuality	0	

Does the Church of England give adequate answers on the following Issues? This is how the bishops responded:

Moral Problems:	IA 14 (38.9%)	DK 6 (16.7%)
Family Life:	IA 17 (48.6%)	DK 4 (11.4%)
Spiritual needs	IA 14 (40%)	DK 6 (17.1%)
Social Problems:	IA 7 (20%)	DK 9 (25.7%)

IA = Inadequate Answers DK = Don't Know

(Source: *Daily Mail*, 14.2.1996:6)

During the 1990s, a debate built up in British political and public life about the moral basis of British society. This was inspired more by issues such as child abuse and violent crime than precisely by religion. However, some politicians cited the importance of religious principles and there was a religious aspect to the debate. This mood of moral concern may evaporate but it further illustrates the danger of both exaggerating secularisation or assuming it is wholly irreversible.

Secularisation: informal, personal religion

Religion as a source of personal meaning and fulfilment survives much more widely and with greater vitality than institutional religion. Interestingly, Thomas Luckmann considers that the primary function of religion is to give personal meaning to life. Although few in Britain go regularly to church, the vast majority believe in 'something', even if no more than a vague force behind the universe. What is more, according to David Hay, 'well over a third of all women and just under a third of all men in Great Britain claim to have had some sort of religious experience'. To use Hay's own terms, almost half of these 'wouldn't touch the church with a

bargepole'. It is worth giving a brief extract from one of the examples of 'mystical' experience cited by Hay:

> *Then it happened. 'I lost all sense of time, of my own body and 'ego'; it was as if I became one with the natural world ... for an unthought passage of time I was filled with the certainty and knowledge of the meaning of life'. Previously he'd been cynical about religion ...*
>
> *(New Society, 12.4.1979)*

No doubt many who could not claim anything resembling a mystical experience routinely pray or 'talk to God in their own way'. For them neither belief in science nor in humanity has been quite enough to make them feel complete. The secularisation thesis is, therefore, less applicable to personal religion of this kind than to formal religion. New age, quasi-religious thinking and lifestyles and even a reputed revival of paganism also offer some challenge to the secularisation hypothesis – albeit difficult to quantify. However, a survey published by the Humanist Association in 1996 claimed that only 43 per cent of Britons believed in God. It may be that even personal religion is beginning to weaken in Britain.

Secularisation: churches and sects

Although sometimes seen as an example of religious fragmentation, the constant rise and fall of religious sects is often cited as evidence that religion is not slowly dying. Ernst Troeltsch first made the distinction between churches and sects in the early 1930s (1981). Churches are large religious organisations. They tend to support the state and generally to be conservative. In contrast, sects are typically smaller religious organisations and often oppose the secular and ecclesiastical establishment. Whereas churches represent orthodoxy in teaching and ritual, sects are frequently innovative and even spontaneous in these matters. In addition to churches and sects, Bryan Wilson has suggested the term denomination to describe religious organisations which do not have the status, power and perhaps size of membership of a church but which have a stable and settled existence. Examples in Britain are the Baptist and Methodist denominations.

Roy Wallis has suggested that there are three main types of sects: world-rejecting, world-accommodating and world-affirming. Just as the 'church, denomination, sect' typology should be regarded as an ideal type rather than a framework into which every religious organisation fits, so should Wallis' typology of sects. World-affirming sects accept the world as it is and members seek to deal with problems and to find fulfilment through spiritual means. An example of such a movement is Transcendental Meditation (TM). TM had its origin in the Hindu religion. It offered spiritual solutions and experience without requiring its members to give up worldly pursuits. It has attracted, in particular, middle class young people who may have been materially satisfied but spiritually deprived.

World-accommodating sects neither accept nor reject worldly pursuits but seek vital spiritual expression as a priority. They are often break-aways from churches which are considered to have 'lost touch with true spirituality'. The Pentecostalists believe that the Holy Spirit is in direct communion with them whereas the ritual and formalism of other churches impedes such communication. World-rejecting sects separate themselves from what they see as a corrupt world, sometimes to prepare for an anticipated second coming. One of the best known contemporary sects of this kind is the 'Unification Church' or 'Moonies' led by the Reverend Moon.

Although accurate statistics on the growth of sects are notoriously difficult to produce, it seems that the increase in popularity of sects which began in the 1960s, is continuing into the 1990s. Although the membership in Britain of the Church of Scientology increased between 1970 and 1990, its own claim of a tenfold increase to 50,000 ought to be treated with scepticism. Table 18.4 gives more reliable information on the overall growth of fundamental Christian 'sects' between 1970-1994 and while this is substantial, it is not quite as spectacular.

Whereas in the 1960s cults tended to develop as splinters from major religions, such as the Jesus People and TM (Hinduism), in the 1990s, paganism and the occult re-emerged as additional influences. The 'new age movement' is an umbrella term covering such cults but also ecological and environmental groups.

Table 18.4 Church membership (United Kingdom)

	1970	1980	1992	1995
		Millions		
Non-Trinitarian churches				
Mormons	0.1	0.1	0.2	0.2
Jehovah's Witnesses	0.1	0.1	0.1	0.1
Other Non-Trinitarian	0.1	0.2	0.2	0.3
All Non-Trinitarian churches	0.3	0.4	0.5	0.6

(Source: *Social Trends*, 1997)

Reasons for the popularity of sects

What accounts for the recurrent and perhaps currently growing popularity of sects? First, a reason often given by members of sects themselves seems highly convincing. They claim to find formal religions cluttered with 'empty' ritual and lacking in the immediate spiritual experience for which they crave. This interpretation is compatible with Troeltsch's analysis that established churches tend to become like other organisations in society – hierarchical, bureaucratic and often impersonal. A second explanation for the appeal of sects, given by Max Weber, is still of relevance. He suggests that 'marginal' social groups may find compensation and explanation for their lack of privilege and status in the life of a sect.

To a considerable extent, the nineteenth century Methodists drew on the working class for its membership. If the Church of England was 'the Conservative party at prayer' the Methodists often had a more radical political as well as religious hue. In the post-war world, black people have sometimes lifted their sense of oppression by joining a religious sect. In addition to fundamental Christianity, the Rastafarian religion in Jamaica and Britain and the Black Muslim religion in America have attracted sizeable membership.

Young middle class people are sometimes associated with sectarian activity. This can hardly be explained by social marginality. Roy Wallis has suggested, however, that they may feel emotionally alienated from society and seek more meaningful experience and a sense of community in a sect. Eileen Barker's *The Making of a Moonie Choice or Brainwashing* (1985) confirms the analysis in relation to the Moonies. Typically, the sect attracted intelligent and idealistic middle class youth who were often repelled by society's materialism. The Moonies, Scientologists, and the neo-hippy Children of God appear to offer a total package of emotional, religious and even intellectual security not available elsewhere. However, the youthful search for community does not exclusively take a religious form. In the1960s, 'the counterculture' (see pp. 456-9) and today an array of 'new age' groups provide closeness and purpose of a non-religious kind. Sometimes alternative secular movements and the religious impulse converge as when psychedelic drugs are taken to achieve a 'short-cut' to mystical experience: a 'sort of' counterfeit infinity.

Bryan Wilson associates the growth of sects with social change. As old orders crumble or appear to, people seek new answers and reassurance. Methodism waxed at a time of considerable social and economic change and the current appeal of sects may reflect the need for explanation and solution to an array of seemingly overwhelming global problems. The uneasy sense, as we approach the millennium, that the human species may be evolving on a course to self-destruction prompts some to find a different way of life.

Liberal intellectuals frequently criticised the radical activity – religious and non-religious – of young people in the 1960s as naive and sometimes dangerous. Contemporary concern frequently focuses on the vulnerability of young people drawn into sects and away from previous family and other ties. The 'dark side' of sectarianism is perhaps less in bizarre belief than in the ability of some sects to deprive members of their possessions, their previous friends and relations, and their independence of thought.

Secularisation: the strength of world religions in Britain

The growth of non-Christian world religions in Britain, particularly Islam (the Muslim religion), has revitalised religious debate in Britain. Their expansion (see Table 18.5) has occurred primarily because of post-war immigration from the new Commonwealth and Pakistan (see pp. 220-2).

Table 18.5 Church membership (active adults)

	1970	1980	1992	1995
		Thousands		
Non-Trinitarian churches				
Muslims	0.1	0.3	0.2	0.6
Sikhs	0.1	0.2	0.1	0.4
Hindus	0.1	0.1	0.2	0.1
Jews	0.1	0.1	0.1	0.1
Others	0.1	0.1	0.1	0.1
All other religions	0.4	0.8	1.1	1.3

(Source: *Social Trends*, 1997)

These religions are central to the lives of relevant minority groups and are a fundamental element of multicultural Britain. They bring difference, diversity and interest into a society in which the Christian religion had perhaps been drifting into irrelevance. The members of these religions differ from most professed Christians in that they regularly observe formal ritual and practice. Inhabitants and citizens of a 'modern' society, many remain traditional in their religious and moral outlook. For some, this means that religious authority and principle overrides that of secular law.

The religious and moral strength of communities based on traditional world religions other than Christianity has both helped and hindered their adjustment to life in Britain. Crime, drug abuse, marital and family break-up tend to be substantially lower than the national average in these communities. However, on certain points of principle, their religions have brought them into conflict with majority opinion. An early example of tension occurred when male Sikhs felt morally unable to wear crash helmets when riding motor-bikes because of their religious custom of always wearing a turban in public. The Rushdie matter will be discussed (see p. 542). One of the most important points that it underlined was the potential conflict among some Muslims of their commitment to Islam and their commitment to observe British law when the two appeared to clash. On the one hand is the principle of free expression enshrined in law and on the other is the injunction by the highest Islamic authority to punish blasphemy. The Gulf War further tested the allegiance of some British Muslims although the 'Muslim world' itself was divided on the issue.

In the 1970s and 1980s evangelical movements – which seek more immediate spiritual experience and communication – grew in popularity in the United States and to a lesser extent in Britain. Their rise survived even the well-publicised sexual and financial scandals that some of their leaders became involved in. Evangelism, like sectarianism, is one answer to the desire for religion with 'heart and soul'.

Secularisation: conclusion

Secularisation has occurred in Britain to the extent that there has been a decline in formal religious observance and in the institutional influence of the church. On the other hand, in a less formal sense, 'there is a lot of religion about' – personal, sectarian and evangelical. The growth of the great world religions in Britain has interrupted any smooth flow towards secularisation even in the area of formal religion. It may be that the secularisation thesis needs to be reformulated to apply only to the major Christian churches and perhaps not to all of these. Secularisation in the sense of the triumph of science and reason over religion and the spiritual has not occurred. Figure 18.3 summarises the arguments for and against secularisation.

**The Secularisation Thesis:
For and against: a summary**

FOR

1 **Formal religious practice** in Britain has tended steadily to decline in the post-war era.

2 The **Institutional influence** of the church has tended to decline over several centuries.

AGAINST

1 **Personal religion** – in terms of a belief in the spiritual and as a source of meaning – appears to thrive (although precise measurement is difficult).

2 The vitality of **religious sects** runs counter to the secularisation thesis (though it undermines formal religion).

3 The growing strength in Britain of several of the great **world religions**, at the least, complicates the secularisation thesis.

4 A **comparison** of religion in Britain with that of another 'modern' society – **the United States** – appears partially to refute the secularisation thesis.

Note: A 'for and against' summary inevitably over-simplifies. Qualifications and counter-arguments to each point can be found in the main text.

Figure 18.3 Arguments for and against the secularisation thesis

Secularisation: should the term be dropped?

David Martin found the evidence for a consistent trend to secularisation so unconvincing that he suggested that the term be abandoned. Larry Schiner found six distinct uses of the term and made the same plea. Jeffrey Hadden argues that the data can neither confirm nor disconfirm 'the historical process predicted by secularisation theory.' Instead of the long obsession with secularisation, Hadden argues for more research of a comparative kind on 'the tumultuous entanglement of religion in politics around the globe'. The next section looks at some work of this kind.

Questions

1 Does the continued strength of personal and informal religion suggest that the secularisation hypothesis is mistaken?
2 In what ways can it be said that secularisation has or has not occurred?

The global picture: religion and modernity

On the basis of his own massive comparative survey, Weber concluded that the effects of religion on society are unpredictable and varied. Sometimes religion might have a conservative effect, whereas in other cases it might contribute to social change. Thus, he thought Buddhism militated against the development of capitalism in China, whereas in Northern Europe, Calvinism had the opposite effect (see p. 531-2).

An overview of religion in the contemporary world similarly shows a pattern of variety and often unpredicted development. With the opening up of the Soviet bloc, it appears that traditional religions, particularly Catholicism and Islam, have remained much stronger in parts of Eastern Europe and the southern Soviet republics than many had suspected. In the United States, the dominant Western nation, religion has remained a much more visibly buoyant part of national life than in Britain. World-wide, 'Eastern' religions flow west and Christianity is well-established in nearly all areas of the world. Figure 18.4 gives the size of membership of the larger world religions.

Liberalism, fundamentalism and secularisation

A potential conflict must be introduced here between liberalism and fundamentalism. Liberalism is associated with Western democracies and is based on mutual toleration of differences between groups (i.e. it is pluralistic). Fundamentalism is associated with opposition to liberalism and a militant and sometimes violent attitude to enforcing 'moral purity' (as defined by the fundamentalist). Frequently, fundamentalists seek to use the state to establish and enforce what they see as morality. In origin, the term fundamentalist applied to Christians who believed that social morality should literally be based on the Bible. More recently, it has also been used by Western academics and the media to describe more militant Muslim societies and individuals, but not all Muslims. Liberal and fundamentalist approaches occur in both religion and politics, and more widely.

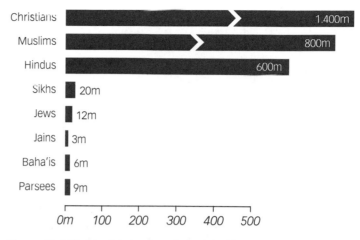

Figure 18.4 World religions: size of membership

The distinction between liberalism and fundamentalism is relevant to the concept of secularisation applied to the global context. Secularisation has occurred in the West in the particular and crucial sense that a division is made between the authority of the church and state. In Islam such a distinction is not established and, indeed, the general assumption is that Islamic law should govern civil as well as religious life. The term theocracy can be used to describe societies ruled by a single version of 'God's law' applied to both public and private life. Despite tendencies to theocracy, a degree of religious and political pluralism occurs in most Muslim states. Nevertheless, theocracy and liberalism are ultimately contradictory.

Islam and modernity: Ernest Gellner

In *Postmodernism, Reason and Religion* (1992) Ernest Gellner raises the question of whether Islam is compatible with the development of a modern society or whether its deep resistance to secularisation also implies an incompatibility with modern institutions. In Weber's terms, is Islam a case of a religion *congruent* with capitalism (and modernity) or not?

According to Gellner, Islam responded to the challenge of the West not by surrendering its own religious and cultural tradition but with 'a vehement affirmation of the puritan version of its own tradition' – namely, the discipline and application of High Islam.

Gellner's answer to his own question is then:

> On the evidence so far, the world of Islam demonstrates that it is possible to run a modern, or at any rate modernising, economy, reasonably permeated by the appropriate technological, educational, organisational principles, and combine it with a strong, pervasive, powerfully internalised Muslim conviction and identification. A puritan and scriptualist world religion does not seem necessarily doomed to erosion by modern conditions. It may, on the contrary be favoured by them.
>
> (22)

The fact that in the Far East, there are a number of other societies – Malaysia, Singapore, Japan – which have developed forms of capitalist economies, without becoming comprehensively secular, gives some support to Gellner's thesis.

Islam has been a particularly powerful and dynamic force both globally and in Britain for the past two decades. The immediate reason for this was the quadrupling of the oil price in 1973 which made several Muslim nations hugely wealthy and greatly increased their importance in global investment and development. The money to finance a Muslim revival was available. Historically, Islam has been an expansionist religion, and new economic power coincided with a feeling among many in the Muslim world that they had suffered from Western 'exploitation and arrogance' for long enough. These sentiments were notably strong in Iran and Iraq whereas the 'West' managed to maintain more friendly relations with the neo-feudal regimes in Saudi Arabia and Kuwait.

In 1979, the Shah of Iran was overthrown in a revolution that was partly inspired by Muslim clerics. The Shah had previously been enthroned as a result of a coup inspired by the United States Central Intelligence Agency (CIA). The so-called 'rule of the mullahs' (clerics) led by Ayatollah Khomeini followed the Shah's overthrow. Internally, Iran became governed on more strictly Islamic principles and externally its relations with the West deteriorated. It was during this period that Western hostages were taken and the notorious fatwa against Salman Rushdie was issued (see p. 542). With the death of Ayatollah Khomeini in 1989 and the rise of Rafsanjani, the Iranian leadership adopted a more pragmatic style, but the influence of Muslim clerics remained strong.

The recent history of Iraq provides another example of the influence of the Islamic religion both in the internal affairs of a country and more widely. Prior to the Gulf War of 1990, Saddam Hussein had seemed a relatively 'modern-minded', if dictatorial leader, in the sense that he appeared to distinguish between the political and religious areas of power. However, during the early stages of the war, he did play the 'religion card' by declaring the war to be a 'jihad' (holy war) against the infidel. In fact, this did not have the effect of uniting the Muslim world against the coalition but, according to press coverage of the war, it seems that Saddam Hussein had more support among the Arab masses than among their leaders.

Undoubtedly, religion is a major element in Muslim opposition to and resentment of 'the West'. However, whether it is a cause or a justification – or both – is debatable. In the following extract, Martin Woollacott first describes the anger of one individual, Sheikh Tamimi, against 'the West', and then broadens his description to suggest that the sheikh's views are widely shared in 'the Arab' or, more precisely, part of the Arab Muslim world.

Sheikh Tamimi is not sure whether Bush is best compared to Charlemagne or Richard the Lionheart, but he is sure that the West is engaged in a new crusade against Islam, 'It is not our holy war against you, but your holy war against us,' says the Sheikh. 'Saddam Hussein has become an agent of God and he has had to face the West and the whole world of the unbelievers.'

The Sheikh is one of scores of such fundamentalist leaders through the Arab world today. They differ in theology, in ability, in sophistication and in political visibility but they share one common characteristic. They see themselves as the inheritors or a pure tradition which compromising and sometimes evil politicians have sullied, and they see themselves as having the right to influence political leaders if not to replace them. This is the great opposition movement - anti-Western, anti-Israeli, anti-modern, and anti-rational - which is waiting in the wings in the Middle East and whose day may come if the Arabs and the West do not learn the right lessons from the disastrous war which has just ended. [i.e. the Gulf War]

(Martin Woollacott, The Guardian, 1991:25)

Islam is a reference point in many countries outside the Middle East for those who feel dispossessed by the West. Arguably, Islam is now a more popular vehicle for opposition to the West than Marxism. For instance, during the early 1990s a rising tide of Muslim fundamentalism occurred in Nigeria. One of its leaders, Mallam Zakzaky, made great emphasis of the complete nature of the Islamic system which, in his view, offers a total political, economic and social programme unlike the Christian religion which he sees as practically irrelevant. It is precisely this failure to separate matters ecclesiastical from matters secular that his critics find threatening.

Islam in Britain

To what extent does Britain's Muslim population feel a conflict of allegiance between commitment to the Muslim faith and loyalty to Britain? The first point to make is that the evidence to answer this question is not available. The second point is that British Muslims vary immensely both in their interpretation of the Muslim faith and of their duties towards Britain. Some find no conflict between their faith and their commitment to British law whereas others seem prepared to obey external Islamic authority even if it conflicts with British law. Vivck Chaudhary and Dave Hill comment interestingly on such differences:

> *The sheer diversity of British Muslims makes the gelling of a cohesive, grass-roots British Muslim identity still seem a long way off. In trying to see the future, it would also be naive to regard Muslims as functioning in isolation from the enduring social mechanisms of Britain as a whole. Social class and economic climate permeate the lives of Muslims as they do everybody else. Islamic culture will not more evolve in a vacuum in Britain than it does in Saudi Arabia.*
>
> *(V Chaudhary and D Hill, The Guardian, 3.5.1991:19)*

Thirdly, however, the years between 1988 and 1991 saw a series of situations arise which sorely tested the judgement of members of the Muslim community. Matters were made worse by a continuing tide of racism against Asian Britons (see p. 220). Again, Chaudhary and Hill express the position well:

> *But the last three years have seen Britain's Muslim communities embroiled in major convulsions of identity, going right to the heart of their role in British life and in the wider world. The Rushdie affair, arguments about Islamic schools and political parties and, most recently, the Gulf War, have dragged abstract issues of social and spiritual identity down from the stratosphere and set them firmly in the discourse of everyday life. The full implications are, as yet, uncertain. But the debate has been loud: and with it have come shifting sensibilities for uncomfortable times.*
>
> *(V Chaudhary and D Hill, The Guardian, May 1991:19)*

More recently, British Muslims have protested against and greatly reduced street prostitution in their neighbourhoods in a part of Leeds and in Balsall Heath, Birmingham. Such conflicts are

Figure 18.5 Battle for Balsall Heath. What is tolerated by one cultural group may not be by another

predominantly local and even neighbourhood in focus, but they occur against a background of real cultural difference and often substantial white racism.

Rushdie: the limits of liberalism?

As well as demonstrating the strength of Islam in Britain – and, therefore, throwing further doubt on the secularisation hypothesis – the Rushdie affair has sharply highlighted some of the key issues in the complex relationship between British Muslims and the dominant culture.

From the point of view of Ayatollah Khomeini and those who followed him, the central issue was that of blasphemy. Rushdie's *The Satanic Verses* was deemed to present the Prophet Mohammed in a highly blasphemous way. Apparently, a number of British Muslims petitioned Khomeini through the Islamic embassy in London to make a judgement on Rushdie. Khomeini issued his fatwa in February 1989 calling for 'all zealous Muslims' to seek to execute Rushdie 'as well as those publishers who were aware of its contents'. There have been several deaths apparently related to the fatwa but so far (1997) Rushdie remains alive.

Liberal views

From the point of view of Rushdie and the overwhelming majority of Western liberals of whatever political persuasion, the central issue of principle was one of freedom of speech and expression. This view is strongly implicit in one of Rushdie's early responses to the fatwa:

> *Frankly I wish I had written a more critical book. A religion that claims it is able to behave like this, religious leaders who are able to behave like this, and then say this is a religion that must be above any whisper of criticism - that doesn't add up.*
> *(Quoted in Appignasi and Maitland)*

In the West, the fatwa was also perceived to contravene British sovereignty. This was linked to the issue of freedom in that the purpose of the contravention was to curtail freedom of speech. Anthony Burgess, the novelist and critic, combines both points in the following reference to the fatwa:

> *It is a declaration of war on citizens of a free country and as such it is a political act. It is to be countered by an equally forthright, if less murderous, declaration of defiance.*
> *(Quoted in Appignasi and Maitland)*

Ernest Gellner likewise saw the Rushdie affair in terms of an irreconcilable conflict of principle between liberalism and Islam which he regards as a *fundamentalist* religion. By fundamentalist he means that the 'points of (religious) doctrine and points of law are not separated, and Muslim learned scholars are best described as theologians/jurists'.

A Muslim perspective

The British Asian scholar, Tariq Modood presents matters somewhat differently. In doing so, he challenges Western liberals to rethink and to extend their values to apply to a conservative but not, he argues a generally fundamentalist British cultural minority. British Muslims, he contends are not the same as other Britons. They live by different norms and beliefs but are entitled to do so. Equal rights includes the right to be different. Can a secular, liberal and reputedly tolerant society extend its tolerance to British Muslims and others of deep religious persuasion?

Modood seeks to persuade liberals to scrutinise whether or not they are fully practising the tolerance and cultural pluralism they preach. The fact that the British blasphemy laws apply to Christianity but not to other major religions is generally supportive of his case (although most liberals would prefer the abolition rather than extension of these laws).

Yet, there are problems with Modood's case. First, he could reasonably be construed to be asking liberals to tolerate intolerance. Whether or not Islam is inherently fundamentalist is doubtful. However, some British Muslims act in a fundamentalist way (i.e., with moral intolerance accompanied by threat) while others – seemingly the overwhelming majority – do not. A precondition of pluralism is *mutual* tolerance. Modood cannot reasonably ask liberals to tolerate aggressive intolerance if that is his intention. Second, liberals in principle cannot accept the breaking of the law and breach of the legal principle of sovereignty explicit in the fatwa. It may be that only a tiny minority of British Muslims seriously supported the implementation of the fatwa but those who do risk breaking British law and also disregard a tradition of opposition to absolutism and intolerance whether secular or religious.

Discussions of conflicts of high principle inevitably run the risk of sounding pompous even though the enunciation and practice of such principles are crucial to forming the character of societies. At a more mundane level, much of the leadership of the minority British Muslim and of the majority British community seem to have approached the problem of the Rushdie affair in a pragmatic way. Sometimes the strategy seems to have been one of benign near-neglect – if the matter cannot be resolved by argument, then perhaps, in time, people will begin to feel less strongly about it. To the extent that this is happening, perhaps British Muslims are being drawn into the liberalism of muddled compromise. Meanwhile, Rushdie is taking his chances carefully and would prefer to have the fatwa rescinded.

Conclusion: beyond the secularisation thesis?

Although framed broadly within the secularisation debate, this chapter has continually threatened to breach the bounds of this issue – vast as it is. As Grace Davie points out there are other questions of relevance to the sociology of religion: 'The role of women within the churches, the ecumenical debate and the European question (ecumenism and Europe are closely linked) ...' (in Obelkevich and Catterall, 165). In the wider context, there is the question of the relationship of Britain and the West to societies and groups which are religious either in a traditional or 'new' sense. Davie indicates the complexities of the relationship of religion to modernity or, for those who prefer the term, postmodern society:

> *In many respects, these confusing tendencies reflect underlying shifts in society though they have been differently interpreted. For some commentators they are associated with what has become known as late capitalism; a post-industrial or postmodern society quite different in mood from the optimistic certainties of the 1960s (a shift in emphasis ushered in by the oil crisis of the early 1970s). The concept of postmodernism remains, however, controversial. For it is equally possible to argue that the re-emphasis of this kind of religious life both within and without the mainline churches is an ongoing part of modernity, rather than a post- or anti-modern reaction to this. For all its optimism and creativity, modernity has – and always will – engender a whole range of unsolved moral, ecological and, surely, religious problems. The religious dimensions must, therefore, be considered an essential part of modernity, though its shapes and forms may be widely diverse (Hervieu-Léger, 1986). Both views – obliged to take the religious dimension into account – challenge the assumptions of the secularisation thesis.*
>
> (169)

Questions

1 To what extent is there a clash between the values of modern liberalism and Islam?
2 Is religion compatible with modernity?

Summary

1 Major sociologists offer a number of key analyses of religion:
   • Durkheim argues that religion functions to reinforce the collective unity or social solidarity of a group.
   • Marx considered religion to be:
   i A form of alienation – from 'real' happiness in the present world.
   ii A form of ideology which developed 'false consciousness' among the oppressed.
   • Freud considered that religion helps to control potentially socially disruptive instincts through sublimation.
   • Marcuse, drawing on both Marx and Freud, describes both religion and the capitalist media as forms of ideological and emotional repression of the working class.
   • Weber analysed religion both in terms of:
   i Its varied contribution to social change and maintaining the status quo.
   ii The process of de-sacrilisation which he perceived as a move from supernatural to rational explanation.
   A number of authorities have linked religious pluralism with modernity.
   Berger and Luckmann argue that religion is only one way in which people try to construct meaning out of their experience.
2 The secularisation hypothesis proposes that religious belief and practice have declined and that science and rationality have increased in importance.
3 Two main points were discussed which generally support the secularisation thesis:
   i Formal religious practice in Britain, as measured by church attendance and observance of the rites of passage, has declined.
   ii The institutional influence of the church on other areas of national life has tended to wane.
4 Four main points were discussed generally argue against the secularisation thesis:
   i Personal belief in the spiritual still appears widespread.
   ii The ebb and flow of religious sects continues apace.
   iii There has been a growth of membership in several world religions in Britain.
   iv The view that secularisation tends to occur in 'modern' societies is severely questioned by the example of the United States.
5 The secularisation thesis was not intended to apply to traditional societies, and certainly world-wide the great religions show few signs of overall decline.
6 There is a fundamental difference between the more secular, liberal, Western societies and those societies in which church and state are scarcely, if at all, differentiated (theocracies). Officially, liberal states are committed to religious and ideological tolerance and pluralism, whereas theocracies, such as Khomeini's Iran, are not. On the contrary, 'true believers' in theocracies are often militantly intolerant of non-believers'. This difference of principle is a recipe for great tension and potential conflict. It is a difference which recurs internationally between liberals and religious fundamentalists, including in Britain.
7 Despite the great tensions created by the Rushdie matter and the Gulf War, the overwhelming majority of British Muslims observe both British law and their normal religious practice. Nevertheless, a surge of racism against Muslims during this period and fundamentalist and uncompromising statements by some Muslims indicated that the elements of potentially greater civil strife exist.
8 The Rushdie affair is discussed as an example of the confrontation of Western liberalism and Islam. The latter is discussed both in its fundamentalist and more tolerant forms.

9 The view that secularisation is not the inevitable accompaniment of modernity is presented through the work of Ernest Gellner and, briefly, Grace Davie.

Research and coursework

Of the many possible areas of study under the topic, the relationship of religion and community could be particularly interesting. You may select an area for study in which one religion predominates. If so, what effect does this have on the community? Does it greatly increase community solidarity as, following Durkheim, one might hypothesise? Is religious leadership in the community dominated by a particular age group, class or sex? What is the experience of those who cease religious practice in a strong religious community? To what extent does the church deal with local social problems?

On the other hand, you may select an area for study in which several religions are practised. Do patterns of leisure sociability tend to be affected by membership of a given church? Are there religious-based rivalries within the locality? Again, are particular religions associated with a given class, ethnic group or even age group (it is unlikely that gender will be a significant variable in this context)? How do you explain these relationships?

A starting point for the type of enquiry suggested above might be a church notice-board and/or calendar of events. These may indicate who leading and active church members are. Prior to examining the links between church and social relationships and activities, the issue of whether to proceed in an overt (possibly using interview) or covert (possibly, using participant observation) way will have to be resolved.

Alternatively, an enquiry – perhaps through depth-interviews – into more 'personal' or New Age 'religion' is feasible.

Further reading

R Bocock and K Thompson eds., *Religion and Ideology* (Manchester University Press, 1985) is a very useful reader. Steve Bruce's *Religion in Modern Britain* (Oxford University Press, 1995) explores newer issues. Books by a protagonist of the secularisation thesis, are Bryan Wilson, *Religion in Sociological Perspective* (Oxford University Press, 1982) and, on the other side, D Martin, *A General Theory of Secularisation* (Blackwell, 1978).

Readings

Reading 1
Religion – the opium of the people

From K Marx and F Engels, *On Religion,* reprinted in R Bocock and K Thompson, eds., *Religion and Ideology* (Manchester University Press, 1985), pp. 11-12

Religious distress is at the same time the *expression* of real distress and the *protest* against real distress. Religion is the sign of the oppressed creature, the heart of a heartless world, just as it is the spirit of a spiritless situation. It is the *opium* of the people.

The abolition of religion as the *illusory* happiness of the people is required for the *real* happiness. The demand to give up the illusions about its condition is the *demand to give up a condition which needs illusions.* The criticism of religion is therefore *in embryo the criticism of the vale of woe*, the *halo* of which is religion.

Criticism has plucked the imaginary flowers from the chain not so that man will wear the chain without any fantasy or consolation but so that he will shake off the chain and cull the living flower. The criticism of religion disillusions man to make him think and act and shape his reality like a man who has been disillusioned and has come to reason, so that he will revolve round himself and therefore round his true sun. Religion is only the illusory sun which revolves round man as long as he does not revolve round himself.

The task of history, therefore, once the *world beyond the truth has* disappeared, is to establish the *truth of this world*. The immediate *task of philosophy*, which is at the service of history, once the *saintly form* of human self-alienation has been unmasked, is to unmask self-alienation in its *unholy forms*. Thus the criticism of heaven turns into the criticism of the earth, the *criticism of religion* into the *criticism of right* and the *criticism of theology* into the *criticism of politics* [...]

The philosophers have only *interpreted* the world, in various ways; the point, however, is to *change* it.

Questions

1 What does Marx mean by the phrase religion 'is the opium of the people'? To what extent would other founders of social science, such as Durkheim and Weber, agree with him?
2 Compare Marx's use of the concept of alienation in the context of religion and work.

Reading 2
Beyond the secularisation thesis

From Grace Davie, 'Religion in Post-war Britain', in J Obelkevich and P Catterall eds., *Understanding Post-war British Society* (Routledge, 1994), pp. 169-70

Quite clearly, the churches – British and otherwise – are operating within a global framework quite different from that which emerged in the immediate aftermath of the Second World War. The framework, moreover, continues to shift in radical and unpredictable ways. The sheer speed of events in 1989, for example, took everyone by surprise; so, too, did the Iraqi invasion of Kuwait (August 1990) and the collapse of the Soviet Union (December 1991). Very few sociologists now deny that the religious dimension is an increasingly important factor in these shifts and in the subsequent reactions of international diplomacy. The politico-religious aspirations of the Islamic countries are perhaps the most obvious example of this shift, but it is by no means limited to the Muslim world. What Robertson calls the politicisation of religion and the religionisation of politics is a global phenomenon.

Such conclusions have serious implications for the secularisation thesis; implications which must, first of all, prompt a degree of questioning concerning the inherent Eurocentrism embodied in this perspective. It is no longer possible to assume that Europe's religious behaviour today will become everyone else's tomorrow. This simply isn't the case. But we also need to look more closely at some aspects of religious life within Britain itself, not least at the rather unexpected prominence of the British churches in the political debates of the 1980s. For even here there has been some politicisation of religion and religionisation of politics.

Up to a point, it is possible to explain this phenomenon in terms of the immediate political context; the churches – and the established Church in particular – filled a conspicuous void in the absence of effective political opposition through much of the Thatcher period. The churches, were, moreover, not only prominent, but undeniably effective in bringing particular social and economic issues to public attention and sustaining a significant level of political debate. A growing awareness of the effects of government policy on the most deprived areas of British society (*Faith in the City*, 1985) was the most obvious example of ecclesiastical pressure in this respect. The problem remained intractable, but the *concept* of an urban priority area could no longer be ignored. The political void explanation was, however, only part of the story. For the continued prominence of religious issues in, for example, the Rushdie affair, in education (notably the content and aspirations of religious education), in medical ethics, in ecological issues, and in the tragically unresolvable Northern Irish question, must, surely lead to a more fundamental reappraisal of the role of religion in contemporary British – and indeed European – life. Society's attitudes towards religion are undoubtedly very different in the 1990s compared with the immediate post-war period. Such attitudes remain, none the less, central to some of the most significant issues facing contemporary Britain, not least to those problematic of a truly pluralist society.

An adequate reappraisal of the religious factor in modern, or postmodern society has become a priority for the sociologist. It requires imaginative thinking and new frames of reference. The emphasis will, necessarily, be different from that which has dominated the subdiscipline in recent years. Not only does the sociology of religion require an improved theoretical input, it needs, above all, to overcome its conviction that secularisation is an inevitable consequence of modernity.

Questions

1 How convincing do you find the evidence cited by Davie that in the 1980s and 1990s 'there has been some politicisation of religion and religionisation of politics'?
2 Do you agree that secularisation is not 'an inevitable consequence of modernity'?

Community and Localities

The urban/rural contrast can be overdone – despite poverty and squalor, twenty per cent of all agricultural produce is produced in urban areas

Aims of this chapter

1 To introduce definitions of community with examples.

2 Critically to present the concept of community (and related concepts) as it appears in classical sociology.

3 To present conflict theory analysis of the socio-economic

forces, including global capitalism, that shape localities.

4 To describe the involvement of capital, politicians, planners and citizens in local processes.

5 Critically to discuss concepts of community current in the 1990s.

The concept of community

Definitions of community

Three main definitions of community should be noted:

1 The term community is employed to describe a *fixed locality* (a given geographic area) as a basis of social organisation. Thus, a traditional rural village where people are born, live and die close to each other fits this usage.

2 Community is used to refer to a local *social system* or set of relationships that centre upon a given locality. Margaret Stacey suggests that, from a sociological point of view, it is the concentration of relationships, rather than the geographical factor that matters. Stacey would prefer to drop the term community in favour of local social system. She considers that the former term has acquired so many meanings that a precise use of it is almost impossible, whereas the latter term simply indicates relationships in a given locality as the topic for study.

3 Community is also used to describe a *quality of relationship* which produces a strong sense of shared identity. This usage does not depend on physical whereabouts or even on people having met each other. Thus, it is possible to refer to the Catholic or Jewish community in a neighbourhood, town, country or, even, throughout the world. Sometimes a shared threat or triumph can produce or intensify a 'feeling of community'. Thus, people in Britain during the Second World War sometimes claim that there was 'a stronger sense of community' then. As Howard Newby points out it is 'loss of community' in terms of shared identity and accompanying experiences that accounts for much of the usage of the phrase.

Since the 1960s, this third sense of community has been widely used. Thus, youth subcultures, especially the hippies, were thought of as lifestyle communities. The commune movement attempted to give territorial reality to 'the search for community'. In the 1980s and 1990s there has been a revised interest in what are perceived as 'ethnic communities' (see pp. 232-6). Often the symbolism of community is emphasised as being the focus for 'feelings of community' e.g. the Koran, a national flag, the image of a culture hero or martyr such as Ché Guevara or Malcolm X. Anthony Cohen's *The Symbolic Construction of Community* (1985) presents

community in this way – 'as a mêlée of symbol and meaning cohering only in its symbolic gloss' (20). In other words, community works as a general focus of sentiment and belief – try to put too much definition and detail on it, and there is a risk that the 'spell' will be broken.

In practice, the above three usages of the concept frequently overlap. The most common application of the term community – to social relations in a neighbourhood or area – has aspects of all three usages.

Activity

We will consider how useful and accurate the notion 'loss of community' is when we have reviewed the literature comparing traditional and modern society. Immediately you might find it helpful to 'test' the above usages of community against your own experience. Usages 1 and/or 2 might apply to your local area whereas usage 3 might apply to some experience you have had.

Problems with the concept of community

'Perfect community' – in the sense of a wholly harmonious community – is hard or impossible to create, although some come closer to achieving it than others. No doubt a Cistercian monastery is closer to perfect community than the average boarding school – though both would probably claim to be communities.

Simply to state the issue of perfect community is to indicate that it is problematic. Sociologists deal with this in two ways. First, most usages of the term build in the notion of conflict within community. Most communities, such as neighbourhoods and youth peer groups are not completely harmonious – although, in some ideal sense, they may seek to be. That leads to the second point: community is a process of building and search rather than a destination – and best studied as such. Experience and realism may tell us that conflict and community co-exist – are even part of each other – but generally members of a community seek solidarity and harmony with each other – sometimes directing hostility outwards. Third – as Anthony Cohen makes clear – community is experienced more in moments, often of a ritual or ceremonial kind, than as a constant. As Durkheim explained, these moments of communion do strengthen social solidarity. Finally, core sociological concepts such as stratification and community are necessarily general in meaning and scope. That is their strength. They are able to illuminate what is common in a variety of different contexts.

Examples of community

It is more fruitful to explore the concept of community in a general way – but aware of its various nuances – rather than to look for cases of each of the three different meanings separately. Some of the following examples emphasise locality more than community of feeling and in others, locality is transcended by feeling (e.g. world ethnic or religious communities). Because of modern communications, the spatial limits to relationships is less important. It is the changing socio-spatial pattern of relationships and networks that this chapter is largely about. All of the examples below are drawn from other parts of this book, to which page references are given.

1 Family – kin

According to Zygmunt Bauman, family is the starting point of the individual's social experience of community (some psychoanalysts argue that the original and ultimate experience of community is within the womb). Close kin can also be part of the web of primary relationships that constitute the child's experience of 'us'. As the child gets older, s/he enters other communities – peer groups, religious groups, tightly-nit neighbourhood groups and clubs. Bauman's understanding of community is exclusive as well as inclusive. Beyond 'us' are 'them' – those excluded from 'our community' (see pp. 150-3 – this section is well worth reading now).

2 Kibbutzim and communes

For members of the Kibbutzim and commune movements, family is regarded as too narrow and restrictive a basis of community. They seek a wider community usually of shared ideology (e.g., gender equality) and practice (see pp. 57-8).

3 Working and middle class communities

Class differentiates families and communities. Residential areas in Britain are more differentiated by class than in most Western societies. In traditional working class communities relations were more geographically confined and socially dense than among the more mobile residents of middle class areas.

Community studies – particularly of working class communities – were extremely popular among sociologists and

Figure 19.1 Sharing community – for a weekend. The Afro-Caribbean Notting Hill Carnival now attracts multiethnic involvement

cultural critics in the 1950s and 1960s. Controversial and sometimes sentimentalised as these studies were, several have deservedly become classics (see pp. 481-4).

4   Youth peer groups/subcultures

The extent to which youth peer groups and subcultures can operate as lifestyle communities has recently been re-emphasised (Förnas, 1995). Although class and ethnicity can divide youth, being the same age appears to provide a potential basis for mutual acceptance and recognition. Perceived or actual closure against older people is an aspect of modern youth peer group and subcultural communities. This is not necessarily a function of biology but probably of differences in authority, status and taste associated with different generations. What Berger referred to as youth 'status spheres' seek to by-pass adult authority and interference. The Who's lyric 'Hope I die before I grow old' is, nevertheless, a statement which is less appealing the more it becomes true (see pp. 469-70).

5   Ethnic communities

The interplay of culture and place or locality is nowhere more obvious than in the case of ethnic community. Particular ethnic groups are often strongly associated with given geographical areas such as Chinatown in London and Harlem the centre of Afro-American culture and community in New York. Such communities tend to exclude others from the fullest level of intimacy and belonging but also to use their uniqueness – say, in cuisine, music, or style – as a commercial and cultural meeting point with others.

The typical desire of ethnic groups for a territory or location is illustrated by the Jewish search for, and attachment to 'their homeland'. An attachment equalled by that of the Palestinians (see pp. 222-4).

6   National communities

For an entity of relatively recent invention, the nation-state has a lot of pulling power. Whereas in medieval times men died for their feudal lord, in modern times, people have marched off in their millions and died in the clash of nation states. Eric Hobsbawn argues that it is the powerful who have provided the dominant meanings of the nation-state – in Britain, the upper class. Ideologies of national superiority and empire have been closely linked in Britain and if those who perpetrated them also believed them, they were all the more effective for that. Nevertheless, whatever nation may be taken to represent, there is no doubt that the idea can capture the popular imagination.

7   Football hooligans

Football hooligans have colonised the concept of nationality and used soccer as a way of pursing violent conflict. Arguably, competition, if not conflict, is inherent in soccer and in nationalism but the 'hoolies' crucially fail to draw the line between violent and non-violent competition. Their revelling in the national flag and other patriotic regalia angers those who imagine nation in other ways than in conflict with supposed 'enemy nations'. Yet, their sense of territoriality, their nationalistic songs and symbols are drawn from mainstream national traditions and practices (See pp. 493-5).

8   Global community?

The globalisation thesis – presented fully in the next chapter – is that the world is becoming more integrated in economic, political and cultural terms. In each of these areas, there are those who espouse a notion of community but, for now, the reality is as much one of struggle and contest. Economically, there is now more talk than for some time of a world free trade community – but that can hardly take place when some national economies are so much stronger than others. Politically, the United Nations stands as a beacon to global co-operation, not least, in the area of human rights – but for the moment the UNs moral strength often counts for little against the military strength of nations and blocs. Culturally, the media – fuelled by capital – has linked the world together much more closely. However, even if a common world cultural community were desirable (and surely it would be Western dominated), it is likely that it would be resisted at national and local levels (see pp. 520-4).

9   The internet

With less than 1/2000th of the world's population in regular use of the internet, it is a little early to speculate about the extent to which it will facilitate the formation of communities. Immediately the most obvious use for the internet seems to be as a means for providing and accessing information quickly and cheaply. Already groups sharing a wide range of interests regularly communicate on the internet and with more and more adults living alone, it is possible that they will communicate more in cyber-space than face-to-face (see p. 503).

From traditional community to urban society?

There have, of course, been great changes in Western society in the last two hundred years. Crudely, we can say that Western society has moved from the traditional to the modern. Poorer societies – nearly all of them in the southern hemisphere – are today going through a similar process of change even though many are trying to control, interpret or even resist it. What we seek, therefore, are concepts and theories that explain and illuminate this near-universal pattern of change.

The shift from traditional to modern is one of the most fundamental developments in world history. Raymond Aron, the French sociologist, remarked that it was not until he visited India that he realised that the significant division in the world was not between communism and capitalism but between the modern, industrially-advanced states and those which remained industrially undeveloped. Over-simplified or not, this comment at least helps to knock aside the cultural blinkers which often obscure the way Westerners see the world.

Much modern sociology is premised on the view that there are fundamental differences between traditional and modern societies. For Marx it was capitalism and for Weber rational thinking and bureaucracy, particularly industrial bureaucracy, that brought about the transition from traditional to modern society. Here, however, it is not the causes of the change from traditional to modern society that concerns us but their respective characteristics. Tönnies, Durkheim and Simmel did much of their work in this area. Their work has been widely interpreted – with some justification – as arguing that 'community' was more characteristic of traditional than of modern societies. To what extent there actually has been a loss of community is an issue we engage directly after discussing the work of these classic sociologists and that of Talcott Parsons.

Ferdinand Tönnies and Emile Durkheim: Gemeinschaft/Gesellschaft and mechanical/organic solidarity

Tönnies and Durkheim sought to understand the change from traditional to modern society. Their major writings on this matter were published before the turn of the century and their focus was European rather than global. Nevertheless, their theories have influenced more recent thinkers, particularly those of a functionalist perspective, who have had a major interest in world development.

Ferdinand Tönnies

Tönnies in *Gemeinschaft und Gesellschaft* (1887), and Durkheim in the *Division of Labour* (1983), contrast the social life of traditional rural communities with that of rapidly developing, industrial urban areas. On the one hand, they stressed family and community as sources of identity and support and, on the other, their relative weakness in the urban context where a more individualistic and impersonal way of life was developing. Tönnies used the terms Gemeinschaft and Gesellschaft to describe this broad sweep of social change. Gemeinschaft means community and Gesellschaft can be translated either as society or association. He considered Gemeinschaft relationships to involve the whole person and to be typical of rural life. Because people related more fully to each other, and not simply in respect of their specific functional roles (shopkeeper, policeman, teacher), greater mutual involvement and caring existed, and so a stronger community was formed. Thus, a policeman was not merely somebody who did a given job, but a friend or at least an acquaintance who had a general concern for

the order and welfare of the community. The difference between the two types of relationships is summed up in the admittedly rather exaggerated and idealised contrast between the 'friendly village bobby' and the modern, car-bound officer.

Gesellschaft relationships are seen as associations or transactions for practical purposes, with little informal content. Dealings with 'modern' professionals such as lawyers or doctors tend to be of this kind. Terms that are virtually interchangeable with the rather cumbersome phrases Gemeinschaft and Gesellschaft relationships are, respectively, holistic (full) and segmental (partial) relationships. Tönnies used his key terms not only to describe relationships but also organisations. gemeinschaftlich ('community-like') organisations such as the church are stronger in traditional societies, whereas gesellschaftlich organisations, such as big businesses, are stronger in modern societies. Churches have a moral and emotional influence, whereas businesses predominate in the practical and economic spheres. These examples illustrate the deep change perceived by Tönnies from the moral/emotional quality of traditional life to the practical/rational quality of modern life.

Durkheim: mechanical and organic solidarity

Durkheim's analysis in *The Division of Labour in Society* (1907) concentrated rather more systematically than did Tönnies on the problem of how societies achieve social order and cohesion or, to use his term, social solidarity. Nevertheless, his terms, mechanical and organic solidarity, overlap and complement Tönnies' Gemeinschaft and Gesellschaft. He described solidarity in traditional societies as mechanical and in industrial societies as organic. Mechanical solidarity is the product of a uniformly accepted and strictly enforced system of belief and conduct and is facilitated by a small, homogeneous (similar) population. Classically, it occurs in so-called 'primitive' or traditional societies in which everybody shares the same religiously inspired beliefs and habits. In such societies, a person would not think of rejecting the moral consensus: personal fulfilment and identity are gained by identifying with the whole group and not through a separate sense of individuality.

A different basis of order and cohesion – organic solidarity – develops as societies become more complex. Organic solidarity is a product not of common beliefs but of shared material interests and practical interdependence. To understand this, we must first describe what Durkheim meant by the division of labour. The division of labour means that work is broken down into specialised tasks performed by different people. It is a particular feature of modern society, and assembly-line production may be considered the prime example of it. Organisationally and humanly, the division of labour divides people but it also makes them more dependent on one another. Thus, a single group of workers, say toolsetters, can bring an assembly-line to a halt by taking disruptive industrial action. Interdependence is broader than this example might imply and encompasses the whole of a modern society – a strike in the gas or electricity industries might bring other forms of industrial production to a halt. Durkheim himself succinctly reconciles the paradox of increased job or role specialisation with increased solidarity:

> *This (organic) solidarity resembles that which we observe among the higher animals. Each organ, in effect, has its special character and autonomy; and yet the unity of the organism is as great as the individuation of the parts is more marked. Because of this analogy, we propose to call the solidarity which is due to the division of labour, 'organic'.*
>
> *(1947)*

Although Durkheim commented on the strength of organic solidarity, he felt that the ultimate stability of modern society depended on finding a new moral basis of solidarity in addition to practical interdependence. He argued that without moral and normative consensus in society, people tend to suffer from anomie – a sense of normlessness or lack of moral guidance to behaviour. In such circumstances, deviant activities such as crime and suicide tend to rise. Durkheim's theory of anomie and deviance was discussed in greater detail in Chapter 12.

George Simmel

The work of George Simmel (1858-1918) echoes many of the sentiments of Tönnies and Durkheim. More than they, he attributed most that is characteristic of modern life, including 'lack of community', almost solely to the growth of the city. His stress on the impersonality and isolation of city life parallels Durkheim's concern with anomie. Simmel's particular interest in the effect of the urban environment on the individual – eloquently expressed in his essay *The Mind and the Metropolis* – places him as much within the tradition of social psychology as sociology. This essay and his work on dyads (two people) or triads (three people) have led some to claim him as a founding father of interactionism, which is the sociological perspective that gives most attention to individual psychology.

Yet Simmel also had a strong sense of structure, as his analysis of the characteristics of urban life shows. He designated urban life as rational in the sense that it involves quick, logical and calculating reactions. This is because of the many practical, money-based relationships that city life depends upon. He contrasted this to the slow, habitual quality of rural life. Quite simply, he argued that the mind became more agile in the city through sheer overstimulation. Crudely, we could say that he gives academic clothing to the popular stereotypes of 'city slicker' and 'country bumpkin.' There is no doubt, however, that like Tönnies and Durkheim, Simmel is on the side of what he sees as a receding rural past, rather than the emerging urban present. He regards the blasé and reserved attitudes necessary to cope in the city as poor change for the involvement and community of rural life, despite the greater material wealth and cultural sophistication of the city. Within it, the values of the market-place so predominate that people often

treat others as things or mere bearers of commodities and services. Like Durkheim, Simmel had great influence on the Chicago School of urban sociologists, whose work we consider shortly.

Comment on the 'community/society' model

Several comments and criticisms can be made about the community/society model. Firstly, it is suffused with conservative romanticism about the past. As a result, it tends to minimise the repressive nature of traditional community and perhaps exaggerate its satisfying aspects.

Secondly, the model largely disregards class conflict, or reduces it to the level of mere 'disequilibrium' in society. There were immense differences in wealth, power, lifestyle and prestige between people before the industrial revolution, as well as after it. The fact that the privileged position of the nobility was sanctioned by custom, tradition and religion never did convince all the peasantry that such glaring inequalities were either natural or justifiable.

Thirdly, a bi-polar or two part model of change is too simple. Durkheim himself constructed a more complex scheme of comparative change but rather than describe this in detail now, we will go on instead to consider more recent and often more complex theories of order and change.

Talcott Parsons: traditional and modern society

Parsons' attempt to analyse the transition from traditional to modern society owes something to both Durkheim and Weber. His lists of *pattern variables* (which categorise pairs of contrasting values and norms) can be regarded as an expansion of Durkheim's mechanical-organic axis of comparison. Accordingly, we can present them as follows:

Pattern variables 'A': characteristic of traditional society	Pattern variables 'B': characteristic of modern society
Ascription: The status etc. a person is given at birth, for example, king.	*Achievement:* The status a person acquires through her/his own efforts, for example, a pop star.
(Role) Diffuseness: relationships are broad or gemeinschaftlich (see above).	*(Role) Specificity:* relationships are for specific purposes or gesellschaftlich (see above).
Particularism: people treat each other in a personal way, so a farm-labourer asks 'the squire' to give his son a job.	*Universalism:* the same rules, principles or laws apply to everybody equally, as in appointing a person to a post in the civil service.

Affectivity: the expression and satisfaction of emotions is felt to be important, e.g. criminals are publicly punished, so the community can express its vengeance.

Collective orientation: shared interests are most important, for example, with the family or community.

Affective neutrality: the affective or emotional side of people is controlled so that it does not interfere with 'the job in hand', e.g. bereaved people must control their grief in public.

Self-orientation: individual interest is most important, as in the pursuit of personal success even if it distances an individual from her/his family.

Having presented Parsons' pattern variables as a contrast between traditional and modern society, we must immediately complicate the picture. First, Parsons fully recognised, as did Tönnies and Durkheim, that there can be considerable overlap between the two types of society. Indeed, it makes sense to think in terms of a graded rural-urban continuum (development) of which pattern variables 'A' and 'B' are the extremes, but which, in practice, are more likely to appear together in various 'mixes'. Further, Parsons considered that though modern society is relatively rational and affectively neutral, people do of course have feelings which they need and want to express. These feelings or 'expressive functional imperatives', as Parsons called them, find their main outlet in the kinship and cultural community sub-systems (see Chapter 21). However, what we want to emphasise here is the continuity of Parsons' model of societal types with those of Durkheim and Tönnies. As such, it hardly does more than offer a useful comparative checklist for locating given societies on a traditional-modern continuum. Thus, an Indian tribe would 'score' high under 'A', a modern state high under 'B', and an industrially developing country, such as Saudi Arabia, would show a mix. We will further evaluate Parsons' pattern variable model in the section on development later in this chapter.

The urban and community studies of the Chicago School of Sociology

The Chicago School of Sociology established an international reputation between the two world wars. Durkheim was a major influence on the urban sociology for which the school became renowned. This showed itself in two ways: first, in the clear cut contrast made between rural, 'folk' society and urban society, and also in the use of the organic analogy to describe the processes of urban life.

Louis Wirth followed Durkheim closely in making a firm distinction between rural and urban society. He defined the city in terms of three fundamental features: population size, density and heterogeneity (Wirth, 1938). These characteristics meant that though the city dweller would experience more human contacts than the rural inhabitant, he would also feel more isolated because of their emotionally 'empty' nature. Social interactions typical of

the city, those required to obtain goods and services, were seen by Wirth as impersonal, segmental (narrow in scope), superficial, transitory, and usually of a purely practical or instrumental kind. These kinds of interactions were referred to as secondary contacts. Wirth considered that secondary contacts had increased at the expense of primary contacts (which are total relationships involving emotional as well as practical content, such as those within a family). Like Durkheim, Wirth saw a partial solution to individual atomisation in the rise of voluntary associations, representative political institutions, industrial organisations and other collective or corporate organisations. However, he too did not think these provided the quality of emotional self-expression characteristic of primary group relations.

It is in the work of another urban sociologist of the Chicago School, S W Burgess, that we find the most faithful application of functionalist theory to the physical and social development of the city. Burgess describes urban processes 'as a resultant of organisation and disorganisation analogous to the anabolic and catabolic processes of metabolism in the body'. More usually, Burgess draws on plant ecology rather than human biology as a model for understanding urban processes. He writes of 'urban ecology' almost as if it is an impersonal and natural phenomenon, rather than a human creation and susceptible to control.

S W Burgess

Burgess presents a model or, as he referred to it, ideal construction, of the tendency of urban areas to expand radially from the central business district. The centre circle of the series of concentric circles in the model is the main business area. Next comes the zone of transition containing the slums and ghettos of the lower working class and immigrant groups. This zone is also characterised by cheap hotels and lodging houses and the easy availability of drink and sex. Other descriptions of this zone used by Chicago sociologists still sometimes employed are 'twilight zone' and 'zone of deterioration'. Earlier we looked in some detail at the analysis of 'lower class deviance' within this zone, developed by sociologists at the University of Chicago (Chapter 12, pp. 351-2). The next zone contains the homes of more successful and respectable working class people: it is an area of escape from the ghetto. Beyond are the higher class residential areas which make up the next zone. Finally, there is the commuter zone interspersed with countryside and farmland and merging into predominantly rural areas.

In his own day, Burgess' model was far from universally applicable – even in the United States. Since the Second World War, residential patterns have become still further complicated, particularly in countries such as England and Holland, where public housing projects have often been built outside the central urban zones. As a guide to the physical location of particular social groups and as a way of understanding why these groups inhabit particular areas, Burgess's work is inadequate. It does make the point, however, that social groups are cut off from one another both spatially and in their way of life or culture. Other urban sociologists, including Hoyt, have argued that a sectoral model provides a more accurate description of the patterns of neighbourhood layout. More recently, B T Robson's carefully researched study of residential patterns in Sunderland found that Hoyt's model applied closely to the south of the city, and Burgess's somewhat less precisely to the north.

Criticisms of the Chicago school

Sociologists now consider other issues to be more important than the functioning of various urban zones as such. One such issue is to explain how physical and spatial environments affect people's social and cultural opportunities and the nature and quality of their interactions. We can refer to this type of analysis as socio-spatial. A further sociological concern is to identify the factors that enable some social and ethnic groups to live in 'desirable' neighbourhoods and which force others to live in slums. A major criticism of the sociologists of the Chicago school is that they largely ignored this problem. Their work is descriptive rather than explanatory. Instead of examining how the free market system in land and property affected socio-spatial systems, they assumed these effects to be 'natural' and therefore did not analyse what caused them. Because they did not adequately examine how the control of wealth and power affects residential patterns and community life, their work can be said to be clearly limited by their own belief in, or ideological commitment to, capitalism.

Further the Chicago School underestimates both the survival of community in the city and the ability of people to express themselves in apparently impersonal contexts such as the modern city.

Anthony Cohen's criticism of the Chicago School

Cohen argues that the Chicago School severely misinterpreted Durkheim. Cohen contends that Durkheim considered that there are elements of organic solidarity in mechanical societies and elements of mechanical solidarity in organic societies. He quotes Durkheim as follows: 'These two societies really make up only one. They are two aspects of one and the same reality'. Cohen goes on to say: 'The complementary of the two modes was, however, largely neglected by the Chicago scholars who used Durkheim's dichotomy as a paradigm for their own distinctions between urban and rural societies' (25).

In fairness, however, the quite sharp distinction between the rural/urban and traditional/modern seems to be a feature of all the sociologists discussed above, including Durkheim, not just the Chicago School.

Community studies: testing the 'loss of community' thesis

The works we have so far discussed have been at the level of 'grand theory'. Perhaps the best way of testing the ideas presented in them is by means of the community study. Of course, it is impossible to go back and examine at first hand what community was once like, but at least the persistent stereotype that community has declined can be measured against real cases. In addition, the world offers many examples of traditional as well as modern communities and these can be studied for comparative purposes. Our first case study is of just such a kind.

Some case studies

Redfield and Lewis

In the 1930s, Robert Redfield published a study of social life in Tepoztlan, a Mexican village. He found a stable, well-integrated and harmonious community. In 1949 an account of the same village appeared, written by Oscar Lewis. He discovered a tense, divided and distrustful community. It seems highly probable that some of the apparent 'change' lay in the eyes of the beholder rather than in the social life of the people of Tepoztlan. More precisely, the two researchers approached the village with different expectations and theoretical perspectives: Redfield was predisposed to find community, and Lewis was conscious of the degradation that poverty can produce in traditional societies. Howard Newby, who has a keen eye for the relationship between sociologists' personal values, their choice of theoretical and methodological approach, and their ultimate 'findings', describes the discrepancy between the reports of Redfield and Lewis as 'unnerving'. It reminds us that despite sociologists' impressive battery of research apparatus, they, like others, sometimes end up seeing what they want to see. With due caution, therefore, it can only be said that Lewis further opened up the doubts about the gemeinschaftlich qualities of traditional communities.

Herbert Gans and Willmott and Young

Studies of urban life, however, have raised questions about the Gesellschaft side of the comparative model. Herbert Gans' *The Urban Villagers* describes the lively, 'village-like' ethnic and working class communities of Boston's West End and New York's Lower East Side. The individual is seldom isolated, but supported by informal groups of family, kin and friends. We have already referred to Willmott and Young's Bethnal Green study which was published in 1957. Some 70 years after Tönnies mourned the passing of community, Willmott and Young found a thriving community in an inner city industrial area. They emphasise especially how 'mum' figures are at the centre of local interactions, creating what they describe as 'matrifocal communities' (see p. 62). The key link in the traditional working class extended family is the relationship between mother and daughter. This continues when the daughter is married because of the likelihood that the newly married couple will live close to the female's family of origin or, in the early days of marriage, actually in her parents' home. Traditionally, men spent much of their leisure time separately from women in pubs and Working Men's or Labour Clubs. This pattern of segregation has long been breaking down, though there are still public bars in some areas where 'respectable' women would not drink, even in male company. Working class children of all ages tend to be left to get on with their own lives much more than middle class children and 'playing out in the backs' or 'on the streets' can be a major activity until well into adolescence, especially for boys. Any 'mischief they get up to' is likely to be met with rougher parental justice than a middle class child would normally expect to receive. Traditional working class community is woven in a web of 'talk' and 'gossip' and in the passing of time together in ways more or less amusing or practically useful. There are reserved areas of personal and family privacy but the whole is or was, relatively open, collective and social.

The waning of the above pattern of life might be regarded as a second phase – and, perhaps, a more genuine one – in 'loss of community'. But the fact that traditional working class community is breaking up does not mean it never existed. Some recent commentators, because they no longer find thriving working class communities of the kind described 40 years ago by Willmott and Young, seem almost to assume that the whole phenomenon is a romantic fiction. But one of the reasons for chronicling traditional working class life was an awareness of its imminent decline.

Another development that has undermined any simplistic rural-urban contrast is the fast growth of commuter villages. In *Urbs in Rure (The City in the Countryside)*, R E Pahl draws our attention to the commuter invasion of rural areas. Some villages are almost wholly occupied by people who work elsewhere. Pahl has also written of the culture clash between indigenous village inhabitants and commuters. The irony is that in their search for community, commuters sometimes destroy what they are looking for. Other studies have shown that class division, business rationality and many of the problems of isolation and anomie frequently associated with urban life also occur in rural Britain.

In addition to the above case studies, it is worth recalling that historical enquiry has also thrown doubt on notions of traditional community, at least in so far as they depended on the predominance of the extended family (see Chapter 3, pp. 61-2).

Some general points of criticism of the 'loss of community' thesis

The empirical data discussed in the previous section provides a tentative basis from which to make some general criticisms of the 'loss of community' thesis.

1 Firstly, it is an oversimplification. At both 'ends' of the continuum we have found evidence to contradict the model.
2 Secondly, a related point: the model seems to underestimate the capacity of people to rebuild community in new circumstances after the break-up of their old communities.
3 Thirdly, the ideological limits of the model need to be criticised. It is characterised by conservative nostalgia. As a result, it tends to miss or minimise the unpleasant aspects of traditional society. From this limited perspective, a crucial theoretical flaw emerges – which brings us to our fourth point.

4 The model has little use for class or class conflict in the analysis of community life. It takes as a 'given' the capitalist system instead of examining how this system shapes social life. More recent work has sought to rectify this imbalance. Indeed, it has tended to argue that it is precisely what the above critics ignored – capitalism and resultant class divisions – that account for the lack of community which so concerned them. Before examining these conflict-based approaches, however, we will briefly review the new towns movement in Britain which, among other things, represented a 'search for' better communities than had developed in the urban environment of industrialism.

The new towns: an attempt to create better communities

The new town concept, first popularised around the turn of the century by Ebenezer Howard, was an attempt to plan social idealism into reality. Howard's 'bread and roses' idealism aimed at providing the city dweller with improved housing in less crowded neighbourhoods with conveniently available facilities, but he also advocated sacrosanct agricultural areas around the town, and wanted to erode class barriers by introducing socially mixed neighbourhoods. Welwyn Garden City, one of the early new towns (1920), probably came closest to the fulfilment of Howard's dream but more recent new town developments tend to have been less ambitiously conceived. Notwithstanding the inevitable crop of mistakes and complaints there is no doubt that, in terms of basic amenities provided, the new towns are a vast improvement on what they replaced. One woman in Milton Keynes said: 'It's like being in paradise compared to where I used to live.' There is no doubt, despite her choice of metaphor, that she was thinking in terms of such things as an upstairs bathroom, spacious lounge, perhaps central heating, and having a toilet which belonged to her own house and which worked properly. Against the backcloth of inner city decay (which we examine shortly), the new towns represented a substantial improvement in the standard of life of most who moved to them. Nevertheless, only a small percentage of migrants from the inner city have gone to new towns. Crucially, from the point of view of the decline of the inner city, these have often been skilled or semi-skilled workers and their families.

As an attempt to tinker with the class system by introducing 'socially balanced' neighbourhoods, the new towns have been less successful. A useful piece of research in this area is B J Heraud's *Social Class and the New Towns – A Detailed Study of Social Class in Crawley*. One of Heraud's crucial findings is that movement out of the originally mixed social class areas was usually to social class defined communities. This was especially true of middle class families. The original balanced areas tended to become socially more working class whereas the middle class moved into the new subsidised housing areas. As Heraud points out, however, the commitment of the town's Urban Development Corporation to social balance seemed to weaken progressively, and it is possible that a more sustained experiment would be more successful. In the middle 1970s, as the total population went into slight decline and it became clear that the inner cities were, if anything, under- rather than over-populated. New town developments tended to slow down or be abandoned. Stonehouse, which was to have been near Glasgow, and the planned central Lancashire new town, reputedly to have been named Red Rose, stayed on the drawing board. It may be that this slackening in momentum will provide opportunity to adjust to, and improve on, the changes that have already taken place.

The new towns, therefore, have provided materially better communities than elsewhere, but not socially very different ones. In particular, they, too, are characterised by class division. Given that they exist in a predominantly capitalist society, this is probably inevitable.

The English and the rural idyll

The new towns are only the best known example of the notorious English obsession with the pastoral. The search for the rural idyll continues as we approach the second millennium. Between 1984 and 1994, the population in the metropolitan areas tended to fall while that in areas such as East Anglia and counties such as Cambridgeshire and Buckinghamshire, grew. It is the non-metropolitan areas that are projected to experience most of the population growth up to 2011.

In seeking to understand why so many English are gripped by the rural idyll, it is important to be clear about which groups tend to leave the cities and which – still in fewer numbers – gravitate towards it. As Pahl noted over a quarter of a century ago, it is still largely the middle class who opt for 'rural life'. To these must be added increasing numbers of the self-employed and retired. Those moving in the opposite direction tend to be younger people – mainly students and young professionals on whom any hope for sustained urban revival probably rests.

The dislike of many English middle class people of living in the city dates back to the industrial revolution and reflects the class basis of English society – occupationally, residentially and culturally. England – the first industrial nation – gave over its inner urban areas to more severe, complete and rapid industrial development than occurred in other European countries. As Engels and Dickens show in their different ways, the mid-Victorian inner city was not one in which the middle class would aspire to live. The very wealthy bourgeorsie had built or bought from declining aristocrats their own country mansions – a process that thrives today in the highly unequal 1990s. The very wealthy have been steadily followed by members of the professional and managerial middle classes. All this is in some contrast to what historically has tended to happen in other major cities of Western Europe. Thus, Paris and Milan – although not without ghettos – and many major provincial French and Italian cities can claim to be 'bourgeoisefied' in a way that has not happened in England. Very recently, the postindustrial landscaping of numerous urban areas in Britain, including some up-market residential developments, has given a face-lift to some inner and central urban areas in Britain. There are even signs of a revival of civic awareness and vitality in a number of cities including Birmingham and Manchester.

Nevertheless, the English preference for the pastoral persists. Robin McKie suggests that, ironically, the English may be damaging precisely that rural beauty that many of them so eagerly seek (see Reading 1). He comments that:

> (U)rban antipathy in now irrevocably damaging our entire landscape, a trend that so alarms planners and geographers that they are pressing for major investment programmes and tight rural planning restrictions to halt the destruction.
>
> (The Observer, 26.5.1996:19)

… and what about Scotland? Who owns it?

Despite the strong impact of the industrial revolution there the development of Scotland's major cities has been somewhat distinct from those of England. Edinburgh is more European in appearance and concept than English cities. The majestic Princes Street is flanked on one side by sloped gardens leading up to the castle and on the other by Georgian streets, partly residential and partly professional and commercial. Glasgow was more shaped and scarred by industry but was revitalised in the 1980s and 1990s partly under the stimulus of being selected as a European City of Culture. Ancient cities such as Perth and Stirling have retained much of their traditional appearance although they are not without areas of commercial modernity and low income housing.

The socio-spatial issue for Scotland is not so much the appearance of or lack of vitality of its urban areas as the question of who owns its land. According to Andy Wightman, author of *Who Owns Scotland?* (1996), about half of Scotland is owned by about 500 people of whom probably less than half are Scots. Figure 19.2 lists the national origin of some recent purchasers of large amounts of Scottish land and property. According to Rachel Kelly the result is 'a sea-change in the ownership of the Scottish Highlands and Islands':

> No longer are vast wildernesses owned by families who have gone hunting, shooting and fishing for generations. In their stead are self-made millionaires from Egypt, the Netherlands, Dubai, Hong Kong and America and a crop of environmental and conservation groups.
>
> (The Times: 6.3.1996:41)

Foreign investment can contribute to raising the general wealth of an area. In 1992, Scotland rose to become the fourth richest region in the United Kingdom, in terms of average personal income per head (see p. 562). However, there is no such individual as the 'average person' and this statistic may actually reflect the great wealth of a relatively few people. Scotland provides a classic case of economic globalisation and the issues of wealth distribution and national independence the process raises.

Conclusion: England; Scotland; global capitalism

The above consideration of the English rural idyll and the question of who owns Scotland both show that the relationship of the urban to the rural is far more complex than earlier accounts indicated. The development of capitalism – industrial and agricultural – has increasingly blurred many of the assumed differences between the rural and the urban. Capitalism restructures rural areas just as readily as it does urban ones – hindered only by government or social movements/local protest. For instance, the owner of the Blackford estate in Perthshire was recently accused by locals of abandoning farms on the slopes of the Ochil Hills – presumably for economic or other reasons. The owner could be virtually anybody but it makes the conduct of protest and opposition more difficult that it happens to be His Excellency Mahdi Mohammed Al Tajur, of the United Arab Emirates.

The other factor which is common between city and countryside is that, to a greater or lesser extent, people do form communities – in the broadest sense – or associations. Frequently, people object to 'development' – using either local government channels or more direct forms of protest – and, again, such action is no respector of geographical boundaries.

But if the processes that drive urban and rural development are fundamentally the same, there are still some differences between city and countryside. These are, as Wirth noted, that the city has more numerous, and more varied, people in a more limited space. This means, as Simmel noted, that aspects of city life are more impersonal because there are more people whom the individual does not know. These factors can exacerbate problems of housing, the environment and crime but it is socio-economic processes that structure both the urban and rural contexts.

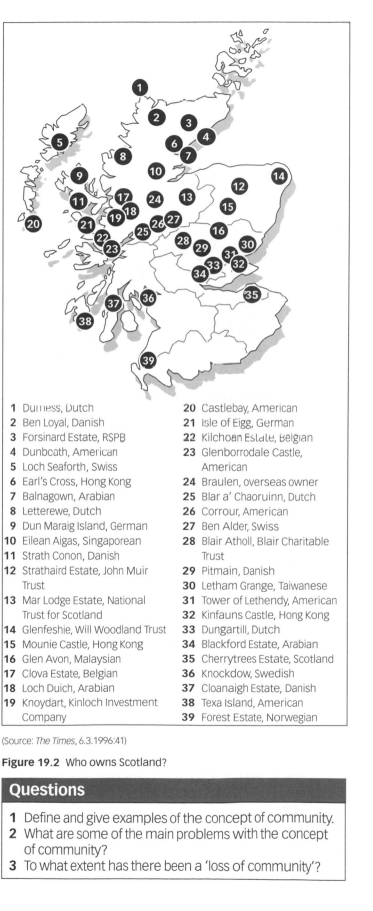

1	Durness, Dutch	20	Castlebay, American
2	Ben Loyal, Danish	21	Isle of Eigg, German
3	Forsinard Estate, RSPB	22	Kilchoan Estate, Belgian
4	Dunbeath, American	23	Glenborrodale Castle, American
5	Loch Seaforth, Swiss	24	Braulen, overseas owner
6	Earl's Cross, Hong Kong	25	Blar a' Chaoruinn, Dutch
7	Balnagown, Arabian	26	Corrour, American
8	Letterewe, Dutch	27	Ben Alder, Swiss
9	Dun Maraig Island, German	28	Blair Atholl, Blair Charitable Trust
10	Eilean Aigas, Singaporean	29	Pitmain, Danish
11	Strath Conon, Danish	30	Letham Grange, Taiwanese
12	Strathaird Estate, John Muir Trust	31	Tower of Lethendy, American
13	Mar Lodge Estate, National Trust for Scotland	32	Kinfauns Castle, Hong Kong
14	Glenfeshie, Will Woodland Trust	33	Dungartill, Dutch
15	Mounie Castle, Hong Kong	34	Blackford Estate, Arabian
16	Glen Avon, Malaysian	35	Cherrytrees Estate, Scotland
17	Clova Estate, Belgian	36	Knockdow, Swedish
18	Loch Duich, Arabian	37	Cloanaigh Estate, Danish
19	Knoydart, Kinloch Investment Company	38	Texa Island, American
		39	Forest Estate, Norwegian

(Source: *The Times*, 6.3.1996:41)

Figure 19.2 Who owns Scotland?

Questions

1 Define and give examples of the concept of community.
2 What are some of the main problems with the concept of community?
3 To what extent has there been a 'loss of community'?

Conflict-based models of urban-rural analysis: Marxist and Weberian

Marxist urban-rural perspectives

It is not only Marxist critics who find the ultimate cause of both urban and rural inequality and decay in the nature of capitalism, but the roots of such an analysis are certainly to be found in the writings of Marx and his colleague Engels. Unlike Durkheim and Tönnies, Marx's starting point for understanding society was not community or lack of it, but the nature of capitalism. Marx believed that national and international community would be part of a genuinely communist world but he did not consider that such community was possible under capitalism: competition and class conflict prevented it. Only within classes did he consider that community and solidarity (a sense of unity and mutual support) were normal, although he envisaged that the capitalist ruling class would seek to produce a 'false' sense of national community so as to reduce class conflict and consolidate its own interests (see Chapters 8 and 11).

Castells: (capitalist) consumer city

The contemporary Marxist, Manuel Castells, contextualises his analysis of urban life within a broad critique of capitalism. Like Marx, he considers that industrial cities in modern capitalist societies developed as a result of the centralisation of production. The early stages of capitalist production required a large, conveniently recruitable labour force. However, Castells regards the capitalist city of the post-Second World War era as increasingly a *location of consumption* rather than just production which has become increasingly geographically dispersed. Much consumption is public – education, health, transport, social services – as well as private. Castells considers that the working class has a particular concern with issues relating to collective consumption i.e. mainly of Welfare State services although he fully recognises that other social classes may become involved in urban issues (or, equally, rural or suburban issues). He refers to any group which sustains an involvement in an urban issue as an urban social movement and his analysis of this phenomenon is one of his major theoretical contributions.

Urban social movements

Stuart Lowe has suggested that there have been three phrases in the development of Castells' analysis of urban social movements (1986). In the first phase, Castells stressed that the primary contradiction in capitalist society is that between capital and labour and that urban social movement based on consumption are of secondary importance to the primary class conflict based on work-place relations. In the second phase of his theoretical development

Castells describes urban social movements as dealing with 'a new source of inequality' based on consumption rather than production which may be independent both of the class system and established political parties. Thus, local movements concerned with the damage to private or public property of, say, transport 'development' often cross both class and party lines in their 'membership'. In his third phase, Castells describes urban social movements as primary sources of change, independent of class and institutional politics. He describes the core characteristics or urban social movements as a concern with issues of consumption, as drawing on community (i.e. cross-class support), and as seeking a high degree of local democratic autonomy and decentralisation of service provision from the central state. Again, it is possible to suggest at least a partial example in the British context in the various locally based movements that opposed central government's cuts in health and other welfare services (and, some would argue, the anti-poll tax campaign).

More recently, Castells has taken further the idea that 'the city' is constantly being reshaped by wider forces: economic (consumption now more than production), financial, demographic and cultural. In *The Information City* (1989) he argues that the increasing volume and speed of information flow accelerates processes of change, the historic emergence of the space of flows, superseding the meaning of the space of places (348). 'Power rules through flows' – on which the city depends, i.e. flows of money, information.

Comment on Castells

Several comments can be offered on Castells' theory of social movements. First, as he is aware, any given movement is unlikely to survive for more than a few years at most, unless it feeds into the institutionalised political system and, in particular, establishes links with political parties. Given this, what Castells is describing as urban social movements are, in fact, essentially contemporary types of pressure groups. Second movements concerned with matters of consumption are not exclusive to the urban context but can also occur in suburban and rural areas. Castells concentrates on the urban context because it remains the primary location of the capitalist economy and government and of the majority of consumers.

Finally, it is possible to draw out of Castells' urban theory a highly non-Marxist conclusion. Indeed, this appears to have been accomplished by one of Castells' British interpreters, Peter Saunders. Saunders argues that as people become more consumer-oriented – notably, in respect to a preference for private home ownership rather than rented tenancies – they are likely to become less politically radical. However, it is equally possible to argue that social movements that reflect the demands of black people, of women, and of the environmentally concerned can most logically be incorporated into a radical agenda and party. Castells argues that one element of social movements is a concern for meaning and values. Racial justice in, for instance, employment and housing, adequate day-care facilities to allow mothers to do paid work, and an adequately protected environment, are all matters which may require radical policies and actions. (For a full account of social movements, see pp. 316-8).

Weberian urban-rural perspectives

According to Weber, the most fundamental and enduring feature of a city is that it functions as a market-place. As he put it: '(t)o constitute a full urban community a settlement must display a relative predominance of trade-commercial relations'. The complexity of urban commercial and other activity requires a local government, administration and law. In other words, like Tönnies, Weber considered that much urban life is directed by associational (rational-functional) and often contractually-based activity. The core urban activity, as Weber saw it, is 'trading-commercial'.

John Rex and Robert Moore: the housing market and housing classes

Writing broadly within the Weberian tradition, John Rex and Robert Moore examined the position of black people in relation to housing allocation (*Race, Community and Conflict*, 1967). They consider 'that the basic process underlying urban social interaction is competition for scarce and desired types of housing' (274). They describe two main modes of housing allocation. First, is allocation through the private market by means of which most of the middle and much of the skilled working class acquire housing. Second, is the allocation of public housing through local government bureaucracy. An individual's strength or weakness in relation to housing allocation places her or him in a particular housing class. In the inner-city area of Sparkbrook, Birmingham, Rex and Moore discerned seven housing classes and considered it likely that the same or similar classes occurred in other inner-city areas. These classes are:

- Outright owners of large houses in desirable areas.
- Owners with mortgages wholly occupying houses in desirable areas.
- Council house tenants.
- Council house tenants in slum dwellings designated for demolition;.
- Tenants wholly occupying houses owned by a private landlord.
- Owners of houses bought with short-term loans who need to let rooms to meet repayments.
- Tenants of rooms in lodging-houses.

Rex and Moore concluded that in the mid 1960s black immigrants, both Afro-Caribbean and Asian, tended to be disproportionately concentrated in lower housing classes compared to the whole population (with the partial exception of Irish immigrants). A main reason for this which applied to both private and public housing was racial discrimination. This could occur as a result of prejudice by estate agents, vendors, mortgage providers, or public housing officials. What Rex later referred to as institutional racism (see p. 219) also played a part in hampering access by black people to public housing. A major example of institutional racism given by Rex is that the length of residency requirement for allocation to council housing automatically prevented recent immigrants from accessing this type of property (although this now applies only to a small percentage of black people).

In a later volume, written with Sally Thompson, Rex argues that it is in the context of neighbourhoods of low-quality housing that a 'black underclass' develops (1979). The other major aspect contributing to this process is the low pay of many black workers, to which racial discrimination is also a factor. The extent to which Rex considers that members of the black 'underclass' are likely collectively to organise to defend and promote their own interests is discussed on pp. 228-9.

Consumption and social movements

Rex and Moore stress that relations to the means of consumption (in this case the consumption of housing) as well as relations to the means of production (i.e. occupation) can structure social relations in the city. Thus, Rex found some evidence that people might organise as housing classes as well as occupational classes, although he thought that this was occurring through existing voluntary organisations such as community associations and churches rather than through new organisations. In his emphasis on consumption and the possibility of social movements arising around consumption issues, Rex is close to the position adopted by Manuel Castells some years later. Some Marxists see this emphasis as a departure from the orthodox Marxist analysis that roots all major social conflict in the relations by social groups to the means of production. Whatever view one takes, it is clear that in an age of increasing consumption, the issue is an urgent one for Marxists to consider. Rex and Moore can claim to have grappled with it some years before even Castells.

The socio-spatial effects of capitalism: rural and urban

The separation here of the social and socio-spatial effects of capitalism is purely for the purposes of presentation and in recognition of the fact that the use of space has been of particular interest to both Marxist and Weberian sociologists in recent years. Clearly, the amount and quality of the space people occupy and enjoy is a major feature of their social life. The spatial question is, therefore, primarily a social rather than a physical issue as far as we are concerned. 'Space' is rather an abstract word, but what is meant is that identifiably different groups of people occupy different 'bits of territory' within a given society. Thus, as we saw, black immigrants are over-represented in inner-city areas as, for that matter, are poor whites. The middle class predominates in suburbia, although, as Herbert Gans has shown, this is something of an oversimplification as far as the United States is concerned. What sociologists seek to do is to explain why some groups occupy more and better space (both environmentally and in terms of amenities) than others. Put as simply as possible, why do some people live in bigger and better houses and less crowded and more attractive neighbourhoods than others?

The answer given to the above question by the social geographer, David Harvey, is the same as that offered by Castells and by Rex and Moore. The problems associated with the city – housing, environmental decay, poverty, crime – are not caused by the city as such, but by the way the socio-economic system affects the city. In other words, the problems are socio-economic rather than essentially urban in nature. It is the unequal way in which the employment, housing and consumer markets work nationally (and internationally) that is the main cause of these problems. Logically, therefore, these problems can also occur outside the urban environment in places where the capitalist system favours some of the expense of others. As we have seen, R E Pahl's appropriately titled *Urbs in Rure* (1965) makes exactly this point: high-income commuters and 'second-house' weekend visitors introduce new class divisions and material and status inequalities into rural society. Raymond Williams, however, makes the point that class divisions, including the glaring juxtaposition of ostentatious wealth and humiliating poverty, have long been a feature of rural life. He stresses that the capitalistic development of agriculture has often been as hard on the peasantry as industrial development has been on the urban proletariat. Indeed, originally it was partly because the peasantry were dispossessed of their land by the agricultural revolution that they spilled into the cities in search of work. This sort of systematic socio-economic analysis is far from either the static concentric circles model of Burgess or the simple rural-urban continuum of Tönnies. The latter are even more remote from Castell's analysis of power in relation to communication 'space'.

Locality and economic restructuring: Britain in global context

It has been a main theme of this section that particular localities or socio-economic areas are fundamentally affected by wider forces largely beyond their control. As Philip Cooke put it, much of local life 'is increasingly, controlled by global political and economic forces' (1989:1). Cooke has edited a book, *Localities*, which examines these 'forces' and the responses to them of people in localities in respect to seven local areas: Thanet; Swindon; Cheltenham; south west Birmingham; Liverpool; Lancaster; and Middlesbrough. The key process studied in the book is the 'restructuring' of the British economy. The term restructuring means reshaping, and in part rebuilding of the economy. It is generally considered that Britain underwent a period of economic restructuring from the 1960s in which the economy was changed decisively from being a predominantly manufacturing one (up to the mid 1950s) to being predominantly a service one. This process is not completed and, indeed, economies continuously change, but its main effects are probably now apparent (see Figure 19.3).

Manufacturing and non-manufacturing employees in employment (United Kingdom)

(Source: *Employment Gazette*, June 1991)

Figure 19.3 Economic change changed the socio-spatial 'shape' of Britain

It is the socio-spatial effects of restructuring that is of primary interest here (the occupational aspects are discussed in Chapter 6 and the technological/work-organisation aspects in Chapter 9). As Cooke remarks, '(b)y showing detailed patterns of change at locality level it is possible to gain some indication of the spatially uneven distribution of advantage and disadvantage as it has developed'. In going on to discuss some of these changes, Cooke is at pains to point out that people are not necessarily helpless victims of such change but interact with, and initiate change themselves:

The most important employment location tendencies in the 1970s were metropolitan deindustrialisation and the urbanisation of the countryside. Substantial shifts of population and employment from cities were in part an effect of the failure by older, city-based UK firms to compete with those from overseas. But movements of this kind may also be an expression of changed preference in residential location, in this case for what may be perceived as a 'rural idyll'*. In the past the process of suburbanisation that produced the urban sprawl of the interwar years arose as jobs followed residential development, especially when employers realised that the suburbs contained sizeable pools of relatively cheap, female labour (Hobsbawn, 1968; Mills, 1973; Scott, 1982). As Scott (1982) points out, though, while a multiplicity of 'factors' are at work in the decentralisation process only a few of these can be seen in operation using information about employment change. To be interested in the changing nature of localities as distinct from local economics involves tracing changes in their

> *social composition and, for example, the extent to which private as against public consumption of services, density of white or blue collar occupation, or level of professional qualification may have varied from place to place over time.*
>
> (Cooke, 1989:4)
>
> * see p. 556 and pp. 571-2

Although Cooke stresses that the seven selected localities are not in any sense statistically representative of the 334 'travel-to-work' areas in the United Kingdom, they were selected to illustrate the restructuring process. Overall, the studies show a prospering south, at the core of which is London's financial, governmental, cultural and tourist-attracting capacity and dynamism (Figure 19.4), and a de-industrialised north (i.e. with a substantially reduced manufacturing capacity and concentration of employment in manufacturing). In addition to London, other southern urban areas such as Swindon and Cheltenham have also attracted investment – significantly for manufacturing as well as service development. Cooke explains this partly in terms of the more 'flexible' suppliers and workforces more common in the south and contrasts these with the entrenched union power and traditional labour and managerial styles associated with northern manufacturing industry. Cooke emphasises that there are variations and exceptions within the contrasting 'north-south' stereotype and that each locality requires specific analysis. Thus, Lancaster in the north had a much higher growth in producer services than the national average between 1971 and 1981 and Swindon in the south grew rapidly in both manufacturing and services employment between 1981 and 1984.

Figure 19.4 London: global financial centre = local wealth

(a) Regional unemployment

Unemployed as percentage of workforce
Oct 1989 (1979 in brackets)

UK Average 5.9 (4.0)
London 4.7 (2.7)

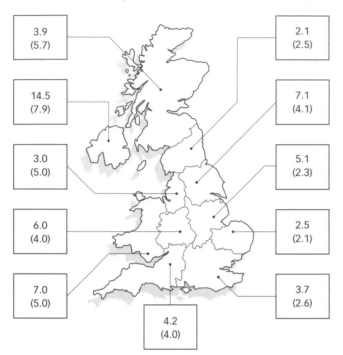

3.9 (5.7)	2.1 (2.5)
14.5 (7.9)	7.1 (4.1)
3.0 (5.0)	5.1 (2.3)
6.0 (4.0)	2.5 (2.1)
7.0 (5.0)	3.7 (2.6)
4.2 (4.0)	

(b) Personal income in Britain's regions

Income per head, 1992

☐ £9,500 and over   ▨ £8,700 – £8,900
▨ £8,900 – £9,500   ■ £8,700 and below

		£6,000	£10,000
UK average		9,493	
Greater London	1	11,577	
South East	2	10,478	
East Anglia	3	10,478	
Scotland	4	9,528	
South West	5	9,405	
East Midlands	6	9,035	
West Midlands	7	8,955	
Yorkshire and Humberside	8	8,858	
West Midlands	9	8,848	
North	10	8,837	
Northern Ireland	11	7,986	
Wales	12	7,980	

(Source: *The Guardian*, 1.6.1994:3)

Figure 19.5 Regional diversity in the UK

As a result of the above trends, more high paying occupations tend to be in London and the south east and more low paying occupations elsewhere. This results in a marked difference in average pay between the south east and the rest (see Figure 19.5 which also shows regional differences in unemployment).

Unequal economic development and inequalities of income and wealth, in turn, cause inequalities of health, educational attainment, and differences in consumption and lifestyle between regions. These differences are discussed in class, gender, racial and age terms elsewhere in this book, but it is important also to remember that they have a regional and economic developmental dimension. Inequalities between regions are also reflected in the tendency for the south to vote Conservative and the north to vote Labour. An extreme example of this is that the ten constituencies with the highest unemployment all returned Labour MPs in 1987, whereas the ten constituencies with the lowest unemployment all returned Conservative MPs (see Chapter 11, p. 323). In the former case all the constituencies were north of the Trent and in the latter case, they were south of it.

Although the general analysis offered in the 'Localities' study is likely to remain relevant to trends in the 1990s, the latest data it draws on are for 1987. Since then there may have been a modest reduction in the differences between north and south. First, there has been an increase in investment (particularly foreign investment) in parts of the north, particularly the north east, and in certain industries in Scotland and Wales (see Table 19.1). In the latter case, there has been no revival in the traditional extractive industries but expansion has occurred in electronics and financial services.

It appears that the national economy is becoming increasingly dominated by the service sector. Second, the economic recession of the early 1990s initially affected the south east more than the north. Indeed, the early 1990s recession affected the service sector perhaps as much as the manufacturing sector. The overall effect of the recession may be slightly to reduce inequalities between south and north.

Table 19.1 Employment changes in Wales

	1978	**1990**	**Percentage**
Electronics	13,000	23,000	+77
Financial services	43,000	68,000	+58
Coal	39,000	4,000	−90
Iron and steel	63,000	18,000	−70

Question

What theory or theories do you consider best explain economic, social and environmental change in urban and rural localities?

Class and group conflict in the local context: capital, politicians, planners and citizens

We now discuss the local context in terms of groups which have power and those which have little or none. The groups we will consider are business people, politicians, miscellaneous 'gate-keepers' and the citizens . Two conflict theories should be noted as reference points for interpretation in this section. First is the pluralist, rooted in Weber, which regards multi (plural) group conflict as essential to liberal democracy. Second, is the Marxist, which places group conflict in what Marxists consider to be the more profound context of class conflict.

Capital

Business people have power to affect the lives of other people. Investment provides work and a basis for prosperity, and lack of it causes unemployment and social hardship. The fact that we tend today to think of business mainly in terms of large national and international companies and institutions may make economic power seem more impersonal, but the effects of it are real enough. When, in 1991, Rolls Royce decided to switch some of its production to Germany, there was relatively little its British employees could do about it. It is worth illustrating again the extent to which Britain's economy is exceptionally global in nature. Britain's companies invest more abroad (outward direct investment) and foreign companies invest more in Britain (inward direct investment) as a percentage of GDP than any other leading industrial country (see Figure 19.6) This gives the multinationals – British and foreign-involved – great flexibility and power. Investment can, of course, raise the living standards of local workforces and of local areas but it does so at the cost of independence – if labour 'misbehaves', capital can withdraw. Of course, matters may be more complex, especially if the foreign company has invested heavily in plant, equipment and training. Nevertheless, the current balance of power lies strongly with capital. All this can greatly affect local development. It is true that trade unionists are beginning to respond to the international nature of many large companies by organising internationally themselves, but they often lack the resources and experience to do so effectively.

Politicians

National and local politicians are a second group whose power affects others. As elected representatives of the people, their policies ought to benefit the public though this does not always seem to happen. Let us look at local government first. Joe Chamberlain, as mayor of Birmingham in the 1870s, was an early urban reformer who successfully sought to improve the public amenities and standard of health of his city. His achievements were a model for

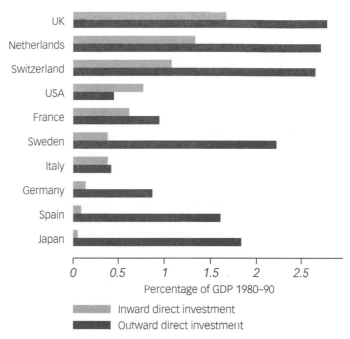

(Source: CBI in *The Independent*, 22.2.1996)

Figure 19.6 International comparison of foreign direct investment (FDI)

other local politicians concerned with the standard of public amenities in their areas and were the prelude to great advances in civic provisions. Not all local authorities, however, have matched what he helped to inspire. Theoretically, government should be 'above' sectional interest and seek to serve the common good. This involves placing checks and controls on the activity of business. There is always a danger, however, that government may favour business 'development' at the expense of others. Sometimes it even happens that the immense revenues controlled by local authorities which are the practical basis of their power and patronage are mis-spent. Much of the design and construction of public works such as the building of roads and houses is contracted out by local authority officials to private companies of builders and architects. Inevitably, this sometimes leads to corruption. An example is the case of T Dan Smith, the leading politician on Newcastle's Labour-dominated Council in the early 1970s. Smith was found guilty of giving contracts to architect John Poulson in return for bribes and favours. Such clear-cut cases of corruption are rarely proven but sometimes Council contracts do seem to favour the interests of commercial developers rather than the public.

In the 1980s, central government partly by-passed local government in the area of urban renewal by setting up Urban Development Corporations. By far the biggest was London's Dockside Corporation. A frequent complaint by local residents was that developers and 'outsider, yuppie' purchasers of property benefited from the development, but they themselves did not. More recent urban policy is reviewed below (see pp.565-7).

Planners

A third 'group' which has power in the city is made up of planners, architects, state and local authority bureaucrats, welfare workers, and managers of banks and building societies, 'gate-keepers' as Pahl refers to them. We include them together mainly as a matter of convenience. The important thing that these various people have in common is that their decisions can profoundly affect the lives of ordinary citizens. They can open or close the door to valuable resources such as public housing, social security payments and help from the social services. More than that, some of these agencies have great power to interfere in, and even radically change, the course of people's lives. Payment of social security will often be made dependent on a visit from an investigator who will ask a range of questions that in normal circumstances would be regarded as constituting an invasion of privacy. In some circumstances, investigation can continue in a secret and lengthy manner. Social security fraud is, understandably, not popular with the majority of the public and so the surveillance of officialdom tends to be grudgingly accepted in this area by the tax-paying majority.

Planning policy, by contrast, is an example of bureaucratic power that has frequently provoked widespread condemnation. For instance, with the support of the politicians who often depend on them for detailed advice, planning officers can make use of wide legal powers to require people to quit their houses which can then be destroyed.

Figure 19.7 'Disney' plan makes old Oxford wince: heritage sites can be put at risk by modern commercial development

The increasing importance of heritage both as an 'industry' and as a focus of leisure activity, can give planners additional problems in certain localities. In the struggle indicated by the photograph captioned ''Disney' plan makes old Oxford wince', all four groups dealt with in this section played a part. The planners seem to be supporting the scheme for a club and cinema for local youth whereas adult local residents were concerned that the development would mar the historical beauty of the area (see Figure 19.7).

A number of key positions which regulate access to various resources controlled by private enterprise ought also to be mentioned here. In particular, money lending institutions of various kinds, notably banks and building societies, can make decisions that affect people's lives radically. Thus, it became very much more expensive to insure inner urban small businesses, including shops, after the urban disorders of the 1980s and 1990s.

Citizens

We now discuss the most important group mentioned above, citizens. Despite the great individual and group differences between people living in the same locality, residents of the same area – by that very fact – share much in common. Despite the landscaping of previous industrial areas, it is highly arguable that the public spaces in Britain's localities – particularly still in some inner urban areas – compare poorly with those of many other European countries. Partly, it is that the destructive effects of industrial development and decay still linger. It may even be that British culture is exceptionally privatised rather than public in nature (in contrast to Italian and Spanish culture). It is also the case that central government shapes local affairs in Britain more than in most European countries – a situation intensified under Thatcherism. Historically, democracy in Britain involves voting for a representative with, perhaps, occasional communications thereafter. Increasingly, people have become more aware of the possible conflict between their own interests and the policies of government and its official representatives. It may be that the new emphasis on citizens' rights will produce mechanisms to enable people to bring government bureaucracies more effectively to account.

Communities are created and recreated in a crucible of power. Decisions taken by business people, politicians and planners affect the lives of individuals and communities. C Wright Mills sought passionately in his writings to make people aware of the relationship between 'private' troubles and 'public' or political issues. It is largely in an attempt to control, or at least to influence and make more accountable, the above powerful groups that community action movements began rapidly to develop in the 1960s. These movements vary widely in kind and purpose. Tenants' Associations are concerned with practical matters of self and group interest such as rents and living conditions. As Castells suggested these movements bear a similar relationship to public consumption as do trade unions to work: they aim to protect the interest of their members. More ad hoc groups may organise around an issue affecting a particular local area at a given time. An example from the provinces is the protest group in Preston's suburb of Ashton, which organised against a plan to drive a road through an avenue of birches in Haslem Park. Where an issue is general rather than local – such as the poll tax – a movement with a wider geographical base of support may develop.

Recent social movements such as the campaigns against the by-pass developments in Bath and Newbury have drawn support from a wide section of their respective communities. Despite their failure, their concern with issues of environment and quality of life may well spread. There may be good reasons for it to do so. By one measure, that of sustainable economic development (as opposed to GDP), Britain is in decline! (see Figure 19.8)

Citizenship and urban crisis

In the 1980s and 1990s, a crisis occurred in the public life of many of Britain's urban areas of a kind that citizens – however they organise – cannot easily hope to solve. There are five obvious aspects to this crisis. First, there is the growing inequality between the inner urban 'have nots' and the suburban and country 'haves'.

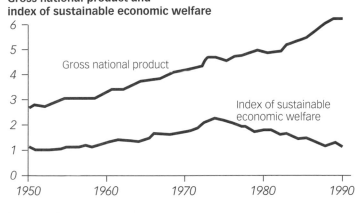

Gross national product and index of sustainable economic welfare

Gross national product

Index of sustainable economic welfare

(Source: *NEF*)

Figure 19.8 Britain: falling sustainable economic welfare

Second, the poorer urban areas can rarely raise the revenue to deal with their problems – difficulty intensified by the overall reduction

Figure 19.9 An episode in a decade of sporadic violence: was deprivation a factor in these outbreaks? In April 1981, 191 people were arrested after rioting and looting in Brixton

in funds provided by central government. Third, the increasing centralisation of economic power in the hands of large, often multi-national companies makes the urban economy very vulnerable to possible disinvestment. Fourth, and not unconnected with the above, a major problem of public order developed in Britain's inner cities in the 1980s and 1990s. Fifth, for whatever reason, government policy has not yet succeeded in releasing the energies needed to revitalise inner urban areas (see Figure 19.9).

In the light of this crisis it is worth considering the viability of the two models of political conflict referred to in Chapter 11. How realistic a description of current urban politics is the liberal model of pluralist democracy? As far as the city is concerned, particularly for the city poor, is liberal democracy working? On the other hand, is there now a basis for an effective traditional, socialist coalition in urban areas? Deindustrialisation, the numerical decline of the manual working class and union membership, and the growth of the lower (under) class are some problems such a coalition would face as, indeed, the Militant-led Liverpool Labour Council did in the mid 1980s. (For a discussion of liberal, Marxist and elite political theories, see Chapter 11).

Inner urban deurbanisation/ urbanisation of the countryside

Drawing mainly on conflict perspective, this section is about the inner city not as a physical entity but as the focal point of the activity of groups of people, the most powerful of whom are probably businessmen, politicians and top civil servants. Sometimes these groups act in concert and sometimes in conflict, but their major decisions affect the lives of the rest of us. More abstractly, we want to show how the capitalist system operates on the inner city – always bearing in mind that government can try to act as a checking or, to use Galbraith's term, countervailing power to control business as well as to smooth its path.

Since the Second World War the inner city or, more precisely, the inner city ring (the area around the business centre) has been inhabited by low income groups and beset by social problems. Once thriving manufacturing areas were hit by the decline of such staple industries as docking, shipbuilding, textile production and heavy manufacturing. Manchester, Liverpool, Glasgow, Belfast, Newcastle and Inner London – all large metropolitan areas – developed 'inner city problem areas'. For instance, the break-up of traditional working class community in East London (see above, Willmott and Young) was due to the decline of the docks and the associated service and distribution trades. In addition, advanced technology and large scale industry made the craft industries and other small scale production units of the East End obsolete and uncompetitive. As described earlier in this chapter much new economic development, notably in the service sector occurred

outside the old, inner-urban industrial areas. People followed in droves. Between 1961 and 1971, almost 100,000 people left the single borough of Tower Hamlets. Those that remained in Inner London were drawn, disproportionately, from the old, socially disadvantaged, unskilled and semi-skilled workers. They were joined by immigrants who were prepared to do unskilled and semi-skilled work in the inner city of a kind that many whites wished to avoid. In the early 1990s, the average overall annual loss of population from urban areas was about 100,000.

The above processes of economic decline of urban areas and of population movement out of them are referred to collectively as *deurbanisation*. On the other hand, the 'urbanisation' of many suburban rural areas occurred. Of course, not all urban areas declined. It is mainly the 'old' industrial cities that have experienced deurbanisation. Many service industry towns such as Southend, Oxford, Swindon and York have undergone a parallel increase in population. Nor is the process of deurbanisation irreversible. Highly urbanised West Yorkshire regained population between 1984 and 1994 and other traditional industrial areas may do so although it is unlikely their populations will again become as densely concentrated as in the mid 1950s.

It would be quite misleading to 'blame' individual business people for inner urban decline. Many of them also suffered as a result of the decline of Britain's traditional industrial base. The point to pursue is a quite different one. It is that when capitalism falters or fails – even if only in the process of change rather than collapse – it is incapable of rectifying the resultant adverse social consequences. The capitalist system works on profit, not philanthropy, and when it fails it is left to the sometimes reluctant hand of government to pick up the pieces.

Class and the urbanites

An analysis of the occupants of the inner city (and in part, the city centre) shows that class factors like income and education mean that people in the same geographical zone lead radically different lives. Inner city occupants can be divided into various disadvantaged groups, immigrants, 'cosmopolites', and some members of the upper class. We have already explained why the disadvantaged and immigrants are disproportionately represented in the inner city (see Chapters 6 and 8). 'Cosmopolites', to use Gans's term, include students, artists, writers, musicians, entertainers as well as other intellectuals and professionals. Though some may be quite poor, this is not the definitive feature of life that it is for disadvantaged groups: for them the city is meaningful because it provides opportunity for self-expression and experience.

The fact that different social groups can live in close physical proximity, yet socially in different 'worlds', is still better illustrated by reference to the very rich who keep a town residence (often in the centre rather than inner city) as well as a country home. A member of the upper class may live a stone's throw from a poor community but is sealed off from its occupants by wealth, privilege and power. The urban environment may be the physical limits of the poor person's world but the rich person is much more geographically mobile, and can escape to the 'country' or abroad, almost at will. On the whole, the upper class do not live or spend time in the countryside to seek community except in some cosmetic or whimsical sense. Their residences are usually well secluded from those of nearby inhabitants, although traditionally-minded landed aristocrats and gentry may still pride themselves on being 'part of the local community', however cushioned their position may be by privilege and by the deference afforded to them. In fact most of these, like the *nouveaux riches* who have bought into rural real estate, tend to have friends of similar social status who, in the nature of things, are unlikely to live close by. The upper class, however, can afford to travel, and visits and meetings are easily arranged. Friendship networks are likely to be national or international and may seem to have an unreal, 'starry' quality to those outside the charmed circle. Members of the upper class know each other but others only know of them. Upper middle and middle class people sometimes buy property in previously working class areas in the inner city. This process is sometimes referred to as 'gentrification'. It has added to the jigsaw-like quality of the social patterns of residence of many of Britain's cities. In fairness, it should be added that the collapse in property prices in the late 1980s and early 1990s bought significant hardship to many middle class people who had bought near the price peak.

National government policy

The role of national government in helping to create the above social and demographic (population distribution) patterns is important. In the post-war period, government and industry co-operated to disperse industry and population away from the old industrial areas. The new town movement was part of this policy. The centre and inner city zones were redeveloped as office and service areas. Some of the new housing, including high-rise flats and large estates, was of poor quality and design. 'Living in the sky' made community virtually impossible and caused families great practical problems. Even so, the new housing was generally a material, if not an aesthetic improvement on what was left undemolished of the old inner city housing stock. Most of this came to be occupied by those groups who, for reasons already mentioned, did not participate in the new 'out of city' expansion. Welfare state expenditure tends to be relatively high in inner city areas although this is a palliative, not a solution to the basic problem. Various government schemes have been adopted to encourage the economic development of these areas. As in similar schemes in the United States, money has tended to disappear often without much seeming to happen to the benefit of locals (see Figure 19.10).

It is now clear that despite some successes, the urban policies of the Thatcher governments (1979-90) have achieved no more substantial an inner urban revival than those of previous governments, particularly as Britain moved into recession as Margaret Thatcher moved out of office. The basis of the Thatcher

Figure 19.10 'If it wasn't for the 'ouses in-between' – Docklands as seen from Greenwich. Docklands development, like other urban developments, has not always benefited long-term local inhabitants

Urban development corps	Jobs created	Cost per job (£)
Birmingham Heartlands	611	48,282
Black Country	11,397	38,598
Bristol	2,250	56,267
Central Manchester	4,667	24,909
Leeds	8,218	10,745
London Docklands	71,889	35,168
Merseyside	10,605	42,763
Plymouth*	0	0
Sheffield	10,096	12,738
Teesside	11,469	35,513
Trafford Park	14,813	17,815
Tyne & Wear	16,242	24,049
Total jobs: 162,267		**Average cost per job: £30,736**

*Created in 1993.

(Source: Department of Environment)

Figure 19.11 Urban development corporations; jobs and cost

approach was to channel more central government money into private enterprise and less through local government and public enterprise. Urban Development Corporations were set up to by-pass local authorities, but where possible to draw together private and public expertise and investment. The construction of residential and commercial property in London's Dockland and less substantial efforts elsewhere were not adequate replacements for traditional industry either in terms of productivity or job creation. However, over 150,000 jobs were created albeit at a highly variable and sometimes expensive cost (see Figure 19.11). Commenting on the period from 1977 to 1992, the Policy Studies Institute stated 'surprisingly little has been achieved' (Urban Trends I). The emphasis of policy changed somewhat in the Major era although the emphasis on the private sector continued and local business and voluntary groups were encouraged to draw up schemes in competition with each other. In 1996, 170 out of over 300 submissions succeeded. Some imaginative and grassroots based schemes received money. However, critics noted overall severe cuts in development funding and that some needy areas got nothing.

Hard city: city of plans

In his essay, *Metropolis: The City as Text* (1992), James Donald explores what he sees as two sides of the modern city. He identifies two groups as typifying these aspects – the planner and the flâneur i.e. the strolling observer of 'the landscapes of the great cities'. Donald usefully focuses on two aspects of the city which require further emphasis here.

The notion that the city or any other sizeable locality can be planned is characteristic of the modern belief in rationality and progress. That optimism partly motivated the new towns movement discussed above. Notions of real improvement if not earthly paradise drove the hard edge of planning. Pre-eminent among modern planners is Le Corbusier (1887-1965) who was hugely influential in the inter-war and post-Second World War periods. Le Corbusier aspired to clear up the chaos and degradation of the large industrial cities. He was contemptuous of architects and planners who wanted to turn-back to the pre-modern age. He aspired to use modern techniques to create a better ordered and functioning city, a city that could meet and shape all demands put upon it.

Le Corbusier's urban concept was ambitious and totalistic. According to Donald:

> They (architects like Le Corbusier) proposed, quite literally to organise and recreate the city as a machine, as 'a working tool'. They therefore adopted a functionalist engineering approach. According to 'The Athens Charter', in which many of the progressivists' principles were laid down: 'The key to city planning are to be found in four functions: housing, work, recreation and traffic' ... It was nothing less than the construction of a new framework of experience that would determine any possible social behaviour, and so create a new type of person.
>
> *(448-9)*

As Donald observes, in very few cases were such plans put fully into practice. In England, towns like Welwyn (1920) and Letchworth (1930) reflected communitarian values and concepts of cultural participation which levened planning totalitarianism.

Today planners and architects do not produce such total schemes. First, is the fact that individuals and groups need to be left space and opportunity to create their own lifestyle and communities. These are not fixed and so the flexibility for grassroots initiated development and change needs to be there. The trick is one of self-absence rather than omni-presence on the planners part. Second, as much of this chapter has demonstrated, the city is less and less a fixed physical entity.

Soft city: city of dreams

According to Baudelaire, to play the flâneur – the urban stroller is:

> to be away from home and yet to feel oneself everywhere at home; to see the world, to be at the centre of the world, and yet to remain hidden from the world. The spectator is a prince who everywhere rejoices in his incognito.
>
> *(Quoted in Frisby, 1985:180-190)*

No planner will be able to direct the gaze and wanderings of the dedicated flâneur . The last thing the flâneur wants to find is an orderly metropolis. It is precisely to see the unplanned, the different, unpredictable and shocking that sets the flâneur off to stroll. The individual and ethnic variety, and startling inequalities of contemporary international cities will rarely disappoint the flâneur.

Jonathan Raban presents a somewhat similar image of the urban landscape in *Soft City* (1975). However, for Raban, the city is as much an invitation to participation and action as to observation. It is a site of opportunity for fun and pleasure, a place to meet people and gain experience. Soft city lights symbolise a kaleidoscope of colourful possibilities not available elsewhere. Soft city is above all enticing to younger people but is also the preferred habitat of many who cannot settle for humdrum routine. For some of these, the city lives as much in the imagination as in anything achieved, a focus of constantly renewed dreams.

Of course, 'soft city' is no more the only version of the city than the planned city. Even for the young, problems of housing, jobs and family rip the urban screen of dreams. For adults – urban-based or otherwise – these daily problems often leave little time to pursue dreams.

Community in the 1990s

In life, community is difficult to find and, in sociology, it is difficult to define. Nevertheless, the word has powerful resonance and the 'search for community' is surely destined to continue. Just as there was something of a revival of the search for community in the 1960s, so there has been in the 1990s. Much of the drive behind this new surge of interest in, and action about, community has come from the United States. However, there has been some distinctive thinking in Britain and also some imitation of what has been happening in the United States. Here I will refer first to two American analysts of community and then deal with what is happening in Britain.

Robert Putnam: 'the culprit is television'

In the opening lines of his essay Robert Putnam muses on the 'strange disappearance of social capital and civil engagement in the United States … – networks, norms and trust – that enable participants to act together more effectively to pursue shared objectives' (1996).

In support of this analysis he cites evidence from the General Social Survey conducted annually by the national opinion research centre in Chicago. The survey shows 'at all levels of education and among both men and women, a drop since 1974 of roughly one quarter in group membership and a drop since 1972 of roughly one third in social trust'. In other words people act less together as citizens and trust each other less.

Putnam sifts through a long list of possible explanations for this decline in civic and communal life. He dismisses the possibility that people are working so hard that they have less time for such activity or the explanation that they are preoccupied by financial pressures. He finds some evidence that the increasing numbers of women in paid work has reduced the time they have available for voluntary activity – group membership among women has declined at twenty to 25 per cent per annum for the 1950s, compared to ten to fifteen per cent among men.

Significantly, a similar trend has occurred in Britain over the same period. A report by Demos, *Where Have All the Women Gone?* (1995) states that in 1954, the Women's Institute had 467,000 members and in 1992, it had 299,000 members. The membership of its urban equivalent, the Townswomen's Guild halved between 1971 and 1992, to 90,000. Demos had previously reported that 86 per cent of working women stated that they did

not have time to do essential things, never mind join voluntary organisations. It is worth recalling that women in paid work still tend to do most of the housework. Ironically, it does seem that the price of women's partial economic liberation – welcome in itself – has been a decline in community.

However, although Putnam once regarded the rise of the (paid) working women, as the main explanation for the decline of civil and communal activity, he no longer does so. Now, he 'blames' television. As he states:

> *The timing fits … It is as though the post-war generations were exposed to some mysterious X-ray which permanently and increasingly rendered them less likely to connect with the community.*

The timing fits for Britain as well. The hours people spend watching television must be at the expense of some other activity. If Putnam is correct, for the post-war generations – those about 50 year old and less – television watching has occurred at the expense of civil and communal activity. An experiment referred to in Chapter 17 gives some support to Putnam's view. A family which removed its television spent more time talking and doing things together (see pp. 517-8). By extension, so might communities.

Putnam is too much of a realist to suggest that television be abolished. He also appreciates that electronic technology provides new means of communication and community. However, television, in particular, seems to have contributed to the privatisation of non-work time and to a loss of a certain kind of community.

Amitai Etzioni: redefining community

Etzioni's *The Spirit of Community: Rights, Responsibilities and the Communitarian Agenda* (1995) is ambitious both in its vision of community renewal and as a rallying call to communitarian action. Etzioni is a distinguished social scientist, but this book and the social movement it represents offer an explicitly political agenda.

As Etzioni sees it, post-war society has become deeply fractured and fragmented. Crime, drug-taking, poverty amid gross affluence, a rising prison population – all alert to the failure of local and national community. He considers that all this was made worse by the 'egoism' of the 1980s. Far from regarding the concern of Tönnies and others about 'loss of community' as misconceived he finds ample long term evidence that they were right. Etzioni's proposal is to start doing something about this by founding, along with others of similar views, a communitarian movement. He describes communitarians as follows:

> *We are a social movement aimed at shoring up the moral, social and political environment. Part change of heart, part renewal of social bonds, part reform of public life.*

(247)

The most important change is 'change of heart' or moral change. As he sees it, it is time for people to take responsibility rather than to seek more rights. Indeed, he suggests a 'moratorium' on rights – there are enough for the moment. Nevertheless, the movement would seek to secure human rights in a Bill of Rights. However, the urgent need is for parents to look after their children, for schools to build character, and for people to rebuild communities. Etzioni spells these matters out in considerable detail. His basic pitch, however, is one of moral and community revival. There have been a number of highly successful social movements in the post-war period. Time will tell whether the communitarianism movement will be another. Etzioni is aware of, and sensitive to the main criticisms of community – it is vague, it can be oppressive, it is against the individualist spirit of the times. His view, however, is that times can change and that a period of social repair is now the priority.

Community in Britain

In the wake of 1980s individualism and frequently associated social atomisation, each of the three major political parties have, in the 1990s, stressed the importance of community. The Liberal Democrats, formerly the Liberal party, have a long tradition of commitment to local politics and community. Paddy Ashdown has continued this vigorously, not least in his efforts to achieve racial harmony in his own constituency of Yeovil. Conservative ideologist, David Willets, after making his name as an advocate of individualism has begun to emphasise the one-nation Tory tradition. His concept of community is voluntaristic. He sees community as the outcome of individual effort and restraint.

The Labour party has come closest to echoing some of the more constraining communitarian ideas and policies from across the Atlantic. Thus, in 1996, in New Orleans and New Jersey a curfew was imposed on under eighteen year olds – with an apparent drop in the crime rate. Jack Straw, a member of the Shadow Cabinet, suggested that some localities in Britain might want to consider this approach. However, there is an independent communitarian tradition within the Labour party fed by both democratic socialism and by a particular interpretation of applied Christianity. Both Tony Blair, the present Labour leader, and his predecessor, John Smith have expressed strong commitment to community in the context of Christian socialism. Tony Blair's particular contribution to the debate on community has been to link the concept with that of individual opportunity. As a statement of principle, the following is as clear as Margaret Thatcher's famous remark that 'there is no such thing as society, there are only individuals and families':

> *I believe the individual will do best in a decent and strong community. We are not individuals set in isolation but members of a community. And we believe freedom, in the broad and not just the legal sense, is best achieved when economic and social conditions help to promote it. Liberty, equality and fraternity (or solidarity). These are all values instantly recognisable to any radical throughout the centuries.*
> (The Independent: 27.3.1996:15) (author's brackets)

These are broad brush words. Success in politics is about making words make a difference.

Conclusion

Schumpeter argues that capitalism develops unevenly: that it destroys as it creates. Britain's localities are a testament to the truth of this. Equally, the state of some areas and the poverty within them, demonstrates that capitalism must be controlled. Most contemporary conflict theorists consider that only central government can hope to control capital and deal with its social consequences. However, equally there is now a strong and widespread body of opinion that local people must effectively and beneficially be involved in any revitalisation of their localities. The Gemeinschaft-Gesellschaft model of Tönnies and the rural-urban framework of Wirth now seem inadequate as a conceptual framework to deal with contemporary urban issues.

Unemployment, poverty, racial conflict and public disorder, have increased the urgency of the debate on urban policy. This debate is part of a wider disagreement about the kind of economy and society Britain might become. The Conservatives believe that only free enterprise – large-scale and small – can provide a secure basis of jobs and prosperity. To varying degrees, Social Democrats argue that the state must step in where private enterprise fails, and indeed sometimes take initiatives in its own right. They certainly consider the condition of the inner cities as a suitable issue for substantial intervention. Marxists argue that capitalism is inherently inegalitarian and unpredictable in its consequences and seek to attack urban problems along collectivist lines. Others accept capitalism but seek to regulate it so that people's lives and localities are energised rather than destroyed by it. Few imagine it is an easy horse to ride.

Questions

1 Critically consider conflict approaches to urban-rural analysis.

2 'Sociologists conceive of the city not so much as a physical object but more in terms of group conflict and as the site of important processes such as economic development and information flows.' Discuss.

3 What factors have undermined social solidarity in Britain in (approximately) the last 25 years? What efforts have been made to revive solidarity and community and how effective might they be?

Summary

From rural community to urban society (1-3).

1 Three definitions of community emphasise, respectively, fixed locality, local social systems, quality of relationships. As *seven* examples of community show, these aspects frequently overlap.

2 Several pairs of contrasting concepts were introduced: Gemeinschaft/Gesellschaft (Tönnies) mechanical/organic solidarity (Durkheim); rural/urban; (Wirth); and traditional/modern society (Parsons). Each of these pairs of concepts contrasts what their authors see as the essence of pre-industrial, largely rural, traditional society with that of industrial, largely urban, modern society.

3 The notion that the transition from 'traditional' to 'modern' society involved a 'loss of community' was critically discussed. A variety of case studies and theoretical analyses establish that a simple notion of 'loss of community' is untenable. The example of the new towns and the English 'myth of the rural idyll' illustrate both the continuing 'search for community' and problems associated with this.

Conflict-based models of urban-rural analysis (4-6).

4 Marxist urban-rural theory is based on the analysis that capitalism is the basic force that structures both urban and rural social and political life. What are seen as simple contrasts between urban and rural life are rejected.

5 The French Marxist Manuel Castells considers that urban areas in capitalist societies developed first as centres of production (centralising capital and labour) and then more as centres of consumption. He argues that a variety of social movements develop in response to issues of mainly public consumption, such as health and welfare and the environment, in capitalist society.

6 Weberian urban-rural perspectives, like Marxist ones, are not based on an assumption of fundamental urban-rural difference. In Weber's case, it is mainly the economic function of providing a market that distinguishes the city, and accounts for many of its characteristics, such as density of population and physical environment. Rex and Moore specifically examine the housing market in the inner-city area of Sparkbrook, Birmingham. The disadvantage of black people within this market led Rex on to examine the concept of a 'black underclass'.

7 The theoretical approach that the formation of social life in both urban, suburban and rural areas is both the product of economic forces and people's response to them occurs in both Marxist and Weberian conflict perspectives. This approach is illustrated and expanded in the sections titled 'The socio-spatial effects of capitalism'; 'Locality and economic restructuring: Britain in the global context'; and 'Class and group conflict in the local context'. The inner-city is analysed as an example of conflict analysis.

8 Significant political and policy differences exist about how to respond to the problems associated with urban areas. Some consider that only capitalism and the enterprise and investment it generates can revitalise these areas whereas others consider that public investment and planning is essential.

9 In the 1990s discussion of the need for community is again current. Two American views and the views typical of the three main political parties are critically presented.

Research and coursework

Community, rural and urban issues offer the opportunity of using one's own local area as the subject of research. Issues of homelessness, the social effects of the closure or opening of a place of work, racial conflict or co-operation, the reasons for and effects of changes in residency patterns, the decline or development of a 'community' are all possible topics for research depending on the area one lives in.

The danger in selecting a local issue is that the resulting research may be merely descriptive and even anecdotal. In fact, this topic area is one of the more theoretical ones and this ought to be apparent in any research into it. Take the example of an analysis of changes in residency patterns in a given area. Let us suppose that evidence suggests that the area has become more 'middle class' as more professional, managerial and administrative employees have moved into the area. It then has to be asked why this is so. It may be that new business ventures or government offices have been established in the area. In the case of the former, there may be foreign capital involved or joint private-public sector money. Such data and explanation should lead to consideration of relevant theoretical perspectives. In this case, both Marxist and Weberian perspectives seem particularly appropriate for consideration as both directly deal with economic development (and underdevelopment) and its social effects (including occupational, class and residential change).

There is no requirement, even in the case of this topic, that research should be locally based (and even if it is, the relationship between the issue as it occurs in the local context to the wider national, and perhaps, international context should be explored). Indeed, two suggestions for studies made by the AEB lend themselves to a wider treatment. The suggestions are: make 'An assessment of government policy and initiatives on inner city development in the 1980s' and make 'A study of ethnic minority groups and housing, e.g. access to location, type'. In the first case, presentation and criticism of Thatcherite ideology as applied to urban policy would be expected, and in the second, a useful starting point might be Rex and Moore's study of housing classes in Sparkbrook referred to above – (although these by no means exhaust the range of theoretical reference).

Further reading

Two books which suggest similar processes are at work in the countryside and the city are Howard Newby, *Green and Pleasant Land? Social Change in Rural England* (Penguin Books, 1980) and Raymond Williams, *The Countryside and the City* (Paladin, 1975). More recently, Philip Cooke ed., *Localities* (Unwin Hyman, 1989) is an excellent survey of socio-economic development in seven areas. David Smith's *Divided Britain* (Pelican, 1989) provides a more general overview.

Readings

Reading 1
The pastoral myth

From Robin Mckie, 'Yet British still seek a Rural Idyll, and ruin it', *The Observer*, 26.5.1996:19

Every day, 300 people abandon city life in Britain. Car exhausts, fouled pavements, asthma, fear of crime, traffic jams and poor housing: all combine to make urban life intolerable.

This exodus represents an annual outflow of 100,000 individuals, an emigration of the disaffected that has gone on for decades. Millions have decamped from UK cities since World War Two.

The basic cause goes beyond simple urban deprivation. That is only a symptom. The real malaise is rooted in British culture, say geographers and planners.

In Western Europe, most citizens have learned how to come to terms with life in conurbations. For example, Parisians, Milanese and Berliners display an enjoyment of cafe society and promenading that contrasts with Britons' sullen hostility to their own cities. We neglect them, let them decay, and hate them even more as a result.

Instead, the British are obsessed with seeking out a rural idyll – in numbers that are turning precious vestiges of the countryside into soulless suburban enclaves. Berkshire – split by the M4 – is almost an entire dormitory county today, and Hampshire, cleft by the M3, faces a similar fate.

In one survey, 81 per cent of respondents said they would prefer to have their home in a village or small English town. Yet more than 70 per cent of the UK population actually lives in a city, despite recent exoduses. 'Most of our population dwell in cities, but have their hearts in the country,' said Geoff Mulgan of the think-tank Demos.

Inexorably, these country-lovers are seeping out of cities and peppering the landscape with motorways, business parks, out-of-town hypermarkets and fringe housing estates. Every year, an area of countryside the size of Bristol is built over in the process.

'People are obliterating the very things they desire,' said Tony Burton, of the Council for the Protection of Rural England (CPRE). 'At the same time, cities are increasingly being left to dereliction.'

And there is no sign of the rot stopping. Environment Secretary John Gummer recently announced that of the 4.4 million new homes to be built in Britain over the next 20 years, half are to be erected outside cities – despite the lethal pressures that already afflict rural land, and the neglect of inner city sites.

In other words, Britain's urban antipathy is now irrevocably damaging our entire landscape, a trend that so alarms planners and geographers that they are pressing for major investment programmes and tight rural planning restrictions to halt the destruction.

'These measures are crucially needed, though we also have to understand why we don't like cities in the first place,' said Charles Landray. In his book, *The Creative City*, he traces much of the country's urban woes to the Industrial Revolution, which occurred first in Britain and had a much more devastating effect than elsewhere. Large tracts of city land were turned into squalid, unhygienic ghettos. On the Continent, developers learnt from our example, and created far less desolate landscapes.

'Cities became places where you could celebrate some sense of liberation, as you can see in the works of Baudelaire and Manet. Dickens merely depicts them as grim points of exploitation, by contrast,' says Landray.

'And merchants who made their fortunes from steam or steel here merely aped the aristocracy – and built country mansions. Cities were for the poor.' In fact, the division is not so much a European-British one, but an English-Continental one. In Scotland, particularly in Glasgow and Edinburgh, where tenement flats provide the dominant form of accommodation, cities are more European in attitude. City dwellers there have made their pact with their environment, unlike their English counterparts.

'In England, city-dwellers have a greater passion for house and gardens,' said Ken Worpole, of the think-tank Comedia. 'They persist in believing this rural myth and have spent years trying to turn cities into the countryside. Now they are turning the countryside into cities.'

A measure of England's urban antipathy is provided by census analyses carried out by Tony Champion, reader in geography at Newcastle University. These show that the net annual surplus of disaffected urbanites (generally the retired, the self-employed or those sick of commuting) over new city-lovers (usually young adults leaving the country to find work or further education) is around 100,000.

'In 1987, during the boom, it was 125,000 a year. Then in 1990, during the recession, it dropped to 65,000 when the property market collapsed. Now it is back up to 90,000. In other words, the urge to leave cities is as strong as ever. Only economics limit the flow.'

If unchecked, this urge is likely to have an immense impact on the nation. If concrete and tarmac spread at the present rate, an area of countryside the size of Greater London will have been built over by the year 2016. Something, say the planners, must be done.

'The root of the problem lies with the city,' said the CPRE's Burton. 'People are being pushed out, rather than being pulled into the country. We have to make cities more attractive places in which to live.'

Transport forms much of the focus for the attentions of groups such as the CPRE, with cars being pinpointed as the main source of misery for city-dwellers. They induce 'urban immobility' for children. Parents are so fearful their children will be knocked down if they walk or ride a bike that they take them everywhere by car themselves. This loss of freedom induces frustration in children.

In addition, exhaust fumes are linked to spiralling asthma rates in children, and gridlocked roads, particularly London's, send travelling times soaring.

Major investment in city public transport is sought as a priority for protecting the countryside, though other measures are also needed. At present, it is still cheaper to build on virgin land than reclaim old inner-city industrial or housing sites. Tax incentives to help the latter, at the expense of the former, are also urged by groups such as the Civic Trust.

The trust points to the soundlessness of many urban areas, which are increasingly monitored by closed circuit television rather than patrolled by police, and also to the remoteness of decision-making in town and city centres, where local bank and store managers have no autonomy, despite their importance to their community.

But perhaps the most important factor is pride and involvement. 'Restoring that to cities would reap enormous dividends,' said Paul Davies, director of the trust's regeneration unit.

In cities such as Glasgow, which has striven to create a unique cultural identity for itself in recent years, and Manchester, with its vibrant pubs and clubs, there is evidence this can be done. The task is elusive. 'The crucial point is that it can be done,' added Davies.

Questions

1 Why do some of the English middle class seek a rural idyll?
2 To what extent and why is the rural idyll a 'myth'?

Reading 2
The concepts of locale, locality and community

From Philip Cooke, 'Locality, Economic Restructuring and World Development', in Philip Cooke ed., *The Changing Face of Urban Britons: Localities* (Unwin Hyman, 1989), pp. 10–12

There is a gap in the social science literature when it comes to a concept dealing with the sphere of social activity that is focused upon place, that is not only reactive or inward-looking with regard to place, and that is not limited in its scope by a primary stress on stability and continuity.

Community is inadequate because it fails to satisfy the second and third conditions. Also, it fails to satisfy the first condition in that it is not strictly denotative of place. It is by no means unusual to speak of community aspatially as in the idea of communities of interest or 'community without propinquity' (Webber, 1964). Community is, therefore, too broad in its spatial reach and too narrow in its social connotations, especially in respect of its external content. 'Locality' is a strong candidate for filling the gap.

Before considering the adequacy of *locality* to the task in hand it is worth briefly considering the value of the apparently cognate concept of *locale* recently introduced by Giddens (1984). As Giddens put it:

Locales refer to the use of space to provide the *settings* of interaction, the settings of interaction in turn being essential to specifying its contextuality … Locales may range from a room in a house, a street corner, the shop floor of a factory, towns and cities, to the territorially demarcated areas occupied by nation-states (Giddens, 1984:118).

There are three reasons for rejecting the notion of locale as a candidate to fill the gap. The first of these is that it is even looser than community in its spatial scope. For, although there are such appellations as the 'community of nations' and, even more formally, the European Community, even common usage seldom extends its application to the scale of the room. The second reason for rejecting locale is that it reproduces the passive connotations of community in the way it refers to setting and context for action rather than as a constituting element in action. Finally, unlike even the inadequate notion of community embodied in the work of earlier theorists of community, locale lacks any specific social meaning. It remains primarily a synonym for space – a particularly old-fashioned one, since it stands for a space which can be *occupied* by socio-political entities such as the nation state.

A better conceptualisation, offered by Savage *et al.* (1987), sees locality as the product of the interactions of supralocal structures. These may, it is proposed, give rise to local specificity, but this never goes as far as to warrant the designation 'local culture' though it does merit the appellation 'locality'. However this approach is too restrictive in its structural determination. It shares with community and locale a blind spot with respect to the active, potentially effective power embodied within both the concept of locality and the practices of its members. If locality is reduced to the interactive outcome of common structural determinations it becomes impossible to explain local variations between otherwise similarly constituted places. Yet we know that historical and contemporary social practices of an innovative character emerge in specific localities, sometimes in more than one, more or less simultaneously.

Historical examples would include the ways in which industrial districts such as Sheffield, Stoke-on-Trent, Limoges, Lyons and Bradford emerged either singularly or sometimes in parallel as localities displaying particularly productive specialisms. Outside the industrial sphere, the development of localities with particular aesthetic specialisms such as Salzburg for opera, Cannes for film appreciation and Nashville for country and western music cannot readily be explained without considerable reference to local initiatives of a collective kind. Returning to industry and the highly contemporary period, new specialisms are being forged in small towns such as Treviso in Italy where clothing production is dominated by, but by no means limited to, the activities of the Benetton company. Meanwhile, Boston in Massachusetts has become an important software and high technology centre and Cambridge (UK) is blossoming as a research and development complex in industrial science and engineering.

Such examples probably have to be understood in terms that include but move beyond the purely structural. Each is a clear illustration of local mobilisation by a few or many individuals and groups taking full advantage of what may be called *pro-active capacity*. What this means is rather straightforward. In sovereign nation states there are two main levels at which collective identification is actively expressed. The first is the national level: individuals are officially accorded a nationality with which as subjects they identify to a greater or lesser degree. The second is the local level where individuals work and live their everyday lives for the most part. At both these levels individuals of the appropriate age have democratic rights and freedoms of expression. Furthermore, the existence of such rights implies, in practice, the distance of the two levels. One of the key attributes of sovereignty is the right to *name* localities, a fact made visible whenever the control of territory is transferred as, for example, when colonising powers annexe it or when emergent nationals win independence. Membership of a locality by birth, or by residence for a qualifying period, admits the individual to the citizenship bestowed on 'nationals' of the sovereign power.

Citizenship is thus a precondition for participation in the range of affairs that may take place in the territory of the nation state. Those lacking citizenship and residing in an alien nation state lack many of the instruments of pro-activity such as welfare or electoral rights, though they may possess certain economic rights. Such groups constitute and fall back upon what is more accurately called their community than their locality, though it is not unreasonable to consider such a community as existing in a particular locale.

Thus the discussion of the status and meaning of locality returns us to the point of departure. Citizenship as a means of social participation implies the existence of the modern nation state, an institution which became generalised only from the period when cultural modernity and industrial capitalism became dominant social paradigms. The modern nation state is one in which citizenship applies at both the local and the central levels. Both levels are key means for social mobilisation and political intervention. For individuals who are *subjects* of the sovereign power of the nation state their citizenship rights are exchanged for their allegiance. Citizen subjects obtain civil, political and social rights (Marshall, 1977) in exchange for certain obligations such as those involving obedience to the law, including acceptance of military conscription in time of war. As Turner (1986) puts it: 'to be a citizen is to be a person with political rights involving liberty and protection in return for one's loyalty to the state' (Turner, 1986:106-7).

That the state can enforce this relationship is the result of modern methods of surveillance (Giddens, 1984) such as the various certificates, licences and numbers by means of which the modern state locates individuals in their localities.

In conclusion, locality is a concept attaching to a process characteristic of modernity, namely the extension, following political struggle, of civil, political and social rights of citizenship to individuals. Locality is the space within which the larger part of most citizens' daily working and consuming lives is lived. It is the base for a large measure of individual and social mobilisation to activate, extend or defend those rights, not simply in the political sphere but more generally in the areas of cultural, economic and social life. Locality is thus a base from which subjects can exercise their capacity for pro-activity by making effective individual and collective interventions within and beyond that base. A significant measure of the context for exercising pro-activity is provided by the existence of structural factors which help define the social, political and economic composition of locality. But the variation between similarly endowed localities can only be fully understood in terms of the interaction between external and internal processes spurred, in societies dominated by capitalist social relations, by the imperatives of collective and individual competition and the quest for innovation.

Question

Critically review the arguments presented by Cooke for and against the use of the terms locale, locality and community. Which term do you find most appropriate?

An image of development/progress? McDonald's opens in Moscow

Aims of this chapter

1 To describe the various organisations and institutions involved in underdevelopment and globalisation.

2 Critically to present the main perspectives on development and underdevelopment.

3 To examine the economic, political and cultural dimensions

of globalisation.

4 To analyse the main theories of globalisation and to appreciate that globalisation provokes 'oppositional tendencies'.

5 To examine key underdevelopment themes and to indicate aspects of globalisation within them.

Terminology: development, underdevelopment and globalisation

Social change can take the form of *development*, *undevelopment* and *underdevelopment*. Development implies some positive progress in a society's condition whereas undevelopment implies decline or stagnation. Underdevelopment is a term used especially by Marxists to indicate that the operation of international capitalism tends to prevent or retard development in the poor world. What is viewed as development varies somewhat from society to society. The goals of socialist societies are not the same as those of capitalist ones. The former tend to stress egalitarian and communal objectives, whereas the latter put greater emphasis on individuality and personal freedom. However, the apparent global triumphs of the capitalist system have swayed opinion throughout the world in favour of capitalist models of development, and there has been a corresponding decline in the popularity of socialist models. While this trend seems likely to be sustained, it need not be regarded as inevitable. There is already in the mid 1990s, something of a resurgence of communism in Eastern Europe albeit of a more democratic kind.

There are some aspects of development on which in practice there is near-universal agreement. These are mainly technological, economic and educational. Nearly all societies seek to improve their technology, increase their wealth and develop the skills of their people. How this should be done and who should most benefit from development are, of course, matters of wide disagreement.

Once we move beyond quantifiable and measurable matters of wealth and technique to consider political and cultural issues, disagreement about what constitutes development becomes more marked. The Western democracies tend to want 'developing' societies eventually to adopt the political and civil liberties common in the West. By contrast, China (and until recently the Soviet Union) looks to the Communist party – theoretically the organ of the working class or peasantry – as the means of political decision and expression. Even so, a number of 'developing' societies have, at different times, attempted to combine Western-style political institutions and civil liberties with broadly socialist

programmes of economic development. Jamaica under Michael Manley's leadership and Chile under Salvador Allende's are examples. In contrast, Singapore has developed rapidly – with a capitalist economy and rather authoritarian political and civil regimes.

There is even less agreement about what constitutes a developed cultural life than about political development. This applies both to the level of popular culture, i.e. the quality of everyday life, and to 'high' culture – classical music, literature and the rest of the arts. Unsurprisingly, capitalist images of socialism and socialist images of capitalism tend towards the uncomplimentary.

The terminology of social change reflects a variety of ideological perspectives, some of which have been indicated above. The term development tends to reflect a liberal-capitalist view that world 'progress' is likely, whereas that of underdevelopment has clearly negative overtones. To avoid the polarisation of these terms, some prefer more developed countries (MDCs) and less developed countries (LDCs). J K Galbraith suggests that the terms rich and poor nations are probably the simplest and truest (see Figure 20.1). The terms, First, Second and Third World are now less frequently used. The First World is the United States and Western European capitalist democracies, the Second World was until recently thought of as the Soviet Union and its former communist bloc allies, and the Third World is the poor or relatively poor countries.

The terms 'North' and 'South' or 'Northern countries' and 'Southern countries' have largely replaced first, second and third worlds. These newer terms avoid the offensive implication of

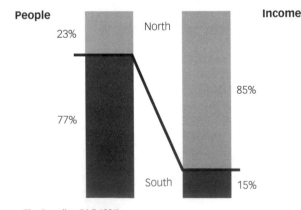

(Source: *The Guardian*, 24.5.1991)

Figure 20.1 North and South: the basic inequality

hierarchy that could be taken as assumed in the older usage. North and South are taken to be divided by a line running between the United States/Mexico, Europe/Africa, Russia/Asia and dipping down to include Japan, Australia and New Zealand.

Not all countries fit neatly into simple categories. Figure 20.2 shows three groups of countries at different levels of development according to income and type of production. A large service sector is usually taken as an indicator of advanced development; such economies, for example the United States, are sometimes referred to as post-industrial though Marxists prefer the terms capitalist/socialist/communist. The figure also gives data about the employed population (usually a smaller proportion of the total population in poorer countries).

Levels of development

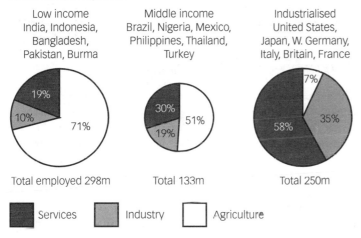

Low income
India, Indonesia, Bangladesh, Pakistan, Burma

Middle income
Brazil, Nigeria, Mexico, Philippines, Thailand, Turkey

Industrialised
United States, Japan, W. Germany, Italy, Britain, France

Total employed 298m   Total 133m   Total 250m

■ Services   ▨ Industry   ☐ Agriculture

Note: The percentages refer to levels of employment in given economic sectors.

(Source: *The Economist* 24.2.1979:32 – slightly adapted to up-date)

Figure 20.2 Breakdown of employment in selected countries

The context of development/underdevelopment has been changed by the process of *globalisation*. Globalisation refers to economic, political and cultural processes which operate beyond or above the national level and which take effect throughout the world or globe (see pp. 594-5). Two examples are the media and the transfer of money.

The West and the world: historical and contemporary overview

Many of the problems and issues of the contemporary world are the product of the impact of the Western powers on the rest of the globe. This impact began in the fifteenth century, intensified in the nineteenth and remains very strong. Of course there is nothing new

or modern in imperial expansion. The Greeks and Romans established large empires which radically changed the economic, political and cultural lives of their subject peoples. The modern European empires have done no less. The major difference is that between them the Western European powers settled. occupied or subdued virtually the rest of the world. The result is that even today world politics, economics and even cultural relations take place within a framework largely created by Western Europe. Societies which have been subjugated by the West have been put in a reactive position, few have attained power and influence comparable to that of the Western nations. Put more technically, the causes of change in Western European societies – particularly, Britain – were largely endogamous (generated from within) whereas in the South they were and are predominantly exogamous ('imported' or imposed from outside). It would be difficult to exaggerate the shock to many traditional societies as they struggled to re-orientate or even survive (for instance, the American Indians) under the impact of the West.

Three phases of Western influence and domination can be indicated. First, is the period of exploration, trade and conquest beginning in the fifteenth century and which included the 'discovery' of the Americas. Second, is the period of the formal empires – when most European colonies were established – of the nineteenth and first half of the twentieth century. Third, is the post-Second World War period during which the formal European empires were broken up. Politically, the United States and the former Soviet Union became the dominant world powers although they have usually tried to avoid (often unsuccessfully) establishing formal occupations of societies they sought to dominate. The world economic power of European corporations (and especially now American) continues, however. The term neo-colonial is widely used to describe a situation in which one country is actually, though not formally, controlled by another (the term can refer to either economic or political control). Finally, during the post-war period, Japan has developed into an economic power of global significance.

What, then for good or ill, has the Western impact on the Third World been? The arguments that surround this question are the substance of the rest of this chapter. Certain key points should be noted here. Economically the issue is whether the West has tended or, at least, tried to stimulate development (economic growth) or whether it has more typically exploited and underdeveloped non-Western societies. Politically, interest has focused on the struggle between the USSR and the United States and the systems they represented and advocated. The current ascendancy of the United States has been accompanied by many developing countries adopting capitalist strategies for growth and usually other aspects of liberal-capitalism.

Historically the European powers have been caught in the contradiction of supporting nationalism and democracy at home but not always in their subject territories. Eventually, however, all of them acquiesced in the political independence of their colonies. Many ex-colonies adopted political systems reflecting the originally European ideologies of liberalism and socialism. The cultural impact of Europe on the rest of the world defies summary. Christianity, liberty and democracy (liberalism), equality (socialism), the idea of linear progress itself, all spread from the West. Currently, the domination of the West, particularly the United States, of the entertainment media raises profound issues of value, and of cultural independence, creativity, quality and taste. The image of members of a Chinese peasant commune avidly watching Western films (shown in the documentary *Heart of the Dragon*) focuses the issue nicely.

The changing institutional context of development and globalisation

Power and purpose

It is not possible to make much sense of the development/ underdevelopment or globalisation debates presented below without knowing the basic institutional framework of post-war international political and economic life. Our interest here is less in institutions in organisational terms than in their power and purposes. Geoffrey Hawthorne has suggested that in the post-war period, the following were major players in the global power game: the United States; the political military blocs of Nato and the Warsaw pact; and trading blocs, such as the European Union.

Political power

After the defeat of Germany and Japan, two new power blocs emerged: the North Atlantic Treaty Organisation (NATO) of the United States and most of Western Europe, and the Warsaw Pact which included the Soviet Union and most of the countries of Eastern Europe. The Warsaw Pact was formally disbanded in 1991 following the break-up of the communist bloc. This has resulted in a relative increase in the power and influence throughout the world of the United States – the only remaining super-power.

The United Nations was established as part of the post-war settlement in an attempt to provide a forum in which international problems and emergencies could be discussed and to some extent acted upon. In practice, the UN was so constituted that the major victorious powers surrendered none of their independence or sovereignty. Nevertheless, the UN is a unique focus of world opinion and cannot be ignored by the major powers. It has frequently been used by representatives of poorer nations – either individually or in concert. It has also fulfilled important, though, in the total world context, minor functions in such areas as health, education, research and peace-keeping. If these kinds of issues are ever to be tackled primarily through a world agency, then the United Nations and its predecessor, the League of Nations, will be seen as the embryo of this approach. However again it is often the United States that is the decisive moving force in any action the UN takes.

Trading associations and agreements

The post-war world was also divided into two main economic blocs paralleling the political. The General Agreement on Tariffs and Trade (GATT) established the framework of international commerce for most of the world. The Soviet Union opted out and instead introduced Comecon for the Eastern European bloc. In practice, there has been a significant amount of trade between the areas and this has increased with the break-up of Comecon. Many Southern nations argue that GATT and its successor, the World Trade Organisation (WTO) favours the manufacturing interests of the North rather than their own agricultural and extractive industries and have sought changes in the Agreement to accommodate this view. If WTO is supposed to be internationally fair and neutral, the other trading agreements and associations shown in Figure 20.3 are open attempts by richer nations to develop trade and prosperity between themselves on a *regional bloc* basis.

World monetary and financial systems

The monetary system established after the war reflected the emergence of the United States as the world's leading economic power and the relative decline of Britain. The dollar became the world's major reserve currency – because much international trade was now conducted in dollars it became necessary for most countries to keep reserves of dollars if they wanted to buy Western products. The lending institutions related to the United Nations, the World Bank and International Monetary Fund (IMF) reflected the dominance of the United States and Britain. The role of the World Bank, whose full title is the International Bank for Reconstruction and Development, was to provide loans for development projects in Europe or elsewhere following the destruction of war. In recent years its lending has been concentrated in the developing countries. The International Monetary Fund had a much wider brief to provide loans for countries in major economic difficulty, including balance of payment deficit, (i.e. when the value of imports exceeds exports). Loans are provided at interest and subject to the borrowing recommendations for economic recovery laid down by the fund.

The multinationals

The American, European and Japanese multinationals dominate global production and trade. The extent of their political and cultural power and influence is more open to debate and these matters are explained throughout this chapter. The larger multinationals such as Microsoft and Shell are often wealthier than many of the countries in which they do business. There are right-wing thinkers as well as Marxists who consider that the multinationals have greater power even than Western governments. Thus, Peter Riddell argues that after their period of high activity in the 1950s and 1960s, governments should recognise that 'real power lies with global business'. Riddell argues that as far as Britain is concerned a Labour government would be unable fundamentally to change this (see Reading 1).

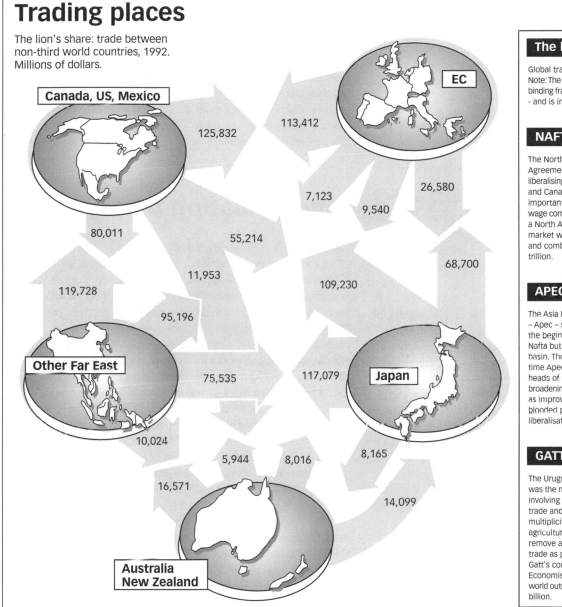

Trading places

The lion's share: trade between non-third world countries, 1992. Millions of dollars.

Canada, US, Mexico

EC

125,832

113,412

7,123

9,540

26,580

80,011

55,214

68,700

11,953

109,230

119,728

95,196

Other Far East

75,535

117,079

Japan

10,024

5,944

8,016

8,165

16,571

14,099

Australia New Zealand

The big three

Global trading agreements
Note: The European Community is a more binding framework than NAFTA and APEC - and is included in the diagram.

NAFTA

The North American Free Trade Agreement or Nafta is the pact liberalising trade between the US, Mexico and Canada – although there are important side agreements limiting low wage competition. The aim is to establish a North American style Euro-Common market with a population of 370 million and combined output of around $7 trillion.

APEC

The Asia Pacific Economic Co-operation – Apec – summit at Seattle represented the beginning of something similar to Nafta but for the countries of the Pacific basin. The Seattle Summit was the first time Apec had assembled its 12 Pacific heads of state, with the aim of broadening its agenda from matters such as improved air-links to a more full blooded programme of trade liberalisation.

GATT (now WTO)

The Uruguay round of trade talks (1993) was the most ambitious ever attempted involving over 100 countries liberalising trade and standardising trade rules in a multiplicity of sectors – ranging from agriculture to textiles. The aim was to remove as many invisible barriers to trade as possible while extending the Gatt's competence and powers. Economists reckon that the gains to world output could eventually reach $270 billion.

(Source: *The Guardian*, 'Globalisation and Society', 16.11.1993 – adapted)

Figure 20.3 Mainly, the rich countries trade between themselves

The West (and Japan) and the rest

The countries of the South often struggle for political, cultural and national identity and for economic development in a world not of their own making. Indeed, some of them, such as Nigeria, were literally put together by Western nations. Others, such as Iran, still cherish aspects of traditional culture as old or older than Western European civilisation. Even apologists for Western imperialism agree that some of the peoples of the South have suffered greatly (as well as, in their view, benefited) at the hands of the West. The slave trade alone proves the point. It is hardly surprising that intense and conflicting feelings of hatred and admiration, rejection and imitation, and of disgust and envy are freely expressed about Europe and the United States in the South. No doubt, if history had been different, and Western Europe had itself been occupied, its inhabitants would have felt similarly about their conquerors.

Conclusion: nations and sovereignty

However one strikes the balance of real power in the world – it is clearly not entirely in the hands of nations, particularly small nations dependent either on aid or the activities of multinationals.

It is almost universally considered desirable that nations remain *legally sovereign* (i.e. independent) but *practical sovereignty* often has to be shared with international agencies, multinational companies and even other nations i.e. crucial political and economic decisions affecting nations are often shared with other agencies. In so far as this is becoming increasingly the case, it illustrates globalisation.

Globalisation: the global system

Although some still dispute it (see p. 596), there is widespread agreement that in certain crucial respects 'globalisation' is occurring or, put more strongly, a 'global system' is emerging. This means that certain key processes are developing at a transnational level which are eroding the independence and 'separateness' of nations and the power of the nation state. Regional identity – European, Asian – is also seen as deeply affected by these developments.

First, the concept of a 'global system' began as an economic theory. It suggested that capitalist economic forces, particularly the major transnational corporations, are creating a situation which challenges and reduces the autonomy and sovereignty of nations. Second, with the continuing collapse of Soviet-style communism, some commentators consider that the triumph of liberal-democracy, as well as the capitalist economic system, is likely to be part of a shared global future. There is disagreement about how far socialism might be part of 'the new world order'. Within Europe there is little support for authoritarian-socialism but still substantial support for democratic socialism. Indeed, the European social chapter contains significant elements of democratic socialism.

There is increasing speculation from both the left and right that global cultural patterns – if not a global culture – are emerging. Most agree that it will be much more varied and individualised than the old 'mass' culture but some fear that style, fashion and consumption will be predominantly producer – rather than consumer-led. Leslie Sklair (1991) argues that an 'ideology of consumerism' fuelled by advertising and the capitalist dominated media is now dominant throughout most of the globe (see p. 599).

Conclusion: globalisation and development

It is vital to appreciate that the process of globalisation does not solve the problems of development faced by poorer countries. Indeed, if fascination with globalisation distracts attention from these problems it may make development more difficult. Nevertheless, there are links between globalisation and development as will become obvious in the rest of this chapter.

Theories of change

Neither theorists nor policy-makers agree on why some regions develop and others do not. The following theoretical section has been divided into four parts: modernisation theory; Marxist theories; two liberal theories – neo conservative (free market) theories and social democratic theories; and a feminist account of change. Many important issues are raised within the theoretical discussions but a number of key themes are further analysed in the next section.

Modernisation theory

Modernisation theorists argued that the pattern of historical change has been from simple to complex, or modern, societies. They differ in their explanations of change but are in agreement in rejecting the Marxist model (see below). Many modernisation theorists also subscribed to convergence theory, i.e. they contended that the advanced industrial societies, whether socialist or capitalist, are growing more alike. Again, this differs from Marxists who see socialist and capitalist societies as at least in potential very different. Many of the concepts of modernisation theorists can be found in the earlier work of Spencer, Durkheim and Weber.

To a large extent, modernisation theory has been superseded by globalisation theory. Despite differences within as well as between these approaches, both see the 'master-pattern' of development occurring essentially along capitalist lines. Modernisation theorists could reasonably claim that the capitalist-dominated contemporary world is basically the world as they predicted it would develop.

Why, then, bother with modernisation theory if it is somewhat dated? First, modernisation theory is or was an *ideology* as well as a theory. It is an excellent example of the kind of optimistic, western-centric thinking typical of those who see the capitalist version of modernity as the embodiment of 'progress'. As such, then, modernisation theory is a key ideological expression of the main period explored in this book – modernity. Second, although the approach taken here is critical, it will be obvious that much of the analysis offered by modernisation theorists of how development does or does not occur remains of use.

Spencer, Durkheim and Weber on change

The view that social development has broadly evolved towards the more complex is apparent in the work of several of the founding fathers of sociology, notably Spencer and Durkheim. Ronald Fletcher usefully distinguishes between the descriptive and explanatory in their work. Thus, Spencer's descriptive criteria were:

the simple society; the compound society (clans, tribes); doubly compounded (city states, kingdoms); and trebly compounded (empires, modern nations and federations). His explanatory typology consisted of the military and industrial types of society. He explained the change from the one to the other partly by the very success of military societies in establishing the conditions for the peaceful development of industry and welfare. Durkheim's descriptive criteria are very similar to Spencer's: the horde; the clan; simple polysegmental; polysegmental simply compounded (confederations of tribes); polysegmental doubly compounded (nations and federations). His explanatory typology proposes an increasing differentiation of society from the mechanical to the organic (see pp. 551-2) and has much more currency among contemporary sociologists than the now largely disregarded typology of Spencer.

Both Spencer and Durkheim were influenced by the strong nineteenth century interest in biology and, in particular, the tendency to find parallels between biological and social evolution. Both employed the concept of structural differentiation to indicate that, as society develops more functions, it becomes structurally more complex. This perspective has been elaborated more recently by Talcott Parsons (see below).

Max Weber's contribution to understanding change does not lie in the development of formal descriptive or explanatory frameworks. Yet, in his 'dialogue with Marx' (see below) he made several observations about the nature of social change which have influenced more recent modernisation theorists and liberal historians. First, Weber stressed the importance of ideas and choice in the process of change (see p. 143). In this respect, Weber is sometimes described as a 'voluntarist'. Second, a related point, he rejected what he took to be Marx's overemphasis on the economic causes of change. Instead of economic 'determinism', he offered a multi-factoral approach to understanding change in which ideas played a major role. Third, he rejected Marx's analysis of class conflict and revolution. Change could be gradual as well as revolutionary and there were other important sources of change than class conflict. Fourth, although he recognised the inequality of capitalist society, he did not attribute it essentially to capitalism. Rather, he thought that large, rational organisations or bureaucracies, including the capitalist corporation, were necessarily hierarchical and unequal. He anticipated that as socialist societies developed large scale industrial and governmental bureaucracies, they would be characterised by inequality. Again, modernisation theorists and liberal thinkers have tended to accept and build on this analysis whilst, in some cases, arguing for the mitigation of the extremes of inequality in their own and other societies. One can see in Weber's analysis of bureaucracy in modern society, the seeds of convergence theory.

Examples of modernisation theory

This section gives examples of modernisation theory. They differ mainly in the extent to which they stress the diffusion (spread) of technology or of ideas as the primary stimulus to development. Although it is recognised that non-capitalist forms of modernisation can occur, the assumption is that capitalist modernisation is best. The focus, then, is on how capitalist modernisation can occur.

Walt Rostow: stages of growth

Walt Rostow's emphasis is on the role of technology, though not exclusively so. Rostow's influential work *The Stages of Growth* was first published in 1960. He argued that it 'is possible to identify all societies, in their economic dimensions as living within one of five categories'. These are:

1 Traditional society
2 Preconditions for take-off
3 Take-off
4 Drive to maturity
5 Age of high mass-consumption

There is a broad similarity between Rostow's categories and the descriptive evolutionary frameworks of Spencer and Durkheim. However, he is little interested in what he calls traditional societies. He uses the term as a catch-all to describe those societies whose productivity is 'limited by the inaccessibility of modern science'. For Rostow, modern science and its practical application in technology is the key to the 'take-off' into development. In Europe the scientific and technological preconditions for take-offs were developed internally, elsewhere it was the 'intrusion by more advanced societies' which 'shocked the traditional society' and began or hastened its undoing and opened the way for change, especially 'economic progress'. In the take-off phase, growth becomes the 'normal condition'. In traditional society, take-off requires not only the availability of capital and technology but the emergence of a modernising, political elite. The 'drive to maturity' is characterised by a high percentage of national income reinvestment 'to extend modern technology over the whole front of its economic activity'. Once this economic infrastructure is laid down, leading economic sectors 'shift towards durable consumers' goods and services'. Higher personal income and greater leisure time stimulate this process. Rostow also notes that in this stage, money available for welfare expenditure increases.

On the relationship between development and democracy, Rostow acknowledges what in a later publication he refers to as 'an important and painful truth' (1971): that it is possible for development to occur under totalitarian leadership. In *Stages of Growth* he devotes a full chapter to attacking communism although he also refers to the Meiji Restoration in Japan and Ataturk's Turkey as non-communist forms of 'peculiarly inhumane ... political organisation capable of launching and sustaining the growth process'. However, he seems to reveal that his primary concern is with communism rather than totalitarianism as such when he argues the need for a partnership between the Western powers 'in association with the non-communist politicians and peoples' to achieve growth and democracy. To be consistent in opposing totalitarianism, he should have written 'non-totalitarian' rather than 'non-communist'. In fact, it has been a criticism of American post-war international policy that its government has been too ready to work with and support right-wing totalitarian regimes merely to oppose communism, as occurred in the case of the Shah of Iran and President Diem of (formerly) South Vietnam. Frequently, the underlying problem is that there is little or no democratic tradition in many poorer countries. This raises the question of whether promoting 'democracy' against communism is a viable basis of political policy in societies in which it has few roots. We return to this controversial and ideologically charged question later.

Parsons and Hoselitz: development and the diffusion of western culture

Talcott Parsons and Bert Hoselitz conceptualise modernisation within a Functionalist framework. Following Weber, they stress that the diffusion of ideas and values (or culture) from the West outwards is the underlying dynamic of modernisation rather than the spread of technology emphasised by Rostow. However, the two approaches are not incompatible. According to Parsons, as society evolves in a more complex direction, so its institutions change and adapt and become more functionally differentiated. Thus, in more modern societies, many of the more formal aspects of socialisation are carried out within the educational system rather than the family. In *Sociological Factors in Economic Development* (1960), Hoselitz draws on Parsons' typology of pattern variables (see p. 552) and uses it as a means to analyse the social factors that contribute to economic growth. He concluded that the values of achievement, universalism and specificity (particularly as applied to the division of labour) are conducive to growth, and those of ascription, particularism and diffuseness to stagnation. Interestingly, he finds that the former three values have accompanied growth in the former Soviet Union as in the West thus indicating some convergence between the two types of society (see below). Finally, he suggests that 'deviant' elites may be more effective agents of modernisation than traditional ones.

David McLelland: development and achievement orientation

The social psychologists David McLelland has also examined the attitudes conducive to development. His work is more empirical than that of Hoselitz. McLelland set out to test whether the need for achievement, or 'Nach' as he termed it, is related to development. Using tests he devised for the purpose, he attempted to relate increases in *Nach* in a given culture to increases in the production of certain relevant commodities. His tests included both historical and contemporary societies and seemed to establish the positive correlation he had hypothesised. Since this was so, McLelland recommended greater socialisation in achievement motivation in Third World countries.

McLelland's work is an interesting piece of cross-cultural social psychology but arguably highly ethnocentric. To those Third World societies struggling against often acute economic difficulties and, as some of them saw it, imperialist exploitation, the advice to take achievement courses must have seemed arrogant. A second criticism is that the correlation he establishes between increases in achievement motivation and production need not be causal. For instance, both could occur as part of a much wider imitation of the West or, in certain cases, both could be imposed by Western powers.

The practical effect of modernisation theory – in so far as it can be gauged – was to underpin a rather simplistic approach to aid and development on the part of the Western powers in the twenty years following the Second World War. 'Modernisation' turned out to be a much less predictable and neutral and a more political process than these theorists seemed to anticipate.

Critique of modernisation theory

In retrospect, perhaps the most damaging criticism of modernisation theory is its ethnocentrism, i.e. it assumes the necessity of 'modern' (in effect, American and Western) values to Third World societies with little consideration of their own cultures. The notion that Third World societies might want to balance modernisation with traditional culture or even reject aspects of modernisation is not adequately appreciated. Instead 'modern man' or rather 'American man' is the presumed ideal goal. What now seems a naive belief in progress supported these chauvinistic attitudes (see also pp. 539-40).

Second, the grand models of modernisation theory lack the feel of historical reality: we are presented with a succession of stages rather than with people acting out of variety of motives with a variety of results. Third, and relatedly, modernisation theorists fail to explore the various class and national conflicts which radically affect development/underdevelopment (see section on underdevelopment theory). The issue of inequality has deeply concerned many in the South but an appreciation of its importance is not apparent in modernisation theory until the 1970s. Marxists particularly criticise diffusionists for not appreciating that the motive of economic exploitation is the key to understanding capitalist expansion.

Fourth, there is a clear tendency to deterministic thinking in modernisation theory both in its more technological and in its more 'value-functionalist' versions. This tendency is at its strongest in convergency theory which is fully presented in the next section. Weber's original emphasis on values was, of course, intended to give due importance to subjectivity and choice. However. Hoselitz's treatment of values, framed within Parson's pattern variable pairs, makes them appear prescriptive and restrictive. Ironically, this is probably the oppositive of Weber's intention although he too struggled systematically to reconcile value subjectivity with the objective effects of social institutions.

Finally, mainstream modernisation theory both in United Nation's development institutions and elsewhere has been steadily moving away from the assumptions of modernisation theory for almost 25 years.

In particular, within the World Bank, it is no longer taken for granted that economic growth will benefit all social groups within the society in which it occurs. There is now much more concern to find strategies for development which immediately meet the basic needs of the poor (see p. 610). However, modernisation theory remains of great interest as an example of how social science can play an ideological role – in this case the support and justification of American liberal capitalism – even to the point where, perhaps, social science and ideology appear barely distinguishable.

Convergence theory

Convergence theory is closely related to modernisation theory. It is usually applied to more industrially developed societies which by virtue of certain technological and organisational imperatives (needs) are seen as moving structurally closer together. In particular, the comparison is made of the United States and the Soviet Union. Thus, Raymond Aron, the French sociologist remarked that it was not until he visited India that he realised that the significant division in the world was not between communism and capitalism, but between modern states and those which remained industrially undeveloped. However, the models of development surveyed above imply an assumption of convergence on an even larger scale, which all societies undergo as they 'modernise'.

Dahrendorf and Bell

Convergence theory focused a number of themes in American and, to some extent, European liberal-social democratic thought during the late 1950s/early 1960s. Together, these themes cohered into a mood which considerably influenced politicians and policy makers. A key work stimulating this climate of opinion was Ralf Dahrendorf's *Class and Class Conflict in an Industrial Society* (1959). Dahrendorf argues that there has been a decline in the 'old' militant working class and in the 'old' individualistic, capitalist class and in traditional class conflict (see p. 167). He observes instead a managed or organised society in which solutions to social (no longer class) problems are technical rather than ideological in nature. Daniel Bell, who acknowledges Dahrendorf's influence, makes this point the central theme of his *The End of Ideology: On the Exhaustion of Political Ideas in the Fifties* (1961). Bell strongly contends that ideological and political 'extremism' such as Fascism and Communism, are not merely redundant but dangerous: their intolerance and contempt of compromise leading almost certainly to inhumanity and bloodshed. He believed he saw a prudent consensus emerging in the West in which the institutions of liberal democracy were accepted as the most mature and realistic means of political expression. With Bell, as with other modernisation

thinkers, it can be difficult to disentangle what he believes is happening from what he wants to happen. Although Dahrendorf and Bell's expectations of immediately convergent trends referred mainly to the Western capitalist democracies, it is arguable that the sharply polarised ideological politics of the 1960s and 1980s (in the West) directly contradict even this limited theses. Again, despite the decline of Communism and crisis of Marxism, the late modern world is still full of ideological conflict. Much of this is cultural in nature – as is the tension between Islam and the West.

Clark Kerr: 'industrial man'

Clark Kerr *et al., Industrialism and Industrial Man* (1959) is probably the most comprehensive statement of convergence theory. Like Dahrendorf he considers that it is the industrial rather than the capitalist nature of modern society which gives it many of its basic characteristics. The same industrial technology produces similar occupational and stratificational systems and in Kerr's view mature industrial society requires higher levels of managerial, technical and labour skills than early industrial society. Both arguments have come in for sharp criticism. John Goldthorpe's view that stratification in socialist 'industrial' societies, notably the former Soviet Union, was produced primarily by political rather than technological or market factors is one noted alternative analysis.

Kerr envisaged that industrial society would be marked by increasing wealth and leisure. Like Bell and Dahrendorf, he argues that, contrary to Marx, protest will not increase in later industrial society: 'Rather, turning Marx on his head, protest tends to peak early'. This is partly because increasing general affluence and the welfare state remove the incentive for protest, particularly based on class. In this case, the 40 years since Kerr wrote do not tend to bear him out. Rather, perhaps what has happened is that in Western Europe and the United States, a substantial and growing minority of unemployed and low paid are not sharing in the now not so general affluence (see Harrington pp. 386-7). The urban riots of the 1960s (USA) and 1980s (Britain) are a form of protest by such groups.

Finally, again echoing Bell, Kerr links industrialism with the development of liberal pluralist democracy and with the consensus about basic values, including a belief in compromise, necessary for it to work. Thus, industrial society 'develops a distinctive consensus which relates individuals and groups to each other and provides a common body of ideas, beliefs and value judgement integrated into a whole'.

Comment on convergence theory

In comment, whilst a general commitment to liberal democracy and values persists in the West, the broader liberal consensus of the 1950s has been split (see pp. 456-9). Social and political life in the West has proved less settled and less easily manageable than Kerr and his liberal contemporaries imagined.

Kerr is somewhat ambiguous in committing himself to the view that either the Soviet Union or countries of the South will finally evolve as the Western industrial democracies have done. Less cautiously, Rostow refers to communism as a 'disease of transition' which popular demand for consumer goods and political freedom (i.e. capitalist democracy) would eventually undermine. The apparent collapse of Soviet communism in 1991 makes Rostow's analysis seem less sweeping than it did, but whether convergence will occur throughout the poor world remains an open question.

A formidable criticism of modernisation/convergence theory has been made by Marxists. They argue that the major impact of the capitalist West on the Third World has not occurred through the diffusion of technology and ideas but through economic and political exploitation. The scant consideration of this perspective among modernisation theorists does seem a failure of imagination. That such a viewpoint is widely held, particularly in the socialist Third World, was made forcefully apparent by the North Vietnamese in the 1960s and by the socialist Sandanista government of Nicaragua in the conflict with the Reagan administration in the 1980s.

Much more recently, Fukuyama has presented an interpretation of the direction of world development which seems to endorse modernisation theory. His book *The End of History* (1992) is a remarkable piece of Western triumphalism. He declares that 'the last man' – and a model the world has enthusiastically accepted – is modern, liberal capitalist man.

Marxist theories (and 'globalisation')

Marxists regard capitalism in its 'mature' stage as a world system. However, for Marxists the emphasis is on capitalism rather than globalisation in the sense that it is the defeat of capitalism and its replacement by socialism that most matters.

The Marxist, Wallerstein's capitalist world system theory is sometimes considered to be the first theory of globalisation (see pp. 598-9). However, it will be obvious from what immediately follows that from Marx onwards, Marxists have developed a world or global dimension to their theories. They argue that capitalism produces inequality at the global as well as national level (see Figure 20.4).

Marx

Like the other founders of sociology, Marx attempted to describe and explain historical change. His descriptive categories are primitive communism, the Asiatic mode of production, the ancient form of society, feudalism, capitalism, and communism (with socialism as an intermediary stage between the last two). Primitive communism is a simple form of hunting and gathering society in which goods are held in common and there is no class

stratification. The Asiatic mode of production occurred mainly in Asia and was not a necessary stage in historical change: it was characterised by state exploitation of labour. The ancient form of society emerged out of primitive communism through tribal warfare; successful tribes established cities and enjoyed the surplus produced by conquered slaves. The Greek and Roman empires are examples. A more recent case of a slave society is the plantation society of the Southern United States. Feudalism is characterised by the legally enforceable control of the land by the minority who exploit the labour of the serfs or peasant majority. Capitalism signals the rise to dominance of the manufacturing middle class over the landed nobility. Marx anticipated that capitalism would be replaced by communism when the urban proletariat overthrew the capitalist class and took over the means of production.

Marx's explanation of historical change is based on class conflict. As he put it, 'the history of all hitherto existing society is the history of class struggle'. He saw class conflict as a 'dialectic' or process which generates change. As the above description indicates, the dominant class is always the one that owns the main means of producing wealth, and the exploited class is the one that provides the labour to work these.

Marx was well aware of the role of imperial expansion in causing change (see Chapter 1, Reading 3). He observed that 'modern industry has established the world market'. He appears to have thought that the impact of capitalism on the non-capitalist world though brutal was necessary to its industrial development However, his own efforts were mainly directed towards analysing capitalist society rather than capitalism's impact on the world.

Lenin

In his essay *Imperialism, the Highest Stage of Capitalism*, Lenin offers a more detailed global analysis. He argues that up to about the last quarter of the nineteenth century, the main purposes of capitalist imperialism were to acquire raw materials and open up markets for manufactured products. From then on – rather earlier for Britain – the nature of imperialism began to change to the extent that a new form – finance imperialism – was already dominant by the First World War. Finance imperialism involved the export to and investment of capital in poorer countries. This provided income and cheap labour.

Lenin regarded finance capitalism as an aspect of a new stage in capitalist development, monopoly capitalism. Monopoly capitalism occurs when production is concentrated increasingly into a few, large-scale enterprises. Lenin cited considerable evidence to suggest that the banks control monopoly capital because they finance it – thus, the term 'finance capitalism'. Much 'surplus capital' is 'exported' abroad where profits are often highest: 'Thus, finance capital almost literally … spreads its net over all countries of the world'. According to Lenin, there develop 'international capitalist monopolies which share the world among themselves'. Supporting this economic 'exploitation' of 'small, or weak nations' is the political activity of 'capitalist' governments which eventually complete the 'territorial division of the whole world'. Lenin referred to the mutual involvement of the state and monopoly capital as 'state monopoly capitalism', and foresaw it as an increasing trend.

In summary, Lenin states: 'If it were necessary to give the briefest definition of imperialism, we should have to say that imperialism is the monopoly stage of capitalism.' Lenin may have under-estimated the continuing need for raw materials and commodity export markets in motivating imperialism but his analysis does accommodate the vital and growing role of the large, international corporation in the world economy – to the extent that he foreshadows the much later commentator, André Gunder Frank.

Baran and Sweezy: the monopoly stage of capitalism

Like Lenin, Paul Baran and Paul Sweezy describe monopoly capitalism as a world system of exploitation. In their book, *Monopoly Capitalism*, they state:

> *From its earliest beginnings in the Middle Ages, capitalism has always been an international system. And it has always been a hierarchical system with one or more leading metropolises at the top, completely dependent colonies at the bottom, and many degrees of superordination and subordination in between.*
>
> *(Baran and Sweezy, 1966)*

They are equally succinct about the purposes of the multinational corporations which in their view dominate American policy:

> *What they want is monopolistic control over foreign sources of supply and foreign markets, enabling them to buy and sell on specially privileged terms, to shift orders from one subsidiary to another, to favour this country or that depending on which has the most advantageous tax, labour and other policies - in a word, they want to do business on their own terms and wherever they choose. And for this what they need is not trading partners but 'allies' and clients willing to adjust their law and policies to the requirements of American big business.*
>
> *(Baran and Sweezy, 1966)*

According to Baran and Sweezy, because of these 'privileged terms' the multinational companies frequently make a much higher profit on investment abroad than in the United States. Accordingly, between 1946 and 1963, foreign direct investments of American corporations increased more than five times. A key concept used by Baran and Sweezy is economic surplus ('the

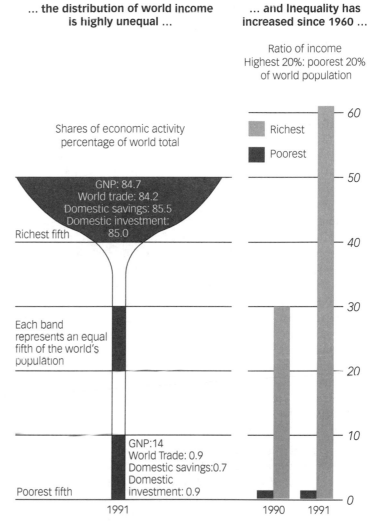

(Source: *The Financial Times*, 26.8.1994:7)

Figure 20.4 Marxists explain the massive income and economic activity inequality between the richer and poorer countries in terms of exploitation ...

difference between what a society produces and the costs of producing it'). The multinationals make more surplus in foreign than domestic investment, most of which they then repatriate, thus depriving the producing country of its use.

An interesting feature of Baran and Sweezy's analysis is their view that 'the rise of a world socialist system as a rival and alternative to the world capitalist system' had occurred. Now, 30 years after they wrote, it is clear that socialism (by which they mean communism) scarcely survives as a world movement. In particular, deep Sino-Soviet divisions developed. More recently, the break-up of the Eastern European Communist bloc and the crisis and steep decline of communism in the Soviet Union itself severely question whether communism will survive as a substantial 'alternative' global system.

Gunder Frank: dependency theory

Two major contemporary analysts of capitalism as a world system are Immanuel Wallerstein and André Gunder Frank. Both argue that the 'dependency' produced by world capitalism has typically created 'underdevelopment' in the South. Development is a myth which obscures the reality of exploitation: rhetoric aside, the capitalist powers have never seriously intended to give up their economic domination of the South. Here I will present only Frank's perspective in detail, occasionally supported by authors of similar views. Wallerstein's views are presented in the 'globalisation' section.

Frank's earlier work concentrated on the history of capitalist 'exploitation' – both imperial and neo-colonial – and in laying down the framework of his analysis of contemporary capitalism. As he put it, his 'approach rests on two fundamental pillars, historicity and structural unity', both of which he attributes to Marx. His historical analysis leads him to the conclusion that wherever capitalism impacts, it transforms the local society by forcing it into the capitalist system – in a dependent capacity. Such is the power of capitalism that other forms of social systems such as slave or feudal systems cannot survive independently of it. Thus, following the black Marxist historian, Eric Williams, he rejects the idea that slavery in the South of the United States, the West Indies, and Brazil was pre-feudal and terms it 'capitalist slavery'. He goes on to say:

> *It extracted immense riches from Africa where the slaves came from, from America where the slave-produced goods came from, and from the slave trade itself, all of which, while serving an undoubtedly important source of the … accumulation of capital in the metropoli, not only decapitalised the populations of peripheral countries but implanted the social, economic, political and cultural structure of underdevelopment among them.*
>
> *(Frank, 1975)*

Similarly, he wrote of Latin America, his major area of detailed analysis, that whatever previous forms of social organisation existed – primitive or feudal – 'they were turned to the [capitalist] metropolitan outside, produced for the outside and were controlled by the outside'.

Core-periphery relations

Frank's historical analysis indicates the nature of his model of the capitalist world system as a unified structure. The basic system is comprised of the core and the periphery, more usually referred to as the metropolis-satellite relationship. Thus, the capitalist metropolis of the United States has many dependent satellites in Latin America, including, for instance, Honduras and Mexico. Within both the metropolis and the satellite, further bi-polar

relationships occur. Thus, London is a metropolis for Britain and Mexico City for Mexico. They enjoy a surplus extracted from the rest of the country. This surplus is syphoned up through regional and local metropolitan centres which also take a share of it. For Frank as for Baran and Sweezy, then, accumulating a surplus – crudely, a profit – is the major purpose of capitalism.

Although the key metropolis-satellite relationship is between the capitalist and 'Third World' countries, the role of the major 'Third World' metropolis in facilitating capitalism is also vitally important. The multinational companies seek a relationship with the central political-military and business elites in the satellite country which enables them to enjoy favourable economic conditions. Thus, in order to attract multinational investment some countries, such as Mexico and the Philippines, have provided tax-free trade zones. Often, 'Third World' elites become wealthy on the basis of such collaboration. Largely to service the needs of the elite and those of rich foreign nations, a small urban middle class also develops. The majority – overwhelmingly peasants – remain poor in a situation of 'uneven' development (see pp. 606-10 for health inequality). Frank refers to the total process of Third World 'exploitation' as 'the development of underdevelopment'.

Semi-peripheral economies

Frank has sometimes been accused of making too rigid a contrast between development and underdevelopment. He goes some way towards meeting this criticism in his twin-volumed study *Crisis: In the World Economy* (1980) and *Crisis: In the Third World* (1981). In the latter volume he introduces a category of 'intermediate, semiperipheral, or subimperialist economies' of Brazil, Mexico, Argentina, India, Saudi Arabia, Iran, Israel and South Africa. Two varying characteristics describe these countries. First, they are generally wealthier than the majority of Third World countries. Most of them practised – with some success – a policy of 'import substitution' by which they replaced First World imports with their own manufactures. Second, these powers sometimes function as control 'intermediaries' between central metropolitan and peripheral areas, such as South Africa on the African continent and Israel in the Middle East. However, Frank emphasises that all these powers are themselves still dependent: several have chronic balance of payment problems, massive debts, or rely on the metropolitan powers for arms, – in some cases all three.

The dynamic nature of Frank's analytical framework is further illustrated by his comments on developing relations among the metropolitan powers. He suggests that Japan, Germany and Russia may be seriously challenging the economic and political dominance of the United States. Mindful of Britain's loan under severe conditions from the International Monetary Fund in 1976, he comments: 'The British economy is now threatened by an absolute decline to semi-peripheral or even underdeveloping near-peripheral status.' No doubt the rise of unemployment in Britain from less than one million to generally over two million since he wrote would help confirm him in his observation.

Multinational 'superexploitation'

In Crisis: *In the Third World*, Frank surveys a range of major Third World problems within the above theoretical framework. He examines what he calls the 'super-exploitation' of Third World labour by multinational enterprises, the enormous debts of many Third World countries, 'political-economic' repression and the role of the state, the international arms trade and warfare in the Third World, and the efforts of certain Third World countries to combine in order to maintain the price of exports – as the Organisation of Petroleum Exporting Countries (OPEC) did with oil. Here these points are discussed as an interconnected piece rather than separately.

The common thread behind these themes is in the relentless pursuit of profit by multinational corporations – supported, on occasions, by metropolitan government pressure or military action. Thus, the drive for profit results in the 'superexploitation'

(a) Weapon suppliers

Percentage of conventional weapons sales to three trouble spots

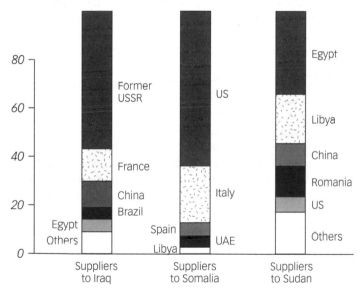

(b) The widening gap

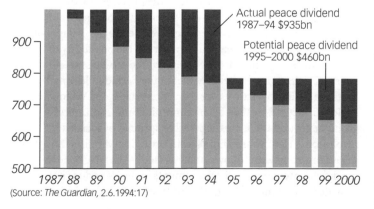

(Source: *The Guardian*, 2.6.1994:17)

Figure 20.5 War and peace

of many Third World workers by which Frank means they are paid at less than subsistence level and are kept alive by assistance from relatives and friends who work in the traditional sector of the economy. Profit also accounts for the billions of dollars of arms sold to Third World countries. Sometimes these are used to quell unrest – as in South Africa; sometimes in nationalist wars, which ruin economies and maintain dependency, as in the Iran-Iraq war. Often these arms are sold to states which, far from being democratically representative, need them precisely because they are not. Since the end of the Cold War, the arms trade has declined but it has contributed to a legacy of injury and maiming, civil disorder and underdevelopment (see Figure 20.5)

Thus, to give a recent example, the British government sold arms to Saddam Hussein of Iraq, despite later condemnation of him and his regime. There are many examples of this kind which lead Frank to conclude that profit is a stronger motive than democracy in the capitalist West. On the same issue, Teresa Hayter claimed (1985) that 'the majority of governments supported by the West are authoritarian, often military regimes of a brutally repressive nature'. Recently, Western governments have shown more sensitivity to this issue but it is far from resolved.

The weakness of opposition to western capitalism

Such is the power of Western capital within the capitalist world system that Frank holds out little hope that OPEC-like strategies could effectively redistribute wealth from the rich to the poor world. He comments that even 'the oil bonanza has been relatively short lived and very localised in a few OPEC countries'. Certainly, in the mid 1990s it is clear that the capitalist countries have been able to diversify or develop their own sources of energy. Further, according to Frank:

> The few OPEC countries that have had a balance-of-payments surplus recycled their money to and through the Western banks and financial markets. The deficit counterpart of the first post 1974 'OPEC surplus' was shifted to the non oil-producing Third World countries, where the state and the bourgeoisie obliged the masses to bear the burden of the higher costs of the world's oil.
>
> *(Frank, 1981)*

In other words, the West raised the money to pay for the increase in the price of oil by lowering the price paid for commodities from poorer, less well-organised Third World countries. Frank suggests that if this was the result of a Third World grouping combining to control the production and marketing of oil – one of the most favourable commodities for such action – the chances of doing better with another commodity are slight. However, he advocates trying.

Another aspect of Frank's analysis which illustrates the power and pervasiveness of world capitalism requires mention. In contrast to Baran and Sweezy, he did not see the Soviet Union (or China) as providing the basis of a genuinely alternative socialist world system to capitalism. Indeed, he cited the growing trade links between the First and Second Worlds as evidence of one world market, not two. He further argues that the profit the Soviet Union gained in exporting rather less sophisticated and cheaper manufactured products to the Third World provides it with the capital to buy more sophisticated items from the West – again illustrating the single market system.

The debts of poorer countries

Frank refers to the huge debts of many poorer countries as 'bondage'. These debts are so enormous that there is no foreseeable prospect of paying them. Indeed, quite frequently debtor nations have to borrow to pay the interest on their debts. Some of these debts are owed to international 'development' agencies such as the World Bank but increasingly to private Western banks which charge higher rates of interest. Frank notes that several of the intermediate level economies have tried to 'grow' their way out of debt dependency by amassing substantial balance of payments surpluses. Several years after Frank wrote, this policy seems to be faltering badly (see Figure 20.6).

Long-term debt stock and arrears for the 32 Severely Indebted Low-Income Countries (SILICS)

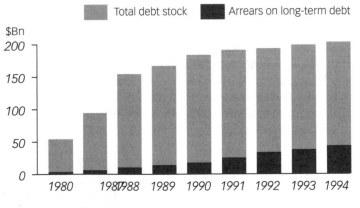

(Source: World Bank in *The Guardian*, 20.2.1996:15)

Figure 20.6 Long-term public debt

Debt and aid

When, as often happens, Third World countries are unable to pay their debts, they usually turn to the International Monetary Fund to borrow money to do so. In many cases the conditions the IMF imposes for the loan are severe and cause unrest. The left-wing critic, Anthony Sampson, describes the case of the socialist government of Michael Manley in Jamaica:

> At first Manley's government kept away from the IMF, but by 1977 they had to ask for help. The fund offered them the biggest loan (per head) in its history, but conditions as usual were strict. After drawing the first loan Jamaica soon failed its 'performance test' and had to negotiate again. The finance minister resigned, the Jamaican dollar was drastically devalued, and in 1978 average wages fell by thirty-five per cent. Wherever their drastic remedies had been applied (one Fund official was quoted as saying) they had either led to the death of democracy or the overthrow of the government. There were riots and demonstrations (or 'social tensions' as the IMF called them), while new disasters visited the island, including floods and the higher oil-price. The only really thriving industry was marijuana. The Government showed no signs of being able to meet its next test, and it had to go back to the Fund …
>
> (Sampson, 1981:339)

In her bitterly titled book, *Aid as Imperialism*, Teresa Hayter makes an analysis of the aid relationship which seems supportive of Frank's perspective on Third World financial dependency. Government aid is usually 'tied' to the purchase of items from the lending country and aid channelled through United Nations institutions is often available only for approved projects which sometimes has more appeal to, for instance, World Bank economic experts than those of recipient countries.

Hayter argues that most aid neither reaches the people who really need it nor goes into the kind of projects likely to ensure long-term development. Instead, it sticks in the hands of Third World governmental and business elites to whom it acts as a kind of bribe to pursue policies compatible with the interests of Western multinationals and governments. Even an apparently successful programme such as the 'green revolution' in India, which greatly improved crop yield, made many rich landowners – some of whom were leading politicians – richer and disenfranchised many poorer peasants from the land.

Frank: solutions

What solution does Frank advocate to the pessimistic world situation as he sees it? His answer is socialism, though he finds little to enthuse about in the Soviet model. Well before the collapse of Soviet communism, he was acutely aware of the possibility of socialist societies being incorporated into the capitalist world system. For instance, he believes that in the period following North Vietnam's military victory over the United States, the Vietnamese leadership actually sought such economic connection. Which group or groups, then, are the possible agencies of socialist revolutions? Here, Frank differs from orthodox Marxists though in a way consistent with his own analysis (see below). He believes that the development of socialist movements in the West does not provide the best model for the Third World. Marx considered the industrial working class to be the agency for change in advanced capitalist societies but in many countries of the South, this group is numerically small. Frank argues that capitalism has been imposed on the Third World from the outside and that the peasantry – many of whom are wage workers – are a potentially anti-capitalist revolutionary force. He hints that a world revolutionary alliance between the peasantry of the South and the Western urban proletariat might be possible. He advocates development independent of the world capitalist system to those countries that achieve socialist revolution. He also favours mutual co-operation between socialist societies. At no point does he suggest that any of this is either inevitable or easy. The 'crisis' of capital accumulation (a falling rate of surplus) he considers characterises contemporary capitalism may be resolved as others have been. He offers not prophecy, but struggle.

Modes of production theory (critique of Frank)

From the point of view of Marxist theory, there is an obvious and major inadequacy in Frank's analysis. In treating capitalism primarily as a market system – *a means of exchange* – he fails to deal with it systematically as a mode of production. Indeed, the concept of production fundamental to Marx's theory of change and class structure – is generally of peripheral importance in Frank's work.

Ernesto Laclau: modes of production

An early and perhaps still the most effective critique of Frank along these lines was Ernesto Laclau's essay, *Feudalism and Capitalism in Latin America* (1971). Laclau demonstrates that there are various modes of production existing in Latin America and elsewhere in the Third World. What this means in terms of class structure and for the prospects of strategies for change needs to be examined in detail, case by case. It cannot be taken for granted that the peasantry are a new global revolutionary proletariat. Significantly, however, Laclau agrees with Frank that there is one world capitalist system. What he insists on is that different modes of production occur within this world system and this makes for much more complex analysis both in particular cases and globally than Frank achieves in his over-simplified scheme.

John Taylor and Ian Roxborough: class formations

Two more recent works deal further with points raised by Laclau. In *From Modernisation to Modes of Production* (1979), John G Taylor argues that to understand Third World economic systems and social formations (his preferred terms to 'societies'), the imposition of the capitalist mode of production on non-capitalist ones is the appropriate framework for analysis. Capitalist imperialism impacting on the non-capitalist world results in economic, social and political effects not found in the West where capitalism developed indigenously. Typically, this produces a highly differentiated, even fragmented, class structure in Third World societies. Thus, the capitalist class is divided into the 'comprador' class supported by multinational money and a 'national' capitalist class seeking more independent development. Sometimes the latter is sufficiently 'progressive' to draw substantial support from the peasantry and urban proletariat. Such a coalition sustained the Christian Democratic government of Edward Frei in Chile between 1964-70. It broke up when the peasantry became sceptical about Frei's proposed land reforms, leading the way for the formation of Salvador Allende's Marxist minority government in 1970. Laclau's account ends here but we can continue it. Allende was overthrown in 1973 by a military coup led by General Pinochet. According to Nathaniel Davis, US Ambassador to Chile, 1971-73, the United States' Central Intelligence Agency spent at least $6 million on covert operations during Allende's period in office. Pinochet called his regime an 'authoritarian democracy' – an otherwise non-existent term. It was, in fact, a military dictatorship.

As Taylor's example indicates, the complexities of Third World class formations are mirrored in the political and ideological spheres. Instability and unpredictability seem to be a general result of the 'imperial' connection. In a similar vein, Ian Roxborough in *Theories of Underdevelopment* (1979) comments on the weakness of the domestic bourgeoisie in Third World societies. They are generally unable to achieve the bourgeois liberal revolution that the much stronger bourgeoisie brought about in Western societies in the nineteenth century. Instead, Third World societies are vulnerable to the power play of elites which are themselves frequently under pressure from outside forces.

The conclusion of the above debate between Frank and his Marxist critics would seem to be that Third World societies must be analysed in terms of internal and external factors or, in Taylor's terms, the interaction between the two. This brings us rather close to the proposition at the beginning of this chapter that change can be analysed in endogamous and/or exogamous terms. Does this mean that the millions of words written on the 'Frank controversy' were a waste. The answer is 'no' because the theoretical and empirical details that have emerged in the debate have led to a fuller understanding of the complexities and unpredictability of change.

Two liberal theories

1 Old liberalism: new conservatism

Milton Friedman and Peter Bauer

Nineteenth century liberal capitalism has made a revival in the late twentieth century in the new conservatism of Thatcherism and Reaganism and their successors. The label is different but the ideology is essentially the same. Adam Smith's *The Wealth of Nations* (1776) was the most influential early statement of capitalist economics. Milton Friedman, the contemporary American economist, refers to Smith's writings often and enthusiastically in his own work, *Free to choose*. Like Friedman, the British development economist, Peter Bauer has been a significant intellectual influence on the new conservatism. Bauer's book, *Dissent on Development* (1975), is also committed to private enterprise and the free market as the means of development, although he does not return to Smith's classical principles to the extent of Friedman.

Friedman wants (virtually) to exclude government from economic life. He cites four functions for government, the first three of which are given by Adam Smith: defence; law and order; the provision of those necessary public works that private enterprise does not find it profitable to provide; and the protection of members of the community who cannot be regarded as 'responsible' individuals. Bauer sees a wider range of functions for government, including 'the provisions of basic health and education services' but the only economic function he mentions is the 'management of the monetary and fiscal system'. Both regard the production, distribution and exchange of goods and services and investment as best left to private rather than public enterprise. Following Smith, Friedman argues that as long as economic exchange is voluntary both parties can benefit because 'no exchange will take place unless both parties do benefit', i.e. people pursue their own interests. Both Friedman and Bauer seem to believe that this principle operates both between individuals and between nations. In addition to their theoretical arguments, they cite empirical illustrations of the success of the free market system in stimulating growth. Friedman gives Hong Kong as 'perhaps the best example'. It has no tariffs and virtually no other restraints on international trade and, according to Friedman, the role of government is interpreted rather narrowly within the 'four duties'. Despite the natural disadvantages of small size and dense population, it has one of the highest standards of living in Asia 'second only to Japan and perhaps Singapore'.

Opposition to planning

Friedman and Bauer's enthusiasm for private enterprise is matched by their opposition to central planning and aid as means to development. Bauer states: 'Comprehensive planning has thus not served to raise general living standards anywhere. There is no analytical reason or empirical evidence for expecting it to do so. And in fact both analytical reasoning and empirical evidence point to the opposite conclusion.' Although this point is made in a typically assertive and authoritative manner by Bauer, it is open to dispute. If we take growth rather than increase in living standards as the basis of assessment, then the former Soviet Union achieved some success under central planning in the post-war period when its rate of growth was for a time greater than that of the United States. Much of this growth was in the military sector but there is no theoretical reason why it could not have occurred in the consumer section of the economy.

A second example which may be regarded as disproof of Bauer's statement is Sweden – only mentioned once and in passing in Bauer's book. It is not clear whether Sweden represents an example of 'comprehensive planning' as indicated by Bauer but it is certainly one of the more planned mixed economies. In the post-war period, it has had as high if not a higher average living standard than that of the United States. The state also played a major role in the industrialisation of Japan and Germany. One of the most notable features of societies with comparably high living standards to the United States – such as Switzerland, Luxembourg, Japan and West Germany – is the relatively small proportion of the economy devoted to armaments products.

Opposition to aid

Both Friedman and Bauer are emphatic in their opposition to aid. Aid here refers not to emergency assistance, as in the Ethiopian famine, but aid as a regular strategy for development. They consider that it distorts the free market process. As Bauer puts it, if the conditions for a viable development project are present then it will be possible to raise money on the commercial market, if not, the project should not be undertaken. Needless to say, this assertion of free market principles would not be considered axiomatic by either socialists or social democrats. A second point made by Bauer is that aid often ends up in the wrong hands and benefits the wealthy rather than the needy. The Marxist Hayter makes the same point. Criticism of aid policies from various quarters suggests a need for radical review.

However, there is little support, even among conservatives, for Friedman and Bauer's precise position. Rather what happened under President Reagan is that aid was more closely tied to political goals. Thus, an aid programme for Caribbean countries was made contingent on the political and economic 'suitability' of recipients. Similarly, aid was sent to the Contra rebels in Nicaragua whilst an American trade embargo was set up to undermine the governing socialist party, the Sandinistas. Aid is the carrot, whilst the embargo and, more usually, the activities of the CIA are the stick. In the 1990s, the policy of linking aid more closely to the acceptance of democratic and free market reforms was adopted by the British government. This linkage is referred to as '*conditionality*'. Multi-lateral agencies such as the IMF have for a long time imposed economic conditions – economic conditionality – in return for aid. However, making bi-lateral aid (i.e. aid involving only a donor and recipient nation) conditional on political reform is a more recent development. It further demonstrates that in contemporary global relations, national sovereignty is vulnerable to external power. A problem with conditionality is that those who most need aid – the poor – are as likely to be in regimes that do not meet conditionality criteria as those that do …

Finally, both theorists make a point which demands serious consideration as the core of their socio-economic philosophy. Friedman makes it most succinctly: 'Economic freedom is an essential requisite for political freedom'. Or conversely, comprehensive central planning is a 'sure recipe for tyranny'. Bauer takes to task the Swedish social scientist, Gunnar Myrdal, on the same issue. In his book, *Asian Drama: An Inquiry into the Poverty of Nations* (1968), Myrdal comes out in favour of strong central planning as a means of 'modernisation'. Bauer is able to show that Myrdal at least implies that the price of such policies is likely to be a decrease in political and civil freedom. Smelling the beginnings of the canker of totalitarianism, Bauer severely condemns Myrdal for believing that the conditions for development can or should be imposed by democratically suspect regimes. Nevertheless, several of the 'Tiger economies' of South East Asia have shown that development can, indeed, occur in authoritarian regimes in which governments are often significantly involved in economic planning. These countries tend to have mixes of economic policy, political and civil liberties (or lack of them), and social welfare not typical of either socialist or Western capitalist societies – *yet*, they have developed. As such, they arguably challenge both socialist and capitalist models of, and assumptions about development (see p. 592).

Comment

In comment, it is a major challenge of modern socialism to reconcile equality and freedom much more effectively than, say, the Soviet Union did. Many social democrats, as well as conservatives such as Bauer and Friedman, make this reservation and consequently choose not to be socialists.

Despite Bauer's criticism of the ideological bias of other development theorists, the conservative-liberal perspective seems equally ideological. Friedman's view that it is human nature to pursue one's interests individually seems neither philosophically nor historically more valid than the view that interests can be pursued collectively. Further, their use of examples is highly selective and both seem to employ the near unprovable generalisation as freely as the Marxists and social democrats they oppose.

2 Liberal/social democratic perspective on a 'new' world order

Many have long been convinced that the huge gap between the rich and poor countries was both morally wrong and politically dangerous: morally wrong because of the poverty and suffering in the Third World, politically dangerous because poverty makes these countries susceptible to 'extremist' political ideologies. This mixture of humanitarianism and pragmatism is what inspired the liberal reform movements in Britain and other Western European countries earlier in the twentieth century. Just as social reform ameliorated the condition of the working classes in the advanced industrial societies, so now certain adjustments in the world trade, finance and aid could help the poor world. These policies would be implemented within the framework of the world capitalist system of trade and finance which they were partly intended to strengthen. The best known expressions of this spirit of liberal reform are the two reports of the Independent Commission on International Development Issues under the chairmanship of Willy Brandt: *North-South: A Program for Survival* (1980), and *Common Crisis: Co-operation for World Recovery* (1983). It is important to add that many of the recommendations of the 'Brandt Reports' are supported by the politically various 'Group of 77' (now closer to 150) Third World nations established in Algiers in 1967. The view of many in the group was that the Brandt package, though not ideal, was the best likely to be offered and worth uniting around (see below).

Both 'Brandt Reports' argue that the rich North and the poor South share mutual interests on which to base co-operation. The North needs the raw materials of the South and the South needs the manufactured products of the North. As the South develops more heavy industry, the North can turn more to high technology and services. More 'equitable' prices for Third World products would fuel the ability of the poorer countries to trade with the richer ones. Protectionism would reduce world trade and have a generally damaging effect.

The recommendations of the two reports are a mixture of idealism and practicality with *Common Crisis* tending more towards the latter. *North-South* states that 'there must be an end to mass hunger and malnutrition' and suggests more international financing of agricultural research and development in the South. Co-operation to avoid the waste of common global resources and of 'irreversible ecological damage' is urged. The Ethiopian famine of 1985 was partly caused by ecological breakdown and underlines the urgency of this issue. *North-South* recommends both population control and anti-poverty programmes. The report also urged an end to the arms race and a reduction in armaments production. Instead resources should be transferred to production for peaceful purposes including the reduction of world poverty. The peace-keeping role of the United Nations would be increased.

Both Reports made recommendations on industrial development, trade and finance. Finance is perhaps the key issue because without it development is not possible. It is the major focus of *Common Crisis*. Essentially, the detailed suggestion for reforms of the IMF and the World Bank amount to more and easier credit for developing countries. More participation in these institutions for countries of the South is recommended. The hope is expressed that, given a lead, the private banks will follow suit. Aid-giving countries were urged to double their contributions by 1985 (although, in fact, Britain reduced its official aid). Beyond these suggestions, *Common Crisis* indicates that a revision of the post-war settlement of the world trade and financial framework at Breton Woods is required largely with a view to strengthening the currently weak and dependent position of the Third World. The free-trade perspective of the reports has already been mentioned and the above financial initiatives were perceived as complementing this approach.

The ascendancy of free market ideas and policies

In reality, the liberal-conservatism described in the previous section has tended to dominate the world economic scene in the 1980s and 1990s rather than the liberal reformism of the 'Brandt Reports'. No consensus has developed among the governments of richer countries to adopt the bulk of the Brandt proposals. The dependency theorist, Wallerstein's comment that capitalism is more dominant at world than national level because of the absence of significant restraining checks, seems increasingly true. The 'Brandt Reports' offered some voluntarily introduced restraints and a marginal redistribution of power and resources. If its major proposals are not adopted, as now seems likely, relative global inequalities are likely further to increase.

In 1985 a report was published claiming both to 'defend' and 'extend' the reasoning of the above two reports. It was the report of the Socialist International Committee on Economic Policy, chaired by Michael Manley, titled *Global Challenge: From Crisis to Co-operation: Breaking the North South Stalemate*. Although firmly based on social democratic principles, the report was more radical than its predecessors. It declared monetarism dead and called for an application of updated Keynesian principles to tackle the needs of the global economy. In addition it demands 'a major redistribution of resources'. *Global Challenge* is sharply critical both of the failure of the United States to pursue fundamental reforms to deal with the debt crisis of the South and of much of the United States' foreign policy. Although the report's 'main proposal is for a multi-lateral solution to the North-South' problem, it also suggests that others should proceed without the United States if that country's leaders are unwilling to move ahead. One of the report's most challenging statements was: 'Without disarmament there can be no genuine development.'

Gender and development

The established perspectives on development, including even underdevelopment theories, tend to ignore both the impact of development on women, and the importance of their labour preceding it. As for strategies for future development it is only in the area of population control that adequate appreciation of women's role is beginning to occur (see p. 609). As Aidan Foster-Cater ironically comments, in development theory, women are 'the satellite that is no one's metropolis'.

Leghorn and Parker's *Woman's Worth: Sexual Economics and the World of Women* (1981) provides a feminist framework for analysing development. For them the main gender issue is simple:

> *In virtually all existing cultures, women's work, though usually invisible to the male eye, sustains the economy and subsidises the profits, leisure time and higher standard of living enjoyed by individual men, private corporations, and male dominated governments. In spite of this, women live almost universally without the corresponding economic, political and social control over their lives that such a crucial role should mean. How does this happen?*
>
> *(Leghorn and Parker, 1981)*

A feminist view of power

An attempt is made to grapple with the issue of why men generally have more power than women (patriarchy) in Chapter 7. Here, the question is the relationship between development and gender. Leghorn and Parker provide three categories which they describe as 'an alternative women-centred way of looking at and understanding the economic organisation of cultures throughout the world'. They are:

1 Minimal power. This involves minimal access to crucial resources, low valuation and freedom in reproduction, high violence against them, and few occasions to share experiences, support and resources. Examples are: Ethiopia, Peru, Algeria and Japan.

2 Token power. This is a more variable situation in relation to the areas indicated in (1) and includes 'some freedom to create networks, though these networks may be undermined when they become effective bases of change'. Examples are: USA, Cuba, the USSR and Sweden.

3 Negotiating power. This involves greater access to resources which may be different to men's and enough economic power to provide a bargaining tool, high valuation and support for reproduction and highly developed networks. Examples are: China (post-revolutionary), Ewé and Iroquois cultures.

It may come as a shock to the reader that the modern societies of the USA, the USSR and Sweden appear only in the second category. In this respect, Leghorn and Parker receive some support from Ivan Illich, though their positions require distinguishing. Illich argues in *Gender* that in many pre-industrial societies male and female roles were often complementary in what he refers to as 'the regime of gender'. Development imposes a cruder sexual division of labour in which patriarchal domination increases. Leghorn and Parker are less inclined to romanticise gender relations in pre-industrial societies and show, for instance, that in many such societies women have been physically mutilated (foot-binding in traditional China, infibulation in parts of Africa – a severe form of female circumcision) as well as socially subordinated. They, therefore, discriminate between those pre-industrial societies in which women have more power (3) than in industrial societies and those which have less (1).

Leghorn and Parker offer no grand theory of gender and development. The impact of development on each society varies. They do argue, however, that:

> Because women's role was secondary in virtually all cultures before colonialism (whether these assumptions and values were overt or subtle), the existing norms and institutions made it possible for Western-based forms of sexual oppression to be superimposed.
>
> (Leghorn and Parker, 1981)

Thus, the imposition of colonial taxes on indigenous inhabitants would often break up the family, requiring the male to work in the urban-industrial economy and leaving the women to do domestic and agricultural work (including what had been the work of their spouses). The assumption that men are 'naturally' better suited to modern industrial and agricultural work has also reinforced the subordination of women. Thus, whilst women in Africa do 70 per cent of the agricultural work, almost all the agricultural aid has gone to men. Most education and training funds also go to men.

They point out that there are occasions when women's status improves as a result of Western influence. Thus, access to work outside the home in Algeria and Japan broke women's traditional seclusion and improved their chances of acquiring some economic and social independence. In Africa, infibulation, although still widespread, is now typically done in more sanitary conditions. Of course, Western female norms are not always accepted wholesale by traditional societies. For instance, women in Iran have long struggled to balance traditional Muslim belief with what they see as the more desirable aspects of Western female behaviour.

Gendered labour

It would be a mistake, in any case, to imagine the liberation, female or otherwise, has been a prime purpose of the Western nations in relation to the South. Although not dealt with by Leghorn and Parker, the working conditions of certain women employed by Western corporations illustrates highly patriarchal attitudes. Thus, in the Philippines, Mexico and elsewhere young women are sometimes employed (until they are 'burnt out') in such areas as assembling electronic components or textiles. The personnel manager of one multinational presented the following recruitment criteria:

> I choose people with elegant figures and thin hands because they are more agile ... I take physical appearance into account; you can tell if people are aggressive by the way they look, so I try to choose people who seem more docile and can be managed more easily.

A businessman from the United States showed a similar level of enlightenment:

> There's no welfare here. You can push Mexican workers. Also there's the 48 hour week. You don't see any horsing around here, no queues for the water-fountain or the bathroom. These girls work.

It is businessmen, remember, along with government and the military, who are mainly responsible for the dealings of the West with the Third World. The people they deal with are usually rich, unrepresentative male elites. As Teresa Hayter says, 'The majority of governments supported by the West are authoritarian'. It is perhaps little wonder that some feminists believe that women would make a better job of running the world than men and that they merit a chance to do so.

The Iroquois cultures of the eighteenth and nineteenth centuries are among those in which Leghorn and Parker consider women have negotiating power. Significantly, women had considerable economic power both in the production and distribution of food. Further, descent was matrilineal and residence upon marriage was the home of the wife's mother. The leading women, the matrons, exercised an indirect political power in selecting the male council of elders. Women worked collectively and had ample opportunity for 'networking' – a process of mutual support which Leghorn and Parker greatly emphasise.

A female global caste?

They conclude that despite differences in women's lack of power across cultures, women are a global caste. They record their impression that within each of their three categories, women overwhelmingly carry the burden of family care and receive a comparably limited amount of time and money from their male partners. They urge women to organise on the basis of a matriarchal concept of power, reflecting values of creativity, co-operation and caring. Institutions would reflect those values and would be organised in a decentralised and collective way rather than hierarchically and individualistically.

Strictly, Leghorn and Parker's view of women as a caste is not reconcilable with the socialist view that the primary category of social analysis is class (see pp. 189–90). However, the values and institutional frameworks they advocate are remarkably similar to traditional libertarian socialist ideals and as such are as applicable to men as to women. Leghorn and Parker recognise this but are not prepared to wait for men to act accordingly. In time, perhaps men will change, but in their view, the immediate task is for women to liberate themselves. In the Third World many feminists are, of necessity, less separatist than Leghorn and Parker, and pool their feminist principles in movements of national liberation and socialism. The goals of national independence and combating poverty may take immediate precedence over reforming

(a) Foreign direct investment inflows as percentage of GDP

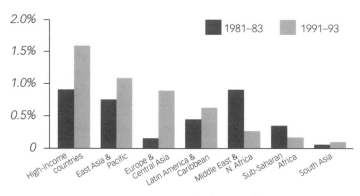

(b) Forecast real GDP growth per capita, 1996–2005

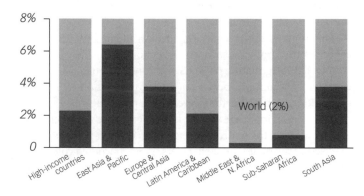

(Source: World Bank in *The Financial Times*, 8.5.1996:6)

Figure 20.7 Growth flows from inward investment

patriarchal structures within a society, as they did in China. Even so, women often acquire new roles, experience and confidence in these movements and in this practical way the principle of gender equality is asserted.

Conclusion: under/development – the future

If any doubt remains, the next section – on globalisation – will confirm that the world is dominated by capitalism – economically, socially and culturally. There are many constraints on and modifications of capitalism at international, bloc and national level but the ascendancy of the capitalist system is clear. The capitalist system is not intended to create economic equality or anything like it. However, is global capitalism, at least, helping to foster development? Figure 20.7 (a and b) does no more than add further data to that already discussed but it is data which indicates current and future trends.

Figure 20.7a shows the level of foreign direct investment into the high income countries (i.e. 'the developed' countries) and into the rest of the world by region. Foreign direct investment is the amount invested in a national economy by foreign nationals. What Figure 20.7a shows is that the high income countries of the North and the fast developing economies of the East Asia and Pacific

region receive higher levels of foreign investment. In other words the rich invest most in the rich – both on a percentage basis and overwhelmingly in absolute terms (not shown here).

The data in Figure 20.7b illustrates a number of issues and must present a dilemma for many Southern country governments. First, the pattern of global inequality will not change greatly in the foreseeable future. Second – nevertheless the growth rate in some poorer countries, particularly in South Asia, is likely to accelerate – and at a somewhat faster rate than in high income countries. So the pattern of inequality of global capitalism can change even though the richer countries have accumulated vast resources. Third, Sub-Saharan Africa and now the Middle East and North Africa will get relatively poorer and absolutely only marginally better off.

What development policies should those countries with indifferent prospects pursue? Should they seek to 'protect' their economies and try to develop fairly independently? Or, perhaps as well, should they seek to form trading blocs with similarly positioned countries? Or should they – as the World Bank argues – liberalise their economies and trading relations and so 'integrate' more into the 'world economy' – which, according to the Bank is what more successful developing economies have done. However, it is debatable whether some of the world's weaker economies could withstand international competition. The only thing the future guarantees is hard choices in difficult circumstances.

Questions

1. Which perspective on development/underdevelopment best explains the extent of world inequality?
2. Which perspective suggests the most convincing solutions to world inequality?
3. 'Marxist theory exaggerates the power and effects of world capitalism'. Discuss.

Globalisation

Terminology and explanation

Like most major sociological concepts, that of globalisation has been defined in various ways. However, Malcolm Waters gives a fairly neutral definition of globalisation. He defines globalisation as:

> *A social process in which the constraints of geography on social and cultural arrangements recede and in which people become increasingly aware that they are receding.*
>
> *(1995:3)*

In other words, physical distance and obstacle have become less important in communication and exchange in social (which includes, political and economic) and cultural matters – and

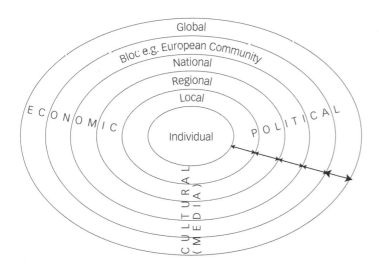

Figure 20.8 Levels (or overlapping spheres) of interaction

people are aware that this is so. It would, indeed, be surprising if they were not. Virtually everybody knows that people and objects are conveyed around the world more swiftly than in the past and that words and images can cross the world in seconds. In David Harvey's phrase 'time and space are compressed'. Thus, a message that 200 years ago took several weeks and considerable physical effort to deliver, now only takes seconds.

Increasing global interconnectedness shows itself in economics, politics and culture. Where one looks at matters from an individual, regional, national or bloc point of view, a global dimension to contemporary life is apparent.

Figure 20.8 illustrates the various levels of interaction and meaning constructed in the contemporary world. Interaction can occur between all levels but globalisation theory argues that there is a greater global component to interaction in the modern world than previously. Although the figure has a rough spatial reference, the point is that communication is no longer limited by space. Events and images can be experienced virtually simultaneously throughout the globe. Communication is two-way or can be networked. Individuals can address each other regardless of where they may or may not be. Individuals or groups of sufficient power and influence can address global populations (occasionally this is done by terrorists or otherwise illicitly when unauthorised access to communication is gained). Crucially important to globalisation theory is that reactions and responses occur at all levels of the global system. Thus, localities might gain grants or aid from the block level or at the global level from the UN. Again, individual, local or national responses to aspects of globalisation – say, the activities of a media multinational – can vary greatly. This point is examined more theoretically later and in Reading 2 (p. 601 and pp. 621-2).

Anthony Giddens: globalisation: three key aspects

There are various explanations and descriptive models of globalisation but at this point it will help to take three concepts of Anthony Giddens to illustrate three key aspects: time-space distanciation, disembedding and reflexivity.

1 *Time-space distanciation.* Giddens uses this term to describe the separation of time and space brought about by modern communications. The term means the same as Harvey's concept of 'time-space compression'. Anyone using the telephone experiences time-space distanciation or compression – the further the call, the greater the compression.

2 *Disembedding.* This term refers to 'the lifting out' of social relations from local contexts by means of mechanisms that enable relationships to occur across a wide range of contexts, and potentially globally. There are two types of disembedding mechanisms: symbolic tokens and expert systems. For instance, money – a token of exchange-value – allows relationships based on economic exchange to take place across the world. Expert systems such as psychiatry or management theory similarly replace personal or local knowledge and has with standard expectations and service. Instead of working things out with a friend, neighbour or colleague, we may 'consult an expert'.

3 *Reflexivity.* This key concept refers to the need in modern society to be conscious of and respond to the innovatory and changing nature of expert systems and society generally. Both modern individuals and modern society itself are reflexive i.e. constantly reconsidering and adjusting. Thus a great deal of reflection is occurring in relation to the welfare state – which will probably be restructured as a result.

Giddens is especially interested in the interplay of the local and global levels of action and identity. This theoretical analysis is clear, if complex, and avoids simplistic formulae (see p. 600).

What has caused globalisation and what is its significance? We will address these questions later. First, it will be helpful further to illustrate globalisation in the economic, political and cultural fields.

Forms of globalisation

Economic globalisation

Geoffrey Barraclough has suggested that by the mid twentieth century, European dominance had been superseded by a global age, the core dynamic of which is, in his view, economic (1978). This new global economic framework involved resurgent Japan, the two superpowers, the European community and a confrontation between the rich and poor worlds. It had its origins in the development of trade routes; in the growth of trade, including economic dependency; and in the massive flow of capital around the world, some of it in the form of investment by the industrial countries in the non-industrialised. The institutional regulation of the post-war world economy was described earlier (see pp. 577-9).

Three aspects stand out in contemporary economic globalisation: globalisation of production; globalisation of products and, therefore, of consumption; and the globalisation of the financial markets. Large multinational companies have branches in several countries and began to integrate production globally from the 1970s. Integration of production involves the assembling of a commodity from components made in different factories in various parts of the world. Because any given component is usually easily produceable in more than one location, the globalisation of production tends to strengthen capital and weaken labour. It also lowers costs as production can be switched to where labour is cheap or efficient or where tax or subsidy incentives exist.

The globalisation of products and consumption involves creating a global market for a single product or variation of a single product. McDonald burgers and Ford's Mondeo (literally 'world' car) are examples. Research costs on the 'Mondeo' and other 'world' cars tend to be extremely high and, although the cars are basically standardised, they are sold on quality and reliability. McDonald's now opens two-thirds of its new outlets each year outside of the USA – where the market for its products is largely saturated. McDonald's can now be found as far apart as Moscow and Hong Kong – where it is positioning itself for expansion into China.

The globalisation of the financial and money markets involves two notable aspects. First, banks and stockbroking houses are increasingly internationally owned and operated, especially in Britain. Thus, the merchant banks Barings and Morgan Grenfell are foreign owned as is the Midland High Street Bank (by the Hong Kong and Shanghai Bank). Second, largely due to computer technology, money can be much more easily and quickly transferred around the world. This can facilitate trade transactions, but it has also created a huge market in money itself – much of it essentially speculating in currency exchange. The downfall of Barings Bank and its transfer to Dutch ownership occurred as a result of the speculations of a young employee, Nick Leeson, who bet lavishly on the direction in which the Japanese yen would move – and got it wrong.

How far has economic globalisation occurred?

The above brief introduction to economic globalisation does not deal with theoretical debates nor with the relationship between economic, political and cultural globalisation. However, one fundament controversy should be presented here: some commentators argue that economic globalisation is not new and that its contemporary extent has been exaggerated. Paul Hirst argues that a globalised economy would have four basic features – none of which the international economy (his preferred term) has.

These are:

1 International processes rather than national economies and governments would dominate at the national level. In fact, argues Hirst, it is at the *bloc* level – Japan; European Community; North Atlantic Free Trade Association – that the international economy is largely regulated.

2 The main players would be genuinely *trans*national rather than merely multinational companies with an international management operating according to global market conditions and without a national base. In few, if any, companies is this actually the case.

3 Capital would dominate labour. In fact, Hirst argues that the blocs are able to protect labour and pursue common strategies of social provision within their boundaries. He suggests that Britain's attempt to opt out of the social chapter will undermine the conditions of labour without greatly helping Britain's long term economic position.

4 Economics and politics would pull apart – with the former being in the ascendancy. Hirst argues that in practice an open world trading system still ultimately depends on the willingness of the United States to police it.

Will Hutton has contended that what he terms 'the myth of globalisation' serves to undermine the confidence of national governments that they can control the activities of multinational companies in the interests of their own people, particularly their labour forces. He suggests that a more robust approach is quite possible, especially in the wider regulatory context of the institutions of international co-operation whose authority is now 'more, not less important' (*The Guardian*, 12.6.1995:17).

Comment

Hirst and Hutton's arguments suggest that it would be simplistic to assume that the world or even the world's economy 'has been taken over by' transnational companies. Blocs, national governments, and international regulatory agencies exercise great – often conflicting and economic counterbalancing – power. Equally, however, it is clear that large companies seek and help to create global markets in key commodities. As a result some achieve great wealth, power and cultural influence especially in poorer countries which become *dependent* on their investment. Further, financial markets have become highly globalised although it remains possible for particular national governments to opt out of this process.

Political globalisation

The basis of the view that political globalisation is occurring is that, on the one hand, there is 'a crisis of the territorial nation-state' (Bell, 1987) and that, on the other, multinational corporations and certain global and bloc-wide inter-governmental institutions have developed a global power and presence.

Daniel Bell famously proposed that the nation-state is 'too small for the big problems of life, and too big for the small problems of life' (1987). To the extent that Bell is right, this may explain the reported widespread apathy among the citizens of Western democracies towards their governments. Thus, problems such as multinational investment/disinvestment, global pollution, and the threat of a rogue nuclear power may be seen as 'too big' for a national government effectively to deal with (this is even more likely to be the case in respect to poor countries). On the other hand, central government control of local systems of, say, schooling or housing policy may be locally resented.

David Held has argued, in effect, that nation-states have ceded some sovereignty to larger entities in order for a range of 'big' problems to be dealt with more effectively. Thus, the European Union deals with a wide range of political, social and cultural issues; NATO with military matters; WTO and IMF with trading and financial matters. It is important to add, that the United Nations is also a key global organisation with a wide remit. It is active in the humanitarian and health fields, in pollution research and in peace keeping.

Held has suggested that the above developments could provide a basis for a supra-national state – a kind of world government to deal with the 'big' issues – which would have legislative and coercive powers. Many consider that if such an institution were to be established it should be guided in its goals and actions by the United Nations Charter of Human Rights. Such a strong centralisation of authority and power would only be justified if directed by fundamental humanitarian principles. Even so, it is easy to imagine that such a supra-national state would struggle to please the poor and rich countries equally.

Aware, perhaps, of the possible abuses of centralised power, Leslie Sklair has outlined an alternative, more direct response to the transnational corporations, the transnational capitalist class (see below), and the culture/ideology of consumerism (1995). This is the disruptive action of social movements which Sklair sees emerging and which he supports. Two examples occurring in 1995 can be cited to exemplify Sklair's argument. First, is the protests against the conditions in which livestock are transported in the European Community. This protest was supported by Animal Rights, generated some local involvement at the ports of transit, and mobilised a wider public opinion. The second example is the successful attempt by Greenpeace to stop Shell disposing of one of its decommissioned oil platforms under the sea. Greenpeace's effectiveness in mobilising public opinion was impressive. Even when Greenpeace acknowledged that it was mistaken in some of its pollution estimates, Shell remained in respectful public dialogue with the organisation (see p. 615). It may be, as Sklair implies, that the disruptive politics of social movements will be more effective in confronting 'transnational power' than the more cumbersome and time-consuming response of political parties and national governments. However, it is difficult to conceive of effective control of transnational corporations without political action at the national and/or transnational political level.

The process of political globalisation: summary

To summarise this section, then, the alleged process of political globalisation develops something like this:

- The power of the modern nation-state declines because of ...
- the rise of transnational corporations and ...
- the emergence of a range of 'big', global problems which, require ...
- the development of global political institutions possibly even ...
- a supra-national state, meanwhile ...
- opposition to TNCs and protest against global problems is mounted by social movements, often in local contexts.

Cultural globalisation

Is there a common culture developing across the globe? This is a huge question. It will help to distinguish between culture in its narrow and in its wider sense. Narrowly culture is often taken to refer to leisure activity including patterns of consumption of media and dress (style). A more general usage of the term regards culture as a whole way of life whether society-wide or limited to a subculture (see p. 476). This usage includes economic and political norms and behaviour as well as leisure and consumption. It is culture in the more general sense that is discussed here. A discussion of cultural globalisation specifically in relation to the media is given earlier (see pp. 420-2). Mike Featherstone in *Consumer Culture and Postmodernism* (1991) usefully suggests a number of ways in which the globalisation of culture may be occurring. They can be summarised as follows:

1 There are certain important trends towards cultural globalisation but cultural differentiation is also occurring (see point 3). Featherstone gives as an example of cultural globalisation the development of global financial markets in which the main actors share many business and lifestyle norms and values, e.g. an international frame of reference in leisure as well as work. Other commentators stress the extent to which certain areas of *consumption* have become globalised at a more popular level e.g. fast food, 'world' cars.

It is worth extending the above examples of cultural globalisation by reference to the *Concise Oxford Dictionary of Sociology*. This particular definition appears to take the view that globalisation is *primarily* a cultural phenomenon and only secondarily an economic and political one:

> *Globalisation theory examines the emergence of a global cultural system. It suggests that global culture is brought about by a variety of social and cultural developments; the existence of a world-satellite information system; the emergence of global patterns of consumption and consumerism; the cultivation of cosmopolitan life-styles; the emergence of global sport such as the Olympic games, world football competitions, and international tennis matches; the spread of world tourism; the decline of the sovereignty of the nation-state (but see qualification – point 3, author's brackets); the growth of a global military system; recognition of a world-wide ecological crisis, the development of world-wide health problems such as AIDS; the emergence of world political systems such as the League of Nations and the United Nations; the creation of global political movements such as Marxism, extension of the concept of human rights; and the complex interchange between world systems.*
>
> *(202)*

The above definition reflects the broad sweep of theories of cultural globalisation which embrace political and social as well as cultural developments more narrowly considered. However, it is on matters of communication, lifestyle and consumption on which cultural globalisation theory tends to focus.

2 Global compression (a key aspect of globalisation) is occurring in that 'the world becomes united to the extent that it is regarded as one place' (146). Featherstone, along with Roland Robertson, considers that many do increasingly see the world as one place. Both the media and increased personal geographical mobility feed this perception. A whole range of 'problems' (e.g., famine in Ethiopia) and events (e.g. the rugby world cup) routinely have a global dimension and, as in the case of the latter example, may be constructed globally as events. Of course, this tendency to think and act within a global *framework* does not mean that either individuals or nations always agree *in detail* – often, they meet precisely to debate or compete.

3 Thirdly, Featherstone sees a possible development away from nationalism towards a kind of global humanism (perhaps based on a concept of human rights) which will allow for local diversity and multi-culturalism which nationalism has tended to repress. Thus, cultural globalisation posits two *alternative* trends: a global framework of competing nation-states; the possibility of the rise of a global frame of reference at the expense of nationalism.

Comment: markets and media

It is not possible to understand the concept of cultural globalisation without linking it to economic globalisation. Increasingly, the key link between the economic and the cultural is the commercial media. By carrying advertisements and other images of 'desirable'

consumer lifestyle, the media helps to make global markets. In order to test the cultural globalisation thesis, it is necessary to examine media globalisation in detail. This has been done in Chapter 17, pp. 420-2 and it is relevant to re-read that section now.

The globalisation thesis again raises the question of the relationship of culture to the economy. Postmodernists such as Featherstone argue that globalisation has greatly increased the relative importance of culture. In contrast, historically, Marxists have usually argued that the economy structures culture. However, it is, in fact, the American Marxist, Frederick Jameson, who has been most influential in analysing the extent to which people have become seduced into accepting capitalism by their obsession with cultural consumption. Somewhat like Baudrillard, he sees capitalism now as virtually a closed system, sealed against radical change.

Theories examining globalisation: the causes

It has been suggested that accounts of modernity can be divided into two theoretical approaches (McGrew, 1992). One approach is monocausal – stressing a single cause of globalisation. The other approach is multi-causal, suggesting that a number of causes are involved. Major figures adopting the first approach are Immanuel Wallerstein, Leslie Sklair and James Rosenau. Anthony Giddens and Roland Robertson are prominent among those who adopt a multi-causal perspective. I will deal with each in turn. There is no firm link between monocausal theory and Marxism and multi-causal theory and Weberianism. However, Wallerstein and Sklair are Marxists and, in many ways Giddens stands in the tradition of Max Weber.

Monocausal explanations of globalisation

1   Immanuel Wallerstein

Wallerstein argues that we now live in a capitalist world system. It is capitalism that drives the process of globalisation. Capitalism operates across national boundaries but the role of the state can be significant in its spread. The capitalist world economy began in one part of the globe (mainly Europe) and gradually 'incorporated' the whole globe. Wallerstein divides the modern capitalist world system into three types of states:

i   Core states: which are developed, rich, have strong national cultures and are globally dominant e.g. the USA; Japan; and the European Union.

ii Peripheral areas which are economically dependent, poor, culturally invaded and weak e.g. Africa, Latin America.

iii Semi-peripheral areas: which are partly dependent on the core states, have moderately strong governments and economies that are likely to be declining (e.g. certain of the former socialist Eastern European States) or rising (e.g. Singapore, Malaysia).

According to Wallerstein, the capitalist world system is characterised by a division of labour in which the core states retain high skill, high investment production, with low skill, low investment production occurring in the periphery and semi-periphery. However, capitalism is seen as a dynamic system of cyclical boom and bust and, as the semi-peripheral areas indicate, change can occur.

Anthony Giddens regards Wallerstein's capitalist world system theory as a precursor of globalisation theory. However, Malcolm Waters suggests that it is almost exclusively an economic theory – lacking the necessary component of cultural globalisation to make it a genuine theory of globalisation. Two points can be made against Waters. First, it is a matter of debate whether economic or cultural (or political) forces are primary in the globalisation dynamic. Second, within the tradition of neo-Marxist thought characterised by Wallerstein, there is a powerful analysis of global, capitalist culture. One such analysis is provided by Leslie Sklair whose work we now consider.

2   Leslie Sklair

Sklair, like Wallerstein, argues that what drives the process of globalisation is capitalism. For him the transnational corporations are the key manifestation of contemporary capitalism. He distinguishes three levels at which transnational practices occur:

Level	Dominant institution
i economic	transnational corporation
ii political	transnational capitalist class
iii cultural	consumerism

Sklair argues that the power of transnational corporations and of the transnational capitalist class exceeds that of nation states although he considers that first the British capitalist class and now the American are hegemonic in promoting global capitalism.

According to Sklair, members of the transnational capitalist class is much wider than the owners of the means of production which make up Marx's 'bourgeoisie'. It is comprised of 'the entrepreneurial elite managers of firms, senior state functionaries, leading politicians, members of the learned professions, and persons of similar standing in all spheres of society' (62). This mixed group of people is seen as accepting, promoting and benefiting from global capitalism. They often do so at the expense of poorer social groups, whether intentionally or not.

Sklair explains the global dominance of capitalism not simply in terms of the economic, political and military strength of capitalist societies but also in terms of the appeal of 'the ideology of consumerism'. Advertising and Western-made popular programmes such as 'the soaps' tantalisingly display mainly Western-made consumer items throughout the world, including much of the Third World. These 'modern things' are what most people seem to 'want' (although Sklair considers that much

consumption is 'induced' by capitalist display). As Sklair put it: '*Modernity*' becomes what global capitalism has to offer' (230). Along with some other radical thinkers, Sklair considers that the new social movements offer the best chance of disrupting the practices and power of transnational capitalism (see pp. 316-8).

3   James Rosenau

Whereas Wallerstein and Sklair see capitalism as the force behind globalisation, for Rosenau:

> *it is technology … that has so greatly diminished geographic and social distances … it is technology … that has fostered the interdependence of local, national and international communities that is far greater than any previous experienced.*
>
> *(1991:17)*

Technology, especially the technology of communication, allows people to by-pass national restrictions and authority. This new level of communication and action is not international but transnational i.e. it is a level of interaction not between but across/above nations. Some examples will clarify what Rosenau sees as a decentralised and multi-centric 'transnational society':

- Transnational organisations e.g. McDonald's, the United Nations.
- Transnational problems e.g. ethnic conflict, pollution.
- Transnational events e.g. the French nuclear bomb tests of 1995 which provoked a worldwide response, the Rugby World Cup of 1995 in which the games were played at times for maximum and optimum media access (i.e. with teams' home audiences in mind).
- Transnational communities e.g. religious (Islam), knowledge (academic), lifestyle (skinheads).
- Transnational structures e.g. global markets.

The scope of transnational action is, then, substantial. However, it does not replace the national level. Rather, Rosenau sees two worlds developing; one, a multi-centric world of diverse, relatively equal actors, and the other a national-centric world of national actors. The two worlds or levels interact. For instance, nation states seek, often with difficulty, to regulate, if not control, the transnational world of communications. In the case of internet, satellite and commercial software, states tend to react well behind the speed of innovation. Similarly, there have been occasions when nation states have seemed fairly powerless before the machinations of global financial markets. Rosenau, then, considers that we now live in a *bifurcated* world, the two levels of which do not mesh together entirely comfortably.

Conclusion: monocausal explanations of globalisation

Wallerstein and Sklair cite capitalism as the key dynamic underlying globalisation. In doing so, they are close to the theoretical analysis of Karl Marx who over 100 years ago described the relentless worldwide search for markets of European capital. In contrast, Rosenau is closer to Weber who also recognised the role of modern technology in helping to set a framework in which modern life would develop. However, Weber's master concept of 'rationality' embraced more than Rosenau's concept of technology and Weber's causality tended much more to the multi-causal than the monocausal. In this key respect, Anthony Giddens seems to stand closer to Weber.

Multi-causal explanations of globalisation

Anthony Giddens

Anthony Giddens considers that globalisation is one of the major consequences of modernity. Rationality and invention – particularly in the areas of production, exchange and communications – have linked localities in a complex web of relationships. Whereas Wallerstein and Sklair attribute globalisation primarily to the expansion of capitalism, Giddens sees four distinct, though related causal dimensions. These are:

- Capitalism
- Industrialism
- The inter-state system, i.e., relations of nations
- Militarism

Giddens agrees that the expansion of the capitalist system substantially contributed to globalisation. However, like Weber, he sees industrialism as contributing independently to both modernity and globalisation. Thus, the former Soviet Union developed a non-capitalist, industrial economy which, with some success, it set up as a global alternative to capitalism. This has, of course, now collapsed.

Malcolm Waters suggests that on the matter of modernity 'Giddens' main message is that a modern society is not defined entirely by its economic base but by the fact that it is a nation-state' (48). The powerful national states of Western Europe and the United States forged global domains by political and military means (Giddens' fourth point). Political and military action could be linked to economic motives but is not necessarily subordinate to them as Marxists suggest. Nation state activity helped to create globalisation and the relationships of nation states is a key aspect of globalisation in the contemporary world. Giddens sees no

necessary contradiction between the existence of nation states and national identities and of globalisation. However, he is keenly interested in the interplay of forces and identities at all levels (see p. 595).

The three aspects considered characteristic of globalisation by Giddens – time-space distanciation, disembedding and reflexivity – were discussed above (see p. 595). Given that he considers that these factors are become increasingly significant, he also believes that the process of globalisation is intensifying. Driven forward by the juggernaut of modernity, globalisation is a process which destroys and undermines as well as creates common experiences. It 'is a process of uneven development that fragments as it co-ordinates' (1990:175).

Roland Robertson

Like Giddens, Robertson sees a number of causes as contributory to globalisation. He considers that the economic, political and cultural developments discussed above (see pp. 595-8), each make distinctive contributions to the globalisation process. However, he himself does not devise a theory which attempts to explain the relationship of these three factors or their precise contribution to globalisation. In his more recent work, Robertson does refer to 'the intensification of consciousness of the world as a whole' (1992:8) and focuses particularly on what he perceives as increasing globalisation at the cultural level. Whereas previously economic and political trends to globalisation were more obvious he considers that since about the late 1960s 'the world *moved* from being merely *in itself* to the problem or possibility of being *for itself*' (1992:55). In other words people are beginning to think and act more in global terms, for instance, in relation to the environment.

Unlike Giddens, Robertson contends that the process of globalisation pre-dates the rise of capitalism and modernity, although both tend to accelerate globalisation. Robertson presents quite a complex periodisation of globalisation, suggesting that the germinal phase occurred between 1400 and 1750 with the gradual dissolution of Christendom and the rise of a scientific understanding of humanity's 'place in the universe'. By the twentieth century, Robertson considers that a complex interplay of cultural forces and meanings have penetrated the previously largely localised lives of individuals. In the contemporary world, individual and national identities are defined partly with reference to the international system of societies and humanity in general. Malcolm Waters usefully summarises Robertson's analysis of these globalised relationships in a passage worth some consideration.

> *Robertson makes numerous careful reservations about his argument. He claims that globalisation, for example, is neither necessarily a good nor a bad thing – its moral character will be accomplished by the inhabitants of the planet. He is also not saying that the world is, as a consequence of globalisation, a more integrated or harmonious place but merely that it is a more unified or systematic place. He means by this that while events in any part of the world will increasingly have consequences for, or be referenced against events in other distant parts, this relativisation may not always be positive. Indeed, the world as a system may well be riven by conflicts that are far more intractable than the previous disputes between nations. However he is saying the following: first that the world is experiencing accelerated globalisation to such an extent that it can be regarded as an accomplishment; second, that we need new concepts to analyse this process; third, that the process is fundamentally cultural and reflexive in character; and fourth that globalisation follows the path of its own inexorable logic.*
>
> (45-6)

Robertson has been criticised for implying that Western humanism is emerging as the globalising philosophical and ethical system. Kavolis has argued, that traditional religion, particularly in the form of Islam, is capable of repulsing Westernisation, including Western humanism, and, indeed, of expanding itself (1988). However, Robertson is careful to avoid the assumption of any inevitable march towards a harmonious, humanistic world nor does he argue that conflict and disagreement will necessarily diminish.

Conclusion: globalisation – a dialectical rather than a unilinear, process

Anthony Giddens has emphasised that the dynamic of globalisation is not proceeding in a single, predictable direction. There is no foreseeable destination which the globe will reach. On the contrary, global trends can spark opposition and counter-movements. Another way of expressing this distinction is that globalisation is a dialectical rather than a unilinear movement. Anthony McGrew has helpfully summarised several 'binary oppositions' or dualities which are 'commonly identified within the discourse of globalisation' (see Reading 2).

These dualities are:

- Universalisation versus particularisation
- Homogenisation versus differentiation
- Integration versus fragmentation
- Centralisation versus decentralisation
- Juxtaposition versus syncretisation

McGrew gives his own examples of these binary oppositions in the reading but others can be offered here. Tourism may now be virtually *universal*, but *particular* localities respond to it

distinctively (see pp. 616-8). A global sameness or *homogenisation* occurs in certain dress styles but these styles are often 'tweaked', or *differentiated* by, for instance producer-consumer youth groups (see pp. 462-3). Globalisation can *integrate* across national boundaries yet fragmentation into perceived ethnic or national identities seems increasingly to be occurring. Globalisation allows for *centralised* surveillance and control but contemporary social movements constantly resist. In late modernity, images and artefacts of every historical period are *juxtaposed* – often via the media – yet groups reclaim or refashion 'their own' self images and identities from the apparent chaos often mixing various styles and traditions.

Questions

1 Describe economic, political and cultural globalisation.
2 What has caused the process of globalisation?

Under/development and globalisation themes

The following themes concerning under/development and globalisation have been selected for more detailed treatment:

1 World population and inequality
2 Urbanisation and industrialisation
3 Development and the environment
4 Media globalisation (Presented in Chapter 17, pp. 520-4).

The importance of these matters is obvious. The first two have long been recognised as key areas of under/development. The second two have been selected because, as well as being relevant to under/development, they relate directly to globalisation. Consideration of them illustrates again that globalisation cannot be properly considered without raising issues of under/development. Who is affected by it? Who controls the images and ideas dominant on the global media? For now and for the foreseeable future, globalisation is not producing 'one world' so much as restructuring the context of conflict and competition.

Theme 1: world population, inequality and under/development

Are development and population size linked?

The relationship between the development of a society and its population size and growth rate is one of the fiercest issues in both public and academic life. At the heart of this debate is a crucial contemporary global issue: *why* do some societies continue to languish in poverty, while others develop rapidly. Does the solution to stimulating development lie mainly in controlling population growth or elsewhere. Initially, three approaches to this question will be indicated here and these will recur throughout the remainder of this chapter.

1 Reduce population growth (plus aid) to create the conditions for development (liberal/social democratic)

It has long been a widely held view in the West that 'there is a population problem in the Third World'. In the 1960s this view was often associated with liberal/social democratic and even radical thinkers who wanted to finance large-scale family planning projects in poorer countries. In addition, they often favoured providing aid (usually in the form of low-interest loans) for infrastructural or basic economic development e.g. roads, dams, factories.

The view that 'population control' is the key to development remains strong. It is a view that historically has been associated with the World Bank. As recently as 1995, Robert McNamara, President of the bank, reiterated this position in undiluted terms:

> *The greatest single obstacle to the economic and social advancement of the majority of peoples in the undeveloped world is rampant population growth ... The threat of unmanageable population pressures is very much like the threat of nuclear war.*
>
> *(Quoted in The Times 16.8.1995:16)*

This view has become severely controversial. First, it is widely interpreted outside the West as blaming poorer countries for the poverty they experience. Often, outside the West, it is exploitation by Western governments and capital that is seen as the root problem of poverty and underdevelopment. Recently, a group of Southern countries at the United Nations tried to have a motion discussing 'excessive population growth' replaced with one discussing 'over-consumption' in the West. The view that it is inequality both global and within poorer societies rather than population growth that explains underdevelopment is widely held outside the West. In addition there is substantial expert opinion which regards reduction in inequality within poorer societies as the key to reduction in population growth.

2 Reduce inequality to reduce population growth (radical/Marxist view)

The view that if the poor had more material and cultural resources, then, they would be less likely to have large families is argued by Susan George and is presented in some detail below (see p. 607).

This approach does not primarily argue that greater equality

Greed and need

Estimates of amounts spent worldwide, $billion per year:

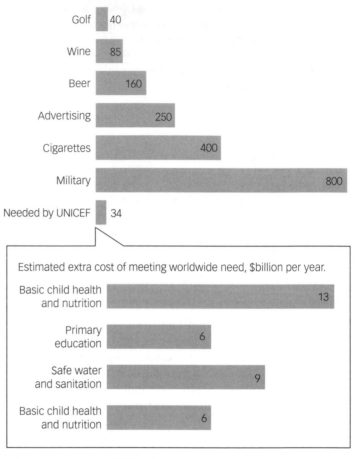

(Source: *The Guardian*, 16.12.1994:10)

Figure 20.9 Underdevelopment – a problem of over-consumption (mainly in the West)?

should be achieved through the distribution of aid. Aid can help deal with crises – such as occurred in war-torn Ethiopia and Rwanda – it can alleviate hunger, and even provide funding and support for development projects. However, it can do relatively little to achieve greater economic production or a more equal distribution of wealth within societies. Aid is also most unlikely to redress the highly unequal balance of trade between rich and poorer countries. Figure 20.9 illustrates the massive inequalities between rich and poor countries. We have already discussed some possible solutions but given the power of the richer countries and weakness of the poorer ones, international solutions look very remote.

3 Population size is unimportant in development (New Right/laissez-faire view)

Peter Bauer's New Right views in relation to development have already been described (see pp. 589-91). Consistently enough, Bauer argues that 'poverty in the Third World is not caused by population pressures'. Bauer goes further, and makes a broad association between population growth and economic growth:

> *Population growth in the Third World has often gone hand-in-hand with rapid material advance. Since the Second World War, a number of countries which used to be considered undeveloped have combined rapid population increases with even faster – indeed spectacular economic growth for decades on end, notably Taiwan, Hong Kong, Malaysia, Kenya, the Ivory Coast, Mexico, Columbia and Brazil. Economic performance depends on personal, cultural and political factors, on people's capacities, attitudes, motivations and social and political institutions.*
>
> *(P Bauer, 'World Numbers Will Look After Themselves', The Times, 16.8.1995:16)*

As we saw, Bauer takes a 'purist' free market view to development as well as to population size. Contrary to Bauer, there are many who adopt a broadly free market approach to the world economy who would still see both a function for aid and for birth-control policy. Government policy under John Major was to provide a modest amount of aid on the basis of *conditionality* i.e. providing certain political and economic reforms were implemented (see p. 590). Aid was also provided on an emergency basis.

The two classic arguments against a completely free market approach apply especially in relation to the global economy. First the competitors are not competing with equal resources. Second, severe losers in economic competition – regardless of why they fail – need welfare or aid. In this case, some of the severest losers – in parts of Africa and South Asia – will die without it.

Population terminology

The birth rate and death rate are key determinants of population size. The birth rate is the number of live births per year per 1,000 people and the death rate is the number of deaths per year per 1,000 people. The fertility rate is the number of live births per 1,000 women of child-bearing age (15-44). The infant mortality rate (IMR) is the annual rate of death of infants 0-12 months per 1,000 live births. The IMR varies internationally mainly according to the quality of childcare and makes a critical contribution to the overall death rate. The difference between the birth rate and death rate gives the rate of natural population increase and, if we adjust for net immigration and emigration, we get the rate of population growth. The concept of dependent population is very important. It refers to non-producing members of the population. The dependency ratio is arrived at by dividing non-producers by producers.

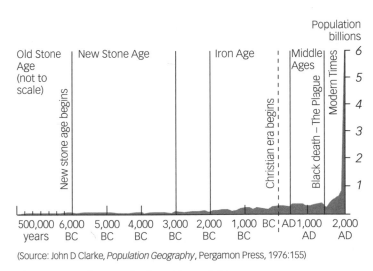

(Source: John D Clarke, *Population Geography*, Pergamon Press, 1976:155)

Figure 20.10 The growth of world population

Population trends

World population trends

In many parts of the world, population growth has outstripped available resources. Millions have died through starvation or ill-health caused by malnutrition. Forecasts used to suggest that crisis of global over-population would escalate beyond control early in the twenty-first century. However, the *State of World Population Report*, published by the United Nations (1982), indicated that a drop in the rate of population increase had at last occurred and that population will level off at about 10.54 billion in the year 2110. The decrease is due to an overall fall in the birth rate. In poorer countries this reflects some success in the policy of governments and development agencies (see below). In countries at an intermediate level of development, parents themselves often opt for smaller families, largely to secure higher living standards. In any case, these global figures conceal an average rate of population growth of about 2.5 per cent in poorer countries compared to less than 1 per cent in developed countries.

The report makes the following estimates of the world population at given times:

1950	1980	2000	2110
2.5 billion	4.4 billion	6 billion	10.5 billion

(Figure 20.10 illustrates earlier population growth trends.)

If the current trends are proved correct, the world should be able to maintain its people adequately if resources are developed, distributed and used for this purpose. That is a big 'if'. The exploitation of resources to create private wealth or their diversion into armaments build up are alternatives.

Regional population trends

The above trends are of concern to the whole species. This section examines briefly specific regional trends.

Population will stop growing and stabilise first in the industrially developed areas of the world. According to the United Nations report, this will happen first in Western Europe in about 2030 when its population will be about 400 million. Next will be North America, levelling off at 320 million, with the area covered by the former Soviet Union at 380 million.

There has been concern in the European Parliament about the combined effects of a falling birth rate and a low death rate. The danger perceived is that there will not be enough workers to cope with the burden of dependency caused by an ageing population.

There are arguments against adopting policies to increase the Community's birthrate. First, Europe, including Britain, is far from employing all of its present population of working age. Secondly, many older people are quite capable of doing productive work. Thirdly, the working population of Europe could be increased indefinitely by changing immigration policies. In view of the continued expansion of population in the South, the latter might be a particularly effective policy. In reality, however, more prosperous European nations are increasingly introducing immigration controls designed severely to limit immigration from poorer societies.

Continued population expansion in the South contrasts with the situation in Europe, The biggest increase in population will come in Africa. It is the one region in which the rate of population increase is barely slowing down. Africa, where millions already die or are disabled through malnutrition, is expected to treble its population by the year 2110. That of South Asia is expected to more than double to 4.2 billion. There the fertility rate is slowing somewhat more quickly than in Africa (see Figure 20.11).

Latin America, which is generally better able to support its people, is also expected to more than double its population. East Asia, however, will level off quickly, rising from 1.2 to 1.7 billion. This is largely because of the success of birth control policies adopted in China.

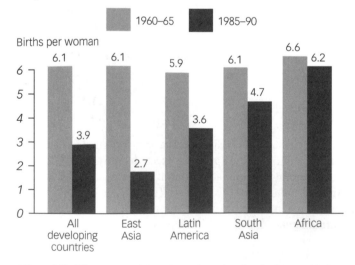

Although fertility rates are falling throughout the developing world, they remain much higher than replacement rates (about two births per woman) except in East Asia.

Figure 20.11 Fertility trends in the developing world, by region

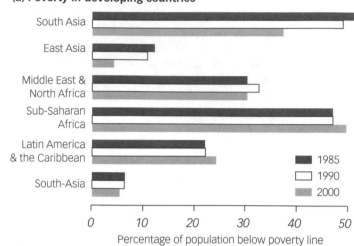

(a) Poverty in developing countries

Percentage of population below poverty line

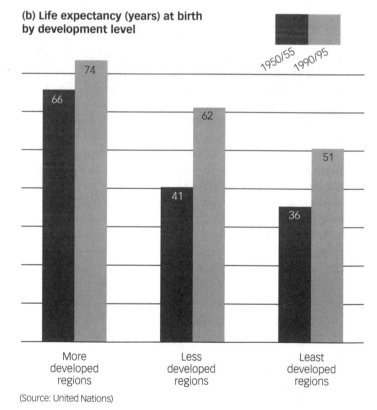

(b) Life expectancy (years) at birth by development level

(Source: United Nations)

Figure 20.12 (a) Poverty in developing countries and (b) Life expectancy in countries at various levels of development

Regional population age structures

In demographic terms, Mozambique and Indonesia are reasonably representative of less developed countries. The data on both indicate three major problem areas. First, the gap between the birth and death rate creates rapid population growth. With many more being born than dying, the population of these two countries is still growing (i.e. births and deaths are out of 'balance'). Ironically, in the short to medium term, an increase in life expectancy can create

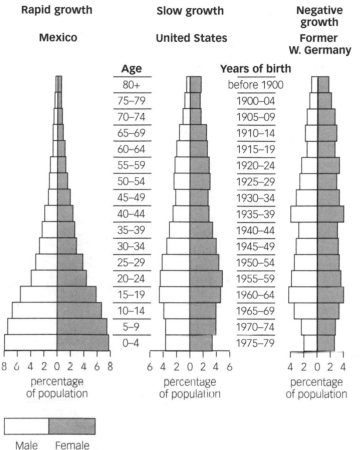

Rapid growth	Slow growth	Negative growth
Mexico	United States	Former W. Germany

Age	Years of birth
80+	before 1900
75–79	1900–04
70–74	1905–09
65–69	1910–14
60–64	1915–19
55–59	1920–24
50–54	1925–29
45–49	1930–34
40–44	1935–39
35–39	1940–44
30–34	1945–49
25–29	1950–54
20–24	1955–59
15–19	1960–64
10–14	1965–69
5–9	1970–74
0–4	1975–79

8 6 4 2 0 2 4 6 8
percentage of population

6 4 2 0 2 4 6
percentage of population

4 2 0 2 4
percentage of population

Male   Female

(Sources: Censuses of Mexico, the United States and West Germany (The Population Institute, Washington DC))

Figure 20.13 Comparative population composition: age and sex

economic problems for a country (see Figure 20.12). Second, though falling, the infant mortality rate is appallingly high. Third, in both countries, over 40 per cent of the population is under the age of fifteen. This puts a heavy burden of dependency on the adult population, even though many older children in Third World countries contribute to family income. The lower death rate in China is a result of success in reducing the rate of infant mortality and to the relatively youthful age structure if its population. The percentages of the population under fifteen are far higher than in advanced industrial countries. However, this situation is rapidly changing in China because of the success of its one child per family policy.

Australia, the USA and the UK are at a similar stage of demographic development. In 1978, the birth and death rates in the UK were actually in balance although in the 1990s there have been slightly more births than deaths. The issue of age dependency for Britain and, to a lesser extent, the USA, is with the group 65 or over – the opposite end to where the problem lies for countries such as Mexico and Indonesia.

Figure 20.13 contrasts the population composition of Mexico,

the USA and former West Germany. The age structures of South Asia, Latin America and Africa are fairly similar to that of Mexico, and that of the former Soviet Union to the USA. The populations of Western Europe are the oldest, and the region has about five per cent fewer aged fourteen or younger than both USA and former USSR. The problem of old age dependency is, therefore, at its most acute in Europe, though it will also be felt sharply in the USA early next century. However, as Figure 20.14 suggests, it is the population imbalances within major global regions, that perhaps gives most cause for thought.

	Developed region	Less developed region
	North America →	Latin America
	Japan →	China/India
	Europe →	Africa
Key characteristics	Nil/low population growth	High population growth
	Low fertility	High fertility
	Rich	Poor(er)

The main regional pressure to migrate is likely to be from Africa on Europe, although there will continue to be pressure from Latin America on North America. The fifteen to 24 age-group is the one most likely to migrate and the numbers in this group are greatly increasing in Africa.

Numbers (in millions) in the fifteen to 24 age group (Actual and projected)

	Latin America	Africa
1960	34	52
1980	74	91
2000	170	300

Whereas Africa annually produces fifteen million more births than needed to replace preceding generations, Europe is 1.2 million short. Migration can, therefore, only be one element in solving Africa's problems. The main solution must be development, including family planning.

Figure 20.14 Areas of global population imbalance

British population, trends and age structure, (compared to the south)

The purpose of this brief section is twofold: first, to establish the historical development of the British population from a demographic point of view; second, to indicate the main demographic issues facing contemporary Britain. Because demography cuts into so many other topics, the reader will be sign-posted elsewhere in this book for detailed discussion of specific points.

Broadly, the population growth of Britain has followed the *pattern* indicated in Figure 20.13. It is not possible to say precisely when slow population growth gave way to more rapid increase but slow growth, interrupted by occasional natural disasters, occurred throughout the middle ages. More rapid growth preceded the industrial revolution but the improvements in public health and nutrition which underlay the increase became more marked in the nineteenth century, especially the latter part (see pp. 421-2). These improvements reduced the death rate but the birth rate barely fell until the last quarter of the nineteenth century: thus, the rapid population growth for the preceding century. Indeed, a high birth rate was necessary to maintain a stable population in traditional society. Given a very high infant mortality rate, families had to have several children to ensure the survival of two or three. Children functioned as breadwinners and later as protectors of their parents, should the latter reach old age. Fertility was regarded as a blessing and had religious sanction. Similar factors explain the persistence of high birth rates in the Third World, especially in poorer, more traditional societies. There are two crucial differences, however. First, Britain's period of rapid population growth was supported by and essentially caused by an even greater increase in wealth and resources. Comparable development is not occurring in the Third World. On the contrary, the population boom in the South was partly triggered by the entirely artificial factor of Western medicine, particularly in the control of infectious disease, which destroyed 'natural' population balance. As a result, poor countries with booming populations tend to become highly dependent on the West. Second, and more optimistically, the modern family planning methods, which only became widely available in the West well after its population boom had passed its peak, are currently available to the South. Arguably, however, the best stimulus to population control is development itself (see p. 607). Figure 20.15 below compares population growth in the developed and underdeveloped world between 1975 and 2000 (projected).

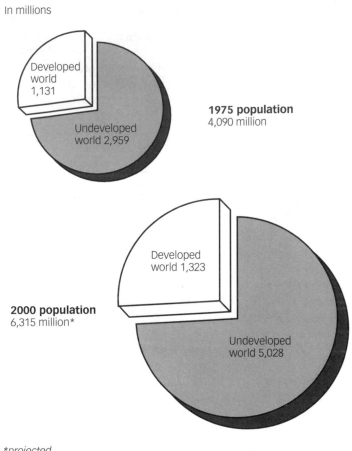

In millions

Developed world 1,131

Undeveloped world 2,959

1975 population 4,090 million

Developed world 1,323

2000 population 6,315 million*

Undeveloped world 5,028

*projected

(Source: *The Global 2000 Report to the President*, Council on Environmental Quality and the Department of State, USA)

Figure 20.15 World population growth 1975-2000

Population, inequality and health

I will review briefly four approaches to population growth and control. The first, that of Thomas Malthus, can fairly be termed a theory on the basis of the historical and comparative evidence he accumulated in support of it. The others concentrate as much on advocating forms of control as on explaining growth and are strongly tinged with ideology. The separation between this section (on perspectives) and the next (on policy) is not precise – there is a particularly large overlap in relation to perspectives (2) and (3).

1   Malthus

Malthus (1766-1834) argued that 'population, when unchecked, increases in a geometrical ratio. Subsistence only increases in an arithmetical ratio.' Thus population increases as follow – 1, 2, 4, 8, 16, 32 … – and food – 1, 2, 3, 4, 5, 6. At the sixth point in this progression, population increase has run ahead of the increase in food production by over 500 per cent. Malthus may not have been precisely correct, but there is no doubt that he observed a general tendency. The one solution he offered to the resultant misery was moral restraint, including postponement of marriage, coupled, with pre-marital chastity until the partners could afford to support

a family. Malthus's policies of control have not proved popular, but this analysis of population control remains influential. R K Kelsall suggests that as far as many Third World countries are concerned 'the factors in the situation are basically those to which he drew attention', i.e. population growth out-running food supplies. However, the relevant frame of reference has undoubtedly been changed by the development of effective contraception and improvements in agriculture.

2   Neo-Malthusianism – family planning

A second approach is sometimes referred to as Neo-Malthusianism. It broadly accepts Malthus's analysis but argues for the adoption of birth control within marriage. Today, many of those involved in the practical urgencies of population policy advocate birth control whenever necessary with little concern for theoretical reference. Malthus did not adequately anticipate the effect of birth control on population growth, nor did he fully appreciate the extent to which improved crop fertilisation and production could sustain larger populations. In fact, human invention in the fields of birth control, health and nutrition and agriculture has produced a pattern of population growth outlined in Table 20.1, rather than repeated cycles of growth and decline back to a stable figure as Malthus indicates.

The theory of population transition presented below, developed at the United Nations, should not be over-generalised. It applies well to most modern societies but it may apply less well to Third World societies if the factors that reduced population growth in the West fail to do so there.

Table 20.1

Type	Birth rate	Death rate	Population growth
1	High	High	Stable
2	High	High-declining	Slight increase
3	High	Low	Large increase
4	Falling	Falling	Falling
5	Low	Low	Low and stable

Type 1 would describe many simple societies unaffected by modern factors and type 5 most modern societies. It should be possible to pick out various types in the chart from the previous section.

In summary, then, the second approach covers those who advocate modern techniques of birth control and improved crop fertilisation to reduce population and improve nutrition in the Third World. (The assumption that technology is the key to progress in population control complements one version of modernisation theory.) Usually now this approach is incorporated along with attempts to raise living standards of which the following approach (3) is an example.

3 Redistribution of resources and population stabilisation (radical perspective)

We now turn to a third approach. Susan George, in *How the Other Half Dies: The Real Reasons for World Hunger* (1977) sharply attacks attempts to deal with the problems of Third World countries primarily in terms of population control. She states her own position clearly:

> *The first thing to realise when trying to think straight about population/food is that hunger is not caused by population pressure. Both hunger and rapid population growth reflect the same failure of a political and economic system.*
>
> *(George, 1977:59)*

George finds a grossly unequal distribution of wealth in world and, in most cases, national terms. Hunger and population growth are symptoms – one is not the cause of the other – of this

inequality. Couples have many children because only children will protect them against poverty. Population decrease tends to follow decrease in poverty. The abolition of poverty is, therefore, what should come first and the resources are there to achieve it. Belabouring the poor about birth control is to appear to blame them for problems that are not of their own making.

In the following quotation, George summarises some of the evidence for her case:

> *The Overseas Development Council Population report quotes a 1971 study by William Rich showing that where decrease in birth rates is concerned, variations between UDCs (UDCs is short for Underdeveloped Countries) with similar gross national products per capita result primarily from differences in the distribution of this GNP. In more egalitarian countries, birth rates tend to decline rapidly, and vice versa. These conclusions are also borne out by the comparative figures for five UDCs published by the New Internationalist ...*
>
> *This [data] shows that if you want to get your natural birth rate from 41 down to 26 (Taiwan) or from 45 to 30 per thousand (Korea), the best way to go about it is not to distribute condoms and IUDs and hope for the best, but to give people effective land reform and more income. They will reward you with fewer babies.*
>
> *(George, 1977:63)*

Importantly from the point of view of practical policy-making, a study by staff of the World Bank and of the Institute of Development Studies at the University of Sussex came to conclusions similar to those of George. First, they argued that the main goal of development should not merely be growth but 'redistribution with growth'. They noted that growth could occur without the majority benefiting. Instead they argued for development strategies that would meet the needs of the majority. This became known as the 'basic needs approach'. Second, they tended to regard population control as secondary to and dependent on more egalitarian policies of development (see below). Incidentally, this marked a sharp departure from the assumptions of the modernisation theorists who believed that the general population would almost automatically benefit from growth. Consequently, they rarely addressed the issue of the redistribution of resources.

4 Population laissez-faire (New Right perspective)

A fourth, quite different perspective on world population growth comes from the political right. It reflects the free market view that became popular in the 1970s and 1980s. One example of this approach is a position paper prepared in the Presidential White House for the United States delegation to the UN International Conference on Population (August 1984; source, Harford Thomas,

The Guardian, 3.7.1985: 21). It argues that population growth is, in itself, as asset. It became dangerous only because in developing countries 'economic statism' interfered with the natural mechanisms of economic incentives and rewards which would have adjusted population growth to rising living standards. The draft document then goes on to argue that the USA 'does not consider abortion an acceptable element of family planning programmes'.

Peter Bauer adds the libertarian argument that if condoms and the pill are not popular in the Third World then that is the choice of the people living there. The West should leave well alone.

Although presented as theory, this approach is highly ideological and speculative. Supposing reduced population control results in population increase rather than decrease? Free market population policies may be no more effective in reducing population than free market economics has so far been (1997) in reducing poverty in Britain. Perhaps a free market 'experiment' in the area of population would be too risky.

Comment

My own view favours a policy combining a redistribution of resources (as Susan George argues) and continued efforts to extend birth control (an up-dated version of approach (2)). Though George's case is well sustained, there is evidence that birth control does have an independent effect in reducing population. In *Human Numbers, Human Needs*, Paul Harrison and John Rowley point out that, in the industrialised world where 70 per cent of couples of reproductive age are using contraception, birth rates are low at sixteen per 1,000. Estimates suggest that if unwanted births were prevented in Bangladesh, Colombia, Jamaica and several other countries, population growth rates could be halved.

Population policy and development

1   Reasons for controlling the rate of population growth

As the previous section suggests, the precise relationship between the rate of population increase and development (and vice versa) is contentious. Fully aware of this, Ozzie G Simmons, nevertheless, attempts to summarise the relationship between rapid population growth and development in the light of existing research. In his article, *Development Perspectives and Population Change*, he briefly examines this relationship in respect to several key areas: health, education and labour absorption, food, and income distribution. Broadly, his perspective reflects the assumptions of (2) and especially (3) of the previous section.

Health

On the matter of health, Simmons observes that high fertility rates have a direct effect on the cost of services 'since obstetric and paediatric care constitute a large part of total demand for health services'. However, he emphasises that there are other causes of inadequate health care of comparable importance in the Third World. In most less developed countries (LDCs), health care tends to be concentrated in the urban areas and available mainly to the urban elites and middle class. He argues for a change from expensive, high-technology, hospital-based medicine to a primary care approach carried out by larger numbers of assessable, though less fully and expensively trained, paramedics (for a fuller discussion of this issue, see p. 610).

Education and labour absorption

The provision of education facilities is the factor which Simmons sees as most negatively affected by rapid population increase. Quite simply, an age structure weighted towards children and teenagers tends to raise the cost and decrease the quality of the educational system. On the matter of labour absorption, he considers rapid population growth to exacerbate rather than cause unemployment and under-employment. He advocates meeting the problem by improving the skills and access to productive assets of the majority (a basic needs approach) and through labour intensive development.

Food

Simmons points out that the world can produce enough food to meet foreseeable needs, taking into account estimates of population growth. However, this calculation depends on the food surplus produced by the developed countries (DCs) which is expensive for LDCs to buy. Alternatively and preferably, Simmons suggests that the LDCs should try to achieve the 3.5 per cent to four per cent increase in food production required to meet their needs and which is physically, technically and economically possible. He concludes that to be successful, this policy would need to be accompanied by income redistribution which would both enable people to buy food and probably reduce population growth (see George above). In short, he sees the food problem primarily as one of production and distribution rather than as a function of over-population.

It is worth adding that the aid and development agencies have had some success at least in the basic matter of reducing starvation and the resultant physical damage. From 1995, UNICEF revealed that 2.5 million fewer children are expected to die annually from malnutrition and disease. Fewer should be disabled, blinded and mentally retarded.

Income distribution

Simmons considers that there is a tendency for rapid population increase adversely to affect income distribution in two main ways. First, in the absence of growth, the more people there are, the more thinly resources – health, education, land – tend to be spread. Second, high fertility increases inequality of income between families because the poor tend to have larger families. Despite hazarding these two points, Simmons stresses that the state of research in the area does not support generalisations. He comments that it is 'just as likely' that inequality causes high fertility among poorer, less educated sections of the population as the reverse.

Conclusion: Simmons

Simmons concludes by arguing that both population control and poverty-focused development strategies are necessary and, carefully pursued, almost certainly complementary. Finally, his emphasis is on eliminating what he refers to as 'the underlying causes of poverty':

> The real solution lies in structural change, in changing the distribution of productive wealth and thus the distribution of economic power, and in increasing the participation of the poor in decision-making and thus enabling them to exercise political power.
>
> (1983)

He offers no detailed blueprint for population policy or development strategy because the factors involved vary and require different responses in different societies. Similarly, he sees no single political road to change – continued resistance to change, reform and revolution are all possible.

2 Population policy in the South with reference to fertility and infant/child mortality

Two issues relating to population are discussed below: the reduction of the fertility rate and infant and child mortality and disease, i.e. child health. These issues, particularly the second, are so urgent that they require immediate response. However, in discussing them, the analysis already made in this section needs to be remembered. These are issues not merely of population policy, but of the development and distribution of resources – both within Third World societies and globally. The education and employment of the young of the Third World is discussed later.

The reduction of the fertility rate

A reduction in the fertility rate is historically a major factor in reducing the rate of population increase. However, a variety of factors make this a more complicated matter than one of contraception education. There is resistance to birth control for both practical and cultural reasons in many countries in the South and, in any case, expert opinion in the West is not certain precisely how key variables such as female education and more equal income distribution affect the fertility rate.

The main practical reason for producing large families in the South, is to provide enough workers to run the family's property and to ensure care and protection for parents in their old age. In the absence of a welfare state this makes sense and even more so given high infant mortality rates among the very poor – three out of ten children die before they reach the age of five. The cultural complement to this is the high status normally associated with having a large family and religious disapproval of 'unnatural' interference with reproduction. For these reasons, it is usually both crude and ineffective for outsiders to impose birth control or to try to bribe people to use it (although China itself seems successfully to have enforced its own one child per family policy).

Factors associated with a reduction in the fertility rate

A better way than imposing birth control is to discover, and where practical to create, the conditions or factors that are associated with a decline in the fertility rate.

1 *Decline in infant mortality*
   One commonly found correlation with a decline in the fertility rate is a prior decline in the rate of infant mortality. This relationship occurred in Britain and other European societies as they developed and in virtually all Southern societies in which the fertility rate has decreased. A decline in infant mortality, then, seems almost a precondition of a decline in the rate of fertility, although the former can occur without the latter. The logic of this correlation appears to be that when there is a high likelihood of children surviving, there is less need to have so many of them.

2 *Increase in income and resources of the poor*
   This brings up a second factor associated with fertility decline which is also strongly associated with a decline in the rate of infant mortality: an increase in the income and resources of the poor. Robert Repetto's *Economic Equality and Fertility in Developing Countries* demonstrates that the more equal the total distribution of income in a society, the lower the overall birthrate will tend to be. Again, this appears to establish a crucial link between development and a reduction in the rate of population growth.

3 *Increase in the paid employment of women*
   Simmons also claims that a fourth factor, the paid employment of women, is ambiguous in its effect on fertility. He cites a range of studies of female work status and fertility in Latin America which shows no consistent inverse relationship between female employment outside the home and fertility. However, the recent *World Fertility Survey* covering the period from 1972 to the mid 1980s appears to re-establish the general connection between both the education and paid employment of women and low fertility. Three-fifths of the world's illiterate are women and this provides an added reason for action.

4 *Education (especially female)*
   According to Ozzie Simmons, the effect of female education on fertility is less certain than is commonly thought. He suggests that '(p)erhaps the most widely accepted generalisation is that of the inverse relationship between education and fertility', i.e. the educated tend to have fewer

children. However, in countries with the lowest rates of female literacy, education is likely to increase fertility possibly by simply increasing the ability to have live births. Otherwise, education is associated with a decline in fertility, especially the education of women and particularly in urban areas (see Figure 20.16).

5 *Family planning*

Finally, the effect of family planning programmes on fertility remains to be considered. The debate centres on the issue of whether family planning programmes are effective in the absence of development and in the presence of strong cultural resistance to them. The balance of opinion is that such programmes tend to be more effective where at least some development has occurred, but in some cases they may also help independently to reduce fertility. The following example of a successful family planning programme was implemented in a society, Indonesia, which had experienced some development.

Case study in family planning: a success story?

With an estimated population of 150 million, Indonesia seems a prime case for an effective planning policy. Its population has been increasing by 2.9 million per year and each year two million more jobs are needed. In the face of these trends, Indonesia has achieved a 'success story unrivalled in family planning history', according to demographers Terence and Valerie Hull, and Masri Singarimbun.

The setting up of the National Family Planning Co-ordination Board in 1970 indicated firm commitment to family planning. Initial funding came from the Indonesian government ($1.3 million) and foreign donors ($3 million). Now the programme's annual budget is over $50 million. The programme has helped to bring down population growth rate from 2.4 per cent in 1964 to around 1.9 per cent in 1981. In the Bali region, for instance, the birth rate fell an astonishing 34 per cent between 1970 and 1975. A lower rate of growth still is the target.

The major reason for the success of the programme is that it has been well organised and implemented. The programme is effective down to the village level. Local part-time field workers and prominent members of the community operate the programme and simple clinics have been established. It is local people, rather than outside experts, who have succeeded in persuading and explaining about birth control. Backing up the field workers are thousands of local volunteers who have helped to set up over 30,000 community family planning posts. Efficient communication between the local administrators and the planning board is crucial. The board evaluates incoming data and advises local workers accordingly.

The success of the above programme goes some way towards undermining the view that there is almost overwhelming cultural resistance to birth control in many traditional societies. Perhaps resistance in the past has been the fault of insensitive administrators, ignorant of local feeling and custom. The Indonesian case suggests that there is another way. Certainly, the

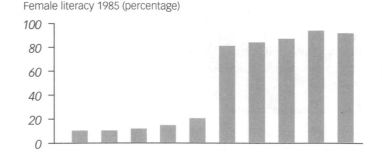

Female literacy 1985 (percentage)

Population growth 1988–2000 (percentage)

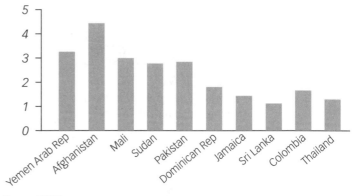

(Source: UNDP)

Figure 20.16 The more education people have, the more likely they are to have small families

case for combining family planning programmes with anti-poverty development strategies seems strong.

Reducing infant and child mortality and disease

Statistics are not, in themselves, 'appalling' but the misery and deprivation behind the figures of infant and child mortality and disease certainly are. The basic or absolute poverty which underlies them is perhaps the major human and social problem in the world today. Only two other issues of survival – the nuclear and environmental – are of comparable importance. It may help to illuminate the personal experience of childhood poverty and starvation if we concentrate briefly on two aspects of it – physical disablement and mental illness – rather than attempt a coverage.

There are about 200 million disabled children in the world, most of them in underdeveloped countries. Malnutrition is a major cause of disablement in the Third World. For instance, every year 250,000 children become blind through lack of vitamin A. Prevention can cost as little as three or four pence per person. In 1979, a survey in the villages of Camp Tinio and Mananac in the Philippines showed that 119 out of 568 children under the age of six were to some extent disabled – over twenty per cent. Of those impaired, 80 per cent were found to be malnourished. The following is an extract from a report by Teresa Tunay on the low cost community-based care programme that followed the survey. It is particularly worth noting the reasons why she thinks the programme was effective:

Today, only a few months later, 46 per cent of those children have shown very significant improvements. The original survey also found Josefina, a ten month old baby girl who was a victim of Down's Syndrome. In other words, she was a mongoloid child. When her home was visited by one of the survey team, Josefina was virtually a wilting head of lettuce in her mother's arms. Her body appeared boneless. She could not even hold her head up. Her eyes were lifeless and she responded to neither the sound of a voice nor to a smiling face.

Today only 16 weeks later, Josefina has put on weight, runs around the house in a baby walker, plays enthusiastically with a string of coloured beads, and is just as responsive as any normal child of her age.

Josefina's 'therapy' did not require institutionalisation or gadgetry. Her mother was shown how and where to 'tickle' her baby to exercise the muscles. The treatment progressed through gentle kneading of the child's limbs to a daily ritual of therapeutic exercise. Soon, the child began to make steady and continued progress ...

The key to low-cost but dramatic improvements in the lives of the majority of the disabled lies in releasing the care and support which is latent in the family and the community. And it was from that point that the 'Reaching and Unreached' programme began. Two young researchers, one trained in occupational therapy and the other in pre-school education, went to live in the village, renting a small hut at a nominal rate, from the village of 'barangay' captain.

In discussion with the community, they agreed to concentrate their efforts on children under the age of six, not only because the young child is the most vulnerable, but also because the earlier the help the more potential there is for improvement and the less damage is done to the normal processes of child development.

Village volunteers were trained. Non-technical indicators were listed for the detection of impairments. And the community as a whole was involved in finding impairments in their children, in discussing their attitudes towards it, and in planning and carrying out the rehabilitation programmes themselves.

(From Teresa Tunay, 'Miracles for the Man'y, New Internationalist, No. 95:13)

It is a myth that mental illness is a 'luxury' of materially rich societies. Different cultures produce different illnesses, but overall, mental illness seems to be as common in the underdeveloped as in the industrialised world. It is not hard to see why. Poverty produces stress and depression; malnutrition can lead to apathy. People in the Third World are more subject to natural disasters, bereavements, rising but often frustrated expectations, enforced migrations and wars than Westerners. All of these are typically emotionally stressful occurrences.

War, of course, causes unequalled physical and emotional damage. The following is a report from Berry Brazleton on a number of Kampuchean children most of whom have been orphaned by war. He is writing about an orphanage in Phnom Penh:

Most infants in these overcrowded orphanages lie around all day, flat on their backs, their heads flattened and the hair worn off the backs of their heads.

The orphans are being physically salvaged in Phnom Penh, but the quality of their future lives is far from assured. We know now that unless a baby is stimulated by his environment to learn and to experience the excitement of learning, he will not be able to learn later. The combination of an undernourished brain coupled with a non-stimulating environment can be critical deprivation to an immature developing child ...

In Phnom Penh and the Thai border camps the babies are well nourished, but the girls taking care of them have been through too much themselves to be able to respond to the psychological needs of small dependants. Everyone in the orphanages means well and they would institute the same kinds of interactive experiences that I did, but they have not thought of them. Their own lives have been too sparse, and they have barely recovered from the mass depression.

(From Berry Brazleton, 'Games that Children Play for Survival', The Guardian, 18.12.1981:7)

Conclusion: population policy and politics

As the above discussion of world population problems and policy progressed, the political issues that underlay all policy decisions should have become increasingly apparent. As Susan George emphasises, at the centre of the political debate about population is development. Birth control policies may help – international aid helps – but development is essential to solving the problems of the South. However, there are deep political and ideological disagreements about how development best occurs. These disagreements are not merely about the 'mechanisms' of development but reflect profound differences of value and preference. At its widest, this debate is about what kind of future world community we will make.

Theme 2: urbanisation and industrialisation

The urban populations of the South are expanding much more rapidly than those of the First and Second World, where indeed the numbers resident in many major cities are decreasing. Already,

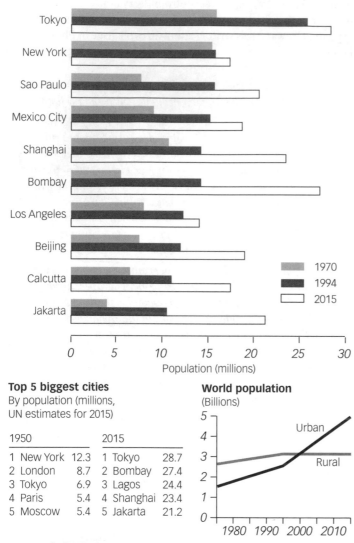

Largest urban agglomerations by population (millions)

Legend: 1970, 1994, 2015

Top 5 biggest cities
By population (millions, UN estimates for 2015)

1950			2015		
1	New York	12.3	1	Tokyo	28.7
2	London	8.7	2	Bombay	27.4
3	Tokyo	6.9	3	Lagos	24.4
4	Paris	5.4	4	Shanghai	23.4
5	Moscow	5.4	5	Jakarta	21.2

World population (Billions)

Urban
Rural

(Source: United Nations)

Figure 20.17 The growth of cities

only two Western cities feature in the ten most populous cities of the world (see Figure 20.17). It is in cities that most of global population increase occurs. What has caused this phenomenon?

First, it is instructive to note a factor which has contributed relatively little to the increase in urban population – industrialisation. This is in stark contrast to what occurred in the developing West, where accelerated urbanisation was largely the result of industrialisation. In the South there is usually only a scant industrial base to sustain the expanding urban masses, though this is less true of some countries at an intermediate level of development such as South Korea, Brazil and Argentina. However, most migrants to the city do not get a (relatively) better paying industrial job. Push as well as pull factors account for the move to the cities. First, population increase means fewer jobs to go round in the traditional agricultural sector. Second, where agriculture is

modernised an absolute reduction in jobs typically takes place.

Of the pull factors, the strongest is the prospect of making a better living than as a rural peasant. Cities, especially international ones, have large formal and informal economies in which the determined or inventive can survive and, in some cases, even prosper. Even begging and the odd official handout are likely to produce a better income in the city. Second, facilities such as clean water and drainage are more likely to be available in the city, as are odd bits of unwanted or 'spare' materials with which to build a shelter. Third, is the cultural attraction of the city – the glamour of the 'modern' way of life. John Roberts in *The Triumph of the West* emphasises the fascination and charisma of Western culture and it is in the cities of the world that the artefacts of the West are most temptingly displayed. No doubt what appeals most is Western wealth and lifestyle, but perhaps, too, there is a deeper desire to 'become' Westernised – to think and feel like Westerners. Modernisation theorists might regard this process as liberating and Marxists as the very trough of ideological dependency, but Roberts is surely right that it is widespread (as, it must be said, is resistance to it).

Neither governments nor the private housing sector in most countries of the South can hope to house all the people flooding into the city. In any case, many could not afford to rent, still less, buy accommodation. What can work well, is the provision of loans, aid or materials by the government or voluntary agencies, for people to build their own houses. In general, however, how people make out in the city, including where they live, depends on what they can earn.

Employment

There has been a severe crisis of unemployment in the advanced capitalist countries, especially among the young. Ironically, in Britain this crisis has coincided with policies to make education more vocationally relevant. Unemployment, in the Third World, is on a far greater scale than in the capitalist West. There are several reasons for this.

Population increase is, of course, a major factor in global unemployment. During the 1970s the size of the labour market in the South increased by 2000 million. It is estimated that by the year 2000 another 200 million will have joined the labour markets. More than 30 million new jobs per year will be needed to absorb this increase. A second important factor contributing to unemployment is lack of investment in agriculture and industry. Many Southern countries are deeply in debt to Western banks and cannot afford extensive development investment. This observation raises the issue of whether the world trading system is so weighted against the Third World that prospects of significant development and higher employment are remote. We will return to this point shortly. Thirdly, economic development in the South, as in the capitalist West, often results in a reduction rather than an increase in employment. This is because some projects are capital rather than labour intensive: machinery replaces people. In such cases, increases in production and profit are likely to benefit the few who own businesses rather than the majority.

The formal economy

All large towns and cities have a formal economy. Generally, the less developed a society, the smaller the formal economies of its cities will be. A formal economy is made up of a public sector (central or local government jobs) and a private sector (longer term jobs in industry or business with some, though greatly varying, employment benefits and security). In capital or international cities, the formal sector can be quite large but is usually smaller than the informal sector.

Multinationals and employment

Frequently, the owners of businesses in the South are Western multinational companies who are attracted by the lower wages they can pay, usually unorganised workforces, lack of legal restrictions, and developing markets. Sometimes multinational companies use Western employees in their Southern operations to avoid the expense of training Third World workers in more technical tasks and to ensure a compliant workforce.

The informal economy

Despite the above difficulties and the fact that employment in the South remains overwhelmingly rural, growing opportunities for work exist in the cities, not least in the informal sector:

> *Many Africans migrating to the cities found themselves without jobs, or unable to get those they aspired to. Some accommodated themselves to a socially disapproved existence as pimps, touts, prostitutes, or thieves, living often at the margins of subsistence or preying, like parasites, on what few pickings a capital city of an impoverished country can offer. Others swelled the ranks of those who staff the industries, small trades and services that blanket the landscape of any African city. This sector for the urban economy, described often nowadays as the 'informal sector', in fact accounts for a considerable degree of urban employment. ... The conditions of employment can be extremely harsh. For three or four years apprentices are bound to their masters in a condition resembling that of servitude. A space on the workshop floor is living accommodation, and pocket money barely covers the means of survival, while the El Dorado to the apprentice, namely a workshop of his own, is difficult to finance and may indeed never materialise.*
>
> (Robin Cohen, 'The emergence of wage labour', in Allen and Williams eds., 1982:39)

Tens of millions of people survive in the 'twilight zone' of the informal sector. Uncomfortable though governments may be about the existence of this kind of enterprise, for many it is likely to be the only work available in the foreseeable future. Even in the West, the failure of the formal economy has forced millions to seek informal means of supplementing their incomes in the so-called 'black economy'. Governments and development planners in the South would do better to accommodate the working and living needs of workers in the informal sector rather than viewing them as a temporary phenomenon.

The city 'lumpen-proletariat'

Workers in the informal sector are not the bottom of the urban 'heap' in the South. As Robin Cohen puts it, 'there exists a group of genuinely unemployed workers, 'job applicants' by self description, but in fact a lumpen-proletariat proper'. A lumpen-proletariat is an ill-defined mass of individuals without any regular employment. One of the major historical causes of the drift to the city in many countries was the seizure of land by white settlers as happened in Kenya and South Africa. Today, rural overpopulation and the hope for material advancement that the city symbolises are important factors.

International labour migration

Increasingly, migration in search of work is not merely internal, but international. The international migrant population of the world is well over twenty million and still increasing. Several millions of these workers are Eastern Europeans who have found temporary jobs in Western European countries. Generally, they receive low pay for doing some of the least attractive work, and do not enjoy the rights of citizenship. In the Third World, migrants across international boundaries frequently do not even find work. Their situation is perilous and many exist in absolute poverty. Their vulnerability was illustrated in Nigeria in 1983. Nigeria is the most prosperous country in West Africa because of its oil and other resources. It attracts many illegal migrant workers. However, it was particularly badly hit by the world recession of the early 1980s because of the drop in the world price of oil. It ordered illegal migrant workers out of the country. As a result, hundreds of thousands had to return to their impoverished homelands.

Education and employment

Many in the South see education as the main hope of escaping from the kind of problems we have been discussing. They are probably right, yet the relationship both between education and individual achievement and between education and development is problematic and unclear. First, there is the question of what priority to give to the various sectors of education. There is a strong correlation between development and an extensive primary (and to an extent secondary) system of education. In other words there is a case for concentrating on mass numeracy and literacy, although typically it is secondary and higher education that gets favoured treatment. Second, there is curriculum content and particularly the question of relevance to development needs. In many ex-colonial countries spectacular examples of irrelevance occurred with youngsters becoming more expert in the history and literature of the former colonial power than their own – an example of cultural neo-colonialism and self denigration at the heart of the socialisation process. In higher education, irrelevance has often taken the form of over-concentration on classical subjects and liberal professional training, such as law and medicine, when the greater need was for practically-trained graduates. Thus, there is a surplus of barristers in the West Indies and of doctors in India but a shortage of trained business people and engineers in both. Curricula can also be over-academic at the secondary level. Thus the promise that all Zimbabwean children would have the opportunity to take 'O' levels came back to haunt the government not only because of its impracticality but because of its irrelevance to the country's economic needs. Third, the principle that 'those who have shall get even more' applies as much to education as to other matters. The offspring of the wealthy can buy an education which will equip them for elite membership whilst distancing them from the struggles and feelings of the great majority. Even so, some elite members educated in the West seem responsive to the principles of democracy and social justice for all, while others seem quite resistant to them.

Theme 3: development and the environment

The opening two chapters of this book raised the question of the environment in the context of late modernity. Ullrich Beck – the sociologist of risk – argues that the characteristic of late modernity is that the unintended and often negative consequences of modern development become apparent. He is referring above all to what he sees, and increasingly others see, as the human destruction of the environment and parts of the eco-system (i.e. the systems of planetary inter-dependence). Modern society itself is now utterly dependent on technical intervention in and technological harnessing of the forces of nature. If this goes wrong in any serious way, then, the consequences are likely to be correspondingly serious. To take what may seem a small example. The British consume about 700,000,000 chickens per annum. These chickens are only produced and consumed to an acceptable level of safety by the use of antibiotics in their feed. Without this, there would be a highly enhanced risk of the spread of salmonella and other diseases to human beings. Supposing chickens widely developed immunity to antibiotics? The resulting scenario would be even more inconvenient than the 1996 'mad cow disease' scare both for consumers and producers. Both of these cases – one imagined, the other real – are intended to indicate that the balance between

humans, technology and nature can be a fine one – and not without risk. Beck argues that the risks from car, industrial and nuclear pollution are far greater than those indicated in the previous paragraph. Many tens of thousands of people have died as a direct result of these risks – the 'acceptable' risks of modernity.

Multinationals and the environment: a case study

This section deals briefly with some of the recent environmental issues raised in relation to the oil giant, Shell. These issues are important in themselves but need to be seen within the broad perspective of political economy adopted throughout this chapter. The value of Shell's annual production is about equal to that of Ghana's. However, it is highly arguable that internationally, Shell's economic power counts for more than the political power of Ghana. Many countries have a vested interest – employment, trade, taxation, whatever – in the activities of Shell. The activities of Shell in relation to the environment and other matters are sometimes contested – and virtually always monitored – by other groups and interests. These include the governments of the countries Shell operates within, the media and public opinion within these countries and internationally, groups such as Greenpeace, and local peoples and individuals affected by Shell's activities.

Figure 20.18 gives details of six international situations concerning a range of issues, nations, and interest groups which Shell has been involved with in recent years. Four of these directly concern the environment and the other two – concerning Burma and South Africa – clearly show that, powerful as Shell is, it has to take into consideration international public opinion about matters such as where it invests and how it treats its labour force. In the case of South Africa under apartheid, Shell continued its business activities arguing, as did some other Western multinationals, that it treated its employees better than indigenous businesses. However, it does seem to be the case that international trade sanctions were crucial to bringing an end to apartheid and Shell's policies worked in a contrary direction. Shell's motivations for withdrawing from Burma are debated but, as John Pilger has re-emphasised, the Burmese government's human rights record certainly offers a powerful reason.

Of the four environmental cases, the first came up in the United States where Shell manufactured pesticides and herbicides. Shell sought to require its insurers to pay for a share of the resulting damage. This case is interesting in that it illustrates Beck's argument about the unintended and unforeseen (or perhaps simply disregarded) consequences of 'modernity' – in this case chemical processing. The damage of pollution to health and to the environment is increasingly resulting in large insurance claims. One of the main reasons why Lloyd's insurance brokers – one of the largest international insurance companies – got into major financial difficulty was the size of the compensation payments it had to make against pollution claims. The second issue, the oil

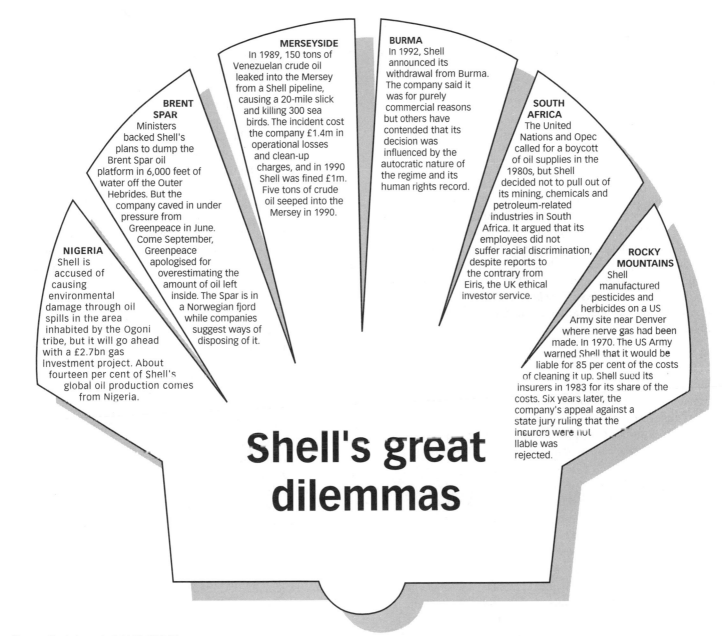

BRENT SPAR
Ministers backed Shell's plans to dump the Brent Spar oil platform in 6,000 feet of water off the Outer Hebrides. But the company caved in under pressure from Greenpeace in June. Come September, Greenpeace apologised for overestimating the amount of oil left inside. The Spar is in a Norwegian fjord while companies suggest ways of disposing of it.

MERSEYSIDE
In 1989, 150 tons of Venezuelan crude oil leaked into the Mersey from a Shell pipeline, causing a 20-mile slick and killing 300 sea birds. The incident cost the company £1.4m in operational losses and clean-up charges, and in 1990 Shell was fined £1m. Five tons of crude oil seeped into the Mersey in 1990.

BURMA
In 1992, Shell announced its withdrawal from Burma. The company said it was for purely commercial reasons but others have contended that its decision was influenced by the autocratic nature of the regime and its human rights record.

SOUTH AFRICA
The United Nations and Opec called for a boycott of oil supplies in the 1980s, but Shell decided not to pull out of its mining, chemicals and petroleum-related industries in South Africa. It argued that its employees did not suffer racial discrimination, despite reports to the contrary from Eiris, the UK ethical investor service.

NIGERIA
Shell is accused of causing environmental damage through oil spills in the area inhabited by the Ogoni tribe, but it will go ahead with a £2.7bn gas investment project. About fourteen per cent of Shell's global oil production comes from Nigeria.

ROCKY MOUNTAINS
Shell manufactured pesticides and herbicides on a US Army site near Denver where nerve gas had been made. In 1970. The US Army warned Shell that it would be liable for 85 per cent of the costs of cleaning it up. Shell sued its insurers in 1983 for its share of the costs. Six years later, the company's appeal against a state jury ruling that the insurers were not liable was rejected.

Shell's great dilemmas

(Source: *The Independent*, 14.10.1996:15)

Figure 20.18 Ethics, environment and the global marketplace

pipeline leakage into the Mersey was relatively straightforward. The Company was found guilty of negligence and was fired and required to pay compensation.

In 1995, two internationally renowned incidents involving Shell occurred, Brent Spar and the case of Ken Saro-Wiwa. Shell planned to dispose of the Brent Spar oil platform in water about one mile deep of the Outer Hebrides. Greenpeace objected claiming that the amount of oil remaining within the structure could cause major environmental damage if it leaked. When Greenpeace activists sailed out to the platform, their cause received widespread publicity. An international boycott against Shell occurred at filling stations – especially in Germany where environmental awareness is strong and standards relatively high. Shell conceded the issue – even though its own estimate on residual oil was proved more accurate than that of Greenpeace. Again, the media battle was crucial and although Shell achieved some impressive representation, Greenpeace played the 'David and Goliath' card effectively to a seemingly sympathetic media and public.

The case of Ken Saro-Wiwa represents the kind of public relations nightmare that a multinational investing in an undemocratic regime fears. Shell itself, withdrew from Burma perhaps to avoid risking such an incident. It also raises a number of crucial issues of power and ethics. Some background is necessary. Shell Development Company of Nigeria which is a unit of the

Royal Dutch Shell Company has had connections with Nigeria for over 60 years. Oil revenues provide about 90 per cent of the government of Nigeria's foreign exchange and about 80 per cent of its overall revenue. The government at the time of the Saro-Wiwa incident was a military dictatorship. One area of Shell's oil extraction was the Ogoni region. Saro-Wiwa was the best known among the local campaigners who objected to the environmental pollution caused by Shell and which was instrumental in Shell's (apparently temporary) withdrawal from the region in 1993. Saro-Wiwa and a group of other prominent campaigners fell foul of both the government and Shell. They wanted a greater share of the oil revenue for the Ogoni region, recognition that the oil was owned by the region, and political self-determination. Saro-Wiwa also called on Shell to pay a compensation sum of $10 billion to the Ogoni people for alleged environmental damage. A company spokesman acknowledged that Shell had caused some environmental problems to the region but said 'these do not add up to devastation' (Quoted in *The Independent*, 14.10.1995:15). The government executed Saro-Wiwa and a group of co-campaigners for 'political insurrection'.

Comment

Could Shell have prevented the execution of Saro-Wiwa and his co-campaigners, assuming its top management had wanted to? Shell still has huge investments in Nigeria and intends to increase them. What, then, is the balance between Shell's economic power against that of one of Africa's largest, richest countries? Yvette Cooper comments:

> *Oil and natural resource companies … cannot make and break contracts at the drop of an executioners axe. Energy projects can take years to plan and years to complete, and it can be decades before you get a return on your investment. Short-term political demonstrations are simply not an option.*
>
> *But alongside the limits on their freedom to manoeuvre, oil companies also have … power and … responsibility. Their power peaks precisely when a government and an economy are in trouble – and the revenue from natural resources becomes the only remaining support for a regime. Right now, the oil revenues from operations by Shell, Elf, Agip and other oil multinationals are helping the Nigerian military government to survive.*
>
> (*The Independent, 14.10.1996:15*)

Eco-tourism: selling 'tradition' and 'nature': a case study in global tourism

According to the World Travel and Tourist Council, tourism is the largest industry in the world and growing at an extremely fast rate. Already about 500 million travel for tourism annually – a figure which could double in the next 25 years. Everybody it seems is travelling around *consuming* everybody else! As Sue Wheat puts it: 'Today, the search for the exotic destination is on with a vengeance'. Undoubtedly, the growth in world tourism is one of the more spectacular examples of the surge in consumption in late modernity. It reflects, on the one hand, increased wealth – and so most tourists are Westerners and Japanese/East Asian – and, on the other hand, it reflects the search for new experience – for someone or something 'different'. Sociologists are increasingly interested in the effects of tourism on the societies and culture visited or consumed. Eco-tourism is usually presented as a form of tourism which aims not merely at visiting natural environments and communities but at getting modestly involved in them and, if possible, contributing to their preservation and care. If this is a case of wanting to have one's cake and eat it, it is in principle possible for some of the money raised through eco-tourism to be channelled back into the sites toured.

For many developing countries, general tourism is a major revenue earner. While attempts are often made to attract tourists, doing so successfully can generate severe problems. First, there is the problem of what John Urry refers to as 'the tourists gaze'. Being constantly 'on show' or asked 'to perform' can be awkward and demeaning – even if people 'get used to it'. Second, the 'tourist-native' relationship tends to be a dependent one for the latter. Gunder Frank explained how this occurs at the macro economic and political levels. Psychologically, dependent attitudes may develop at the individual and national levels given that what indigenous people most want from tourism is 'the dollar'. Thirdly, tourists can cause wear and damage to natural environments and historic sites and movements.

On the other hand, *superficially* at least, tourism might appear to provide a stimulus to local culture – to difference. It is, after all what is different about the local culture that the tourist has paid to see (usually, on assurance of doing so at a minimum level of familiar comfort!). From 'Bronte country' in Yorkshire to the ancient Greek remains of Crete, the globetrotting tourist is looking for the historically, ethnically or locally 'authentic'.

Eco-tourism in Belize

Eco-tourism in Belize illustrates the issues raised above in relation to promoting the natural environment and historical sites. Belize became independent from Britain in 1981. It has a population of less than 200,000 people who speak several languages and is becoming increasingly cosmopolitan. The country has a long beautiful coastline along the Caribbean, a rich inland habitat, and several cites of ancient Maya civilisation. Tourism is the country's second industry after agriculture. As Rich Wilk observes with some irony:

RECOMMENDED ITINERARY No.1
14 Days

Snorkelling on the Belize Barrier Reef from north to south

With over 170 miles of barrier reef, Belize has a plethora of underwater attractions to keep the keen marine naturalist occupied for long periods. This tour of fourteen days enables the avid snorkeller to sample the barrier reef in three locations. In the north at Ambergris Caye, a lively island with the reef just a quarter of a mile away; in the middle reef on St George's Caye, a small private island with important historical connections; and finally in the south at Placencia peninsula, with the most beautiful offshore islands and the least visited part of the reef – here one can also take optional adventurous inland excursions to Mayan ruins, down jungle rivers and to the Cockscombe Jaguar Preserve.

Day 1 Depart LONDON. O/n UNITED STATES (HOUSTON or MIAMI).

Day 2 Arrive BELIZE INTERNATIONAL AIRPORT. Met and tfr to boat. Tfr to ST GEORGE'S CAYE. Stay 4 nts in ISLAND RESORT, FB. Snorkelling offshore, or by boat (to be arranged at resort).

Day 6 Tfr to BELIZE CITY. Take taxi (not inc) to BELIZE CITY MUNICIPAL AIRPORT. Catch scheduled flight to SAN PEDRO, AMBERGRIS CAYE. Stay 3 nts AIR-CONDITIONED HOTEL, RO. Snorkelling to be arranged at hotel or with one of the many boat operators along the waterfront.

Day 9 Catch scheduled flight via BELIZE CITY to PLACENCIA PENINSULA airstrip. Met and tfr to the beachfront. Stay 4 nts in DIVING INN with wood and thatch cabins, BB. Snorkelling trips or inland excursions to be arranged at the Inn.

Day 13 Catch scheduled flight to BELIZE INTERNATIONAL AIRPORT. Depart BELIZE.

Day 14 Arrive LONDON.

Price: £893   *Departures:* Flexible

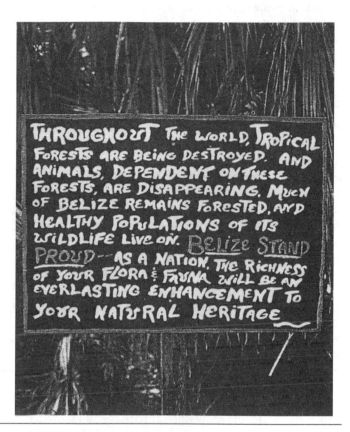

On the one hand …   **and on the other …**

(Source: Open University, D103, SS MOD 6, S3:8)

Figure 20.19 Eco-tourism in Belize

> *When Belizeans turn off the TV they can look out of the window at a parade of foreign tourists, resident expatriates, and students in search of authentic local experience, traditional medicine, untouched rainforests and ancient ruins.*
>
> *(Learning to be local in Belize: global systems of common difference)*

A BBC2 film about eco-tourism in Belize, *Cashing in on Paradise* illuminates many of the difficulties and compromises that can face the various groups involved in such 'development'. Both Belize's marine environment, including its magnificent barrier reef, and its still not wholly explored inland territories are marketed to western tourists. The government attempts to do this in a controlled way but faces considerable difficulties both in protecting the environment and in ensuring that ownership of many of the country's economic assets, including land, is predominantly in the hands of Belizeans.

Thus, despite restrictions on snorkelling and tourist sea-traffic in the barrier reef area, the reef has been significantly damaged. The independent, non-profit making organisation, Coral Lay Conservation also reports that the numbers of many species, including turtles, have declined because of threats to their habitat resulting from developments along the reef.

Question

What are the arguments for and against each of the approaches to Belize's environment shown in Figure 20.19?

Controversy, around a proposed eco-tourist site near the small town Punta Gorda in southern Belize illustrates the possible gains and losses – economic and cultural – associated with eco-tourist development. The town is located in a beautiful natural environment close to Mayan remains. An American company would like to establish a small (initially!) residential eco-tourist base in the town. The company would employ local labour and substantially use local produce in the enterprise. In other words, the company offers economic development of a certain sort and provided it did not withdraw or go bankrupt, it probably would boost local living standards. To varying degrees local people, conservation groups, central and local government officials favour or oppose the plan mainly depending on how they balance economic advantage against possible environmental damage and disruption to their culture and independence.

Comment: 'having to be different'

Despite the 'caring' philosophy of eco-tourism its potential danger to local environments is evident. Less obvious is the effect of eco-tourism on local cultures. As was noted above, it is, after all, the expectation of tourists that the locals will be 'different'. At one level, therefore global capitalism in the form of the tourist industry is not steam-rolling local people into being the same as Westerners but encouraging difference. However, matters are not so simple. First, having to display local culture for money endangers the authenticity of the culture itself – in Marxist terms it commodifies it. Second, although the intent of tourism, including eco-tourism, is to offer the local (e.g. 'ethnic' culture) for consumption, Western tourists and the Western media provide enticing examples and images of Western wealth and patterns of consumption. The revenue tourism generates provides the means for locals to imitate Western patterns of consumption and lifestyle and often they do. Ironically, this undermines the local culture which is what is being sold to the tourist. Richard Wilks illustrates this process in relation to beauty contests in Belize. Contests at local level still reflect ethnic style and concepts of beauty whereas at national level, Western standards increasingly impinge. Third, although the international tourist trade demands local and ethnic difference, this occurs within a common global framework of economic and cultural exchange: what Richard Wilks refers to as a 'structure of common difference'.

Wilks' own view is that local culture is not inevitably swamped or commodified by the global but that it is certain to be changed. He sees a genuine contest between the various groups and levels involved and further comments that the Belizeans have been involved in a similar contest or unequal exchange for hundreds of years:

> And a place like Belize has never had very much range for autonomous action; not under British colonialism and not under cold war discipline. But the growth of a global order of communication and of systems of common difference forces us to think about autonomy and dependency in very different ways. The same processes that destroy autonomy are now creating new sorts of communities, new kinds of locality and identity ...
>
> (130)

This is obviously true. People survive external pressures and forge different identities – individual and collective – in circumstances not of their own choosing. However, in stressing change and difference, the questions of fairness and quality should not be dodged. How far does the West still exploit the rest? Is the 'gift' of modernity better than the traditional ways of life it inevitably changes?

Conclusion: global citizenship? Local character?

The scope of this chapter has been so wide that there is a danger of concluding it with empty generalisation. Taking that risk, it seems to me that the globe is still more an arena of struggle than of community. Out of the complexity of exploitation and aspirations to liberation and greater equality, most would look for a wider spread of both human rights and material prosperity. Historically, in the West, these have been achieved through struggle and implemented through the state. The state has been the guardian of citizen's rights and implemented welfare reforms and modest wealth redistribution.

More recently, the prosperity and rights agenda – has moved to the world stage. For all its flaws, the United Nations has consistently tried to pursue common minimum standards on a global communal basis. Within Europe, human rights are increasingly secured at the Community as well as at the national level. It would be ironic if the Western nation-states faltered in their commitment to extending citizen's rights and a fairer basis of national community when, world-wide this agenda seems to be gaining greater acceptance.

Of course, the Western legacy to the world is deeply flawed. First, is the economic exploitation that characterised much capitalist and imperialist activity. Second, is the abuse of many indigenous societies and cultures around the world – an abuse verging at times on the genocidal.

Inevitably, societies and cultures experiencing the impact of the West have had mixed reactions. Over time they have variously rejected, accepted and modified aspects of Western culture and institutions and reclaimed and often reassessed their own cultures in the light of Western impact. These processes are apparent in the following quotation about Africa and the West. No people, place or culture have been more exploited and changed by the West than Africa. None has found the West more alien and different. The following quotation from Yashin Alibhar-Brown give an indication of how contemporary African thinkers are reassessing the meaning of the tribal, the national and the pan-African and of development itself, as they take more measured consideration of the West and of their own heritage:

The African academic Professor Ali Mazrui is also posing iconoclastic questions. Has the time come, he asks to move the 'Imperial soul' from where it has resided, from Europe, and latterly the USA, to Africa? Should the Organisation of African Unity, say, intervene – even with force – under the banner of Pax African in countries that are out of control and use sovereignty as a shield? And why are we so dogmatic, he wants to know, about the way we think about Africa: 'Tribalism is not necessarily a pathology. This excessive enthusiasm we have had for the nation state has just encouraged hatred. So why don't we take two steps back and re-tribalise countries and then create federal structures? Perhaps if we succeed in giving people back a secure identity, they can learn to live with ethnic diversity which is a challenge for the whole world.'

Soyinka advocates another radical alternative. He thinks that the borders which have made countries dysfunctional ought to be redrawn as a matter or urgency.

The historian Basil Davidson wrote earlier this year about the need for Africa to make organic connections with its past, instead of trying to live up to the expectations foisted on it by colonisation and decolonisation …

The new leaders are thinking in terms of power transfer, regional co-operation and human rights, too. So conscious are they of the need to put their houses in order, that few of them glibly talk of neo-colonialism or Western bias. Professor Kirya, for example, believes the image of Africa will not change in the eyes of the Western media until they see positive transformations.

Others argue that it is not Western interference, but indifference that will prove to be a catastrophe for Africa. But the West, afraid these days of refugee flows and needing new markets would be unwise to be indifferent. Too much is at stake, says Samuel: 'Africans are changing, we have suffered too much and people in your country must help us to move forward.'

Source: Yashin Alibhar-Brown, 'For Africa the only answer lies within', The Independent, 26.10.1994:14)

Questions

1 To what extent does 'overpopulation' hinder development?
2 Critically discuss development and underdevelopment in relation to one major issue or theme of your choice.

Summary

1 Development implies some positive progress in a society's condition whereas undevelopment implies decline or stagnation. The historical and contemporary overview section is crucial in that it describes the key groups involved in global economic, political and cultural power-play. These include the multinationals which Marxists consider the most powerful. In any case, the activities of these groups largely determines the pattern of under/development.

2 In a global context, three main theories of under/development change occur:
   • Modernisation theory.
   • Marxism.
   • Liberal/Social Democratic.

3 Modernisation theorists argue that the pattern of historical change has been from simple to complex or modern societies. Among the main explanations for development are that adopting 'Western attitudes and values' and/or 'Western' technology can promote development.

4 There are two distinct Marxist theories of underdevelopment. André Gunder Frank argues that the 'dependency' produced by world capitalism has typically created 'underdevelopment'. He considers that the global economy is a unified world capitalist system. In contradiction, Marxist modes of production theory argues that there remain various non-capitalist modes of production within societies in the 'Third World'; and that this is crucial to understanding them economically, politically and socially.

5 The two liberal theories of development have as their common core a commitment to development through the 'free' capitalist market. However, whereas the traditional liberals (often modern Conservatives) want to leave the market essentially unregulated, liberal social democrats argue that governments or international bodies should regulate both the functioning and effects of the free market, including the inequalities it creates.

6 The contribution made by the work of women to development has been frequently ignored. The position of women within patriarchal systems in various societies differs greatly in terms of power and status and is not 'better' in all respects in capitalist societies.

7 Globalisation refers to the process by which the world is bound more closely and immediately together in economic, political and cultural terms. There is disagreement about the main causes of globalisation and even whether it is occurring in any significantly new sense.

8 Three under/development themes are discussed here and one elsewhere (see pp. 520-4) and their relationship to globalisation indicated. These are:

i *World Population and inequality*
The main issue here is whether population should be controlled directly through planning, not at all, or , indirectly, through resource redistribution.

ii *Urbanisation and industrialisation*
The structure of and influences on cities in Southern countries are discussed. These differ in many ways from Western cities.

iii *Development and the environment*
The impact of Western multinationals and tourists on the environment of Southern hemisphere countries is discussed in the context of globalisation and under/development.

Research and coursework

Under/development is not the easiest topic on which a British based student could attempt even a small piece of primary research. An exception might be black British students who can draw on material from developing countries or who might be able to interview people who know such societies well. However, such research would have to be as systematic as any other project as it would be assessed by the same criteria. Another possibility – now that globalisation has become a syllabus topic – would be to look at the 'global in the local' i.e. how globalisation has affected some aspect or aspects of your own locality. These might include, patterns of consumption, employment/unemployment and the social or organisational aspects of foreign investment/ development.

Further reading

Malcolm Waters, *Globalisation* (Routledge, 1995) and Anthony McGrew, *A Global Society,* in S Hall *et al.* eds., *Modernity and its Futures* (The Open University, 1992) are excellent, up-to-date introductions to this area – but demanding.

Readings

Reading 1
A question of power: national politicians and the multinationals

From Peter Riddell, 'Leaders in Cloud-Cuckoo-Land', *The Times*, 28.9.1995:14 (adapted)

Politicians know that real power lies with global business, says Peter Riddell.

There are obviously differences between the parties, but they are not nearly as large as they pretend. Politicians have less and less room for manoeuvre.

Modern politics has had three broad phases. The first, lasting up to the end of the last century, was when the State took little or no responsibility for economic and social conditions. Government was about diplomacy, running colonies and paying for an army and navy, while maintaining law and order. The second phase, starting in the 1900s and reaching its high point in the 1950s and 1960s, was when the State took direct responsibility for the economy, levels of unemployment and welfare.

Politics seemed to have no limits as ministers became involved in a wide range of decisions affecting people's lives and the affairs of business. National governments could tax, spend and change the fortunes of even the largest company. While this era has mistakenly been viewed as an era of consensus, there were clear choices between the main parties on issues of both production and distribution.

But politics has entered an era of increasing limits over the past decade. National governments no longer have as much power as they did. What is fashionably known as 'globalisation' – free movements of capital, skilled labour and information – restricts the sovereignty of individual nations far more than any ceding of powers to European institutions under formal treaties. The volume of transactions in foreign exchange markets severely limits the power of any national government to influence its own country's exchange rate or long-term interest rates, while the margin for altering short-term rates is, in practice, narrow.

Most large companies have become so multinational that their nominal base in a particular country accounts for less and less of their assets and profits. They are above the actions of any particular government. The chief executive officers of these companies are as much politicians as any elected minister.

Professor Susan Strange, of Warwick University, argues in the summer issue of the journal *Government and Opposition* that the decisions of companies, not of governments, have brought about the most important changes in the patterns of trade and production. In all the hype ... over the global launch of Windows 95 by Microsoft, governments were irrelevant.

Similarly, rapid technological change and liberalisation of State monopolies has put many media and telecommunications giants outside the control of any government. Shell's abrupt change of mind two months ago over the Brent Spar platform showed that international pressures produced by Greenpeace's campaign mattered far more than the views of the British government (see pp. 614–6).

This shift in the balance between states and markets has dramatically altered the context in which politicians operate. Governments can no longer direct industry, but rather are suitors, competing in offering subsidies to attract the investments of multinational companies which could be made in several countries. When Siemens announced its plans for a major new microchip factory in Tyneside ... Michael Heseltine was rightly delighted. But the German company had done the Government, and Britain, a favour, not the other way round.

No party seriously interested in power would now advocate the large-scale intervention which was officially Labour policy during the 1970s and early 1980s. A radical assault on capital via either nationalisation or controls is no longer feasible for any industrialised country. The last attempt at socialism in one country, by the Mitterrand Government in the early 1980s, quickly had to be reversed.

National governments can no longer set levels of corporate or personal taxation which are significantly out of line with international trends, while public borrowing is limited by international capital markets, as Tony Blair explicitly recognised ...

The replacement of the Tories by Labour would still make a difference in some areas: for example, the distribution of taxation and spending. These changes could matter for some individuals, but they are likely to be pretty marginal in terms of the overall tax and spending burden. Any increase in spending and taxes under a Labour Government would probably be much less than has occurred over the past few years under the Tories. To base an election campaign on whether or not income tax should be cut by 2p is largely a diversion.

The need for caution in promises is underlined by Andrew Britton, in the *National Institute Economic Review*, who is broadly sympathetic to many of Labour's aspirations. He argues that 'the optimistic assumptions underlying Labour's policy presentation ought to be questioned'. In particular, he highlights the conflict between moving towards full employment and improving the pay and conditions of the average worker.

Mr Blair has raised Labour's hopes but these are mainly for an end to the long period of Tory rule rather than recreating the high expectations and 'New Jerusalem' mood which Harold Wilson projected in 1963-64. As Professor Strange argues: 'When the next election comes, who really believes there will be major changes in the way Britain is governed?' One result is 'disillusion bordering on disdain so widely felt for politicians. People know that their promises of lower unemployment, more job creation, are not to be relied on.'

Questions

1 What are the 'three broad phases' of modern politics, Riddell refers to? Briefly mention a couple of characteristics of the second two.
2 What does Riddell mean by the 'shift in balance between states and markets'? Briefly, do you agree that this alleged shift 'has dramatically altered the context in which politicians operate'?
3 Describe and briefly comment on Riddell's analysis of the scope for change that a Labour government might have.

Reading 2
Binary oppositions in global dynamics

In addition to reading the text below, look again at Figure 20.8 and the surrounding text before attempting the following questions.

From Anthony McGrew, 'A Global Society', in S Hall *et al.* eds., *Modernity and Its Futures* (The Open University, 1992), pp. 74-6

It should be apparent by this stage that the discourse of globalisation – 'global babble' or 'globe talk' – is characterised by considerable complexity. This may well reflect the 'real' nature of globalisation, or it may simply issue from the nature of the discourse itself. In exploring the dynamics of globalisation, a more intense sense of complexity, and even ambiguity, surfaces. This arises because, within the existing literature, globalisation is understood as a process which is essentially *dialectical* in nature and *unevenly* experienced across time and space.

Sophisticated accounts of globalisation are not teleological in the sense that they assume the existence of an inexorable historical process leading to a universal human community. Rather, globalisation is generally understood to be a *contingent* and *dialectical* process; dialectical in the simple sense of embracing contradictory dynamics. As Giddens explicitly acknowledges, globalisation ' is a dialectical process because…' it does not bring about '… a generalised set of changes acting in a uniform direction, but consists in mutually opposed tendencies' (Giddens, 1990:64). But what is the substantive form which these 'opposed tendencies' take? Several 'binary oppositions' or dualities are commonly identified within the discourse of globalisation:

Universalisation versus particularisation

In the same way that globalisation universalises aspects of modern social life (e.g. the nation-state, assembly line production, consumer fashions, etc.) it simultaneously encourages particularisation by relativising both 'locale' and 'place' so that an intensification (or manufacturing) of uniqueness (or difference) is thereby fostered (e.g. the resurgence of nationalism and ethnic identities) (Robertson, 1990; Wallerstein, 1991; Harvey, 1989).

Homogenisation versus differentiation

In as much as globalisation brings about an essential 'sameness' to the surface appearance and institutions of modern social life across the globe (e.g. city life, religion, McDonalds, the existence of human rights, bureaucratisation, etc.), it also involves the assimilation and re-articulation of the global in relation to local circumstances (e.g. human rights are interpreted in very different ways across the globe; the practice of Islam is quite different in different countries, etc.) (Hannerz, 1919).

Integration versus fragmentation

Whilst globalisation creates new forms of global, regional and transnational communities or organisations which unite people across territorial boundaries (e.g. the transnational corporation, international trade unions, transnational class formations), equally, it also divides and fragments communities, both within and across traditional nation-state boundaries. For example, labour becomes increasingly divided along local, national and sectoral lines; and ethnic and racial divisions become more acute as the 'others' become more proximate (Bull, 1977; Bozeman, 1984).

Centralisation versus decentralisation

Although globalisation facilitates an increasing concentration of power, knowledge, information, wealth and decision-making authority (e.g. the European Community, transnational companies), it also generates a powerful decentralising dynamic as nations, communities, and individuals attempt to take greater control over the forces which influence their 'fate' (e.g. the activities of new social movements, such as the peace, women's, or environmental movements) (Rosenau, 1990; Wallerstein, 1991).

Juxtaposition versus syncretisation

By compressing time and space, globalisation forces the juxtaposition of different civilisations, ways of life, and social practices. This both reinforces social and cultural prejudices and boundaries whilst simultaneously creating 'shared' cultural and social spaces in which there is an evolving 'hybridisation' of ideas, values, knowledge and institutions (e.g. the mixing of cuisines, New Age lifestyles, architecture, advertising images, etc.) (Perlmutter, 1991; Jameson, 1991).

These contradictory tendencies are inscribed in the very dynamics of globalisation; a process which is by definition dialectical. For the participants in 'globe talk', the contradictory nature of globalisation serves to remind us of its essential contingency and complexity. This is further reinforced by the *unevenness* with which globalisation has been experienced across time and space.

Questions

1 Pick any two of the five suggested binary oppositions below and provide and explain an example of each.
2 Present and explain reasons why globalisation is occurring in a way that produces 'opposed tendencies' or 'binary oppositions'.

21

CHAPTER

Sociological Theory: Paradigm or Paradigms?

Sociology now adopts a global perspective

1 Critically to discuss the classic sociological perspectives and the so-called 'perspectives approach' to sociology popular in the 1970s and 1980s.

2 To review a number of attempts to theorise the

agency/structure dualism in sociology.

3 Critically to examine some more recent sociological theory, including postmodernism, and to discuss the issue of whether or not there is a 'new sociology' addressing 'new' questions.

Introduction

This chapter discusses sociological theory at a more advanced level than Chapters 1 and 2. As was the case in Chapter 1, each of the main perspectives is discussed in turn and here there is in addition a section on phenomenology. The underlying theme of the chapter is whether sociology is moving towards a relatively unified approach or generally shared perspective or whether, on the contrary, it is destined to reflect many perspectives – some perhaps contradictory – as poststructuralists would argue (see p. 643).

Let us begin, however, with some key established sociological questions which have given focus to the discipline.

Key questions in sociology

Charles Wright Mills had the work of Marx, Durkheim, Weber and other 'classic' sociologists in mind when he suggested that such thinkers 'have consistently asked three sorts of questions'. Essentially these questions are:

1 What is the structure of this particular society as a whole? (or how is a given society made up?)

2 What is the relationship between the individual or self – including particular types of individuals – and this society?

3 Where does this society stand in human history?

Taken together, questions 1 and 2 return us to the relationship between self and society raised in Chapter 1. However, let us consider the questions separately as Mills proposes them. Before the question 'what is the structure of a particular society?' can be addressed, we need to know what is meant by structure. The structure of society refers to its institutions, particularly major institutional systems such as the economy, the political system and the family. Institutions have a physical aspect, e.g. banks are part of the economy, and a normative and behavioural aspect, i.e. behaviour within given institutional areas is governed by a range of norms, e.g. the professional regulations governing banking. Mills himself uses the term 'components' to describe institutions and emphasises the importance of analysing how they relate to each other and why and to what extent they change. He also stresses that much can be learnt through comparing the social structures of societies.

Mills' second concern, the relationship between the individual and society, is central to sociology. Mills is aware of the power of

society to mould individual behaviour (he describes 'human nature' as seemingly 'plastic') but, as we have seen, he also stresses that knowledge and understanding can motivate and facilitate personal action. Mills also considers it to be an important sociological question why certain types of character – say, fascist or materialistic or idealistic – appear more prominently in certain social circumstances than in others. Here he is raising the issue of the relationship between group character and social structure.

Mills' third question 'where does this society stand in human history' suggests that perspective and a sense of context can be gained on a society by knowing how and why it has changed and how it compares to other societies. Such comparative and historical work has enabled sociologists to categorise societies into types, and thus map out the panorama of human social experience.

Mills' questions cover – from a marginally more general standpoint – much the same ground as those used at the beginning of Chapter 1. The latter were intended to focus the fundamental concerns of sociology and to introduce the main elements of the thought of Marx, Weber and Durkheim. These were the questions:

1 How is society constructed?

2 How does society 'operate' or function?

3 Why are some groups in society more powerful than others?

4 What causes social change?

5 Is society normally in orderly balance or in conflict?

6 What is the relationship of the individual to society?

7 What is the primary purpose of sociological study?

Question 1 – 'How is society constructed?' – roughly equates to Mills' – 'What is the structure of this particular society as a whole?' Questions 2, 3 and 5 are subsidiary to question 1. Question 6 – 'What is the relationship of the individual to society?' roughly equates to Mills' – 'What is the relationship of the individual or self … and this society?'. Rather less closely, question 4 – 'What causes social change?' roughly equates to Mills' – 'Where does this society stand in human history?'. Mills' question more precisely targets the centrality of the comparative and historical in sociological methodology and imagination. My question 7 subsumes the other 6 – 'What is the primary purpose of sociological study?'. The answer is to explore the meaning of social actors and their relationship to society.

Searching for the answers to the above questions – or questions like them – has certainly sustained the development of sociology over its relatively brief period as a distinct discipline. After all, these questions are wide enough and important enough to generate endless research and theory.

With a little adjustment Mills' questions can still stand as relevant today (see p. 647). However, such questions were applied by Weber, Marx and Durkheim to a *particular historical period*. Perhaps the most powerful argument that sociology needs to be radically rethought is that the *more specific* questions asked by the classical sociologists were appropriate to their own time but not quite so appropriate to our own. One way of putting this proposition is to state that the classical sociologists were seeking to explain the transition from traditional to modern (or modern capitalist) society whereas now the main issue is to explain the transition from modern to late modern or postmodern society. Others argue that the fundamental sociological issues have not greatly changed and that in so far as change has occurred, it was largely anticipated by the classical sociologists.

Before confronting this fraught debate, it will help to review the basic achievement of sociology up to the early 1960s when there was something of a challenge to established perspective.

Sociological perspectives: structural and interpretive perspectives, 1880s to 1960s

Any adequate sociological perspective must address the relationship between the self and society indicted above. However, in the period under discussion a difference of emphasis within sociology between those perspectives which concentrate mainly on structure and those which concentrate on the interaction of self and others: roughly, the large-scale and the small-scale, respectively. The more structural perspectives are functionalism and Marxism. The collective term used to refer to the other perspectives – interactionism and ethnomethodology – is interpretive. This indicates that they are primarily concerned with how the self (in relation to others) interprets society and finds meaning in doing so. Weber's sociology contains significant elements of both structural and interpretist perspective.

Structural sociology

Marxist, Tom Bottomore and the functionalist, Robert Nisbet, describe the 'central core of sociological theory' as:

> ... so many attempts to define the fundamental elements of social structure – both those which are universal and those which have particular historical character – and to provide some explanation or interpretation of the unity and persistence of societies, as well as their inner tensions and their potentialities for change.
>
> (Bottomore and Nisbet, 1979:viii)

This nicely sums up the approach of structural sociology which tends to concentrate on questions 1 and 3 proposed by Mills, the structural and historical/comparative.

Bottomore and Nisbet go on to locate the founders of 'sociological structuralism':

> It is our view that sociological structuralism arose in the works of Auguste Comte in France and Karl Marx in Germany. In France the pre-eminent sociological structuralist has been Durkheim.
>
> (Bottomore and Nisbet: 559)

Functionalism (consensus theory)

Functionalist perspective studies the structure and functioning of society. It is sometimes referred to as structural-functionalism. The concept of structure has already been sufficiently introduced. A function is simply an effect or outcome of the working of a social institution. Thus, a function of the economy is to produce goods and services for consumption. A description is given below of the structure and functioning of society as understood by leading post-Second World War functionalist, Talcott Parsons. Functionalism, in general, and Parsons' work in particular emphasises the importance of value consensus (agreement about fundamental values) as a condition for the effective functioning of a society. Both Weber and, especially, Durkheim influenced functionalism but little if any of Marx's thought has been adopted into the perspective.

Influences on functionalism: Comte, Durkheim, Weber

Both Comte and Durkheim distinguished between social statics and social dynamics. Social statics refers to the relatively 'given' structure of society (i.e. norms/rules) whereas social dynamics refers to the active relationships between the various parts of society. This distinction parallels that made by functionalists between structure and functioning. A more general influence of Comte and Durkheim on functionalism is their commitment to produce a science of society comparable in rigour to the natural sciences.

Comte and Durkheim left a legacy to functionalism which reflected their view that society has enormous power to form and structure the thought and behaviour of its members. Durkheim argued that sociology is the study of a 'category of facts (which consists of ways of acting, thinking, and feeling, external to the individual, and endowed with a power of coercion, by reason of which they control him'. So for Durkheim, sociology was largely about establishing what the 'rules or norms of a society are and how behaviour is controlled by them. He considered that the resulting order is essential for society to function well. He acknowledged that individuality exists but stated that it is not the object of sociology to study it. Rather, sociology is the study of the effect of social conditions on behaviour: such as economic crisis on the rate of suicide (see p. 361).

In contrast to Durkheim, his contemporary, Max Weber, did not attempt to separate the study of the individual from the study of society. Indeed, he would have considered such a separation impossible because in his view, the individual and society exist not independently but in a state of interaction in which they can change each other. People's values and ideas are influenced by society but they also change society. His theory of social action posits that the starting point of sociology is meaningful action. Weber's study of organisation (p. 293) shows his appreciation of the power of what Durkheim called 'social facts' to structure people's lives, but equally his analysis of charismatic figures such as Luther and Napoleon indicates that he believed individual personality and ideas can have a major impact on society.

Talcott Parsons

Talcott Parsons is the founder of modern functionalism (Durkheim and Weber did not use the term to describe their orientations). His social systems theory attempted to synthesise Durkheim's social structural and Weber's social action perspectives together with the insights of other social scientists, notably Freud. Parsons considered that people learn basic values, norms (rules) and roles through socialisation. He saw the successful internalisation of society's values, norms and roles as a precondition of social order, and the failure to learn or accept them as a problem of deviance .

The figure of Parsons' social system model needs explanation (see Figure 21.1). The concept of social system encompasses both structure and functioning. Each of the four subsystems in the model meets a given essential human need. These needs are referred to by Parsons variously as imperatives or prerequisites. The economy meets the imperative of adaptation (i.e. material needs); the political sub-systems or polity provide an institutional framework for collective goal attainment; kinship institutions provide pattern maintenance (of accepted ways of behaviour) and tension management (of emotions); and the cultural and community sub-systems provide integration (co-ordination and control of the various parts of the system), and goal attainment.

The integrating function of the cultural community sub-system is particularly important in functionalist theory. This is achieved by reinforcing values and socially acceptable behaviour – familiar functions of church and school. These values permeate the whole system and are the basis of the social consensus that underpins social order. For Parsons, as for Durkheim, society is a moral entity which requires conformity from its members to function effectively. Like his contemporary Edward Shils, Parsons sees a major role for the elite of society to maintain the 'central value system'. Their tendency to equate elite values with society's values has been criticised by conflict theorists who point to class, racial and other opposing values between groups.

How adequate is the organic analogy?

In Chapter 1, we introduced the functionalist comparison of society to a biological organism. In later chapters, we examined several applications of the organic analogy. The application examined in greatest detail was the way in which societies are considered to develop from the simple to the complex, just as growing bodies do. This approach stresses the evolutionary aspect of the analogy, and is apparent in the work of Durkheim and Parsons, but can be traced back to the British sociologist, Herbert Spencer (1820-1903), who was substantially influenced by Darwin's theory of biological evolution. We will consider shortly whether the concept of evolution provides an adequate basis for understanding social change.

Apart from applications of the organic analogy based on evolutionary perspective, others reflect the view that society is structured and functions like an organism. This emphasis finds its strongest expression in the writings of the British anthropologist, Radcliffe-Brown, (1881-1955), but it also partly underlies the more sophisticated social systems theory of Talcott Parsons. The basic notion here is that the various parts of society work in relation to one another (see the family-society model, Chapter 3, p. 54) and that society can best be understood by analysing these inter-relations (see Parsons' social systems model, p. 626). Functionalists consider that just as some parts of the body are functionally more important than others, so too, must society be hierarchically arranged for functional purposes. This view is apparent in the work of Davis and Moore (Chapter 5, p. 154) and Michels (Chapter 10, p. 294). Another major concept is that of social equilibrium by which society is assumed to seek balance and orderly functioning in the same way that the body does. Consensus on norms and values is considered a necessity for healthy functioning, although the analogy is rarely pursued as literally as this. Deviant behaviour, however, is often compared to physical 'pathology' by functionalists, not least by Durkheim himself.

Criticisms of functionalism (particularly the organic analogy)

We now turn to a critical appraisal of functionalism.

An over-socialised conception of human beings

Firstly, in reference to the organic analogy, organs do not think, whereas people do, or to put it more technically, the organic analogy contains no parallel for intentional social action. Biological processes are not generally achieved through the use of will, reason and imagination but mainly take place below the level of conscious awareness. Despite attempting to balance individuality with the effect of social structure, Parsons is widely considered to have produced a model of society which tends much more to the social structuralism of Durkheim than to the social action emphasis of Weber. Whatever his intention, Parsons treats values almost as though they are 'things' socially imposed upon the individual rather than partly the product of his or her own considered choice. As Figure 21.1 indicates, values are presented predominantly as the property of systems rather than of individuals and groups.(For an example of functionalist analysis of values, see Bert Hoselitz, p. 582). As Anthony Giddens remarks 'recognisably human agents seem to elude the grasp of his scheme: the stage is set, the scripts written, the roles established, but the performers are curiously absent from the scene'. The result of this is that functionalism present what Dennis Wrong calls an oversocialised conceptualisation of human beings.

An exaggeration of the role of consensus

A second criticism frequently made of functionalism is that it exaggerates the role of consensus and underestimates that of conflict in the functioning of society. It should be added that the concepts of consensus and equilibrium are linked, in that functionalists regard the former as a precondition of the latter. This emphasis on stability and order is reflected on the organic analogy itself in that organic bodies, particularly animals, strive to maintain internal balance (partly through an often complex process of homeostasis or adaptation) but there is no proof – indeed, it is most unlikely – that societies as entities are inherently endowed with similar adjustment mechanisms. Social order and equilibrium may be maintained through the conscious action of individuals and groups, but that is a different matter. Although consensus does contribute to social order, it too, must in part be intentionally created and maintained. It certainly cannot be regarded as automatically self-regulating or perpetuating. In other words, social equilibrium and consensus occur in a different way from organic equilibrium. There is no adequate explanatory parallel between the organic and social fields.

To the extent that Parsons does incorporate conflict into his scheme, he tends to assume that 'the system' has the capacity to neutralise it. Thus he allows that 'tension' can arise within society but the fact that he sees this as being 'managed' within the family and kinship sub-system suggests he sees it mainly as an individual problem. Conflict between classes, racial groups, and the two sexes gets scant consideration in his work. Robert Merton, working within the functionalist tradition, has introduced the concept of dysfunction which indicates that a social structure may function in

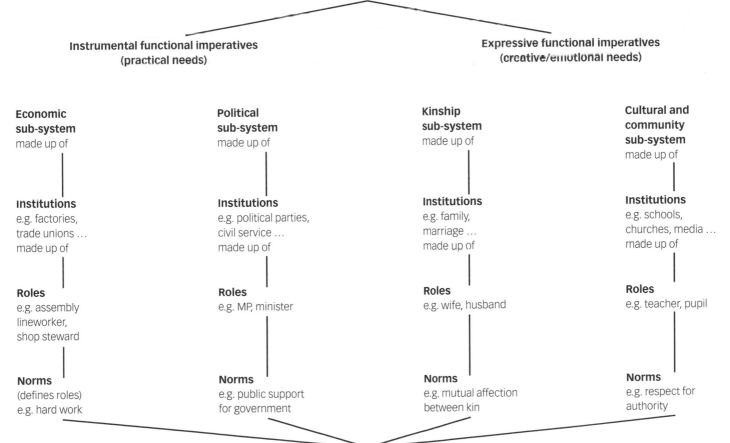

Figure 21.1 Society as a social system

a way that has a negative or maladaptive effect on society. Thus, it can be argued that means testing the poor is dysfunctional in so far as it puts off some of them from applying for needed social security.

A misleading separation of structure and system

A third criticism of the organic analogy is that it produces a misleading separation of structure (society's parts or institutions) and system (society's functioning). In particular, it leads only to a partial conceptualisation of the problem of social change. By contrast, this division seems to work well in the natural sciences. In biology, it helps to examine the structure of a plant or animal (anatomy) and then to describe how the various parts function in relation to one another and the whole. In a limited descriptive sense, the same approach is useful in sociology although, significantly, society cannot be similarly 'laid out' anatomically for examination. In real life, society 'functions' through the more or less organised actions of individuals and groups, not in the manner of an unreflecting organism. Nor does change occur solely through evolution and adaptation, although it may to some extent. Equally important in the history and development of nations and cultures are revolutions and drastic breaks with the past. Parsons' notion of dynamic equilibrium, but which social balance adjusts to accommodate new phenomena within the system, still stresses continuity at the expense of change and severance. It also underestimates the role of people in making history. For him, systems change and almost 'make' people, not the other way around.

In retrospect, Robert Merton's attempts to use the concept of function to embrace a wide variety of social events looks like the death throes of a theory stretched beyond its inherent capacity. In particular, his concept of manifest function which he uses to describe intended, as opposed to unintended (latent) consequences of institutional functioning does not adequately conceptualise the role of choice in social life. The basic problem is that it is not possible to provide an adequate account of consciously directed action within a framework that takes as its model the unconscious functioning of the organism.

Tautology

A final criticism of functionalism is that it is teleological, or tautological, as Chris Brown has referred to it. In other words, because functionalists see certain functions being performed by given institutions, they conclude that there must be need for these institutions – that is, they explain causes by their consequences. Actually, many institutions exist, the 'need' for which can be doubted. Inevitably, opinions will differ as to which institutions qualify: some will suggest the class system, others the nuclear family. Further, people create organisations and institutions not only to fulfil social needs but to pursue their own purposes and interests – sometimes at the expense of others.

Finally, although nobody can take exception to a descriptive account of the functions institutions perform, including those

many of us may not be aware of, this is only an aspect, and a rather obvious one, of sociological analysis. Who made things as they are, and in whose interest, are equally important questions which functionalists tend to underestimate.

The issue is not whether functionalism is an 'incorrect' perspective but how useful and illuminating it is. It is certainly helpful as a descriptive, if limited, account of what institutions 'do' – and, as such, it has some appeal to students. Further, the functionalist analysis of socialisation warns us, usefully, of what is 'done' to us individually in order to make us conforming members of society. Both these aspects of sociological analysis, however, are fairly obvious and well dealt with in other perspectives. Functionalism must stand or fall on the fruitfulness of its central concepts as presented in the biological analogy, or in Talcott Parsons' more recent, and, admittedly, more sophisticated systems theory. In either case, it seems to smack too much of evolutionism and not enough of intentionality.

Functionalism's evolutionary content is nowhere more obvious than in modernisation theory. It is functionalism's conceptualisation of universal progress – towards the American way – that marks it out not only as a sociology of modernity but as a perspective limited by the optimistic assumptions of modernity. Functionalism's message to poorer countries was – adapt and you, too can become like us.

Marxism (conflict theory I)

Whereas functionalism is based on the assumption that value consensus and social order are normal to society, Marxists consider that conflict over values and material issues is normal in class-divided societies. This is because, in Marx's view, different groups or classes of people have different needs or wants which ultimately brings them into conflict. However, Marxists recognise that even societies divided by classes may remain basically stable and orderly for long periods.

Structure and ideology

Marx's analysis of the structure of society begins with the issue of human survival: the need to produce goods. The area of society concerned with the production of goods is the economy. Marx referred to the forces of production, the means of production, the social relations of production, and the mode of production. The forces of production are all the factors, including scientific and technological which contribute to production. The means of production are included within the forces of production and are the concrete instruments of production (such as land in feudal societies and factories in capitalist-industrial societies). The social relations of production refers to the way in which production is socially organised – in all non-communist societies, there is a class which owns the means of production and a class which works the means of production. In nineteenth century capitalist society – the society he lived in – Marx described the class which owned the means of production as the capitalist class or bourgeoisie and the class which sold its labour as the working class or proletariat. The mode of production is the most general description of the main type of production in a given society, such as the feudal, capitalist or socialist modes of production.

Considered a s a whole, the economy and classes are referred to as the base or infrastructure of society. The other areas of society are collectively termed the superstructure. As presented in Figure 5.1, the superstructure covers politics and culture/ideology (see p. 141) – roughly the area of 'ideas'. Marx stated that:

> *The ideas of the ruling class are in every epoch the ruling ideas: i.e. the class which is the ruling material force of society is at the same time its ruling intellectual force. The class which has the means of material production at its disposal, has control at the same time over the means of mental production.*
> *(The German Ideology, cited in Bottomore and Rubel, 1961:93)*

Marx's phrase 'religion … is the opium of the people' summarises his view that religion has functioned primarily to befuddle dominated or 'exploited' groups and persuade them to believe that they should conform to societies which exploit them. Marx refers to these misguided (in his view) conformist beliefs, as 'false consciousness'. Contemporary Marxists tend to point to education and the media as the main agencies of ideological control. The French Marxist, Althusser, particularly stresses the power of the ruling or dominant class to achieve widespread acceptance of its ideological beliefs among other classes, including the working class. This analysis is referred to as 'the dominant ideology thesis'.

However, other Marxists, including Nicholas Abercrombie, have stressed another aspect of Marx's analysis of ideology. This is that the working class has the basis of an alternative ideology to the dominant capitalist one, in its own experience of work. Marx argued that their shared experience of 'exploitation' at work could promote working class solidarity and collective action. In short, lead them towards socialism. So, Marx indicates both a potential for ideological conformity and for an alternative ideology among the working class.

Contradiction and change

It is important to note, however, that Marx did not consider that ideas alone can fundamentally change a society. He argued that the underlying condition of change in a society exists when a fundamental contradiction or contradictions develop to such a point that the existing social order becomes threatened with break-up. The most basic contradiction a society can develop is when its mode of production and its social relations become antagonistic.

By this he meant that the balance of economic power can pass to a new group even though formally the old social order appears intact. Thus, Marx argued that eventually capitalists would become unable to control the system of capitalist production because they would be unable to maintain their domination of the working class (just as the feudal nobility had lost its capacity to control the emerging bourgeoisie). Marx described a complex network of contradictions underlying the basic contradiction described above: these centred upon the falling rate of profit for capitalists, increased competition between them, and increased exploitation (immiseration) of the working class leading to a revolutionary response. Many contemporary Marxists have attempted to explain why Marx's outline or scenario for revolution has not yet occurred (see below p. 630). Some ex-Marxists have decided that it is unlikely to occur.

Marx's theory that historical change occurs through the synthesis of contradictions within a system is known as dialectical materialism. It is materialistic in that he sees economic forces and development as providing the dynamic that underlies historical change. Contradictions emerge from the antagonistic economic and social relations of classes.

Criticisms of 'crude' Marxism

The Marxist heritage is profoundly ambiguous: Marx has left two legacies, although it is unlikely that he intended to do so. The first is based on the belief that class conflict and socialist revolution are historically inevitable, and the other is based on the view that, to achieve a social revolution, it is necessary to work for a change in the consciousness of the working class (as they come to realise the nature of capitalist exploitation, they will surely organise to end it). It is the first of these two legacies of thought which has been the most severely criticised. We now examine some criticisms of Marxism, particularly 'crude' Marxism.

1 The belief that proletarian revolution is inevitable

The belief that a revolution of the proletariat is inevitable on account of certain economic 'contradictions' in capitalism, has been criticised repeatedly as crudely deterministic. This means that its adherents consider that 'the future is known from the past', and, they state, certain major future events are bound to happen because of 'the laws of history'. We examined Karl Popper's comments on this issue earlier, in Chapter 2. Marx's application of dialectical theory to historical change is sometimes cited as an attempt to uncover such laws. The principle of the dialectic is that opposite elements (thesis and antithesis) combine to produce a synthesis (new phenomenon). The concept comes from natural science, but as applied by Marx to recent history, it means that the clash of the capitalist class with the proletariat will produce a new synthesis: the classless society. It is doubtful whether Marx intended this model to be accepted as rigidly inevitable, but if he did, it is, indeed, an example of crude determinism. Perhaps Marx has suffered as much from the ideas of some of his followers as from his critics. No wonder he once said 'I am not a Marxist'. The major refutation of determinism, which modern Marxists do generally accept, is that, within the structural realities of their time, people make their own history and, for that reason, the future cannot be predicted.

2   The over-stress on conflict

A second criticism of Marxism is the reverse of that made against functionalism, that it over-stresses conflict and under-estimates the extent of consensus in society. This criticism needs to be qualified. Marx's concept of 'false consciousness' fully recognises that what he would see as a 'false consensus' masking the deeper reality of class conflict, can occur. However, the possibility that many people might consciously and intelligently seek consensus and agreement across class-lines runs counter to his theoretical model. Marx's critics on this point argue that many people quite normally and rationally do act in this way. If they are right, then the basis of Marx's model of society and social change are undermined.

3   The gap between ideals and practice

A third criticism of Marxism is that it is idealistic in theory but can frequently be cruel and repressive in practice. When commentators say this they have in mind primarily the example of Soviet totalitarianism and imperialism. They argue that the Soviet record of human rights and foreign policy is not attributable simply to the wickedness of the Soviets, but is a basic feature of Marxist 'dogma' itself. They contend that 'in the real world' it is not possible to combine material equality with a high level of personal freedom and expression. When the state is controlled by an unrepresentative group, it may use its power to repress not only political opposition but also to organise, control or repress a wide range of other activities, not least those of a cultural kind. Many European and American Marxists accept these criticisms, but deny that the former Soviet regime represented a fair picture of Marxism. We now examine some of their ideas on the subject.

Recent trends in Marxist thought

1   Marxist humanism

First is the trend towards Marxist humanism. This aspect of Marxism concentrates on the repression of human potential in capitalist society and the prospect of its release in communist society. The sources of humanism within Marx's own workers are his early writings on human potential and his analysis of alienation, discussed in the last chapter. In Britain, Raymond Williams and E P Thompson are major representatives of Marxist humanism (see pp. 481-4), and in the United States C Wright Mills achieved international influence.

2   The Frankfurt school

Critical theory, as its name suggests, raises the possibility of criticising the way things are from another point of view. Herbert Marcuse was a critical theorist until his death in 1979. He attacked capitalist 'reality', particularly from the point of view that it is culturally repressive – especially, although not exclusively, of the working class (see Chapter 15, p. 458). Before fleeing to America from Nazi Germany, Marcuse worked at Frankfurt University, the 'home' of critical theorists. Like other philosophers and sociologists of the Frankfurt school, Marcuse was greatly influenced by Freud as well as by Marx, and effected a synthesis of the two that captured the imagination of many student radicals of the 1960s. He took Freud's concept of psychological repression and applied it to capitalist society. He argued that capitalism is not interested in full human expression and development, but primarily in exploiting labour. In doing this, it represses human potential and reduces people to the level of a machine. Habermas is now the most influential member of the Frankfurt school. Whereas Marcuse, stressed the emotional, sexual and artistic repression of capitalism, Habermas has argued that capitalism fails to promote truthful and rational dialogue (see p. 317). Like Marcuse, Habermas holds out the possibility of a more liberated and rational society. His work, as well as that of Williams, Thompson and Mills, shows that the interest of Marxists is not narrowly sociological but extends to the whole range of human cultural expression.

3   Marxist structuralism

A third contemporary trend in Marxism is Marxist structuralism, associated particularly with the French Marxists, Althusser and Bourdieu. We discussed their thinking in the context of socialisation, especially education, and referred again to Althusser in Chapters 4 and 16. Structuralists tend to see a rather tight fit between the base and the superstructure. In other words, they see culture less as free expression and more as an area in which ideological conformity to capitalist society is created. In this sense they are rather like structural functionalists, although whereas the latter generally approved of conformity to capitalist society, Marxist structuralists certainly do not.

4   A stress on agency and action

Fourthly, developments in Marxist thought have also been forged in political practice as well as in the studies of academics. Lenin, Mao and the Cuban revolutionary, Che Guevara, were men of action as well as intellectuals. They were all successful revolutionaries and it is not surprising that they emphasise the need for Marxists to organise in order to create the change they wanted rather than to assume that history was inevitably on their side. They stressed the role both of the revolutionary party and of committed leadership in helping to bring about revolution. The danger in this was that the leadership would lose touch with the majority of the people on whose behalf revolution was supposed to take place. Having 'imposed' revolution, post-revolutionary change might also 'have to be' imposed on a population whose 'consciousness' might be far from communist. Marxists differ on whether such imposition is justifiable. The alternative is to seek fundamental change only with mass support, either gradually or through revolution. The difficulty here is that the forces of the system preventing the growth of such support are immense; one way of measuring support is through the ballot box. Zimbabwe has an elected neo-Marxist government, but it remains to be seen whether it has struggled to maintain socialist policies against the opposition of the powerful countries and international business interests. The elected Marxist government of Allende in Chile was prevented from doing this.

It is not easy to classify neatly the theoretical contributions of Marxist activists. The three revolutionaries mentioned above all stressed the need for people to force the historical issue in order to bring about socialist change. To that extent they were humanists. Whether the violence they used in pursuit of change contradicts their humanism is a point that could long be debated. In the 1990s, most Marxist activitsts in the West, tend to be more involved with alternative political and lifestyle movements rather than with the rhetoric of violent revolution. They are more likely to be inspired by Gramsci (see pp. 485-6) than Lenin.

5 Marxism, culture and postmodernism

Much of the treatment of Marxism in the current edition of this book has been about Marxist analysis of culture. In general Marxists have a low opinion of culture in capitalist society – a society that is now global in certain major respects. Marxists such as Jameson argue that the ideology of consumerism had enabled capitalism to reconcile even the poor to the capitalist system. Even those exploited by capitalism are offered the hope of consumer satisfaction via the media. In their often close dialogue with postmodernism, Marxists tend to argue that things *could* and *should* change but are increasingly perplexed as to how this might happen.

Conclusion: a crisis of Marxism

Even before the rise of President Gorbachev and the collapse of Eastern European communism, contemporary Marxism was in a ferment of debate: some issues are becoming clear. Few Marxists now are historical determinists, although a case could be made that the French structuralists have merely substituted cultural mechanics for economic. Few Western European Marxists support the use of violent means to achieve change in Western Europe (although it is seen as a legitimate means to overthrow unrepresentative and exploitative regimes in the Third World). Most Western Marxists are now democratic in the sense that they no longer support one party rule. These observations prompt the questions – 'Are Marxists with such beliefs really Marxists?' and 'Are they essentially any different from democratic socialists?' The

answer to these questions, upon which the future of Marxism depends, is likely to emerge in the next decade or so. The issue both theoretically and practically is whether there is a distinctly Marxist solution to the inequalities and exploitation produced by capitalism which does not diminish personal and civil freedom.

Max Weber: social action theory (conflict theory II)

Max Weber has greatly contributed to both the interpretive and structuralist traditions in sociology. However, according to Weber's own claim, his point of departure and ultimate goal was to analyse the individual person:

> Interpretive sociology considers the individual and his action as the basic unit, as its 'atom' … In this approach, the individual is also the upper limit and sole carrier of meaningful conduct … In general, for sociology such concepts as 'state', 'association', 'feudalism', and the like, designate certain categories of human interaction. Hence it is the task of sociology to reduce these concepts to 'understandable' action, that is, without exception to the actions of participating individual men.
>
> (Quoted in Gerth and Mills eds., 1970:55)

A clearer commitment to interpretive sociology, a sociology of social action, would be difficult to find. Yet, despite this important statement of principle on interpretive sociology, Weber's main theoretical contributions to sociology probably lie in the area of structural analysis.

Four types of social action

Weber divided social action into four types:

- Instrumentally rational action (action geared to 'the attainment of the actors own rationally pursued and calculated ends').
- Value-rational action (action 'determined by a conscious belief in the value for its own sake of some ethical, aesthetic, religious or other form of behaviour, independently of its prospects of success').
- Affectual action ('determined by the actors' specific affects and feeling states').
- Traditional action (determined by ingrained habituation).

In short, he categorised as motivated by reason, values, emotion, or tradition – or by some combination of the four. Weber intended his typology of action to cover the range from the rational to the non-rational.

Weber's typology of social action appears to be the preliminary to developing a sociology that will have the self at the centre of it. However, both Charles Wright Mills and Alan Dawe have commented that he did not achieve this. Dawe argues that this is because Weber uses his action typology to define particular types of social order, e.g. bureaucratic, religious, rather than to analyse the complexity of subjective (individual) motivation and action. Individuals are categorised as members of particular types of society, institutions or movements rather than in terms of their individual complexity. As Mills implies, Weber's turning away from strictly interpretive to more structural sociology is hardly surprising. No sociologist has yet solved the mammoth task of being 'true to' the subjectivity of members of society, except, perhaps, in very small-scale research, let alone effectively linking such analysis to broader influences and issues. Perhaps the problem is simply not solvable.

Rational action, bureaucracy and modernity

Weber considered that the type of action most characteristic of capitalist society is instrumentally rational action, i.e. logically organised action to achieve given goals. He argued that large-scale organisations characterised by a hierarchical and complex division of labour were the main embodiment of rational action in capitalist society. He went further than this, however, and argued that rational action is also the dominant type of action in socialist societies. Indeed, he believed that rational action is characteristic of modern societies themselves. Bureaucracy is the way rational and 'scientific' thinking is expressed in organisational form (see p. 289). Weber considered that religious and traditional thought and action were likely to decline against the relentless march of reason and science. He referred to this process, with a touch of poetic pathos, as disenchantment (see p. 532).

Despite his apparent belief in the triumph of bureaucracy, Weber never lost his concern for the individual – even if he sometimes expressed this in a gloomy and even arrogant manner:

> This passion for bureaucracy is enough to drive one to despair. It is as if we were deliberately to become men who need order and nothing but order, who become nervous and cowardly if for one moment this order wavers, and helpless if they are torn away from their total incorporation in it. That the world should know no men but these; it is in such an evolution that we are already caught up, and the great question is not how we can promote and hasten it, but what we can oppose to this machinery in order to keep a portion of mankind free from this parcelling-out of the soul, from this supreme mastery of the bureaucratic way of life.
>
> (Cited by Dawe in Bottomore and Nisbet, 1979:391)

Structure, pluralism and individuality

Weber's theory of action and, particularly, his analysis of bureaucracy as institutionalised rational action, never became the

rigid dogma that the concept of class has in the hands of crude Marxists. The above quotation shows him typically trying to understand the tension and interplay between individuality and social structure – an attempt he never surrendered for a more simplistic approach.

In general, Weber's structural analysis involves consideration of a variety of factors, the precise relationship of which cannot be predicted. As Mills says, his approach to 'social dynamics' (interaction and change) is 'pluralistic'. He sees many (i.e. a plurality of) groups, rather than merely two main classes, as involved in social interaction. Thus, he examines stratification in capitalist society mainly in terms of the relationship between class, status and political groups which he characterises as one of controlled conflict or competition (for this reason Weber is described as a conflict theorist). The precise relationships between the groups varies between capitalist societies: the only way to understand how they relate in a given society is by close and specific analysis. In order to establish and explain patterns of similarity and difference between societies, Weber advocates use of the comparative method (see p. 25) but he also insists that each society or 'case' is in certain respects, historically unique and must be analysed as such.

For Weber, the uniqueness of societies and the complexity of social processes and structures reflects the uniqueness of individuals and groups of individuals. His use of the concept of 'charisma' illustrates his view that the individual may greatly affect society. Literally, charisma means 'gift of grace' and Weber uses it to refer to self-appointed leaders who are seen as extraordinary (sometimes as 'saviours') by their followers. In the contemporary world such leaders as Nelson Mandela and Saddam Hussein appear charismatic. But Weber also considered that more ordinary people could make meaningful choices. Again, his view of society is pluralistic, it reflects the unpredictable conflict of ideas and values. Nor are these merely the reflection of self or class interest as he believed Marx tended to see them but they are partly the product of people's personal ideas, values and beliefs.

Comment on Weber

Whereas other sociological perspectives can be criticised for over-emphasising one or other side of the self/structure relationship, perhaps the more precise criticism of Weber is that he did not achieve the immense task of 'blending' the two aspects together but rather oscillated between them. If anything, as both Mills and Dawe suggest, his practical work tended more towards structural sociology, whereas his statements of intent implied he would attempt to develop a sociology of individual or subjective meaning. A second criticism of Weber is that his perception of the dominance of bureaucracy in modern society under-estimated both the relevance and frequency of other organisational forms and the ability of people within bureaucracies to find less formal and often more satisfying and effective ways of working. This is ironic, given his own commitment to understanding individuality.

However, paradox is at the heart of Weber's imagination and of his sociology. Shortly, we will consider some more contemporary attempts to engage with the problematic relationship between agency and structure – a relationship which remains central to sociological theory.

Interactionism (and structural perspective): towards a synthesis?

There is no need to outline again the basics of the interactionist perspective. Instead a more specific matter is considered below. However, one way of over-viewing the interactionist perspective is to *consider its core* concepts.

The list of interactionist concepts given below could almost be used as a basis of describing the interactionist perspective. While most of these concepts occur within other perspectives, their total usage within the interactionist perspective is distinctive and largely defines interactionist theory.

Some key concepts within the interactionist paradigm

- Self: significant other: generalised other
- Meaning: interaction: negotiation
- Labelling: stereotyping: self-fulfilling prophecy
- Career: signification: amplification

Figure 21.2 Key interactionist concepts

Since Mead, symbolic interactionism has progressed theoretically as much through practical application as through abstract theorising. Accordingly, we have been able to examine in some detail recent interactionist analyses of work, deviance and organisation. There is no need to review this research now. Instead, we will discuss the criticism frequently made of interactionism – that it lacks a structural dimension. In particular, we will assess Tom Goff's comparison of Mead's sociology to that of Marx. In his book, *Marx and Mead* (1980), Goff attempts to show that the work of Marx and Mead is, essentially, complementary rather than contradictory. To the extent that he is successful, his analysis has implications for the theoretical reconstruction of sociology. In particular it can be considered as one of several examples of attempts to link structural and interpretist theory reviewed in this chapter.

Firstly, both Marx and Mead emphasised that the individual is formed in society, and give comparable emphasis to the influence of social structure on people. Mead went into far greater detail about how this takes place and his social psychology has been very useful in much practical interpretist research. Marxists such as Paul Willis appear to have been influenced by it or, at least, by other compatible currents within phenomenology. Secondly, both Marx

and Mead describe people as conscious beings with the potential to change and recreate their own social environment. Neither the individual human being nor the group is ever 'reduced' to society. If Mead conveyed much more of the psychology of individual choice and understanding than did Marx, Marx presented a much more urgent message of emancipation from social repression and an alternative and freer way of life. A third point of convergence can be derived from the other two. For both of them, social structure and human creativity are not separate, but dialectically related – that is, people and social environment interact and can change each other. This leads to the fourth agreed point – that human thought is located in a social context, and informed by experience. In that sense, it is practical in nature and, for Marx at least, can be directed most rationally towards radically improving the quality of human life.

Goff has indicated Marx's concept of alienation as a major possible area of difference between him and Mead. Certainly, Mead had no particular sense that the division of labour in capitalist society was especially alienating: in fact, he was inclined to argue that the process of productive fragmentation was likely to continue and seemed none too distressed by it. He did, however, have a vivid appreciation of the way social institutions can smother individuality – a sentiment which accords with a Marxist-Weberian notion of alienation (see Chapter 9, pp. 262-3). The following quotation shows this:

> *Oppressive, stereotyped and ultra-conservative social institutions – like the church – ... by their more or less rigid and inflexible unprogressiveness crush or blot out individuality or discourage any distinctive or original expressions of thought and behaviour in the individual selves or personalities implicated in and subjected to them ...*
>
> *(Mead, first published 1934, 1962)*

It is not too much to conclude, therefore, that Mead's framework of social analysis can be adapted to accommodate the concept of alienation.

Although the above considerations indicate that Mead's social thought is compatible with, and even complementary to, the structural aspects of Marxist theory, it remains true that the former is more suited to the micro-level of analysis and the latter to the macro-level. Mead developed the more detailed conceptual tool-kit for small-scale interaction and Marx the more detailed one for institutional analysis and class conflict, although in so far as these two levels overlap there is room for synthesis. Even accepting that the two perspectives are most effective at different levels of social analysis, and that theory and research will reflect this, it is inaccurate to present them as radically opposed: the above discussion shows that they need not be.

Phenomenology and ethnomethodology

Phenomenology

Phenomenology was originally a philosophical perspective but it has 'fed into' sociology through ethnomethodology. Edmund Husserl, the most influential philosopher of phenomenology, wanted to develop a philosophy which presented human action in terms of the meanings of actors rather than as the product of 'external' influences. Husserl argued that there is no knowable objective reality 'out there' but that each individual makes her or his own reality by categorising or 'sorting out' their own experience. Thus, what one individual may explain as illness, another may explain as punishment 'by the spirits' and another, still, as just bad luck (see pp. 416-7). It is only when individual or subjective definitions 'agree' that shared meanings or a shared definitions of reality occur.

Husserl considered that it is one of the main purposes of philosophy to establish what meanings a given group might have in common and how these relate to its wider culture. Thus, to refer again to the example given above, an explanation of a particular experience as 'illness' or 'disease' characterises Western, scientific culture whereas an explanation in terms of punishment 'by the spirits' better fits a magical frame of reference (for a fuller analysis of differing perspectives on health, see Chapter 14).

Alfred Schütz (1899-1959) applied and developed Husserl's approach in relation to sociology. Like Husserl, Schütz 'bracketed' (set aside) the issue of the nature of objective reality and concentrated on how social actors make sense of and categorise their own experience, including interpreting the actions of others. That for him is the purpose of sociology – not to explain human behaviour as the effect of certain external causes.

Schütz did not consider that actors create and interpret meaning without reference to others. On the contrary, he argued that over time, given groups produce a shared stock of meanings which enable members more or less to understand each other and to anticipate each others' actions. A key concept in understanding the notion of a shared stock of meanings, is typification. A typification is a conceptual category used by a given group to describe phenomena (things) which are perceived as similar enough to be put in the same descriptive grouping. Thus, in British culture most would know who to categorise as a goalkeeper as opposed to a scrum-half or what to typify as a sausage as opposed to a plum-pudding. Different typifications develop in different cultures. Thus, whereas white Americans typify annual seasonal changes into four groupings (typifications), several American Indian tribes describe as many as eighteen changes (one such example is the Abernake Indians of the North Eastern states). Such different typifications reflect a different way of perceiving or constructing given phenomena. Typifications shared within a given group enable its members to make sense to each other and

create a reasonably orderly social life.

Schütz distinguishes between the naturalistic perspective of the member of a social group and the phenomenological perspective of the outside observer (adopting the phenomenological perspective). The term naturalistic describes the taken-for-granted, 'commonsensical' approach taken by members of a given social group. They regard their way of life as 'normal' and are generally not aware of the extent to which it reflects only their own subjective experience. By contrast, the phenomenologist seeks to describe the way of life of a given group. However, s/he does so from the point of view of the actors involved and not from an external explanatory perspective. This leads to a different choice of methodology from structural sociology. In order 'to get close to' social actors, phenomenologists adopt qualitative methods such as observation, rather than more quantitative methods.

Schütz requires comparison with both Weber and the interactionists. He argued that Weber failed to produce a sociological approach fully based on the meanings of social actors. He regarded Weber's types of social action (see pp. 631-2) as too remote from what actors actually think and do to provide the basis of a genuinely interpretive sociology. Similarly, a more recent group of sociologists – mainly influenced by Schütz – the ethnomethodologists also consider that interactionism does not deliver a genuinely inter-subjective sociology i.e. a sociological perspective based exclusively on how actors create, interpret and share meanings. Schütz himself was a theorist rather than an applied researcher. Whether his own approach successfully provided the basis for an effective interpretative and inter-subjective sociology must be assessed through the contribution of the group of sociologists he influenced most, the ethnomethodologists.

Ethnomethodology

The Californian sociologist, Harold Garfinkel founded ethnomethodology in the late1950s and early 1960s. It is convenient to think of him as practically applying and developing Schütz's phenomenological approach. Crudely, ethnomethodology is phenomenological sociology.

In Chapter 1, ethnomethodology was referred to as an attempt to describe how individuals make sense of, or give explanatory accounts of, their experience. We need to extend this point here before returning to the broader issue of the relationship between ethnomethodology and structural perspective. Two concepts used by ethnomethodologists need to be introduced. Unfortunately, both reflect the extreme verbosity with which ethnomethodology is commonly associated, but they are capable of simple definition and illustration. The terms are the *documentary method* and *indexicality*. The documentary method is employed by all of us and involves the assumption that a given event or occasion can be made sense of by seeing it as just one example, or document, of a general type. Thus, to take Cicourel's previously cited study of delinquency, a police officer may see a particular youth with what s/he regards as delinquent characteristics and accordingly place him within the general category of delinquent, that is, s/he reacts to the 'documentary' evidence, perhaps a skinhead haircut and tattooed arms. S/he could, of course, be mistaken. The concept of indexicality means that sense can only be made of any object or event by relating it back to its context, or the circumstances of its occurrence. Thus, the word 'five' makes sense as an answer to the question, 'What time is it?' but not as an answer to 'How many players are there in a cricket team?' Similarly, to continue with the kind of example that appeals to Harold Garfinkel, the founder of ethnomethodology, a police officer in the outfit of a clown would make sense in the context of a fancy dress ball but not in the context of a drugs raid. We can agree, then, that meaning depends on context. The inter-relatedness of meaning and event – almost to the point of equation – is referred to as *reflexivity* by the ethnomethodologists, and is a third key concept of the perspective. Because of their respect of the uniqueness and unpredictability of personal meaning, ethnomethodologists examine social activity with careful reference back to context and the various verbal descriptions (conveyors of meaning) given of it by social actors. Study in this depth of detail has, necessarily, to be on a small scale, as was Cicourel's study of the social organisation of juvenile delinquency, and Atkinson's research into coroners' definitions of suicide.

Comment on ethnomethodology

Three critical comments can be made about ethnomethodology. First, in confining themselves to describing rather than explaining the meanings of social actors, ethnomethodologists are begging an important question i.e. why do members of a particular cultural group reason in the way they do. As the next point illustrates, this question becomes even more urgent when put in a comparative context. Second, it is doubtful whether ethnomethodology is quite as original as some of its adherents appear to think. Arguably it is very little different to descriptive cultural anthropology – the careful observation and accounts of the social life of a particular cultural group.

Comparative cultural anthropology inevitably forces the question – a classic sociological one – 'why do cultural groups behave differently?' Ethnomethodologists do not attempt to answer this question because it may involve explanations not shared by members of the cultural groups under examination. Third, despite the commitment of ethnomethodologists to describing social life only in terms of members' subjective and inter-subjective meanings, the concepts of typification and shared meaning bear comparison with the structural ones of norms, values and beliefs. Presumably, the 'external' influence of socialisation is part of the process by which individuals come commonsensibly to accept typifications and shared meanings. Yet, this is another issue which they fail to address.

Both structural perspectives and symbolic interactionism offer theories of social order and structure. For the former, order and structure lie in the institutional framework which constrains

members of society, and for the latter order exists through the creation of shared meanings. Ethnomethodologists go a stage further back, as it were, by examining how individuals cope with, and make sense of, existing situations (whether 'orderly' or not). This interest need not, in my view, be incompatible with structural perspective. Presumably, it is not unlikely that the underlying patterns and taken-for-granted assumptions which individuals seek and find reinforced in experience (reflexivity) can be widely shared. If so, this fact structures interaction. Otherwise, there would be chaos.

The New Right: Peter Saunders

Taken as a whole, the recent work of Peter Saunders outlines a fairly comprehensive New Right theory of sociology. Saunders argues that the most efficient (and fairest) type of society is based on the free market and *equality of opportunity*. In these respects, Saunders is not original but reflects the thinking of the Austrian economist, Frederick von Hayek, and the American economist, Milton Friedman. They, and Saunders, argue that equal access to the free market enables individuals to compete on the basis of ability and character. The rewards of successful competition act both as an incentive to effort and productivity, and recognise hard work and merit. The free market or capitalist system is so economically efficient that the general standard of living is steadily raised, not just that of the successful.

While Saunders is committed to equality of opportunity, he also firmly believes in natural or *biological inequality* i.e. individuals are endowed with different and unequal intellectual and other capacities. Controversially and contrary to what has been the consensus among most social scientists, Saunders considers that the system of unequal class stratification in Britain is a fair reflection of people's natural inequality. He argues that British society is sufficiently open for the able of lower class origins to move upwards and that relatively low downward mobility among the higher classes can be explained by their generally greater intelligence. He contends, then, that Britain is already a *meritocracy*. This brings him into sharp disagreement with Marxist and Weberian sociologists who argue that this is far from the case (see pp. 175-81).

Like other New Right thinkers, Saunders does not believe in *equality of outcome* – a situation in which everybody has equal access to the same material and cultural resources. However, there are very few theorists who *are* committed to complete equality in this sense. Even Marx argued 'only' for the principle of – from each according to their means, to each according to their needs. In practice the real argument about material and cultural 'equality' is one of extent – how much or how little is it acceptable for individuals to have in relation to others. Saunders and the New Right in general consider that substantial inequality is socially desirable and functional. This analysis is reinforced by their argument that state interference to achieve much greater material and/or cultural equality invariably has negative consequences. However, the New Right is not opposed to policies to deal with 'real' poverty although its critics argue that it is inadequate in this respect.

In his *Capitalism: A Social Audit* (1995), Saunders reviews the current state of the capitalist system and, predictably, gives it a ringing endorsement. He tests the capitalist system in relation to three demanding issues:

Does it have the ability to bring prosperity to poor countries?

Can capitalist growth continue without further serious environmental destruction?

Does capitalism provide a better framework than other social systems for the pursuit of human happiness?

Briefly, his answers are 'Yes, yes and yes'. However, a fundamental basis of his arguments is that capitalism has defeated socialism. Capitalism is now the 'only game in town' and so it is even more important that the capitalist system achieves its positive potential in these three areas. However, Saunders does not consider that capitalism will inevitably achieve these three outcomes in the absence of individual effort and moral choice. For him, the free market is one side of the New Right philosophy but the other is a complementary but restraining wider 'framework':

> *No less than any other socio-economic system, capitalism needs a shared framework within which to operate. It needs individuals to be motivated to act in certain ways: it needs symbols to legitimate the inequalities of condition which arise from market transactions, and it needs a core set of values which can bind people together through ties of mutual obligation and social responsibility. Nineteenth century liberals such as John Stuart Mill believed that such a morality would be secure in a society of strong and free individuals, for he could not believe that educated and rational human beings would fail to understand how individual freedom depends upon respect for others and how the self-interest of each demands a recognition of social duty and obligation by all.*
>
> *(119)*

Roughly précised, Saunders is saying that for capitalist individualism and self-interest to work, it is necessary for people to believe that they should act in conformity to the system (motivation); for them to be exposed to cultural signs (symbols) that inequality is socially rightful (legitimate) e.g. some would 'legitimately' possess certain consumer possessions, others not; and to share a common system of values (notably active mutual respect to balance self-interest). Saunders considers that John Stuart Mill also took this point of view.

A key point to note about Saunder's perspective is that it is genuinely sociological. The 'framework' which he considers capitalism 'needs' is clearly a *societal* (or social) one. He is saying, what virtually all sociologists would agree with, that unless people

are socialised into and to some extent practise shared values and behaviour, there will be social chaos – virtually, no society. This distinguishes Saunders from extreme New Rightists who argue that there is individual action but 'no such thing as society'.

The main criticism of Saunders is that he shows little appreciation of the necessity for the planned, rule-bound and institutionalised nature of much of modern capitalist society but continues to argue – in classic nineteenth century liberal style – that individuals should be mutually respectful and dutiful because it is the right thing to do. In fact, Saunders is very pessimistic that in contemporary society many people are not doing the right thing and that society is in decline. Yet, he can offer no more than, in effect, to say that people should do better. However, in all modern societies (so far!), both human relationships (e.g. marriage/divorce) and human needs (e.g. of those in poverty) are highly regulated and institutionalised. It is difficult to see how this could be otherwise in a world in which people, left to themselves, might be unable to agree (e.g. in divorce) or might perhaps not sufficiently help each other (e.g. in poverty). Again, it could be argued that the real issue in relation to state legislation and planning in modern societies is one of degree – what is the best balance at any given time between external social constraints (planning, rules, institutions) and individual freedom. It is arguable that the framework of the state as it has evolved throughout the twentieth century is now part of that very societal framework that Saunders acknowledges as necessary. Certainly, seventeen years of New Right ideology and Conservative rule failed to roll back the state (although it did rearrange it).

Questions

1 Describe and explain what you consider to be the most important developments in Marx's thought since Marx's time.
2 To what extent do you consider Max Weber successfully combined the concepts of structure , action and meaning?

The battle of the perspectives: 1970s to 1980s

As we saw earlier, in a book published in 1960 Charles Wright Mills attempted to outline what he saw as 'the classic tradition' in sociology. In doing so, he was in no way seeking to impose a detailed model of society on his colleagues. He knew that models of society had differed and would continue to do so. However, as described above, he also considered that the classic theorists had addressed a common core of concerns.

For about a quarter of a century after Mills' death in 1962, sociology became notorious for its internal theoretical squabbling. Although some real theoretical progress was made during this period, much of the debate involved a seemingly endless rehearsal of the flaws and merits of Marxism, functionalism and symbolic interactionism. Arguably, Mills himself fired some of the first shots in this debate in his famous attack on what he saw as the inflated theoretical prose of Talcott Parsons (Mills helpfully 'translated' Parsons's *The Social System* into a few lucid sentences). However, it is doubtful whether, had Mills lived, he would have got much involved in the rather circular perspectives debate.

As it happens, the debate between the three major perspectives, proved to be quite an effective way of teaching introductory sociology at various levels. The first edition of this book and other textbooks published in the early 1980s adopted the perspectives approach as a way of presenting sociology to students.

Arguably, one effect of the perspectives debate was to slow down theoretical advance in sociology. Practitioners and teachers of sociology did justice to Marx, Weber and Durkheim and the generation following them but perhaps paid them too much respect. It is true that the revival of Marxist sociology in the 1960s and 1970s and a body of empirical work inspired by symbolic interactionism represented significant achievement but by working within given paradigms, sociologists perhaps missed some of the new 'big' questions.

Late modernity and new questions for sociology: 1990s

Although sociology has, in part, become a vehicle for all kinds of postmodernist thinking, initially postmodernism crept up on sociology somewhat unawares. The founders of poststructuralism and postmodernism – Foucault, Baudrillard, Lyotard – thought across the disciplines but were more philosophers than sociologists. It is true that Bell's theory of postindustrial society did occur within social science. However, influential as this concept has been, it perhaps took some time for the full significance of what Bell was saying to sink in. His was an early emphatic statement that information culture was to become the dynamic sector of society, driving even the economic.

Since then, postmodernism has seeped into much sociological thinking. It is worth repeating the new – or newish – questions it has brought to the fore:

Key questions of late modernity (or postmodernity)

1 Is postmodernity a period when the 'price of progress' e.g. environmental damage, is more important than further material progress itself?

2 Have culture/knowledge issues replaced economic and material ones as definitive of (postmodern society)?
3 Has globalisation occurred i.e. is there a crucial sense in which forces of communication have produced a global society?
4 Have class questions declined in importance compared to those of gender, 'race'/ethnicity, nationality and other bases of identity?
5 Have leisure/consumption become more significant than work/*production*?

All these questions have been explored recurrently throughout this book. It is not the place of a textbook to give single, dogmatic answers – the more so since these questions are relatively new and controversial. But do they represent a radical change in the focus of sociology?

I would argue that the fundamental sociological perspective remains intact. That is, to summarise Mills, an exploration of the relationship of the individual to the social in a comparative context. The one fundamental thing that Mills' definition does not encompass and which he could not really have anticipated is the extent to which many sociologists now regard global society rather than national society as their widest routine frame of reference. The elision of nation-state and society is less and less made. 'Society' now means the interplay of various 'levels' of social, economic, political and cultural forces (in no necessary order of priority) each and all of which the individual is likely to interact with (see p. 595).

The importance of the global frame of reference indicates the direction of the paradigm shift that, in effect, postmodernists imply has occurred with the decline of the Marxist and liberal 'meta-narratives' and the emergence of a new cluster of interests – roughly indicated by the above five questions. This level of concern is more specific than that indicated by Mills. Whereas he was describing the basic outline of the discipline, postmodernists are asking different questions in relation to a world they see as greatly changed from that confronted by Marx, Weber and Durkheim.

'The new sociology'

Michelle Barrett

Michelle Barrett has been prominent among those who have been trying to integrate the insights of postmodernism into sociology (ATSS Annual Conference, 1995). While I would reject any implication that the 'new' sociology should replace established sociology lock, stock and barrel (or Weber, Marx and Durkheim!), there is no doubt that Barrett intends to be radical and challenging. She puts forward five propositions of the 'new sociology':

• Social activity takes place in a global context.
• Identity and the self are central to sociology.
• Social meaning is culturally produced.

• Power and advantage have several sources.
• Ethics determine political choices.

The first four of these propositions have been extensively explored in this book. Barrett would not claim that they are original to her but what is relevant here is that she is piecing them together as a provisional framework for a new sociology. The fifth proposition reflects Barrett's concern that too often sociologists have deduced political 'truths' from their sociological perspectives. What she is reasserting is that a person's values or ethics are what should be the basis of political choices. What she is warning against is using sociology for political, biased purposes.

Barrett goes on to present three key postmodernist (or poststructuralist as she prefers to call them) ideas or critiques which she considers can usefully be applied to established sociology. Postmodernism criticises the following common sociological assumptions:

• Universalism.
• Materialism.
• Rationalism.

Again, these points of concern will not strike readers of his book as new – Foucault and Lyotard have made them the common currency of sociological discussion. However, they clearly need to be addressed in the context of an overall review of sociology such as Barrett's. Many would now agree that the goals of a single universal sociological theory – the unified paradigm discussed in previous editions of this book – is neither desirable nor likely. The overarching metanarratives, the 'big stories' or perspectives, are simply too big – they fail to encompass diversity, unpredictability and the complexities of change. Barrett's own example of this point is that feminism cannot expect to produce 'one voice' for all women. For instance, black women have and will sometimes speak differently than white women. Related to her rejection of universalism, is Barrett's opposition to 'essentialism'. There are no essential or static and unchanging gender, ethnic or class identities that can be set up and defended or promoted. These broad identities will doubtless continue as vital reference points for individuals and groups but it is they, not sociologists, who will make their own meanings and alliances.

Barrett's objection to the dominance of a materialist perspective in sociology is also widely shared. She associates this perspective with crude Marxist economism which asserts that the most influential (determining?) part of society is the economy. She contends that Foucault has reversed Marx's hierarchy, placing culture at the centre of social processes – 'objects emerge in discourse'. Stuart Hall takes a less polarised 'either/or' approach, suggesting that currently within sociology, culture is more to the fore than structure – a situation he appears to agree with. However, if his implication is that the relationship could change, I would agree with him.

In her critique of rationalism, Barrett again cites Foucault. As much as anybody, the latter has explored the dark side of modern rationality, including the coercion intrinsic to the liberal project of reform, discipline and improvement. Barrett cites Bauman's study of the holocaust as an example of rationality severed from moral moorings – the bureaucratic production of genocide.

Comment on Barrett

Barrett's reframing of sociological theory comes down heavily on the side of culture rather than structure. For her identity, self and meaning are at the centre of sociology and these are studied primarily within the context of culture and agency rather than socio-economic 'determinants'.

Arguably, Barrett's cultural voluntarism understates the capacity of 'power structures' to define, constrain and limit' personal and group opportunity and development (intellectual and imaginative as well as practical). This point of criticism will perhaps be clearer when a recent theoretical work by Derek Layder has been considered.

Derek Layder and sociological dualisms: moving the debate forward

Much sociological debate has tended to emphasise one or other side of either *individual* 'freedom' or *social* determination. In so far as positions have tended to harden and camps form on one or other side of this dualism, sociological debate has sometimes tended to be repetitive. Further, the reiteration of two views – often presented fractiously and as mutually contradictory – has inhibited the cumulative development of sociological theory and research.

In the above debate, functionalism and Marxism have often been seen as 'taking the side' of social or structural determinism and symbolic interactionism as 'taking the side' of individual 'freedom' and meaning. Weber tried to integrate both perspectives in his social action theory. Weber, of course, was only the most explicit in his attempt to reconcile individuality and social structure. Other sociologists have to various degrees attempted to come to terms with 'the other point of view'. Although the 'perspectives battle' of the 1960s and 1970s rather caricatured the above division, the differences were genuine enough. Since the 1970s, there have been a number of attempts to move beyond the rather circular nature of the above debate. One of the best general summaries of these efforts is Derek Layder's 'Understanding Social Theory' (1994).

Before looking at Layder's contribution in more detail, it is worth briefly discussing the implication of the phrase 'social theory' in the title of his book: *Understanding Social Theory*. The choice of the term 'social theory' can be taken to indicate two things: first, in the past quarter of a century, many worthwhile contributions to understanding society have come from outside sociology; second, and relatedly, the boundaries between sociology and certain other disciplines have tended to blur. To an extent, this marks a return to earlier practice when Marx and Weber utilised a range of social sciences in their work.

Three core dualisms of social theory

Layder suggests that social theory has tended to be organised around three core and related dualisms (see Figure 21.3). Each of the two columns can be thought of as clusters of related concepts.

Micro	Macro
Agency (Action)	Structure
Individual	Society

(Source: Layder: 3)

Figure 21.3 Core conceptual dualisms in sociology

Layder observes that the individual/society dualism 'is perhaps the oldest and represents a persistent dilemma about the fitting together of individual and collective needs' (3). At root, what is at issue is the freedom/determinism debate referred to above although there are other proposed attributes of individuality (such as the capacity to create meaning) and of society (such as the provision of opportunity) which enter debates about this dualism.

Layder regards agency (action)/structure and individual/society as closely related dualism. An advantage in using the former rather than the latter is that agency (action) and structure 'focuses on the *mutual* influence of social activity and the social context in which it takes place' (4) (author's stress on 'mutual'). In other words, agency is part of the weave of social structure. Layder's use of the two terms in this dualism is, then, as follows:

> ... *agency will refer to the ability of human beings to make a difference in the world ... structure ... (to) social relationships ... (which) provide the social context or conditions under which people act.*
>
> *(5)*

Distinguishing between agency-structure and micro-macro, Layder points out:

> *whereas agency-structure can in principle refer to both large-scale and small-scale features of social life, the macro/micro distinction deals primarily with a difference in level and scale of analysis ... for example, micro phenomena deal with more intimate and detailed aspects of face-to-face conduct (e.g. labelling in a classroom), while macro phenomena deal with more impersonal and large-scale phenomena (e.g. the relationship of the education system to the economy).*
>
> *(5-6) (author's brackets)*

Layder's summary of these three core dualisms is well worth consideration in its own right but a further purpose in referring to them here is to introduce the growing body of theory that has addressed the 'divide' or 'divides' between these often polarised dualisms (although, as Layder comments, the dualism of agency (action)/structure rather invites bridge-building).

Theoretical approaches to the dualisms

Layder's categorisation of how major social theorists and theories relate to these dualisms is partly summarised below. However, I have selected only authors referred to previously in this book – so that what follows can serve a genuine summary function as well as, in some cases, limited further exploration of theory. Their approaches to the dualism of agency/structure will be used as a general indicator of where they stand in relation *to the dualisms* in general.

Emphases on agency or structure of established sociological perspectives

	Agency	Emphases	Structure
Marxism			✓
Functionalism			✓
Symbolic Interactionism	✓		

Figure 21.4 Sociological perspectives: their emphases within the agency/structure dualism

More recent theorists are categorised by Layder into those who attempt to go 'beyond the dualisms' by welding them together in an integrated whole and those who accept that they are separate but attempt to link them. Only Elias and Habermas are discussed in any detail below but there follows a brief list of where some other major figures fit.

Beyond the dualisms

Foucault (poststructuralism) Attempts to 'transcend' the dualisms 'by analysing the 'middle ground' of social practices and how they express relations of power' (9) (see pp. 98-100 and pp. 366-7).

Elias (figuration sociology) sees society in terms of figurations or chains of relationships thus dualisms are rendered irrelevant.

Giddens (structuration theory) replaces the concept of dualism with duality (which sees agency/structure in complementary rather than oppositional terms) (see pp. 592-3 and p. 601).

Linking the dualisms

Bourdieu (theory of social practice) attempts to link objective and subjective aspects of social life.

Habermas (critical theory) The everyday or *lifeworld* is crossed (organised, manipulated) by the public world of systems (*produced and operated by* experts e.g. the media).

Elias and Habermas contrasted

Something more can be said here about Norbert Elias's attempt to go 'beyond the dualisms' and Habermas's attempt to link what he, unlike Elias, sees as *distinct* if overlapping levels of social activity. The other sociologists in the above two categories have been sufficiently referred to elsewhere in this book. Elias and Habermas can stand as examples of the above two approaches to a less polarised sociology.

Elias: figurational theory

Elias (1897-1990) was fiercely critical of functionalism and structuralism because he considered that they reified individuals and treated social processes as mechanistic. Instead, he attempted to develop a figurational or processual sociology which would adequately embody individuality. Thus, he studied social *processes* rather than a supposed social system which he did not consider existed externally to people. Elias argued that a widespread perception of the individual/society split occurred as part of the civilising process – Elias's central research concern (see pp. 493-4). The *process* of civilisation *developed* as external, public restraints on behaviour were gradually replaced by internal, individual moral regulation. However, Elias contends that sociology should regard and research individual behaviour as part of chains of social interdependencies. As the chains or networks become more remote from the individual, they become more impersonal. However, the chain or networks are interlinkings of action, not systems separate from people.

Layder acknowledges that Elias has lent insight to our understanding of individuality in *developmental* historical context. However, he suggests that Elias's figuration sociology is not substantially adequate at either the micro or macro level. He argues that Elias misses both the intricacies of *subjective* meaning and the power of *institutions*.

Habermas

In a period when the enlightenment project has come in for severe criticism, Jurgen Habermas remains a champion of reason and a believer in the potential for individual and human progress. Indeed, he works to complete the project of modernity. His central concept is that of 'communicative rationality', which is concerned with the way in which people in interaction are preoccupied with reaching an understanding' (189). Habermas argues that the main intention of 'people in interaction' is to communicate effectively with each other. On that basis, co-operative action can take place. The disposition to achieve 'communicative rationality' permeates the whole of society which itself is divided into distinct but overlapping 'worlds'.

Habermas refers to the life-world ('world one') and to the technical world of science including social science ('world' two)

each of which exercise different criteria for *validity* in relation to communicative rationality. The *Penguin Dictionary of Sociology* gives as clear a distinction as any between these two 'worlds':

> *(The life-world) refers to the everyday world as it is experienced by ordinary men and women. For phenomenological sociology … the life-world is the 'paramount reality' and the main object of sociological inquiry. Its chief characteristic is that it is unproblematic and taken for granted, and is therefore to be contrasted with the world of scientists and sociologists in which natural objects and social interactions are not taken for granted.*
>
> (238)

Habermas has attempted to link the life-world with society as a social system ('world' three). Like Giddens, who in this respect has drawn from Habermas, the latter argues that more and more functions have been 'uncoupled' from the life-world and taken over by the social system. Thus, many economic and political functions that occurred within kinship have been taken over by public systems. Further, Habermas considers that not only has the life-world lost functions, it is increasingly 'colonised' by the social system – largely through the media and consumerism. He sees the new social movements as an attempt to regain lost quality of life, including rights and personal and political freedoms (see p. 317).

While sympathetic both to Habermas's distinction between the micro (life-world) and macro (social system) levels and to his attempts to link them, Layder feels that Habermas tends to 'compact the world of everyday interaction into the wider social context' (205). Layder suggests that Goffman's work on 'interaction order' might provide the necessary linking level of analysis (see p. 478).

Conclusion

Layder's own preference in solving the agency/structure and related polarities is to accept that the distinctions exist and to forge links between them. In other words he is broadly sympathetic to Habermas's approach. However, it is the postmodern solution of transcending or conflating the previously polarised concepts that has made the greatest impact in recent years. We shortly consider postmodernism in detail.

Social constructionism: Vivien Burr

The above theoretical approaches could all be referred to as broadly social constructionists. Throughout this book frequent reference to what is increasingly referred to a social constructionist perspective has been made. Arguably, the widespread acceptance of this approach in sociology (and other social sciences, especially psychology) has been the major theoretical development in recent years. I will first present a notably clear outline of social constructionism and then add comments.

Without suggesting that all social constructionists necessarily adopt all or even most of them, Vivien Burr cites the following four points as characteristic of the social constructionist approach (see Reading):

1 A critical stance towards taken-for-granted knowledge.
2 Historical and cultural specificity.
3 Knowledge is sustained by social processes.
4 Knowledge and social action go together.

All these points are developed in the reading extract from Burr but they can be briefly put in the context of this book here. On the first point, it will be obvious enough by now that sociologists do not accept as 'truth' everyday stereotypes and knowledge. A large part of the discipline is in exploring the less obvious reasons for why people think and behave as they do. The second point about historical and cultural specificity is increasingly accepted in all the social sciences. It is part of sociological method to look at institutions – such as families (see pp. 57-60) – and social practices – such as diet and hygiene (see pp. 435-7) – in specific, often comparative cultural context.

The third point – knowledge is sustained by social processes – has become central to much sociological and historical work. The extract from Burr explains this concept very well but the basic idea is that cultural life is created by people – it has to be lived before it can be 'discovered' by experts.

The notion that 'knowledge and social action go together' is not an invitation to equate sociology with politics but simply restates the truism that 'knowledge is power' – in the sense that it can inform action. Thus, in part, knowledge about particular social institutions and the way they work has inspired some of the great social movements of our time. It *is* possible to study gender inequality and racism without seeking to take action against them but it is hardly surprising that many women and black people have chosen to link the two. Again, it needs to be said, that there is a frontier between academic knowledge and social action but it is a frontier that can legitimately be crossed.

Social constructionism has its roots in symbolic interactionism and in poststructuralism, particularly the work of Foucault. It has become widely accepted as an approach that combines both analysis of social/culture context and human agency. At the broadest level, the term could be used to describe the work of the sociologists presented in the previous section.

Postmodernism and sociology

Given the huge impact of postmodernism on sociology and its frequent appearance throughout this book, it is appropriate to make a critical assessment of this influential theory and to try to gauge its relationship to sociology.

Postmodernism: summary

Critique of modernity (negative)

1 Totalistic theories ('metanarratives') are rejected.
2 Postmodernism is not a totalistic theory.

Propositions/characteristics of postmodernism (positive)

1 Culture has become the dominant aspect of social life.
2 Globalisation, especially of the media, shapes the 'explosion' of culture.
3 Postmodernism can be characterised as a romantic theory/movement.
4 Postmodernism emphasises identity, difference and pluralism.

The postmodernist critique of totalistic theory ('metanarratives')

However superficial aspects of postmodernism may seem, there is no doubt about the substantial nature of its targets of criticism. Lyotard's famous declaration that great metanarratives, including Marxism and the liberal project of the enlightenment, are exhausted was not likely to pass without extensive refutation (1984). Yet, now that the dust begins to settle on the ensuing debates, it is clear that in their more grandiose and totalising formulations, both Marxism and liberalism have lost credibility. Surely few now believe in the inevitable march of progress in either its crude Marxist or crude liberal variations. Neither revolution nor evolution will produce utopia. So much, I take as common ground. Unfortunately, as far as Marxism is concerned many postmodernists tend to leave the matter there and fail to re-evaluate what may be of continuing relevance in that perspective. Liberalism gets fairer treatment – partly because the liberal theory of pluralism closely coincides with postmodern pluralistic analysis. I will return to these matters after considering some of the main tenets of postmodernism itself and, in particular, the extent to which these are new and original.

Postmodernism is not a totalistic theory

Postmodernism is not a totalistic (or universalistic) theory i.e. it does not attempt to explain everything about social life. In this respect it is unlike the 'grand theories' of Marxism and functionalism which do set up models of the social world as a total and self-regenerating system. Postmodernists consider that the social world is made up of many and different individuals, groups and cultures whose behaviour and identities are changeable and not precisely predictable. There is, therefore, no point in attempting to create a theory that seeks to explain what all of the people do all of the time – it cannot be achieved. Postmodernists cite a further reason for avoiding 'total theory'. They consider that any sociological theory will reflect the priorities and concerns of the sociologist constructing it. While these priorities and concerns may be shared by others (as, for instance, some Marxists share a common perspective), it is not intellectually justifiable to insist that there is only one way of seeing or theorising social life.

Some have suggested that postmodernism is a metanarrative itself, to which Lyotard has replied that it is the 'metanarrative to end metanarratives'. This is tongue in cheek and the fact is that – at its best – postmodernism is open, pluralistic and provisional – very different principles from those which totalistic theory reflects.

It may be that the main contribution of postmodernism is that it provides a critical perspective on modernity itself, including modernist theories such as Marxism and functionalism. For Zygmunt Bauman, postmodernism is largely a reflection on modernity. He considers that postmodernism itself shares the key modern characteristics of rationality and critical reflexivity. In other words, postmodernity is (as yet) still part of modernity. Similarly, Anthony Giddens regards what many refer to as 'postmodernity' as a phase of modernity, although he himself prefers the terms 'late' or 'high' modernity to that of postmodernity. Nevertheless, it is highly arguable that postmodernism is more than a diagnosis of a faltering modernity. As Krishan Kumar argues, both postmodernists and leading Marxist critics of 'late capitalism' such as Jameson and Harvey seem to be pointing to the onset of what may be a 'new era' (1995:139). If so, what do they consider are its main positive characteristics?

A postmodern (or merely late modern) epoch?

In the following discussion of postmodernism, two points need to be kept in mind. First, it is an enormous claim to suggest that humanity is entering a new historical epoch – however that may be defined. To put matters in perspective, if we think of history so far as being characterised by ancient, medieval and modern epochs, then, postmodernity would be a fourth. There would need to be substantial and convincing justification before it could be widely accepted that an historical break into a new epoch or era is occurring. Many postmodernists and theorists of late modernity hesitate to assert that change on this scale is occurring, preferring to see postmodernity occurring within the modern epoch. On the other hand the flurry of 'post' theories – post-industrial society theory, post-Fordism, poststructuralism and postmodernism – can be taken to imply the end of one period and the beginning of another, especially when they are linked to each other as Kumar does.

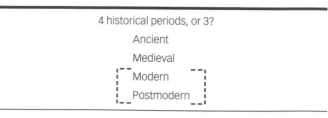

Figure 21.5 Has there been a transition from the modern to a postmodern period?

The second point to bear in mind in the following discussion, is that if a new historical period is emerging, that of postmodernity, it is still very much in the making. For those who believe in the power of human agency, this means that people – individually and collectively – can still shape and change postmodern society. Such an interventionist and creative approach is generally within the spirit of postmodernism (although the French poststructuralists, particularly Foucault and Derrida, have bequeathed a strand of determinism to postmodernist thought). We can now turn to analyse the positive or 'new' content of postmodernism.

Culture has become the dominant aspect of social life

Postmodernists argue that as a result of advanced communications technology, culture has become the dominant aspect of social life and saturates every aspect of it. Dominic Strinati gives a summary version of this view:

> First, postmodernism is said to describe the emergence of a social order in which the importance and power of the mass media and popular culture means that they govern and shape all other forms of social relationships. The idea is that popular cultural signs and media images increasingly dominate our sense of reality, and the way we define ourselves and the world around us.
>
> (1995:224)

If postmodernists are right, then, in postmodernity culture rules. Of course, postmodernists appreciate that the dominance of culture could not have come about without communications technology. What they see as definitive, however, is the sheer scale of the explosion of culture and communication that the technology enables. In emphasising the primacy of the cultural over the technological and economic, postmodernists differ radically from traditional Marxists who do the reverse.

Globalisation shapes the 'explosion' of culture

A second point of which there is consensus among postmodernists is that the primacy of culture and communication is occurring within and is deeply affected by the global context. Much cultural output is projected by media operating in a global market financed by capital likewise operating in a global market. Coca Cola and the Mondeo are, respectively, a world drink and a world car. Both are economic products but the status, style and meaning that can be read into them (by advertisements and audiences) are cultural in nature. Generally, postmodernists also appreciate that cultural production can and does occur at other levels than the global, including the local and individual. Nor do they deny that audience members can be actively involved both in contributing to and interpreting the meaning of media messages. However, what they seek to emphasise is the growing global dimension of culture.

Postmodernism – a romantic theory/movement

A third distinctive feature of postmodernist thinking is its romantic nature and emphasis on the subjective and emotional. This is the reverse side of the rejection of the more grandiose claims of science and reason. In its celebration of individuality and emotion, Krishan Kumar has located postmodernism within the tradition of romantic movements which exist in a tense but mutually dependent relationship with 'rational modernity'. Such movements include the English romantic poets and more recently, Dadaism and surrealism through to the 1960s counterculture. The implication is that what was alternative then is now becoming much more widespread. Postmodernists are not opposed to science and reason any more than they are opposed to technology. Their reservations pertain to how science and reason are employed. For instance, Marxism claimed to be 'scientific' and to have discovered the logic of historical change. Similarly, the liberal enlightenment boasted that the application of reason could solve all social problems and bring about the perfectibility of 'man'. It did not quite work out either way because too much was claimed and expected in both cases. In their eagerness to achieve their goals some Marxists and Marxist regimes became embroiled in bloody totalitarianism. On the other hand, the liberal ideal of well-engineered modernity may be in danger of polluting the planet beyond recovery. The unintended consequences of apparently scientific and rational behaviour have in both cases been highly destructive.

Postmodernists suggest that science and reason should not be regarded as neutral means to achieving desired ends but that their use should always be carefully weighed in relation to their effects on human beings and other organic life. Science should be guided by moral and aesthetic criteria. Zygmunt Bauman has made this argument most eloquently in relation to the holocaust (1992). He maintains that the technology of mass execution enabled the executioners to distance themselves from the moral and human reality of their actions. Genocide could be rationalised as 'just doing my job'.

Postmodernism emphasises identity, difference and pluralism

A fourth aspect of postmodernism, highly complementary to those previously mentioned, is its emphasis on identity, difference and pluralism. I will take pluralism first, as its link with the above is most obvious and because it provides the necessary context for analysing identity and difference as understood by postmodernists. Pluralism refers to a society and political system made up of many different and varied groups – no single group or party has total dominance of control. Postmodernists both believe in the desirability of pluralism and tend to consider that the world is becoming more pluralistic. Their commitment to pluralism is a logical consequence of their analysis that the grand metanarratives – the large schemes of how society 'should' be – are exhausted. Logically, if there is not to be just one vision of society, there must be the potential for many. Thus, postmodernists endorse the liberal commitment to democracy and tolerance (although they arrive at this point by a somewhat different route). Additionally, postmodernists argue that pluralism in a wider cultural sense is increasingly characteristic of the contemporary world. This is partly made possible by increasing average personal wealth and, therefore, capacity to consume and by the increasing variety of goods available.

Traditionally, sociologists have frequently explained collective, communal and even personal identity in terms of differences of class, gender, socially constructed age stages and ethnicity. In contrast, postmodernists tend to regard these areas of difference as too broad, adequately to explain the variety and complexity of identities (although postmodernists, along with other observers, acknowledge the continuing powerful pull of ethnic and national identities). Many postmodernists see the class system as fragmenting and declining as a basis of identity. A person's consumer and lifestyle choices are seen as more central to identity than class position (whether defined in Marxist or Weberian terms). This analysis fits in well with the culturalist bias of postmodernism. Individuals, sometimes coalescing as lifestyle groups, are seen as constructing their identities from a vast and constantly replenished supply of media images and consumer products. Paul Willis develops such an analysis in *Common Culture* (1990) – a book which marks a shift for him away from Marxism towards postmodernism.

Different gender, youth and ethnic identities

Angela McRobbie, a former colleague of Willis's at the Centre for Contemporary Cultural Studies in the 1970s, has also more recently taken a postmodern turn. In *Postmodernism and Popular Culture* (1994), she moves away from large structural categories such as gender and youth culture (or even subculture). These categories may be adequate starting points for theoretical analysis but the individuals 'within' them are seen as potentially very varied and different and subject to a wide range of influences. Thus, McRobbie refers to 'changing modes of femininity' and 'different, youthful subjectivities' (178-9). In other words, there are many different ways of being 'feminine' and of being 'youthful'. The search for a shared or consensual feminism has been overwhelmed by the sheer variety of 'feminine' identities and aspirations. Similarly, although young people continue to enjoy much age-based activity, they seem deliberately to avoid solidified subcultural 'uniform' identities, preferring instead constantly to play variations on 'their own' individual identity. However, for McRobbie there is no core identity, 'no real me' as she puts it. Rather, she sees individuals as constantly subject to a barrage of texts and symbols which partly constitute their subjectivity.

'Ethnicity' appears to have held up better than the other three major, global categories of stratification. Undoubtedly, ethnic and national identities have focused popular enthusiasm in many parts of the world in the first half of the decade – albeit it often in a crude and bloody way. However, as far as the postmodern argument about the 'break up' of the large categories of stratification – identity is concerned, this development is somewhat misleading. When Stuart Hall cautiously welcomed an emerging sociological interest in 'new ethnicities' (1992), his point of departure was that previously non-white ethnic groups had all been allocated to the category 'black' by most sociologists. Hall was acknowledging that within this broad (political) category, there are groups of enormous difference and variety. In doing so, Hall, like Willis and McRobbie, takes a postmodern turn. In fairness, it should be stated that the exploration of ethnicities by sociologists and cultural theorists influenced by postmodernism has been generally sophisticated. Ethnic and national identities are seen as socially constructed or 'imagined' rather than as cultural or, still less, as biological givens. In her recent collection, McRobbie herself provides an interesting, if provisional analysis, of 'inter-ethnic friendship' among the young in which she suggests that initiative is often held by Afro-Caribbeans (1994). Paul Gilroy's ambitions, *The Black Atlantic: Modernity and Double Consciousness* (1993) moves far beyond his earlier consideration of generally cruder, flag-waving forms of ethnic identity (1987). The black cultural diaspora triangulating between Africa, the Americas and Europe is presented at its best as far transcending narrow nationalistic concerns.

The recent work of Gilroy, Hall and McRobbie, then, appears to adopt an approach to culture that looks for and records difference, variety and change. They no longer apply established Marxist (or feminist or 'black') perspective to the links between stratification and culture but seem to assume a much closer merging of the two areas, if not the dominance of the latter.

Criticisms of postmodernism

There has been no lack of criticism of postmodernism (see below). Both liberal defenders of enlightenment rationality and Marxists committed to a continuing critique of capitalism (rather than 'modernity') have reasserted their basic positions and often ridiculed the pretensions of postmodernism. In particular, the late Ernest Gellner sharply refuted what he saw as the *cognitive relativism* of postmodernism (1991).

The following criticisms of Postmodernism are made:

1 It is relativistic (Gellner).
2 It is deterministic.
3 Contemporary society remains capitalist (Jameson, Harvey).
4 Postmodernist theory is not adequate to the task of analysing contemporary society.

1   Liberal criticism

Gellner makes no secret of his contempt of postmodernism as the following quotations indicates:

> *It is almost impossible to give a coherent definition or account of postmodernism … All one can say is that it is a kind of hysteria of subjectivity…*
>
> *(1991:29)*

He abhors what he sees as the failure of postmodernists to accept rational discourse or any concept of external institutional (structural) constraint:

> *In the end, the operational meaning of postmodernism … seems to be something like this: a refusal (in practice, rather selective) to countenance any objective facts, any independent social structures, and their replacement by a pursuit of 'meanings' …*
>
> *(29)*

In contrast, Gellner reasserts the validity and usefulness of the core commitment of the enlightenment to science and reason:

> *It is committed to the view that there is external, objective, culture-transcending knowledge: there is indeed 'knowledge beyond culture'. All knowledge must indeed be articulated in some idiom, but there are idioms capable of formulating questions in a way such that answers are no longer dictated by the internal characteristics of the idiom or the culture carrying it but, on the contrary, by an independent reality.*
>
> *(75)*

My own view is that not all and, in fact, probably only a minority of postmodernists are relativistic in the sense that Gellner asserts. Most do consider it their task to discover subjective meanings but few want to discard the established framework of (social) scientific theory and method. Their interest in subjectivity leads them to adopt predominantly qualitative methods of enquiry and some have been quite innovative in this respect (thus, autobiographical data on both subjects and author are now often considered relevant in the interplay of meanings and interpretations). I will return to this issue later.

A second and related criticism of much postmodernist theory is that it is deterministic and anti-humanistic. Gellner has commented on contradictory tendencies in postmodern thought, one of which emphasises individuality and difference and the other of which argues that individuality (subjectivity) is constituted by 'discourse' or ideologies which are generally not fully understood by those believing and practising them. Foucault is particularly associated with the latter view but a version of it has been influentially promulgated by Baudrillard in relation to the media. It must be said that Foucault and other French poststructuralists did precisely intend to take an anti-voluntaristic and anti-humanistic stand. There is no final resolution to the voluntarism versus determinism debate although some sort of balanced position between the two extremes seems the most sustainable perspective. On this issue, I strongly agree with Gellner that Foucault and, indeed, a long line of French structuralists and poststructuralists have tended to adopt the gloom and doom theoretical position. Given the choice, Habermas's commitment to human emancipation through employing 'communicative reason' seems to offer more.

However, as Gellner himself grudgingly accepts, there is a strong stand of postmodernist thought which emphasises and, indeed, celebrates freedom and creative diversity. Christopher Jencks describes this more positive strand as follows:

> The Postmodern Age is a time of incessant choosing. It's an era when no orthodoxy can be adopted without self-consciousness and irony, because all traditions seem to have some validity … Pluralism, the 'ism' of our time, is both the great problem and the great opportunity: where Everyman becomes a Cosmopolite and Everywoman a Liberated Individual.
>
> (Jencks, 1989:7)

2   Marxist criticism

The main Marxist criticism of postmodernism also argues that it lacks a firm anchoring in socio-economic (as opposed to cultural) theory. Thus, Jameson (1992) and Lash (1990) describe Western (and global) society as, respectively, in a stage of 'late capitalism' and 'disorganised capitalism' i.e. they type it according to what they see as its economic nature. They use the term postmodernism to describe the culture of late capitalism. For them, therefore, postmodernism is an aspect of late capitalist society. To this point, their thinking remains within the orthodox Marxist framework of base/superstructural analysis and thus they apparently distance themselves from postmodernists. However, like the postmodernists, both Jameson and Lash argue that in 'late' or 'disorganised' capitalist society the cultural has become of much greater significance. The following quotation from Jameson seems impeccably postmodernist except perhaps that he veers away from saying so. He comments on

> a prodigious expansion of culture throughout the social realm, to the point at which everything in our social life – from economic value and state power to practices and to the very structure of the psyche itself – can be said to have become 'cultural' in some original and yet untheorised sense'. Elsewhere he states that the term 'economic' and 'cultural' collapse back into each other and say the same thing, in an eclipse of the distinction between base and superstructure.
>
> (Quoted, Kumar, p. 115-116)

In pursuing their interest in cultural analysis – and, thus, being drawn onto the chosen ground of the postmodernists – Jameson and Lash arguably underplay perhaps the strongest point that Marxists could make against the postmodernists *viz.,* that they largely disregard the brute fact that capitalism continues to produce massive inequalities at the national and global levels. In the last twenty years inequality has greatly increased within Britain and between the West and the poor world. Marxists and conflict theorists in general could make this rather unfashionable and unromantic issue much more central to their concern (as, indeed, some do – see Westergaard (1994) and Goldthorpe and Marshall (1992)). The sources of inequality in late capitalist society have shifted somewhat but remain essentially related to work. No doubt inequality does have new and important cultural dimensions but it is primarily a material matter to those on the wrong end of it. Any revival of radical, conflict sociology is likely to occur around a renewed concern about inequality. Whether or not it is helpful to retain the concepts of social structure and, in particular, that of structural inequality in pursuing such an agenda is less important than laying bare the generation, incidence and effects of continuing inequality.

Conclusion how theoretically adequate is postmodernism?

The fourth and final criticism of postmodernism to be raised here relates to its theoretical adequacy. Does postmodernist theory offer or, at least, begin to offer a theoretical and conceptual framework that illuminates the nature of contemporary society? The first point to make here is that postmodernists do not claim to explain on the same scale or in the same way that the grand theorists of sociology aspired to. On the former point, they explicitly argue that total explanations of social life are impossible and misleading. On the matter of *how* they go about explaining the contemporary world, postmodernists seek significantly to modify the traditional approach which relies exclusively on rational enquiry. Postmodernists do not react to their scepticism about the capacity of the scientific approach to explain everything by resorting to irrationality. Rather, they tend to supplement rational analysis with moral, emotional and aesthetic reference. The morality, emotions, and sense of beauty and image of both sociological authors and their subjects seem to be allowed a larger part in postmodernist than traditional sociological analysis (including even interpretist approaches). Of course, such 'data' has always been used by sociologists but postmodernists employ such material not just as evidence but as a way of reining back and contextualising the more totalistic claims of science and reason.

So, postmodernism is neither a total theory of society nor does it adopt an entirely traditional approach to social scientific enquiry. Where does that leave us in terms of understanding the place of postmodernism 'within' or in relation to sociology? At the least, postmodernism offers an interesting array of analysis and insight on the contemporary world. In a recent review of a number of books on postmodernism, Ali Rattansi suggests that established sociology and postmodern approaches can be used together. He even anticipates that 'A'-level texts will soon incorporate 'postmodernism' as a 'perspective' in sociology (1995: 348) (Heaven forbid!). Similarly, Krishan Kumar finds much of relevance in postmodernist (and the other 'post') theories – although he retains a critical attitude to them.

> I hope I have shown that these theories do speak to our current condition. Like all theories they are one-sided and exaggerated. That is why they are useful and stimulating. No doubt they leave out much of what needs to be considered …
>
> Nevertheless, what seems to me remarkable is how much of the present state of the world they manage to capture.
>
> *(1995:201)*

Coming from such an authoritative source, that is an impressive, if qualified, endorsement. There is a place within sociology for postmodernist theory and concepts. That said, it is doubtful whether any of the postmodernist propositions and concepts discussed above are wholly original (although the analysis of difference and identity is distinctive). Viewed from the longer vantage point, it may be that postmodernism will somewhat shift sociology towards more qualitative and humanistic issues (Foucault notwithstanding). Kant's trilogy of the moral, aesthetic and rational have tended to be developed as separate spheres. Sociology has had a long history of pursuing the rational-scientific paradigm. In part, postmodernism can be viewed as a continuation of the 1960s project of forcing a re-evaluation of the relationship of reason to morality and aesthetics (notably pursued by Herbert Marcuse). There is at the heart of postmodernism a deep concern about the negative effects of the application of science and reason.

Nevertheless, postmodernists have presented no good reason to discard core sociological concepts such as structure, agency, power, inequality and alienation. Some of the most impressive developments of 'postmodernist' analysis have been generated by sociologists such as Harvey and Jameson and by Giddens who have a firm grasp of classical theory. However much they may re-theorise the concept of social structure and its effects, they are not about to abandon it. We will have to see how the new emphasis on

culture meshes with established sociological concerns.

Likewise, it is too early to judge whether or not we have entered upon a postmodern age with comparably distinctive and important characteristics as those of the modern, medieval and ancient, epochs. For some postmodernists this would, in any case, be a rather modernist way of looking at matters.

Conclusion: sociology – the state it's in

In earlier editions of this book, I have discussed the possibility that out of sociology's various perspectives there might emerge a 'unified sociological paradigm'. This seems unlikely now and I do not propose to make that issue the centrepiece of this concluding discussion. However, it is worth reiterating that the various efforts to 'thread together' what Layder refers to as the dualisms are a unifying exercise albeit more modest than 'total paradigm theory'. The fact that a unified paradigm is not emerging also seems to matter much less than it did although some might disagree. Lyotard and Foucault have carried the argument that 'big pictures' of reality are beside the point. Reality is not static but in constant *process*. However, what actually is happening in sociology and social science is interesting and exciting enough, if at times a little difficult to follow.

In the previous edition, I suggested that both the theory and methods of the subject lent themselves to pluralistic usage. Those who seek to study, for the purposes of generalisation, the effects of structure on individuals and groups are likely to combine structuralist theory with quantitative methods. Those who want to understand meaning, experience and feelings are likely to prefer interpretist theory and combine it with qualitative methods. Many studies combine both approaches. Thus, Marshall *et al.* in their highly empirical and statistically based *Social Class in Modern Britain* still sought to explore *subjective* class consciousness.

The impact of postmodernism and related 'isms' on sociology has taken sociology further in the direction of theoretical and methodological pluralism (although the detailed implications have not yet been fully worked out). A major and probably irreversible aspect of this is the acceptance that the global level and other socio-spatial levels (such as the bloc) now affect everyday social experience. The other central aspect of the postmodernist effect is the importing into sociology of an array of cultural concepts – many of which have their roots in semiotics (see p. 487). The combination of these two influences in the study of media globalisation has been immensely powerful.

When A H Halsey writes '(s)ociology is no longer one subject', he has mainly in mind the two traditions of, on the one hand, the empirical study of society of the kind Goldthorpe, Marshall and Halsey himself have undertaken, and on the other, the interpretist tradition as well as cultural studies as practised by Hoggart, E P

Thompson and the younger Stuart Hall. To quote Halsey more fully:

> *Sociology is no longer one subject. Those who define it as cumulative and explanatory in its aspirations with due (but not slavish) respect for natural science models and attempts at quantification and comparison have one credible answer. Similarly, those who assimilate the subject to the arts as intellectual history, and theoretical interpretation have a related, but different, and also credible solution.*
>
> (A H Halsey, 'Subject to Change', The Times Higher Education Supplement, 14.61996:i5)

Halsey is reluctant to include postmodernism within sociology. He likens it to what he sees as the over-political, excessively subjective 'tendencies of the late 1960s and early 1970s' which affected sociology and other social sciences. My own main concern about postmodernism is that voiced by Gellner – its thread of dangerous anti-humanism. However, on balance, postmodernism or, at least, the analysis of late modern society by such as Giddens, Beck and Barrett has made a substantial contribution to sociology. Arguably, it has done even more than that.

Postmodernism or the analysis of late modern society has brought into play a series of related theoretical insights and concepts which, for those who choose to adopt them, have shifted the focus of the discipline. Lyotard's burial of 'metanarratives' perhaps make talk of a paradigm shift in sociology seem too grandiose. However, many sociologists are exploring a different range of issues and in a different way from those which exercised the founders of sociology. The essential substructure of the discipline, as described by Mills, remains intact but the application and content have changed considerably in the work of, for instance, Giddens, Stuart Hall and W R Connell. Moreover, although Halsey, with some justification, emphasises the split in sociology, this chapter has shown that there is a wide range of impressive work attempting to integrate aspects of the discipline.

It almost seems that sociology is its own worst enemy. Sociology is always lending to, or borrowing from other subjects. Borrowings from sociology have stiffened the theoretical content of, for example management studies and development studies. On the other hand, sociology owes much to cultural studies and philosophy. This busy ebb and flow now seems more vital than either constant theoretical in-fighting or the search for the grail of a unified paradigm. Long may it run.

Questions

1 Critically consider various attempts to combine a sociology of structure with a sociology of action/agency.
2 On balance, has the contribution of postmodernism to sociology been positive or negative?

Summary

1 Three key issues focus the basic concerns of sociology:
   i The nature of social structure.
   ii The relationship between self and society.
   iii The historical development of society.
2 Functionalism analyses the functions and dysfunctions of society almost as though society were an impersonal organism. Functionalism is criticised for underestimating both intentionality and social conflict.
3 Marxism occurs in a variety of forms all of which are premised on the concept of class conflict. Marxism is criticised for being deterministic and for being superseded by actual historical developments.
4 Max Weber attempted to develop a sociology which linked social action and institutional formative power. He is criticised for over-emphasising the latter and failing to achieve a convincing synthesis.
5 Interactionism approaches society by attempting to understand the shared meanings of social actors. It can be strongly argued that interactionism and structural sociology are complementary rather than contradictory.
6 Phenomenology and ethnomethodology are related perspectives which analyse society in terms of the attempts of members to create social order. They are criticised for ignoring the formative power of institutions.
7 The battle of the perspectives has given way to a much more interesting if equally intense period of sociological debate in which genuinely challenging ideas on globalisation and culture are being asked.
8 A number of social theorists are confronting the agency (action)/structure divide in sociology and contributing to the reshaping of the discipline.
9 The basic propositions of postmodernism are presented with liberal and Marxist criticisms.
10 The 'state' of sociology is reviewed. Although no 'unified paradigm' is on the horizon, there is some cause for optimism.

Research and coursework

A project of 'pure theory' would seldom be appropriate at introductory level and, in any case, should only be attempted in close discussion with the project supervisor. That said, a critical review of a theoretical perspective or of the work of a major sociologist such as Ann Oakley or Charles Wright Mills might be feasible for a student sufficiently 'fired up' to do the reading and analysis required.

Further reading

Mary Maynard's *Sociological Theory* (Longman, 1989) is crisp and accessible. A succinct and authoritative entrée into many recent leading sociologists' ideas is John Lechte, *Fifty Key Contemporary Thinkers From Structuralism to Postmodernity* (Routledge, 1994).

Reading

Key characteristics of social constructionism

'Key Characteristics of Social Constructionism' from Vivien Burr, *An Introduction to Social Constructionism* (Routledge), 1995, pp.2-5

There is no one feature which could be said to identify a social constructionist position. Instead, we might loosely group as social constructionist an approach which has at its foundation one or more of the following key assumptions (from Gergen, 1985). You might think of these as something like 'things you would absolutely have to believe in order to be a social constructionist':

1 A critical stance towards taken-for-granted knowledge:

Social constructionism insists that we take a critical stance towards our taken-for-granted ways of understanding the world (including ourselves). It invites us to be critical of the idea that our observations of the world unproblematically yield its nature to us, to challenge the view that conventional knowledge is based upon objective, unbiased observation of the world. It is therefore in opposition to what are referred to as positivism and empiricism in traditional science – the assumptions that the nature of the world can be revealed by observation, and that what exists is what we perceive to exist. Social constructionism cautions us to be ever suspicious of our assumptions about how the world appears to be. This means that the categories with which we as human beings apprehend the world do not necessarily refer to real divisions. For example, just because we think of some music as 'classical' and some as 'pop' does not mean we should assume that there is anything in the nature of the music itself that means it has to be divided up in that particular way. A more radical example is that of gender. Our observations of the world suggest to us that there are two categories of human being – men and women. Social constructionism would bid us to question seriously whether even this category is simply a reflection of naturally occurring distinct types of human being. This may seem a bizarre idea at first, and of course differences in reproductive organs are present in many species, but we should ask why this distinction has been given so much importance by human beings that whole categories of personhood (i.e. man/woman) have been built upon it. Social constructionism would suggest that we might equally well (and just as absurdly) have divided people up into tall and short, or those with ear lobes and those without.

2 Historical and cultural specificity:

The ways in which we commonly understand the world, the categories and concepts we use, are historically and culturally specific. Whether one understands the world in terms of men and women, pop music and classical music, urban life and rural life, past and future, etc. depends upon where and when in the world one lives. For example, the notion of childhood has undergone tremendous change over the centuries. What it has been thought 'natural' for children to do has changed, as well as what parents were expected to do for their children (e.g. Aries, 1962). It is only in relatively recent historical times that children have ceased to be simply small adults (in all but their legal rights). And we only have to look as far back as the writings of Dickens to remind ourselves that the idea of children as innocents in need of adult protection is a very recent one indeed. We can see changes even within the timespan of the last 50 years or so, with radical consequences for how parents are advised to bring up their children.

This means that all ways of understanding are historically and culturally relative. Not only are they specific to particular cultures and periods of history, they are seen as products of that culture and history, and are dependent upon the particular social and economic arrangements prevailing in that culture at that time. The particular forms of knowledge that abound in any culture are therefore artefacts of it, and we should not assume that *our* ways of understanding are necessarily any better (in terms of being any nearer the truth) than other ways.

3 Knowledge is sustained by social processes:

If our knowledge of the world, our common ways of understanding it, is not derived from the nature of the world as it really is, where does it come from? The social constructionist answer is that people construct it between them. It is through the daily interactions between people in the course of social life that our versions of knowledge become fabricated. Therefore social interaction of all kinds, and particularly language, is of great interest to social constructionists. The goings-on between people in the course of their everyday lives are seen as the practice during which our shared versions of knowledge are constructed. Therefore what we regard as 'truth' (which of course varies historically and cross-culturally), i.e. our current accepted ways of understanding the world, is a product not of objective observation of the world, but of the social processes and interactions in which people are constantly engaged with each other.

4 Knowledge and social action go together:

These 'negotiated' understandings could take a wide variety of different forms, and we can therefore talk of numerous possible 'social constructions' of the world. But each different construction also brings with it, or invites, a different kind of action from human beings. For example, before the Temperance Movement, drunks were seen as entirely responsible for their behaviour, and therefore blameworthy. A typical response was therefore imprisonment. However, there has been a move away from seeing drunkenness as a crime and towards thinking of it as sickness, a kind of addiction. 'Alcoholics' are not seen as totally responsible for their behaviour, since they are the victims of a kind of drug addiction. The social action appropriate to understanding drunkenness in this way is to offer medical and psychological treatment, not imprisonment. Descriptions or constructions of the world therefore sustain some patterns of social action and exclude others.

Questions

1 Give your own examples of each of the above four characteristics of social constructionism.
2 To what extent are the four characteristics found or not found in other sociological perspectives? Give examples.

Bibliography

Allen, C and Williams, G (eds.), *Sociology of Developing Societies: Sub-Saharan Africa*, Macmillan, 1982

Allen, S, 'Gender, Race and Class in the 1980s', in C Husband, *Race in Britain*, Hutchinson, 1987

Anderson, A, *A Family Structure in Nineteenth Century Lancashire*, Cambridge University Press, 1971

Arber, S, 'Class and the Elderly', in *Social Studies Review*, Vol.6, No.3, January 1990

Ariès, P, *Centuries of Childhood*, Jonathan Cape, 1973

Arnot, M and Weiner, G, *Gender and the Politics of Schooling*, Hutchinson, 1987

Atkinson, J, 'The Changing Corporation', in D Clutterbuck, (ed.), *New Patterns of Work*, Gower, 1985

Ball, S J, *Beachside Comprehensive: A Case Study of Contemporary Schooling*, Cambridge University Press, 1981

Banfield, E, 'The Imperatives of Class', in J Raynor and E Hams (eds.), *Urban Education: The City Experience*, Ward Lock, 1977

Banks, M *et al.*, *Careers: Identities*, Open University Press, 1992

Baran, P A and Sweezy, P M, *Monopoly Capital*, Penguin, 1966

Bates, I and Riseborough, G, *Youth and Inequality*, Open University Press, 1993

Bauer, P, *Dissent on Development*, Harvard University Press, 1975

Bauman, Z, *Intimations of Modernity*, Routledge, 1992

Bauman, Z, *Thinking Sociologically*, Blackwell, 1990

Beck, U, Giddens, A and Lash, S, *Reflexive Modernisation: Politics, Tradition and Aesthetics in the Modern Social Order*, Blackwell, 1994

Becker, H, *Outsiders; Studies in the Sociology of Deviance*, Macmillan, 1966

Becker, H, *Social Problems: A Modern Approach*, John Wiley and Sons, 1966

Bell, C and Newby, H, *Community Studies*, Allen and Unwin, 1971

Bell, D, *The End of Ideology*, The Free Press, 1960

Bell, N W and Vogel, E F (eds.), *A Modern Introduction to the Family*, The Free Press, 1968

Beynon, H, *Working for Ford*, Penguin, 1973

Blau, P M, *On the Nature of Organisations*, John Wiley, 1974

Blauner, R, *Alienation and Freedom*, University of Chicago Press, 1964

Bott, E, *Family and Social Network*, Tavistock, 1957

Bottomore, T B and Nisbet, R (eds.), *A History of Sociological Analysis*, Heinemann, 1979

Bottomore, T B and Rubel, M (eds.), *Karl Marx: Selected Writings in Sociology and Social Philosophy*, Penguin, 1961

Bowles, S and Gintis, H, *Schooling in Capitalist America*, RKP, 1979

Braverman, H, *Labour and Monopoly*, Monthly Review Press, 1974

Breugel, I, 'Sex and Race in the Labour Market', in *Feminist Review*, No.32

Bronfenbrenner, U, *Two Worlds of Childhood: USA and USSR*, Allen and Unwin, 1971

Brown, C, *Black and White Britain: The Third PSI Survey*, Heinemann, 1984

Brown, J, 'Poverty in Post-war Britain', in J Obelkevich and P Catterall, *Understanding Post-War British Society*, Routledge, 1994

Brown, P, *Inequality, Unemployment and the New Vocationalism: Schooling Ordinary Kids*, Tavistock, 1987

Bruce, S, *The Sociology of Religion*, Oxford Paperbacks, 1996

Burnham, T, *The Managerial Revolution*, Putnam, 1943

Burns, T and Stalker, G, *The Management of Innovation*, Tavistock, 1966

Burr, V, *An Introduction to Social Constructionism*, Routledge, 1995

Butler, D and Stokes, D, *Political Change in Britain*, Macmillan, 1974

Campbell, A, *Delinquent Girls*, Basil Blackwell, 1981

Carradine, D, *The Decline and Fall of the British Aristocracy*, Yale University Press, 1990

Cashmore, E and Troyna, C, *Black Youth in Crisis*, Allen and Unwin, 1982

Cashmore, E, *Rastaman: The Rastafarian Movement in England*, Counterpoint, 1979

Cashmore, E, *The World of One Parent Families: Having to,* Counterpoint, 1985

Castles, S and Kosack, G, *Immigrant Workers and Class Structure in Western Europe,* Oxford University Press, 1973

Chambliss, W J and Mankoff, M, *Whose Law? What Order?,* John Wiley and Sons, 1976

Chodorow, N, *The Reproduction of Mothering,* University of California Press, 1978

Cicourel, A V, *The Social Organisation of Juvenile Justice,* Heinemann, 1976

Clarke, J, Cochrane, A and McLaughlin, E, *Managing Social Policy,* Sage Publications, 1994

Clegg, S and Dunkerley, D, *Organisation, Class and Control,* RKP, 1980

Cloward, R A and Ohlin, L E, *Delinquency and Opportunity,* The Free Press, 1961

Clutterbuck, D, *New Patterns of Work,* Gower, 1985, Heinemann, 1976

Coates, K and Silburn, R, *Poverty: The Forgotten Englishman,* Penguin, 1970

Coates, K and Topham, T, *Trade Unions and Politics,* Blackwell, 1986

Cohen, A K, *Delinquent Boys,* The Free Press, 1965

Cohen, A P, *The Symbolic Construction of Community,* Routledge, 1985

Cohen, G (ed.), *Social Change and the Life Course,* Tavistock, 1987

Cohen, S, *Folk Devils and Moral Panics,* Martin Robertson, 1980

Cohen, S, *Visions of Social Control: Crime, Punishment and Classification,* Polity Press, 1985

Coles, B, 'Gonna Tear Your Play House Down: Towards Reconstructing a Sociology of Youth', in *Social Science Teacher,* Vol.15, No.3

Coles, B, *Youth and Social Policy: Youth Citzenship and Young Careers,* UCL Press, 1995

Connell, R W, *Gender and Power,* Polity Press, 1987

Connell, R W, *Masculinities,* Polity Press, 1995

Cooke, P et al., *Localities,* Unwin Hyman, 1989; *Common Crisis: Co-operation for World Recovery,* Pan, 1983

Cootes, A, 'Labour: The Feminist Touch', in *Marxism Today,* Vol.29, No.22, 1985

Corrigan, P, *Schooling the Smash Street Kids,* Macmillan, 1979

Cowgill, D O and Holmes, L, *Ageing and Modernisation,* Appleton-Century-Crofts, 1972

Crewe, I, 'Why Mrs Thatcher was Returned with a Landslide', in *Social Studies Review,* Vol.3, No.2, September 1987

Crompton, R and Jones, G, *White-Collar Proletariat,* Macmillan, 1984

Curran, J, 'Rethinking the Media as a Public Sphere', in P Dahlgren and C Sparks (eds.), *Communication and Citizenship,* Routledge, 1991

Dahl, R, *A Preface to Political Theory,* University of Chicago, 1968

Dahrendorf, R, *Class and Class Conflict in Britain,* RKP, 1959

Daniel, W W and Millward, N, *Workplace and Industrial Relations in Britain,* Heinemann, 1983

David, H and Howard, H, *Beyond Class Images,* Groom Helm, 1979

Davis, K and Moore, W E, 'Some Principles of Stratification', in R Bendix and S M Lispet, *Class, Status and Power,* RKP, 1967

Dean, H and Taylor-Gooby, P, *Dependency Culture: The Explosion of a Myth,* Harvester Wheatsheaf, 1992

Deem, R and Salaman, G (eds.), *Work, Culture and Society,* Open University Press, 1985

Delmar, R, 'Looking Again at Engel's 'Origins of the Family, Private Property and the State'', in J Mitchell and A Oakley (eds.), *The Rights and Wrongs of Women,* Penguin, 1977

Delmar, R, 'What is Feminism?', in J Mitchell and A Oakley (eds.), *What is Feminism?,* Basil Blackwell, 1986

Ditton, J, 'Absent at Work: or How to Manage Monotony', in *New Society,* 21 December 1972

Doyal, L and Pennell, I, *The Political Economy of Health,* Pluto Press, 1979

Drew, D and Gray, J, *The Black-White Gap in Exam Achievement. A Statistical Critique of a Decade's Research,* QQSE Research Group, Sheffield University

Dunleavy, P and Husbands, C T, *British Democracy at the Crossroads,* Allen and Unwin, 1985

Dunleavy, P and O'Leary, B, *Theories of the State,* Macmillan, 1987

Durkheim, E, *Suicide: A Study in Sociology,* RKP, 1970

Durkheim, E, *The Division of Labour in Society,* The Free Press, 1967

Edwards, R, *Contested Terrain, The transformation of the Workplace in the Twentieth Century,* Heinemann, 1979

Ehrenreich, B and J, 'The Professional-Managerial Class', in P Walker (ed.), *Between Capital and Labour,* Harvester Wheatsheaf, 1979

Eisenstadt, S N, *From Generation to Generation: Age Groups and Social Structure,* Collier Macmillan, 1956

Ellis, W, *The Oxbridge Conspiracy,* Penguin, 1995

Engels, F, *The Origin of the Family, Private Property and the State,* Lawrence and Wishart, 1972

Erikson, E, *Childhood and Society,* W W Norton, 1963

Etzioni, A, *Modern Organisations*, Prentice-Hall, 1963

Etzioni, A, *The Spirit of Community*, Fontana, 1995

Evans, D, *Sexual Citizenship: The Material Construction of Sexualities*, Routledge, 1993

Evans-Pritchard, E, *Witchcraft, Oracles, and Magic among the Azande*, Oxford University Press, 1937

Featherstone, M (ed.), *Global Culture: Nationalisation, Globalisation and Modernity*, Sage, 1990

Firestone, S, *The Dialectic of Sex*, Paladin, 1972

Fitzgerald, M, 'Are Blacks an Electoral Liability?', in *New Society*, 8 December 1983

Fletcher, R, *Sociology: The Study of Social Systems*, Batsford, 1981

Fletcher, R, *The Family and Marriage in Britain*, Penguin, 1966

Förnas, J and Bolin, G, *Youth Culture in Late Modernity*, Sage Publications, 1995

Frank, A G, *Crisis in the World Economy*, Homes and Meier, 1981

Frank, A G, *On Capitalist Development*, Oxford University Press, 1975

Freeman, D, *Margaret Mead and Samoa: The Making and Unmaking of an Anthropological Myth*, Harvard University Press, 1983

Friedman, A, *Industry and Labour: Class Struggle at Work and Contemporary Capitalism*, Macmillan, 1977

Friedman, M and Friedman, R, *Free to Choose*, Avon Books, 1983

Fuller, M, 'Young, Female and Black', in E Cashmore and B Troyna (eds.), *Black Youth in Crisis*, Allen and Unwin, 1982

Gallie, D, *In Search of the New Working Class*, Cambridge University Press, 1978

Gans, H, *The Urban Villagers*, Free Press, 1962

Garfinkel, H, *Studies in Ethnomethodology*, Prentice-Hall, 1967

Gellner, E, *Postmodernism, Reason and Religion*, Routledge, 1992

Gerth, H H and Mills, C W, *Character and Social Structure*, Harcourt Brace, 1953

Giddens, A, 'An Anatomy of the British Ruling Class', in *New Society*, 4 October 1979

Giddens, A, *Modernity and Self-Identity*, Polity Press, 1991

Giddens, A, *The Consequences of Modernity*, Polity Press, 1990

Giddens, A, *The Transformation of Intimacy: Sexuality Love and Eroticism in Modern Societies*, Polity Press, 1992

Gill, R, 'Altered Images: Women in the Media', in *Social Studies Review*, September 1988

Gilroy, P, *The Black Atlantic: Modernity and Double Consciousness*, Verso, 1993

Gilroy, P, *There Ain't No Black in the Union Jack*, Hutchinson, 1987

Glasgow, D, *The Black Underclass*, Vintage Books, 1981

Glasgow University Media Group, *Bad News*, RKP, 1976

Glasgow University Media Group, *War and Peace*, Open University Press, 1985

Goffman, E, *Asylums*, Penguin, 1968

Goffman, E, *Stigma*, Penguin, 1971

Golding, P and Murdock, G, 'The New Communications Revolution', in J Curran, *Bending Reality: the State of the Media*, Pluto, 1986

Goldthorpe, J H *et al.*, *The Affluent Worker in the Class Structure*, Cambridge University Press, 1969

Goldthorpe, J H, Llewellyn, C and Payne, C, *Social Mobility and Class Structure in Britain*, Oxford University Press, 1980

Goode, W J, *World Revolution and Family Patterns*, The Free Press, 1965

Gould, J and Kolb, W (eds.), *A Dictionary of Social Sciences*, Tavistock Publications, 1964

Gouldner, A W, *Wildcat Strike*, RKP, 1957

Gregory, J, *Sex, Race and the Law: Legislating for Equality*, Sage, 1987

Griffin, C, *Typical Girls, Young Women from School to the Job Market*, RKP, 1985

Griffin, C, *Representations of Youth*, Polity Press, 1993

Habermas, J, *Legitimation Crisis*, Heinemann, 1971

Hall, S, Critcher, C, Jefferson, T, Clarke, J and Roberts, B, *Policing the Crisis*, Macmillan, 1979

Hall, S and du Gay, P, *Questions of Cultural Identity*, Sage Publications, 1996

Hall, S and Jefferson, T (eds.), *Resistance through Rituals*, Hutchinson, 1976

Hall, S *et al.*, *The Empire Strikes Back*, Hutchinson, 1981

Halsey, A H, *Change in British Society*, Open University Press, 1995

Halsey, A H, Introduction in N Dennis and G Erdos, *Families Without Fatherhood*, IEA Health and Welfare Unit, 1992

Ham, C, *The New National Health Service: Organization and Management*, Radcliffe Medical Press, 1991

Hargreaves, D, *Social Relations in a Secondary School*, RKP, 1967

Harrington, M, *The New American Poverty*, Rinehart and Winston, 1984

Harrington, M, *The Other American*, Penguin, 1963

Harris, C C, *The Family and Industrial Society*, Allen and Unwin, 1983

Hart, A, 'Images of the Third World', in *Looking Beyond the Frame*, Links Publications, 1989

Hart, N, *The Sociology of Health and Medicine*, Causeway, 1986

Hartmann, P and Husbands, C, *Racism and the Mass Media*, Davis Poyner, 1974

Harvey, D, *Social Justice and the City*, Edward Arnold, 1973

Hayter, T, *Aid: Rhetoric and Reality*, Pluto Press, 1985

Heath, A, Jowell, R and Curtice, J, *How Britain Votes*, Pergamon, 1985

Hebdige, D, *Subculture: The Meaning of Style*, Methuen, 1979

Himmelweit, H T et al., *How Voters Decide*, Academic Press, 1987

Hoggart, R, *The Uses of Literacy*, Penguin, 1957

Husbands, C (ed.), *Race in Britain: Continuity and Change*, Hutchinson, 1982; 2nd edition, 1987

Hutton, W, *The State We're In*, Jonathan Cape, 1995

Hyman, R, *Strikes*, Fontana, 1984

Illich, I, *The Limits of Medicine: Medical Nemesis*, Calder and Boyars, 1975

Inequalities in Health, *The Black Report and The Health Divide*, Penguin, 1988

Jenks, C, *Culture*, Routledge, 1993

Johnson, T J, *Professions and Power*, Macmillan, 1972

Jones, B, *The Moving Target: Job Flexibility in Britain*, Seminar, Johns Hopkins University, 1988

Jones, G and Wallace, Y, *Youth Family and Citizenship*, Open University Press, 1992

Keenoy, T, *Invitation to Industrial Relations*, Basil Blackwell, 1985

Kelly, J, *Trade Unions and Socialist Politics*, Verso, 1988

Kerb, C et al., *Industrialisation and Industrial Man*, Heinemann, 1962

Kincaid, J C, *Poverty and Equality in Britain*, Penguin, 1973

Kirby, M, *Investigating Political Sociology*, Collins Educational, 1995

Kuhn, T S, *The Structure of Scientific Revolutions*, University of Chicago Press, 1970

Kumar, K, *From Post-Industrial to Postmodern Society*, Blackwell, 1995

Lane, T and Roberts, K, *Strikes at Pilkington*, Fontana, 1971

Laslett, P, *The World We Have Lost*, Methuen, 1971

Layder, D, *Understanding Social Theory*, Sage Publications, 1994

Le Grand, J and Robinson, R, *Privatisation and the Welfare State*, Allen and Unwin, 1984

Lea, J and Young, J, *What is To Be Done About Law and Order*, Penguin, 1984

Lechte, J, *Fifty Contemporary Thinkers*, Routledge, 1994

Leghorn, L and Parker, K, *Women's Worth: Sexual Economics and the World of Women*, RKP, 1981

Lenin, V I, in H Christman (ed.), *Essential Works of Lenin*, Bantam, 1969

Lewis, O, *The Children of Sanchez*, Random House, 1961

Lockwood, D, *The Blackcoated Worker*, Allen and Unwin, 1958

Lowe, S, *Urban Social Movements*, Macmillan, 1986

Lyotard, J-F, 'The Postmodern Condition', in J C Alexander and S Seidman, *Culture and Society: Contemporary Debates*, Cambridge University Press, 1990

Mac an Ghaill, M, *The Making of Men: Masculinities, Sexualities and Schooling*, Open University Press, 1985

Mac an Ghaill, M, *Young, Gifted and Black*, Open University Press, 1988

Mack, J and Lansley, S, *Poor Britain*, Allen and Unwin, 1985

Malinowski, B, *The Sexual Life of Savages*, RKP, 1957

Mannheim, K, *Essays on the Sociology of Knowledge*, RKP, 1952

Marcuse, H, *Eros and Civilisation*, Sphere, 1969

Marcuse, H, *One Dimensional Man*, RKP, 1964

Marshall, G, *In Praise of Sociology*, Hyman, 1990

Marshall, G, Newby, H, Rose, D and Vogler, C, *Social Class in Modern Britain*, Hutchinson, 1988

Martin, D, *The Religious and the Secular*, RKP, 1969

Martin, E, *The Women in the Body*, Open University Press, 1987

Marx, K and Engels, F, *The Communist Manifesto*, Penguin, 1981

Maslow, A, 'A Theory of Motivation', in *Psychological Review*, Vol.50

Mason, D, *Race and Ethnicity*, Oxford University Press, 1995

Matza, D, *Delinquency and Drift*, Wiley, 1964

Maynard, M, 'Contemporary Housework and the Housework Role', in Graeme Salaman (ed.), *Work, Culture and Society*, Open University Press, 1988

Maynard, M, 'Current Trends in Feminist Theory', in *Social Studies Review*, Vol.2, No.3, January 1987

Maynard, M, *Sociological Theory*, Longman, 1989

McIntosh, M, 'The State and the Oppression of Women', in A Kuhn and A Wolpe (eds.), *Feminism and Materialism*, RKP, 1978

McIntosh, M and work group, 'Work and Leisure', in Alan Tomlinson (ed.), *Leisure and Social Control*, Brighton Polytechnic, 1981

McKenzie, R and Silver, A, *Angels in Marble*, Heinemann, 1968

McRobbie, A, 'Teenage Girls: Jackie and the Ideology of Adolescent Femininity', in B Waites *et al., Popular Culture, Past and Present*, Groom Helm, 1985

McRobbie, A, *Postmodernism and Popular Culture*, Routledge, 1994

Mead, G H, *Mind, Self and Society*, University of Chicago Press, 1962

Mead, M, *Coming of Age in Samoa: A Study of Adolescence and Sex in Primitive Societies*, Penguin, 1971

Mears, R, 'Debates about Health Inequalities', in M O'Donnell, *A New Introductory Reader in Sociology*, Nelson, 1993

Merton, R K and Nisbet, B, *Contemporary Social Problems*, Harcourt, Brace, Javanovich Inc., 1976

Merton, R K, *On Theoretical Sociology*, The Free Press, 1967

Miles, R, *Racism*, Routledge, 1989

Miles, R, 'Racism, Ideology and Disadvantage', in *Social Studies Review*, March 1990

Miliband, R, *Divided Societies*, Oxford Paperbacks, 1991

Miliband, R, *The State in Capitalist Society*, Weidenfeld and Nicolson, 1969

Miller, D (ed.), *Acknowledging Consumption*, Routledge, 1995

Miller, D, *On Nationality*, Clarendon Press, 1995

Miller, D, *Worlds Apart*, Routledge, 1995

Miller, W, 'Lower Class Culture as a Generating Milieu of Gang Delinquency', in *Journal of Social Issues*, Vol.14

Millet, K, *Sexual Politics*, Doubleday, 1970

Mills, C W, *The Power Elite*, Oxford University Press, 1956

Mills, C W, *The Sociological Imagination*, Oxford University Press, 1959

Mills, C W, *White Collar: the American Middle Classes*, Oxford University Press, 1951

Mirza, H F, *Young, Female and Black*, Routledge, 1992

Mishler, G E, *Social Contexts of Health, Illness and Patient Care*, Cambridge University Press, 1981

Mitchell, D A, *A New Dictionary of Sociology*, RKP, 1979

Mitchell, J and Oakley, A (eds.), *What is Feminism*, Blackwell, 1986

Mitchell, J, *Women's Estate*, Penguin, 1971

Modood, T, 'The Indian Economic Success', in *Policy and Politics*, Vol.19, No.3, 1991

Modood, T, Beishon, S and Satnam, V, *Changing Ethnic Identities*, P.S.I., 1994

Morgan, D H, *Socialisation and the Family: Change and Diversity*, in M Woodhead and A McGrath (eds.), Open University Press, 1988

Morley, D and Robins, K, *Spaces of Identity*, Routledge, 1995

Moser, C and Kalton, G, *Survey Methods in Social Investigation*, Heinemann, 1979

Muggleton, D, *From Subculture to 'Neo-tribe': Identity, Paradox and Postmodernism in Alternative Style*, 'Youth 2000' Conference Paper, University of Teeside, 1995

Muncie, J and McLaughlin, E, *The Problem of Crime*, Sage Publications, 1996

Murdock, G and Golding, P, 'Capitalism, Communication and Class Relations', in J Curran *et al., Mass Communication and Society*, Edward Arnold, 1977

Murdock, G and Golding, P, 'Ideology and the Mass Media: The Question of Determination', in M Barrett *et al.* (eds.), *Ideology and Cultural Production*, Croom-Helm, 1979

Murdock, G and Golding, P, 'The New Communications Revolution', in J Curran *et al.* (eds.), *Bending Reality: The State of the Media*, Pluto, 1986

Murdock, G and Phelps, P, *Mass Media and the Secondary School*, Macmillan, 1973

Murdock, G P, *Social Structure*, Macmillan, 1949

Murray, C, 'Underclass: A Disaster in the Making', in *Sunday Times Magazine*, 26 November 1989

Navarro, V, *Medicine Under Capitalism*, Prodist, 1976

North-South, *A Programme for Survival*, Pan, 1981

O'Donnell, M (ed.), *A New Introductory Reader in Sociology*, Nelson, 1988

O'Donnell, M, *Age and Generation*, Tavistock, 1985

O'Donnell, M, *Race and Ethnicity*, Longman, 1991

Oakley, A, *The Captured Womb*, Blackwell, 1984

Oakley, A, *The Sociology of Housework*, Pantheon, 1974

Pahl, J, *Private Violence and Public Policy*, RKP, 1985

Pahl, J, *Urbs in Rure*, Weidenfeld and Nicolson, 1965

Parker, S, *The Sociology of Industry*, Allen and Unwin, 1972

Parkin, F, *Class Inequality and the Political Order*, Paladin, 1972

Parkin, F, *Marxism and Class Theory*, Tavistock, 1979

Parsons, T, 'The Family its Function and Destiny', in R N Ansden (ed.), *The Social Structure of the Family*, Harper and Row, 1949

Parsons, T, *The Social System*, The Free Press, 1951

Patrick, J A, *Glasgow Gang Observed*, Methuen, 1973

Paxman, J, *Friends in High Places: Who Runs Britain?*, Michael Joseph, 1990

Peach, C, *West Indian Migration to Britain*, Oxford University Press, 1968

Pearson, G, *Hooligan: A History of Respectable Fears*, Macmillan, 1983

Pelletier, K, *Mind as Healer, Mind as Slayer*, Allen and Unwin, 1979

Phillipson, C, *Capitalism and the Construction of Old Age*, Macmillan, 1982

Piore, M and Sabel, C F, *The Second Industrial Divide: Possibilities for Property*, Basic Books, 1984

Pollert, A, 'Dismantling Flexibility', in *Capital and Class*, No.34, 1988

Pryce, K, *Endless Pressure*, Bristol Writers Press, 1986

Raynor, J and Harris, E (eds.), *The City Experience*, Open University Press, 1977

Reich, C, *The Greening of America*, Allen Lane, 1970

Renvoize, J, *Going Solo: Single Mothers by Choice*, RKP, 1985

Rex, J and Tomlinson, S, *Colonial Immigrants in a British City: A Class Analysis*, RKP, 1979

Rex, J, *Race and Ethnicity*, Open University Press, 1986

Roberts, K, *Contemporary Youth Unemployment*, Paper to British Association for the Advancement of Science, 1982

Roberts, K *et al.*, *The Fragmentory Class Structure*, Heinemann, 1977

Roberts, K, *Youth Employment in Modern Britain*, Oxford University Press, 1995

Rostow, W, *The Stages of Economic Growth*, Cambridge University Press, 1960

Rowbotham, S, *Women's Consciousness: Man's World*, Penguin, 1973

Rustin, M, 'The Politics of Post-Fordism', in *New Left Review*, No.175, 1989

Rutter, M, *Fifteen Thousand Hours: Secondary Schools and Their Effects on Children*, Open Books, 1979

Sampson, A, *The Money Lenders: Bankers in a Dangerous World*, Hodder and Stoughton, 1981

Saunders, P, *Capitalism: A Social Audit*, Open University Press, 1995

Saunders, P, *Social Class and Stratification*, Tavistock, 1990

Scase, R, *Class*, Open University Press, 1992

Scott, J, *Poverty and Wealth: Citizenship, Deprivation and Privilege*, Longman, 1994

Scott, J, *The Upper Classes: Property and Privilege in Britain*, Macmillan, 1982

Scott, S and Morgan, D, *Essays on the Sociology of the Body*, The Falmer Press, 1993

Seidler, V J, *Recreating Sexual Politics*, Routledge, 1991

Sharpe, S, *Just Like a Girl*, 2nd edition, Penguin, 1994

Sharpe, S, 'The Role of the Family in the Oppression of Women', in *New Edinburgh Review*, 1972

Shorter, E, *The Making of the Modern Family*, Fontana, 1977

Sillitoe, A, *Saturday Night and Sunday Morning*, Allen and Unwin, 1958

Silverman, D, *The Theory of Organisations*, Heinemann, 1970

Silverstone, R, 'Television and Everyday Life: Towards an Anthropology of the Television Audience', in M Ferguson (ed.), *Public Communication: The New Imperatives*, Sage Publications, 1990

Simmel, G, 'The Metropolis and Mental Life', in K Wolf (ed.), *The Sociology of George Simmel*, Free Press, 1950

Simmons, O G, 'Development Perspectives and Population Change', in *Papers of the East-West Population Institute*, 1983

Sinfield, A, *What Unemployment Means*, Martin Robertson, 1981

Skellington, R, *'Race' in Britain Today*, 2nd edition, Open University Press, 1996

Sklair, L, *Sociology of the Global System*, Harvester Wheatsheaf, 1991

Smith, D, Tomlinson, S and Stanworth, M, 'Women and Class Analysis: a reply to Goldthorpe', in *Sociology*, 18, 1984, pp.159-170

Solomos, J, *Race and Racism in Contemporary Britain*, Macmillan, 1989

Solomos, J and Back, L, *Race, Politics and Social Change*, Routledge, 1995

Steinberg, I, *The New Lost Generation; the Problems of the Population Boom*, Martin Robertson, 1982

Stewart, A *et al.*, *Social Stratification and Occupations*, Macmillan, 1980

Stone, M, *The Education of the Black Child*, Fontana, 1981

Strinati, D, *An Introduction to Theories of Popular Culture*, Routledge, 1995

Sumner, C, *The Sociology of Deviance: An Obituary*, Open University Press, 1994

Taylor, J G, *From Modernisation to Modes of Production*, Macmillan, 1991

Taylor-Gooby, P, *Public Opinion, Ideology and the Welfare State,* TKP, 1985

Thompson, E P, *The Making of the English Working Class,* Penguin, 1968

Thompson, G, *Markets, Hierarchies and Networks: The Co-ordination of Social Life,* Sage, 1991

Thompson, K, *Key Quotations in Sociology,* Routledge, 1996

Tizzard, B et al., *Young Children at School in the Inner City,* Lawrence Erlbaum, 1988

Tönnies, F, *Community and Society,* Harper and Row, 1957

Townsend, P, *Poverty in the United Kingdom,* Penguin, 1979

Tuchman, G et al., *Hearth and Home: Images of Women in the Media,* Oxford University Press, 1978

Tumin, M, *Social Stratification: The Forms and Functions of Social Inequality,* Prentice-Hall, 1967

Urry, J, *Consuming Places,* Routledge, 1995

Walters, V, *Class Inequality and Health Care: The Origins and Impact of the National Health,* Croom Helm, 1980

Warde, A, 'Consumption, Identity-formation and Uncertainty', in *Sociology,* 28, 1994, pp.877-98

Wedderburn, D and Crompton, R, *Workers' Attitudes and Technology,* Cambridge University Press, 1972

Westergaard, J and Resler, H, *Class in Capitalist Society,* Penguin, 1976

Whale, J, *The Politics of the Media,* Fontana, 1977

Whyte, W F, *Street Corner Society,* University Of Chicago Press, 1955

Wilding, P, *The British Welfare State: Thatcherism's Enduring Legacy in Politics and Policy,* Vol. 20, No. 3, 1992

Wilkinson, H, *No Turning Back: Generations and Genderquake,* Demos, 1994

Willis, P, *Learning to Labour,* Saxon House, 1977

Willis, P et al., *Common Culture,* Open University Press, 1990

Willmott, P, *Adolescent Boys in East London,* Penguin, 1966

Willmott, P, 'Urban Kinship Past and Present', in *Social Studies Review,* November 1988

Willmott, P and Young, M, *Family and Kinship in East London,* Penguin, 1962

Willmott, P and Young, M, *The Symmetrical Family,* RKP, 1973

Wilson, B R, *Religion in a Sociological Perspective,* Oxford University Press, 1982

Wirth, L, 'Urbanism as a Way of Life', in *American Journal of Sociology,* Vol.44, No.1

Wood, S, *The Transformation of Work,* Unwin Hyman, 1989

Wright, E O, *Classes,* Verso, 1985

Yule, V, 'Why are parents so tough on children?', in *New Society,* 27 September 1986

Author index

Subject index